Endorsed by

International Webmasters Association Mission Statement

The International Webmasters Association (http://www.irwa.org/) is the first individual membership association to represent the Web Professionals of the World. Our mission is to provide individual Web Professionals with global networking opportunities at the chapter, regional and international levels; we are also the first professional organization to embrace the internationality of the Web with our Language Centre.

HTML 4

Professional Reference Edition

Rick Darnell, et al.

201 West 103rd Street
Indianapolis, IN 46290

UNLEASHED

Trademarks

Publisher	Jordan Gold
Executive Editor	Beverly M. Eppink
Managing Editor	Patrick Kanouse
Brand Director	Alan Bower

Acquisitions Editor
David B. Mayhew

Development Editor
Bob Correll

Software Development Specialist
Patty Brooks

Production Editor
Lisa M. Lord

Indexer
Rebecca Salerno

Technical Reviewer
Will Kelly

Editorial Coordinators
Mandie Rowell
Katie Wise

Technical Edit Coordinator
Lorraine E. Schaffer

Marketing Coordinator
Linda B. Beckwith

Resource Coordinator
Charlotte Clapp

Editorial Assistant
Rhonda Tinch-Mize

Cover Designer
Jason Grisham

Book Designer
Gary Adair

Production Team Supervisor
Andrew Stone

Production Team
Chris Livengood
Becky Stutzman

Overview

Contents

Part V Programming Languages for HTML

Part VII   Effective Web Page Design

31   Creating an Effective Interface   561

32   Navigation and Layout   585

Dedication

To Jane, Margaret, and Elizabeth.
—Rick Darnell

Acknowledgments

While I've been breathing for the past several years, I've been able to develop this interesting phenomenon called a "writing career." For my in-laws, it usually evokes the story of an early immigrant through Ellis Island. The customs agent asked for his occupation, and the young man replied, "Writer." The customs agent paused for a moment, then wrote "Unemployed" on the processing form.

I'm happy to say that the reality is somewhere in between working a full-time job and lying on the couch watching Oprah. I have a lot of freedom during the day, which includes the chance to spend half of it with my two daughters, work as a volunteer firefighter/EMT, and hang out in the yard and pull weeds. I also get the chance to work mornings, nights, and weekends when the deadline crunch is on.

There are two really neat aspects about writing. The first is seeing your name in print. It's probably vain and self-serving, but I get great satisfaction from seeing my name attached to a comprehensive work such as this one.

Second is the people you meet along the way, who make the whole process possible and enjoyable. Writers are pretty pointless without editors, and vice versa. It's one of those dichotomies that results in a certain tension, but also holds incredible satisfaction when both sides reach the end of the process and another book is born.

Acquisitions Editor David Mayhew was the guiding hand that negotiated the contracts, set the deadlines, hired the writers, and made sure we delivered the goods. An acquisitions editor has a thankless job and doesn't get nearly the glory we writers do, but David certainly puts in every bit as much work.

Development Editor Bob Correll keeps everyone honest. He's the one responsible for making sure we authors stick to our subjects and cover them in a competent way. If we start to cut corners or hedge around a topic because we don't understand it, Bob calls us on the carpet to set it straight. For being former military intelligence, he's even quite polite and non-threatening about it.

Production Editor Lisa Lord has a job similar to Bob's, except she's making sure we obey the laws of proper grammar, punctuation, spelling, and all those other details I and others have been known to ignore on occasion. It's humbling and rewarding to work with someone like Lisa, who reminds me that no writer ever outgrows the need for a good English teacher.

Last, but certainly not least, our Executive Editor on this project is Her Majesty Beverly Eppink, who also deserves a great deal of gratitude. She continues to maintain a generous and supportive attitude towards the authors, even though her contact with us is now buffered through the front-line editors. She's certainly encouraged my development with editors at Sams.net in the last year and is responsible for a great deal of my success.

Many other people on the payroll at Macmillan make these projects happen, from the publisher and lawyers, to technical editors and proofreaders, designers, lawyers, secretaries, custodians, and many others. Although I don't know everyone's name, everyone makes a contribution to the finished product. Many thanks to you all.

Then, there are the other authors who participated in this project. I was the lead author on this book, but it still couldn't be a book without the contributions of the others. It's good to be in the company of people working fervently toward the same goal, even though we're in different states and on different continents.

In addition to the folks who worked directly on this project, there are many people who have fostered me during my early attempts at writing, giving me the needed guidance so I could learn how to put the right words in the right order. This list includes Bonnie Montgall, David MacFarland, John Braden, and influences such as Edward Abbey, Kenneth Grahame, and A.A. Milne.

Last in this list of acknowledgments, but certainly not least, is you, the reader. Your investment in this book just made my bank account a few cents bigger. (Royalties aren't all they're cracked up to be.) I hope you find the book useful and worth the money you shelled out for it. If it makes your job easier or gives you new ideas for communicating with your fellow humans, then we've done our jobs on this end. Thank you.

—*Rick Darnell*

About the Authors

Rick Darnell hails from the flatlands of Kansas, although he currently finds his view blocked by a bunch of mountains while living with his wife and two daughters in western Montana. He graduated from Kansas State University with a degree in broadcasting, became confused, and started writing for two small energy industry magazines and a local weekly newspaper. While spending time as a freelance journalist and writer, Rick has seen the full gamut of personal computers since starting out with a Radio Shack Model I in the late 1970s. When not in front of his computer, he serves as a volunteer firefighter/EMT and member of a regional hazardous materials response team. Rick has authored several books for Sams.net Publishing and Que Corporation, including *HTML 4 Unleashed* and *Teach Yourself Dynamic HTML in a Week*. His Web page is at `http://people.montana.com/~darnell/`, and he can also be reached by e-mail at `darnell@montana.com`. For this book, he wrote Parts I, II, and IV, as well as Chapters 16, 26, 27, and Appendix C.

Bruce Campbell (`bdc@hitl.washington.edu`) lives in Seattle, WA and works with technologies related to Web-based 3-D collaborations, such as VRML. When he's not writing, he is either teaching for Catapult training centers or Central Seattle Community College, performing VR-related research at the Human Interface Technology Laboratory at the University of Washington, or running around somewhere in North America. Bruce's writing credits include being a co-author of the Sams.net books *Teach Yourself VRML 2.0 in 21 Days*, *HTML 4 Unleashed*, and *Teach Yourself Dynamic HTML in a Week*. His home page URL is at `http://www.hitl.washington.edu/people/bdc`. Bruce wrote Chapters 28, 29, and 30.

David and Rhonda Crowder were hypertext pioneers and have been involved in the online community for over a decade. Their company, Far Horizons Software, a Web site design firm, created the award-winning LinkFinder and NetWelcome sites. They and their cats live in Miami, Florida. David and Rhonda wrote Chapters 12-15 and contributed to Appendix G.

Molly E. Holzschlag is an instructor, designer, and the author of numerous books on Web design and Internet technologies, including *The Laura Lemay Guide to Sizzling Web Site Design* and *Laura Lemay's Web Workshop: Guide to Designing with Style Sheets, Tables, and Frames*. Molly teaches Web design to graduate media studies students at the New School for Social Research. You can visit her Web site at `http://www.molly.com/`. Molly wrote Part VII of this book, "Effective Web Page Design."

Will Kelly (`willk@tiac.net`) is a freelance technical writer and consultant in the Washington, DC area. He has written documentation and courseware on projects for companies such as WordPerfect (when it was still WordPerfect!), MCI, Oracle, Corporate Software and Technology, and Concert. As a frequent technical editor for Sams Publishing, he is more used to kvetching about chapters than writing computer book chapters. However, for this book, Will was also a contributor to Appendix A.

Dmitry Kirsanov graduated in 1996 from St. Petersburg (Russia) University, Faculty of Languages. He worked first as a translator, then pursued a career as freelance writer and published two books and numerous magazine articles on the Internet and the Web, all in Russian. Recently, he started to write for the Web in English by opening the *Design Lab* monthly column at `http://www.webreference.com/dlab/`. Dmitry wrote Part IX, "Advanced Techniques."

Robert McDaniel is an Internet technology enthusiast who has been active with the Web since its early days. Some of his other works include the *CGI Manual of Style*, *PC Magazine Webmaster's Ultimate Resource Guide*, *Late Night Microsoft Visual J++*, and *How to Program Microsoft Visual Basic Scripting Edition*. He is currently working on an intranet project at Walt Disney Imagineering Research and Development. Robert wrote Chapters 24 and 25.

Kelly Murdock (`murdocks@itsnet.com`) works as a full-time programmer and spends much of his spare time exploring the graphics frontier. He especially enjoys dabbling in 3-D. He is the lead author of *Laura Lemay's Web Workshop: 3D Graphics and VRML 2* and has contributed to several other titles. He also writes a regular column, "Kel's Eye Inside Reviews," for `www.3dreview.com`. Kelly wrote Chapter 23.

Simon North's background includes working as a helicopter repair technician, a software quality assurance engineer, and a technical translator. He is an experienced technical writer, specializing in online, multimedia, and interactive delivery methods. He is one of the authors of the Dutch national standard for consumer documentation and is co-author of *Presenting XML*. Simon has been involved with SGML since 1989, and was an active participant in Dutch CALS/SGML standardization activities. Simon is an avid Internet surfer, having built his first intranet in 1993. His latest hobby (since giving up free-fall parachuting) is collecting e-mail accounts, but Simon can be contacted at `sintac@xs4all.nl`.

Lee Anne Phillips is one of the "old hands" in the networking business, having skipped straight from the University of California at Berkeley into the mainframe world in 1977. Since that time, she's worked for a variety of companies, dabbling in one aspect of networking or another. She finally stumbled onto the World Wide Web itself in 1994, after a brief flirtation with ARPAnet during her carefree student days and a long-term romance with the Internet. She now resides in her place of birth, the San Francisco Bay area of California, after many years in exile and on the road. She holds a bachelor's degree in computer science and is a card-carrying computer nerd. Her current interests are electronic mail systems, user interfaces, and the continuing development of HTML and SGML as universal communications media. She wrote Appendixes B and G of this book and was a major contributor to Appendix A.

Tell Us What You Think!

As a reader, you are the most important critic and commentator of our books. We value your opinion and want to know what we're doing right, what we could do better, what areas you'd like to see us publish in, and any other words of wisdom you're willing to pass our way. You can help us make strong books that meet your needs and give you the computer guidance you require.

As the team leader of the group that created this book, I welcome your comments. You can fax, e-mail, or write me directly to let me know what you did or didn't like about this book—as well as what we can do to make our books stronger. Here's the information:

Fax: 317-817-7070

E-mail: html@mcp.com

Mail: Mark Taber
            Comments Department
            Macmillan Computer Publishing
            201 W. 103rd Street
            Indianapolis, IN 46290

Introduction

The Internet has progressed extremely fast in recent years. Once the realm of academics, researchers, and defense agencies, the Internet and its associated parts are rapidly becoming a mainstream media conduit for communication between individuals, companies, and global dwellers.

As part of the Internet, the World Wide Web is the predominant force in the growth of the global computer network. Its language is simple, its interface is attractive and friendly, and it's adaptable to a wide variety of uses. There are Web sites for selling products, selling ideas, maintaining appearances, informing publics, continuing education and knowledge, and just plain wasting time, and the World Wide Web concept is being adapted to internal communications by establishing intranets inside companies.

HTML (Hypertext Markup Language) is the language that puts the face on the Web. It consists of a variety of elements called *tags*, which are used for everything from defining type styles and headings to inserting specialized content, such as images, sounds, virtual reality worlds, and Java applets.

One of the main drawbacks to working with HTML is that many Web page editors don't display a page the way it will look on a browser. Instead, HTML authors and designers must contend with the content of their page intermixed with the tags that control how the content appears to the user. The good news is that this situation is changing rapidly, with the advent of new WYSIWYG editors that display a page using the standard accepted by most browsers.

So, with the introduction of graphical editors, why learn the intricacies of HTML? There are several reasons. First, HTML is as much an organizational tool as a design tool. The tags give structure and purpose to each part of the page and explain how it relates to the rest of the page. Learning the organization behind the page leads to better designs for your readers.

Second, even some of the best WYSIWYG editors don't support all the tags that are part of HTML at any given time. Sometimes it's necessary to directly modify the source of the page to add or change tags and attributes. To do this, you need to know how the tags relate to each other.

The final reason for learning HTML is simply for the fun of it. You gain a certain satisfaction from building a Web page from the ground up. You'll know about every brick and board that went into it, and you'll have the know-how to tweak each one so that the result is just what you wanted. On the other side of that is the fun of seeing other Web pages and knowing how the page author and designer worked to develop the intended effect.

HTML AS GENERAL CONVERSATION

The World Wide Web is becoming more and more common as a topic of conversation at the dinner table, at cocktail parties and banquets, in car pools, and around the water cooler at work. After reading this book, we're sure you'll discover HTML is one of the most fascinating things on the planet and will want to discuss the nuances of each tag with those around you.

Don't do it. It's more than enough in general company to know what *HTML* means. If you try to discuss HTML in any detail, you'll get blank stares and suddenly find yourself standing in a corner by yourself holding a small plate of vegetables and runny ranch dressing with the host's dog hanging on your every word.

How This Book Is Organized

This book is divided into nine different sections, plus eight appendixes. The book begins with basic concepts and foundations of HTML and then delves into the details of standard tags and their attributes, advanced features, and extensions. After the details of the language are covered, additional related topics are covered, including design, supporting technologies, and new forms of markup language, such as Extensible Markup Language.

Here's a section-by-section look at what's in store:

- **Part I, "Introducing HTML 4.0":** The chapters in this section cover the foundation and history of HTML, beginning with the concept of hypertext and extending into document types, document structure, and how different browsers and platforms fit into the Web picture. As part of the introduction, Chapter 5, "Get Started Now", was added to get you up to speed quickly if you already have a grasp of HTML 3.2.

- **Part II, "Structural and Navigational Elements of HTML 4":** This section covers the standard tags supported by the latest HTML 4.0 specification, and includes widely used items such as divisional and organizational tags, lists, and tables. It also includes items that should be used and aren't, such as document type declarations.

- **Part III, "Basic HTML 4.0 Interactivity":** There's more to a Web page than just reading the words. This section covers some of the foundations of building interactivity into a page, using elements such as anchors, image maps, forms, and objects like applets and embedded controls.

- **Part IV, "Presentation Techniques":** After the previous two sections covering the structure and function of a Web page, this section shows how to use the latest techniques for making the page look the way you want. It starts with the tag-based formatting options, such as <B> for bold and <I> for italics, and then progresses to Cascading Style Sheets, JavaScript Style Sheets, element positioning, frames, and layers.

- **Part V, "Programming Languages for HTML":** HTML's capabilities are extended a great deal through the support of technologies that add interactive features to otherwise lifeless pages. These technologies include Common Gateway Interface (CGI) scripts for data transfer, JavaScript, and VBScript (Visual Basic Script).

- **Part VI, "Dynamic HTML":** Dynamic HTML is a new way of integrating HTML, scripting, and style sheets to create interactive Web pages without working through the Web server, applets, or other add-on solutions. Best of all, correctly implemented Dynamic HTML can be viewed on any browser, with the dynamic features activated only on compatible browsers.

- **Part VII, "Effective Web Page Design":** With the tools and bricks in place from the previous sections, you have the requisite technical knowledge to build Web pages with HTML. However, a technically correct page is not necessarily a user-friendly page. This section shows you how to build attractive, usable pages by including concepts and examples for designing user interfaces and navigation tools.

- **Part VIII, "XML":** Extensible Markup Language is the new kid on the block in the world of the Internet, and its use is growing because of its inherent flexibility. In effect, XML allows you to create pages with your own customized markup tags. This feature is already in use for one of the latest features of the Web—Web casting and channel subscriptions. This section explains what XML is and how to implement it in your Web site.

- **Part IX, "Advanced Techniques":** The chapters in this section discuss the evolution of standards for character sets and page representation in an international arena. Issues of standardization among browsers and platforms, and HTML's use in non-Web environments, such as indexing and search engines, are also covered. Plus, there's an entire chapter devoted to accessibility issues—for more and less capable browsers and people.

The appendixes in the back of the book include more reference information to help you with your day-to-day work using HTML. In addition to a quick reference of HTML tags, the appendixes also include references for HTML 4.0, Cascading Style Sheets Level 1, Extensible Markup Language, and scripting languages. Additional information is also provided for cross-browser comparisons, color and character values, and online information resources.

We hope the combination of information in the chapters and references in the appendixes makes *HTML 4 Unleashed, Professional Reference Edition* the most complete HTML reference book you have in your collection.

How to Use This Book

Whether you're an old hand or a newbie, Chapters 1 through 5 are a good introduction and explanation of why HTML looks and acts the way it does, and how it works within the framework of the Internet and intranets.

Chapters 6 through 16 are the meat and potatoes of HTML 4.0. Every tag in the HTML specification is covered in this area, along with their attributes and behaviors. If you're a beginner, working through this section will give you a solid foundation for working with HTML. These chapters are augmented by Chapters 17 through 22, which give you a host of techniques for controlling the Web page's appearance.

Chapters 31 through 35 offer added reinforcement to the presentation techniques. This course in Web design will quickly get you up to speed in building Web pages with examples of good page structure. If you've already worked with HTML, you should review this area to see new ways of presenting information to your users in a way that looks good and gets your point across.

For advanced users, Chapters 23 through 30 and 36 through 39 show how to extend HTML beyond the elements illustrated in the previous chapters. Advanced concepts, including programming languages, Dynamic HTML, and XML are explained and illustrated here.

The last section, Chapters 40 through 42, is another good place to go regardless of your experience with HTML. It shows ways of making your HTML pages friendlier for an international audience. It also helps you create pages that are accessible by more than the "big two" from Netscape and Microsoft, including disabled users with special-purpose browsers. As a last step, strategies for indexing your pages and adding them to search engines is also covered.

COMMON ATTRIBUTES

Most of the elements in this book share some common attributes. Rather than list all of them for each element every time, I've identified them here and referred to this list in several chapters. The first set of attributes are referred to as the core attributes:

id: This value serves as document-wide identification, and should be unique among any other IDs in the document.

title: This attribute supplies additional information about the element and can be used or ignored at the browser's discretion.

class: Style sheets use this attribute to apply a style to a set of elements associated with this class. See Chapter 18, "Using Cascading Style Sheets," for more information.

style: This attribute is used to include inline style information for the current instance of the element. See Chapter 18 for more information.

The next two are international attributes (see Chapter 40, "Internationalizing Your HTML"):

lang: This attribute specifies the primary language for the document text, with the default as unknown. For more information, consult "Tags for the Identification of Languages," available at ftp://ds.internic.net/rfc/rfc1766.txt.

dir: The direction of weak or neutral text, which carries the value LTR (left-to-right) or RTL (right-to-left). The browser determines the default direction, although for the English and European languages, it's safe to assume left-to-right.

Next come the alignment attributes, which determine how text is justified within the document. The values are `left`, `right`, `center`, or `justify`. The default is `left` for `LTR` paragraphs and `right` for `RTL` paragraphs. Many browsers don't support `justify` (both left and right), in which case the alignment defaults to the value based on the `dir` attribute.

The last attributes are the event handlers—`onclick`, `ondblclick`, `onmousedown`, `onmouseup`, `onmouseover`, `onmousemove`, `onmouseout`, `onkeypress`, `onkeydown`, and `onkeyup`—which are covered in more detail in Chapter 28, "Working with the User: Events."

Conventions Used in This Book

Sams.net has spent many years developing and publishing computer books designed for ease of use and containing the most up-to-date information available. With that experience, we've learned what features help you the most. Look for these features throughout the book to help enhance your learning experience and get the most out of HTML.

- Screen messages, code listings, and command samples appear in `monospace type`.
- Uniform Resource Locators (URLs) used to identify pages on the Web and values for HTML attributes also appear in `monospace type`.
- Terms that are defined in the text appear in *italics*. Italics are sometimes used for emphasis, too.
- In code lines, placeholders for variables are indicated by using *`italic monospace type`*.

TIP

Tips give you advice on quick or overlooked procedures, including shortcuts.

NOTE

Notes present useful or interesting information that isn't necessarily essential to the current discussion, but might augment your understanding with background material or advice relating to the topic.

CAUTION

Cautions warn you about potential problems a procedure might cause, unexpected results, or mistakes that could prove costly.

> **WARNING**
>
> Warnings are like Cautions, only with more attitude. They let you know about actions that could seriously disrupt or damage someone's system.

Who Should Read This Book?

This book has been planned and designed to meet a wide variety of needs, depending on your level of experience and knowledge with HTML.

For beginners, we offer an introduction into the basics of HTML, including basic page structure and all the tags needed to build the page. Each HTML element is presented with its corresponding attributes, along with its default behavior and the minimum information it needs to function.

Both casual and accomplished users will find it easier to jump around to the specific topics they need, such as tables, frames, or design. Remember that this book is a comprehensive resource for HTML 4.0, so you'll still want to glance at the other chapters to see what else you might be missing.

For experts, this book serves as an excellent reference to answer specific questions. The syntax, attribute listings, and examples give you plenty of opportunities to see variations on HTML implementation. The references at the back of the book put the technical information you require within easy reach.

We've worked hard to put together the most comprehensive HTML book available, and we hope you'll agree that it's not only an important addition to your collection, but also a valuable tool you'll use every day.

From all of the authors, thank you for choosing *HTML 4 Unleashed, Professional Reference Edition.*

—*Rick Darnell*

(darnell@montana.com)

IN THIS PART

Introducing HTML 4.0

PART

I

HTML 4.0 Overview

by Rick Darnell

CHAPTER

1

Welcome to the brave new world of the latest HTML recommendation from the World Wide Web Consortium (W3C). Although it's hard for a lot of casual Web users to understand, this set of specifications is really pretty exciting.

HTML 4.0 picks up the pieces left behind at HTML 3.2. HTML 3.2 started life as HTML 3.0, which included proposals for many of the features found in HTML 4.0. However, the timing wasn't right for HTML 3.0—it got bogged down in the approval process and was never formally accepted as a standard. There was a lot of disagreement on how the new features should be represented in the standard and how different browsers would interpret them. So, HTML 3.2 was developed as a new standard that dropped most of the advanced features originally proposed for HTML 3.0, including advanced table settings, events, and other items. Instead of leading the evolution of HTML, the standards process became a reflection of currently accepted practice and adoption of proprietary markup.

Now the members of the W3C HTML Working Group and the other groups and subcommittees have had a chance to regroup and refocus their efforts. The result is a new HTML specification that returns to the roots of a structured markup language, while implementing powerful means to control appearance and allowances for up-and-coming dynamic behavior.

NOTE

This book covers the latest information available on the draft HTML 4.0 specification, known as *WD-html40-970917*. This abbreviation stands for "Working Draft of HTML 4.0 as of September 9, 1997." It's an essentially stable draft, which shouldn't change significantly before its acceptance as an official recommendation. For more information on its status, check the W3C Web site (see the following Tip).

TIP

The Web site of the World Wide Web Consortium is `http://www.w3.org/`. It includes draft recommendations, final proposals, and information on other W3C projects, such as the Amaya Web browser.

But all of this background is just generalities. Take some time during the next few pages to see what's happened since HTML 3.2.

New Features

There are several new tags and new features in HTML 4.0. One of the first notable differences is the support of identification and event capturing for practically every element in the body of a Web page. The id attribute is supported for everything from headings to tables to form elements to blockquotes and all points in between. By assigning a unique name to an element, you can reference it for anchors and Dynamic HTML features.

The expanded event coverage was introduced by Netscape in its Navigator 2.0 release with JavaScript, except the events were limited to a handful of tags—primarily hyperlinks and form elements. With the advent of Dynamic HTML and document-wide scripting, events are now supported for virtually every element that contains any sort of content, including images, anchors, paragraphs, tables (including individual rows, cells, and columns), and other inline and block elements.

Another big piece of news for HTML 4.0 is the shift from tag-based appearance features (such as <B> for bold) to style sheets. This shift is the result of a long-standing debate between HTML purists and Web page designers. The purists insist that tags should indicate structure and content only—given the incredible variety of applications and platforms for viewing pages, the author should not be able to dictate a page's appearance. On the other side are the designers, who take advantage of every quirk and idiosyncrasy of various HTML implementations to make their pages look just right; it's a competitive world and they want to make sure their pages are on the cutting edge.

By deprecating the tags and attributes that affect appearance (see the next section, "Deprecated Features"), the purists return to a kinder, gentler HTML that doesn't allow both <EM> and <I> to create emphasis in a document. By adding style sheets, designers now have a whole new set of tools in their page-creation grab bag, including advanced font specification, background colors for individual elements, and global styles. One advantage of this development is that the coolest pages can be viewed by both Lynx and Internet Explorer 4.0, and users of both browsers will get the full benefit of the content without a bunch of extra proprietary tags getting in the way.

The <OBJECT> tag was also expanded to encompass virtually any external file you could possibly place on a Web page, including applets, embedded controls, plug-ins, images, sounds, and anything else that comes to mind. With its expanded attribute list and support for parameters and alternative text, the <OBJECT> tag is shaping up to usurp the use of several tags, including <EMBED>, <APPLET>, and <IMG>. One faction is also arguing to use <OBJECT> in place of <IFRAME> for inline frames.

Beyond the global implications of the new attributes and style sheets, HTML 4.0 also introduces several new structure tags, listed in Table 1.1.

Table 1.1. New structure tags in HTML 4.

Tag	Description
<Q>	For inline quotes. <Q> is a cousin to <BLOCKQUOTE>, with <Q> being an inline element and <BLOCKQUOTE> acting as its own paragraph.

continues

Table 1.1. continued

Tag	Description
`<INS>` and `<DEL>`	For documents under current revision, when maintaining the history of changes is important. `<INS>` marks inserted text with the date of insertion, and `<DEL>` provides the same service for deleted text.
`<ACRONYM>`	A new structure tag similar to `<ADDRESS>`. It marks a group of letters that stand for something else, such as *SCBA* for *self-contained breathing apparatus.*
`<COLGROUP>`	Identifies a collection of columns in a table for formatting. It allows designers to easily select entire columns of a table for setting width and alignment properties.
`<FIELDSET>`	Groups form elements into logical groups. This new tag also comes with a companion called `<LEGEND>` to provide a visible label for the group of form controls.
`<BUTTON>`	A feature-rich button for forms. This button serves as a jack-of-all-trades beyond the usual Submit and Reset buttons. It can submit forms, calculate totals, invoke scripts, interact with objects, and include rich formatting, such as colors, different fonts and sizes for text, and images.

The last big addition, and one of the most controversial, is frames. HTML 4.0 will include frame sets and frames as part of the official standard, much to the chagrin of many Web users and authors who can't stand the things. However, the W3C decided that frames were in broad enough use, so it would be a good idea to at least standardize what's there so they could work on a better implementation of the frames idea. Love frames or hate them—they're now an official part of HTML.

Of course, with all the new bells and whistles, there are also some tags and attributes that didn't fare so well. These are the *deprecated* elements—they're still in the standard, but not for long.

Deprecated Features

What is a *deprecated feature*? It's a tag or attribute that has been part of previous HTML standards, but is no longer needed or is detrimental to HTML's further growth. These items are left in the standard for the current revision, but will probably be removed as obsolete by the next revision of HTML.

> **TIP**
>
> If you're using deprecated elements with the strict HTML 4 Document Type Definition (see Chapter 4, "The HTML Document Type Definition") and process your documents through HTML validation at the W3C site, your page will generate errors. The deprecated elements are part of the "casual" HTML Document Type Definition only.

Remember all the hoopla about style sheets? The appearance and structure of a document are finally separated and placed in separate locations where they belong. However, this separation also means that tags such as <FONT> have come to the end of their usefulness because their behavior is now handled by the style sheet. The appearance tags that are now deprecated include <CENTER>, <FONT>, <BASEFONT>, <STRIKE> (also <S>), and <U>. It's a fairly safe bet that the other appearance tags, such as <B> and <I>, are also headed for obsolescence by the next version of HTML.

In the meantime, see Chapter 17, "Simple Style with Text," to see how to work with what's left, and Chapter 7, "Text Alignment and Formatting," for information on working with logical styles.

In addition to the deprecated appearance tags, the appearance attributes for many elements are also on their way out. They include the color information that could be included with the <BODY> tag, such as bgcolor, color, and link. The align attribute for paragraph and other block tags is also deprecated for the same reasons.

Other elements slated for disposal include the following:

- **<APPLET>:** Introduced by Netscape to support Java applets, this tag's role is now filled by the <OBJECT> tag, which has been expanded to serve all file insertion tasks (see Chapter 16, "Embedding Objects in HTML").

- **<ISINDEX>:** This tag is used to generate a text field to input a search term for a Web index. This function has now been shifted to forms and CGI scripts (see Chapter 15, "Building and Using HTML Forms").

- **<DIR> and <MENU>:** Essentially, these elements duplicate the functions of the unordered list tag <UL> (see Chapter 8, "Using Lists to Organize Information"). They were placed in this category because most browsers really don't distinguish between these two tags and an unordered list.

Dead Features

This is the boneyard of obsolete elements no longer found anywhere in the HTML standard. In a year or so, you'll be lucky to find a current browser that still supports them.

The three elements that were axed in HTML 4.0 are <XMP>, <PLAINTEXT>, and <LISTING>. All three produced the same result—preformatted text that presented characters, punctuation, and spaces in a monospace font. This function is the same one served by the <PRE> element, which is still an active part of HTML. All three elements were deprecated in HTML 3.2, and their removal is official with HTML 4.0.

Summary

You've read about the changes in a nutshell. Is HTML 4.0 the "perfect HTML?" Of course not. As long as there's more than one person working on it, there are going to be differences over what it should and shouldn't do and what should and shouldn't be a part of the standard.

The general consensus in the Web community is that HTML 4.0 is a solid step forward from HTML 3.2, with its style sheet implementation of appearance control, an expanded model for tables, support for the emerging Dynamic HTML technologies, and enhancements to forms.

As appearance elements are deprecated and removed in the future, HTML will continue to focus on structure markup, and new appearance controls will develop within the confines of the <STYLE> tag.

All in all, it's a solid standard that was thoroughly evaluated and implemented. It has its flaws, but the worst of the HTML evolution is over for now. As a result, authors and developers have gotten a new and more efficient set of tags to build their Web pages.

And I'm glad you're here to learn about it! There are only 41 more chapters to go, so let's get started...

What Is Hypertext Markup Language?

by Rick Darnell

IN THIS CHAPTER

CHAPTER 2

Although many people think hypertext markup language (HTML) consists of the tags put into a World Wide Web page, the concepts behind HTML have a long history. This chapter presents a glimpse of some of the people and ideas that have led to our Web of text, images, animation, sound, and other features.

I'll begin with a concept—nonlinear information—to give you a starting point for learning about the HTML that's used to build current Web pages. Take heart—it's not as technical and dry as it sounds.

Working with Nonlinear Information

What is *nonlinear information*? To answer that question, let's take a step back and consider linear information. It's one of the most common ways we communicate with each other. *Linear*, by its root *line*, is an adjective that means relating to or resembling a straight line. So linear information must be information that progresses in a straight line, beginning at point A and ending at point B with a set path in between.

A novel is an example of linear information. You begin at page one and proceed to the end. This type of reading presents the information in a line, and you receive the plot and characters in the order they were intended, so by the end everything makes sense.

Could you read a novel in a nonlinear fashion? Certainly. Just pick pages at random until you've read the entire book. The novel has been read, but because the information has been taken out of its intended order, chances are you'll have no real concept of what the book was about.

Does this mean nonlinear information creates confusion? Not necessarily. It depends on how it's used. A magazine is a good example of a resource set up to take advantage of a nonlinear structure. Using the table of contents, you can turn to the page of an article that interests you. You'll probably come across a phrase such as "continued on page 58" that leads you to the end of the article several pages later (after some important advertisements) or near the back of the magazine. This form of reading is nonlinear because you didn't have to read everything between the table of contents and the beginning of the article to make sense of what the article was about. Likewise, you didn't have to read the intervening pages between the point where the article leaves off and where it's completed.

A similar analogy exists in musical formats. A cassette tape of music is a linear format. It's designed to be heard from one end of the tape to the other. You can try to skip directly to your favorite song at the end of the tape, but you still have to fast-forward through all the other songs that come before. However, a compact disc is a nonlinear format. You can select any track on the CD and hear it instantly, without waiting to move through the other tracks on the disc.

Early Attempts at Nonlinear Information Systems

Entire philosophies and concepts of nonlinear information systems have been put on paper, but the paper itself was the shortcoming of all the suggested systems. The requirement that nonlinear information systems be affixed to paper doomed the majority of them to eventual failure. A few hangers-on are still with us, such as 3×5 notecards in a box and filing cabinets, but most have disappeared.

People have tried to make these nonlinear systems even more user-friendly, such as the invention to help organize research notes on index cards. One company made the cards with holes along the edges, allowing users to cut notches in the cards. The holes were numbered so that researchers could assign certain topics to certain numbers. A person could put a knitting needle through a deck of cards at the appropriate hole and shake the deck, causing the notched cards to fall out and the selected cards to remain on the knitting needle. Those cards could be sorted again by subsequent rounds of poking and shaking to eventually place the cards in a usable order for translating into a research paper.

Of course, there was a lot of legwork to be completed first. The researcher and various assistants had to compile the information onto the cards, create the index, notch where appropriate, and so on to have a usable system. If they wanted to share cards among a group, then everyone had to use the same indexing and notching scheme, and any cards pulled for use by one researcher were unavailable to the others.

Enter Vannevar Bush, the director of the Office of Scientific Research and Development under Franklin Roosevelt during World War II. Bush had worked with optical devices on machines for rapid selection of specified spools of microfilm, and used his tenure in the Roosevelt administration to refine his ideas on storing and retrieving vast amounts of data using links to the user. He used terms such as *trails* and *footprints* to describe the path of a user through different sources of information.

After World War II, Bush described the hardware of what could be called the first browser. It was an incredibly complicated affair, which consisted of a desk with translucent projection screens embedded in the top, a keyboard, buttons, and levers. The "content"—such as books, magazines, and papers from other researchers—was purchased on microfilm. The desk also had the capability to record original work, such as notes and diagrams, on microfilm for later display. Books were called up by typing a code, then projected on the screens while using a lever to control the speed of changing pages. When new material was created, it was assigned a code, which was stored in an index along with the codes for all the other available content.

Bush also took the next leap in indexing by allowing associative indexing. Users could cause any item at any time to immediately select another item. The concept was that the user could build a trail where items are joined and immediately recalled by merely tapping a button. The trails could also overlap and interconnect, so that once created, a user could follow the trail at will, including tangents and side excursions.

Origins of Hypertext Markup Language

From the fabulous interactive desk, we take a jump to the 1960s and a man by the name of Ted Nelson. Nelson held a degree in philosophy and had returned to school to earn a master's in sociology. While taking a computer class designed for humanities students, he realized the potential of computers in the areas of thinking and writing. This was still the era of big mainframes, punchcards, and tape readers, so the connection wasn't an obvious one at the time.

Nelson continued to pursue the idea and ended up with a vision of a system he called Xanadu, which included the first use of the word *hypertext*. In this and subsequent works, he proposed nonsequential writing, saying that writing had always been sequential because pages were sequential and there was no alternative. Nelson proposed using the computer to propel our minds into the hyperspace of thought. He called the new realm of immediately available text and graphics *hyperworld* and the storage system *hyperfile*.

Despite its creative and innovative approach, Xanadu was never carried out. Nelson announced releases due in 1976, 1988, 1991, and 1995, all of which went unfulfilled. *DATAMATION* magazine called Xanadu the first example of vaporware.

Among the problems delaying Xanadu are the coinages of terms and the changes in terminology that have marked its progression. Nelson has used terms such as *xanalogics*, *humbers*, *docuverses*, and *tumbler arithmetic*. Understanding what everything means and keeping up with the new names makes any broad acceptance of Xanadu an uphill battle. Although his concepts are alive and well in today's World Wide Web, Xanadu itself seems to have sunk to the depths to rest with its namesake.

In another fabulous arena was Bill Atkinson, who created a lot of wonderful software for Apple's Macintosh computer, including MacPaint and MultiFinder. In 1987, Apple Computer introduced Atkinson's HyperCard to the world. HyperCard uses the graphics abilities of the Macintosh computer to show a virtual deck of cards on its screen. The cards themselves can contain text, sound, video, or pictures, along with buttons and other navigation aids for the user to go from one card to the other.

HyperCards are created in an interpreted language called *HyperTalk*, which is similar to English and can be read and understood without a great deal of study. Using HyperTalk, script authors can create cards, accept keyboard or mouse input from the user, act on the input, and display the results. People have scripted complex programs and games using HyperTalk, although it can be relatively slow.

HyperCard suffers from several drawbacks, including the lack of links. The only option an author has for links are clickable buttons, which must be placed so they don't obscure any text on the screen. Adding text to a card might require the author to rewrite the location of all the navigation buttons. Originally, HyperCard supported only one card size in black and white, with just one card visible at a time. Like Bush's "integrated desktop" of the late 1940s, the HyperCard was still constrained to the universe of the computer it resided on.

Despite their limitations, the cards filled a need at the time and became very popular. The HyperCard concept has matured, thanks to development by other vendors. It's currently sold as a separate product from Macintosh.

The next real step was to tie the functions of HyperCard with the concepts of Xanadu, which finally occurred at the European Laboratory for Particle Physics (CERN).

The World Wide Web: The First Practical Nonlinear Information System

With many of the ideas, hardware, and software in place for the first time, nonlinear information systems have become workable. The solution came from Tim Berners-Lee, an English scientist at the European Laboratory for Particle Physics. He saw the difficulties that scientists from different countries had in communicating with each other. Although he had been hired to work on a high-energy particle accelerator, he became involved in an effort to facilitate communication between scientists.

Earlier in his career, he wrote a program called Enquire that allowed him to create associations in his personal notes, in an effort to make notetaking and notekeeping work more closely with the way we think. That idea carried over into his new concept for using computers to help users look at a database of ideas with hypertext as the query mechanism. In Berners-Lee's model, the "mcta" database is made up of as many databases as necessary on as many computers as necessary, with no single person in charge of the data or the database. Everybody could keep his or her data current and make the results available by computer. Everybody would have access to all the data and could build relationships by linking and bookmarking links. There would be no chasm between different disciplines; interdisciplinary knowledge would be readily available and easily searched and viewed. Building bridges between disciplines would be as easy as making a link.

In developing his idea, Berners-Lee also made several other developments that led to the World Wide Web as we know it. First, he realized that a hierarchical system of information would collapse under its own weight. He also saw that the information on a system would not be limited to text and that indexing would limit access to information and hide it from those who needed data from a different context. His answer to the problems was distributed hypertext, where people kept their data on their computer, but the computers were linked on a network with the data publicly available on the network.

Berners-Lee wrote the server and client software on his computer, and then distribution began among his fellow scientists. Along with his colleagues, he grappled with the protocols and ended up with URLs (Uniform Resource Locators), HTTP (Hypertext Transport Protocol), and HTML.

The Creation of HTML

When Tim Berners-Lee was faced with many options for implementing his concepts, he chose Standard Generalized Markup Language (SGML). This decision has led to the Web's independence from any individual operating system or language. He also set the stage for the ongoing debate over just what HTML is supposed to be used for.

SGML is an internationally recognized standard for text information processing that provides an organized way to structure content for broad use. Documents marked according to rules outlined in SGML have two basic elements—the content and information about the content.

This structured approach to markup was ideal for Berners-Lee's purpose. A scientist could create content, SGML markup could be added later, and the resulting document could be made available through the network to anyone with network access. Sound familiar?

SGML is platform independent, requiring only a computer and the appropriate software to parse (analyze) the documents to make sense of the data. The parsing software was somewhat customized for each user to take advantage of the machine he or she happened to be using at the time. It was up to each individual parsing program to display the markup text in an appropriate fashion for the platform—so a Heading 1 was different from a Heading 2, and an Emphasis looked different from a Strong. Because the markup identified only the nature of the content, it was the reader's responsibility to decide how to represent the particular levels of meaning for the platform.

Before HTML, a document author didn't have to care how the document would appear on someone's monitor. It was accepted that appearance was the province of the user. HTML authors couldn't specify font names or sizes, margins, white space between elements, or any other graphical feature.

PRACTICAL HYPERTEXT MARKUP THEORY

The author of a nonlinear information system must furnish a method of linking related ideas and a search mechanism for specific queries that might not have obvious answers. Ultimately, a nonlinear information system can have no bounds. With a uniform linking mechanism, the reader isn't restricted to an author's work, but can follow links to source documents anywhere in the world. These benefits are also drawbacks if they are poorly implemented. Maintaining context in a hypertext world is difficult but necessary.

With that said, here is the basis of the hypertext world we call the World Wide Web. To prepare hypertext, information is chunked into small, manageable units called *nodes*. *Hyperlinks* leading to different nodes are then embedded into the nodes. The process of navigating among the nodes by using their links is called *browsing*. A collection of nodes interconnected by hyperlinks is called a *web*, which makes the World Wide Web a global hypertext system.

Effective design for hypertext documents that are part of a nonlinear system is more difficult than designing for narrative text. This problem has led to several methods that are useful for designing Web pages. One method is dividing the text into chunks that deal with one theme, topic, or idea. After the material is "chunked," it must be written so that it can be read as a standalone node by a reader who might have come to that node from any of several links supplied by the author or from a search engine.

The author can't assume that the reader has any information from "earlier" passages, as is the case with narrative text writing. Poorly chunked nodes can result in a procession of information bits with no context and little content, or in a node that's an unreadable collection of links shouting for attention and overwhelming the content.

Linear text develops its context from everything that has come before. In nonlinear information systems such as the Web, words such as *later* or *previous* become context traps for the author. In a hypertext situation, "later" might never come and "previous" might never have been. A reader can even follow a link to another node before finishing the current node and never return to the original node.

Each node must not only be correctly chunked, but it must also be written so that it supplies a set of context clues that a reader with no prior link to that node can use to become oriented to the information being presented.

One option is to provide links to a hierarchy where readers can orient themselves, if they must, and connect to other relevant nodes. In addition, links within the document must have a purpose that's obvious to people coming into the node from other Web sites.

The Evolution of HTML

One of the requirements for creating a usable nonlinear information system is to make the system easy for nonexperts to understand and use. Unlike AppleScript, HyperTalk, and WinHelp files, marking up text for presentation on the Web uses a limited set of tags that are simple and easy to understand. This simplicity was difficult to come by and is rapidly disappearing under the onslaught of new attributes for graphical interfaces.

Level 0 HTML

In using SGML to describe how to format content, Berners-Lee made use of another aspect of SGML—its ability to define other languages. Berners-Lee and his colleagues used SGML to describe the rules for hypertext markup language in a document type definition (DTD), the basis for the structure of documents on the World Wide Web. DTDs are discussed in greater detail in Chapter 4, "The HTML Document Type Definition."

In its first implementation, HTML followed the SGML rules of platform-independent content markup with no provisions for representing the document in HTML itself. Users had to provide formatting through their browser-platform combination (the client), and the client wasn't known at the time of document creation.

HTML was at Level 0 in its first implementation in 1990. At that time, the means of communication over the Internet included e-mail, FTP (file transfer protocol), and Telnet, all using TCP/IP (transmission control protocol/Internet protocol). Gopher was becoming a popular means of indexing information, and Gopher servers were being introduced to the Internet along with Archie, Veronica, and Jughead. WAIS (Wide Area Information Server) was also being introduced as a means of providing access, especially to students on college campuses. To allow worldwide access to HTML documents, Berners-Lee and his associates introduced the idea of HTTP and URLs to supply addresses and a means of locating the data.

At Level 0, HTML offered a platform-independent means of marking data for interchange. The concept was that servers would store and supply data and clients would retrieve and display it. Therefore, the HTML nodes could provide access not only to other HTML nodes, but also to Gopher space, FTP, Network News, and so on.

HTML 0.0 was very close to SGML. The only required element was the TITLE element, and many older pages still start with a title and then go straight into the text. There's no HTML, no HEAD, no BODY. A <P> tag was often used at the end of each paragraph to separate paragraphs. There were six levels of headings, but with the expectation that each level would be used only once and that the levels would be used sequentially.

Level 0 allowed a <BODY> tag, and authors could include addresses, anchors, blockquotes, line breaks, headings, images, lists, paragraphs, and preformatted text.

Level 1 HTML

Discussions over HTML 0 brought to light several shortcomings, so in 1992, Dan Connolly began developing HTML 1.0, which was released on the Internet the same year. The idea of an HTML container was added, with a HEAD element separate from the BODY element. Opening and closing tags were required for some elements.

Along with TITLE, the HEAD element could contain the attributes of ISINDEX, LINK, and BASE, giving the document a context within a larger universe. Along with the ANCHOR element, the IMAGE element allowed GIF (graphics interchange format) files to be displayed within the text if the browser supported that format. The horizontal rule was also introduced, beginning the slide down the slippery slope of giving the author some control over the document's final appearance to the user.

Level 1 also introduced forms, which make it possible for authors to have input fields on their nodes that allow feedback from users and open the door to considering interaction through Common Gateway Interface (CGI) scripting. The potential of forms and CGI scripts is still evolving, even with the addition of new form capabilities in HTML 4 (see Chapter 15, "Building and Using HTML Forms" and Chapter 25, "Understanding the Common Gateway Interface").

Other tags introduced with Level 1 included the CITE and CODE elements, along with style elements that implied usage and not appearance: KBD (keyboard), SAMP (sample output), STRONG (strong emphasis), and VAR (variable or program argument). It also included elements for B (bold),

I (italic), and TT (teletype monospace). While Level 1 was under discussion, additional elements and capabilities were being proposed as HTML+ waited in the wings.

HTML+ and the Advent of Graphics

Another early pioneer of the Web, Dave Raggett, proposed another extension of HTML called HTML+, which incorporated graphical and display elements into HTML. By incorporating these elements, HTML+ could take advantage of the capabilities of Mosaic and other graphics-based browsers becoming available. HTML+ offered a means for linking to and accessing PostScript documents, JPEG images, MPEG movies, and sounds. MIME (Multipurpose Internet Mail Extensions) was used to allow the extension of HTML file types; the data available over the Web wasn't restricted by the 7-bit ASCII conventions of the Internet. This proposal removed the limits to the types of data available on the Internet. With the developments that came before, there was no limitation on the number of computers, number of users, or amount and type of data.

HTML+ was an important step forward for HTML. Raggett included elements and attributes for superscripts and subscripts, footnotes, margins, inserted and deleted text, alignment of content, tabs, tables, mathematical formulas, extended sets of character entities, and figures.

With HTML+, Raggett sought to extend HTML beyond the concept of an article with hyperlinks placed on a computer. He introduced HTML+ as the means to link beyond text to sound files, moving images, PostScript, and any other format introduced with MIME extensions.

Even with his introduction of elements for visual formatting and control, Raggett wouldn't deal with instructions on appearance and kept his proposal within the constraints of SGML. Elements, attributes and values remained case insensitive in accordance with SGML rules. HTML+ parsers ignored tags they didn't recognize, allowing authors and users to use other SGML markup in HTML documents for indexing and other processing outside HTML. To make sure browsers would detect HTML+ and render it correctly, it was suggested that a document identifier be used that preceded all other information in the document, including the <HTML> tag. This identifier is still part of the HTML standard, appearing as the <!DOCTYPE> tag.

HTML 2

Increasing demands on HTML led the newly formed World Wide Web Consortium (W3C) to introduce HTML 2 (see the section "The World Wide Web Consortium" later in this chapter for more information about W3C). Level 2 used the FORM element with INPUT, SELECT, OPTION, and TEXTAREA, plus the BR element for line breaks.

HTML 2 also added the META element for detailed document description and an avenue for indexing and cataloging the contents. It also changed the descriptions of the head and body sections and the anchor, base, lists, image, link, and title elements.

The W3C development group for HTML 2 crafted a draft specification that maintained backward compatibility with existing HTML standards. The DTD also provided for optional container tags, such as the <P> tag.

HTML 2 didn't break any new ground as far as HTML's capabilities. Rather, it carried on and made official the status quo. It was workable for all current user agents because it followed the rules established by SGML, and it didn't require extensive debate because there was no controversy over whether the proposed elements were necessary.

> **TIP**
>
> You will see the term *user agent* occasionally in this book. For these discussions, you can consider *user agent* synonymous with *browser*. In reality, a user agent is any application that can process an HTML document.

With an official ruling by the W3C, the world now had a standard HTML to serve as a benchmark against which browsers and markup could be measured.

HTML 3

HTML 3 was proposed as an attempt to address the competing demands for a markup language that operated across all platforms and for a page description language that was acceptable to software companies besides Netscape. The theory was that HTML 3 would be fully SGML compliant, but allow hints to browsers on how to display certain text. HTML 3 was developed under the stewardship of Dave Raggett, who also supplied the impetus behind HTML+ and contributed to HTML 2.

Elements proposed for HTML 3 included a FIG element that supported text flow around figures. Support was also suggested for mathematical equations, and a TABLE element to help format tabular data without the hassle of the PRE element.

The ALIGN attribute was added to several elements, including IMG, P, and HR, allowing authors to provide for left, right, or center justification. On the character level, HTML 3 also proposed some new logical elements, including tags for definitions, quotations, language, inserted text, and deleted text. Some of the proposed physical tags were underlined text, bigger and smaller text, subscript, and superscript. Additional attributes were also proposed for background images, tabs, footnotes, and banners.

Consideration was also given to style sheets in HTML 3. By removing the majority of display-oriented elements from HTML and placing them in style sheets, the purity of an SGML language could be preserved while still offering a way for authors to incorporate graphical design on the Web.

Several books were written about the migration from Level 2 to Level 3 and the dangers of using markup not yet approved as a standard. HTML 2 existed as a standard, but HTML 3 languished in the draft process as Microsoft and Netscape both pushed ahead with browser developments. By the time the HTML 3 draft had expired, Microsoft had introduced its Internet Explorer, and Netscape Navigator had advanced to another version—and neither browser was limited to the current or proposed standard. With all the different forms of HTML available, confusion and aggravation reigned.

HTML 3.2

In the end, HTML 3 was too ambitious. HTML 3.2 was drafted in acknowledgment of reality and incorporated many of the tags already in heavy use on Web pages. It added the SCRIPT and STYLE tags to make room for scripting languages and style sheets. It formalized practices such as colors for backgrounds, text, and links and sizing, alignment, and spacing for images.

HTML 3.2 was the new standard, replacing HTML 2. It offered new elements and attributes that enlivened Web pages with animation, colors, and sound. It made it possible to create attractive, dynamic Web pages that complied with an established standard. There was some disagreement on who was setting the standards, but at least a formally recognized DTD was now available.

HTML 4

The latest version of HTML uses some of the ideas and changes proposed for HTML 3 that were abandoned with HTML 3.2. HTML 4 allows separating physical styles from the content markup by relying more on style sheets. Many see the style sheet solution as the best way to suggest a document's appearance yet still allow full use of HTML as an SGML-compliant method of bridging the chasm between users and operating systems.

HTML 4 also serves some of the same purpose as HTML 3.2 by acknowledging current practice. The FRAME element is now formally defined somewhere other than Netscape or Microsoft. To address the competing interests between applets, plug-ins, and ActiveX controls, the W3C has introduced the OBJECT element, along with enough flexibility to serve in other roles in the future.

The new standard for HTML also makes use of other W3C proposals for the Web. Rather than incorporate all the functionality for a Web page into one standard, HTML 4 works with interfaces to many other standards. The HTML 4 standard includes the STYLE, DIV, and SPAN elements for incorporating style sheets, but the actual style sheet specification is a separate entity, as in Cascading Style Sheets 1.

The World Wide Web Consortium

During a workshop in July 1993, Berners-Lee proposed founding a consortium to handle the problems of establishing standards for HTML and HTTP. He and his employer weren't the proper group to maintain the standards, so a consortium was suggested as the body to establish a reference model for the standards, test proposals to determine compliance, and award a stamp of approval.

The W3C Charter

As a result of Berners-Lee's proposal, the World Wide Web Consortium (W3C) was formed in 1994 to try to bring some much needed order to the HTML world. Founded as an industry consortium, W3C's goal is developing common standards for the evolution of the World Wide Web. Members of the consortium may propose standards for adoption; once adopted, those standards are used by members in their software, whether server or client. The W3C is also trying to develop faster, more efficient Web protocols for images, sounds and video.

The Work of the W3C

How does the W3C get its work done? The first step is identifying an issue or technology that affects the World Wide Web. The W3C governing body, called the Advisory Committee, appoints a working group that consists of experts gathered to work together toward resolving a particular well-defined technical issue, such as HTML standards.

The working group develops a series of *working drafts* until they've reached a stable consensus and agreement. Then, if the W3C director approves, the draft is promoted to a *Proposed Recommendation*, also called a *Draft Recommendation*, which is sent to all W3C members for comment. Depending on the number and nature of the comments, the W3C director can issue the result as a *Recommendation* as-is or with minor changes, return it to the working group, or scrap it altogether.

If it's any consolation, W3C doesn't work with a blind eye to the industry it affects. The W3C is hosted by Massachusetts Institute of Technology, but the members of its committees are representative of World Wide Web companies, including organizations such as Microsoft, Netscape, Sun Microsystems, IBM, and others. Although it costs a lot of money for an organization to join W3C, no single organization or company has more influence in the W3C's final recommendation than any other.

With both Netscape and Microsoft as members of the W3C, the W3C has become the battleground for the heart and soul of the Web. The charter of the consortium—to bring order to the growth of HTML and HTTP protocols—has taken a back seat to the commercial interests and posturing of some of the consortium's members. Although many had predicted that bringing Netscape into the fold would force the company to give up its renegade ways, the tide of commerce inexorably flows into the conference room. Even as attempts are made to pull standards back from software vendors, new HTML standards still include items that bow to the reality of proprietary tags introduced by Microsoft and Netscape, such as frames.

Summary

A combination of three factors made Berners-Lee the creator of the Web. First, he worked during a time when computers were powerful enough, small enough, and cheap enough to be used as the infrastructure of the World Wide Web. That was an occurrence Berners-Lee couldn't have orchestrated.

The second factor was his ability to see beyond a particular need and a particular solution, to see instead the realization of a great theme reaching down through time to the right moment with the right tools—an efficient way to store and retrieve nonlinear information. The third factor was chance: Berners-Lee was in the right place at the right time to have the tools that Vannevar Bush lacked.

Berners-Lee used the tools he had at hand, invented what he didn't have, wrote software, drafted proposals, and coordinated the efforts of many people to get his idea into working order. The rest, as they say, is history.

Structure of an HTML Document

by Rick Darnell

IN THIS CHAPTER

The Hypertext Markup Language is all about structure. Yes, there have been some inroads by appearance-oriented material, but at the heart, HTML is about defining the structure of a document.

After all, a markup language is used to describe what purpose each piece of the document fills in relation to the others. It can indicate that one piece of text is a third-level heading, that the section below is a paragraph, and that the last piece is an address. Within the paragraph, you can mark citations, acronyms, and other special pieces of text. The result is a document in which you can see the *purpose* of each piece of text, instead of the intended appearance.

In contrast, the publishing programs most computer users are familiar with (Microsoft Word and Publisher, Aldus Pagemaker) emphasize the document's appearance rather than its structure. Instead of indicating the text's purpose, authors directly select type faces, colors, margins, and borders to precisely control what the final page looks like.

This chapter takes a look at the structural aspect of an HTML document, beginning with its big pieces, and descending down into the details. The appearance aspect of an HTML document is controlled with style sheets, which are mentioned in this chapter as a piece of the structure. Detailed explanations and examples are found in Part IV, "Presentation Techniques," and Part VII, "Effective Web Page Design."

HTML TERMINOLOGY

Before you take a look at the structure of HTML and its related issues, it's important to establish a common ground for terms. Here's a list of definitions of terms that are used throughout this chapter and book.

- **Attribute:** An attribute supplies additional instructions to the browser about a tag. The information varies from tag to tag and can include such items as file locations, size, name, or style.

- **Browser:** A Web browser is a special type of parsing engine that evaluates the tags and content of an HTML file and displays it according to the capabilities and rules of the file's own capabilities and platform. For example, a text-only browser displays the alternative text for an image, but a graphical browser displays the actual image. A browser for a monochrome platform ignores the color settings from a style sheet or renders them as shades of gray.

- **DTD (Document Type Definition):** A collection of rules written in Standard Generalized Markup Language (SGML) that define the syntax and structure of a specific type of document, such as HTML (see Chapter 4, "The HTML Document Type Definition").

- **Element:** A distinctive component of a document's structure, such as a title, paragraph, or list. When referred to in its applied form within a document, an element is also called a *tag*. In this book, *element* is used interchangeably with *tag*.

> ■ **Tag:** A code that identifies an element so that a browser or other parser knows how to display its contents. Tags are surrounded by special delimiter characters (angle brackets). In this book, *tag* is used interchangeably with *element*.

There are three basic levels to the structure of an HTML document. First is the document structure, where the document is divided into major sections depending on their purpose, such as the head, body, and script components.

Second is the divisions within each of the major sections. This level primarily applies to the head and body, as each one has its own unique groups of content, such as titles, metadata, divisions, paragraphs, forms, and headings.

The third level exists primarily within the body. It's the substructure of elements and their children, such as lists and list items, forms and form elements, and tables with table rows and data cells.

You'll explore each of these major sections, their purposes, and their contents in this chapter.

The Structure of a Document

Every HTML document, by its very creation, has two main parts: a head and a body. Even if they're not explicitly identified, HTML assumes their existence. HTML also offers the chance to add additional functional components to the page in the form of style sheets, scripts, and frame sets.

However, I'm getting a bit ahead of myself. Although they are part of the definition of an HTML document, two tags exist outside the document structure: `<!DOCTYPE>` and `<HTML>`. The first tag identifies the version of HTML used for the current page and the rules it has agreed to follow. The latter tag identifies a global language and text direction for the document, in addition to serving as a container to mark the beginning and end of the HTML contents. Both elements are explained in more detail in Chapter 6, "Structuring Text."

With these two tags in hand, you could create an HTML document with the following three lines:

```
<!DOCTYPE HTML PUBLIC "-//W3C//DTD HTML 4.0//EN">
<HTML>
</HTML>
```

It wouldn't look like much on a browser. As a matter of fact, it wouldn't display anything at all. However, a browser that conforms to HTML standards is going to automatically view the document as though it were written like this:

```
<!DOCTYPE HTML PUBLIC "-//W3C//DTD HTML 4.0//EN">
<HTML>
<HEAD>
```

```
</HEAD>
<BODY>
</BODY>
</HTML>
```

As I said, every HTML document is assumed to have a head and a body, even if they aren't explicitly defined.

> **TIP**
>
> At this point, I'm going to recommend that you not depend on the browser to define the beginning and end of the head and body. You should take the time to include these elements as part of every document you create. It's the professional thing to do, and it saves time and effort in later revisions and editing.

The HEAD element includes a variety of information for the browser, including a title for the document, keywords, link information, and other information that's not necessarily for the user to experience directly. For more information on composing the HEAD element, see Chapter 6.

The BODY is what the end user sees when the document is rendered on the browser. It includes text and objects, such as images and applets, along with markup tags to define their structure and relationship to each other.

There are three more optional components in the HTML document structure: style sheets, scripts, and frame sets. These elements must be defined explicitly, or the browser won't assume their existence.

A style sheet, created with the STYLE element, is a new addition to HTML. It gives you a new way to define how a document looks, including a choice of typeface and font, colors, borders, margins, and alignment. In the past, this formatting was handled by adding attributes or tags directly to the body. By adding the style sheet as a structural element to the document, the appearance and content are separated to give browsers more precise control. Style sheets are covered in much more detail in Chapters 18, "Using Cascading Style Sheets," 19, "Cascading Style Sheets and Element Positioning," and 21, "Using JavaScript Style Sheets."

The SCRIPT element encloses a section of programming code included directly on the Web page. This element gives the user a way to interact directly with a document, without relying on interaction with a Web server. A document could include more than one script in more than one language. Current popular choices for scripting languages are JavaScript (Chapter 23, "JavaScript at a Glance") and VBScript (Chapter 24, "Using VBScript"). Other choices include Python and Perl.

The last optional element is FRAMESET, which gives the browser directions on subdividing its window into a set of smaller windows, each with its own unique content. In essence, each window becomes its own "mini-browser" that can host a new HTML document. The FRAMESET element is closely related to the BODY element. On frames-capable browsers, the FRAMESET element supersedes the BODY element. On nonframe browsers, the FRAMESET element is ignored and the BODY element is used. Implementing frame sets is covered in Chapter 20, "Creating Frames."

The Structure of a Section

Of the major HTML document elements, each has its own unique structure and requirements, reflected in the purpose defined for that element. Two of the document elements listed in the previous section, STYLE and SCRIPT, are unique in that their structure depends on their content.

In the case of STYLE, the formatting, syntax, and order of style definitions vary, depending on whether the author has selected Cascading Style Sheets (Chapter 18) or JavaScript Style Sheets (Chapter 21). For SCRIPT, the same exceptions apply, depending on which scripting language is used. A script can contain one function, several functions, or stand alone as an application unto itself.

HEAD and BODY Structure

The structure of the head and body of an HTML document are similar in that a specific order or layout is not dictated. The difference is that the elements of the head exist as siblings, but the body can create a hierarchy of parents and children.

Remember that the head contains information about the document that can affect the display of the body, but isn't necessarily displayed to the user directly. No element in the head is more important than any other—TITLE is as important as LINK is as important as META. They are treated differently only according to their purpose.

On the other hand, there's the BODY element. It typically contains a hierarchy of elements. Consider this simple body content:

```
<BODY>
<H1>Packing a first aid kit</H1>
<P>When you pack a first aid kit, you don't need to bring everything for
every possibility. Only concentrate on the probable, combined with enough
supplies to match your skills for the possible.</P>
</BODY>
```

The body includes two children, an H1 element and a P element. If you imagined BODY as a tree, then the two elements would come out of the trunk at the same spot. You can also nest elements, as shown here:

```
<P>When you pack a first-aid kit, you don't need to bring everything
for every possibility. Only concentrate on the <EM>probable</EM>,
combined with enough supplies to match your skills for the possible.</P>
```

The EM element is a branch of the P element, which is a branch of the BODY. As elements are nested within the body of an HTML document, a hierarchy is established between the elements that will be different for each document, depending on the tags used by the author.

FRAMESET Structure

A <FRAMESET> is a special type of body element that, by its definition, can contain frames and frame sets only. Its contents are much more controlled than the body. However, the hierarchy established by the placement of a <FRAMESET> evolves in the same way as a <BODY> element.

In the following lines, each of the two FRAME elements are siblings and children of the FRAMESET element:

```
<FRAMESET>
  <FRAME>
  <FRAME>
</FRAMESET>
```

If you add another frame set with another frame to the configuration, you get something like this:

```
<FRAMESET>
  <FRAME>
  <FRAME>
  <FRAMESET>
    <FRAME>
  </FRAMESET>
</FRAMESET>
```

Now there are two FRAME elements and one FRAMESET, which are siblings and children of the first FRAMESET. The sibling FRAMESET also has a FRAME child of its own, making it a grandchild of the first FRAMESET. HTML recognizes this kind of hierarchy as it's implemented in browsers and allows elements in configurations such as this to work with each other based on their relationships.

The Substructure of Other Elements

In the body of an HTML document, some elements have their own internal structure to help define their use and appearance. A good example of this is the TABLE element (discussed in more detail in Chapters 9, "Organizing Data with Tables," and 10, "Table Layout and Presentation").

An HTML table is constructed as at least one row with at least one data cell, much as an HTML document needs at least one head and one body:

```
<TABLE>
  <TR>
    <TD>Data
</TABLE>
```

Each table can also have a caption, a header, a footer, and body content:

```
<TABLE>
  <CAPTION> Caption </CAPTION>
  <THEAD>
    <TR>
      <TD>Data
```

```
<TFOOT>
   <TR>
      <TD>Data
<TBODY>
   <TR>
      <TD>Data
</TABLE>
```

Each table becomes a mini-document with a form and structure of its own. There are other elements similar to TABLE within the body, including the different types of lists (ordered, unordered, definition), forms, and field sets.

Summary

At its heart, HTML is about structure. Authors are given a set of tools to mark the purpose and intent of each piece of text within a Web page. It's then up to the browser to decide how to display the content to the end user.

For the last two revisions of HTML (HTML 2.0 and 3.2), non-structure tags have wormed their way into HTML, including tags and attributes for font colors and sizes, justified text, and bold, italic, or underlined text. With HTML 4.0, the appearance tags and attributes are being deprecated in favor of style sheets—a way to define appearance without the direct use of elements. The body of HTML is returning to a structure-only use.

An HTML document is composed of parts in a descending hierarchy, beginning with the head, body, style sheet, script, and frame set. The head includes information about the document that's implemented by the browser or used by search engines, and the body includes all the content meant for display by the user. The style sheet defines how the document should appear on the browser. The script sets up a way to interact with the user by using a simplified programming language. The frame set divides the browser window into a set of smaller windows that can each hold its own HTML document.

By working with structure separately from appearance, HTML comes closer to achieving true independence from the proprietary demands of specific browsers or platforms.

3

STRUCTURE OF
AN **HTML**
DOCUMENT

The HTML Document Type Definition

by Rick Darnell

CHAPTER 4

In many of the examples you see in this book, you'll see a special markup tag at the very beginning of the document that looks something like this:

```
<!DOCTYPE HTML PUBLIC "-//W3C//DTD HTML 4.0//EN">
```

This amazing little line refers to a special document called the *Document Type Definition* (*DTD*), which contains all the information about the tags, entities, and overall document structure. It's the master blueprint of every HTML document.

The DTD comes with some good news and bad news. The good news is it's freely available for review and examination from the World Wide Web Consortium (W3C). The bad news is that it's way too long to review from top to bottom in this chapter. Therefore, I'll discuss the major concepts and syntax features of the DTD for HTML 4 by looking at the actual pieces from the original definition. In this way, you'll gain an understanding of the entire DTD without spending days of your life reviewing a bunch of technical notation.

SGML: The Structure Behind HTML

SGML is an international standard for the description of marked-up electronic text. That sounds like an awful lot to grasp, so I'll break it down further. SGML is a way to describe a language in formal terms—markup languages, in particular.

A parallel to SGML is the grammar you learned in school. In grammar classes, you learned about nouns, verbs, subjects, predicates, and a host of other features of the language. These items aren't the language itself—they only describe the language and how its pieces fit together.

Historically, the word *markup* has been used to describe marks within text intended to let the typist, typesetter, or whoever know how a particular passage should be printed or laid out. We've seen markup as editing marks, such as wavy underlining to indicate boldface, a line through text to indicate deletion, or a single underline to indicate italics. As the formatting and printing of texts was automated, the term *markup* was extended to cover all sorts of special markup codes inserted into electronic texts to govern formatting, printing, and other processing.

Generalizing from that history, *markup* is defined as any means of creating an explicit interpretation for a piece of text. At their lowest level, such as ASCII text documents, all printed texts contain markup: punctuation marks, capitalization, and spaces between words can be regarded as a kind of markup. These basic elements help the reader determine where one word ends and another begins, or how to interpret a sentence (question or exclamation), or where a dependent clause begins and ends.

Now take this concept to the next level as a *markup language*, which is a set of markup conventions, separate from the content, that are used to encode text or other content. A markup language must specify how the markup is distinguished from the content, what markup is required, what markup is allowed, and what the markup means.

A BRIEF SGML HISTORY

The roots of SGML go back to the late 1960s when the concept of descriptive markup saw the light of day for the first time. After companies started using computers for document processing, it soon became obvious that a storage format should have not only formatting codes interpreted by the computer, but also descriptive, human-legible information about the role of every element in a document.

The first working system that used these concepts was the generalized markup language (GML) developed by a team at IBM. This original system was the direct predecessor of SGML and contained prototypes for many of its major features, such as hierarchical document structure and Document Type Definition. IBM built mainframe publishing systems based on GML that were widely used to produce technical documentation in the corporation.

In 1978, the American National Standards Institute (ANSI) started research in the field of generic document markup to establish a nationwide standard for information interchange. This effort was joined by some of the original GML developers from IBM. The first ANSI draft was published in 1980 and finalized as an industry standard in 1983.

In 1984, the International Standards Organization (ISO) joined the activity and started preparing an international version of the standard. The first draft was published in 1985, and the final version was released a year later under the name *ISO 8879:1986 Information Processing—Text and Office Systems—Standard Generalized Markup Language.*

SGML is generally best used in large corporations and agencies that produce a lot of documents and can afford to introduce a single format for internal use. Besides IBM, other applications of SGML include projects developed by the Association of American Publishers and the U.S. Department of Defense. In 1992, another project was started at the European Laboratory for Particle Physics (CERN) for hypertext markup language, but that's another story in Chapter 2, "What Is Hypertext Markup Language?"

4

THE HTML DOCUMENT TYPE DEFINITION

Why Use SGML?

There are several very good reasons for developing a markup language. First, it's needed to focus on the structure of a document instead of its formatting. The markup system should allow you to build a hierarchy of descriptive tags so that they can not only separate and describe different parts of the document, such as chapters and paragraphs, but also formally prescribe its structure.

Another important requirement of markup is that it allows easy extension and modification. Ideally, a user should be able to define a completely new set of tags if the need arises. Finally, the markup shouldn't be proprietary; it should let anyone create and use markup tools based on the system and produce software implementing the tools.

SGML, designed with these markup needs in mind, is strictly descriptive and has no means to mark up a document's visual or design-oriented aspects. However, it can easily work with external procedural markup systems, such as style sheets.

SGML accomplishes the goals and needs of a markup system not by existing as a markup system, but by being an ordered way to create markup languages for particular types of documents. SGML's flexible syntax makes it possible to build markup languages such as HTML to meet a wide range of demands.

Defining an SGML Application

A document created with SGML exists as a hierarchical structure of nested elements. An *element* can be a chapter, section, paragraph, table, heading, or any other component of the document. Even though there might be some common notions about the appearance of these items, SGML has no means or desire to specify any aspects of their appearance. The author can give direction or suggestions through comments in the SGML application, but they can be ignored by user agents and parsers.

There are four basic parts to an SGML application:

- First is the SGML declaration that tells which characters and entities are allowed in the application.

- The Document Type Definition, which outlines the syntax of the markup tags. It can also include other definitions, such as numeric and character entities. All documents marked up with the same hierarchy of elements are said to belong to a certain *document type*. Rather than describe a set of tools to mark up a document, SGML defines the structure of a particular type of document through the DTD.

- A specification that describes the semantics of the markup, in addition to syntax that can't be expressed through the DTD.

- Instances of documents that contain content and markup tags. Each document must have a reference to the DTD that's used to interpret it.

The first three parts are explained in this chapter, and the rest of the book covers creating documents that fit the last part.

> **NOTE**
>
> SGML syntax is very close to HTML syntax. SGML statements, like HTML tags, are enclosed in angle brackets (< >) and contain a keyword or name followed by one or more parameters separated by spaces. The only consistent difference is that SGML statements typically include an exclamation point between the opening bracket and the statement keyword, as shown:
>
> ```
> <!ELEMENT IMG - O EMPTY -- Embedded image -->
> ```

The other feature of SGML syntax is using comments within the statements. The comment is the last item in a statement and begins and ends with a double dash (--).

The SGML Declaration for HTML 4

The SGML declaration is a formal construct used to specify some general information about an SGML application and is associated with its document type. It includes several parts, including the level of SGML standard, the character set, an estimate of needed system resources, syntax, scope, and features.

The first part of the SGML declaration is SGML "ISO 8879:1986", which identifies the ISO version of SGML that the declaration conforms to. In case you hadn't noticed, this is the same original standard developed by ISO after the work by ANSI and IBM.

After the standard comes a brief comment that identifies the declaration and its use, in this case, SGML Declaration for HyperText Markup Language version 4.0.

Next comes the CHARSET section that specifies which character set to use by any document conforming to the document type. A specific character set is identified because of the differences between characters and the values used to represent them on different computers and operating systems. Here is the CHARSET declaration for HTML 4:

```
CHARSET
        BASESET   "ISO Registration Number 177//CHARSET
                  ISO/IEC 10646-1:1993 UCS-4 with
                  implementation level 3//ESC 2/5 2/15 4/6"
```

The SGML declaration defines exactly what character set it uses—the values or codes allowed in a conforming document and what characters they're intended to represent. Instead of reinventing the wheel, SGML typically uses character sets that have already been adopted by standards bodies, such as ISO.

4

THE HTML
DOCUMENT TYPE
DEFINITION

NOTE

Because HTML is used around the world with a variety of languages, it must be flexible enough to allow non-Latin characters. This is done through HTML internationalization, described in the RFC 2070 recommendation (ds.internic.net/rfc/rfc2070.txt). RFC 2070 describes an extended character set that makes use of the Unicode standard, which uses 16-bit codes instead of the traditional 8-bit codes. More information about this issue is found in Chapter 40, "Internationalizing Your HTML."

After CHARSET comes the CAPACITY section, which provides a rough estimate of the system resources needed by an SGML parser to process the DTD. It's described in terms of different types of memory, as shown:

```
CAPACITY          SGMLREF
                  TOTALCAP      150000
                  GRPCAP        150000
                  ENTCAP        150000
```

This information isn't very reliable because memory usage largely depends on the parsing program's internal architecture. Most SGML parsers don't take these values into account, and the people who write the declaration just assign big enough numbers to make sure DTD processing isn't aborted because a capacity value is exceeded.

After CAPACITY is one line for the SCOPE declaration:

SCOPE DOCUMENT

This line's purpose is to specify that the following syntax section is for use by both conforming SGML documents and the DTD of this particular application.

Next comes the SYNTAX section, which defines syntax features of the SGML application, such as naming rules, delimiters and control characters, and reserved names.

The FEATURES section of the SGML declaration has parameters that control the use of some SGML syntax features. There are three SGML features used in the HTML 4 DTD:

- ■ MINIMIZE: This class contains markup minimization features intended to facilitate SGML markup and make it more readable and easier for people to use. Minimization features allow you to omit some tags and other markup instructions in certain situations when the context would resolve any ambiguity.

  The first feature allowed for HTML is OMITTAG YES to permit certain elements to exist without either a beginning or an ending tag. The other feature is SHORTTAG YES, which isn't supported by current popular browser selections. It allows the use of empty tags, omitted attribute names, and other typographical oddities, with the missing information implied by the parser through simple and effective rules.

- ■ LINK: This class contains features that affect processing attributes of elements. They are specific to SGML and are not allowed in HTML.

- ■ OTHER: The last class contains miscellaneous features that don't fit in any other class. The notable feature is FORMAL YES, which indicates that the PUBLIC entity declarations should use the formal syntax of public identifiers to enable a parser to automatically substitute external sources.

With the SGML declaration out of the way, it's time to turn your attention to the meat and potatoes of the SGML application—the Document Type Definition.

The Document Type Definition for HTML 4

The Document Type Definition for HTML 4 (HTML DTD) is too long to print in its entirety in this chapter. For those of you who really enjoy that level of detail, you can find the current DTD at www.w3.org/TR/WD-html140-970708/HTML4.dtd. In this chapter, I'm going to present bits and pieces of the DTD, with the hope that by taking a look at some of the details, you can look at any part of the whole and understand what you're looking at.

> **NOTE**
>
> Besides the consecutive versions of HTML, there are several HTML variations that deviate from the standard set of supported features, including the Microsoft and Netscape versions of HTML with their host of proprietary tags, such as <MARQUEE> and <LAYER>. It's general industry practice to document the extension in the form of a DTD, which should be available from the developer who introduced the element.
>
> Actually, quite a few DTDs for variations on HTML standards are available. You can find a large collection of DTDs and other HTML resources at www.webtechs.com/html/.

A DTD is expressed as a series of declarations that identify each element and its possible content and context. This identification is done primarily by using two basic tools: *entities* and *declarations*.

Entities

If you've ever used a word processor for very long, then you've probably figured out how to use macros. Macros are those great little shortcuts to do things like insert your name and address at the end of a letter or include frequently used phrases, such as "Where color is expressed as a hexadecimal triplet," or even whole paragraphs.

SGML *entities* are similar to word processing macros—they are shorthand pieces of text that expand into strings or markup instructions within the DTD.

In HTML documents, entities are used to invoke characters that are either absent on a computer keyboard (such as é for é) or have a special meaning and can't be typed directly into the document (such as < and > for < and >, used to contain tag information). In the DTD itself, entities play a more important role in helping to make declarations more concise and readable. The entities used in DTD are called *parameter entities* as opposed to *general entities* intended for use in HTML documents.

To begin, the first declaration in the HTML DTD is a parameter entity:

```
<!ENTITY % HTML.Version "http://www.w3.org/TR/WD-html40-970708/HTML4.dtd"
  -- Typical usage:

    <!DOCTYPE HTML SYSTEM "http://www.w3.org/TR/WD-html40-970708/HTML4.dtd">
    <html>
    ...
    </html>
  --
>
```

First, note the delimiter syntax, which is the same for an ENTITY and an ELEMENT. It begins with the angle bracket and an exclamation point and ends with an angle bracket. After the ENTITY keyword comes the `%` character, indicating that the entity in question is a parameter entity rather than a general entity.

Separated by one or more spaces from the percent character is the entity name used to invoke the entity:

```
HTML.Version
```

Note that the name contains a period, making use of the NAMING section settings of the SGML declaration, and that the entity names are case-sensitive.

The last obligatory component of an entity declaration is the string enclosed in quotation marks that shows what this entity stands for and what it will expand to when invoked. This is called the *data string*:

```
"http://www.w3.org/TR/WD-html40-970708/HTML4.dtd"
```

This is the syntax to invoke the entity within the SGML document:

```
%entityName;
```

So, the first entity of the HTML DTD will be seen again as this:

```
%HTML.Version;
```

The last part of the `HTML.Version` entity declaration is the comment that's a reminder about the necessity to start any HTML document intended as a valid SGML document with a DOCTYPE declaration. This comment allows an SGML parser to know at once that the structure and tags of the document it's about to process are described in the DTD identified in the URL. Of course, HTML browsers could also make use of this information to select the level of HTML support needed for the document, although only a few of them really do.

NOTE

Using a URL as a DTD identifier is rather unusual. It's explained by the fact that at the time of this writing, the HTML 4 DTD is still evolving toward a final specification. More often, to refer to external information sources, SGML documents use *public identifiers* of a special form.

For example, the HTML 3.2 DTD has an `HTML.Version` entity that expands to `-//W3C//DTD HTML 3.2 Final//EN`, which is the public identifier of the HTML 3.2 DTD. When HTML 4 reaches its final incarnation, its public identifier will be `-//W3C//DTD HTML 4.0 Final//EN`. An alternative short form of the final public identifier is `-//W3C//DTD HTML 4.0//EN`.

Another example is the identifier string of a character set standard used for the BASESET parameter in an SGML declaration. Any DTD or related standard has a unique public identifier assigned to allow a reference from other SGML documents. These references are usually made with parameter entities.

If the data string in an entity declaration is preceded by the additional keyword `PUBLIC`, then the string is not the entity value but a public identifier pointing to an external information source. For example, the HTML 4 DTD is accompanied by a set of general entities for accessing characters of ISO Latin-1—which is a standard isolated in a separate document (`www.w3.org/pub/WWW/Markup/Cougar/ISOlat1.ent`) that's identified by its own unique public identifier (`-//W3C//ENTITIES Latin1//EN//HTML`). This information is incorporated into the HTML DTD like this:

```
<!ENTITY & HTMLlat1 PUBLIC "-//W3C//ENTITIES Latin1//EN//HTML">
```

Now, instead of the string containing a URL, it contains the public identifier of the external resource whose contents are substituted for each occurrence of the entity `%HTMLlat1;`. The formal rules for constructing public identifiers aren't given here, but more information and a catalog of identifiers can be found at `www.webtechs.com/html-tk/src/lib/catalog`.

On the other hand, we have *general entities*. They are declared in the DTD similarly to parameter entities, but there are some important differences:

- A general entity is used only in documents conforming to the document type. In this case, it's an HTML document.
- A general entity doesn't have the `%` character in its declaration.
- A general entity is invoked by using the `&` (ampersand) character. For example, `&lt;` identifies a less-than character (`<`). Because this makes the ampersand a special character, a separate entity (`&amp;`) is needed to include an ampersand for other uses.
- A general entity usually contains the `CDATA` (character data) keyword in its declaration before the data string. The keyword indicates that the string isn't interpreted as SGML data. In other words, any markup instructions it might contain should be ignored and treated as ordinary text characters.

As an example, look at these entity declarations that define how to access four special characters:

```
<!ENTITY amp    CDATA  "&#38;"   -- ampersand     -->
<!ENTITY gt     CDATA  "&#62;"   -- greater than  -->
<!ENTITY lt     CDATA  "&#60;"   -- less than     -->
<!ENTITY quot   CDATA  "&#34;"   -- double quote  -->
```

This example shows a special kind of entity called a *character reference* that doesn't require any declaration. If the entity opening delimiter `&` is immediately followed by the `#` character and a number, this number is interpreted as a character code from the document character set defined in the SGML `CHARSET` section, and the whole entity is replaced by the character having this code. This method is one of the two used to access characters beyond the reach of a computer keyboard; the method uses mnemonic character entities such as `&amp;` or `&lt;`.

You might wonder how the entities in the preceding example could expand to special characters if the `CDATA` keyword prohibits any SGML instructions from having an effect in the data string. The answer is that this string is read twice—the first time when the entity declaration is interpreted, and the second when the data string itself is interpreted as part of the document. The CDATA keyword affects only the first reading. As a result, the DTD is protected from the special characters, and the document receives expanded references and the resulting characters.

Elements

A document marked up with an SGML application is basically a hierarchy of nested elements. A marked-up element is usually enclosed in a pair of start and end tags. The ELEMENT statement in SGML defines both start and end tags, but not their attributes, and prescribes the content of the element by defining its content model. This is an example of an element declaration:

```
<!ELEMENT P -O (%text)*>
```

Here, P is the element name and is shorthand for *paragraph*. The two characters following the element name are *minimization indicators*, specifying whether it's possible to omit start or end tags for this element. The first indicator refers to the start tag and the second to the end tag. The two possibilities for this notation are a hyphen or an O. A hyphen means a tag is required, and an O means it can be omitted. So, in the previous example, a P element is required to have an opening <P>, but an ending </P> is optional.

It's possible for both tags to be optional. For example, take a look at the element declaration for the HTML element:

```
<!ELEMENT HTML OO (%html.content)>
```

Both start and end tags are marked as optional. Does this mean you can create a technically accurate Web page without an opening or closing <HTML> tag? You bet—it's completely legal. For clarity's sake, I still recommend using it, but the DTD says you don't have to. The same is true for closing tags on table data cells <TD>, paragraphs <P>, and other items.

Now, take a look at the last component in both of the previous element declarations. The P element includes

```
(%text)
```

and the HTML element has

```
(%html.content)
```

These items constitute the *content model* specification. Here, it's done with parameter entities, and to see what they expand to, you should find the corresponding ENTITY statements in the DTD. The content model declares what can, what must, and what can't go inside the element.

The simplest type of content model is specified by a single keyword from Table 4.1.

Table 4.1. Content model keywords.

Keyword	Description
CDATA	Stands for *character data*, and means the SGML parser suspends processing for the element content. Any tags or entities in the element won't have any effect on the parsing and are treated as ordinary text characters. The only tag that an SGML parser reacts to when skipping over CDATA content is the end tag of the element that switched on CDATA mode.
EMPTY	Indicates that the content of the element is empty. Naturally, this keyword is always accompanied by permission to omit the end tag, such as: `<!ELEMENT IMG -O EMPTY -- Embedded image -->`
RCDATA	Stands for *replaceable character data*, and introduces a content model that's different from CDATA in that it expands all general entities and character references, but ignores markup statements. RCDATA isn't used in the HTML DTD.
ANY	Allows any markup and data characters in the element. ANY isn't used in the HTML DTD.

Sometimes it's necessary to be more specific in defining the content model of an element. In that case, a *content model group* is used, which is one of the primary ways of defining the content of an element. It's explained in the following section.

Content Model Groups

The simplest model group is one element name enclosed in parentheses, which means the element being defined must have one occurrence of the element specified in the content model and nothing else. Unfortunately, this happens only rarely; more often, a model group contains two or more element names, as shown:

```
<!ELEMENT DL - -  (DT¦DD)+>
```

This is the element declaration for a definition list. If you'll remember from the previous section, the element name is DL, and both a starting <DL> and ending </DL> are required. The next part says that within the DL element, the user can place a DT (term) element, a DD (definition) element, or both. How do you figure this out? The key is the separator between the elements, called a *connector*. It can be one of three characters:

- A comma, which indicates the elements in the content model *must* appear in the order specified. There are very few uses of this separator in the HTML DTD; the most notable use is in the TABLE element.

- A vertical bar is the "or" connector. It indicates that either element can appear, but not both. In the DL example, this connector is used to allow both types of content in the list.

- An ampersand is the "and" connector. It indicates that all the elements listed must occur before the closing tag, but unlike elements separated with the comma, the elements can appear in any order.

The plus sign following the group in the example is an *occurrence indicator*; it defines how many times the elements in the content group may occur. An occurrence indicator is one of three characters:

- A question mark means that the element can occur once or not at all, such as in the caption for a table:

  ```
  <!ELEMENT TABLE - - (CAPTION?, …
  ```

- A plus sign means that the element must occur at least once, and can include many more occurrences. For example, a SELECT element in a form is used to create a drop-down or multiple-selection list. As such, it can include any number of options, but must have at least one, as shown:

  ```
  <!ELEMENT SELECT - - (OPTION+)>
  ```

- An asterisk means that the element can occur any number of times or not at all. For example, an applet could have none, one, or more parameters.

  ```
  <!ELEMENT APPLET - - (PARAM¦%inline)*>
  ```

The model groups can be nested and grouped by using additional parentheses with connectors and occurrence indicators applied to individual elements or entire groups.

Besides element names, the #PCDATA keyword is also available for model groups. It refers to "usual" characters of the document without any markup tags. It's used to explicitly allow or disallow plain text in an element.

Using the #PCDATA keyword with connectors and occurrence indicators can limit the set of elements allowed inside another element, without prohibiting plain text from appearing there. For example, here's how the %text; entity is defined through some subordinate entities:

```
<!ENTITY % font
 "TT ¦ I ¦ B ¦ U ¦ S ¦ STRIKE ¦ BIG ¦ SMALL">

<!ENTITY % phrase "EM ¦ STRONG ¦ DFN ¦ CODE ¦
                  SAMP ¦ KBD ¦ VAR ¦ CITE ¦ ACRONYM">

<!ENTITY % special
   "A ¦ IMG ¦ APPLET ¦ OBJECT ¦ FONT ¦ BASEFONT ¦ BR ¦ SCRIPT ¦
   MAP ¦ Q ¦ SUB ¦ SUP ¦ SPAN ¦ BDO ¦ IFRAME">

<!ENTITY % formctrl "INPUT ¦ SELECT ¦ TEXTAREA ¦ LABEL ¦ BUTTON">

<!-- %inline covers inline or "text-level" elements -->
<!ENTITY % inline "#PCDATA ¦ %font ¦ %phrase ¦ %special ¦ %formctrl">
```

Here, each entity is built with a series of possible elements until the inline entity, which is defined as character data and/or any of the font, phrase, special, or formctrl elements—in plain English, "possibly a chunk of text, in addition to possibly one of the other listed defined elements."

After the entities are defined, they can be used to create additional content models, as shown:

```
<!ELEMENT (%font¦%phrase) - - (%text)*>
```

This particular declaration means that a font or phrase element must have a starting and ending tag and can include any number of text characters.

One other interesting feature of the content groups is the use of characters for adding or subtracting model groups. For instance, the FORM element is allowed to contain anything that can occur within a block-level element, except for another FORM element. Because this means forms can't be nested, the subtraction operation is used:

```
<!ELEMENT FORM - - %block.content -(FORM)>
```

Now you have the elements in hand, but as you know, many tags also include attributes. That's the topic of the next section.

Attributes for Elements

An element is not fully described by its name and content model. Many elements have assorted *attributes* that provide additional information about rendering the element. Attributes for each element are declared in the DTD with the ATTLIST statement.

Here is the attribute list for the horizontal rule element:

```
<!ATTLIST HR
  %coreattrs;                      -- id, class, style, title --
  %events;
  align (left¦right¦center) #IMPLIED
  noshade    (noshade)  #IMPLIED
  size       %Pixels    #IMPLIED
  width      %Length    #IMPLIED
  >
```

The first two attributes listed are named entities that expand to a generic set of attributes available for virtually all elements. The core attributes (coreattrs) are used primarily for style sheet implementation, and the event attributes (events) cover the standard document events.

Next come the attributes that are unique to the HR element. Each entry begins with the attribute name, such as align, then proceeds to the type of value the attribute can take and the default value. Continuing with the first entry, the three possible values are left, right, or center.

Some attributes default to a certain value based just on their appearance. This happens in the HR element with the noshade attribute:

```
noshade    (noshade)  #IMPLIED
```

In effect, this statement gives two possible ways of specifying the attribute when it's used in markup: `<HR noshade=noshade>` or `<HR noshade>`. Like the content groups for elements, the single value within the parentheses of the attribute definition indicates that only one value is possible. If the attribute is used without assigning an explicit value, the required value is substituted.

In addition to the named values listed in the parentheses, the value can also be one of five keywords.

- **CDATA:** This keyword means that the value of the attribute can be any string of characters and should be ignored by the parser. CDATA is used in situations where it would be impossible to impose stricter limitations on the value of an attribute, such as in the name of a division or form element.

- **NAME:** This keyword indicates that the value of the attribute is a name conforming to SGML naming rules as defined by the SGML declaration.

- **NMTOKEN:** This keyword is similar to NAME, except there's no requirement to start the name with the name start character (typically, a Latin character).

- **NUMBER:** This keyword allows the parameter to take numeric values, such as the starting number for an ordered list:

```
<!ATTLIST OL -- ordered lists --
...
  start  NUMBER  #IMPLIED  -- starting sequence number --
...
>
```

- **ID:** The last keyword indicates that the attribute value is an *identifier* that meets two requirements. First, it is a valid SGML name, and second, it's unique across the document (not assigned to any other attribute). This value is specified for the ID attribute for style sheets.

The last part of the attribute definition assigns a default value to the attribute. In most of the previous examples, it has been the keyword #IMPLIED; however, it can be a specific value. Consider this excerpt from the FORM element:

```
<!ELEMENT FORM - - %block -(FORM)>
<!ATTLIST FORM
...
  method      (GET¦POST) GET       -- HTTP method used to submit the form --
...
>
```

The attribute called method is forced to the default value of GET if it's not explicitly identified, although it can have a value of GET or POST.

Most attributes, however, have one of three keywords as their default value:

- **#FIXED:** This keyword must precede the actual default value and is used to specify that the value can't be changed by the user. It's used only once in the HTML DTD:

```
<!ATTLIST HTML
        VERSION CDATA #FIXED "%HTML.version;"
    …
    >
```

▨ **#IMPLIED:** This keyword indicates that the attribute is optional. The browser can optionally use its own default value, although a default value isn't specified in the DTD.

▨ **#REQUIRED:** This keyword indicates that the attribute must be included. For example, take a look at this line from the FORM attribute list:

```
action        %URL         #REQUIRED -- server-side form handler --
```

This line indicates that the action attribute must have a URL specified as a form handler.

Deprecated Features

The HTML DTD includes several *deprecated features*, which are elements and attributes that are no longer recommended for use, but are included in the DTD anyway for backward compatibility with other versions.

> **TIP**
>
> Avoid using deprecated features in your documents. Although they might still be supported in many browsers, being deprecated means they're on their way out. Chances are, there's a better way to use the feature you want, such as an unordered list for a directory listing.

Deprecated elements are sometimes processed differently from the rest of the document. To do this, SGML offers a way to identify *marked sections* that makes it possible to isolate any markup statements and declarations to control their processing:

```
<![ %HTML.Deprecated [
   <!ENTITY % preformatted "PRE ¦ XMP ¦ LISTING">
]]>
```

The %HTML.Deprecated entity expands into a special keyword that tells the parser what to do with the contents of the section. If the word is IGNORE, then the marked section is ignored entirely. If the word is INCLUDE, then the marked section is processed on equal terms with the rest of the DTD. So, to get a "strict" version of the DTD that includes only the recommended elements, the HTML.Deprecated entity can be changed from

```
<!ENTITY % HTML.Deprecated "INCLUDE">
```

to

```
<!ENTITY % HTML.Deprecated "IGNORE">
```

Summary

I've covered a lot of ground in this chapter, but I hope you now have a handle on what the Document Type Definition is and how to read it. I've used the W3C standard in this chapter's examples, but if you were to review any of the DTDs for other HTML variations (such as the DTDs available at www.webtechs.com/html), the same standards and syntax would apply.

In a nutshell, the HTML DTD is an SGML application broken into two major parts: the declaration and the DTD. The declaration takes care of housekeeping issues, such as which character set to use and which version of SGML the rest of the document is based on. The DTD includes the definitions for all legal HTML elements and their attributes, using a syntax that looks very much like HTML. Special characters and separators help specify the content and structure of the elements' usage.

Do you need to read the DTD in its entirety if you want to create HTML documents? No, all you need is a good book like this one. However, if you're trying to create pages according to specific types of HTML, or a new HTML standard is released and you want to see if there are any important changes, you can go straight to the DTD to see what's going on.

Get Started Now

by Rick Darnell

IN THIS CHAPTER

CHAPTER 5

The rest of this book is going to delve into each element and attribute in the HTML 4.0 specification, but right now, I'm going to give you a sneak peek at what's included in HTML and how to build Web pages. If you've never worked with HTML before or are just looking for a few new ideas, this chapter is for you.

This chapter focuses on building several HTML pages that incorporate most of HTML's standard features. Also, I give an introduction to basic HTML design that's continued in Part VII ("Effective Web Page Design"), which covers Web page design in much more detail.

Basic Page Layout Issues

Before beginning to create your page, you must answer two important questions:

- What do you want to say?
- To whom do you want to say it?

Although these are two separate questions, they are hard to separate. What you want to say depends on whom you want to say it to. As you try to answer these two questions, you will probably come up with more questions as you start to plan your Web pages. These questions help sharpen your focus even more:

- Are you targeting your pages to potential customers?
- Do you want to offer unique information on a special topic or issue?
- Is this page a method of keeping employees and other personnel informed of company developments and news?

If you don't have an audience or a message, there's a good chance you'll end up saying nothing to anyone. This advice is also important in Chapter 15, "Building and Using HTML Forms." Form follows function, and the lack of one shows up in the other.

After you know what your basic message is and how it should be organized for delivery to your audience, it's time to plug the individual parts of the message into the framework. If the Web site is the bell, the pages are the clappers that work to make the sound.

Before you start a new page, remember that the overall design and layout of your page is how your message is communicated to the user. Good design and layout aren't ends in themselves. If you look at many pages on the Web, you'll see the full gamut—from bland pages with no thought given to their appearance to pages whose only message is to show off how artistic a designer can be. As you start to play with the design, remember one cardinal rule of layout: Self-indulgence is a message-killer.

It's a good idea to flip through magazines, books, and brochures before you start. Web page design develops from printed page design, and the printed page is a good place to start looking for ideas.

Although the number of formatting options and capabilities are growing for Web pages, these features are still limited in comparison to those of their printed cousins. With a little creativity, however, you can make your page stand out from the run-of-the-mill pages.

A FEW WORDS ABOUT A LOT OF SPACE

Space is an important part of every page. It gives breathing room in the midst of a crowd of information. Effective use of space can help a page as much as ineffective use can hurt a page.

Having too much space on a page causes the user to waste time by constantly scrolling to get to the next piece of information. Having too little space makes everything run together like gumbo. An extra set of eyes can help judge the overall effect. Enlist the help of friends and co-workers to critique your work. It's some of the best advice you can get for free.

The following five layouts use the default font the browser provides and the same image and headline size. Even with this limitation, different uses of headline, text, images, and white space result in a very different look for each layout. Depending on how you use and place the four page elements, each layout can take on its own personality that you can harness to help reinforce your message.

A Conventional Page

The first page style is one that's seen all too often on the Web. It's also the easiest to construct and doesn't really require any knowledge of design or HTML. Although the conventional page doesn't take advantage of any of HTML's formatting capabilities, it's the most compatible with all browsers and platforms. It consists of a heading at the top, followed by the bulk of the text, and perhaps an image included at the end or somewhere else along the way. (See Listing 5.1 and Figure 5.1.)

Listing 5.1. A conventional page layout.

```
<!DOCTYPE HTML PUBLIC "-//IETF//DTD HTML 4.0//EN">
<HTML>
<HEAD>
 <TITLE>Conventional</TITLE>
</HEAD>
<BODY>
<H1>The Alberton Canyon Derailment</H1>
<P>In the early morning hours on Thursday, April 11, 1996, an east-bound
Montana Rail Link (MRL) train derailed in western Montana approximately
two miles west of Alberton,  and immediately adjacent to the Clarks Fork
River and I-90.  Eighteen cars derailed from the 71-car train, including six
Cars carrying hazardous materials. Four contained chlorine; one contained
Potassium cresylate; and the sixth contained sodium chlorate.</P>
<P><IMG SRC="/mrfd/Alberton/albert8.jpg" WIDTH="300" HEIGHT="197"></P>
<P>To compound the problem further, another MRL train derailed near Noxon,
```

5

GET STARTED NOW

continues

Listing 5.1. continued

```
Mont., spilling 1,000 gallons of diesel fuel and overturning another chlorine
car.  The additional confusion caused by the diversion and rerouting of
resources slowed the initial response of personnel and equipment.</P>
<P>One of the chlorine cars and the potassium cresylate car were breached,
resulting in the release of approximately 100,000 lbs. of deadly chlorine gas.
The cloud drifted over the highway and through the town of Alberton forcing
the evacuation of more than 1,000 people in a 100 square-mile area. Half of
these were kept out of their homes for 17 days.  An estimated 350 people were
treated for health and respiratory problems in Missoula hospitals, 35 miles to
the east. A lone fatality occurred when a transient riding in a box car walked
into the cloud after surviving the crash.</P>
</BODY>
</HTML>
```

FIGURE 5.1.

A conventional page: heading at the top, text-heavy middle, and picture at the bottom.

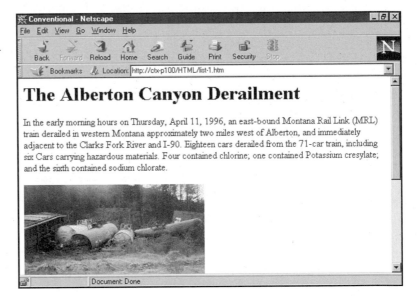

Although you wouldn't want all the pages in your site to look like this one, it's a quick-and-dirty way of putting a page together to disseminate information until you can put something else together. It's also a good alternative if you're developing a mirror for older browsers that might not support HTML 4.0 advanced features.

A Modern Layout

A modern layout is similar to the text-heavy conventional layout but makes use of horizontal rules to mark the beginning and end of the page and images that extend into the text. (See Listing 5.2 and Figure 5.2.) A true modern layout would also include extra space between each of the text lines, which you'll see how to do in Chapter 18, "Using Cascading Style Sheets." The main feature of a modern layout is the use of left- and right-alignment on images, allowing text to flow around the picture instead of staying inline.

Listing 5.2. A modern layout.

```
<!DOCTYPE HTML PUBLIC "-//IETF//DTD HTML 4.0//EN">
<HTML>
<HEAD>
 <TITLE>Modern</TITLE>
</HEAD>
<BODY>
<HR NOSHADE STYLE="width:75%; height:8px; text-align:left">
<H1>The Alberton Canyon Derailment</H1>
<P>In the early morning hours on Thursday, April 11, 1996, an east-bound
Montana Rail Link (MRL) train derailed in western Montana approximately
two miles west of Alberton,  and immediately adjacent to the Clarks Fork
River and I-90.  Eighteen cars derailed from the 71-car train, including six
Cars carrying hazardous materials. Four contained chlorine; one contained
Potassium cresylate; and the sixth contained sodium chlorate.
<IMG SRC="/mrfd/Alberton/albert8.jpg" ALIGN="RIGHT"
➡STYLE="width:300px; height:197px"></P>
<P>To compound the problem further, another MRL train derailed near Noxon,
Mont., spilling 1,000 gallons of diesel fuel and overturning another chlorine
car.  The additional confusion caused by the diversion and rerouting of
resources slowed the initial response of personnel and equipment.</P>
<P>One of the chlorine cars and the potassium cresylate car were breached,
resulting in the release of approximately 100,000 lbs. of deadly chlorine gas.
The cloud drifted over the highway and through the town of Alberton forcing
the evacuation of more than 1,000 people in a 100 square-mile area. Half of
these were kept out of their homes for 17 days.  An estimated 350 people were
treated for health and respiratory problems in Missoula hospitals, 35 miles to
the east. A lone fatality occurred when a transient riding in a box car walked
into the cloud after surviving the crash.</P>
<HR noshade style="width:75%; height:8px; text-align:right">
</BODY>
</HTML>
```

FIGURE 5.2.

A more modern layout that uses horizontal rules and pictures integrated into the text.

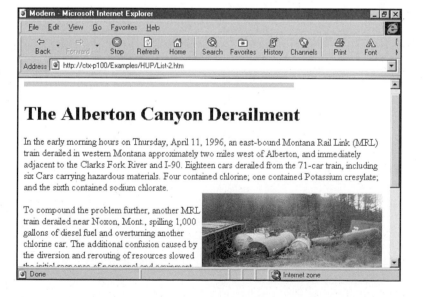

5

GET STARTED NOW

You can easily convert a conventional layout to a modern layout by simply adding left or right to the image's align attribute. It noticeably improves the appearance of the page without a lot of effort.

A Classic Layout

Adding columns to a page does two things. First, it shortens line length, making it easier for the user to read the text. This benefit is especially important on a Web page, where most users are looking at a screen, which causes more eye strain than reading a printed page.

Second, columns conserve space in large documents. Although it seems as though columns take up more space, they actually reduce the document's total length, which is one reason newspapers use multiple columns.

A classic layout is one of the simplest uses of columns in a Web page. (See Listing 5.3 and Figure 5.3.) Because HTML doesn't directly support columns, however, tables fit the purpose quite nicely to get the same effect.

Listing 5.3. A classic layout that uses tables to create columns.

```
<!DOCTYPE HTML PUBLIC "-//IETF//DTD HTML 4.0//EN">
<HTML>
<HEAD>
 <TITLE>Classic</TITLE>
</HEAD>
<STYLE type="text/css">
<!--
.center {text-align:center}
-->
</STYLE>
<BODY>
<H1 CLASS="center">The Alberton Canyon Derailment</H1>
<HR STYLE="width:75%; height:8px" CLASS="center" NOSHADE>
<TABLE WIDTH="100%" BORDER="0" CELLSPACING="15">
 <TR VALIGN="TOP">
  <TD WIDTH="50%">
   <P>In the early morning hours on Thursday, April 11, 1996, an east-bound
   Montana Rail Link (MRL) train derailed in western Montana approximately
   two miles west of Alberton,  and immediately adjacent to the Clarks Fork
   River and I-90.  Eighteen cars derailed from the 71-car train, including six
   Cars carrying hazardous materials. Four contained chlorine; one contained
   Potassium cresylate; and the sixth contained sodium chlorate.
   <P><IMG SRC="/mrfd/Alberton/albert8.jpg" STYLE="width:300px; height:197px"></P>
  <TD WIDTH="50%">
   <P>To compound the problem further, another MRL train derailed near Noxon,
   Mont., spilling 1,000 gallons of diesel fuel and overturning another
   chlorine car. The additional confusion caused by the diversion and rerouting
   of resources slowed the initial response of personnel and equipment.</P>
   <P>One of the chlorine cars and the potassium cresylate car were breached,
   resulting in the release of approximately 100,000 lbs. of deadly chlorine
   gas. The cloud drifted over the highway and through the town of Alberton
   forcing the evacuation of more than 1,000 people in a 100 square-mile area.
```

```
    Half of these were kept out of their homes for 17 days.  An estimated 350
    people were treated for health and respiratory problems in Missoula
    hospitals, 35 miles to the east. A lone fatality occurred when a transient
    riding in a box car walked into the cloud after surviving the crash.</P>
</TABLE>
</BODY>
</HTML>
```

This layout, shown in Figure 5.3, makes use of tables to create columns on a Web page. The headline is placed outside the table and centered to give it extra prominence.

Figure 5.3.

This classic layout is a simple, two-column format with a centered headline and image set into the text.

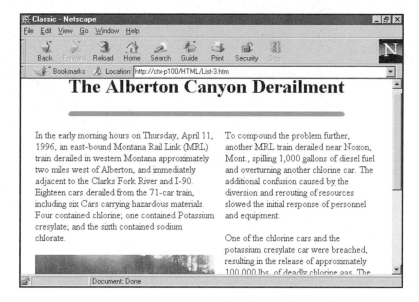

The two columns should be of equal width, and only one requires the width attribute. However, both <TD> tags include the width specification, which helps you avoid ambiguity later when you're reviewing and revising the page.

A Technical Information Page

The layout for technical documents developed from a need for practical features. Originally, many of these pages looked more like a conventional design. This layout meant a lack of space to make notes or comments about the contents, however. By shifting to a three-column format and leaving one of the outside columns open for diagrams and illustrations, the page gained additional white space.

The resulting design is very angular, and the ample white space results in a clean, strong appearance. (See Listing 5.4 and Figure 5.4.)

Listing 5.4. The technical page layout.

```
<!DOCTYPE HTML PUBLIC "-//IETF//DTD HTML 4.0//EN">
<HTML>
<HEAD>
 <TITLE>Technical</TITLE>
</HEAD>
<BODY>
<TABLE BORDER="0" WIDTH="100%" CELLSPACING="15">
 <TR>
  <TD>
  <TD COLSPAN="2" WIDTH="33%">
   <H1>The Alberton Canyon Derailment</H1>
 <TR VALIGN="TOP">
  <TD VALIGN="MIDDLE">
   <P><IMG SRC="/mrfd/Alberton/albert8.jpg" STYLE="width:225; height:148"></P>
  <TD WIDTH="33%">
   <P>In the early morning hours on Thursday, April 11, 1996, an east-bound
    Montana Rail Link (MRL) train derailed in western Montana approximately
    two miles west of Alberton, and immediately adjacent to the Clarks Fork
    River and I-90. Eighteen cars derailed from the 71-car train, including
    six cars carrying hazardous materials. Four contained chlorine; one
    contained potassium cresylate; and the sixth contained sodium chlorate.</P>
   <P>To compound the problem further, another MRL train derailed near Noxon,
    Mont., spilling 1,000 gallons of diesel fuel and overturning another
    chlorine car.  The additional confusion caused by the diversion and
    rerouting of resource slowed the initial response of personnel and
    equipment.</P>
  <TD WIDTH="33%">
   <P>One of the chlorine cars and the potassium cresylate car were breached,
    resulting in the release of approximately 100,000 lbs. of deadly chlorine
    gas. The cloud drifted over the highway and through the town of Alberton
    forcing the evacuation of more than 1,000 people in a 100 square-mile area.
    Half of these were kept out of their homes for 17 days. An estimated 350
    people were treated for health and respiratory problems in Missoula
    hospitals, 35 miles to the east. A lone fatality occurred when a transient
    riding in a box car walked into the cloud after surviving the crash.</P>
   </TABLE>
</BODY>
</HTML>
```

The technical page design, shown in Figure 5.4, is similar to the two-column classic, except a third column is added to the table to hold images, comments, diagrams, and so forth.

A Formal Page

Formal pages aren't necessarily the most space-efficient designs in the world, but they do have a certain style that fits the bill for announcements, such as a local fire department naming a new chief or getting a new fire truck.

The design is created by using a table with three columns. The width of each of the outside two columns is 25 percent of the table width, leaving half the table width for the center column and the text (as shown in Listing 5.5 and Figure 5.5). Then, each content element is placed in its own cell—first the headline, then the image, and last, the text.

Figure 5.4.

This design combines some of the features of conventional and modern layouts but uses more white space.

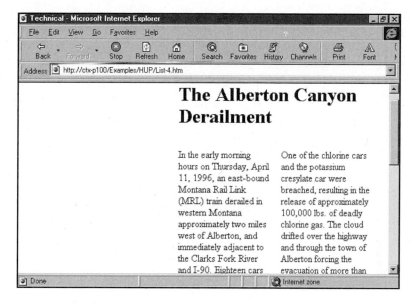

Listing 5.5. A formal page layout.

```
<!DOCTYPE HTML PUBLIC "-//IETF//DTD HTML 4.0//EN">
<HTML>
<HEAD>
 <TITLE>Formal</TITLE>
</HEAD>
<STYLE type="text/css">
.center {text-align:center}
.initial {font-size:+3}
</STYLE>
<BODY>
<TABLE BORDER="0" WIDTH="100%" CELLSPACING="3">
 <TR>
  <TD WIDTH="25%">
  <TD>
   <H1 class="center">The Alberton <BR>
    Canyon Derailment</H1>
  <TD WIDTH="25%">
 <TR>
  <TD>
  <TD>
   <P class="center">
    <IMG SRC="/mrfd/Alberton/albert8.jpg" STYLE="width:300px; height:197px"
    ➥VSPACE="24">
   </P>
  <TD>
 <TR>
  <TD WIDTH="25%">
  <TD>
   <P><SPAN class="initial">I</SPAN>n the early morning hours on Thursday, April
   ➥11,1996, an east-bound Montana Rail Link (MRL) train derailed in western
```

continues

Listing 5.5. continued

```
      Montana approximately two miles west of Alberton, and immediately adjacen
      to the Clarks Fork River and I-90. Eighteen cars derailed from the 71-ca
      train, including six cars carrying hazardous materials. Four containe
      chlorine; one contained potassium cresylate; and the sixth containe
      sodium chlorate.</P
   <P>To compound the problem further, another MRL train derailed near Noxon
      Mont., spilling 1,000 gallons of diesel fuel and overturning anothe
      chlorine car.  The additional confusion caused by the diversion an
      rerouting of resources slowed the initial response of personnel an
      equipment.</P
   <P>One of the chlorine cars and the potassium cresylate car were breached
      resulting in the release of approximately 100,000 lbs. of deadly chlorin
      gas. The cloud drifted over the highway and through the town of Alberto
      forcing the evacuation of more than 1,000  people in a 100 square-mile area
      Half of these were kept out of their homes for 17 days.  An estimated 35
      35 miles to the east. A lone fatality occurred when a transient riding i
      a box car walked into the cloud after surviving the crash.</P
         <TD WIDTH="25%"
 </TABLE
 </BODY
 </HTML
```

In a formal design, three columns create the space to the left and right of the text and contro the headline and initial image space. The formal layout is particularly fitting for those moment in which dignity is everything. In Figure 5.5, large initial capital letters, central placement o text and image, and lots of space give this page its grace and simplicity

FIGURE 5.5.

An example of formal design.

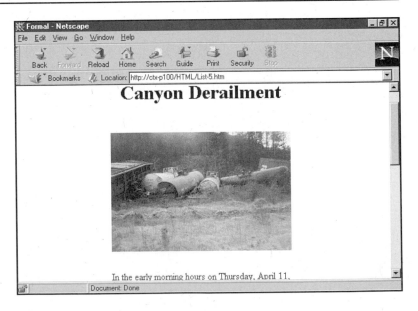

As an added touch, you can increase the size of the first letter in the text by using a style sheet, which could also implement additional text formatting and fonts.

Page 1: A Template

With some of this basic layout information in hand, it's time to roll up your sleeves and get to work. Using the Missoula Rural Fire District site as an example, you'll begin with a template, which will become the basis for your other pages.

NOTE

An HTML template serves as a guide to other HTML pages, as does a pattern for sewing or tracing outlines. Templates are useful for maintaining the same design and image across multiple pages, without guesswork, by providing much of the underlying structure and formatting before you begin.

The Fire District uses its site to communicate a variety of information to the public, including safety tips and date-dependent news. The Fire District also uses the site to develop general awareness of its varying roles and responsibilities in the community. The Web pages need to have a professional look, yet offer information in a friendly manner.

For this purpose, choose a design that's a cross between the classic and technical layouts. It includes ample white space on the left side, interrupted only by hanging headlines and an appropriate image, combined with a bold banner across the top.

Construction on the page begins with the basics—a structure for the document (as shown in Listing 5.6).

Listing 5.6. The beginning of the template for a set of Web pages.

```
<!DOCTYPE HTML PUBLIC "-//IETF//DTD HTML 4.0//EN">
<HTML>
<HEAD>
<TITLE>MRFD - a title</TITLE>
</HEAD>
<STYLE type="text/css">
<!--
BODY {background:"white"}
-->
</STYLE
<BODY>
</BODY>
</HTML>
```

Structure does not a page make, but even a castle needs a foundation before the flags fly from the towers. In short, every Web page should start at the beginning and work from there. In addition to the structure, you'll specify a default background color with a style sheet. A placeholder <TITLE>, which contains the format for the Web page titles, is also added so you don't forget to add a title for other pages later on.

TIP

It's a good idea to begin a page title with a common identifier for your site. This identifier makes it easier for users to spot it if they include a bookmark for the page on their home browsers.

Now that the first bit of detail is finished, it's time to move to formatting for the top of the document. For consistency, give every page the same banner across the top by using a simple table with text and an image. (See Listing 5.7 and Figure 5.6.) This technique is described in more detail in Chapter 10, "Table Layout and Presentation."

Listing 5.7. The first part of the page includes a two-column table with one row.

```
<!DOCTYPE HTML PUBLIC "-//IETF//DTD HTML 4.0//EN">
<HTML>
<HEAD>
<TITLE>MRFD - a title</TITLE>
</HEAD>
<STYLE type="text/css">
<!--
BODY {background:white}
TABLE.banner {background:black}
H1.banner {color:white}
-->
</STYLE>
<BODY>
<TABLE class="banner" border="0" cellspacing="15" width="100%">
 <TR>
  <TD align="RIGHT" valign="BOTTOM" width="75%">
   <H1 class="banner">...Subject Title...</H1>
  <TD align="LEFT" valign="BOTTOM">
   <IMG src="/mrfd/images/fire2.jpg" HEIGHT="158" WIDTH="149">
</TABLE>
</BODY>
</HTML>
```

You should note several things about the opening table tag. First, the borders are invisible (border="0"), which ensures that only the formatting itself is apparent to the user; the method of the formatting remains hidden. Next, the cellspacing attribute uses a larger-than-normal figure to help pad the contents of the two data cells. The table will always occupy 100 percent of the available window width, and when classified as a banner, will have a black background (background:black).

The first cell's contents are forced to the bottom and right margins and occupy 75 percent of the available table width. Then, the page title is added in white to contrast against the black background. Because it's the main title, you use the <H1> tag.

FIGURE 5.6.

The template as it appears so far, with a document title and heading for the top of the document.

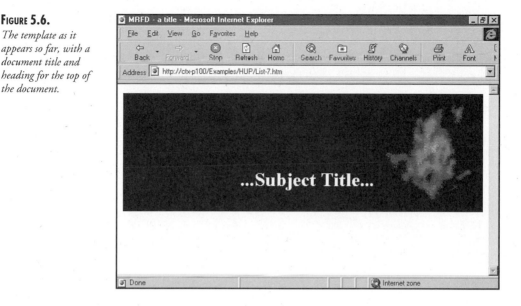

The second cell's contents are aligned to the bottom and left margins. The `width` attribute is not used because the browser will automatically assign it the remaining 25 percent of the table. Its content is a JPEG image with a specified `height` and `width`. (For more information on these attributes, refer to Chapter 11, "Adding Images to Your Web Page.")

Because there's no way of telling where a document based on the template could appear, it uses a `src` URL, which is relative to the document root of the Web page.

TIP

The `height` and `width` for the image are the same as its actual dimensions. These attributes help speed the page display time by alerting the browser to how much space is needed before the image begins to download.

TIP

The image of the flame could just as easily be an animated GIF or a Shockwave animation, as described in Chapter 16, "Embedding Objects in HTML." Place the special content in a common directory so the browser cache can recognize the file, no matter what page it appears on. This method dramatically speeds download time for subsequent pages.

After the banner for the page is finished, indicate where the content will appear. To do this, use another table with opposite column width settings to add interest and balance to the layout, as shown in Listing 5.8 and Figure 5.7. In this content area, 25 percent of the width is allotted for a headline, and the balance is used for the body text.

Listing 5.8. Add the area for content by using another table.

```
<!DOCTYPE HTML PUBLIC "-//IETF//DTD HTML 4.0//EN">
<HTML>
<HEAD>
<TITLE>MRFD - a title</TITLE>
</HEAD>
<STYLE type="text/css">
<!--
BODY {background:white}
TABLE.banner {background:black}
H1.banner {color:white}
-->
</STYLE>
<BODY>
<TABLE class="banner" border="0" cellspacing="15" width="100%">
 <TR>
  <TD align="RIGHT" valign="BOTTOM" width="75%">
   <H1 class="banner">...Subject Title...</H1>
  <TD align="LEFT" valign="BOTTOM">
   <IMG src="/mrfd/images/fire2.jpg" HEIGHT="158" WIDTH="149">
</TABLE>
<TABLE BORDER="0" CELLSPACING="15" WIDTH="100%">
 <TR>
  <TD WIDTH="25%" VALIGN="TOP">
   <H2>Topic Title
     <IMG SRC="/ClipArt/Earth/Landscp/Wildrnss.jpg" WIDTH="162" HEIGHT="122">
   </H2>
  <TD VALIGN="TOP">
   <P>Body text...</P>
</TABLE>
</BODY>
</HTML>
```

With the two main elements in place, the Web page template shown in Figure 5.7 begins to take shape. Notice the placeholder text, which will be replaced for each Web page as it's developed from the template.

Now the structure tags are in place, the page has a banner heading, and the table is formatted to receive content. The last step is to add a couple of details to finish the job, including a horizontal rule at the bottom of the page and a link back to the home page. The completed template file, with all these pieces in place, appears in Listing 5.9.

Listing 5.9. The `template.htm` file includes all the components for the other Fire District Web pages.

```
<!DOCTYPE HTML PUBLIC "-//IETF//DTD HTML 4.0//EN">
<HTML>
<HEAD>
```

```
  <TITLE>MRFD - a title</TITLE>
</HEAD>
<STYLE type="text/css">
<|--
BODY {background:white}
TABLE.banner {background:black}
H1.banner {color:white}
.right {text-align:right}
-->
</STYLE>
<BODY>
<TABLE class="banner" border="0" cellspacing="15" width="100%">
 <TR>
  <TD align="RIGHT" valign="BOTTOM" width="75%">
   <H1 class="banner">...Subject Title...</H1>
  <TD align="LEFT" valign="BOTTOM">
   <IMG src="/mrfd/images/fire2.jpg" HEIGHT="158" WIDTH="149">
</TABLE>
<TABLE BORDER="0" CELLSPACING="15" WIDTH="100%">
 <TR>
  <TD WIDTH="25%" VALIGN="TOP">
   <H2>Topic Title
    <IMG SRC="/ClipArt/Earth/Landscp/Wildrnss.jpg" WIDTH="162" HEIGHT="122">
   </H2>
  <TD VALIGN="TOP">
   <P>Body text...</P>
</TABLE>
<HR>
<P class="right">
<A HREF="/mrfd/index.htm"><STRONG>MRFD Home</STRONG>
 <IMG SRC="/mrfd/Images/cross.gif" WIDTH="113" HEIGHT="97" ALIGN="MIDDLE">
</A></P>
</BODY>
</HTML>
```

FIGURE 5.7.

The Web page template after adding a content area.

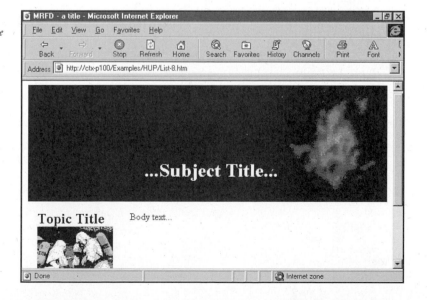

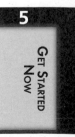

The completed file, `template.htm`, illustrates the basic appearance of any Web page created for the Missoula Rural Fire District. By using invisible borders for the table, advanced formatting techniques can be used without distracting the visitor.

> **NOTE**
>
> If a picture is worth a thousand words, it can seem to take at least a thousand minutes to load. For that reason, most of the pages in the Fire District site have only three relatively small images—one in the banner, one under the document title, and one for the link to the home page.
>
> Because the banner image and home page image are the same on practically every page, the user's browser should maintain its respective files in a cache that further speeds download time. The only new file the browser needs to download for each page is the one under the document title.
>
> Why all this emphasis on limiting images? Because a lot of ISDN and 28.8K modems are on the market, not to mention all the 14.4K and 9600 modems still being used. This limit is an attempt to be sensitive to the download time for all users while still including enough images to make the pages interesting.

Save the template as `template.htm`. Every time a new page is needed, you can place a copy of `template.htm` in the appropriate directory and rename it. Then, when you open it for editing, you can simply replace the placeholder contents with the real thing. Because it's a utility file not meant for display to users, it's kept on the local drive, not on the Web site.

Creating a Real Page from the Template

After the template is created, make copies that are then modified to create the real pages for your users. The first copy is destined to become one of the district's safety pages. First, rename it, and then add the content. Other than changing the information in the <TITLE> tag and adding the appropriate content in the body, no other modifications to the page are needed. (See Listing 5.10 and Figure 5.8.)

Listing 5.10. Only the <TITLE> and body content were changed in this page based on `template.htm`.

```
<!DOCTYPE HTML PUBLIC "-//IETF//DTD HTML 4.0//EN">
<HTML>
<HEAD>
 <TITLE>MRFD - Living in the Wildland/Urban Interface</TITLE>
</HEAD>
<STYLE type="text/css">
<!--
BODY {background:white}
TABLE.banner {background:black}
H1.banner {color:white}
.right {text-align:right}
```

```
.maroon {color:maroon}
-->
</STYLE
<BODY>
<TABLE class="banner" BORDER="0" CELLSPACING="15" WIDTH="100%">
 <TR>
  <TD ALIGN="RIGHT" VALIGN="BOTTOM" WIDTH="75%">
   <H1 class="banner">...Summer Fire Safety...</H1>
  <TD ALIGN="LEFT" VALIGN="BOTTOM">
   <IMG SRC="/mrfd/images/fire2.jpg" HEIGHT="158" WIDTH="149">
</TABLE>
<TABLE BORDER="0" CELLSPACING="15" WIDTH="100%">
 <TR>
  <TD WIDTH="25%" VALIGN="TOP">
   <H2>Living in the wildland/urban interface
   <IMG SRC="/mrfd/images/Wildrnss.jpg" WIDTH="162" HEIGHT="122"></H2>
  <TD VALIGN="TOP">
   <P>Wildfire is a natural element in all ecosystems and environments, and
    Montana is no different. Our climate conditions lead to flammable ground
    cover such as grass, brush and trees. Everyone who has lived in Missoula
    County for any length of time can attest to smoky summer days, or may even
    have seen some of the larger wildfires visible from the valley. Fire is
    a part of our history and a naturally occuring element where we live.</P>
   <P>A new dimension is added to wildfires by the presence of homes. Wildfire
    quickly threatens homes and homeowners, and create a new set of issues for
    firefighters.</P>
   <P><SPAN class="maroon">Missoula Rural Fire District</SPAN> has firefighters
    trained for containing fires in the wildland/urban interface. But compared
    to a wildfire, they are very limited in manpower and equipment, and in the
    distances and terrain they protect. The first homes to burn in the recent
    Pattee Canyon fire were lost while firefighters were still enroute to the
    scene.</P>
   <P>If you're in an area which has a potential for wildfire, you can call
    for a representative from <SPAN class="maroon">Missoula Rural Fire
    District</SPAN> to come to your home and make
    <A HREF="/mrfd/Seasonal/Summer/Wildfire_Tips.htm">suggestions for creating
    defensible space</A> around your structures. <CITE>Defensible space</CITE>
    is an <DFN>area of reduced fuel</DFN> which gives your home greater odds
    of surviving a fire. This is a service provided free of charge to district
    homeowners. For more information, call 549-6172 or
    <A HREF="mailto:mrfd@montana.com">send us a note</A>.</P>
</TABLE>
<HR>
<P class="right">
<A HREF="/mrfd/index.htm"><STRONG>MRFD Home</STRONG>
 <IMG SRC="/mrfd/Images/cross.gif" WIDTH="113" HEIGHT="97" ALIGN="MIDDLE">
</A></P>
</BODY>
</HTML>
```

Several features were included within the content. First, any mention of "Missoula Rural Fire District" was highlighted in maroon to subtly emphasize who is providing the information. Red or pink would stand out more, but could also distract the user from trying to read. This use of the <SPAN> tag and style sheets is covered in Chapter 18.

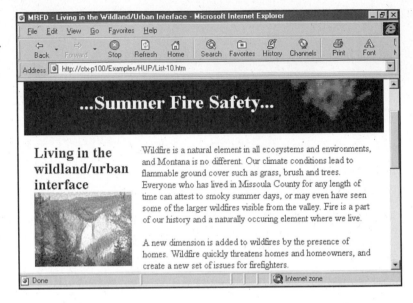

Next, two hyperlinks were added within the text, following the syntax in Chapter 13, "Hyperlinking and Anchors." The first was a link to a related page, `/mrfd/Seasonal/Summer/Wildfire_Tips.htm`. To get more information on this topic, users can click the hyperlink. The second was a link to send e-mail, `mailto:mrfd@montana.com`. If users want to provide feedback, they have the option of doing it immediately instead of looking for a feedback page somewhere else on the site.

Another feature used the logical tags for citations and definitions. The `<CITE>` tag was used to highlight the term *defensible space*, and the `<DFN>` tag was used to mark the definition in the same sentence. In most browsers, these tags would probably look the same—appearing in italics. These two tags, like the other logical tags, indicate the purpose or role of text and make it easier to edit the page at a later time.

This page is simple, but it represents most of the content on this site. The total time to create it—including copying and renaming the template, typing the text, and finding an appropriate image to use under the document title—was 10 minutes.

A Page with a List

The next page created with `template.htm` is a directory of the fire stations that are part of the district. After you copy the template, change the banner headline and page title and add the lists for the body text. (See Listing 5.11 and Figure 5.9.) You also add a set of nested lists. More detail on adding lists is in Chapter 8, "Using Lists to Organize Information."

Listing 5.11. The outer list in this set is a definition list that includes an ordered list as a part of each definition (<DD>).

```
<!DOCTYPE HTML PUBLIC "-//IETF//DTD HTML 4.0//EN">
<HTML>
<HEAD>
 <TITLE>MRFD -- Station Directory</TITLE>
</HEAD>
<STYLE type="text/css">
<!--
BODY {background:white}
TABLE.banner {background:black}
H1.banner {color:white}
.right {text-align:right}
.maroon {color:maroon}
-->
</STYLE
<BODY>
<TABLE CLASS="banner" BORDER="0" CELLSPACING="15" CELLPADDING="1" WIDTH="100%">
 <TR>
  <TD ALIGN="RIGHT" VALIGN="BOTTOM" WIDTH="75%">
   <H1 class="banner">...Directory...</H1>
  <TD ALIGN="LEFT" VALIGN="BOTTOM">
   <IMG SRC="/mrfd/images/fire2.jpg" HEIGHT="158" WIDTH="149">
</TABLE>
<TABLE BORDER="0" CELLSPACING="10" CELLPADDING="5" WIDTH="100%">
 <TR>
  <TD WIDTH="25%" VALIGN="TOP">
   <H2>Missoula Rural Fire District Station Directory</H2>
  <TD WIDTH="75%" VALIGN="TOP">
   <DL>
    <DT><STRONG>Station 1</STRONG> (Administration and Maintenance)
    <DD><EM>2521 South Ave. West, Missoula<BR>
     (406) 549-6174</EM>
     <OL>
      <LI>Engines 311, 312, 316
      <LI>Water Tender 317
      <LI>Staff vehicles 301, 302, 303, 305
     </OL>

    <DT><STRONG>Station 2</STRONG>
    <DD><EM>6550 Highway 10 West, Missoula<BR>
     (406) 549-3601</EM>
     <OL>
      <LI>Engines 321, 326
      <LI>HazMat Response 328
      <LI>Staff vehicle 304
     </OL>
    </DD>

    <DT><STRONG>Station 3</STRONG>
    <DD><P><EM>Closed June 1995</EM></P>

    <DT><STRONG>Station 4</STRONG>
    <DD><EM>9480 Highway 10 East, Bonner<BR>
     (406) 258-6061</EM>
     <OL>
```

continues

Listing 5.11. continued

```
       <LI>Engines 341, 346
       <LI>Water Tender 347
       <LI>Truck 348
      </OL>

   <DT><STRONG>Station 5</STRONG>
   <DD><EM>12221 Highway 93 South, Lolo<BR>
     (406) 273-2551</EM>
    <OL>
     <LI>Engines 351, 356
     <LI>Water Tender 357
    </OL>
   </DD>

   <DT><STRONG>Station 6</STRONG>
   <DD><EM>8455 Mullan Road, Missoula<BR>
     (406) 542-0366</EM>
    <OL>
     <LI>Engines 361, 366
    </OL>
   </DD>
  </DL>
</TABLE>
<P class="right"><A HREF="/mrfd/index.htm">
<STRONG>MRFD Home</STRONG>
<IMG SRC="/mrfd/Images/cross.gif" WIDTH="113" HEIGHT="97" ALIGN="MIDDLE">
</A></P>
</BODY>
</HTML>
```

FIGURE 5.9.

In this directory pages, definition list tags are used when additional information is needed for each list entry.

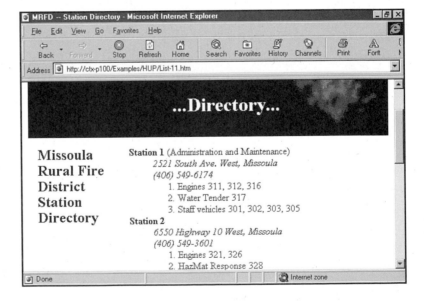

Each list entry consists of two parts: the name of the station and its address, and assigned apparatus. The only list available in HTML that fits a term-definiton relationship is the definition list. The list of apparatus is created by using a numbered list within the definition.

Summary

This chapter has given you a look into the way one organization uses HTML 4.0 to build its Web pages. The process began with experimenting with the four basic design elements: headlines, text, images, and space. These elements led to a simple design that fit the needs of the Fire District and became the basis of a Web page template.

From there, HTML elements—including hyperlinks, font sizes and colors, lists, and inline images—were added to the pages. The result is a uniform look to the Web site that doesn't require much time to implement. This feature is especially useful because this site is maintained by people with other demands on their time.

It's possible to use combinations of graphics, tables, and frames to build more elaborate and fancy page designs, but you should get a feel from these examples for what's possible while still remaining within the constraints of the standard HTML elements. Part IV, "Presentation Techniques," covers extended HTML design features beyond what I've discussed in this section. Part VII focuses on design, showing you how to make better use of HTML's capabilities to deliver your message to an eager audience.

II

PART

Structural and Navigational Elements of HTML 4

Structuring Text

by Rick Darnell

IN THIS CHAPTER

CHAPTER 6

As explained in Part I of this book, "Introducing HTML 4.0," HTML documents are created by combining special markup codes called *tags*. Tags define the structure of the document and provide the framework for holding the actual content, which can be text, images, or other special content.

The elements covered in this chapter are called *structural* elements because their primary purpose is to create the form of the document. These elements include the document itself, the head and body sections, page titles, and other basic document identifiers.

NOTE

Actually, all HTML tags are structural in their purpose of defining the relations of elements to each other within the document. The reason this particular set is referred to as *structural* is because these elements really have no formatting purpose for what appears on the screen. All other tags control the appearance of the page in one form or another.

The easiest way to illustrate the purpose and form of structural tags is to begin with a page, shown in Listing 6.1, with no structure.

Listing 6.1. This HTML document lacks any HTML structural form.

```
Missoula Rural Fire District Home Page
Welcome to the MRFD Home Page
Thank you for visiting our home page. From here, you can
link to several destinations, including fire safety
information, district budget, minutes from board meetings
and upcoming training.
```

If the code in Listing 6.1 were displayed on a browser, it would look something like the page in Figure 6.1. Note the complete lack of organization. It could also generate an error in a non-standard Web browser because the type of content isn't identified.

Good page design begins with good organization, and that's what the structural tags provide.

COMMON ATTRIBUTES

Most of the elements in this chapter share some common attributes. Rather than list all of them for each element every time, I'll identify them here and refer to this list in the text. The first set of attributes are referred to as the *core attributes*:

id: This value serves as document-wide identification, and should be unique among any other IDs in the document.

title: This attribute supplies additional information about the element and can be used or ignored at the browser's discretion.

class: Style sheets use this attribute to apply a style to a set of elements associated with this class. See Chapter 18, "Using Cascading Style Sheets," for more information.

style: This attribute is used to include inline style information for the current instance of the element. See Chapter 18 for more information.

The next two are *international attributes* (see Chapter 40, "Internationalizing Your HTML"):

lang: This attribute specifies the primary language for the document text, with the default as unknown. For more information, consult "Tags for the Identification of Languages," available at `ftp://ds.internic.net/rfc/rfc1766.txt`.

dir: The direction of weak or neutral text, which carries the value `LTR` (left-to-right) or `RTL` (right-to-left). The browser determines the default direction, although for the English and European languages, it's safe to assume left-to-right.

Next come the *alignment attributes*, which determine how text is justified within the document. The values are `left`, `right`, `center`, or `justify`. The default is `left` for `LTR` paragraphs and `right` for `RTL` paragraphs. Many browsers don't support `justify` (both left and right), in which case the alignment defaults to the value based on the `dir` attribute.

The last attributes are the *event handlers*—`onclick`, `ondblclick`, `onmousedown`, `onmouseup`, `onmouseover`, `onmousemove`, `onmouseout`, `onkeypress`, `onkeydown`, and `onkeyup`—which are covered in more detail in Chapter 28, "Working with the User: Events."

FIGURE 6.1.

Without some basic structural elements, this Web page is formless and pointless.

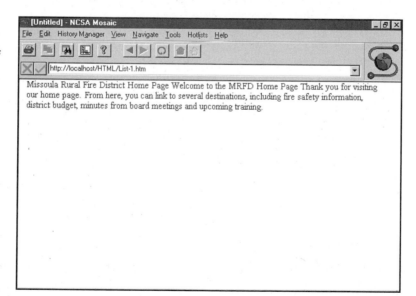

The `<!DOCTYPE>` Declaration

Theoretically, the `<!DOCTYPE>` tag should be the first tag in your HTML document. This tag tells the Web server what it's dealing with when it delivers the document; in turn, the server informs the browser what kind of tags it can expect inside.

Here's how the `<!DOCTYPE>` tag is used:

```
<!DOCTYPE HTML idString>
```

In this declaration, `idString` specifies the version of HTML used in the document. For example, the following code identifies a document built according to the standards laid out for HTML 4.0:

```
<!DOCTYPE HTML PUBLIC "-//W3C//DTD HTML 4.0//EN">
```

> **TIP**
>
> You can find a reasonably complete list of DOCTYPE declarations at the following address:
>
> `http://ugweb.cs.alberta.ca/~gerald/validate/lib/catalog`

In reality, using `<!DOCTYPE>` is difficult. Many variations of HTML are in use, the standards are continuously evolving, and browser implementations continue to change the rules. The mix of extensions in a document can include tags from HTML 2.0, 3.2, and 4.0, along with customized extensions from both Netscape and Microsoft. This situation is where universal standards and the rules of the marketplace meet head-to-head. As a practical matter, many browsers ignore `<!DOCTYPE>` or just ignore the tags they don't understand, regardless of whether they're part of the standard expressed for the document.

> **NOTE**
>
> The `<!DOCTYPE>` tag is also used in customized forms by applications, such as Microsoft FrontPage, that need to identify product-specific content.

With this bit of preamble out of the way, it's time to move on to the document itself.

Setting the Boundaries with `<HTML>`

The first tag to learn about is `<HTML>`, which is the next line in a document after `<!DOCTYPE>`. It's paired with `</HTML>` to encase all the other tags in an HTML page; the two mark the absolute beginning and end of the file.

This is the syntax for using the <HTML> tag:

```
<HTML [version=URL][international]>
...document and tags...
</HTML>
```

In this declaration, *URL* is the URL of the Document Type Definition that applies to this document, and *tags* are the rest of your HTML document. Elements allowed within the <HTML> tag are the <HEAD> tag followed by a <FRAMESET> or <BODY>.

Using the <!DOCTYPE> and <HTML> tags is the first step in providing a structure for the first example in this chapter, and results in the code shown in Listing 6.2.

Listing 6.2. Marking the beginning and end of an HTML document.

```
<!DOCTYPE HTML PUBLIC "-//W3C//DTD HTML 4.0//EN">
<HTML>
Missoula Rural Fire District Home Page
Welcome to the MRFD Home Page
Thank you for visiting our home page. From here, you
can link to several destinations, including fire safety
information, district budget, minutes from board meetings
and upcoming training.
</HTML>
```

There are a couple of good reasons to use the <HTML> tag. First, HTML isn't the only markup language on the Web. There are cousins to HTML, such as extensible markup language (XML), that are interpreted in slightly different ways and gaining in acceptance and use. Second, using the <HTML> tag is good style and shows that whoever built the document had some idea what to do—and because you're taking the time to read this book, you know what to do.

> **NOTE**
>
> The opening and closing <HTML> tags are optional, and most browsers still know what to do with the document after it's loaded, especially if it still conforms to the DTD and uses the DOCTYPE element. However, some browsers might become confused when handed a document without any clear indication of type with either DOCTYPE or HTML, resulting in a page that's displayed unpredictably or that might refuse to load at all.

The appearance of Listing 6.2 won't change on the browser with the addition of the opening and closing <HTML> tags, but at least now its boundaries are delineated and the browser knows how to interpret the file after it's loaded.

Now that the document's type and boundaries are marked and identified, it's time to divide the HTML page into two operational parts: the header and the body. The tags and their compatriots that govern these two major sections are explained next.

The HEAD Element

Theoretically, every document has a header and a body. The header of the document is where global settings are defined; it's contained between the `<HEAD>` and `</HEAD>` tags.

Here's how the `<HEAD>` tags are used:

```
<HEAD [profile=URLlist][international]>
header content
</HEAD>
```

The `URLlist` contains one or more URLs separated by spaces that specify files with metadata profiles for the document. The `profile` is discussed in more detail in the section "Using `<META>` to Give More Information," later in this chapter. The *header content* includes one or more items from the six tags used exclusively within the header portion of an HTML document. It's also a favorite place to include scripting language function definitions.

The addition of these tags to the sample HTML document results in Listing 6.3.

Listing 6.3. Getting an extra boost of structure with the `<HEAD>` tag.

```
<!DOCTYPE HTML PUBLIC "-//W3C//DTD HTML 4.0//EN">
<HTML>
<HEAD>
Missoula Rural Fire District Home Page
</HEAD>
Welcome to the MRFD Home Page
Thank you for visiting our home page. From here, you
can link to several destinations, including fire safety
information, district budget, minutes from board meetings
and upcoming training.
</HTML>
```

Displayed on a browser, the results are made slightly clearer by the elimination of the first line, which has disappeared completely. It's destined for use in the next header tag.

Headers also serve another important function. Using the HTTP protocol, it's possible to download the header information only. Most users aren't aware of this capability and probably don't care. It's used primarily by search engines and automated robots, which can download a header and get some basic information about the page—title, file format, last-modified date, keywords—without spending the extra time to load or look at the rest of the document.

Giving Your Page a `<TITLE>`

Probably the most commonly used HEAD feature in HTML is the `<TITLE>` tag. It's a required element in the HEAD, and this is its syntax:

```
<TITLE [international]>text</TITLE>
```

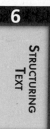

In this tag, *text* is a short, one-line name for the document that's displayed in the browser's title bar. Without a title, most browsers default to the HTML filename. Because filenames aren't always terribly descriptive and are sometimes long and clunky, it's good practice to supply a title for all HTML documents.

The addition of the <TITLE> tag to your HTML document reinforces its structure; the results are shown in the code in Listing 6.4 and the page in Figure 6.2.

Listing 6.4. Adding a title to the HTML document.

```
<!DOCTYPE HTML PUBLIC "-//W3C//DTD HTML 4.0//EN">
<HTML>
<HEAD>
<TITLE>Missoula Rural Fire District Home Page</TITLE>
</HEAD>
Welcome to the MRFD Home Page
Thank you for visiting our home page. From here, you can
link to several destinations, including fire safety
information, district budget, minutes from board meetings
and upcoming training.
</HTML>
```

FIGURE 6.2.

The Web page after adding some structural elements and a title (shown in the browser's title bar).

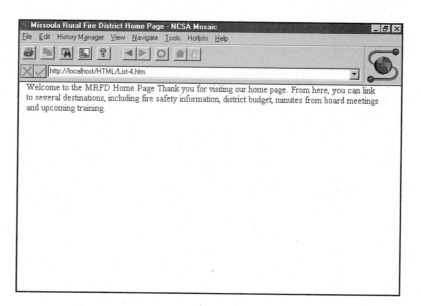

Only one title is allowed per document (as explained in the following Tip), and its size is limited by the size of the user's browser window. You can include a title that's as long as you want, but it's truncated in the browser's title bar if it stretches beyond the limits.

TIP

To make your titles easier for the user, make sure they are short and to the point, but not so short as to be vague. For example, "MRFD" is not a good title. What does MRFD mean? Where are we? What are we doing here? On the other hand, "Missoula Rural Fire District Home Page" is a good title. You've identified the page and its purpose, which is what the user needs to know.

Keep in mind that many browsers keep their name in the title bar along with your title, leaving less space for your page's title. Keep the title long enough to be useful but short enough to fit.

ONE TITLE ONLY, PLEASE

Once upon a browser, when Netscape 1.0 was the biggest show in town, there was a slight glitch with the <TITLE> tag. You could stack up a series of tags, like this:

```
<TITLE>M</TITLE>
<TITLE>MR</TITLE>
<TITLE>MRF</TITLE>
<TITLE>MRFD</TITLE>
<TITLE>MRFD H</TITLE>
<TITLE>MRFD Ho</TITLE>
<TITLE>MRFD Hom</TITLE>
<TITLE>MRFD Home</TITLE>
<TITLE>MRFD Home </TITLE>
<TITLE>MRFD Home P</TITLE>
<TITLE>MRFD Home Pa</TITLE>
<TITLE>MRFD Home Pag</TITLE>
<TITLE>MRFD Home Page</TITLE>
```

The result would be a title that gradually built up across the title bar. This aberrant behavior was fixed in Navigator 2.0, and the result was pages with some strange behavior. Different browsers interpret multiple titles in different ways. For example, Navigator 4.02 picks the first title from the list, but Internet Explorer 4.0 uses the last tag. For the preceding example, your document would appear to have a title of "M" or "MRFD Home Page," depending on which browser the user preferred.

The moral of this little story? Use one title in your document so that the browser won't have to guess, and your users won't have to wonder what's going on.

A <BASE> for Hyperlinks

The <BASE> tag controls the actions of relative hyperlinks in the body of the document. By default, relative links in a document refer to the same server where the page is located. However, with the <BASE> tag, you can specify that the relative links are resolved in relation to a different location, whether it's another directory on the host or a completely different server. (For more information on hyperlinks and anchors, see Chapter 13, "Hyperlinking and Anchors.")

The <BASE> tag takes a single attribute, HREF, with the following syntax:

```
<BASE href="protocol://servername/path/"[target=targetFrame]>
```

The URL in the href attribute specifies an absolute URL for use in resolving hyperlinks, and the *targetFrame* identifies the frame that will receive the contents of the hyperlink.

> **NOTE**
>
> In the <BASE> tag, *protocol* is a valid Internet communication standard, such as HTTP; *servername* is a server name or address, such as www.wossamotta.edu or 89.123.32.21; and *path* is any additional mapping on the server. The path is an optional value to the URL. If the path is included by itself, it refers to the host server.

For example, a page for an educational institution is located on the server at www.frostbitefalls.org. The page is copied straight off the university's server at www.wossamotta.edu and placed in the new location. Any relative links will no longer work because they're referring to locations at the home location.

If the user clicks on a link to look at the football schedule, then the browser takes the content of the link, /football/schedule.html, and combines it with the host, www.frostbitefalls.org, to create http://www.frostbitefalls.org/football/schedule.html. But, alas, Frostbite Falls doesn't have this directory, and the user gets the dreaded 404 Not Found error.

The <BASE> tag circumvents this problem, like so:

```
<BASE HREF="http://www.wossamotta.edu/">
```

Now, when a user clicks on a link for the football page, the base information is substituted for the host information, which results in http://www.wossamotta.edu/football/schedule.html— and now the information on the match-up against Tick Tock Tech is easily accessed.

Showing Relationships with <LINK>

The <LINK> tag has been around since the early days of HTML, although it has yet to earn acceptance or implementation from many browsers. In its current definition, <LINK> provides a media- and platform-independent method for defining relationships between the current HTML page and other documents and resources. All popular browsers, with the exception of Mosaic 3.0, still ignore the tag.

In theory, <LINK> is used to create document-specific toolbars or menus, to control how collections of HTML files are connected when printed, and to link associated resources, such as style sheets and scripts. In addition to the core, international, and event attributes, there are five other attributes used with LINK:

href   The URL of the linked document. It's provided in standard URL format, but is typically a relative URL.

rel   This attribute and its value indicate the relationship of the current document to the document referenced in href. The values that are used include Contents, Index, Glossary, Copyright, Next, Previous, and Help. For example, the following line indicates that a glossary for the current document is located in a file called glossary.html:

```
<LINK rel=Glossary href="glossary.html">
```

This attribute is also used to specify linked style sheets, described in Chapter 18. Another possible value is Alternate, which indicates another version of the document. It's commonly paired with the language attribute to specify the same document in a different translation.

rev   This attribute is similar to rel, except it indicates a reverse relationship between the document and the URL. For example, the following line indicates that the current document has a glossary for the document specified in the URL:

```
<LINK rev=Glossary href="chapter1.html">
```

It accepts the same values as rel.

type   This attribute describes the type of input control to create. The possible values are: text, password, checkbox, radio, submit, reset, file, hidden, image and button. It is not currently supported by any major browser.

media   This attribute specifies what kind of medium the information will be displayed on. It can include a single media type, or a list separated by commas. These are the possibilities:

- **screen:** The default output, intended for a computer monitor.
- **print:** Either a hardcopy format or a print-preview mode on a screen, such as a Postscript file.
- **projection:** Projection onto a large-format screen.
- **braille:** Output is translated for a Braille feedback device.
- **speech:** Output is interpreted through a speech synthesizer.
- **all:** Output applies to all devices.

target   The name of a current frame to display the content of the link.

Currently, the only use for <LINK> in Internet Explorer (3.0) or Navigator (4.0) is to specify style sheets as external to the document. Mosaic (3.0) supports the use of <LINK> to create a custom button bar just above the document. (See Figure 6.3.)

FIGURE 6.3.

NCSA Mosaic uses `<LINK>` *tags to create a navigation bar at the top of the document.*

Buttons created by `<LINK>` tags

For more information on using `<LINK>` with cascading style sheets, see Chapter 19.

Using `<META>` to Give More Information

Web servers send their own header with HTML documents to help clients interpret the document. This header is separate and different from the header you've been working on in this section.

Like the `<!DOCTYPE>` tag, the `<META>` tag is used to pass additional information about how the document should be handled, and it's often used with add-on content supplied by applications such as Microsoft FrontPage and Macromedia Backstage. In addition, it's used to give extra information about the document that can be used by search engines to classify and identify the document without downloading the entire document. This is the syntax:

```
<META [http-equiv][name][content][scheme][international]>
```

The `http-equiv` and `name` attributes serve the same basic purpose, with one important difference. Any `<META>` tag using `http-equiv` is added to the response header supplied to the browser. If the tag uses the `name` attribute, the information is available for reference in the document header, but not included in the server-generated response header.

Keep in mind one important consideration when using the `http-equiv` attribute. It should never override a standard header value, such as `last-modified` or `contenttype`. Doing so could result in a conflict with the server that prevents delivery of the document by the server or interpretation by the browser. Here are some examples of `http-equiv`:

```
<META HTTP-EQUIV=refresh CONTENT=60>
<META HTTP-EQUIV=keywords CONTENT="fire department public safety">
<META HTTP-EQUIV=reply-to CONTENT="mrfd@montana.com">
```

This example covers three of the most used variables for `http-equiv`:

- **refresh** implements a process called *client-pull*, in which the browser is directed to reload the document after the number of seconds specified in `content`. It's used when the document is updated on a periodic basis. `content` can also take the form `N; URL=url`; `N` is the number of seconds to wait, and `url` is the new URL to load.

- **keywords** specifies a list of words separated by spaces, which is used by some search engines to classify the document for quicker retrieval. Many search engines load only the head and not the body, so it's important to include the keywords in the `<META>` tag so the engine knows what is found in your document.

- **reply-to** provides an e-mail address that users can use to respond to the author or responsible party for the page. Its display is typically triggered by the server, which adds it as a server-side include. This attribute is not commonly used.

NOTE

A *server-side include* (SSI) is a direction placed in the HTML document that tells the server to insert a piece of text on the page when the page is delivered to the browser. Its use is typically for things that might change from hit to hit, such as the last-modified date, hit counter value, document size, or Webmaster address. The syntax for inserting and activating an SSI differs with each Web server, so you'll need to check your documentation or system administrator for more information.

WHAT IS CLIENT PULL?

Client pull provides a way for pages to automatically reload after a certain amount of time has passed, or for a series of pages to automatically load themselves with a pause between them. If you wanted the browser to reload the current page in four seconds, you would add this tag to your HTML page:

```
<META http-equiv="Refresh" content=4>
```

If the value of `content` is 0, the page is refreshed as fast as the browser can retrieve it, which may be a little slow if the user has a slow or poor-quality connection. It's definitely not fast enough for any sort of quality animation.

After the `refresh` value is added to `http-equiv`, the browser will reload it ad infinitum. To stop the process, you need to supply a hyperlink to another page without a client pull tag.

Continuously loading the same page is useful for pages that are updated constantly, such as documents with stock quotes or sports scores. However, you can also use client pull to load a different page. Continuing the process of loading a new page allows you to automatically lead a user through a series of slides or instructions. The `content` attribute is modified to provide this capability:

```
<META http-equiv="Refresh"
content="8;URL=http://www.mrfd.com/safety/tip2.html">
```
The URI must be a full URL. Relative URLs consisting only of pathnames aren't allowed. Inside the target page, you can include a pointer to the next page, and so on. This technique allows you to load any number of pages in a sequence. However, it's still a good idea to supply a link out of the automatic process so your readers aren't forced to sit through the entire show.

The `name` attribute is used to provide other information about the document that might be useful to someone looking at it but not critical to deliver in the header. Here are some examples:

```
<META NAME=author CONTENT="Dave Herzberg">
<META NAME=description CONTENT="Home page for MRFD">
<META NAME=copyright CONTENT="Copyright 1997, Missoula Rural Fire Dist.">
```

The attributes for these examples are used more often by HTML editors:

- **author** identifies the person who created the page, and sometimes includes the name of the HTML editor.

- **description** gives a one-line explanation of the page or its use. It's sometimes used by search engines to provide a summary of the page when it displays search results to a user.

- **copyright** is the official copyright notice for your page. Anything you create is subject to protection by copyright law, whether or not it has this statement. However, including it prevents ignorance excuses ("I didn't know") from would-be plagiarizers.

As seen in the preceding examples, `content` is the actual value contained in the tag. Although most browsers and servers don't require quotation marks around the value, it's good practice to use them. They remove ambiguity and the possibility of misinterpretation, especially for values requiring more than one word.

The `scheme` attribute is used to identify a method or template that should be used to evaluate the content attribute. It's included to support efforts, such as the Dublin Core profile, to define properties for electronic bibliographies.

The BODY Element

Like the `<HEAD>` tag, the `<BODY>` tag's primary purpose is to delineate the main portion of the document—the part seen by the user. Here's how it's used:

```
<BODY [bgcolor=value][onload=action][onunload=action][core][international][events]>
...document contents...
</BODY>
```

In this tag, `bgcolor` is the name of a color to use for a background in the document. The color can also be defined as a hexadecimal triplet (see the following Note). The *document contents* are any valid HTML content, including text, forms, graphics, special content, and so on.

NOTE

There are 16 color names recognized by HTML 4.0: black, silver, gray, white, maroon, red, purple, fuchsia, green, lime, olive, yellow, navy, blue, teal, and aqua. These color names should be recognized by any browser supporting color on its respective platform.

You can also specify the color with a hexadecimal triplet. The triplet is formed by three two-digit hexadecimal numbers representing the red, green, and blue mix of the color. Decimal digits begin with 0 and end with 9, but hexadecimal digits begin with 0, continue with 9, and end with the letters A through F. A two-digit hexadecimal number ranges in value from 00 (decimal 0) to FF (decimal 255).

So the color red would be defined as complete saturation of red (FF, or 255 parts out of a possible 255) with the complete absence of green (00, or 0 parts out of a possible 255) and blue (00, same as green). As a triplet, red is written as FF0000. To let HTML know it's dealing with a hexadecimal value and not a name, the pound character (#) is added to the beginning, making the complete value #FF0000. Gray would be an equal mix of all three colors, represented as #C0C0C0 (192 parts out of 255 for each of the colors), and fuchsia is made by combining pure red with pure blue and represented as #FF00FF.

In the previous version of HTML, it also included five attributes to describe default values for the body of the document: background (background image), text (text color), link (normal link color), alink (link color during a click), and vlink (visited link color). These attributes are deprecated in HTML 4.0 in favor of specifying their values with style sheets (see Chapter 18).

TIP

If omitted, the <BODY> tag is assumed by the browser after the <HEAD> tag. If the <HEAD> tag is also absent, the <BODY> tag is assumed immediately after the opening <HTML> tag.

The onload and onunload event handlers are unique to the <BODY> tag. Although they're discussed in more detail in Chapter 28, I'll give a quick overview here.

The onload event specifies a script or other action to take when the entire contents of the document have been loaded, but not yet rendered by the browser. This event allows the page author to display alerts or take other action before the user has a chance to interact with the page. Note that the entire content of the page doesn't include images or other objects. The content of the page for this attribute is composed solely of the HTML file's contents.

The onunload event is similar to onload, except it happens when the user has made an action to leave the current page and load a new one. Page authors can take several actions in reaction to this event, with one important exception—they can't prevent the user from leaving.

6

More on creating scripts to respond to the user is found in Chapter 23, "JavaScript at a Glance," and Chapter 24, "Using VBScript."

Breaking a Body into Pieces: <DIV> and <SPAN>

The <DIV> element is used to structure an HTML document into a series of divisions. This is its syntax:

```
<DIV [core][international][events]>Content</DIV>
```

In this element, *Content* is one or more lines of text and other HTML markup that make up the division.

The <DIV> tag is a block element that acts much like a <P> tag. If a <P> tag doesn't have a closing </P>, <DIV> effectively closes it and starts a new paragraph. Other than this behavior, <DIV> doesn't generate paragraph breaks before or after its placement.

USING <CENTER> INSTEAD OF <DIV align=center>

The <CENTER> tag is identical to <DIV align=center>. This duplication occurred because the <CENTER> tag was introduced by Netscape at about the same time the <DIV> element was added to the HTML 3.0 specification.

Using the align attribute of <P> or <DIV> is the preferred way to center text. The <CENTER> tag is still in the HTML 4.0 specification because of its widespread use, although it has been deprecated and slated for eventual removal.

The <SPAN> tag is similar to the <DIV> tag, except it's used to mark content inline rather than create a new block. Because it's an inline element, it doesn't make use of the alignment attribute:

```
<SPAN [core][international][events]></SPAN>
```

The most common use that has developed for both <DIV> and <SPAN> is marking sections of text for formatting or positioning with style sheets. As you'll discover in Part VI, "Dynamic HTML," these two structural elements are important to some of the interactive style and positioning abilities for dynamic documents.

The STYLE Element

The STYLE element holds a place in your document for setting all the properties that control its appearance, including font selection, color, alignment, and borders. The <STYLE> tag is supported by a separate W3C recommendation on cascading style sheets.

You can find more about style sheets and using the <STYLE> tag in Chapters 17, 18, 19, and 21 ("Simple Style with Text," "Using Cascading Style Sheets," "Cascading Style Sheets and Element Positioning," and "Using JavaScript Style Sheets"), which cover cascading style sheets (CSS) and their use, JavaScript-based style sheets, and other alternatives to CSS.

The SCRIPT Element

The SCRIPT element is a bit of a free spirit, and it's used in two ways. In either application, it indicates a specific scripting language being used in the document. Two scripting languages are currently in widespread use on the World Wide Web: JavaScript and Visual Basic Script (VBScript). Here is this element's syntax:

```
<SCRIPT [type=MIMEtype][language=language][src=URL>
…script content…
</SCRIPT>
```

In this element, *MIMEtype* is an Internet MIME type for the language, such as text/vbscript; *language* is typically either VBScript or JavaScript, and *URL* identifies an external source for the script. More information on specifying and creating scripts is in Chapters 23 and 24.

In its typical usage, <SCRIPT> contains a section of programming code. If this code is placed in the header, it's interpreted before the rest of the document is loaded. This practice is common for segments of code that serve as functions, when it's imperative to have the function loaded and available before anything in the document has a chance to invoke it.

Browsers that don't support scripting languages probably won't recognize the <SCRIPT> tag. If this happens, the tag's contents are displayed as regular text, which results in a lot of strange reading for the user. To avert this problem, there's a simple workaround:

```
<SCRIPT>
<!--
script stuff
-->
</SCRIPT>
```

By encasing the script with HTML comment tags within the <SCRIPT> tags, a noncompatible browser will ignore the script contents. The script will then ignore the comment tags and process normally.

TIP

Here's another method of defining a script that's supported by Microsoft and Netscape but not yet sanctioned by the HTML standard:

```
<SCRIPT language=language for=id event=eventHandler>
...script commands for this function...
</SCRIPT>
```

In this method, *id* identifies the id attribute for the element on the page the function is created for, and *eventHandler* is the action that triggers the function.

For example, the following snippet of code creates a script to react to a click on the nextPage button:

```
<SCRIPT language=javascript for=nextPage event=onClick>
...script commands for this function...
</SCRIPT>
<BODY>
...HTML stuff...
<INPUT type=button value="Move On" id=nextPage>
...HTML stuff...
</BODY>
```

Summary

Structure tags set the stage for the rest of your HTML and provide its basic framework. They mark the beginning and end of the file, header, and body sections. Additional tags and attributes in the header set basic behaviors, define a title, and pass information to the browser. By using the <BODY> tag, you can also set background images and colors and set default colors for text items on the page.

Although these tags serve an important purpose in your HTML document, they're not the visible part that's fun to play with. Coverage of the elements that give purpose to your text is next in Chapter 7, "Text Alignment and Formatting."

Text Alignment and Formatting

by Rick Darnell

IN THIS CHAPTER

CHAPTER 7

In Chapter 6, "Structuring Text," you saw how to build a frame for an HTML document. The basic structure includes the boundaries of the HTML page, a header and body, and a handful of other items to provide a framework for the page content. With that little bit of HTML, you have more than enough to build a Web page.

You could put all your text between the two body tags, and the user could read it. There's a small problem, however. It would appear as one long unbroken paragraph, no matter how you typed it or how many lines you placed in between the paragraphs. Web browsers don't look at text the way a person does. When the browser sees the end of a line in your document, it adds a space and keeps right on going. The result is one long string of words on the page that is neither attractive nor easy to read.

The HTML elements covered in this chapter are designed to add some basic alignment and formatting to your page. There are tags for headings, addresses, and quotations; there are tags to begin new paragraphs and start new lines; and there are tags to add horizontal lines to help divide the page.

This chapter explains the workhorses for organizing and formatting your document. You'll find that practically every page on the Web uses at least one or two of these tags, and many make liberal use of more than that. Read on to find out how to use HTML text formatting elements to give visual and logical structure to your pages.

COMMON ATTRIBUTES

Most of the elements in this chapter share common HTML attributes, such as items that control identification, style, language, and event handling. Because the common attributes are so pervasive in HTML 4 (that's why they're called "common"), you will find an overview of them in the introduction of this book. You can also find more information about these often-used features and their associated elements in Appendix A, "HTML 4.0 Reference."

Meanwhile, in this chapter, I'll refer to the common attributes by using these keywords: *core*, *international*, and *event*.

Additionally, many of the elements can accept other elements within their borders. These are referred to as the *inline elements*, and include the following options:

font elements: These elements include tags for bold (`<B>`) and italics (`<I>`) and are covered in Chapter 17, "Simple Style with Text."

phrase elements: These elements include tags such as emphasis (`<EM>`), code (`<CODE>`), and address (`<ADDRESS>`) and are covered in this chapter.

special elements: This collection is a hodgepodge of elements that includes all the following items: applets and objects (Chapter 16, "Embedding Objects in HTML"), images (Chapter 11, "Adding Images to Your Web Page"), anchors (Chapter 13, "Hyperlinking and Anchors"), image maps (Chapter 14, "Creating Menus with Image

Maps"), scripts (Chapters 23, "JavaScript at a Glance," and 24, "Using VBScript"), fonts, superscripts, and subscripts (Chapter 17), line breaks and short quotes (this chapter), and inline frames (Chapter 20, "Creating Frames").

form elements: This set of elements is used to add elements to a form, including buttons, text fields, and checkboxes.

Headings <H1> Through <H6>

You don't begin a newspaper story with the lead paragraph; you begin it with a headline. And that's where this chapter begins—with the text formatting tags. The six HTML heading styles are a way of showing the level of importance among different parts of your page, much like this book uses different levels of headings to visually organize the information.

This is the syntax:

```
<Hn [core][international][events]>Heading Text</Hn>
```

Here, *n* is an integer from 1 to 6 indicating the level of heading used, with 1 being the most important and 6 being the least. All the attributes are optional.

Although browsers vary in the size and typestyle given to the six heading levels, every browser follows the basic rule of giving the biggest and boldest style to <H1>, and the smallest and most unobtrusive style to <H6>. (See Figure 7.1.)

> **TIP**
>
> On some browsers, the lowest heading levels are actually smaller than the body text. The result looks slightly odd.

Headings allow any of the inline elements within their boundaries. You can set the style (bold, italic, or underlined), typeface, and size within a heading to give it additional emphasis, as shown in this example:

```
Next on our site is <H1>Reflections on <I>The Devils
of Loudun</I></H1> followed by pictures of my cat.
```

Changing the style is possible in any of the heading styles, regardless of their level, to further control the heading's appearance. (See Figure 7.2.)

In Figure 7.2, note how the browser handles the text before and after the heading tags. A heading is always placed on its own line, even if it's placed inline with other material. A new paragraph is started for the heading, and any material following it is placed on the next new line.

FIGURE 7.1.
HTML heading styles show a descending level of emphasis and importance.

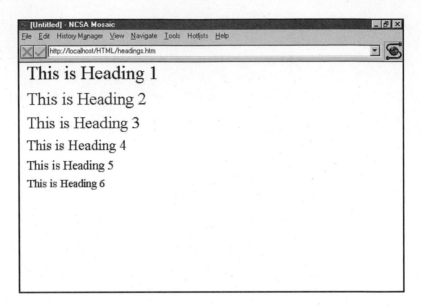

FIGURE 7.2.
You can use physical formatting to control all or part of the text in a heading.

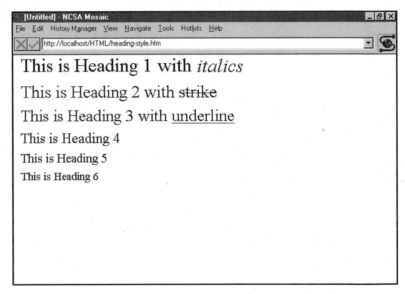

Basic Text Formatting

Now that the headings are in place, it's time to turn your attention to the rest of the document. The next step is to start breaking the text into paragraphs. Listing 7.1 appears to be a Web page broken into logical paragraphs, but look at Figure 7.3 to see how a browser interprets it.

Listing 7.1. Trying to use extra hard returns to force each statement to its own line.

```
<HTML>
<HEAD>
<TITLE>Hot Water Safety</TITLE>
</HEAD>
<BODY>
Hot water is dangerous.

Turn down the hot water heater thermostat.

Always supervise children in the bathtub.

Don't encourage children to play around the tub.
</BODY>
</HTML>
```

FIGURE 7.3.

The browser has ignored the extra line breaks and run the lines together into one long paragraph.

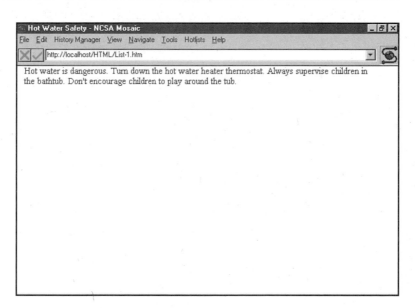

This result obviously isn't what the designer had in mind, so check out the next three elements for methods to make the page conform to the way it should look.

A New Paragraph: <P>

The first way to break text into paragraphs is to use the paragraph tag: <P>. The syntax looks like this:

```
<P [core][international][events]>...Text...</P>
```

Text is a line or paragraph text, which should begin on a new line and remain together. The closing tag is optional and can be omitted. If used with a style sheet, however, the closing tag is required to apply the style properties.

Using this tag on the preceding listing results in the code shown in Listing 7.2 and the page shown in Figure 7.4.

Listing 7.2. Defining each line as its own paragraph.

```
<HTML>
<HEAD>
<TITLE>Hot Water Safety</TITLE>
</HEAD>
<BODY>
<P>Hot water is dangerous.</P>

<P align=right>Turn down the hot water heater thermostat.</P>

<P>Always supervise children in the bathtub.</P>

<P align=right>Don't encourage children to play around the tub.</P>
</BODY>
</HTML>
```

FIGURE 7.4.

The <P> tag marks each sentence as its own paragraph, although the extra return between lines is still ignored.

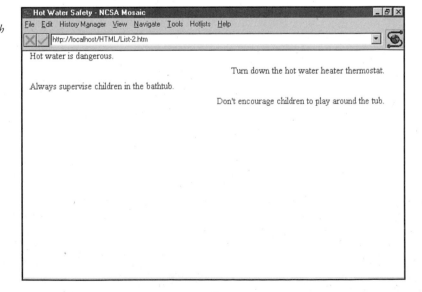

Notice the behavior of the alignment. A new paragraph supersedes any alignment settings in the previous paragraph. Also, if an alignment isn't specifically set, it defaults back to the left.

Any of the inline elements can be used in the <P> tags without causing a new line to begin. Other block-level elements, such as forms and headings, force the end of the paragraph and begin on a new line.

A New Line:

A line break tag, <BR>, is similar to a paragraph tag, but it behaves slightly differently. It starts a new line within the current paragraph, but it doesn't start a new paragraph. This is the syntax:

```
<BR [clear=left¦all¦right¦none][core]>...Text...
```

Text is the material that should appear on the next line, and the optional `clear` attribute defines how the following material should flow around floating images. An ending tag is not used.

Used with the preceding example, this tag creates the same basic effect as using a paragraph tag and keeps all the text within the same paragraph. (See Listing 7.3 and Figure 7.5.)

Listing 7.3. Instead of new paragraphs, each line is started with a line break tag.

```
<HTML>
<HEAD>
<TITLE>Hot Water Safety</TITLE>
</HEAD>
<BODY>
<P>Hot water is dangerous.

<BR>Turn down the hot water heater thermostat.

<BR>Always supervise children in the bathtub.

<BR>Don't encourage children to play around the tub.</P>
</BODY>
</HTML>
```

In Figure 7.5, notice that the lines are slightly closer together because they're still within the same paragraph.

The big difference you'll notice between line breaks and new paragraphs is line spacing. (See Figure 7.6.) A line break uses the same spacing as though the line had just scrolled down from the preceding line. A new paragraph typically uses an extra half-line of space because the first line of a paragraph is not indented.

Any alignment or other text formatting that's set before the line break within the same paragraph is carried to the new line.

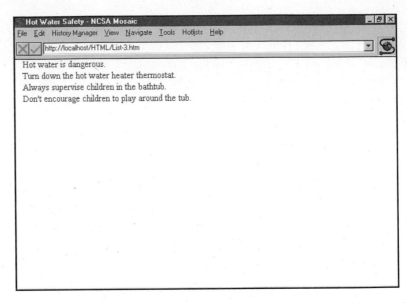

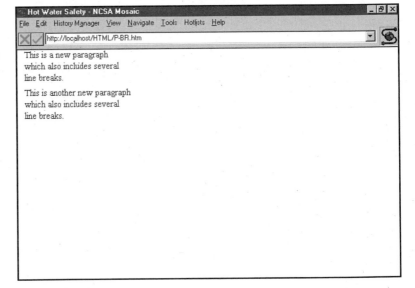

The clear attribute is used to move past floating images on either margin. A value of left moves the text after the line break past any floating images on the left margin (as shown in Figure 7.7), and a value of right performs the same function for floating images on the right. As you might expect, all does the same for floating images on either margin. Other options for causing text to flow around an image are covered in Chapter 11.

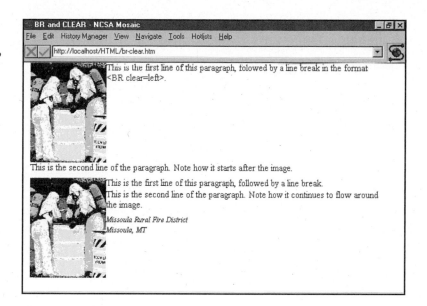

FIGURE 7.7.

Using the clear *attribute allows text to move past a floating image.*

Standard inline images don't "float," so they're not affected by the clear attribute. An inline image, by definition, appears only on the line where it was inserted.

Preformatted Text, Spaces and All: <PRE>

The last method for making your four lines of text appear the way you want is to mark the whole section as preformatted text. The syntax looks like this:

```
<PRE [width=number][core][international][events]>...Text...</PRE>
```

Text is any text, including returns, spaces, and other hard formatting. The width attribute tells the browser how many characters wide it should allow for the content, and lets the browser choose an appropriately sized font or indent as necessary so that the text is properly displayed. The width attribute is not supported by many browsers.

There are several key differences between this method and the two preceding tags. Look at Listing 7.4 and Figure 7.8. All the text is contained by the <PRE> tags, which causes the browser to display everything in between *exactly as it finds it*. It also uses a monospaced font for display, which helps format the text into rows and columns for data presentation.

Listing 7.4. The <PRE> tag tells the browser to present the text within exactly as typed.

```
<HTML>
<HEAD>
<TITLE>Hot Water Safety</TITLE>
</HEAD>
<BODY>
<PRE>Hot water is dangerous.
```

continues

Listing 7.4. continued

```
Turn down the hot water heater thermostat.

    Always supervise children in the bathtub.

        Don't encourage children to play around the tub.</PRE>
</BODY>
</HTML>
```

Notice in Figure 7.8 that the monospace font preserves character spacing for accurate display of indents and other formatting.

FIGURE 7.8.

Preformatting displays the lines exactly as they were typed in the file.

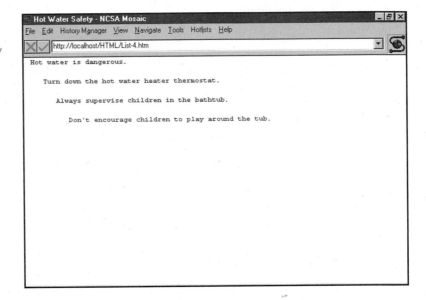

TIP

For browsers that aren't compatible with tables, preformatted text is an effective way to display a table made out of textual elements representing the border lines.

The monospaced font helps when preserving the line breaks and spaces inserted by the user. If you start a new line, insert five spaces, and then start typing, that's exactly how your text appears when using the <PRE> tag. Browsers disable automatic word wrap to further ensure that your text is displayed exactly as you typed it.

> **CAUTION**
>
> Before HTML 4.0, there were three other tags that were also used for preformatting: `<XMP>`, `<LISTING>`, and `<PLAINTEXT>`. With the release of HTML 4.0, these three tags are now obsolete. Browsers will probably continue to support them for a while, but if you want to maintain conformity with current HTML standards, then it's best to shift to the `<PRE>` tag now.

Formatting Text by Its Usage

As discussed in Part I, "Introducing HTML 4.0," one of the primary uses for HTML is to mark up text so its meaning and structure, rather than just the appearance, are immediately apparent. Remember that in the traditional world of word processing and publishing, people tend to think in physical styles—font, size, bold, italic, and so on.

However, HTML is a way of defining structure as much as appearance. HTML is a simple markup language used to create hypertext documents that are portable from one platform to another (see Chapter 2, "What is Hypertext Markup Language?"). Within this limitation, each browser is given a lot of latitude in how it interprets tags. The HTML 4.0 specification includes recommendations on preferred appearances, but browsers can deviate from them based on the needs and limitations of their respective platforms.

With that bit of review out of the way, it's time to introduce the logical style tags. These tags describe the use for a piece of text, instead of the physical attributes it should have. It's much the same as defining a style on your word processor for addresses. Every time you have an address, you apply the "address" style. You cease to think about the text in physical formatting by substituting the new style.

The big difference between your word processor and the browser is that the combination of browser and platform decide how you should see text, instead of relying solely on the author's whims.

> **NOTE**
>
> For each of the following styles, the preferred browser interpretation is listed, even though it could vary across applications and platforms.

The Phrase Elements

The first set of elements to look at are the HTML phrase elements, used to add structure information to text fragments, rather than entire lines or paragraphs.

Basic and Strong Emphasis: <EM> and <STRONG>

Sometimes you need to make sure the reader doesn't miss the point of your message. To do that, you need to emphasize a word or words in a sentence. HTML provides the emphasis tag (<EM>) to fill this need. This is the syntax:

```
<EM [core][international][events]>...Text...</EM>
```

Text is the word or words you want to emphasize. Italics are the recommended rendering of emphasized text.

Related to the emphasis tag is the strong emphasis tag (<STRONG>), which should convey a higher level of importance to the reader. The syntax looks like this:

```
<STRONG [core][international][events]>...Text...</STRONG>
```

Text is the word or words needing extra emphasis. Boldface type is the preferred rendering of strong text. The difference between these two tags is illustrated in Figure 7.9.

Figure 7.9.

Emphasized text is usually displayed with italics, and strong text uses boldface type.

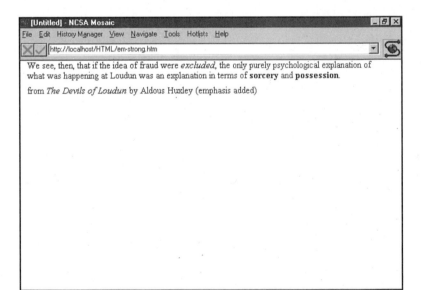

OTHER OPTIONS FOR EMPHASIZING

In Chapter 17, you'll also see how the italic (<I>) and bold (<B>) tags are used to generate the same effects as emphasis and strong emphasis. So why should anyone use the logical styles? They're longer and aren't as clear about their final appearance.

Remember that part of HTML's purpose is to show structure and meaning within a document, and that's the role the two emphasis tags play. Using the physical bold or italics tag would produce the same visual effect, but using the logical tags also shows the intention and is stable across all platforms—not just the ones that support a variety of type styles.

Noting a Source: <CITE>

Sometimes when you're composing pages, you'll want to attribute facts to their sources or call attention to an acronym. Once again, HTML supplies tags that identify how the text is being used and leaves the details of its physical appearance to the browser.

The citation tag, <CITE>, is used to identify sources of information outside the current document. It's used most often in research and professional papers, although you might find its uses in other areas, such as book reviews and Frequently Asked Questions. This is the syntax:

```
<CITE [core][international][events]>Source</CITE>
```

Source is the name of the citation. The usual rendering for <CITE> is italics.

Defining Terms: <DFN> and <ACRONYM>

When you think about terms and definitions, a dictionary or glossary is the image that usually comes to mind. HTML offers one way of presenting this type of information through different types of lists, which are covered in Chapter 8, "Using Lists to Organize Information." Although HTML lists are the usual method for presenting terms and definitions, there's another alternative.

The other option for showing a definition term is using the <DFN> tag. Its syntax is the following:

```
<DFN [core][international][events]>Term</DFN>
```

Term is the word that's defined. It's used to identify words within a body of text that includes the definition in the same sentence. (See Figure 7.10.) The typical rendering for a defined term is italics.

The <ACRONYM> tag is used to highlight the alphabet soup of letters and numbers that seem to be so popular with computer people and government officials, such as WWW, W3C, ASCII, OSHA, DoD, IRS, and others. Its use looks like this:

```
<ACRONYM [core][international][events]>allTheLetters</ACRONYM>
```

Here, *allTheLetters* is the acronym.

FIGURE 7.10.

The italicized words "Entry Team" are the definition term.

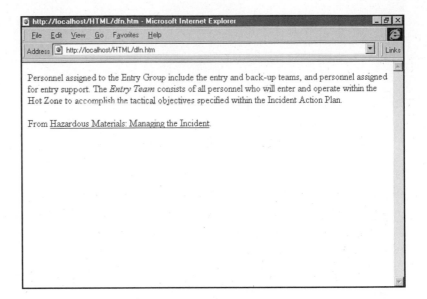

NOTE

<ACRONYM> is a new tag that's not currently supported by any browser, although it's fair enough to expect it from the next release of Navigator or Internet Explorer. Until that time, there's no suggested or preferred representation, but it's safe to assume it will probably be either italics or boldface.

Indicating Program Code: <CODE> and <VAR>

You've seen examples of syntax and usage of HTML code throughout this chapter, and you will continue to see them throughout the rest of the book. Sams.net Publishing uses a special monospaced typestyle to show these examples so that they stand out from the rest of the text.

HTML has a similar feature in the <CODE> tag that it uses to format programming or other similar code lines. The syntax is shown here:

```
<CODE [core][international][events]>...CodeLine</CODE>
```

CodeLine is the line or lines of code samples. If multiple lines of code are included, the line-break tag <BR> is also needed.

It's important to note that although the typical display of this element uses monospace text similar to the PRE element, <CODE> still requires the <BR> or <P> tags to force new lines. Other than the appearance of the text, anything within the <CODE> container behaves the same as other HTML text.

The <VAR> tag is often used with the <CODE> tag to help explain the code. Its syntax is the following:

`<VAR [core][international][events]>Variable</VAR>`

`Variable` is the name of a variable being described, much like <DFN> works for definition terms. The typical representation is italics, which is also the same as <DFN>.

<VAR> is similar to <DFN> in use; it explains a variable or argument of a piece of code within the context of a normal sentence or paragraph. Figure 7.11 includes an example of using <CODE> and <VAR> together. After the code listing, there's a brief explanation of two of the variables.

FIGURE 7.11.

The lines of Java code are displayed in a monospaced type to separate them from the explanatory text.

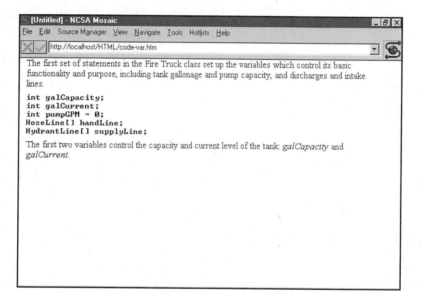

Two more companions to the code elements are used in similar situations: <SAMP> and <KBD>.

These two tags identify things the computer would say to the user and examples of what the user should say to the computer. Like <CODE> and <VAR>, they are hangers-on from the old days of the Internet, when just about everyone worked from a text-based UNIX system. This is the syntax for the <SAMP> tag:

`<SAMP [core][international][events]>SampleOutput</SAMP>`

`SampleOutput` is an example of a message the user might receive from the computer.

This is the syntax for the <KBD> tag:

`<KBD [core][international][events]>KeyboardInput</KBD>`

`KeyboardInput` is an example of something the user might type on the keyboard. The typical representation of sample output is monospaced text, and keyboard input is usually displayed with bold monospaced text, although this representation varies across browsers. (See Figure 7.12.)

FIGURE 7.12.

The computer's output is presented in bold monospaced type on a separate line; the user's response is presented as italicized type.

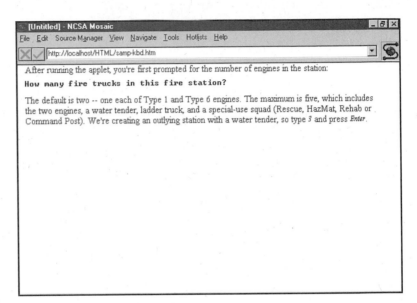

Other Special Text Formatting

In the world of HTML text formatting, some tags don't fit well into one category or another. The following styles are not included as phrase elements or as the style elements presented in Chapter 17. Instead, these tags include some additional formatting based on content.

Documents with Changes: <INS> and <DEL>

One of the new additions to HTML 4 is the ability to mark up a document to show the changes that have been made to it. This feature is intended for use by several people who might be working on the same document. When someone enters a new bit of text or content, he or she places it between the <INS> tag, and content to be deleted is marked with <DEL>. This type of markup is often used by lawyers working through changes on a document or authors and editors revising a book.

When documents are going through many hands and multiple revisions, this mechanism is very useful for letting people see the history of the document's revision.

These two elements are unusual for HTML because their nature is neither block-level nor inline elements. They can contain one or more words in a paragraph, or span one or more block-level elements, such as paragraphs, lists, and tables.

> **TIP**
>
> The <INS> and <DEL> tags aren't currently supported by any browser, but can be expected soon in the next significant release from Netscape or Internet Explorer. A possible solution is underlined text for <INS> and strikethrough for <DEL>. Other possibilities listed by the W3C include special fonts, not showing deleted text at all, or other special markings.
>
> For the time being, it would be a good idea to include a style to represent the text in a recognizable fashion for browsers that are at least compatible with style.

This is the syntax for the <INS> tag:

```
<INS [cite=URL][datetime=date][core][international][events]>Content</INS>
```

URL points to a source document that indicates why the material was changed, and the *date* indicates the date and time the change was made. The syntax is identical for the <DEL> tag.

> **TIP**
>
> The date and time of insertion must be entered according to the ISO8601 standard, which dictates a format of YYYY-MM-DDThh:mm:ssTZD, as follows:
>
> ■ YYYY is a four-digit year.
>
> ■ MM is a two-digit month; 01 represents January, and so on.
>
> ■ DD is a two-digit day of the month.
>
> ■ T is a separator to mark the beginning of the time element.
>
> ■ hh are two digits of the hour in 24-hour time only (00 through 23).
>
> ■ mm are two digits for the minute.
>
> ■ ss are two digits for the second.
>
> ■ TZD is the time zone designator, which is Z for Universal Coordinated Time (UTC), or a number of hours and minutes (hh:mm) ahead or behind UTC, represented as +hh:mm or -hh:mm.
>
>   UTC was once known as Greenwich Mean Time (GMT), the local time at the Greenwich median at zero degrees longitude. The initials for Universal Coordinated Time are based on the French translation of the term.
>
> Each of the elements *must* be present to represent the time. For example, August 27, 1997 5:42 p.m. in Mountain Standard Time is presented as 1997-08-27T17:42:00-07:00.

Address Information: <ADDRESS>

The <ADDRESS> tag is used to mark contact information for the current document, whether it's an e-mail address or a complete mailing address and phone number. It behaves much like the paragraph tag, forcing the text within its confines to be separated from surrounding material by additional line spacing. The syntax looks like this:

```
<ADDRESS [core][international][events]>...ContactInformation...</ADDRESS>
```

`ContactInformation` is the address information, along with any paragraph-level formatting such as line breaks. It's typically displayed as italic body text.

You can nest other items within the address tag, including hyperlink information. For example, here's one option for displaying e-mail contact information:

```
<ADDRESS><A href="mailto:sam@fairdeals.com">Sam Beauregard</A><BR>
Fair Deal Sam's Used Cars<BR>
"With Sam B., it's a guarantee"<BR>
Great Falls, MT
</ADDRESS>
```

This code would create a hyperlink to connect to the user's e-mail software while maintaining the formatting for address information. (See Figure 7.13.) For more ideas on working with hyperlinks and mailto destinations, see Chapter 13.

FIGURE 7.13.

Text formatted with the `<ADDRESS>` *tag; a nested tag for defining a hyperlink is included.*

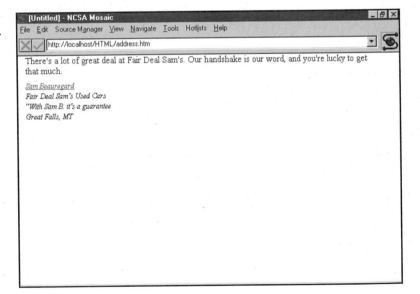

Working with Long and Short Quotations: <BLOCKQUOTE> and <Q>

For shorter quotations, it's certainly fine to use quotation marks or the `<Q>` tag and leave the text inline with the rest of the content. However, if the amount of text to quote exceeds more than a couple of sentences, it's easier for the reader to take note of the quote if it is separated from the rest of the text. This is when the `<BLOCKQUOTE>` element is used. The syntax looks like this:

```
<BLOCKQUOTE [cite=URL][core][international][events]>...Text...</BLOCKQUOTE>
```

Text is the quotation that should be separated from the rest of the surrounding material, and *URL* points to the source for the quote. The <BLOCKQUOTE> tag creates a separate paragraph for the text and, in most browsers, indents the entire paragraph from the left. (See Figure 7.14.) Some browsers also include a slight indent from the right or set the blockquote in italics.

Figure 7.14.

A block quotation; the citation for the quote's source is marked in italics.

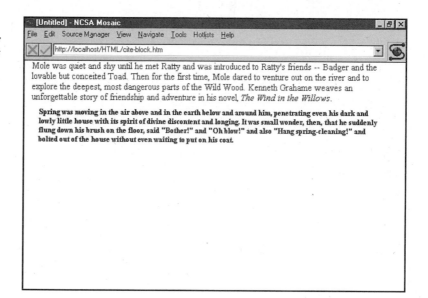

The block quotation allows other formatting within its borders, including paragraphs, line breaks, and headings. Individual browsers vary in their handling of special formatting. Most will indent special formatting, such as headings, along with the rest of the block quotation.

Keep in mind that not all browsers handle the block quotation the same way, especially in regards to the type style (regular or italics). If you include formatting such as italics within a block quotation, and the browser normally displays blockquotes in italics, then your added emphasis is lost to the reader. In some cases, the browser might change the type style of the rest of the block quotation.

TIP

For safety and consistency, try to avoid the use of other formatting within a block quotation.

The <Q> tag is intended for use on shorter quotes that don't require an offset from the rest of the text, as the BLOCKQUOTE does. The blockquote is a block element that includes paragraph breaks before and after, but the Q quotation is an inline element. Its syntax looks like this:

```
<Q [cite=URL][core][international][events]>...Text...</Q>
```

Text is the quotation that should be separated from the rest of the surrounding material, and *URL* points to the source for the quote. This is a new tag that's not yet implemented by the major browsers.

Drawing a Line on the Page: <HR>

Horizontal lines are an easy-to-use element for dividing a page into logical sections. They signal the reader to be alert for a change in subject or style, or they can separate figures and captions from body text. Depending on your design needs, <HR> also includes several attributes to fine-tune its appearance. This is the syntax:

```
<HR [align][width=lineWidth][size=lineThicknes][noshade][core][events]>
```

Here, *lineWidth* and *lineThickness* set the basic appearance of the line. The height of a horizontal rule is set in pixels, such as size=8. The width is set either in pixels or as a percentage of the browser window width. If you're using the percentage value, include a percentage sign (%) after the value. The typical defaults for height and width are 3 pixels high and 100 percent of page width. (See Figure 7.15.)

Figure 7.15.

The first line on this page uses the browser size defaults. The subsequent lines adjust the height *and* width *values for varying effects.*

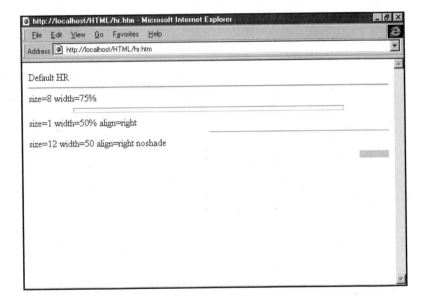

The default alignment for a horizontal rule is typically left-justified. Full justification is not supported for lines—just try setting the width to 100%.

The last attribute is noshade. Normally, a browser displays a horizontal rule in some form of three-dimensional shading. This shading varies from browser to browser; some show it as depressed, some raised, some as an outline. Using noshade forces the horizontal rule to appear as a thick line with no additional highlighting. Again, this appearance can vary among browsers. Some use black for the rule, and others use shades of gray.

A Quick Review of Logical Styles

You might have noticed a lot of overlap in the way different HTML logical elements are represented in a browser. Although there's no set standard for these items, there are some commonly accepted conventions. Table 7.1 lists the logical styles and their known typical renderings.

Table 7.1. Logical element styles.

Element	Style
<ADDRESS>	*Italics*
<BLOCKQUOTE>	Normal with indent
<CITE>	*Italics*
<CODE>	Monospace
<DFN>	*Italics*
<EM>	*Italics*
<KBD>	**Bold Monospace**
<SAMP>	Monospace
<STRONG>	**Bold**
<VAR>	*Italics*

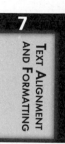

Browsers might interpret these items in a variety of ways, but remember that this is okay. Part of HTML's purpose is to make documents that are platform independent. The end user really shouldn't care which style is used for which item, as long as it's consistent.

When you use the logical styles, the browser can decide how to display a certain type of text based on the platform's capabilities, reducing your concerns about where your document can be viewed.

Summary

This chapter is designed to give you a head start in formatting text on your Web pages so that you can give your message the maximum impact. With the exception of a couple of tags for hyperlinks and images, this chapter includes all of the most frequently used tags in HTML.

First, and most important, are the tags to break the text into paragraphs and lines. Without them, every HTML document would be just one long, hard-to-read document. They give the basic structure to the page for the reader.

After breaking the document into paragraphs, HTML 4 offers a set of tags that carry logical and structural meaning, rather than explicit appearance information, to format the page. These tags format the text based on its purpose and usage, such as citations and addresses. They are typically supported across platforms and browsers, although the actual rendering might be atypical.

A multitude of other HTML tags also control text appearance and formatting, but they are unique enough to deserve treatment by themselves. They include the list tags (Chapter 8, "Using Lists to Organize Information"), style tags (Chapter 17), hyperlinks and anchors (Chapter 13), tables and frames (Chapters 10, "Table Layout and Presentation," and 20, "Creating Frames"), and forms (Chapter 15, "Building and Using HTML Forms").

Using Lists to Organize Information

IN THIS CHAPTER

Lists are everywhere. On the refrigerator for groceries, on a scratch pad for to-do lists, in the front of books as a table of contents, in lists of directions for accomplishing tasks. Lists are one of the most natural ways to organize information.

HTML has a special set of tags just for displaying lists with a host of special attributes to give you greater control over their appearance.

At the most basic level, lists are divided into two categories:

- **Ordered lists:** These lists are typically used to indicate a sequence of events or priorities. They're also used to specifically identify sections and relationships when creating outlines.

- **Unordered lists:** An unordered list is typically used to display a group of items that are somehow related, but are not necessarily displayed in a hierarchical fashion. Three special HTML subsets of unordered lists are illustrated later in this chapter—definitions, directories, and menus.

The next sections look at each type of list and the ways to customize them to your own specific circumstance.

Ordered (or Numbered) Lists: <OL>

A list is defined by its opening and closing tags. For ordered lists, they are <OL> and </OL>. However, you'll need more than the opening and closing tags—you'll need something to put in them. Look at Listing 8.1, which is a list encased with the ordered list tags.

Listing 8.1. A simple ordered list enclosed with <OL> tags.

```
<!DOCTYPE HTML PUBLIC "-//W3C//DTD HTML 4.0//EN">
<HTML>
<HEAD>
<TITLE>Basic CPR</TITLE>
</HEAD>
<BODY>
Basic CPR
<OL>
Use Body Substance Isolation Precautions
Determine Unresponsiveness
Open Airway
Look, Listen and Feel for Breathing
Ventilate Twice
Check for Pulse
If No Pulse, Begin Compressions
</OL>
</BODY>
</HTML>
```

If the list is viewed on a browser, you can see where the text was indented in preparation for a list, but no actual numbering took place. (See Figure 8.1.)

FIGURE 8.1.

A list of information enclosed with the list tags doesn't result in an HTML list.

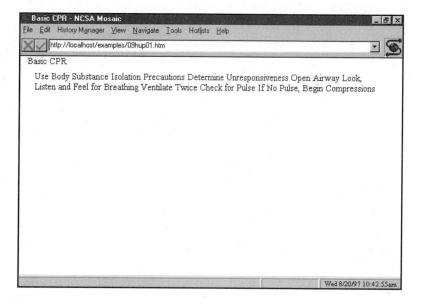

How come the list doesn't have numbers? Remember that HTML doesn't recognize line breaks unless it's told explicitly where they occur with the `<P>` or `<BR>` tags. The same principle applies to lists, although a different tag is used to tell the browser where each specific item begins. This tag is the list item tag, `<LI>`.

With the `<OL>` and `<LI>` tags in hand, the basic syntax for an ordered list is as follows:

```
<OL>
<LI>ListItem1
<LI>ListItem2
...
<LI>ListItemN
</OL>
```

`ListItem` is each separate item in the list. See Listing 8.2, which shows the same list used in Listing 8.1, for an example of how to use these tags.

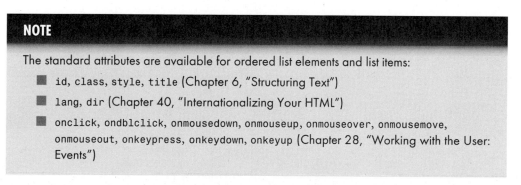

NOTE

The standard attributes are available for ordered list elements and list items:

- `id`, `class`, `style`, `title` (Chapter 6, "Structuring Text")
- `lang`, `dir` (Chapter 40, "Internationalizing Your HTML")
- `onclick`, `ondblclick`, `onmousedown`, `onmouseup`, `onmouseover`, `onmousemove`, `onmouseout`, `onkeypress`, `onkeydown`, `onkeyup` (Chapter 28, "Working with the User: Events")

8

USING LISTS TO ORGANIZE INFORMATION

Listing 8.2. Marking the beginning of each separate item with a list item tag.

```
<!DOCTYPE HTML PUBLIC "-//W3C//DTD HTML 4.0//EN">
<HTML>
<HEAD>
<TITLE>Basic CPR</TITLE>
</HEAD>
<BODY>
Basic CPR
<OL>
<LI>Use Body Substance Isolation Precautions
<LI>Determine Unresponsiveness
<LI>Open Airway
<LI>Look, Listen and Feel for Breathing
<LI>Ventilate Twice
<LI>Check for Pulse
<LI>If No Pulse, Begin Compressions
</OL>
</BODY>
</HTML>
```

For each item identified with <LI>, the browser starts a new line, indents, and adds a number. (See Figure 8.2.)

FIGURE 8.2.

After each item is marked with a list item tag, the browser indents it and adds automatic numbering.

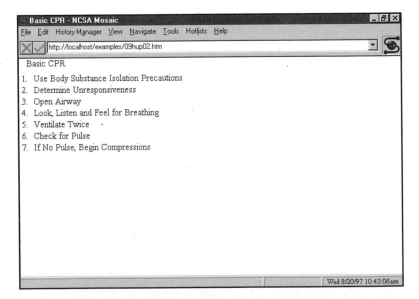

TIP

You can also include an optional closing tag, </LI>, to the list item. It's not required because the beginning of the next list item implies the end of the previous list item.

However, if you're going to use style sheets (see Part IV, "Presentation Techniques") or dynamic HTML features (see Part VI, "Dynamic HTML") with the list, the closing tag is required.

The line break tags—<P> and
—are also allowed within the body of a list to further control its appearance and formatting, as shown in Listing 8.3.

Listing 8.3. Organizing your list into headings and subtext with the <BR> and <P> tags.

```
<!DOCTYPE HTML PUBLIC "-//W3C//DTD HTML 4.0//EN">
<HTML>
<HEAD>
<TITLE>Basic CPR</TITLE>
</HEAD>
<BODY>
Basic CPR
<OL>
<LI>Use Body Substance Isolation Precautions<BR>
If available, be sure to use latex or vinyl gloves,
goggles and a barrier device with one-way valve.<P>
<LI>Determine Unresponsiveness
<LI>Open Airway
<LI>Look, Listen and Feel for Breathing
<LI>Ventilate Twice
<LI>Check for Pulse
<LI>If No Pulse, Begin Compressions
</OL>
</BODY>
</HTML>
```

When viewed on a browser (as shown in Figure 8.3), the tags affecting line breaks don't affect the line numbering. When the list begins with the <OL> tag, only an <LI> tag causes the browser to start a new line with the next number. You can force other lines to begin with the line break tags, but because it doesn't begin a new list item, the browser treats it like a continuation of the current item and doesn't add a number for the next item in the sequence.

> **NOTE**
>
> The standard formatting elements are available in <LI> elements:
>
> ■ **font elements:** TT, I, B, U, S, STRIKE, BIG, SMALL (Chapter 17, "Simple Style with Text ")
>
> ■ **phrase elements:** EM, STRONG, DFN, CODE, SAMP, KBD, VAR, CITE, ACRONYM (Chapter 7, "Text Alignment and Formatting")
>
> For cleaner code and later revisions, make sure any other formatting tags opened in a list item are closed before the next item begins.

FIGURE 8.3.

Additional text formatting and page breaks don't affect the basic list numbering or style.

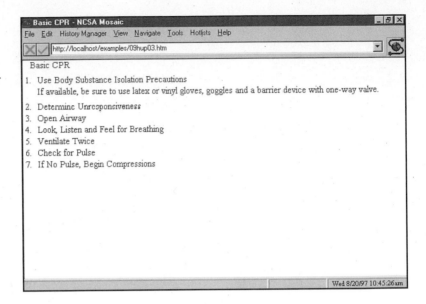

In addition to the formatting you can apply to individual list items, there are two other ways to customize an ordered list: choosing a new beginning for list numbering (start) and selecting the numbering characters used (type). These two attributes are covered in the following sections.

Where to start a List

Sometimes it's necessary to interrupt a list for some explanatory text or other material where indenting isn't needed. Look at Listing 8.4, which shows two ordered lists interrupted by some explanatory text, and its corresponding Figure 8.4.

Listing 8.4. Interrupting an ordered list with some explanatory text that you didn't want indented.

```
<!DOCTYPE HTML PUBLIC "-//W3C//DTD HTML 4.0//EN">
<HTML>
<HEAD>
<TITLE>Basic CPR</TITLE>
</HEAD>
<BODY>
<H2>Basic CPR</H2>
<H3>Airway and Breathing</H3>
<OL>
<LI>Use Body Substance Isolation Precautions<BR>
If available, be sure to use latex or vinyl gloves,
goggles and a barrier device with one-way valve.<P>
<LI>Determine Unresponsiveness
<LI>Open Airway
<LI>Look, Listen and Feel for Breathing
<LI>Ventilate Twice
</OL>
```

```
<P>Look for chest rise and listen for exhalation while ventilating.
If no air enters, reposition the airway and try again. If the
airway is blocked, attempt to clear it using appropriate airway
obstruction maneuvers. If you can't get air into the patient,
circulation won't help. If the airway won't clear, you'll remain
in steps 3 through 5 until you can successfully ventilate the
patient, or they are transported to a hospital.</P>
<H3>Circulation</H3>
<OL>
<LI>Check for Pulse
<LI>If No Pulse, Begin Compressions
</OL>
</BODY>
</HTML>
```

In Figure 8.4, list numbering isn't consecutive between individual lists. A new list starts the numbering process over from the beginning.

FIGURE 8.4.

Without a start *attribute, numbering isn't consecutive between lists.*

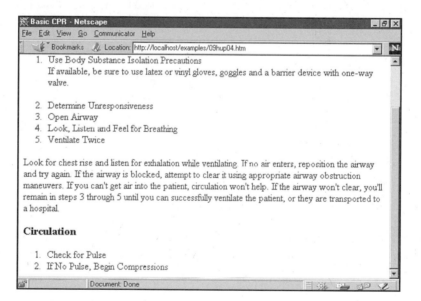

Two sets of <OL> tags are used—one for the first half of CPR (airway and breathing), and another for the second half (circulation). Because each portion of the list is contained within its own pair of ordered list tags, the browser treats each portion as a separate list and begins numbering from 1 for the second list. The browser doesn't know it's really a continuation of the first list.

To work around this problem, use the start attribute for the <OL> tag to start numbering anywhere you want. This attribute can be used to override default list numbering when a list is broken into multiple parts. (See Listing 8.5 and Figure 8.5.)

Listing 8.5. Using the `start` attribute.

```
<!DOCTYPE HTML PUBLIC "-//W3C//DTD HTML 4.0//EN">
<HTML>
<HEAD>
<TITLE>Basic CPR</TITLE>
</HEAD>
<BODY>
<H2>Basic CPR</H2>
<H3>Airway and Breathing</H3>
<OL>
<LI>Use Body Substance Isolation Precautions<BR>
If available, be sure to use latex or vinyl gloves,
goggles and a barrier device with one-way valve.<P>
<LI>Determine Unresponsiveness
<LI>Open Airway
<LI>Look, Listen and Feel for Breathing
<LI>Ventilate Twice
</OL>
<P>Look for chest rise and listen for exhalation while ventilating.
If no air enters, reposition the airway and try again. If the
airway is blocked, attempt to clear it using appropriate airway
obstruction maneuvers. If you can't get air into the patient,
circulation won't help. If the airway won't clear, you'll remain
in steps 3 through 5 until you can successfully ventilate the
patient, or they are transported to a hospital.</P>
<H3>Circulation</H3>
<OL start=6>
<LI>Check for Pulse
<LI>If No Pulse, Begin Compressions
</OL>
</BODY>
</HTML> parts
```

FIGURE 8.5.

Using the start
attribute with the
<OL> tag.

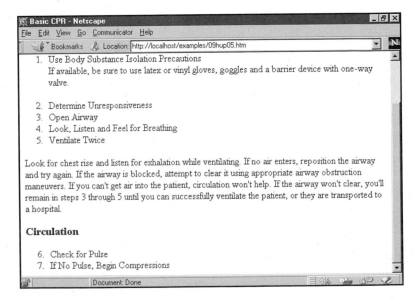

Using the `start` attribute makes it possible to create lists that are interrupted by blocks of text or other material and then resumed with appropriate numbering in a subsequent list. This is the syntax for `start`:

```
<OL start=number>
```

In this attribute, *number* is any integer from 2147483647 to –2147483648. Be sure not to use commas in your numbers because they will be misinterpreted by the browser.

> **TIP**
>
> If numbers outside this range are used, the numbers "roll over" to the beginning. For example, if a list begins with 2147483647, the next number displayed in line is –2147483648. If your lists are hampered by a numbering system that extends only to two billion and some change in either direction, you probably have too much time on your hands.

What type of List Is Needed?

In the early days of HTML, there was only one type of ordered list, with numbers beginning at 1 and ending wherever the list stopped. Then, as people began stretching the use of lists to things such as online books, they began wanting to use something other than numbers. The `type` attribute was developed to meet this need; here is its syntax:

```
<OL type=numberingSystem>
```

In this attribute, *numberingSystem* is one of five characters: `1`, `A`, `a`, `I`, or `i`. Examples of the latter four numbering units are illustrated in Table 8.1.

Table 8.1. Values and styles for the type attribute.

Value	Style	Example
1	Arabic	1, 2, 3…
A	Uppercase alpha	A, B, C…
a	Lowercase alpha	a, b, c…
I	Uppercase Roman	I, II, III…
i	Lowercase Roman	i, ii, iii…

The ability to use something other than numbers leads to a useful feature of ordered lists: *nested lists*, which are lists within lists that can extend several levels. To create a nested list, include a new set of ordered list tags within the current list tags (as shown in Listing 8.6). The browser begins a new list for the new tags, while remembering where the parent list left off after the nested list ends. (See Figure 8.6.)

Listing 8.6. Creating a nested list.

```
<!DOCTYPE HTML PUBLIC "-//W3C//DTD HTML 4.0//EN">
<HTML>
<HEAD>
<TITLE>Patient Assessment</TITLE>
</HEAD>
<BODY>
<!--BEGIN MAIN LIST-->
<OL type=A>

<LI>Safety Considerations
<OL type=1>
  <LI>Body substance isolation
  <LI>Scene safety
  <LI>Initial size-up
</OL>

<LI>Initial Patient Assessment
<OL type=1>
  <LI>General Impression
  <LI>Unresponsiveness
  <OL type=i>
    <LI>Alert to person, place and time
    <LI>Verbal response to audible stimuli
    <LI>Pain evokes verbal or physical response
    <LI>Unresponsive to all stimuli
  </OL>
</OL>

<LI>Patient Critical Needs
<OL type=1>
  <LI>Airway
  <LI>Breathing
  <OL type=i>
    <LI>Use oxygen if indicated
    <LI>Consider use of assisting with bag valve mask
  </OL>
  <LI>Circulation
  <LI>Bleeding
</OL>

<!--END MAIN LIST-->
</OL>
</BODY>
</HTML>
```

One of the main problems with nesting lists is the confusion they can generate. It's easy to lose track of which list is which and what's subordinate to what after the second or third embedded set of items. Remember that extra leading and trailing spaces are stripped from HTML along with extra carriage returns. Feel free to use extra returns and indenting with comment tags to make your page's source code easier to read and edit.

FIGURE 8.6.

Using the type *attribute with nested lists results in text formatted into outline form.*

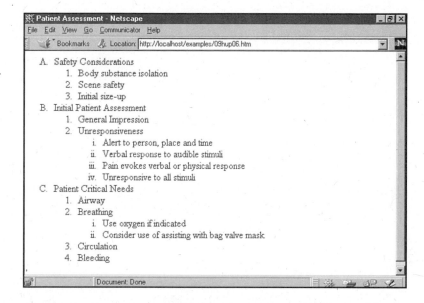

> **TIP**
>
> If you use type with start, be sure to use an integer with start regardless of the type specified.
>
> For example, if you're including an ordered list that uses capital letters and begins at the letter *D*, the opening tag should be <OL type=A start=4>. The browser will translate the starting position into the appropriate letter.

Now that you've worked through the types and variations of an ordered list, it's time to take a look at its half sister—the unordered list.

Unordered Lists: <UL>

Unordered lists are typically used to represent a set of items that are somehow related to one another, but don't necessarily need to follow a specific order. The syntax is similar to that of the ordered list:

```
<UL>
<LI>ListItem1
<LI>ListItem2
...
<LI>ListItemN
</UL>
```

ListItem is each separate item in the list. See Listing 8.7 for an example.

> **NOTE**
>
> The standard attributes are available for unordered list elements and list items:
>
> ■ id, class, style, title (Chapter 6)
> ■ lang, dir (Chapter 40)
> ■ onclick, ondblclick, onmousedown, onmouseup, onmouseover, onmousemove, onmouseout, onkeypress, onkeydown, onkeyup (Chapter 28)

> **NOTE**
>
> The standard formatting elements are available within unordered list <LI> elements:
>
> ■ **font elements:** TT, I, B, U, S, STRIKE, BIG, SMALL (Chapter 17)
> ■ **phrase elements:** EM, STRONG, DFN, CODE, SAMP, KBD, VAR, CITE, ACRONYM (Chapter 7)
>
> For cleaner code and later revisions, make sure any other formatting tags opened within a list item are closed before the next item begins.

Listing 8.7. Substituting <UL> for <OL> in the unordered list.

```
<!DOCTYPE HTML PUBLIC "-//W3C//DTD HTML 4.0//EN">
<HTML>
<HEAD>
<TITLE>Jump Kit Inventory</TITLE>
</HEAD>
<BODY>
EMS Jump Kit Contents
<UL>
<LI>Rescue Scissors and Penlight
<LI>Stethascope and Sphygmanometer
<LI>Oxygen Bottle
<LI>Non-Rebreather Mask and Nasal Cannula
<LI>Oral and Nasal Airways
<LI>Gauze and Trauma Dressings
<LI>Sterile Saline and Water
<LI>Oral Glucose and Activated Charcoal
</UL>
</BODY>
</HTML>
```

As you can see in Figure 8.7, the unordered list is typically represented the same way as an ordered list, except bullets are used instead of numbers.

FIGURE 8.7.

An unordered list uses bullets instead of numbers.

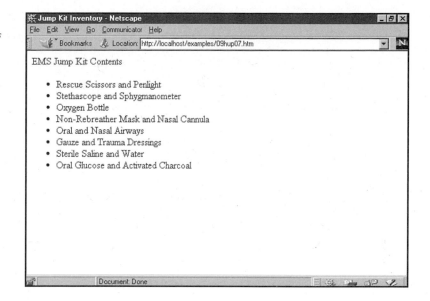

The actual appearance of the bullet varies from browser to browser. Internet Explorer uses small text bullets, and NCSA Mosaic uses a graphical bullet.

Numbering is obviously not an issue for an unordered list. However, HTML 4 offers some additional choices for the default bullet appearance with the `type` attribute.

What type of Bullet Do You Want?

Three basic types of bullets are supported by HTML 4, although not all browsers support all three. If a browser doesn't recognize the attribute, the default bullet representation is used. This is the syntax for `type`:

```
<UL type=bulletType>
```

In this attribute, *bulletType* is one of three values: `circle`, `square`, or `disc`. Their representations are shown in Figure 8.8.

Also like the ordered list, an unordered list can contain other lists within a list. This nesting helps show the relationship among items, even though there isn't an underlying hierarchy. It's implemented in the same manner, with another set of list tags replacing a list item. (See Listing 8.8.) The `type` attribute helps to graphically differentiate the relationships.

FIGURE 8.8.

Three styles of bullets are supported by HTML 4.

Disc bullet ———

Square bullet ———

Circle bullet ———

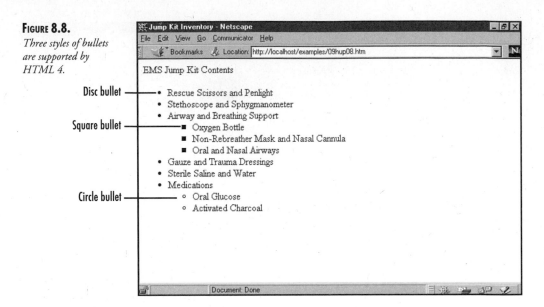

Listing 8.8. Using different types of bullets helps to graphically separate sublists.

```
<!DOCTYPE HTML PUBLIC "-//W3C//DTD HTML 4.0//EN">
<HTML>
<HEAD>
<TITLE>Jump Kit Inventory</TITLE>
</HEAD>
<BODY>
EMS Jump Kit Contents
<UL type=disc>
<LI>Rescue Scissors and Penlight
<LI>Stethoscope and Sphygmanometer

<LI>Airway and Breathing Support
<UL type=square>
<LI>Oxygen Bottle
<LI>Non-Rebreather Mask and Nasal Cannula
<LI>Oral and Nasal Airways
</UL>

<LI>Gauze and Trauma Dressings
<LI>Sterile Saline and Water

<LI>Medications
<UL type=circle>
<LI>Oral Glucose
<LI>Activated Charcoal
</UL>
</UL>
</BODY>
</HTML>
```

Notice that the list item preceding the embedded list is also a heading for the list. This item helps the reader because it identifies how the sublist relates to the main list.

> **NOTE**
>
> One additional attribute is allowed for both types of lists, although its implementation in browsers is sparse at best, and its use is now deprecated by HTML 4. This attribute is compact, which signals the client to try to display the list in the most space-efficient manner possible. Given the other possible variables in a list, most browsers ignore this attribute.

A Definition or Glossary List: <DL>

The last specialty list tag is <DL>, which stands for definition list. This tag is used to create a glossary-style listing, which is handy for items such as dictionary listings and Frequently Asked Questions pages.

The <DL> tag is used similarly to the unordered list tag, except that it doesn't use the <LI> tag to mark its entries because a definition list requires two items for every entry: a term and its definition. Marking these two items is done with the corresponding <DT> and <DD> tags. This is the syntax for the <DL> tag:

```
<DL>
<DT>Term1<DD>Definition1
<DT>Term2<DD>Definition2
...
<DT>TermN<DD>DefinitionN
</DL>
```

In this tag, *Term* is the word requiring a definition, and *Definition* is the block of text that supplies the definition. Another form of including the tags on the page places each <DT> and <DD> tag on separate lines, although the first method is a bit more clear in purpose. The browser presents the content in the same fashion (on separate lines), whichever way you choose.

> **NOTE**
>
> The standard attributes are available for definition list elements:
>
> - id, class, style, title (Chapter 6)
> - lang, dir (Chapter 40)
> - onclick, ondblclick, onmousedown, onmouseup, onmouseover, onmousemove, onmouseout, onkeypress, onkeydown, onkeyup (Chapter 28)

The <DL> tag's implementation can vary a bit from browser to browser, but a common method of displaying the content is shown in Figure 8.9.

FIGURE 8.9.

Using a series of hanging indents to separate terms from definitions.

Term ——

Definition ——

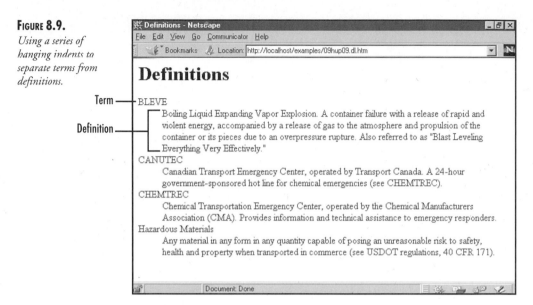

Like the other list tags and styles, it's also possible to include additional physical formatting tags in the terms or definitions:

```
<DT><B>Term</B>
<DD><I>Definition</I>
```

A popular method of implementing the definition list is to give the term a bold style and use regular or italic type for the definition (as shown in Figure 8.10). Neither the <DT> nor the <DD> tag includes any attributes of its own, beyond the standard options (see previous note).

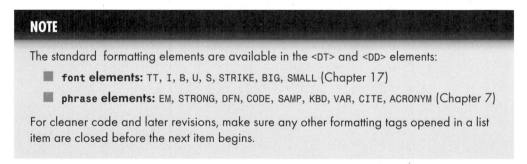

NOTE

The standard formatting elements are available in the <DT> and <DD> elements:

- **font elements:** TT, I, B, U, S, STRIKE, BIG, SMALL (Chapter 17)
- **phrase elements:** EM, STRONG, DFN, CODE, SAMP, KBD, VAR, CITE, ACRONYM (Chapter 7)

For cleaner code and later revisions, make sure any other formatting tags opened in a list item are closed before the next item begins.

Now that you've seen the major styles for creating and displaying lists, it's time to take a look at the last two styles.

FIGURE 8.10.
Additional formatting in the definition list helps emphasize the graphical separation between term and definition.

Italicized term in definition

Bold term

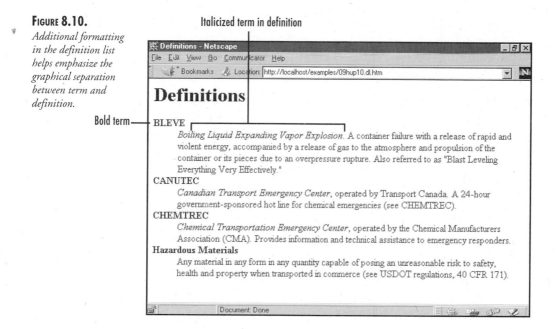

Using the DIR and MENU List Styles

The last set of list tags supported by HTML 4 are `<DIR>` and `<MENU>`, originally designed for directory listings and user menus. However, their use has fallen by the wayside, and they are deprecated in the HTML 4 standard.

> **TIP**
>
> Because the `<DIR>` and `<MENU>` are deprecated, the W3C encourages using the `<UL>` tag in their place.

Both `<DIR>` and `<MENU>` use the `<LI>` tag to mark each separate item, except for the definition list. The syntax for the two lists is the same as for an unordered list (which is part of the reason they are slated for eventual removal from the HTML standard):

```
<MENU> <!-- or DIR -->
<LI>ListItem1
<LI>ListItem2
<LI>ListItemN
</MENU> <!-- or /DIR -->
```

Both items are typically rendered by the browser as unordered lists. (See Figure 8.11.) Note that slightly different typefaces are used in Mosaic. Previous recommendations from the W3C included a multicolumn directory list rendering for the `<DIR>` tag, although browsers have rarely followed this recommendation. A list of choices, such as those used with submitting a form or selecting a response to a question, was recommended for `<MENU>`. This tag is typically rendered the same as an unordered list. Neither item has any attributes, other than the often ignored and now deprecated `compact`.

NOTE

The standard attributes are available for the `<DIR>` and `<MENU>` elements:

- `id`, `class`, `style`, `title` (Chapter 6)
- `lang`, `dir` (Chapter 40)
- `onclick`, `ondblclick`, `onmousedown`, `onmouseup`, `onmouseover`, `onmousemove`, `onmouseout`, `onkeypress`, `onkeydown`, `onkeyup` (Chapter 28)

NOTE

The standard formatting elements are available in these elements:

- **font elements:** TT, I, B, U, S, STRIKE, BIG, SMALL (Chapter 17)
- **phrase elements:** EM, STRONG, DFN, CODE, SAMP, KBD, VAR, CITE, ACRONYM (Chapter 7)

For cleaner code and later revisions, make sure any other formatting tags opened in a list item are closed before the next item begins.

FIGURE 8.11.

The basic representation of a menu and directory list is still an unordered list.

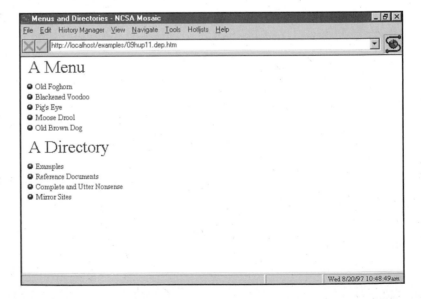

Summary

Two main categories of lists are used with HTML. First is an ordered list, which can be used with its attributes to create a variety of formats for your information. Second is the unordered list, with its options for displaying unprioritized information.

The actual implementation of list item attributes varies from browser to browser, so be aware of differences. In Netscape Navigator, for example, setting an <LI> attribute in the middle of a list also affects the following list items. This behavior doesn't exist in Microsoft Internet Explorer.

Definitions are another list type. They are unique in that they don't require a list item tag, but instead use a pair of tags—a definition term and the actual definition—to accommodate the paired list items.

Two additional tags, now virtually obsolete but still part of the standard, are for menus and directory listings. Their preferred implementation is ignored by most browsers, which tend to represent the two as simple unordered lists.

The next two chapters, "Organizing Data with Tables" and "Table Layout and Presentation," add more options for displaying text. With the text formatting tags in the preceding chapter and the types of lists in this chapter, you're developing quite an arsenal to get your point across with HTML 4.

Organizing Data with Tables

by Rick Darnell

IN THIS CHAPTER

CHAPTER 9

In the world of the Web, HTML tables have become one of the most used and powerful tools for formatting Web pages. In this chapter, you'll learn about tables in their original use of making formatting tabular data, such as spreadsheet and database information, easier.

As you begin to explore the nuances of the table tags and their attributes in this chapter, you'll probably begin to see additional applications. In the next chapter, "Table Layout and Presentation," you'll use tables to create a variety of page layouts not directly supported by HTML.

On the downside, table tags are also some of the most complicated to understand and use. In the linear space of a page of HTML coding, you must define a two-dimensional form. It's hard to keep track of which row belongs to which information and how a particular cell will look in its final form. A table-enabled browser is crucial if you're not using a visual HTML editor.

COMMON ATTRIBUTES

Most of the elements in this chapter share common HTML attributes, such as items that control identification, style, language, and event handling. Because the common attributes are so pervasive in HTML 4 (that's why they're called "common"), you will find an overview of them in the introduction of this book. You can also find more information about these often-used features and their associated elements in Appendix A, "HTML 4.0 Reference."

Meanwhile, in this chapter, I'll refer to the common attributes by using these keywords: *core*, *international*, and *event*.

Additionally, many of the elements can accept other elements within their borders. These are referred to as the *inline elements*, and include the following options:

font elements: These elements include tags for bold (`<B>`) and italics (`<I>`) and are covered in Chapter 17, "Simple Style with Text."

phrase elements: These elements include tags such as emphasis (`<EM>`), code (`<CODE>`), and address (`<ADDRESS>`) and are covered in Chapter 7, "Text Alignment and Formatting."

special elements: This collection is a hodgepodge of elements that includes all the following items: applets and objects (Chapter 16, "Embedding Objects in HTML"); images (Chapter 11, "Adding Images to Your Web Page"); anchors (Chapter 13, "Hyperlinking and Anchors"); image maps (Chapter 14, "Creating Menus with Image Maps"); scripts (Chapters 23, "JavaScript at a Glance," and 24, "Using VBScript"); fonts, superscripts, and subscripts (Chapter 17); line breaks and short quotes (this chapter); and inline frames (Chapter 20, "Creating Frames").

form elements: This set of elements is used to add elements to a form, including buttons, text fields, and checkboxes.

Setting a Basic Table

Like other block elements discussed in previous chapters, a table is marked at its beginning and end with a `<TABLE>` tag and can contain a variety of row and column definitions. At its simplest level, a table consists of the `<TABLE>` tags and one row with one cell:

```
<TABLE>
<TR> <!-- table row -->
<TD>Content <!-- table data -->
</TABLE>
```

In a word, this simple form is called "pointless." However, there are a few things to note. First, only the `<TABLE>` tag needs to be closed with `</TABLE>`; otherwise, the browser doesn't know when to stop table formatting. Second, the table row (`<TR>`) and table data (`<TD>`) cells can accept their respective closing tags, but they're not required. A new row or data cell automatically marks the end of the previous row or data.

> **TIP**
>
> If you plan on formatting the contents of your rows and cells by using a style sheet, you'll need to use closing tags for those elements. A style sheet doesn't work with an open-ended tag.

As you might expect, there are a few attributes that apply to the three basic table tags. First, take a look at `<TABLE>`. In addition to the core, `international`, and event attributes, a table has the following options:

- **`align:`** This is the standard alignment attribute, which accepts values of `left`, `right`, or `center` to control placement on the page. Most browsers default to a left or center alignment.

- **`width:`** The width of the table, expressed in pixels or as a percentage of the browser window width. (See Figure 9.1.) For example, a table that occupies half of the available window is marked with `width=50%`, and a table 500 pixels wide is expressed as `width=500`. The default is just wide enough to handle the longest content in each column.

  As a general rule, use the percentage value to ensure compatibility across a variety of displays and platforms. The pixel value is useful when you need a fixed width for content such as images.

- **`cols:`** This attribute is new in HTML 4. It tells the browser how many columns are included in the table. In the past, the browser had to wait until the entire table was loaded to begin rendering it.

- **frame:** This attribute, a companion to the `border` attribute, determines where a frame surrounding the table should appear. Its possible values are `void` (none), `above` (top side), `below` (bottom side), `hsides` (horizontal sides), `lhs` (left-hand side), `rhs` (right-hand side), `vsides` (vertical sides), and `box` or `border` (all sides).

- **border:** This attribute sets the width of a border around the table in pixels. The default varies with each browser, but is typically 2 or 3 pixels. If you don't want a border, use a value of `0`.

- **rules:** This attribute determines where lines are used to separate cells within the table itself. Its possible values are `none` (no lines), `groups` (between logical groups such as `TBODY` and `THEAD`), `rows` (between each row), `cols` (between each column), and `all` (between all cells).

- **cellspacing:** Identified in pixels, this attribute determines the amount of space between cells. As a side-effect, it sometimes determines the width of the rules between cells, too.

- **cellpadding:** Similar to `cellspacing` and also identified in pixels, this attribute sets the amount of space between the edge of the cell and the actual cell content. The difference between the two is shown in Figure 9.2.

FIGURE 9.1.

Each table column is sized to accommodate its widest element.

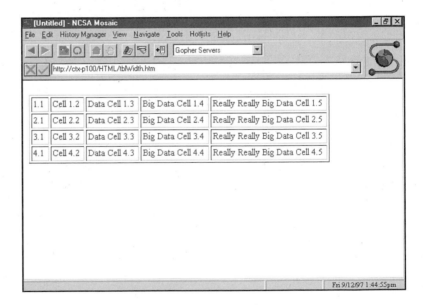

With the basic parameters defined for the table, take a look at the table row and table data tags, covered in the next two sections.

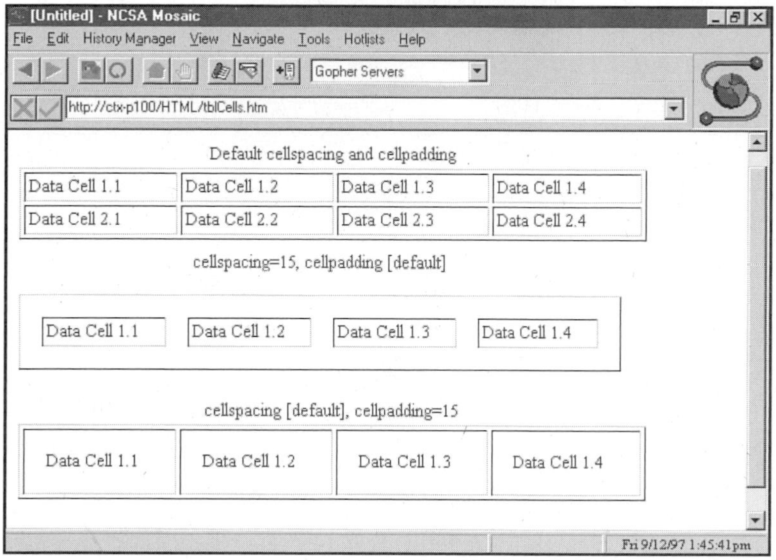

Figure 9.2.

These table variations include a version with default values, one with increased cell spacing, and another with increased cell padding.

Where the Row Starts: <TR>

The beginning of a row is marked by using the <TR> tag with this syntax:

```
<TR [align=horizontalAlign] [valign=verticalAlign]
    [core][international][events]>
```

<TR> marks the beginning of a row of cell definitions and can set default display settings for its cells. The align attribute sets the horizontal spacing of cells on the row and can be one of the following values: left, right, justify, or char.

> **NOTE**
>
> The last value, char, is a special setting that formats textual content around a specific character. The default for English-speaking browsers is the decimal point for formatting numerical information, but French language browsers use the comma. You can use the char attribute to set the character to another value, such as char="*".

The valign attribute sets the vertical placement of information in the cell and takes one of these values: top, middle, or bottom. The <TR> tag doesn't require a closing tag, although you can use one to help make the boundaries of each row easier to identify. In addition, the <TR> tag also accepts the core, international, and event attributes.

There are two attributes for <TR> that set the default behavior for all cells in that row, but individual cells can override the values of <TR>. The first attribute is align, which is similar to align in the <TABLE> tag, but it's limited to controlling the horizontal alignment of the material in cells. The available values are left (default), right, or center. Figure 9.3 shows a table with these three options.

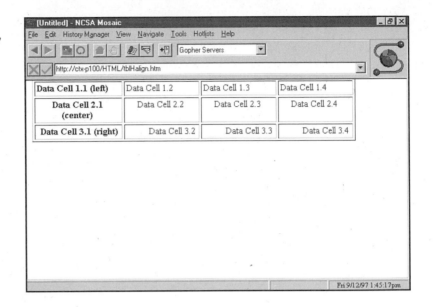

Defining Table Cells: <TD> and <TH>

With the beginning of the row marked with <TR>, it's time to finally get down to the work of filling each cell. Two types of cell tags are used in a table. The first, <TH>, marks a header cell, which is similar to a heading tag on a Web page. The other is a data cell tag, <TD>, used for the body of the table.

After the beginning of the row is identified, you can begin adding each cell for content. This is the syntax for <TD>:

```
<TD [rowspan=numRows][colspan=numCols][axis=headerName][axes=axisNames]
    [alignment][nowrap][core][international][events]>cellContent
```

The attributes for <TD> are discussed in the following sections. A closing </TD> or </TH> isn't required for individual cells, although many HTML designers and editing programs use them for clarity.

> **NOTE**
>
> Depending on the number of cells and their contents, there are two conventions for <TD> tag placement. The first placement is on the same row as the container <TR> tag, which means you'll have one line of HTML beginning with <TR> for every row in your document.

> However, if you have many cells, or if they include items such as hyperlinks or images, you'll probably want to go with placing each cell definition on its own line, with a closing </TR> tag and an extra carriage return at the end of every row.
>
> With either placement method, the code behaves the same way. It's up to you to choose a format that helps clarify the code for future editing and revision.

When you're considering formatting options for each cell, think of the <TD> and <TH> tags as <BODY> tags. Any tag valid for the body of an HTML document is valid in a cell, which means you can embed text, graphics, forms, plug-ins and objects, applets, and even other tables. This feature is what gives tables their power when used to format a page.

The attributes for table cells are divided into two broad categories: those that affect the cell's size, and those that affect the cell's contents.

A special kind of table data cell is the header cell, <TH>. Most browsers include a different font style for header cells to help emphasize their purpose to the user. (See Figure 9.4.)

FIGURE 9.4.

The first row is defined with the <TH> tag, and the second, with the <TD> tag.

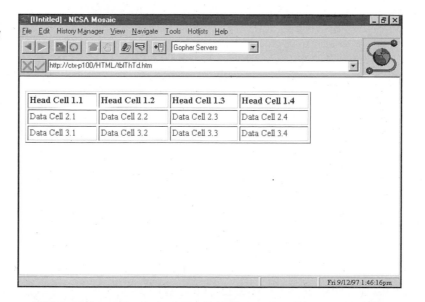

9

ORGANIZING DATA WITH TABLES

TIP

Header cells are a logical definition, not a physical one. Interpretation of the <TH> tag is left up to the browser, and it varies across platforms and applications.

Here's the syntax for <TH>:

```
<TABLE>
<TR><TH TDattributes>Cell Header
</TABLE>
```

In this tag, `Cell Header` is the cell's header content, and `TDattributes` are any or all of the legal attributes for <TD>.

Cell Size Attributes: `rowspan` and `colspan`

The first set of attributes determines its capability to merge with an adjacent cell. The `rowspan` and `colspan` attributes are used to combine adjacent cells into larger cells. It's important to note that when you're using these attributes, the adjacent cells aren't eliminated; they're just "hidden" while the acquiring cell uses their space. This is the syntax:

```
<TD rowspan=numRows colspan=numCols >
```

In this attribute, *numRows* is the number of rows, including the current cell, that are joined. Likewise, *numCols* is the number of columns joined together. The default for both values is 1.

Spanning is a little tricky to plan and carry out. For example, start with a 3×3 table, which requires three rows with three cells each. (See Listing 9.1.)

Listing 9.1. Basic HTML for displaying a 3×3 table.

```
<!DOCTYPE HTML PUBLIC "-//W3C//DTD HTML 4.0//EN">
<HTML>
<BODY>
<TABLE border=3 width=75%>
 <TR> <TD>Cell 1.1   <TD>Cell 1.2   <TD>Cell 1.3
 <TR> <TD>Cell 2.1   <TD>Cell 2.2   <TD>Cell 2.3
 <TR> <TD>Cell 3.1   <TD>Cell 3.2   <TD>Cell 3.3
</TABLE>
</BODY>
</HTML>
```

Now you can begin merging cells by combining Cells 1.1 and 1.2. Because this method reaches across columns, it's called a *column span*. (See Listing 9.2 and Figure 9.5.) To do this, `colspan=2` is added as an attribute to the table data tag for Cell 1.1.

Listing 9.2. A column span across Cells 1.1 and 1.2 results in adding the `colspan` attribute.

```
<!DOCTYPE HTML PUBLIC "-//W3C//DTD HTML 4.0//EN">
<HTML>
<BODY>
<TABLE border=3 width=75%>
 <TR> <TD colspan=2>Cell 1.1   <TD>Cell 1.2   <TD>Cell 1.3
 <TR> <TD>Cell 2.1              <TD>Cell 2.2   <TD>Cell 2.3
 <TR> <TD>Cell 3.1              <TD>Cell 3.2   <TD>Cell 3.3
</TABLE>
</BODY>
</HTML>
```

FIGURE 9.5.

The revised table with a column span.

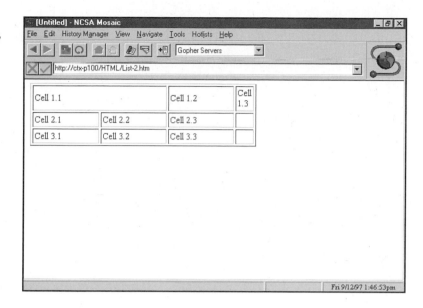

Notice the bottom two rows of cells in Figure 9.5. As you can see, spanning cells isn't quite as simple as just adding the span attributes. Here's what happened. When the browser encountered colspan=2, it knew Cell 1.1 needed to take up the space of two cells, and it provided the space accordingly. Then, it continued across the row and finished adding the next two cells. The result was space for a total of four cells (two joined and two individuals).

At the next row tag, the browser started a new row by adding three cells. The browser didn't encounter a fourth <TD> tag, even though there was room in the table for one. Instead of adding a cell that the user didn't specify, it simply filled in with blank space. The final result was a 3×4 table with the bottom two rows only partially defined.

This feature of cell spanning can cause many headaches when you're working with tables. For each cell you span, you need to remove the corresponding cell definition. (See Listing 9.3 and Figure 9.6.)

Listing 9.3. A column span across Cells 1.1 and 1.2 requires adding the colspan attribute and removing the adjoining tag.

```
<!DOCTYPE HTML PUBLIC "-//W3C//DTD HTML 4.0//EN">
<HTML>
<BODY>
<TABLE border=3 width=75%>
 <TR> <TD colspan=2>Cell 1.1              <TD>Cell 1.3
 <TR> <TD>Cell 2.1        <TD>Cell 2.2  <TD>Cell 2.3
 <TR> <TD>Cell 3.1        <TD>Cell 3.2  <TD>Cell 3.3
</TABLE>
</BODY>
</HTML>
```

FIGURE 9.6.
*With the adjoining
data cell removed, the
table retains its original
3×3 appearance.*

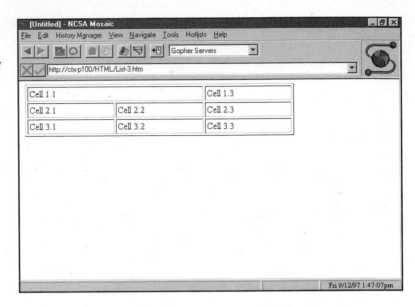

> **TIP**
>
> It might be a bit awkward to edit tables in the graphical manner shown in Listings 9.2 and
> 9.3, but it's useful for determining which cells should be removed for spanning.

The same rules also apply for the rowspan attribute, except cells below the originating tag should
be removed. In Listing 9.4, for example, three adjoining cell tags are removed. It's also possible
to combine the two attributes for other effects. (See Figure 9.7.)

Listing 9.4. Combining the first cell with the next row and next column.

```
<!DOCTYPE HTML PUBLIC "-//W3C//DTD HTML 4.0//EN">
<HTML>
<BODY>
<TABLE border=3 width=75%>
 <TR> <TD colspan=2 rowspan=2>Cell 1.1          <TD>Cell 1.3
 <TR>                                            <TD>Cell 2.3
 <TR> <TD>Cell 3.1              <TD>Cell 3.2  <TD>Cell 3.3
</TABLE>
</BODY>
</HTML>
```

When spanning in two directions at once, you need to delete all the data cells in the path of the
merge, which means removing cells from the right, left, and diagonal directions.

FIGURE 9.7.

Four adjoining data cells have been combined into one large cell, but the table keeps its original 3×3 appearance.

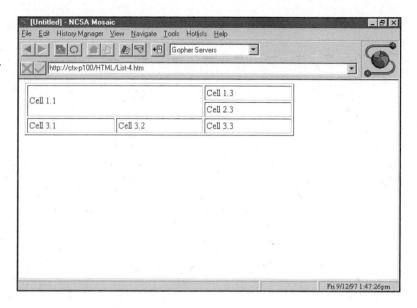

Identifying Header Cells: axis and axes

The axis and axes attributes tell the browser which row and column headers apply to a particular cell. Here's how they are used:

```
<TD axis="cellName" axes="cellName1, cellName2"
```

In these attributes, the names relate to another cell that acts as a header for the current cell. Normally, the name is the same as the value of the id attribute for a cell. If the id attribute isn't used, then the name of a cell defaults to its contents.

For example, take a look at this table:

```
<TABLE>
  <TR>
    <TH>Name <TH>Department <TH>Certification
  <TR>
    <TD axis="Beree" axes="Name">Russ Beree <TD>MFD <TD>Technician
  <TR>
    <TD axis="Colwell" axes="Name">Bill Colwell <TD>MRFD <TD>Technician
  <TR>
    <TD axis="Lanier" axes="Name">Marty Lanier <TD>MRFD <TD>Technician
</TABLE>
```

The axis value for the first table cell is the same as the name for that cell, but the axes value relates to the column and is the same for each cell in that column.

Although not supported by popular browsers yet, these two attributes were included for general browser database support.

Cell Content Alignment: `align` and `valign`

The next group of attributes controls how text and other content are placed in the cell. This is the syntax for these attributes:

```
<TD align=left¦center¦right valign=top¦middle¦bottom nowrap>
```

In these attributes, `align` controls horizontal justification, `valign` controls the vertical justification, and `nowrap` forces text content in the cell to remain on one line.

The values and behavior for `align` and `valign` are the same as the `<TR>` tag, and they override its values for the current cell only.

One other attribute, `nowrap`, disables automatic word wrap within the cell's borders depending on other table settings, such as fixed or proportional width of a cell or the entire table. It's a deprecated attribute in HTML 4.0, and using a style sheet with the `white-space` attribute is now preferred.

If the table doesn't have a specified width, the affected cell expands horizontally to accommodate the text. The same is true if the table width was specified as a percentage of the browser window; in that case, the table's width expands to accommodate the larger cell.

If the `nowrap` attribute is used with any `width` settings specified in pixels, the `width` settings have priority, and line wrapping is reinstated.

A similar effect is produced by omitting `nowrap` and using nonbreaking spaces (` `) between words that should remain together on the same line. This technique allows you to keep certain words together and lets others flow to a new line as needed.

Giving the Table a Name: `<CAPTION>`

The last basic element for a table is a caption to identify it. The `<CAPTION>` tag is to the table what the `<TITLE>` tag is to the `<HEAD>` of the document, except you can specify whether the caption appears at the top or bottom of the table.

If included, a caption must appear immediately after the opening `<TABLE>` tag before any table rows or cells are defined. This is the syntax:

```
<TABLE>
<CAPTION [align=alignment][core][international][attributes]>
captionText
</CAPTION>
...table contents...
</TABLE>
```

The `align` attribute is used slightly differently from other elements. In this case, it indicates where the caption is placed in relation to the table. Its possible values are `top`, `bottom`, `left`, or `right`.

Grouping Rows and Columns

HTML 4.0 now includes support for groups of rows and columns to further define a table's structure. Although not widely supported yet, these new tags for a table will help the browser display essential identifying material within cells and give authors more flexibility in structuring information.

Row Groups: <THEAD>, <TBODY>, and <TFOOT>

The row grouping tags—<THEAD>, <TBODY>, and <TFOOT>—are probably going to be used often by those people who need to display tabular data and other raw forms of information. Here's the syntax for using the three tags:

```
<TABLE>
<THEAD [alignment][core][international][events]>
...rows and cells...
<TFOOT [alignment][core][international][events]>
...rows and cells...
<TBODY [alignment][core][international][events]>
...rows and cells...
</TABLE>
```

Using opening and closing tags for row groups relies a lot on inference from other parts of the table. For example, </THEAD> isn't required if it's followed by a </TFOOT> or </TBODY>. The same is true for using </TFOOT>. If either <THEAD> or <TFOOT> is used, you need to specify the beginning of the body content with <TBODY>. If neither <THEAD> nor <TFOOT> is used, then <TBODY> is assumed and you don't need an opening or closing tag.

How a browser uses the groups will be up to the browser developer, but one of the more common assumptions is that the <THEAD> and <TFOOT> rows will remain visible on the screen while the user scrolls the <TBODY> up and down. There's also the possibility of the browser's assigning default appearances to the head and foot of a table, although the W3C standard doesn't make any recommendations about a preferred display.

> **TIP**
>
> Because of its potential uses in displaying a table, <TFOOT> must appear before <TBODY>. This placement gives the browser a chance to load and evaluate what to do with the foot before processing the rest of the table.

Column Groups: <COLGROUP> and <COL>

<COLGROUP> and <COL> are another attempt to help define the parts of a table more easily. Before these tags, you had to keep track of how many <TD> cells were in each row to know how many columns were in your table, which cells were in the same column, and how to format the cells in a given column.

The syntax for the column group tag is as follows:

```
<COL [span=][width=][alignment][core][international][events]>
```

For <COLGROUP>, this is the syntax:

```
<COLGROUP [span=][width=][alignment][core][international][events]>
```

A closing tag is optional for <COLGROUP>, although recommended until browsers begin to recognize it. Otherwise, browsers such as Navigator 4.02 might choose not to display the rest of the table at all. Its brother <COL> is an empty element, so it doesn't use a closing tag.

You can include a series of columns in a column group for easy identification and overriding of attributes. For example, this table includes possible definitions for five columns:

```
<TABLE>
  <COL>
  <COL>
  <COL>
  <COL>
  <COL>
  <TR>
    ...table contents...
</TABLE>
```

If you wanted to put the first three in a group and format them the same way, you would use <COLGROUP> like this:

```
<TABLE>
  <COLGROUP width="10%">
    <COL>
    <COL>
    <COL>
  </COLGROUP>
  <COL>
  <COL>
  <TR>
    ...table contents...
</TABLE>
```

By definition, every table has at least one column, although it doesn't need a <COL> tag to identify it. The span attribute of the column tags identifies how many columns are in the current group, with a default of 1. The width and align attributes set the basic appearance of the column's cells. In the previous example, you could omit the three column tags in the column group and add the span attribute:

```
<TABLE>
  <COLGROUP span=3 width="10%">
  </COLGROUP>
  <COL width="40%">
  <COL>
  <TR>
    ...table contents...
</TABLE>
```

> **TIP**
>
> If there aren't at least five <TD> tags or their equivalent (<TD colspan=5>) in the body of the document, then the extra column tags or column group spanning is ignored.

The width attribute is no longer associated with individual cells. By shifting it to a column element, you now have three ways to specify cell width: absolute, percentage, and relative.

The first method, *absolute*, is specified by a single integer to indicate the number of pixels. This method is useful for inserting items such as images and other elements that require exact sizes, but discouraged for general use because it's impossible to know what size the user's display area is. The second method, *percentage*, defines the column width as a percentage of the table's entire width and is identified as an integer from 0 to 100 followed by a percent sign (%).

The last option, *relative*, is a new method of defining the width by assigning a proportion of the available width. Take a look at the following column group specification:

```
<COLGROUP width="1*">
<COLGROUP width="4*">
<COLGROUP width="1*">
<COLGROUP width="2*">
```

This set of four tags defines four columns with a proportional width of 8 units. The first and third columns are 1/8 of the width of the table, the second is 4/8, and the last is 2/8. If the overall width of the table is 100 percent of the browser window, then the first and third columns would be 12.5 percent, the second would be 50 percent, and the third 25 percent. A special value for this method is 0*, which indicates that the browser should use the least amount of space possible to hold that column's widest contents.

To see why <COLGROUP> is a handy tool to add to your tool box, look at this table built according to HTML 3.2 specifications:

```
<TABLE>
  <TR>
    <TD width="20%">content <TD width="20%">content <TD width="20%">content
    <TD width="10%">content <TD width="10%">content
    <TD width="10%">content <TD width="10%">content
  <TR>
    <TD width="20%">content <TD width="20%">content <TD width="20%">content
    <TD width="10%">content <TD width="10%">content
    <TD width="10%">content <TD width="10%">content
</TABLE>
```

To make sure each column maintains its proper proportion, you have to include the width attribute with every data cell. However, with <COLGROUP>, if you add two lines to the top of the table that identify column settings, you can eliminate the width attribute in the body of the table and make the result much more readable:

```
<TABLE cols="7">
  <COLGROUP span="3" width="20%">
  <COLGROUP span="4" width="10%">
```

```
<TR>
  <TD>content <TD>content <TD>content
  <TD>content <TD>content <TD>content <TD>content
<TR>
  <TD>content <TD>content <TD>content
  <TD>content <TD>content <TD>content <TD>content
</TABLE>
```

With all the tools in place for building tables, it's time to step back and see how all the tags and attributes interrelate.

Whose Default Overrides Whose?

As you've seen in the tags leading to the actual cell data tag, there have been several opportunities to influence a cell's width. So whose attribute take precedence?

As a general rule, the last attribute encountered sets the standard for the rest of the table, although that's not always the case. Take a look at the following table definition:

```
<TABLE width=400>
<CAPTION>Table width=400, Cell width=500</CAPTION>
<TR><TD width=200>200 pixel-wide cell <TD width=300>300 pixel-wide cell
</TABLE>
```

In its definition, the table is set to 400 pixels wide. However, in the first two data cell definitions, the width is forced to 500 pixels. What happens? The last tag wins in Mosaic, and the <TABLE> tag wins in Netscape.

Here's what happens in Figure 9.8. The width setting in the <TABLE> tag sets its physical width. When the browser encounters the data cells with their width attributes, it looks at the total pixels requested for the row. When it sees the disparity, it decides the individual cells know what they want, so it adjusts the overall table width to match.

FIGURE 9.8.

The first table ends up wider by expanding to the sum of the data cell widths, but the second doesn't have width settings for the data cells.

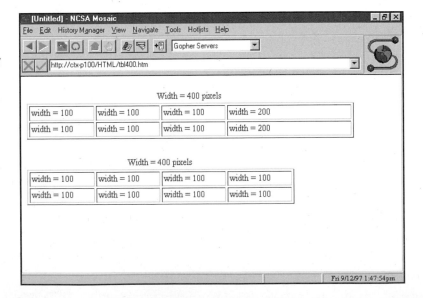

In Figure 9.9, Netscape does just the opposite. It assumes the <TABLE> tag holds the absolute limits of the outer boundary, so it shrinks the first table to fit in the space allotted by ignoring the request in the last cell.

FIGURE 9.9.

In Netscape, the first table remains at 400 pixels—the same as the second table.

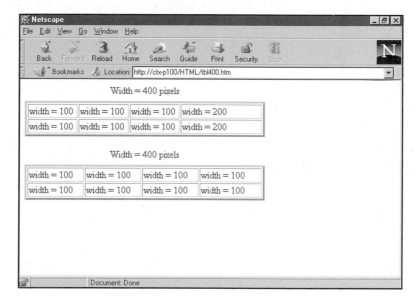

The moral of this story? Make sure everything adds up, and you won't have a problem. If you test with different browsers and see dramatically different results, it's time to go back and try adding up the widths again.

Now, look at another example—this time involving text alignment:

```
<TABLE>
<CAPTION>Align=right Valign=bottom</CAPTION>
<TR align=right valign=bottom>
  <TD>Cell 1 (TR default)
  <TD align=left>Cell 2 (align=left)
  <TD valign=top>Cell 3 (valign=top)

</TABLE>
```

The first cell in the table accepts the defaults from the <TR> tag. Cell 2 overrides the horizontal alignment and forces the text to the left, and Cell 3 overrides the vertical alignment and forces the text to the top. (See Figure 9.10.)

Note that the next cell in a row doesn't inherit any settings from the preceding cell. Each data cell starts with the defaults defined in the <TR> tag until an attribute is specifically overridden in the <TD> tag.

Alas, the world is full of exceptions to rules. In this case, the height attribute used in the first data cell also sets the height for all other cells in that row. Making the cells' heights consistent ensures the integrity of the borders used to outline the cells. If each cell had its own height, the

result would be a mishmash of zigzags and stairsteps as a line was drawn around each unique cell.

FIGURE 9.10.
Although cell alignment is set to the bottom right, each of the next two cells overrides one of the defaults.

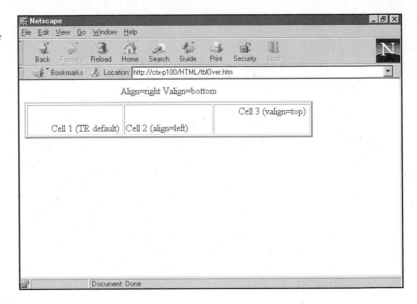

Displaying Real Data with a Table

Now that you've been through the syntax for tables, it's time to look at a practical example of how a data table is used on the World Wide Web.

The exhibit is a basic table for displaying tabular data. (See Figure 9.11.) In this case, it's a list of events for a single user generated from a database with a CGI script. Although this isn't a human-generated page, the table formatting follows the HTML standard. (See Listing 9.5.)

Listing 9.5. This HTML page was generated by a CGI script and includes a table for displaying tabular information.

```
<!DOCTYPE HTML PUBLIC "-//W3C//DTD HTML 4.0//EN">
<HTML>
<HEAD>
<META HTTP-EQUIV="Content-Type" CONTENT="text/html">
<TITLE>Incident Log</TITLE>
<BASE HREF="http://localhost/IncidentLog/">
</HEAD>
<BODY>
<H1>Volunteer Time Record</H1>
<TABLE BORDER="0" WIDTH="75%" CELLSPACING="0" CELLPADDING="0">
<CAPTION ALIGN="TOP">Prepared for the month of February 1997</CAPTION>
<TR ALIGN="CENTER" VALIGN="CENTER">
  <TD WIDTH="50%" NOWRAP="NOWRAP">Firefighter ID: 294</TD>
  <TD WIDTH="50%" NOWRAP="NOWRAP">Report Date: 11-Mar-97</TD>
</TR>
<TR>
```

```
   <TD COLSPAN="2"><P>F=Fire   E=Emergency Medical   H=HazMat  
   T=Training</P>
   </TD>
</TR>
</TABLE>
<HR>
<TABLE COLS="3">
<THEAD>
<TR>
  <TH>Incident Date
  <TH>Incident Time
  <TH>Incident Type
</THEAD>
<TBODY ALIGN="LEFT" VALIGN="TOP">
<TR ALIGN=LEFT>
  <TD>Feb 01, 1997
  <TD>09:00
  <TD>T
<TR ALIGN=LEFT>
  <TD>Feb 01, 1997
  <TD>22:00
  <TD>E
<TR ALIGN=LEFT>
  <TD>Feb 03, 1997
  <TD>19:00
  <TD>T
<TR ALIGN=LEFT>
  <TD>Feb 05, 1997
  <TD>19:00
  <TD>T
<TR ALIGN=LEFT>
  <TD>Feb 06, 1997
  <TD>15:10
  <TD>F
<TR ALIGN=LEFT>
  <TD>Feb 10, 1997
  <TD>19:00
  <TD>T
<TR ALIGN=LEFT>
  <TD>Feb 12, 1997
  <TD>19:00
  <TD>T
<TR ALIGN=LEFT>
  <TD>Feb 14, 1997
  <TD>18:00
  <TD>T
<TR ALIGN=LEFT>
  <TD>Feb 15, 1997
  <TD>09:00
  <TD>T
<TR ALIGN=LEFT>
  <TD>Feb 17, 1997
  <TD>12:30
  <TD>E
</TBODY>
</TABLE>
<HR>
</BODY>
</HTML>
```

9

ORGANIZING
DATA WITH TABLES

FIGURE 9.11.

*This page demonstrates
one of the more
traditional uses of
tables—displaying raw
data in table form.*

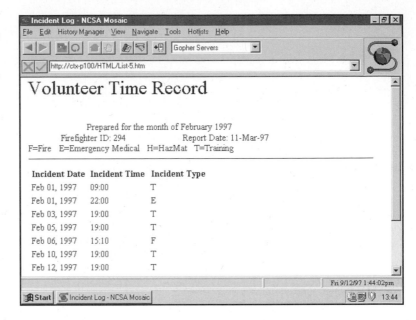

A table was used to format the top of the page (which is covered more in the next chapter). Then, the data table makes use of the <THEAD> and <TBODY> tags to differentiate between the two sections of the table. Some browsers that support <THEAD> would render the table so that the information in the head row was also displayed while the contents of the <TBODY> section scrolled.

Notice the use of the table header tag, <TH>, in the first row to identify the contents of each column. Other than alignment, no other text formatting is used in any of the cells; the difference between the <TH> and <TD> cells comes entirely from the browser's interpretation of each.

Summary

Tables are a series of nested tags, beginning with the initial <TABLE> tag, descending to the first <TR> tag, and culminating with a series of <TD> tags, with lots of options for defining a caption and groups of rows and columns. Building a table requires using a fistful of tags and their associated attributes, but keeping the basic order in mind makes the process easier.

Tables are one of the container classes in HTML that have the most associated tags and attributes, which also makes tables one of the hardest HTML elements to master. However, if you take the time to build up your tables row by row and cell by cell with your goal clearly in mind, you'll find them to be one of the most powerful and useful tags in the HTML arsenal.

Table Layout and Presentation

by Rick Darnell

CHAPTER 10

Tables aren't just a convenient way to display all kinds of obscure data, as you read in the previous chapter. HTML tables are also a very powerful tool for formatting Web pages. Designers are using tables to create multiple columns, hanging indents, sidebars, and other features previously reserved for the printed page.

There's even more good news. When used for page design, tables typically require fewer tags and attributes than when they're used for displaying data. If you maintain the standard HTML formatting in each cell, such as enclosing body text in <P> tags, they also degrade quite nicely on noncompatible browsers—sometimes even better than their data-displaying counterparts.

> **TIP**
>
> With the advent of style sheets, you can create styles that simulate columns, hanging indents, and other display features without using a table. The W3C recommends using style sheets for all appearance-oriented features on a page. For this reason, tables aren't recommended by the W3C for creating page layouts because that would make the <TABLE> tag the same as an appearance tag (like <FONT> or <STRIKE>). However, for those designers and authors who are used to working with tables, the <TABLE> tag is going to remain the preferred option. The choice, of course, remains in your hands. As a matter of practicality, I'd recommend still using tables to compensate for the weakest features of style sheets (such as columns) and using style sheets where they're stronger (margins, hanging headings, and so forth).

With that preamble and warning out of the way, it's time to get out the angle iron, nuts, and bolts to build the basic frame for your new vehicle.

A Quick Review of Table Syntax

A table is marked at its beginning and end with the <TABLE> and </TABLE> tags, with three basic divisions of content allowed within the table. The syntax for tables used for page layout resembles this:

```
<TABLE>
  <TR>
    <TD>Cells</TD>...
    ...additional cells as needed...
  </TR>
  ...additional rows as needed...
</TABLE>
```

An ending </TABLE> tag is required, although the closing tags for <TR> and <TD> are optional—they're automatically closed by a new <TR> or <TD> or the closing </TABLE>. Closing tags for rows and cells are required for use with style sheets, and recommended for help in troubleshooting and later revisions.

Each of the tags and its attributes were explained in the previous chapter, but here's a quick look at them again:

- ■ `<TABLE>` marks the beginning and ending of a single table.
- ■ `<TR>` marks the beginning of a new row in the table.
- ■ `<TD>` defines the contents of a single cell in the table.

Using only these three tags, you can create a wide variety of attractive and practical layouts for your pages.

A Simple Two-Column Layout

One of the easiest layout tables is a two-column layout that has one column with an index to the contents and another column to hold the actual content. (See Figure 10.1.)

FIGURE 10.1.

A simple table with contents listed on the left and text on the right.

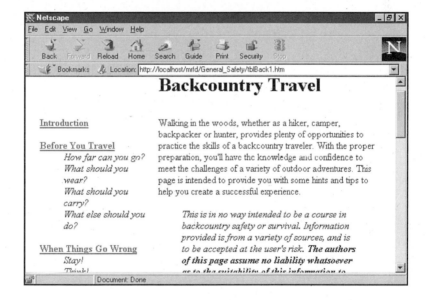

Building this page is a straightforward task; it begins with the basic required tags for a table with rows for header and content and columns for index and body:

```
<TABLE width=100% cellspacing=15 border=0>
  <TR>
    <TD>
      <!-- Empty cell to keep header from index column -->
    </TD>
    <TD>
      <!-- HEADER CELL -->
    </TD>
  </TR>
  <TR>
```

```
<TD>
  <!-- INDEX CELL -->
</TD>
<TD>
  <!-- BODY CELL -->
</TD>
</TR>
</TABLE>
```

The width attribute has been added to the <TABLE> tag so that it occupies the maximum amount of space on the page. After all, you're using this table to format the page, so it should occupy all the space it can. Also, 15 pixels of cellspacing have been added to give a little breathing room between columns, and the border has been hidden so that the page formatting stays invisible.

Now you need to adjust the table rows so they display their contents correctly. You want the content to begin at the top of the cells and the index column to be half as wide as the body column:

```
<TR valign="top">
  <TD width="33%">
    <!-- Empty cell to keep header from index column -->
  </TD>
  <TD width="67%" id="tblTitle">
    <!-- HEADER CELL -->
  </TD>
</TR>
<TR valign="top">
  <TD id="tblIndex">
    <!-- INDEX CELL -->
  </TD>
  <TD id="tblBody">
    <!-- BODY CELL -->
  </TD>
</TR>
```

An id attribute has been added for each of the two main cells and the header cell in case you decide to apply other formatting or style sheets in a later revision of the document.

Adding Content to the Two-Column Layout

With the shell of the table in place, you can start adding some content. A definition list on the left supplies an index to the contents, and the body contents have been placed in the right-hand column. (See Listing 10.1.)

Listing 10.1. The table shell is filled with content.

```
<!DOCTYPE HTML PUBLIC "-//IETF//DTD HTML 4.0//EN">
<TABLE width=100% cellspacing=15 border=0>
  <TR valign="top">
    <TD width="33%">
    </TD>
    <TD width="67%" id="tblTitle">
      <H1>Backcountry Travel</H1>
    </TD>
```

```
<TR valign="top">
  <TD>
    <DL>
      <DT><STRONG><A href="#intro" alt="Introduction">Introduction</A></STRONG>
    </DL>
    <DL>
      <DT><STRONG><A href="#prepare" alt="Preparation">Before You Travel</A>
      ➥</STRONG>
      <DD><EM>How far can you go?<BR>
       What should you wear?<BR>
       What should you carry?<BR>
       What else should you do?</EM>
    </DL>
    <DL>
      <DT><STRONG><A href="#lost" alt="In To Trouble">When Things Go Wrong</A>
      ➥</STRONG>
      <DD><EM>Stay!<BR>
       Think!<BR>
       Observe!<BR>
       Plan!</EM>
    </DL>
  </TD>
  <TD>
    <P><A name="intro">Walking in the woods,</A> whether as a hiker, camper,
    ➥backpacker or hunter, provides plenty of opportunities to practice the
    ➥skills of a backcountry traveler...</P>

    <BLOCKQUOTE><EM>This is in no way intended to be a course in backcountry
    ➥safety or survival. It's you against the world, and we're not taking any
    ➥responsibility for the outcome. </EM></BLOCKQUOTE>

    <H2><A name="prepare">Before you travel</A></H2>
    <H3>How far can you go? </H3>
    <P>When choosing a location and route, take into account your physical
    ➥condition, the reason for hiking, and the terrain and weather you could
    ➥possibly encounter...</P>

    <H3>What should you wear?</H3>
    <P>Proper foot gear is one of the most important parts of your journey.
    ➥Sturdy running shows are good for hiking on relatively smooth surfaces,
    ➥such as maintained trails...</P>

    <H3>What should you carry?</H3>
    <P>For short trips, a fanny pack or day pack should include at least one
    ➥quart of water per person, map, flashlight, first aid kit, rain gear,
    ➥high-energy snack, toilet paper...</P>

    <H2><A name="lost">When things go wrong</A></H2>

    <BLOCKQUOTE><EM>The worst thing you can do is to get frightened. The
     truly dangerous enemy is not the cold or the hunger, so much as the
     fear. It robs the wanderer of his judgment and of his limb power; it
     is fear that turns the passing experience into a final tragedy ...
     Keep cool and all will be well ... Use what you have, where you are,
     right now.</EM><BR>
    <CITE>Ernest Thompson Seton, 1906</CITE></BLOCKQUOTE>
```

continues

Listing 10.1. continued

```
<P>So you've planned, you've prepared, and now you're on the trail. And
   the worst part is, you don't know where you are. There's a four-step
   process to follow, and all you have to do is <EM>STOP</EM> --
   <STRONG>S</STRONG>tay-<STRONG>T</STRONG>hink-<STRONG>O</STRONG>bserve-
   <STRONG>P</STRONG>lan.</P>


   <EM>...More stuff here...</EM>

   </TD>
  </TR>
</TABLE>
```

This table example is a very basic way to handle the page. It includes one row for the heading and one row for the content. If you wanted to further divide your content into logical sections, you could add additional rows for each part—one row for the introduction, one for getting ready, one for getting lost, and so forth.

As you look through the listing, you'll notice something else about the content in the cells. Each piece of content is marked up as though it weren't part of a table. Paragraph tags and other items are still used to preserve the formatting, even if the table isn't rendered by the user's browser. (See Figure 10.2.)

Now that you've had a little taste of what's possible, take a look at an example that's a bit more advanced.

FIGURE 10.2.

Even viewed on an old browser such as Mosaic 1.0, the page still retains much of its form because of structure tags besides <TR> *and* <TD>.

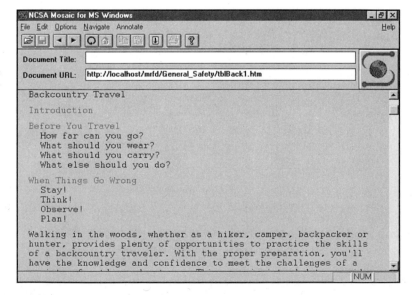

A Staggered Body with an Index

The next design is a little more visually interesting. At each break on the two columns for the text, the content shifts to the other column. (See Figure 10.3.) The resulting teeter-totter effect graphically separates each section on the page, without interrupting the flow of text within those sections. An index running down the left side provides a road map without interfering with the flow of text, and a hyperlink in the unused cell supplies a quick path back to the index for top-down navigation.

FIGURE 10.3.

The content alternates between the two columns at logical breaks.

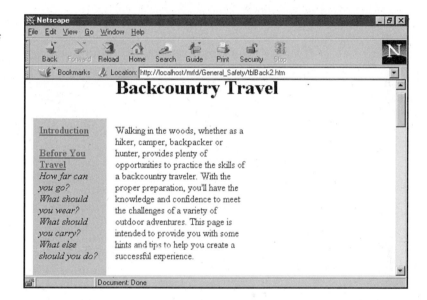

The framework for this table includes one row for the heading, followed by an initial three rows for the content. Note that the span attributes are used to confine the heading to the two heading columns, and another span attribute encompasses the rows for the index.

```
<TABLE border="0" width="100%" cellspacing="5" cellpadding="10">
  <TR>
    <TD>
      <!-- Empty cell to keep header from index column -->
    </TD>
    <TD colspan="2">
      <!-- HEADER CELL -->
    </TD>
    <!-- <TD> Unused cell from header span </TD> -->
  </TR>
  <TR>
    <TD width="16%" rowspan="3" valign="top" bgcolor="#C0C0C0">
      <!-- INDEX CELL -->
    </TD>
    <TD width="42%" valign="top">
```

```
          <!-- FIRST BODY CELL -->
      </TD>
      <TD width="42%" valign="bottom">
        <!-- Empty cell, ready for hyperlink at bottom -->
      </TD>
    </TR>
    <TR>
      <!-- <TD> Unused cell from index span </TD> -->
      <TD width="42%" valign="bottom">
        <!-- Empty cell, ready for hyperlink at bottom -->
      </TD>
      <TD width="42%" valign="top">
        <!-- SECOND BODY CELL -->
      </TD>
    </TR>
    <TR>
      <!-- <TD> Unused cell from index span </TD> -->
      <TD width="42%" valign="bottom">
        <!-- THIRD BODY CELL -->
      </TD>
      <TD width="42%" valign="top">
        <!-- Empty cell, ready for hyperlink at bottom -->
      </TD>
    </TR>
</TABLE>
```

Fortunately, the framework just *looks* complicated. Comments in each of the cells let you see what's needed in each one. The first row is for a header only, which spans just the body columns. The second row begins with the index cell, and then includes a content cell followed by an empty cell. The last row's first cell is absorbed by the index column, the second is empty, and the third remains empty.

You might be wondering at this point why the index column isn't placed on the right side of the table. That's because the page is rendered on a browser without tables. As the browser starts ignoring the table tags, the first real content it comes across is the header and then the index, which makes it appear first in the document, as a user would expect.

If you placed the index on the right side, then a user without table capability would see the header, then the first body cell, followed by the index, and the rest of the document—a rather confusing order for the poor user to figure out.

WHEN TO PLACE THE SKINNY COLUMN ON THE RIGHT

There is a situation in which you would place the index column on the right—if you turned the column into a sidebar or note. Then, the basic table framework would look like this:

```
<TABLE border="0" width="100%" cellspacing="5" cellpadding="10">
  <TR>
    <TD colspan="2">
      <!-- HEADER CELL -->
    </TD>
    <!-- <TD> Unused cell from header span </TD> -->
```

```
      <TD>
        <!-- Empty cell to keep header from sidebar column -->
      </TD>
    </TR>
    <TR>
      <TD width="42%" valign="top">
        <!-- FIRST BODY CELL -->
      </TD>
      <TD width="42%" valign="bottom">
        <!-- Empty cell, ready for hyperlink at bottom -->
      </TD>
      <TD width="16%" rowspan="2" valign="top" bgcolor="#C0C0C0">
        <!-- SIDEBAR CELL -->
      </TD>
    </TR>
    <TR>
      <TD width="42%" valign="bottom">
        <!-- Empty cell, ready for hyperlink at bottom -->
      </TD>
      <TD width="42%" valign="top">
        <!-- SECOND BODY CELL -->
      </TD>
      <!-- <TD> Unused cell from index span </TD> -->
    </TR>
</TABLE>
```

If this frame were filled with content and then viewed on an incompatible browser, the user would see the header, then the first body cell of content, followed by the sidebar, and then the next body cell. This framework maintains a logical order for users as they read your page.

Adding Content to the Staggered-Body-with-Index Layout

With the index-plus-two-column table in place, it's now time to fill it with content, as shown in Listing 10.2. You'll use the content from the example in the previous section.

Listing 10.2. Adding content to the index-plus-two-column table.

```
<!DOCTYPE HTML PUBLIC "-//IETF//DTD HTML 4.0//EN">
<TABLE border="0" width="100%" cellspacing="5" cellpadding="10">
  <TR>
    <TD>
      <!-- Empty cell to keep header from index column -->
    </TD>
    <TD colspan="2">
      <!-- HEADER CELL -->
      <H1>Backcountry Travel</H1>
    </TD>
    <!-- <TD> Unused cell from header span </TD> -->
  </TR>
  <TR>
    <TD width="20%" rowspan="3" valign="top" bgcolor="#C0C0C0">
```

continues

Listing 10.2. continued

```
      <!-- INDEX CELL -->
      <A name="index"></A>
      <P><STRONG><A href="#intro" alt="Introduction">Introduction</A></STRONG></P>
      <P><STRONG><A href="#prepare" alt="Preparation">Before You Travel</A>
      ➥</STRONG><BR>
       <EM>How far can you go?<BR>
       What should you wear?<BR>
       What should you carry?<BR>
       What else should you do?</EM></P>
      <P><STRONG><A href="#lost" alt="In To Trouble">When Things Go Wrong</A>
      ➥</STRONG><BR>
       <EM>Stay!<BR>
       Think!<BR>
       Observe!<BR>
       Plan!</EM>
    </TD>
    <TD width="40%" valign="top">
      <!-- FIRST BODY CELL -->
      <P><A name="intro">Walking in the woods,</A> whether as a hiker, camper,
      ➥backpacker or hunter, provides plenty of opportunities to practice the
      ➥skills of a backcountry traveler...</P>

      <P><EM>This is in no way intended to be a course in backcountry safety or
       survival. It's you against the world, and we're not taking any
      ➥responsibility for the outcome.</EM></P>
    </TD>
    <TD width="40%" valign="bottom">
      <!-- Empty cell, ready for hyperlink at bottom -->
      <A href="#index">Return to Index</A>
    </TD>
  </TR>
  <TR>
    <!-- <TD> Unused cell from index span </TD> -->
    <TD width="40%" valign="bottom">
      <!-- Empty cell, ready for hyperlink at bottom -->
      <A href="#index">Return to Index</A>
    </TD>
    <TD width="40%" valign="top">
      <!-- SECOND BODY CELL -->
      <H2><A name="prepare">Before you travel</A></H2>
      <H3>How far can you go? </H3>
      <P>When choosing a location and route, take into account your physical
      ➥condition, the reason for hiking, and the terrain and weather you could
      ➥possibly encounter...</P>

      <H3>What should you wear?</H3>
      <P>Proper foot gear is one of the most important parts of your journey.
      ➥Sturdy running shows are good for hiking on relatively smooth surfaces,
      ➥such as maintained trails...</P>

      <H3>What should you carry?</H3>
      <P>For short trips, a fanny pack or day pack should include at least one
      ➥quart of water per person, map, flashlight, first aid kit, rain gear,
      ➥high-energy snack, toilet paper...</P>
    </TD>
  </TR>
  <TR>
```

```
<!-- <TD> Unused cell from index span </TD> -->
<TD width="40%" valign="top">
  <!-- THIRD BODY CELL -->
  <H2><A name="lost">When things go wrong</A></H2>

  <P><EM>The worst thing you can do is to get frightened. The
   truly dangerous enemy is not the cold or the hunger, so much as the
   fear. It robs the wanderer of his judgment and of his limb power; it
   is fear that turns the passing experience into a final tragedy ...
   Keep cool and all will be well ... Use what you have, where you are,
   right now.</EM><BR>
  <CITE>Ernest Thompson Seton, 1906</CITE></P>

  <P>So you've planned, you've prepared, and now you're on the trail. And
   the worst part is, you don't know where you are. There's a four-step
   process to follow, and all you have to do is <EM>STOP</EM> --
   <STRONG>S</STRONG>tay-<STRONG>T</STRONG>hink-<STRONG>O</STRONG>bserve-
   <STRONG>P</STRONG>lan.</P>
  <EM>...More stuff here...</EM>
</TD>
<TD width="40%" valign="bottom">
  <!-- Empty cell, ready for hyperlink at bottom -->
  <A href="#index">Return to Index</A>
</TD>
</TR>
</TABLE>
```

There are some variations to the content as it's presented in this table. Primarily, the definition list was removed for the index and the blockquotes were removed for the disclaimer and Seton quote. With narrower columns, the indents force the text into even narrower spaces, and the page just doesn't look right.

You'll reuse this content for one more example in this chapter, so you can see one more way of creating interesting pages with a simple tool.

A Traditional Newspaper Layout

The last example is a bit of a departure from the two previous ones you've seen in this chapter. It creates a grid with a table that can then be used in a more traditional fashion for layout. (See Figure 10.4.)

This type of layout is done with a rather intimidating table structure. The base set of tags creates a 5×5 grid—three content columns and two gutter columns—along with a header row. When it's time to add content, you'll use column and row spanning to add the content and headings. The following section of code creates a header row, followed by five rows divided into five cells each:

```
<TABLE border="0" width="100%" cellspacing="0" cellpadding="0">
 <TR>
  <TD colspan="5">
   <!-- HEADER CELL -->
  </TD>
```

```
<!-- 4 unused <TD> cells here -->
</TR>
<TR valign="top">
 <TD width="30%"> </TD>
 <TD width="5%">
 <TD width="30%"> </TD>
 <TD width="5%">
 <TD width="30%"> </TD>
</TR>
<TR valign="top">
 <TD width="30%"> </TD>
 <TD width="5%">
 <TD width="30%"> </TD>
 <TD width="5%">
 <TD width="30%"> </TD>
</TR>
<TR valign="top">
 <TD width="30%"> </TD>
 <TD width="5%">
 <TD width="30%"> </TD>
 <TD width="5%">
 <TD width="30%"> </TD>
</TR>
<TR valign="top">
 <TD width="30%"> </TD>
 <TD width="5%">
 <TD width="30%"> </TD>
 <TD width="5%">
 <TD width="30%"> </TD>
</TR>
<TR valign="top">
 <TD width="30%"> </TD>
 <TD width="5%">
 <TD width="30%"> </TD>
 <TD width="5%">
 <TD width="30%"> </TD>
</TR>
</TABLE>
```

This type of layout is best created in an editor with a visual interface so you can see the results as you edit. The major drawback to this layout is that it doesn't necessarily degrade well in a browser that doesn't support tables. If you're going to use this style, it's a good idea to supply a traditional version that presents the material in the correct order.

TIP

The easiest way to figure out how a table is presented to a non-table browser is to read the HTML sequentially. Each set of content appears on the Web page in the order the browser encounters it. In other words, the cells in each row are rendered from left to right, in the order that the rows are presented.

FIGURE 10.4.

A traditional newspaper layout uses a grid of cells.

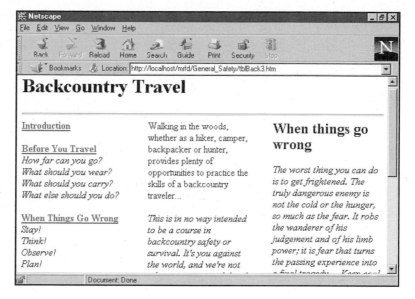

Adding Content to the Newspaper Layout

The heading cell is easy enough to understand, so start with the first bit of content—the index. This part of the text should occupy the upper-left area of the layout, so put it in the first row after the header in the first cell:

```
<TD width="30%">
  <P><STRONG><A href="#intro" alt="Introduction">Introduction</A></STRONG></P>
  <P><STRONG><A href="#prepare" alt="Preparation">Before You Travel</A>
    ➥</STRONG><BR>
   <EM>How far can you go?<BR>
   What should you wear?<BR>
   What should you carry?<BR>
   What else should you do?</EM></P>
  <P><STRONG><A href="#lost" alt="In To Trouble">When Things Go Wrong</A>
    ➥</STRONG><BR>
   <EM>Stay!<BR>
   Think!<BR>
   Observe!<BR>
   Plan!</EM></P>
</TD>
<TD width="5%">
```

Next, add the introduction to the next adjacent cell:

```
<TD width="30%">
  <P><A name="intro">Walking in the woods,</A> whether as a hiker, camper,
    ➥backpacker or hunter, provides plenty of opportunities to practice the
    ➥skills of a backcountry traveler...</P>
  <P><EM>This is in no way intended to be a course in backcountry safety or
   survival. It's you against the world, and we're not taking any
    ➥responsibility for the outcome.</EM></P>
</TD>
<TD width="5%">
```

The information about what to do when you're lost occupies all of the third column, so add it with a rowspan attribute. You need to work through the other rows, too, and make sure the last cell in each row is deleted or commented out so it doesn't affect the table display:

```
<TD WIDTH="30%" ROWSPAN="5">
  <H2><A NAME="lost">When things go wrong</A></H2>
  <P><EM>The worst thing you can do is to get frightened. The
    truly dangerous enemy is not the cold or the hunger, so much as the
    fear. It robs the wanderer of his judgment and of his limb power; it
    is fear that turns the passing experience into a final tragedy ...
    Keep cool and all will be well ... Use what you have, where you are,
    right now.</EM><BR>
    <CITE>Ernest Thompson Seton, 1906</CITE></P>
  <P>So you've planned, you've prepared, and now you're on the trail. And
    the worst part is, you don't know where you are. There's a four-step
    process to follow, and all you have to do is <EM>STOP</EM> --
    <STRONG>S</STRONG>tay-<STRONG>T</STRONG>hink-<STRONG>O</STRONG>bserve-
    <STRONG>P</STRONG>lan.</P>
  <EM>...More stuff here...</EM>
</TD>
```

Now you're ready to start on the next row, which contains the heading for the body text about getting ready. It should extend across the entire article (two columns), so it includes the colspan attribute to combine the first and second columns with the gutter. A horizontal rule is added to separate the header from the preceding content, and the valign attribute is set to bottom to force it closer to its text. Because the last column is occupied with the body text from the previous row, it's already commented out:

```
<TD width="30%" colspan="3" valign="bottom">
  <HR>
  <H2><A name="prepare">Before you travel</A></H2>
</TD>
<!-- unused cells <TD width="5%"><TD width="30%"> -->
<TD width="5%">
<!-- <TD width="30%"> </TD> -->
```

The next row contains two columns of content for the header, along with another commented column tag for the third column:

```
<TD width="30%">
  <P><STRONG>How far can you go?</STRONG>
  When choosing a location and route, take into account your physical condition,
  ➡the reason for hiking, and the terrain and weather you could possibly
  ➡encounter...</P>
</TD>
<TD width="5%">
<TD width="30%">
  <P><STRONG>What should you wear?</STRONG>
  Proper foot gear is one of the most important parts of your journey. Sturdy
  running shows are good for hiking on relatively smooth surfaces, such as
  ➡maintained trails...</P>
</TD>
<TD width="5%">
<!-- <TD width="30%"> </TD> -->
```

The last two rows remain the same in case you need to expand the content later. The last two cells in the last two rows are removed to make room for the third column of text, which extends to the bottom of the table.

The finished table is shown in Listing 10.3. It's not the prettiest or easiest table to put together, but done correctly, it can mimic the appearance of a newspaper while still offering meaningful content and be interpreted by as many browsers as possible.

Listing 10.3. The completed newspaper layout.

```
<!DOCTYPE HTML PUBLIC "-//IETF//DTD HTML 4.0//EN">
<TABLE border="0" width="100%" cellspacing="0" cellpadding="0" valign="top">
  <TR>
    <TD colspan="5">
      <!-- HEADER CELL -->
      <H1>Backcountry Travel</H1>
      <HR>
    </TD>
    <!-- 4 unused <TD> cells here -->
  </TR>
  <TR valign="top">
    <TD width="30%">
      <P><STRONG><A href="#intro" alt="Introduction">Introduction</A></STRONG></P>
      <P><STRONG><A href="#prepare" alt="Preparation">Before You Travel</A>
      ➥</STRONG><BR>
       <EM>How far can you go?<BR>
       What should you wear?<BR>
       What should you carry?<BR>
       What else should you do?</EM></P>
      <P><STRONG><A href="#lost" alt="In To Trouble">When Things Go Wrong</A>
      ➥</STRONG><BR>
       <EM>Stay!<BR>
       Think!<BR>
       Observe!<BR>
       Plan!</EM>
    </TD>
    <TD width="5%">
    <TD width="30%">
      <P><A name="intro">Walking in the woods,</A> whether as a hiker, camper,
      ➥backpacker or hunter, provides plenty of opportunities to practice the
      ➥skills of a backcountry traveler...</P>
      <P><EM>This is in no way intended to be a course in backcountry safety or
       survival. It's you against the world, and we're not taking any
      ➥responsibility for the outcome.</EM></P>
    </TD>
    <TD width="5%">
    <TD WIDTH="30%" ROWSPAN="5">
      <H2><A NAME="lost">When things go wrong</A></H2>
      <P><EM>The worst thing you can do is to get frightened. The
       truly dangerous enemy is not the cold or the hunger, so much as the
       fear. It robs the wanderer of his judgment and of his limb power; it
       is fear that turns the passing experience into a final tragedy ...
       Keep cool and all will be well ... Use what you have, where you are,
       right now.</EM><BR>
      <CITE>Ernest Thompson Seton, 1906</CITE></P>
```

continues

Listing 10.3. continued

```
          <P>So you've planned, you've prepared, and now you're on the trail. And
          the worst part is, you don't know where you are. There's a four-step
          process to follow, and all you have to do is <EM>STOP</EM> --
          <STRONG>S</STRONG>tay-<STRONG>T</STRONG>hink-<STRONG>O</STRONG>bserve-
          <STRONG>P</STRONG>lan.</P>
          <EM>...More stuff here...</EM>
        </TD>
      </TR>
      <TR valign="top">
        <TD width="30%" colspan="3" valign="bottom">
          <HR>
          <H2><A name="prepare">Before you travel</A></H2>
        </TD>
        <!-- unused cells <TD width="5%"><TD width="30%"> -->
        <TD width="5%">
        <!-- <TD width="30%"> </TD> -->
      </TR>.
      <TR valign="top">
        <TD width="30%">
          <P><STRONG>How far can you go?</STRONG>
          When choosing a location and route, take into account your physical
          ➥condition, the reason for hiking, and the terrain and weather you could
          ➥possibly encounter...</P>
        </TD>
        <TD width="5%">
        <TD width="30%">
          <P><STRONG>What should you wear?</STRONG>
          Proper foot gear is one of the most important parts of your journey. Sturdy
          running shows are good for hiking on relatively smooth surfaces, such as
          ➥maintained trails...</P>
        </TD>
        <TD width="5%">
        <!-- <TD width="30%"> </TD> -->
      </TR>
      <TR valign="top">
        <TD width="30%"> </TD>
        <TD width="5%">
        <TD width="30%"> </TD>
        <TD width="5%">
        <!-- <TD width="30%"> </TD> -->
      </TR>
      <TR valign="top">
        <TD width="30%"> </TD>
        <TD width="5%">
        <TD width="30%"> </TD>
        <TD width="5%">
        <!-- <TD width="30%"> </TD> -->
      </TR>
    </TABLE>.
```

Summary

Tables were originally designed for the simple display of information and data in an orderly and tabular form (see Chapter 9, "Organizing Data with Tables"). But, the same flexibility that allows for efficient data display also allows tables to create a host of different page layouts.

You've seen three examples of layouts in this chapter, and there are even more ideas in Part VII, "Effective Web Page Design," that use tables and style sheets. They should get you started on creating pages that go beyond the normal default Web page display.

With new capabilities, however, come new responsibilities. Remember that not all browsers support tables—which means it's your job to make sure your tables will work well across browsers and platforms whether the user has a table-enabled browser or not.

When your page is displayed by a browser without tables, the browser displays the information in the same sequence it's found within the table tags. If you haven't included container tags (paragraphs, divisions, or other block-level formatting) for the content in your cells, then everything will run together as one continuous paragraph.

If you keep these ideas in mind as you work on your own creative layout solutions, you'll produce Web pages that are both attractive and Web friendly.

10

TABLE LAYOUT AND PRESENTATION

Adding Images to Your Web Page

by Rick Darnell

IN THIS CHAPTER

Images are as common on Web pages as they are in magazines. Yes, there are some sites that don't include images, but they're few and far between. Even most text-heavy sites include an image of a company logo or other icon graphic.

As prevalent as they are, images are a relatively new feature of the Web. The Web's roots lie in academia and defense industries, which didn't have much of a need for pictures on the computer. However, as the Web expanded into the realm of the casual user, page developers wanted the ability to include graphics.

Enter the National Center for Supercomputing Applications at the University of Illinois (NCSA). It assembled a browser called Mosaic that supported the display of images right on the page with the rest of the text. With Mosaic, the graphical browser was born, and this first work became the basis for almost every other browser created since, including Netscape Navigator and Microsoft Internet Explorer.

NCSA accomplished the addition of graphics to HTML with a tag called <IMG>. This tag allowed authors to insert a picture inline with the rest of the text. That tag is still around, and it has some brand-new tricks, which I show you in this chapter. This chapter also includes some friends and relations of the tag that are associated with images. This feature has come a long way since its inception, and you'll learn a multitude of ways to fine-tune appearance and placement.

As much as the <IMG> tag has become one of the stalwarts of HTML, it seems to have entered its twilight. The <OBJECT> tag introduced with HTML 4 includes the capability to insert images, plug-ins, applets, and other media types, along with expanded possibilities for optional content when the content isn't supported or displayed for other reasons.

The Basic <IMG>

The <IMG> tag is an empty element used to insert inline images, from small icons and graphics to large image maps that occupy most of the browser window. Because the tag is a single resource element (one tag for one image), an ending tag is not supported.

In addition to identifying which image to use, the tag also has attributes for defining its position in relation to the surrounding text and Web content. These positions include floating the image in the left or right margin, or placing it above, below, or centered on the text line it appears on.

This is the syntax for an image tag:

```
<IMG src=URL [alt=textDescription][core][events][alignment]>
```

The src attribute identifies the image *filename* with a physical or relative URL and filename. The alt attribute defines a brief text description of the image or its use for browsers that don't load the image. The *core* and *events* attributes are explained in the sidebar in this book's introduction.

TIP

Browsers don't load images for a variety of reasons. First, the browser could be a nongraphical browser, such as Lynx. Second, the user might have image auto-loading turned off to speed up download time. Supplying a value for alt ensures that the user has some idea of what's supposed to be going on with that big blank space.

The alt attribute is vital for interoperability with speech-based and text-only user agents. For disabled people, the alt attribute can provide a brief description of what the image is. For text-only browsers, it's the only indication that the user is missing any content.

The src attribute is required for every image. It identifies the specific image to use and its type. The two most popular image file types are GIF (Graphics Interchange Format) and JPEG (Joint Photographic Experts Group, also used as JPG), although PNG (Portable Network Graphic) images are starting to gain acceptance and be more widely used.

The second attribute in the syntax definition, alt, is optional but recommended. It provides a text description of the image and is the only portion of the <IMG> tag used by browsers that don't support inline images.

WHERE TO ALIGN THE IMAGE

Like many other appearance attributes, the align attribute is deprecated in HTML 4.0 in favor of appearance control through style sheets. In the interim, align is still supported for compatibility with older browsers, but its use is on the way out. A more complete discussion of align is covered in Chapter 17, "Simple Style with Text." As a quick reference, here's how align works to position images in relation to the line of text in which they occur. Unlike other alignment attributes for items such as tables, align controls both the horizontal and vertical placement. Here's its syntax:

```
<IMG src="URL" align="position">
```

In this line, *position* is one of five values: top, middle, bottom, left, or right. The specific action of each value is as follows:

- **top:** Positions the top of the graphic with the top of the current text line. If the text line is formatted with a tag such as <H1>, the image appears to occupy more space in the line itself than if it occured in a line of standard body text. Browsers differ on whether the line immediately preceding or following the image is used to determine alignment.

- **middle:** Similar to top, but the vertical midline of the image is aligned with the baseline of the current line. (See Figure 11.1.) Its interpretation is consistent across browsers.

continues

continued

- **bottom:** The default value if align is omitted from the <IMG> tag. In this case, the bottom of the image rests on the baseline of the current text line.

- **left:** Forces the image to the current left margin, and any text following the image flows around the image's right margin. Its interpretation depends on whether any images or other material with left alignment appear earlier. Preceding text generally forces the image to wrap to a new line, with the subsequent text continuing on the line preceding the image.

- **right:** Similar to left, but the image is forced to the right margin. Any following text is wrapped along the image's left side. It exhibits the same behavior as left but in the opposite direction, depending on the alignment of preceding text and other material. (See Figure 11.2.)

Some browsers introduce extra line spacing with multiple images that use left or right alignment, but don't depend on the spacing to be uniform across all browsers and all platforms. For more information on controlling text flow, see Chapter 7, "Text Alignment and Formatting."

When placing an image on a page, remember that it's an inline feature displayed right along with any text on the same line. If it's not separated from surrounding material with a line break or paragraph, the image is placed on the same line as the current line of text according to the align attribute. This placement can lead to some rather undesirable looks for images, as shown in Figure 11.3.

FIGURE 11.1.

The text for the icon is aligned with the center of the image.

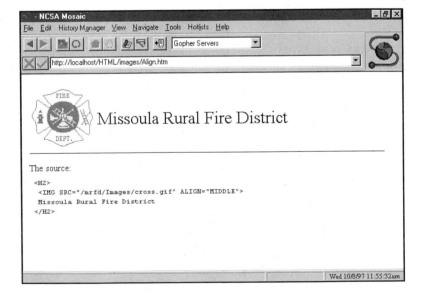

FIGURE 11.2.

The image is aligned right, with the text that follows it flowing around it to the left.

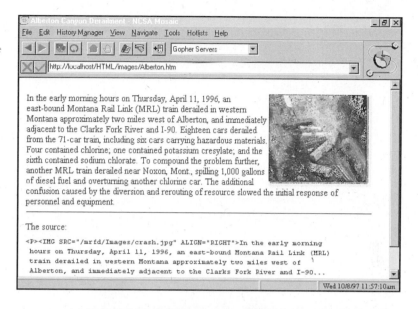

FIGURE 11.3.

Even though the images are small, they still affect line spacing, giving the paragraph a slightly askew look.

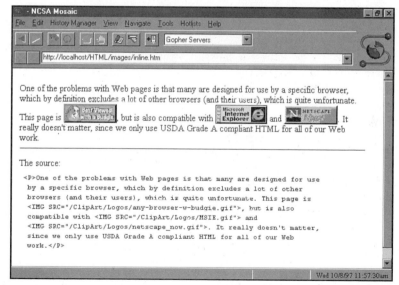

Making Space with the `width` and `height` Attributes

The two image size attributes—`width` and `height`—set the horizontal and vertical space for the image in pixels. They are typically used as a pair to reserve space in the browser window before the image is loaded. This is the syntax:

```
<UMG src="URL" width=pixels height=pixels>
```

`URL` is the image name and `pixels` is the amount of space reserved for the image.

For consistent and predictable results, images should be used at actual size. However, that's not always possible for a variety of reasons. In most browsers, the width and height attributes take precedence over the actual image size, giving you an easy way to force the image into a different-sized space.

However, there are some drawbacks to this method of resizing an image. First, if a small image is enlarged, the overall image quality suffers. If a large image is reduced, download time is increased for a larger file than what's needed. If the values specified in the <IMG> tag don't maintain the height-to-width ratio of the original, the image will look distorted on the Web page, as shown in Figure 11.4.

FIGURE 11.4.

The first image is in its original form; the other two are modified through their width *and* height *attributes.*

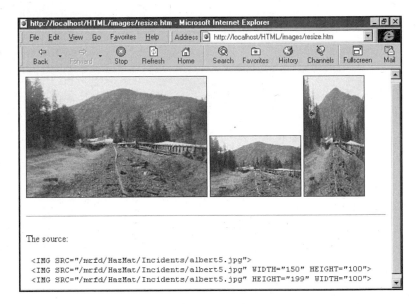

There are a couple of reasons why you'll want to specify a size for your image. The first, already mentioned, is that it can speed display time for the rest of the page. When size information is omitted, some browsers set aside a minimal amount of space and then begin downloading the first bit of the image, which includes its size information. While the browser is working on that, it doesn't work on downloading any more of the body of the page.

Depending on the browser settings, the rest of the page might not be displayed until it knows how much space each image needs, or the display might update and reload as each piece of information is acquired. Using the width and height attributes removes the guesswork for the browser.

The two attributes also preserve page formatting. If your page's overall appearance depends on the size and relation of the images to the text (like a newspaper or magazine), specifying the image size makes sure the proper amount of space is blocked. Although the image still won't appear, the right amount of space is held open to ensure the effect you want.

Would You Care for a Border with That Image?

When an image appears as part of a hypertext link, the browser usually responds by drawing a colored border (typically blue) around the image. The width of this border is set by using the border attribute. Here's the syntax:

```
<IMG src="URL" border=pixels>
```

URL is the path and name of the image file, and pixels is the width of the border in pixels. Use a value of 0 to hide the border. The color of the border is controlled by the link color attributes in the style sheet or <BODY> tag.

Most browsers also indicate a hyperlink image by changing the mouse pointer when it passes over the graphic, so that the user doesn't have to guess whether a borderless image is a hyperlink.

Give the Image a Little hspace and vspace

The space attributes set up a *buffer zone* around the perimeter of the image, which is very useful when white space is needed immediately next to the image. The hspace and vspace attributes set the width of this white space in pixels. This is the syntax:

```
<IMG src="URL" hspace=pixels vspace=pixels>
```

URL is the image file, and pixels is the number of pixels added to the appropriate side. By default, both space attributes' values are small, non-zero numbers, which supply just enough white space to keep the image from touching adjacent text.

> **NOTE**
>
> *White space* is a design term for "space without anything in it." It doesn't necessarily have to be white. Depending on the page's background color, white space could also be green, blue, pink, or any other color.

The space is added to both sides of the attribute. Therefore, if you include a value of 40 for hspace, 40 pixels of space are added to the right and left sides of the image. However, this amount of space makes the image look as though it's not in alignment with the other margins on the page. (See Figure 11.5.)

FIGURE 11.5.

The horizontal space around this image gives it a different apparent margin from the surrounding text.

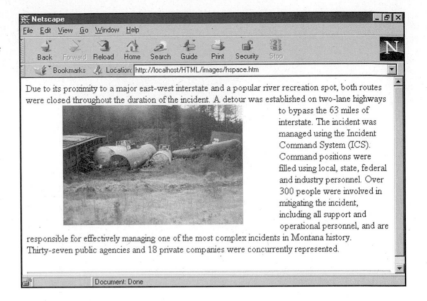

The `ismap` Attribute for Server-Side Maps

The `ismap` attribute identifies the image as an image map, used to associate specific areas of an image with hyperlinks to other documents.

To have validity, an `<IMG>` tag with `ismap` is encased with a hypertext anchor tag. When the user clicks on the image, the `ismap` attribute passes the x and y location of the click to the server. This is the syntax:

```
<a href="URL/file.map"><img src="imageURL" ismap></a>
```

`URL/file` is the name of the file with the image map coordinates (using a `.map` extension), and `imageURL` is the name of the actual image. This is called a *server-side* image map because all the hyperlink information is processed by the Web server.

TIP

The `ismap` attribute is used only with server-side image maps. To function, the server must have the appropriate CGI software to process the image map information and the file that defines each of the hot spots.

The location on the image where the user clicks is passed to the server by creating a new URL from the URL specified in the anchor tag. A question mark is added to the end, followed by the value of the x and y coordinates separated by a comma. The link is then followed, using the new URL. For example, if the user clicks at the location x=10 and y=27, the URL sent to the server is `/cgibin/navbar.map?10,27`.

Adding Images to Your Web Page

Chapter 11

177

11

ADDING IMAGES
TO YOUR WEB
PAGE

TIP

It's a good idea to use border=0 with the image and use graphical clues to let the user know that the image is a clickable map. Otherwise, it's easy to confuse an image map with a one-shot hyperlinked image. Graphical clues include techniques such as bold shapes with descriptive text, or a long horizontal shape in the traditional navigation bar layout.

A recent feature added to browsers is the capability to interpret an image map without any help from the server. Called *client-side image maps*, they include all the necessary information to process their hyperlinks without further communication from the server. This type of image map is covered with the next attribute: usemap. You can find more information on image maps in Chapter 14, "Creating Menus with Image Maps."

usemap for Client-Side Image Maps

The usemap attribute marks an image as a client-side image map that's used with a <MAP> tag. In most cases, a client-side map is preferable to a server-side map because it requires no communication across network lines and no additional support from the server to operate. This is the syntax:

```
<IMG src="URL" usemap="[mapURL.html]#mapName">
```

URL is the image file, and [mapURL.html]#mapName is an incomplete URL specifying the location of the <MAP> element that has the coordinate and hyperlink information and is identified similarly to a target anchor. If the filename is omitted, the <MAP> element is assumed to be in the current HTML file.

NOTE

Note the difference between the extension of the file specified for the hyperlink anchor on ismap and the source of the coordinates for usemap. The former requires a MAP file, which consists of a collection of coordinates and hyperlinks. The latter is a block of HTML tags within an HTML file. The file can contain other content, or it can exist solely for storing the map information.

The active regions of the image map are described for the browser by using <MAP> and <AREA> tags. This information is usually placed inside the HTML file with the <IMG> tag that requires it, although it can be placed in a separate file if the same map is used on several pages.

To ensure compatibility across browsers and platforms, ismap and usemap can be used on the same image, which allows the browser to choose which way it wants to interpret the image map, giving the document the maximum chance for compatibility. More information about both attributes is in Chapter 14.

Including an Image as an <OBJECT>

Once the exclusive realm of Microsoft ActiveX controls, the <OBJECT> tag has been adopted by the World Wide Web Consortium as a general-purpose tool to insert any type of content on a Web page, including applets, plug-ins, embedded controls, and yes, Virginia, images. You can read more about all these uses in Chapter 16, "Embedding Objects in HTML," but right now I'll cover just images.

This is the simplest syntax for adding an image with the <OBJECT> tag:

```
<OBJECT src="imgURL">alternateContent</OBJECT>
```

The *imgURL* is the URL for the image file. Instead of the alt attribute for alternative content in the standalone <IMG> tag, the <OBJECT> tag allows you to nest almost any HTML content within its borders for display by incompatible browsers. For example, the following code displays the enclosed text and its formatting if the browser doesn't recognize the <OBJECT> tag:

```
<OBJECT src="festus.gif">
A picture of <STRONG>Festus</STRONG>,
black panther of the north and <EM>my cat</EM>.
</OBJECT>
```

WARNING

Unfortunately, this use of the <OBJECT> tag is not yet supported by any of the major browsers. Navigator will ignore the tags and default properly to the alternative content, where you should include the <IMG> tag. Internet Explorer will balk when it doesn't find its .OCX file and display a faulty content icon (a graphic that looks like a page with a red ✕), which you can't work around.

Keep an eye on Internet Explorer—when it includes full support for the <OBJECT> tag, you can start using this technique to include images. In the meantime, it's useful information for the future.

There are several other attributes you can use with images inserted in this way. For new image formats that aren't necessarily supported by all browsers, such as PNG, you can specify a MIME type. This method gives the browser the option to bypass loading the content and move to the alternative text, as shown:

```
<OBJECT src="festus.png" type="image/x-png">
  <OBJECT src="festus.gif" type="image/gif" standby="Loading large image of my
  ➥cat.">
    A picture of <STRONG>Festus</STRONG>,
    black panther of the north and <EM>my cat</EM>.
  </OBJECT>
</OBJECT>
```

Adding Images to Your Web Page
CHAPTER 11

179

11

ADDING IMAGES
TO YOUR WEB
PAGE

Here, the outer tag specifies a PNG image. If the browser decides it can't handle that type of image, it can disregard the tag and move to the next tag, which include a GIF image. In this case, you've assumed it's a large inefficient GIF that's going to take some time to load, so you've provided a standby message to display in the image's space while the file loads from the server. Last, if the user has a text-based browser that doesn't support images, some alternative text is supplied.

The <OBJECT> method of inserting images gives you the most flexibility for including images on your page and should prove even more useful as the Web progresses.

Using Images as Substitute Content

With the wide variety of browsers and capabilities on the Web, it's increasingly hard to make one page work for everyone. This is especially true when you're including content such as Java applets, ActiveX controls, and Netscape plug-ins. If a browser doesn't recognize your special content, it ignores it and leaves either a big hole or a blank space in your layout.

You can use browser tag incompatibility to your advantage by placing an image tag just before the closing tag of the specialized content. Here's what the format looks like:

```
<APPLET attributes height=contentHeight width=contentWidth>
<PARAM attributes>
...other applet-specific lines...
<IMG src="URL" height=imageHeight width=imageWidth>
</APPLET>
```

The <APPLET> tag is any of the specialized content container tags, and the <PARAM> tags are any of the tags subordinate to the container. As a matter of style and convention, the <IMG> tag is placed immediately before the closing container tag, and the content and image size attributes have the same value.

When this set of tags is encountered by a browser that doesn't support applets, this is what happens:

1. The opening container tag is not understood, so the browser ignores it and does nothing.

2. Likewise, the subsequent tags that support the container tag are ignored. So far, the browser has done nothing but throw away the material it doesn't understand.

3. When the <IMG> tag is encountered, the browser suddenly has something it can work with. It interprets this tag and loads the image into the document in the space that was originally designed for the specialized content.

4. The closing container tag is reached. Because it closes something the browser never understood, it's ignored, too.

This technique ensures that everyone who views your page has something to see, even if it's a large graphic that says, "You need a Java-compatible browser for this page." Another common method is to use a screen capture from a video or a VRML (Virtual Reality Modeling Language) file for the image. Even though the image is static, the user still gets a taste of what was intended. More information about this technique is found in Chapter 16.

Summary

Using inline images in Web pages is part of what made the World Wide Web such a popular place to spend time. To add these images, you have the <IMG> tag; its use depends on only one attribute, src, to identify the graphics file. Although plug-ins and different browsers support a wide variety of image formats, GIF and JPEG are the most popular and are supported in almost every setting.

With the advent of HTML 4.0, additional capabilities in the <IMG> tag have been officially extended to make it easier to control the appearance and behavior of graphics on the Web page, along with the fine-tuning you can do with style sheets. In the same breath, the beginning of the end is heralded for <IMG> with support for inserting images with the <OBJECT> tag.

Mapping attributes set the graphics as an image map. Graphical image maps are one of the more popular uses for graphics files, including menu bars and full-screen images for site navigation.

III

PART

IN THIS PART

Basic HTML 4.0 Interactivity

Understanding Uniform Resource Locators

by David and Rhonda Crowder

IN THIS CHAPTER

CHAPTER

12

A *Uniform Resource Locator*, commonly abbreviated URL, specifies the exact location of a resource (usually a file) on the Internet. URLs are a subset of a larger plan for Universal Resource Identifiers (URIs). So far, URLs are the only development that has been instituted under the URI concept, so the terms are often used interchangeably.

> **NOTE**
>
> In the original plan, *URI* was reserved for future addressing schemes, and *URL* was supposed to refer to only those addressing schemes currently in common use for accessing Internet resources. To further confuse the terminology of Internet addressing, Universal Resource Identifiers are sometimes called "Uniform Resource Identifiers," and Uniform Resource Locators are sometimes called "Universal Resource Locators," even in official documentation. In addition to the more common URI and URL, *Universal Document Identifiers* (UDIs) and *Uniform Resource Names* (URNs) are occasionally used, too, although the latter acronym technically refers only to URLs that are persistent objects.

There are three different types of URLs: absolute, relative, and fragment.

Absolute URLs

Absolute URLs use a complete Internet address to give the location of a resource. To do this, they specify the transfer protocol first, then the particular server on which the file is located, and finally, the actual path to the file on the server. The following URL, for example, would be interpreted by a Web browser as an instruction to use the Hypertext Transfer Protocol (HTTP) to go to the Macmillan Computer Publishing Web server (www.mcp.com) and retrieve the home page from the Sams Publishing Company directory (/sams/home.html):

```
http://www.mcp.com/sams/home.html
```

In the terms of the official specification (RFC 1738), the transfer protocol is referred to as the "scheme" by which information is transferred. The server is referred to as the resource's "network host" and can be addressed by either domain name or numerical IP (Internet Protocol) address. Therefore, the Web address used in the preceding example could also be written as shown in the following line and still be a valid URL:

```
http://206.246.150.10/sams/home.html
```

> **NOTE**
>
> With the advent of virtual servers, the host need not be a separate computer. As far as URLs are concerned, a domain name or IP address, which is one of many virtual servers on a single real server, is no different from an Internet address that's the only one on a dedicated machine.

Relative URLs

Relative URLs (sometimes called "partial URLs") are used for accessing files when the full Internet address is unnecessary. This is the case with most Web sites, where most hyperlinks point to documents and other files located on the same site and, often, in the same directory on that site. Relative URLs are so called because the address is taken to be relative to the URL of the document in which they're embedded (called the "base document"). When relative URLs are accessed, the base part of the URL is automatically concatenated to the relative URL by the browser (or other client agent), so it doesn't have to be separately specified. Relative URLs can be used in any place an absolute URL can be used (anchor tags, image sources, and so on).

Say you have browsed to the home page of a Web site at the absolute URL of `http://something.com/index.html`. Although that page could indeed be linked to another page on the same site with the absolute URL of `http://something.com/nextpage.html`, a more economical method is simply linking with the relative URL of `nextpage.html`.

The browser strips everything to the right of the last `/` in the current document's address, then adds the relative URL to the end of the resulting base URL. In this case, it would remove the `index.html` portion from the absolute URL `http://something.com/index.html` to get a base URL of `http://something.com/` and replace the removed portion with the relative URL `nextpage.html`. The result is the full URL of `http://something.com/nextpage.html`. The browser can then find the correct page just as though the absolute URL of the second page had been coded into the calling Web page.

> **TIP**
>
> Relative URLs are an absolute necessity if you want your Web site to be completely portable. An instructional site, for example, that's compressed and available for download and installation on a visitor's own system would be essentially useless if it used absolute URLs for each of its internal links because that would require access to the original server whenever a link was followed. You'd also want to use relative URLs in any similar situation. Mirror sites, for instance, need to make duplicate files available without causing hits on the original server. Also, if you move your home page to a new server, it's certainly easier to change your own Internet address if you don't have to recode every internal link.
>
> If, on the other hand, you want to prevent your site from being portable, you should avoid relative URLs and stick with absolute URLs.

Relative URLs can refer to files in the same directory as the calling document, in a subdirectory, or in a parent directory. You can't, of course, use relative URLs to point to a resource that's not located at the same base URL as the calling document.

To code a relative URL for a file in the same directory as the calling document, simply use the name of that file as described at the beginning of this section.

For a relative URL to a file (in this case, `lowerdoc.html`) in a subdirectory of the one containing the calling document, the procedure is the same, except that you must also add the name of the subdirectory (in this case, `lowerdir`), with, of course, a dividing slash between the subdirectory and the filename, as in the following example:

```
lowerdir/lowerdoc.html
```

To make a relative URL to a file (in this case, `upperdoc.html`) in the parent directory of the calling document, do the same as for a subdirectory, but use the path component `..` for the directory name, as in the following example:

```
../upperdoc.html
```

Although these examples used HTML files as the resources, all addressable resources are identified in the same way. An image file called `face.gif`, for instance, in a subdirectory called `images`, would be located by the relative URL `images/face.gif`.

Establishing the Base URL

The base URL from which relative URLs are calculated is usually not specified by the HTML author, but simply defaults to the location of the calling document or takes the URL from the `Content-Base` entity header in the HTTP header (see the section "Hypertext Transfer Protocol (HTTP)").

However, HTML authors can and do change the base URL, both implicitly and explicitly. If you use `"Refresh"` as the value for the `http-equiv` attribute of the `META` element to load a new page, then the URL specified in that element establishes the new base URL. For instance, say you have a page that has moved from `http://www.oldsite.com/index.html`, and you have set up a redirection from the old site to the new one at `http://www.newsite.com/index.html`. You would then have source code something like the following at the old site:

```
<HEAD>
<META http-equiv="Refresh" content="3; url=http://www.newsite.com/index.html">
</HEAD>
```

This code would switch the browser over to the new site three seconds after the old site was loaded, and the base URL would, of course, be altered as well.

> **CAUTION**
>
> The W3C specification for HTML 4.0 incorrectly states that the preceding code should read as follows:
>
> ```
> <META name="refresh" content="3,http://www.newsite.com/index.html">
> ```
>
> However, it has never been done this way, and this method doesn't work with either Netscape Navigator or Internet Explorer. Stick with the `http-equiv` approach.

There are also a couple of ways in which you can explicitly declare the base URL for a document. The META element's http-equiv attribute can be used to override existing HTTP header entities, so you could code something like the following:

```
<HEAD>
<META http-equiv="Content-Base" content="http://www.newsite.com/">
</HEAD>
```

However, this is most definitely *not* a good approach. Although adding your own custom headers is not a problem, and will be handled well by most servers, any attempt to override the headers generated during normal interaction between the client agent and the HTTP server (even if the server will allow it, which it might not) is likely to result in unpredictable behavior.

A much better approach to establishing the base URL is to use the BASE element, which is specifically designed to perform just this task. Each document can have its own BASE element because the scope is limited to the document containing it. The BASE element is contained in the HEAD element and is used as follows:

```
<HEAD>
<BASE href="http://www.thissite.com/">
</HEAD>
```

Note that BASE has no end tag; there's no such thing as </BASE>.

12

UNDERSTANDING
URLs

> **NOTE**
>
> Although it's difficult to imagine why anyone would have more than one BASE element in the HEAD, the W3C specification states that the last BASE element is the one that establishes the new base URL. It's worth noting, though, that a META http-equiv="Refresh"—whether it comes before or after any BASE element—makes this point moot because redirecting the browser overrides the BASE element.

In addition to href, BASE also has one other attribute, target, which denotes the frame in which the called document will be displayed. This attribute doesn't need to be specified unless you are using frames and want to load the resources linked with relative URLs into a particular frame. If (as is usually the case) it isn't specified, then target defaults to _self, meaning that a linked document will occupy the frame from which it was called (if you haven't used frames, then the linked document will occupy the entire browser window).

Using _blank as the target, whether you're using frames or not, results in a new browser window being opened and the called document being loaded into it. The HTML code needed to do this is as follows:

```
<HEAD>
<BASE target="_blank">
</HEAD>
```

There are two other reserved names that you can name as the target. These remaining reserved names are _parent and _top. _parent causes the called document to be displayed in the FRAMESET that contains the calling frame, and _top causes the called document to be displayed in the full browser window, thus eliminating all frames.

You can also, of course, use any custom names you might have assigned to your frames as the target. The same HTML code used previously for the _blank target is used with any of these names, either reserved or custom.

The two approaches can be combined, specifying both the base URL and the target frame. You could even, by using a base URL other than the one where the calling document resides with a pair of custom-named frames, set up a menu of links in one frame that would use relative URLs to call only pages from another site to be displayed in the second frame.

The BASE element in that case would look something like the one in the following example:

```
<HEAD>
<BASE href="http://www.anothersite.com/" target="display_window">
</HEAD>
```

Any target specified in the BASE element can be overridden on a case-by-case basis by specifying a different target in an anchor, link, image map, or form.

CAUTION

If you explicitly declare the base URL in the HEAD section, you're making the site nonportable, just as though you had coded every relative URL as an absolute URL. If you want the site to work on other servers or local systems, you should remove the explicit base path information from the HEAD section on the version you make available for download or adjust the path information if you move your site to a new Internet address.

Fragment URLs

Using either the name attribute of an <A> element or the id attribute of any element creates an anchor. These anchors can be referenced in bookmark fashion as a fragment URL. For example, an anchor could be declared in either of the following manners:

```
<A name="candybar">This is the candy bar anchor.</A>
<H1 id="candybar">This is the candy bar anchor.</H1>
```

NOTE

You can't use both methods with the same fragment identifier because both name and id occupy the same name space. That means any variable assigned to one can't be assigned to the other.

The fragment URL to access such an anchor might look like this example:

```
http://www.fragdemo.org/chocolate.html#candybar
```

The portion following the Web page address and beginning with the hash mark (#) is called a "fragment," hence the name *fragment URLs*. The part of the fragment after the hash mark (in this case, `candybar`) is called a *fragment identifier*, and is the same as the `name` or `id` of the referenced anchor.

Neither the # nor the following fragment identifier are technically part of the URL because they were never officially part of the HTTP scheme. In fact, fragment URLs, because they have this nonstandard portion tacked onto the end, aren't officially URLs, although they are treated as such by Web browsers and can be considered as such for all practical purposes by HTML authors.

Fragment URLs can be either absolute, as in the preceding example, or relative, as in this example:

```
chocolate.html#candybar
```

The fragment identifier has scope only within the document it's found in. That means there's a special kind of unofficial "relative within the document" URL, which can be performed only with such an anchor. Just as a relative URL doesn't need to have the base URL explicitly declared, neither does a fragment URL need any preface *if the link to it is within the document where it's found.* Such a "document-relative" URL would simply look like this:

```
#candybar
```

Types of URL Schemes

Although there are several different transfer protocols or schemes, ranging from older ones like Gopher and WAIS to obscure ones like Prospero, HTML authors are generally concerned with only the few URL schemes currently in common use. The most commonly used are HTTP (for Web pages), `mailto` (for e-mail), `news` (for newsgroups), and, to a lesser extent today, because files can be transferred through HTTP, FTP (for file transfers). In the interests of completeness, we will also give some coverage to ones that are less common, either because of limited usefulness or because they're outdated, including `file` and `telnet`. We will also mention some, like the TV protocol, that are designed to take advantage of emerging, but not yet available, technologies.

Most of the URL schemes have optional elements, which you won't normally use. Ports, for example, aren't usually specified because most network administrators simply accept the default ports. Therefore, a Web server is almost always on port 80 (although you occasionally find an odd one on another port, such as 8001).

Hypertext Transfer Protocol (HTTP)

The URL scheme of greatest interest to HTML authors is, of course, HTTP (Hypertext Transfer Protocol), which is the Web's native protocol. It's used to access HTML pages through Web browsers and other client agents. HTTP uses URLs in a couple of interesting ways.

The actual URL scheme for HTTP looks like this:

```
http://<host>:<port>/<path>?<searchpart>
```

The first part (http://) defines the protocol used to access the host. The *host* is either a domain name like www.mcp.com or a numerical IP address like 206.246.150.10. As we mentioned, the *port* for Web servers defaults to 80. The *path* defines the location of the requested HTML document on the host. The *searchpart*, which is optional, includes parameters for CGI processing.

In HTTP processing, the client agent (usually a Web browser such as Netscape Navigator) sends a request to the HTTP server. The first component in that request is the *method,* which is followed by other header information. The most common methods are GET, HEAD, and POST. GET is perhaps the most used method because it's the way to request a Web page. A simple GET request header looks something like the following:

```
GET /sams/home.html HTTP/1.1
Connection: Keep-Alive
User-Agent: Mozilla/3.01Gold(Win95;I)
Host: www.mcp.com
Accept: image/gif, image/jpeg
```

The first line asks the HTTP server to send an HTML page to the browser. It also supplies the HTTP version. Asking the server to hold the line open, it also tells it what browser (User-Agent) and ISP are being used and informs the server what other types of files it will accept.

The /sams/home.html portion is called the Request-URI. In this case, it's a relative URL composed of the path from the URL, which is the complete local path to it on the server. This is the most common form of a GET request to a server. A GET request that must pass through a proxy is required to use the absolute URL of the resource, which would include the host information and be prefaced by http://.

The server then responds by sending back a header with similar identifying information along with the requested file (which is called the *entity body*) or, if things don't work out, an error message. For instance, if the requested page doesn't exist, your screen displays the 404: Not Found response.

The HEAD method is of less interest to HTML authors. It works the same way as the GET method, but no file is returned from the server, only information about the specified file. This method is used by client agents to determine, for instance, the last revision date of an HTML page to decide whether to use a cached version or, if the cached version is outdated, request a new one from the server.

The GET method can also be used to activate a CGI program at the server by using the searchpart of the URL. Typically, searchpart is used with form input (see Chapter 15, "Building and Using HTML Forms"). In this case, the first line of the header would look something like this:

```
GET /cgi-bin/cats.pl?breed=shorthair&age=4 HTTP/1.1
```

Instead of having an existing HTML page sent back, this method invokes a Perl CGI program called cats.pl in the server's cgi-bin directory. That program would then process the information on breed and age. Next, it would create a new HTML page in response to the input and send that page back to the server, which would relay it to the browser from which the request was sent.

The POST method performs a similar task, but in a different way. The GET method sends the variable input as part of the URL itself, but the POST method works a bit differently. As you will no doubt recall, a request using the GET method consists of the method line followed by other information. A request using the POST method adds a third part, the entity body. You have already met the entity body in the form of the HTML page returned from a normal GET request. A POST entity body is the same idea, but going in the other direction. Instead of an HTML page, the POST entity body consists of the variable parameters being sent to the CGI program, and the URL in a POST request doesn't contain a searchpart.

> **NOTE**
>
> Of the three commonly used methods, only GET and HEAD are actually required to be supported by all HTTP servers. It's possible, though unlikely, that an HTTP server would not support the POST method.

Mailto

You commonly use mailto URLs for invoking e-mail programs (as in the usual Contact the Webmaster link found at the bottom of most Web pages). The URL scheme is as follows:

```
mailto:<e-mail address>?<subject=>
```

Note that there are no double slashes after the colon, as there are in HTTP URLs.

The effect when invoked is to launch an e-mail program with the To field filled in with the value from e-mail address. Just as with an HTTP URL's searchpart, you can specify an optional addition—in this case, subject. If a subject is specified in the URL, then the Subject field in the e-mail is filled in with that value, too.

Therefore, a mailto URL of mailto:john@smith.com?subject=Happy Birthday would create an e-mail message ready to send birthday greetings to the person at that address.

> **TIP**
>
> Internet Explorer does not handle `mailto` URLs and might even crash when it encounters them.

There is no port specified in a `mailto` URL. Currently, there's some discussion about expanding the `mailto` URL to include other options, such as `<body=>`, which would act the same way as `<subject=>` but actually place the e-mail message itself automatically. This feature would be very useful for mailing list owners because it would allow easy—and errorless—subscription and unsubscription commands to be sent from a Web page.

News

You might also want to use the news URL so that visitors to your site can access linked Usenet newsgroups. Although you supply the URL on your site, visitors' chances of actually getting the newsgroup depends on their own access to a news server (generally provided by their ISP). A news URL simply provides their news reader software with the parameters to locate either a particular newsgroup or even a particular article, if you have the message ID for it. The news URL scheme has two versions:

```
news:<newsgroup-name>
news:<message-id>
```

The first version is the one generally used. To connect to the Archaeology newsgroup, for example, you would code the following into a link:

```
news:sci.archaeology
```

The second version specifies individual articles rather than the whole newsgroup. However, this version is of limited usefulness because the life of an article is ephemeral and getting its message ID involves some extra effort.

As with the `mailto` URL, there's no port involved, and there are no double slashes after the colon.

Network News Transfer Protocol (NNTP)

As an alternative for specifying a Usenet newsgroup, you can use the Network News Transfer Protocol (NNTP) for newsgroup access. This is the URL scheme for NNTP:

```
nntp://<host>:<port>/<newsgroup-name>/<article number>
```

However, most news servers won't accept just anybody dropping in on them, so this URL has very limited use. The port defaults to 119. The newsgroup name is handled the same as with a news URL, and the article number is the message ID. Also, if the article has expired, the link is useless, anyway.

File Transfer Protocol (FTP)

The File Transfer Protocol is still in use for retrieving files from FTP servers, though not as much as in earlier days because HTTP is capable of transferring files. This is the URL scheme for specifying a resource on an FTP server:

```
ftp://<user>:<password>@<host>:<port>/<cwd1>/<cwd2>/.../<cwdN>/
<name>;type=<typecode>
```

An HTML author, of course, does not supply the user name or password when coding a link to an FTP URL. In most cases, they aren't required, anyway, because most FTP sites you add links to would be anonymous FTP sites that are open to all. The port defaults to 21. The *cwd* parts are the directory path to the file, and *name* is the filename to be retrieved.

Generally speaking, all you, as an HTML author, have to do is supply the file's protocol, host, and file address and the software takes care of the rest. Therefore, you could simplify the preceding syntax to the following:

```
ftp://<host>/<cwd1>/<cwd2>/.../<cwdN>/<name>
```

You don't have to specify a particular file. You can simply supply the host, as shown in the following example, which causes a directory listing of the site to be retrieved:

```
ftp://ftp.microsoft.com
```

File

File URLs are rarely seen except when accessing a Web page you have downloaded onto your local drive. In fact, file URLs don't have any officially established protocol associated with them, yet they will work as a viable substitute for FTP and can be used to retrieve files from anonymous FTP servers.

Here's the file URL scheme:

```
file://<host>/<path>
```

An example of using the file URL scheme like FTP would look like the following:

```
file://ftp.microsoft.com/
```

File URLs do not have a real place in HTML authoring, although they play a tangential role if you want to use Web technology outside the World Wide Web. A Web page located on, for example, a CD-ROM, has a file URL. However, you don't need to code this information into any of your pages because the page would be accessed by using a Web browser's file-opening methods. In that case, the file URL simply shows up in the Location box at the top of the browser.

Telnet

Telnet is a means of logging onto a remote computer system. The `telnet` URL scheme is as follows:

```
telnet://<user>:<password>@<host>:<port>/
```

As with FTP, you do not specify the user name or password in a link. The port defaults to 23. Here's an example of using a `telnet` URL scheme to find the Library of Congress site:

```
telnet://locis.loc.gov
```

Reserved and Unsafe Characters

There are a handful of characters that shouldn't be used in a URL, either because they can cause conflict in the interpretation of URLs or because they're reserved by various URL schemes. The hash mark (#), for example, because it's used to denote a fragment URL, should never be used in any other manner. A URL of `http://www.unsafe.com/index#1.html`, for instance, could cause problems if it was interpreted as a fragment URL. There's really no reason why a character shouldn't be used in its proper place. However, if a character is going to be used in a URL differently from its reserved use in the URL scheme, it must be encoded with an *escape code* using %HH (hexadecimal) notation. The following table lists these characters and their encoded equivalents.

Table 12.1. Escape codes for unsafe or reserved characters.

Character	Escape Code
Space	%20
"	%22
#	%23
%	%25
&	%26
/	%2F
:	%3A
;	%3B
<	%3C
=	%3D
>	%3E
?	%3F
@	%40
[	%5B

Character	Escape Code
\	%5C
]	%5D
^	%5E
'	%60
{	%7B
¦	%7C
}	%7D
~	%7E

12

UNDERSTANDING URLs

Future Trends

New URL schemes are being proposed all the time. Many are obscure or of no interest to HTML authors, but two particularly interesting schemes will doubtless come into play soon. One is the TV URL scheme for reception of television programs. Its format is as follows:

```
tv:<broadcast>
```

Here are some examples of its proposed use:

- **tv:cnn** For use with netword IDs
- **tv:wsvn** For use with call signs
- **tv:10** For use with channel numbers

The other future URL scheme, similar to the `mailto` URL scheme, is the `callto` URL for telephone communication. It has several proposed variations, including voice, fax, or data communication; accommodating pauses; and adding dialing extensions after connecting. This is the basic format for the `callto` URL:

```
callto:<phone number>
```

Summary

Uniform Resource Locators, known by a variety of similar names, are techniques for establishing Internet addresses where files and other resources can be located. There are three kinds of URLs: absolute, relative, and fragment. Absolute URLs contain the full address, including protocol, host, path, and filename. Relative URLs don't need the host or, in some cases, the path specified. Fragment URLs refer to named elements in a particular HTML page. There are several types of URL formats, called "schemes," including HTTP, mailto, news, and FTP. Several characters are reserved by URL schemes or could conflict with the proper interpretation of URLs, so they need to be encoded with escape codes. You have also been introduced to some proposed URL schemes that might affect HTML authors. A thorough understanding of the different URLs and their proper use is essential for good Web design. In the next chapter, "Hyperlinking and Anchors," we'll take a look at the practical application of URLs.

Hyperlinking and Anchors

by David and Rhonda Crowder

IN THIS CHAPTER

Hypertext is the very essence and heart of the World Wide Web. Without hyperlinks (hypertext links), the Web would be nothing but a bunch of separate and unrelated files, instead of the coherent, interlocking whole that it is. Linking different files into a single unit can be seen on a small scale in the composition of an HTML page, on a larger scale in the construction of a Web site, and on the macro scale in the totality of the Web itself.

COMMON ATTRIBUTES

Most of the elements in this chapter share common HTML attributes, such as items that control identification, style, language, and event handling. Because the common attributes are so pervasive in HTML 4 (that's why they're called "common"), you will find an overview of them in the introduction of this book. You can also find more information about these often-used features and their associated elements in Appendix A, "HTML 4.0 Reference."

Meanwhile, during this chapter, we'll refer to the common attributes by using these keywords: *core*, *international*, and *event*.

Additionally, many of these elements can accept other elements within their borders. They are referred to as the *inline elements* and include the following options:

font elements: These elements includes tags for bold (<B>) and italics (<I>) and are covered in Chapter 17, "Simple Style With Text."

phrase elements: These elements includes tags such as emphasis (<EM>), code (<CODE>), and address (<ADDRESS>) and are covered in Chapter 7, "Text Alignment and Formatting."

special elements: This is a hodgepodge of elements that includes all the following items: applets and objects (Chapter 16, "Embedding Objects in HTML"), images (Chapter 11, "Adding Images to Your Web Page"), anchors (this chapter), image maps (Chapter 14, "Creating Menus with Image Maps"), scripts (Chapters 23, "JavaScript at a Glance," and 24, "Using VBScript"), fonts, superscripts, and subscripts (Chapter 17), line breaks and short quotes (Chapter 7), and inline frames (Chapter 20, "Creating Frames").

form elements: This set of elements is used to create the various elements on a form, including buttons, text fields, and checkboxes.

Uses of Hyperlinks

Hyperlinks are used in several different ways::

- ■ Connecting with other HTML pages that are part of the Web site, or to related material from other Web sites. This use is most often implemented by using the ANCHOR element, although the LINK element might eventually see more use (see Chapter 7 for detailed information on the LINK element).

- Embedding objects, such as images and sounds, in an HTML page (see Chapter 16).
- Connecting to non-HTML resources.
- Supplying additional information, used for elements like Q, BLOCKQUOTE, INS, and DEL (see Chapter 7) to provide a link to other documents that have more information about the use of the element in question. The informational use is new and largely unimplemented.

Hyperlinks are often used so that a Web site can be broken up into several different HTML pages, all of which are interlinked. The alternative of having only a single, very long page would be unwieldy and have an objectionably long download time.

The Structure of Hyperlinks

Every hyperlink has two ends: the source anchor and the destination anchor. (See Figure 13.1.) For instance, in the link denoted by the HTML code `<a href="http://www.linkfinder.com/">`, the destination end of the link is the LinkFinder Web site. The source end of the link is whatever HTML document contains this code. All hyperlinks are two-way streets; for a link between two HTML pages, the source and destination ends are equally available by clicking the Back and Forward buttons of your Web browser.

FIGURE 13.1.
Link structure.

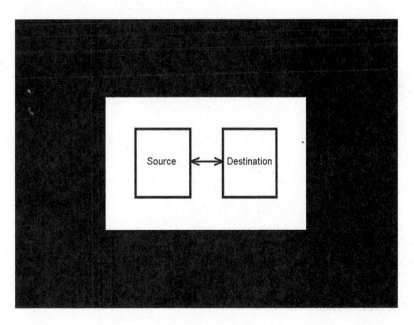

> **NOTE**
>
> The A in the `<A>` tag stands for "anchor." However, there's some dispute about the correct terminology. The official W3C documentation for HTML 4.0 says that an anchor is "a named zone within an HTML document" and that the `<A>` tag is used to define a link. Although it's possible to assign a name to an ANCHOR element, it's not required. Because anything with an `<A>` tag is commonly referred to as an "anchor" by most HTML authors, we will use that terminology and refer to an ANCHOR element with a name attribute assigned to it as a *named anchor* in this chapter.

Although most links are to other HTML pages, either within or outside the Web site where they originate, links are often made to other types of files, the most common being image files (GIFs, JPEGs, or PNGs). Although it might not seem at first glance that there is a two-way relationship in such a case, it does exist; it's what allows you to view the image separately if you want, and then return to the Web page in which it's embedded.

The two-way connection also exists in places where it's not so obvious, and where the user finds it impossible to explore the bidirectional connection, such as when a Java applet is linked to a page. Nonetheless, it is there, for the applet must not only be located, but must know where to execute itself.

The ANCHOR Element

The ANCHOR element, which appears only in the body of an HTML page, is generally rendered in a special way in a Web browser. If it contains just text, it's usually colored blue and underlined, but no other changes are made to the text. Of course, this formatting could be changed by using style sheets to define the element's style differently, but to do so would risk confusing visitors to your site, who are used to finding the standard representation. If the anchor contains an image, either with or without accompanying text, the image is usually outlined in blue.

> **CAUTION**
>
> Both the starting tag (`<A>`) and end tag (`</A>`) are required in an ANCHOR element. Failure to include the end tag results in a *very* long hyperlink.

The href (hypertext reference) attribute is the only absolute necessity in an ANCHOR element. Without it, there's no hyperlink. An ANCHOR element without a specified href does nothing at all. In fact, it's not even recognized by a Web browser as an anchor. Code such as `<A>This is not an anchor</A>`, when rendered in either Netscape Navigator or Internet Explorer, doesn't even turn blue.

Once the `href` attribute is added, however, the anchor becomes functional. Its proper use is as follows:

```
<A href=URL>Anchor text or image goes here.</A>
```

The URL can be a fully qualified absolute address, a relative URL, or even a fragment URL, and it must be enclosed in quotation marks. Any of the following are valid hyperlinks:

```
<A href="http://www.someaddress.com/index.html">A link to a full URL.</A>

<A href="/index.html">A link to a partial URL.</A>

<A href="#middle">A link to a fragment URL (named anchor).</A>

<A href="http://www.someaddress.com/index.html"><img src="image.gif">Image
➡ link - optional text goes here.</A>
```

Interestingly, although the `href` attribute must be present for a hyperlink anchor to be recognized by Web browsers, the URL value doesn't have to be specified. In Netscape Navigator, the following code is enough to cause the anchor to be recognized:

```
<A href>An improper link.</A>
```

Internet Explorer still won't recognize the anchor under these circumstances, but adding the equals sign (=) causes the same effect as the preceding code does in Netscape Navigator:

```
<A href=>Another improper link.</A>
```

Both of these are, of course, examples of very bad HTML code. The only reason they work at all is that Web browsers are designed to be very forgiving. The minimum to meet the proper standard would be the following:

```
<A href="">An empty URL.</A>
```

The link created by this code defaults to the base URL. Therefore, the preceding code, if found in a page at `http://www.mycompany.com/clocks.html`, would default to `http://www.mycompany.com/` and would, again by default, load the home page.

If you're using frames, then the `target` attribute can be used to specify which frame the linked resource will be displayed in. If you have established a frame called `main_window`, for instance, then you could specify that a linked HTML page be loaded into it by using the following code:

```
<A href="bagua.html" target="main_window">Feng Shui</A>
```

You have several different options when specifying the target frame. The `target` attribute in the `ANCHOR` element works the same way as the same attribute in the `BASE` element. For a full explanation of the `target` attribute, see Chapter 12, "Understanding Uniform Resource Locators."

The `rel` and `rev` attributes serve exactly the same function in the `ANCHOR` element as they do for the `LINK` element (see Chapter 7). The `accesskey` attribute is covered in Chapter 41, "Creating Widely Accessible Web Pages."

Named Anchors

Named anchors are those elements that contain either an <A> tag with a name attribute or any element with an assigned ID. Either the name or id attributes can be used because they aren't just similar—they're the same. For example, you can't define an anchor for one element and an ID for another element, such as the following two, without conflict:

```
<A name="netscape" href="http://www.netscape.com">Netscape Home Page</A>

<IMG id="netscape" src="navigator.png">
```

Both name and id occupy the same namespace, which means they are the same variable within the scope of the HTML document where they are found. You can use the same variable in a different HTML document without creating conflict, though, because that would be outside the scope of the first document.

> **TIP**
>
> Both NAME and ID are case-insensitive, so Netscape, NETSCAPE, NetSCape, and netscape are the same variable.

Although the official HTML specification allows anchors that have only a name or id attribute, this doesn't work in practice. As mentioned in the section "The ANCHOR Element," anchors must have an href attribute, or they aren't recognized by either Netscape Navigator or Internet Explorer.

Named anchors are generally used for creating links within the document where they exist. Menus, for example, can be created quite easily by identifying different sections of a Web page with named anchors and then setting up a series of links to the fragment URLs in the beginning of the HTML page. This method is illustrated in the following sample code and in Figure 13.2:

```
<H1>Menu Choices</H1>
<P><A href="#meat">Meat Dishes</A></P>
<P><A href="#fish">Seafood Dishes</A></P>
<P><A href="#veggies">Vegetable Dishes</A></P>
<P><A href="#fatcity">Desserts</A></P>
<H2 id="meat">Meat Dishes</H2>
...
<H2 id="fish">Seafood Dishes</H2>
...
<H2 id="veggies">Vegetable Dishes</H2>
...
<H2 id="fatcity">Desserts</H2>
...
```

In this example, users who select an option from the menu choices will find those sections of the page immediately displayed, without having to scroll through the entire page to reach them. Note that, in this case, the named anchors aren't done with the ANCHOR element and the name attribute, but with the `id` attributes of several H2 elements. Therefore, the fragment URLs refer to the beginning of the section, and the top line of the resulting display is the section's title heading.

FIGURE 13.2.

A menu with named anchors.

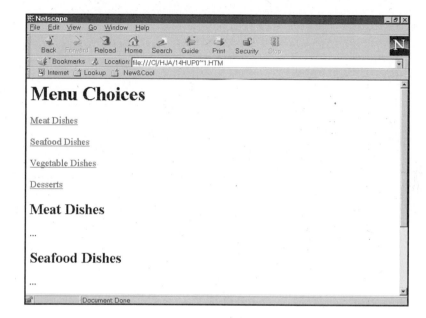

Named anchors and fragment URLs, however, can also be used with links from other documents. You could reach the dessert section of the same menu we just described from another document by using a link to the menu document and appending the fragment to it, as shown:

```
<A href="http://www.eatfood.com/feedme.html#fatcity">Desserts</A>
```

By selecting this link, you access the referenced page. The display begins with the page already scrolled down to the point where the named anchor is, instead of beginning at the top of the page as usual.

It's possible to have an ANCHOR element that performs a dual role as both a link source and a named anchor destination. You just have to use both the `href` and `name` (or `id`) attributes, as in the following example:

```
<A name="navigator" href="http://www.netscape.com/">Netscape Home Page</A>
```

Because the `name` and `id` attributes are equivalent, you could also write this code as follows:

```
<A id="navigator" href="http://www.netscape.com/">Netscape Home Page</A>
```

Either way, a link to it would have the following code:

```
<A href="#navigator">Netscape Link</A>
```

Image Links

Images can be used to create nontextual links by using the ANCHOR element. All that's required is substituting the textual portion of the link with an image URL. You can do that with the original approach from earlier HTML versions, as in the following code:

```
<A href="http://www.hamburger.com/index.html"><img src="hamburger.gif"></A>
```

Or, the link can be coded with the newer OBJECT element approach, as in the following code:

```
<A href="http://www.hamburger.com/index.html"><OBJECT data="hamburger.gif"
➥ type="image/gif"></A>
```

With either approach, the final result looks like the image in Figure 13.3.

FIGURE 13.3.

An image link.

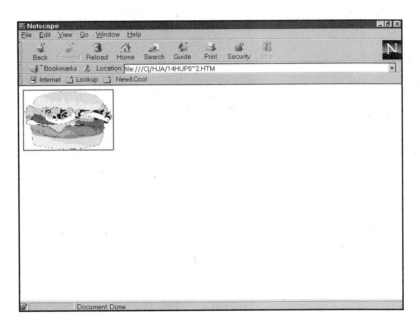

You can also have both text and an image in the same link, as shown in the following variation, illustrated in Figure 13.4:

```
<A href="http://www.hamburger.com/index.html"><img src="hamburger.gif">
➥Hamburgers</A>
```

In fact, there's no technical reason why several images couldn't be included in a single link. However, having a multiple-image link doesn't seem to offer any particular advantage because clicking on any of the images leads to the same result. It's possible this type of link could be useful, though, so the technique is shown in the following code and the results in Figure 13.5:

```
<A href="http://www.hamburger.com/index.html"><img src="hamburger.gif">
➥<img src="fries.gif">Burger and Fries</A>
```

FIGURE 13.4.

An image link with text.

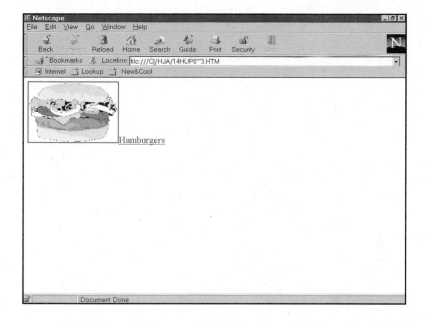

FIGURE 13.5.

A dual-image link with text.

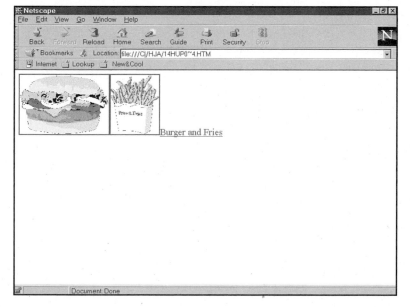

Links to Specialized Content

Some links to specialized content are accomplished in the same manner as links to regular HTML resources. For example, a link to an Adobe Acrobat file would look like this:

```
<A href="http://www.specialized.org/readme.pdf">README file in Acrobat format</A>
```

However, to read Acrobat `.pdf` files in a Web browser, your users must have the Acrobat reader plug-in. If they don't already have it installed, then they will have to download it and install it before they can access your file. Remember the potential extra time and effort for your users when deciding whether to use nonstandard files on your Web site. This one download-and-install operation, for example, could delay their initial access to your file by about half an hour—a serious strain on the patience of the average Web surfer. Many people do have the most popular plug-ins already installed, but it might be better to take advantage of the new capabilities offered by cascading style sheets, which allow you to produce a Web page with the same precise control over fonts and positioning as you have with external products. Using style sheets will make your site visitors happier and, because pure HTML frees you from reliance on external products and plug-ins, will also reduce the expense and complexity of producing your Web site.

The simplest way to add a sound file is to just set up a regular hyperlink to the sound resource, as in the following code:

```
<A href="themsong.wav">Play our theme song!</A>
```

The drawback to this approach is that the sound file must be downloaded to the client before it's played. Real-time streaming audio, however, is available with special software, such as RealAudio servers.

RealAudio sound files, unlike the straight link approach, require a special invocation method. Instead of linking directly to the sound resource, your HTML page links to a special metafile that contains information about the sound resource. This information is then passed back to a user's Web browser, which relays it to either a standalone player or a plug-in for processing.

The metafile contains just the URL of the sound resource. A RealAudio metafile looks like the following example:

```
pnm://www.yourserver.com/themesong.ra
```

As with any URL scheme, the first part is the protocol (in this case, pnm, which is specific to RealAudio files), followed by the server address and the path to the file. RealAudio files always have an `.ra` extension.

Multiple resources can be stacked together in a single metafile if you want them to be played one after the other, as in the following example:

```
pnm://www.yourserver.com/themesong.ra
pnm://www.yourserver.com/tada.ra
pnm://www.yourserver.com/introsong.ra
```

There's no header information or any HTML coding in a RealAudio metafile. Although some other data (such as copyright statements) can be added, it's added to the URL itself. These metafiles are saved as "plain vanilla" ASCII files. The extension for the metafile depends on whether it's intended for use with a plug-in or a standalone player. For plug-ins, the file extension is .rpm, and for standalone players, it's .ram.

There's no way for you to know if a visitor to your site has the plug-in or the standalone player, so you should save the same metafile with both file extensions. As you might have suspected, there are also two different methods of invoking the sound resource, and you need to use them in tandem to cover all the possibilities.

The link for a simple invocation of a RealAudio sound resource for the standalone player is simply the usual ANCHOR element, and the URL for the href attribute is the address of the metafile. A typical example would look like this:

```
<A href="themesong.ram">Play our theme song!</A>
```

The link for invoking a RealAudio file for a plug-in, however, uses the EMBED element, which is not standard HTML. The following code would embed a RealAudio player object in the HTML page:

```
<EMBED SRC="themesong.rpm" width=300 height=134>
```

To cover both options, use the NOEMBED tag with the other two approaches outlined previously:

```
<EMBED SRC="themesong.rpm" width=300 height=134>
<NOEMBED><A href="themesong.ram">Play our theme song!</A></NOEMBED>
```

This code displays a RealAudio player object in those browsers that support that option and a regular hyperlink in those that don't.

A full explanation of installing and using RealAudio servers and files is beyond the scope of this book; for further information, you can find full explanations at RealAudio's Web site at http://www.real.com/.

Summary

Hyperlinks are the most important elements of the World Wide Web; without them, the Web couldn't exist. They are most commonly used to interconnect HTML pages, both within a Web site and among different sites. However, they are also used when images and other objects are added to an HTML page.

Hyperlinks are bidirectional, having both a source anchor and a destination anchor. Most hyperlinks are invoked with the <A> tag, representing the ANCHOR element, and the destination anchor is specified with the href (hypertext reference) attribute, which is the only absolutely required attribute in a link. Named anchors are destination anchors that can be used to specify hyperlinks to a particular section of an HTML page. They are composed of either an ANCHOR element that uses the name attribute or any other element using an id attribute. Hyperlinks, either from the same page or another page, can refer to them with a fragment URL, and this capability is often used in creating menus. Links can contain text, images, or both. Hyperlinks can also be set up to non-HTML resources, such as Adobe Acrobat files or RealAudio sound files. Some non-HTML resources use exactly the same link syntax as any HTML link, but others require variations in the procedure. Hyperlinks are also used in image maps, which are covered in the following chapter.

Creating Menus with Image Maps

by David and Rhonda Crowder

IN THIS CHAPTER

CHAPTER 14

Perhaps because we're born with the ability to interpret visual images, but language is something we have to be taught, image maps have a universal appeal over textual menus. Whatever the reason, image maps have taken over as the first choice for menu development on the World Wide Web.

What exactly is an image map? You will no doubt recall from Chapter 13, "Hyperlinking and Anchors," that a hyperlink can be either textual or image-based. An *image map* is an extended version of an image hyperlink. Instead of having only one possible link no matter where you click on an image, it offers several different possibile links, depending on where you click on the image map. A single picture can replace a large textual menu.

A single-link image anchor poses no particular processing difficulty, but image maps, with their multiple hyperlinks, require a method for determining which link to follow. The method decided on was to keep track of the position of the mouse pointer in relation to the upper-left corner of the image. That corner was given the coordinates 0,0 in x,y notation. The x coordinates, running from left to right, increase as you go farther to the right; the y coordinates, running from top to bottom, increase the farther down you go. (See Figure 14.1.) A list of links is keyed to coordinates that originally represented only rectangular shapes. If the pointer is between 0,0 and 20,10, then a different hyperlink is activated than if the pointer is between 0,11 and 20,20.

FIGURE 14.1.
Image map coordinates.

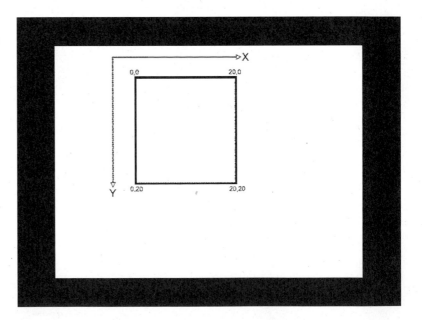

As image map technology improved, two more kinds of shapes that could be keyed to hyperlinks were added. Modern image maps support not only the original rectangular areas, but also circular and polygonal areas.

COMMON ATTRIBUTES

Most of the elements in this chapter share common HTML attributes, such as items that control identification, style, language, and event handling. Because the common attributes are so pervasive in HTML 4 (that's why they're called "common"), you will find an overview of them in the introduction of this book. You can also find more information about these often-used features and their associated elements in Appendix A, "HTML 4.0 Reference."

Meanwhile, during this chapter, we'll refer to the common attributes by using these keywords: *core*, *international*, and *event*.

Choosing Appropriate Image Maps

Of course, you can't use just any old image without regard for its content; the image has to make sense as a hyperlink map. For example, say you're hired to design a Web site for a home builder. The client wants the site to show views of different rooms in a model house. The exact method is left up to you.

You could simply use a textual menu, something like the one in Figure 14.2, and the following code:

```
<P>Choose from the following links to view pictures of the rooms:
<P><A href="masterbedroom.html">Master Bedroom</A>
<P><A href="recroom.html">Recreation Room</A>
<P><A href="kitchen.html">Kitchen</A>
...
```

Such a design would simply call up a new Web page for each listed room. Those pages would likely have embedded images of the rooms in question, followed by a description of them that included, perhaps, information on square footage and available furnishing options.

This design is primitive, though, and probably won't impress the client. Opting for a more elegant and graphical design, you decide to make the page into a pair of frames. The top frame will be an image map; the bottom one will display the image of the room and the information pertaining to it.

There are several images of the house to choose from, but the exterior views don't suit your purpose because not all the rooms could be selected from one of them. Among the materials available from the client, though, there are floor plans for the model. This solution is perfect for the problem of finding an image that lets you duplicate that particular textual menu because it includes a visual representation of every room in the house. The resulting Web site would look something like Figure 14.3.

This case is typical of the use of actual maps for image mapping. Any time a geographical representation is involved, a standard type of map will do the job. To show the layout of the house,

use a map of the house. If you need to show the distribution of a company's offices around the United States, use a map of the country.

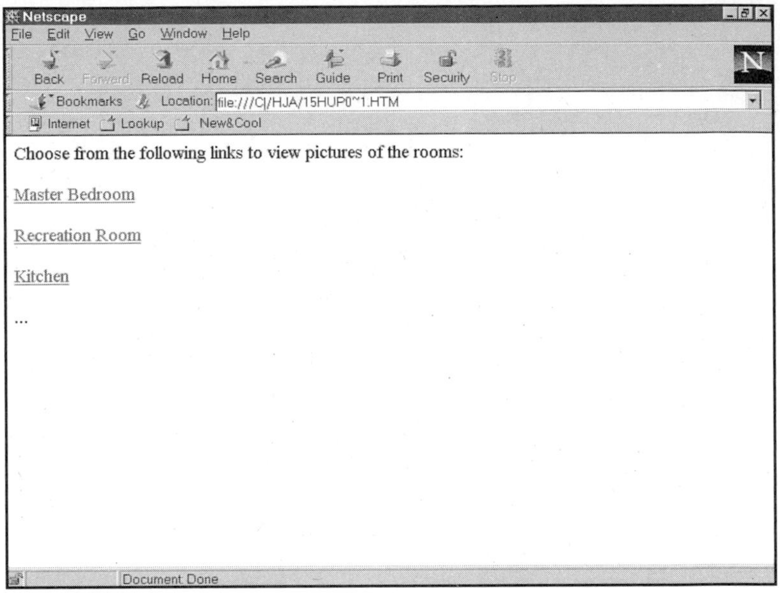

FIGURE 14.2.

A textual menu.

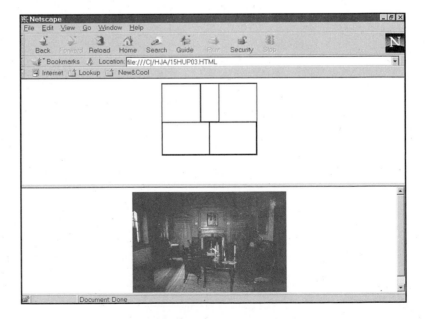

FIGURE 14.3.

An image map menu.

There are other types of "maps," though, that express visual representations of constituent elements or relationships. The purpose of an image map menu is to provide a comprehensible set of links to further information. In this sense, a circuit design is a map to its components. (See Figure 14.4.) A photograph of a meal on a dining room table could be a map to different recipes, as shown in Figure 14.5, and a class group portrait could be a map to biographical information on the graduates. (See Figure 14.6.)

FIGURE 14.4.

A component map.

FIGURE 14.5.

A recipe map.

FIGURE 14.6.
A biographical map.

Of course, text can be used in an image map, too, as shown in Figure 14.7. The lettering is simply treated as another part of the image.

FIGURE 14.7.
A textual map.

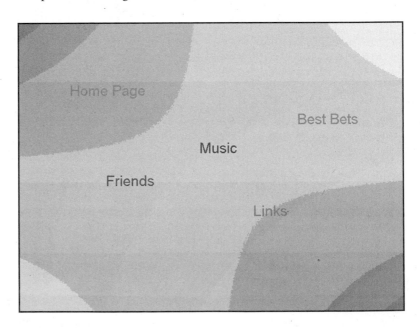

Client-side or Server-side?

Once you have the perfect image for your image map, you must make a decision about the method you will use for it; image maps can be client-side or server-side. Server-side image maps are processed by a CGI program at the server where the Web site is located, and client-side image maps are processed by the Web browser or other client agent.

Server-side, the older method, is definitely on the decline because client-side image maps have the tremendous advantage of shifting the computing burden to the individual user's system, instead of adding to the existing server load that, on any popular Web site, is probably already jammed beyond endurance.

Client-side image maps are also easier to code and offer functional advantages to the user as well as the server administrator. When the user moves a pointer over a server-side image map, there's no feedback. Client-side image maps, on the other hand, display the URL of the link in the same manner as a textual anchor link does, by showing it in the Web browser's status line. One other advantage is that client-side image maps can use partial URLs, but server-side image maps require full URLs.

As far as speed is concerned, client-side wins hands-down over server-side. When a user clicks on a server-side image map, the Web browser sends the coordinate information to the HTTP server, which passes it to the CGI program that accesses the URL information from a separate .map file. After processing this data, the CGI program sends the URL back through the server to the Web browser, which then sends it back to the server as a standard hyperlink request. Client-side image maps are simply handled within the HTML document itself. No outside files or server access at all are required; the first time the HTTP server is involved in the process is when the hyperlink is activated by the Web browser. Compared with the cumbersome server-side method, the pure HTML client-side method is the clear victor.

Client-side Image Maps

The first thing you need for a client-side image map is, of course, an image. The image used for the image map is inserted into the HTML page just like a normal image, but with one important difference: the usemap attribute. Here's an example of inserting an image map into an HTML page:

```
<img src="sporting_goods.gif" usemap="#sportsmap">
```

The usemap attribute is what makes this image usable as an image map. It not only tells the client agent that this is an image map, but directs it to a named anchor on the HTML page where the coordinate and URL information for this image map can be found.

That named anchor will be a MAP element, which basically contains the same textual menu the HTML page would if you had done things the old-fashioned way. It's a list of links, but these links have something else added to them: a definition of the area on the image map that will activate them.

MAP elements, which are contained within the BODY element, have only one attribute, name. The name attribute is used to identify the particular MAP element so that it can be accessed through the IMG element's usemap attribute. Only one item is permitted between the start and end tags of a MAP element: the AREA element.

The AREA element is where the actual links and coordinates are found. It first defines the particular shape of the area on the image, then gives its coordinates, and then specifies the URL of the hyperlink that will be activated if the mouse button is clicked while its pointer is within that area. There are three different shapes that can be defined with the shape attribute: rect, circle, and poly. They refer to, respectively, rectangles, circles, and polygons. If you don't specify a shape, then the attribute defaults to rect.

Rectangles (see Figure 14.8) require two sets of coordinate pairs. The first pair gives the coordinates of the upper-left corner, and the second pair gives the coordinates of the lower-right corner:

```
<AREA shape=rect coords="upper_left_x,upper_left_y,lower_right_x,lower_right_y"
➥ href="hyperlink_URL">
```

FIGURE 14.8.
Rectangle shapes.

Circles require one set of coordinate pairs—which gives the coordinates of the center point—and a third number that gives the radius of the circle:

```
<AREA shape=circle coords="center_x,center_y,radius" href="hyperlink_URL">
```

Polygons (see Figure 14.9), by definition a much more complex shape than either rectangles or circles, require a series of coordinate pairs that define points along the outline of the figure:

```
<AREA shape=poly coords="first_point_x,first_point_y,second_point_x,
➥second_point_y,...,last_point_x,last_point_y" href="hyperlink_URL">
```

NOTE

You probably learned in geometry class that polygons are any shape with many sides. In that sense, a rectangle is a polygon. In image map terminology, though, polygons are a bit different. It's true that you could use a polygon to define a rectangle, but there's no need to do so because a specialized tool already exists for that purpose. Polygons are generally used to create a series of short lines closely outlining any odd shape that can't easily be encompassed by a circle or rectangle.

FIGURE 14.9.
Polygon shapes.

The shape attribute has a fourth possible value, but it's not actually a shape. That value is default, which establishes a URL that will be activated if a user clicks inside the image map, but outside any of the other areas.

CAUTION

The default value of the shape attribute is rect, not default. This is just a rather unfortunate choice of phrasing.

The following example shows the MAP element for the image map in Figure 14.10. The URLs have been named to show which piece of sporting equipment they correspond to in the image map, so you can readily compare the code with the figure:

```
<MAP name="sportsmap">
<AREA shape=circle coords="65,129,57"
➥ href="http://www.sportgoods.com/baseball.html">
<AREA shape=rect coords="185,186,251,328"
➥ href="http://www.sportgoods.com/golf.html">
<AREA shape=poly coords="396,231,403,219,405,202,400,188,390,175,376,162,357,
➥152,337,151,324,153,317,157,314,162,309,170,309,184,317,204,326,216,337,224,
➥348,232,358,234,374,237,389,234,398,226,398,228,396,231"
➥ href="http://www.sportgoods.com/football.html">
<AREA shape=poly coords="183,94,257,96,300,42,270,11,245,11,215,39,215,53,177,
➥53,169,72,148,93,181,95,184,98,183,94"
➥ href="http://www.sportgoods.com/bowling.html">
<AREA shape=default href="http://www.sportgoods.com/index.html">
</MAP>
```

FIGURE 14.10.

A sports image map.

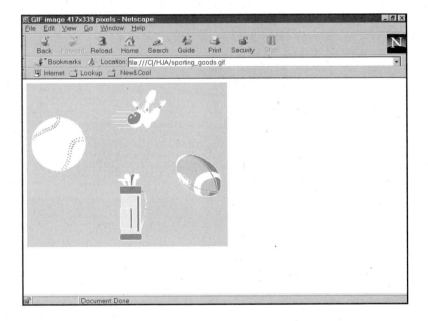

The circle shape, of course, was chosen for the baseball. Because of the irregular shapes of many images, such a perfect fit isn't often possible. Although the golf bag isn't a perfect rectangle, its shape could be fully enclosed and closely outlined with a rectangle, which is considerably easier than using a polygon. If a user were to click very near, but not on the golf bag, the effect would be the same as a click directly on it because the rectangle is a little larger than the golf bag, encompassing the handle and clubs. The football and bowling images had to be done with polygons, since neither a circle nor a rectangle could come anywhere near properly outlining them. Of the two, the football has the most coordinate pairs because its shape was followed most closely by the outlining. The polygon around the bowling scene is considerably looser, but still functional.

> **NOTE**
>
> As with plain images, a large image map can slow download time tremendously. Although it's impossible to set an arbitrary size limit for all image maps, you should use the smallest image that's both easy to see and easy to use. The sports image map uses an image that's 417×339, and you probably shouldn't go much over that.

As you can see, the major problem in developing a MAP element is establishing the coordinates (not to mention typing them in without any errors!). One way to do this is to load the image you're going to be using for the image map into a graphics program, most of which display the pointer coordinates. Then, while moving the mouse pointer around the edges, note the coordinates at critical points. When you're done, take your handwritten list of numbers and type them all in. However, this method is tedious, frustrating, and prone to all kinds of mistakes, any one of which can ruin your image map's functionality and undo all your hard work.

The solution most HTML authors have turned to is using programs specifically designed for creating image maps. That's how we created this example. These programs are explored in detail in the section "Image Map Tools."

The AREA element has some other interesting attributes. If you're using frames, you can specify which frame the link is displayed in by using the target attribute. If you have established a frame called link_frame, for instance, then you could specify that a linked HTML page should be loaded into it by using the following code:

```
<AREA shape=rect coords="185,186,251,328"
➥ href="http://www.sportgoods.com/golf.html" target="link_frame">
```

You have several different options when specifying the target frame. The target attribute in the AREA element works the same way as the target attribute in the BASE element. For a full explanation of the target attribute, see Chapter 12, "Understanding Uniform Resource Locators."

The nohref attribute is available for those odd situations when you want to define a shape, but prevent a link from being made from it. It is applied as follows:

```
<AREA shape=rect coords="185,186,251,328" nohref>
```

The alt attribute is used to supply information about the link for nongraphical client agents, and works the same way as it does for a normal image with the IMG element (see Chapter 11, "Adding Images to Your Web Page.")

The AREA element also supports the tabindex and accesskey attributes for keyboard use, which are discussed in Chapter 15, "Building and Using HTML Forms," and in Chapter 41, "Creating Widely Accessible Web Pages."

> **TIP**
>
> If two different areas overlap, and a user clicks on the overlapping part, then the one listed earliest in the MAP element is the link that will be activated. That's because the Web browser reads the listing from the top down, looking for an AREA element that encompasses the coordinates that were clicked; once it finds a match, it stops looking and will never try the other ones.

The Object Image Map Method

HTML 4.0 introduced an alternative approach to adding client-side image maps to Web pages. They can be coded with the OBJECT element instead of the MAP element. With this method, there's no separate IMG element with a usemap attribute pointing to the MAP element. Instead, the AREA elements are contained solely within the OBJECT element itself.

The following example shows the same image map used in the preceding example, but coded as an OBJECT instead of a combination of IMG and MAP elements:

```
<OBJECT data="sporting_goods.gif" shapes>
<AREA shape=circle coords="65,129,57"
➥ href="http://www.sportgoods.com/baseball.html">
<AREA shape=rect coords="185,186,251,328"
➥ href="http://www.sportgoods.com/golf.html">
<AREA shape=poly coords="396,231,403,219,405,202,400,188,390,175,376,162,357,
➥152,337,151,324,153,317,157,314,162,309,170,309,184,317,204,326,216,
➥337,224,348,232,358,234,374,237,389,234,398,226,398,228,396,231"
➥ href="http://www.sportgoods.com/football.html">
<AREA shape=poly coords="183,94,257,96,300,42,270,11,245,11,215,39,215,53,177,
➥53,169,72,148,93,181,95,184,98,183,94"
➥ href="http://www.sportgoods.com/bowling.html">
<AREA shape=default href="http://www.sportgoods.com/index.html">
<OBJECT>
```

The core of the system is the AREA elements, which are used identically in both approaches. The key to making an OBJECT element into an image map lies in the shapes attribute in its start tag, which tells the HTML parser that image map coordinates will follow.

> **CAUTION**
>
> Be careful to note that the OBJECT element's attribute for defining itself as an image map is shapes (plural); it's not the same thing as the AREA element's shape (singular) attribute, which is used to specify exactly what kind of shape (rect, circle, or poly) the area is composed of.

Server-side Image Maps

Server-side image maps require an outside file to hold the map coordinates. It's called, as you might imagine, a .map file. However, .map files aren't as simple as they could be. You need to determine whether your HTTP server follows CERN or NCSA image map file standards. Both types of servers handle .map files, but each requires a slightly different format for them, and each uses a different program to handle them.

The CERN .map file for the earlier sample image map would look like the following:

```
default http://www.sportgoods.com/index.html
circ (65,129) 57 http://www.sportgoods.com/baseball.html
rectangle (185,186) (251,328) http://www.sportgoods.com/golf.html
polygon (396,231) (403,219) (405,202) (400,188) (390,175) (376,162) (357,152)
➡ (337,151) (324,153) (317,157) (314,162) (309,170) (309,184) (317,204)
➡ (326,216) (337,224) (348,232) (358,234) (374,237) (389,234) (398,226)
➡ (398,228) (396,231) http://www.sportgoods.com/football.html
polygon (183,94) (257,96) (300,42) (270,11) (245,11) (215,39) (215,53)
➡ (177,53) (169,72) (148,93) (181,95) (184,98) (183,94)
➡ http://www.sportgoods.com/bowling.html
```

Note that, in contrast to the HTML AREA element's order of things, the CERN format lists the shape first, then the coordinate pairs, each in parentheses, and then the URL of the hyperlink. There's also a difference in how it describes the shapes themselves; "circle" becomes "circ," "rect" becomes "rectangle," and "poly" becomes "polygon," although "default" remains "default." The coordinates for the circle shape are separated from the radius, which isn't enclosed in parentheses.

The NCSA .map file for the same sample image map would look like the following:

```
default http://www.sportgoods.com/index.html
circle http://www.sportgoods.com/baseball.html  65,129 65,186
rect http://www.sportgoods.com/golf.html 185,186 251,328
poly http://www.sportgoods.com/football.html 396,231 403,219 405,202 400,188
➡ 390,175 376,162 357,152 337,151 324,153 317,157 314,162 309,170 309,184
➡ 317,204 326,216 337,224 348,232 358,234 374,237 389,234 398,226 398,228 396,231
poly http://www.sportgoods.com/bowling.html 183,94 257,96 300,42 270,11 245,11
➡ 215,39 215,53 177,53 169,72 148,93 181,95 184,98 183,94
```

Note that the same terminology is used as with HTML's AREA element. Therefore, "circle" is "circle," "rect" is "rect," "poly" is "poly," and "default" is "default." The only real difference is that the coordinate pairs are separated by spaces. The circle shape is defined by its center point and a point on its circumference.

With each of these methods, it's necessary to use the IMG element; there's no OBJECT element approach to server-side image maps because they represent different levels of technology. However, the usemap attribute isn't used in this case. The older ismap attribute is used instead, as in the following example:

```
<A href= http://www.sportgoods.com/cgi-bin/htimage/sports.map>
➡<img src="sporting_goods.gif" ismap></A>
```

This line would invoke the built-in CERN image map handler, which is called `htimage`. To use the NCSA image map handler, which is called `imagemap`, it would need to be modified to read:

```
<A href= http://www.sportgoods.com/cgi-bin/imagemap/sports.map>
➥<img src="sporting_goods.gif" ismap></A>
```

Mixing Client-side and Server-side

If you want to support both kinds of image maps, it can be done. Of course, it requires some extra work. You have to make both kinds of map data: a `.map` file and a `MAP` element. Once that's done, all you have to do is code the image map link just as you would for a server-side approach, and then add the `usemap` attribute, too.

The dual image map technique with the CERN server would look like this:

```
<A href= http://www.sportgoods.com/cgi-bin/htimage/sports.map>
➥<img src="sporting_goods.gif" ismap usemap="#sportsmap"></A>
```

The dual image map technique with the NCSA server would look like this:

```
<A href= http://www.sportgoods.com/cgi-bin/imagemap/sports.map>
➥<img src="sporting_goods.gif" ismap usemap="#sportsmap"></A>
```

Image Map Tools

As mentioned earlier, gathering and coding the coordinate pairs for the points that define the shapes in an image map is a daunting task. Fortunately, this problem has been solved by some specialized programs with simple interfaces that allow HTML authors to draw clickable areas right over the image. These programs then translate those drawn lines into the code necessary for implementing the image map and allow you to save it in any of the image map file formats.

The sports image map in the earlier example (see Figure 14.10) was developed by using a freeware program named Map This!. Several other similar programs are listed in Appendix G, "Development Resources."

To begin, you must already have an image (in either GIF or JPG format) that you intend to make into an image map. You can either use one of your own for this example, or you can load `sporting_goods.gif` from this book's companion CD-ROM.

To load an image into Map This!, click the New File button (or choose File | New from the menu) to open the Make New Image Map dialog box (see Figure 14.11), which simply reminds you that you must use existing GIFs or JPGs. If you want to set this dialog box so that it doesn't come up every time you load a new image file, select the checkbox that says `Don't show this message....` Click the Okay button to proceed.

FIGURE 14.11.

The Make New Image Map dialog box.

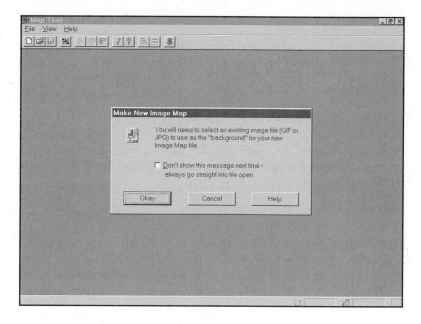

The next thing to come up is a standard file open dialog box (see Figure 14.12), which is set to show only GIF and JPG (or JPEG) files. Select the name of the file you want to load for your image map. In this example, we're using `sporting_goods.gif`. Click the Open button (you can also just double-click on the filename instead of clicking once to select the file and then clicking the Open button).

FIGURE 14.12.

Opening an image file in Map This!.

The file you will use is now loaded. Click on the maximize button in the upper-right corner of the window containing the image to bring it up to full size, as shown in Figure 14.13.

FIGURE 14.13.

The expanded image.

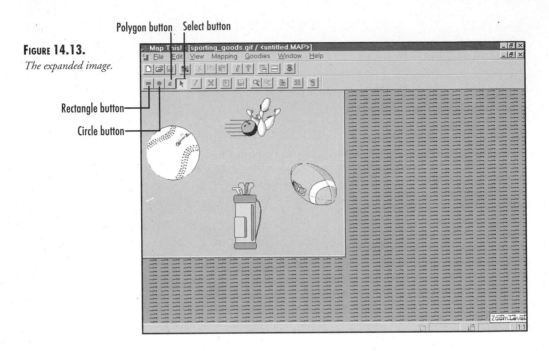

There are buttons on the toolbar for each of the three shapes: rectangle, circle, and polygon. Another button, next to the shape buttons, is for selecting areas after you create them.

To set up a clickable image map area for the baseball, click the Circle button, then move the pointer to the center of the baseball. Hold down the left mouse button and move the pointer out until the resulting circle is the size of the baseball. It doesn't matter if it's not perfectly centered. Next, click the Select button and move the pointer to any place within the blue circle. While holding the mouse button down, drag the blue circle until it covers the baseball entirely. (See Figure 14.14.) The blue circle changes into a crosshatched pattern during this operation, which is normal for any selected area. Release the mouse button.

If the size is imperfect, you have two options. The first is to simply ignore it. Most users click in the center of an image map link, so it probably won't matter much if the size of the area is just a little bit off. If you want to adjust it, though, just move the mouse pointer until it's over one of the grab handles along the periphery of the circle. When the pointer changes to a double arrow, hold the left mouse key down and drag in or out until the circle is the exact size you want. Repeat if necessary. Use the selection technique you just learned to reposition the area, if needed.

Next, click the Rectangle button. Place the mouse pointer at the lower-left corner of the golf bag. Hold down the left mouse button and move the pointer to the upper right until the entire golf bag, handle included, is enclosed within the rectangle. (See Figure 14.15.) If you need to resize the rectangle, use the same technique as with the circle. The only difference is that the grab handles on a rectangle affect only the side they're on; if they are on a corner, they affect only the two sides that meet at that corner.

FIGURE 14.14.
The covered baseball.

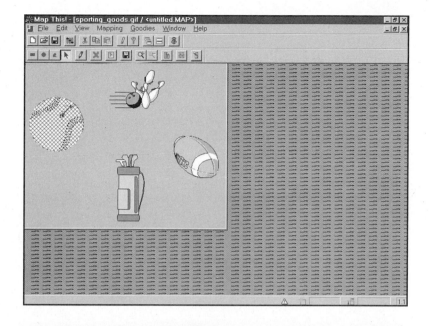

> **NOTE**
>
> We chose the lower-left corner of the golf bag as the starting point in this example because it was a clearer reference point than the right side of the bag, which has the handle poking out. However, you can actually start a rectangle at any point and move the mouse pointer in any direction; you don't have to go from lower left to upper right.

The next shape to use is the polygon. Drawing a polygon is somewhat more complex than a circle or rectangle, but it consists of only a single step, repeated several times. That procedure is to click the left mouse button to establish a point, move the pointer to the next place you want to put a point, click again, move on, and so forth. As you do this, a moving line follows your actions, one end anchored at the last point you established and the other end at the pointer's current position. It might sound complex, but it's very simple to do.

Click the Polygon button, then place the mouse pointer at the lower-left corner of the bowling scene. Move the pointer to the right (without holding the button down) until you reach a point to the right of the base of the bowling scene, and click the left mouse button to establish a point there. Next, move the pointer at an angle up to the right until you clear the rightward-leaning pin, click again, move up and left until you reach a spot above the highest bowling pin, and click again. Now, move the pointer left and down until you reach a point above the horizontal lines, click again, and move the pointer straight left until you reach a point above the starting point. Double-click the left mouse button to complete the polygon. Figure 14.16 shows the same polygon, but it has been selected so that the underlying image shows through for instructional purposes.

Figure 14.15.

The covered golf bag.

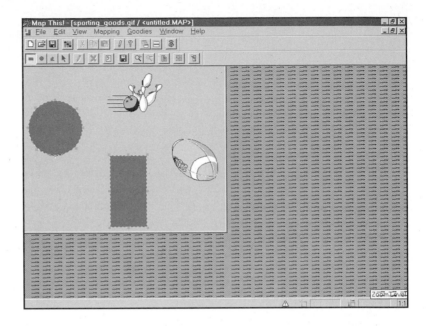

Figure 14.16.

The selected bowling scene.

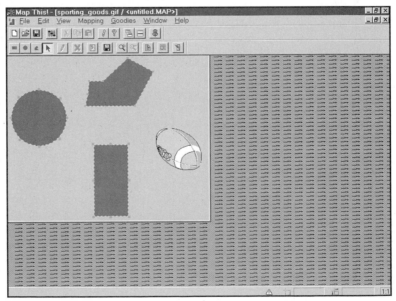

> **NOTE**
>
> Although Map This! automatically adds the final line connecting the end point with the start point, that's just a nice extra touch. A polygon doesn't have to be fully closed to define an area. The Web browser or other client agent automatically connects the first and last points to close it. Therefore, a polygon actually requires only a minimum of three points to fully enclose the area within the two lines they make (of course, this minimal number of points creates only a triangular shape; you'd need to add more points for a more complex shape).

Resizing a polygon, strictly speaking, is impossible. You can, however, move the points one by one. Doing so affects the shape of the polygon, so it can be adjusted to more closely fit the form of the underlying object, if necessary. This method works pretty much like the rectangle's grab handles, except that the pointer changes to an open crosshair instead of double arrows. Holding down the left mouse button and moving the underlying point affects only the two lines anchored to that point. Moving the polygon, as opposed to changing its shape, works exactly the same way as moving the other two shapes.

Finally, apply a polygonal shape to the football. Unlike the bowling scene, which you followed only approximately, carefully follow the outline on this shape. After clicking the Polygon button, place the mouse pointer at one tip of the football and click the left mouse button to establish a point there. Now, move the pointer along the edge of the football until the line between the first point and the mouse pointer closely matches with the edge of the football. If you go too far, the straight line will become too long and not follow the outline of the football. If that happens, simply move the mouse pointer back until the line fits better, then click the left mouse button. Continue to do this until you have totally outlined the football (which will take many points), and then double-click the left mouse button. The result should look something like Figure 14.17.

Now you need to add the URLs for each area. Click the Select button and then the baseball. Press the right mouse button to bring up the popup menu (see Figure 14.18), and choose Edit Area Info to open the Area Settings dialog box. (See Figure 14.19.) Fill in the URL to be activated for this area and any comments you would like included, then click the OK button. Repeat this for all the other shapes.

At this point, save the image map you have drawn. Click the Save button on the toolbar or choose File | Save from the menu to open the Settings for this Mapfile dialog box shown in Figure 14.20. Fill in the default URL (for all parts of the image map outside the defined areas), select which type of image map you want to create (CERN, NCSA, or client-side image map [CSIM]), and then click the OK button.

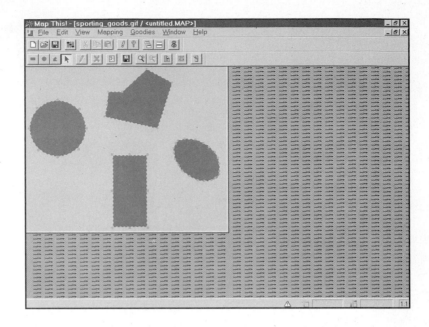

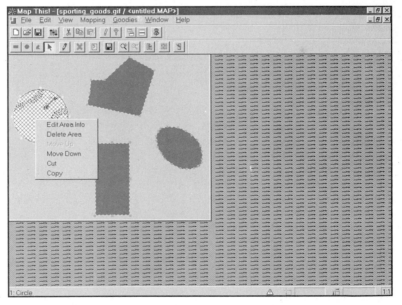

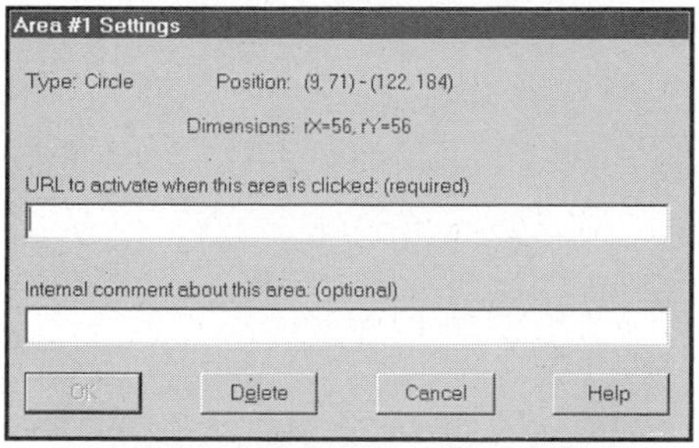

FIGURE 14.19.
The Area Settings dialog box.

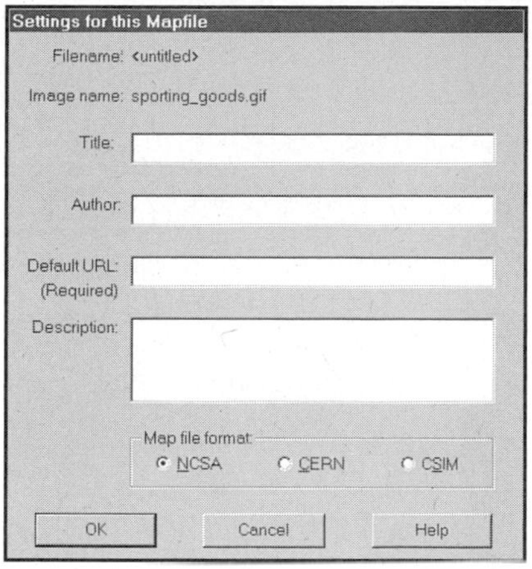

FIGURE 14.20.
The Settings for this Mapfile dialog box.

This opens the Save the Image Map File dialog box. In Figure 14.21, the HTML setting is selected because we chose CSIM in the previous dialog box. You can still choose one of the other types of files, however (CERN or NCSA). Pick whichever is appropriate, and then click the Save button.

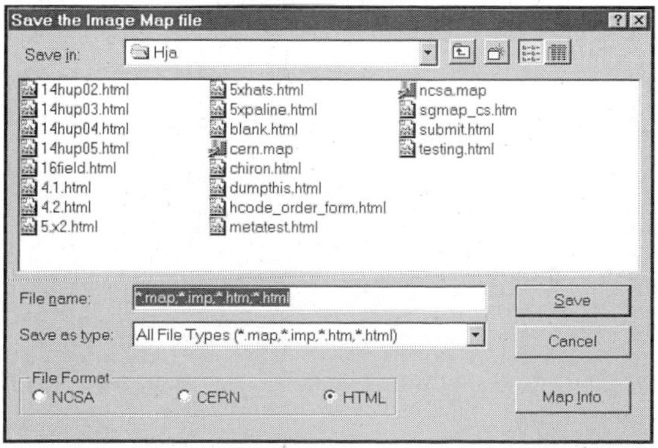

FIGURE 14.21.
The Save the Image Map file dialog box.

Here's a listing of image-mapping tools available on the Web:

Coffee Cup Image Mapper++

http://www.coffeecup.com/mapper/

Live Image

http://www.mediatec.com/

Map Edit (WIERD COMPANY)

http://www.boutell.com/mapedit/

Map This! (NO LONGER AVAILABLE HERE. 12/15/99)

http://www.download.com/PC/Result/TitleDetail/0,4,0-16965,501000.html

MapMaker32

http://members.tripod.com/~mharing/mapmaker.html

Summary

Image maps are the most popular method for creating menus on the World Wide Web. In essence, they're extended versions of standard image-based hyperlinks. The best images to use for image maps are those with a graphical representation of existing information. Image maps can be either client-side or server-side, but there are tremendous advantages to the current technology of client-side image maps. Both, however, can be mixed in a single Web site.

Image maps use three kinds of shapes: rectangles, circles, and polygons. Polygons are any multisided shapes that aren't rectangles. Image maps are usually covered by the IMG element, but there's a new technique involving the OBJECT element. The complexity of setting the parameters for image map shapes can be made easier by using one of the many different image-mapping software tools available.

Building and Using HTML Forms

IN THIS CHAPTER

CHAPTER 15

COMMON ATTRIBUTES

Most of the elements in this chapter share common HTML attributes, such as items that control identification, style, language, and event handling. Because the common attributes are so pervasive in HTML 4 (that's why they're called "common"), you will find an overview of them in the introduction of this book. You can also find more information about these often-used features and their associated elements in Appendix A, "HTML 4.0 Reference."

Meanwhile, during this chapter, we'll refer to the common attributes by using these keywords: *core*, *international*, and *event*.

Additionally, many of these elements can accept other elements within their borders. They are referred to as the *inline elements* and include the following options:

font elements: These elements includes tags for bold (<B>) and italics (<I>) and are covered in Chapter 17, "Simple Style with Text."

phrase elements: These elements include tags such as emphasis (<EM>), code (<CODE>), and address (<ADDRESS>) and are covered in Chapter 7, "Text Alignment and Formatting."

special elements: This is a hodgepodge of elements that includes all the following items: applets and objects (Chapter 16, "Embedding Objects in HTML"); images (Chapter 11, "Adding Images to Your Web Page"); anchors (Chapter 13, "Hyperlinking and Anchors"); image maps (Chapter 14, "Creating Menus with Image Maps"); scripts (Chapters 23, "JavaScript at a Glance," and 24, "Using VBScript"); fonts, superscripts, and subscripts (Chapter 17); line breaks and short quotes (Chapter 7); and inline frames (Chapter 20, "Creating Frames").

form elements: This set of elements is used to create the various elements on a form, including buttons, text fields, and checkboxes.

Forms, which allow visitors to your site to give you input, are used for a variety of purposes. For instance, they can be used for order processing on a retail site, or they can be set up to get customer feedback by e-mail.

The FORM element contains several other elements, called "controls," that have a variety of methods for gathering information. When a form is completed and submitted, the information in its active controls is passed to a program that takes whatever action the form has been designed to perform. Each element in the form has both a name and a value, so the data that's passed for processing is in the form of name/value pairs.

Often, processing the data is done with a CGI program. These programs are usually written in Perl, but may be in any language that can run on the server, such as C. (See Chapter 25, "Understanding the Common Gateway Interface," for more information.)

Another possibility for form data handling is to pass the information to a JavaScript or VBScript program, which takes care of the processing on the client system, thus freeing up server resources. (See Chapters 23 and 24 for more information.)

The results of a form can also be e-mailed to the Webmaster (or another designated recipient) by using the `mailto` action in the form definition.

The FORM Element's Attributes

```
<FORM [action=URL][method=get¦post][enctype=MIMEType][onsubmit=script]
➥[onreset=script][accept-charset=charset][core][international][events]>
➥FormElements</FORM>
```

The `FORM` element has two main attributes: `action` and `method`. The `action` attribute takes a URL as its argument. Usually, it's an HTTP URL and gives the address of the program used for processing the data, as in the following example:

```
<FORM action="http://www.sellstuff.com/cgi-bin/getmoney.pl" method="post">
...
</FORM>
```

Although using the HTTP URL is the normal approach, it's not uncommon to use a mailto URL for the `action` instead, as shown in the following code:

```
<FORM action="mailto:webmaster@somewhere.com" method="post">
...
</FORM>
```

> **CAUTION**
>
> Internet Explorer crashes when faced with a mailto URL.

The `method` attribute can have either GET or POST as its value. GET is officially deprecated, and POST is the preferred action. GET submits the name/value pairs to the URL specified in the `method` attribute as an appendage to the URL itself, but POST sends them as a separate section following the HTTP header; this separate section is called the "entity body."

The `enctype` attribute is used to state the encoding type of the form content. It's not usually specified because forms use the `application/x-www-form-urlencoded` content type by default. However, there's an advantage to specifying it when using the mailto URL for the `action` attribute. With the mailto approach, the results of a form are e-mailed to a specified address. If the form data is mailed in URL encoding, it arrives in your mailbox in a nearly incomprehensible form, as in the following example:

```
firstname=John&lastname=Smith&jobdesc=This%20job%20isn%27t%20fun.
```

You can just barely read through this gibberish to translate the encoded characters.

15

BUILDING AND USING HTML FORMS

There's also the option of running the form data through a word processor, exercising infinite patience while using the search-and-replace function. If you haven't memorized all the possible character encodings, and you value your sanity, you can use a utility like DeFORM to translate the message into human-readable format.

You can also have the data mailed as plain text to begin with, which is where the `enctype` attribute comes into its own. Simply set it as follows:

```
<FORM action="mailto:webmaster@somewhere.com" method="post"
➥ enctype="multipart/form-data">
...
</FORM>
```

Two attributes are specifically geared toward use with scripting languages: `onsubmit` and `onreset` are intrinsic event attributes specific to the FORM element. The `onsubmit` event occurs when the form is submitted (typically by clicking on the Submit button). The `onreset` event is triggered when the form is reset (usually by activating the Reset button). For details on using scripting languages with HTML, see Part V, "Progamming Languages for HTML."

Finally, the new `accept-charset` attribute is used to specify the character sets the server must accept to handle the form, such as ISO-8859-9.

The INPUT Element

```
<INPUT [type=text¦password¦checkbox¦radio¦submit¦image¦reset¦button¦hidden
➥¦file][name=controlName][value=controlValue][checked][disabled][readonly]
➥[size=controlWidth][maxlength=wordLength][src=URL][alt=altText][usemap=URL]
➥[align=left¦center¦right¦justify][tabindex=tabNum][accesskey=keyCombo]
➥[onfocus=script][onblur=script][onselect=script][onchange=script]
➥[accept=charset] [core][international][events]>
```

The INPUT element is the most critical to using forms. It's entirely possible to build an entire form using no other elements (see Figure 15.1) because this one includes such a wide array of controls, which are specified by using the type attribute. Acceptable values for the type attribute are listed in Table 15.1.

Table 15.1. Values of the INPUT element's type attribute.

Form Controls	*Values for the* type *Attribute*
Custom push buttons	`button`
Checkboxes	`checkbox`
Included files	`file`
Hidden elements	`hidden`
Images	`image`
Password entry boxes	`password`
Radio buttons	`radio`

Form Controls	*Values for the* type *Attribute*
Reset button	reset
Submit button	submit
Text entry boxes	text

FIGURE 15.1.

A form built with only the INPUT *element.*

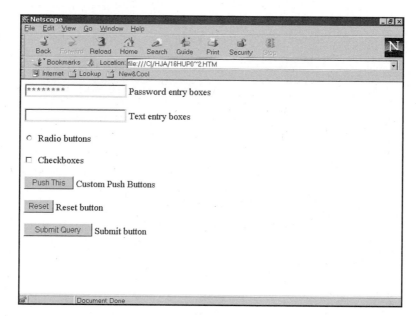

The button Value

The button value for the type attribute is new. Before HTML 4.0, the only buttons were the Submit and Reset buttons, whose meaning and actions were predetermined. The button input type, however, has no default function; its function is defined by you in a script. A typical button declaration looks like this:

```
<INPUT type="button" name="custom_button_01" value="Push This"
onclick="runprocess()">
```

Each control is assigned a unique identifier with the name attribute; without this identifier, it would be impossible to tell which control was assigned what value. The name attribute has scope only within the FORM element where it's found.

As you can see in Figure 15.2, the value attribute's text is displayed on the button. The value of the onclick attribute is the name of the script that's activated when the button is clicked.

FIGURE 15.2.

The button *value of the* type *attribute.*

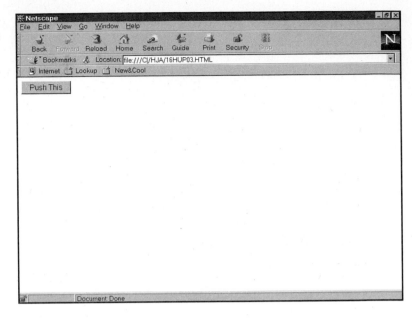

The reset Value

The reset value of the type attribute creates a button with only one purpose: When it's clicked, it clears the form of all entries, leaving it blank and returning all entries to their default settings. (See Figure 15.3.) It's declared with the following code:

```
<INPUT type="reset">
```

FIGURE 15.3.

The Reset button.

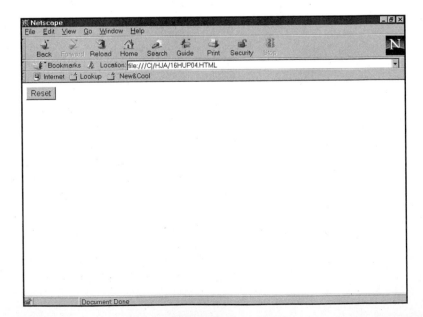

The submit Value

The submit value of the type attribute creates a button, shown in Figure 15.4, that, like the Reset button, has only a single purpose. In this case, it's to send the name/value pairs of the active form elements to the URL specified in the FORM declaration. Strangely enough, the HTML specification allows multiple Submit buttons to exist. The Submit button is declared with the following code:

```
<INPUT type="submit">
```

FIGURE 15.4.

The Submit button.

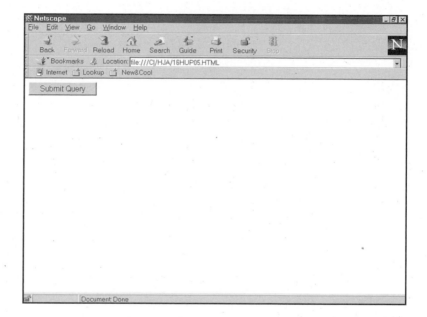

The image Value

The image value of the type attribute has only one difference from the submit attribute: It replaces the stark Submit button with an image. (See Figure 15.5.) Otherwise, it has the same function. The code to declare it looks like this:

```
<INPUT type="image" src="submit_image.gif">
```

The checkbox Value

The checkbox value of the type attribute is a Boolean input device; it's either off or on. It looks like a hollow box that, when selected, is filled with a checkmark to indicate its active state. (See Figure 15.6.) Checkboxes are extremely versatile and can be used in several different ways. The basic code for declaring a checkbox is as follows:

```
<INPUT type="checkbox" name="choice1" value="cards" checked>
```

FIGURE 15.5.

An image button.

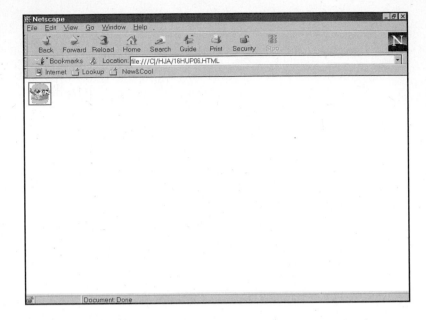

FIGURE 15.6.

The checkbox *value for the* type *attribute.*

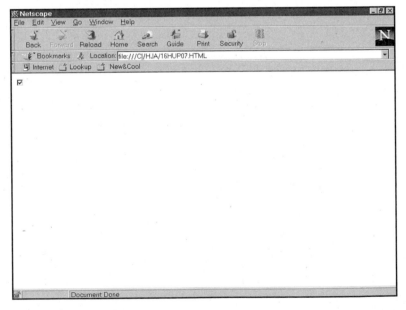

The checked attribute is optional; it causes the checkbox to be "on," or filled with a checkmark, when the form is first created. Of course, if a user clicks the filled checkbox, it switches to its empty state. The checked attribute doesn't establish a permanent state; it just sets the default state of the checkbox.

Depending on your purposes, the value attribute doesn't necessarily need to be used, either. If you're using only a single checkbox, its name attribute alone is enough. All you need to know is whether that one box was checked because no user action can possibly alter the contents of the value attribute in a checkbox (unless you go to a great deal of trouble to work up some really strange JavaScript). Therefore, the simple fact of its on or off state should tell you all you need to know. For example, if you wanted to ask whether someone wanted to be added to the subscriber list for your newsletter, the following code would suffice:

```
<INPUT type="checkbox" name="addsub">
```

If a user checked the box, you would be notified when the form was submitted. If he or she didn't, then you would get no results at all for addsub because the results of empty elements aren't included when the form is submitted.

> **CAUTION**
>
> The official HTML specification states that the value attribute is required for both radio buttons and checkboxes, so the use described in this section isn't technically proper HTML.

If, on the other hand, you wanted a user to be able to make multiple selections on the same topic, the value attribute becomes more important. You might, for instance, have differing publishing schedules for your newsletter, in which case you would want to set up something like this:

```
<INPUT type="checkbox" name="sub" value="yes" checked>
<INPUT type="checkbox" name="sub" value="daily" checked>
<INPUT type="checkbox" name="sub" value="weekly">
<INPUT type="checkbox" name="sub" value="monthly">
```

This code sets the form up so that the default order would be for a subscription to the daily edition. (See Figure 15.7.) However, the user could also subscribe to the weekly or monthly versions—or even to any combination of the three because checkboxes aren't mutually exclusive.

The name attribute in this example is the same for the entire range of choices. Instead of creating a conflict as would normally be the case, this technique causes a series of name/value pairs, each pair bearing the same name, but a different value, to be sent when the form is submitted.

Of course, it's perfectly okay to use multiple checkboxes with different names, too.

The radio Value

The radio value of the type attribute is very similar to the checkbox type. The difference between the two is that radio buttons are mutually exclusive. Therefore, if you were to render the choices outlined in the section on checkboxes with radio buttons, the user could choose only daily, weekly, or monthly subscriptions, as shown here:

```
<INPUT type="radio" name="sub" value="yes" checked>
<INPUT type="radio" name="version" value="daily" checked>
<INPUT type="radio" name="version" value="weekly">
<INPUT type="radio" name="version" value="monthly">
```

FIGURE 15.7.

Multiple checkboxes.

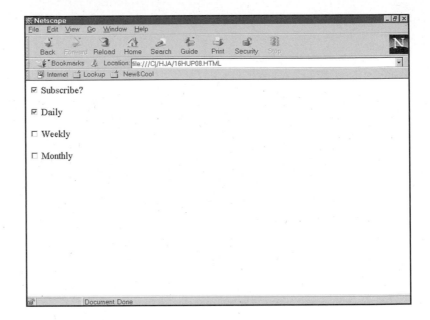

You will no doubt have noticed that there's a difference in the names of the INPUT elements. As with the checkbox example, the user must choose to receive the subscription—hence the sub name. The version name, however, is restricted to those radio buttons that define the version the user wants to receive. Because radio buttons are mutually exclusive, the selected one turns the other ones off, so only the final selection is sent along with the other form data when the form is submitted.

Of course, radio buttons look different from checkboxes. Instead of an empty or a checked box, the user sees an empty circle or one with a solid dot in it. (See Figure 15.8.)

The file Value

The file value of the type attribute has never had popular support. The official specification dedicates five sentences to describing it. First outlined in RFC 1867 back in 1995, it's a method for adding the contents of user-defined uploaded files to form output. In theory, the user is prompted for the name of a file. When the form is submitted, the specified file is accessed and the contents added to a multipart form submission response.

RFC 1867 suggests the following invocation:

```
<FORM encytpe="multipart/form-date" action="_URL_" method="post">
File to process: <INPUT name="userfile1" type="file">
```

```
<INPUT type="submit" value="Send File">
</FORM>
```

The `file` attribute would be used with the `accept` attribute, which limits the kinds of files allowed in a file upload. The `accept` attribute takes as its argument a comma-delimited list of MIME types.

FIGURE 15.8.

Radio buttons.

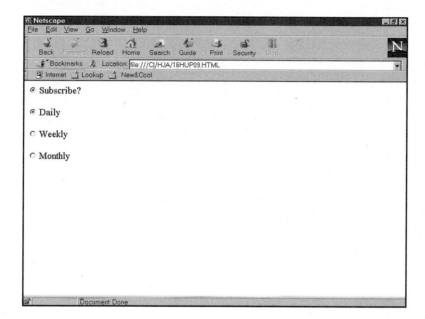

The `hidden` Value

The `hidden` value of the `type` attribute allows you to submit form information that's invisible to the user. Here's the basic code to invoke it:

```
<INPUT type="hidden" name="cantsee" value="from_my_form">
```

This would cause the name/value pair `cantsee`/`from_my_form` to be submitted along with all the other information from the form.

The `text` Value

The `text` value of the `type` attribute asks for input in the form of a single line typed response of a given length. The code for adding text response for a user's first name is as follows:

```
<INPUT type="text" name="firstname">
```

A number of text responses could be strung together to create a meaningful form, as shown in the following code and illustrated in Figure 15.9:

```
<INPUT type="text" name="firstname" size="40">
<INPUT type="text" name="lastname" size="40">
```

15

BUILDING AND
USING HTML
FORMS

```
<INPUT type="text" name="address1" size="40">
<INPUT type="text" name="address2" size="40">
<INPUT type="text" name="city" size="40">
<INPUT type="text" name="state" size="2">
<INPUT type="text" name="zipcode" size="10">
```

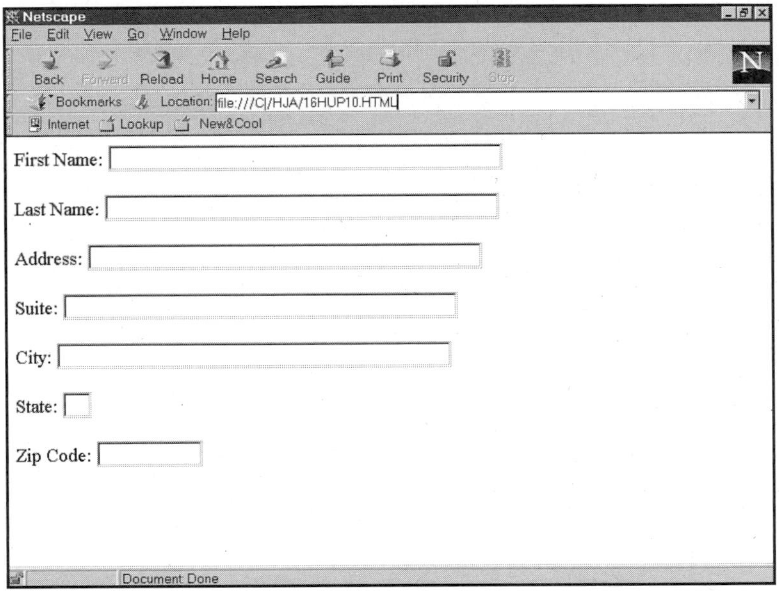

FIGURE 15.9.

Text boxes.

The `size` attribute sets the length of the text box in characters. You can also set the maximum number of characters that can be entered by using the `maxlength` attribute. If `maxlength` exceeds `size`, then the client agent should scroll the input. The default for `maxlength` is unlimited. The code for setting `maxlength` looks like this:

```
<INPUT type="text" name="lastname" size="20" maxlength="40">
```

Text can be set to be unalterable by the user with the `readonly` attribute. The value of such text is included along with the values of other active elements when the form is submitted. Read-only elements are—even though they can't be changed by the user—capable of receiving focus and are included in tabbing navigation. There would seem to be little use for this attribute because the `hidden` attribute already allows HTML authors to include unalterable name/value pairs, with the added advantage that they can't even be seen by the user. It's possible, through scripting, to dynamically alter the `readonly` state of a text element, making it writable again.

The password Value

The `password` value of the `type` attribute is exactly like the `text` attribute, except that the visible response on the form is in the form of asterisks, so that no one can read the secret password while looking over the user's shoulder. (See Figure 15.10.) Here's an example of the code for setting `password`:

```
<INPUT type="password" name="secret" size="30">
```

As with the `text` attribute, you can set the `maxsize` and `readonly` attributes.

FIGURE 15.10.
Creating a password field.

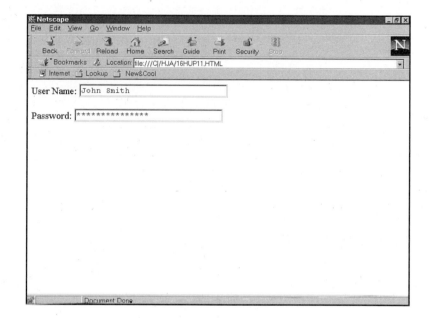

Other Attributes

Closely related to `readonly` is the `disabled` attribute. When an element is disabled, its contents are not only unalterable, but unusable, so it's taken out of the tab order. When a form is submitted, the name/value pairs of disabled form elements are not included. If the disabled element is a button (whether Custom, Reset, or Submit), then the button can't be activated. The disabled state can be altered through scripting.

Although `readonly` is limited to the `text` and `password` types within the `INPUT` element, `disabled` can be applied to any `INPUT` type, as well as to the `TEXTAREA`, `SELECT`, `OPTION`, `OBJECT`, `LABEL`, and `BUTTON` elements.

The `alt` attribute is used for those few Web browsers that can't accept forms. It serves the same function as the `alt` attribute in images and displays an explanation of the element for the users of such limited browsers. Exactly what the functional use of this is supposed to be is a mystery because it just lets people see what elements the form is composed of, but not interact with those elements in any way. However, the code for setting it looks like this:

```
<INPUT alt="This is a submit button." type="submit">
```

15

BUILDING AND
USING HTML
FORMS

The usemap attribute can be used to include a client-side image map into the INPUT element (see Chapter 14, "Creating Menus with Image Maps"). This use has never been widespread and has limited utility in a form. The syntax is as follows:

```
<INPUT usemap="#mapx">
```

> **NOTE**
>
> The ISINDEX element is now deprecated in favor of the INPUT element. It was used during interactive searches of a Web page. Generally, it was placed in a document built by a special CGI script, and generated a prompt for the user to enter a search string. The text supplied by the user was appended to the document's URL and passed back to the CGI script for processing in the form URL?search1+search2+...+searchN. The ISINDEX element has one attribute, prompt, which changes the default message for the text field. The syntax is <ISINDEX prompt="string">.

The BUTTON Element

```
<BUTTON [name=controlName][value=controlValue][type=button|submit|reset|
➥[disabled][tabindex=tabNum][accesskey=keyCombo]
➥[onfocus=script]
➥[onblur=script] [core][international][events]>ButtonText</BUTTON>
```

The BUTTON element takes three possible values for the type attribute: submit, reset, and button. These values are all totally duplicative; their counterparts already exist in the INPUT element, with types of the same names. Just as with those three values for the INPUT element, submit causes the form to be submitted, reset causes the form to be reset, and button creates a script-defined push button.

It's hard to say what purpose this duplication of effort is supposed to serve. Perhaps the W3C plans, at some future date, to eliminate the button types from the INPUT element.

The SELECT and OPTION Elements

```
<SELECT [name=controlName][size=controlWidth][multiple][disabled]
➥[tabindex=tabNum][onfocus=script][onblur=script][onchange=script][core]
➥[international][events]></SELECT>

<OPTION [selected][disabled][value=controlValue][core][international]
➥[events]></OPTION>
```

The SELECT element is used to create a list of choices, either as a drop-down menu or a list box. Each of the choices in the list is an OPTION element. To create the selection list shown in Figure 15.11, use the following syntax:

```
<SELECT name="testlist">
<OPTION>Choice 1</OPTION>
```

```
<OPTION>Choice 2</OPTION>
<OPTION>Choice 3</OPTION>
<OPTION>Choice 4</OPTION>
<OPTION>Choice 5</OPTION>
<OPTION>Choice 6</OPTION>
</SELECT>
```

FIGURE 15.11.

The SELECT *element.*

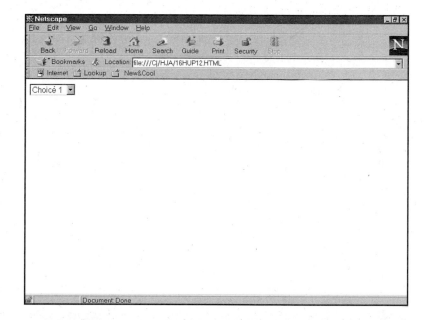

> **TIP**
>
> Selection lists are most useful when there are many choices to be made. If there are only a few, then either checkboxes or radio buttons might be a better choice.

The end tags on the OPTION element are optional. If they're not used, the element automatically terminates at the beginning of the next OPTION element or the end of the SELECT element that contains it.

The OPTION element can also have a specified value assigned to it, but that's not required. If it's absent, the contents of the OPTION element will become the "value" part of the name/value pair. Therefore, the implied value in the preceding example would be Choice 1 for the first option, even though it doesn't have a specific value attribute assigned. The following code demonstrates the syntax for assigning a value attribute:

```
<OPTION value="large_monitor">45 Inch Diagonal Monitor</OPTION>
```

15

BUILDING AND USING HTML FORMS

If you want to specify a default selection, then you can use the `selected` attribute with options. This choice causes the selected element to be highlighted. The user can accept it or deselect it at will, and more than one option can be selected. The following code and Figure 15.12 illustrate the use of the `selected` attribute:

```
<OPTION selected>Choice 1</OPTION>
```

FIGURE 15.12.

The selected *attribute.*

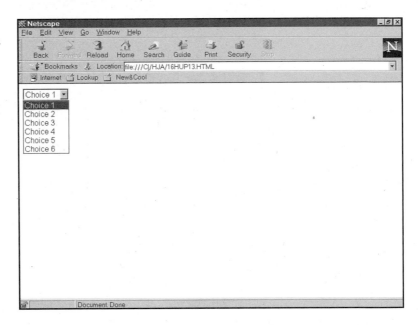

By default, the `SELECT` element displays a drop-down menu in which only the first element is displayed. However, you can use the `size` attribute to make more of the options visible. Changing the first line of the preceding example by adding this attribute, as shown in the following code line, results in the selection list shown in Figure 15.13:

```
<SELECT name="testlist" size="3">
```

Users can select only a single choice from a drop-down menu, but you can use the `multiple` attribute to allow them to select a range of choices. Of course, they can still choose only one if that's their wish, but they can now choose any or all available options. If more than one option is chosen, then multiple name/value pairs are sent when the form is submitted. Each has the same name, but a different value.

Using the `multiple` attribute changes the format of the selection list from a drop-down menu to a list box. Figure 15.14 illustrates the same example after using the following first line:

```
<SELECT name="testlist" multiple>
```

Figure 15.13.
The size *attribute.*

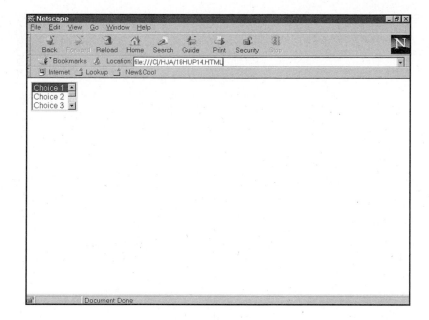

Figure 15.14.
The multiple *attribute.*

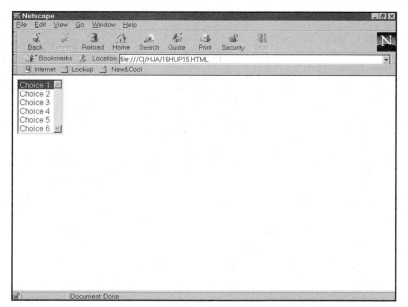

> **NOTE**
>
> You can't get a list box by setting the `size` attribute to the same number as the number of options. That setting just generates a drop-down menu with a grayed-out scrollbar. The only way to get a list box is by using the `multiple` element.

The TEXTAREA Element

```
<TEXTAREA [name=controlName][rows=numRows][cols=numCols][disabled][readonly]
➥[tabindex=tabNum][onfocus=script][onblur=script][onselect=script]
➥[onchange=script][core][international][events]></TEXTAREA>
```

The TEXTAREA element is similar to the INPUT element's `text` type. The difference is that users can type in a larger section of text than they can with text boxes. Instead of a single line of text, there's a large window where multiline responses can be typed. It's typically used for comments or "delivery" instructions—anything that requires more than a simple response. The dimensions of the window are specified with the `rows` and `cols` attributes. These attributes, of course, refer to the number of rows and columns in the text window. The following code illustrates the use of the TEXTAREA element; the results are shown in Figure 15.15:

```
<TEXTAREA name="comments" cols="40" rows="10">
Content, if any, goes here.
</TEXTAREA>
```

FIGURE 15.15.

The TEXTAREA *element.*

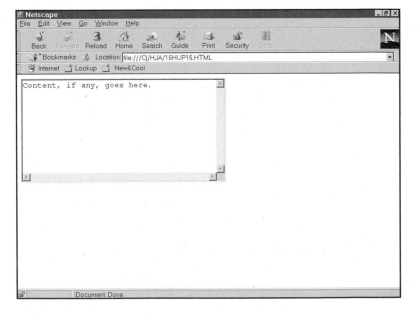

TEXTAREA requires both start and end tags. As with the INPUT element's text and password types, TEXTAREA elements can use the readonly attribute. If it's specified, then any initial content you provide can't be altered by the user.

The LABEL Element

```
<LABEL [for=control-name][disabled][accesskey=keyCombo][onfocus=script]
➥[onblur=script][core][international][events]></LABEL>
```

The LABEL element is new to HTML 4.0. As the name implies, it's the text that labels a control. Unlike normal text, however, the label and its associated control both share the same focus. In other words, if you click on or tab to the label, it has the same effect as though you had clicked on the control itself.

Labels are associated with controls in one of two ways, either implicitly or explicitly. In the implicit association method, the associated element is contained in the LABEL element as illustrated in Figure 15.16 and the following code:

```
<LABEL>Say Yes.<INPUT type="checkbox" name="yesbox"></LABEL>
```

FIGURE 15.16.
An implicit label.

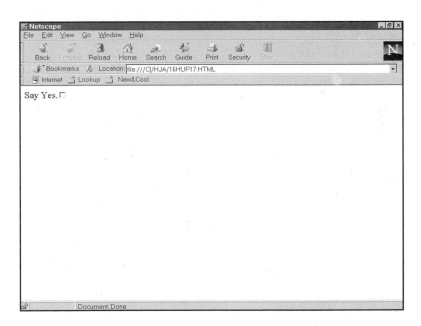

With an explicit association, the label is tied in by using the control element's id attribute. The for attribute of the LABEL element is assigned the value of the control element's id attribute, as shown in the following code:

```
<LABEL for="nope">Say No.</LABEL>
<INPUT type="checkbox" name="nobox" id="nope">
```

The LABEL element must still come before the control for the display to look right; a logical association has nothing to do with visual placement. The preceding explicit code produces the same appearance as the implicit code, whose results you saw in Figure 15.16.

One advantage of the explicit association approach is that the LABEL and control elements are separate, so their placement can be structured separately in a table.

The HTML 4.0 draft specification doesn't address the possibility of conflict between the name and id attributes.

> **CAUTION**
>
> LABEL is very new, and not yet fully implemented. Netscape Navigator 4.03 doesn't support it, and Internet Explorer 4.0, although it supports explicit label declarations, doesn't support the implied label relationship.

The FIELDSET and LEGEND Elements

```
<FIELDSET [core][international][events]></FIELDSET>

<LEGEND [align=left¦center¦right¦justify][accesskey=keyCombo][core]
➥[international][events]></LEGEND>
```

The FIELDSET and LEGEND elements are also new to HTML 4.0. Field sets create boxes around grouped controls, just as panels do in standard programming, and legends are labels that refer to the overall field set. Both elements require start and end tags. The use of field sets and their legends is illustrated in Figure 15.17 and the following code:

```
<FIELDSET>
<LEGEND align="left">This is first legend.</LEGEND>
Check this one: <INPUT type="checkbox" name="firstbox">
Unless you want to check this one: <INPUT type="checkbox" name="otherbox">
</FIELDSET>
<FIELDSET>
<LEGEND align="right">This is second legend.</LEGEND>
Type your name: <INPUT type="text" name="typename">
Type your age: <INPUT type="text" name="typeage">
</FIELDSET>
```

The possible values for the align attribute are top, bottom, right, and left. The alignment in this case is relative to the field set, not the page.

There is no provision in the HTML 4.0 specification for controlling the size of field sets; they stretch across the entire screen, regardless of the space taken up by the controls they contain.

FIGURE 15.17.

The FIELDSET *and* LEGEND *elements.*

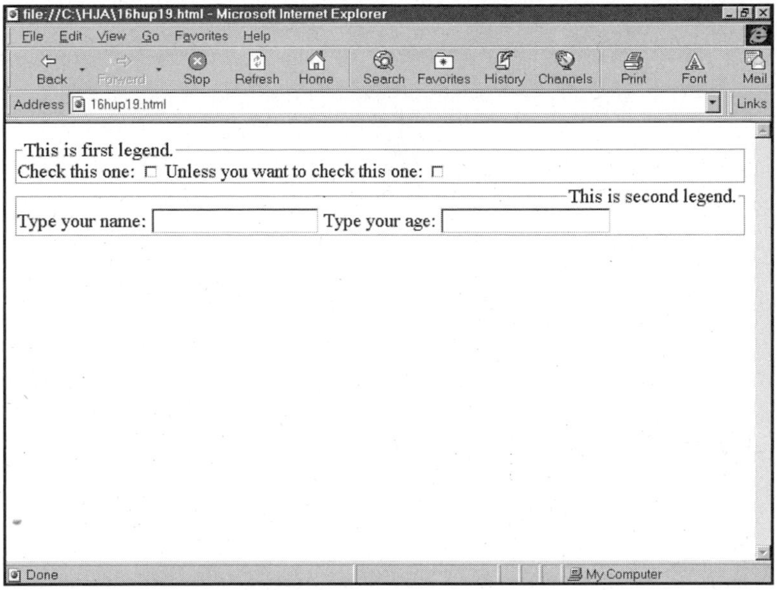

CAUTION

FIELDSET and LEGEND are very new, and not yet fully implemented. Netscape Navigator 4.03 does not support them, and Internet Explorer 4.0 doesn't properly align legends. Although `right` places the legend at the upper-right area of the field set, `top`, `left`, and `bottom` all send the legend to the upper-left area of the field set.

Tab Navigation

The `tabindex` attribute is for navigating through a form by using the Tab key to move from one element to the next. You don't need to use `tabindex` if you want the form to be navigated in the order that the elements appear, as is usually the case. If `tabindex` isn't specified, then that's the default behavior of the Tab key.

However, if you want to navigate in some other order, or if you want some elements to be left out of the tab order, then this attribute becomes useful. To set the tab order for a pair of text input boxes, you would use the following syntax:

```
<INPUT tabindex="1" type="text" name="firstname">
<INPUT tabindex="2" type="text" name="lastname">
```

15

BUILDING AND USING HTML FORMS

If two elements have the same `tabindex` value, then the navigation order is the order in which they appear. The following code, then, would have the same effect as the preceding example:

```
<INPUT tabindex="1" type="text" name="firstname">
<INPUT tabindex="1" type="text" name="lastname">
```

It's not necessary for the assigned values to be sequential; all that's required is that they be in ascending order corresponding to the navigation pattern you want to set. Therefore, the following code has the same effect as the two previous examples:

```
<INPUT tabindex="11" type="text" name="firstname">
<INPUT tabindex="32" type="text" name="lastname">
```

In fact, it would be wise to give nonsequential number values to the `tabindex` attributes of successive elements. This technique was widely used in the old days of BASIC programming when each line was given its own number, the purpose being to leave room for adding new lines of code as needed without having to renumber everything. If you have assigned 1 and 2 as the `tabindex` values for two elements, and then you decide to add another element between them, you have created extra work for yourself. If, on the other hand, the `tabindex` values are 100 and 200, you can add all the elements you could possibly need without having to renumber the existing ones.

To remove an element from the tab navigation order, you could use the `disable` attribute. If you want it out of the order entirely without disabling it, though, you can simply assign it a negative `tabindex` value, as in the following example:

```
<INPUT tabindex="-1" type="text" name="firstname">
```

The `tabindex` attribute is supported by the BUTTON, INPUT, SELECT, and TEXTAREA elements (it's also supported by the ANCHOR, AREA, and OBJECT elements, but they aren't form elements).

Access Keys

Access keys are covered in Chapter 41, "Creating Widely Accessible Web Pages." They are used to give direct keyboard access to, in this case, form elements. An element is assigned a particular hot key, and when that key is pressed in tandem with the Alt key (for IBM users) or the Cmd key (for Apple users), the FORM element gets focus. Users are already familiar with this technique, which is commonly used for menu selection, among its many other uses.

To set an access key for a form element, use the `accesskey` attribute; for its value, specify the character of the key you want to assign to the element. Here's an example of setting an access key:

```
<INPUT type="text" name="address" accesskey="A">
```

You should keep careful track of the access keys you assign so that there's no duplication to cause conflict between elements.

> **CAUTION**
>
> Access keys are very new, and not yet fully implemented. Netscape Navigator 4.03 doesn't support them, and Internet Explorer 4.0 sometimes has trouble recognizing access keys if they aren't coded as capital letters. There is also a fundamental design flaw of access keys—they override the browser's own access keys. Therefore, if you code an access key of *F*, it will prevent you from using the keyboard to select the File menu on the browser.

Summary

Forms allow you to easily get input from visitors to your site. Uses of forms are, for all practical purposes, limited only by your creativity in applying them. The overall FORM element is used to contain several other elements, which are called "controls." Information in the controls (in the form of name/value pairs) is processed by a separate program when forms are submitted. Often, this processing is handled by a CGI program, but it can also be done by a scripting language, such as JavaScript. The data can also just be e-mailed to a predetermined address.

Controls have a wide variety of capabilities. The INPUT element, for instance, can be coded as text boxes, push buttons, checkboxes, radio buttons, and so on. The Reset and Submit buttons (which, respectively, clear the form and submit its contents for processing) are also examples of uses of the INPUT element. With the SELECT and OPTION elements, you can build a selection list, in the form of a drop-down menu or a list box, for choosing different options. The TEXTAREA element lets you set aside an area of the form where users can type in long pieces of text; it's typically used for a "comments" section. The LABEL element creates a text label that, unlike normal text, is keyed to the same focus as the control it's associated with. The FIELDSET and LEGEND elements graphically separate form sections in the same way panels do in other programs. The field set delimits the group of elements around which the line is drawn, and the legend gives a label to the entire field set.

Forms already have default tab navigation from top to bottom, but you can establish the order in which tabbing will bring focus to elements, if you want to change it. You can also assign access keys to form elements, allowing users to bring focus to an element by hitting a particular key combination.

15

BUILDING AND USING HTML FORMS

Embedding Objects in HTML

by Rick Darnell

If you want to present something other than text and horizontal lines in HTML, you're going to have to insert it on the page from another file. This is a fact of life with HTML that isn't going to change for a long, long time.

HTML 3.2 is limited to two tags for inserting special content beyond text: the <APPLET> tag for adding Java applets and the <IMG> tag for inserting graphic images. HTML 4.0 has moved beyond the original two tags by adding Microsoft's <OBJECT> tag and modifying it for use by all special content, including images, applets, plug-ins and more. This addition also means that Netscape's <EMBED> tag will never get official recognition from the World Wide Web Consortium (W3C).

This chapter explores ways to use the <OBJECT> tag to insert the most popular types of content now available on the Web and shows how the tag can be used to add new types of content in the future with no further revision by the W3C.

Adding Specialized Content to a Web Page

With the advancement of browsers and supporting applications, the list of items you can add to a Web page is growing week by week. This content includes items directly supported by a browser, such as animated GIFs, Portable Network Graphics (PNG), Java applets, and virtual reality. It also includes items supported through helper applications and plug-ins, which are special applications that the browser allows to run in the browser window. Both Netscape plug-ins and Microsoft ActiveX components are examples of this kind of content. With these tools, you can view spreadsheets and word processor files and listen to live sound and video, for example.

Depending on the browser's capabilities, each object on a Web page may in turn be handled internally by the browser or by a helper application that's invoked. Whichever is the case, the content remains as part of the rest of the Web page.

HOW DOES A BROWSER KNOW WHAT TO DO?

When your browser loads any particular file—whether it's an HTML file, an image, or multimedia—how does it know what to do with it? The browser's reaction is determined by two things: the filename extension and the file's content type.

You'll see a lot of file extensions tossed around in examples throughout this book, including .html (Web pages), .gif (images), .dcr (Shockwave), and .wrl (virtual reality). The browser uses the file extension to determine what to do when it retrieves a file from your local disk.

The content type is used when the browser receives a file from a Web server because the Web server doesn't always send a filename. In some cases, the server sends only data with no file information. Instead of a filename and extension, it sends a special code called the *content type*, which identifies the information it's sending. Content types include text/html, image/gif, application/mpe, application/msword, and so on.

Both the browser and server contain lists of file extensions and content types. The server uses the list to determine which content type to send with a given file. The browser's list includes an additional entry for helper applications that corresponds to content types.

Basic <OBJECT> Tag Use

The <OBJECT> tag is nothing new to the Web. Microsoft introduced the tag with the advent of its ActiveX technology as a way to insert embedded controls on a Web page. The HTML 4.0 version of <OBJECT> has been expanded to work with all special content, including applets, plugins, ActiveX, images, and any future type of embedded content.

This is the basic proposed syntax:

```
<OBJECT data=URL type=MIMEtype height=pixels width=pixels>
  <!--Parameters-->
  <!--Alternative content, including other objects-->
</OBJECT>
```

Here, the `data` attribute tells the name of the file, such as `image.gif`, and the `type` attribute is the Internet content type, such as `image/gif`, followed by the height and width of the object's area in pixels. It's followed by any number of parameter tags for additional control of the content, alternative content for browsers incompatible with the object, and a closing `</OBJECT>` tag.

CAUTION

Inserting images and other objects with the HTML 4.0 <OBJECT> tag remains largely unimplemented on most browsers. The one exception is ActiveX controls, which are still supported with <OBJECT> on Internet Explorer.

Using the tag for applets or plug-ins on Internet Explorer could cause the browser to lock up. On Navigator, the <OBJECT> tag is ignored altogether, and the alternative content is used.

I recommend waiting until Navigator and Internet Explorer are up to speed with the standard before you try any large-scale implementation of <OBJECT> on your site.

For example, say you want to include a video file of your cat on your Web page, and it's located in a QuickTime movie file called `festusOfTheNorth.mov`. You can do that by using the `<OBJECT>` tag in this manner:

```
<OBJECT data="festusOfTheNorth.mov" type="video/quicktime" alt="My cat">
</OBJECT>
```

This method inserts the file and identifies its MIME type to the browser. If the browser doesn't know how to handle a QuickTime movie, then it won't display anything. But say you're a conscientious Web author who wants to provide some alternative content for browsers that don't support QuickTime, so you insert a Microsoft animation, as shown here:

```
<OBJECT data="festusOfTheNorth.mov" type="video/quicktime" alt="My cat">
  <OBJECT data="festusOfTheNorth.avi" type="video/msvideo" alt="My cat">
  </OBJECT>
</OBJECT>
```

Now, if the browser doesn't support a QuickTime movie, it will try the Microsoft animation. Suppose you want to offer a few more options, though—a Portable Network Graphic, a plain old interlaced GIF, and some text for nongraphical browsers. Then you just keep right on nesting the tags until you come down to the lowest common denominator content:

```
<OBJECT data="festusOfTheNorth.mov" type="video/quicktime" alt="My cat movie">
  <OBJECT data="festusOfTheNorth.avi" type="video/msvideo" alt="My cat movie">
    <OBJECT data="festusOfTheNorth.png" type="image/png" alt="My cat image">
      <OBJECT data="festusOfTheNorth.gif" type="image/gif" alt="My cat image">
      You should see my cat, Festus of the North. He's a fat black cat with white
      ➡toes.
      </OBJECT>
    </OBJECT>
  </OBJECT>
</OBJECT>
```

> **TIP**
>
> As another option for the interior default content for images, you could include the `<IMG>` tag with the `alt` attribute to guarantee support with older browsers that don't support the multiple-use version of the `<OBJECT>` tag yet. In the previous example, the innermost object and text would be replaced with `<IMG src="festusOfTheNorth.gif" alt="My cat, Festus of the North.">`.

So far, so good…but how does `<OBJECT>` work with applets, plug-ins, and ActiveX controls? You'll take a look at that in the next section.

Adding Dynamic Content Through `<OBJECT>`

In addition to static content, such as images, animations, and audio, you can also use the `<OBJECT>` tag to add interactive content, such as applets, plug-ins, and embedded controls with a special attribute called `classid`.

> **TIP**
>
> In this chapter, I'm defining "dynamic content" as anything that can interact with the user, which pretty well limits the field to applications. Although video and audio files (MPEG, AVI, AU, WAV) might seem dynamic, they typically can't be controlled or changed by the user.

This is the basic syntax for adding the application content to a Web page:

```
<OBJECT classid="protocol:fileName" codetype="type/subtype">
  <!--Alternative content for noncompatible browsers-->
</OBJECT>
```

The `classid` contains the protocol and the filename or identifier of the content separated by a colon, and `codetype` tells what kind of application it is. Between the opening and closing tags, you can also include additional `<OBJECT>` tags, alternative content, or parameters to pass to the application.

Parameters are included with the `<PARAM>` tag. This is the basic syntax for using it:

```
<PARAM name="paramName" value="paramValue">
```

Here, *paramName* is the name of the parameter, and *paramValue* is its associated value. There are two additional attributes for this tag: `valuetype` and `type`.

- **valuetype:** This attribute defines how the `value` attribute should be interpreted. The possible values for this attribute are `data` (default), `ref`, and `object`. The default sends `value` to the object as a string. With the next value type, `ref`, the `value` attribute is treated as a URL pointing to a resource. The last value type, `object`, identifies another `<OBJECT>` tag on the current page by the object's `id` attribute.

- **type:** This attribute, used only when the value type is set to `ref`, identifies the MIME type of the resource identified in the `value` attribute.

With the basic object and parameters in hand, it's time to tackle the main three types of content the tags were developed for: applets, plug-ins, and controls (oh, my).

Java Applets

You can use the `<OBJECT>` tag to insert one of the most popular forms of embedded content on the Web—Java applets. Java can implement sound, animation, and other user interactivity regardless of platform. Java is currently supported by at least four browsers: HotJava from Sun (which is written in Java), Netscape Navigator 2.0 or later, Microsoft Internet Explorer 3.0 or later, and the W3C's beta version of the Jigsaw Web server.

> **WARNING**
>
> Internet Explorer 4 and Navigator 4 still do not support the `<OBJECT>` tag for a Java applet. You'll still want to use the `<APPLET>` tag within the `<OBJECT>` tag as optional content, or refrain from using the `<OBJECT>` tag until the browser implementations catch up with the standard.

This is the simplest syntax to include a Java applet with `<OBJECT>`:

```
<OBJECT classid="java:fileName.fileExtension">
</OBJECT>
```

Here, *className* is the name of the Java class file, and *fileExtension* is the extension of the class file, typically `class`. This simple syntax requires that the Java file be located in the same directory as the Web page. To help the browser decide if it's capable of running the applet as executable content, the W3C also recommends using the `codetype` attribute:

```
<OBJECT classid="java:className" codetype="application/octet-stream">
</OBJECT>
```

Now the browser will look at the code type first. If it can't run basic executable content types, it will quit trying to load the applet and move on to other tasks. Otherwise, it will look at the protocol on the `classid`. If the browser can run an application and support Java, then it will continue to load the class for execution.

If your applet files are in a separate location from your Web page files, then use the `codebase` attribute to identify their directory with an URL:

```
<OBJECT classid="java:className" codetype="application/octet-stream"
        codebase=URL>
</OBJECT>
```

When the browser tries to load the applet, it prefixes the class name with the URL to find the needed file.

Some applets can also accept other parameters to control their behavior. For a ticker applet, it might be the scrolling message and a background image. For an image map applet, it could be a list of URLs and image coordinates. You get the idea. All this extra information is included with the `<PARAM>` tag, covered earlier in this chapter.

The parameter of the name is case sensitive and must exactly match the parameter name in the applet. The value of a parameter is a different matter. All parameters passed from an HTML page to an applet are passed as strings, no matter what they are or how they're reformatted on the page. Any conversion to other types (integer, Boolean, date) must happen within the applet itself.

THE `<APPLET>` TAG

The `<APPLET>` tag is still an official part of HTML, although its use has been deprecated with the development of the `<OBJECT>` tag. If you're feeling nostalgic and still want to include applets on your Web page with the `<APPLET>` tag, follow this syntax:

```
<APPLET code="appletName.class"[codebase="pathToClass"]
        width=pixelWidth height=pixelHeight[align=alignment]>
  <!-- optional parameters -->
  <!-- alternative content -->
</APPLET>
```

The required line of code identifies the name of the applet and the size it will appear on the page. You must include the `class` extension for the code attribute, and the Java Virtual Machine associated with the browser should automatically assume that the first method to call is `init`.

Embedding Objects in HTML

CHAPTER 16

261

16

EMBEDDING
OBJECTS IN
HTML

If the applet is in a separate directory from the Web page, then you need to give the browser a URL to the location of the applet with `codebase`. Also, you might want to set the applet's size and alignment with the appearance attributes.

Like the `<OBJECT>` tag, the `<APPLET>` tag can also use the parameters through the `<PARAM>` tag.

ActiveX Controls

The `<OBJECT>` tag was originally designed for Microsoft's ActiveX control technology. It's another option Web page designers have for delivering specialized content to the user. This standard, developed by Microsoft, is a bit of a cross between Java and plug-ins. Like Java, it's loaded automatically when it encounters the browser; like a plug-in, it stays loaded on the user's system for future use and doesn't have to be reloaded.

Currently, only Java Internet Explorer and Netscape Navigator support ActiveX. Other browsers might follow their lead, but there's no indication of that happening any time soon.

ActiveX controls also offer a variety of content options, including Shockwave, spreadsheets, and Windows-type controls. To include an ActiveX control, use the `<OBJECT>` tag with this syntax:

```
<OBJECT classid="clsid:identifier" data="contentFile">
</OBJECT>
```

Identifier is a 36-character string that identifies the control, and `data` identifies the URL of the file that contains the content.

TIP

If you use the `codetype` attribute for your control, the appropriate value for ActiveX is `application/x-oleobject`.

The `codebase` attribute has a slightly different use for ActiveX. Instead of automatically going to the source, the browser checks the user's system to see whether the control is already loaded on the machine. If it is, the browser uses the local version; if it's not, the browser uses `codebase` to load and install it from the network.

Netscape Plug-Ins

In the early days of Mosaic and other early Web browsers, for new additions to Web technology, you had to wait for a new version of the browser. If a new type of content was introduced, such as video or virtual reality, you had to wait until a new version of the browser that supported it was introduced. Then Netscape introduced plug-ins, which expanded the browser's capabilities without waiting for a new release.

One of the most popular multimedia plug-ins available is Shockwave from Macromedia, which allows page authors to display multimedia content developed using Shockwave Director. This content can take the form of animations, electronic books, games, or other items requiring synchronized sound and video with interactivity.

TIP

One key problem with plug-ins is that they require users to have a browser that supports plug-ins and have the proper plug-in installed. Many plug-ins are available for only one or two platforms, leaving another chunk of users out in the cold. Also, you must coordinate with your system administrator to make sure the Web server knows how to deliver the goods.

Netscape includes several of the more popular plug-ins, such as those for virtual reality and Web chat, with its standard software release. Microsoft is also including ActiveX controls in Internet Explorer to detect and implement plug-ins.

Embedding plug-in content in your Web page with the `<OBJECT>` tag is similar to adding an image. Begin with the name of the plug-in content file and the type:

```
<OBJECT data="filename" type="contentType/contentSubtype">
</OBJECT>
```

This syntax should serve for most plug-in content that's stored in the same directory as the source page. For a plug-in file stored elsewhere on the Web site, you could also add the `codebase` attribute. The other basic appearance attributes also apply, including size and alignment.

For example, a Macromedia Shockwave plug-in could be inserted as the following:

```
<OBJECT data="movingEye.dcr" type="application/x-director" codebase="/specialStuff"
      height=244 width=200>
  This animation requires <A href="www.macromedia.com"
  title="Macromedia">Macromedia Shockwave</A>.
</OBJECT>
```

The browser would attempt to load the file at `/specialStuff/movingEye.dcr`, which is a MIME type `application/x-director`. If the browser doesn't support the MIME type, then the alternative content is displayed, which directs the user to the Macromedia Web site.

THE `<EMBED>` TAG

The old way to put a plug-in on a page is to use the `<EMBED>` tag. Three attributes are required, with this syntax:

```
<EMBED src="URL" width=wPixels height=hPixels>
```

Embedding Objects in HTML

CHAPTER 16

263

16

EMBEDDING
OBJECTS IN
HTML

Here, src is the location of the plug-in file, and width and height define how much space the plug-in will occupy on the Web page. For plug-ins that need additional parameters, add attributes to the <EMBED> tag. Check the documentation for the specific plug-in you're using to see what it requires.

To support users who aren't using plug-in–capable browsers, use the <NOEMBED> tag immediately following the <EMBED> tag. This tag pair creates a place for a snapshot of the plug-in in action, alternative text, or a hyperlink to the application home page. This is the syntax:

```
<EMBED src="URL" width=wPixels height=hPixels>
<NOEMBED>
...substitute content...
</NOEMBED>
```

Plug-in–compatible browsers ignore everything between the <NOEMBED> tags. If a browser doesn't recognize the <EMBED> tag, it won't recognize the <NOEMBED> tag or display anything within its borders.

Working with Other Objects and Special Features

In addition to all the interesting things possible with the <OBJECT> tag, there are several other options for adding interactivity and special features to your Web page. Many of these items are proprietary, so they work on only one or two browsers.

Animated GIF Files

Animated GIF files are supported indirectly through HTML 4.0 by using the <IMG> and <OBJECT> tag for inserting standard GIF files. An animated GIF file contains several images combined into one package; these images are then displayed in turn to create a simple animation.

There are some good and bad points to this technology. The good news is that it's even simpler to implement than the Java Animator, although you lose the sound component. The bad news is that it creates very large GIF files, which can take a long time to download. In a GIF animation, all the images it includes are saved in the same file, along with the instructions about how many times to display it.

An animated GIF also works with browsers that don't support the animation portion by displaying only the first image in the file. Of course, the user still has to wait for the other images included in the animation package to download.

To create an animated GIF, you need the set of image files and a utility to assemble them. You have the following options, depending on your platform:

■ Windows: The most popular tool is Alchemy Mindworks GIF Construction Set, which also supports creating transparent and interlaced images. It's available from www.mindworkshop.com/alchemy/.

- Macintosh: GIFBuilder is a freeware utility you can use to assemble a set of GIF, PICT, or TIFF files into an animated GIF file. It's available from www.mid.net/INFO-MAC/.

- UNIX: With a command-line utility called whirlGIF, you can assemble a set of GIF files into an animated GIF. It includes a variety of options for the animation, which are explained at www.msg.net/utility/whirlgif/.

At this point, you might be wondering why you can't just use your old reliable image editor. Animation has been a capability of GIF files for quite a while, but it hasn't been supported in very many places. Its newfound popularity on the Web has caught graphics programs unprepared.

After you assemble the animation, try to load it with your browser. If nothing happens, you need to make sure you're using the latest version of Navigator, Internet Explorer, or Mosaic.

Video with `dynsrc`: Internet Explorer

Microsoft has equipped Internet Explorer to handle its native AVI video files by adding the `dynsrc` attribute to the `<IMG>` tag. The syntax for an image then becomes the following:

```
<IMG src="imageURL" dynsrc="video.avi">
```

If the browser doesn't support `dynsrc`, it ignores the attribute and uses the image identified in `src`.

Microsoft added several other attributes to go along with `dynsrc` to help control its display, including the following:

- **controls:** This set of controls added to the bottom of the video frame direct fast-forward, rewind, stop, and play.

- **loop:** This value determines how many times the video should replay. For example, a value of 3 causes the video to repeat three times and then stop. A value of -1 or INFINITE causes it to play in an endless loop.

- **start:** There are two ways to start the video. The first is FILEOPEN, which causes the video to begin as soon as the entire HTML page and AVI file are loaded. The other option is MOUSEOVER, which prevents the video from starting until the user passes the mouse over the top of the frame.

Background Sounds: Internet Explorer

Another option Microsoft added for its browser is the ability to play a sound file as a soundtrack for a page. This feature is possible with the `<BGSOUND>` tag, which has the following syntax:

```
<BGSOUND src="soundURL" loop=##¦INFINITE>
```

In this syntax, the src is a WAV, MIDI, or AU sound file, and loop specifies how many times the sound should play. If loop is omitted, the default is one time. Otherwise, select -1 or INFINITE to play the sound in an endless loop.

Summary

In HTML 4.0, you can expect the <OBJECT> tag to replace all the other current tags used to insert inline content, including images, sounds, Java applets, plug-ins, and ActiveX controls. The tag as proposed by W3C includes all the attributes needed by all these items so you'll retain the same control over their appearance and behavior.

However, the only browser that currently supports <OBJECT> for anything is Internet Explorer, which uses it to implement ActiveX controls. Trying to use <OBJECT> for anything else in IE causes the program to hang as it tries to figure out what you mean. Navigator ignores the <OBJECT> tag and moves on to the alternative content within, as will virtually all other browsers.

In short, the multiple-use <OBJECT> tag is a good idea that's included in the standard, but it's not in use yet by the favorite browsers. You'll need to use the deprecated <APPLET> and non-standard <EMBED> tags for Java and plug-ins, respectively, in addition to the other proprietary attributes for inline video and sound. I encourage you to use the proprietary methods at least until the next major revision of the popular browsers.

IV

PART

Presentation Techniques

Simple Style with Text

by Rick Darnell

IN THIS CHAPTER

CHAPTER 17

Formatting Text with Physical Styles

Much of this book has been spent on structural HTML, which defines how portions of text are used, instead of how they should appear. Admittedly, there is a de facto relationship between the two, although the ultimate choice still remains in the browser—a Brand-X browser can choose to present <EM> in bold smallcaps rather than italics. The first choice to make sure that <EM> is displayed the way you want is through a cascading style sheet, which is discussed in Chapter 18, "Using Cascading Style Sheets."

If most of your users aren't equipped with a style sheet–capable browser, such as Internet Explorer 3.02 or Netscape Navigator 4.02, then you do have one more option. You can force style through the use of special HTML tags.

With the discovery of HTML by page designers and other appearance-minded people on the Web, HTML's shortcomings quickly became apparent when it came to controlling the details of page appearance. The logical styles don't cover all the possibilities that designers and page authors seem to thrive on. Designers started clamoring for more control and were rewarded with tags and attributes from Microsoft and Netscape. Using physical styles allows a page designer to take control over many details of the page's appearance, including type style, size, and color.

CAUTION

Many of the tags and attributes mentioned in this chapter have been deprecated in HTML 4.0 in favor of style sheets. I have indicated which elements are current and which are deprecated. Documents built with deprecated features will validate only according to the loose HTML definition and fail on the strict definition.

COMMON ATTRIBUTES

Most of the elements in this chapter share common HTML attributes, such as items that control identification, style, language, and event handling. Because the common attributes are so pervasive in HTML 4 (that's why they're called "common"), you will find an overview of them in the introduction of this book. You can also find more information about these often used features and their associated elements in Appendix A, "HTML 4.0 Reference."

Meanwhile, during this chapter, I'll refer to the common attributes by using these keywords: *core, international,* and *event.*

Basic Text Formatting Styles: <I>, <B>, <U>

The first three text-formatting elements are standards in almost all text-processing environments. They set the basic appearance of text (as shown in Figure 17.1) and are derived from many of the logical styles, such as italics (<I>) for emphasized text (<EM>) and bold (<B>) for strong text (<STRONG>).

FIGURE 17.1.

The three basic physical styles are italics, bold, and underline.

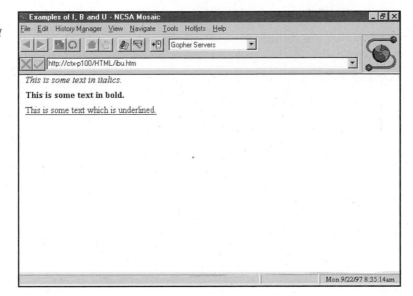

This is the syntax for each of the elements:

```
<I>...Text...</I>
<B>...Text...</B>
<U>...Text...</U>
```

<I> stands for italics, <B> stands for bold, and <U> stands for underline. Each of the elements also accepts core, international, and event handler attributes.

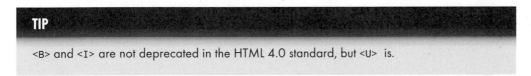

TIP

<B> and <I> are not deprecated in the HTML 4.0 standard, but <U> is.

In addition to using the tags individually, you can also nest them for a combined effect, like this:

```
This is <B>bold text with <I>bold and italics text</I></B>.
```

From the days of typesetting and proofreader marks, underlined text was used to indicate items that should be set in italics, including book and magazine titles. Another possible use of underlined text has been introduced with the <INS> tag (see Chapter 7, "Text Alignment and Formatting"). The <INS> tag, used to mark text that has been inserted into the document, is helpful for a document in the midst of revising and editing. Because <INS> is still largely unsupported, you can use <U> as backup markup in this fashion:

```
<U><INS datetime="1997-09-21T19:38:00Z">This was a good idea and
was inserted.</INS></U>
```

Remember that underlined text can confuse readers in the context of a Web page because it's also used to mark hyperlinks to other documents, especially when the text color is different from the surrounding text.

Variations on Basic Size: <BIG> and <SMALL>

Included in the HTML 4.0 specification are these two fine little tags, which indicate that text should be bigger or smaller than the default size. The browser has the option of picking whatever size text it feels appropriate for both of these elements—their value is relative to the base font size of the document.

So, if a user is using a large font size (18 pt) to compensate for a vision impairment, then the browser might choose to render text within the <BIG> tag as 24 pt and <SMALL> as 14 pt. Or, it might choose to ignore the tags altogether.

> **TIP**
>
> Generally, you get the best results with these two tags when there's no other style associated with the document or when they have their own style definitions to complement the base size of the text.

Strikethrough Text: <STRIKE> and <S>

Strikethrough text is used more often in traditional word processing than in HTML pages. It indicates text that has been deleted but is still left on the page for review. This way other readers can review the changes and know how the revision of the document has progressed. The syntax can use one of the following forms:

```
<STRIKE>...Text...</STRIKE>
```

```
<S>...Text...</S>
```

Both attributes accept the core, international, and event attributes. The traditional purpose of <STRIKE> is being replaced by the <DEL> tag, which is described in more detail in Chapter 7.

Because <DEL> is still largely unsupported, however, you can use <STRIKE> as backup markup in this fashion:

```
<STRIKE><DEL datetime="1997-09-21T19:38:00Z">This was a bad idea and
was deleted.</DEL></STRIKE>
```

Both <STRIKE> and <S> are deprecated in the HTML 4.0 standard.

Teletype or Monospaced Text: <TT>

Several logical text styles take advantage of monospaced text. Simply stated, in monospaced text, each character takes up the same width on the screen. Normally, graphical browsers use adjustable-width fonts, which means an *m* takes up more space than an *i*, which takes up less space than a *j*. In a monospace font, all three take up the same amount of space along with all the other characters, including spaces, periods, and other punctuation marks. (See Figure 17.2.)

FIGURE 17.2.

The difference between normal and monospace fonts isn't very evident until they are seen next to each other.

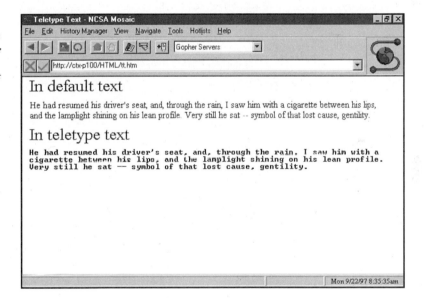

This is the syntax for using the <TT> tag:

```
<TT>...Text...<TT>
```

Text is the font to display in monospace font. This attribute accepts the core, international, and event attributes.

The <TT> designation in the tag hearkens back to the days of teletype machines. Essentially, they were typewriters hooked up to networks that delivered news and bulletins. As was standard for typewriters at the time, they used a monospace type style.

Superscripts and Subscripts: <SUP> and <SUB>

Next in the list of physical styles are the two tags for creating superscripts and subscripts. A *superscript* is text set slightly higher than the base text, and a *subscript* is set slightly lower. Both typically use a smaller typeface. Here is the syntax for both:

```
<SUP>Text</SUP>
```

```
<SUB>Text</SUB>
```

Both attributes accept the core, international, and event attributes. Normally, a superscript or subscript is used for only a character or two. The following snippet uses these features to indicate an endnote source (superscript) and a notation for a chemical formula (subscript). (See Figure 17.3.)

```
The chemical formula<SUP>1</SUP> for Glacial Acetic acid
is C<SUB>2</SUB>H<SUB>4</SUB>O<SUB>2</SUB>.
<BR><SUP>1</SUP>Chemical Hazards Response Information System.
```

FIGURE 17.3.

Superscripts and subscripts are typically used for small pieces of text, such as endnotes and other special notations.

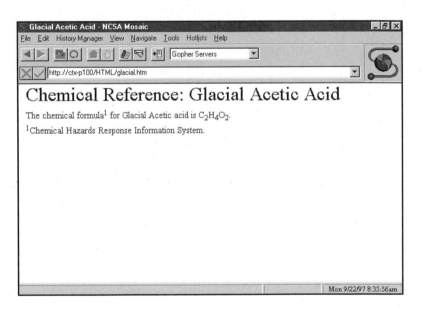

Like the other elements, you can nest these tags for additional usefulness. For example, you can make a reference to an endnote superscript also serve as a link to the actual endnote, like this:

```
The chemical formula<A HREF="#1"><SUP>1</SUP></A> for Glacial Acetic acid
is C<SUB>2</SUB>H<SUB>4</SUB>O<SUB>2</SUB>.
<BR><A NAME="1"><SUP>1</SUP></A>Chemical Hazards Response Information System.
```

Clicking on the superscript for the endnote moves the user to that location in the document. For more information on working with anchors and hyperlinks, see Chapter 13, "Hyperlinking and Anchors."

Working with the Letters: `<FONT>`

The FONT element is used to change the basic font characteristics—typeface, size, and color—of blocks of text. Its use in HTML 4.0 is deprecated.

The face attribute is used to specify one or more typefaces to use for the text selection. To specify the Garamond typeface as the first choice and Arial as the second, the tag would look like this:

```
<FONT face="Garamond,Arial">...text...</FONT>
```

If neither typeface is found on the user's browser, the default typeface for that particular application is used. If you choose to use the attribute, be sure that your page still displays correctly even if the user's browser doesn't support it.

Setting the Size: `size` and `<BASEFONT>`

An important attribute of `<FONT>` is size. It sets the size of the tag's contents to a specific or relative size. This is the syntax:

```
<FONT size=number>...Text...</FONT>
```

Here, *number* is the desired size expressed as an integer from 1 to 7 or as a relative value from -6 to +6. If a relative value is used, it's added to the current setting for `<BASEFONT>`. (This method is covered later in this section.) Unlike the headings, where `<H1>` represents the largest heading and `<H6>` is the smallest, the size attribute uses 1 for the smallest type size and 7 for the largest. (See Figure 17.4.)

FIGURE 17.4.

This is how different text sizes are represented using the FONT element.

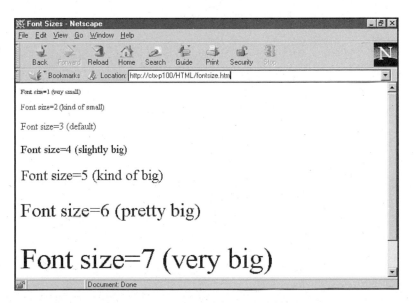

For people used to dealing with type sizes represented in points, the range of sizes for HTML text doesn't seem practical. After all, a line of 1-point type creates fine print not even a lawyer could understand.

HTML type sizes do correspond to physical sizes, but the actual physical size varies between browsers and platforms. So, don't try to think of size 1 being equal to 6-point text. Instead, just think of size 1 as "really small," size 7 as "really big," and 2 through 6 as a range of "fairly small" to "fairly big."

As a companion to the size attribute of <FONT>, the BASEFONT element gives you a way to set the base size of the body text. Here is its syntax:

```
<BASEFONT [size=number]>
```

In this element, *number* is the size of the base font, expressed as an integer from 1 to 7. If omitted, it defaults to 3. It sets the base size for all text following it and does not have a closing tag.

In addition to specifying an absolute text size, you can also use a relative number for <BASEFONT>. The syntax is the same, but a plus or minus sign is placed in front of the number. This method uses the default base size (3) and adds the value of the size attribute. (See Figure 17.5.)

FIGURE 17.5.

No matter what the size of the previous font is, a relative value for the base font size is always added to the default size.

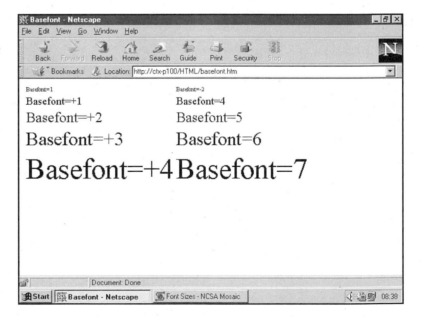

Using relative sizes, the range of values for the base size attribute is -2 to +4. For both <BASEFONT> and <FONT>, relative values that result in a size less than 1 or more than 7 default to the minimum and maximum values for physical sizes.

A Different Shade of Text: color

You can control the color of a block of text by using the color attribute, which has the following syntax:

```
<FONT color=name¦RGBValue>...Text...</FONT>
```

Here, the value of color is a *name* of one of the 16 standard colors or an RGB hexadecimal triplet that specifies the mix of colors to use. Remember that default text colors for the entire document are set with attributes of the <BODY> tag, which was covered in the previous chapter.

> **NOTE**
>
> You can define a color in two ways. The first is the RGB hexadecimal triplet, which is very specific but not that easy to remember.
>
> Or, you can use the name of the color. It's much easier, but you can't use just any name. Personally, I really liked the color of my friend John's car. It was taupe. Unfortunately, I can't type <FONT color="taupe"> and expect the browser to understand.
>
> If you want to use color names, you'll need to stick to one of the 16 standard values: black, green, silver, lime, gray, olive, white, yellow, maroon, navy, red, blue, purple, teal, fuchsia, and aqua. Some browsers use other names. To be safe, use one of these names, or get out a scientific calculator and start figuring 32 percent blue as a hexadecimal number (it's #000020).

Be careful when changing text colors, especially when using a non-default background, such as an image or other color. Some colors don't work well together, such as green text on red or red text on purple. The resulting effect will do more to drive your readers away than to illustrate your point.

Summary

The tags in this chapter are indeed a simple way to add style to your Web page. By quickly inserting a tag or two, you can easily change the appearance of a block of text. However, most of them have been deprecated in HTML 4.0 in favor of style sheets.

The elements that remain current in HTML 4.0 include the following:

TT	Teletype
I	Italic
B	Bold
BIG	Bigger than default
SMALL	Smaller than default

SUP   Superscript

SUB   Subscript

The elements that are deprecated in HTML 4.0 include the following:

STRIKE, S   Strikethrough

U   Underline

FONT   Typeface, size, and color

BASEFONT   Default text size

Although any of the tags in these two lists can be used to fine-tune the appearance of your text, you get the best results with style sheets, which are covered in the following chapter.

Using Cascading Style Sheets

by Rick Darnell

IN THIS CHAPTER

In the previous chapter, you had a chance to change the appearance of a document by using HTML tags on pieces of text. This method is effective, but not necessarily the easiest. After all, every time you want to make some red text, you have to bracket the text with `<FONT text="red">`.

Cascading style sheets (CSS) offer the tools to fine-tune your Web pages to the nth degree, while still maintaining backward compatibility with older browsers. CSS is an accepted standard from the World Wide Web Consortium.

In a nutshell, style sheets control how HTML tags are formatted. The ranks of Web authors are increasingly filled with people from graphic design or desktop publishing backgrounds, and controlling the nuances of style is a part of the natural approach to design. However, a common tool to control style was missing from HTML in its first incarnations and limited in subsequent advancements.

So, with all this introduction, I still haven't addressed what CSS is. The word *cascading* means that multiple styles can be used in an individual HTML page, and the browser will follow an order—called a *cascade*—to interpret the information. Of the three types of style sheets, a designer can use all three simultaneously, and the browser will deliver the goods in an orderly, predictable fashion. Style sheets in general, and CSS in particular, are an important method of controlling how text is displayed and moved around on the page, and this chapter shows you how it's done.

Style Control with Style Sheets

Historically, style control with HTML is clumsy at best and nonexistent at worst. However, with cascading style sheets, a Web designer has dramatically improved ways of working with important style elements, such as fonts, and specific features, such as font face, font size, font weight, font style, and leading (pronounced "led-ing"). Style controls extend beyond basic typographic functions to margins, indents, colors, graphics, and a myriad of other options.

The World Wide Web Consortium (W3C) has released a definitive standard for style sheets, which is now reflected in Microsoft Internet Explorer 3.0 and later versions, and Netscape Navigator 4.0 and later versions. With both major browsers now on board with implementations, you can expect style sheets to become an integral part of many Web pages.

NOTE

From the are-we-moving-forward-or-sideways file, when a page using style sheets exclusively is viewed by older versions of Netscape (3.0 or earlier) or Internet Explorer (2.0 or earlier), the Web page reverts back to the prison-gray background. Older browsers demote fonts and other styles to their bare-bones defaults. (See Figures 18.1 and 18.2.)

FIGURE 18.1.

A page using cascading style sheets as it appears in Internet Explorer 4.0 is presented in all its glamour.

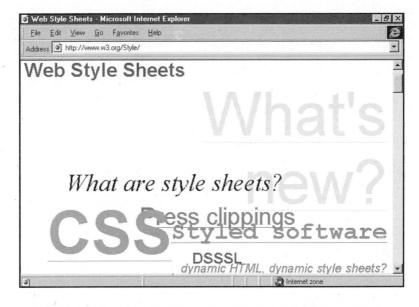

FIGURE 18.2.

The same page reverts to a bare-bones default in a non-CSS browser, such as Mosaic.

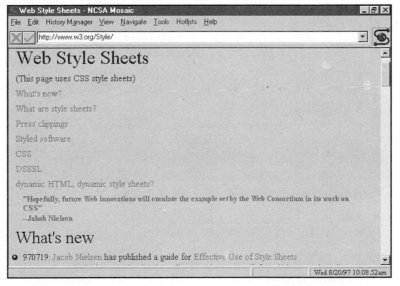

18

USING
CASCADING
STYLE SHEETS

With all their promise, there are still some challenges in using style sheets, such as problems with the difference in the fonts each user selects on his or her machine. My selection of fonts is different from yours, your selection is different from your co-worker's, and your co-worker's selection is different from his or her neighbor's. A style sheet can call for a specific typeface, but if the font and font weight aren't on the visitor's machine, the browser can't interpret the style you've set up.

And, as mentioned in the preceding Note, a page that deals exclusively in style sheets won't get the desired results in a noncompatible browser. Without some allowance for the many other types of browsers on the Web, a page can look like it was created to be as ugly and unreadable as possible.

Fortunately, there are workarounds for the problems. Wise designers stack information into the style argument strings and back the style up with attributes in the HTML tags, which allows the browser to seek out the information it can interpret. This is good, but the designers still lose some control as a result, because they're never assured that a page is going to remain consistent regardless of where it's viewed. Old rules remain true—use prudence and caution, and, whenever possible, test the results of your work by viewing it in a variety of browsers on a variety of platforms.

Essential Style Sheets

There are three primary ways to use style sheets: the inline method, the individual page or embedded method, and linking to a master or external style sheet.

- **Inline style sheet:** This approach takes advantage of existing HTML tags in a standard HTML document and adds a specific style to the information controlled by those tags. An example of using inline style sheets is controlling the indentation of a single paragraph by using the `style="someStyle"` attribute within the `<P>` tag. Another method of doing this is by combining the `<SPAN>` tag and the `style="someStyle"` attribute.

- **Embedded style sheet:** With this method, the designer can control individual pages by using the `<STYLE>` tag, along with its companion tag, `</STYLE>`. This information is placed between the `<HTML>` tag and the `<BODY>` tag; the style attributes are inserted within the full `<STYLE>` container.

- **External (linked) style sheet:** This is a master style sheet stored in an external file. It uses the same syntax you would use with an embedded style. This file uses the `.css` extension. Then, simply make sure all the HTML documents that will require those controls are linked to that document.

Inline and embedded style sheets are usually much more common because having all the styles and their attributes in the same file for easy review and modification is very convenient.

> **NOTE**
>
> The attribute syntax for embedded and linked style sheets is somewhat different from standard HTML syntax. For CSS, attributes are placed within curly brackets. Where HTML places an equals (=) sign, CSS uses a colon (:) instead. In HTML, individual attributes are separated by a space, and CSS uses a semicolon. A style sheet string would look like this:
>
> ```
> {font-style: arial, helvetica; margin-left}
> ```

Still, as with HTML, style sheet syntax is very logical. As you work with the examples in this chapter, you should become quite comfortable with the way style sheets work.

When you refer to the style attributes as properties of an object, the hyphen disappears and the first letter of the second word is capitalized. So, `font-style` becomes `fontStyle`, and `text-decoration` becomes `textDecoration`.

The following sections should serve as an introduction for newcomers and a review for old hands on the basics of each type of style sheet. Although you'll be using some style sheet syntax to create the examples, detailed syntax is covered later in the chapter and in Appendix C, "Cascading Style Sheets Level 1 Quick Reference."

Using Inline Styles

An inline style is included with the tag it affects. It doesn't affect any other HTML tags on the page, whether they're the same type or not. For example, if you place an italic style with an `<H1>` tag, the style won't apply to any other `<H1>` tags on the page. An inline style is created by adding the `style` attribute to each affected element.

To create an inline style, begin with a blank page in your HTML editor.

NOTE

I'm not going to make any assumptions about which HTML editor you're using. There are a lot to choose from, and you should use whatever you're comfortable with. There are a couple of requirements, however.

First, it should allow nonstandard tags, such as `<STYLE>`. Some browsers automatically validate HTML and some don't, and those that do differ in how they handle nonstandard items. If your editor doesn't directly support HTML 3.2, HTML 4.0, or CSS1 (Cascading Style Sheets Level 1), make sure your editor still lets you insert items that aren't standard to earlier versions of HTML.

The second requirement follows from the first. If you're going to add nonstandard elements, you'll need a way to modify the document's source code. In addition to adding new tags, you'll also need a way to add attributes to existing tags.

If your editor doesn't support this kind of activity and you can't find an editor you like, then you can always fall back on the old faithful text editor. It might not be pretty, but it works.

Next, include the following lines of HTML. Pay attention to the extra `style` attributes in the `<BODY>`, `<P>`, and `<SPAN>` tags.

```
<!DOCTYPE HTML PUBLIC "-//IETF//DTD HTML 4.0//EN">
<html>
<head>
```

```
<title>An Inline Style</title>
</head>
<body style="background: white">

<p style="font-size: 14pt" id="p14">
This came from a P tag with a style.
I know not how it was--but, with the first glimpse of the building, a sense
of insufferable gloom pervaded my spirit. </p>

<p>
This came from a P tag without a style.
I know not how it was--but, with the first glimpse of the building, a sense
of insufferable gloom pervaded my spirit.</p>

<p>
<span style="font-size: 18pt" id="span18">
This came from a SPAN tag with a style.
I know not how it was--but, with the first glimpse of the building, a sense
of insufferable gloom pervaded my spirit.</span>

<span>
This came from a SPAN tag without a style.
I know not how it was--but, with the first glimpse of the building, a sense
of insufferable gloom pervaded my spirit.</span></p>

</body>
</html>
```

Save the file as inline.html.

Figure 18.3 shows the finished page as it appears in Internet Explorer 4.0.

As you can see from the example, the inline style for a tag has no effect on any other tag around it. Its effect is very localized.

FIGURE 18.3.

The results of inline style sheet commands.

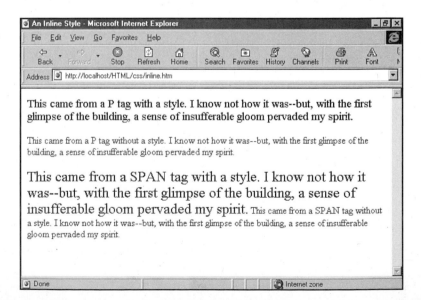

TIP

The <DIV> (division) tag can be used like the <SPAN> tag for inline control. The <DIV> tag is especially helpful for longer blocks of text, but <SPAN> is most effective for adding style to smaller stretches of information, such as sentences, several words, or even individual letters within a word.

In one sense, an inline style defeats the ultimate purpose of cascading style sheets. The main point of the technology is to control the style for an entire page or sets of pages. For this reason, the inline method typically is used only where touches of style are required. Besides, adding style to each tag requires a lot of typing, so it has the potential to generate a lot of errors.

An Embedded Style for a Page

The next style you'll work with is an embedded style. An *embedded style sheet* is a set of style definitions placed within <STYLE> tags and found between the head and body of the document. It sets the style attributes for the entire page where it's located and is created by following these steps:

Begin with a blank page in your HTML editor. Type the following text. Be sure you place the <STYLE> tags in the proper place—immediately after <HTML> and before <BODY>. The style is similar to what you just saw in the inline styles. The exact syntax is covered in more detail as you work through the chapter.

```
<!DOCTYPE HTML PUBLIC "-//IETF//DTD HTML 4.0//EN">
<html>
<head>
<title>An Embedded Style Sheet</title>
</head>

<style>
BODY {background:#0000FF; color: #FFFF00; margin-left:0.5in; margin-right:0.5in}
H2 {font-size:18pt; color:#FF0000; background:#FFFFFF}
P {font-size:12pt; text-indent:0.5in}
</style>

<body>

<h2 id="h2_1">This heading in red on a white background.</h2>

All text is yellow on a blue background.<BR>

This text is not indented, except for the margins. During the whole
of a dull, dark, and soundless day in the autumn of the year, when the clouds
hung oppressively low in the heavens, I had been passing alone,
on horseback, through a singularly dreary tract of country; and at length
found myself, as the shades of the evening drew on, within view of the
melancholy House of Usher.

<p id="p_1">
This text is indented. During the whole of a dull, dark, and soundless day
```

18

USING CASCADING STYLE SHEETS

in the autumn of the year, when the clouds hung oppressively low in the heavens, I had been passing alone, on horseback, through a singularly dreary tract of country; and at length found myself, as the shades of the evening drew on, within view of the melancholy House of Usher.</p>

```
</body>
</html>
```

Save the file as `embedded.html`.

> **NOTE**
>
> The text for the examples in this chapter were taken from "The Fall of the House of Usher" by Edgar Allan Poe as reprinted by the Gutenberg Project. The Gutenberg Project is dedicated to scanning, transcribing, and other methods of converting public domain books and other written works into "plain vanilla" electronic text. You can access the complete text to Poe's classic, in addition to a host of other classics, at the project's home page:
>
> `www.promo.net/pg/.`

Figure 18.4 shows the finished page as it appears in Internet Explorer 4.0.

FIGURE 18.4.

The results of individual, or embedded, style sheet commands.

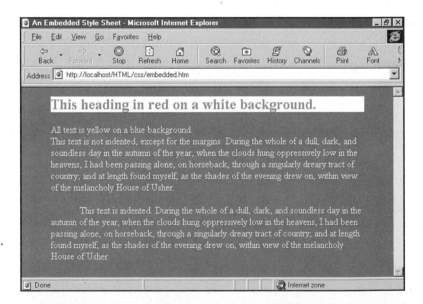

> **NOTE**
>
> You might have noticed by now that I'm using paragraph tags as containers, with a beginning <P> and an ending </P>. This is part of the HTML 4 specification, although it's

not required. However, if you're going to work with cascading style sheets, you need to get into the habit of using closing tags with elements such as paragraphs, table cells, and similar items. A style sheet won't recognize a new paragraph until you specifically mark it with <P> and </P>. This is true even if it's a new paragraph by default, such as the first line following a heading.

When you begin using style sheets, the embedded variety is probably the one you'll find yourself using most often. Its page-by-page control lets you modify the look and behavior of each page in a site. However, if strong uniformity is required for a set of pages or the entire site, a link to a master style sheet is called for.

A Linked Cascading Style Sheet

Creating a style sheet that can be linked to and used by any number of other pages is really a simple task. It's called a *linked* style sheet because all the style definitions sit in one file, and the actual HTML page creates a link to it when the page is loaded. Creating a linked style is similar to an embedded style. Begin with a blank page in your HTML editor.

NOTE

Many editors automatically include the basic HTML structure tags when you create a new document, including the <HTML>, <HEAD>, and <BODY> tags. Because a linked style sheet doesn't require anything, you will probably find this task easier with a text editor.

Place the style definitions between the tags the same way you did for the embedded style sheet:

```
BODY {background:#0000FF; color: #FFFF00;
➡margin-left:0.5in; margin-right:0.5in}
H2 {font-size:18pt; color:#FF0000; background:#FFFFFF}
P {font-size:12pt; text-indent:0.5in}
```

Now, instead of saving your work as an HTML file, save it with the extension .css. For this example, the entire name is master_style.css.

Next, integrate the master style file with an HTML page. Repeat this process for any pages that use the same style definitions. To do this, first select an existing HTML page to which you want to apply the master style. For now, use a stripped-down version of the page from the embedded style sheet example:

```
<!DOCTYPE HTML PUBLIC "-//IETF//DTD HTML 4.0//EN">
<html>
<head>
<title>A Linked Style Sheet</title>
</head>

<body>
```

```
<h2>This is a heading.</h2>

It was a mystery all insoluble; nor could I grapple with the shadowy
fancies that crowded upon me as I pondered.

<p>
I was forced to fall back upon the unsatisfactory conclusion, that while,
beyond doubt, there are combinations of very simple natural objects which
have the power of thus affecting us, still the analysis of this power lies
among considerations beyond our depth.</p>

</body>
</html>
```

Open the file in your HTML editor, and then place the following line within the <HEAD> tag, below the <TITLE>:

```
<link rel=stylesheet href="master_style.css" type="text/css">
```

The <LINK> tag identifies another file that's related in some way to the current page and is also used to create navigation buttons on browsers such as Mosaic. In this case, it identifies a cascading style sheet in the same directory as the Web page. If this were a JavaScript Accessible Style Sheet (JASS), the type would be text/jass. Creating styles with JASS is covered in Chapter 21, "Using JavaScript Style Sheets."

The complete header now looks like this:

```
<head>
<title>A Linked Style Sheet</title>
<link rel=stylesheet href="master_style.css" type="text/css">
</head>
```

Save the file as linked.html.

All the affected tags in the Web page will be interpreted according to the styles you've set forth in the .css file. The results of the sample page using an externally linked style sheet are shown in Figure 18.5. The page doesn't contain any other style sheet information, other than the location of the .css file.

> **NOTE**
>
> Some Web servers require registering a MIME type for style sheets before the server can deliver the linked style sheet to the browser. The Web administrator needs to know that the suffix is .css and the MIME type is text/css.

With the style information in its own file, you can use it on any number of pages by simply adding the <LINK> tag in the document header.

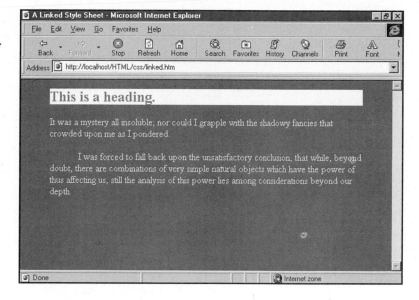

FIGURE 18.5.

This page includes a link to an external style sheet.

Combining Style Sheet Techniques

Sometimes one style sheet solution isn't enough, so designers with complex requirements benefit from mixing style sheet techniques. Mixing takes full advantage of the cascading feature of style sheets. Multiple techniques are resolved by the browser in the following manner:

- First, linked style sheets are applied globally.
- If an embedded style sheet is encountered on the same page with a linked style sheet, the embedded style overrides the linked style if there's a conflict.
- Inline styles override both embedded and linked styles.

This orderly and predictable implementation lets you define a single style sheet for an entire site, modify individual pages to support specific tasks with an embedded style, and use inline styles to tweak the details of specific lines.

18

USING
CASCADING
STYLE SHEETS

NOTE

If your site includes a multitude of pages, linked styles, and embedded styles, it's easy to lose track of what uses what and where any one style is overridden. To make your life easier, keep the linked styles as generic as possible, and then apply other style sheet techniques only when they're required to create specific effects, such as formatting for tables or margins for a set of images.

> **TIP**
>
> Style sheet syntax is temperamental—everything has to be in the right place for it to function well. If your page doesn't display the style you specified, check your syntax carefully. A misplaced curly bracket, colon, semicolon, or other punctuation in the style definition could render your style useless. If you find no problems with the syntax, then look for problems with any tables, such as closing tags for all rows, cells, and other elements.

Text-Specific Style Attributes

The face of the Web can't change for the better if designers don't understand some text-based fundamentals before putting style sheets to use. Some graphic designers spend entire careers dedicated to the study of typography. It's undeniably an art, requiring a familiarity not only with countless font faces, but also related attributes, such as weight, size variations, styles, families, and how to artistically use all these aspects in attractive combinations.

The good news is, you don't have to spend a lifetime learning all these things. All you need are a few simple guidelines to keep your page attractive and readable.

> **NOTE**
>
> Everything you want to know about type and more is covered in *TypeStyle* by Daniel Will-Harris (Peachpit Press). It covers the issues that affect anyone who works with words—how to combine different typefaces to make pages easier to read and, more important, how to avoid ugly and embarrassing mistakes.

The following text and text-related attributes are available for use in all methods of style sheets:

- `font-family:` This attribute controls the face of the font by setting arguments for either of the following:

  The name of the typeface you want to use. Here is a sample style specification for Times:

  `{font-family: times}`

  Because an individual computer might not have the installed font of your preference, you might want to add a similar alternative:

  `{font-family: times, garamond}`

  If a font name in your style definition is more than one word, such as Goudy Old Style, you'll need to put quotations around it, such as `font-family: times "goudy old "style", garamond`. Otherwise, quotes aren't necessary.

Most computers, including all with Microsoft Windows, come equipped with standard fonts, such as Times and Helvetica. They might have different names, like Dutch or Arial, but they're essentially the same thing. You can find a lot more typefaces on inexpensive CD-ROMs or professional-quality fonts from companies like BitStream (`www.bitstream.com`) or Image Club (`www.imageclub.com`).

As a last resort, you can add a generic family name that tells the browser to pick a typeface that at least shares the same basic attributes as your other choices:

```
{font-family: serif}
```

The following type families are recognized with style sheets:

serif   Serif fonts are a good choice for long sections of text. Popular serifs include Times New Roman and Garamond.

sans serif   This font family includes popular choices such as Arial, Helvetica, and Avante Garde. Sans serif fonts are often used for headings to complement serif body text.

cursive   These are script fonts—fonts that look as though they have been handwritten. They include faces such as Zapf Chancery and Park Avenue.

fantasy   Fantasy fonts are decorative and useful for stylish headings and titles. Typically, however, they're not practical for body text or long headings. Examples include Blippo, Hobo, and Broadway.

monospace   This type family is a throwback to the days of typewriters and teletype machines. *Monospace* means every letter takes an equal amount of space—an *i* takes as much space as an *m*. Most fonts are proportional, which means each letter takes up a space that's proportional to the individual letter's size and style, instead of being forced to fit in an exact amount of space. In proportional fonts, an *i* takes about a fourth of the space an *m* does. Examples of monospace include Courier or American Typewriter; they're used to represent lines of code or things the user should type.

The traditional guideline for selecting serif versus sans serif fonts is to use serif fonts for body text and sans serif fonts for headings or small blocks of text.

There's a good reason for this choice. Research and experience indicate that serif fonts are easier to read. However, sans serif fonts are becoming increasingly popular as body text fonts in Web browsers, partly because serifs don't always translate well across a variety of

continues

continued

screens and screen resolutions. Sans serif faces don't have the extra ornamentation to worry about.

It all comes down to good judgment. You need to base the use of serif or sans serif fonts on whether the pages are attractive and easy to read.

TIP

Use a typeface family as the last item in a `font-family` list, because it covers your font choices as completely as possible. Even if a specific typeface is unavailable on a given computer, a similar one in the same category is likely to be available. A savvy designer includes a list of choices, from top choice through last choice, and ends with the category. For example, if you prefer three specific serif typefaces, then the final attribute appears as follows:

`{font-family: garamond, goudy, times, serif}`

■ **`font size:`** Sizing in style sheets offers the designer five measurement options:

points To set a font in point size, use the abbreviation `pt` immediately next to the numeric size: `{font-size: 12pt}`. This standard is the one most designers use.

pixels Pixels are specified with the `px` abbreviation: `{font-size: 24px}`. A pixel is one dot on a screen; the number of pixels varies with the size of the screen. Many people use a screen 800×600 pixels in size, although there are still a lot of 640×480 screens. Incidentally, 640×480 was used for the screen images captured for this book.

TIP

Most Web designers are more comfortable with the point and pixel values for setting font sizes. However, if you prefer another method and find it easy for you to use, that's fine, too. The best advice I can give is to choose a method and stick with it. Consistency is a smart approach to creating styles and makes it easier to adjust the style to fit changing demands.

---

inches If you'd rather set your fonts in inches, simply use `in` and the numerical size, in inches, of the font size you need: `{font-size: 1in}`.

centimeters   Some people might prefer centimeters, represented by `cm` and used in the same way as points and inches: `{font-size: 5cm}`.

percentage   As a last resort, you might want to set a percentage of the default point size: `{font-size: 150%}`.

- **font-style:** This attribute typically dictates the style of text, such as placing it in italics. The following is the appropriate syntax to do this:

  `{font-style: italic}`

  You might think that another value for `font-style` would be bold, but that's covered by `font-weight`. The other legal values for this attribute are `normal` and `oblique`; `normal` reverts the text to its default status, and `oblique` is similar to `italic`, except that it's slanted manually instead of relying on the true italic version of the typeface.

- **font-weight:** The thickness of a typeface is referred to as its *weight*. As with font faces, font weights rely on the existence of the corresponding font and weight on an individual's machine. A range of values are available in style sheets, including the following: `extra-light`, `demi-light`, `light`, `medium`, `extra-bold`, `demi-bold`, and `bold`.

  Before you assign font weights, make sure the font face you're applying the weight to has that weight available. Always check your work on a variety of platforms and machines, when possible, to see whether you have been able to get a strong design, even though some machines might not support the font or the font weight in question. As a general rule, `bold` is always available.

- **text-decoration:** This attribute decorates text; it includes the values `none`, `underline`, `italic`, and `line-through`.

NOTE

The `text-decoration` attribute is a favorite of people who dislike underlined links. You can use the `A {text-decoration: none}` style definition to globally shut off underlined hyperlinks. For an inline style, place the value within the link you want to control:

```
<a style="text-decoration: none" href="nowhere.html" alt="Nowhere">
Link to nowhere</a>.
```

- **line-height:** Another important text-related aspect is *leading*, which is the amount of line spacing between lines of text. This space should be consistent, or the result is uneven, unattractive spacing. You can use the `line-height` attribute to set the distance between the baselines, or bottoms, of lines of text.

  To set the leading of a paragraph, use the `line-height` attribute in points, inches, centimeters, pixels, or percentages in the same way you describe `font-size` attributes:

  `P {line-height: 14pt}`

TIP

When using leading with the `line-height` attribute, your headings can still have plenty of space before the following text. This spacing is possible because leading works in style sheets by referring to the baseline of a piece of text. To avoid placing extra space between heading and body attributes, set the paragraph top margins to 0. You'll still get some space, but it'll be a natural amount rather than the leading equivalent. Another trick is to make sure your leading is less than your body-text point size.

In the next section you'll work on margins, indents, and other text alignment attributes. They will help add some texture and white space to your pages.

Margins, Indents, and Text Alignment Attributes

Despite what the standard version of HTML would have you believe, pages don't exist just to have you place text from border to border with a minimum of white space. Creating a good design includes setting margins and indents so the reader's eye is guided from one element to the next, and having enough white space to give the reader a break in between thoughts. The next set of attributes serve this noble purpose:

- **`margin-left`:** To set a left margin, use a distance in points, inches, centimeters, or pixels. The following sets a left margin to three-fourths of an inch:

  `{margin-left: .75in}`

- **`margin-right`:** For a right margin, select from the same measurement options provided for the `margin-left` attribute:

  `{margin-right: 50px}`

- **`margin-top`:** You set top margins by using the same measurement values as for other margin attributes:

  `{margin-top: 20pt)`

- **`text-indent`:** Again, points, inches, centimeters, or pixel values can be assigned to this attribute, which indents any type of text:

  `{text-indent: 0.5in)`

  Internet Explorer also allows negative margin and text indent values, which you can use to create interesting and unusual effects, such as overlapping text and hanging indents (an "outdent") for a contemporary design.

- **`text-align`:** With this long-awaited feature, you can justify text. Values include `left`, `center`, and `right`.

  `{text-align: right}`

  Text alignment is a powerful layout tool, and as a designer, you will enjoy being able to place text in a variety of alignments without having to rely on tables, divisions, or other, less graceful HTML workarounds of the past. Remember, text justification requires a fine eye. Left justification is the only reasonable choice for long blocks of text because it's more readable and easier for the eye to follow. Right justification comes in handy for short bursts of text, such as pull-quotes. Use centered text sparingly. Even though it seems natural to want to center text, it's actually more difficult to read and looks clichéd and ungainly.

> **TIP**
>
> Full justification (to the right and left margins at the same time) isn't available yet. The only available workaround is to create the text as a graphic image, and then load the graphic where you want the justified text. It's an awkward way of accomplishing the task, but full justification should be added as an option in a later HTML revision. For now, make sure your Web pages use generous margins and white space to lead the reader's eyes where you want them to go.

With these attributes in hand, it's time to work on another example to see how they work in an HTML page.

Margins and Justification Controls

To control margins in a style sheet, begin with a simple HTML page that includes a basic style sheet, such as this one:

```
<!DOCTYPE HTML PUBLIC "-//IETF//DTD HTML 4.0//EN">
<html>

<head>
<title>Styles</title>
</head>

<style>
<!--
BODY {background: white}
H1 {font-family: verdana, helvetica, arial, san-serif ;
➥font-size: 18pt; font-style: normal}
H2 {font-family: verdana, helvetica, arial, san-serif ;
➥font-size: 14pt; font-style: normal}
P {font-family: garamond, goudy, times, serif;
➥font-size: 12pt; font-style: normal; line-height: 14pt}
A {text-decoration: none; font-weight: bold}
-->
</style>

<BODY>
<H1>The Destination</H1>

<P>Nevertheless, in this <A href="mansion.html">mansion of gloom</A>
I now proposed to myself a sojourn of some weeks. Its proprietor,
```

```
Roderick Usher, had been one of my boon companions in boyhood; but
many years had elapsed since our last meeting.</P>

<H2>Why I Came</H2>

<P>A <A href="letter.html">letter</A>, however, had lately reached me
in a distant part of the country--a letter from him--which, in its
wildly importunate nature, had admitted of no other than a personal
reply.  The MS gave evidence of nervous agitation.</P>

</body>

</html>
```

Add the following margin syntax for the BODY attribute in the <STYLE> tag section:

```
BODY {margin-left: 0.75in; margin-right: 0.75in; margin-top: 0.25in;
➡background: white}
```

You use the BODY style as the base for other elements. For example, setting the typeface to Garamond for the body makes Garamond the base typeface for paragraphs, hyperlinks, and other items.

Save the file as margin.html and view it in a browser. The results on Internet Explorer are shown in Figure 18.6.

FIGURE 18.6.

Margins create attractive white space around the page, giving it "breathing room" from the edges of the browser window.

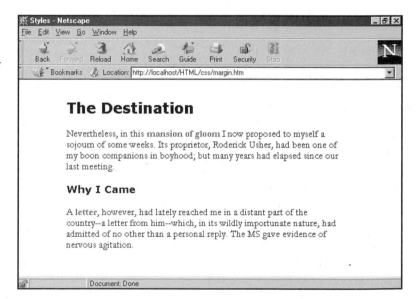

In this example, margin values for the entire page were changed by using the BODY attribute. You can also add margins to any other HTML tag. For example, if you want to set different margins for the headers, place the margin values in the string next to the header of your choice. Similarly, you can adjust margins on individual paragraphs by adding the margin values you want to the paragraph string.

If you're including margins for the BODY style definition as well as in the P style definition, be sure your paragraph margins are larger than those you've selected for the body of the text. Otherwise, you won't be able to see the difference. The browser ignores the lesser margin and uses the largest value available between the two.

Next, add justification to create more visual interest on the page. Alignment, or *justification*, plays an important part in design. This next example illustrates how to change the justification to affect the text.

Beginning with the margin.html example, add the text-align attribute to the two heading tags:

```
BODY {margin-left: 0.75in; margin-right: 0.75in; margin-top: 0.25in;
➥background: white}

H1 {font-family: verdana, helvetica, arial, san-serif;
➥font-size:18pt; font-style:normal; text-align:left}
H2 {font-family: verdana, helvetica, arial, san-serif;
➥font-size:14pt; font-style:normal; text-align:right}
P {font-family: garamond; font-size: 12pt; font-style: normal;
➥line-height: 11pt}
A {text-decoration: none; font-weight: bold}
```

Because you're justifying paragraphs separately, add those attributes with inline style. The entire file should look like this:

```
<!DOCTYPE HTML PUBLIC "-//IETF//DTD HTML 4.0//EN">
<HTML>

<HEAD>
<TITLE>Text Styles</TITLE>
</HEAD>

<STYLE>
<!--
BODY {margin-left: 0.75in; margin-right: 0.75in; margin-top: 0.25in;
➥background: white}
H1 {font-family: verdana, helvetica, arial, san-serif;
➥font-size:18pt; font-style:normal; text-align:left}
H2 {font-family: verdana, helvetica, arial, san-serif;
➥font-size:14pt; font-style:normal; text-align:right}
P {font-family: garamond; font-size: 12pt; font-style: normal;
➥line-height: 11pt}
A {text-decoration: none; font-weight: bold}
-->
</STYLE>

<BODY>
<H1>The Destination</H1>

<P>Nevertheless, in this <A href="mansion.html">mansion of gloom</A>
I now proposed to myself a sojourn of some weeks. Its proprietor,
Roderick Usher, had been one of my boon companions in boyhood; but
many years had elapsed since our last meeting.</P>

<H2>Why I Came</H2>
```

```
<P>A <A href="letter.html">letter</A>, however, had lately reached me
in a distant part of the country--a letter from him--which, in its
wildly importunate nature, had admitted of no other than a personal
reply. The MS gave evidence of nervous agitation.</P>

</BODY>

</HTML>
```

Save this page as justify.html and view it in your browser. The look of the page is becoming more interesting, as shown in Figure 18.7.

FIGURE 18.7.

Justification helps make a Web page more visually interesting, even without pictures.

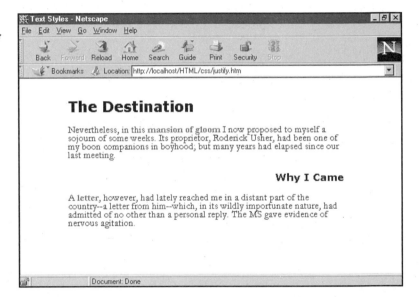

So far, you've learned how to change the typeface and its related attributes, change its style, and add some spacing and justification around the page. Now it's time to get out a paintbrush and see what can happen with color.

Color and Background

Take a look at the BODY style definition and you'll notice a background attribute used to set the background color of the entire page. You can also use the bgcolor attribute with the <BODY> tag, although its use is deprecated in HTML 4.0. The background style attribute wasn't always used in early implementations of CSS, and bgcolor was used as a workaround.

> **TIP**
>
> Now that CSS is a stable part of both Navigator and Internet Explorer, you can drop using the bgcolor attribute.

You can add background color to other styles besides BODY. For example, you can throw a splash of color behind a paragraph or a header simply by placing the background attribute with that tag. In addition, you can change the text color for any tag, which is particularly satisfying for Web designers who are constantly seeking to use browser-based color to enliven pages rather than rely on time-consuming graphics solutions.

The syntax required to create background color is the style attribute background convention and a hexadecimal color value:

```
{background: #FFFFFF}
```

The value for the color is a hexadecimal triplet, which is the standard Web convention for defining a color. It works like this: Begin with red, green, and blue (the three basic colors for an additive system). If you put the maximum value of all three together, you get white. Take away all three, and you get black. Increase or decrease all three by the same value, and you get shades of gray.

With that bit of housekeeping out of the way, each pair of digits in the value stands for one of the colors—in order, red, green, and blue. The two digits are a hexadecimal number, represented in our decimal numbering system as 0 (hexadecimal 00) to 255 (hexadecimal FF). So, green is represented by 00FF00, yellow is FFFF00, and so on.

> **NOTE**
>
> Internet Explorer allows color names for the color and background attributes. Color names include black, silver, gray, white, maroon, red, purple, fuchsia, green, lime, olive, yellow, navy, blue, teal, and aqua.

Similarly, you can invoke background graphics by replacing the hex argument with a URL:

```
{background: http://myserver.com/cool.gif}
```

You change the text color by using the color attribute and a color value or name:

```
{color: #FF6633}
```

When you use color and background, make sure you're working with compatible combinations or you'll end up with an unreadable mess. For example, red text on a blue background is virtually impossible to read, but yellow on blue works very well.

Adding Color

For the next example, you'll add a background color to a heading, leaving the rest of the page with its default color.

Open the justify.html file (used in the previous example) in your HTML editor. Add background:#99CCCC to the H2 style variable so that it now reads as follows:

```
H2 {font-family: verdana, helvetica, arial, san-serif; font-size:14pt;
➥font-style:normal; text-align:right; background:#99CCCC}
```

Save the file as `color.html` and view it in your browser. The result is shown in Figure 18.8.

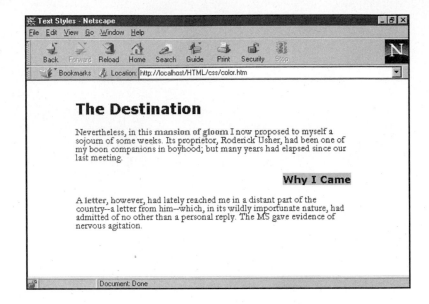

The contrast you gain by using different colors can be very effective, but you must be careful and consistent with your choice of color palettes. If it's done well, the color contrast can add an extra bit of emphasis and style to a Web page.

The same process works with sections of text by following the same guidelines as `background` and using the `color` attribute:

1. Open `color.html` in your editor.

2. Add `color:#FF0033` after the `background` tag for the `H2` style:

   ```
   H2 {font-family: verdana, helvetica, arial, san-serif;
   ➥font-size:14pt; font-style:normal; text-align:right;
   ➥background:#99CCCC; color: #FF0033}
   ```

3. Save the file as `color2.html` and view it in a browser. The result is a page with a lot of style, completely controlled by using an embedded style sheet.

With some basic appearance and style treatments under your belt, it's time to move on to the more mundane matters of organization. The next section shows how to define style sheets as groups and create subclasses of different styles.

Organizing the Style

There are two organizational techniques that can help make style sheets easier to use. The first is *grouping*, which reduces the amount of typing needed by creating logical groups of styles. If you need variations on a style, you can use *classes*. This technique lets you assign different styles to the same HTML tag.

Grouping Style Sheets

The first grouping technique assigns the same style attributes to the same set of tags. Without groups, the syntax would look like this:

```
H1 {font-family: arial; font-size 14pt; color: #000000}
H2 {font-family: arial; font-size 14pt; color: #000000}
H3 {font-family: arial; font-size 14pt; color: #000000}
```

Here's the same example grouped:

```
H1, H2, H3 {font-family: arial; font-size 14pt; color: #000000}
```

In addition to grouping styles, you can also group attributes within a style by using a string of values in an attribute category. Using the syntax from previous examples, here's the long way of writing a style for BODY:

```
BODY {font-family: arial, san-serif; font-size: 12pt; line-height: 14pt;
➡font-weight: bold; font-style: normal}
```

With attribute grouping, all the variables are lumped together under font. The result looks something like this:

```
BODY {font: bold 12pt/14pt arial, san-serif}
```

The same process applies for other groups of attributes. For example, use margin followed by the top, right, and left margin values:

```
BODY {margin: .10in .75in .75in}
```

If you use two variables, then the second number is applied to both the right and left margins. If one number is used, then it's applied to all three margins.

Note that the variables are separated only by a space. Be sure not to use commas, or the page might generate an error or display in unpredictable ways.

When you're grouping attributes, be sure to remember that attribute order is important. Font weight and style must come before other font attributes; the size of the font comes before the leading; and then you can add additional information to the string. Note that there are no commas between the attributes, except in the case of font families. More information on the correct order is in Appendix C.

Assigning Classes

Additional variations on a style are possible by assigning classes to individual HTML tags. You do this by adding an extension name to any HTML tag. This name can be almost anything, such as `BobText`, `hippo`, `topText`, `footerStuff`, or anything else that comes to mind. Using the preceding examples, there are two styles for paragraphs—one justifies left and the other right. In the example, you used inline styles to get the effect you wanted, but by using classes, you can define it ahead of time:

```
P.left {font-family:garamond; font-size:12pt; font-style:normal;
➥line-height:11pt; text-align:left}

P.right {font-family:garamond; font-size:12pt; font-style:normal;
➥line-height:11pt; text-align:right}
```

In the first definition, a new `<P>` style is created called `left`. This style is used in the document as `<P class="left">`. It uses 12-point Garamond text that's aligned to the left margin. The second definition creates a new `<P>` style called `right`. It's used as `<P class="right">` and is the same as the previous style definition, except it justifies text to the right margin.

TIP

This is a good time to use both kinds of grouping to simplify creating and later editing the styles. Begin with a foundation for the `<P>` tag:

```
P {font:garamond 12pt/11pt normal}
```

After the common ground has been defined, you can add the class descriptions for the two variances:

```
P.left {text-align:left}
P.right {text-align:right}
```

When the whole batch is put together, it looks like this:

```
P {font:garamond 12pt/11pt normal}
P.left {text-align:left}
P.right {text-align:right}
```

When you go back to review the style for changes or troubleshooting later, you can see where the classes share common traits and where they're different. It's much cleaner and much easier to read than the original method.

When you use the style in the document, use the `class` attribute to identify which version of the tag is applied:

```
<P class="left">His reserve had been always excessive and habitual.</P>
<P class="right">His reserve had been always excessive and habitual.</P>
```

All the `<P>` tags that include `class="left"` use the `P.left` style attributes, and the `<P>` tags with `class="right"` use the `P.right` attributes defined for that class.

If you use the new definitions with grouping for the `justify.html` file, the style section now looks like this:

```
<STYLE>
<!--
BODY {margin-left: 0.75in; margin-right: 0.75in; margin-top: 0.10in}

H1, H2 {font-family: verdana, helvetica, arial, san-serif}
H1 {font-size:18pt; text-align:left}
H2 {font-size:14pt; text-align:right}

P {font:garamond 12pt/11pt normal}
P.left {text-align:left}
P.right {text-align:right}

A {text-decoration: none; font-weight: bold}
-->
</STYLE>
```

The completed file is saved as `group.html`, with each line of style much shorter and succinct, and easier to read and understand. The visual result is still the same. (See Figure 18.9.)

`Group.html` uses the same styles as `justify.html`, but styles are defined in a different way. Although the definitions use different syntax, you won't notice any difference between the image in Figure 18.9 and the one in Figure 18.7.

18

FIGURE 18.9.

Using style and attribute grouping creates the same page as justify.html.

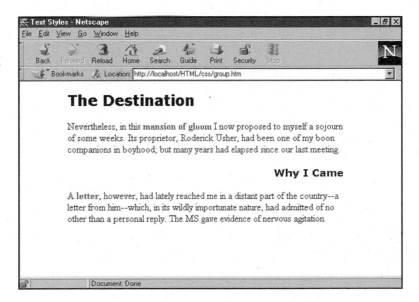

The Destination

Nevertheless, in this mansion of gloom I now proposed to myself a sojourn of some weeks. Its proprietor, Roderick Usher, had been one of my boon companions in boyhood; but many years had elapsed since our last meeting.

Why I Came

A letter, however, had lately reached me in a distant part of the country--a letter from him--which, in its wildly importunate nature, had admitted of no other than a personal reply. The MS gave evidence of nervous agitation.

Style Sheets Everywhere: A Host of Examples

Because style sheets are so flexible, now is a good time to spend some time working with a variety of templates to get a better feel for the types of effects that are possible. You'll notice that most of the examples don't involve big complicated style sheets. My own personal opinion is that the simpler it is, the easier it is to understand and maintain.

The following examples change only a few attributes of the given styles, such as fonts, colors, and alignment. The range of tags affected is also limited, including headers and paragraph styles. However, they are the basis of style sheets you can modify and use on your own Web pages.

All the examples use embedded style sheets. As an added feature, the sample code is also shown so you can see how it would appear as a linked style—useful for using the same style sheet on multiple pages. Also note that style sheets aren't the only method used to control the page appearance. There's also ample use of tables, HTML tags, and attributes.

> **TIP**
>
> It needs to be said again and again and again: Know your audience. It's much more important to get your message across than to prove how incredibly clever you can be with style sheets, especially when you're working with business clients. If the choice is between the client's business interests and a designer's best judgment, choose the business interest. It pays better for everyone involved.

What I hope to accomplish with these examples is to inspire you to take some time and work with style sheets. It's a good evening project when the thought of watching television reruns again makes your stomach churn. Success with style sheets will give you power over your pages and make working with Dynamic HTML much more enjoyable.

But enough of this lecturing from the soapbox. Here's what you came for...

Example 1: A Report Cover Page

Start off with a simple cover page for an online report. When you start working with layers later this week, you could use it as a top layer, with other pages (layers) beneath it.

Open a new page in your HTML editor, and begin with the basic structure of an HTML document.

```
<!DOCTYPE HTML PUBLIC "-//IETF//DTD HTML 4.0//EN">
<HTML>

<HEAD>
<TITLE>Knee Deep in the Green Stuff</TITLE>
</HEAD>

<STYLE>
<!--
```

```
-->
</STYLE>

<BODY>
</BODY>

</HTML>
```

Notice the comment tags used within the <STYLE> tags to make sure that style-incompatible browsers won't display the contents as other HTML text.

Because this is a cover page, keep it simple. There's no use cluttering up the screen with a bunch of superfluous graphics or text. Have a title, subtitle, and organization name, along with one image. Add all these items to the body of the page:

```
<BODY bgcolor=white>
<H1>Knee Deep</H1>
<IMG SRC="/mrfd/images/cleanup-r.gif">
<H2>Incident Analysis:<BR>Post Creek Poison Spill</H2>
<H3>Missoula Regional<BR>Hazardous Materials</H3>
</BODY>
```

As a default for all the examples, set the page background color to white.

> **TIP**
>
> Don't forget, you can also use the hexadecimal triplet method of specifying colors. I just used the color keywords to make it easier to read. The hexadecimal value for white is #FFFFFF.

You're off to a fine start, if slightly bland, as shown in Figure 18.10. This is how the page appears on a browser without styles. It's your job to do something more with it.

The treatment for this page begins by adding white space around the borders of the page:

```
BODY {margin:.25in .5in}
```

This definition adds a quarter-inch of space to the top and bottom of the page, and a half-inch to the left and right sides. It uses attribute grouping to eliminate the need to use margin-top, margin-bottom, margin-left, and margin-right, which require a lot more typing.

Next, set the typeface for the first three headings:

```
H1, H2, H3 {font-family:helvetica, arial, sans-serif}
```

Because this is the first page of a report, assume that the rest of the pages will be added through layering on the same page. You can also assume that the rest of the document doesn't need right-aligned headings. To use right-alignment for the first page only, create a new class called page1 with the desired alignment for the cover:

```
H1.page1, H2.page1, H3.page1 {text-align:right}
```

Figure 18.10.

*The initial title page is
serviceable, but doesn't
have a very interesting
design.*

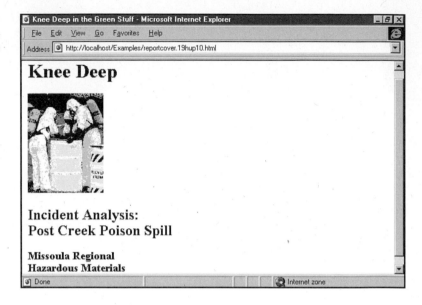

Now, finish the work on your three headings by setting the margins to accommodate your image, which would force part of the cover off the bottom of the page:

```
H1.page1 {margin-bottom:-.15in}
H2.page1 {margin-top:-.15in; margin-bottom:0in}
H3.page1 {color:white; background-color:black; margin-top:0in}
```

Notice the use of negative numbers. Instead of adding space, they subtract space, so whatever comes after `H1.page1` and before `H2.page1` can come .15 inches closer to those respective elements.

To emphasize the section of the page marked with `<H3>`, its text is reversed in white against a black background. The finished style section now looks like this:

```
<STYLE>
<!--
BODY {margin:.25in .5in}

H1, H2, H3 {font-family:helvetica, arial, sans-serif}
H1.page1, H2.page1, H3.page1 {text-align:right}

H1.page1 {margin-bottom:-.15in}
H2.page1 {margin-top:-.15in; margin-bottom:0in}
H3.page1 {color:white; background-color:black; margin-top:0in}
-->
</STYLE>
```

To finish the job, you need to make additional modifications to the body of the page. For this, you need to add only a `class` attribute to each of the heading tags:

```
<H1 class="page1">Knee Deep</H1>
<IMG SRC="/mrfd/images/cleanup-r.gif">
<H2 class="page1">Incident Analysis:<BR>Post Creek Poison Spill</H2>
<H3 class="page1">Missoula Regional<BR>Hazardous Materials</H3>
```

Save the file as ReportCover.html. It should match Listing 18.1.

Listing 18.1. ReportCover.html.

```
<!DOCTYPE HTML PUBLIC "-//IETF//DTD HTML 4.0//EN">
<HTML>

<HEAD>
<title>Knee Deep in the Green Stuff</title>
</HEAD>

<STYLE>
<!--
BODY {margin:.25in .5in}

H1, H2, H3 {font-family:helvetica, arial, sans-serif}
H1.page1, H2.page1, H3.page1 {text-align:right}

H1.page1 {margin-bottom:-.15in}
H2.page1 {margin-top:-.15in; margin-bottom:0in}
H3.page1 {color:white; background-color:black; margin-top:0in}
-->
</STYLE>

<BODY bgcolor=white>
<H1 class="page1">Knee Deep</H1>
<IMG SRC="/mrfd/images/cleanup-r.gif">
<H2 class="page1">Incident Analysis:<BR>Post Creek Poison Spill</H2>
<H3 class="page1">Missoula Regional<BR>Hazardous Materials</H3>
</BODY>

</HTML>
```

When you view the final work in Internet Explorer, it looks like Figure 18.11. This cover can be reused for the same purpose, as long as the image remains close to the same size. If it gets too tall, then it will force the text off the bottom of the page and hide part of the design on smaller screens.

To make this example into a linked style sheet for use by other report covers, cut the <STYLE> tags and their contents and paste them into a new file called ReportCover.css. Now, in the header of the original ReportCover.html, add a new line below the closing </TITLE>:

```
<LINK rel=stylesheet href="ReportCover.css" type="text/css">
```

It will work exactly the same as the embedded style, but now it's easily accessible by other pages that want to use the same set of attributes.

18

USING
CASCADING
STYLE SHEETS

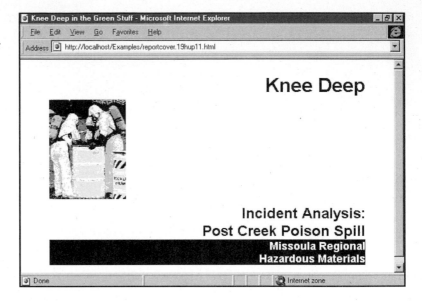

Example 2: Fun Stuff for Kids

This example is another fairly simple style implementation. The changes are few, but they do perk up a page geared toward kids and their parents. The format is an electronic newsletter, so the emphasis is on content rather than interactivity.

Begin with the basic HTML document in your editor (as you did in the previous example). The newsletter is composed of four basic parts: masthead, banner, headlines, and text. The first two appear only once on each page.

The masthead is set in a smaller heading font, the banner is set in the largest, and both elements are centered on the page:

```
<H5 align=center>Summer news and reviews * Where to find fun at Usher</H5>
<H1 align=center>KIDZ ZONE</H1>
```

Now supply headlines for each story, with the content roughly balanced across three columns. Use tables to give the three-column format enough padding so the text has "breathing room." A horizontal rule marks the end of a story:

```
<TABLE cellpadding="15">
<TR valign="top">
<TD>
<H2>A little about woodwork</H2>
In this there was much that reminded me of the specious totality of old
wood-work which has rotted for long years in some neglected vault, with no
disturbance from the breath of the external air.  Beyond this indication of
extensive decay, however, the fabric gave little token of instability.
</TD>
<TD>
```

```
Perhaps the eye of a scrutinizing observer might have discovered a barely
perceptible fissure, which, extending from the roof of the building in
front, made its way down the wall in a zigzag direction, until it became
lost in the sullen waters of the tarn.
<HR>
</TD>
<TD>
<H2>The arrival</H2>
Noticing these things, I rode over a short causeway to the house.  A
servant in waiting took my horse, and I entered the Gothic archway of the
hall.  A valet, of stealthy step, thence conducted me, in silence, through
many dark and intricate passages in my progress to the studio of his
master.
<HR>
</TD>
</TR>
</TABLE>
```

So far, the newsletter looks like Figure 18.12, which isn't bad—it just isn't that good.

FIGURE 18.12.

The start of the newsletter highlights the need for visual help, primarily in the masthead and banner.

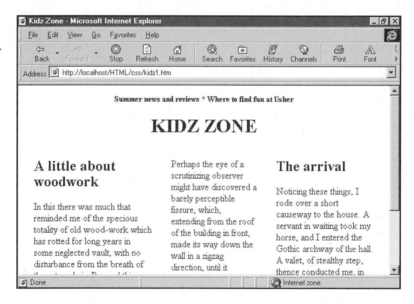

Now work on adding some pizzazz to make the page a little more interesting. First, add some white space to the top and sides to give your layout some freedom from the browser window. Then, continue with the masthead, banner, and headlines. Set all three in Comic Sans, a slightly playful but still very readable typeface:

```
BODY {margin-left:36pt; margin-right:36pt; margin-top:24pt}
H1, H2, H5 {font-family:"comic sans ms", verdana, sans-serif;
➥text-align:center}
```

The details for the masthead and banner are next. Set the masthead on a yellow background, and set the banner in yellow on a blue background:

```
H1 {font-size:60pt; color:yellow; background-color:blue;
➥margin-top:0pt; margin-bottom:18pt}
H5 {font-size:12pt; background-color:yellow;
➥margin-top:36pt; margin-bottom:0pt}
```

Provide extra spacing between the banner and the table below by using the margin-bottom attribute.

> **TIP**
>
> You're probably wondering why you didn't use blue on yellow in the masthead as an
> opposite to the banner's yellow on blue. That's because blue on yellow looks pretty close
> to black, and black is actually a little easier to read. So you left the masthead text with the
> default black and just added a yellow background.

Make the headlines similar to the masthead and banner, but set them flush left so they're easier
to read. Also, give the horizontal rules at the end of each story a little extra touch by coloring
them green and making them thick enough to be noticed. The green is a nice accent to the
blue and yellow at the top of the page. Define a big black line for the normal horizontal rule to
mark the end of the page:

```
H2 {font-size:18pt; text-align:left}
HR {color:black; height:16}
HR.green {color:green; height:8}
```

Last on the list is the body text. Instead of using paragraph tags, take advantage of the table
data tag. In some uses, the <TD> tag isn't used with a closing tag. For this style to work, the
</TD> tag is required:

```
TD {font-family:tahoma, arial, sans-serif; font-size:12pt; width:33%}
```

The width attribute at the end sets the width of the table cell, which is the same as using <TD
width="33%">. The finished style definition now looks like this:

```
<STYLE>
<!--
BODY {margin-left:36pt; margin-right:36pt; margin-top:24pt;
➥background:white}
H1, H2, H5 {font-family:"comic sans ms", verdana, sans-serif;
➥text-align:center}
H1 {font-size:60pt; color:yellow; background-color:blue;
➥margin-top:0pt; margin-bottom:18pt}
H2 {font-size:18pt; text-align:left}
H5 {font-size:12pt; background-color:yellow;
➥margin-top:36pt; margin-bottom:0pt}
TD {font-family:tahoma, arial, sans-serif; font-size:12pt; width:33%}
HR {color:black; height:16}
HR.green {color:green; height:8}
-->
</STYLE>
```

All that's left is to add the class name to the horizontal rule tags at the end of the stories:

```
<HR class="green">
```

When you're finished, save the file as Kidz.html. It should look something like Listing 18.2.

Listing 18.2. Kidz.html.

```
<!DOCTYPE HTML PUBLIC "-//IETF//DTD HTML 4.0//EN">
<HTML>

<HEAD>
<title>Kidz Zone</title>
</HEAD>

<STYLE>
<!--
BODY {margin-left:36pt; margin-right:36pt; margin-top:24pt;
➥background:white}
H1, H2, H5 {font-family:"comic sans ms", verdana, sans-serif;
➥text-align:center}
H1 {font-size:60pt; color:yellow; background-color:blue;
➥margin-top:0pt; margin-bottom:18pt}
H2 {font-size:18pt; text-align:left}
H5 {font-size:12pt; background-color:yellow;
➥margin-top:36pt; margin-bottom:0pt}
TD {font-family:tahoma, arial, sans-serif; font-size:12pt; width:33%}
HR {color:black; height:16}
HR.green {color:green; height:8}
-->
</STYLE>

<BODY>
<H5>Summer news and reviews * Where to find the fireworks</H5>
<H1>KIDZ ZONE</H1>
<TABLE cellpadding="15">
<TR valign="top">
<TD>
<H2>A little about woodwork</H2>
In this there was much that reminded me of the specious totality of old
wood-work which has rotted for long years in some neglected vault, with no
disturbance from the breath of the external air.  Beyond this indication of
extensive decay, however, the fabric gave little token of instability.
</TD>
<TD>
Perhaps the eye of a scrutinizing observer might have discovered a barely
perceptible fissure, which, extending from the roof of the building in
front, made its way down the wall in a zigzag direction, until it became
lost in the sullen waters of the tarn.
<HR class="green">
</TD>
<TD>
<H2>The arrival</H2>
Noticing these things, I rode over a short causeway to the house.  A
servant in waiting took my horse, and I entered the Gothic archway of the
hall.  A valet, of stealthy step, thence conducted me, in silence, through
```

continues

18

USING
CASCADING
STYLE SHEETS

Listing 18.2. continued

```
many dark and intricate passages in my progress to the studio of his
master.
<HR class="green">
</TD>
</TR></TABLE>
<HR>
</BODY>

</HTML>
```

When you view the page in Internet Explorer, it looks like Figure 18.13. It's really a simple style, but the extra color and sizing on the type make a big difference in its impact, even without the use of images.

FIGURE 18.13.

Using two typefaces and three colors to get an effect with much more visual appeal than the original model.

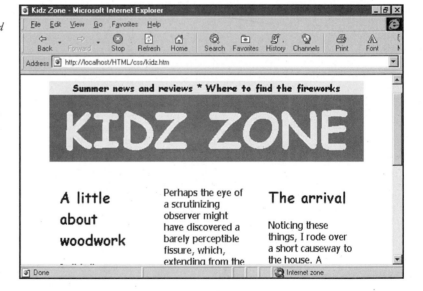

Example 3: A Variation on a Brochure

This example is called a brochure, but it could fit a lot of purposes on a Web site, such as a directory, one in a series of FAQs, or even a confirmation page. It uses negative margins as the first example does.

Begin with a foundation page in your HTML editor (as you did in the first example). This design is based on a two-column format, with the heading on the left and the text on the right. You want plenty of space between the two elements, so set the padding to 20 pixels. By the same token, this page should look the same no matter what kind of monitor the user has, so take the liberty of setting the width of the columns in pixels, also:

```
<TABLE cellpadding="20">
<TR>
<TD width="150">
<H2>Wild</H2>
<H2>flowers</H2>
</TD>
<TD width="300">
<P>I looked upon the scene before me--upon the mere house, and the simple
landscape features of the domain--upon the bleak walls--upon the vacant
eye-like windows--upon a few rank sedges--and upon a few white trunks of
decayed trees--with an utter depression of soul which I can compare to no
earthly sensation more properly than to the after-dream of the reveller
upon opium--the bitter lapse into everyday life--the hideous dropping off
of the veil.</P>
</TR>
</TABLE>
```

First are the routine tasks. Define a quarter-inch margin for the top and bottom and a half-inch for either side. Then, set the basic typeface for the heading and give the page a white background (I'm not very picky on this one):

```
BODY {margin:.25in .5in; background:white}
H2 {font-family:serif; font-size:14; text-align:center}
```

To get the effect you're after, split the heading tag into three separate classes: base, reverse, and large. The base is the same as the H2 definition in the last step, so move on to the reverse style. It should be white on black, with extra letter spacing to fill up the horizontal space:

```
H2.reverse {letter-spacing:1.25em; color:white;
➥background-color:black}
```

Next comes the big class. It includes a large initial letter, which you can take care of with an inline style a little bit later. For now, increase its size to 30 points, make it italic, and force it to the right margin. The negative top margin forces it close to the element that will appear above it (H2.reverse):

```
H2.big {font-style:italic; font-size:30; text-align:right;
➥margin-top:-48pt}
```

The last item is the body text of the brochure. Set it in a sans serif font to contrast with the heading; add extra space between the lines and slightly increased spacing between the letters. The effect is slightly reminiscent of seeds planted in a vegetable garden or a very ordered flower garden:

```
P {font:8pt verdana, tahoma, sans-serif; line-height:12pt;
➥letter-spacing:.1em}
```

Take a quick break from styles, and add the class information to the two headings:

```
<H2 class="reverse">Wild</H2>
<H2 class="big">flowers</H2>
```

Can you see where this is headed? The word *Wild* appears in a reversed banner over *flowers* in much bigger text. But what about that big first letter? Read on.

Use the <SPAN> tag to mark the first letter. This tag works well for marking individual letters or entire blocks of text. It's a great multipurpose style tag. Set the large letter in a different color (red) to stand out from the rest of the heading and add a striking spot of color to the page:

```
<H2 class="big">
<span style="font-size:72pt; color:red; font-weight:normal">f</span>
lowers</H2>
```

The *f* was separated from the rest of the word *flowers* in this line so it's easier to see the <SPAN> tag. When the page is displayed, the *f* will appear in line with the rest of the word.

Save the file as `DirtyFingernails.html` and display it on a browser. If your file is the same as Listing 18.3, then your browser should reveal something close to Figure 18.14.

Listing 18.3. `DirtyFingernails.html`.

```
<!DOCTYPE HTML PUBLIC "-//IETF//DTD HTML 4.0//EN">
<HTML>

<HEAD>
<title>Dirty Fingernails -- Wildflowers</title>
</HEAD>

<STYLE>
<!--
BODY {margin:.25in .5in; background:white}
H2 {font-family:serif; font-size:14; text-align:center}
H2.reverse {letter-spacing:1.25em; color:white; background-color:black}
H2.big {font-style:italic; font-size:30; text-align:right; margin-top:-48pt}
P {font:8pt verdana, tahoma, sans-serif; line-height:12pt; letter-spacing:.1em}
-->
</STYLE>

<BODY>
<TABLE cellpadding="20">
<TR>
<TD width="150">
<P> </P>
<H2 class="reverse">Wild</H2>
<H2 class="big">
<span style="font-size:72pt; color:red; font-weight:normal">
f</span>lowers</H2>
</TD>
<TD width="300">
<P>I looked upon the scene before me--upon the mere house, and the simple
landscape features of the domain--upon the bleak walls--upon the vacant
eye-like windows--upon a few rank sedges--and upon a few white trunks of
decayed trees--with an utter depression of soul which I can compare to no
earthly sensation more properly than to the after-dream of the reveller
upon opium--the bitter lapse into everyday life--the hideous dropping off
of the veil.</P>
</TR>
</TABLE>
</BODY>

</HTML>
```

FIGURE 18.14.

This brochure uses a negative margin and a big letter to create the effect of text overlapping other text.

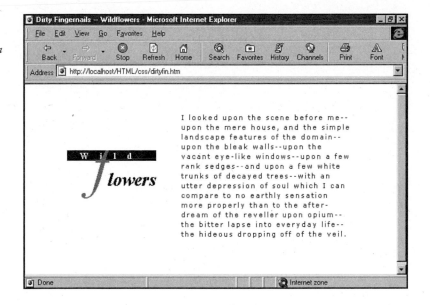

The downside of this example is that when it appears in a browser that's incompatible with style sheets, the whole effect is lost. However, it's still in a presentable enough form to be readable and acceptable to the user.

Summary

The concept of style sheets is very advanced for HTML. They give you designer tools to do things that were never even thought of in the early days of the Web. However, the actual implementation is still rather crude and unwieldy. Like most technologies associated with the Internet, don't expect the situation to last long. Between the collaborative processes at the World Wide Web Consortium and the intense competition between Microsoft and Netscape, you can expect more changes and advancements in the months and years to come.

As you begin to use style sheets to design your pages and then begin fine-tuning your creations, you'll certainly come head-to-head with the limitations of browsers. Remember, the concept and technology is new, and the stumbling blocks and brick walls will fall away as time progresses.

Cascading Style Sheets and Element Positioning

by Rick Darnell

IN THIS CHAPTER

One of the great drawbacks of using HTML up to this point has been its lack of tools for precise layout. This limitation has forced page authors to resort to tricks with tables, frames, and images to accomplish their design goals.

With the initial standard for Cascading Style Sheets (see the previous chapter, "Using Cascading Style Sheets"), many of the design problems were addressed, including margins, alignment, and text size. However, most of the CSS properties relate to appearance, not to actual positioning on the page.

Through the World Wide Web Consortium (W3C), Netscape and Microsoft put their heads together to create an addition to the CSS standard that provides a new set of style properties just for moving elements around on a page (`http://www.w3.org/TR/WD-positioning`)—and that's what you're going to explore in this chapter.

Relative Versus Absolute Positioning

One of the first issues to address in positioning is geography—how do you determine where on the page to place an element? Placement requires a coordinate system with predictable starting points. Actually, CSS positioning offers two systems.

The first is *relative*. You should recognize relative because it's been the default positioning system since HTML was created. Using traditional HTML relative positioning, each element's starting point depends on the previous element. For example, look at this snippet:

```
<H1>Here's the title</H1>
<P>Now is the time for <BR>someone to do something.</P>
```

The paragraph is placed one line down on the page *relative* to the heading above it, and the start of the text after the line break tag is placed *relative* to the preceding line. In this case, that means placing it on the next line at the same horizontal point as the beginning of the paragraph.

The second positioning system is *absolute*. Any element using absolute positioning can be placed anywhere on the page independently of any other element. The absolute system begins numbering at the top-left corner of the document as it's presented in the browser window. Therefore, the top-left corner coordinates are 0,0. On a 640×480 pixel display, the bottom-right corner would have the coordinates of 620,440, or somewhere in that neighborhood.

> **NOTE**
>
> Why isn't it possible to know the exact bottom-right coordinates? For several reasons. First, the size of the user's display can't be determined, so his or her display could just as easily be 1024×768 as 640×480. Then, if the browser is maximized in the display, there's still extra space needed for scrollbars, menus, status bars, and other features that eat into the available space. Or, the browser might be sharing the screen with other applications, or the page itself could be occupying a smaller frame within the current browser window.

In Windows 95/NT or Microsoft Office, for example, you might also have a taskbar or toolbar floating around on the screen that the browser has to work around. Last, the browser might not be maximized.

Because of the nature of HTML and browsers, there's no ironclad way of knowing where the bottom-right corner of your user's display is. Therefore, all coordinates begin with the top-left corner of the display.

With a basic definition of absolute and relative positioning systems in hand, you're left wondering why you should even bother with relative positioning. After all, absolute positioning allows you to put an element anywhere you want on the page, and it should be the same consistent spot on the same browser with the same resolution. With relative positioning, the location of the element is always going to depend on another element, which means you have less control.

However, remember that elements using absolute positioning are ignorant of each other, so it's harder to control which element is in line with other elements. Using relative positioning allows you to place other elements based on the location of specific points in the content, as you'll see in the last example of the section on relative positioning.

With a little theory under your belt, it's time to tackle some examples of positioning, beginning with absolute methods.

Absolute Positioning

I'll begin with a bit of HTML that will illustrate what's moving around on the page. Here is one paragraph that includes two spans in sequence:

```
<!DOCTYPE HTML PUBLIC "-//IETF//DTD HTML 4.0//EN">
<BODY>
<P>Here is the beginning of the contents.
 <SPAN id="frontside">Here is the beginning of the frontside span.
 Here is the end of the frontside span.</SPAN>
 <SPAN id="backside">Here's the backside span...and the end of the
 backside span.</SPAN>
 Here is the end of the contents.</P>
</BODY>
```

TIP

The <SPAN> element is an inline element. There won't be any additional paragraph breaks in the document, even though I've added some here to make the code easier to read.

When viewed in a browser, the result is just what you would expect. (See Figure 19.1.) It begins with the contents, followed inline by the outside span, which is followed inline by the inside span, and closed with the contents. Each element is placed inline relative to its predecessor on the page.

Figure 19.1.

The traditional representation of HTML is inline, relative to the previous element.

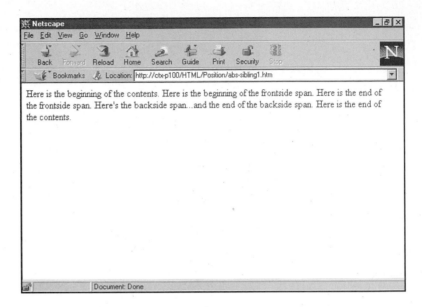

To alter this behavior, I'm adding a style sheet that moves the inside span:

```
<STYLE type="text/css">
#frontside {position:absolute; top:150px; left:250px;
        border-style:solid; border-width:thin; border-color:black}
</STYLE>
```

I added a border around the element so you can see the space it occupies on the screen. Putting the style together with the text results in what you see in Figure 19.2.

Now add one more style definition to use absolute positioning on the inside span:

```
#backside {position:absolute; top:100px; left:50px;
        border-style:solid; border-width:thin; border-color:black}
```

When the new document is displayed in the browser, the `backside` span appears above the `frontside` span (See Figure 19.3), even though the latter appears first in the code.

Now modify the code so that the second span is inside the confines of the first:

```
<BODY>
<P>Here is the beginning of the contents.
 <SPAN id="frontside">Here is the beginning of the frontside span.
 <SPAN id="backside">Here's the backside span...and the end of the
 backside span.</SPAN>
 Here is the end of the frontside span.</SPAN>
 Here is the end of the contents.</P>
</BODY>
```

FIGURE 19.2.

Using absolute positioning, the outside element is placed in a lower-right corner.

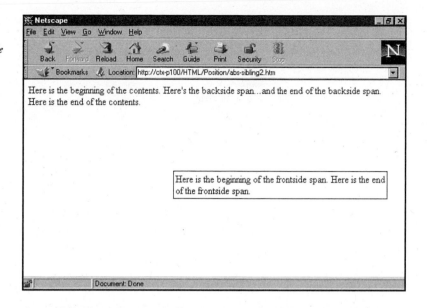

FIGURE 19.3.

The two sibling spans have been placed in absolute positions on the body of the document.

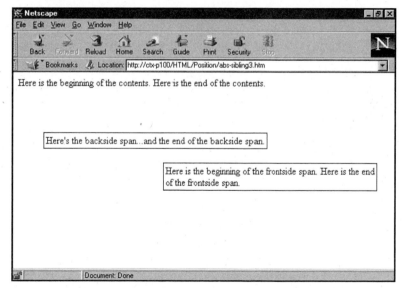

19

CSS AND ELEMENT POSITIONING

This code makes backside a child of frontside; before, the two were both equal siblings to the document body. The result is shown in Figure 19.4.

This is not what you would expect. The backside span has now moved below the frontside span. Here's the catch: Absolute positioning is still relative to the element's *parent*. In Figure 19.2, both <SPAN> tags are children of the <BODY> tag. Therefore, their absolute positions are based on the starting point of the body of the document (top-left corner of the browser window). In Figure 19.3, the second span becomes a child of the first. So, the first <SPAN> (frontside) is placed in an absolute position relative to the body, and the second <SPAN> (backside) is placed in an absolute position relative to the top-left corner of the first.

FIGURE 19.4.

The two sibling spans have been placed in absolute positions on the body of the document.

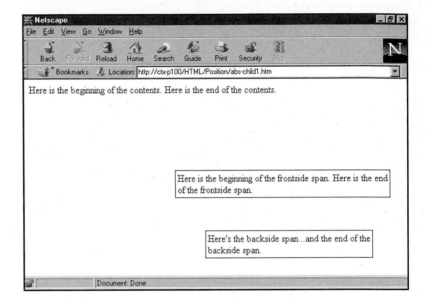

At this point, you've seen the basic behaviors of absolute positioning:

- It defines a new starting point for the contents of the element.
- The physical location of the starting point is defined by the top-left corner of the element's *parent*.
- It defines a new coordinate system, beginning with 0,0 at the top-left corner of the element.

As a default, the height of the positioned element is just tall enough to accept its contents, although you can increase or decrease it with the `height` style property. The width of the element is limited by the right edge of the parent element, although it can also be increased with the `width` style property.

Now that you have a grasp of absolute positioning, it's time to move on to relative positioning.

Relative Positioning

To illustrate relative positioning, I'm going to begin with an example similar to the first example from the previous section:

```
<!DOCTYPE HTML PUBLIC "-//IETF//DTD HTML 4.0//EN">
<BODY>
 <SPAN id="frontside">Here is the beginning of the frontside span.
```

```
Here is the end of the frontside span.</SPAN>
<SPAN id="backside">Here's the backside span...and the end of the
backside span.</SPAN>
</BODY>
```

Then I'll create a new style sheet, beginning with simply defining the type of positioning for the second span. The result is shown in Figure 19.5.

```
<STYLE type="text/css">
#backside {position:relative}
</STYLE>
```

Figure 19.5.

Defining the first span's positioning as relative doesn't change the document. Everything flows inline as it should.

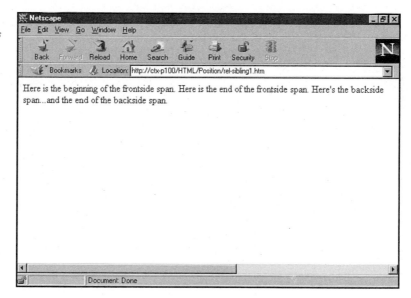

Now adjust the style to shift the text down 10 pixels and right by 30 pixels, and redisplay the results, shown in Figure 19.6:

```
#backside {position:relative; top:10; left:30}
```

Here's what's happening in Figure 19.6. The relative position of the backside span tells the browser to move the element to the right of and below where it would have started normally—it does *not* place the element relative to the origin of the parent element (<BODY>). Take a look at Figure 19.7 to see what happens when you make backside a child of frontside.

You can use this behavior to interesting effect. Take a look at Listing 19.1. You want to make sure the reader sees the school name that's cited in the text. To do that, shift the paragraph to the right by 25 pixels, using relative positioning to give you some space on the left-hand side to mark the paragraph. Then, define a style to display makeshift arrow symbols in the empty space by defining an absolute position to the left of the paragraph. (See Figure 19.8.)

19

CSS AND ELEMENT POSITIONING

FIGURE 19.6.

FIGURE 19.6.

The second span is shifted to the right, relative to where it should have started.

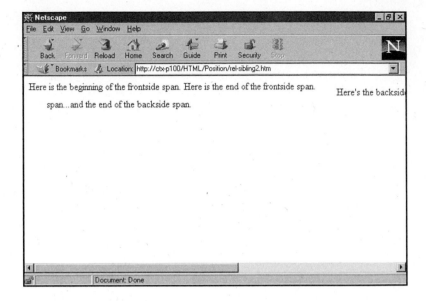

FIGURE 19.7.

Both sides of the outside parent span are placed normally, while the inner span is shifted down and to the right.

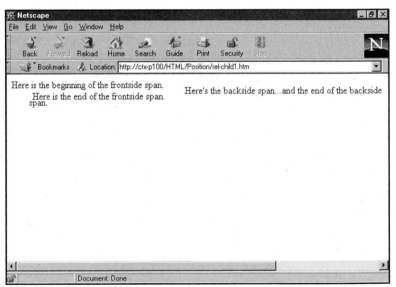

Listing 19.1. Using positioning to place paragraph markers in text.

```
<!DOCTYPE HTML PUBLIC "-//IETF//DTD HTML 4.0//EN">

<STYLE type="text/css">
P {position:relative; left:25px}
.mark {position:absolute; left:-25px; color:white; background:gray}
</STYLE>
```

```
<BODY>
<P>We want to issue congratulations to the latest members of the
HazMat team who returned from the <SPAN class="mark">--&gt;</SPAN>
<CITE>National Fire Academy</CITE>
this summer with 80-hour certificates in Site Operating Practices of
Hazardous Materials Incidents.
</P>
</BODY>
```

The document shown in Figure 19.8 displays a text arrow next to the cited word in the empty space to the left of the paragraph.

FIGURE 19.8.

Whatever the dimensions of the browser window, the text arrow always appears to the left of the paragraph next to the citation.

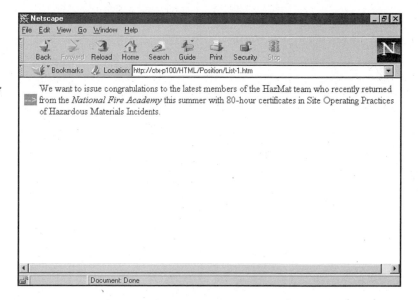

Now you've seen how relative positioning behaves and how it can be used with absolute positioning. However, this example has been just the start of positioning—now it's time to take a look at some of the other behaviors of positioned elements.

Other Properties of Positioned Elements

Now that you've played with moving a couple of elements around on the page in relation to each other, it's time to see a couple of other things that positioned elements can do. To start with, try working with the overlapping blocks in Listing 19.2. The results are shown in Figure 19.9.

Listing 19.2. This document uses overlapped elements.

```
<!DOCTYPE HTML PUBLIC "-//IETF//DTD HTML 4.0//EN">
<STYLE type="text/css">
#block1 {position:absolute}
#block2 {position:absolute; top:25; left:25}
</STYLE>
<BODY>
<DIV id="block1">
  <H1>This is Block 1<BR>
  This is Block 1<BR>
  This is Block 1<BR>
  This is Block 1<BR>
  This is Block 1</H1>
</DIV>
<DIV id="block2">
  <H1>This is Block 2<BR>
  This is Block 2<BR>
  This is Block 2<BR>
  This is Block 2<BR>
  This is Block 2</H1>
</DIV>
</BODY>
```

FIGURE 19.9.

Block 2 is placed over Block 1, but you can still see Block 1 showing through.

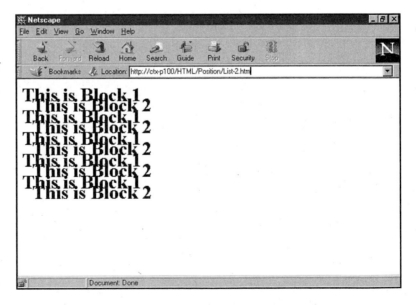

By default, positioned elements are transparent. To override this behavior and make Block 2 act more like a wall and less like a window, a background color is added to Block 2, as shown in Figure 19.10:

```
#block2 {position:absolute; top:25; left:25; background:silver}
```

FIGURE **19.10.**

The background color of Block 2 makes it opaque, covering the contents of Block 1.

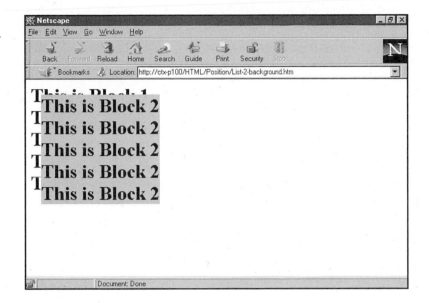

You can also change the order in which the blocks are stacked by using the z-index style property.

TIP

The term z-index is a throwback to your junior high geometry days. Remember the x, y, and z coordinates of three-dimensional space? The x coordinate is for the horizontal, the y coordinate is for the vertical, and the z coordinate is for the depth.

To illustrate this little trick, add two more blocks to your page, using the same format as the first two, and add some contrasting background colors so you can tell each one apart. Each block overlaps a section of the others, but the last block displayed (Block 4) always gets to be on top and Block 1 is always on the bottom. (See Figure 19.11.)

Now add the z-index property to each of the styles. The numbering for this property relates to the order in which the blocks should be displayed on the browser. The lower the number, the further down the element is in the stack. Using this information, reverse the stacking order of the blocks with this style sheet (see Figure 19.12):

```
#block1 {position:absolute; z-index:4; background:silver}
#block2 {position:absolute; z-index:3; background:gray;
         top:50; left:100}
#block3 {position:absolute; z-index:2; background:silver;
         color:white; top:150; left:150}
#block4 {position:absolute; z-index:1; background:black;
         color:white; top:100; left:25}
```

19

CSS AND
ELEMENT
POSITIONING

FIGURE 19.11.

The blocks are placed on the page in the order they're found in the document, with Block 1 on the bottom and Block 4 on the top.

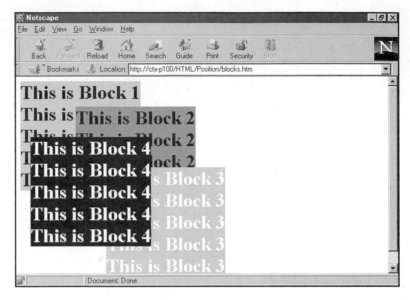

FIGURE 19.12.

Block 1 now has a front-row seat, and Block 4 is pushed to the back.

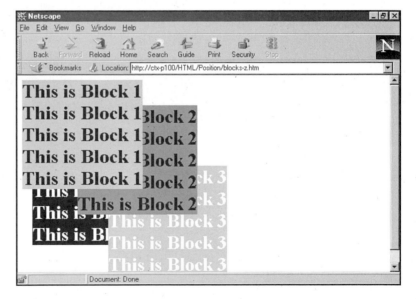

Combining Positioning and Scripts

This use of positioning and scripts is a feature that crosses lines between CSS and Dynamic HTML (covered in Part VI, "Dynamic HTML"). You can use positioning to display and hide CSS elements on a page. In Listing 19.3, I've used the <DIV> tag with a style sheet to stack each division, and then controlled which one is on top with the z-index property. The results are shown in Figure 19.13

> **NOTE**
>
> In this section, I use the terms *layers, divisions,* and *elements* interchangeably. This usage doesn't imply that I'm also using Netscape's <LAYER> tag because I'm not. However, the same rules for positioning a <DIV> or a <SPAN> apply to <LAYER>—it's just that Navigator 4.0 is the only browser that will recognize it.

Listing 19.3. Using a script to display the desired division and hide the current division.

```
<!DOCTYPE HTML PUBLIC "-//IETF//DTD HTML 4.0//EN">
<HTML>
<HEAD>
<TITLE>Multiple Layers</TITLE>
</HEAD>

<STYLE type="text/CSS">
<!--
.card {position:absolute; top:75px; left:75px; width=150; background:white}
-->
</STYLE>

<SCRIPT language="javascript">
<!--
lastDiv='four';
function showLayer( thisDiv ) {
  document.all[lastDiv].style.zIndex = 1;
  document.all[thisDiv].style.zIndex = 4;
  lastDiv = thisDiv;
}
//-->
</SCRIPT>

<BODY>
<FORM>
<INPUT type="button" value="Show Layer 1" onClick="showLayer('one')">
<INPUT type="button" value="Show Layer 2" onClick="showLayer('two')">
<INPUT type="button" value="Show Layer 3" onClick="showLayer('three')">
<INPUT type="button" value="Show Layer 4" onClick="showLayer('four')">
</FORM>
<DIV id="one" class="card">
<P>This is layer number 1.
This is layer number 1.
```

continues

Listing 19.3. continued

```
This is layer number 1.</P>
</DIV>
<DIV id="two" class="card">
<P>This is layer number 2.
This is layer number 2.
This is layer number 2.</P>
</DIV>
<DIV id="three" class="card">
<P>This is layer number 3.
This is layer number 3.
This is layer number 3.</P>
</DIV>
<DIV id="four" class="card">
<P>This is layer number 4.
This is layer number 4.
This is layer number 4.</P>
</DIV>
</BODY>
</HTML>.
```

FIGURE 19.13.

Using CSS, scripting, and <DIV> tags, you've created a simple Dynamic HTML effect with CSS positioning.

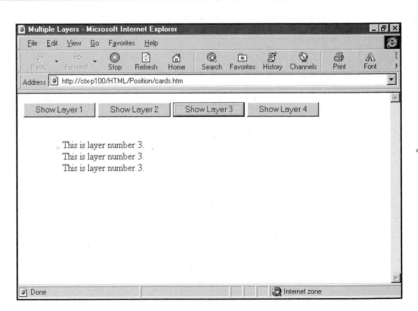

When a button (such as Show Layer 2) is clicked, a JavaScript function (showLayer) is invoked to assign a low z-index to the currently displayed division (1, if the page was just loaded) and a high z-index to the new division (in this case, 2). The same process continues with the new division and the division that's selected by clicking a button.

Summary

CSS positioning gives authors one more element of control over their Web pages. No longer are they bound by the constraint of where in the order of the document a piece of text appears. Using positioning, you can make the element appear almost anywhere you want.

There are two types of positioning: relative and absolute. Relative positions depend on where the element would have been rendered in the natural flow of the document. Absolute positions are based on the top-left corner of the parent element.

All coordinate systems in CSS positioning are based on the top-left corner of the parent element, beginning with the body of the document. That's because the top-left corner is the one fixed point you can depend on in a document. The bottom-right corner always depends on the user's browser, platform, and individual settings.

Using positioning in a document also allows you to overlap elements on a page. Once overlapped, the order of stacking can be changed with the z-index property. By combining positioning and stacking with scripting, it's possible to produce elementary Dynamic HTML effects.

Creating Frames

by Rick Darnell

IN THIS CHAPTER

CHAPTER 20

Frames are the implementation of a concept first introduced by Netscape in 1995 with their Navigator 2.0 release. After much debate and hand-wringing, the World Wide Web Consortium (W3C) has decided to include frames in the HTML 4.0 standard.

Frames, in case you haven't experienced them, allow you to divide the browser window into smaller segments and display a different Web page in each one. (See Figure 20.1.) The frames can interact with each other, with actions on a page in one frame affecting the contents and behavior of another frame.

FIGURE 20.1.

The Netscape DevEdge Online site has three frames to create an attractive, easy-to-use site.

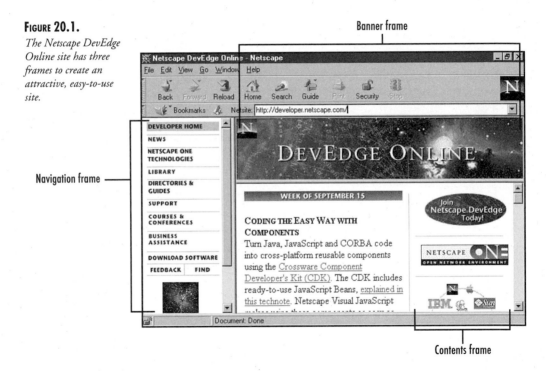

This chapter introduces you to the mechanics of creating frames in their two basic incarnations: as an intrinsic part of the browser window and as inline content.

The Great Frames Debate

The W3C has taken a lot of flak for supporting frames as part of the HTML 4.0 standard. Most authors and users have a love/hate affair with frames. Many authors love them for the extra flexibility they offer in delivering volumes of content to the user, but many users don't like them because of the extra time and resources they require, not to mention the limitation on browsers that support frames.

The biggest argument against frames is that they control the appearance of the user's browser, which runs counter to the HTML goal of a device- and presentation-independent standard.

One of the alternatives to frames that was supported in HTML 3.0 and dropped in HTML 3.2 is the <BANNER> tag. This tag would be used to specify a frame-like element at the top or bottom of the screen that could be used for advertising or links, without committing a lot of browser resources to the effort.

The argument for <BANNER> and against <FRAME> actually has less to do with their implementation and more to do with their current implementations on many Web sites. Frame detractors claim that most sites that incorporate frames do so in a very reader-unfriendly manner by forcing the author's layout preferences onto the reader.

Seen as adding insult to injury, opponents also claim that many Web authors refuse to incorporate meaningful <NOFRAMES> data in their documents, other than "You Need a Netscape/ Microsoft Product" comment, which doesn't help people on some platforms or with accessibility issues.

Given all these arguments and more, are frames an inherently evil addition to HTML? In my humble opinion, no. Their pitfalls might be more apparent to the end user, but for responsible Web authors, there are plenty of ways to make sure a frames page degrades for non-compatible browsers.

The methods to accomplish graceful degradation are included with the description of each frame element and its use in the following sections.

Creating a Set of Frames

As you begin to create a set of frames for your Web site, it helps to take a few minutes to step back and consider why you're using them in the first place. Frames are a useful tool, but just as you wouldn't use a sledgehammer to build a doll house, frames aren't always called for on every Web site.

Remember, frames are still a relatively new addition to the Web. Some common browsers, such as Mosaic and Lynx and older versions of Navigator and Internet Explorer, don't support frames. As a result, if you use frames exclusively on your Web site, users of incompatible browsers are going to have a heck of a time navigating your site.

But let's assume you've pondered the matter, and now decided you want to create a Web navigation experience with frames. That's fine and dandy—all you need to do is add a frame set with some frames to your site, and you'll be off and running.

<FRAMESET>

Adding a frame set is a simple matter of including the <FRAMESET> container tags after the head of the document in lieu of the body:

```
<!DOCTYPE HTML PUBLIC "-//IETF//DTD HTML 4.0//EN">
<HTML>
<HEAD>
  <!--Header material-->
```

20

CREATING FRAMES

```
</HEAD

<FRAMESET>
  <!--Frame definitions-->
</FRAMESET>

</HTML>
```

For browsers that support frames, the frame set content is parsed and interpreted accordingly. For non-frame browsers, the result is a blank page, which we'll address in just a moment with <NOFRAMES>. For now, this is the syntax for the frame set element:

```
<FRAMESET [rows=rowWidths][cols=colWidths][loadEvents]>
  ...Frame or Frameset definitions...
</FRAMESET>
```

Here, *rowWidths* and *colWidths* are a comma-delimited list of sizes for their respective frame rows or columns. If not included, each value defaults to one row and one column, no matter the number of frames that are included in the definition. The <FRAMESET> tag also accepts the onLoad and onUnload events to detect when all the frames have been loaded, and when the user is leaving this set of frames, respectively.

> **TIP**
>
> It's important to note here that a <FRAMESET> can include one or more additional <FRAMESET> tags within its boundaries. These additional tags let you create more complex frame layouts, as you'll see in the next section on the <FRAME> tag.

For example, a frame set including three rows that occupy 20, 20, and 60 percent of the available window space would be defined as follows:

```
<FRAMESET rows="20%,20%,60%">
  ...Frame definitions...
</FRAMESET>
```

Or, you could define the row spaces by using proportional notation:

```
<FRAMESET rows="1*,1*,3*">
  ...Frame definitions...
</FRAMESET>
```

This code specifies a frame set with three rows that respectively occupy 1/5, 1/5, and 3/5 of the available space. To define the space in pixels, omit all suffixes to the measurements.

Because I mentioned the possibility of nested <FRAMESET> tags earlier in this section, take a look at how that's accomplished. For an example in the next section, you're going to create a page that includes a small horizontal frame over a narrow column frame and a wide column frame. To define this structure, begin with the rows:

```
<FRAMESET rows="20%,80%">
</FRAMESET>
```

Then, add a frame for the first row and two columns in the second row. Don't worry about the attribute on the <FRAME> tag—it's covered in the next section.

```
<FRAMESET rows="20%,80%">
  <FRAME scrolling="yes">
  <FRAMESET cols="25%,75%">
    <FRAME scrolling="yes">
    <FRAME scrolling="yes">
  </FRAMESET>
</FRAMESET>
```

Note that the frames don't have a source file for their content yet. Your browser should just create an empty set of frames. You'll see how to specify the source in just a moment. The finished result is seen in Figure 20.2.

FIGURE 20.2.

The result of the nested frame sets is one long row over one narrow column and one wider column.

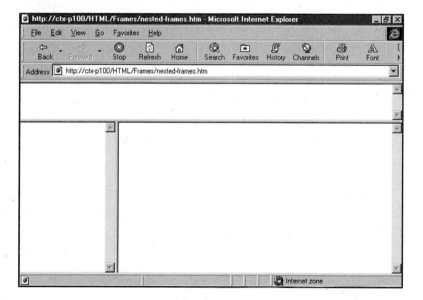

To review, this example first divides the browser into two rows; the top row occupies 20 percent of the space and the bottom row has 80 percent of the space. Then, the second row is divided into columns, with the left column occupying 25 percent of the space and the right column getting 75 percent of the space. That means the bottom-right frame is the biggest, at 60 percent of the total window area (75 percent of the horizontal space times 80 percent of the vertical space).

NOTE

Actually, the available space for display is a little smaller because there are allowances for scrollbars.

If you include a <FRAMESET> tag on your page, you can continue to nest additional <FRAMESET> tags until you're blue in the face and there's no room left on the screen. Eventually, you're going to need to add a <FRAME> tag to tell the browser what the contents of each space should be.

<FRAME>

The relation of <FRAME> to <FRAMESET> is much like the relation of a list item to the list container (see Chapter 8, "Using Lists to Organize Information"), except that frames also define visible space on the browser.

This is the syntax of the <FRAME> tag:

```
<FRAME [name=][src=][behavior][appearance]>
```

Here, name is a user-specified name for the particular frame, and src is the initial URL to display within the frame. To further modify a frame to get custom behavior, see the next two sections for the attributes that affect it.

Basic Frame Behavior

Two attributes control the fundamental behavior of a frame: scrolling and noresize. These attributes set whether the frame provides scrolling ability for the user and whether the user can adjust the frame's proportions.

- **scrolling:** Controls the use of scrollbars on the frame. If the content of the frame exceeds the frame's width, then most browsers add scrollbars so that the user can see the full content. This feature is useful when the content page uses images or other formatting that causes it to extend beyond its set boundaries (see the next section, "Frame Appearance," for information on setting frame size and margins).

  The three choices for scrolling are yes, no, and auto. The default value is auto. For scrolling=yes, the browser always provides scrollbars or other tools as appropriate, whether they're really needed or not. If they're not needed for the content, then the browser should disable them. A value of no means that scrolling devices are never used, which means oversize content is clipped from view, displaying as much as will fit beginning with the file's top-left corner.

- **noresize:** The use of this attribute prevents a user from resizing individual frames. This feature is effective if the content depends on the frame existing at a specific size, such as a frame containing images. Otherwise, the browser defaults to resizable frames.

These two attributes cover the basics of a frame. However, for extended control over these items, you might want to consider using the appearance attributes defined in the next section.

Frame Appearance

Three attributes control the appearance of the frame to the user: frameborder, marginwidth, and marginheight.

■ `frameborder:` Controls whether the frame is surrounded by a border to visually separate it from the rest of the content. To include a border, use `frameborder=1`; otherwise, use `frameborder=0`. Most browsers use a border by default. If you add the `frameborder` attribute to the nested frame set example to hide the borders, you end up with an example that has scrollbars but no dividing lines. (See Figure 20.3.)

FIGURE 20.3.

The nested frame set includes scrollbars but no borders.

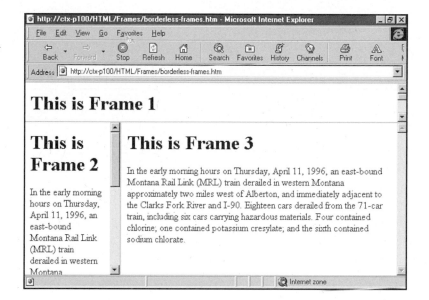

■ `marginwidth:` This attribute sets the amount of space, specified in pixels, between the left and right edges of the frame and the frame contents. The value set with this attribute must be an integer of 1 or greater. The default value is set by the individual browser.

■ `marginheight:` Similar to `marginwidth`, this attribute sets the space between the top and bottom frame edges and the frame content. It accepts the same values as `marginwidth`.

Now that you've set the basic behavior and appearance for the frames, it's time to set up a way for the frames to actually talk and interact with each other.

Communicating Between Frames

The primary method of allowing one frame to communicate with another is through the use of the `target` attribute. This attribute is available for tags that affect hyperlinks (such as `<A>` and `<LINK>`), image maps (`<AREA>`), forms (`<FORM>`), and the HEAD element (`<BASE>`).

To understand the `target` attributes and how to work between frames, you'll use a simple frame set called `frames.htm`. (See Listing 20.1.)

20

CREATING FRAMES

Listing 20.1. The HTML source for `frames.htm`.

```
<!DOCTYPE HTML PUBLIC "-//IETF//DTD HTML 4.0//EN">
<FRAMESET rows="50%,50%">
  <FRAME name="toprow" src="page1.htm">
  <FRAME name="botrow" src="page2.htm">
</FRAMESET>
```

No, it's not a degradable frames page, but that's not the purpose right now. Next, you'll need some source code for the first two pages, shown in Listings 20.2 and 20.3.

Listing 20.2. The HTML source for the initial `toprow` frame: `page1.htm`.

```
<!DOCTYPE HTML PUBLIC "-//IETF//DTD HTML 4.0//EN">
<BODY>
<H1>This is page 1.</H1>
<P><A href="page2.htm">This is a link to page 2.</A></P>
<P><A href="page3.htm">This is a link to page 3.</A></P>
<P><A href="page4.htm">This is a link to page 4.</A></P>
</BODY>
```

Listing 20.3. The HTML source for the initial `botrow` frame: `page2.htm`.

```
<!DOCTYPE HTML PUBLIC "-//IETF//DTD HTML 4.0//EN">
<BODY>
<H2>This is the end of page 2.<H2>
<H2>This is the end of page 2.<H2>
<H2>This is the end of page 2.<H2>
</BODY>
```

The HTML source code for pages 3 and 4 are the same as `page2.htm`, except for the filenames and page numbers. When `frames.htm` is initially loaded into a browser, the result is what you see in Figure 20.4. Note what happens when you click on any of the hyperlinks in the top frame. The top frame changes, but nothing happens with the bottom frame. (See Figure 20.5.)

The way you want this page to work is for the target of a hyperlink in the top frame to load in the bottom frame—and this is where the `target` attribute comes into play. Modify `page1.htm` by adding the `<BASE>` tag with a named target to the head of the document:

```
<HEAD>
<BASE target="botrow">
</HEAD>
```

Now, when you reload the frame set and click on a hyperlink in the top window, the bottom window receives the contents. (See Figure 20.6.)

FIGURE 20.4.

The result of loading frames.htm *into Internet Explorer.*

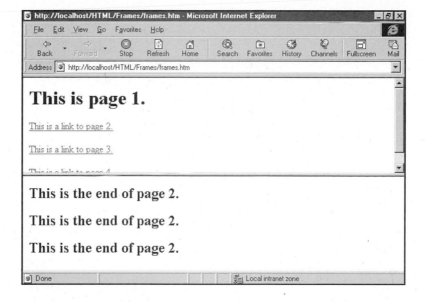

FIGURE 20.5.

The target of a hyperlink is loaded into the top frame, where it was selected.

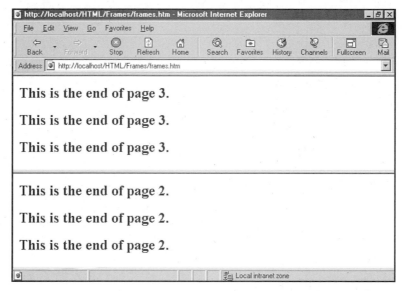

20

CREATING FRAMES

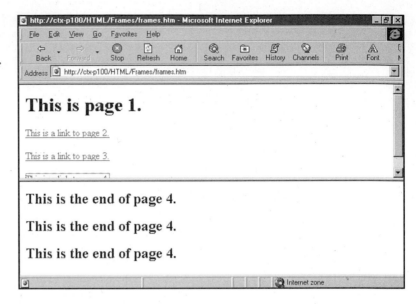

FIGURE 20.6.

The target of a hyperlink in the top frame is loaded into the bottom frame.

The `target` attribute could have been added individually to each hyperlink in the first page, but adding it once to the BASE element was more than enough. Some additional rules govern the behavior of targets and frames:

- If the `target` attribute of an element is an existing frame, then that frame receives the target of the element.

- If an element doesn't have the `target` attribute, but the <BASE> tag does, then the <BASE> tag determines the destination of the content.

- If both the element and <BASE> tag include the `target` and each has different values, then the element's value is used and the <BASE> is ignored.

- If neither the element nor the <BASE> tag of the document specifies a target, then the current frame containing the activated element receives the content.

- If the named frame specified in `target` doesn't exist, then a new window is created and assigned the previously unknown name, and the content is loaded into the new window.

There are some special `target` names you can use, also, which are identified by their beginning underscore character (_). They are reserved names, which can't be used with the `name` attribute. Reserved names identify the relationships between frame sets, their frames, and nested frame sets. Here are the names and their effects when used as `target` attributes:

- `_blank:` Loads the document into a new window without a name.
- `_self:` Loads the document in the same frame as the element that used this name.

- **_parent:** Loads the document into the frame set that contains the current frame.
- **_top:** Loads the document into the original window, canceling all other frames.

You'll see the various uses of target to create nested hierarchies of frames in the last section of this chapter, "Two Common Frame Layouts."

Providing Alternative Content in Frames

Now that you've defined your frame sets and frames, it's time to take into account the great teeming hordes of people who don't have browsers that support frames.

> **NOTE**
>
> The W3C strongly urges authors to provide alternative content for browsers that don't support frames or that are configured to ignore them. I couldn't agree more. Using the latest features is great, but don't forget—people who use the latest and greatest are still one of the smallest segments of the browsing community.

There are two methods to accommodate non-frame browsers. The first is using the <FRAMESET> tag itself. Remember that the frame set replaces the body of the document. Users without frames-compatible browsers will see nothing when they load your page. However, you can add content for noncompatible browsers with the <NOFRAMES> tag placed after the last <FRAME> tag. You can insert any valid HTML inside a set of <NOFRAMES>, including an alternative home page or a link to another starting point on your Web site.

```
<FRAMESET cols="25%,75%">
  <FRAME name="toc" src="home-toc.htm">
  <FRAME name="content" src="home.htm">
  <NOFRAMES>
    Thanks for stopping at our Web site. To view this site without
    frames, check out our <A href="home.htm">no-frame Home Page</A>.
  </NOFRAMES>
</FRAMESET>
```

If the starting point for your no-frames site is also one of the sources for one of your frames, then you can use the <NOFRAMES> tag to include portions of content from your other frame pages.

Consider the previous frame set snippet. If you left the table of contents (TOC) and the home page separate, then the user without a frames browser wouldn't have the benefit of using the page with the TOC. Using <NOFRAMES>, you can include the TOC on the home page without displaying it when frames are in use. The following snippet is from the fictional home page:

```
<!-- the home page -->
<BODY>
<NOFRAMES>
```

20

CREATING FRAMES

```
...table of contents here...
...table of contents here...
...table of contents here...
</NOFRAMES>
<H1>The Home Page</H1>
...the main home page content goes here...
</BODY>
```

When the page is viewed on a frame-compatible browser, everything fits according to plan, as you've seen in the previous frame examples, and the table of contents on the page is hidden. When it's seen on a non-frames browser, the table of contents embedded on the page is revealed.

CAUTION

Although the preceding use of the <NOFRAMES> tag meets the HTML 4.0 standard, it isn't currently supported by the vast majority of browsers, including Navigator and Internet Explorer.

Using these two features of frame pages, you can create a Web site that's functional and usable by *all* your users—not just the ones using the latest version of Navigator or Internet Explorer.

There is one more option for frames to cover in this chapter—frames as content within a Web page.

Beyond Divided Windows: The Inline Frame

Inline frames are a relatively new advancement in the world of frames. An inline frame is treated essentially the same way as an inline image or object; it takes up a block of space on the page for inserting specialized content (in this case, another Web page).

CAUTION

Currently, Internet Explorer (versions 3 and 4) is the only browser that supports inline frames. All other browsers ignore this element.

Inline frames are a useful place to put things like indexes or sidebars that contribute to the current document, but aren't crucial. Using inline frames for accessory information also makes it easier to provide alternative content for noncompatible browsers.

This is the syntax of an inline frame (<IFRAME>):

```
<IFRAME [name=frameName][src=URL][frameborder=1or0][marginwidth=numPixels]
    [marginheight=numPixels][scrolling=yesOrNo][align=verticalOrHorizontal]
    [height=frameHeight][width=frameWidth]>
</IFRAME>
```

The `name` is used to assign a name to the frame that may be used by other hyperlinks in the current document, and `src` is the URL of the Web page or other content that will fill the frame. The rest of the attributes for an inline frame are covered under the `<FRAME>` tag earlier in this chapter, with the exception of `align`, `height`, and `width`.

The `align` attribute is an old friend from the days of working with `<IMG>`. The possible values are `bottom`, `middle`, `top`, `left`, or `right`. The default value is `bottom`, which aligns the bottom of the frame with the current text baseline where it's located.

Likewise, `middle` aligns the frame's vertical midpoint with the baseline of the text, and `top` aligns the top of the frame with the top of the text line. The last two, `left` and `right`, force the frames to their respective margins and cause text to flow around the frames.

> **NOTE**
>
> Although `align` has been deprecated in virtually all other elements in HTML 4.0, it appears to remain in standard use for `<IFRAME>`. The HTML 4.0 Document Type Definition draft does not include support for `class` or `style`. However, it's my guess that browsers such as Navigator and Internet Explorer will still support these options, and the W3C will correct this apparent oversight in the next HTML revision.

If no value is specified for `height` and `width`, then the browser does its best to allocate enough space for the content. Otherwise, you can specify a value for either one or for both by using the three standard measurement techniques: pixels (`height="100"`), percentages (`width="20%"`), or a ratio (`width="2*"`).

As an example of an inline frame, the following HTML code gives you a source document that includes a bit of additional information in an inline frame. (See Figure 20.7.) If inline frames are not supported, then the browser ignores the `<IFRAME>` tag and displays the hyperlink for the content. (See Figure 20.8.)

```
...content...
<IFRAME src="techRequirements.htm" width="50%" height="200"
        scrolling="auto" align="right" frameborder="1">
  <!--User agent does not support frames-->
  Interested in being a HazMat Technician? Then check out the
  <A href="techRequirements.htm" title="Technician Requirements">
HazMat Team Requirements</A>.
</IFRAME>
...more content...
```

20

CREATING FRAMES

FIGURE 20.7.

On a frame-compatible browser, such as Internet Explorer, the inline frame is presented in the midst of the page's other content.

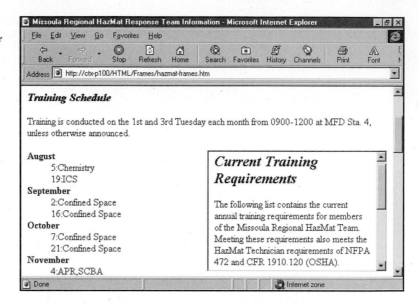

FIGURE 20.8.

On a non-frame browser, such as Mosaic, the page degrades by providing a link to the page that would have appeared in the frame.

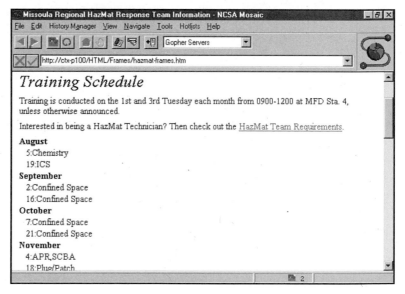

Two Common Frame Layouts

When you're starting out with frames, it can be hard to figure out how to implement them effectively. The following sections cover several of the more useful and common frame layouts.

Navigation Bar with Content

The navigation bar with content frame set consists of a narrow row or column containing site navigation links and a larger main content frame (see Figure 20.9):

```
<!--navbar at top, content on bottom-->
<FRAMESET rows="15%,85%">
  <FRAME name="navbar" src="navbar.htm">
  <FRAME name="content" src="page2.htm">
</FRAMESET>

<BODY>
Welcome to the XYZ Web site. To continue, please go to our no-frames
<A href="index-noframe.htm" title="Frameless Home Page">Home Page</A>.
</BODY>
```

FIGURE 20.9.

One of the most basic layouts for a frame set: index on the top and contents on the bottom.

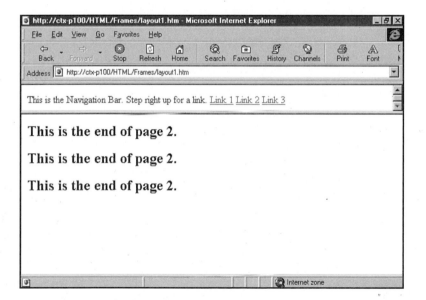

The navigation frame can occupy any side around the content, which can also change its use. For example, placing the `navbar` frame at the bottom of the frame set is useful for including a set of footnotes for the current document. The `navbar.htm` file needs to have `<BASE target="content">` in the head of the document to maintain the navigation frame while displaying contents in the content frame.

To present this frame set as vertical columns, replace the rows attribute with the cols attribute. Additional uses for this layout include placing an advertisement in the narrow column or including an index to the main frame's document.

Table of Contents, Chapter Overview, and Contents

Building on the framework of the previous example, you're going to add one more frame as a column underneath the banner at the top. This structure gives you a nested hierarchy in which the top frame controls the content of the column on the left, and the column on the left controls the column on the right. (See Figure 20.10.)

FIGURE 20.10.

These frames are a nested hierarchy; the top controls the left and the left controls the right.

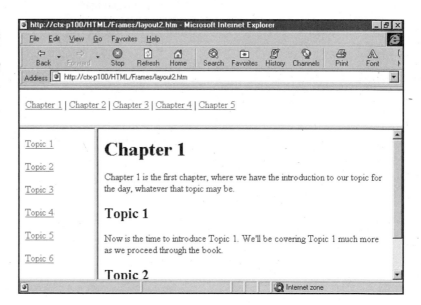

This frame layout is created in two steps. First, divide the frame into two rows:

```
<!--toc at top, chapter file on bottom-->
<FRAMESET rows="20%,80%">
  <FRAME name="toc" src="toc.htm">
  <FRAME name="chapter" src="ch1-top.htm">
</FRAMESET>
```

Then, each chapter file begins with a frame set to set the two columns. This way, when the top frame loads a new page in the bottom frame, the two old columns are automatically dumped and loaded with two new columns:

```
<!-- ch1-top.htm, with chapter index on left, content on right -->
<FRAMESET cols="20%,80%">
  <FRAME name="index" src="ch1-index.htm">
  <FRAME name="content" src="ch1-content.htm">
</FRAMESET>
```

The content for each of the source files in the two frame sets requires a `target` attribute as part of the `<BASE>` tag in the head for this collection to work properly:

```
toc.htm                        <BASE target="chapter">

ch1-index.htm                  <BASE target="content">
```

Also, each chapter index file needs the same `<BASE>` tag in the head for the set to work properly.

Summary

Frames are a useful, albeit controversial, tool to build navigation and display functionality into Web sites. A set of frames is really quite easy to build, beginning with a `<FRAMESET>` container and then working down into the definition for each `<FRAME>` and the content it specifies.

In addition to subdividing a browser's window, you can also include inline frames by using the `<IFRAME>` tag. An inline frame is essentially the same as other specialized content, such as images or objects, and is inserted and controlled similarly.

Using the `target` attribute in content pages gives you the ability to let one frame control the contents of another frame. This feature is very useful for creating nested frames that supply descending levels of navigational detail.

Now that you've seen the official ways to control Web page appearance, from Chapter 17, "Simple Style with Text," through this chapter, it's time to take a look at some other methods, beginning with JavaScript Style Sheets.

Using JavaScript Style Sheets

by Rick Darnell

IN THIS CHAPTER

CHAPTER 21

After exploring the many possibilities with cascading style sheets (CSS) in Chapters 18, "Using Cascading Style Sheets," and 19, "Cascading Style Sheets and Element Positioning," it's time to move on to a different way of defining style—JavaScript Style Sheets (JSSS), from Netscape.

With JSSS, you can use a style sheet to query the browser about its platform, the size of its window, color compatibility, and other items before assigning values to its tags and classes. This approach allows a JSSS page to customize itself to its environment instead of taking a one-size-fits-all approach.

If you're not familiar with style sheets, what they do, and how to include them on your Web pages, go back and take a look at Chapter 18.

JSSS Versus CSS

In Chapter 18, you looked at the Cascading Style Sheet standard from the World Wide Web Consortium (W3C). This standard is slightly different from Netscape's JSSS, beginning with the type declaration.

At this point, I must say that JSSS isn't a mutually exclusive feature for Netscape users. Netscape supports both CSS and JSSS. In both style models, each style attribute is associated with a property, although it's represented slightly differently. For example, `text-align` in CSS is the same as `textAlign` in JSSS. As a rule, a hyphenated word in CSS becomes a single word in JSSS, with the first initial of the second word capitalized.

> **TIP**
>
> JavaScript is case-sensitive, so remembering how to convert two-word values into one word is important to make sure your styles work.

Another important difference appears when you need to mark the style sheet with the `<STYLE>` tag. Where CSS uses `text/css`, JSSS uses `text/javascript`. For example, to link to an external JavaScript style sheet, use this tag:

```
<LINK REL=stylesheet type="text/javascript" href="/styles/mod.js">
```

Although cascading style sheets work in both Netscape Navigator and Microsoft Internet Explorer, JavaScript style sheets currently work exclusively with Navigator 4.0. In spite of their differences, JSSS and CSS share one important trait—every style attribute in CSS is also reflected in JavaScript. The only difference is the syntax used to define the style.

Using JavaScript Style Sheets

CHAPTER **21**

353

21

USING
JAVASCRIPT
STYLE SHEETS

It might help to mention at this point what JavaScript is. JavaScript is a scripting extension to HTML that improves your ability to control the HTML page and respond to user events without the need for client-server communication or CGI scripting. JavaScript is more closely related to a programming language than to HTML tags. It can't exist outside HTML, however. To function, JavaScript must be included as part of a Web page in a browser that understands JavaScript. However, although Microsoft recognizes JavaScript through its own implementation of JScript, it doesn't recognize the JSSS style syntax. No one ever said the world of the Internet was an easy place to get along in.

Netscape developed JavaScript with Sun's Java. JavaScript isn't a watered-down version of Java for beginning programmers. Although it's related to Java, JavaScript offers a solution for client-side scripting for users with high-powered machines who get bogged down by client-server communication. You can read a lot more about JavaScript in Chapter 23, "JavaScript at a Glance."

Creating Style Sheets with JSSS

Following the introduction to JavaScript, it's only logical to begin with the objects that represent the style on your Web page. Netscape 4.0 introduces three new objects for changing styles.

JSSS Objects

Three objects used with JSSS represent the three basic parts of style: tags, classes, and IDs. You'll remember them from Chapter 18.

- **Tags:** The actual mark-up elements used in HTML, tags are children of the document object, so the syntax to access them is document.tags.*tagname*, in which *tagname* is one of the valid HTML tags, such as H1, STRONG, or A.

- **Classes:** These objects are a further division of tags—for example, the left and right versions of a <P> tag. It's important not to confuse the style classes with Java classes, which are the building blocks of Java code.

  Classes are also children of document, so their syntax is document.classes.*classname*[.*tagname*], in which *classname* is the identifier for your class, and *tagname* is an optional identifier for the specific tag to which it applies. A special value for *tagname* is all, which indicates that the class can be used with any tag on the page.

■ **IDs:** They are the unique identifiers for each individual tag. Think of IDs as the name for each tag—the first `<H1>` could be "Ed" (`<H1 id="Ed">`, the second `<H1>` could be "Bob" (`<H1 id="Bob">`, and so on.

The ID is also a child of `document` and uses the syntax `document.ids.`*idname*, in which *idname* is the name of the `id` attribute. In the first preceding example, it is `document.ids.Ed`.

By using all three of these new JavaScript objects, you can set the value of any style attribute in the document. The caveat to all this is that you can modify JSSS only when the page loads. After the browser is finished parsing the page, the styles are set—you can't go back with Netscape Navigator 4.0 and change attributes as you can with the Microsoft Internet Explorer 4.0 model.

In addition to these three objects, there are also a method and a property used with JSSS that you'll want to use.

A JSSS Method and Property

The world of JSSS offers a method to help set contextual styles and a property useful for assigning conditional styles. *Conditional styles* are applied depending on the status of other variables, whether they are other styles or the value on a form. For example, you could check for the existence of color combinations that are hard to read (such as red on blue) and change the colors to more palatable choices.

The `contextual` method allows you to specify styles based on their relation to the position of other tags. Its purpose is the same as the contextual syntax for CSS. You can set all `<P>` tags under an `<H1>` tag to a 14-point typeface and all `<P>` tags under an `<H2>` tag to a 12-point typeface. This use is applied based on the paragraph's relationship to the heading tags, not on classes.

The preceding example is represented like this:

```
<style type="text/javascript">
contextual(tags.h1, tags.p).fontSize = "14pt";
contextual(tags.h2, tags.p).fontSize = "12pt";
</style>
```

> **TIP**
>
> You'll notice that after talking about the new objects as children of `document`, I didn't use `document` in the style definitions. Why not?
>
> Because `document` is one of the top-level documents for a Web page, its use is understood. You can use it for clarity, but it's not required.

The `apply` property is used as shorthand to set the style of a tag or group of styles using a function. For example, consider the following function, which sets a background color for an unspecified tag based on the value of its color:

Using JavaScript Style Sheets

CHAPTER 21

355

21

USING
JAVASCRIPT
STYLE SHEETS

```
function setBackground(thisTag) {
   with (thisTag) {
      if (color == "yellow") {
         backgroundColor = "blue"; }
      else
         if (color == "white") {
            backgroundColor = "black"; }
   }
}
```

Nothing changes. All this processing happens when the `apply` property is referenced during style processing.

The following code snippet first sets the color of three heading tags:

```
with (tags) {
   H1.color = "white";
   H2.color = "yellow";
   H3.color = "purple";
}

tags.H1.apply = setBackground(tags.H1);
tags.H2.apply = setBackground(tags.H2);
tags.H3.apply = setBackground(tags.H3);
```

Then, it takes each of the tags and applies the rules set forth in the function. Listing 21.1 shows the complete page; the text color is set first, then the background is changed by using the `setBackground` method with the `apply` property.

Listing 21.1. Using the `apply` property in a JSSS definition.

```
<!DOCTYPE HTML PUBLIC "-//IETF//DTD HTML 4.0//EN">
<HTML>

<HEAD>
<TITLE>Apply and JSSS</TITLE>
</HEAD>

<STYLE type="text/javascript">
<!--
function setBackground(thisTag) {
   with (thisTag) {
      if (color == "yellow") {
         backgroundColor = "blue"; }
      else
         if (color == "white") {
            backgroundColor = "black"; }
   }
}

with (tags) {
   H1.color = "white";
   H2.color = "yellow";
   H3.color = "purple";
}
```

continues

Listing 21.1. continued

```
tags.H1.apply = setBackground(tags.H1);
tags.H2.apply = setBackground(tags.H2);
tags.H3.apply = setBackground(tags.H3);

//-->
</STYLE>

<BODY bgcolor="white">
<H1>This is white on black (H1)</H1>
<H2>This is yellow on blue (H2)</H2>
<H3>This is purple on the default background color (H3)</H3>
</BODY>

</HTML>
```

When the page is displayed (see Figure 21.1), each heading gets the appropriate background color, even though it wasn't set explicitly during the style definition.

FIGURE 21.1.

Using the apply *property is a quick way to create conditional styles.*

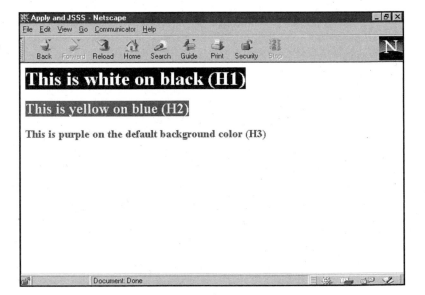

Applying JSSS to a Web Page

Now that you've had a peek at the different objects used to represent style in JavaScript, it's time to actually put JSSS to work on a real Web page. As you've seen with the objects, creating a page with JSSS is similar to creating a page with CSS, except for the syntax.

To begin, you'll work with a page constructed using CSS (see Listing 21.2 and Figure 21.2), and then re-create the style line by line with JSSS.

Using JavaScript Style Sheets

CHAPTER 21

357

21

USING
JAVASCRIPT
STYLE SHEETS

Listing 21.2. This is the file that uses CSS, which you'll replace with JSSS.

```
<HTML>

<HEAD>
<TITLE>A new style</TITLE>
</HEAD>

<STYLE type="text/CSS">
<!--
BODY {margin-left: 0.75in; margin-right: 0.75in; margin-top: 0.10in;
      background: white;}
H1, H2 {font-family: verdana, helvetica, arial, sans-serif}
H1 {font-size:18pt; text-align:left}
H2 {font-size:14pt; text-align:right}
P {font:garamond 12pt/11pt normal}
P.left {text-align:left}
P.right {text-align:right}
A {text-decoration: none; font-weight: bold}
-->
</STYLE>

<BODY>
<H1>More about the House of Usher</H1>
<P class="left">Shaking off from <A href="spirit.html" title="Poe's Spirit">
 my spirit</A> what must have been a dream, I scanned more narrowly the real
 aspect of the building.  Its principal feature seemed to be that of an
 excessive antiquity. The discoloration of ages had been great.</P>
<H2>Not a nice place</H2>
<P class="right">Minute <A href="fungi.html" title="Fungi">fungi</A> overspread
 the whole exterior, hanging in a fine tangled web-work from the
 eaves.  Yet all this was apart from any extraordinary dilapidation.  No
 portion of the masonry had fallen; and there appeared to be a wild
 inconsistency between its still perfect adaptation of parts, and the
 crumbling condition of the individual stones.</P>
</BODY>

</HTML>
```

Begin with the style tags. The basic container for JSSS is the same as for CSS, except for the type and the closing comment tag to hide the styles from incompatible browsers:

```
<STYLE type="text/javascript">
<!-- Begin hiding from incompatible browsers

// Finish hiding from incompatible browsers -->
</STYLE>
```

Note the two slashes before the closing comment tag. In JavaScript, two slashes mark the beginning of a comment. Use them to keep JavaScript from looking at the closing HTML comment tag (-->), which it would try to interpret as a JavaScript statement.

Next comes the body style. The original CSS version called for a left and right margin of 0.75 inches and a top margin of 0.10 inches. You'll do the same with JSSS using the tags.BODY object:

```
with (tags.BODY) {
    marginLeft = ".75in";
    marginRight = ".75in";
    marginTop = ".10in";
    background = "white";
}
```

The three values are set, but what about the `with (tags.BODY)` line at the top? This special feature of JavaScript lets you specify an object for a set of statements. Anything that falls within the curly brackets after the `with` statement is interpreted as though it began with `tags.BODY`.

FIGURE 21.2.

The page constructed with CSS style.

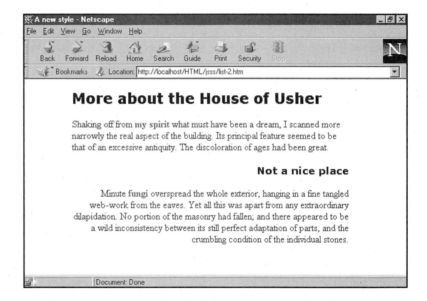

NOTE

Before style sheets, the `with` statement was used primarily with JavaScript's `Math` object. The `Math` object contains several constants, such as `Pi` and `e`, and a range of scientific methods, such as `sin` and `log`. Instead of continually typing `Math.Pi`, `Math.e`, `Math.sin`, or `Math.log`, developers can preface a mathematical section with this statement:

`with (Math)`

The programmer can follow that statement with a set of statements enclosed in curly brackets. With this method, the `Math` object is understood, and a lot of typing and potential typos are eliminated.

Next, you'll work on the two heading tags. These two tags used CSS grouping as a shorthand to make defining the tags easier. Unfortunately, grouping is not something that JSSS handles

Using JavaScript Style Sheets

CHAPTER 21

359

21

USING
JAVASCRIPT
STYLE SHEETS

particularly well. You will use the `apply` property to set the common attributes for both styles, but the end result is still a lot of additional typing.

```
function eval_Heading(thisTag) {
    thisTag.fontFamily = "verdana, helvetica, arial, sans-serif";
    if (thisTag == tags.H1) {
        thisTag.fontSize="18pt"; }
    else thisTag.fontSize="14pt";
}


tags.H1.apply = eval_Heading(tags.H1);
tags.H2.apply = eval_Heading(tags.H2);
```

Compared with the same code required to implement these styles with CSS, it's a bit of additional work. Such is the joy of working with two completely different forms of syntax. One version's drawback is another's strong point, and vice versa.

Notice, too, that you haven't set the left and right text alignment yet. I'll cover that next with the paragraph style. The first part of the `<P>` is straightforward—a font style with a typeface and size:

```
tags.P.font = "garamond, serif 12pt"
```

This code is all you need for the paragraph. You'll specify the text justification with classes that you can use with the heading and paragraph tags. Like CSS, you can use JSSS and the `classes` object to define a class independent of a tag:

```
classes.left.textAlign = "left";
classes.right.textAlign = "right";
```

You can use these two classes with any of the tags to force right or left justification, which is what you'll do later when the HTML is created for the page.

The last style to create is for the anchor. It's a straightforward affair in which you remove the default underline attribute and add bold formatting:

```
with (tags.A) {
    textDecoration = "none";
    fontWeight = "bold";
}
```

The completed JSSS style section is shown in Listing 21.3.

Listing 21.3. The completed JSSS style sheet looks quite different from its counterpart in CSS.

```
<STYLE type="text/javascript">
<!-- Begin hiding from incompatible browsers

with (tags.BODY) {
    marginLeft = ".75in";
    marginRight = ".75in";
    marginTop = ".10in";
    background = "white"; }
```

continues

Listing 21.3. continued

```
function eval_Heading(thisTag) {
   thisTag.fontFamily = "verdana, helvetica, arial, sans-serif";
   if (thisTag == tags.H1) {
      thisTag.fontSize="18pt"; }
   else thisTag.fontSize="14pt";
}

tags.H1.apply = eval_Heading(tags.H1);
tags.H2.apply = eval_Heading(tags.H2);

with (tags.P) {
   fontFamily = "garamond, serif";
   fontSize = "12pt";
}

classes.justleft.all.textAlign = "left";
classes.justright.all.textAlign = "right";

with (tags.A) {
   textDecoration = "none";
   fontWeight = "bold";
}
// Finish hiding from incompatible browsers -->
</STYLE>
```

When the body of the document is created, as shown in Listing 21.4, it changes very little from the CSS version. The notable difference is in the two classes, left and right, which are added to the two heading tags to set their alignment. (See Figure 21.3.)

Listing 21.4. The body of this document includes the addition of classes to the heading tags.

```
<!DOCTYPE HTML PUBLIC "-//IETF//DTD HTML 4.0//EN">
<HTML>

<HEAD>
<TITLE>A new style</TITLE>
</HEAD>

<STYLE type="text/javascript">
<!-- Begin hiding from incompatible browsers

with (tags.BODY) {
   marginLeft = ".75in";
   marginRight = ".75in";
   marginTop = ".10in";
   background = "white";
}

function eval_Heading(thisTag) {
   thisTag.fontFamily = "verdana, helvetica, arial, sans-serif";
   if (thisTag == tags.H1) {
      thisTag.fontSize="18pt"; }
   else thisTag.fontSize="14pt";
}
```

Using JavaScript Style Sheets

CHAPTER 21

361

21

USING
JAVASCRIPT
STYLE SHEETS

```
tags.H1.apply = eval_Heading(tags.H1);
tags.H2.apply = eval_Heading(tags.H2);

with (tags.P) {
   fontFamily = "garamond, serif";
   fontSize = "12pt";
}

classes.justleft.all.textAlign = "left";
classes.justright.all.textAlign = "right";

with (tags.A) {
   textDecoration = "none";
   fontWeight = "bold";
}
// Finish hiding from incompatible browsers -->
</STYLE>

<BODY>

<H1 class="justleft">More about the House of Usher</H1>
<P class="justleft">Shaking off from <A href="spirit.html" title="Poe's Spirit">
my spirit</A> what must have been a dream, I scanned more narrowly the real
aspect of the building.  Its principal feature seemed to be that of an
excessive antiquity. The discoloration of ages had been great.</P>
<H2 class="justright">Not a nice place</H2>
<P class="justright">Minute <A href="fungi.html" title="Fungi">fungi</A>
overspread the whole exterior, hanging in a fine tangled web-work from the
eaves.  Yet all this was apart from any extraordinary dilapidation.  No
portion of the masonry had fallen; and there appeared to be a wild
inconsistency between its still perfect adaptation of parts, and the
crumbling condition of the individual stones.</P></BODY>

</HTML>
```

FIGURE 21.3.

The finished JSSS page with style appears to be identical to the CSS version after which it was modeled.

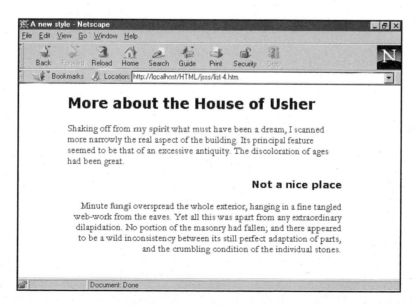

So what have you proved by re-creating a CSS page with JSSS? One important fact—the syntax might be different, but the outcome is the same. CSS and JSSS are different roads to the same result.

> **TIP**
>
> Now that you've created your first style sheet with JSSS, you can use it in an external style sheet, similar to CSS linked style sheets. First, save the style section of the document as its own document with a `.js` file extension. Then, include the `<LINK>` tag in the header of the document to apply the style:
>
> ```
> <LINK rel="stylesheet" type="text/javascript" src="JSSS_style.js">
> ```
>
> That's all there is to it. When the page is loaded, the browser will retrieve the style and apply the tags to it.

Combining Styles

For most of this chapter, I've talked about CSS and JSSS as though they were mutually exclusive implementations of styles. Now that you're approaching the end of the chapter, it's time to tell the truth: You can use both CSS and JSSS on the same page.

How does it work? It works like just about everything else in HTML—whoever has the last word wins. It's the same way style sheets cascade if you include all three types (linked, embedded, inline) on the same page. First, the browser loads the linked style sheet because it's the first style the browser encounters when parsing the page.

Then, the browser comes to the embedded style sheet. Any settings that conflict with the linked style take precedence because it's the last value the browser has encountered.

Last comes the inline style, which trumps both of the others. Neither of the other two styles has a chance to get the browser's attention again before the text is displayed, so the inline style is applied.

The same process works with the two methods of creating style. Instead of including one set of `<STYLE>` tags, you include two. If there's any difference in the styles, the last style in line gets the last say on what the style will be. To see how this works, look at Listing 21.5. After the header, the first style sheet uses CSS to set a heading and paragraph of text to reverse color (white on black). The next style uses JSSS to set the paragraph style back to black on white.

Listing 21.5. This page uses the two different style sheet models to set text and background color.

```
<!DOCTYPE HTML PUBLIC "-//IETF//DTD HTML 4.0//EN">
<HTML>

<HEAD>
```

Using JavaScript Style Sheets

CHAPTER 21

363

21

USING
JAVASCRIPT
STYLE SHEETS

```
<TITLE>CSS and JSSS</TITLE>
</HEAD>

<STYLE type="text/css">
<!--
BODY {background:white}
H1 {color:white; background:black}
P {color:white; background:black}
-->
</STYLE>

<STYLE type="text/javascript">
<!--
with (tags.p) {
    color = "black";
    backgroundColor = "white";
}
// -->
</STYLE>

<BODY>
<H1>Browsers with style show white on black</H1>
<P>Internet Explorer shows this paragraph style in white on black. Navigator
shows it in black on white.</P>
</BODY>

</HTML>
```

When a user views the page in Netscape Navigator, as shown in Figure 21.4, the result is a white-on-black heading and black-on-white paragraph. The initial black-on-white value for the paragraph was overridden by the style assignments in the JSSS section.

FIGURE 21.4.

Between two style sheets on the same page, the last style sheet wins, regardless of the type of style sheet syntax used.

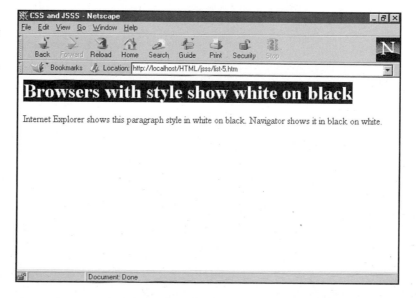

When the user views the same page in Internet Explorer (see Figure 21.5), both the heading and paragraph are displayed with white-on-black text because Microsoft's browser doesn't know how to interpret the JSSS section. It ignores those style values and stays with the CSS version of the style sheet.

FIGURE 21.5.

The same page viewed in Internet Explorer displays the heading and paragraph the same way because the JSSS section is ignored.

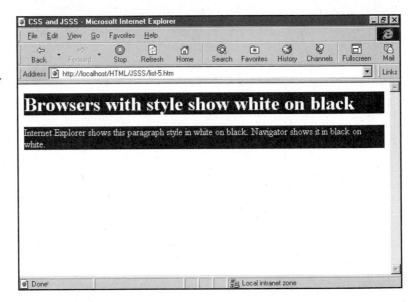

As a general rule, this type of mixing isn't recommended for most pages when you're applying a general style. Mixing the style sheets is useful if you need to generate a style or an effect for a specific browser, however. Put the default style first in the document, followed by the tags needed to create the effect.

Summary

In this chapter you have learned about JavaScript Style Sheets (JSSS), another way of defining the look of a page. JSSS is essentially identical in use to Cascading Style Sheets. The syntax for JSSS is very different, however—not to mention incompatible—when used with Internet Explorer. So far, the only browser that supports JSSS is Navigator, although there's a proposal pending with the W3C.

Although you might choose to use CSS instead of JSSS on your Web pages for compatibility with the most browsers, you'll probably find that you use JavaScript as your scripting language for the same reason. By the same token, CSS and JSSS can co-exist on the same page peacefully. Following the practice of Web browsers, the last style definition encountered has precedence. You can put your CSS defaults for all browsers first in line, and then follow it with Navigator-specific JSSS in the next style. On a non-JSSS browser, the JSSS section is ignored.

Layers, a new part of Navigator, can also be worked with through JSSS. A layer is simply a section of a Web page—whether it's most of the body or a few lines of text—that you can position, move, or display independently of other elements on the page. It's covered in the next chapter, "Layers."

Layers

by Rick Darnell

IN THIS CHAPTER

CHAPTER 22

Layers are Netscape's way of positioning HTML elements with style sheets, which is part of a proposed W3C standard (www.w3.org/pub/WWW/TR/WD-positioning). This means that, like the elements proposed in Cascading Style Sheet positioning, a *layer* is a section of an HTML page that's handled as an independent unit. Layers are *not* a part of the HTML 4 standard.

In a layer-compatible browser, each section can be displayed, hidden, moved, or otherwise manipulated independently of other sections. In Netscape, layers are delineated on the Web page with the <LAYER>, <DIV>, or <SPAN> tags, and Microsoft supports the <DIV> and <SPAN> implementations.

TIP

The <LAYER> tag is proprietary to Netscape and is not compatible with any other browser.

What does all this mean? Layers give you a whole new set of tools for controlling the position and visibility of entire segments of a Web page. You can overlap up to 10 layers and then reveal each one in turn to create an animation, or you can slide layers around for other transition effects.

An Introduction to Layers

Begin by looking at a simple example, shown in Listing 22.1 and Figure 22.1. It's a basic HTML document that includes a paragraph for the body text and a layer that contains an image.

Listing 22.1. This page includes a simple layer with no controls.

```
<HTML>
<HEAD>
<TITLE>Working with layers</TITLE>
</HEAD>
<BODY>
<P>Here's some main text which is part of a paragraph.</P>
<LAYER>
<H1><FONT color="red">HERE'S SOME REALLY BIG TEXT</FONT></H1>
</LAYER>
</BODY>
</HTML>
```

TIP

You'll notice the lack of the HTML 4 <!DOCTYPE> declaration at the beginning of the listings in this chapter. That's because layers aren't part of the HTML 4 standard, so it would be incorrect to tell a browser or SGML parser that the documents conform to that specification.

FIGURE 22.1.

With no other formatting in this simple layer example, it's displayed as any other HTML document would be.

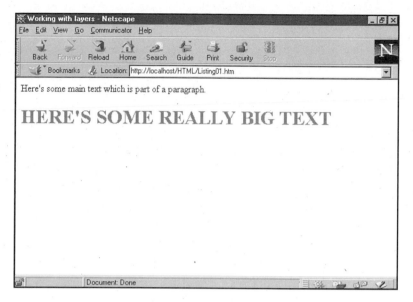

From a design standpoint, this layer isn't very interesting. It would be more useful if you could position it somewhere other than inline with the rest of the document.

To position a layer, you need a coordinate system that can describe any position in the browser window, no matter the size or shape. For this reason, all coordinates are based from the top-left corner of the browser window.

To ensure compatibility with all possible measurements used in style sheets, a layer supports figures in pixels, inches, centimeters, and percentages. If no measurement system is designated, a layer defaults to pixels.

You can see the result of positioning based on a common starting point in Listing 22.2 and Figure 22.2.

Listing 22.2. The new page includes both text items starting from the top-left corner.

```
<HTML>
<HEAD>
<TITLE>Working with layers</TITLE>
</HEAD>
<BODY>
<P>Here's some main text which is part of a paragraph.</P>
<P>Here's some main text which is part of a paragraph.</P>
<P>Here's some main text which is part of a paragraph.</P>
<P>Here's some main text which is part of a paragraph.</P>
<P>Here's some main text which is part of a paragraph.</P>
<LAYER top=0 left=0>
<H1><FONT color="red">HERE'S SOME REALLY BIG TEXT</FONT></H1>
</LAYER>
</BODY>
</HTML>
```

FIGURE 22.2.

This page uses absolute positioning to place the layer with the image at the same starting point as the rest of the page.

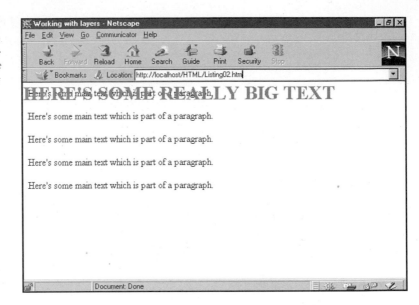

Here's what happens. First, there's a bunch of body text to display, just to make sure there's plenty in the background when you get around to the layer. The layer specifies an absolute position at the top-left corner of the browser window, supplied in the top and left attributes. This is the same starting point used by all pages, but by using the two placement attributes, you've forced the heading text to the same starting point as the beginning of the page.

In addition to placement, you can also control the width of a layer. Listing 22.3 is similar to Listing 22.2, but with two text elements instead of text and graphics. Note the difference in the width of the text between the two paragraphs on the page. (See Figure 22.3.)

Listing 22.3. A new layer is added to the Web page to control the width of the body text.

```
<HTML>
<HEAD>
<TITLE>Working with layers</TITLE>
</HEAD>
<BODY>
<P>Here's some text which is not a part of any layer anywhere, and includes
a rather long sentence which stretches clear across the page.</P>

<LAYER top=150 left=150 width=100>
<P>Here's some main text which is part of another paragraph.
Here's some main text which is part of another paragraph.
Here's some main text which is part of another paragraph.
Here's some main text which is part of another paragraph.
Here's some main text which is part of another paragraph.</P>
</LAYER>

</BODY>
</HTML>
```

Figure 22.3.

This page uses layer width control to set margins for the text in the layer.

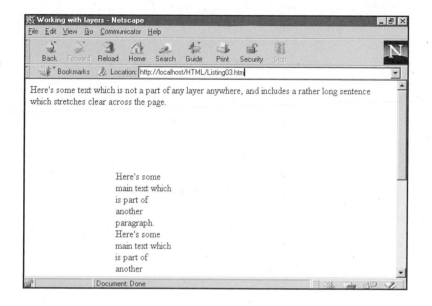

The first paragraph extends all the way across the browser window and is broken according to the rules of the browser—when the line's too long, it continues to the next line. The second paragraph is contained by a layer. Its position begins further down the page, indented from the left. Then, its width is constrained to 100 pixels, forcing a long narrow column down the middle of the page.

Working with Other <LAYER> Attributes

Like every other element in HTML, layers have some default behavior that you should consider. First, as I mentioned earlier, layers are displayed within the normal flow of a document unless additional attributes control their placement.

The second behavior has to do with backgrounds and transparency. If no background color or graphic is specified for a layer, the layer is transparent by default. You saw this effect illustrated in Figure 22.2 when the body text showed through the heading text that was placed over it. Any other setting for the background renders it opaque. (See Listing 22.4 and Figure 22.4.)

Listing 22.4. A background color is added to the layer to make it opaque.

```
<HTML>
<HEAD>
<TITLE>Working with layers</TITLE>
</HEAD>
<BODY bgcolor="white">
<P>Here's some main text which is part of a paragraph.</P>
<P>Here's some main text which is part of a paragraph.</P>
<P>Here's some main text which is part of a paragraph.</P>
<P>Here's some main text which is part of a paragraph.</P>
```

continues

Listing 22.4. continued

```
<P>Here's some main text which is part of a paragraph.</P>
<LAYER top=0 left=0 bgcolor="gray">
<H1><FONT color="white">HERE'S SOME REALLY BIG TEXT</FONT></H1>
</LAYER>
</BODY>
</HTML>
```

FIGURE 22.4.

The black-on-white body text is obscured by the white-on-gray heading text in the layer.

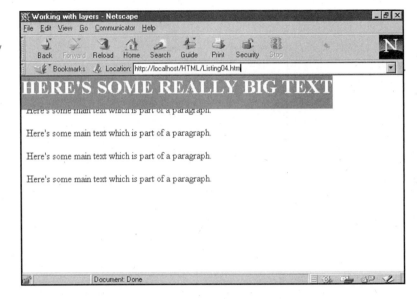

In this page, the background color of the page is set to white, and then the five lines of body text are displayed. This is followed by our faithful layer, now set in a white-on-gray color scheme. By setting a background attribute, the layer is forced to become opaque and obscures all the text underneath it. You can get the same effect by using the background attribute and specifying a URL for a graphic image.

Using More than One Layer

The preceding examples have been sticking to one layer so you can see some of the basic behavior of a layer. It's possible to add more than one layer, however, by adding more layer tags. In Listing 22.5 and Figure 22.5, four layers with absolute positioning have been added so you can see how they stack up on a page.

Listing 22.5. Positioning four layers in four separate positions on the page.

```
<HTML>
<HEAD>
<TITLE>Multiple Layers</TITLE>
</HEAD>
<BODY>
<LAYER top=0 left=0 width=150>
<P>This is layer number 1 located in the top left corner of the window.
This is layer number 1 located in the top left corner of the window.
This is layer number 1 located in the top left corner of the window.</P>
</LAYER>
<LAYER top=0 left=200 width=150>
<P>This is layer number 2 located in the top right corner of the window.
This is layer number 2 located in the top right corner of the window.
This is layer number 2 located in the top right corner of the window.</P>
</LAYER>
<LAYER top=200 left=0 width=150>
<P>This is layer number 3 located in the bottom left corner of the window.
This is layer number 3 located in the bottom left corner of the window.
This is layer number 3 located in the bottom left corner of the window.</P>
</LAYER>
<LAYER top=200 left=200 width=150>
<P>This is layer number 4 in the bottom right left corner of the window.
This is layer number 4 in the bottom right corner of the window.
This is layer number 4 in the bottom right corner of the window.</P>
</LAYER>
</BODY>
</HTML>
```

FIGURE 22.5.

More than one layer is placed on a page, and each is placed in its own position on the page.

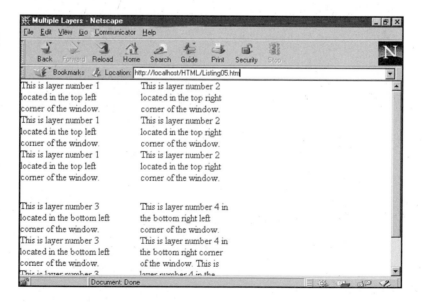

By now, your imagination must be running wild. Next, you'll take the next big step for layers—overlapping and changing the display order at will, which involves adding one more attribute, called `visibility`. (See Listing 22.6 and Figure 22.6.) To gain additional control over each section, you also must give each layer a name. Each layer in Listing 22.6, then, has the same position information and includes a name and `visibility` attribute.

Listing 22.6. Controlling a layer's display status in the stack.

```
<HTML>
<HEAD>
<TITLE>Multiple Layers</TITLE>
</HEAD>
<BODY>
<LAYER name=one top=0 left=0 width=150 bgcolor=white>
<P>This is layer number 1.
This is layer number 1.
This is layer number 1.</P>
</LAYER>
<LAYER name=two top=0 left=0 width=150 visibility=hide below=1 bgcolor=white>
<P>This is layer number 2.
This is layer number 2.
This is layer number 2.</P>
</LAYER>
<LAYER name=three top=0 left=0 width=150 visibility=hide bgcolor=white>
<P>This is layer number 3.
This is layer number 3.
This is layer number 3.</P>
</LAYER>
<LAYER name=four top=0 left=0 width=150 visibility=hide bgcolor=white>
<P>This is layer number 4.
This is layer number 4.
This is layer number 4.</P>
</LAYER>
</BODY>
</HTML>
```

Using the same position and background information for each layer overlaps each layer, blocking the view of any layer underneath. By setting the second through fourth layers as hidden, they are blocked from view and only the first layer is seen.

Now that you have set the layers so that only the first layer is visible, you can attach a script to the document to control which layer is displayed at any given time. You'll control the layer with a form and four buttons. The script calls one function that hides the current layer and displays the selected layer, as shown in Listing 22.7 and Figure 22.7.

Listing 22.7. Including a script to display the selected layer and hide the current layer.

```
<HTML>
<HEAD>
<TITLE>Multiple Layers</TITLE>
</HEAD>

<STYLE type="text/javascript">
```

```
<!--
with (document.classes.cardStack) {
   all.top = 0;
   all.left = 0;
   all.width = 150;
}
//-->
</STYLE>

<SCRIPT language="javascript">
<!--
var topLayer = 0 //the initial layer on top
function showLayer( newTop ) {
  document.layers[newTop].visibility = "show";
  document.layers[topLayer].visibility = "hide";
  topLayer = newTop;
}
function initializeLayers () {
   for (i = 1; i<document.layers.length; i++) {
      document.layers[i].visibility = "hide";
   }
   document.layers[0].visibility = "show";
   document.layers["form"].visibility = "show";
}
//-->
</SCRIPT>

<BODY onLoad="initializeLayers()">
<LAYER name="one" class="cardStack">
<P>This is layer number 1.
This is layer number 1.
This is layer number 1.</P>
</LAYER>
<LAYER name="two" class="cardStack">
<P>This is layer number 2.
This is layer number 2.
This is layer number 2.</P>
</LAYER>
<LAYER name="three" class="cardStack">
<P>This is layer number 3.
This is layer number 3.
This is layer number 3.</P>
</LAYER>
<LAYER name="four" class="cardStack">.
<P>This is layer number 4.
This is layer number 4.
This is layer number 4.</P>
</LAYER>
<LAYER name="form" top=150>
<FORM>
<INPUT type="button" value="Show Layer 1" onClick="showLayer('one')">
<INPUT type="button" value="Show Layer 2" onClick="showLayer('two')">
<INPUT type="button" value="Show Layer 3" onClick="showLayer('three')">
<INPUT type="button" value="Show Layer 4" onClick="showLayer('four')">
</FORM>
</LAYER>
</BODY>
</HTML>.
```

FIGURE **22.6.**

Each layer is stacked on top of the other. Because all the other layers are hidden from view, layer 1 is the only visible layer.

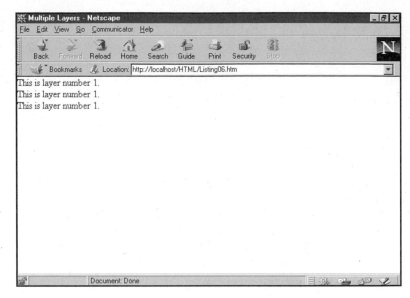

In Figure 22.6, layer 1 was visible, but in Figure 22.7, layer 1 is hidden and layer 3 is visible after clicking the Show Layer 3 button.

FIGURE **22.7.**

Clicking one of the buttons shows the respective layer.

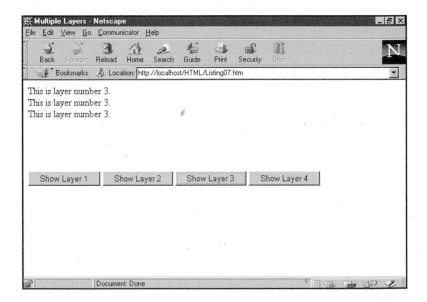

As you can see, you've added a bit to this page to make it more modular. Here's what has happened. First, you've made a generic style for each of the layers in the stack. If you wanted to change the position, text color, or other style attribute, it's now much easier to change the style than to change each tag individually.

When the page loads, a script is called to initialize the visibility of all the layers. This script uses the layers object to work through each layer and set its attribute to hide, then returns to set the other layers to show.

After all this happens, the user sees the initial screen. The form is straightforward, consisting of four buttons. When a button is clicked, the function showLayer is called with one argument— the name of the layer that the user wants to see. The first two lines of the function change the selected layer's visibility attribute to show and the previous visible layer to hide. Then, the user's choice is marked as the current visible layer.

Moving a Layer Around on the Page

The last trick I'll show for layers is the ability to move a layer around on a Web page. This gives you the opportunity for some interesting, albeit superfluous, effects, such as curtains opening or graphics sliding into place. (See Listing 22.8 and Figure 22.8.)

Listing 22.8. By moving a layer across the screen in increments, you get the same effect as a curtain opening to reveal a stage.

```
<HTML>
<HEAD>
<TITLE>Multiple Layers</TITLE>
</HEAD>
<SCRIPT language="javascript">
<!--
function leftMove() {
  document.layers["curtain"].moveAbove(document.layers["thetext"]);
  curtainWidth = 800;
  var moveBy = -1;
  while ( curtainWidth> -1) {
    document.layers["curtain"].offset(moveBy,0);
    curtainWidth += moveBy;
  }
document.layers["curtain"].visibility = "hide";
}
//-->
</SCRIPT>
<BODY>
<LAYER name=curtain bgcolor="red" top=0 left=0>
<H1> This is a heading.</H1>
</LAYER>
<LAYER name=thetext top=5 left=5>
<P>This <A href="tempor.html" title="Eveniet">hyperlink</A>
is part of some
text. It's here so you can see what's happening with the layer moving
across the screen like the curtain on a stage.</P>
</LAYER>
<script language="javascript">
<!--
leftMove();
//-->
</SCRIPT>
</BODY>
</HTML>
```

FIGURE 22.8.

The curtain with the heading text is moved across the screen from left to right to reveal the body text underneath.

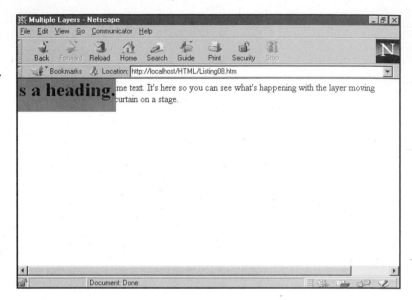

This page begins with a heading in a layer. Because it's the first element on the page, it automatically occupies the top-left position and fills the window from left to right. The red background makes the curtain opaque. The next layer is the body text, positioned at the top-left corner of the window behind the heading text.

> **TIP**
>
> This page is also an example of planning for nonlayer browsers. If this page were displayed on any non-Netscape browser, the user would just see the heading over the body text in the normal HTML presentation of the elements.

Next, take a look at the script. To begin, get the windowWidth property from the current window, which lets you know the width of the space the curtain will be working in. Then, begin with an offset value, which is decremented to move the curtain in a left-to-right motion by using the layer's moveTo method. After the layer is moved over, the offset is decremented by 10 pixels and the loop continues until it has traversed the screen.

As an added safety measure to make sure the curtain moves out of the way, set the visibility property of the layer to hide to make sure it's completely hidden from view on the page.

Two Pages in One with Layers

As the last part of working with layers, you'll see how to combine JSSS (JavaScript Style Sheets) and layers to build two HTML pages that are combined into one. Then, you'll add a form so that the user can pick one page he or she wants to view. The combined pages will take a bit longer to load than either page as it originally existed, but the load time for the combined pages is less than the total time for loading two pages separately from the server.

Both pages are initially constructed from a template using standard HTML. You combine the content from both pages by inserting them in their own layers, along with the addition of some extra text formatting with JSSS, and then add the layers to encompass each one.

The first page is an overview of wildland fire hazards. Begin with the body of the document, shown in Listing 22.9.

Listing 22.9. The basis of the two-in-one page includes a header, a footer, and a table in the middle for content.

```
<BODY BGCOLOR="white">
<!-- Heading for the whole document -->
<TABLE BORDER="0" CELLSPACING="0" WIDTH="100%"
       BGCOLOR="#000000" CELLPADDING="10">
 <TR>
  <TD ALIGN="RIGHT" VALIGN="BOTTOM">
   <H1><FONT COLOR="White">...Summer Safety...</FONT></H1>
  </TD>
  <TD ALIGN="LEFT" VALIGN="BOTTOM" WIDTH="110">
   <P><BR>
    <IMG SRC="/mrfd/Images/pointsource-posterized_92x139.jpg"
        HEIGHT="139" WIDTH="92"></P>
  </TD>
  <TD WIDTH="25"> </TD>
 </TR>
</TABLE>
<!-- Beginning of the actual content -->
<TABLE BORDER="0" CELLSPACING="15" WIDTH="100%">
 <TR>
  <TD WIDTH="25%" VALIGN="TOP">
   <H2>Living in the wildland/urban interface
    <IMG SRC="/mrfd/Images/Wildrnss.jpg" WIDTH="162" HEIGHT="122"></H2>
  </TD>
  <TD VALIGN="TOP">
   <P>Wildfire is a natural element in all ecosystems and environments, and
   Montana is no different. Our climate conditions lead to flammable ground
   cover such as grass, brush and trees. Everyone who has lived in Missoula
   County for any length of time can attest to smoky summer days, or may
   even have seen some of the larger wildfires visible from the valley. Fire
   is a part of our history and a naturally occurring element where we live.</P>
   <P>A new dimension is added to wildfires by the presence of homes. Wildfire
   quickly threatens homes and homeowners, and create a new set of issues for
   firefighters.</P>
   <P><FONT COLOR="Maroon">Missoula Rural Fire District</FONT> has firefighters
   trained for containing fires in the wildland/urban interface. But compared
```

continues

Listing 22.9. continued

```
to a wildfire, they are very limited in manpower and equipment, and in the
distances and terrain they protect. The first homes to burn in the recent
Pattee Canyon fire were lost while firefighters were en route to the
scene.</P>
<P>If you're in an area which has a potential for wildfire, you can call
for a representative from <FONT COLOR="Maroon">Missoula Rural Fire
District</FONT> to come to your home and make
<A HREF="/mrfd/Seasonal/Summer/Wildfire_Tips.htm">suggestions for creating
defensible space</A> around your structures. <CITE>Defensible space</CITE>
is an <DFN>area of reduced fuel</DFN> which gives your home greater odds of
surviving a fire. This is a service provided free of charge to district
homeowners. For more information, call 549-6172 or
<A HREF="mailto:mrfd@montana.com">send us a note</A>.</P>
  </TD>
 </TR>
</TABLE>
<!-- This is the footer for the document -->
<HR>
<P ALIGN="RIGHT">
 <A HREF="/mrfd/index.htm"><STRONG>MRFD Home</STRONG>
 <IMG SRC="/mrfd/Images/cross.gif" WIDTH="113" HEIGHT="97" ALIGN="MIDDLE">
</A></P>
</BODY>
```

The first task is to create some styles for the document to spice it up a bit. This style sheet creates three styles: one for the fire department name and one each for the citation (<CITE>) and definition (<DFN>) tags:

```
<STYLE type="text/javascript">
<!--
with (classes.MRFD.all) {
  color = "red";
  fontFamily = "Helvetica, sans-serif";
  fontStyle = "bold";
}
with (tags.CITE) {
  color = "green";
  fontWeight = "bold";
  fontStyle = "normal";
}
with (tags.DFN) {
  color = "green";
  fontWeight = "normal";
  fontStyle = "italic";
}
//-->
</STYLE>
```

The class for the fire department name is added to the <FONT> tag, which ensures that the text is still highlighted, even if JSSS isn't supported:

```
<FONT COLOR="Red" CLASS="MRFD">Missoula Rural Fire District</FONT>
```

The other tags will be displayed according to their default representations in noncompatible browsers and with green bold or italic text in JSSS browsers.

Your next step is to add a layer to encompass the content of the document. First, add the following layer tag to the top of the content, and complete it with a closing </LAYER>:

```
<LAYER name="content_0" bgcolor="gray">
```

Doing so gives the layer a name you can use to reference it in a script and makes the background opaque so it will block anything else underneath it. Now, pull the content from the second document and add it immediately after the first, along with another set of layer tags. The content portion of your page appears in Listing 22.10.

Listing 22.10. The lion's share of the page includes the content from two pages put on one page and contained in individual layers.

```
<LAYER name="content_0" bgcolor="gray">
<TABLE BORDER="0" CELLSPACING="15" WIDTH="100%">
 <TR>
  <TD WIDTH="25%" VALIGN="TOP">
   <H2>Living in the wildland/urban interface
    <IMG SRC="/mrfd/Images/Wildrnss.jpg" WIDTH="162" HEIGHT="122"></H2>
  </TD>
  <TD VALIGN="TOP">
   <P>Wildfire is a natural element in all ecosystems and environments, and
   Montana is no different. Our climate conditions lead to flammable ground
   cover such as grass, brush and trees. Everyone who has lived in Missoula
   County for any length of time can attest to smoky summer days, or may
   even have seen some of the larger wildfires visible from the valley. Fire
   is a part of our history and a naturally occurring element where we live.</P>
   <P>A new dimension is added to wildfires by the presence of homes. Wildfire
   quickly threatens homes and homeowners, and create a new set of issues for
   firefighters.</P>
   <P><FONT COLOR="Maroon" CLASS="MRFD">Missoula Rural Fire District</FONT>
   has firefighters trained for containing fires in the wildland/urban
   interface. But compared to a wildfire, they are very limited in manpower
   and equipment, and in the distances and terrain they protect. The first
   homes to burn in the recent Pattee Canyon fire were lost while firefighters
   were en route to the scene.</P>
   <P>If you're in an area which has a potential for wildfire, you can call
   for a representative from <FONT COLOR="Maroon" CLASS="MRFD">Missoula Rural
   Fire District</FONT> to come to your home and make
   <A HREF="/mrfd/Seasonal/Summer/Wildfire_Tips.htm">suggestions for creating
   defensible space</A> around your structures. <CITE>Defensible space</CITE>
   is an <DFN>area of reduced fuel</DFN> which gives your home greater odds of
   surviving a fire. This is a service provided free of charge to district
   homeowners. For more information, call 549-6172 or
   <A HREF="mailto:mrfd@montana.com">send us a note</A>.</P>
  </TD>
 </TR>
</TABLE>
</LAYER>

<LAYER name="content_1" bgcolor="gray" visibility="hide">
<TABLE BORDER="0" CELLSPACING="15" WIDTH="100%">
 <TR>
  <TD WIDTH="25%" VALIGN="TOP">
   <H2>Wildfire...Are you prepared?
```

continues

Listing 22.10. continued

```
<IMG SRC="/mrfd/Images/flashover_small_100x118.jpg" WIDTH="160" VSPACE="10">
  </H2>
 </TD>
 <TD VALIGN="TOP">
  <P>More and more people are making their homes in woodland settings -- in
or near forests, rural areas or remote mountain sites.  There, homeowners
enjoy the beauty of the environment but face the very real danger of
wildfire.</P>
  <P>Wildfires often begin unnoticed.  They spread quickly, igniting brush,
trees and homes.  Reduce your risk by preparing now -- before wildfire
strikes.  Meet with your family to decide what to do and where to go if
wildfires threaten your area. Follow the steps listed here to protect your
family, home and property.</P>
 </TD>
</TR>
<TR>
 <TD WIDTH="25%" VALIGN="TOP">
  <HR>
  <H2>Creating defensible space...</H2>
 </TD>
 <TD VALIGN="TOP">
  <HR>
  <UL>
   <LI>Design and landscape your home with wildfire safety in mind. </LI>
   <LI>Select materials and plants that can help contain fire rather than
fuel it. </LI>
   <LI>Use fire resistant or non-combustible materials on the roof and
exterior structure of the dwelling. </LI>
   <LI>Treat wood or combustible material used in roofs, siding, decking
or trim with UL-approved fire-retardant chemicals. </LI>
   <LI>Plant fire-resistant shrubs and trees. For example, hardwood trees
are less flammable than pine or spruce. </LI>
  </UL>
 </TD>
</TR>
<TR>
 <TD WIDTH="25%" VALIGN="TOP">
  <HR>
  <H2>Practice wildfire safety...</H2>
 </TD>
 <TD VALIGN="TOP">
  <HR>
  <P>Find out how you can promote and practice wildfire safety around your
home and property.</P>
  <UL>
   <LI>Contact your local fire department, health department or forestry
office for information on fire laws. </LI>
   <LI>Make sure that fire vehicles can get to your home. </LI>
   <LI>Clearly mark all driveway entrances and display your name and
address. </LI>
   <LI>Report hazardous conditions that could cause a wildfire. </LI>
   <LI>Teach children about fire safety. Keep matches out of reach. </LI>
   <LI>Post fire emergency telephone numbers. </LI>
   <LI>Plan several escape routes away from your home -- by car and by
foot.</LI>
   <LI>Talk to your neighbors about wildfire safety.  Plan how the
```

```
    neighborhood could work together after a wildfire. </LI>
<LI>Make a list of your neighbors' skills such as medical or
    technical. </LI>
    <LI>Consider how you could help neighbors who have special needs such
    as elderly or disabled persons. </LI>
    <LI>Make plans to take care of children who may be on their own if
    parents can't get home. </LI>
    </UL>
    </TD>
  </TR>
</TABLE>
</LAYER>
```

Now you need a way to select a page to view. Use a drop-down list in a form near the top of the page that calls a function to display the appropriate page:

```
<FORM name="topic">
Choose a topic:
<SELECT name="choice" onChange="showPage(this.selectedIndex)">
  <OPTION>The Wildland/Urban Interface</OPTION>
  <OPTION>Preparing for Wildfire</OPTION>
</SELECT>
</FORM>
```

There are two important items in the argument for the call to showPage. The first is this, which refers to the current element in the current form. The second is selectedIndex, which returns a number corresponding to the item chosen. Because you're working with computers, the first option is 0, the second is 1, the third 2, and so on.

The last step is to create the script to hide and display each of the layers (more information on scripting is in Chapter 23, "JavaScript at a Glance"):

```
<SCRIPT language="javascript1.1">
<!--
visibleLayer = "content_0";
function showPage ( layerIndex ) {
  chosenLayer = "content_" + layerIndex;
  document.layers[ visibleLayer ].visibility = "hide";
  document.layers[ chosenLayer ].visibility = "show";
  visibleLayer = chosenLayer;
//-->
</SCRIPT>
```

Start this script by initializing the pointer to the current visible layer. Then, the function will accept the index from the selection list and use it to build the name of the selected layer. The current layer is hidden, the selected layer is displayed, and the pointer to the current layer is updated.

When you combine the style, script, and content, the result is a drop-down list with which users can select either page at their whim. (See Figure 22.9.) You can also easily extend it by adding additional layers and options to the form. If users view this page on an incompatible browser, each of the layer tags is ignored, and the combination is viewed as one big page.

FIGURE 22.9.

When the user picks a page from the list, it's automatically displayed in the window without any work from the browser.

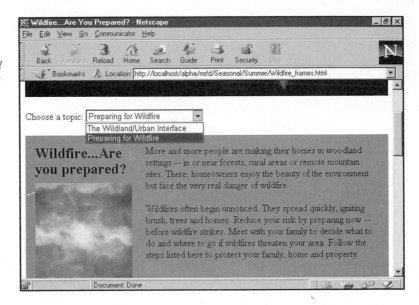

There is one last item. Did you see the hyperlink in the first layer? It was used to point to the page that contained the second layer. You can make this compatible with any browser, however. First, add an anchor immediately following the second layer tag:

```
<A name="fire_tips"></A>
```

Then, modify the hyperlink to work with your script on compatible browsers and to jump to the anchor on incompatible browsers:

```
<A HREF="#fire_tips" onClick="showPage(0)">suggestions for creating
defensible space</A>
```

When a user clicks this link on a compatible browser, the `click` event handler catches the user action before an attempt is made to jump to the anchor. On an incompatible browser, the `onClick` part of the tag is ignored, and the browser jumps to the anchor.

Summary

Netscape's `<LAYER>` tag is used much like element positioning with Cascading Style Sheets (discussed in Chapter 19, "Cascading Style Sheets and Element Positioning"). It can be used to create advanced layouts in your HTML document, create simple animation effects (such as a curtain that unveils content), or combine pages in a "flipchart" arrangement.

Even with its similarity to other positioning schemes, there are no plans for the W3C to include the `<LAYER>` tag as part of the HTML standard. Layers remain unique to Netscape Navigator 4.0, with no support from Microsoft, Mosaic, or any other browser.

Just the same, for intranets or other sites that exclusively use Netscape, layers provide a method for custom HTML layout and simple Dynamic HTML effects.

PART

V

IN THIS PART

Programming Languages for HTML

JavaScript at a Glance

by Kelly Murdock

IN THIS CHAPTER

With each new version, HTML is becoming more and more powerful, but some tasks still require more than what the basic HTML tags can provide.

HTML is designed to format and display items to the screen. However, if you want your Web pages to interact with the user, in the past you needed to write a CGI script to be placed on the server. CGI scripts are quite capable, but they often require some tricky programming and server knowledge.

Another alternative is to use JavaScript, which is easy to learn and use. JavaScript runs on the client and is embedded within the HTML code, so it's ideal for people comfortable with HTML. In this chapter, you get a brief look at what JavaScript is, learn how it can be used to enhance your Web pages, and work through a simple example.

JavaScript: What Is It?

JavaScript is a simple, interpreted, object-oriented scripting language that can be used to add simple interactive behaviors to an HTML page by means of a script of keywords inserted into a Web page.

JavaScript is sometimes considered a subset of the programming language Java. Actually, when looking at its origin, you can see that this isn't true. As Sun was working on defining Java, Netscape was creating a scripting language for their LiveWire product called LiveScript.

As development continued, Java was released to much acclaim. Netscape realized that LiveScript would be useful as a way to interface with Java and contacted Sun with the idea. Sun helped Netscape rework LiveScript and called it JavaScript. Although it does have some syntax that's similar to Java, JavaScript is not a derivative of Java.

It's Simple

With JavaScript, you can embed scripts directly within HTML pages. These scripts can be used to program the Web page to respond and react to the viewer's actions, without your having to learn a complex programming language. JavaScript occupies that middle ground between programming and HTML markup that makes it accessible to everyone.

> **NOTE**
>
> Those familiar with programming concepts will find JavaScript very easy to pick up. However, they will quickly find that it lacks the power of a full-featured programming language.
>
> If you're unfamiliar with such concepts, learning JavaScript is a bit trickier, but not impossible. Start by dissecting some simple examples. With HTML 4, JavaScript is becoming more of a requirement than a luxury.

It's Interpreted

Programming languages such as Java are *compiled*—converted into a form the computer can understand before execution. JavaScript is different. It's an interpreted language, which means the conversion into machine-understandable code takes place as the script is run.

Being an interpreted language makes JavaScript easier to use, but it also increases the chance of including a script with an error. It's critical that you check all your scripts before placing them on your Web pages.

It's Object-Oriented

Stating that the language is object-oriented is important; it means that the language is designed to be modular, with reusable, extendable sections of code. Each object has properties, methods, and event handlers associated with it. By understanding how each of these elements work, you can use them for any object you encounter.

Object *properties* are simply the defining attributes that make up the object. For example, the button object has a name and a value. These are properties that help define what the button is.

Methods are the actions you can do to the object, such as clicking on a button or making a string object all uppercase letters. You can also send parameters to methods to alter the results.

Event handlers are used to mark the commands to execute when something happens. For example, the onClick= event handler tells the browser what to do when a click on the object happens.

How Is It Used?

JavaScript scripts can be embedded within HTML pages quite easily by using the <SCRIPT> tag. One of the attributes of the <SCRIPT> tag, LANGUAGE, is used to specify the scripting language the browser should expect. It should look like this:

```
<SCRIPT LANGUAGE="JavaScript">
<!-- Javascript code goes here -->
</SCRIPT>
```

The <SCRIPT> tag should be located in the <HEAD> section of your HTML code. This isn't a requirement, but it helps create cleaner code. For sections of JavaScript code that display data to the screen, you need to place the code in the <BODY> section.

> **NOTE**
>
> There are other scripting languages besides JavaScript—most notably, VBScript, which is based on Microsoft's Visual Basic. There are many similarities between these two scripting languages, but the syntax is different. See Chapter 24, "Using VBScript," for more information.

For JavaScript to work on the client, it must be run on a JavaScript-compliant Web browser. Netscape Navigator 2.0 and later and Internet Explorer 3.0 and later are both JavaScript-compliant.

To make sure that non–JavaScript-compliant browsers don't try to display the JavaScript code, you should place comment markers around the script, as shown in the preceding code line. These comment markers hide the code from other browsers.

JavaScript can be written directly within an HTML file by using the `<SCRIPT>` tag, but you can also reference an external script file with the `SRC` attribute, as shown:

```
<SCRIPT LANGUAGE="JavaScript" SRC="http://www.myScripts.com/coolScript.js">
```

Notice how JavaScript files have the `.js` extension.

JavaScript's Current State

JavaScript was introduced as version 1.0 along with Netscape Navigator 2.0. Version 1.1 was developed for Navigator 3.0. Now with Netscape Communicator, JavaScript has been updated again to version 1.2.

With each new version, several more objects have been added to the language. These new objects mainly let you control the new features in the browser. For a look at the additions to version 1.2, visit the What's New in the JavaScript 1.2 page at `http://developer.netscape.com/library/documentation/communicator/jsguide/js1_2.html`.

Microsoft has created an implementation of JavaScript for its Internet Explorer browser called JScript. The differences between JavaScript and JScript are very subtle, but do exist. If you plan on creating JavaScript scripts for Internet Explorer, check out Microsoft's JScript information page at `http://www.microsoft.com/jscript`.

> **CAUTION**
>
> Some JavaScript functions are incompatible with Internet Explorer. If you're writing scripts for both browsers, be sure to check the code on both.

What Is It Good For?

Now that you understand what the language is and where it came from, I imagine your bigger question is What is it good for? You can find the answer to this question by taking a quick look at the types of scripting functions that are possible.

Form Validation

Form controls are common throughout the Web. They are easily implemented by using standard HTML tags. However, controlling the data entered into forms can be difficult. Traditionally, this was done by means of a CGI script that resided on the server. As the data was entered, the CGI script queried the server to check whether the data was valid. If it wasn't, then the server had to communicate back to the client that the data wouldn't work. The data had to be re-entered and returned to the server. This laborious process tied up valuable server resources.

JavaScript can internally check the data from within the browser without bothering the server. Then, only if the data is valid, would the information be sent to the server.

Form validation was one of the first uses of JavaScript on the Web and still remains very popular.

Responding to Input

As data is entered into JavaScript form controls, the Web page can respond to this input.

A common use of JavaScript across the Web is to create simple games, such as the Mastermind version found at www.dreamlink.se/mastermind. In this game, the user selects colors in the pull-down menu boxes. The script responds by computing the choices and displaying hints on which ones are correct. Figure 23.1 shows a game in progress.

FIGURE 23.1.

A JavaScript version of Mastermind.

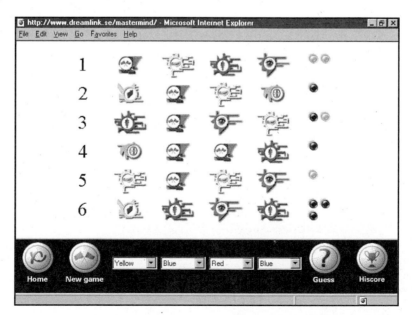

Dialog Boxes

One of the ways that JavaScript sends messages to the user is through dialog boxes. Figure 23.2 shows the conclusion of the Mastermind game with a dialog box announcing the victorious result.

FIGURE 23.2.

Dialog boxes display messages to the viewer.

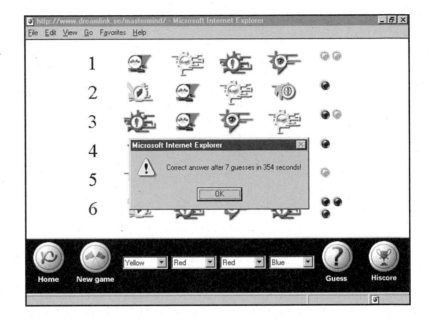

Detecting Browser Characteristics

Another powerful feature of JavaScript is the ability to find out information about the browser environment. A script in an HTML file could determine which browser is being used by the viewer and change the content appropriately.

A good example of browser detection is the Guitar Chord Computer found at `http://web.ukonline.co.uk/alastair.vance/gcc.htm`. As you enter the site with Internet Explorer, a dialog box shows up informing you that you will be routed to a version that works with your browser. (See Figure 23.3.)

Updating the Browser Properties

Not only can JavaScript detect which type of browser the viewer has, but it can also change the properties of the browser on demand. Figure 23.4 shows a Color Picker script that lets users change their browser color scheme on the fly by clicking or moving their mouse over the color palette.

FIGURE 23.3.
JavaScript has detected that the browser is incompatible.

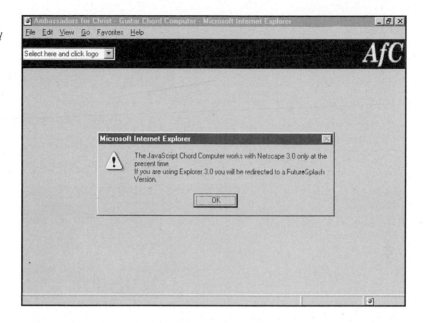

FIGURE 23.4.
The browser colors can be changed as the user moves the mouse over the color palette.

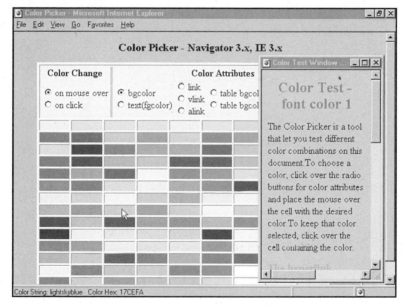

This useful tool also displays the hex values for the chosen colors, which is very helpful when designing Web pages.

Math Capabilities

JavaScript has elaborate mathematical capabilities, also. These math functions include simple arithmetic and complex trigonometric functions. In addition to games and live browser updates, the Web offers a host of calculators for figuring everything from temperature conversion to calorie intake.

In addition to games and calculators, you'll find a lot of educational scripts on the Web, like the algebra tutorial created by Robert Bunge, shown in Figure 23.5. You can find this script at `http://www.pacificrim.net/~rbunge/Algebra/Algebra.html`.

FIGURE 23.5.

This algebra tutorial takes advantage of JavaScript's math *object.*

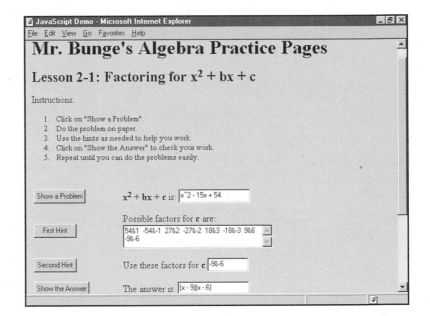

Using Cookies to Keep Visitor Information

Cookies are simple data files that hold visitor information. You can create and control them by using JavaScript. With cookies, you can gather information about visitors, such as their names, and hold onto it until the next time they visit, when you can greet them personally.

Figures 23.6 and 23.7 show a generalized cookie in action. During my first visit to the JavaScript Forum, `http://members.tripod.com/~JavaScriptForum`, (Figure 23.6) the script detects that I'm a new visitor. It records in a cookie my visitor information and the time that I stopped by. Then, during my second visit, the script reads my browser information and looks at the date to present a customized message to me.

FIGURE 23.6.
*My first visit to the
JavaScript Forum.*

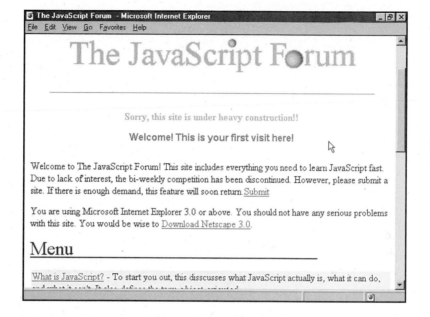

FIGURE 23.7.
*A cookie keeps track of
how often I visit the
site.*

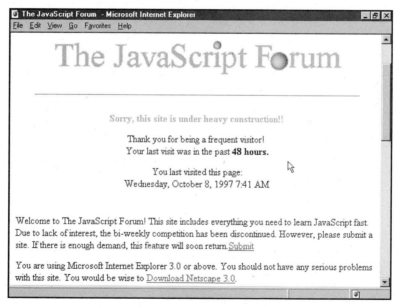

Date and Time Information

Another feature of JavaScript is the ability to query the system for the date and time. Notice the time stamp in Figure 23.7. This feature is handy for keeping track of time and has been used to create online calendar scripts, such as the one shown in Figure 23.8.

FIGURE 23.8.

This calendar script shows how JavaScript can determine dates and times.

Integrating with Java

Although JavaScript is different from Java, the two languages can still communicate with one another. You can include applets written in Java on a Web page and send information to a JavaScript script on the same page. This method helps reduce the limitations of JavaScript.

In the ColorCenter example shown in Figure 23.9, the color grid at the bottom is actually a Java applet. The applet passes the selected color values to the script, which displays that color along with its hex values.

> **NOTE**
>
> JavaScript can interface with other technologies, too. It can be used, for example, to create simple behaviors and motions for VRML worlds.

Basic Graphics

For advanced graphics functions, you really need the power of Java, but for simple graphics control, such as displaying bitmaps or drawing lines, JavaScript is enough.

FIGURE 23.9.

ColorCenter shows how Java applets and JavaScript can be used on a single Web page.

DoodlePad, created by Bill Dortch, is created entirely in JavaScript. It can draw simple shapes and lines. (See Figure 23.10.)

These simple scripts shown in the preceding figures are just a small sampling of the many JavaScripts that can be found online. In the following resources section, you will find many archives full of JavaScripts.

FIGURE 23.10.

DoodlePad shows JavaScript's simple drawing features.

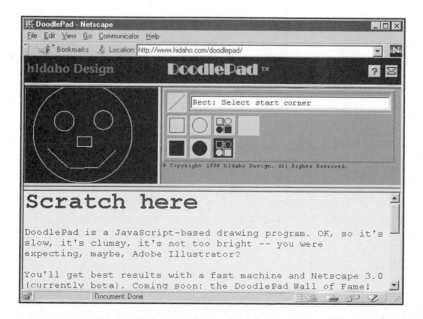

Dynamic HTML

With the latest version of HTML—HTML 4—scripting plays a critical role in controlling the look of Web pages. Dynamic HTML uses the power of scripting to add functionality, such as absolute positioning and responding to events. Part VI, "Dynamic HTML," covers these topics in more detail. You will find more information on JavaScript in Chapters 28, "Working with the User: Events" and 29, "HTML and Scripting: The DHTML Combination."

JavaScript Resources

There are many resources on the Web for learning and experiencing JavaScript. One of the best compilations of JavaScript examples can be found at Gamelan, `http://javascript.developer.com`. (See Figure 23.11.)

FIGURE 23.11.

The Gamelan site is a major source for Web programming information.

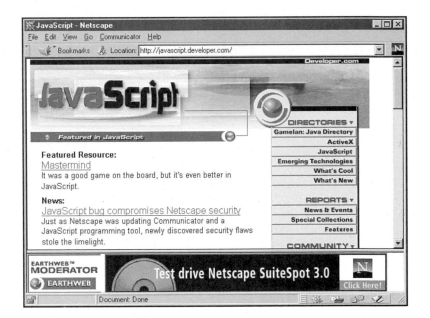

Another good site is JavaScript World at `www.jsworld.com`. This site includes an extensive archive, as well as news and discussion groups. (See Figure 23.12.)

Many JavaScript sites on the Web offer general-purpose scripts that you can include in your own pages. They can be very handy and don't require any programming. One such site is Cut-N-Paste JavaScript (see Figure 23.13), `www.infohiway.com/javascript`. Their scripts range from simple scripts to scroll text to complex calculators and graphic slideshows.

In addition to these sites, Netscape has several good resources for information on learning and using JavaScript.

FIGURE 23.12.

JavaScript World is another good resource.

FIGURE 23.13.

Cut-N-Paste JavaScript offers an easy way to get into scripting.

The official JavaScript 1.1 language specification can be found at: `http://home.netscape.com/eng/javascript/index.html`. The additions to the 1.2 specification are found at `http://developer.netscape.com/library/documentation/communicator/jsguide/js1_2.html`.

Netscape also has an authoring guide, which is invaluable to script writers just starting out. You can find it at `http://home.netscape.com/eng/mozilla/3.0/handbook/javascript/index.html`.

Finally, the DevEdge Newsgroup FAQ on JavaScript can be found at: `http://developer.netscape.com/support/faqs/champions/javascript.html`.

JavaScript Tools

To help developers with their scripting tasks, Netscape has created several tools that can make creating scripts easier.

The Netscape JavaScript Debugger, found at `http://search.netscape.com/eng/Tools/JSDebugger/relnotes/relnotespr1.html`, can help users track down bugs by allowing them to walk through the code step-by-step and examine values.

In addition to the debugger, Netscape is working on a visual development environment for JavaScript. This powerful tool will help you create scripts by means of a layout editor with drag-and-drop capability. You can find the latest on Visual JavaScript 1.0 at `http://search.netscape.com/eng/Tools/VisualJS/relnotes/relnotespr2.html`.

Now that I've covered the resources available and mentioned some tools to help, take a quick look at coding in JavaScript with a simple example.

A JavaScript Example

In this chapter, I've concentrated on presenting an overview of JavaScript and explaining what's possible rather than giving the details of the language. However, before you leave, you'll get a brief look at an example of working with the language.

First, you need to create an HTML structure. The JavaScript code should be inserted where it says `place code here`:

```
<HTML>
<HEAD>
<TITLE>JavaScript Example</TITLE>
<SCRIPT LANGUAGE="JavaScript">
<!-- this code is only for JavaScript-capable browsers
//place code here.
// end of JavaScript code -->
</SCRIPT>
</HEAD>
<BODY>
</BODY>
</HTML>
```

After the structure for the HTML file is built, the first JavaScript command you want is to have visitors enter their names. You get this information by using the prompt dialog box. The inserted value is stored in the variable `Name`, as shown:

```
Name = prompt("Enter Your Name:","Name");
```

You can then recall the value of Name and enter it on the screen with the document.write statement:

```
document.write("<H1>" + Name + "'s Litigation Simulation</H1><HR>");
```

You could have used normal HTML to display the example's title, but by using JavaScript, you can include the user's name to customize the page.

There's more code to add in the <SCRIPT> tag later, but for now, move to the <BODY> tag where you will use HTML form elements to create some text boxes.

First, include some instructions for the activity:

```
For this simulation, you start out with $500,000 dollars. Read the news
➡and select one of the buttons below. The fees or rewards will
➡automatically be added or deducted from your money.
```

The next step is to create three form fields—one that shows your money, one that shows your lawyer's money, and one for news:

```
<FORM METHOD=POST>
Your Money (in hundred thousands): <INPUT TYPE=text NAME="litsmoney"
➡VALUE="5">
<BR>
Your Lawyer's Money (in hundred thousands): <INPUT TYPE=text
➡NAME="lawsmoney" VALUE="0">
<BR>
News: <INPUT TYPE=text NAME="news" SIZE=50 VALUE="You were bit by
➡the neighbor's dog.">
<BR><HR>
```

The NAME attributes are variable names that JavaScript can use to control the values of these fields.

Next, you need three action buttons. They are created by using standard HTML form syntax. The onClick= command is an event handler that tells the code where to go when the button is clicked. You end this section with the </FORM> tag:

```
<INPUT TYPE=button NAME="settle" VALUE="Settle Out of Court"
➡onClick="payment1(this.form)">
<INPUT TYPE=button NAME="sue" VALUE="Take it to Court"
➡onClick="payment2(this.form)">
<INPUT TYPE=button NAME="drop" VALUE="Drop Case"
➡onClick="payment3(this.form)">
<BR>
</FORM>
```

Payment1, payment2, and payment3 are functions that you will include in the <SCRIPT> tag that changes the field values when the buttons are clicked.

Each of these functions is pretty similar to the others. The form keyword is passed in as a parameter so that the functions can have access to change the form's values. Each payment function changes the value of the money fields in a different way:

```
function payment1(form){
     form.litsmoney.value++;
     form.lawsmoney.value++;
     newnews(form,index);
     index++;
}
function payment2(form){
     winorlose = Math.abs(Math.sin(form.lawsmoney.value));
     if (winorlose > 0.5)
         form.litsmoney.value++;
     else
         form.litsmoney.value--;
     form.lawsmoney.value++;
     newnews(form,index);
     index++;
}
function payment3(form){
     form.litsmoney.value--;
     form.lawsmoney.value++;
     newnews(form,index);
     index++;
}
```

Notice that the `payment2` function includes a series of mathematical functions to compute a semirandom result that's saved in a variable called `winorlose`. `If`-`else` statements are used to change the money values based on the result of `winorlose`.

After the field values are modified, another function called `newnews` is called to update the `news` field. It also receives the `form` parameter and another variable called `index` that helps it step through the news entries.

To use the `index` variable, you need to initialize it at the start of the script. The `var` keyword specifies it as a variable and its initial value is set, as shown:

```
var index=1;
```

All the payment functions alter the `index` variable by increasing its value by one. The `newnews` function changes the `news` field depending on the value of `index`:

```
function newnews(form,index){
     if (index==1)
         form.news.value = "You were fired for sleeping on the job.";
     else if (index==2)
         form.news.value = "You were run over by a bus.";
     else if (index==3)
         form.news.value = "You were injured by a defective product.";
     else if (index==4)
         form.news.value = "Your publisher stole your copyright.";
     else if (index==5)
         form.news.value = "Your insurance won't cover your house fire.";
     else if (index==6)
         form.news.value = "That's all the news, you can keep going
➡if you want.";
}
```

You can see the final results by opening this example from the book's CD-ROM. It's a simple example, but it shows several uses of JavaScript. Figures 23.14 and Figure 23.15 show the example in action.

FIGURE 23.14.

A dialog box from the example that lets users enter their names.

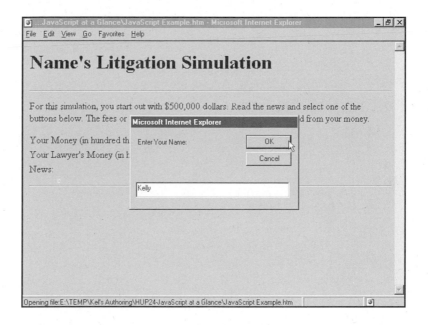

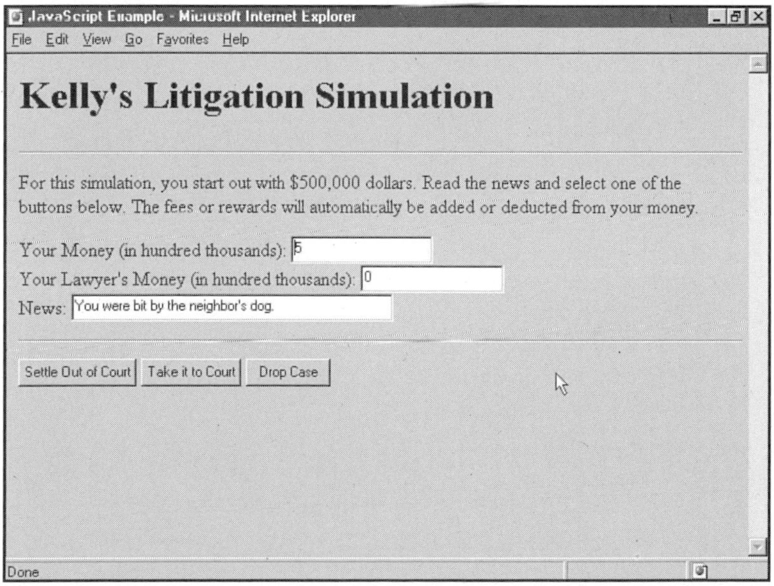

FIGURE 23.15.

Litigation simulation, a JavaScript example.

The complete code for this example is included here in Listing 23.1.

Listing 23.1. Litigation simulation JavaScript example.

```html
<HTML>
<HEAD>
<TITLE>JavaScript Example</TITLE>
<SCRIPT LANGUAGE="JavaScript">
<!-- this code is only for JavaScript-capable browsers
Name = prompt("Enter Your Name:","Name");
document.write("<H1>" + Name + "'s Litigation Simulation</H1><HR>");
var index=1;
function payment1(form){
     form.litsmoney.value++;
     form.lawsmoney.value++;
     newnews(form,index);
     index++;
}
function payment2(form){
     winorlose = Math.abs(Math.sin(form.lawsmoney.value));
     if (winorlose > 0.5)
          form.litsmoney.value++;
     else
          form.litsmoney.value--;
     form.lawsmoney.value++;
     newnews(form,index);
     index++;
}
function payment3(form){
     form.litsmoney.value--;
     form.lawsmoney.value++;
     newnews(form,index);
     index++;
}
function newnews(form,index){
     if (index==1)
          form.news.value = "You were fired for sleeping on the job.";
     else if (index==2)
          form.news.value = "You were run over by a bus.";
     else if (index==3)
          form.news.value = "You were injured by a defective product.";
     else if (index==4)
          form.news.value = "Your publisher stole your copyright.";
     else if (index==5)
          form.news.value = "Your insurance won't cover your house fire.";
     else if (index==6)
          form.news.value = "That's all the news, you can keep going
➥if you want.";
}
// end of JavaScript code -->
</SCRIPT>
</HEAD>
<BODY>
For this simulation, you start out with $500,000 dollars. Read the news
➥and select one of the buttons below. The fees or rewards will
➥automatically be added or deducted from your money.
<FORM METHOD=POST>
Your Money (in hundred thousands): <INPUT TYPE=text NAME="litsmoney"
```

```
➥VALUE="5">
<BR>
Your Lawyer's Money (in hundred thousands): <INPUT TYPE=text
➥NAME="lawsmoney" VALUE="0">
<BR>
News: <INPUT TYPE=text NAME="news" SIZE=50 VALUE="You were bit by
➥the neighbor's dog.">
<BR><HR>
<INPUT TYPE=button NAME="settle" VALUE="Settle Out of Court"
➥onClick="payment1(this.form)">
<INPUT TYPE=button NAME="sue" VALUE="Take it to Court"
➥onClick="payment2(this.form)">
<INPUT TYPE=button NAME="drop" VALUE="Drop Case"
➥onClick="payment3(this.form)">
<BR>
</FORM>
</BODY>
</HTML>.
```

Summary

JavaScript is just one of several scripting languages that are making Web pages interactive. It's a quick and easy alternative to complex programming languages such as Java. In this chapter, you've been given a brief look at JavaScript.

One of the best ways to learn JavaScript is to find good examples on the Web and dissect them. Using someone else's code can springboard you into advanced techniques quickly. You've looked at several sample scripts taken from the Web to see what types of function are available. Also, you now have a list of resources to help you improve your scripting capabilities.

If you've invested time in learning the complexities of HTML and you believe your pages could benefit from the types of features that JavaScript makes possible, then I encourage you to dive into the possibilities.

Using VBScript

by Robert McDaniel

IN THIS CHAPTER

CHAPTER 24

In early 1996, Netscape Communications Corporation unveiled the first client-side scripting language. Originally termed LiveScript, Netscape altered both the name and some of the syntax following the introduction of the Java programming language. Netscape understood that the power and flexibility of Java wasn't without limitations, including slow execution, longer download times for applets, and lack of interaction between Java and the other HTML elements on the Web page. Therefore, Netscape collaborated with Sun Microsystems to provide the same look and feel of Java in a lightweight scripting language.

Netscape also correctly understood that Java was a difficult programming language to learn, especially for Web designers with little or no programming experience. Even to program simple tasks in Java required skills far beyond those of coding basic HTML. At the same time, though, Web page designers wanted the ability to add interactive elements, which perform actions automatically and respond to user actions.

Along with this fundamental understanding of the needs of Web page designers, Netscape also saw the media hype associated with Java. By incorporating similar syntax and using a similar name, they could leverage some of the media frenzy associated with Java. When Netscape Navigator 2.0 was released, they announced the inclusion of JavaScript, an easy-to-learn client-side scripting language with the power and flexibility of a full-featured programming language, but lightweight enough to embed within the source code of HTML pages.

After Netscape introduced JavaScript, the first client-side scripting language, Microsoft realized the necessity of incorporating client-side scripting in its own browser. Because of its embrace-and-extend approach, they wanted to provide support for JavaScript in Internet Explorer. However, Netscape had copyrighted both the name JavaScript and its implementation in Navigator 2.0. Therefore, Microsoft had to create its own implementation of the JavaScript syntax, which they named JScript.

Having accomplished the "embrace" portion of their mantra, Microsoft set its sites on extending the abilities of client-side scripting. This goal led to the introduction of VBScript 1.0 with Internet Explorer 3.0. Because JScript tries to have the same syntax as JavaScript, VBScript is the second client-side scripting language.

Although VBScript is a full-featured scripting language, it isn't often used by Web page developers primarily because of the lack of support for it. Currently, only Microsoft's Internet Explorer has native support for VBScript scripts. And, because virtually everything you can do in VBScript you can also do in JavaScript, most developers choose JavaScript as their scripting language.

So, should you use VBScript? The answer to that depends mostly on what you're trying to accomplish. If you are building an Internet Web site, and you don't want your users having to download plug-ins, you're better off using JavaScript. However, if you are developing an intranet site for a company that uses Internet Explorer exclusively, then VBScript is a good option, especially if you already know Visual Basic.

In this chapter, you get an introduction to VBScript. You will learn the following:

- What VBScript is
- How to use VBScript with your HTML pages
- What VBScript is good for
- Resources for more information

What Is VBScript?

VBScript stands for *Visual Basic Scripting Edition.* As its name suggests, it contains the same language structure, and much of the same syntax, as Microsoft's popular Visual Basic language. By creating VBScript, Microsoft wanted to allow Web page developers to leverage their existing Visual Basic skills when creating client-side scripts.

Although VBScript does have roots in Visual Basic, you don't need to know Visual Basic to learn VBScript. In fact, learning VBScript should be much easier than learning Visual Basic. Also, to use VBScript, you don't need the development environment and compiler, which are necessary with Visual Basic.

VBScript and Visual Basic

VBScript inherits its syntax and structure from Microsoft's Visual Basic programming language. However, there are some differences between the two. Because VBScript programs were designed to be embedded in Web pages, several changes needed to be made to the Scripting Edition of Visual Basic.

First, because VBScript is an interpreted language, it naturally runs slower than compiled Visual Basic applications. To address this, Microsoft made a significant language change to make VBScript execute more quickly. They made VBScript a *loosely typed* programming language.

Programming languages that have many distinct types of data structures require that you use the correct data type in all statements. For example, in a statement requiring a character data type, using an integer returns an error. These types of programming languages are called *strongly typed* languages. Languages that aren't strongly typed are referred to as being *loosely typed.*

VBScript is not a strongly typed programming language. It contains only a single data structure: the variant. You can store any type of data—such as Booleans, integers, decimal numbers, characters, and strings—in variants. By using only a single data structure, Microsoft removes all the overhead required at runtime to verify that the correct data types are being used.

In addition to removing all other data types from VBScript, Microsoft also had to remove many of the Visual Basic commands that were operating-system dependent. Because VBScript is designed to run in a Web browser on any platform, Microsoft had to make sure that any VBScript function would work on all platforms. Therefore, it removed any of the Visual Basic built-in functions that were specific to a single operating system and platform.

For security reasons, VBScript has had all Visual Basic file input and output and operating system commands removed as well. Running programs that have been downloaded from the Internet can be a great risk to the well-being of your machine. These programs can contain hidden viruses that can do a lot of damage to your machine, from removing key files to completely reformatting your hard drive. Visual Basic has all the commands a malicious programmer would need to perform any number of harmful acts to an unknowing user's machine.

VBScript applications are intended to be downloaded from other Web sites across the Internet, so a very real concern is whether these applications might contain malicious actions. To prevent this, Microsoft removed all the Visual Basic file input and output and operating system commands, which are at the heart of virus programs. If an application doesn't have access to the file system or the operating system for the machine on which it's running, it can't make changes to the file system, such as removing files, or invoke operating system commands, such as formatting hard drives. By removing these statements, Microsoft is assuring users that they can download and run VBScript applications without fear of damaging attacks against their computers.

Along with removing many of the Visual Basic commands from VBScript, Microsoft also added a few new features to the Scripting Edition. Because of the unique environment in which VBScript is run, constants and functions not found in the full Visual Basic product were needed. Some of these functions are included to reduce programming time for developing VBScript applications.

For example, the `Split` function is a VBScript function that's not in Visual Basic. When used, it splits apart a string at all occurrences of a specified character, such as a comma. This function is very useful for client-side scripts because much of the environment data is in strings that are delimited by some special character. You can use the `Split` function to quickly break apart this data and work with the portion that's of interest to your application.

VBScript Platforms

Microsoft's first implementation of VBScript was in beta releases of Internet Explorer 3.0 for Windows 95 and Windows NT machines. With the final release, VBScript was supported in versions of Internet Explorer 3.0 for all Windows platforms and Power Macintoshes. Microsoft is working with other companies to develop support for VBScript in Internet Explorer for UNIX platforms.

NCompass, a third-party developer, has created a Netscape plug-in that provides support for VBScript in Netscape Navigator browsers. This plug-in, called ScriptActive, is primarily designed to give Navigator users the ability to work with ActiveX controls. It also offers a conversion tool, which will make Web pages containing VBScript compatible with the Navigator browser.

To extend the uses of VBScript, Microsoft allows licensing VBScript for use in other applications. Third-party developers creating other client or server applications now have the option of building a VBScript interpreter into their applications, enabling the use of VBScript. There's no fee to license VBScript for use in other applications, but the terms of the license do require mention of Microsoft and the appropriate copyrights.

VBScript and Your HTML Pages

The whole point of VBScript was to make a lightweight, easy-to-use scripting language for use in Web pages. That means the scripting language must not only be embedded in an HTML page, but also be aware of that page to interact with it. Microsoft had the benefit of Netscape's earlier developments with JavaScript, so it could embrace the existing definitions for embedding client-side scripts in Web pages. It also extended the functionality by defining and making available objects from the Web page and Web browser to the script.

The <SCRIPT> Tag

Netscape had already defined the method for embedding client-side scripts within HTML documents: the <SCRIPT> tag. By using this tag and its associated </SCRIPT> tag in your HTML, compatible Web browsers understand that the text placed between these tags is application code, not document text.

The <SCRIPT> tag has the following syntax:

```
<SCRIPT LANGUAGE=[scripting language]>
```

For VBScript, you must use the LANGUAGE attribute and set it equal to VBScript, as shown:

```
<SCRIPT LANGUAGE="VBScript">
```

> **CAUTION**
>
> By default, the Web browser uses JavaScript for all client-side scripts. If the LANGUAGE attribute is not present, the application code is interpreted as JavaScript. Therefore, to use the VBScript language in any of your client-side scripts, you must explicitly inform the Web browser that you are using VBScript, not JavaScript. Of course, it's good style to include the LANGUAGE attribute every time you use the <SCRIPT> tag, even if your application code is in JavaScript. If the LANGUAGE attribute is used, and the Web browser that loaded the page doesn't support that scripting language, the contents of the script are ignored.

You can have as many occurrences of the <SCRIPT> tag in your HTML page as you want. You can also use different languages for different occurrences of the <SCRIPT> tag. However, it's typical to have a single large <SCRIPT> section where you have most of your application code, such as subroutines, functions, and variable declarations. Use other occurrences of the <SCRIPT> tag only when you need a function performed at a certain location in the document, such as writing data to the HTML page itself.

24

Hiding Client-Side Scripts from Incompatible Browsers

Most Web browsers in use today support one of the client-side scripting languages. However, that doesn't include everyone; some people visiting your site would see a very garbled Web page if you were to include VBScript in your HTML. Because you want your pages to be cross-platform, cross-browser, and viewable by everyone, you don't want this to happen.

Thankfully, when Netscape introduced the <SCRIPT> tag and implementation in its Navigator 2.0 browser, it built in backward compatibility. It did this by simply using the existing HTML comments tag and teaching newer browsers with support for client-side scripting to ignore this specific occurrence of the HTML comments tag.

The standard syntax for a <SCRIPT> tag in your Web pages would look like this:

```
<SCRIPT LANGUAGE="VBScript">
<!--

    Your Code Goes Here

//-->
</SCRIPT>
```

Notice the second line:

```
<!--
```

This line is the first part of an HTML comment. Browsers supporting client-side scripting always ignore the beginning of an HTML comment. However, browsers not supporting client-side scripting treat everything they encounter, until the ending part of the HTML comments tag, as a comment and don't display it in the Web page.

The ending part of the HTML comment is the next to last line:

```
//-->
```

It's preceded by two slashes, which in client-side scripting denotes a comment line. In other words, the ending HTML comments tag is commented out for Web browsers supporting client-side scripting. Only browsers not supporting client-side scripting use this portion of the HTML comments tag.

By using the opening and closing HTML comments tag, you can successfully hide your application code from Web browsers that don't support client-side scripting. Those types of browsers also completely ignore all occurrences of the <SCRIPT> and </SCRIPT> tags because all Web browsers are designed to ignore HTML tags they don't recognize.

Placing Your Script in Your HTML Code

There are two ways you can embed your VBScript scripts in a Web page. The first way is by using the <SCRIPT> and </SCRIPT> tags anywhere in your HTML document to define the enclosed text as a client-side script and not document text. The second way is to embed the

VBScript code directly in another HTML tag. Of course, this method works only with tags in which embedding script code is supported.

You have already been introduced to the opening and closing <SCRIPT> and </SCRIPT> tags in the section "The <SCRIPT> Tag" earlier in this chapter. In that section, you learned that you can place your <SCRIPT> and </SCRIPT> tags anywhere in your HTML text. The most common place to put your client-side script is in the header section of your HTML, as defined by the <HEAD> and </HEAD> tags. You would then place other scripts in the body section of your HTML document when you want specific text written to the Web page in that location.

For example, you could have a subroutine in the header section of your HTML document that would display a string to the status bar whenever it was called. The VBScript code for the function, complete with the HTML tags, is shown in Listing 24.1.

Listing 24.1. A sample VBScript subroutine in the HTML header section.

```
<HEAD>
<TITLE>VBScript Example</TITLE>

<SCRIPT LANGUAGE="VBScript">
<!--

    Sub Status_Change(Status_String)

        status = Status_String

    End Sub
//-->
</SCRIPT>

</HEAD>
```

The subroutine takes a single string parameter called Status_String. It then places the contents of the string in the Web browser's status bar.

The second method of embedding VBScript code in your HTML text is placing the code into supported HTML tags. The most common HTML tags where you would place VBScript code are the <A> tag, the <BODY> tag, and the <AREA> tag. You can also have VBScript code in the HTML tags for creating forms.

Regardless of which HTML tag you choose to embed VBScript in, the syntax is always the same. You define both the client-side scripting language you're using and the action to take for a specified event. For example, the following is a <BODY> tag that contains some VBScript code:

```
<BODY LANGUAGE="VBScript" onLoad="status='Finished'">
```

As with the <SCRIPT> tag, you always need to specify your choice of language when you use VBScript. Otherwise, the Web browser defaults to JavaScript and uses the JavaScript or JScript interpreter.

24

USING VBSCRIPT

The second part of adding VBScript to a HTML tag is to use defined event handlers for that tag and assign some VBScript code to it. Event handlers are defined for certain HTML tags as part of the Internet Explorer Object Model, which is discussed in the section "Internet Explorer's Object Model for Scripting" later in this chapter.

In this case, the onLoad event handler is being used with the <BODY> tag. The Load event is associated with the document window. When a new Web page is loaded into the Web browser, the Load event is triggered. By using the onLoad event handler, you can define some VBScript code that executes every time the Load event occurs.

With the following code, you're instructing the Web browser to place the string Finished in the Web browser's status bar when it has finished loading the Web page:

```
onLoad="status='Finished'"
```

You could also simply place a call to a subroutine or function in the event handler, as shown:

```
onLoad="Status_Change('Finished')"
```

It would then call the Status_Change subroutine shown earlier in Listing 24.1.

Running your Client-Side Scripts

Your VBScript programs will be run automatically by the Web browser that loads them, depending on how you integrated them into your Web page. Normally, all scripts contained with the HTML <SCRIPT> tag are parsed and executed when the Web page is first loaded. The scripts would have the following form:

```
<SCRIPT LANGUAGE="VBScript">
<!--

    status = "Thanks for visiting!"

//-->
</SCRIPT>
```

The most common use of this form of scripting is to initiate variables and produce data that you want written directly to the Web page. Using the document.write object method, you can write data from your client-side scripts to the Web page for display to the user. However, you can write only to the currently loaded Web page while it's being parsed when loading. Therefore, you should have all your document.write statements in this form:

```
<SCRIPT LANGUAGE="VBScript">
<!--

    document.write("You are using a Web browser that supports VBScript.")

//-->
</SCRIPT>
```

The statements are then executed while the document is being parsed and the data is written to the Web page.

The other option you have when writing code for your `<SCRIPT>` and `</SCRIPT>` tags is to put your code in subroutines and functions. The Web browser doesn't automatically run subroutines and functions when the Web page is being parsed. Instead, you have to call your subroutine or function in another script for it to be run.

For example, with the script shown in Listing 24.1, you have defined the subroutine `Status_Change`. This subroutine isn't automatically run when the Web browser loads the Web page. Instead, you need to call this subroutine somewhere else in another script. Typically, you would have your second script associated with an event. When the event happens, the event handler would call your subroutine to perform the action, such as in the `<BODY>` tag:

```
<BODY LANGUAGE="VBScript" onLoad="Status_Change('Finished')">
```

CAUTION

The `onLoad` event handler is triggered when the Web page completely loads. If you simply place a script that gets executed as the Web page is loaded to display the status message, it gets sent to the status bar while the page is still being parsed. This usually results in your message getting overwritten by the Web browser, which places the message `Done` in the status bar when the page has finished loading.

Internet Explorer's Object Model for Scripting

In an effort to make client-side scripts more powerful, Microsoft defined an object model for its Internet Explorer browser. This object model, formally known as the Internet Explorer Object Model for Scripting, defines an object hierarchy, with objects and their associated properties, methods, and events. You can then make use of the properties, methods, and events in your VBScript applications to develop more robust applications.

The Internet Explorer Object Model for Scripting defines 10 objects:

- Window
- Frame
- History
- Navigator
- Location
- Document
- Link
- Anchor
- Form
- Element

Most of these objects should sound familiar. They represent an object version of the elements making up a Web page document. For example, you have a Web browser window. Each window can contain multiple frames. Each Web page is commonly referred to as a document, which contains links, anchors, forms, and form elements.

Some of the other objects define items you might not otherwise work with except in client-side scripts. Each browser window also has a history list associated with it, which makes the use of back and forward buttons possible. You might want to control movement in the history list, for example, from your client-side scripts.

The Location object simply represents the URL of the document currently loaded in the Web browser. You have full access to this information. You can take it as the entire URL or break it apart into the associated parts, such as the protocol, server name or IP address, and document name.

Also, the Navigator object gives you information about the Web browser being used. It allows you to find out the name of the browser, the version, and the platform on which it's running. You can then use this information to present customized content, depending on these parameters.

Because of the Object Model, Microsoft introduced an alternative implementation for the Script object that allows you to use the <SCRIPT> and </SCRIPT> tags to define event handlers for specific objects. This new implementation defines two new attributes for the <SCRIPT> tag and is in this form:

```
<SCRIPT LANGUAGE=[language] FOR=[object] EVENT=[object's event]>
```

To use this form, you assign the name of the object to the FOR attribute and the object's event that you want to handle in the EVENT attribute. Internet Explorer then executes the contents of this script only when that object's event gets triggered.

For example, you could define a text input field with this line:

```
<INPUT TYPE="text" NAME="txtName" SIZE=30>
```

You could then define a script to handle the Change event, which gets triggered anytime the user makes a change to the contents of the text field. The script could have the following form:

```
<SCRIPT LANGUAGE="VBScript" FOR="txtName" EVENT="onChange">
<!--

    [Your script goes here]

//-->
</SCRIPT>
```

You're already familiar with being able to place event handlers directly in the HTML tag of the object that's generating the event. You could handle this same event by using this syntax:

```
<INPUT TYPE="text" NAME="txtName" SIZE=30 onChange="[Your script goes here]">
```

Either way, the action that takes place is the same. The event gets triggered, and Internet Explorer looks for a valid event handler. If one is found, the contents of the event handler's script get executed.

What Is VBScript Good For?

VBScript gives Web page authors a way to build more interesting and functionally rich Web pages than they could with HTML alone. HTML is a great way to develop lightweight documents for cross-platform viewing. However, it's not a programming language, so it produces static pages.

VBScript, on the other hand, is a full-featured programming language with conditional statements, data structures, and control structures. With them, you can build Web pages that interact with the user and perform a variety of tasks. Some common tasks performed with VBScript are validating form data, displaying messages in the browser window's status bar, setting and checking cookies, manipulating frames, and interacting with ActiveX controls. These tasks are described in the following sections.

Validating Form Data

One of the most common applications of VBScript is validating the user's entries for form data before the entries get sent to the Web server. This form validation is nothing more than the type of validation you would normally have performed with a CGI script, such as verifying that required fields contain the same data and making sure data that should fall within certain ranges is indeed within certain ranges. Basically, you use VBScript to make sure the data entered by the user meets any criteria you have set for it.

For example, suppose you were gathering feedback from your users, and you wanted to collect their names and ages. You could put together a simple form for the user's first name, last name, and age. You could then create a VBScript program that verifies the user has entered data in all three fields, and that the age is in a reasonable range, such as between 1 and 150.

First, you need to create the Web page that contains the HTML form. Listing 24.2 shows the HTML code for this sample Web page.

Listing 24.2. A form validation example.

```
<HTML>
<HEAD>
<TITLE>VBScript Form Validation Example</TITLE>
</HEAD>
<BODY BGCOLOR="#00CC99" TEXT="#000000">
<TABLE BORDER=0 WIDTH=100% HEIGHT=100%>
<TR>
<TD VALIGN=center ALIGN=middle>
<H1>Form Validation Example</H1>
Please Enter your First and Last Name<BR>
```

continues

Listing 24.2. continued

```
and your age in the fields below.<BR>
<P>
Your First Name: <INPUT TYPE="text" NAME="Firstname" SIZE=40>
<P>
Your Last Name: <INPUT TYPE="text" NAME="Lastname" SIZE=40>
<P>
Your Age: <INPUT TYPE="text" NAME="Age" SIZE=20>
<P>
<INPUT TYPE="button" NAME="Send" VALUE="Send">
<INPUT TYPE="button" NAME="Reset" VALUE="Reset">
</TD>
</TR>
</TABLE>
</BODY>
</HTML>
```

Notice the absence of the <FORM> and </FORM> tags in the HTML code of Listing 24.2. You won't need to use these tags for this example because you will be using the intrinsic text input fields and buttons built into Internet Explorer. Internet Explorer has built-in form elements you can make use of instead of building your form in the typical HTML way. Figure 24.1 shows this Web page loaded into Internet Explorer.

FIGURE 24.1.

The form validation example in Internet Explorer.

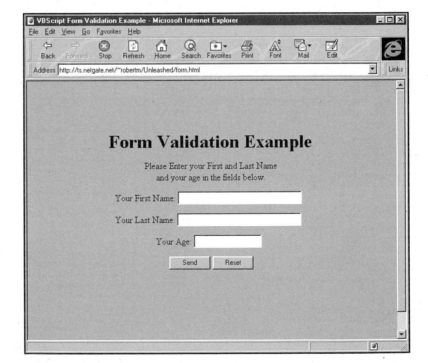

Because you're not using the <FORM> tag to build your HTML form, you have no location for the ACTION attribute for the HTML form. However, this isn't a problem because you will be developing a VBScript application to verify the form data and return the data to the Web server after verification.

Now that you have the HTML page containing the form elements, you need to develop the VBScript application to verify the data. You don't need your script to perform any actions until the user clicks either the Send or Reset button. Therefore, you need to add event handlers, one for when the Send button gets clicked and one for when the Reset button gets clicked. The code for these event handlers is in Listing 24.3.

Listing 24.3. The VBScript script for the form validation example.

```
<SCRIPT LANGUAGE="VBScript">
<!--

    Sub Send_OnClick()

        If Firstname.Value = "" Or Lastname.Value = "" Or _
            Age.Value = "" Then

            MsgBox "You must enter values in all the fields", _
                16, "Empty Field!"

        Else

            If Age.Value >= 1 And Age.Value <= 150 Then
                MsgBox "Thank you for the information.", 0, "Thanks!"

                'Note: The following statement will send the data
                '       to the CGI script cgiscript.pl on the Web
                '       Server machine.
                location.href = "/cgi-bin/cgiscript.pl?Firstname=" & _
                    Firstname.Value & "&Lastname=" & Lastname.Value & _
                    "&Age=" & Age.Value

            Else

                MsgBox "Please enter a valid age!", 16, "Invalid Age!"

            End If

        End If

    End Sub

    Sub Reset_OnClick()

        Firstname.Value = ""
        Lastname.Value = ""
        Age.Value = ""

    End Sub

//-->
</SCRIPT>
```

These functions illustrate another feature of VBScript. When an event for one of the objects in the Object Model gets triggered, VBScript looks for a subroutine with the name in the following form:

```
[object name]_On[object's event]()
```

If VBScript finds a subroutine matching this naming convention, it executes it as the event handler for that event.

So when the user clicks the Reset button, VBScript executes the `Reset_OnClick` subroutine. This subroutine is fairly basic. It resets all the fields to being blank.

When the user clicks the Send button, the `Send_OnClick` subprocedure is run. The first section of this subroutine checks whether data has been entered in all three fields. If not, an error message box is displayed notifying the user that data must be entered in all the fields. This message box is shown in Figure 24.2.

FIGURE 24.2.

The Empty Field!
message box.

When the user has entered data in all the fields, the `Else` portion of the `If...Then...Else` statement is executed. The first statement in this block is another `If...Then...Else` statement that checks the range of the value entered by the user in the `Age` field. If the data is not between the numbers 1 and 150, an error message box is displayed prompting the user to enter a valid age.

Finally, when the user has entered valid data for all the fields, the Thanks message box is displayed to the user and the data is sent to a CGI script on the Web server with the following statement:

```
location.href = "/cgi-bin/cgiscript.pl?Firstname=" & _
    Firstname.Value & "&Lastname=" & Lastname.Value & _
    "&Age=" & Age.Value
```

This statement actually works as a redirection, requesting that the Web browser loads the requested URL. In this case, the requested URL is a CGI script, and the user's form data is added to the end of the URL as a query string.

CAUTION

If you use a similar procedure to validate users' form data and send it to your CGI script, be aware that your CGI script will get the data with the GET request method, not POST.

Displaying Status Bar Messages

Another common use of VBScript is to provide feedback to your users in the browser window's status bar. These messages are often just short blurbs of information having to do with the Web page, links on the page, or the Web site in general. One popular application is to use the status bar as a scrolling marquee message.

In some of the previous examples in this chapter, you have already seen how to place a message in Internet Explorer's status bar. However, there wasn't much explanation about what was really being done. In the previous examples, you saw lines similar to this one:

```
status = "Status Bar Message"
```

This is actually just a shorthand way of setting the window's status bar message. The formal syntax looks like this:

```
window.status = "Status Bar Message"
```

This syntax better illustrates the use of the Internet Explorer Object Model. As you learned in the section "Internet Explorer's Object Model for Scripting," Window is an object in the object hierarchy. One of the properties associated with the Window object is the status property, which stores the contents of the status bar message. By assigning a new value to the property, you change the message that's displayed.

The shorthand version used earlier is another way you can set status bar messages. When used in the shorthand version, Internet Explorer uses the current window by default. The shorthand version is used in the status bar scrolling marquee, which is shown in Listing 24.4. Figure 24.3 shows how Internet Explorer displays this Web page.

Listing 24.4. The status bar scrolling marquee.

```
<HTML>
<HEAD>
<TITLE>A Status Bar Scrolling Marquee</TITLE>
<SCRIPT Language="VBScript">
<!--

    Dim preceding_spaces
    Dim scrolling_message
    Dim current_message

    preceding_spaces = Space(130)
    scrolling_message = "This message will move from " & _
        "the right to the left side of the status bar..."
    current_message = ""

    Sub Scroll_Message()
        If Len(preceding_spaces) > 1 Then

            preceding_spaces = Right(preceding_spaces, Len(preceding_spaces) - 1)
```

continues

Listing 24.4. continued

```
                    If Len(current_message) < Len(scrolling_message) Then
                        current_message = current_message & _
                            Mid(scrolling_message, Len(current_message) + 1, 1)
                    End If

            Else

                If Len(current_message) = 1 Then

                    preceding_spaces = Space(130)
                    current_message = ""

                Else

                    current_message = Right(current_message, _
                        Len(current_message) -1)

                End If

            End If

            status = preceding_spaces & current_message
            MyID = setTimeout("Scroll_Message", 150, "VBScript")

    End Sub

//-->
</SCRIPT>
</HEAD>
<BODY BGCOLOR="#FFCC00" LANGUAGE="VBScript" onLoad=" Scroll_Message">
<TABLE BORDER=0 WIDTH=100% HEIGHT=100%>
<TR>
<TD VALIGN=center ALIGN=middle>
<FONT FACE="COURIER" SIZE=+1>This page contains an example<BR>
of placing a scrolling marquee<BR>
message in Internet Explorer's<BR>
status bar.</FONT>
</TD>
</TR>
</TABLE>
</BODY>
</HTML>
```

The script portion of Listing 24.4 begins by defining three variables with the Dim statement:

```
Dim preceding_spaces
Dim scrolling_message
Dim current_message
```

Following their declarations, they are each given an initial value. The preceding_spaces variable contains the amount of spaces to place before the message. To get the message to scroll across the status bar, your script starts with a lot of preceding spaces and then repeatedly reduces the amount of spaces by one until there is only one left.

FIGURE 24.3.

The status bar scrolling marquee example in Internet Explorer.

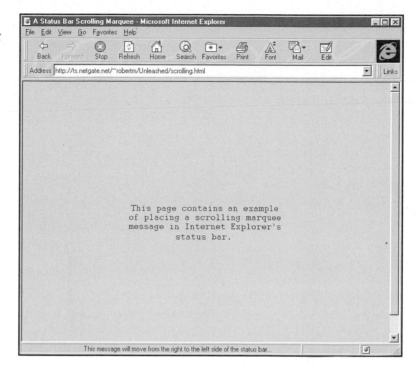

To have the message seem to come in from the right side of the status bar and disappear to the left, you also need to add only a portion of the message at a time until the message is completely in the status bar. Then, when the preceding spaces are all gone, you begin removing characters from the beginning of the string until it's empty, too. To do this, the current_message variable is used to store the portion of the scrolling message that's currently in the status bar. The entire message to be scrolled is stored in the scrolling_message variable.

The Scroll_Message subroutine is used to determine the new portion of the message that will be displayed in the status bar. For the message to scroll, a combination of preceding spaces and characters from the scrolling message have to be displayed repeatedly. It's up to the Scroll_Message subroutine to determine the combination and display the message. After displaying one iteration of spaces and characters from the scrolling message, it uses the following line:

```
MyID = setTimeout("Scroll_Message", 150, "VBScript")
```

This statement causes the VBScript program to pause for 150 milliseconds. After the pause, the subroutine Scroll_Message is executed again. If you don't have your VBScript program pause between iterations, the message will scroll too fast, and your users won't be able to read it. If you want to speed up or slow down the scroll rate, either reduce or increase the 150 number in this statement.

24

USING VBSCRIPT

Working with Cookies

The ability to set and check cookies directly on the client's machine is an important benefit of client-side scripts. Previously, you had to use a CGI script on the Web server machine to set or view cookies. Simple Web page requests had to be funneled through a CGI script if you wanted to use a cookie with that page. Now, with client-side scripts, each Web page is empowered to control cookies itself.

Like JavaScript and JScript, VBScript applications can set and check cookies for the Web page in which they're embedded. You can use this information to then display dynamic data based on the current value of the cookie.

For example, the code in Listing 24.5 produces a Web page with an embedded VBScript application that uses a cookie. This example checks whether the cookie has been set. If not, a message box is displayed, thanking the user for visiting the site. The cookie is set to expire one month after it's set, so the user sees the message box only once a month. Figure 24.4 shows this Web page and message box.

Listing 24.5. Using cookies to determine content.

```
<HTML>
<HEAD>
<TITLE>Using Cookies to Determine Web page Content</TITLE>
<SCRIPT LANGUAGE="VBScript">
<!--

    cookie_index = Instr(Document.Cookie, Visited)

    If cookie_index = 0 Then
        Document.Cookie = Visited & "=" & "1;expires=" & DateAdd("m", 1, Now)
        MsgBox "Thank you for visiting our site!"
    End If

//-->
</SCRIPT>
</HEAD>
<BODY BGCOLOR="#00CCFF">
<TABLE BORDER=0 WIDTH=100% HEIGHT=100%>
<TR>
<TD VALIGN=center ALIGN=middle>
<FONT FACE="COURIER" SIZE=+1><B>Have you been here before?</B><BR>
This page displays a message box<BR>
if you have not previously<BR>
visited this site.</FONT>
</TD>
</TR>
</TABLE>
</BODY>
</HTML>
```

FIGURE 24.4.

The cookie example in Internet Explorer.

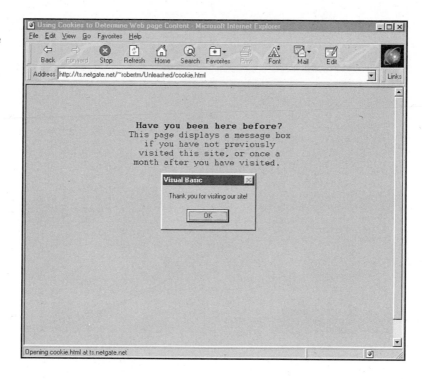

Working with ActiveX Controls

You'll realize the real power of VBScript when you use it with ActiveX controls. VBScript, although able to do some basic applications by itself, does have some major limitations. Most of these limitations are because of its inability to access the operating system or file system. Naturally, these limitations are necessary because opening these systems up to VBScript would be a big security risk.

ActiveX, on the other hand, doesn't have these limitations. ActiveX controls can make changes to the file system and access the operating system to perform its tasks. Through the use of authentication certificates with ActiveX controls, Microsoft asserts that users can feel confident with the security of ActiveX controls published by reputable sources.

What Are ActiveX Controls?

ActiveX is actually the name of a set of technologies developed by Microsoft. These technologies are designed to be multiplatform, extensible, and optimized for the Internet. This optimization consists of small size, automatic downloading, and authentication certificates for security purposes.

ActiveX actually reuses an existing technology. It's the next incarnation of Microsoft's OLE technology, which was first introduced in 1991. OLE allowed users to embed objects of other types in a single file. Using OLE, you could embed Excel spreadsheets in Word documents or, conversely, embed Word documents in Excel spreadsheets, for example.

The underlying technology of both ActiveX and OLE is Microsoft's Component Object Model (COM). COM is a standard by which objects communicate with each other. By building on COM, developers can create objects that communicate with each other without having to bother with the details about how the communication works.

Although Microsoft intended ActiveX to be multiplatform, it's currently available on only a single platform, Windows. Microsoft is working with other companies to port ActiveX to the other popular platforms, such as UNIX and Macintosh.

VBScript and ActiveX controls

VBScript and ActiveX controls are complementary technologies. You can develop low-level ActiveX controls using programming languages such as Java, C, C++, and Visual Basic. After you have developed your control, you can use VBScript to access and modify the control's properties, methods, and events in the user's Web browser.

The real benefit of working with ActiveX controls in your VBScript program is that there's no new VBScript techniques you need to learn. You access the ActiveX controls in the same way you access the objects defined in the Internet Explorer Object Model for Scripting.

For example, suppose you had an ActiveX control named schedule with a property named todays_date, a method named assign_task, and an event named meeting_time. Then, in your VBScript code, you could access the value in the todays_date property with this syntax:

```
schedule.todays_date
```

You would execute the method assign_task with this line:

```
schedule.assign_task()
```

And, if you wrote an event handler subroutine for the meeting_time event, the name of the subroutine would be the following:

```
schedule_Onmeeting_time
```

This is exactly the same way you access properties, methods, and events for the other objects defined in the Internet Explorer Object Model. Naturally, the actual properties, methods, and events vary depending on the ActiveX control. To script for them, you must know their names for the ActiveX control you want to use.

Resources for More Information

This chapter has offered just a small sampling of the VBScript scripting language and what you can accomplish with it. This section covers how to get more information about using VBScript in your Web pages. It's divided into two sections: one on online VBScript resources and the other section on offline resources.

Online Resources

All the information you need to get started developing VBScript applications for your Web pages is online in one form or another. Most of the information can be found on Microsoft's VBScript Web pages. However, many other Internet resources offer useful VBScript and related technology information.

Web Sites

By far, the largest form of online information about VBScript and its related technologies are Web sites. Most of the sites provide tutorials, language references, and a lot of sample scripts. The following is a list of useful Web pages for VBScript and the related HTML, JScript, ActiveX, and cookie technologies:

HTML Quick Reference

`http://www.cc.ukans.edu/info/HTML_quick.html`

HyperText Markup Language

`http://www.w3.org/pub/WWW/MarkUp/`

A Beginner's Guide to HTML

`http://www.ncsa.uiuc.edu/General/Internet/WWW/HTMLPrimer.html`

Special Characters

`http://www.utoronto.ca/webdocs/HTMLdocs/NewHTML/entities.html`

ISO8859-1 (Latin-1) Table

`http://www.uni-passau.de/~ramsch/iso8859-1.html`

Microsoft's VBScript Web Pages

`http://www.microsoft.com/vbscript/`

Scribe - The VBScript Writers Resource

`http://www.km-cd.com/scribe/`

NCompass Labs

`http://www.ncompasslabs.com/products.htm`

Ask the VB Pro

`http://www.inquiry.com/techtips/thevbpro/`

Rollins & Associates Home Page

`http://www.rollins-assoc.com/`

Microsoft's JScript Web Pages

`http://www.microsoft.com/jscript/`

Comparability Issues of Using JavaScript with Microsoft Internet Explorer 3.0

`http://www.gmccomb.com/javascript/ie30.html`

Microsoft's ActiveX Pages

`http://www.microsoft.com/activeplatform/default.asp`

ZDNet's ActiveX Files

`http://www5.zdnet.com/zdwebcat/content/activex/`

C|Net's ActiveX Resources Pages

`http://www.activex.com/`

Netscape's Persistent Cookies Documentation

`http://home.netscape.com/newsref/std/cookie_spec.html`

Malcolm's Guide to Persistent Cookies

`http://www.emf.net/~mal/cookiesinfo.html`

Andy's Netscape HTTP Cookie Notes

`http://www.illuminatus.com/cookie`

New Web pages are cropping up all the time, so a static listing in a published book isn't the best place to have a comprehensive reference list of Web site resources. Therefore, if you're looking for VBScript-related information not found in the preceding sources, you should make use of one of the Internet search directories, such as the following:

Yahoo! (`http://www.yahoo.com/`)

Infoseek (`http://www.infoseek.com/`)

AltaVista (`http://www.altavista.digital.com/`)

Excite (`http://www.excite.com/`)

Lycos (`http://www.lycos.com/`)

C|Net's Search.com (`http://www.search.com/`)

Hotbot (`http://www.hotbot.com/`)

Newsgroups and Listservs

In addition to the wealth of Web-related resources, the Internet also has areas for questions to be posted and answered by other knowledgeable users. These areas are newsgroups and listserv mailing lists. Both are excellent resources for finding out specific answers to questions you have about VBScript. The following is a list of related newsgroups and listservs that you might find useful:

`comp.infosystems.www.authoring.html`

`comp.infosystems.www.browsers.mac`

`comp.infosystems.www.browsers.ms-windows`

`comp.infosystems.www.browsers.x`

`comp.infosystems.www.browsers.misc`

`http://www.dejanews.com/` (Deja News is a service that searches Usenet newsgroups by keywords.)

VBScript Mailing List

To subscribe, send e-mail to: `Listserv@listserv.msn.com`.

In the body of the message, type `Subscribe VBScript Firstname Lastname`.

ActiveX Controls Mailing List

To subscribe, send e-mail to `Listserv@listserv.msn.com`.

In the body of the message, type `Subscribe ActiveXControls Firstname Lastname`.

Advanced HTML Discussion List

To subscribe, send e-mail to `listserv@ua1vm.ua.edu`.

In the body of the message, type `Subscribe ADV-HTML Firstname Lastname`.

Offline Resources

Most of the VBScript resources currently available are online resources, such as Web sites, newsgroups, and listservs. They are your best sources for current information and examples dealing with VBScript.

For those who prefer offline information sources, the best resource would be the various computer books being written on VBScript. Some of the more notable titles include the following:

> *Special Edition, Using VBScript*, QUE
>
> *Laura Lemay's Web Workshop ActiveX and VBScript*, Sams.net Publishing
>
> *How to Program Microsoft Visual Basic Scripting Edition*, Ziff-Davis Press
>
> *The Comprehensive Guide to VBScript: The Encyclopedic Reference for VBScript, HTML, & ActiveX*, Ventana Communications Group Inc.
>
> *VBScript Unleashed*, Sams.net Publishing
>
> *Teach Yourself VBScript in 21 Days*, Sams.net Publishing

If you're interested in purchasing a book on VBScript, check for any one of these titles, or for other titles, in the computer books section of your nearest bookstore. You can also search for and buy VBScript books from the popular online bookstores, such as Amazon (`http://www.amazon.com`) and Barnes and Noble (`http://www.barnesandnoble.com`).

Summary

Visual Basic Scripting Edition, or VBScript, is a client-side scripting language that uses much of the same syntax and structure as Microsoft's popular Visual Basic programming language. Microsoft introduced VBScript to give experienced Visual Basic programmers an easy way to write applications for Web pages.

VBScript isn't just a scripting version of Visual Basic. Because of security issues, some Visual Basic features aren't supported in VBScript. Additionally, because of the unique environment in which VBScript applications run, there are some new features specific to VBScript that aren't

24

USING VBSCRIPT

part of the Visual Basic product. However, whenever possible, Visual Basic features were supported in VBScript to make the languages as similar as possible.

Like other client-side scripting languages, VBScript is intended to be embedded within the HTML source code of Web pages. It supports the same `<SCRIPT>` and `</SCRIPT>` tags for embedding the code in the HTML document. VBScript code can also be embedded within several HTML tags that represent objects in the Internet Explorer Object Model for Scripting.

There are a wide variety of applications for VBScript. Some of the more common applications of VBScript are for form validation, status bar messages, and manipulating frames. Although useful, the true power of VBScript comes through in the ability to work with ActiveX controls. Similar to VBScript's ability to manipulate objects in the Object Model, VBScript can also be used to script for ActiveX controls, allowing Web page authors to dynamically control their embedded ActiveX controls.

Understanding the Common Gateway Interface

by Robert McDaniel

IN THIS CHAPTER

The early World Wide Web consisted of static hypertext documents, which, in their original form, did not even support inline images. The Web browsers displayed the text page with the limited formatting afforded by the early HTML tags. In those early days, nobody realized the impact the Web would soon have on the world. However, even in its rough early stages, the Web began getting a lot of notice.

As more people became interested in this new technology, more and more suggestions were put forth for features to add. Many of the new features were integrated on the client side in the Netscape Navigator browser. These features included adding inline GIF images, more layout tags, and tables. A lot of features, though, couldn't be implemented on the client side. Early on, it was recognized that there was a need to be able to integrate applications into the Web server. By allowing developers to do this, the programmers coding the Web server software wouldn't have to make all the changes developers wanted; developers could add in custom applications themselves.

The Common Gateway Interface, or CGI, was the first way you could integrate applications into your Web site. Through the CGI, developers could write their own applications, custom-built for the task they wanted to perform. They could then easily integrate these applications into their Web site, regardless of the Web server software being used.

Although the CGI has been around for some time now, it's still a viable means of developing applications for use with a Web site. In this chapter, you're introduced to the CGI through the following topics:

- What the Common Gateway Interface is
- How to integrate CGI applications and your HTML pages
- What CGI is good for
- When you should use CGI
- Resources for more information

What Is the Common Gateway Interface?

First, understand that the CGI is not a programming language. It's a gateway through which Web servers and other applications communicate. The CGI defines a standard way in which data can be passed from a Web server to a CGI application and then back to the Web server after the CGI application is finished.

CGI applications run as separate applications from the Web server, so they don't have access to all the information the Web server does, such the Web browser's version and name or any form data the user is sending to the Web server. However, your application must have access to this information to perform its assigned task.

Also, after the CGI application has finished executing, it usually needs to return the results of its task to the user's Web browser. Therefore, there must be a way for data to go from the CGI application to the user's Web browser. At the very least, the CGI application must be able to send the data back to the Web server, which then forwards it on to the user's Web browser.

The flow of data between your Web server and your CGI application is the core of CGI programming. Once you know how to do that, you're ready to begin developing your own CGI applications. This topic is discussed in the section "Integrating CGI Applications into Your Web Site" later in this chapter. Before you actually start developing CGI applications, though, you do need to choose a programming or scripting language for writing your CGI applications.

Programming Language Choices

Because CGI isn't a programming language, you must choose one to use for coding your CGI applications. Your choices of a programming language are limited only by the available languages that will create an executable application that can be run on your Web server machine. On a practical level, though, there are some considerations to take into account when choosing your CGI application language.

The first point you should consider is to choose a language that's commonly used by other CGI developers. These languages include Perl, C, C++, UNIX shells, Java, TCL, Visual Basic, and AppleScript. By choosing one of these languages, you can take advantage of the support of the existing Web developer community when developing your own applications.

There are also many CGI application archives that have ready-to-use CGI applications and library files, which you can freely use on your own site. These archives usually contain scripts in the languages mentioned. Using this existing code whenever possible will cut down on your development time.

The next consideration when choosing a programming language is to pick one that's appropriate for the task you need to perform. If you're doing processor-intensive actions, such as searching and sorting on millions of records, you should use a compiled programming language, such as C or C++, which gives you much better performance than an interpreted language like Perl. However, if performance isn't an issue for the application you are coding, then a scripting language like Perl can greatly reduce your development time because most programmers can write similar code in Perl much faster than code in C.

Keep in mind, too, the intended platform on which your application will run. Obviously, if you're going to be running your application on a UNIX machine, than AppleScript is not an option for you. However, you might not want to use a supported language on a given platform because of issues specific to that platform. For example, Java runs reasonably well on UNIX machines. On Macintosh machines, however, it runs painfully slow. Therefore, if your intended platform is a Macintosh, Java would not be a good choice of languages to use.

The same holds true for operating systems. Some operating systems don't run interpreted languages very well. For example, Perl is a popular choice for writing CGI applications. However, when run on a machine with the Windows NT operating system, the performance can be very poor. Therefore, you might want to choose a different language.

Integrating CGI Applications into Your Web Site

As you start developing CGI applications, you will soon realize that to integrate an application into your Web site, two things must happen. First, your application must be able to receive data from the Web browser and Web server. This is imperative to properly perform most functions. Second, your application must be able to send results back to the user's Web browser after it has finished executing.

The CGI defines how to do both of these tasks. To receive data from the Web browser and Web server, your CGI application doesn't have to do anything to make sure this data is available. The Web server automatically sends this information to your CGI application when it gets started. As for sending data back to the Web browser, that's equally easy. All you have to do is create a valid header, as defined in the CGI specification, and output the results.

HTTP Connections and Headers

At the core of all Web interactions is the Hypertext Transfer Protocol, or HTTP, connection. Through the HTTP connection, Web browsers request documents, which the Web servers then return. When a Web browser requests a document, it sends an HTTP request to the Web server on which the document resides. When the Web server receives an HTTP request, it returns the document in an HTTP response, if it exists and the user is allowed to have access to it. The HTTP request and response make up an HTTP connection.

All HTTP requests and responses contain a section known as the *HTTP header*. The HTTP header includes information about the document, the Web server, the Web browser, and other related items. This information is stored in individual fields within the header. HTTP headers aren't the same for the request and the response; however, some of the fields could be the same.

The HTTP request header fields are shown in Table 25.1. They are the fields that are defined for a Web browser to send in an HTTP request header.

Table 25.1. HTTP request headers.

Request Header Field	Meaning
ACCEPT	The ACCEPT field contains a list of media types, in MIME format, that the Web browser can accept from the Web server.
ACCEPT-ENCODING	The ACCEPT-ENCODING field is used to specify to the Web server the document encoding methods the Web browser supports.
ACCEPT-LANGUAGE	ACCEPT-LANGUAGE specifies to the Web server the Web browser's preferred language for a response.
AUTHORIZATION	AUTHORIZATION stores the authentication information sent by the Web browser to identify itself to the Web server.
CHARGE-TO	The CHARGE-TO field is not currently implemented.

Request Header Field	Meaning
FROM	FROM indicates the e-mail address of the user whose Web browser sent the HTTP request. Most current Web browsers don't supply a value for this field.
IF-MODIFIED-SINCE	The IF-MODIFIED-SINCE is a date value that tells the Web server to return the document only if it has been modified since the given date.
PRAGMA	The PRAGMA field contains any special instructions for the Web server. For example, the no-cache PRAGMA directive instructs Web servers not to send cached versions of the requested document.
REFERER	The REFERER supplies the URI of the previous document where the user clicked a link to navigate to the current document.
USER-AGENT	The USER-AGENT stores the name and version of the Web browser making the request. For example, Mozilla/4.01 [en] (Win95; I) is the user agent for Netscape 4.0 on Windows 95.

Naturally, most of the information in the request header deals with the Web browser. Because the Web browser is making the request, it needs to send relevant information to the Web server. When the Web server responds, it formats an HTTP response header, made up of the fields listed in Table 25.2.

Table 25.2. HTTP response headers.

Response Header Field	Meaning
ALLOWED	Tells the Web browser what request methods are allowed, such as the GET method.
CONTENT-ENCODING	Notifies the Web browser of the encoding method used on the returned document.
CONTENT-LANGUAGE	Specifies the language of the returned document.
CONTENT-LENGTH	Contains the size, in bytes, of the document being returned.
CONTENT-TRANSFER-ENCODING	Contains the encoding of the data between the Web server and the Web browser, such as binary or ASCII.
CONTENT-TYPE	Specifies to the Web browser the MIME type of the data being returned.
COST	This field is not currently implemented.
DATE	Contains the date the returning document was created.
DERIVED-FROM	This field is not currently implemented.

25

UNDERSTANDING THE CGI

continues

Table 25.2. continued

Response Header Field	Meaning
EXPIRES	Specifies a date when the returning document expires.
LAST-MODIFIED	Specifies the date when the returning document was last modified.
LINK	Contains information, such as the URL, of the document being returned.
MESSAGE-ID	A unique identification number for the HTTP connection.
PUBLIC	Contains allowed request methods. It's similar to the ALLOW field, but applies to all Web browsers, not just the one the header is being sent to.
TITLE	Specifies the title of the returning document.
URI	Contains the URI of the returning document.
VERSION	This field is not currently implemented.

The HTTP response headers focus more on the document being returned. This information is used by the Web browser to properly display the document once the Web browser has finished downloading it.

When the Web server gets an HTTP request for a CGI application, it executes the program, instead of returning the contents of the file. The Web server then passes on all the information it receives in the HTTP request headers to the CGI application by placing the data in environment variables.

Before a CGI application has finished running, it needs to return a response to either the Web server or directly to the Web browser. If the results are to be sent to the Web server, the CGI application just needs to send a server directive to the Web server. The Web server then creates an HTTP response header and sends the data and header back to the user's browser. If the CGI application sends the data directly back to the user's Web browser, it must first create a valid HTTP response header and precede the data with the header.

Sending Data to Your CGI Application

Most of the data available to your CGI application comes from the environment variables set by the Web server. The Web server places all the HTTP request header fields in environment variables, which are the names of the field preceded by HTTP_. In addition to all the HTTP request headers, the Web server also sets other CGI environment variables, which are shown in Table 25.3.

Table 25.3. CGI environment variables.

Environment Variable	Meaning
AUTH_TYPE	Specifies the authentication method (if any) used by the Web browser, such as username/password.
CONTENT_LENGTH	Contains the length, in characters, of the user-supplied data, if any.
CONTENT_TYPE	Specifies the MIME type of the user-supplied data.
GATEWAY_INTERFACE	Designates the version of the CGI specification being used. (The current version is 1.1.)
PATH_INFO	Contains any additional path information appended to the requesting URL.
PATH_TRANSLATED	Contains the Web server's translation of the virtual path information, appended to the URL, to the actual path on the server machine.
QUERY_STRING	Contains any information appended the URL with a question mark.
REMOTE_ADDR	Supplies the IP address of the client machine.
REMOTE_HOST	Contains the domain name, if available, of the client machine.
REMOTE_IDENT	Stores the user's login name, if one was used for authentication with the Web server.
REMOTE_USER	Contains the remote user name, as supplied to the Web server.
REQUEST_METHOD	Specifies the request method used by the browser, either GET or POST.
SCRIPT_NAME	Contains the virtual path and filename of the CGI script.
SERVER_NAME	Contains either the domain name or IP address of the Web server machine.
SERVER_PORT	Indicates the port being used by the Web server.
SERVER_PROTOCOL	Specifies the protocol being used between the Web server and Web browser, typically HTTP.
SERVER_SOFTWARE	Contains the name and version of the Web server software.

The environment variables are the primary source of information available to your CGI application, and in some cases, they are the only source. The only other bit of information that may be sent to the CGI application comes from any form data supplied by the user. This form data can be sent to the Web server in one of two ways, with the GET or POST request methods.

25

UNDERSTANDING THE CGI

The GET and POST terms should already be familiar to you from creating HTML forms. They are the values you assign to the method attribute of the <FORM> tag. As far as your CGI application is concerned, the difference between these two request methods is the location from where the CGI application can access the form data. With the GET method, the form data is placed in the QUERY_STRING environment variable. The POST method, on the other hands, causes the data to be sent to the CGI application through standard input.

Regardless of which request method is used, the Web browser always places all form data in one long URL-encoded string of name/value pairs. A *name/value pair* is the name of a form element and the corresponding data entered by the user in that form element. All the name/value pairs for the entire form are joined together, separated by an ampersand (&), and then URL encoded. *URL encoding* is the process of changing some characters to placeholders and replacing other characters with their hexadecimal ASCII value. Before you can begin working with the user-supplied data sent to your CGI application, you need to decode the data and split apart the name/value pairs.

> **TIP**
>
> When processing form data, you should always follow the same sequence of events: Split apart name/value pairs, change placeholders to their respective values, and then convert hexadecimal values back into their character equivalents.

Returning Data from Your CGI Application

After your CGI application has finished its task, it should return a value to the user's Web browser. This process can be done directly, by creating a valid HTTP response header and sending the header and the data to the Web browser, or by sending the data and a server directive to the Web server. Either method is accomplished by the application sending the results to its standard output.

When you send a server directive to the Web server, along with the results to be returned to the user's Web browser, the header your CGI application needs to create is called a *parsed header*. That's because the Web server parses the header you send, makes it a complete HTTP response header, and sends the results back to the Web browser.

At a minimum, a valid parsed header can contain just a server directive, which is one of the three defined in Table 25.4. In addition to the server directive, your CGI application can also send any of the HTTP response headers shown in Table 25.2. The HTTP response header fields sent by the CGI application as part of a parsed header are then integrated into the full HTTP response header the Web server creates and sent back to the Web browser.

Table 25.4. Web server directives.

Directive	Meaning
Content-type	Designates the MIME type of the data being returned.
Location	Designates the virtual or absolute URL to which the Web browser should be redirected.
Status	Contains an HTTP status code, such as 404 Not Found.

When a CGI application is sending its results directly back to the user's Web browser, it must create a non-parsed header to be returned with the data. A *non-parsed header* is an HTTP response header that your CGI application creates and sends to the Web browser. Because the Web server isn't parsing the header and supplying missing fields, the non-parsed header must be complete. Valid HTTP response headers do not have to contain all the HTTP response fields shown in Table 25.2. For example, the following is a valid non-parsed header:

```
HTTP/1.0 200 OK
Server: Netscape-Communications/3.0
Content-type: text/html
```

Whether you return a parsed or non-parsed header from your CGI application, you must return a blank line immediately after the header has finished. That blank line is how the Web server or Web browser identifies the end of the header and the beginning of the returned data. If you don't supply the blank line, your CGI application will cause a server error.

Calling CGI Applications

Once you have developed a CGI application, you're ready to call it from one of HTML documents. There are a variety of ways in which you can call your application. The method you use depends on the task your CGI application is designed to perform.

The most common way CGI applications are called is from the action attribute in the <FORM> tag. These CGI applications are referred to as *form handlers,* and are called when the form is submitted by the user. When a form is submitted, the form data is sent to your CGI application by using the QUERY_STRING environment variable or standard input, depending on whether the request method is GET or POST.

CGI applications can also be called directly in <A>, <IMG>, and server-side include tags. When the URL for a CGI application is assigned to the href attribute of an <A> tag, it will be requested whenever the user clicks on the related link in the Web browser. CGI applications referenced in <IMG> and server-side includes, on the other hand, are executed automatically by the Web server when the user requests the Web page in which these links are embedded.

For example, you could use the image tag:

```
<IMG SRC="/cgi-bin/image">
```

25

UNDERSTANDING THE CGI

The Web server would execute the image CGI application and display the results as an image in the Web browser. To use this form of referencing your CGI application, you need to be sure the CGI application returns the binary data for an image.

Server-side includes are similar in that they are automatically executed by the Web server when the Web page is requested. Server-side includes have this general syntax:

```
<!--#command tag1="value1" tag2="value2" -->
```

For CGI applications, you must use the `#exec` command to have the Web server execute your CGI application. You then specify includes the name of the CGI application by using the `cgi` attribute. For example, take a look at this server-side include:

```
<!--#exec cgi="/cgi-bin/run_me.pl" -->
```

It causes includes the Web server to run the CGI script `run_me.pl`, embedding the results returned from the CGI script in the HTML document where the server-side include was placed.

One final way in which you can call your CGI applications is from client-side scripts. Client-side scripts can request any document that has a URL. Having a client-side script request a CGI application is similar to using the `<A>` tag mentioned earlier; in both methods, the Web browser will send a simple HTTP request for the CGI application, causing the Web server to execute the application. However, the advantage of using a client-side script over a simple anchor tag is that your client-side script controls when the CGI application gets requested. With the `<A>` tag, you have to wait for the user to click on the link.

What Is CGI Good For?

The CGI is good for allowing you to write server-side applications, which extend the functionality of your Web server. By using a server-side application, you gain several advantages, such as cross-platform and cross-browser support, more tasks you can complete, increased processing power, and code integrity.

As you have probably already experienced, every browser on every platform displays HTML pages slightly differently. All browser are not the same; they support different versions of HTML, plug-ins, and client-side scripting languages and versions. Naturally, you can create generic HTML pages that work well on all platforms and browsers. However, you might want to have dynamic, interactive Web pages. Client-side scripting gives you some of these options, as does some of the advanced HTML, but you pay the price when it comes to supporting all browsers and machines.

Server-side applications don't have this same problem, as long as they return their results in displayable HTML code. Of course, you still have some of the same HTML and advanced HTML issues, but you can develop complex applications that dynamically generate custom Web pages for your users. You don't have to be concerned about whether your application is compatible with their browser because it's running on the server machine.

On the server side, too, you have more options for tasks you can perform. Many resources that are popular to integrate into Web sites are server-side resources, such as databases. You can also make use of the abilities of higher level programming languages that can run on the server machine, but not in the user's Web browser.

You also have the added processing power of the Web server machine. Although client-side machines are becoming more powerful, server machines are still a good deal faster than their client counterparts. This extra power lets you develop processor-intensive tasks, such as complex searches and sorts, without degrading the performance of your Web site too much.

Finally, by creating the application on the server side, you don't have to worry about the exposure of your source code. All client-side scripting languages supply the source code to the end user right in the browser window. No special effort or ability is required to get it. Even Java applets and ActiveX controls are somewhat vulnerable because your users hold the actual executable on their machines. The more talented ones can reverse-engineer these programs to get the source code.

Server-side applications, on the other hand, reside on the server the entire time. Whether they are programmed in a scripting language or compiled into an executable, the source code never gets sent to the user's Web browser. Instead, the server machine always executes the program, when it receives a request for it, and returns only the results of the applications.

When Should I Use CGI?

Now that you know some of the basics about CGI applications, and the advantages to using them, you might be wondering when you should use them. The simple answer is when you need to. CGI applications offer a wealth of power for adding features to your Web site. However, unless you have a need for a given feature, it won't benefit you.

This section discusses several common implementations of CGI applications. Some of them might be tasks you need to do on your site, and others might have no benefit for you. It's up to you to determine what you need to accomplish and then implement appropriately.

Search Engines

Search engines are applications that allow your users to search through the documents on your Web site for keywords or phrases. Search engines can be relatively simple or highly complex, depending on the features you want to support. For example, a keyword search is a lot more complicated than searches using predefined choices.

Search engines need the CGI to function correctly. They must be able to receive input, such as a keyword to search for, from the user's Web browser and then return the search results to the browser for display.

Even a basic search engine can be a huge strain on a machine's processor. A basic search consists of two of the most processor-intensive tasks an application can perform—searching and sorting. Because of this, a Web site search engine needs to be highly optimized to provide the level of performance your users will demand.

Developing your own search engine can be a tedious task, even for a simple search. Unless you want the challenge or are trying to develop a better level of technology, you might want to consider avoiding it. A better option would be to license search technology from another company that specializes in creating that kind of software. You can then spend your time developing other areas of your Web site.

One of the best search engines available for licensing on Web sites is Excite's Excite for Web Servers. It supports complex keyword searches and displays the results in a hierarchical format. The current version even has a new technology, which returns related documents that don't even contain the user's keywords.

Excite offers a free license of Excite for Web Servers. The terms of the license call for certain mentions of Excite's name and logo in your Web site. You can check out the current license agreement and download the latest version from Excite's Web site (`http://www.excite.com/navigate/`).

Access Counters

Access counters are a popular feature of many Web sites. They use a CGI application that keeps track of the number of times a Web page has been requested and then displays that total somewhere on the page in either a text or graphical format.

Simple text-based access counters aren't difficult to implement. In fact, most of the code required is to perform the tasks of opening the counter file (which stores the current number of requests for the Web page), reading in the contents, incrementing the number, and storing it back into the file. Beyond that, the CGI application just needs to display the current number on the Web page.

Graphical access counters naturally require a little more coding. You still need to open the counter file and increment the number of requests. However, you also need to create a graphic that represents the number of requests for the Web page. The CGI application then displays the graphic, rather than simple text, in the Web page.

The Perl code in Listing 25.1 contains a CGI script version of a text-based access counter. This code has one subroutine, `Increment_Counter`, that performs the following tasks:

- Opens the counter file for input
- Reads in the contents
- Closes the counter file
- Increments the count
- Opens the counter file for output
- Stores the incremented count value in the counter file
- Closes the counter file

Listing 25.1. A text-based access counter script.

```perl
#!/usr/bin/perl

$file = "/users/robertm/count.dat";

$access_number = &Increment_Counter;
print "Content-type: text/html\n\n";
print $access_number;

sub Increment_Counter {
  local ($count);

  # Get the current value of the access counter.
  open(COUNT, "$file") || die "Content-type: text/html\n\nCannot open counter
  ➥ file!";
$count = <COUNT>;
  close(COUNT);

  # Increment the access counter
  $count++;

  # Store the value of the counter in the counter file.
  open(COUNT, ">$file") || die "Content-type: text/html\n\nCannot open counter
  ➥ file!";
  print COUNT $count;
  close(COUNT);

  return $count;
}
```

With the `Increment_Counter` subroutine, all the rest of your script needs to do is call the subroutine and send the returned value to the Web browser. This is done with the following lines of Perl code:

```perl
$access_number = &Increment;
print "Content-type: text/html\n\n";
print $access_number;
```

Now that you have your access counter CGI script, you're ready to implement it. The first thing you should do is create the `count.dat` file. Be sure and put this file in the directory you assigned to the `$file` variable in your script. Otherwise, the script won't be able to find the file. If you want to start your counter at 1, you need to place a 0 in the file because the value is always incremented before being displayed in the Web browser.

With the CGI script finished and the counter file initialized, you're ready to add the counter to your HTML page. The best way to do that is with a server-side include, as shown:

```html
<!--#exec cgi="/cgi-bin/counter.pl" -->
```

Simply place this line of HTML code at the exact location in your HTML page where you want the counter number to appear. For example, the HTML file shown in Listing 25.2 contains this server-side include. Figure 25.1 shows what this page looks like when it's loaded into Netscape.

25

UNDERSTANDING
THE CGI

Listing 25.2. The text-based access counter HTML file.

```
<HTML>
<HEAD>
<TITLE>Including a Text Access Counter</TITLE>
</HEAD>
<BODY BGCOLOR="#CCFFCC">
<TABLE BORDER=0 WIDTH=100% HEIGHT=100%>
<TR>
<TD VALIGN=center ALIGN=middle><FONT FACE="COURIER" SIZE=+1>thank you
for visiting our site!<BR>you are visitor number</FONT> <FONT FACE="TIMES"
➥ SIZE=+2><B>
<!--#exec cgi="/cgi-bin/access.pl" -->
</B></FONT></TD>
</TR>
</TABLE>
</BODY>
</HTML>
```

FIGURE 25.1.

A text-based access counter.

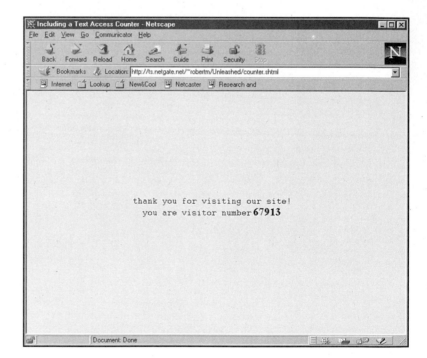

Form Handlers

Form handling is the most common task for CGI applications to perform. By using HTML forms on your Web site, you can get direct feedback from your users. However, unless you want to receive all form submissions by e-mail, you need a CGI application to handle form submissions.

For example, the HTML code in Listing 25.3 contains a Web page form that's used on the unGROOM'd Web site (http://www.ungroomd.com) to get demographics about its users. Figure 25.2 shows what this page looks like in Netscape Navigator.

Listing 25.3. The unKNOW'n survey.

```
<HTML>
<HEAD>
<TITLE>unGROOM'd: unKNOW'n</TITLE>
</HEAD>
<BODY BACKGROUND="../background2.gif" BGCOLOR="#000000" TEXT="#FFFFCC"
➥ LINK="#FFA500" VLINK="#F7007B">
<TABLE BORDER="0" CELLPADDING="0" WIDTH="100%">
<TR>
<TD ALIGN=LEFT VALIGN=TOP>

<IMG SRC="../1pixel.gif" ALIGN=TOP WIDTH="165" HEIGHT="75" BORDER="0"><BR>
<MAP NAME="upperbar">
<AREA SHAPE="rect" COORDS="-6, 178, 133, 201" HREF="../../unarchivd.html">
<AREA SHAPE="rect" COORDS="6,127,135,178" HREF="../columns/columns.html">
<AREA SHAPE="rect" COORDS="6,103,135,127" HREF="../hiscastle/hiscastle.html">
<AREA SHAPE="rect" COORDS="6,75,135,103" HREF="../incout/incout.html">
<AREA SHAPE="rect" COORDS="6,53,135,75" HREF="../mom/mom.html">
<AREA SHAPE="rect" COORDS="6,29,135,53"
HREF="../tyingtheknot/tyingtheknot.html">
<AREA SHAPE="rect" COORDS="6,2,135,29"
HREF="../nowfeaturing/nowfeaturing.html">
<AREA SHAPE=DEFAULT HREF="../toc.html">
</MAP>

<IMG SRC="../upperbar.gif" ALT="navigation bar" ALIGN=TOP WIDTH="135"
HEIGHT="229" BORDER="0" USEMAP="#upperbar"><BR>

<MAP NAME="level1bar">
<AREA SHAPE="rect" COORDS="6, 146, 131, 174" HREF="mmg_pr/pr.html">
<AREA SHAPE="rect" COORDS="6,124,135,147" HREF="mmg_pr/mmg.html">
<AREA SHAPE="rect" COORDS="6,99,135,125" HREF="staff/credits.html">
<AREA SHAPE="rect" COORDS="6,73,135,99" HREF="unlinkd.html">
<AREA SHAPE="rect" COORDS="6,52,135,74" NOHREF>
<AREA SHAPE="rect" COORDS="6,28,135,53" HREF="unlistd/unlistd.html">
<AREA SHAPE="rect" COORDS="6,3,135,28" HREF="uneditd/unedited.html">
<AREA SHAPE=DEFAULT HREF="../toc.html">
</MAP>

<IMG SRC="../level1bar.gif" Alt="alternate navigation bar" ALIGN=top
WIDTH="135" HEIGHT="208" BORDER="0" USEMAP="#level1bar">

</TD>

<TD ALIGN=LEFT VALIGN=TOP>

<TABLE BORDER="0" CELLPADDING="0" WIDTH="400">
<TR>
<TD ALIGN=LEFT VALIGN=TOP >
<IMG SRC="unknown.gif" ALIGN=MIDDLE WIDTH="200" HEIGHT="50" BORDER="0"><BR><BR>
</TD>
```

continues

25

UNDERSTANDING
THE CGI

Listing 25.3. continued

```
<TD ALIGN=LEFT VALIGN=TOP ></TD>
<TD ALIGN=RIGHT VALIGN=TOP >
<A HREF="../toc.html"><IMG SRC="../150plogo.gif" ALIGN=TOP WIDTH="150"
HEIGHT="63" BORDER="0"></A><SMALL><SUP>TM</SUP></SMALL></TD>
</TR>
<TR>
<TD ALIGN=LEFT VALIGN=TOP COLSPAN="3"><BR><HR>
<IMG SRC="../1pixel.gif" ALIGN=TOP WIDTH="400" HEIGHT="1" BORDER="0">
<B>unGROOM'd<SMALL><SUP>TM</SUP></SMALL></B> is dedicated to providing men with
an on line service to help with your "engagement, marriage, and what
follows......" Please take the time to fill out our survey so we can better
understand our readers and what topics are most important to you. We thank you
for your time and support!<BR>
<P><HR>
</TD>
</TR>
<TR>
<TD ALIGN=LEFT VALIGN=TOP COLSPAN="3">
<A NAME="top"></A>
<FORM ACTION="/ungroomd/cgi-bin/survey.pl" METHOD="POST">
<P><INPUT TYPE="text" NAME="name" VALUE="" SIZE=40>Name
<P><INPUT TYPE="text" NAME="email" VALUE="" SIZE=30>E-mail address
<P><B>Are You:</B>
<P><B>Married?</B> <INPUT TYPE="radio" NAME="married" VALUE="Yes">Yes
<INPUT TYPE="radio" NAME="married" VALUE="No">No
<P>If yes, how many years? Years:<INPUT TYPE="text" NAME="yearsmarried"
VALUE="" SIZE=3 MAXLENGTH=3>
<P><B>In a relationship?</B> <INPUT TYPE="radio" NAME="relationship"
VALUE="Yes">Yes <INPUT TYPE="radio" NAME="relationship" VALUE="No">No
<P>If yes, how many years? Years:<INPUT TYPE="text" NAME="yearsrelationship"
VALUE="" SIZE=3 MAXLENGTH=3>
<P><B>Are your parents still married?</B>
<P><INPUT TYPE="radio" NAME="parents" VALUE="yes">Yes
<INPUT TYPE="radio" NAME="parents" VALUE="no">No
<P><B>Would you rather?</B>
<P><INPUT TYPE="radio" NAME="howmarried" VALUE="elope">Elope
<INPUT TYPE="radio" NAME="howmarried" VALUE="have wedding">Have Wedding
<P><B>Do you read any books on marriage/relationships?</B>
<P><INPUT TYPE="radio" NAME="readbooks" VALUE="yes">Yes
<INPUT TYPE="radio" NAME="readbooks" VALUE="no">No
<P>If no, any interest in them? <INPUT TYPE="radio" NAME="booksinterest"
VALUE="yes">Yes <INPUT TYPE="radio" NAME="booksinterest" VALUE="no">No
<P><B>Have you ever cheated sexually on your partner?</B>
<P><INPUT TYPE="radio" NAME="cheated" VALUE="yes">Yes
<INPUT TYPE="radio" NAME="cheated" VALUE="no">No
<P><B>For those who have taken the plunge:</B>
<P><B>How long were you engaged for?</B>
<P><INPUT TYPE="radio" NAME="timeengaged" VALUE="less than a year">Less than a
year <INPUT TYPE="radio" NAME="timeengaged" VALUE="1-2">1-2 Years <INPUT
TYPE="radio" NAME="timeengaged" VALUE="2+">2+ Years
<P><B>Did you feel part of the wedding planning process?</B>
<P><INPUT TYPE="radio" NAME="planning" VALUE="yes">Yes
<INPUT TYPE="radio" NAME="planning" VALUE="no">No
<P><B>Did you attend bridal events?</B>
<P><INPUT TYPE="radio" NAME="bridalevents" VALUE="yes">Yes
<INPUT TYPE="radio" NAME="bridalevents" VALUE="no">No
<P><B>How much did you spend on the engagement ring?</B>
```

```
<P><INPUT TYPE="radio" NAME="ring" VALUE="1-3">$1,000 -3,000
<INPUT TYPE="radio" NAME="ring" VALUE="3-5">$3,000 -5,000
<INPUT TYPE="radio" NAME="ring" VALUE="5-8"> $5,000 - 10,000
<INPUT TYPE="radio" NAME="ring" VALUE="10+">$10,000 +
<P><B>How much did you/are you spending on your wedding?</B>
<P><INPUT TYPE="radio" NAME="weddingcost" VALUE="1-5">$1,000-5,000
<INPUT TYPE="radio" NAME="weddingcost" VALUE="5-8">$5,000-10,000
<INPUT TYPE="radio" NAME="weddingcost" VALUE="10-15">$10,000-15,000
<INPUT TYPE="radio" NAME="weddingcost" VALUE="15-25">$15,000 - 25,000
<INPUT TYPE="radio" NAME="weddingcost" VALUE="25+">$25,000+
<P><B>Who organized the Honeymoon Details?</B>
<P><INPUT TYPE="radio" NAME="honeymoondetails" VALUE="her">Her
<INPUT TYPF="radio" NAME="honeymoondetails" VALUE="you">You
<INPUT TYPE="radio" NAME="honeymoondetails" VALUE="both">Both
<P><B>Did you see a travel agent?</B>
<P><INPUT TYPE="radio" NAME="travelagent" VALUE="yes">Yes
<INPUT TYPE="radio" NAME="travelagent" VALUE="no">No
<P><B>How long was your honeymoon?</B>
<P><INPUT TYPE="radio" NAME="honeymoonlength" VALUE="1 week">1 week or less
<INPUT TYPE="radio" NAME="honeymoonlength" VALUE="2-3 weeks">2-3 Week
<INPUT TYPE="radio" NAME="honeymoonlength" VALUE="4 weeks+">4 weeks or more
<INPUT TYPE="radio" NAME="honeymoonlength" VALUE="none">No honeymoon
<P><B>How much was your honeymoon?</B>
<P><INPUT TYPE="radio" NAME="honeymooncost" VALUE="less than 1000">$1,000 or
less
<INPUT TYPE="radio" NAME="honeymooncost" VALUE="2,000-4,000">$2,000 - 4,000
<INPUT TYPE="radio" NAME="honeymooncost" VALUE="4,000-6,000">$4,000-6,000
<INPUT TYPE="radio" NAME="honeymooncost" VALUE="7,000">$6,000 or more
<P><B>Did you have any marriage counseling prior to marriage or now that you
are married?</B>
<P><INPUT TYPE="radio" NAME="counseling" VALUE="yes">Yes
<INPUT TYPF="radio" NAME="counseling" VALUE="no">No
<P><B>A little about yourself:</B>
<P><B>Age:</B><INPUT TYPE="radio" NAME="age" VALUE="18-24">18-24
<INPUT TYPE="radio" NAME="age" VALUE="25-30">25-30
<INPUT TYPE="radio" NAME="age" VALUE="31-35">31-35
<INPUT TYPE="radio" NAME="age" VALUE="36-40">36-40
<INPUT TYPE="radio" NAME="age" VALUE="40+" CHECKED>40+
<P><B>Sex: </B><INPUT TYPE="radio" NAME="sex" VALUE="male">Male
<INPUT TYPE="radio" NAME="sex" VALUE="female">Female
<P><B>Estimated yearly income?</B>
<INPUT TYPE="radio" NAME="income" VALUE="0-20">0-$20,000
<INPUT TYPE="radio" NAME="income" VALUE="20-40">$20,000-$40,000
<INPUT TYPE="radio" NAME="income" VALUE="40-60">$40,000-60,000
<INPUT TYPE="radio" NAME="income" VALUE="60-100">$60,000-$100,000
<INPUT TYPE="radio" NAME="income" VALUE="100+">$100,000+
<P><B>Education:</B>
<INPUT TYPE="radio" NAME="education" VALUE="High School">High School
<INPUT TYPE="radio" NAME="education" VALUE="Some College">Some College
<INPUT TYPE="radio" NAME="education" VALUE="College Degree">College Degree
<INPUT TYPE="radio" NAME="education" VALUE="Graduate Degree">Graduate Degree
<INPUT TYPE="radio" NAME="education" VALUE="other">Other
<P><B>Weekly internet usage:</B>
<INPUT TYPE="radio" NAME="internet" VALUE="less than an hour">1 Hour or less
<INPUT TYPE="radio" NAME="internet" VALUE="2-3">2-3 Hours
<INPUT TYPE="radio" NAME="internet" VALUE="3-5">3-5 Hours
<INPUT TYPE="radio" NAME="internet" VALUE="5+">5 Hours or more
<P><B>What do you use the web for?</B>
```

continues

Listing 25.3. continued

```
<INPUT TYPE="checkbox" NAME="webusage" VALUE="business">Business
<INPUT TYPE="checkbox" NAME="webusage" VALUE="Entertainment">Entertainment
<INPUT TYPE="checkbox" NAME="webusage" VALUE="Research">Research
<P><B>Favorite types of magazines (you may check more than one box):</B>
<P><INPUT TYPE="checkbox" NAME="magazines" VALUE="music">Music
<INPUT TYPE="checkbox" NAME="magazines" VALUE="entertainment">Entertainment
<INPUT TYPE="checkbox" NAME="magazines" VALUE="business">Business
<INPUT TYPE="checkbox" NAME="magazines" VALUE="adult entertainment">Adult
Entertainment
<INPUT TYPE="checkbox" NAME="magazines" VALUE="sports">Sports
<INPUT TYPE="checkbox" NAME="magazines" VALUE="mens">Men's Publications
<INPUT TYPE="checkbox" NAME="magazines" VALUE="financial">Financial
<INPUT TYPE="checkbox" NAME="magazines" VALUE="computer">Computer
<P><B>Favorite types of Internet sites (you may check more than one box):</B>
<P><INPUT TYPE="checkbox" NAME="internetsites" VALUE="music">Music
<INPUT TYPE="checkbox" NAME="internetsites" VALUE="entertainment">Entertainment
<INPUT TYPE="checkbox" NAME="internetsites" VALUE="business">Business
<INPUT TYPE="checkbox" NAME="internetsites" VALUE="adult">Adult Entertainment
<INPUT TYPE="checkbox" NAME="internetsites" VALUE="sports">Sports
<P><B>What section of unGROOM'd<SMALL><SUP>TM</SUP></SMALL> is of most interest
to you? (you may check more than one box):</B>
<P><INPUT TYPE="checkbox" NAME="ungroomdsection" VALUE="now featuring">Now
Featuring
<INPUT TYPE="checkbox" NAME="ungroomdsection" VALUE="tying the knot">Tying the
Knot
<INPUT TYPE="checkbox" NAME="ungroomdsection" VALUE="mind over marriage">Mind
Over Marriage
<INPUT TYPE="checkbox" NAME="ungroomdsection" VALUE="income's outcome">
Income's Outcome
<INPUT TYPE="checkbox" NAME="ungroomdsection" VALUE="his castle">His Castle
<INPUT TYPE="checkbox" NAME="ungroomdsection" VALUE="last bachelor/MM">The Last
Bachelor/The Marrying Man
<P><B>What topics related to marriage would you like to see covered in
unGROOM'd<SMALL><SUP>TM</SUP></SMALL>? (you may check more than one box):</B>
<P><INPUT TYPE="checkbox" NAME="topics" VALUE="finacial">Financial Issues
<INPUT TYPE="checkbox" NAME="topics" VALUE="Psychology">Psychology Issues
<INPUT TYPE="checkbox" NAME="topics" VALUE="Wedding Day">Wedding Day Issues
<INPUT TYPE="checkbox" NAME="topics" VALUE="Becoming a father">Becoming a
Father Issues
<INPUT TYPE="checkbox" NAME="topics" VALUE="Infidelity">Infidelity Issues
<INPUT TYPE="checkbox" NAME="topics" VALUE="Religious">Religious Issues
<P><B>How did you hear about unGROOM'd<SMALL><SUP>TM</SUP></SMALL>?</B>
<P><INPUT TYPE="checkbox" NAME="hearaboutus" VALUE="internet search">Internet
Search
<INPUT TYPE="checkbox" NAME="hearaboutus" VALUE="Followed a link"> Followed a
link
<INPUT TYPE="checkbox" NAME="hearaboutus" VALUE="Print article">Print article
<INPUT TYPE="checkbox" NAME="hearaboutus" VALUE="Word of mouth">Word of mouth
<INPUT TYPE="checkbox" NAME="hearaboutus" VALUE="Radio">Radio
<INPUT TYPE="checkbox" NAME="hearaboutus" VALUE="Advertisement">Advertisement
<INPUT TYPE="checkbox" NAME="hearaboutus" VALUE="Flyer/hand out">Flyer/hand out
<P><B>Any Additional Comments?</B>
<TEXTAREA NAME="comments" ROWS=4 COLS=40></TEXTAREA>
<P><INPUT TYPE="submit" NAME="Submit" VALUE="Submit"><INPUT TYPE="reset"
VALUE="Reset">
<P><CENTER><B>THANK YOU FOR YOUR TIME &amp; INPUT TO
unGROOM'd<SMALL><SUP>TM</SUP></SMALL>!!!</B>
```

```
</CENTER>
</FORM>
</TD>
</TR>
</TABLE>
</TD></TR></TABLE>
</BODY>
</HTML>
```

FIGURE 25.2.

The unKNOW'n survey.

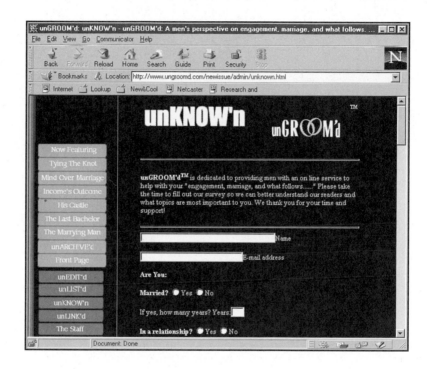

Notice this line from Listing 25.3:

```
<FORM ACTION="/ungroomd/cgi-bin/survey.pl" METHOD="POST">
```

This is the <FORM> tag, which specifies the CGI application to be called when the form gets submitted.

All form handler CGI applications have to do two tasks. The first task is to receive and decode the form data sent by the Web browser. The second task varies widely, depending on the purpose of your CGI application. For example, you might want to place the data in a database for easy access. In that case, the second task your CGI application would perform is to place the data in the database.

This section focuses on the first task—receiving and decoding the form data—for the survey.pl CGI script. The second task is explained in the next section, "Database Integration."

Because the Web browser URL encodes all form data before it's sent to the Web server, your CGI script must decode the data before you begin working with it. The Perl subroutine shown in Listing 25.4 reads in the user's form data and then removes all the URL encoding.

Listing 25.4. The User_Data subroutine.

```perl
sub User_Data {
  local (%user_data, $user_string, $name_value_pair,
         @name_value_pairs, $name, $value);

  # If the data was sent via POST, then it is available
  # from standard input. Otherwise, the data is in the
  # QUERY_STRING environment variable.
  if ($ENV{'REQUEST_METHOD'} eq "POST") {
    read(STDIN,$user_string,$ENV{'CONTENT_LENGTH'});
  } else {
    $user_string = $ENV{'QUERY_STRING'};
  }

  # This line changes the + signs to spaces.
  $user_string =~ s/\+/ /g;

  # This line places each name/value pair as a separate
  # element in the name_value_pairs array.
  @name_value_pairs = split(/&/, $user_string);

  # This code loops over each element in the name_value_pairs
  # array, splits it on the = sign, and places the value
  # into the user_data associative array with the name as the
  # key.
  foreach $name_value_pair (@name_value_pairs) {
    ($name, $value) = split(/=/, $name_value_pair);

    # These two lines decode the values from any URL
    # hexadecimal encoding. The first section searches for a
    # hexadecimal number and the second part converts the
    # hex number to decimal and returns the character
    # equivalent.
    $name =~
      s/%([a-fA-F0-9][a-fA-F0-9])/pack("C",hex($1))/ge;
    $value =~
      s/%([a-fA-F0-9][a-fA-F0-9])/pack("C",hex($1))/ge;

    # If the name/value pair has already been given a value,
    # as in the case of multiple items being selected, then
    # separate the items with a ":".
    if (defined($user_data{$name})) {
      $user_data{$name} .= ":" . $value;
    } else {
      $user_data{$name} = $value;
    }
  }
  return %user_data;
}
```

Notice the order of tasks in Listing 25.4. First, the user's data is obtained from either the QUERY_STRING environment variable or standard input, depending on which request method was used. Next, all plus signs are changed back into spaces, followed by splitting all name/value pairs.

The remainder of the subroutine is a loop that iterates once for every name/value pair. Once inside the loop, the name/value pairs are split and placed in separate variables. Then, any hexadecimal numbers are changed back into their character equivalents. Finally, the name and value are placed into an associative array with the name portion acting as the index of the array element. For example, the associative array is %user_data. The value the user entered in the Email input field on the form would be stored in the array element $user_data["email"].

Notice that if there is already an index in the associative array with the same name, a semicolon and the new value are appended to the existing array element. This addition is made when multiple options can be sent by the user, such as with checkboxes and selection elements.

The User_Data subroutine decodes the user's form data and places the results in an associative array. After decoding the data, it's a good idea to remove any server-side includes the user might have entered. Typically, the only users entering server-side includes are doing so to try to compromise your machine's security, so you should check for and remove any that have been entered. The No_SSI subroutine, shown in Listing 25.5, performs this task.

Listing 25.5. The No_SSI subroutine.

```
sub No_SSI {
  local (*data) = @_;

  foreach $key (sort keys(%data)) {
    $data{$key} =~ s/<!--(.|\n)*-->//g;
  }

}
```

In the next section, you develop the rest of the survey.pl CGI script to handle the unKNOW'n Survey form. As you put the finishing touches on the survey.pl file, the two subroutines you developed in this section will be integrated into it.

Database Integration

Integrating your Web site with a database is another popular application of the CGI. By doing so, you can store much of your data in a database and regenerate your Web pages whenever the data changes, thereby keeping your Web pages up to date. Another common use of a database is to store responses you get from users submitting forms on your Web site. You can then easily generate up-to-date reports from all the responses you have received.

Many large companies use databases in some way with their Web sites. These databases are often the full-featured, commercial relational database management systems, such as Oracle,

Informix, or Sybase. For databases with a lot of records, these systems are the preferred solution.

However, for smaller projects, text file databases are often enough for the needs of the Web site. These databases are simply text files, with each record on a separate line in the file. Fields in each record are delimited by some character, such as commas or semicolons. You could also have single records occupy multiple lines in the file, and delimit the beginning or ending of a record with a special character sequence.

In the previous section, you developed the first part of the `survey.pl` CGI script, which will handle the form input sent by the unKNOW'n survey, shown in Listing 25.3. Now that the form data has been decoded, you can format this information and store it in a text file database for simple access. The code to add the formatted data, along with the two subroutines developed in the previous section, is shown in Listing 25.6.

Listing 25.6. The `survey.pl` file.

```perl
#!/usr/local/bin/perl5

#*********************************************************
# This script maintains a flat-file database of
# ungroomd.com survey responses.
#*********************************************************

$HOME = (getpwnam("www03640"))[7];
$path = "$HOME/survey";
$database_file = ">>$path/unKNOWn.dat";
$quote = "\"";
$ASCII_ten = pack("c", 10);
$ASCII_thirteen = pack("c", 13);
$space = " ";

# Format the Web data received and make sure
# it does not contain any server-side includes
%data_received = &User_Data;
&No_SSI(*data_received);

# Make sure all mandatory fields are full and
# truncate all strings to a maximum of 255 characters
# Also make sure no new-line characters.
foreach $key (keys(%data_received)) {

    $data_received{$key} =~ s/$ASCII_ten//ge;
    $data_received{$key} =~ s/$ASCII_thirteen/$space/ge;

}

open(DATABASE,"$database_file") ||
    die "Content-type: text/html\n\nCannot open database.";

# Lock the database file now.
flock(DATABASE, 2);

print DATABASE $quote . $data_received{"name"} . $quote . "," .
        $quote . $data_received{"email"} . $quote . "," .
```

```
                  $quote . $data_received{"married"} . $quote . "," .
                  $quote . $data_received{"yearsmarried"} . $quote . "," .
                  $quote . $data_received{"relationship"} . $quote . "," .
                  $quote . $data_received{"yearsrelationship"} . $quote . "," .
                  $quote . $data_received{"parents"} . $quote . "," .
                  $quote . $data_received{"howmarried"} . $quote . "," .
                  $quote . $data_received{"readbooks"} . $quote . "," .
                  $quote . $data_received{"booksinterest"} . $quote . "," .
                  $quote . $data_received{"cheated"} . $quote . "," .
                  $quote . $data_received{"timeengaged"} . $quote . "," .
                  $quote . $data_received{"planning"} . $quote . "," .
                  $quote . $data_received{"bridalevents"} . $quote . "," .
                  $quote . $data_received{"ring"} . $quote . "," .
                  $quote . $data_received{"weddingcost"} . $quote . "," .
                  $quote . $data_received{"honeymoondetails"} . $quote . "," .
                  $quote . $data_received{"travelagent"} . $quote . "," .
                  $quote . $data_received{"honeymoonlength"} . $quote . "," .
                  $quote . $data_received{"honeymooncost"} . $quote . "," .
                  $quote . $data_received{"counseling"} . $quote . "," .
                  $quote . $data_received{"age"} . $quote . "," .
                  $quote . $data_received{"sex"} . $quote . "," .
                  $quote . $data_received{"income"} . $quote . "," .
                  $quote . $data_received{"education"} . $quote . "," .
                  $quote . $data_received{"internet"} . $quote . "," .
                  $quote . $data_received{"webusage"} . $quote . "," .
                  $quote . $data_received{"magazines"} . $quote . "," .
                  $quote . $data_received{"internetsites"} . $quote . "," .
                  $quote . $data_received{"ungroomdsection"} . $quote . "," .
                  $quote . $data_received{"topics"} . $quote . "," .
                  $quote . $data_received{"hearaboutus"} . $quote . "," .
                  $quote . $data_received{"comments"} . $quote . "\n";

flock(DATABASE, 8);
close(DATABASE);

# Output success message
print "Location:http://www.ungroomd.com/newissue/admin/unknown-success.html\n\n
➥";

# User_Data
# This procedure receives form input from a Web
# page form and formats it into an associative
# array. The keys of the associative array are
# the names of the form elements. The associative
# array is returned from the procedure.
sub User_Data {
  local (%user_data, $user_string, $name_value_pair,
         @name_value_pairs, $name, $value);

  # If the data was sent via POST, then it is available
  # from standard input. Otherwise, the data is in the
  # QUERY_STRING environment variable.
  if ($ENV{'REQUEST_METHOD'} eq "POST") {
    read(STDIN,$user_string,$ENV{'CONTENT_LENGTH'});
  } else {
    $user_string = $ENV{'QUERY_STRING'};
  }
```

25

UNDERSTANDING
THE CGI

continues

Listing 25.6. continued

```perl
# This line changes the + signs to spaces.
$user_string =~ s/\+/ /g;

# This line places each name/value pair as a separate
# element in the name_value_pairs array.
@name_value_pairs = split(/&/, $user_string);

# This code loops over each element in the name_value_pairs
# array, splits it on the = sign, and places the value
# into the user_data associative array with the name as the
# key.
foreach $name_value_pair (@name_value_pairs) {
  ($name, $value) = split(/=/, $name_value_pair);

    # These two lines decode the values from any URL
    # hexadecimal encoding. The first section searches for a
    # hexadecimal number and the second part converts the
    # hex number to decimal and returns the character
    # equivalent.
    $name =~
      s/%([a-fA-F0-9][a-fA-F0-9])/pack("C",hex($1))/ge;
    $value =~
      s/%([a-fA-F0-9][a-fA-F0-9])/pack("C",hex($1))/ge;

    # If the name/value pair has already been given a value,
    # as in the case of multiple items being selected, then
    # separate the items with a ":".
    if (defined($user_data{$name})) {
      $user_data{$name} .= ":" . $value;
    } else {
      $user_data{$name} = $value;
    }
  }
  return %user_data;
}


# No_SSI
# This procedure checks form data entered by
# a user, and removes any SSI (server side
# includes) fields. It receives an associative
# array as the input.
sub No_SSI {
  local (*data) = @_;

  foreach $key (sort keys(%data)) {
    $data{$key} =~ s/<!--(.|\n)*-->//g;
  }

}
```

These are the first few lines of code in Listing 25.6:

```perl
$HOME = (getpwnam("www03640"))[7];
$path = "$HOME/survey";
$database_file = ">>$path/unKNOWn.dat";
```

```
$quote = "\"";
$ASCII_ten = pack("c", 10);
$ASCII_thirteen = pack("c", 13);
$space = " ";
```

This block assigns values to some variables to be used later in the program.

In the next group of statements, the subroutines developed in the previous section are called. The first line calls the User_Data subroutine and stores the returned data in the %data_received associative array:

```
%data_received = &User_Data;
```

Next, the No_SSI subroutine is called, with the %data_received associative array being passed to the subroutine.

After these two subroutines are called, the user's form data has been received and decoded. The CGI script can now focus on the second task, which is to add the user's data to the text file database.

The first step in this process is to do any special formatting to the data that might need to be done. In this case, the only formatting needed is removing any carriage returns or newline characters that the user might have entered. This formatting is done with the following lines of Perl:

```
foreach $key (keys(%data_received)) {

    $data_received{$key} =~ s/$ASCII_ten//ge;
    $data_received{$key} =~ s/$ASCII_thirteen/$space/ge;

}
```

They loop over each element in the %data_received associative array, checking for and removing any carriage returns or newline characters.

The next step is to open the database file, which is done with the following Perl statement:

```
open(DATABASE,"$database_file") ||
    die "Content-type: text/html\n\nCannot open database.";
```

Because the Web server could receive several requests for a CGI script at the same time, many copies of the survey.pl script could be running at any given moment. Therefore, you need to make sure only one instance of your CGI script modifies the database file at a time. To prevent other instances of the survey.pl file from modifying the database file, you should place a lock on the file immediately after opening it. This is done with the Perl flock statement:

```
flock(DATABASE, 2);
```

The second parameter to the flock function, which in this case is 2, is a code that determines the type of lock to be placed on the file. The number 2 designates setting a write lock on the specified file stream.

25

UNDERSTANDING
THE CGI

With the database file opened and locked, the next step is to write the user's data to the database file. This step is done with the `print` statement in Listing 25.6, with each element in the `%data_received` associative array being printed one at a time, surrounded by quotes and separated by commas.

The only remaining step after placing the record in the database file is to remove the lock on the file and close the file stream, which is done with the following lines:

```
flock(DATABASE, 8);
close(DATABASE);
```

Removing the lock involves another call to the `flock` function, this time with the second parameter set to 8. The number 8 designates removing all locks from the specified file stream. The file stream is then closed by using the Perl `close` statement.

As with all CGI applications, the `survey.pl` file needs to return a result to the user's Web browser. For this situation, the easiest way to do return a result is to redirect the user's Web browser to an existing Web page, which contains a message letting the user know the data sent was successfully received. This redirection is done by sending the `Location` server directive to the Web server with this Perl statement:

```
print "Location:http://www.ungroomd.com/newissue/admin/unknown-success.html\n\n
➡";
```

Resources for More Information

The discussion of CGI in this chapter gives you a basic overview of how CGI works and how you can implement it. There are many sources available to you for more information on creating CGI applications. Most of these resources are available in online versions, but there are some offline versions, too.

Online Resources

When looking for information about an online technology, the many information areas on the Internet are a great place to turn to. With Web sites, newsgroups, and mailing listservs, many choices are available to you. For reference information, the best place to look is related Web sites. For answers to questions, though, it's often more useful to turn to newsgroups and mailing lists to get quick answers from other knowledgeable users.

Web Sites

Many Web sites have information about creating CGI applications, including tutorials, reference manuals, and even script archives. The following is a list of some of the better CGI-related Web sites:

Overview of HTTP

```
http://www.w3.org/hypertext/WWW/Protocols/
```

Object Headers

`http://www.w3.org/hypertext/WWW/Protocols/HTTP/Object_Headers.html`

Names and Addresses, URIs, URLs, URNs, URCs

`http://www.w3.org/hypertext/WWW/Addressing/Addressing.html`

Uniform Resource Locators

`http://www.w3.org/hypertext/WWW/Addressing/URL/Overview.html`

HTML Quick Reference

`http://www.cc.ukans.edu/info/HTML_quick.html`

Hypertext Markup Language

`http://www.w3.org/pub/WWW/MarkUp/`

A Beginner's Guide to HTML

`http://www.ncsa.uiuc.edu/General/Internet/WWW/HTMLPrimer.html`

Special Characters

`http://www.utoronto.ca/webdocs/HTMLdocs/NewHTML/entities.html`

ISO 8859-1 (Latin-1) Table

`http://www.uni-passau.de/~ramsch/iso8859-1.html`

The Common Gateway Interface

`http://hoohoo.ncsa.uiuc.edu/cgi/`

W3C httpd CGI/1.1 Script Support

`http://www.w3.org/hypertext/WWW/Daemon/User/CGI/Overview.html`

Perl Home Page

`http://www.perl.com`

Perl Basics

`http://briet.berkeley.edu/perl/perl_tutorial.txt`

Perl for Win32

`http://www.perl.hip.com`

Index of Perl/HTML Archives

`http://www.seas.upenn.edu/~mengwong/perlhtml.html`

Boutell.com Archive Resources

`http://www.boutell.com/`

Matt's Script Archive

`http://www.worldwidemart.com/scripts/`

Selena Sol's CGI Script Archive

`http://www.extropia.com/`

25

UNDERSTANDING
THE CGI

C++ CGI Class Library

`http://www.ncsa.uiuc.edu/People/daman/cgi++/`

cgi-lib.pl Perl CGI Library

`http://www.bio.cam.ac.uk/cgi-lib/`

CGI.pm Perl 5 CGI Library

`http://www-genome.wi.mit.edu/ftp/pub/software/WWW/cgi_docs.html`

CGI Manual of Style

`http://www.mcp.com/zdpress/features/3970/`

WDB - A Web Interface to SQL Databases

`http://arch-http.hq.eso.org/bfrasmus/wdb/wdb.html`

Free Database Gateway List

`http://cuiwww.unige.ch/~scg/FreeDB/FreeDB.list.html`

WWW-DBMS Gateways

`http://grigg.chungnam.ac.kr/~uniweb/documents/www_dbms.html`

GSQL - A Mosaic-SQL Gateway

`http://www.ncsa.uiuc.edu/SDG/People/jason/pub/gsql/starthere.html`

With Web sites moving and being shut down, it doesn't take long for a static list like this one to have some out-of-date links, and new sites are popping up all the time, offering more resources and other helpful information. If you're looking for information not found on one of the sites listed here, you should use one of the following Internet search directories:

Yahoo! (`http://www.yahoo.com/`)

Infoseek (`http://www.infoseek.com/`)

AltaVista (`http://altavista.digital.com/`)

Excite (`http://www.excite.com/`)

The Lycos Directory (`http://www.lycos.com/`)

C|Net's Search.com (`http://www.search.com/`)

HotBot (`http://www.hotbot.com/`)

Newsgroups and Listservs

Newsgroups and listservs are great sources of information for CGI and related technologies. Although Web sites supply excellent reference material and archives, newsgroups and listservs are much better for getting answers to specific questions. You can post your questions to a newsgroup or send an e-mail message to everyone subscribing to the mailing list, and you will get tips, suggestions, and sometimes even actual code in answer to your question. The following are some of the CGI-related newsgroups and listservs:

```
comp.infosystems.www.authoring.cgi
```

```
comp.infosystems.www.authoring.html
```

```
comp.infosystems.www.authoring.misc
```

`http://www.dejanews.com/` (A search utility for searching through Usenet newsgroups)

Common Gateway Interface List

To subscribe, send e-mail to `listserv@vm.ege.edu.tr`.

In the body of the message, type `subscribe CGI-L Firstname Lastname`.

Advanced CGI Discussion List

To subscribe, send e-mail to `listproc@lists.nyu.edu`.

In the body of the message, type `subscribe ADV-CGI Firstname Lastname`.

Advanced HTML Discussion List

To subscribe, send e-mail to `listserv@ua1vm.ua.edu`.

In the body of the message, type `subscribe ADV-HTML Firstname Lastname`.

Offline Resources

In addition to the wealth of online resources available on CGI and related technologies, you can also find many offline materials, most of which are technical books written on the subject. The following are some of the more popular books on CGI topics:

CGI Bible, IDG Books Worldwide

Teach Yourself CGI Programming with Perl 5 in a Week, Sams.net Publishing

Special Edition Using CGI, QUE

CGI Manual of Style, Ziff-Davis Press

The CGI Book, New Riders Publishing

Instant Web Scripts with CGI Perl, M & T Books

CGI Programming in C & Perl, Addison-Wesley Publishing Company

In addition to these titles, many other CGI books are available. If none of them fits your needs, check out the computer book section of your local bookstore, or visit the `Amazon.com` (`http://www.amazon.com`) or Barnes and Noble (`http://www.barnesandnoble.com`) online bookstores.

Summary

The Common Gateway Interface, or CGI, is a standard that applications you develop use to communicate with your Web server. By using this communication gateway, you can integrate your applications directly into your Web site, thereby extending the functionality of your Web server. CGI is not a specific programming language, so you need to select a language with which to write your CGI applications. Common choices are Perl, C, C++, Visual Basic, Java, TCL, AppleScript, and any UNIX shell.

25

UNDERSTANDING
THE CGI

Much of the CGI revolves around the HTTP headers sent with every HTTP connection. When a Web browser requests a document from a Web server, it sends an HTTP request to the Web server. This request contains a header with specific fields of information. When the Web server then responds to the request, usually by returning the requested document, it also sends an HTTP header along with the HTTP response.

Most of the data available to your CGI applications comes from these HTTP request headers. Form data sent by the user's Web browser is sometimes sent to your CGI application by standard input, when the request method being used is the POST method.

After your CGI application has completed its task, you need to have it send a response back to the Web browser. To do so, an HTTP response header must precede the data being sent to the Web browser. You can add the response header in one of two ways. Your CGI application can create this header itself and send the data directly back to the Web browser. Or, the CGI application can send the data and a directive to the Web server, which then forms the HTTP response header and sends all the information back to the Web browser.

Because the CGI is a server-side interface, the applications you develop will run on a server-side machine, which allows you to take advantage of the benefits of creating server-side applications. Some of these benefits are full cross-platform/cross-browser support, increased flexibility in the tasks you can perform, increased processing power, and source code integrity.

On a practical level, you should use the CGI anytime you need to integrate an application you have developed and your Web site. Actual applications you use the CGI for will vary greatly, depending on the scope of your Web site and what you need accomplished. Some common applications are using CGI applications to add search engines, access counters, form handlers, and database integration.

VI

PART

Dynamic HTML

In Search of a Standard

by Rick Darnell

Dynamic HTML—it's all the rage, but does anyone really know what it means? In all the talk about Dynamic HTML (DHTML), the one thing that's lacking is an identifiable standard—or, more accurately, a standard that everyone can agree on.

Here's the problem: Microsoft and Netscape both have their own ideas about what DHTML should look like, even beginning with the name. Microsoft calls its implementation Dynamic HTML (with a capital *D*), and Netscape refers to its implementation as dynamic HTML (lowercase *d*). The history of the two companies happily working hand in hand to the common good of all Web users is not part of our reality.

In the case of DHTML, both Microsoft and Netscape are using a lot of the same terminology and are referring to the same set of proposed standards in their work toward interactive and dynamic Web pages. Both companies talk about the capability for pages to change without extra trips to the server and more extensive control of styles. But, here's the rub—the actual implementations aren't very compatible.

Netscape has added a new tag, and Microsoft has added new attributes for existing tags. Netscape added load-on-the-fly typefaces, and Microsoft added ActiveX controls for database access. Between the two, the waters are getting muddier, not clearer.

Speaking of standards, now is a good time to mention the World Wide Web Consortium (W3C). The W3C is developing its own recommendation for DHTML. However, true to the spirit of working by committee, the W3C standard existed for months as a list of capabilities, which means all the work put forth so far by Microsoft and Netscape is based only on their best guess of what the finished standard will look like.

So where does that leave you? In the same place you've probably been in before—trying to develop pages that are accessible to as many people as possible while working with implementations that, although not mutually exclusive, have strong tendencies toward incompatibility. To help you understand where this whole technology is headed, here's a description of the players and the rules you'll look at in this chapter:

■ The W3C has developed a wish list of some capabilities for DHTML, which they refer to as the *Document Object Model* (DOM). Although it sounds large and foreboding, the DOM is really just a way for the browser to identify every markup tag and page element and make it accessible for inspection or change. More information on the W3C's DOM plan, and DOM's preliminary implementations in Microsoft and Netscape, are covered Chapter 27, "The Document Object Model."

■ Netscape created its own document object model a couple of years ago with Navigator 2.0. More recently, Netscape has tried other methods of creating dynamic behavior, primarily through the use of a nonstandard <LAYER> tag. However, Netscape started playing down the new tag almost as soon as it released the final version of Netscape Communicator, and is now working toward an implementation that expands on its original document object model. This approach brings Netscape closer to the W3C and Microsoft in this aspect of DHTML.

■ As part of the Internet Explorer 4.0 release, Microsoft has released its version of what it thinks the W3C Document Object Model will look like. Microsoft's version appears to follow the wish list provided by W3C, although it includes some proprietary font and database features that depend on ActiveX controls.

> **NOTE**
>
> This divergent approach is typical for both major browser software companies as they try to anticipate how the DHTML standards will develop. For instance, in 1996 both Microsoft and Netscape released their respective version 3 browsers, which implemented the HTML 3.2 standard that wasn't formally accepted until 1997.

Before you get into the nuts and bolts of DHTML in Chapter 27, take some time in this chapter to explore some different visions of what DHTML could look like when its first official standard is approved by the W3C.

The World Wide Web Consortium

Even though it doesn't resemble a final or usable form, the final word on DHTML's functionality rests with the World Wide Web Consortium and its Document Object Model (DOM) Working Group. There is a bit of irony in this situation because one of the first acts of the group's chair was to issue a statement that labeled the term *Dynamic HTML* as "just marketing."

The DOM Working Group issued a statement of purpose, which states that its goal is not to extend HTML or develop a standard specific to any scripting language. According to the home page for DOM on the W3C Web site, the group is working on a "platform- and language-neutral interface which allows programs and scripts to dynamically access and update the content, structure and style of documents."

That's a mouthful, but what does it mean?

The W3C has received several submissions from member companies, primarily Microsoft and Netscape, on how the various elements of HTML documents should be exposed to scripts. It's important to note that none of the submissions proposes new HTML tags or changes to existing style sheet technology. One of the W3C's most important and hardest goals is to make sure any solution doesn't favor one company's technology to the exclusion of all others.

As mentioned earlier in this chapter, the W3C standard revolves around the Document Object Model, discussed in greater detail in Chapter 27. In a nutshell, the W3C model has two basic requirements:

■ The Document Object Model can be used to take apart and build the document, even after it's loaded by the browser. Individual elements and their attributes can be added, removed, or changed within the document. This model also includes a way to determine and change the content of a page, whether it's text, images, applets, or plug-ins—which is the dynamic part everyone is talking about.

- The DOM won't require a graphical user interface for implementation, owing to the W3C's goal of supplying standards that provide access to Web content for all types of browsers, including those based on Braille and audio technologies. Remember, DOM is a way of opening the structure and contents of a Web page to the page developer so the page can interact with the user—it's not a standard for graphics or animation, although it can be used that way.

> **NOTE**
>
> The W3C is working very hard to develop standards that don't exclude any platform or browser. This focus is part of an ongoing goal to provide World Wide Web standards that support specialized browsers for disabled persons, such as the blind and deaf. For this reason, each new tag or way to manipulate a tag is being developed with an eye toward offering a textual substitute that can be interpreted by browsers for special needs.
>
> To support this effort, the W3C launched the Web Accessibility Initiative (WAI) to promote and achieve Web functionality for people with disabilities. The initiative involves establishing an International Program Office (IPO), which, according to a W3C press release, is responsible for "developing software protocols and technologies, creating guidelines for the use of technologies, educating the industry, and conducting research and development." Because the IPO office is part of the W3C, it will also ensure that all new W3C standards and technologies meet or exceed accessibility goals.
>
> For more information on HTML and accessibility, see Chapter 41, "Creating Widely Accessible Web Pages."

All other requirements of the DOM follow from the manipulation and accessibility guidelines, including each of the major areas required by the DOM Working Group:

- **Structure navigation:** This is the capability to locate elements in a document, such as the parents or children of an object, and it's how Netscape started its document model in Navigator 2.0. It begins with window, then moves down to document, followed by the various children of document, including form, link, applet, and other page elements. Using the DOM model, all tags are exposed for the browser, including unknown tags and elements.

- **Document manipulation:** The standard provides a way to add, remove, or change elements and tags—including attributes of tags—within the document.

- **Content manipulation:** This is the capability to add, change, or delete the content in a document or individual tag. It also includes a requirement for determining, from any part of the document, which tag affects text.

- **Event model:** The event model is comprehensive enough to generate completely interactive documents. It includes the capability to respond to any user action within the document, including moving in and out of form fields, detecting mouse movements and clicks, and determining individual keystrokes. Although the W3C is committed to accessibility for people with disabilites, some of the events will apply only to a graphical interface (such as Windows) that's designed for the average user.

- **Style sheet object model:** This is similar to document manipulation, mentioned earlier. Under the DOM, cascading style sheet attributes are also exposed for modification. With an eye toward the future, the W3C includes a provision to extend the style sheet model to other formats. This might be the loophole Netscape needs to include JavaScript Style Sheets while maintaining compliance with W3C standards.

- **General document and browser information:** The W3C has left no stone unturned. Part of the DOM includes the capability to examine embedded objects, such as cookies and the date a document was created. Other information available includes the user agent (browser) brand and version and the MIME types it supports.

The complete set of requirements for the DOM runs about three pages and includes all the preceding items, plus document type definitions and error reporting. Essentially, all the requirements boil down to this: *Everything* in a document should be available to the user interface for manipulation.

The first step toward creating the standard is to figure out what the current object model is. This step uses the models implemented by Internet Explorer 3.0 and Navigator 3.0 that resulted in the Level 0 standard, which was not released to the general public. It was used only for internal reference by the committee's members.

After the Level 0 standard was established, the Working Group began working toward its long-term goal of building a consensus as to what should and shouldn't be part of the Document Object Model standard, which will become Level 1. Level 1 includes all of the DOM's basic structure and content manipulation features. Other features, such as DTD manipulation and a comprehensive set of events, will be a part of the Level 2 release.

How long will all this head scratching and note passing take? Working Group Chair Lauren Wood said a final version of DOM Level 1 could be released by the print date of this book (December 1997), and Level 2 should be formed by late 1998 or early 1999.

This discussion leads back to the original question: What's a developer to do? The answer from the W3C is to write your DHTML pages to the lowest common denominator of compatibility until the consensus begins to form. This advice is hard for developers to swallow, especially when you want to write with the "latest and greatest" tools on the Web.

My recommendation is similar to the W3C's—if you're writing to a general audience, be wary of anything proprietary, including tags or attributes that are the sole domain of one browser or another. You learn more about this later, but what you'll probably start with is some combination of style sheets and JavaScript. To make sure your implementation is solid, test it with a wide variety of browsers—new and old versions of Navigator and Internet Explorer, no-frills versions such as Mosaic, and text-only applications such as Lynx. This precaution is a reasonable one to take to make sure your dynamic pages won't crater someone else's nondynamic browser.

If you want to write to the emerging standard while using the most advanced tools available, put it someplace separate on your Web site and mark it as "for demonstration only," along with a notation of which browser it was written for.

In short, it's still a long road to an implementation that's going to work well across all browsers, especially the major offerings from Netscape and Microsoft. If you write to the capabilities of most of your users and include safety nets for the rest, you won't go wrong.

Netscape's Story

Netscape got the whole DHTML object rolling back in the old days (about 1995) with its Navigator 2.0 release. That release included a feature called JavaScript, which offered a basic document object model that provided access to elements such as forms, hyperlinks, colors, and various browser attributes.

That first object model was created with an instance hierarchy, which reflected the construction of the HTML page. At the top of the hierarchy was `window`—the parent of all other objects. This object included four children: `location`, `history`, `frames`, and `document`. The `document` object also included children representing specific information about the document:

```
alinkColor

bgColor

fgColor

linkColor

vlinkColor

cookie

lastModified

location

anchors

referreru

forms

links

title
```

An instance hierarchy is built from actual instances, rather than general classes, of objects. For example, suppose the only elements allowed on a page were headings, and a particular page had three H1s and an H4. A class hierarchy would have an object for each possible header—H1 through H6—even the unused H2, H3, H5, and H6. In an instance hierarchy, the same

page would include an object only for the headings that actually appeared on the document—
H1 and H4.

As you can see, the Netscape DOM implementation was a mishmash of page attributes (color settings), META information (last modified date and referring page), and physical elements (anchors, forms, and links) on the page. In the next version of Navigator (3.0), the object model was extended to include applets and other embedded objects.

Netscape had the right idea, but it was still pretty limited in scope and usage. Only a few of the items, such as form elements and some of the colors, could be changed without reloading the document. It was also possible to modify the rest of a page's contents, but only by reloading it with the `javascript` protocol, which is used in the same way as other Internet protocols, such as `http` or `ftp`. It allows the browser to reload a page by invoking a JavaScript method, which results in redefining the page's contents. The user still sees the page go blank and then reload. However, it's much faster than retrieving a new version from the server because the page is created by a process within the browser.

Speaking of the protocol, I would be remiss not to mention JavaScript as the other half of Netscape's big breakthrough in Navigator 2.0. By using JavaScript, developers can write small applications that run on the user's browser, instead of processing through the server. The syntax was related to Java, and with Netscape 3.0, the two languages could talk back and forth across the Web page. This development was a big breakthrough because it gave Java direct access to data on a Web page and provided a way to control Java from outside an applet.

In the early days of JavaScript, developers primarily used it and the Netscape document object model to verify form contents or make fun little 1040EZ calculators. A few hardy folks used it to create some neat effects, such as expanding and contracting outlines and Web sites with custom controls, but most of the uses were limited in scope and utility.

Netscape's Communicator release doesn't extend the document object model in any new and dramatic directions as its ancestors did, but that doesn't mean Netscape doesn't have its eye on the DHTML bandwagon. Here are the three components of Netscape's vision of DHTML:

■ The use of layers to move, hide, and show blocks of HTML on the Web page. The layers can be manipulated in response to user events, making it the only portion of Netscape's solution that meets the definition of *dynamic* that was adopted earlier in this chapter.

A Netscape *layer* is a set of HTML that's displayed, hidden, moved, and altered in different ways. Essentially, it converts your HTML document into a set of slides that you can shuffle and display in any order, singly or in combination.

■ Precise control over formatting, fonts, layout, and other aspects of page behavior through style sheets. Netscape includes support for the W3C's CSS1 (Cascading Style Sheets, Level 1) specification, which Microsoft uses, and JavaScript Style Sheets (JSSS). JSSS doesn't allow changes to the document after it's loaded, but it does allow a style sheet to ask the browser about its environment. The style sheet can then make changes to its implementation to match its specific situation.

> **NOTE**
>
> Although JSSS isn't explicitly supported by the W3C, part of the W3C's position on the Document Object Model is to extend the CSS1 style sheet model to other style sheet formats.

- Dynamic fonts, which are attached to a Web page instead of dependent on the options available on a user's computer. In the past, developers had to guess what typefaces were available on a user's machine, and then supply a list of the preferred choices for a page in the style sheet font attribute or use the <FONT> tag. The dynamic fonts feature uses a new method to check for the existence of the desired typeface, and, if it's not found, download it from the server.

  A dynamic font standard is under development by the W3C that will let Web browsers quickly download a copy of the fonts used in a Web page. This feature would eliminate some of the problems with font availability that have become more noticeable with style sheets.

A little more needs to be said about layers. With the initial betas of Navigator 4.0, Netscape decided to use a new tag—<LAYER>—to implement precise positioning of elements. This decision caused a bit of a problem because Microsoft wasn't going to include the tag on its browser, so the W3C decided not to develop the <LAYER> tag to work on other approaches to DHTML. Given a less-than-warm reception, Netscape is including more emphasis on layers implemented through the Document Object Model with the <DIV> tag. Netscape is also downplaying the <LAYER> tag, although it's still part of the Netscape Communicator release.

The ultimate fate of Netscape's <LAYER> tag is unclear at this point. It doesn't seem as though the W3C is including any support for it in its proposed HTML 4.0 specification, although the tag appears to fulfill many of the features of the W3C draft on positioning HTML elements by using style sheets (www.w3.org/pub/WWW/TR/WD-positioning), which Netscape helped to develop with Microsoft.

In DHTML, Netscape appears to be moving closer to working with the W3C, instead of trying to set its own standards and have W3C follow its lead. Netscape Communicator is fully compatible with existing W3C recommendations or standards for HTML 3.2, plus some from HTML 4, including Cascading Style Sheets. It's also trying to maintain compatibility with working drafts on positioning, object models, and dynamic fonts.

Other than the implementation of JavaScript Style Sheets, covered in Chapter 21, "Using JavaScript Style Sheets," and the <LAYER> tag, covered in Chapter 22, "Layers," Netscape seems to be working on a version of DHTML that doesn't depend exclusively on proprietary or platform-specific controls.

Does this mean that a DHTML page that works on Netscape will also work with Microsoft if both browsers are claiming to meet the upcoming standards? Not necessarily. There are several issues at work here. First, the W3C is not tying DHTML to any specific scripting language. For example, suppose Microsoft makes VBScript and Netscape makes JavaScript completely with the DHTML standard. If a Netscape browser loads a page made dynamic with VBScript, it's not going to work because Navigator still doesn't support that specific language.

Second, both companies view the standard in different ways and are claiming the exclusive privilege of being the only "real solution." This difference in viewpoints is why there's an expanded document object model on one side and layers on the other. These solutions aren't compatible across browsers, even if they both meet the letter or intent of the W3C's work. Currently, neither browser is being written to support anyone else's views on the topic, even though everyone is claiming to be "standard compliant."

Microsoft

As has become the standard operating practice in the ongoing browser battles, Microsoft is boldly going where no standard has gone before with its definition and implementation of DHTML in Internet Explorer 4.0. You can read all about Microsoft's vision of DHTML at `www.microsoft.com/workshop/author/dhtml/`.

Internet Explorer 4.0 (IE4) isn't just a collection of support for a few new tags and a new user interface. Microsoft completely overhauled the HTML parsing engine. The parsing engine in a Web browser looks at HTML documents to see what's inside them. It looks at the tagged text and the content, and then formats the content based on what it finds in the tags. In simpler terms, a parser simply breaks large units of information (like a Web page) into smaller pieces (like markup tags), which are easier to interpret and process, the same way you read a book.

The extended IE4 parsing engine takes the individual tags and document elements and integrates them with a Document Object Model that's supported by any scripting language available. As a matter of practicality, the two choices are JavaScript and VBScript, which are provided as components of IE4. The examples in this book for both Netscape and Microsoft are created with JavaScript.

TIP

IE4 is a component-based application that allows adding other scripting languages through the use of third-party programs linked to the browser. So if you can find the extra modules, you can also add languages such as Python to your browser and expand your scripting options.

Microsoft's vision of DHTML includes four components, which are similar to Netscape's:

■ The Document Object Model allows any element on a page to be shown, hidden, changed, or rearranged without reloading the page from a server. One of the surprises in Microsoft's implementation of the DOM is that it isn't specific to Windows or ActiveX. It's as though the Microsoft model were completely built into the HTML parser as part of the browser. By implementing the DOM with any scripting language on the browser, developers can use the scripting languages to examine or control practically any page element.

■ A way to control elements on a page through scripts, including JavaScript and VBScript. The scripting languages include objects that relate to the elements on the page as defined by the Document Object Model. Using the language's comparison and assignment features, page developers can examine and change the attribute or content of any element on the page referenced by the DOM, including headings, links, text, and other items. This ability also includes controlling and manipulating embedded Java applets, ActiveX controls, and plug-ins.

■ Multimedia ActiveX controls for animation and other effects, such as filters and transitions, without relying on downloading large files or pages. These controls have been implemented through Cascading Style Sheets with the use of filters for fade-in, fade-out, and other types of effects.

■ A way to bind data to an HTML page, including automatic generation of tables, sorting tabular data, and querying local tables. This component uses a special set of HTML attributes enabled with ActiveX to display "live" database records in the same way you would display an applet or plug-in. In the old HTML school, displaying database records required working with CGI scripts and advanced Perl, C, or Java programming. Because DHTML supports immediate changes to page content, the database can update automatically in reaction to user typing, or the table can display live updates from third-party changes to the database.

Like Netscape, Microsoft is working with W3C standards and proposals, trying to anticipate the future of DHTML through the work of the consortium.

The Microsoft DOM is very similar to the Netscape Navigator 2.0 model. It begins with the core objects representing the page and browser (such as window and document), and then branches into more detail (such as form, applet, and link). Microsoft has further expanded the model to include every element on the page. From headings to paragraphs to images to tables to horizontal rules—it's no-holds-barred access to everything on the page.

One of the big strengths touted by Microsoft is compatibility with other browsers that don't support the Internet Explorer 4.0 DHTML implementation. Microsoft calls its compatibility with other browsers *graceful degradation*. Developers and authors writing specifically to the Microsoft version of DHTML won't need to produce alternative versions for Netscape or anyone else, according to Microsoft (see the sidebar "The Reality of Graceful Degradation"). The scripting and tags used by Microsoft are accepted technologies in use by other browsers and blessed by the W3C.

THE REALITY OF GRACEFUL DEGRADATION

Every silver lining has a dark cloud, and the DHTML story is no different. Microsoft DHTML doesn't gracefully degrade when placed on Navigator 4.0, especially when it depends on style sheets. Look at Figures 26.1 through 26.3. In Figure 26.1, you see the DHTML overview from Microsoft's site as viewed on Internet Explorer 4.0. Click on a heading, and the contents underneath appear.

The first test of graceful degradation is the old reliable Mosaic from NCSA. The same page loaded on it (see Figure 26.2) degrades quite nicely. Mosaic doesn't understand style sheets or scripting, so it just ignores all the extra tags and attachments and displays the page in a clean, straightforward, predictable manner to make everything accessible to the user.

In Figure 26.3, you see the same page on Navigator 4.0 (Preview Release 4). Microsoft uses the `display:none` attribute to hide the contents until the user clicks the heading, where it depends on a JavaScript method to remove the attribute so the contents can display. Here's the problem: Netscape doesn't support changing CSS1 style sheets with JavaScript, so there's no way to reveal the hidden elements without loading a new page from the server.

Why does the bulleted list appear, even though it's associated with the content under the headings? Because Navigator doesn't think it belongs with the rest of the hidden text and assumes that the `<UL>` display attribute is set for display. The effect is a list without an explanation, which is still not an acceptable interpretation of the page.

FIGURE 26.1.

Click on a heading in the Microsoft DHTML page, and the contents below it appear.

Previously hidden text —

Hidden text is associated
with these headings

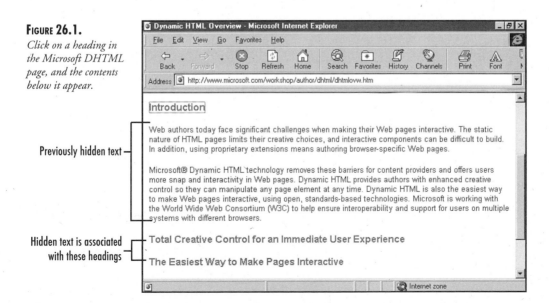

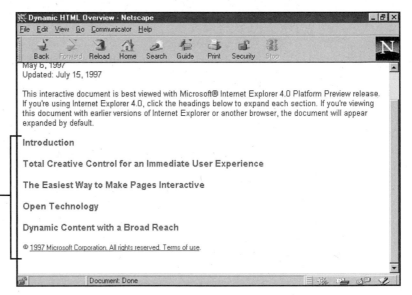

FIGURE 26.2.
Graceful degradation on a browser that's not compatible with CSS1 style sheets or JavaScript.

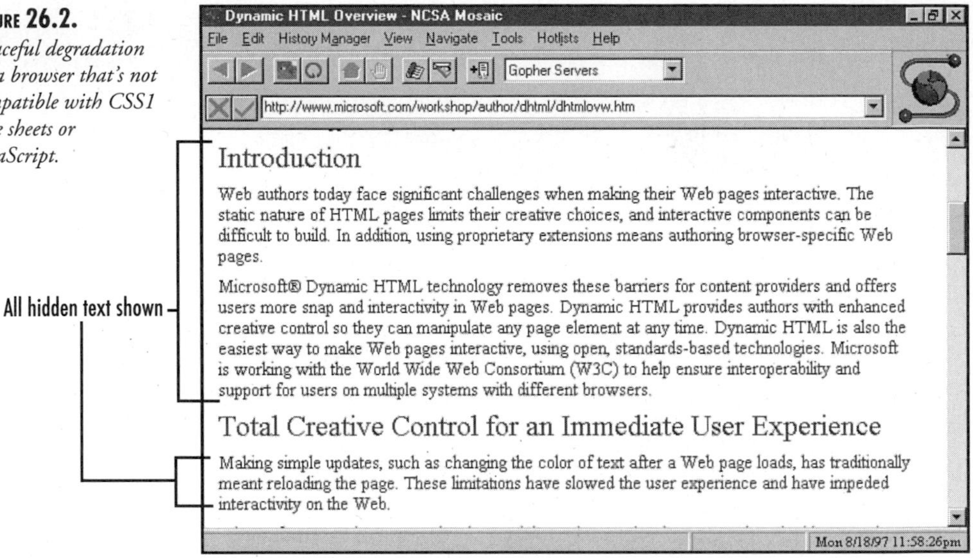

All hidden text shown →

FIGURE 26.3.
Because Netscape is compatible with CSS1 but not with JavaScript's modification of CSS1, it doesn't degrade gracefully.

Hidden text associated with headings isn't shown →

Summary

A Dynamic HTML standard should remain a moving target through 1998, as the software developers continue to revise their products to meet the rules outlined by the W3C. For the time being, there are three slightly different schools of thought on what DHTML is.

The three main players—the World Wide Web Consortium, Netscape, and Microsoft—all seem to agree that an expanded Document Object Model is at the center of the solution. The expanded document model will allow access to every element, along with its attributes and its content, through a scripting language. With unbridled access and control over the contents, HTML pages will bear a closer resemblance to Silly Putty than to tablets of stone.

From the DOM, the views start their divergence. The W3C doesn't use DHTML as part of its vocabulary at all, except to acknowledge the term's use by software vendors. Its work is almost exclusively centered on developing the Document Object Model and its relation to style sheets, scripting languages, and other existing technologies.

Netscape includes JavaScript Style Sheets and layers in its bundle of DHTML capabilities. Layers and JSSS appear to be the result of an implementation of the W3C working draft on positioning HTML elements, although the <LAYER> tag isn't included as part of the proposed HTML 4.0 specification.

In addition to the Document Object Model, Microsoft is also stressing multimedia effects and data awareness with its vision of DHTML. However, the Microsoft solution also depends on proprietary items, such as ActiveX controls, to implement access to the DOM.

Unlike a year or two ago, when the two companies sought to build Web standards around their respective visions, both Netscape and Microsoft seem more eager to work with the World Wide Web Consortium in developing standards for their browsers. The days are gone, it's hoped, when each company will create its own tags and technologies in an attempt to force standards to conform to its respective software. Although competition between the two remains fierce, the user is no longer subjected to getting caught between incompatibilities.

It appears as though Netscape and Microsoft might come closer together than either would like to admit. For the time being, you might want to pick the lowest common denominator between the two—a combination of the W3C Document Object Model, cascading style sheets, and scripting—and hang with it until the W3C recommendation is finalized and the differences between browsers shake out. It's still too early in the game to depend on anything that appears to be too proprietary.

Meanwhile, I'll take a wild guess and say the W3C's final recommendation will be closer to Microsoft than Netscape, and the common areas between the two won't be completely compatible. At that point, both companies will need to make sure that whatever their implementation of DHTML is, it's in full compliance with the standard. However, the W3C seldom moves quickly compared to the rest of the World Wide Web, so subsequent browser releases from Microsoft and Netscape should allow enough time for these companies to adjust to the W3C standard—whatever it looks like.

The Document Object Model

by Rick Darnell

The Document Object Model (DOM) sounds pretty intimidating, conjuring visions of programmers in smoke-filled rooms gleefully rubbing their hands together over cauldrons of melted 8088 processors and chanting strange incantations. No, wait a minute—those were the witches in Macbeth.

In this chapter, it's my job to dispel the voodoo surrounding DOM and reveal it for what it is—a structured way of accessing HTML elements and content on a Web page. There's no new set of tags or attributes to learn because the DOM's goal is to work within existing HTML, style sheets, and scripting languages.

In this chapter, you'll take a look at the history of DOM with Netscape and Microsoft, what the World Wide Web Consortium (W3C) envisions for the future, and what you're going to work with in the rest of the book.

Some DOM History

DOM is not a new concept. In fact, it has been around since one of the first implementations in Netscape Navigator 2.0 in 1995. Up to this point, Netscape's version didn't generate a lot of interest except in relation to using JavaScript with forms. A new implementation of DOM in Microsoft Internet Explorer 4.0 extends the model originally created for Netscape.

Breaking New Ground: Netscape

Netscape was the first company to develop a DOM with the creation of its JavaScript scripting language. For its first attempt, the model offered a lot of functionality for developers. Initially, the DOM was described as an *instance hierarchy* of *JavaScript objects*, defined like this:

- Instance: No objects are created until they appear on a Web page. For example, if no hyperlinks were on a page, the link object would be empty. Instance hierarchy is different from a general class hierarchy, in which an object is created for every class whether it's included as part of the Web page or not.

- Hierarchy: Not all objects are created equal. Each exists in a set relation to other objects. (See Figure 27.1.) In the case of a Web browser, the highest spot on the hierarchy food chain is the window object. Under the window is a document object, which is the current HTML page loaded in the browser. In its initial presentation, there are three objects underneath document: anchor, link, and form. Individual form elements are found under the form object.

- JavaScript: JavaScript is a scripting language for HTML documents. Scripts are triggered after the user manipulates something on the document, such as placing the mouse over a hyperlink, clicking a button, or changing the content of a form field.

- Objects: An object is a construct with associated properties and methods. Think of a house—its properties could include items such as bedrooms, bathrooms, floors, and square feet. The first three properties could also be objects with properties of their own, such as closets, tubs, showers, flooring, and windows. Although properties describe the house, methods change it. For example, a home addition method could affect the other properties by adding rooms and square footage. You can learn more about JavaScript in Chapter 23, "JavaScript at a Glance," and Chapter 21, "Using JavaScript Style Sheets."

FIGURE 27.1.

The first JavaScript object hierarchy.

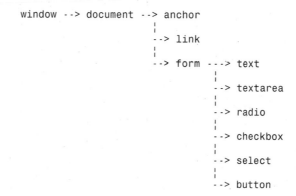

```
window --> document --> anchor
                     |
                     --> link
                     |
                     --> form ---> text
                               |
                               --> textarea
                               |
                               --> radio
                               |
                               --> checkbox
                               |
                               --> select
                               |
                               --> button
```

Now that you've seen each term, you can put the whole picture together. The first DOM was a collection of certain page elements that existed in a descending relation to each other with the JavaScript language. The topmost parent in the relationship was the browser window, and the hierarchy continued down to individual elements on the page. Only the selected elements were accessible—you were out of luck if you wanted to work with tags such as headings or blockquotes.

With that out of the way, Netscape decided to improve on a good thing with the release of Navigator 3.0. The main feature of the new JavaScript was additional objects representing plug-ins, applets, and images. Other elements on the page, such as headings and blockquotes, remained inaccessible to JavaScript programmers.

With the introduction of Netscape Communicator with Navigator 4.0, Netscape hasn't extended the JavaScript DOM in any tangible fashion. You can access forms, applets, plug-ins, images, layers, frames, anchors, and hyperlinks on a page—the major page components—but nothing else.

Navigator 4.0 also includes support for JavaScript Style Sheets (JSSS), however, which uses a slightly different document object. JSSS uses JavaScript syntax to control a document's style (read more in Chapter 21). When used in <STYLE> tags, the document object picks up a whole new set of objects that aren't available when used in <SCRIPT> tags. The new objects are based on a general class hierarchy in which each HTML element is represented, along with style classes and individual identifiers. (See Figure 27.2.)

27

THE DYNAMIC
OBJECT MODEL

FIGURE 27.2.
*The JavaScript
document hierarchy for
style sheets.*

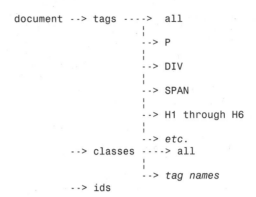

```
document --> tags ----> all
                         |
                        --> P
                         |
                        --> DIV
                         |
                        --> SPAN
                         |
                        --> H1 through H6
                         |
                        --> etc.
         --> classes ----> all
                         |
                        --> tag names
         --> ids
```

Using this object hierarchy, you can access and modify every HTML element, whether or not it appears on a page. It lets the page developer create functions to evaluate the user's browser and environment and to create a style based on that knowledge.

With that in mind, it's time to walk up the West coast to Washington and see what Microsoft has accomplished with the DOM.

Extending the Idea: Microsoft

With Internet Explorer 3.0, Microsoft jumped on the JavaScript bandwagon, adding its own scripting language (Visual Basic Scripting Edition, commonly called VBScript) as another option. The DOM, which was part of this release, matched Netscape's implementation in Navigator 2.0, which meant that Internet Explorer lacked some of the new JavaScript objects, such as those representing applets and images.

This meant continued incompatibilities between the two versions of JavaScript and, by extension, the DOM. VBScript followed a DOM implementation compatible with Microsoft's version of JavaScript.

NOTE

It's hard to tell where VBScript is headed. Although it reaches many users just because it's a Microsoft product, it still misses many more users because Microsoft is the only company currently implementing it with its browser (although a VBScript plug-in is available for Netscape). VBScript's fate seems to be relegated to a minor role until more browsers support it. If you're choosing between languages and want to reach a larger audience, use JavaScript.

27

THE DYNAMIC OBJECT MODEL

OLD JAVASCRIPT, NEW ECMASCRIPT

In early 1997, Netscape handed JavaScript to the European Computer Manufacturer's Association (ECMA) for development as a standardized language. ECMA responded in summer 1997 with ECMAScript–JavaScript in a standard form.

ECMAScript was originally designed to be a Web scripting language. However, the ECMAScript standard provides core scripting capabilities for a variety of host environments. For this reason, the specification doesn't tie the language to any particular host environment.

For the time being, Netscape and Microsoft are both pledging to fully support the ECMAScript standard, which should give the two browsers additional common ground when developing scripting and DHTML (Dynamic HTML) applications. Will they be 100 percent compatible? Not likely. Like many other technical standards, ECMAScript includes the great caveat, "A conforming implementation of ECMAScript is permitted to support program syntax not described in [the] specification." And the world still turns.

With Internet Explorer 4.0, Microsoft stopped trying to play catch-up in the JavaScript object model game by extending the DOM to include every tag and content on the page. The new DOM that Microsoft offers is accessible to JavaScript or VBScript and not simply relegated to the page's style sheet sections. It includes a new object called `all`, which is really an array of all the elements on a page. (See Figure 27.3.)

FIGURE 27.3.

The Microsoft DOM looks similar to Netscape's DOM but offers access to every element through the document's `all` *property.*

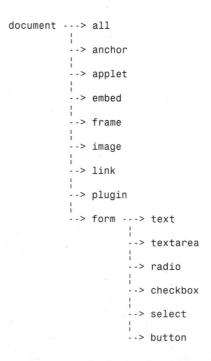

```
document ---> all
         |
         --> anchor
         |
         --> applet
         |
         --> embed
         |
         --> frame
         |
         --> image
         |
         --> link
         |
         --> plugin
         |
         --> form ---> text
                   |
                   --> textarea
                   |
                   --> radio
                   |
                   --> checkbox
                   |
                   --> select
                   |
                   --> button
```

The other thing that the Microsoft DOM does that Netscape's doesn't do is open the world of *events* to every element. Events are how a browser detects and responds to user events, such as mouse movements or keyboard actions, and are covered in more detail in the next chapter, "Working with the User: Events." With Netscape's version of the DOM, events are restricted to specific objects. For example, the only events that are affected by clicks are hyperlinks and buttons. The Microsoft model opens all page elements to practically all events, however. For example, you can detect a user clicking a heading or moving the mouse over a blockquote.

Using the IE4 model, you can also access each attribute in an element, including settings affecting size, color, font, background, and anything else that's legal for the particular page tag. Then, to take the model one step further, Microsoft's DOM also allows you to examine and change the content between each set of tags.

Microsoft's approach is definitely in line with the W3C's list of DOM requirements, although it's still a Microsoft solution, not a standard. So far, Microsoft is the only company to include this type of DOM in its browser. It's good to work with it and to see how to access it using scripts, but don't depend on it as the final word.

In Search of a Standard Revisited

The final judge in developing a universal standard is in the hands of the World Wide Web Consortium. What the W3C decides will probably be adopted in major portions, if not entirely, by Netscape, Microsoft, and the other browser developers.

> **NOTE**
>
> Unfortunately, the W3C isn't known for its lightning speed when making decisions. A preliminary Level 1 DOM specification (think of it as version 1.0) is scheduled for release by the time of this book's printing. DOM Level 1 will fulfill only some of the requirements set forth by the W3C. An extended set of specifications isn't expected until late 1998 or early 1999.

The following sections take a look at what the W3C has identified as the key requirements of a universal DOM, including an emphasis on the parts that will be addressed in the preliminary Level 1 specification.

General Requirements

As you've learned several times, one key component of the W3C DOM is that it should be universal—users shouldn't be required to use a specific browser or computer to take advantage of the DOM. The DOM should also be language independent. Remember that Netscape's version began life tied to JavaScript. What the W3C wants is to separate the DOM from languages so that a language can access the properties of the document object, but not dictate its structure.

Another important feature is tied to the W3C's commitment to creating accessibility for all users on the Web—therefore, a graphical user interface isn't required for conforming to the DOM.

> **NOTE**
>
> Several nongraphical browsers are currently available—most noticeably, the text-only Lynx. Other versions are designed for people who are blind or have other disabilities that prevent them from using what we tend to think of as a "typical browser," such as the graphical interface of Navigator or Internet Explorer. Specialty browsers can interpret HTML as speech, Braille, or special typefaces.

The ability to work in both graphical and nongraphical environments can create some confusion for developers. This section explores using the DOM to create decidedly graphical effects. If the DOM is used for so much graphical behavior, why go to the trouble of saying it doesn't require a graphical user interface? Because not everyone can use a graphical user interface, most notably people with vision disabilities. The W3C is committed to standards that promote HTML and DOM accessibility for as many people as possible.

The last general requirement is that the DOM must not open the user's browser to problems with security, validity, or privacy. This requirement has already generated some discussion among the group working on the DOM recommendation. Although one part of the DOM says all attributes on a page must be accessible and modifiable, this requirement can lead to problems for portions of the object model, especially when it relates to the user agent and history list.

Some pages are designed to work with specific browsers. Browsers identify themselves with a user_agent attribute, which would be accessible and available for scripts to modify. Unscrupulous page designers could use this attribute to change the way a browser views a page so that it would appear incompatible. The result would cause an incorrect interpretation of the page or crash the browser.

The other problem is with the history object. Why should access to the history list be a security issue? It depends on the sites you browse to. Web pages with forms that ask for information such as a user name, password, credit card information, or other private information, often pass that information to the server embedded in a URL.

The history object could give those with less-than-honorable intentions yet another way to peruse private information for ill-gotten gain. For this reason, both Microsoft and Netscape have disabled or plan to otherwise change this part of the DOM.

Structure Navigation

This set of DOM capabilities refers to ways of moving within a document, such as finding the parent of an element or what children are contained in an element.

PARENTS AND CHILDREN IN HTML

What constitutes a parent and child? Go ask your mom or dad—that discussion is beyond the scope of this book. Beyond the birds and the bees, the parent-child relationship concerns nested tags. Look at the following snippet of HTML:

```
<DIV id=parent1>This is Division 1.</DIV>
<DIV id=parent2>This is Division 2 which leads to
<BLOCKQUOTE id=child1>block quote 1 which ends with</BLOCKQUOTE>
the end of Division 2.</DIV>
```

The first division, parent1, is not a parent of the second division, parent2. It stands on its own, because the closing tag of the first precedes the opening tag of the second. The blockquote, child1, is a child of the second division, parent2. It sits completely within the confines of the division's opening and closing tags.

Here's another parent-child relationship you might recognize:

```
<OL>
  <LI>Item 1</LI>
  <LI>Item 2</LI>
  <LI>Item 3</LI>
</OL>
```

Each of the list items is a child of the ordered list tag, which makes the list items siblings to each other. If you nested another list by adding a new list container with its own set of list items, the new list would be a child of the outer list and a sibling to the other list items:

```
<OL id=outerlist>
  <LI>Item 1</LI>
  <LI>Item 2</LI>
  <LI>Item 3</LI>
  <UL id=innerlist>
    <LI>Sub item 1</LI>
    <LI>Sub item 2</LI>
    <LI>Sub item 3</LI>
  </UL>
</OL>
```

Using JavaScript notation, here's one way you could express the structure of the preceding snippet as a series of objects:

```
document.outerlist
document.outerlist[0] //Item 1
document.outerlist[1] //Item 2
document.outerlist[2] //Item 3
document.outerlist.innerlist
document.outerlist.innerlist[0] //Sub item 1
document.outerlist.innerlist[1] //Sub item 2
document.outerlist.innerlist[2] //Sub item 3
```

The structure of the notation reflects the structure of the document, requiring a reference to the outer list to reach the inner nested list. Each sibling then exists in a parallel relationship with its neighbor.

Parent-child relationships in HTML do several things for you. First, they allow you to reference tags by their relationship to each other, as outlined in the sidebar "Parents and Children in HTML." By defining a specific way to identify elements in their relationship to the document and to each other, you are given a method for expressing the document's unique structure.

After each element is identified and expressed as part of the document structure, some additional structure navigation requirements fall into place, including exposing attributes and unknown tags.

You handle unknown tags the same as you would other elements. If it has an `id`, you could use that value to reference it within the DOM. If it doesn't, you could identify it by its relative position to other elements.

Document and Content Manipulation

Document and content manipulation follow the structure navigation standards. Document and content manipulation are used with the event model to supply the "Dynamic" part of Dynamic HTML.

First, document manipulation allows you to change tags. For example, you could change an `H1` heading into an `H3` heading or into a new paragraph with `P`. Second, it lets you add or remove tags from the document. The hard part of all this is that adding or removing page tags should still result in a valid document. Therefore, the DOM should have a way to prevent you from turning a set of `LI` tags into orphans by removing the parent `UL` or `OL` tag, or remove the `LI` tags at the same time. The W3C has given no indication on what the preferred method will be on this issue.

With content manipulation, the page designer can script for changes to the content of any part of a document. This DOM requirement has two parts. First, like the structure navigation, you should be able to determine which element is surrounding any particular piece of text or determine the text within any given element.

After you're able to reference the content, you can add, change, or delete content at will. Microsoft added this feature to its Internet Explorer 4.0 browser with the `innerText` property. For example, with an `H1` heading named `mainHeading`, you can determine its content this way:

```
var textContent;
textContent = document.mainHeading.innerText;
```

This code creates a new string called `textContent`, which now contains all the text between the tags identified as `mainHeading`. To change this content, use the same property:

```
textContent = "This is a new heading";
document.mainHeading.innerText = textContent;
```

In addition to the content, you can use the property to add new tags or elements. You could also change the preceding line to the following one:

```
textContent = "<H2>This is a new heading</H2>";
document.mainHeading.innerText = textContent;
```

Because you're affecting only the content, the elements that surround the content do not change. Add the new content within the existing tags, resulting in HTML that now looks like this:

```
<H1 id=mainHeading><H2>This is a new heading</H2></H1>
```

If you wanted to replace the `<H1>` tags with `<H2>` tags, you can use the `outerText` property, which returns the string inside the `mainHeading` element, including the elements themselves. The code would look like this:

```
TextContent = document.mainHeading.outerText;
textContent = "<H2 id='mainHeading'>This is a new heading</H2>";
document.mainHeading.outerText = textContent;
```

And the resulting HTML would look like this:

```
<H2 id=mainHeading>This is a new heading</H2>
```

Because the DOM has a variety of ways to examine and change your document, it also needs a way to find out what the user is doing so it can react appropriately; this subject is covered in the next section.

Event Model

To permit completely interactive documents, the event model must include a wide variety of possible activities for the user, including mouse movements, mouse clicks, combinations of mouse movement and clicking (drag-and-drop), key presses, and actions revolving around forms. More information about events and event handlers is in Chapter 28.

In Netscape's versions of object models, specific events were tied to specific objects. You could detect the user moving the mouse pointer over a hyperlink, but not a heading; you could detect a click on a button, but not a blockquote. A key part of the W3C requirement for the DOM is that every element will accept every applicable event. Any piece of text will be able to respond to mouse activities, including clicks, double-clicks, and pointers moving over and out of its area.

This requirement also produces a certain amount of difficulty, however, when it's merged with the user accessibility issues also stressed by the W3C. What if the user interface doesn't support a mouse? That removes many potential events from the range of possibilities for a page when it's viewed on a unconventional browser. This issue hasn't been addressed yet in the requirements, but you can expect browser developers to supply other events, such as pressing specific keys to substitute for mouse activities.

One new idea provided for HTML in the event model is a concept known as *event bubbling*, which recognizes that an event that affects an element can also affect its parent. Through scripting constructs, the event handler can let the system know whether the event was handled completely. If it wasn't, the event is passed up to the next level of the document.

For example, the user clicks an ordered list item, and the event handler for the list item does its work. If the event handler is finished and the event has been completely fulfilled, the event handler returns true and the event is complete. If the event handler returns false, however, the event is passed to the parent element. The ordered list container now has the chance to perform additional actions to complete the event. If it returns true, the event is finished. If it returns false, the event is sent to the document for any default handling dictated by the user's browser.

Summary

On its simplest level, the Document Object Model is a way of defining how browsers can express their structure and content, regardless of the platform or scripting language. It has its roots in Netscape's JavaScript Object Model, introduced in Navigator 2.0. The early Netscape model included a limited number of objects and events that provided access to some of the key components on a page, such as forms and hyperlinks, but ignored almost all other formatting tags. Netscape's original idea is now expanded in scope and capabilities in Microsoft's Internet Explorer 4.0, which includes an object model that is closer in intent to requirements outlined by the W3C.

This isn't to say that Microsoft's solution is the final word on the Document Object Model. The W3C's requirements aren't standards—they're only a list of the capabilities they expect from a DOM. The problem with conforming to this sort of list is that it doesn't create a standard—it just expresses a wish list.

A preliminary version of the DOM with the key components in place (structure navigation, document and content manipulation, and event model) is expected at press time. Any formal W3C ruling on a complete implementation of the full DOM requirements isn't expected for another year or more. After a standard is developed, it will probably take the software developers up to another year to modify their browsers to make sure they work with the brave new world envisioned by W3C.

In the meantime, keep an eye on both Netscape and Microsoft. Their future browser revisions are a good indicator of which way W3C's flag is blowing, because both companies are part of the W3C committee working on the issue. Even if they don't meet the final W3C DOM exactly, you'll be close enough to make an easy transition when both browsers come closer to compatibility with each other.

Working with the User: Events

by Bruce Campbell

IN THIS CHAPTER

CHAPTER 28

Intrinsic Events

An important enhancement to the HTML 4 standard is the addition of *intrinsic events* to HTML documents and HTML 4–compliant user agents. Although handling events on Web pages means you must write code to create HTML documents, the added functionality of standard user events opens up Web documents to infinite possibilities for new and flexible Web content. With the addition of a standard event model, Web pages become dynamic and more responsive to user interaction. The current working draft of the World Wide Web Consortium (W3C) standardizes 18 events that you, as a Web page author, can use to write scripts to handle and create interactive Web pages.

> **NOTE**
>
> Remember that the W3C uses the term *user agent* as a superset of Web browsers. The word *browser* conjures up the requirement of sight to use the application. The W3C wants HTML user agents to be created for everyone, including the sight-impaired. I use the term *user agent* often in this chapter.

Web-based HTML 4 documents download a sophisticated Web page to a client once in an initial state. After the document finishes loading in the user agent, an HTML 4 Web page can dynamically change without returning to the Web to request additional information, which reduces the Web server page demand significantly. HTML 4 events supply the impetus for dynamic changes. As an event takes place, the user agent recognizes the event and processes Web page changes as instructed by code within the HTML document. This chapter discusses the HTML 4 intrinsic event list in detail. The word *intrinsic* refers to the user agent already being aware of the events, whether a Web page author uses them to dynamically change Web pages or not.

Yes, to use the intrinsic events of the HTML 4 specification, you will have to write scripting code and include the code in your HTML documents or in additional files referenced in your HTML documents. The details of adding scripts to your Web pages is covered in Chapter 29, "HTML and Scripting: The DHTML Combination." This chapter, a setup chapter to Chapter 29, covers the promise of dynamic Web pages made possible by a standard event list. In a static Web browser, those strictly adhering to the HTML 3.2 specification, there's no way for a Web author to provide dynamic content without returning to the Web server and loading another Web page. Web servers have to handle more page requests under the static document model. HTML 4's intrinsic event list is the launching point for adding interactive and dynamic functionality to your Web pages.

Why Standardize Events?

If each user agent developer invents his or her own event list, a Web author would have to write code specifically for each user agent. Two developers might provide the same functionality, but if they give different names to their events, content you created for one user agent would not work on the other.

The reasons for standardizing the events list are mostly the same as those for standardizing HTML tag and attribute names: standardization in the HTML document-parsing routine within the user agent and consistency in the reliable minimal feature set of compliant user agents.

How Events Work

A strong symbiotic relationship between the user agent developer and the Web page author is required for events to be enabled on a Web page. The HTML 4 specification standardizes the user agent–Web page relationship. The developer writes code within the user agent that listens for any one of a finite list of events to take place, while the site visitor uses the user agent application. Programmers refer to the event-recognizing code object as an *event listener*.

On the other hand, the Web page author reviews the list of available events and writes code to make something happen for each event he or she wants to enable on the Web page. The code the Web author writes is called an *event handler*. As a Web author, you can tie each event handler to as much of the Web page as you want. For example, on today's computers, most applications handle a click event whenever a user clicks on an active application. HTML 4 is no exception. You can write separate event handlers to handle clicks on different images on your Web page or any visible HTML element, for that matter, or you can write a single event for the whole HTML document. Event handlers have a scope, too, and by the time you finish reading this chapter, you will discover how you define their scope.

The creative part of the process is deciding what to do within your event handlers. When a user clicks on an image on your Web page, you can change the image, expand a paragraph of text, change the attributes of text somewhere else on the page, start an animation, go elsewhere on the Web to get more information, or do something no one has ever thought to do before. The possibilities seem endless as you consider 18 events and tens of possible actions for each event.

In Chapter 29, you'll see more detailed examples of event handlers. This chapter focuses more on setting up events properly within the tag structure of your HTML 4 documents. You initialize events as attributes of HTML tags by using the standard event name as the attribute name and supplying a value, which is the appropriate script function name. For example, to enable a click event for an image on your Web page, this is how you specify the image tag:

```
<IMG NAME="image1" SRC="image1.gif" onClick="Function1();">
```

Then, you write a script routine called `Function1()`, or you can handle the event within the `<IMG>` tag itself by including the appropriate code as the value for the `onClick` attribute. Handling events completely within an HTML tag is called *inline event handling*. This chapter includes an inline event-handling routine as an example in the section "Inline Text Attribute Changes" later in this chapter.

The rest of this chapter looks at the Web author's job in making events work. Before you get immersed completely in your Web page authoring responsibilities, consider all the work the user agent developer has to have done to make the events work for you. Of course, there's no reason why you can't be the user agent developer as well. Forgive me for assuming you plan to create content for Netscape's Communicator or Microsoft's Internet Explorer Web browsers, if you are writing your own user agent as well. As you surely have realized by now, writing a fully compliant HTML 4 Web browser is significantly more difficult than writing a fully compliant HTML 1, 2, or 3.2 Web browser.

Most of the events an HTML 4 user agent listens for would be very difficult or impossible to write if the underlying operating systems didn't already provide the basic data for the event. For example, the Windows, NT, UNIX, and Mac operating systems all make pointing device clicks available to applications written on that platform. Operating systems pass on to the user agent at least the x and y location of a click and which button was clicked.

The user agent developer is responsible for mapping the raw event data from the underlying operating system to its significance on the loaded Web page. For the click event, the user agent must know where each HTML element has been placed on the Web page and then consider how an operating system mouse click translates to a Web page element. The user agent then must refer to the loaded Web page to see the implications of that event. If the Web page author hasn't written a specific event handler for that event on that element, the user agent then increases the event's scope. If no event handler exists within the scope for that event on the Web page, the user agent can drop the event details and move on to the next event in the event queue.

> **NOTE**
>
> By writing a user agent in Java, the user agent developer can take advantage of the Java Virtual Machine doing the specific operating system work itself.

The user agent event listener keeps adding new events into the event queue, and the user agent considers each event in the queue in the order of arrival. For each event, the user agent performs the appropriate functionality that's specified by the Web page author. If at any time the user loads another Web page, the event queue is cleared and begins accepting new events for the newly loaded page. As you get familiar with the standard events of HTML 4, consider the implications of making the event work from the user agent developer's perspective. Some events are much more easily enabled than others. For each event added to the HTML 4 specification, the user agent developer has a lot of work to do.

Setting the Scope of an Event Handler

By taking advantage of the natural hierarchy of Web pages, event-handling routines can be more specific in defining their scope. HTML 4 pages are very hierarchical. A character on a Web page is part of a word on a Web page, which is a part of a sentence that's part of a paragraph, which can be part of a division that's a part of the whole document.

Figure 28.1 demonstrates the hierarchy of elements on a Web page. By using the <SPAN></SPAN> tag pair, you can create the letter a as a valid character element, the word ideas as a valid word element, and the sentence with the word *ideas* as a valid sentence element. The paragraph with the word *ideas* is a valid paragraph element you can create by using the <P></P> tag pair. Finally, the first two paragraphs create a valid division element, if contained in a <DIV></DIV> tag pair.

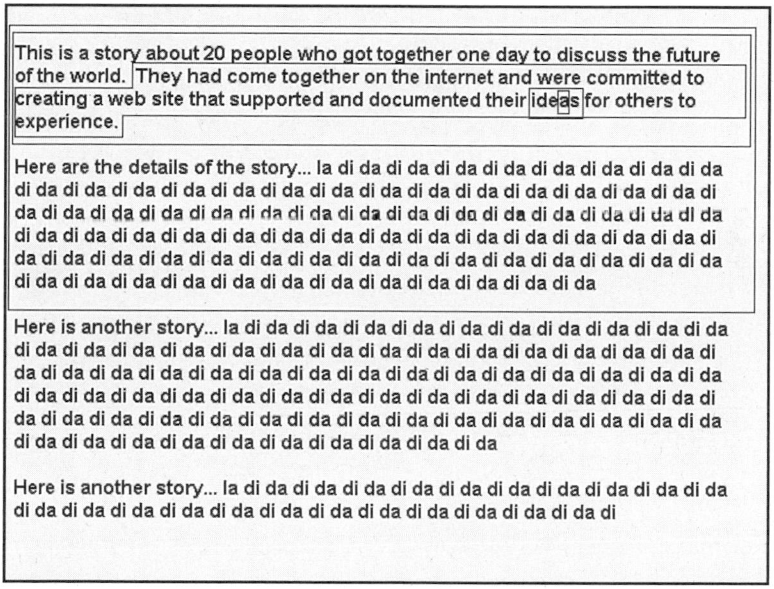

FIGURE 28.1.

The HTML element hierarchy.

In hierarchy terms, the letter *a* element is the lowest level element, and the division element is the highest level element. When a user clicks on the letter *a* in the word *ideas,* he or she is really clicking on five elements, not including the Web page document itself, if all the tags were included as suggested in the previous paragraph.

You can enable your event handlers within any of the tag pairs for which that event is valid. You set the appropriate scope based on the tag in which you place the event as an attribute. For example, consider the following HTML document snippet:

```
<DIV>
   <IMG SRC="image1.gif">
   <IMG SRC="image2.gif">
   <IMG SRC="image3.gif">
</DIV>
```

This code creates a division with three images placed within the division tag pair. You can enable an onClick event for a specific image by placing an onClick attribute in the <IMG> tag, as shown here:

```
<IMG SRC="image1.gif" onClick="RunMe();">
```

Or you can place the onClick attribute within the opening <DIV> tag to enable a single onClick event for all three images:

```
<DIV onClick="RunMe();">
```

If you place an onClick attribute within the <IMG> tag and the opening <DIV> tag, the user agent should use only the attribute of the lowest element in the Web page element hierarchy. In this case, the onClick attribute of the <IMG> tag would be enabled, if it exists, before considering an onClick attribute of the opening <DIV> tag. The <IMG> tags are lower in the hierarchy because they are embedded within the <DIV></DIV> tags. Once a user agent finds an enabling event in a lower level tag, it doesn't consider the same event attribute in higher level tags.

> **NOTE**
>
> Microsoft calls the process of the user agent looking first at the lowest tags and then moving up the element hierarchy *event bubbling*. In Internet Explorer 4.0, you can specify that the user agent not look to higher tags by canceling the event bubbling. However, at the time of this writing, the mechanism for canceling event bubbling isn't standardized in the W3C's latest HTML 4 working draft.

For many standard HTML 4 events, you can specify an event handler for the document as a whole. HTML 4 user agents associate the active Web page with a document object. You can think of the document object as the highest level object of every Web page in the element hierarchy. When you write an event handler for the document, you ensure that an event-handling routine will be run for that specific event as a last resort by the user agent. The document object also gives you an opportunity to simplify your Web pages by writing a single routine, instead of separate routines for each element on the page. If you need specific routines for certain elements, place the appropriate attributes within those tags. You can still create the document event handler to handle events related to all other elements. Chapter 29 explains the specifics for creating document event handlers.

The HTML 4 Event List

Now that you grasp the big picture of events, event listeners, and event handlers, it's time to look at the specifics of the events standardized by the W3C's latest working draft of HTML 4. There are 18 events to consider, listed here:

```
onload          onmouseover     onkeydown

onunload        onmousemove     onkeyup

onclick         onmouseout      onsubmit

ondblclick      onfocus         onreset

onmousedown     onblur          onselect

onmouseup       onkeypress      onchange
```

The following sections explain each event in this list.

The onload Event

The onload event occurs when the user agent finishes loading a window or all frames within a FRAMESET. This attribute may be used with BODY and FRAMESET elements.

The onload event gives you a wonderful opportunity to create Web pages that vary based on information that changes elsewhere on the Web or changes based on current information on your Web server. With the onload event, you can write an event handler that puts together the Web page piece by piece from dynamic sources, such as a stock server, weather server, or news server. The onload event triggers only once per Web page, so the user agent doesn't have to continually adjust for the effects of its script routine. You should also note that the onload event fires without any specific additional behavior by the user.

The onunload Event

The onunload event occurs when the user agent removes a document from a window or frame. This attribute may be used with BODY and FRAMESET elements.

The onunload event is part of the HTML 4 event list to allow sophisticated processing between a Web server and the active user agent application. Obviously, a user isn't immediately going to notice the effect of the onunload event handler routine because the page is no longer active in the user agent. However, the page could be altered in the cache in case it's visited again, or the server could be made aware that the user is no longer on that page.

In an integrated Web page application that networks multiple users, the onunload event could be handled to inform other users that currently a user is no longer participating in that Web page application. For a single user, the onunload event could enact changes in another frame of a frame set.

28

WORKING WITH
THE USER: EVENTS

The onclick Event

The onclick event occurs when the pointing device button is clicked over an element. This attribute can be used with most elements.

The onclick event will probably end up being the one handled most often. It makes a Web user an active participant instead of a passive reader of information. Almost all computer users have a pointing device at their disposal. With the onclick event, you can make dynamic changes happen on a Web page whenever a user clicks somewhere on it.

The ondblclick Event

The ondblclick event occurs when the pointing device button is double-clicked over an element. This attribute may be used with most elements.

The ondblclick event opens up a Web page element to multiple event possibilities. A user can distinguish between single and double clicks to interact with a Web page. The Web page author can write two separate event-handling routines based on the same element. A double click is more difficult for a user to perform, so usually the option selected less often should be assigned the ondblclick event handler and the more popular choice assigned the onclick event.

Usually, you consider the ondblclick event when an onclick event-handling routine already exists for an element or when you intend the event to be triggered only by experienced users you expect to be trained in the use of your Web page. Web surfers are apt to go clicking on every part of a Web page, yet less likely to go double-clicking just for the fun of it.

The onmousedown Event

The onmousedown event occurs when the pointing device button is pressed over an element. This attribute may be used with most elements.

Like the onclick event, the onmousedown event involves a user pressing down on a pointing device button. However, the onmousedown event allows for dynamic Web page changes that are active only while the pointing device button is pressed down; these changes can be reversed by writing a separate event handler for the onmouseup event.

The onmousedown event can be used with drag-and-drop behaviors by users to trigger an event when they begin the drag operation.

The onmouseup Event

The onmouseup event occurs when the pointing device button is released over an element. This attribute may be used with most elements.

Like the onclick event, the onmouseup event involves a user releasing a pointing device button, but it also allows for dynamic Web page changes that aren't active until the user releases the pointing device button.

The onmouseup event can be used with drag-and-drop behaviors by users to trigger an event when they end the drag operation by dropping a movable Web page element.

The onmouseover Event

The onmouseover event occurs when the pointing device enters the area of a Web page element. This attribute may be used with most elements.

Use the onmouseover event when you want to trigger an event for a Web page element without the user having to press a pointing device button. The event triggers each time the user moves the pointing device cursor over the element associated with the event-handling routine.

Event-handling routines for onmouseover usually provide more information about the element of interest by expanding a section or adding new information to the Web page. Or, the event-handling routine might change the attributes of an element to give it emphasis over other similar elements on a Web page.

The onmousemove Event

The onmousemove event occurs when the pointing device is moving over an element. This attribute may be used with most elements.

The onmousemove event differs from the onmouseover event in that it triggers multiple times as the mouse moves over an element. The onmouseover event fires only once upon entering the area of a Web page element, but the onmousemove event continually triggers as long as the user's pointing device is moving over an element. The frequency of triggering is somewhat conditioned by the user agent's event-processing logic, as each developer can make a different decision on how often the event fires.

The onmousemove event can be used in with a user's drag-and-drop behavior to update the object being dragged.

28

WORKING WITH
THE USER: EVENTS

NOTE

Be sure to understand how the onmouse family of events interacts with the onclick family of events for the user agents you target. The HTML 4 working draft says nothing about which event fires first when a user behavior is potentially one of two or more events. For example, a click entails both a mouse down and mouse up event. If you include two or more event attributes within an element's tags, you need to know the user agent specifics of which events trigger in which order. Look to Microsoft's Web site (www.microsoft.com) for details about their implementation in Internet Explorer 4.0.

The onmouseout Event

The onmouseout event occurs when the pointing device is moved away from an element. This attribute may be used with most elements.

Use the onmouseout event when you want to trigger an event for a Web page element without the user having to press a pointing device button. The event triggers each time the user moves the pointing device cursor off the element associated with the event-handling routine.

Event-handling routines for the onmouseout usually collapse additional information about the element of interest by removing a section from the Web page. The event-handling routine might also change an element's attributes to emphasize it over other similar elements on a Web page, showing explicitly that the element had already been visited.

The onfocus Event

The onfocus event occurs when an element receives focus either by the pointing device or by tab order navigation. This attribute may be used with the following elements: LABEL, INPUT, SELECT, TEXTAREA, and BUTTON.

In theory, the onfocus event works similarly to the onmouseover event, which you use often with text and image elements, but it's specifically used with form-related elements.

The onblur Event

The onblur event occurs when an element loses focus either by the pointing device or by tab order navigation. This attribute may be used with the following elements: LABEL, INPUT, SELECT, TEXTAREA, and BUTTON.

The onblur event works in theory similarly to the onmouseout event that's used often with text and image elements. However, the onblur event is specifically used with form-related elements.

The onkeypress Event

The onkeypress event occurs when a key is pressed and released over an element. This attribute may be used with most elements.

The onkeypress event is similar to the onclick event, except that it offers many more conditional possibilities. A pointing device might typically have three buttons to press, but a keyboard might have over a hundred distinct keys. The onkeypress event triggers whenever a user presses any key on a keyboard, yet triggers for the element the pointing device cursor is currently positioned over.

The onkeydown Event

The onkeydown event occurs when a key is pressed down over an element. This attribute may be used with most elements.

The onkeydown event is similar to the onmousedown event except that it, too, offers many more conditional possibilities because a keyboard has more keys than a pointing device has buttons.

The onkeydown event allows for dynamic Web page changes that are active only while the key is pressed down; these changes can be reversed by writing a separate event handler for the onkeyup event.

The onkeyup Event

The onkeyup event occurs when a key is released over an element. This attribute may be used with most elements.

The onkeyup event is similar to the onmouseup event, except that it gives you many more conditional possibilities because the keyboard has more keys than a pointing device has buttons.

However, the onkeyup event allows for dynamic Web page changes that aren't active until the user releases the pointing device button. The onkeyup event-handling routine can also reverse dynamic changes made by the onkeydown event.

The onsubmit Event

The onsubmit event occurs when a form is submitted. It applies only to the FORM element.

Use an onsubmit event-handling routine to perform tasks based on the submission of an HTML form, such as changing the form's background color to indicate it has been submitted.

The onreset Event

The onreset event occurs when a form is reset. It applies only to the FORM element.

Use an onreset event-handling routine to perform tasks based on resetting an HTML form, such as changing the form's background color to indicate it has been reset.

The onselect Event

The onselect event occurs when a user selects some text in a text field. This attribute may be used with the INPUT and TEXTAREA elements.

You write onselect event-handling routines to handle advanced form processing on a field-by-field basis and potentially communicate with a database. Your routine might update information on the Web page based on the form field of interest or dynamically give the user more information about valid data to be entered into that field.

The onchange Event

The onchange event occurs when a control loses the input focus and its value has been modified since gaining focus. This attribute applies to the following elements: INPUT, SELECT, and TEXTAREA.

28

WORKING WITH
THE USER: EVENTS

Onchange event-handling routines are used to handle advanced form processing on a field-by-field basis and potentially communicate with a database. Your routine could update information on the Web page based on the form field of interest or dynamically perform a validity check on the changed data in that field.

> **NOTE**
>
> You will learn more about the importance of the onselect and onchange events in Chapter 30, "Data Binding."

Other Events of Interest

Just as user agent developers have created and promoted their own HTML tags and attributes beyond the W3C's working drafts and recommendations, user agent developers are sure to extend the event list beyond the one supported by the W3C.

To date, Microsoft has been the most aggressive in recommending new events and incorporating them into the Internet Explorer 4.0 Web browser. Microsoft has aligned new HTML events with the available event model in Visual Basic for applications written in Visual Basic. The event model in Visual Basic has been a great timesaver for programmers, so why not include those same features for Web pages? Really, HTML 4 events make Web pages function more as applications than encyclopedia-like pages of static information, and Visual Basic is a successful platform for many applications.

In fact, most of the examples in Chapter 29 currently work only in Internet Explorer 4.0. Microsoft uses the standard 18 events suggested by the W3C in its HTML 4 working draft, but it adds new events as well to the technology it calls *Dynamic HTML*. The following list includes 15 additional events made available for event handling when writing code for the Internet Explorer Web browser.

onhelp	onafterupdate	ondatasetcomplete
onscroll	onbeforeupdate	onerrorupdate
onrowenter	onbeforeunload	onfinish
onrowexit	ondatasetavailable	onreadystatechange
onabort	ondatasetchanged	onstart

The onhelp event triggers when a user selects the Help feature while the pointing device is positioned over an element. The onscroll event triggers when a user scrolls the contents of a scrollable Web page element or the whole Web page document. The onrowenter and onrowexit events work similarly to the onmouseover and onmouseout events, except that they're specific to table row elements and can be triggered by using the Tab key.

The other 11 events in the preceding list are specific to advanced forms processing in data-bound data forms. In fact, the onrowenter and onrowexit events work especially well with data fields in a dynamically created table. Chapter 30 covers data binding and describes these events.

As the HTML 4 event model settles in as a standard, expect Netscape to develop innovative new events, too. Check Netscape's Web site for details at http://www.netscape.com.

Examples of Using Intrinsic Events

Chapter 30 presents detailed examples of scripting event handlers that allow available HTML 4 intrinsic events to create dynamic Web pages. There's no inherent limit to the size of an event-handling script routine. Event handlers can contain detailed conditional logic and call multiple subprocedures—all in the same HTML file as the HTML tags and body text.

This chapter does give you an example of simple event handlers that don't require sophisticated script functions. Handling events within an HTML tag is called *inline event handling*. After the inlining example, other examples show you how to set up events for some interesting dynamic Web page changes. The event-handling script routines aren't covered in this chapter, but you will have a better understanding of the possibilities before you read the details in Chapter 29.

Inline Text Attribute Changes

To create simple dynamic text effects, you can set up your events and text attribute changes from within the HTML tags themselves. Any dynamic change to a Web page that you create solely within a single HTML tag is called an *inline change*. Inline changes are very straightforward.

As an example, take a look at Listing 28.1, which dynamically changes a heading's font size in response to user interaction. The HTML file is quite short.

Listing 28.1. An inline text attribute change.

```
<HTML>
<HEAD>
<TITLE>Test</TITLE>
</HEAD>
<BODY BGCOLOR=#FFFFFF>
<H1 onmouseover="this.style.fontSize=128"
    onmouseout="this.style.fontSize=32">
Hello World
</H1>
</BODY>
</HTML>
```

In Listing 28.1, you see two event attributes on the open <H1> tag. The onmouseover attribute sets up an event to trigger when readers places their pointing devices over the contents of the heading. When the pointing device rests over the heading, the text of the heading changes to 128 points in size. The `onmouseout` attribute sets up an event to trigger when readers move the pointing device off the heading. When the mouse leaves the heading area, the heading's text changes to a much smaller 32 points.

To change text attributes dynamically within an HTML tag, you take advantage of built-in features of the HTML 4 object model. The `this` keyword refers to the HTML element identified by the tag where the `this` keyword is contained. All text elements have a style object you can dynamically change. You then add the appropriate style property name and assign a new value to the property. You could dynamically change color by assigning the `this.style.color` property a value such as `Red`.

Figure 28.2 shows the Web page in Listing 28.1 after the user has placed the mouse over the heading.

FIGURE 28.2.

The text is enlarged in response to the onmouseover *event.*

Figure 28.3 shows the same Web page after the user moves the mouse off the Hello World heading.

Inlining is concise, but not especially robust. For inline dynamic changes, you don't need to create any scripts for your Web pages, yet scripts are a feature that allows you to add conditional logic to your Web pages. To save download time for sophisticated event handlers, you certainly want to include the code only once on the document. Create the event-handling routine as a script and refer to the script several times from multiple HTML tags. Chapter 29 covers scripting.

FIGURE 28.3.

In response to the onmouseout *event, the heading's text is reduced.*

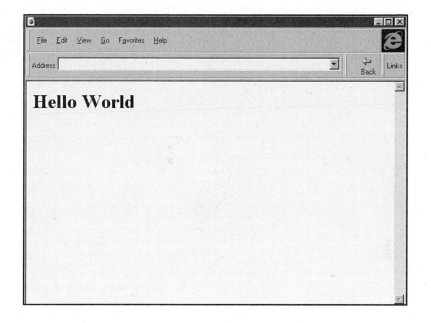

Hello World

Event Attribute Examples

The following event attribute examples are valid HTML 4 tags that set up event handlers without actually presenting the script-handling routines. In each case, the event-handling script routine is named RunMe(). The example identifies under which conditions the script would be run. When the event triggers, the user agent runs the RunMe() script function it encountered when the HTML file was initially parsed.

As a first example, consider an online multiple choice exam delivered to a user through HTML 4 Web pages. Each question has four possible answers shown as bitmap images. As a user clicks on an answer, the image changes to a bitmap that identifies a correct or incorrect answer. The events could be set up as follows:

```
<DIV><IMG ID=Answer1 SRC="Answer1.gif" onClick="RunMe();"></DIV>
<DIV><IMG ID=Answer2 SRC="Answer2.gif" onClick="RunMe();"></DIV>
<DIV><IMG ID=Answer3 SRC="Answer3.gif" onClick="RunMe();"></DIV>
<DIV><IMG ID=Answer4 SRC="Answer4.gif" onClick="RunMe();"></DIV>
```

The RunMe() script function determines which answer the user selected with the pointing device. The function then compares the selected answer with the correct answer. If the user selected the correct answer, the script directs the appropriate <IMG> tag to change its SRC attribute value to correct.gif. If the user selected the wrong answer, the SRC attribute value is changed to wrong.gif.

The RunMe() function runs when the onclick event triggers. Remember, the onclick event triggers whenever a user clicks on an element with a pointing device button.

For the second example, I've used a map of Eastern Europe that allows a user to pass the pointing device over a country to learn more about its geography. Each country could be set up with the appropriate division tags, as follows:

```
<DIV><IMG ID=Poland SRC="Poland.gif" onMouseOver="RunMe();"></DIV>
```

The RunMe() script function determines which country the pointing device moves into. As the user selects a country, the script passes a long text string to a paragraph named in its paragraph tag and replaces the paragraph's current contents with explanatory text about the selected country. Changing a tag's contents without an additional request to a Web server is called *dynamic HTML content replacement*. The contents of the explanatory paragraph dynamically change to text that always matches the current location of the pointing device cursor.

The RunMe() function runs when the onmouseover event triggers. Remember, the onmouseover event triggers whenever a user moves the pointing device onto an element.

For the third example, I've used a furniture placement application for an office environment. The user opens a Web page and moves top-view bitmaps of office furniture to create the cubicle orientation of his or her dreams. Each furniture item could be set up with the appropriate division tags, as follows:

```
<DIV><IMG ID=Chair SRC="Chair1.gif" onMouseMove="RunMe();"></DIV>
```

The RunMe() script function determines which piece of furniture the pointing device is moving over. As the user selects a piece of furniture, the script updates its position based on where the user moves the mouse. The script also updates a depth index for the item the user is moving to make that piece of furniture always appear on top of all the others.

The RunMe() function runs when the onmousemove event triggers. Remember, the onmousemove event continually triggers as a user moves the pointing device over that element. This is different from the Eastern Europe example, in which the onmouseover event triggered only once as the mouse first entered the physical area covered by the element's location.

> **NOTE**
>
> These three examples of dynamic Web pages all use images as the source elements of the events, but text elements are just as valid as source elements. The inline example you saw earlier uses a text element—a heading—as the source element. These three examples could just as easily use headings, or any other text element, instead of images.

Summary

This chapter gives you a diving-off point for creating dynamically changing HTML 4 Web pages: *intrinsic events*. User agent developers build intrinsic events into their applications so Web authors can rely on them to work. As far as the Web author is concerned, the events are *intrinsic* to HTML 4. Web authors create event-handling routines to specify what action should take place when the user agent application notices an event has taken place.

Currently, there are 18 events specified in the W3C's HTML 4 working draft. An author identifies which events the user agent should handle by identifying them as attributes of the appropriate HTML tags. For example, an `ondblclick` event is enabled by including an `ondblclick` attribute within the tag of the element receiving the double-click, and an `onload` event is enabled by including an `onload` attribute within the opening `<BODY>` tag of the HTML 4 document. Most of the time, the event attribute placement is easy to figure out, but remember that not all event attributes are valid in all HTML 4 tags. This chapter has given you a concise explanation of the validity and use for each HTML 4 event in the section "The HTML 4 Event List."

Once events are set up properly within the HTML 4 tag structure of a Web page, event-handling routines dictate what action takes place when an event triggers. You can write event-handling routines as separate script functions, as they appear in Chapter 29, or you can write your event-handling routines within the HTML 4 tag structure itself. In either event, the power of event-handling routines opens up your Web pages to exciting, dynamic, and animated possibilities.

HTML and Scripting: The DHTML Combination

by Bruce Campbell

IN THIS CHAPTER

Dynamic HTML

In the previous chapter, you learned about the HTML 4 event model. HTML 4 specifies 18 events for use in creating dynamic and interactive Web pages. This chapter rounds out your knowledge by showing you how to use scripts to specify your event-handling routines.

You learned in Chapter 28, "Working with the User: Events," how standardizing events requires coordination between the user agent developer and the HTML 4 Web page author. Once the user agent application incorporates the HTML 4 event model, the author writes event-handling routines to set up actions on the Web page. Then, for many events, event triggers depend on the actions of the Web surfer. For example, the onclick event requires the user to press a button on his or her pointing device for the onclick handling routine to run for the clicked-on element.

This chapter covers the technical and creative requirements you must meet to make your Web pages more responsive to and interactive with your Web-based audience. You will read about the technical details to consider when creating dynamic Web pages in accordance with the HTML 4 specification, while considering additional Web browser developers' innovations. The technology you use to create dynamic Web pages, although a subset of HTML 4, still stands out as a self-contained technology under the generally accepted name *dynamic HTML*.

Dynamic HTML deserves its own label because it brings features to Web pages that users demand in other current applications. Although the Web has grown up with HTML 1, 2, and 3.2, which helped Web page authors create somewhat sophisticated, encyclopedia-like pages, many users prefer Web pages to behave the same as other applications they use on a daily basis.

As mentioned in the previous chapter, many of the working draft's HTML 4 events take advantage of events that are already being kept track of by an operating system. Dynamic HTML communicates those events to the Web page. An event becomes significant to a Web page only if you, as the Web page author, specifically identify its effect within your HTML document. This chapter looks at complete examples of event-handling script functions you can extend or learn from to create Web pages that capture the essence of dynamic HTML.

Why Dynamic HTML?

Besides helping Web pages grow up to a mature status on today's sophisticated computers and helping engage users with increased responsiveness and interactivity, dynamic HTML also lends efficiency to what some technologists consider deficiencies in how the Web delivers documents. Web documents are delivered to Web users by using HTTP (HyperText Transport Protocol). The version of HTTP predominantly used on the Web today requires a lot of overhead for each file a Web server delivers to a client.

Just as your neighborhood mailperson would be inefficient if he or she had to go back to the post office each time to pick up the mail for the next address on the route, delivering Web sites one file at a time can be inefficient. Sure, the HTTP standard is being rehashed to work out some of its inefficiencies, but dynamic HTML gives Web authors an opportunity to deliver more information in a single file. In fact, you could deliver the equivalent of a whole Web site's worth of text as a single file. However, your graphics files are still delivered one at a time when you use dynamic HTML, as they were with HTML 3.2.

Dynamic HTML offers benefits to the Web server and reduces the network protocol communications overhead. Using dynamic HTML, Web servers require fewer connection requests than they do with HTML 3.2–compliant documents. Perhaps you have considered similar trade-offs when you design your Web sites to have many small hyperlinked documents or a few large heavily bookmarked documents. In some regards, the issues are similar when looking at the trade-offs of using dynamic HTML or HTML 3.2.

You can use dynamic HTML to send a large file of information once to a user, instead of many smaller Web pages. HTML 3.2 requires similar planning. The big new benefit, though, is that with dynamic HTML, the user doesn't have to be inundated with the whole page's information from the get-go. You can present the information incrementally in response to a user's actions. The actions result from your event-handling routines.

Suffice it to say that dynamic HTML offers different Web page delivery strategies and trade-offs than HTML 3.2 does. This chapter is more concerned with helping you use dynamic HTML correctly and creatively. Even if you don't value the new opportunities for reduced communications and Web server connection loads, you will enjoy the opportunity to bring your Web pages to life more easily.

Creating Dynamic Web Pages

You create dynamic Web pages by adding event-handling scripts to your HTML documents. Remember that your event-handling scripts become active when an event is triggered through an element on the Web page. The rest of this chapter offers complete examples of dynamic Web pages. As you master each example, play creatively with the code to change events, add new functions, and combine effects.

Event Handling Scripts

You write event-handling scripts with an appropriate scripting language. The HTML specification says nothing about standardizing scripting language within its domain. Instead, most scripting languages authors use to create dynamic Web pages have developed a following over the past few years. Scripts included on HTML 2 or HTML 3.2 Web pages run when the Web page initially loads. Popular Web page–scripting languages include JavaScript, VBScript, and TCL. The W3C provides event-handling script routine examples for all three languages.

Including Scripts in an HTML Document

Unless you use only simple inline event handling as discussed in Chapter 28, you place your event-handling routines within a script element. The SCRIPT element consists of a <SCRIPT> </SCRIPT> tag pair, appropriate attributes within the <SCRIPT> opening tag, and one or more script functions placed between the opening and closing tags. The SCRIPT element can appear any number of times within the HEAD element or BODY element of an HTML document.

You also have the option of supplying your script functions in an external file and using the src attribute of the SCRIPT element to reference the functions. In consideration of user agents that can't or won't handle scripts, authors can include alternative content by using a NOSCRIPT element.

An opening <SCRIPT> tag commonly contains one or more of three attributes: type, language, and src. The type attribute identifies the content type for the scripting language whose syntax is followed in the script functions within the script element. The value for a type attribute must be an Internet Media Type. There is no default value for the type attribute. The language attribute is another way to identify a scripting language, but the W3C prefers that you use the type attribute instead. The src attribute specifies the location of an external script. The value for the src attribute can be a relative or absolute URL. If the src attribute has a URL value, user agents must ignore the element's contents and retrieve the script by using the URL.

The scripting language must be explicitly identified on each Web page to be HTML 4 compliant. If you provide multiple script functions in a single HTML file, you can identify your scripting language once by placing the appropriate <META> tag within the <HEAD></HEAD> tag pair. For example, you can define JavaScript as your scripting language with a HEAD element, as shown:

```
<HEAD>
<META http-equiv="Content-Script-Type" content="text/javascript">
</HEAD>
```

Here, the content attribute value is a valid Internet Media Type.

The W3C calls a scripting language defined in one <META> tag the *default scripting language* because that scripting language syntax is expected by the user agent in the absence of any other type attributes in opening <SCRIPT> tags. You can use multiple scripting languages on the same Web page as long as you package the script routines within the appropriate <SCRIPT></SCRIPT> tag pairs; each pair identifies its scripting language. There are two ways you can identify a scripting language for a script element. You can use the type attribute of the script element:

```
<SCRIPT type="text/javascript">
```

Or you can use the language attribute of the script element:

```
<SCRIPT language=javascript>
```

However, the W3C recommends you use the type attribute to be parallel with the <META> tag specification. The local declaration of scripting language effectively overrides the default declaration, if any. Remember, HTML 4 documents that contain neither a default scripting language declaration nor a local one for a script element are incorrect. User agents might still try to interpret the script but aren't required to.

Each scripting language has its own conventions for referring to HTML objects from within a script. The HTML 4 specification doesn't define a standard mechanism for referring to HTML objects. However, scripts should refer to an element according to its assigned name. Scripting engines should observe the following precedence rules when identifying an element: A name attribute takes precedence over an id if both are set. Otherwise, one or the other may be used. The content of the SCRIPT element is a script, so it must not be evaluated by the user agent as HTML markup. The user agent must pass it on as data to a script engine.

USING HTML MARKUP TAGS IN SCRIPTS

As you write sophisticated scripts, you might want to actually reference HTML markup tags in your script code. The W3C is very specific about how a user agent should define where a script begins and where it ends within the script element. The W3C explanatory warning is reproduced here:

"HTML parsers must be able to recognize script data as beginning immediately after the start tag and ending as soon as the ETAGO (</) delimiters are followed by a name character ([a-zA-Z]). The script data does not necessarily end with the </SCRIPT> end tag, but is terminated by any </ followed by a name character.

Consequently, any HTML markup that is meant to be sent to a script engine (which may do whatever it wants with the markup) must be 'escaped' so as not to confuse the HTML parser. Designers of each scripting language should recommend language-specific support for resolving this issue."

Here's an illegal example:

The following code is invalid because of the presence of the </EM> characters found inside the SCRIPT element:

```
<SCRIPT type="text/javascript">
  document.write ("<EM>This won't work</EM>")
</SCRIPT>
```

A conforming parser must treat the </EM> data as the end of script data, which is clearly not what the author intended.

In JavaScript, this code can be expressed legally by making sure the apparent ETAGO delimiter doesn't appear immediately before an SGML name start character:

```
<SCRIPT type="text/javascript">
  document.write ("<EM>This will work<\/EM>")
</SCRIPT>
```

continues

29

HTML AND SCRIPTING

continued

In TCL, you can write this code legally as follows:

```
<SCRIPT type="text/tcl">
  document write "<EM>This will work<\/EM>"
</SCRIPT>
```

In VBScript, the problem can be avoided with the Chr() function:

```
"<EM>This will work<\" & Chr(47) + "EM>"
```

Scripts can be used with HTML 4 documents to produce highly responsive and interactive Web pages. The W3C places potential script-enabled features in the following four categories:

1. Scripts that are evaluated as a document loads to modify the contents of the document dynamically.

2. Scripts that accompany a form to process input as it's entered. Designers can dynamically fill out parts of a form based on the values of other fields. They can also make sure input data conforms to predetermined ranges of values, that fields are mutually consistent, and so on.

3. Scripts that are triggered by events that affect the document, such as loading, unloading, element focus, mouse movement, and so on.

4. Scripts that are linked to form controls (such as buttons) to produce graphical user interface elements.

This chapter continues with sample event-handling routines for each of the four preceding categories. As you read each example, think creatively and abstractly about how you might use part of the example or extend the example to create new features on your HTML 4 Web pages.

Examples of Dynamic Web Pages

Dynamic Web pages consist of HTML tags, body text, event attributes, and script-handling routines. The HTML tags and attributes have developed from their humble beginnings in the HTML 1 specification. Event attributes are a new HTML 4 feature associated with the list of intrinsic events covered in Chapter 28. Script-handling routines are enclosed within <SCRIPT> </SCRIPT> tag pairs. Any other text in an HTML file that's not within the < and > symbols of each HTML tag or within a script element is considered body text.

You will notice all four components (HTML tags, body text, event attributes, and script-handling routines) in each example in this section. Make sure you're comfortable identifying each component. Last, consider ways of combining the components of each example in new and exciting ways. The five examples that follow represent the four category types of the previous section: a load time dynamic example, a form processing example, two user action examples, and a user interface example.

A Load Time Dynamic Example

Dynamic Web pages have been available for some time now to Web authors who write for Netscape Navigator and Internet Explorer. In pre-HTML 4 compliant browsers, all scripts are run at load time and completed before the Web page finishes loading. Examples are Web pages that access dynamic Web servers to determine a changing value under the server's control. For example, Web pages can access a stock server, a weather server, a game server, or a news server to get information that's changing on a regular basis. The Web page updates a variable in the script and writes the appropriate value on the Web page. The value becomes static text until the next time the page loads. A Web server that continually updates a Web page from the server end uses what's called *push technology*. Push technology puts much of the burden on the server, but today's typical home computer is equipped with significant processing power.

Dynamic HTML takes advantage of the client computer's processing power. A great example of a load time dynamic Web page is an animated Web page that begins automatically at load time. The example in Listing 29.1 is a dynamic HTML Web page that runs an animation of the sonar tracking process used by marine biologists when tracking aquatic life.

The example runs under Internet Explorer 4.0 by using ActiveX controls that load as part of a standard install. All the HTML tags should be familiar to you if you have read the earlier chapters in this book that cover the HTML 4 specification. Pay particular attention to the onload event attribute and the cycle() event-handling script. Take a look at Listing 29.1 to see the HTML file syntax and Figure 29.1 to see the file loaded in a Web browser.

Listing 29.1. A load time animation.

```
<HTML>
<HEAD>
</HEAD>
<BODY BACKGROUND="water.jpg"  onload="cycle();"
 TEXT=#FFFFFF LINK=FFFF22 VLINK=FF22FF>
<H2>Squid Tracking -- How Do They Do It?</H2>
<TABLE>
<TR><TD WIDTH=320>
<DIV ID=AnimDiv STYLE="position:relative;width:320px;height:320px">
<IMG SRC="sonard.gif" ID=sonard BORDER=0
 STYLE="container:positioned;position:absolute;
 TOP:0pt;LEFT:150px;WIDTH:32px;HEIGHT:32px;ZINDEX:0;">
<IMG SRC="sonaru.gif" ID=sonaru BORDER=0
 STYLE="container:positioned;position:absolute;
 TOP:0pt;LEFT:150px;WIDTH:32px;HEIGHT:32px;ZINDEX:0;">
<IMG SRC="squid2.gif" ID=squid1 BORDER=0 onclick="Guess();"
 STYLE="container:positioned;position:absolute;
 TOP:170pt;LEFT:20px;WIDTH:64px;HEIGHT:64px;ZINDEX:1;">
<IMG SRC="squid2.gif" ID=squid2 BORDER=0 onclick="Guess();"
 STYLE="container:positioned;position:absolute;
 TOP:190pt;LEFT:20px;WIDTH:64px;HEIGHT:64px;ZINDEX:2;">
<IMG SRC="squid2.gif" ID=squid3 BORDER=0 onclick="Guess();"
 STYLE="container:positioned;position:absolute;
 TOP:180pt;LEFT:0px;WIDTH:64px;HEIGHT:64px;ZINDEX:3;">
```

29

HTML AND SCRIPTING

continues

Listing 29.1. continued

```
<IMG SRC="boat.jpg" BORDER=0 STYLE="container:positioned;position:
absolute; TOP:0pt;LEFT:0px;WIDTH:320px;HEIGHT:50px;ZINDEX:5;">
</DIV></TD><TD>
<FONT COLOR=#FFFF00><I>To track squid, they use a sophisticated sonar
device that emits sound waves down into the ocean from the surface.
The sound waves will either bounce off the ocean floor or bounce off
the squid if they get between the emitting boat and the ocean floor.
In this manner, they get very precise images of each squid that gets
in the way of the sound waves.</I></FONT><BR>
</TD></TR></TABLE>
<OBJECT ID="pathone"
     CLASSID="CLSID:E0E3CC60-6A80-11D0-9B40-00A0C903AA7F">
<PARAM NAME=XSeries
     VALUE="0,20;10,50;20,80;30,115;40,150;50,185;60,220;70,255;80,300">
<PARAM NAME=YSeries
     VALUE="0,170;10,170;20,170;30,170;40,170;50,170;60,170;70,170;80,170">
</OBJECT>
<OBJECT ID="pathtwo"
     CLASSID="CLSID:E0E3CC60-6A80-11D0-9B40-00A0C903AA7F">
<PARAM NAME=XSeries
     VALUE="0,20;10,55;20,80;30,110;40,135;50,170;60,200;70,230;80,270">
<PARAM NAME=YSeries
     VALUE="0,190;10,190;20,193;30,195;40,197;50,194;60,192;70,190;80,190">
</OBJECT>
<OBJECT ID="paththree"
     CLASSID="CLSID:E0E3CC60-6A80-11D0-9B40-00A0C903AA7F">
<PARAM NAME=XSeries
     VALUE="0,0;10,20;20,50;30,80;40,100;50,128;60,148;70,178;80,210">
<PARAM NAME=YSeries
     VALUE="0,180;10,182;20,185;30,190;40,185;50,181;60,179;70,176;80,179">
</OBJECT>
<OBJECT ID="pathfour"
     CLASSID="CLSID:E0E3CC60-6A80-11D0-9B40-00A0C903AA7F">
<PARAM NAME=XSeries
     VALUE="0,150;10,150;20,150;30,150;40,150;50,150;60,150;70,150;80,150">
<PARAM NAME=YSeries
     VALUE="0,20;10,50;20,90;30,135;40,180;41,0">
</OBJECT>
<OBJECT ID="pathfive"
     CLASSID="CLSID:E0E3CC60-6A80-11D0-9B40-00A0C903AA7F">
<PARAM NAME=XSeries
     VALUE="0,150;10,150;20,150;30,150;40,150;50,150;60,150;70,150;80,150">
<PARAM NAME=YSeries
     VALUE="40,0;41,180;50,135;60,90;70,50;80,20">
</OBJECT>
<SCRIPT language="vbscript">
function cycle()
        dim itimer
        pathone.Target = squid1.Style
        pathtwo.Target = squid2.Style
        paththree.Target = squid3.Style
        pathfour.Target = sonard.Style
        pathfive.Target = sonaru.Style
        squid1.style.visibility="visible"
        squid2.style.visibility="visible"
```

```
            squid3.style.visibility="visible"
            sonard.style.visibility="visible"
            sonaru.style.visibility="visible"
            pathone.Play
            pathtwo.Play
            paththree.Play
            pathfour.Play
            pathfive.Play
            itimer = setTimeout( "Moves()", 50)
End function

Sub Moves
            dim itimer
            pathone.Tick
            pathtwo.Tick
            paththree.Tick
            pathfour.Tick
            pathfive.Tick
            if currentTick < 9 then
                itimer = setTimeout("Moves()", 50)
            end if
End Sub
</SCRIPT>
</BODY>
</HTML>
```

Figure 29.1 shows the squid sonar-tracking animation as the sonar waves are heading back toward the ocean surface. At this point in the animation sequence, the sonar waves have already bounced off the moving squid.

FIGURE 29.1.

A load time animation.

The <BODY> opening tag includes the sole event attribute in this example. To run a script immediately after the Web page loads, you place an onload attribute in the <BODY> tag and supply a script function name as its value. Only the onload event belongs inside an open <BODY> tag. In Listing 29.1, the animating script function's name is cycle(), which is written using the VBscript scripting language. The Web browser processes the script properly because the open <SCRIPT> tag contains the necessary language="vbscript" attribute.

> **NOTE**
>
> All the examples in this chapter and the next have been tested using the Internet Explorer 4.0 Web browser. As the HTML 4 specification changes over time, you can continue to use these examples to get a general understanding of what dynamic HTML offers to Web authors. Surf the Web, especially the Netscape (www.netscape.com), Microsoft (www.microsoft.com), and the W3C (www.w3c.org) Web sites, for any syntax, object model, or event model changes.

The cycle() function calls a subfunction named Moves. In the cycle() function, each squid and sonar image is associated with a timing object through a line such as this one:

```
pathone.Target = squid1.Style.
```

Each squid and sonar object has a Play method that is called to start the timing sequence. The Play method is activated for each squid and sonar image with a line like this one:

```
pathone.Play
```

The timing objects also have a Tick method that increments the index into the timings. The Tick method is called in the Moves subfunction, which provides the looping construct an animation requires. The timing sequences and path targets are communicated to the Web browser through ActiveX objects. The ActiveX objects are loaded through <OBJECT></OBJECT> tag pairs.

Each open <OBJECT> tag contains a CLASSID="CLSID:E0E3CC60-6A80-11D0-9B40-00A0C903AA7F"> attribute that identifies the appropriate ActiveX control to the Web browser. The animation control requires two parameters. The XSeries contains multiple pairs of times and x coordinates; the YSeries contains multiple pairs of times and y coordinates. The combination of x and y coordinates define the animation sequence for each animated image object.

With the Web page created from Listing 29.1, the animation begins as soon as the Web page loads. Once the animation has finished, the user needs to reload the page to rerun the animation. You could add an onclick attribute to the image with the SRC="boat.jpg" attribute to start the animation whenever the user clicked on the boat at the surface of the water. The event-handling script would remain exactly the same and handle both the onload and onclick events.

A Form Processing Example

As the Web investigates its promise as a technology that supports information brokering and commercial transactions, more and more electronic forms are appearing on Web pages to request information from Web surfers. Dynamic HTML helps make forms more interactive by providing events such as onblur and onchange that a Web page author can use to verify and validate form field input.

Listing 29.2 is a simple example of forms processing using dynamic HTML and the onchange intrinsic event. The two data fields included in the Web page in Listing 29.2 create a concert ticket order transaction in which a user can order only 10 tickets at a time. The form calculates the appropriate order total based on the quantity entered, while keeping the quantity ordered at 10 or less. Each ticket costs $8.88, and there are no applicable sales taxes. Take a look at Listing 29.2 and Figure 29.2, and then continue reading for more explanation of this example.

Listing 29.2. A form processing example.

```
<HTML>
<HEAD>
<FONT FACE="verdana,arial,helvetica" SIZE=2>
<TITLE>Form Example</TITLE>
</HEAD>
<BODY BGCOLOR="#FFFFFF">
<H1>Concert Ticket Order Form</H1>
Maximum 10 tickets per order
<HR>
<TABLE>
<TR><TD>Quantity</TD>
<TD><INPUT NAME="qty" onChange="checkNum();" VALUE="0">
</TD></TR>
<TR><TD>Price</TD>
<TD><INPUT NAME="price" VALUE="">
</TD></TR>
</TABLE>
<P><I>See you on the 17th !!!!!</I>
<SCRIPT language=javascript>
function checkNum() {
  if (qty.value >= 10) {
     qty.value=10;
  }
  price.value=qty.value*8.88;
}
</SCRIPT>
<HR>
</BODY>
</HTML>
```

Figure 29.2 shows the concert ticket order form after a user tries to enter a quantity of 15 tickets. The form accepts a maximum quantity of only 10 tickets, so the user's input is changed to 10 and a price of $88.80 is calculated for the total order price.

FIGURE 29.2.

A form processing example.

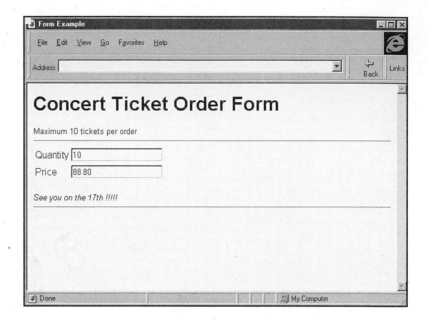

The example in Listing 29.2 is an elementary example compared with the animation example in Listing 29.1. Keep in mind that dynamic HTML Web pages can be as complicated or as simple as your needs dictate. The interactivity is provided by the onchange event attribute, which is part of the <INPUT> tag with the NAME="Qty" and VALUE="0" attributes. The onchange attribute has a value of checkNum(), which identifies an event-handling script function for the onchange event.

> **NOTE**
>
> The rest of the examples in this chapter all use JavaScript as the scripting language. As this book went to press, JavaScript was by far the most generally accepted scripting language in use by Web developers who write for multiple user agents. VBScript syntax is different, but it's also a simple translation from JavaScript for all the JavaScript examples in this chapter.

The checkNum() function is embedded within a <SCRIPT></SCRIPT> tag pair. The open <SCRIPT> tag specifies the script language with the language=javascript attribute. The checkNum() function determines the current value of the text field named Qty and compares it to the maximum of 10. If the quantity entered is greater than 10, the script sets the value to exactly 10. The script then calculates a total price for the order and sets the value of the Price text field to the quantity of tickets ordered times $8.88.

The script could also actually forward the order information off to the appropriate process to get the tickets mailed to the user, if the user had already logged in with an account number. HTML 4–based forms are no longer solely dependent on a submit button, but be aware that your users might still expect to confirm their input before it gets processed.

Two User Action Examples

At the heart of dynamic HTML is the excitement of letting your Web audience play with your Web pages. The event model allows you to deliver pages that users click on, pass their pointing device cursor over, or even speak to, should they have the appropriate voice-enabling technology. Your event-handling routines can be highly responsive to your audience's inquisitiveness. In fact, by the time a user is done interacting, the Web page might not remotely resemble its initial load state.

User action scripts are so exciting that this section has two examples. The first expands and collapses news items for different towns in a rural valley. The second provides a model for distributing interactive trivia over the Web. The first example is enabled by the mouseover event, and the second example returns you to the onclick event.

Listing 29.3 shows you the HTML file for a rural valley news Web page. The Web page loads with all six town names visible, along with the projected high temperature for the day. As a user passes his or her pointing device cursor over a town name, the day's top news story for that town expands to the right of the town name. Figures 29.3 and 29.4 show Listing 29.3 as loaded in a Web browser.

Listing 29.3. An expand and collapse example.

```
<HTML>
<BODY BGCOLOR=#FFFFFF>
<HEAD>
<FONT FACE="verdana,arial,helvetica" SIZE=3>
<TITLE>Today's High Temperatures</TITLE>
</HEAD>
<BODY>
<STYLE>
.redPlain     {color:rgb(255,0,0);
               font-size:10pt;
               font-style:normal;}
.redSmall     {color:rgb(255,0,0);
               font-size:2pt;
               font-style:normal;}
.blackPlain  {color:rgb(0,0,0);
               font-style:normal;
               font-size:16pt;}
</STYLE>
<H3>The Verentian Valley News</H3>
<HR>
<TABLE>
<TR>
```

continues

29

HTML AND
SCRIPTING

Listing 29.3. continued

```
<TD WIDTH=200>
<P ID=T1 CLASS="redPlain" onmouseover="redP();">Argunk      71
<P ID=T2 CLASS="redPlain" onmouseover="redP();">Henders     63
<P ID=T3 CLASS="redPlain" onmouseover="redP();">Krikett     69
<P ID=T4 CLASS="redPlain" onmouseover="redP();">Lowville    68
<P ID=T5 CLASS="redPlain" onmouseover="redP();">Viennes     75
<P ID=T6 CLASS="redPlain" onmouseover="redP();">Yinsburgh   75
</TD>
<TD>
<P ID=PG1 CLASS="redSmall">
The mayor here, Cora James, announces a new plan for curtailing the
current trend of juvenile delinquency: an evening curfew at 9PM.
<P ID=PG2 CLASS="redSmall">
500 community residents continue to keep a lid on the details of
the theme for this year's Solstice Day Festival yet smile smugly
when asked about it.
<P ID=PG3 CLASS="redSmall">
This year farmers suggest a winter wheat crop may be a good idea.
It has been 6 years since the last attempt.
<P ID=PG4 CLASS="redSmall">
Once again, the boy wonder, Jimmy Westen, has made statewide news
for his latest invention.
<P ID=PG5 CLASS="redSmall">
Our regional professional baseball squad wins its fifth straight
and takes solid hold of second place.
<P ID=PG6 CLASS="redSmall">
Actress Jennifer Urgent returns home to find community support before
considering her next effort.
</TD>
</TR>
</TABLE>

<SCRIPT LANGUAGE=JavaScript>
var source
function redP() {
    source = window.event.srcElement;
    T1.className="redPlain";
    T2.className="redPlain";
    T3.className="redPlain";
    T4.className="redPlain";
    T5.className="redPlain";
    T6.className="redPlain";
    PG1.className="redSmall";
    PG2.className="redSmall";
    PG3.className="redSmall";
    PG4.className="redSmall";
    PG5.className="redSmall";
    PG6.className="redSmall";
    source.className="blackPlain";
    if (T1.className=="blackPlain")
        PG1.className="blackPlain";
    if (T2.className=="blackPlain")
        PG2.className="blackPlain";
    if (T3.className=="blackPlain")
        PG3.className="blackPlain";
    if (T4.className=="blackPlain")
        PG4.className="blackPlain";
```

```
    if (T5.className=="blackPlain")
        PG5.className="blackPlain";
    if (T6.className=="blackPlain")
        PG6.className="blackPlain";
}
</SCRIPT>
</FONT>
</BODY>
</HTML>
```

Figure 29.3 shows the rural valley news Web page immediately after it has loaded in a Web browser. At that point, all news stories are collapsed.

FIGURE 29.3.

The mouseover *event before triggering.*

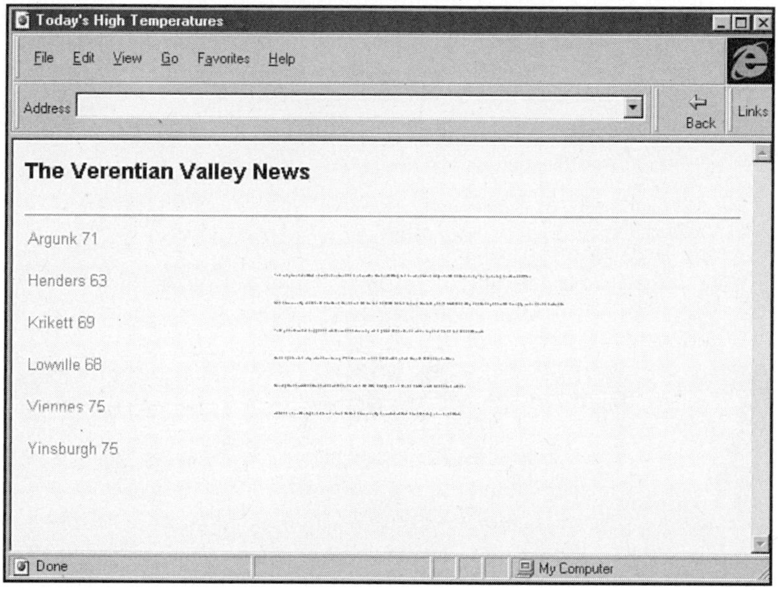

Figure 29.4 shows the rural valley news Web page immediately after a user moves his or her pointing device cursor over the Lowville 68 text. At that point, the Jimmy Westen news story expands so it can be easily read.

The rural valley news dynamic Web page takes advantage of the Cascading Style Sheet specification (CSS), which is a part of HTML 4. Three styles are set up in the <STYLE></STYLE> tag pair. The .redPlain class style is a 10-point, red text style, the .redSmall class style is a 2-point, red text style, and the .blackPlain class style is a 16-point, black text style.

The first six <P> tags, T1 through T6, initially load with the .redPlain class style. Each paragraph contains a town name and high temperature for the day. All six <P> tags include the onmouseover event attribute with a value of redP(). The redP() function is the event-handling script function name for the onmouseover event.

Figure 29.4.

The mouseover *event after triggering.*

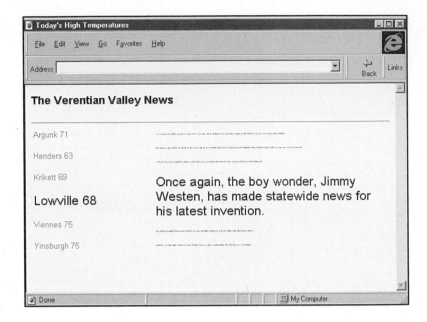

The next six `<P>` tags, named `PG1` through `PG6`, initially load with the `.redSmall` class style. Each paragraph contains a top news story.

> **NOTE**
>
> You have probably noticed inconsistencies in the use of case in this chapter's examples. I believe in showing different uses of case when the technology is not case sensitive. On the whole, JavaScript is more case sensitive than VBScript. So wherever you see me varying case in these examples, the variation would work fine in VBScript examples, too.

The `redP()` script function exists in a `<SCRIPT></SCRIPT>` tag pair. Again, Listing 29.3 uses the `javascript` scripting language as identified as an attribute of the open `<SCRIPT>` tag. The `redP()` script has a very useful feature of the Internet Explorer object model. After declaring a variable named `source`, the script assigns the event source of the `mouseover` event to the source variable:

```
source = window.event.srcElement;
```

This line identifies which town name the user is currently passing the pointing device cursor over.

The rest of the script sets the appropriate text style to each paragraph on the Web page, based on the current position of the pointing device cursor. If you were scripting for a Web browser that doesn't include the `srcEvent` property for an `event` object, you would write six separate script functions for each town name that set the paragraph text styles accordingly.

Listing 29.4 shows an example of an interactive trivia question, which looks great as a Web page. The example asks the user a question about the planets of the solar system and evaluates his or her answer when the user clicks on a planet bitmap image. The example has only a single question, but with dynamic HTML 4, you could deliver a whole exam as a single Web page and calculate and present test results through script functions. Take a look at Listing 29.4 and Figures 29.5 and 29.6, and then continue reading for additional details.

Listing 29.4. A click and replace example.

```
<HTML>
<HEAD>
<FONT FACE="verdana,arial,helvetica" SIZE=2>
<TITLE>Planetary Trivia</TITLE>
</HEAD>
<BODY BGCOLOR="#FFFFFF">
<H2>Planetary Trivia</H2>
<HR>
<BR>
<H3><P ID=Q1 STYLE="color:Blue">
<B>Question 1: </B>
</H3><P>
Which of the following planets reflects the highest percentage
of light it receives from the sun?
<BR>
<TABLE>
<TR><TD><IMG SRC="mars.gif" ID=A11 onclick="Answer1();"></TD>
<TD><IMG SRC="venus.gif" ID=A12 onclick="Answer1();"></TD>
<TD><IMG SRC="saturn.gif" ID=A13 onclick="Answer1();"></TD>
<TD><IMG SRC="uranus.gif" ID=A14 onclick="Answer1();"></TD></TR>
</TABLE>.
<P ID=A1></P>

<SCRIPT LANGUAGE=JavaScript>
var srcElement
function Answer1() {
  srcElement = window.event.srcElement;
  if (Q1.style.color=="blue") {
     if (srcElement.id=="A12") {
        srcElement.src = "correct.gif";
        Q1.style.color= "Green";
     } else {
        srcElement.src = "wrong.gif";
        Q1.style.color= "Red";
     }
     A1.innerHTML="<B>Venus</B> has an albedo of 59% " +
        "which is much higher than the other answers";
  }
}
</SCRIPT>
<HR>
</BODY>
</HTML>
```

Figure 29.5 shows the planetary trivia Web page immediately after it loads in a Web browser. The user has yet to click on an answer.

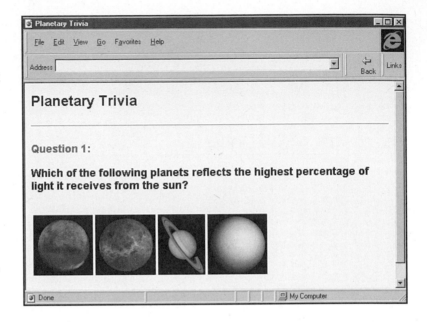

Figure 29.6 shows the planetary trivia Web page immediately after a user has guessed that Venus is the right answer. Venus is indeed the correct answer, so the user is rewarded with a smiley face image. The color of the question heading turns green to indicate a correct answer, too.

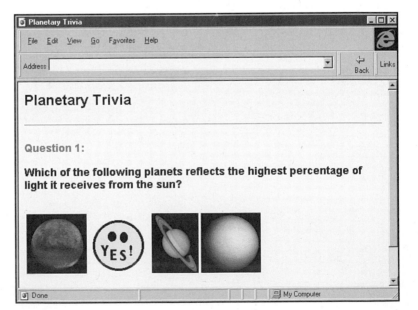

The question number appears in a heading-enclosed paragraph named Q1 with a STYLE="color:Blue" attribute that makes the question header text blue. Images of Venus, Mars, Saturn, and Uranus are provided in <IMG> tag elements and given the names A11 through A14. These planet images all include onclick="Answer1()" attributes, which set up an event to trigger with a user click on the element. The answers are evaluated in an Answer1() script function.

The last line before the script element creates an answer paragraph where text appears to explain the correct answer. The paragraph is named A1 within its <P> tag in the ID=A1 attribute.

The Answer1() event-handling script function is placed in the <SCRIPT></SCRIPT> tag pair. Similar to Listing 29.3, the script uses a variable named source to keep track of which planet image the user has clicked on. If the question header paragraph is any color but blue, the script does nothing because the user has already made a guess at the answer.

If the event source element is the A12 image (Venus), the script replaces Venus's image with a correct answer image. The script also changes the question header color to green. If the event source element is any other image but A12, the script replaces the selected image with a wrong answer image and changes the question header color to red. In either a right or wrong answer, the script finishes by replacing the contents of the answer paragraph (A1) with text that explains the correct answer. When writing code for the Internet Explorer 4.0 Web browser, scripts replace text by changing the innerHTML property of any text element.

A User Interface Example

Currently, the name of the game in effective application design is easily understood user interfaces. HTML 4 gives you the ability to design your own simple user interfaces on Web pages. The example in this section adds a simple user interface to the concert ordering form of Listing 29.2. Listing 29.5 supplies the HTML file contents, and Figure 29.7 shows the file loaded in a Web browser.

Listing 29.5. A user interface example.

```
<HTML>
<HEAD>
<FONT FACE="verdana,arial,helvetica" SIZE=2>
<TITLE>Form Example</TITLE>
</HEAD>
<BODY BGCOLOR="#FFFFFF">
<H1>Concert Ticket Order Form</H1>
Maximum 10 tickets per order
<HR>
<TABLE><TR><TD>
<BUTTON ID=1 onClick="FillQty();">1</BUTTON>
<BUTTON ID=2 onClick="FillQty();">2</BUTTON>
<BUTTON ID=3 onClick="FillQty();">3</BUTTON>
<BUTTON ID=4 onClick="FillQty();">4</BUTTON>
```

continues

Listing 29.5. continued

```
<BUTTON ID=5 onClick="FillQty();">5</BUTTON>
<BUTTON ID=6 onClick="FillQty();">6</BUTTON>
<BUTTON ID=7 onClick="FillQty();">7</BUTTON>
<BUTTON ID=8 onClick="FillQty();">8</BUTTON>
<BUTTON ID=9 onClick="FillQty();">9</BUTTON>
<BUTTON ID=10 onClick="FillQty();">10</BUTTON>
</TD><TD></TD><TD>
<BUTTON ID=Red onClick="Colorize();">Red</BUTTON>
<BUTTON ID=White onClick="Colorize();">White</BUTTON>
<BUTTON ID=Blue onClick="Colorize();">Blue</BUTTON>
</TD></TR><TR><TD>--------------</TD></TR>
<TR><TD ID=Qtylbl><B>Quantity</B></TD>
<TD><INPUT NAME="qty" VALUE="0" SIZE=4>
</TD></TR>
<TR><TD ID=Pricelbl><B>Price</B></TD>
<TD><INPUT NAME="price" VALUE="" SIZE=4>
</TD></TR>
</TABLE>
<P><I>See you on the 17th !!!!!</I>
<SCRIPT language=javascript>
function FillQty() {
  srcElement = window.event.srcElement;
  qty.value=srcElement.id;
  price.value=qty.value*8.88;
}
function Colorize() {
  srcElement = window.event.srcElement;
  Qtylbl.style.background=srcElement.id;
  Pricelbl.style.color=srcElement.id;
  if(srcElement.id=="White") {
      Pricelbl.style.background="Red";
  } else Pricelbl.style.background="White";
}
</SCRIPT>
<HR>
</BODY>
</HTML>
```

Figure 29.7 shows the concert ordering Web page after the user has clicked on two buttons: the button with the label 1 and the button with the label White. Similar to Figure 29.2, the total price has been calculated by the event-handling script and displayed in the Price text field.

In Listing 29.5, a simple user interface is created from 13 button elements. The first 10 buttons have the names 1 through 10 and set up an onclick event through an onclick="FillQty();" attribute. The next three buttons have the names Red, White, and Blue and set up an onclick event through an onclick="Colorize();" attribute.

Both the FillQty() and Colorize() script functions are placed within the same <SCRIPT></SCRIPT> tag pair. The two functions could just as easily have their separate script elements, but if you want to use the same scripting language for two script functions, why not place them in the same script element?

FIGURE 29.7.

Adding a simple user interface.

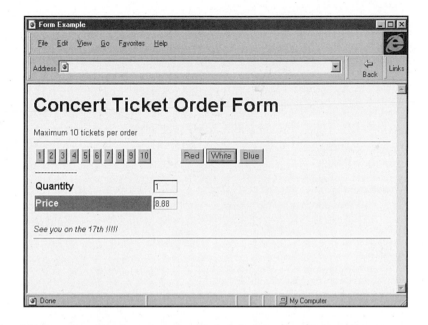

> **NOTE**
>
> Also remember that <SCRIPT></SCRIPT> tag pair placement is not bounded by the HEAD or BODY elements. As long as you don't break any of the rules for embedding tags within tags, script placement is quite flexible.

The FillQty() script function fills both the Quantity text field and Price text field when a user selects a quantity by clicking on a numbered button. The Qty input element's VALUE attribute is assigned the id name of the numbered button that was clicked. The Price input element's VALUE is calculated by multiplying the quantity by $8.88, the price of a ticket.

The Colorize() script function changes the color of the Quantity and Price labels. First, the script changes the background color of the Qtylbl text element to the id name of the color button that was clicked. Then, the script changes the text color of the Pricelbl text element to the same color as the Qtylbl text element color. To avoid a white-on-white situation, the script changes the background color of the Pricelbl text element if the White button is chosen by the user.

The <NOSCRIPT></NOSCRIPT> Tags

This section covers issues about lack of support for scripting that authors should consider when designing good HTML documents. The <NOSCRIPT></NOSCRIPT> tag pair lets authors provide alternative content when a script is not executed. The W3C specifies that the contents of a

NOSCRIPT element should be rendered only by a script-aware user agent in the following two cases:

- The user agent is configured not to evaluate scripts.
- The user agent doesn't support a scripting language invoked by a SCRIPT element earlier in the document.

The HTML 4 specification also requires user agents that don't support client-side scripts to render the contents of <NOSCRIPT></NOSCRIPT> tag pairs as though it were the contents of a BODY element.

The Planetary trivia example in Listing 29.4 offers a good example of appropriately including a <NOSCRIPT></NOSCRIPT> tag pair. After the line <P ID=A1></P>, the Web page could be considerate to older user agents by adding the following additional HTML syntax:

```
<NOSCRIPT>
<P>
The correct answer is <B>Venus</B>, the second image from the left.  Venus
has an albedo of 59% which is much higher than the other answers.
</NOSCRIPT>
```

This content would be rendered by a Web browser only when one of the two conditions specified previously were true. True, without a script-capable Web browser, users couldn't interactively take the test, but they could learn from the Web page because the answer would be presented along with the question.

Commenting Out Scripts

User agents that don't recognize <SCRIPT></SCRIPT> tag pairs will likely render the script element's contents as text. The W3C provides a discussion of comments in their HTML 4 working draft. The rest of this section reproduces the W3C's discussion of commenting out scripts almost verbatim.

Some scripting engines, including those for the languages JavaScript, VBScript, and TCL, allow the script statements to be enclosed in an SGML comment. User agents that don't recognize script elements will thus ignore the comment, but smart scripting engines will understand that the script in comments should be executed.

Another solution to the problem is to keep scripts in external documents and refer to them with the src attribute.

The JavaScript engine allows the string <-- to occur at the start of a SCRIPT element, and ignores further characters until the end of the line. JavaScript interprets // as starting a comment extending to the end of the current line. This is needed to hide the string --> from the JavaScript parser.

```
<SCRIPT type="text/javascript">
```

```
<--  to hide script contents from old browsers
  function square(i) {
    document.write("The call passed ", i ," to the function.","<BR>")
    return i * i
  }
  document.write("The function returned ",square(5),".")
// end hiding contents from old browsers  -->
</SCRIPT>
```

In VBScript, a single quote character causes the rest of the current line to be treated as a comment. It can therefore be used to hide the string --> from VBScript, for instance:

```
<SCRIPT type="text/vbscript">
  <--
    Sub foo()
      ...
    End Sub
  '  -->
</SCRIPT>
```

In TCL, the # character comments out the rest of the line:

```
<SCRIPT type="text/tcl">
<--  to hide script contents from old browsers
  proc square {i} {
    document write "The call passed $i to the function.<BR>"
    return [expr $i * $i]
  }
  document write "The function returned [square 5]."
# end hiding contents from old browsers  -->
</SCRIPT>
```

> **NOTE**
>
> Some browsers close comments on the first > character, so to hide script content from such browsers, you can transpose operands for relational and shift operators (for example, use y < x rather than x > y) or use scripting language–dependent escapes for >.

Summary

Dynamic HTML is an enhancement to HTML 4 that adds interactivity and dynamic changes to the Web page. Using dynamic HTML syntax, Web authors can compete with CD-ROM titles and traditional business applications to offer the value on the Web that home and office markets demand. Dynamic HTML instantiates Web page elements as objects through the ID or NAME attribute. After an element is instantiated, user events can trigger changes to the element, such as font, style class, size, color, and location changes. Events are set up as attributes of each event's source element. For example, an onload="Function1();" attribute sets up an onload event within a <BODY> tag.

Dynamic HTML is sure to expand quickly once users accept the new functionality of Web pages and demand more. The W3C has chosen an appropriate set of 18 events to standardize initially. Chapter 30, "Data Binding," covers additional events outside the W3C's working draft specification for HTML 4, but in the same spirit syntactically. Data binding is yet another opportunity to make Web page information delivery more efficient, given the current delivery mechanism of the HTTP standard. Yet, as you will see, data binding also shows promise for making Web page maintenance less costly.

Data Binding

by Bruce Campbell

IN THIS CHAPTER

CHAPTER 30

Data Binding and Data-Awareness

A document is *data-aware* if it associates itself with a specific data source, and *data binding* is the process of connecting a data source to a Web page. Data-awareness is a feature of a computer application that allows it to access data and keep a reference to that data source. The application, in effect, continues to be aware of the data. Data-awareness through data binding isn't part of the W3C's (World Wide Web Consortium's) working draft, but is a component of Microsoft's Dynamic HTML technology. Data binding works through a process very similar to the HTML event-handling process, so your understanding of Chapter 29, "HTML and Scripting: The DHTML Combination," is a foundation for understanding the material in this chapter. This chapter covers the data-binding process.

A video game is data-aware if it has access to high scores and earlier game states that you saved while playing. Such data-awareness is a great feature for an adventure game. As you play and realize that you have gone down an unfortunate path, you can reload an earlier position in the game and resume from that place. When a video game is data-aware, it can access the data immediately and restore the game to a requested state.

Now, imagine you're playing a dynamic HTML–based Web page game, and you would like to have the game downloaded once so that it runs locally on your machine. As you begin to save game states, you shouldn't have to ask the Web server to save the game state for you. A good Internet citizen knows that there's no need to create unnecessary Web traffic. Instead, a data-bound, state-saving data source can be accessed from a loaded Web page and updated on the client.

In the case of a Web browser, data-awareness is a feature of a user agent that requests all the possible data for a Web page once, disconnects from the Web server, and then interacts with the data locally for as long as the user wants to interact. Data binding makes a Web page aware of a data source.

Why Use Data Binding?

To understand why you should bind data sources to data-aware HTML 4 Web pages, look at a real-world example. Suppose you're shopping for Christmas gifts for your family and friends. As you flip through your favorite mail order catalog, you're amazed at how easily you find 10 items that should make your loved ones happy. Your sister's birthday is coming up on December 18th, and you're celebrating the holidays early with your in-laws on the 21st.

You have a decision to make. To you, there's no difference between requesting three different shipments to arrive for the three different dates you need presents (the 18th, 21st, and 25th) or having them all shipped at the same time. However, having a delivery truck stop by on three different occasions is using up additional natural resources, not to mention creating additional paperwork (or database record entries) for the mail order company. You might make others wait longer for their deliveries as the delivery truck stops at your home before going on to theirs.

Your simple actions related to a mail-order purchase have an effect on many other things and people.

Data delivery on the Web is similar to goods delivery by mail. Today, you jump from one page to another, and the server delivers the next page's data each time you click a link. All the examples from Chapter 29 deliver Web pages in this manner. Other Web visitors wait for their Web page delivery (albeit microseconds) while the server distributes other people's pages.

With a data-aware Web browser, all the data can be delivered with a single Web server visit, and the browser stays aware of the data. With dynamic HTML, the Web page can dynamically change to present the data based on interactive user actions. In fact, a reader could add new data to the data source, if needed. The data can be uploaded again at the end of the Web page's use. By now, you should see the benefit of adding data-awareness to the Web browser and Dynamic HTML specification. Now throw in the benefit of better management of Web page maintenance. Web authors are finding Web page maintenance much easier (and therefore less expensive) when the variable data is maintained separately from the fixed text and graphics on a Web page.

> **NOTE**
>
> The biggest drawback to data binding is that often more data is delivered than what's actually used by the recipient. Extra data uses up network bandwidth that could be used for data that's actually consumed. However, as data compression methods for data sources keep getting better, it appears that the trade-off is usually worth it for the Web server's sake.

Data Delivery Today

Today, much data is delivered to corporate data consumers through local area networks (LANs), and most corporate data is stored in relational databases. Relational database theory has been incorporated into computing environments for its ability to deliver data efficiently and non-redundantly. Usually, data is delivered to a PC in a manner that can be efficiently presented by a relational database front-end tool, such as Access, Paradox, or FoxPro, to name just a few.

Corporate consumers can request data from data servers by creating a query through a query language. *Query* is just a fancy word for a request for information in a specific format from the database where the information is stored. The Structured Query Language (SQL) is the standard language of relational data requests and manipulation. Almost all data servers understand SQL. A data server accepts a query, runs it, and sends back the query result set over the corporate network. Only recently has the business world considered using the Internet as part of its network.

> **NOTE**
>
> As you think about the benefits of a standard, structured way of requesting database information, you begin to see all the benefits the HTML standard has for Web presentation. With HTML, you can use one of many browser software applications to request a Web page from any one of many server applications. With SQL, you can use one of many data-analysis tools to request data from any one of many data server applications. The standard (HTML or SQL) is the go-between for independent technology improvements at either end.

Not every data consumer in the business world knows how to properly request data to be most efficient with shared computing and networking resources. Public Web consumers can't be expected to understand the trade-offs, either. Every time I request relational data over a corporate network, I make a decision. Should I request more data than I currently need so I have it on my PC when the time comes to use it? Or should I request only the summary information I need now?

Data access decisions have been around for a long time. For the business community, technologists have worked on both ends of the spectrum to deliver the best of both worlds. Data-analysis tools are ready to accept all the data at once and supply the tools to analyze it in pieces locally on a PC. Web servers are optimized to simultaneously analyze, calculate, and deliver data requests from tens to hundreds of simultaneous requests. Because the technologists have been working on these same fundamental opportunities for decades, many believe it's proper to provide the same benefits to the rest of the world on the Web.

The more technologists look to apply the time-honored benefits of relational data theory to the Web, the more readers are confronted with wanting to have the best of both worlds within the Web page. Again, you arrive at a point where you should consider data-aware Web pages and Web browsers.

The User Agent's Role

For a data-aware Web page delivery strategy to work, a Web browser must be able to understand the data format the Web server delivers. The browser must put the data in a place in memory from which the browser can easily retrieve it. The Web browser also must remember where it put the data when the Web page wants to display more of the data.

The Internet Explorer 4.0 Web browser can handle the receiving, placing, calculating, and presenting needs of data-aware Web pages. For Microsoft, I would assume that adding the necessary data-aware functionality wasn't very difficult because it has been creating the Access data-analysis tool for several years, and it has developed the data-binding process for the Visual Basic application environment. Yet, without Dynamic HTML, adding data-awareness to Web pages would be awkward because there would be no simple way to communicate a reader's desire for more data with the data source that had been delivered.

Dynamic HTML's event model offers more than enough interactivity on a Web page to provide clean, easily understood data presentation and alteration strategies. You can click a button to see the next row of data in the data source. You can enter a date in a text box to see the information for a particular day. You can pass your pointing device over a particular image file to request that image's data. You can click on a table of data to sort the table by that row. In other words, you can perform many of the same data analysis functions as in popular relational data-manipulation tools.

The Data Form

You create a data form to present data in a Web page. A *data form* is a presentation object that contains labels defining the significance of each piece of data and fields in which to display the data for a particular piece of the data source. Usually, a piece of the data source that refers to a specific data object is called a *record*. You use a data form to present each record one at a time. Displaying only a subset of records at a time is called *filtering*. Dynamic HTML gives readers the chance to indicate they would like to see a different record.

Data forms can look very glamorous as you add graphics and color by using the appropriate HTML tags. So, each record can be presented in a way that resembles traditional Web pages. I don't want my readers to suspect they're not getting each record from the Web one at a time. Of course, a trained eye will know the difference, but I want the untrained eye to not have to worry about the details.

Adding Data-Awareness with Dynamic HTML

So far, this chapter has been mainly definitions and vision. The data analyst community is constantly thinking up new terms and coming up with visions for the future—and they like doing both. This section covers the technical details of how to add a data source to a Dynamic HTML Web page intended for viewing with the Internet Explorer 4.0 Web browser.

To add data-awareness to a Web page, supply an `<OBJECT></OBJECT>` tag pair with all the appropriate attributes. Look at an example:

```
<OBJECT ID="townnews"
    CLASSID="clsid:333C7BC4-460F-11D0-BC04-0080C7055A83"
    BORDER="0" WIDTH="0" HEIGHT="0">
    <PARAM NAME="DataURL"   VALUE="towndata.txt">
    <PARAM NAME="UseHeader" VALUE="True">
</OBJECT>
```

The opening `<OBJECT>` tag contains an `ID` attribute that gives the data source a name. In this case, the data source contains news for several towns. The `CLASSID` attribute references the ActiveX control that provides data-awareness to an Internet Explorer 4.0 Web page. The data-awareness ActiveX control comes with the standard Internet Explorer 4.0 installation.

30

DATA BINDING

Note that the data source object takes up no space on the Web page; instead, components of the data source are accessed and presented in other tags on the Web page. The nested <PARAM> tags and their attributes are required because the Web browser uses the parameters to set up the data source properly. The NAME=DataURL parameter provides a VALUE that identifies the data source's filename. The UseHeader parameter identifies whether to use the first row in the data source as a header for the rest of the records in the data source. A VALUE of True tells the Web browser to refer to each column in the data source by the name at the top of the column.

To create the data form in your Web page, associate a label and data field with each column in your data source. The following example creates a label in which a <LABEL></LABEL> tag pair is used to define it:

```
<LABEL FOR=hightemp>Today's High Temperature: </LABEL>
```

The opening <LABEL> tag contains a FOR attribute that identifies the field for which the label is intended. You put the text for the label between the <LABEL></LABEL> tag pair.

You create a field similarly to the following, where an <INPUT> tag contains the appropriate attributes that create the form field:

```
<INPUT ID=hightemp TYPE=text DATASRC=#townnews DATAFLD="High">
```

The ID attribute names the field. The TYPE attribute defines the type of data the field holds. The DATASRC attribute associates the field with the right data source object, and the DATAFLD attribute associates the field with the correct column of data in the data source.

Examples of Data-Aware Web Forms

This chapter gives you two examples of data-aware Web forms that you can embed into a Web page. The first one shows a sports page that's organized around the locker room concept. A reader can point and click on the Web page to visit each team's locker room and see statistics specific to that team. The second example shows an interactive, geographical Web page.

A First Example of Data Binding

In the example from Listing 30.1, the locker rooms are pages for the teams of the Web Baseball League, a fictitious baseball league playing games on the Web. Each locker room page shows the number of team wins and losses, the team batting average, and the team ERA through the last game played for each team in the league. Initially, when the page loads, the Tigers team locker room is presented as shown in Figure 30.1. Readers can use the two buttons marked < and > to move forward or backward through the different locker rooms.

Almost all the big sports information providers on the Web use a locker room concept so readers can navigate directly to their favorite teams. If a reader then decides to go to another team's locker room, a second request is made to the Web server to deliver that team's information.

With the example in Listing 30.1, however, all the data is delivered at once in a single file. As readers browse through the different teams, they don't have to depend on any additional data delivery from the Web.

FIGURE 30.1.

The Tigers team locker room.

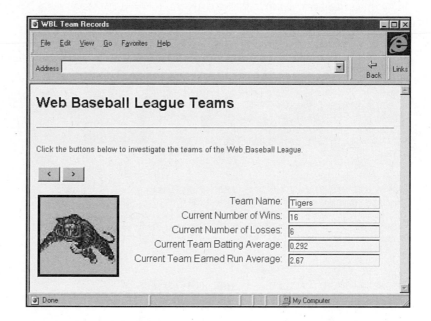

Look at Listing 30.1, and then continue reading for a detailed explanation. Figure 30.2 shows the locker room for the Frogs team as displayed in Internet Explorer 4.0.

Listing 30.1. An example of dynamic record presentation.

```
<HTML>
<HEAD>
<FONT FACE="verdana,arial,helvetica" SIZE=2>
<TITLE>WBL Team Records</title>
</HEAD>
<BODY BGCOLOR="#FFFFFF">
<H2>Web Baseball League Teams</H2>
<HR>
<P>Click the buttons below to investigate the teams of the Web Baseball
League.</P>
<P>
<OBJECT ID="teamlist"
        CLASSID="clsid:333C7BC4-460F-11D0-BC04-0080C7055A83"
        BORDER="0" WIDTH="0" HEIGHT="0">
  <PARAM NAME="DataURL" VALUE="wblteam.txt">
  <PARAM NAME="UseHeader" VALUE="True">
</OBJECT>
```

continues

Listing 30.1. continued

```
<TABLE>
  <TR>
    <TD ALIGN=RIGHT><INPUT TYPE=BUTTON ID=backward VALUE="   <   "></TD>
    <TD ALIGN=LEFT><INPUT TYPE=BUTTON ID=forward VALUE="   >   "></TD>
  </TR>
</TABLE>
<P>
<IMG ID=Picture SRC="Tigers.jpg" BORDER=4 HEIGHT=128 WIDTH=128 ALIGN=LEFT>

<TABLE ALIGN=CENTER CELLSPACING=0 CELLPADDING=0>
<TR>
<TD ALIGN=RIGHT VALIGN=TOP><LABEL FOR=team>Team Name: </LABEL></TD>
<TD ALIGN=LEFT VALIGN=TOP WIDTH="10"></TD>
<TD ALIGN=LEFT VALIGN=TOP><INPUT ID=team TYPE=text
DATASRC=#teamlist DATAFLD="Team"></TD>
</TR>

<TR>
<TD ALIGN=RIGHT VALIGN=TOP><LABEL FOR=wins>
Current Number of Wins: </LABEL></TD>
<TD ALIGN=LEFT VALIGN=TOP WIDTH="10"></TD>
<TD ALIGN=LEFT VALIGN=TOP><INPUT ID=wins TYPE=text
DATASRC=#teamlist DATAFLD="Wins"></TD>
</TR>

<TR>
<TD ALIGN=RIGHT VALIGN=TOP><LABEL FOR=losses>
Current Number of Losses: </LABEL></TD>
<TD ALIGN=LEFT VALIGN=TOP WIDTH="10"></TD>
<TD ALIGN=LEFT VALIGN=TOP><INPUT ID=losses TYPE=text
DATASRC=#teamlist DATAFLD="Losses"></TD>
</TR>

<TR>
<TD ALIGN=RIGHT VALIGN=TOP><LABEL FOR=BA>
Current Team Batting Average: </LABEL></TD>
<TD ALIGN=LEFT VALIGN=TOP WIDTH="10"></TD>
<TD ALIGN=LEFT VALIGN=TOP><INPUT ID=BA TYPE=text
DATASRC=#teamlist DATAFLD="BA"></TD>
</TR>

<TR>
<TD ALIGN=RIGHT VALIGN=TOP><LABEL FOR=ERA>
Current Team Earned Run Average: </LABEL></TD>
<TD ALIGN=LEFT VALIGN=TOP WIDTH="10"></TD>
<TD ALIGN=LEFT VALIGN=TOP><INPUT ID=ERA TYPE=text
DATASRC=#teamlist DATAFLD="ERA"></TD>
</TR>
</TABLE>

<SCRIPT LANGUAGE=JavaScript>
function documentClick() {
    Picture.src = team.value + ".jpg";
}
```

```
document.onclick = documentClick;

</SCRIPT>

<SCRIPT LANGUAGE=JavaScript>
function backwardClick() {
  if (teamlist.recordset.AbsolutePosition > 1) {
     teamlist.recordset.MovePrevious();
  } else {
     alert("Already at first team");
  }
}

backward.onclick = backwardClick;

function forwardClick() {
  if (teamlist.recordset.AbsolutePosition != teamlist.recordset.RecordCount) {
     teamlist.recordset.MoveNext();
  } else {
     alert("Already at last team");
  }
}

forward.onclick = forwardClick;

</SCRIPT>
</FONT>
</BODY>
</HTML>
```

FIGURE 30.2.

A dynamic record presentation of the Frogs team locker room.

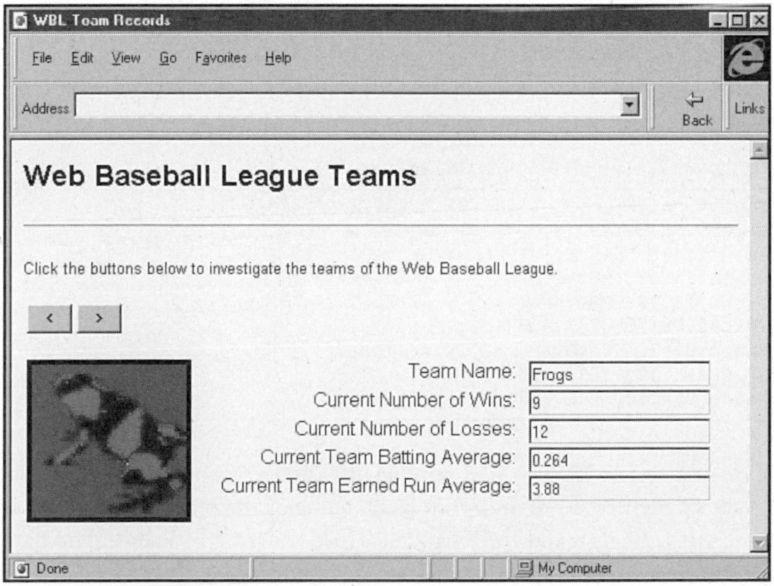

The data control object used in this example is an ActiveX control you can download once from the Internet to extend the capabilities of your Web browser. In fact, Internet Explorer 4.0 includes the data-awareness control in its standard package. The same control is used for all the data-aware examples in this chapter. The data control object is included in the HTML page by way of the `<OBJECT></OBJECT>` tag pair. The ActiveX control identification lines from Listing 30.1 follow:

```
<OBJECT ID="teamlist"
        CLASSID="clsid:333C7BC4-460F-11D0-BC04-0080C7055A83"
        BORDER="0" WIDTH="0" HEIGHT="0">
  <PARAM NAME="DataURL" VALUE="wblteam.txt">
  <PARAM NAME="UseHeader" VALUE="True">
</OBJECT>
```

The `ID` attribute value instantiates `teamlist` as the data source object. The `CLASS_ID` attribute value of the `<OBJECT>` tag is a sophisticated string with embedded security used to select the appropriate ActiveX control for data source management. The control requires two parameters identified in the `<PARAM>` tags with `NAME` and `VALUE` attributes. The `DataURL` parameter supplies the URL of the data source to the Web browser. The `UseHeader` parameter identifies whether the header row of the data set should be used as column name information. A table with two buttons is added to the Web page to give the user controls for moving from team to team. Both are instantiated as objects with the `ID` attribute. One button is instantiated as `backward` and the other as `forward`.

The bitmap image for the Tigers team logo is placed on the page in an `<IMG>` tag instantiated as an object with the `ID=Picture` attribute. The team logo image will change through the `document_onclick()` function declared later within a script. The Tigers team information is the first row of the data source `wblteam.txt`. Listing 30.2 shows the `wblteam.txt` file's contents.

Listing 30.2. Contents of `wblteam.txt`.

```
Team,Wins:INT,Losses:INT,BA:FLOAT,ERA:FLOAT
Tigers,16,6,.292,2.67
Bears,14,8,.244,2.87
Robins,13,8,.267,2.67
Lions,11,10,.282,4.07
Rhinos,10,10,.255,3.55
Frogs,9,12,.264,3.88
Sharks,8,12,.251,4.15
Spiders,4,14,.212,3.86
```

The first line in Listing 30.2 contains the header information for the data source. `Team` is the name of the first field, and `Wins` is the name of the second. The `Wins` and `Losses` fields are of type `INT` (integer), and the `BA` and `ERA` fields are of type `FLOAT`. The data types are used by the Web browser when presenting data to a reader. The details for each team then follow in the data source file as separate team records.

NOTE

You might have noticed that the `wblteam.txt` file is in a simple comma-separated values (CSV) format. With all the expertise Microsoft has gained over the years in file formats, you can be sure you will have lots of options for the file format of delivered data to a Web surfer. I use CSV because it's very straightforward and easy to use for debugging, and almost all personal data software applications allow a database table to be exported in that format.

After you add the team logo image to the page, you create the data form. The team data form has five labels and five fields. Create each label with a `<LABEL></LABEL>` tag pair, as follows:

```
<LABEL FOR=team>Team Name: </LABEL>
```

Each field is created with an `<INPUT>` tag, like this:

```
<INPUT ID=team TYPE=text DATASRC=#teamlist DATAFLD="Team">.
```

The tags for each data form label and field are similar. For the team field, the `TYPE` attribute identifies the presentation type for the field. The `DATASRC` attribute identifies the source of the data (which has the same value as the data source object name that points to the `wblteam.txt` file). The `DATAFLD` attribute identifies the field in the data source from which the input box expects to get data. The field name is obtained from the first row of the `wblteam.txt` file.

NOTE

For the example in Listing 30.1, I chose to present the data form in a table for a more organized look. The table tags are straight out of the HTML 3.2 specification. Listing 30.3 gives you an example that shows a less organized method of presenting data.

The first `<SCRIPT></SCRIPT>` tag pair includes a script with the `documentClick()` function, which is available to any Web page loaded in a user agent that supports dynamic HTML. In this case, the `documentClick()` function is used to keep the locker room team logo in agreement with the current data row being shown on the Web page. This single line handles every mouse click on the page for every team:

```
Picture.src = team.value + ".jpg";
```

It changes the `SRC` attribute for the `Picture` object based on the `Team` field of the current data row. The `Team` field is instantiated with the `ID=team` attribute of its `<INPUT>` tag.

Within the other `<SCRIPT></SCRIPT>` tag pair, two functions handle the user's button clicks. The `backwardClick()` function moves the user back up the data set, one row at a time, until the first row is encountered; the `forwardClick()` function moves the user down the data set rows, one row at a time, until the last row is encountered. The function names *must* start with the same string as existing, instantiated objects. Without using the exact same strings of `backward` and `forward`, the function would not work as intended.

A Second Example

The second example shows a geography Web site where data is presented more as a continuation of body text than in a neat and orderly table. Instead of moving through the data sequentially one record at a time, a reader can click an image to see information about that particular item. The data form presents the specific, absolute record related to the selected land mass.

This example uses the five states of the Pacific Northwest in the United States. Figure 30.3 shows the presentation for the state of Washington. A user can see the information for Washington by clicking on the Washington State image that's part of the map.

FIGURE 30.3.

A presentation on the state of Washington.

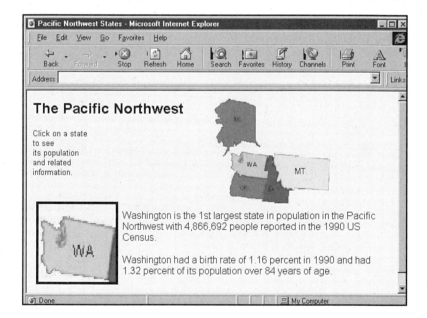

NOTE

To get population and area figures for the United States, I visited the United States government's census Web site. There is so much information available online at http://www.census.gov/ that it's overwhelming even to a statistics addict like me. I used the map facility at http://www.census.gov/datamap/www/ to get the statistics for this example.

If you visit the census Web site, notice how parts are organized as data forms in which you request certain information and wait for the request to be served back to you. As of September 1997, the census Web site is still using CGI scripting to communicate with a CD-ROM reader on its server. Therefore, the census Web site is a great example of the old way of interacting with a data source.

The Dynamic HTML syntax needed to create the data-binding example in Listing 30.3 is similar to Listing 30.1. Take a look at Listing 30.3 and Figure 30.3 and then continue reading for more details.

Listing 30.3. A point-and-click dynamic record presentation.

```
<HTML>
<HEAD>
<FONT FACE="verdana,arial,helvetica" SIZE=2>
<TITLE>Pacific Northwest States</title>
</HEAD>
<BODY BGCOLOR="#FFFFFF">
<H2>The Pacific Northwest</H2>

<P ID=ne>Click on a state <BR>
to see <BR>
its population <BR>
and related <BR>
information.</P>
<P>
<OBJECT ID="statelist"
        CLASSID="clsid:333C7BC4-460F-11D0-BC04-0080C7055A83"
        BORDER="0" WIDTH="0" HEIGHT="0">
  <PARAM NAME="DataURL" VALUE="pacnw.txt">
  <PARAM NAME="UseHeader" VALUE="True">
</OBJECT>
<P>
 <IMG ID="alaska" STYLE="container:positioned;position:absolute;
TOP:10pt;LEFT:300px;WIDTH:96px;HEIGHT:96px;ZINDEX:1;" src="alaska.jpg">
 <IMG ID="idaho" STYLE="container:positioned;position:absolute;
TOP:80pt;LEFT:390px;WIDTH:48px;HEIGHT:84px;ZINDEX:5;" src="idaho.jpg">
 <IMG ID="washingt" STYLE="container:positioned;position:absolute;
TOP:70pt;LEFT:338px;WIDTH:64px;HEIGHT:48px;ZINDEX:4;" src="washingt.jpg">
 <IMG ID="oregon" STYLE="container:positioned;position:absolute;
TOP:100pt;LEFT:338px;WIDTH:64px;HEIGHT:48px;ZINDEX:2;" src="oregon.jpg">
 <IMG ID="montana" STYLE="container:positioned;position:absolute;
TOP:76pt;LEFT:410px;WIDTH:96px;HEIGHT:64px;ZINDEX:3;" src="montana.jpg">

<TABLE><TR><TD>
<IMG ID=Picture SRC="alaska.jpg" BORDER=4 HEIGHT=128 WIDTH=128 ALIGN=RIGHT>
</TD><TD>
<SPAN ID=state DATASRC=#statelist DATAFLD="State"></SPAN>is the
<SPAN ID=pr DATASRC=#statelist DATAFLD="Pop_Rank"></SPAN> largest state in
population in the Pacific Northwest with
```

continues

Listing 30.3. continued

```
<SPAN ID=pop DATASRC=#statelist DATAFLD="Population"></SPAN> people reported in
the 1990 US Census.
<P>
<SPAN ID=state2 DATASRC=#statelist DATAFLD="State"></SPAN> had a birth rate of
<SPAN ID=ar DATASRC=#statelist DATAFLD="Birth_Rate"></SPAN> percent in 1990 and
had <SPAN ID=area DATASRC=#statelist DATAFLD="Over_84"></SPAN> percent of its
population over 84 years of age.
</TD></TR></TABLE>
<SCRIPT language=JavaScript>
var srcElement
function documentClick() {
    srcElement = window.event.srcElement;
    if (srcElement.id=="alaska") {
       statelist.recordset.AbsolutePosition = 1;
    } else {
       if (srcElement.id=="washingt") {
          statelist.recordset.AbsolutePosition = 2;
       } else {
          if (srcElement.id=="oregon") {
             statelist.recordset.AbsolutePosition = 3;
          } else {
             if (srcElement.id=="idaho") {
                statelist.recordset.AbsolutePosition = 4;
             } else {
                if (srcElement.id=="montana") {
                   statelist.recordset.AbsolutePosition = 5;
                }
             }
          }
       }
    }
    Picture.src = srcElement.id + ".jpg";
}

document.onclick = documentClick;

</SCRIPT>
</FONT>
</BODY>
</HTML>
```

The <OBJECT></OBJECT> tag pair that sets up the data source is identical to the pair in Listing 30.1, except that the data source name and file are changed to statelist and pacnw.txt, respectively.

The five state images are included through <IMG> tags, each with an SRC attribute that identifies the URL for each image file, an ID attribute that gives each object image a name, and a STYLE attribute that places and sizes each image on the Web page.

Similar to Listing 30.1, a larger image object is added to the page to provide an image of the state the reader selects with a mouse click. Initially, the image is set to the state of Alaska. When a reader clicks a different state, the larger image is replaced with that state's.

Each data record field is set up as a separate form field on the Web page. For the Pacific North-west States data form, I use `<SPAN></SPAN>` tag pairs, instead of the `<INPUT></INPUT>` tag pairs I used in Listing 30.1. The difference for Listing 30.3 is that the data form fields are placed within free-flowing body text, instead of in a neat and orderly table. Remember that the difference between division tags and span tags is that span tags don't include a line feed. Because you're creating a free-flowing presentation, you don't need to create labels.

As for the script function created to tie everything together, the `scrElement` feature from Chapter 29 is used. I determine the source element of a reader's mouse click with the following line in the function `documentClick()`:

```
srcElement = window.event.srcElement;
```

The `documentClick()` function is always available as a part of dynamic HTML.

Next, the `ID` attribute of the image selected by the user is determined. Depending on which image a reader clicks, the data source record is set to that row with a line in the function like the following:

```
statelist.recordset.AbsolutePosition = 2.
```

Here, the row indicator is set to row 2 (its absolute position), which contains the information for the state of Washington. Five such lines are created in the script function because there are five states.

Finally, the larger image's source is set to the bitmap image file of the state that the reader selects. The following line is used to change the image:

```
Picture.src = state.value + ".jpg";
```

The Pacific Northwest specific data comes from the data source file named `pacnw.txt`. Listing 30.4 shows the contents of the file. Note that the file format is CSV (comma-separated values). Also note that the string data includes a space character at the end of each string to provide appropriate spacing on the Web page.

Listing 30.4. Contents of the file `pacnw.txt`.

```
State,Pop_Rank,Population,Birth_Rate,Over_84
Alaska ,5th ,"550,043 ",".23 ","1.78 "
Washington ,1st ,"4,866,692 ","1.16 ","1.32 "
Oregon ,2nd ,"2,842,321 ","1.37 ","1.24 "
Idaho ,3rd ,"1,006,749 ","1.13 ","1.41 "
Montana ,4th ,"799,065 ","1.34 ","1.28 "
```

NOTE

All the examples in this chapter have used data forms for data presentation only. Microsoft has implemented an architecture in their Internet Explorer 4.0 Web browser that permits you to create data form Web pages that your readers can use to update data as well. Microsoft's Dynamic HTML architecture includes form field validation events you can use to check a Web-based form's contents before or after you update a database. The validation events build on the W3C's intrinsic event list given in Chapter 28.

Dynamic Table Generation

Dynamic table expansion is a feature of a data presentation tool that allows variable-length data sources to automatically be displayed in a table of any length. For Web browser presentation, dynamic table expansion means that you, the Web author, must identify only the first row of the table with the appropriate headers and then identify which column from the data source belongs with which header field. The Web browser does the rest, dynamically creating the necessary table tags to show the complete contents of the data source.

The dynamic table expansion feature works especially well with variable-length data sources that change over time. You don't have to change the Web page because the Web browser does all the work of creating the appropriate tags depending on the number of records in the data source. Only the data source changes to present more recent data.

For example, imagine you offer a New Snow Page on a daily ski report Web site. Every day you list in a table on a Web page all the mountains that got new snow in the past 24 hours. For each mountain, there is a mountain name column, a new centimeters of snowfall column, and a current centimeters of snow base column. To present the information each day, you could take advantage of dynamic table expansion on a data-aware Web page. The HTML file you create can stay the same day after day. Only the data source that includes a variable number of records (depending on the number of mountains that got snow in the past 24 hours) must change daily. The Web browser knows how to present the variable information in a table based on the first row you identify with the appropriate HTML tags.

You use dynamic table expansion for its simplicity and flexibility in presenting changing data. With this feature, you can use multiple data sources on the same Web page by repeating the code for each data source. For example, perhaps you want to show on a Web page daily baseball standings for all the Major League, AAA, and AA teams in the United States and Canada. Every night, each league commissioner could send you a data source of the team standings for that league.

Daily, on the Web server, you would replace each data source's file with a file of the same name. A reader who downloads the standings page then would get the latest standings for each team.

Dynamic expansion means that each league's standings are already expanded and visible on the page when the Web browser finishes loading the Web page. The Internet Explorer 4.0 Web browser also comes with the capability to dynamically sort data in a dynamically generated table.

The Web browser reads the definition of the first table row from the `<TABLE>`, `<TR>`, and `<TD>` HTML tags that define the row. Then, by using the attributes associated with a second row of table tags, the Web browser associates the appropriate columns from the data source with the different cells in the table. After that, the browser reads through all the data and expands the table to make room for each row of data in the data source.

The Web browser must contain the different file translation logic that's needed to interpret different data source file types. The Web browser must also contain any sorting logic to dynamically sort a data source before displaying a table.

To add dynamic table expansion to your Web pages, you insert into your HTML file the same `<OBJECT></OBJECT>` tag pair you use to present data-aware data forms. Then, you create the first row of the table by using a `<THEAD></THEAD>` tag pair. You nest the table header within a `<TABLE></TABLE>` tag pair. The opening `<TABLE>` tag needs a few attributes such as the following, in which an `ID` attribute gives the table the name `mytable` and a `DATASRC` attribute associates the appropriate data source object with the table:

```
<TABLE BORDER="1" ID="mytable" DATASRC="#mydata">
```

The `BORDER` attribute defines the thickness of the border to be used between cells in the table.

You then create three lines after the opening `<TABLE>` tag to look like the following, which begins the table head with a `<THEAD>` tag, begins the first row with a `<TR>` tag, and begins the first column header cell with a `<TD>` tag:

```
<THEAD>
<TR>
<TD><FONT COLOR="#0000FF"><B><U><DIV ID=col1>Name</DIV></U></B></FONT></TD>
```

Of all the tags nested within the `<TD></TD>` table cell tag pair, the `<DIV ID=col1>Name</DIV>` sequence is the most critical. The division creates an object with the name `col1`. Remember that *division* is just another word for a section, but a division is a section that can be much smaller than a typical word processing section. You can reference `col1` from any script function to modify the division's appearance or contents.

The text `Name` actually appears within the table cell on the Web page. You should recognize the `<FONT>`, `<B>`, and `<U>` tags as older HTML tags that affect the appearance of the text. In this case, the table headings are colored blue and are boldfaced and underlined. I recommend adding some form of text formatting to the header row to make it stand out from the rest of the table.

30

DATA BINDING

> **NOTE**
>
> In Chapter 29, you learned to vary text format or style as a way to give feedback to a user. Table headers are a great example of where you should vary text attributes to draw attention to their availability for interaction. If you add dynamic sorting to your table, be sure to make the headers stand out. Users are more apt to click on a header if it jumps out at them.

For each column in your data source, add an additional `<TD></TD>` tag pair similar to the preceding example. After you declare all the column headers, close off the first table row with a `</TR>` tag, and close off the table head with a `</THEAD>` tag.

After the table head, you create a table body identifier by using a `<TBODY></TBODY>` tag pair. In a table with four columns, the table body identifier might look like the following:

```
<TBODY>
<TR>
<TD><DIV DATAFLD="Col1"></DIV></TD>
<TD><DIV DATAFLD="Col2"></DIV></TD>
<TD><DIV DATAFLD="Col3"></DIV></TD>
<TD><DIV DATAFLD="Col4"></DIV></TD>
</TR>
</TBODY>
```

Each cell in the table body identifier contains a division with a `DATAFLD` attribute. The value of the `DATAFLD` attribute is the column name specified in the data source you identified in the opening `<TABLE>` tag. In this case, you are using the `mydata` data source.

> **NOTE**
>
> As a review, don't forget that the `mydata` data source identifier is the object `ID` attribute name for the `<OBJECT></OBJECT>` tag pair. You add the object tag pair to the page to supply the appropriate ActiveX control the Web browser uses to handle the dynamic data-aware functionality of the Web page.

That's all you need to do to add dynamically expanding tables to a Web page that follows Microsoft's approach to data-awareness. The Web browser does the rest.

This chapter gives you two examples of how to dynamically generate tables from a data source. The first one demonstrates the flexibility of a dynamic Web page in handling variable-length data sources. The second example shows how to provide the dynamic sorting feature to your readers.

An Example of Dynamic Table Generation

As I mentioned earlier, you take more advantage of dynamic table generation when you provide a variable-length data source often over a period of time. A daily New Snow Report Web page is one example, and Listing 30.5 gives you another one.

For this first example, imagine you're offering a Web site that announces new births for a busy city hospital. Any town citizen can visit your Web page daily to see information about babies who have been delivered by the hospital's staff. You want to provide the mother's name, the baby's name if available, the baby's sex, the baby's weight and length, and the mother's comments, if any, all within a dynamic table on the Web page.

Look at Listing 30.5 and Figure 30.4, and then continue reading for a detailed explanation.

Listing 30.5. Hospital births Web page.

```
<HTML>
<HEAD><TITLE>Recent Hospital Births</TITLE></HEAD>
<BODY BGCOLOR= "#FFFFFF">
<H2>This Month's Births</H2>
<HR>
<P>
<OBJECT ID="babylist"
     CLASSID="clsid:333C7BC4-460F-11D0-BC04-0080C7055A83"
     ALIGN="baseline" BORDER="0" WIDTH="0" HEIGHT="0">
     <PARAM NAME="DataURL" VALUE="babies1.txt">
     <PARAM NAME="UseHeader" VALUE="True">
</OBJECT>

<TABLE BORDER="1" ID="elemtbl" DATASRC="#babylist">
<THEAD>
<TR>
<TD><B><U><DIV ID=mom>Mom</DIV></U></B></TD>
<TD><B><U><DIV ID=name>Baby</DIV></U></B></TD>
<TD><B><U><DIV ID=sex>Sex</DIV></U></B></TD>
<TD><B><U><DIV ID=weight>Weight</DIV></U></B></TD>
<TD><B><U><DIV ID=length>Length</DIV></U></B></TD>
<TD><B><U><DIV ID=comment>Comment</DIV></U></B></TD>
</TR>
</THEAD>
<TBODY>
<TR>
<TD><DIV DATAFLD="Mom"></DIV></TD>
<TD><SPAN DATAFLD="Baby"></SPAN></TD>
<TD><DIV DATAFLD="Sex"></DIV></TD>
<TD><DIV DATAFLD="Weight"></DIV></TD>
<TD><DIV DATAFLD="Length"></DIV></TD>
<TD><DIV DATAFLD="Comment"></DIV></TD>
</TR>
</TBODY></TABLE>
<HR>
</BODY>
</HTML>
```

FIGURE 30.4.

Births for three days in May.

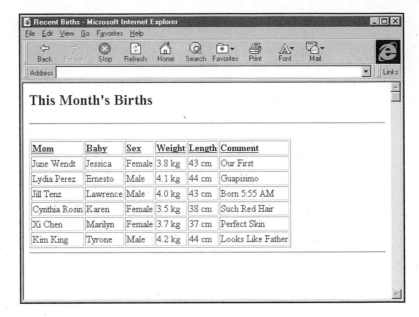

Before you review Listing 30.5 in detail, focus on the benefits of using dynamically generating tables. Figure 30.4 shows the This Month's Births Web page as it displays the data source in Listing 30.6. After the column header row, the table dynamically expands to include six additional rows, each with a separate baby record.

Listing 30.6. Contents of the `babies1.txt` file.

```
Mom,Baby,Sex,Weight,Length,Comment
June Wendt,Jessica,Female,3.8 kg,43 cm,Our First
Lydia Perez,Ernesto,Male,4.1 kg,44 cm,Guapisimo
Jill Tenz,Lawrence,Male,4.0 kg,43 cm,Born 5:55 AM
Cynthia Rosin,Karen,Female,3.5 kg,38 cm,Such Red Hair
Xi Chen,Marilyn,Female,3.7 kg,37 cm,Perfect Skin
Kim King,Tyrone,Male,4.2 kg,44 cm,Looks Like Father
```

Go ahead and edit the `babies1.txt` file to include two new births for May 4. You can change the file, save it, and then reload the Web page. If you're short on creativity, just copy and paste or type the bottom two rows from the `babies2.txt` file from Listing 30.7. The table will automatically generate two new rows as it expands for the new data source. Remember that any computer process could automatically generate the baby births data source by accessing a database on the hospital's network and running a query. Also, keep in mind that you don't need to re-create the Web page each time the data source changes.

Listing 30.7. Contents of the `babies2.txt` file.

```
Mom,Baby,Sex,Weight,Length,Comment
June Wendt,Jessica,Female,3.8 kg,43 cm,Our First
Lydia Perez,Ernesto,Male,4.1 kg,44 cm,Guapisimo
Jill Tenz,Lawrence,Male,4.0 kg,43 cm,Born 5:55 AM
Cynthia Rosin,Karen,Female,3.5 kg,38 cm,Such Red Hair
Xi Chen,Marilyn,Female,3.7 kg,37 cm,Perfect Skin
Kim King,Tyrone,Male,4.2 kg,44 cm,Looks Like Father
Jen Georgeson,Lyle,Male,4.1 kg,42 cm,First on Fourth
Tin Xin,Yu,Male,3.9 kg,42 cm,Very Easy Birth
```

The result of adding two new lines to the data source is shown in Figure 30.5. The data from Listing 30.7 is presented in Microsoft's Internet Explorer 4.0 Web browser. This time, the table displays eight rows for the eight baby records in the data source plus one for the column headers.

FIGURE 30.5.

Births for four days in May.

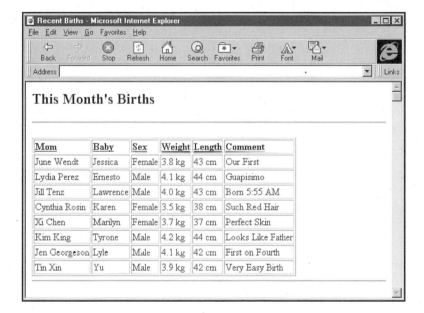

Return review your focus to Listing 30.5. You have probably noticed that Listing 30.5 doesn't require a script. In fact, you didn't even need to use the `onLoad()` event-handling function to start the table generation process. The browser starts the table and generation process solely from the other HTML tags on the Web page.

First, you add the object tags to activate the ActiveX control that handles table generation and expansion. Next, you name the object with the `ID="babylist"` attribute. You will refer to the `babylist` name whenever you want to use the data source object in the other HTML tags on the page. The `CLASSID` attribute defines the proper value for the control. You need no physical

30

DATA BINDING

space on the Web page for the data-awareness control, so you set the BORDER, WIDTH, and HEIGHT attributes to 0. You add an ALIGN attribute and set it to baseline, which aligns each row along the baseline for the table.

The two <PARAM> tags are expected by the ActiveX control. The first parameter the ActiveX control expects is a DataURL for the data source. The data is saved in a comma-separated value (CSV) file named babies1.txt. You want to use the first row in the data file as a header record, so set the UseHeader parameter to True.

When you're finished, the data source object looks like this:

```
<OBJECT ID="babylist"
    CLASSID="clsid:333C7BC4-460F-11D0-BC04-0080C7055A83"
    ALIGN="baseline" BORDER="0" WIDTH="0" HEIGHT="0">
    <PARAM NAME="DataURL" VALUE="babies1.txt">
    <PARAM NAME="UseHeader" VALUE="True">
</OBJECT>
```

After you define the data source object, refer to the data source ID attribute value within the table. The opening <TABLE> tag includes a DATASRC attribute, which has been set to be the name of the babylist data source object. The leading pound symbol (#) is required syntax when you're referring to a data source name.

Next, create the first two rows of the table. The first is nested within a <THEAD></THEAD> tag pair. The first row is a row of column headers for the table. You create the first row with simple HTML tags, and the second row is nested within a <TBODY></TBODY> tag pair. The second row is just as clean, but includes a DATAFLD attribute for each opening <DIV> tag. The DATAFLD attribute value for each division had better agree with the header row in the data source. If not, the Web page won't present the correct data in the column as the table expands.

An Example of Dynamic Table Sorting

As an example of dynamic table sorting, this section presents a simplified baseball statistics Web page that provides dynamic sorting. You can extend this page to include more interesting statistics, such as team home runs, team stolen bases, team shutouts, and team home winning percentage.

Take a look at Listing 30.8, and then continue reading for the details. Of most interest to you should be the script functions near the bottom of the listing.

Listing 30.8. A sortable baseball statistics Web page.

```
<HTML>
<HEAD><TITLE>WBL Current Standings</TITLE></HEAD>
<BODY BGCOLOR= "#FFFFFF">
<H2>WBL Current Standings</H2>
<HR>
<P>
<OBJECT ID="teamlist"
```

```
        CLASSID="clsid:333C7BC4-460F-11D0-BC04-0080C7055A83"
        ALIGN="baseline" BORDER="0" WIDTH="0" HEIGHT="0">
        <PARAM NAME="DataURL" VALUE="wblteam.txt">
        <PARAM NAME="UseHeader" VALUE="True">
</OBJECT>

This Table is Sortable By Clicking on the Column Header<P>
<TABLE BORDER="1" ID="elemtbl" DATASRC="#teamlist">
<THEAD>
<TR>
<TD><FONT COLOR="#0000FF"><B><U><DIV
    ID=team>Team</DIV></U></B></FONT></TD>
<TD><FONT COLOR="#0000FF"><B><U><DIV
    ID=wins>Wins</DIV></U></B></FONT></TD>
<TD><FONT COLOR="#0000FF"><B><U><DIV
    ID=losses>Losses</DIV></U></B></FONT></TD>
<TD><FONT COLOR="#0000FF"><B><U><DIV ID=BA>
    Batting Avg</DIV></U></B></FONT></TD>
<TD><FONT COLOR="#0000FF"><B><U><DIV ID=ERA>
    ERA</DIV></U></B></FONT></TD>
</TR>
</THEAD>
<TBODY>
<TR>
<TD><SPAN DATAFLD="Team"></SPAN></TD>
<TD><DIV DATAFLD="Wins"></DIV></TD>
<TD><SPAN DATAFLD="Losses"></SPAN></TD>
<TD><DIV DATAFLD="BA"></DIV></TD>
<TD><DIV DATAFLD="ERA"></DIV></TD>
</TR>
</TBODY></TABLE>
<SCRIPT LANGUAGE="JavaScript">
function teamClick() {
  teamlist.Sort = "Team";
  teamlist.Reset();
}

team.onclick = teamClick;

function winsClick() {
  teamlist.Sort = "Wins";
  teamlist.Reset();
}

wins.onclick = winsClick;

function lossesClick() {
  teamlist.Sort = "Losses";
  teamlist.Reset();
}

losses.onclick = lossesClick;

function baClick() {
  teamlist.Sort = "BA";
  teamlist.Reset();
}
```

30

DATA BINDING

continues

Listing 30.8. continued

```
ba.onclick = baClick;

function eraClick() {
  teamlist.Sort = "ERA";
  teamlist.Reset();
}

era.onclick = eraClick;

</SCRIPT>
<HR>
</FONT>
</BODY>
</HTML>
```

Other than the functions inside the <SCRIPT></SCRIPT> tag pair, Listing 30.8 is very similar to Listing 30.5. The data source used for this example is the same wblteam.txt file used for the team locker room example given earlier in Listing 30.1.

The following are the changes you need to make in Listing 30.5 to create Listing 30.8:

- Change the data source object ID attribute to teamlist, and change the DataURL parameter to wblteam.txt.
- Change any DATASRC attributes from #babylist to #teamlist.
- Change the text in the table header row (added also is the blue font color).
- Change any DATAFLD attributes to the appropriate values supplied in the data source header line.

A script function was then added to handle a reader's mouse click on each table header cell. All the functions were placed within the same <SCRIPT></SCRIPT> tag pair. Each function adds the suffix Click() to the ID value of the column header opening <DIV> tag to define a function name. For example, the function for the wins column is named winsClick().

Each function contains two simple lines. The first line tells the Web browser to re-sort the table based on the column the reader clicked with the mouse:

```
teamlist.Sort = "Wins";,
```

All sorts are done in ascending order. The second line tells the Web browser to regenerate and re-expand the table, which is done with the new sort:

```
teamlist.Reset(),
```

NOTE

That's right, the sort script function events aren't referenced as attributes of the table row <DIV> tags, but instead are automatically associated through the ID attribute value. I think that's a clever way of associating an element with an event, but it puts more burden on the browser to implicitly notice the connection. For documentation purposes, I like adding the event attribute to the HTML element that initiates the event. You can decide whether you agree.

Adding dynamic sorting to your Web pages is simple when the data binding is done properly. You might want to point out to your readers that they can sort the table dynamically. In Figure 30.6, text has been added to the page to indicate that the table can be sorted. I sorted the table you see in Figure 30.6 by team earned run average by clicking the ERA column heading.

FIGURE 30.6.
Dynamic standings sorting.

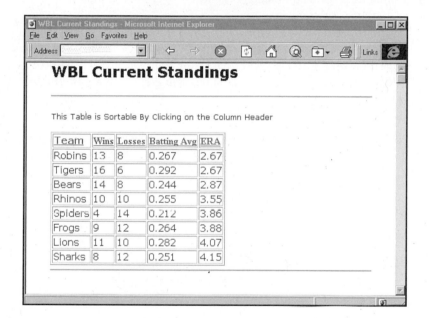

DATAFORMATAS and DATAPAGESIZE

You can use the DATAFORMATAS attribute in the same tag pair as a DATAFLD attribute to distinguish between two different types of data in a database: text and html. If you store HTML tags in the text of a database field and create a Web page data field with a DATAFORMATAS=html attribute, the Internet Explorer 4.0 Web browser formats the text using the HTML tags. In fact, you can even specify an image by storing an <IMG></IMG> tag pair in your database field. If you don't identify a DATAFORMATAS attribute, the browser uses the text type as default.

As an example of using the DATAFORMATAS attribute, consider the following <DIV></DIV> tag pair, which accesses a data source dynamically:

```
<DIV DATAFLD="Element" DATAFORMATAS=html></DIV>
```

You might have an `Element` column field that looks like this:

```
<B>Na</B> is the symbol for <I>Sodium</I>
```

The field would appear on the Web page as follows:

Na is the symbol for *Sodium*

On the other hand, the `DATAFORMATAS` attribute might be set to `text` or not appear at all, as in this example:

```
<DIV DATAFLD="Element"></DIV>
```

In that case, the field would appear on the Web page as follows:

```
<B>Na</B> is the symbol for <I>Sodium</I>
```

In the latter case, the tags actually appear as text. No doubt, you want to avoid having tags appear on your Web page as text. Still, the ability to store HTML tags in a database and let a Web browser present the formatted text and graphics is a powerful feature. More and more, Web authors will store changing data in a database. Why? Because the cost of maintaining Web pages drops significantly if the dynamically changing facts are kept separate from the static text.

You can use the `DATAPAGESIZE` attribute to identify how many rows of data you want to present to users at one time. For very long tables, users might want to manage how many rows they see at one time. You can create the controls that allow users to manage table presentations.

As an example of using the `DATAPAGESIZE` attribute, consider the following dynamic table's open `<TABLE>` tag:

```
<TABLE DATAPAGESIZE=10 id=Periodic DATASRC="#ElementTable"
```

Now a user will see only 10 records at a time when the table generates. In your scripts, you can move forward in the table by using the `.nextPage` method, or dynamically change the page size by using the `.dataPageSize` property of the table name object.

When a user clicks on a button you provide, your `onmouseclick` event can execute a script function with the following line:

```
Periodic.nextPage
```

You can change the table size dynamically to 15 records with this line:

```
Periodic.dataPageSize=15
```

Both `DATAFORMATAS` and `DATAPAGESIZE` are new Dynamic HTML attributes with powerful capabilities.

Summary

This chapter has introduced the concepts of data binding and data-awareness. Data binding is a feature of the Internet Explorer 4.0 Web browser that allows flexible data delivery by a Web author. Once a data source is bound to a Web page, a data-aware Web page stays aware of a data source that's downloaded at the same time as the page. Using dynamic HTML, you then provide a way for the reader to interact with the Web page and filter or sort the data. The data is then presented anew.

The advantages of using data-awareness include eliminating multiple Web server requests and eliminating readers' wait time. The disadvantage lies in the initial download time of the data source. The corporate world has been accessing data over a network for years, and Information Services (IS) specialists are always considering data delivery strategy trade-offs when providing new applications. Web page data-awareness brings those same trade-off decisions to the Web author. With multiple delivery strategies available, the Web author can control the best way to deliver Web page data to the user.

With Internet Explorer 4.0, you can present more than one record at a time from a data source within a Web page. Displaying only a subset of records at a time is called filtering. If you want to present the entire data source, you can set up an automatically generating and expanding table by using the appropriate Dynamic HTML tags. The table will automatically fill up with the data from the data source file you identify.

After a Web page automatically loads a data source in a file, you can indicate by which columns readers can sort the table. Readers sort a column by clicking on it with their mouses. When a sort is requested, the table dynamically regenerates and re-expands the table in the row order of the sorted column.

VII
PART

Effective Web Page Design

CHAPTER 31

Creating an Effective Interface

by Molly E. Holzschlag

IN THIS CHAPTER

Just as your smile and outward appearance help others identify what's interesting and appealing about you, a user interface is what allows Web visitors to want to stop and enjoy the bounty your site offers.

Interfaces welcome, guide, and provide the functional elements needed to help your visitor get to the information or experience he or she is seeking. Considered a critical aspect of multimedia design, a well-built interface is particularly important for the Web. If someone isn't finding the necessary information, or isn't having a meaningful adventure on your pages, he or she can simply choose to take a sharp turn off the road and visit another site—one, perhaps, that's more interesting and informative for the visitor and profitable to your competitor.

One step to avoid creating sites that act as pit-stops or U-turns on the Web's highways and byways is to be sure that the sites you build make the visitor feel comfortable and give that visitor the goods he or she is after. There are several methods for building such sites, including intelligent design as well as an attractive and *useful* site interface.

In this chapter, I'll introduce you to the basic principles of interface design and show you how to analyze your site's intent, conceive of a design that will address your audience's concerns, and create a corresponding interface using HTML techniques. The concepts and techniques in this chapter are designed both to inspire your individual creativity and to be applied immediately to your current projects.

Principles of User Interface Design

Several time-honored principles of user interface design can be applied to your Web site plans. These guidelines are drawn from other media, such as interactive CD-ROMs, kiosks, and even television! The hypermedia environment of the Web—with its links to here, there, and everywhere in the vast and complex Internet world—is often bereft of these foundational principles. The results are ill-designed interfaces that confuse and frustrate rather than inform and assist the people who visit those Web sites.

The reason for the abundance of problems with user interfaces on the Net has a lot to do with Web sites often being built by computer engineers, high school students—even fine artists—all of whom have much to contribute content-wise to the Web environment, but little or no experience in what it takes to communicate in the unusual, nonlinear structure of the Web.

TIP

Want to give me a KISS? That's right—make me happy and follow that wise, if not very nicely said, acronym for *keep it simple, stupid!* User interfaces might be complicated technologically, but they should be easy for any user to understand.

Creating an Effective Interface

CHAPTER 31

563

31

CREATING
AN EFFECTIVE
INTERFACE

The following principles can help you avoid the potholes inexperienced Web designers can find themselves driving into. Apply these ideas to the sites you build, and you stand a much better chance of a smooth ride toward your Web success.

Metaphor

In design, *metaphor* refers to the symbolic representation of the structure you're attempting to build. A metaphor acts as a familiar visual aid around which you build the entryway, interiors, windows, doors, and exits of your environment.

In fact, I used metaphor to write the previous paragraph. I defined a Web site as though it were a building—with a selection of the elements you expect to find in a building. Metaphor helps people feel comfortable because they're familiar with the rules of the setting. You can find a good example of using metaphor in the Microsoft Network, which uses a TV or radio-style metaphor by calling its areas "channels," as you can see in Figure 31.1. Users know what a channel is, so they relate easily to the concept and can interact with the interface without having to think too much about *how* to do so.

FIGURE 31.1.

The familiar TV "channel" metaphor is used on the Microsoft Network's 1997 2.0 build.

Metaphor should use common, everyday concepts that people from any part of the globe who come upon your site can understand immediately. Achieve metaphor, and you're one step closer to helping people make themselves comfortable and visit with you a while.

Clarity

To increase a visitor's desire to stay, you want to make sure he or she understands the elements in your pages. None of the critical pieces should be abstract or difficult to decipher. That's not to say abstraction as an art form isn't allowed—a good designer can use abstract art in a very clear Web site. What a good designer can't do is use abstractions when it comes to those elements needed to navigate the site, locate information, or return to important areas in the site.

Elements that fall into this category include any buttons, image maps, or links needed for site navigation. A button that leads the visitor left shouldn't have an arrow that faces up, and a link that offers a mail option shouldn't pull up your newsreader. It's that simple and that clear. Clarity is a must for precise communication.

Consistency

Consistency is not only of the utmost importance in interface design, it's also one of the skeletal necessities of a Web site. All too often, I find myself landing on a Web page and thinking "Wow, this looks great!" Then, as I move to the next page, I find myself wondering what happened to the inviting design and promise that first page offered. If I stay long enough to move through the site, backgrounds change, font styles are inconsistent, headers and navigation are completely irregular—in short, I can't tell from one page to the next where the heck in the Web world I am!

Being consistent with design elements allows for a cohesive presentation. A consistent look to your site keeps your visitors calm instead of tense, confused, and ready to take a hard left—right off of your site.

Orientation and Navigation

Following closely along with each of the previous concepts is the idea that a site visitor must know where he or she is at any given time. This principle is *orientation*. If I'm deep into a site that has hundreds of pages, it helps to know where in that site I am. It's also helpful if I have quick access to other areas of the site and can go back to where I came from if I find out I'm somewhere I really don't want, or need, to be.

Orientation is achieved by making sure each site either has a header that defines that page's purpose or another, familiar element that instantly tells me where I am. You have probably seen a variety of methods used to ensure orientation. One example can be found on the Wilde Rose Coffee Roastary site, `http://desert.net/wilderose/`. Note that an empty coffee cup helps define my location. (See Figure 31.2.) As you can tell, navigation is not only connected with orientation, but also with every individual user interface premise I've outlined. I'll explain this issue in much more depth in Chapter 32, "Navigation and Layout."

Creating an Effective Interface

CHAPTER 31

565

31

CREATING
AN EFFECTIVE
INTERFACE

31

FIGURE 31.2.

Notice that the empty coffee cup corresponds with my orientation to the current page.

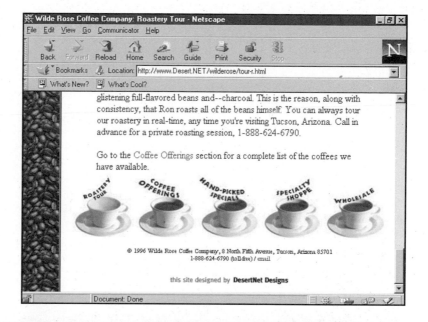

TIP

It's one, two, three clicks away! If you make your visitor click more than three times to get to the information he or she is after, you run the risk of disorienting them. Ideally, no piece of data on your site should be more than three clicks away from a related piece of data.

For now, I'll simply say that navigation is an integral part of interface design and a critical element of any Web site. It's all about getting from way over there to right where you want to be—logically, quickly, and easily.

Analyzing a Site's Intent

As with any project, one of the most important steps is to analyze your goals and plan to meet them. A good Web site is almost always well planned, or the results can be haphazard and confusing.

NOTE

Developers who have worked in corporate organizations are already familiar with the audience and intent process. However, many Web designers come to Web design by different routes. Regardless of the type of site—whether it's a corporate page or a personal one—the guidelines discussed here are always beneficial.

A good place to begin is by detailing the site's intent and then defining the audience. The comparison will let you know what directions to take in terms of short- and long-term planning, what types of technology you will need to support the design, and, of course, what kind of interface and site design will best meet your needs.

Design Intent

Begin by asking the following questions:

- What is your primary reason for having this Web site?

  Is the site's purpose point-of-sales? Or, perhaps you're interested in providing customer service or product technical support for your company. Other possible intentions for Web sites include entertainment, product advertising and promotions, information and education, news, and special-interest communities.

- What current information and content do you have and consider important to include on the site?

  Company brochures, product photos and illustrations, previous advertising campaigns, interesting programs and games, news copy, art, URLs for existing, similar-interest Web sites, and a range of other materials you already have will help define the content of your site.

- What are your short- and long-term goals for the site?

  The best way to think about short- and long-term goals for Web sites is by already knowing what your most immediate goal is. If your site intends to offer customer service for its line of notebook computers and the pressure's on to provide online support to consumers immediately, first determine which notebook models require the most services and support.

  Then, look beyond the immediate demand into the site's long-term vision. This analysis will help determine the structure of the site. You'll begin by providing what your customers need today, but you'll also save yourself a lot of headaches by planning for what they're going to want tomorrow.

Audience Intent

Now, define your audience:

- What is your demographic?

  Are you trying to sell rare books to collectors? Maybe you want to create a site that raises funds for multiple sclerosis. You might have a newspaper that caters to educated 30-somethings, or perhaps you want to create an interactive Web site for members of a particular city's gay community. No matter what your intent is, *who* you're creating for is going to affect the *way* your interface is designed.

■ What experience or information should the audience walk away with?

The answer to this question is particularly important. If you have analyzed and planned to meet every other concern, but then fail to give your visitor a specific experience, activity, or resource as he or she leaves the site, you've missed your mark. Knowing that you want a visitor to walk away armed with knowledge about family planning options or with a vacation itinerary in hand allows you to design your site to achieve that goal.

Once you've successfully answered the questions, consider your goals in the context of the demographic. This step is extremely important, because when you sit down to design and code your site, you'll have a clear idea of what type of interface to design! If your site is well-planned and organized, your efforts will be more coordinated and efficient.

Examining the information you've collected, you'll find that you now know several important things. First, you're aware of your site's intent and long-term goals. That knowledge relates to the practical design of your interface because it tells you what you need to design and how much you need to design.

Also, you know what current information is available for content, and you know who the audience is, which determines the type of interface you'll use to deliver that information to them. Finally, you know what you want your audience to gain from your Web site. You are now poised to consider the project's look and feel, breadth and scope, and page-by-page content.

A Case in Point: Microsoft Site Builder Network

A fine example of the results of defining the audience and the site's intent can be found on Microsoft's Site Builder Network. This active, continually growing site offers information, community activities such as bulletin boards and chats, and training for Web site designers. Visit the site by pointing your browser to `http://www.microsoft.com/sitebuilder/`.

In this case, the site's intent is to deliver information and services to people like you, who might be designing sites on the Internet or for your company's intranet or extranet. There are short-term goals, such as offering the latest-breaking industry news (Figure 31.3), and there are long-term goals, such as building lasting resources and a sense of community, which are provided by the site's newsgroups and feedback services. By addressing these issues, interface clarity can be achieved, too, because a clear goal results in a clearer communication of that goal.

NOTE

Internet, intranet, and extranet—oh my! What's the difference? Simply put, Internet Web sites are those found in the commonly trafficked areas of the Net. They are Web sites available to anyone with a Internet connection and Web browser. Intranets sit behind

continues

continued

boundaries, called *firewalls,* that keep the information inside a designated area. They are used to supply internal information to companies and organizations from the terminals and computers used by employees. An extranet lies in the virtual space between the Internet and an intranet. It's part of an intranet that is open to broader, but still controlled, traffic. A publishing company who sets up a special area for book buyers, other publishers, and industry-only individuals who need access to regulated facts and figures is an example of an extranet.

FIGURE 31.3.

The What's New page on the Microsoft Site Builder Network.

Microsoft's content is often generated from an internal slew of authors and designers. However, ample links to external resources are available throughout the site, which shows community spirit and offers alternatives for Web designers who are likely to be designing for platforms other than those supported by Microsoft.

The site's audience is very specific, which is the definitive issue of the success of the site's interface design. Because the audience is made up of designers, the design can be flexible and use frames and programming technologies, such as Visual Basic Script (VBScript), to deliver the goods. (See Figure 31.4.) The reason the site can use these techniques is because a Web designer is more than likely going to be equipped with the most recent browsers and higher-end hardware, plug-ins, and services.

To show how audience plays a role in how Microsoft decided to design the site interface, look at Figure 31.5. This is a screen shot of Microsoft's main company page, at http://www.

Creating an Effective Interface

CHAPTER 31

569

31

CREATING
AN EFFECTIVE
INTERFACE

microsoft.com/. The audience for this page is computer users, and perhaps can be slightly more defined by the assumption that these computer users have an interest in Microsoft products. That's pretty broad! So the interface is simpler, and although it's designed attractively with tables and graphics, it avoids using more high-end technologies, such as the interface using frames and VBScript found on the Site Builder Network's main page.

FIGURE 31.4.

The Site Builder Network's interface is built with tables, frames, and drop-down menus using VBScript.

FIGURE 31.5.

Although tables are used in Microsoft's home page, the interface avoids frames or scripts because of the broader audience base.

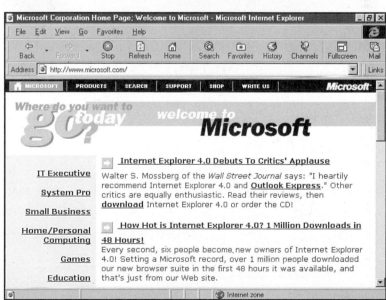

Finally, not only is the information well organized and accessible, but there's plenty of it. Visitors to this site looking for information on the latest technology, HTML, ActiveX, Java—if it's of interest to the Web designer—are going to find it and leave the site with resources galore.

Conceiving a Design

With an understanding of what user interface design consists of, what is required of you to analyze the site and audience intent, and an example of a successful interface in hand, you're ready to begin thinking about how to implement a design.

How you actually express the knowledge you've gained in terms of Web technology depends largely on what skills you have and what human and technological resources are available to you. Not everyone reading this chapter is going to have advanced HTML or design skills, but some will. Another issue is the extent of the material you intend to provide. Some reader might simply want to promote his or her professional services as a massage therapist, but someone else reading the material in this book is looking for information on how to create interfaces for a daily newspaper with feedback and chat features.

To consider these varying circumstances and supply information to help you conceive the design you have in mind, I'm first going to go over some of the site elements you'll be working with. Then I'll introduce two practical approaches to interface design: a standard-level interface that requires basic HTML and graphic skills and an advanced interface design requiring tables for layout.

> **NOTE**
>
> In Chapter 32, I'll give you even broader and more sophisticated examples of interfaces.

Common Pages in a Web Site

Here's a list of common pages in a Web site:

- Welcome page
- Content pages
- Feedback page

Other aspects you might need to accommodate include the following:

- Downloadable media (programs, files, sound, and video)
- Inline media (audio, video, and multimedia presentations that run within the browser's parameters)

■ Search functions

■ Chat rooms, bulletin boards, and newsgroups

The challenge now is to incorporate the common elements and special aspects into a single, integrated format. A welcome page can be very different in look and feel from a content-laden page, and content pages are different from those that need to support inline media, such as a Surround Video presentation of the new car your company is unveiling.

By using the foundations you've learned, such as consistency, clarity, orientation, and well-designed navigation, you should have little trouble keeping even the largest site conceptually joined from page to page.

The Front Door

The first part of interface design is deciding what the virtual front door of your site is going to look like, and how that front door will integrate with the site's content pages. Some designers prefer to have a page that's predominantly graphical, much like a traditional magazine cover. Other designers like a functional greeting, or *splash page*, with graphics as well as navigational options available, but some designers take the stance that because people want to get to the information fast, a splash page is a waste of time.

Each individual client and site is going to have unique needs, so I advise you to use the research you've conducted on goals and audience to determine what's going to work best in a given scenario. Some designers choose to have a splash page; others don't. Either way, it's critical that you're consistent with your design.

> **CAUTION**
>
> The glue of a site is integration, so if you do have a splash page, and that page looks nothing like your internal pages, you have no interface. Be sure to keep a cohesive look and feel between your pages!

A good splash page should convey the site's identity as well as introduce some of the site's design elements, such as color, shape, typography, and texture. (See Figure 31.6.)

If you choose not to have a splash page, it's wise to make sure a visitor is welcomed on your home page. Even if you have a lot of information and detailed navigation on that first page, be sure to let your visitor know who you are and why you are there. It's also handy to tell or suggest to the site visitor what you hope he or she will experience or gain from the visit.

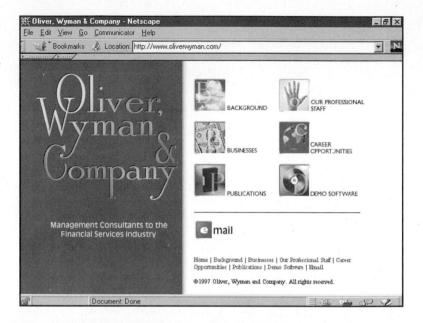

NOTE

Are there any exceptions to rules such as "Always have a welcome" or "Identify yourself on a splash page?" Yes, but they're determined by your audience and intent, and any exceptions tend to be for entertainment, games, or artistic sites rather than corporate, consumer, or customer service sites.

Remember, your front door is the first opportunity you have to make people feel welcome and interested in the content to come. Think carefully and apply the principles of user interface design to get an instant rapport with your visitors!

Content Pages

As a visitor continues to move through a site, each page should offer a combination of consistent and new features. Traits such as color palettes and fonts can provide consistency, and fresh components can be added by using a variety of layouts, graphics, and other multimedia options.

In Figure 31.6, the stage is set for the Oliver Wyman site. The color palette is introduced, as are metaphors such as the newspaper icons for news and the sky background icon for company background information.

The objective in terms of an interface is to keep each page interesting so that visitors are compelled to see what's coming next, not just in terms of the information you have to impart, but also in terms of the visual panorama that unfolds as they move throughout the site. By the time

31

CREATING
AN EFFECTIVE
INTERFACE

a visitor moves to an internal page of the Wyman site, he or she has already been introduced to specific traits. With that as a foundation, the designer can add new layouts and design elements. This progressive addition of information protects consistency and avoids causing the visitor problems with orientation. (See Figure 31.7.)

FIGURE 31.7.

The Oliver Wyman content pages maintain a consistent but interesting look, keeping visitors engaged with the site.

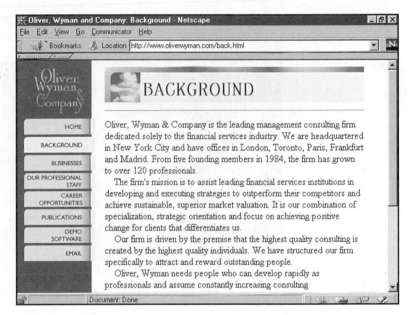

Feedback Forms

You should also consider feedback forms as part of a design. Many good designers keep a consistent look and feel in a site and suddenly lose that consistency because they didn't design the feedback form to be neat, attractive, and reflective of the site's concept.

Keep your colors, fonts, and layouts intact when dealing with forms. Wherever possible, align the right end of feedback fields with one another. This alignment creates a neat, tidy appearance, which addresses the issue of clarity. Web site visitors might not consciously be aware of why your forms are so easy to use, but they will appreciate it and remember your site as a convenient one they'll use again and even recommend to interested friends.

Special Considerations

The three elements covered so far—welcome pages, content pages, and feedback pages—are the most commonly used in Web sites. However, there's an increasing demand both by the competitive industry and hungry audiences to provide a variety of highly interactive content using advanced scripting, database, multimedia, and Web programming techniques.

Figure 31.8 shows an example of a multimedia exhibit on the Arizona-Sonora Desert Museum Web site (`http://desert.net/museum/`), which requires a good-sized chunk of the page's space. Therefore, the interface design might have to adjust to accommodate the media. How do you maintain cohesion in your interface's design when so much of the space is being used by an object?

FIGURE 31.8.

Multimedia events can take up large chunks of a page's available space.

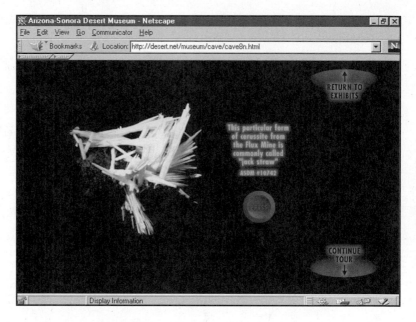

If you jumped to answer that question and your responses involved consistency, clarity, and maintenance of similar elements from other parts of the site, you're on the track to addressing the greatest challenge in interface design. Specific examples would include sticking to the color palette and font choices, keeping the visitor oriented, and maintaining consistent navigation media within these pages.

Interface Design: Standard HTML

Now that you have the theoretical and planning-oriented concepts behind you, it's time to start applying your creative ideas and research results to the practice of Web site design. In step with the KISS method, the idea is to start simple and build from there.

An attractive and practical interface can be built from standard HTML. I'm not talking fancy tables, frames, or complex graphic and multimedia techniques; I'm describing accessible, straight-forward design that even a Web design novice can accomplish well. The trick, aside from un-derstanding interfaces, is knowing what goes into a standard page.

In this section, I'll show you three important elements necessary for a content page and give you a few tips and tricks along the way to make sure your page, although simple, looks really good. Next, I'll integrate that information with the concepts you've already learned about splash pages, attach a simple form to the final product, and voilà! You'll have yourself a Web interface. In fact, you have the concept of a basic Web site.

Standard Page Elements

To address the issues of navigation, orientation, clarity, and providing functional information in your pages, begin by ensuring they contain the following elements:

- **Header:** A header states the page's name or purpose. Headers can be created very simply with text, but preferably use a graphic that incorporates some style element of the page design. Headers allow for clarity and orientation by telling the visitor exactly where in the site he or she is.

- **Body text:** The text in a page fulfills the concern of content, interest, and site experience. For the sake of clarity, it should be well-written, concise, and use a voice appropriate to the subject.

- **Navigation:** Whether you use buttons, an image map, text navigation, or a combination of these methods, what's important is to always make sure your site visitor can get anywhere in the site within three clicks of the mouse.

- **Site identification:** Each page should have some element that lets the visitor know the name of the site, reinforcing orientation and clarity. A good place to do this is in the <TITLE> tag, so that the site's name and the specific page in question are identified at the top of the browser. Another good—and practical—method of identifying the site is supplying the copyright information at the bottom of the page. This information identifies the site and supplies a legal demonstration of your copyright.

- **Contact:** Accessibility to the site's owner or appropriate contact personnel is very important. By creating a simple mailto link on each of your pages, you've immediately strengthened your user interface design in terms of function. For more information on mailto links, refer to Chapter 12, "Understanding Uniform Resource Locators."

That's all, you say? The answer, in terms of a simple page, is a simple "yes!"

Case Study: Cornucopia

Given these components, examine Figure 31.9, where I've created a fictitious content page based on all the interface concepts introduced earlier in this chapter, as well as the elements described in the previous section. Using simple HTML and free clip art from Caboodles (http://www.caboodles.com/), the page illustrates what can be done even by a novice who has some creative ideas and good foundations.

FIGURE 31.9.
Cornucopia's Herb Garden.

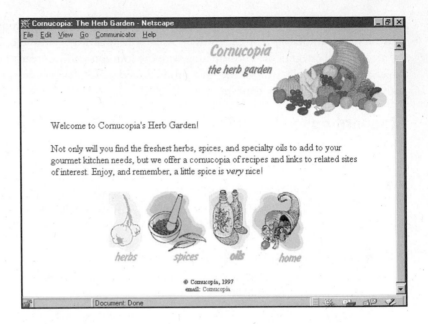

This site's intent is primarily to sell the specialty gourmet products the company offers. The audience is quite broad—people of all nationalities love to cook, as do both men and women and people from a range of age groups, including children to more mature people. Because of my broad demographic, a standard, simple site design and interface is the best way to go.

I'm going to examine the site's interface components, and then discuss them in terms of application. A look at the underlying HTML will also help you to see first-hand what the underpinnings of a standard HTML user interface look like.

- **Metaphor:** This page's example shows the use of metaphor quite clearly. Because the site is a retail gourmet foods shop, I went for the concept of a cornucopia, suggesting abundance, color, and zest, as well as the natural relationship to all the individual herbs, spices, and products visually represented in the headers and navigation.

- **Clarity:** Note that my choice of metaphor is very simple. There are no abstractions here; every graphic choice is a globally identifiable element. This cornucopia metaphor ensures that the site visitor is absolutely clear about what I'm trying to express in this site.

- **Consistency:** I've achieved consistency by making all the images logical, using one style font for the headers and navigation, and staying within a range of colors. Although you can't see the colors in this example, I do go into more depth on palette control in Chapter 33, "Managing Web Color and Graphics." Another consistent aspect of this site example can be found a bit later on, when I add a splash page and a feedback form. You'll see how I repeat elements to get the cohesion required of effective user interfaces.

■ **Orientation and navigation:** The header identifies not only the name of the site, but also the specific subject of the page, "The Herb Garden." You can get the same end-result by using the `<TITLE>` tag. Each navigation element is clearly named and represented visually. Finally, I've included a copyright notice that identifies the site at the bottom of the page.

Cornucopia: The HTML Structure

Not only is the site intentionally simplistic for the sake of the audience, it's also an example of what can be done with very little working knowledge of HTML. Granted, the site isn't likely to win a prize for its cutting-edge design, but that's not what this example is trying to show. In fact, a more contemporary or aggressive design might get in the way of the broad-based audience and the easy experience I want my site visitors to have.

Here's the code for the sample page. Pay special attention to the way I've used the title, provided `alt` arguments for images, and made sure to code the copyright and `mailto` elements.

Listing 31.1. HTML structure example: Cornucopia.

```
<html>
<head>
<title>Cornucopia: The Herb Garden</title>
</head>
<body bgcolor="#FFFFFF" text="#000000" link="#CC0000" vlink="#66FF00"
alink="#FFFFFF">

<img src="corn-hed.gif" width=315 height=140 border=0 align="right"
alt="cornucopia header">
<br clear="all">

<blockquote>

Welcome to Cornucopia's Herb Garden!
<p>

Not only will you find the freshest herbs, spices, and specialty oils to add
to your gourmet kitchen needs, but we offer a cornucopia of recipes and links
to related sites of interest. Enjoy, and remember, a little spice is
<i>very</i> nice!
<p>

<blockquote>

<div align="center">

<nobr>

<a href="herbs.htm"><img src="herb.gif" width=57 height=120 border=0
➥ alt="herbs"></a>

<a href="spice.htm"><img src="spice.gif" width=103 height=120 border=0
➥ alt="spices"></a>
```

continues

Listing 31.1. continued

```
<a href="oils.htm"><img src="oils.gif" width=67 height=125 border=0
alt="specialty oils"></a>

<a href="home.htm"><img src="home.gif" width=91 height=120 border=0
alt="return home"></a>

</nobr>
<p>

<font size=1>
&copy Cornucopia, 1997<br>
email: <a href="mailto:corny@cornucopia.biz">Cornucopia</a>
</font>

</div>

</body>

</html>
```

Adding a Splash Page and Feedback Form

To round out the example and give you a good visual sense of what a simple interface can do, I've also created a splash page for Cornucopia and a feedback form for folks to get in touch.

The splash page, shown in Figure 31.10, uses a simple cornucopia, which is a colorful visual introduction. Beneath that, I've placed a subtitle indicating the site's intent. Finally, I've included text links to main sections of the site, including the content page examined earlier. I've chosen to place these links on the splash page to ensure clarity, and I've opted to use text rather than graphical links because I want to reinforce the types of products and information available in the site.

In Figure 31.11, you can see that I've created a feedback form. Note that I've kept the same header used earlier intact, although I've changed the subtitle for page identification. I've also aligned the left edges of input fields and kept the right edges to a minimum.

The end result is a site interface that's easy to use, simple to make, and accomplishes its intent.

> **NOTE**
>
> To create margins on pages where I'm not using tables, I always make use of the <BLOCKQUOTE> tag. This method ensures that my text has margins around it by providing *white space*, an important part of effective visual design.

FIGURE 31.10.
Cornucopia's splash screen.

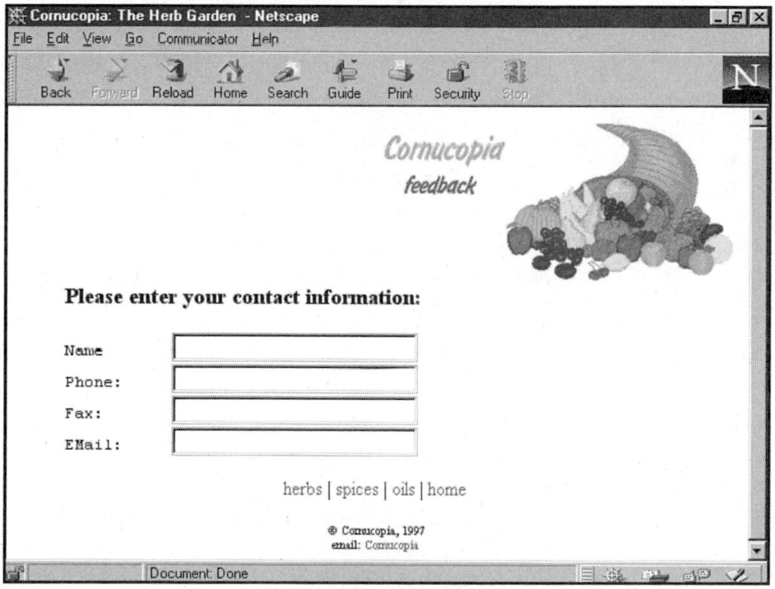

FIGURE 31.11.
A well-designed feedback form.

Designing Advanced Interfaces

As you become more adept at using HTML, you can begin trying advanced techniques, such as tables and frames, for an effective site interface. As you saw previously with the Microsoft examples, this approach can be very effective for the right audience.

In this section, I'm going to show an example of a table-based interface and step it through the same analysis as the standard interface. The reason I'm repeating that step is to let you compare and contrast two different interfaces that are successful because they're made of the *same* conceptual components.

Case Study: Molly.Com

I'm using one of the incarnations of my own Web site, which can be found by pointing your browser to `http://www.molly.com/`. Because my audience is a bit more specific than the one for the previous example, I knew that I could use tables, as well as a more abstract look to the site, as shown in Figure 31.12, which is a content page in the site. This shows how important the preliminary questions of audience and intent are, regardless of the type of site you're working on.

FIGURE 31.12.

A content page from molly.com.

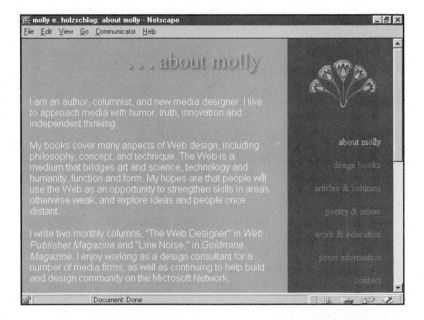

- **Metaphor:** Note that there are only two graphics on this page. One is the page header, and the other is a hand-drawn lotus blossom. The blossom, appearing in the same place on every content page, is an abstract, yet consistent, element in the site. The metaphor expresses a feminine touch and relates to my work in aesthetics (design) and creative expression (writing and music).

- **Clarity:** Although my use of metaphor is subtle, each page is clearly defined, and the content of each page is straightforward. This clarity lets people relate to the information on the site without having questions as to what the site is about.

- **Consistency:** The look of all the internal pages is the same, and the splash page, as shown in Figure 31.13, contains color and navigation elements that are found on each page of the site. These elements, along with carefully selected font styles for headers and text, make the site consistent.

FIGURE 31.13.

The splash page from `http://www.molly.com/.`

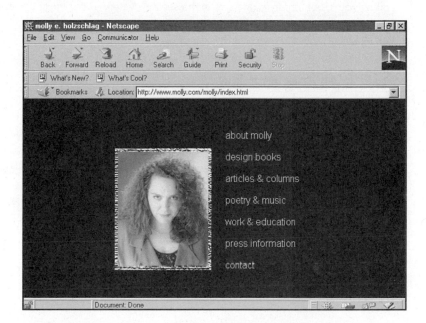

- **Orientation and navigation:** I use no graphical navigation in this site. Every page is accessible from the right-hand margin list of links. Headers clearly mark the individual page's content, and every main page is one click away from another within the site.

molly.com: The HTML Structure

Working with tables can be a Web designer's first entrance into high-style design. The combination of interface issues, such as consistency, and visual texture with table styles is an excellent starting point. This combination will ultimately give you the most effective tools available for your site creation.

The code in this site, shown in Listing 31.2, is a bit more complex than that of the Cornucopia example, but an intermediate or accomplished coder can get similar results quite easily.

No matter what your level of skill is, pay close attention to the `<TITLE>` tag and the `alt` attribute in images, which help add clarity and identify them for nongraphical browsers, and take a peek at the font face attributes. Note that I use a Times font for navigation, and an Arial font for the text. The graphical headers use Times, too, which creates nice visual texture but also lends consistency.

TIP

If your fonts look too large or too small, you can adjust them by simply selecting Font options from the View menu on the toolbar. Both Netscape and Internet Explorer browsers allow you to set font style and size in the sections where you set user preferences; however, it's wise to leave them at their default settings.

Listing 31.2. Code sample from molly.com.

```
<!-- molly e. holzschlag: molly@molly.com -->

<html>
<head>
<title>molly e. holzschlag: about molly</title>
</head>
<body bgcolor="#000000" text="#FFFFCC" link="#996666" vlink="#CCCC99"
background="images/mol-bak.gif">

<table border=0 width=600 cellpadding=5 cellspacing=0>
<tr>

<td valign=top width=400>

<img src="images/ab-hed.jpg" alt="about molly header" width=300 height=50
➥align=right>
<br clear="all">
<pre>

</pre>

<font face=arial,helvetica>.

I am an author, columnist, and new media designer. I like to approach media
with humor, truth, innovation and independent thinking. <p>

My books cover many aspects of Web design, including philosophy, concept, and
technique. The Web is a medium that bridges art and science, technology and
humanity, function and form. My hopes are that people will use the Web as an
opportunity to strengthen skills in areas otherwise weak, and explore ideas
and people once distant.
<p>

I write two monthly columns, "The Web Designer" in <i>Web Publisher
Magazine</i> and "Line Noise," in <i>Goldmine Magazine</i>. I enjoy working as
a design consultant for a number of media firms, as well as continuing to help
build and design community on the Microsoft Network.
<p>

Other writing interests include music features, profiles, and reviews. I also
write poetry, prose, and exploratory fiction.
<p>
```

Music is not only a writing interest--I'm a singer, songwriter, and guitar
player with one solo album credit "Mysteries Involving Circles and Rings"
(Kept in the Dark Records, 1991). For the past several years I have been a
member of the duo Courage Sisters with Patty Sundberg.
<p>

As time goes on I realize I particularly enjoy teaching, and I am currently
developing an online masters-level course in Web design at
The New School for Social Research in New York.
<p>.

I have a B.A. in writing, and an M.A. in media studies from The New School.
I am about to pursue a Ph.D. in the humanities. My studies focus on the
consciousness of cyberspace and the use of nonlinear environments as tools
for human evolution.
<p>

Travel, cats, elephants, esoteric studies, philosophy, healing arts, and the
relationship between art and science are among my personal interests.
</font>

</td>

<td valign=top align=right width=200>

<img src="images/lotusm.gif" alt="Lotus Blossom" width=125 height=125>
<p>

<a href="molly.htm">about molly</a>
<p>.

<a href="books.htm">design books</a>
<p>

<a href="write.htm">articles & columns</a>
<p>

<a href="poems.htm">poetry & music</a>
<p>

<a href="work.htm">work & education</a>
<p>

<a href="press.htm">press information</a>
<p>

<a href="contact.htm">contact</a>
<p>

<a href="index.html">home page</a>

</td>
</tr>
</table>

</body>
</html>.

> **TIP**
>
> Always use height and width values in image strings. They are an essential aid to the browser's ability to logically deliver information.

Summary

The concepts and examples in this chapter should set you well on your way to being able to design effective interfaces with HTML. The next chapter will introduce you to concepts and methods that will advance your interface design skills.

Remember that understanding the parts of something is important to relating to it as a whole. This approach is clearly demonstrated when you study user interface design. By thinking carefully about concepts such as metaphor, clarity, and orientation, you can strengthen the parts of an interface. Analyzing audience, intent, and the type of experience you want your site visitors to have give you perspective on the big picture, leading you to more cohesive, easier to use, and, ultimately, more professional Web sites.

Navigation and Layout

by Molly E. Holzschlag

Navigation and layout are as critical to a site's design as the interface is and, in fact, are an extension of user interface design. They form the way people get to and experience the content you're offering—and if a Web visitor can't do that, you might as well not even have a Web site! Navigation and layout should be considered early in the planning stages of your sites, along with the interface. The combination, when successful, creates the groundwork for the most effective sites around and makes their site designers the most desirable in the business.

In fact, designers who have made groundbreaking discoveries in how to use the Web's nonlinear, interactive potential as a basis for navigation techniques have gotten a lot of attention for those efforts. Similarly, designers who understand the constraints of a site's visual area and create designs that maximize the computer screen's potential place themselves ahead of the game.

Why is navigation so important, you might be asking? Isn't it just a matter of offering up site section options and allowing people to go to those areas with links? Well, that's true, but there are several complications—or perhaps the better word is *opportunities*—involved in creating navigation for the Web.

The first issue is pretty straightforward: Many Web sites are enormous! They hold thousands, if not tens or even hundreds of thousands of individual pages of data. If you aren't convinced, look at a site such as Microsoft's at `http://www.microsoft.com/`.

Another issue, and one you'll see deconstructed and examined in this chapter, involves online publications. Newspapers and magazines are challenged by how to manage back issues—issues that often hold relevant information. As the content pages add up, so does the need to find a way to manage all that data, both behind the scenes and in front of them.

Finally, the Web's nonlinear environment provides a unique problem for designers accustomed to page-by-page design. With the opportunities available to a Web designer through hypermedia, linking, and multiple forms of navigation, the choices for the designer and the end-user become diverse. A Web site isn't a book, so you don't page forward or occasionally turn back a page to get to the information. Well, you *can* present information that way, but you don't necessarily want to! You want to harness that nonlinearity and offer options and excitement to your site visitors.

> **NOTE**
>
> Another example of a nonlinear environment is an interactive CD-ROM, such as an encyclopedia. Much like a Web site, specific words and images are hyperlinked to other information.

Along with navigation issues, site designers must consider how Web pages are actually laid out. Pick up that book, or a newspaper, brochure, or advertising flyer, and you'll see that the words and images are set on the paper in a variety of ways. If you look at television commercials, you'll begin to notice differences in the ways visual information is presented on the screen.

32

NAVIGATION AND
LAYOUT

Laying out Web designs isn't conceptually different from any of these familiar forms of media. What is different is the particular constraints of computer screens and the technological environment in general.

In the previous chapter, "Creating an Effective Interface," I introduced the idea that an interface is the method by which you communicate and interact with the information on the screen. I touched on issues of navigation, which are not only important when studying interface design, but also relevant to Web page layout.

The reason navigation affects layout is that not only do Web designers have to learn to create logical interfaces and familiar but interesting layouts, they must also incorporate navigation elements into the page. A newspaper or television commercial doesn't have this requirement at all, and it creates a new challenge for designers of the Web medium.

This chapter introduces you to important layout basics and focuses on navigation media and methods. Keep the ideas you've learned with your study of interfaces in mind as you read through and study the examples here, and you'll begin to see how they come together to create not only the parts of a Web page, but also a full-service site.

Designing for the Computer Screen

As you might be aware, there are many computer platforms, with two dominating the commercial market, the Macintosh and the PC. Beyond that, there are a slew of video cards and monitors. The end result is that you can never be sure who is looking at your sites and how they are viewing them.

Professional Web designers use a variety of tricks to deal with these cross-platform issues. One way to begin is by figuring out where the most common individual sits and trying to design with that in mind.

At this point, it's generally true that most people view the Web at a resolution of 640×480. That means the total viewing space available is 640 pixels wide and 480 pixels long. However, this space really isn't the design area you have to lay out your work because your browser takes up some of that space! In fact, open up your browser to any page. With the full toolbar showing, you'll see that there is space taken away from the top, the sides, and the bottom of the screen. That makes your actual width quite a bit smaller than 640, and your page length shorter.

TIP

Designers need to set their screen resolution to 640×480 and use that environment for creating and testing pages. It's wise to look at your pages in higher resolution, too, but do so only *after* making sure you've worked well within the 640×480 bounds.

Horizontal and Vertical Design

Along with the constraints browsers place on space, there's the issue of horizontal and vertical design. Anything longer than 600 pixels or so is going to either force a horizontal scrollbar (as shown in Figure 32.1) or become jumbled and not at all the design you set out to create. So the rule of thumb for horizontal layout is to set your sites on that 600-pixel width. Although some designers are venturing out and designing on the horizon, it takes a very skilled designer to do that, so I can't recommend it for most Web page creators.

FIGURE 32.1.

A horizontal scrollbar where one should not be—something good designers try to avoid.

> **NOTE**
>
> Sometimes designers can get away with horizontal design, but they must have a really good reason and excellent skills to pull it off. One interesting example of this kind of design can be found at http://www.circleoffriends.org/. (See Figure 32.2.)

Yes, 600-pixel width total does seem tight, particularly if you're used to viewing the Web at higher resolutions. Until there's a change in the common resolution, however, you're going to want to reach as many people as possible. The one normal exception here is that if you're confident everyone visiting your site is using a higher resolution—well, in that case you're free to design to those dimensions. An example of this might be an intranet environment, where the users all have the same hardware and software settings.

Vertical design is somewhat more flexible, particularly because it's more natural for Web users to scroll down to see more information. There are really only two concerns with vertical design.

FIGURE 32.2.

A horizontal scrollbar that makes sense because the site is designed to demonstrate that many spinal cord injury patients view the world differently.

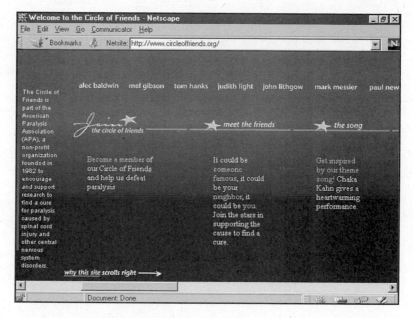

The first is that with any introductory "splash" style pages, you want to fit the important information on one screen before scrolling. In other words, a graphic that's very long and requires a visitor to scroll down to view it can look awkward and unsightly on a main page. (See Figure 32.3.) You have more flexibility with internal pages, where text and graphics mix together in a more fluid, less static fashion.

FIGURE 32.3.

This splash graphic is cut off because of the vertical constraints.

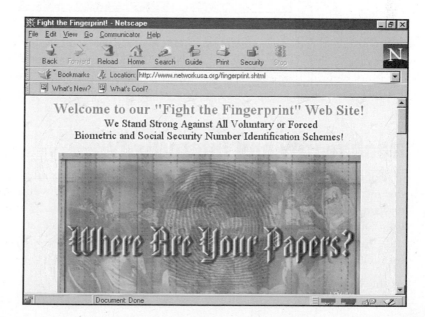

The other vertical issue is how many screens you should allow to scroll. My suggestion is that usually more than three is getting too long; at that point, you should consider moving information to another page. If you do have a long page, offering links back to the top is a nice way of making life easier on your users. (See Figure 32.4.) This is especially true as navigation works its way into the picture because convenient access to the navigation options makes your site visitor's experience a good one.

FIGURE 32.4.

Offering links back to the top is a nice thing to do for Web visitors.

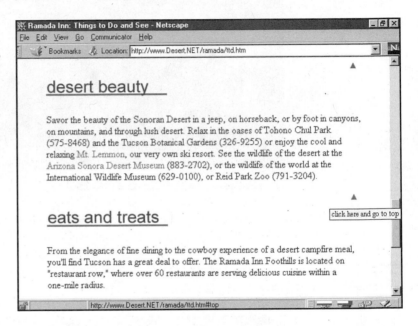

Although layout considerations are important, you can get by on the basics just described. It's pretty much a fixed area for now, although that doesn't mean there aren't more advanced layout issues you will learn, such as those introduced in Chapter 34, "Using Space, Shape, and Type." It's important to get an idea of the area you're working with and understand how navigation fits into the big picture first.

Nonlinearity and Interactivity

One of the most potent aspects of the Web is that it's a nonlinear, interactive medium. What this means is that, unlike newspapers, radio, and television, the Web isn't built on a page-forward, page-back delivery system. A newspaper in English and many other languages is read from left to right. Radio and TV provide information in a package and serve it to you with little involvement from you. Your only current, interactive choices with radio and TV are to turn them on, change the volume, switch the channel, and turn them off.

As the Web and related technologies converge, there will probably be a change in the dominant, nonlinear arrangement. But for now, instead of this limitation of choice resulting from linear thinking, many navigation choices can harness this nonlinear structure and offer up a highly interactive, individual experience for the Web visitor.

From a conceptual standpoint, linearity is like your morning drive to work. Usually you take the same road because you know it gets you there quickly, the traffic is lighter than another route, and its rhythms are familiar to you. Nonlinearity would be taking a different route to work every day—turning down an unfamiliar road just for the heck of it, maybe even going in a completely different direction for a while because the scenery is so attractive.

This example helps you see how linearity and nonlinearity both have advantages and disadvantages. It's no accident that many societies have been based on the linear. To survive and thrive, the straightest, most effective route has been necessary. It's worked to the advantage in many ways, but what's lost with this rigidity is the opportunity for new vistas and possibilities that can be found when that side road is explored.

Philosophically, this cultural phenomenon points to the possibility that a combination of linear and nonlinear methods might be the strongest way to approach a problem. If you have a bit of extra time, you might just take a different route to work this morning. Who knows what the results will be?

Because we're accustomed to the linear, the nonlinear tangents on the Web—through hyperlinks that take us off of one site and drop us in the middle of another one and multiple-choice navigation options that make each drive down the information highway a different experience—challenge the Web designer. He or she must harness the Web's tangential nature to express a given site's intent and logic to the visitor. However, making a Web site linear is denying the possibilities of the Web and the unusual places and experiences it can offer.

Navigation Media

Although there are many navigational possibilities, the graphical media and HTML methods required to carry out navigation are limited. The following elements are considered standard navigation media:

- **Text links:** These are the familiar HTML-based anchors that allow you to select a piece of text and hyperlink it to another Web document. (See Figure 32.5.) Here's an example of a text link:

  ```
  <a href="nextpage.html">Follow this link to go to the next page!</a>
  ```

- **Bullets and individual graphics:** Individual graphics can be hyperlinked by placing them within an HTML anchor. The designer can choose to create bullets (Figure 32.6) or a decorative graphic (Figure 32.7) for this purpose. The code for a hyperlinked graphic appears as follows. Note that in this case, the graphic code literally takes the place of placing the text shown in the preceding standard text link example:

  ```
  <a href="nextpage.html"><img src="images/nextpage.gif"></a>
  ```

Figure 32.5.

Here's a text link example.

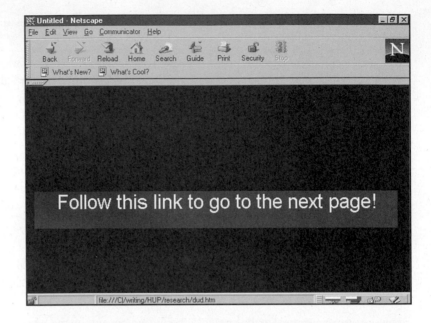

Figure 32.6.

Graphical bullets alert for hotlinks.

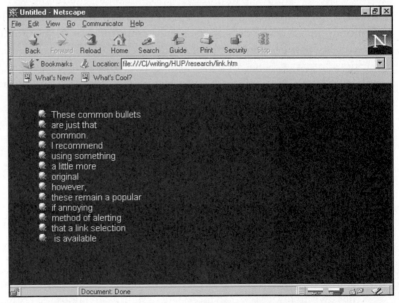

FIGURE 32.7.
Decorative buttons—
a much more
sophisticated approach.

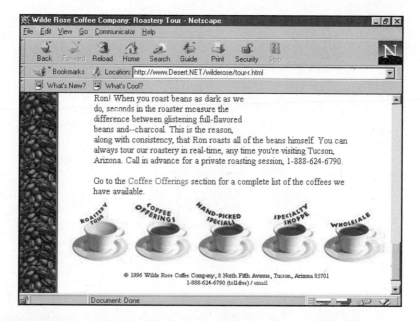

NOTE

Creating area identification by changing your navigation graphics helps differentiate the page you're on from other pages. This common design trick plays into the relationship of navigation to the orientation concept found in interface design. Notice how one of the coffee cups in Figure 32.7 is empty, signifying the page's identity.

■ **Image maps:** An image map is essentially a single graphic with the HTML anchor code matched up to specific coordinates in the map's design. Using this method means that only a single graphic—but one that has multiple navigation options—must be loaded.

The two most common types of image maps are server-side maps, which rely on the server to process the coordinate data, and client-side maps, which use the browser to process the map's information. Client-side maps, shown in Figure 32.8, are faster because they don't require a conversation with the server, so they have become the standard. Here's a sample of the client-side code from the preceding image map:

```
<MAP name="marcmap">

<AREA shape="rect" coords= "0,0,53,30" href="index.htm">

<AREA shape="rect" coords= "53,0,162,30" href="about.htm">

<AREA shape="rect" coords= "162,0,255,30" href="products.htm">
```

```
<AREA shape="rect" coords= "255,0,327,30" href="events.htm">

<AREA shape="rect" coords= "327,0,410,30" href="contact.htm">

<AREA shape="rect" coords= "0,0,440,46" nohref>

</MAP>
```

FIGURE 32.8.

A client-side image map—the text, arrow, and shadowing are all part of one graphic.

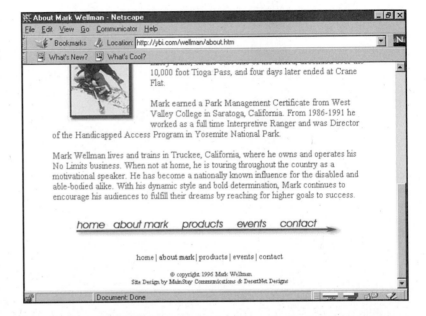

TIP

For details on server-side mapping, check with your systems administrator or Internet Service Provider (ISP) for the components necessary to create such maps. Client-side map information can be found at `http://www.spyglass.com/techspec/tutorial/img_maps.html`.

■ **Enhanced media:** Other methods of hyperlinking involve using a variety of media that perform the same function as text links or buttons, but are more similar to the code found in image maps. Enhanced media techniques include Macromedia Flash and Shockwave, in which buttons and maps can be animated and created with the link coded right into the media (Figure 32.9) and a codebase embedded into the HTML, as follows:

```
<object classid="clsid:D27CDB6E-AE6D-11CF-96B8-444553540000"
➥codebase="fsplash.cab" align="baseline" border="0" width="70" height="35">
<param name="Movie" value="button.swf">
<param name="Loop" value="False">
```

```
<param name="Play" value="True">
<param name="BGColor" value="ffffff">
<param name="Quality" value="high">
<param name="Scale" value="Showall">
</object>
```

FIGURE 32.9.

This animated button has been created with Macromedia Flash.

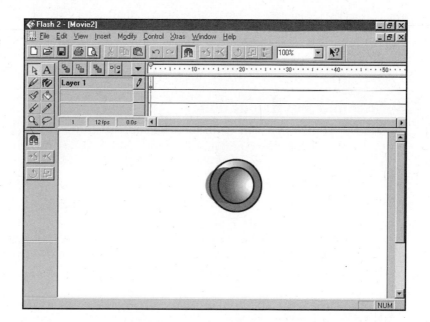

Other enhanced media can be created with advanced programming applications, such as Java, VBScript, ActiveX, and VRML (Virtual Reality Modeling Language). These sophisticated techniques require considerably more training than the straightforward text, graphic, and mapping options. However, the results can be very rewarding because they add new levels of functionality to the more conventional methods of navigation seen in most Web sites.

TIP

Looking for more information on enhanced media navigation options? For Flash and Shockwave, visit http://www.macromedia.com/. Java information abounds at its parent site, Sun Microsystems, at http://www.javasoft.com/. VBScript and ActiveX resources can be found on the Microsoft Sitebuilder Network at http://www.microsoft.com/sitebuilder/.

Navigation Options

Along with media selection, a Web designer must also choose where on the page to place navigation options. As the control of layout through HTML becomes more flexible, so do the options available to the designer.

Typically, a designer chooses to have one primary route of navigation, such as top, bottom, left-margin, or right-margin positioning. Then, he or she might add other options, which result in more choice for the Web site visitor—and, therefore, added interactivity!

Bottom and Top Navigation

Bottom-based options are perhaps the most common navigation system. You can create them with any of the standard navigation media, with a traditional layout approach, or with tables and frames. These choices give you maximum flexibility when deciding how to approach a given Web project.

Why use top navigation? The reason is to create a navigable interface *without* cutting into the precious content space found on the first screen of a Web page. However, top-aligned navigation must always be approached with care because the top area is one of the first places the eye naturally falls. If you have elements there that distract the visitor from the site's main intent, you run the risk of losing that visitor's interest.

> **NOTE**
>
> For some great reading about the Internet from those who live and work with it daily, visit Start Reading. Not only do the articles cover several visionary and vocal topics, but the page is a prime example of top navigation that doesn't interfere with other page elements. You can find it at `http://home.microsoft.com/reading/voices.asp`.

This caution doesn't mean you shouldn't use top-aligned navigation. However, you should do so carefully, so as not to interfere with other important information that should be placed at the top of the page. Make sure the navigation is easy to use and integrated well into the site's architecture. If you integrate elements and have other, immediate items to pull the eye away from the navigation, you'll get a better balance of navigation and content-related items.

> **TIP**
>
> How do you make top-aligned margins flush with the top of the browser? You can do this by controlling top margins in the `<BODY>` tag, but only Microsoft's Internet Explorer (IE) can read that. Style sheets are a method that both the IE 3.0 and Netscape 4.0 browsers support, and you can use style sheets to set your top margins to 0.

The "how" aspect of top-aligned navigation is as straightforward as it is for bottom-based options, both in layout and in media such as text links, graphic buttons, and image maps. You can do it most successfully by using frames or tables, covered in the following section; each method has unique potential and the usual package of quirks.

Top Navigation: Methods

Tables are often used on pages where control of placement is critical. They allow a designer to designate where he or she wants each piece of a design to go. Buttons can be fixed in position, as can image maps and even text.

Frames are often used for top navigation, too. The advantage of frames is that they create a navigation area that remains static throughout a visit to the Web site. Instead of pages reloading information, the top frame stays in place. Not only does this feature allow for a constant reference point, but it also decreases pages' load times because the focus is now on loading only content, not navigation.

> **TIP**
>
> Two good sources for navigation information using tables and frames are at the browser's home sites. Netscape can be found at `http://home.netscape.com/` and Microsoft has the vast SiteBuilder Network for Web developers at `http://www.microsoft.com/sitebuilder/`.

One common mistake in using frames for navigation is creating a small frame for a lot of information. In other words, if you're making a frame that's only 75 pixels in height, make sure your content fits inside those boundaries with some white space to cushion it. Otherwise, you end up forcing people to read data in a tiny space. Cramped content is unattractive from a design standpoint and impractical and inconvenient for your Web site visitors.

Bottom Navigation: Methods

Standard navigation methods use simple HTML, text, and graphics or image maps to achieve the design. These methods are straightforward and often elegant but don't offer as much control as table- or frame-based methods.

When using tables to control bottom navigation, I like to remember the lessons on designing interfaces. How can you best achieve an attractive design? Tables give you a lot of control over individual elements—graphics, text, and navigation—so think of the entire page as an integrated whole. Bottom navigation should work in concert with the other page elements to create a true interface.

For the frame-based method, the advantages are similar to those for top-based navigation. First, your navigation is fixed; it can be on any page you want it to without reloading, and it maintains a consistent presence even as you switch from content page to content page. You also have the flexibility of creating frames with or without borders. (See Figure 32.10.) And, as with a frame-based, top alternative, a bordered frame gives you the option of offering resizing for maximum screen control.

FIGURE 32.10.

This page uses tables and borderless frames to control its tight, stylish interface.

Tables

Borderless frame

Left and Right Margin Navigation

A popular method of designing navigation is by using standard, table-based, or frame-based methods to control margin navigation.

As with top and bottom options, the standard right- or left-sided examples allow great flexibility in terms of media. Frame-based navigation keeps that portion of the page static, while the targeted section loads the information. Using tables gives you maximum control of design.

Left and Right Margins: Methods

It's important to focus on one of the most common Web conventions: the table-based margin background. You've seen this technique often—a strip along the left or right margin of color and design, followed by a solid color or textured field that holds the body of text. (See Figure 32.11.)

As mentioned in the previous section on layout, the designer must consider the constraints of cross-platform design. There are several considerations for backgrounds.

FIGURE 32.11.
A standard table-based margin background.

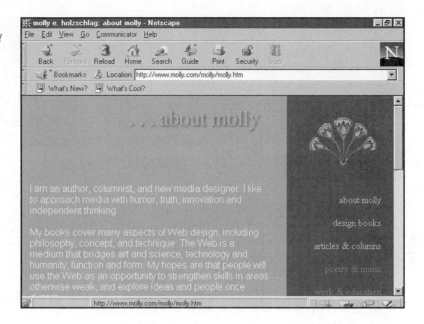

I recommend building all your backgrounds to a pixel width of 1024 or higher! Am I contradicting myself, you ask? Not exactly. Consider that most computer users are using a 640-pixel width, but the *next* most common width on the Web is probably 800 pixels. The higher resolutions, such as 1280 or above, aren't that common. However, if I don't anticipate the possibility of those higher resolutions when it comes to backgrounds, I'm going to end up with a repetition problem, as shown in Figure 32.12.

FIGURE 32.12.
A too-narrow background will repeat.

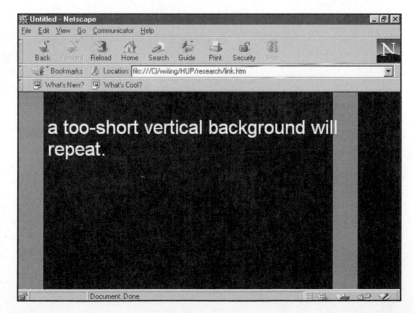

> **NOTE**
>
> Want to know more about backgrounds? The Background FAQ maintained by Mark Koenen is available at `http://www.sci.kun.nl/thalia/guide/color/faq.html`.

Next, place your margin within a field you can control. For a left margin, that means starting at the extreme left and ending where you've left enough natural space for content at low resolution. The total margin is then usually no wider than 200 pixels, with 400 or so remaining for the text and content in the right field.

Conversely, a background created for a right margin must allow the text and content field to run the appropriate width (approximately 400–450 pixels). The right margin design begins at that point, continuing on for the remaining amount of the total 1024. By doing this, you've solved part of the problem causing horizontal scrollbars and avoided repeating background designs.

Frame Navigation for Right and Left Margins

As with top and bottom navigation, the advantage of frame-based navigation is that there's a static section. Whether you choose to use a right or left margin frame, with or without borders, is entirely up to your own design and layout requirements and tastes.

The same spatial issues are true for all navigation options, and considering the design space is an imperative. How much room do you have? Aside from working within pixel limitations, you need to test your work in a variety of browsers to see if there are any slight differences from example to example.

> **NOTE**
>
> Looking for more information on how to build sites with tables and frames? *Laura Lemay's Web Workshop: Guide to Designing with Style Sheets, Tables, and Frames* by Molly E. Holzschlag (Sams.net Publishing) is a great place to walk through individual tasks. In that book, I teach you how to use these techniques in a step-by-step method that makes the process understandable for anyone with a basic knowledge of HTML.

You now have the information to prepare you to select navigation for all margins, as well as create interfaces with navigation and appropriate layout. The next step is to examine how these techniques are used in a variety of examples to clearly demonstrate the power of layout and navigation in the Web medium.

> **NOTE**
>
> Navigation isn't the only use for a frame- or table-based section. You can use the areas however you'd like—you're not limited to what you've learned here. Advertising is one common example of how a frame or table section is set aside for a use other than navigation.

Multiple Navigation in Action

Now I'm going to show you a highly successful method of harnessing and taking advantage of the opportunities of nonlinear structures and interactivity. It might be a familiar example to those of you who have followed my work because I use it often to demonstrate nonlinear, choice-driven design.

The Tucson Weekly remains the best example on the Web for demonstrating multiple methods of navigation. In fact, the publication has actually expanded its interactivity over time. Perhaps this publication's early entrance into the Web medium, combined with the innovative mind of its designer, Wil Gerken, has given it the edge over other publications and Web sites that attempt, but have difficulty in achieving, nonlinearity.

> **NOTE**
>
> Visit the Tucson Weekly at `http://www.tucsonweekly.com/tw/`.

The intention of this section is to offer the inner workings to you, showing you why the navigation is so extraordinary at giving the Web visitor an effective site that captures, but doesn't control, the Web's underlying tangential environment.

The primary way the Tucson Weekly has achieved this "capture without control" concept is by supplying many methods of navigating the site, as well as offering ways of jumping off to other related, but out-of-house, sites.

Here's an overview of the paper's structure and navigation and what it accomplishes:

- **Splash page entrance:** The splash page is the main access to the paper and its sections. It changes each week to accommodate the current cover. (See Figure 32.13.)
- **Table-based right-margin navigation:** The primary sections of the paper are offered up in a right-margin image map, so no matter what section of the paper you're in—a section or content page—you can jump to another. (See Figure 32.14.)

Figure 32.13.

The Tucson Weekly splash page.

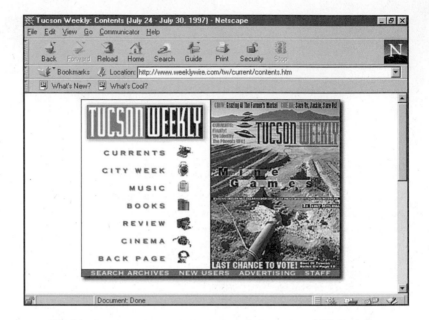

Figure 32.13.

The Tucson Weekly splash page.

Figure 32.14.

The right-margin image map, used for jumping to other areas of the site.

A right-margin image map

■ **Bottom-based text option of right-margin navigation:** The primary sections can be reached through a text option at the bottom of the page. (See Figure 32.15.)

FIGURE 32.15.

Bottom-based text links to get to the site's primary sections.

Bottom-based text links

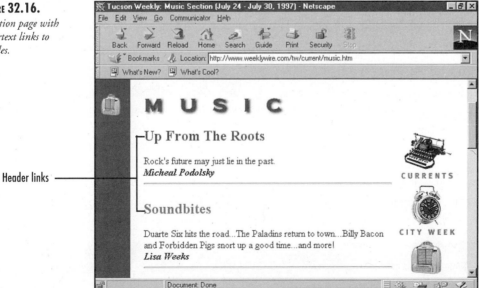

Text-based links to internal pages: Sections are broken down into links to articles and related online forums within the Tucson Weekly site. (See Figure 32.16.)

FIGURE 32.16.

A section page with hypertext links to articles.

Header links

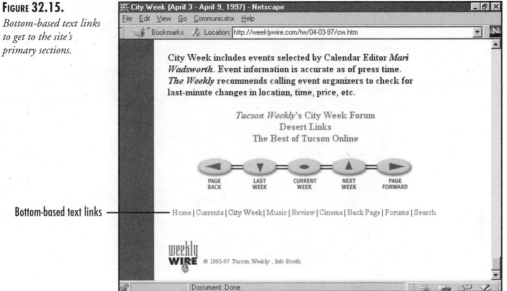

■ **Internal page links:** Text links within articles jump out to the Internet to offer related information on a given subject discussed in the article, as shown in Figure 32.17.

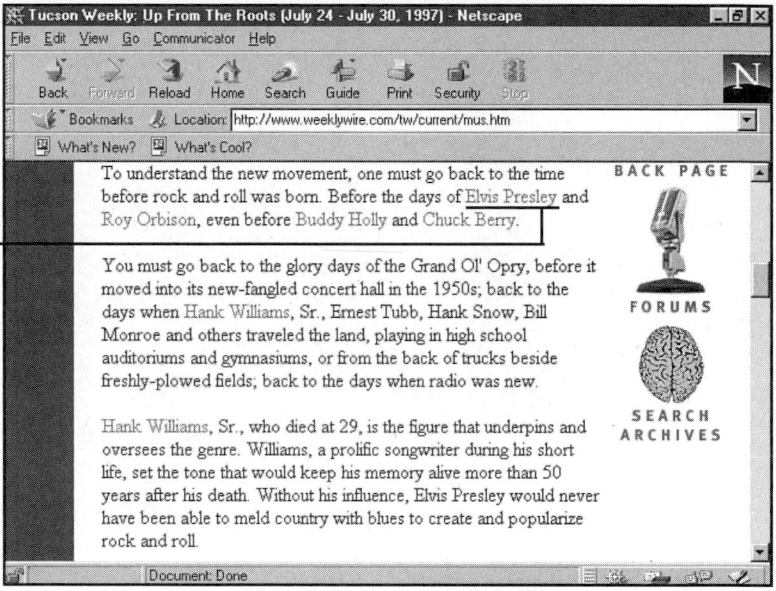

FIGURE 32.17.

An article with hypertext links to the Internet.

Text link

■ **Internal page main menu:** This menu is the shining glory of the Weekly's navigation. It offers a linear option in the guise of page-forward and page-back. Then, it adds nonlinear tangents to last week's issue, and next week's issue (if you're in an archived section of the paper), as well as a "jump" to the current week's edition. No matter where you are in terms of time and space—the date or place of the publication—you can get to any other spot in the paper with a few clicks of the mouse. (See Figure 32.18.)

■ **Weekly Wire menu:** A side-by-side graphic menu to take you to other offerings of this unparalleled online publishing company, including The Weekly Wire home page and sister projects. (See Figure 32.19.)

■ **Advertising:** At the top of Tucson Weekly pages, local and national advertisers are given ad space. (See Figure 32.20.)

NOTE

For another look at nonlinear navigation created by the same designers for another paper, visit the Albuquerque Alibi at http://www.desert.net/alibi/.

FIGURE 32.18.

The Tucson Weekly's shining example of nonlinear navigation.

An internal page main menu

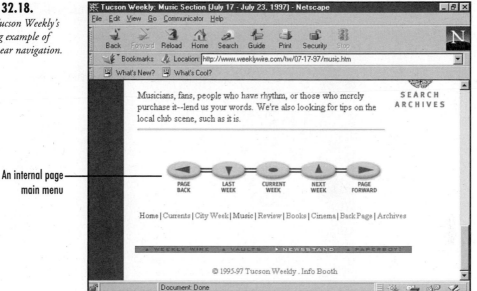

FIGURE 32.19.

The Weekly Wire Menu.

A navigation graphic

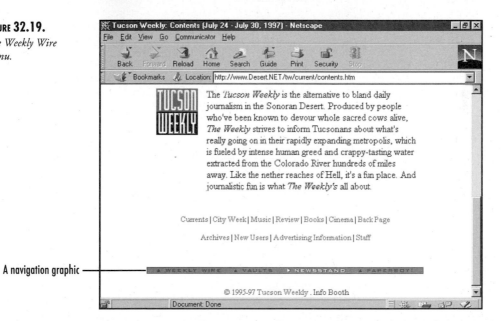

FIGURE 32.20.
Advertising on the Tucson Weekly.

An advertising link —————

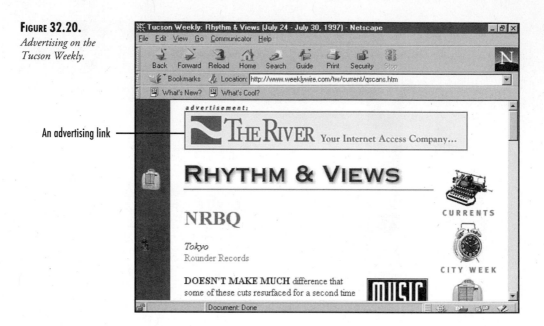

Exhausted yet? I am! Keep in mind that the Tucson Weekly is processed every week, delivered to the Web site the Wednesday evening *before* the print paper is available, and—here's the magic—takes only several hours per week to put together. The way that's done remains a trade secret, but should inspire you to think big and think originally. Use the example of layout and imaginative navigation in this section to push yourself to new levels of design.

Summary

It's easy to see how so many options might actually detract from the enjoyment of a Web site. The Tucson Weekly demonstrates what you learned in this chapter by showing a sophisticated, multiple-method approach to navigation. The nonlinear environment is captured, with the relationship between it and the linear thought process helping the visitor experience interactivity without getting lost.

Using standard elements such as a right navigation menu, bottom menus, text and graphical links, the blue margin background—each of these things serve as visual grounding because you understand them. They aren't foreign to you. However, it's the *way* in which they're combined and used that's unusual and even visionary. The main thing to remember is that none of these efforts are beyond your talents; in fact, they could inspire fresh and unique ways of approaching Web design.

Managing Web Color and Graphics

by Molly E. Holzschlag

IN THIS CHAPTER

I enjoy being described as colorful. I take it to be a compliment because color is vibrant, energetic, and interesting. Web sites should also be vibrant, energetic, and interesting to make them lively and engaging for your site visitors.

Color is an essential element of design. However, successfully using it on the Web is a challenge for most designers. Color control on the Web is limited because of differences in computer platforms, video monitors, and Web browsers.

But rest easy! Careful Web designers can follow some specific—and easy—guidelines that will help them make good, stable choices in terms of visual style and technical know-how. This chapter introduces you to both the concepts *and* techniques necessary to making your Web sites colorful.

Color Palettes: Individual Style

Begin by planning your site's individual color palette to give you a strong foundation for selecting HTML-based background colors, text colors, link colors, and the colors you'll use in graphics. Your color selections for a specific site should be drawn from your knowledge of the audience, the subject matter, and the client's desires. Remember that color communicates emotion, so choose with that in mind.

A hip magazine (see Figure 33.1) is going to have a distinctly different individual color palette than a more sedate but still attractive daily newspaper (see Figure 33.2). Wired's audience enjoys the neon colors, which tend to evoke action, movement, and an on-the-edge sensation, much as primary colors do. This vibrant look is right-on when it comes to Wired's audience, but wouldn't be appropriate for a more traditional publication. The Arizona Daily Star's design uses more subtle color, focusing on black, white, and blue with touches of reds. These colors give a sense of a crisp, clean environment. Visitors to the site naturally shift their focus to the content, without paying too much attention to the design—and this effect is exactly what you want for a daily newspaper.

However, you certainly wouldn't want to switch the color schemes! Neon colors on a relatively conservative daily paper simply won't cut it. If a individual client loves the look of Wired but has an audience of older adults, it might be wise to let him or her in on how these colors could affect their visitors.

Safe Color

The next step is to understand the "safe" palette. This is a palette with 216 colors that are going to remain stable from one browser to another, between platforms, and at different monitor resolutions. Photoshop 4.0 users are in luck—a safe palette is built right into the program. Those with other versions of Photoshop can transfer a safe palette and install it right into the program from Web graphic guru Lynda Weinman's site, `ftp://luna.bearnet.com/pub/lynda/`. Look for the filename `bclut2.aco`.

FIGURE 33.1.

*Wired magazine,
at* http://www.
wired.com/,
uses neon colors.

FIGURE 33.2.

*A more sedate approach
is seen in the Arizona
Daily Star, at* http://
www.azstarnet.com/.

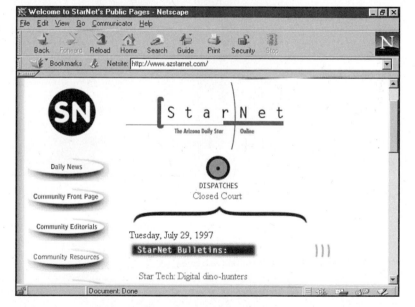

You'll also want to grab `nvalue.gif`, which gives you the entire range of browser-safe colors with their corresponding RGB (red, green, blue) *and* hexadecimal values. RGB values are derived from a method that numerically determines how much red, green, and blue make up the color in question. Hexadecimal is the base sixteen number system, which consists of the numbers 0–9 and the letters A–F. A byte (8 bits) can be represented by using two hexadecimal characters, which make any combination of binary information less cumbersome to understand. In relation to Web color, hexadecimal values *always* appear with six characters.

You can find the hexadecimal value of any color on your own by using a scientific calculator. In Photoshop, pass your cursor over any color. The "info" pop-up displays the individual red, green, and blue values of the color in the form of numbers. (See Figure 33.3.) Simply enter each of these values into the scientific calculator (because I'm using Windows 95, I can use the scientific calculator right on my machine, as shown in Figure 33.4; just choose Scientific from the calculator's View menu), and switch to the radio button marked Hex. The calculator then gives you an alphanumeric combination for the corresponding color value.

FIGURE 33.3.

RGB values as displayed by PhotoShop 4.0.

Say I have a palette that includes a medium gray. The red value in my example is 153; the hexadecimal value is 99. Now I'll complete the same process for the green and blue values. Note that a 0 for a red, green, or blue value is going to be written as 00 for these purposes. You should always end up with a total of six characters. The result of my RGB-to-hexadecimal conversion for the medium gray color is 999999 because all the values were 153. Different colors will get different combinations; some with all the same numeric values, and others in pairs, such as CC9900.

Creating the Individual Palette

To create an individual palette, select between three and five colors from the safe palette; a sample is shown in Figure 33.5. Be sure you have at least one light color and one dark color in your chosen spectrum. Ideas can be drawn from nature, your surroundings, or from a variety of design books. Knowing in advance which colors dominate your site will give your site a cohesive, stylish look.

FIGURE 33.4.

Use the scientific calculator in Windows 95 for quick hex conversions.

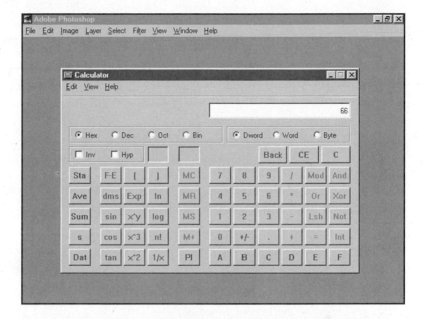

FIGURE 33.5.

I've used grayscale colors to demonstrate the palette in this book, but you'll want to be more adventurous!

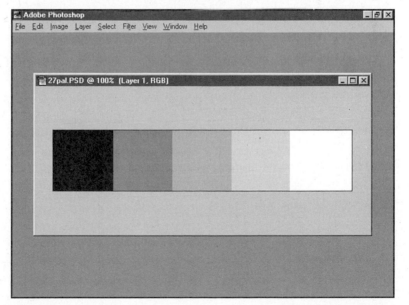

> **TIP**
>
> A great resource for color inspiration is the book `Color Harmony: A Guide to Creative Color Combinations` by Hideaki Chijiiwa. Published by Rockport Publishers, it's a very handy guide to selecting color combinations.

Create individual palettes in PhotoShop, and save them as PhotoShop files so you can maintain the integrity of the palette. Also, be sure to write down the hexadecimal values for each of your colors. This will come in handy when you're coding.

Your individual palette is now ready to go to work!

HTML Color Basics

The hexadecimal values of the palette you've just created will be used for graphics and in your HTML. It's in the HTML that you can get maximum color control because the browser interprets the hexadecimal information quickly and efficiently.

> **TIP**
>
> An excellent article on the technical aspects of Web color by Dmitry Kirsanov can be found at `http://www.webreference.com/dlab/9704/`.

You'll want to use these values to design creative color combinations for backgrounds, links, and text. The most basic, and immediate, application for designers is found within the `<BODY>` tag, where you can define backgrounds, text, and link styles.

The `<BODY>` tag allows for the following color attributes:

> **NOTE**
>
> The HTML 4.0 standard recommends using cascading style sheets as a method of achieving browser color. However, because most designers are working for audiences that don't use style sheet–compliant browsers, these are considered the time-honored methods. If you do choose to use style sheets, it's wise at this time to include *both* methods.

- `bgcolor=x`: This value in hex indicates the background color of the entire page.
- `text=x`: The `text` attribute creates the color for all standard, nonlinked text on the page.
- `link=x`: The color entered for this attribute will appear wherever you've linked text.

- **vlink=x**: A visited link will appear in the color you choose for this attribute.
- **alink=x**: An *active* link—one that's in the process of being clicked—will appear in the color you supply for this attribute.

A <BODY> tag with these attributes appears as follows. You'll note that I've simply placed the hexadecimal value into the quote field. I begin each individual attribute with the # sign:

```
<body bgcolor="#FFFFFF" text="#000000" link="#CCCCCC" vlink="#CCCCCC"
➥alink="#999999">
```

Figure 33.6 shows the results. Note how there are gradation differences in the background color, body text, and link attributes.

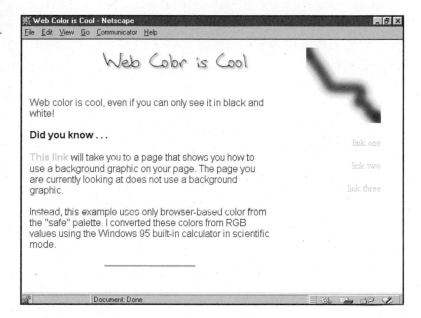

FIGURE 33.6.

The grayscale results of my link attributes.

You might decide to use a background graphic on your page, in which case you use the `background="url"` attribute in the preceding string. This value alerts the browser to load the graphic from the specified location. If you're using a background graphic, I highly recommend including a background color value as well. With this technique, your background color will load instantly, and your graphic will then load over that color. The end product is less jarring and creates a cohesive visual effect.

Here's the syntax for the same page with a two-column, two-color background graphic laid on top of the background color:

```
<body bgcolor="#FFFFFF" text="#000000" link="#CCCCCC" vlink="#CCCCCC"
➥alink="#999999" background="wc-bak.gif">
```

The results of this effect can be seen in Figure 33.7.

Figure 33.7.

Adding a background graphic to the page shown in Figure 33.6.

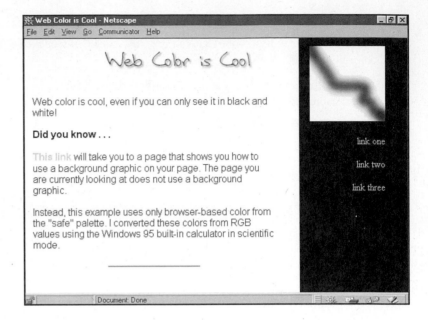

Hexadecimal Alternatives

Some of you might have seen HTML color attributes that use the name of the color rather than the hex value, as shown:

```
<body bgcolor="red" text="white" link="yellow" vlink="green" alink="white">
```

This method was introduced by Microsoft's Internet Explorer browser and is compatible with some versions of other browsers. I suggest avoiding this technique. It's not a standard or stable method of ensuring the most accurate colors across platforms and browsers. It's also limited, and if you want to use colors from the complete 216-color safe palette, you'll end up having combinations of color names and hexadecimal values. In the end, that looks inconsistent and therefore unprofessional.

Using Unsafe Color

Although I recommend using the safe palette whenever possible, it can be restrictive because it has so few colors available. Designers might naturally become frustrated, so the following situations are ones in which you can deviate from the safe palette:

■ You have a good idea that your audience has sophisticated end-user technology, as is often the case with intranet applications. When you know the type of computers, browsers, and monitors the majority of your audience uses, you have much more flexibility in color choice. If most people are accessing your pages with high-end browsers and monitors, by all means use color as you see fit!

■ If you're less certain about your audience, but still interested in using unsafe color, test the colors for dithering at lower resolutions. To do this, set your monitor resolution to 256 colors. If the color *dithers* (moves to the closest color within the system palette), you might discover that your soft yellow becomes a glowing neon color! This isn't going to make you or your client too happy. Ideally, you should test your work on several other computers at a variety of resolutions with different browsers. If your results are stable enough to suit your tastes, you can feel somewhat confident that the colors will look good.

Browser-Based Color

Planning, preparing, and using color with the methods described in this chapter put you at a design advantage by giving you strong foundations in basic Web color theory. By understanding simple color-management techniques, and how to use HTML to control them, you can create rich, colorful sites that get their energy and vibrant look *without* the use of graphics. If you use entirely browser-based colors, the browser never needs to query the server, so you can offer your visitors fast load times without sacrificing aesthetic appeal.

Designers should rely on browser-based colors as much as possible. This can be done by using the simple techniques in this chapter to create background and link colors. As you become more adept with HTML, you'll learn how to add table cell background color or the various color attributes available with cascading style sheets. The primary idea is to help you move color away from graphic images that take time to download.

That's not to say that graphics won't play a role in your design—of course they will! But with proper planning and an understanding of when and how to use safe color, you can add graphics to your already attractive sites with less concern about load times. Browser-based colors free you to use your allotment of downloadable files for truly necessary, higher quality graphics. This method is an effective way of adding professional style to your work.

33

MANAGING WEB
COLOR AND
GRAPHICS

> **TIP**
>
> Macintosh and PC users will appreciate this easy-to-follow color article in May 1997's *MacUser*, http://www.zdnet.com/macuser/mu_0597/bob/webcolor.html.

Web Graphic Technology

There's no excuse for thinking small and looking bad. That a Web site's graphics have to be small and visually less than attractive is a myth. No, I'm not saying you should burden site visitors with impossibly long downloads. In fact, I'm encouraging all Web designers to learn how to design graphics so well that their sites load fast and look great.

Figure 33.8 demonstrates an example of technical expertise combined with design savvy. Even though Paperboy takes up one half of a screen's width and a full screen length, this page loads in a snap! The designers of this page knew how to envision the design and then apply learned technology, such as palette reduction and table-based layout, to it to make it shapely, interesting, and out of the ordinary.

FIGURE 33.8.

Good planning combined with graphics techniques can ensure quality results.

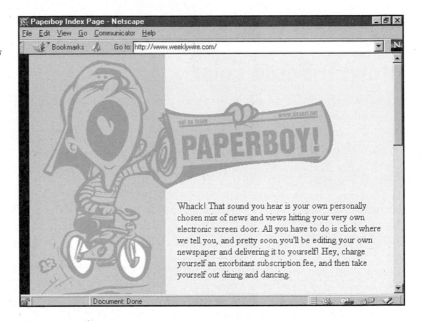

Evaluating Your Skills: The Professional Graphic Designer

Some of you reading this chapter come from a computer graphics design background. You have the edge of having a lot of skills; you also keep up with available materials and resources and understand how to use most of the software programs you'll need for Web design.

If you're a traditional graphic artist, the danger zone is not readjusting your thinking to the Web's low-resolution environment. If you can adjust your thinking, you're almost guaranteed sure success because the skills, knowledge, and personal style you've worked long and hard to develop can be expressed in this medium. If you don't study how to readjust that thinking, however, you can end up having graphics that take too long to download or a design that doesn't fit the constraints of the computer screen, resulting in your frustration level shooting through the roof.

The wise graphic designer interested in designing for the Web will have to bite the bullet—yes, you're going to have to sacrifice high resolution, broad spectrum palettes, and wide, horizontally oriented design in most cases. On the other hand, you'll end up challenging your design skills because limitations sometimes force you to come up with creative, innovative solutions.

Graphic designers new to this environment need to remember this: Keep an open mind, read as much as you can, and practice the techniques.

Evaluating Your Skills: The Web Technologist or Novice

Other readers are interested in becoming Web designers, or are already working in the design environment, but have little or no education in the field of design. For you, the challenge is learning the methods and simultaneously gaining art skills—no easy task! Fortunately, resources abound, and with a little motivation and a lot of savvy you can come up with some very good methods of addressing this challenge.

However, some of you are totally frustrated or simply not interested in the graphic elements of Web design. If you're one of these people and are responsible for setting up Web sites, you can hire graphic designers, photographers, and illustrators by the hour or permanently to help you reach your goals. Check out `http://www.portfolios.com/graphic_designers/` for a look at who in the Web world is offering high-quality graphic design services.

Graphics Tools

If you've ever tried to use a screwdriver to hammer in a nail, you know the right tool for the job is simply a necessity. I have students who constantly complain about the high price of Web graphics tools. The reality is that in the long run, the 1,200–1,500 dollars you're going to shell out for Photoshop and DeBabelizer is very low compared to the high-quality results you're going to want—and require—to compete in this industry.

Web graphic design can be considered as a science unto itself, but the actual requirements to do the job well can be simplified into a handful of programs. Although I'll mention some graphics software in this chapter, remember you'll need a very good computer with plenty of RAM, a top-line graphics card, and good video monitor. A color flatbed scanner is a must for the serious Web designer, as is a high-speed CD-ROM drive, because much of your source material and special effects come on CD-ROMs.

Graphics Software

The following software can be used to work with Web graphics:

Photoshop: With training, a Web page designer can learn how to use Photoshop to do almost anything—from creating to modifying to optimizing graphics. What's more, Photoshop is extremely well supported in terms of third-party plug-ins and specialty applications. (See Figure 33.9.) It's available for both Macintosh and PC platforms. The price might seem daunting at $895.00 for standard licensing. However, for the serious designer, there's simply no substitute for this powerful program.

Paint Shop Pro: I like this program for the first-time, Windows-based page designer who wants to create nice-looking graphics on a budget. The product is shareware and available for download at `http://www.jasc.com/`; registration is $69.00, but the program has been included on this book's CD-ROM.

FIGURE 33.9.

This photograph's professional look has been created completely with Photoshop and a related plug-in, Auto F/X.

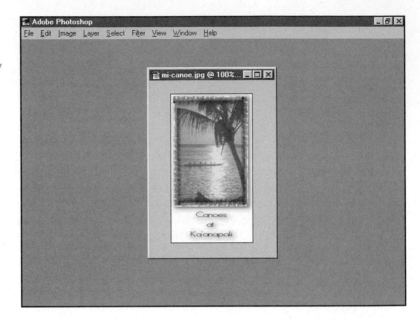

Corel PhotoPaint: Many people who already have Corel products installed will find that Corel PhotoPaint meets many of their Web application needs. I don't recommend it for new purchase, however, because Photoshop is a far superior product for the money, and Paint Shop Pro is just as powerful at a much more reasonable price. More information on Corel products is available at `http://www.corel.com/`.

DeBabelizer Pro: This program is another heavy-weight contender that serious Web page designers need to consider for their suite of tools. DeBabelizer's strength for Web applications lies in its ability to optimize graphics by selecting the best color palette to get small file sizes yet retain as much visual appeal as possible. A particularly powerful aspect of DeBabelizer is its ability to batch-process hundreds of files to a single palette. This feature is useful for people creating large Web sites. Check out `http://www.equilibrium.com/` for more information.

LView Pro: This shareware program is a handy tool for PC-based graphic conversions and transparency creation. You can check it out at `http://www.lview.com/`.

Stock Materials and Special Effects

Beyond these software requirements are other expenses for specialty graphics tools and stock source material. These resources can get costly, but again, the results are worth it. Also, think smart—if you're doing a specific project, write the cost of the specialty goods you need for that project into the specs. That way, you get the materials paid for *and* have them available for future projects!

Where do you go to find source material? For those of you starting out, I highly recommend visiting the Internet Baglady's Web site, `http://www.dumpsterdive.com/`. She has lots of free "stuff" and plenty of links to resources with more things you can practice with, at no cost.

For professional projects, make sure you have stock photography, clip art, and fonts. Visit Image Club (`http://www.imageclub.com/`) for excellent lines on quality stock materials. Also, visiting Photodisc (`http://www.photodisc.com/`) will give you a shopping source for plenty of stock photos, backgrounds, and links to other sites of interest.

Don't forget that old acronym GIGO (Garbage In, Garbage Out)—spend the time to look at what you have, determine what you need, and prepare to shell out the bucks so you're in the best position for success!

Working with Graphics

Okay, so now that you have a good idea of where you're at and where you'd like to go, I can get down to the nitty-gritty of working with graphics. A good place to begin is with what I call "The Five S's of Image Production":

1. Start with quality resources and tools.
2. Scan the image.
3. Size images appropriately.
4. Select attractive treatments, such as matting, filters, borders, and edge effects.
5. Save files in the proper format—GIF or JPG—depending on the file size and quality you're trying to achieve.

Starting with Quality

You're probably tired of hearing this already, but it truly applies to every step of the design process! I'm repeating myself only to ensure that if you take only one lesson away from this chapter, it's that *quality counts*. Start with good materials, and your chances of getting good results are much greater, even when aggressively optimizing your graphics for speed.

Figure 33.10 is an example of good photographic material. Note how the image is clean and crisp. On the other hand, a photocopied, unclear image will require much more time and effort but yield only satisfactory results. (See Figure 33.11.)

Scanner Savvy

There are two main considerations when scanning graphics for use on the Web: source material and scanning resolution.

Source material refers to *what* you're trying to scan. Photos should be clear, clean, and of the highest quality possible. Hand-drawn or printed materials should also be very clean; look carefully for speckles or dust. Anything that you can clean up *before* you scan, do so.

FIGURE 33.10.
This photo of the author is scanner-ready.

FIGURE 33.11.
A crumpled, old photocopy is going to take much more effort to clean up.

Something that many graphic artists like to do is scan real objects. This is part of "organic" design—drawing actual elements from the real world and using them to inspire computer-based graphics. In Figure 33.12, I used this method of incorporating everyday objects by taking a few things off my desk and scanning them. Be creative with this! The only caution is to be sure your scanning surface is nice and clean.

Figure 33.12.

I've taken some three-dimensional objects from my desk and scanned them directly into Photoshop.

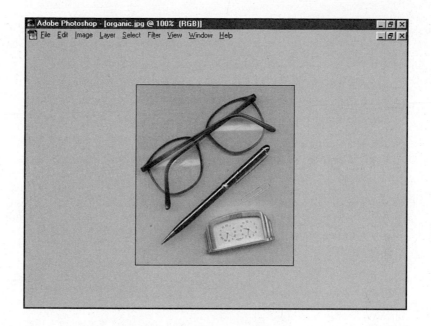

Scanning resolution for the Web can begin higher, but should always end up at 72 dpi (dots per inch). I can hear the groans of print graphic artists as I write that line—yep, it's the lowest resolution on the totem pole. Remember, though, this isn't print media. You don't need high resolution to make an image *seem* like it's high-resolution in the computer graphics environment.

Whether you choose to scan at 72 dpi or scan at a higher resolution, like 300 dpi, and reduce is really a personal call. I've noticed that it's sometimes possible to get better end results by scanning at 300 dpi and then reducing to 72 dpi later on. On other occasions, that doesn't hold true. The difference in quality is often very slight, the type of difference that normally won't be seen when a figure is optimized for the Web.

I personally haven't found a tried-and-true rule, so you'll have to find out what works best for your type of scanner and appeals to your sensibilities. Either way, the end result is going to be 72 dpi.

Sizing Images

Make sure the literal dimensions of your graphics are proportionately appropriate for the Web environment. I'm not referring here to the kilobyte size of the image; I mean the image's width and height. I'm also not discussing background graphics, which I covered in Chapter 32, "Navigation and Layout." The concern here is spot graphics and detail pieces, such as buttons and rules.

Remember again that you're working for standard computer screens, with a common resolution of 640×480 pixels. That means that to keep your designs within the dimensions of that resolution, the actual parts have to be smaller, particularly where width is concerned. There's actually *less* visible space than the 640×480 resolution because your Web browser's interface takes up some of that space.

Horizontal designs are rarely wise, unless you're really thoughtful about the design or have an important reason to design that way. Width-wise, images should always be less than an absolute maximum of 600 pixels.

The length of graphics is really determined by the overall layout of your individual page. Typically, it's best to keep the length of your images approximate to each screen length. In other words, I want to be able to see the entire image without having to scroll down.

Finally, proportion to other elements on the page is paramount. You want to achieve a nice balance among the text, other images, and the image in question. Certainly, there's room for variation in size; just be sure that the ultimate look isn't out of balance. In Figure 33.13, you can see an all-too-common pitfall that good design balance helps you overcome.

FIGURE 33.13.

The large header graphic on this page cuts off the menu below it.

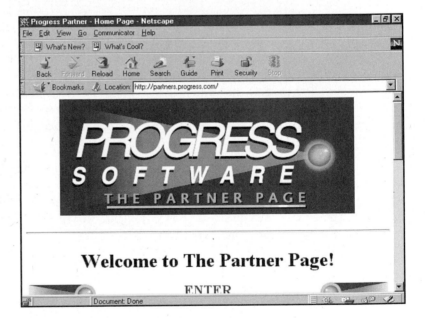

Selecting Graphic Treatments

Adding light sources, special filters, drop shadows, matting, or edge effects can bring life and dimension to your graphics. These effects also help make your site look more professional.

Some of the methods I'll be demonstrating in future chapters are native to Photoshop, which has many great filters and lighting techniques to add liveliness to your images. I also recommend Kai's Power Tools for the very serious Web graphic designer; this package comes with some terrific plug-ins that ramp up options for your design work. Edge effects are also a valuable plug-in to have. I like the suite from Auto F/X (http://www.autofx.com/).

Figure 33.14 shows how a drop shadow adds a nice text effect. In Figure 33.15, I've used an edge effect from Auto F/X to get the sophisticated look for this photograph.

FIGURE 33.14.
A drop shadow adds dimension to this page's header.

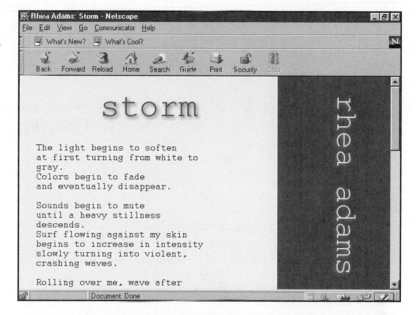

FIGURE 33.15.
Edge effects around photos can offer sophisticated design elements to an otherwise simple page.

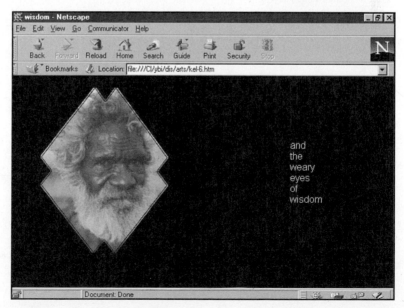

33

MANAGING WEB COLOR AND GRAPHICS

Saving Files Properly

Saving files properly is one of the most critical steps in Web graphics optimization. How you save a file makes an enormous difference in how big it is in kilobytes and how good it looks. There are two primary file types used on the Web: GIF and JPG (also spelled *JPEG*).

When do you use one over the other? The answer is pretty simple, based on the way GIFs and JPEGs work with color palettes and compression. A basic rule of thumb is use GIFs for simple graphics and JPEGs for photographs and graphics in which high-resolution but smaller file size are necessary.

GIFs

The GIF format was developed to create small graphics. The way it works is by reducing a graphic's color palette down to 256 or fewer colors. Often, what you see as one color is really many; for example, yellow is made up of various pigments or, in the case of digitized colors, pixels of individual color. GIF technology reduces colors by *dithering* anything that doesn't fit into the 256-color standard GIF palette to the closest color in that palette.

JPGs

Also written as *JPEG*, the JPG format uses a completely different technology, known as *lossy compression*, to produce smaller file sizes. The unique strength of JPGs is that less dithering occurs, so you can get truer color while retaining a smaller file size.

GIFs, because of the dithering, are best used in graphics with fewer colors, little gradation in color (sky schemes are notoriously bad for GIFs), or few light variations (such as in metallic or 3-D graphics styles).

JPGs are best used for photographs, especially of skies, people, and for high-resolution, light-variable graphics.

Other Graphics Techniques

Other graphics techniques help you maximize graphics while minimizing file sizes and problems inherent to the computer screen. These techniques include progressive rendering and transparency.

Interlaced GIFs and Progressive JPGs

Progressive rendering is the gradual appearance of graphics, a handy technique for keeping people's attention while graphics are loading. You see the entire graphic appear in a "fuzzy" fashion, and then become progressively more clear.

You have two methods for producing progressive rendering on the Web. The most popular and effective is the use of interlaced GIFs. This technique can be applied to any GIF, and usually there are options in your graphics program or plug-in tools that help you do the job during the creation process.

Progressive JPGs are the JPEG answer to interlacing. You can't interlace a JPG, but there are programs that create what's known as a progressive JPG. Photoshop 4.0, for example, includes a progressive rendering option for JPGs. I'm personally not too fond of progressive JPGs because I believe the technology is somewhat preliminary and the quality is fairly inconsistent. Standard, non-progressive JPGs scroll rather than render progressively, but if you've done your optimization, layout, and coding sensibly, it's not an obvious problem, particularly because the results are so attractive.

Transparency

Transparency allows you to create textured backgrounds and "tape" a graphic over them without disrupting the background design. It involves making a color "transparent" in the graphic. That transparent color then disappears when placed over a textured page. This technique takes a little bit of patience and time to learn, but can be done with shareware tools such as Lview Pro, as well as in Photoshop.

Keep in mind that transparency can be done only with GIFs, so if you're looking for a transparent effect with high-quality photographs, you should consider not using textured backgrounds with top-rate photography.

Images and HTML

Images are placed on a page using HTML. Several handy attributes in image tags allow maximum control over how an image is placed on the page. Furthermore, using tables to control graphics is an extremely effective method of layout control. For more specifics on layout, be sure to read Chapter 34, "Using Space, Shape, and Type."

For your immediate purposes, I'll give you a look at the standard image tag and its attributes. An image tag with common attributes looks like this:

```
<img src="header.gif" alt="example header graphic" width=300 height=50>
```

I'll examine the individual parts of this example before going on to more complex attributes.

- **img:** This stands for *image*; the img attribute alerts the browser and server that an image is to be placed at this point in the HTML structure.
- **src=x:** This stands for *source*; the src attribute refers to the location of the image on the server.
- **alt=x:** The alt attribute allows a text alternative to the image to be set within the image string. This attribute is particularly handy for people who use text-only browsers or turn off the images option; it can help with image identity because the text "pops" up as the mouse passes over the image. (See Figure 33.16.)

FIGURE 33.16.

The alt *attribute is what creates this pop-up text comment when the mouse passes over the image.*

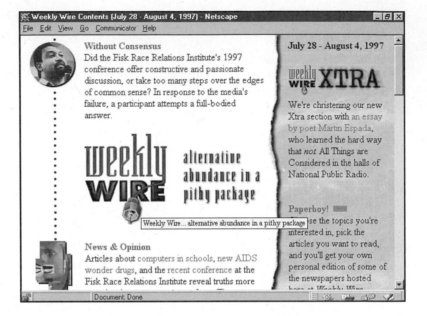

- **width=x:** This is the width of the image. Specifying the width allows the browser to prepare the appropriate amount of horizontal space for the image.

- **height=x:** The height of the image refers to the image's vertical length. As with width, setting the height helps the browser work more effectively.

Other commonly seen attributes that can be used in an image tag are as follows:

- **border=x:** A numeric value of 1 or higher creates a border around the image. Most designers stay away from this attribute, however, and I recommend you do as well. Images look more professional without constraining borders. Set borders to 0 to get a borderless effect.

- **hspace=x:** This refers to *horizontal space* and determines how much space is placed between the image and any text or other images along the horizontal line.

- **vspace=x:** Vertical space, like horizontal space, is the amount of space placed between the image and any other information on the vertical axis.

- **align=x:** Alignment allows an image to be set to various locations in the image space. The most commonly used alignment values for an image include:

  - **right:** This value aligns the image to the right margin.

  - **left:** This value aligns the image to the left margin.

> **NOTE**
>
> There are other alignment options, which you can read about elsewhere in this book, including Chapter 11, "Adding Images to Your Web Page," and Chapter 7, "Text Alignment and Formatting."

Summary

In this chapter, you learned how to put together palettes, work with safe color, and use HTML to give those graphics the best positioning on a page. These techniques put you ahead of the pack when it comes to Web design because they're frequently overlooked. Not paying attention to these methods is part of the reason so much chaos reigns on the Web!

The next chapter looks more closely at alignment issues, as well as how images and text interact on a page. Graphics are a foundation of visual Web page design. They offer opportunities to increase the aesthetic experience by not only adding pictographic representations, but also color, shape, and typography. Read on for more information on how to put your newfound graphics knowledge to use in the context of these important design issues.

Using Space, Shape, and Type

by Molly E. Holzschlag

Space, shape, and type are essential elements of design. This chapter will help you learn some of the HTML techniques necessary to achieve them, as well as give you an overview of the design theory behind the techniques. This information will help you use HTML to design Web sites that have more style and impact.

I hate feeling confined. There's nothing more frustrating than the small space of a Web page that's so jammed with stuff I get claustrophobic. It reminds me of the way my grandmother's house was—you couldn't move in any direction without bumping into some knickknack or knocking over a sentimental but totally unnecessary accessory. Space is essential.

The shape of things is important, too. Shape helps free up space and adds visual interest to a page. You've probably noticed that most Web pages are filled with rectangles. Well, enough of that! This is not to say that rectangles aren't desirable or even downright necessary, but in this chapter, I'll take a look at not only how to free up your space, but why you'd want to add other shapes to your site.

Another element of Web design that adds visual intrigue and helps create space and shape is type. Changes to HTML are beginning to give designers a lot of control over how to manage type, so you'll learn a bit here about the how and why of Web typography.

Give Me My Space!

Look at your computer screen. What shape is it? It's a rectangle. Technically, it's a rectangle that offers up a specific width and height, determined by the number of pixels. Depending on the type of monitor and graphics card that you have, the value of your visual real estate might be 640×480, 800×600, or higher. This value is referred to as your *resolution*, or *res*, for short.

Resolution is an issue that good Web designers will pay close attention to, for it determines how much literal space you have to work with. It's thought that most people have or view the Web at 640×480 resolution, which is the lowest resolution for a typical monitor. I highly recommend using this resolution as a starting point when thinking about spatial design.

What this means in simple terms is that you have a maximum of 640 pixels in width and 480 pixels in length per screen of information. Most Web pages scroll, so length determination is not as critical, unless you want your page to be fixed, as with a splash, or introductory, page. (See Figure 34.1.) But your width is another story. Horizontal scrollbars are rarely used effectively, so you want to keep your widths nice and tight. That means your graphics, your tables, and any other technique you use to set up your page space will make sure that 640-pixel-width maximum isn't overrun.

I say *maximum* because there are other factors that play into your space-making decisions. Open your Web browser. Depending on your personal tastes, you might have any number of toolbars open, taking up vertical space. There could also be a vertical scrollbar to the right and a status bar along the bottom. (See Figure 34.2.) All these factors reduce the amount of literal pixels you have to work with.

FIGURE 34.1.
Introductory splash pages are often fixed, with no vertical scrolling.

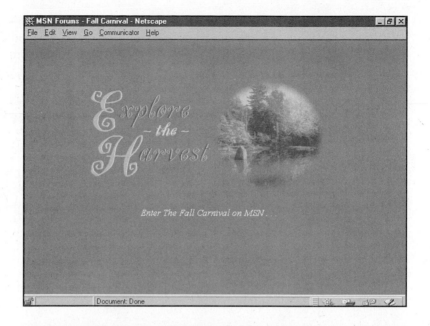

FIGURE 34.2.
The Netscape Web browser with full toolbars and status bars showing—all of this takes up space.

34
USING SPACE,
SHAPE, AND TYPE

Simply put, you *really* have a maximum of 600 pixels widthwise and 400 pixels or less lengthwise to set up your space, but keeping these measurements in mind actually frees rather than constricts you.

Think about that small room in your house, the one with no windows. How do you open the space up? Well, one trick is to paint it white or another light color. Another method is to reduce the amount of furniture in the room—and what furniture and accessories you *do* decide to put in the room are well-chosen and light in color and weight. Finally, you can add mirrors or pictures that expand the room's visual horizons.

Opening up space on your Web page is similar. By following one, or all, of several methods that get the same effects as making that room seem larger, you end up making that page look airier, lighter, and cleaner.

Knowing the constraints you're dealing with *before* designing your page frees rather than limits your ideas. You know what you're working with, so you can make better, sharper choices, enhancing your pages and making your visitors more comfortable.

White Space

On a newspaper or magazine page, the area that's free of text or graphics is referred to as *white space*. Of course, this space might not actually be white, but it's empty space. Often, what you *don't* have on a page is as important as what you do have.

For a Web page, white space is imperative, but sadly, it's often overlooked. White space guides the eye toward the upcoming information, rests the eye by providing a space free and clear of information, and cushions text and graphics, making them seem less like grandma's crowded room.

The following HTML methods will help you get white space on your page, enhancing the visitor's experience. Even though it doesn't seem immediately apparent, a crowded Web site conveys tension. You don't want your visitors to run off—the goal here is to create an environment that's pleasing to them! Space helps decorate your page in an inviting manner.

Margins

There is one standard method for controlling margins with HTML: using the <BLOCKQUOTE> tag. The <BLOCKQUOTE> tag and its companion, </BLOCKQUOTE>, placed around page content instantly create margins and give you precious white space to the left and right of that content. Here's a sample of the code:

```
<html>
<head>
<title>Blockquoting = White Space!</title>
</head>

<body>

<blockquote>
Duis autem vel eum iriure dolor in hendrerit in vulputate velit esse molestie
consequat, vel illum dolore eu feugiat nulla facilisis at vero eros et
accumsan et iusto odio dignissim qui blandit praesent luptatum zzril delenit
```

```
augue duis dolore te feugait nulla facilisi.
<p>

<img src="seattle.jpg">
<p>

Nam liber tempor cum soluta nobis eleifend option congue nihil imperdiet doming
id quod mazim placerat facer possim assum. Accumsan et iusto odio dignissim
qui blandit praesent luptatum zzril delenit augue duis dolore te feugait nulla
facilisi.
<p>

</blockquote>
</body>
</html>
```

Figure 34.3 shows the results. Compare this image with Figure 34.4, where I've removed the blockquotes. Quite a difference!

NOTE

There are two <BODY> tag attributes you can use when designing for Internet Explorer. They are the `leftmargin=X` and `topmargin=x` attributes, which give you control over the left and top margins of a page. For example, if I wanted to have about 30 pixels of white space to the left, and make my page flush with the top of the browser's available page space, I would use the following syntax:

`<body leftmargin=20 topmargin=0>`

FIGURE 34.3.

Blockquotes help create attractive margins, so your text doesn't run end-to-end.

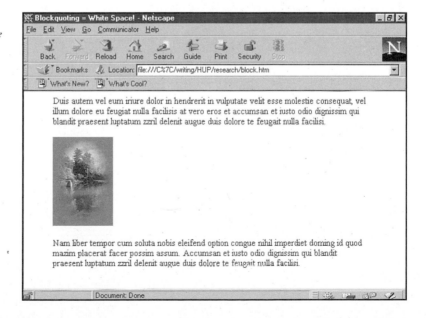

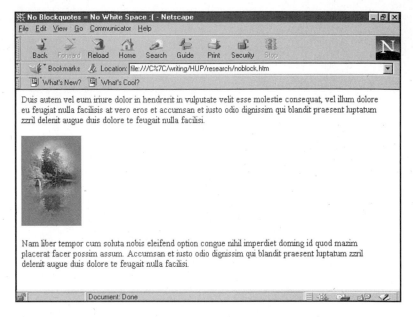

Alignment

Alignment is where, and how, text, images, and objects are placed on a page. Where text is concerned, alignment is often referred to as *justification*. There are a variety of methods to handle alignment using HTML.

Aligning Text and Blocks of Data

Aligning text and images helps supply white space and adds some visual fun to your pages. From a design standpoint, you want to align text where it's appealing, not just to get a different look. For example, standard body text should remain in its most familiar left alignment. Shorter bursts of text can be right-aligned, and centering text and objects should be done very carefully.

> **CAUTION**
>
> Centering text is a common practice, and the untrained eye *thinks* it looks better on a page than plain old left-aligned text. The reason it looks better is because centering text creates white space! This space is what the eye is craving—not centered text, which is actually more difficult to read overall. Centering should be reserved for very specific, condensed sections of text, such as subheadings. Otherwise, reduce the urge to center text by looking at other alignment and space-creating options.

The following HTML tags and attributes allow you to control alignment in a variety of ways:

■ **<DIV>...</DIV>:** The <DIV>, or *division*, tag is one of the most powerful ways to divide blocks of information and align them. Anything within this tag will follow one of these alignment attributes:

center: This attribute centers all information between the <DIV> and </DIV> tag, as shown:

```
<div align=center>

Duis autem vel eum iriure dolor in hendrerit in vulputate velit esse molestie
consequat, vel illum dolore eu feugiat nulla facilisis at vero eros et
accumsan et iusto odio dignissim qui blandit praesent luptatum zzril delenit
augue duis dolore te feugait nulla facilisi.
<p>

<img src="seattle.jpg">
<p>

</div>
```

Figure 34.5 shows the results.

FIGURE 34.5.

Centered alignment using the <DIV> tag.

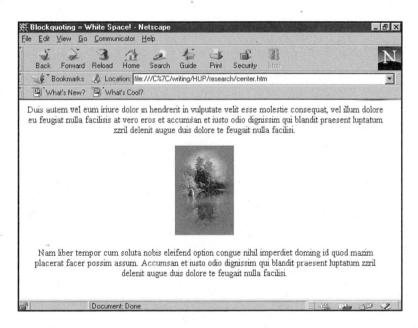

left: All the data will be aligned to the left. Left-alignment is a page's default, so unless you're in a table or another tag, you'll rarely use this attribute.

right: This attribute right-aligns your data:

```
<div align=right>
```

```
Duis autem vel eum iriure dolor in hendrerit in vulputate velit esse molestie
consequat, vel illum dolore eu feugiat nulla facilisis at vero eros et
accumsan et iusto odio dignissim qui blandit praesent luptatum zzril delenit
augue duis dolore te feugait nulla facilisi.
<p>

<img src="seattle.jpg">
<p>

</div>
```

In Figure 34.6, you can see how the text and image are justified to the right.

FIGURE 34.6.

Right-justification with the <DIV> tag.

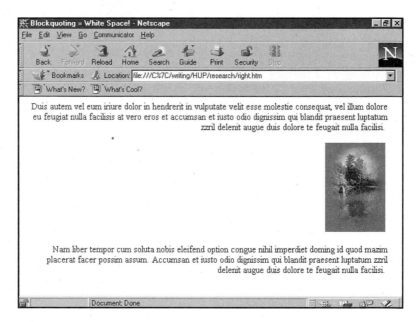

<P>...</P>: Using the paragraph pair of tags with the same attributes found in the <DIV> tag creates the exact same type of alignment.

center: All the text in the following example will be centered:

```
<p align=center>

Duis autem vel eum iriure dolor in hendrerit in vulputate velit esse molestie
consequat, vel illum dolore eu feugiat nulla facilisis at vero eros et
accumsan et iusto odio dignissim qui blandit praesent luptatum zzril delenit
augue duis dolore te feugait nulla facilisi.
</p>
```

left: Once again, left is the standard default for paragraphs, so you will rarely, if ever, use this attribute with a paragraph tag.

right: The following data will be right-aligned:

```
<p align=right>
```

```
Duis autem vel eum iriure dolor in hendrerit in vulputate velit esse molestie
consequat, vel illum dolore eu feugiat nulla facilisis at vero eros et
accumsan et iusto odio dignissim qui blandit praesent luptatum zzril delenit
augue duis dolore te feugait nulla facilisi.
</p>

<p align=right>
<img src="seattle.jpg">
</p>
```

TIP

As you can see from the preceding code example, paragraph alignment requires an opening and closing tag for each section of data that needs alignment. Therefore, if you're trying to align more than just one section on a page, it's quicker and neater to use the <DIV> option.

A common method of centering text is using the <CENTER> tag and its companion closing tag, </CENTER>. I personally advise against this because using the <DIV> tag is much more elegant and cross-browser compatible.

Aligning Images

Images can be aligned on both the horizontal and vertical axes. Aligning images is done right in the image <IMG> tag, with the align=X attribute. A left-aligned image syntax looks like this:

```
<img src="my-face.gif" align=left>
```

To align images vertically, use the following alignment values (see Figure 34.7):

top: Text will align to the top of the image.

absmiddle: The middle of the text line aligns with the middle of the image.

baseline: The base of the text line aligns with the base of the image.

TIP

The baseline and absmiddle attributes are used much less frequently than the others described here. However, designers use them to get more precise placement where necessary.

NOTE

There are several other horizontal alignment options that are quite redundant to those listed here. For more information on all the available horizontal alignment options, check with Appendix A, "HTML 4.0 Reference."

Figure 34.7.

Vertical alignment in action.

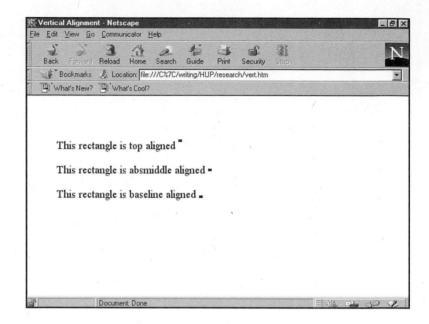

Aligning images horizontally relies on the following attributes (see Figure 34.8):

> **left:** This attribute aligns the image to the left.
>
> **right:** This attribute results in a right-alignment.

Images can be aligned next to text. You can gain more control over this alignment by using the `<br clear=x>` tag and attribute.

> **`<br clear=right>`:** Use this tag after a left-aligned image to force the body of text to the right, as shown in Figure 34.9.
>
> **`<br clear=left>`:** If you've right-aligned an image, this tag forces the body of text to the left of the image, as shown in Figure 35.10.
>
> **`<br clear=all>`:** Use this tag to clear all information away from the image. (See Figure 34.11.)

NOTE

It's important to bear in mind that the HTML 4.0 standard advises the use of style sheets rather than alignment attributes for placement. However, this is expressed in the context of browsers that support style sheets. Currently, the only popular browsers that support style sheets are IE 3.0 and above and Netscape 4.0. These programs are used by a minority of the Web population, so it's wise to always consider your audience before adopting the HTML 4.0 standard for commercial Web design projects.

FIGURE 34.8.
Horizontal alignment.

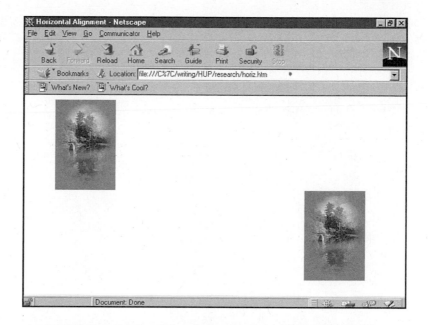

FIGURE 34.9.
Breaking to the right.

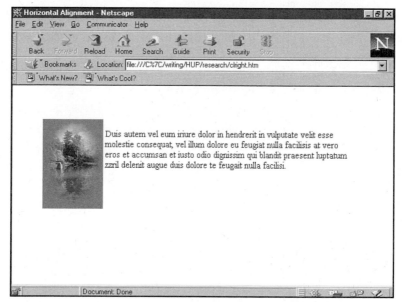

FIGURE 34.10.
Breaking to the left.

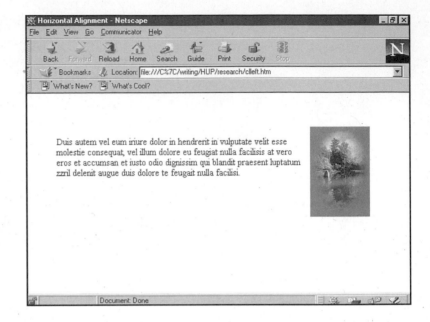

Floating Images

There's another important, somewhat more advanced method available for aligning images. It's a more dynamic alignment that relies on the relationship of blocks of text to an image within that text. The technique is important in the context of alignment and space because it's a powerful way to naturally create space on a page.

Floating images are created by eliminating any breaks after the image. For example, if I have an image and I want to float it within a paragraph, I'll first place and align the image, and then place the paragraph, without using any break between the image and paragraph:

```
<img src="my-face.gif" align=right>
Duis autem vel eum iriure dolor in hendrerit in vulputate velit esse molestie
consequat, vel illum dolore eu feugiat nulla facilisis at vero eros et accumsan
et iusto odio dignissim qui blandit praesent luptatum zzril delenit augue duis
dolore te feugait nulla facilisi.
<p>
```

Figure 34.12 shows the results. Note how the text wraps around the image. This is called *floating,* but those of you with a quick eye will notice something missing. You guessed it—white space!

You can add white space around a floating image by using the following attributes:

> **hspace:** This is *horizontal space.* It controls how much white space is placed horizontally, around the left and right sides of the image.

> **vspace:** *Vertical space* places white space vertically, around the top and bottom of the image.

FIGURE 34.11.
*Clearing the informa-
tion.*

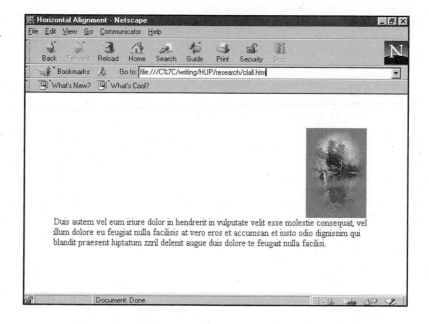

FIGURE 34.12.
*A floating image, before
white space is added.*

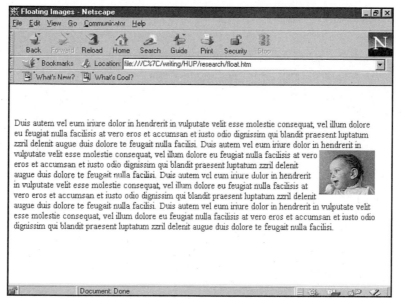

If I change the image code in the preceding example to the following, you'll see in Figure 34.13
that I have created a nice amount of white space around my image:

```
<img src="my-face.gif" align=right hspace=20 vspace=20>
```

FIGURE 34.13.

A floating image with hspace *and* vspace *used.*

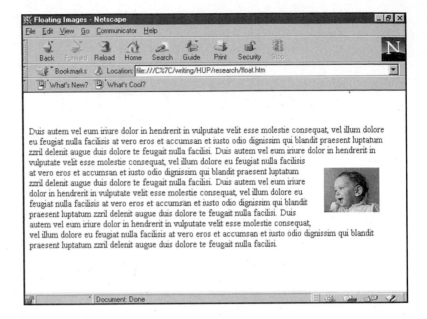

Proportion and Proximity

Another important issue regarding space has to do with proportion and proximity. *Proportion* is how large a given image, object, or section of text is in relation to the other images, objects, and sections of text on the page. Proportion can be understood by thinking about different body types. Some people have very long legs and short torsos; others might have short legs and long torsos. Some faces are round, others are elongated. Although diversity in people is part of what makes them aesthetically interesting, designers strive to keep a balance between the parts. In other words, a good design could be compared to a very even, or "well proportioned," body type.

Proximity means how close one object is to another. If someone's eyes are too close-set or wide apart, you're likely to notice his or her appearance as being somewhat unusual. Again, balancing is the key to good design here, with the distance between objects kept fairly even rather than too close or too distant.

Figure 34.14 shows a page that has ill-proportioned objects that are out of balance in terms of proximity. In Figure 34.15, I've fixed the problem by resizing and placing images on the page in a balanced fashion.

Keep aware of proximity and proportion as you design sites. The more balance you achieve with each, the more natural space you get, and the happier you—and your site visitors—are going to be with the results.

FIGURE 34.14.

Ill-proportioned and out-of-balance page elements.

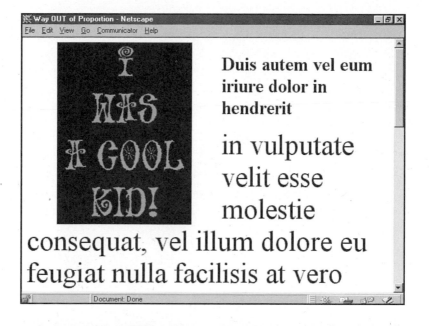

FIGURE 34.15.

The same page with proximity and proportion applied.

Controlling Layout with Tables and Frames

Working with tables and frames, you can lay out pages, control images and text, and ultimately get the space, proportion, and proximity of Web page elements in order. The actual application of layout and frames involves fairly extensive HTML, so I'll demonstrate a simple instance of each to whet your appetite here. Then, I recommend you review Part II of this book, "Structural and Navigational Elements of HTML 4." Also, Chapter 20, "Creating Frames," goes into details of how to use frames effectively.

A Simple Layout with Tables

In this layout, I have four elements: two images and two sections of body text. I want to create an interesting look with plenty of white space between the elements. To do this, I add an appropriate table width combined with the table attributes of cellpadding and cellspacing, which give me added space around the elements. I also used alignment, relying on the `<ALIGN>` tag *within* the table cell instead of using standard, non-table HTML.

```
<html>
<head>
<title>A Simple Table Layout</title>
</head>

<body>

<table border=0 width=590 cellpadding=10 cellspacing=10>
<tr>

<td>
Duis autem vel eum iriure dolor in hendrerit in vulputate velit esse molestie
consequat, vel illum dolore eu feugiat nulla facilisis at vero eros et accumsan
et iusto odio dignissim qui blandit praesent luptatum zzril delenit augue duis
dolore te feugait nulla facilisi.
Duis autem vel eum iriure dolor in hendrerit in vulputate velit esse molestie
consequat, vel illum dolore eu feugiat nulla facilisis at vero eros et accumsan
et iusto odio dignissim qui blandit praesent luptatum zzril delenit augue duis
dolore te feugait nulla facilisi.
</td>

<td>

<img src="images/seattle.jpg" width=100 height=148 border=0 alt="seattle fall">

</td>

<td>

Duis autem vel eum iriure dolor in hendrerit in vulputate velit esse molestie
consequat, vel illum dolore eu feugiat nulla facilisis at vero eros et
accumsan et iusto odio dignissim qui blandit praesent luptatum zzril delenit
augue duis dolore te feugait nulla facilisi.
```

```
Duis autem vel eum iriure dolor in hendrerit in vulputate velit esse molestie
consequat, vel illum dolore eu feugiat nulla facilisis at vero eros et accumsan
et iusto odio dignissim qui blandit praesent luptatum zzril delenit augue duis
dolore te feugait nulla facilisi.

</td>

</tr>
</table>

</body>
</html>
```

As you can see in Figure 34.16, the results are sophisticated, and there's plenty of white space to make me happy!

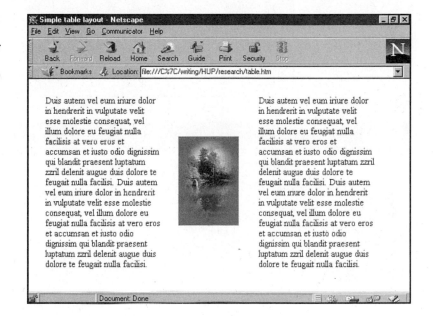

A Layout with Frames

When most people think of frames, they think of bordered frames. In this case, the borderless technique was used to get the results you see in Figure 34.17.

As you can tell from the figure, you don't know that frames are necessarily what gives this page its look, feel, and functionality. Because frames were used, the navigation to the left remains static, with the information pages loading on the right as the visitor clicks on the navigation options.

FIGURE 34.17.

Borderless frames can create attractive and functional interfaces.

> **NOTE**
>
> One of the titles I've written for Sams.net Publishing is *Laura Lemay's Web Workshop: Guide to Designing with Style Sheets, Tables, and Frames.* This workshop offers a very good hands-on starting place for those interested in working with table and frame layouts, as well as learning about style sheets, which I'll address in a bit.

Shape

Think about the word *shape* for a moment. You've all heard people say things like the following:

"He's in excellent shape."

"She's very shapely."

"What kind of shape is this used car *really* in?"

Shape is not incidental in our world. It bears the responsibility of referring to literal geometric forms and aesthetic appearance as well as the quality of an item. Moreover, shape has archetypal meanings—ancient remnants of our cultural legacy that affect us on a subconscious, yet extremely powerful, level.

Students of media, advertising, and design are often taught about the power of shape, but you don't read about it too often in Web design books. I personally can think of no more powerful place to use shape effectively because the Web itself is such a potent medium. Add to that smart, well-thought-out design, and your Web sites are going to have dramatic impact.

While car shopping in the not-too-distant past, I went surfing around to different car sites. The experience was powerful because I saw shape working not only in the ad campaigns for the cars, but also in the design of the cars themselves!

Follow along as I describe the archetypal meaning of shape and then demonstrate how effectively shape is used in the Web page examples I've provided:

> **The Circle:** Circles provide a sense of motion, as well as relating historically to comfort, the feminine, community, and wholeness. Figure 34.18 shows how circular designs for the Honda page exhibit a sense of movement and freedom.

FIGURE 34.18.
Circular design elements at http://
www.honda.com/.

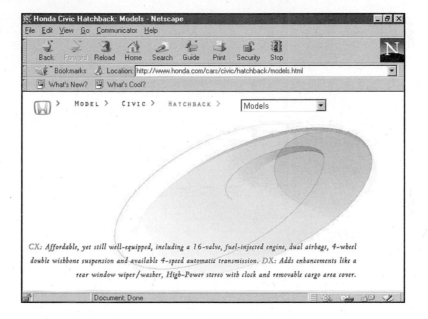

> **The Triangle:** Triangles serve to alert people or create a sense of upward movement and are symbolically linked to power, science, and religion. Saturn cars use the triangular shape in their design. (See Figure 34.19.) Is it any wonder that Saturn has an almost religious following of fans?

> **The Rectangle:** Stability and permanence are the hallmark expressions of the rectangle. The big problem with rectangles on the Web is that they're everywhere! That doesn't mean you shouldn't use them, but learning to integrate other shapes and combinations of shapes can work to your benefit.

So how do you get shape on your Web page? Mostly, shape is going to be provided by graphics. However, white space and the issues discussed earlier, such as proximity and proportion, all play a role in the less obvious shapes that appear on a page. The most important take-home lesson of this section is that shape is powerful. You should think carefully about what you want to express to your audience, and then use shape as a tool for improving your Web site design.

FIGURE 34.19.

Triangles abound in Saturn's design at `http://www.saturncars.com/`.

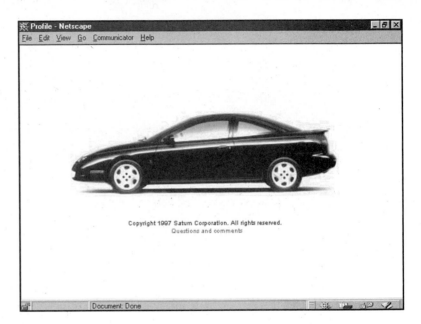

Typography

I know graphic designers who spend their entire careers studying type. No joke—it's that complex, and that much of a fine art.

HTML has until recently been very limited in terms of what can be done with type. Designers wanting to use typographic styles have relied heavily on graphics to deliver the type styles. Fortunately, this is beginning to change.

First, there's the `<FONT>` tag, which has many considerations in terms of widespread compatibility, but it does help designers address type techniques through HTML. The `<FONT>` tag has several attributes, including face, size, and color.

More recently, style sheets have come into vogue, and they deliver even more control for the font fanatic. I'll focus primarily on using the `<FONT>` tag in this chapter, make some references to style sheets, and recommend a variety of resources for you to learn more about Web typography and style sheets. For more information on using style sheets, visit Part IV of this book, "Presentation Techniques," which focuses on more aggressive HTML 4.0 presentation techniques.

NOTE

Of course, to view fonts or style sheets at all, you'll need a compatible browser. Those using Internet Explorer 3.0 or Netscape 4.0 will be able to view fonts and style sheets.

Typeface

A typeface is a font: a special style of type with unique characteristics on its "face." Typefaces add visual interest, identity, and style to a page.

There are several categories of typefaces, known as "families." Within a family are many actual faces, each with a unique personality. If you choose to study typography in more depth, you'll find that there are many variations within individual faces, too, which is one reason the study of typography is such a serious one!

The following families of type will be important to you as you design your Web site:

Serif: These fonts have strokes on the letters. An example of a serif font is the popular Times Roman. Serif typefaces are believed to be good for readability, probably because the strokes create a line for the eye to follow, but no one really knows why readability tests have shown serif fonts to be superior for body fonts—and those tests were made *before* the Web was around. You'll find a lot more sans serif fonts used for body text on the Web these days—an interesting trend.

Sans Serif: This font family doesn't have strokes on the letters; in fact, sans serif letters are rounded and smooth. Popular sans serif fonts include Arial and Helvetica. These fonts are easy on the eye and have been traditionally useful for headers rather than body text. Again, their use in the Web environment is causing a shift in this tradition.

Decorative: Decorative fonts have added features, such as unusual strokes, calligraphic influences, variations in dimension, and unique shapes. Decorative type tends to be used best just as the name expresses: for decoration and enhancement. They rarely, if ever, make good body text, as they look cluttered and busy.

Script: Script fonts resemble cursive handwriting. They are poor choices for body text, but can make wonderful enhancements to headers and areas where text is used as a design element.

Monospace: In these fonts, each individual character takes up exactly the same amount of space as another character. An *M* is usually different from an *I* in width, but in a monospace font, the width is adjusted to be equal for every character in that font. Monospace fonts have been especially popular choices for both body or header text in the past several years.

Figure 34.20 shows a sample of each of these fonts.

FIGURE 34.20.

Samples of different font families.

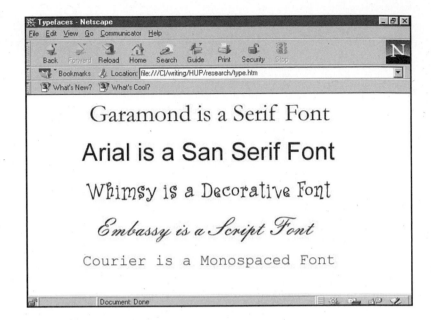

CAUTION

Mixing font faces is a lot of fun and can produce professional, attractive results. However, many beginning designers try too hard, not realizing that less is often more when mixing fonts. Beginners without typographic experience should avoid mixing fonts from the same family—don't mix Garamond and Times, for example, because they are both serif fonts. Fonts from the same family are often too similar to create contrast—which you want—and too dissimilar to allow for continuity, which is necessary.

Using the face Attribute

If you want to add a font face to a selection of text, you can do so by using the face attribute and then defining the font name. Sounds easy enough, and it is. The caveat is that if the font isn't on your visitor's machine, he or she isn't going to see the font you've specified! Therefore, it's wise to keep to common fonts when setting <FONT> tag attributes.

Here's an example of the <FONT> tag with the face attribute included:

```
<font face="arial">This text will appear in the Arial face</font>
```

Most people with PCs running Windows will see the preceding text in Arial fonts, but Macintosh users don't have the Arial font. The common sans serif font for Macs is Helvetica. Fortunately, the <FONT> tag allows you to stack both fonts into the argument. The browser will look for the first font, and if it doesn't find it, will move on to the next named font:

```
<font face="arial,helvetica">This text will appear as Arial or Helvetica,
depending upon which font is available</font>
```

Now you've catered to both your PC and Macintosh friends. It's the right thing to do!

CAUTION

Remember that if a font face isn't available on a given machine, the default face will appear. The default is almost always a serif font, such as Times, unless the user has selected another font for his or her default. So if you're mixing fonts, bear in mind that your sans serifs might appear as serifs, and vice-versa. This lack of control can seem maddening! You can always forgo using a particular type, but then you run the risk of appearing ho-hum. The main caution here goes back to the idea of knowing your audience; that will help you make the best possible choices in every case.

An interesting development in Web typography is embedded fonts. This technique automatically downloads the font characters needed to view a given page. During the summer of 1997, Microsoft released a Web Embedding Font Tool preview. This program analyzes a given site's fonts, compresses the correct font characters, and provides the author with the code to embed the compressed fonts as objects within the HTML code. Sound confusing? It is, a little—but the results are going to be much sounder font control. For more information, check out `http://www.microsoft.com/typography/`. This site offers a lot of great information on Web typography in general.

Type Size

Another consideration when working with fonts is their size, which is important to style and design. A font's size can help indicate what role it's playing on the page: Larger fonts are used for headers, medium-sized fonts for body text, and small fonts for notes and less emphasized information, such as copyright notices.

Varying type size on a page is important, but just as important is keeping that variation consistent. You're looking for the visual interest and practical results that having different sizes of fonts on a page provide; however, you don't want to overwhelm your visitor with too much contrast, which can look like complete chaos!

Using the size Attribute

Font sizing is pretty rudimentary, with whole-number values determining the size of the font. The default, standard size is 3. Obviously, anything higher is going to be bigger, and anything lower will be smaller. You can also use negative numbers, such as -1, to get a very small type size. Here's an example of a header using font face and size attributes:

```
<font face="times,garamond" size=5>
```

Anything much bigger than a size 5 is ungainly. Small fonts, such as 1, are good for notes and copyrights. Anything smaller usually can't be seen by people with average to poor eyesight.

> **NOTE**
>
> Cascading style sheets solve the limitation of font size control by offering up the ability to use points and pixels (as well as inches and centimeters!) to size a font. Chapters 18, "Using Cascading Style Sheets," and 19, "Cascading Style Sheets and Element Positioning," of this book focus on using style sheets for professional presentations.

Figure 34.21 shows an example of a header, body text, and copyright notice, each using a different sized font. Also note the font faces. The header appears in Times, and the copyright notice is in Times set in italics. The body font is Arial. This page looks nice and neat, unlike Figure 34.22, which shows what happens when a coder runs amok. The "wave" effect came into vogue when setting font size first became available. Although fun at the time, it quickly became cliché. It's not very design-savvy either; no one will stick around too long if they have to read a page like that!

FIGURE 34.21.

Attractive, appropriate use of font sizing.

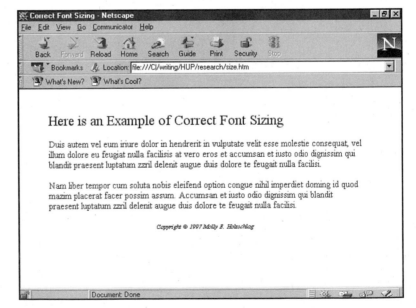

FIGURE 34.22.

Font chaos!

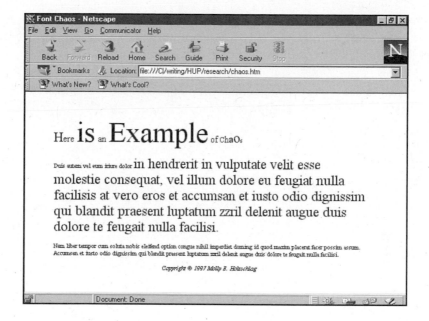

Font Color

Adding color to fonts can help give a page distinction. As with size and face, a light touch is important; you don't want to overwhelm your site visitors with 10 different colors on a page. In fact, sticking to two colors—one for headers and auxiliary text and one for body text—is plenty. Remember, you add colors with the link and visited link colors defined in your <BODY> tag, so more than two text colors and you start going overboard.

An example of the <FONT> tag with the color attribute added looks like this:

```
<font face="Times,Garamond" size=5 color="#003300">
```

Using hexadecimal code, the base 16 equivalent of RGB (Red, Green, Blue) values, I've selected a forest green for my header. You can also use the literal name of standard colors, such as blue, green, red, and the like. I'm not too fond of this technique because it's very limiting. For a nice hexadecimal color chart, visit http://sdc.htrigg.smu.edu/HTMLPages/RGBchart.html or download the nvalue.gif or nhue.gif from http://www.lynda.com/files/. These charts put color selection and hexadecimal values right at your fingertips.

Other Typographic Considerations

There are other considerations when it comes to typography. The good news is that some of them are addressed by new or upcoming technologies. The bad news is that some of them can be accomplished only by using graphics where those fonts would occur. Here's a short course in some of these considerations:

■ Altering the direction of the text can produce an interesting effect. Figure 34.23 shows a font running vertically. This effect was accomplished by using a graphic because it would have been impossible to do with standard HTML.

FIGURE 34.23.

The vertical header on this page was achieved with a graphic.

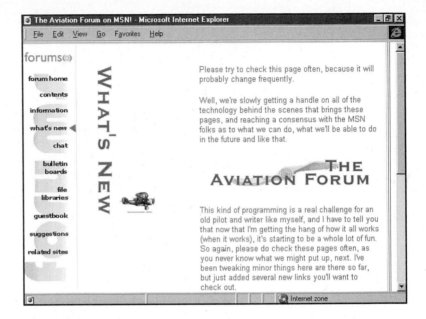

■ Typography also concerns itself with the space between lines, which is called *leading* (pronounced *led-ing*). Leading can be set with a style sheet attribute called *line height*. There still isn't a good option in standard HTML to achieve leading.

■ Kerning is the space between individual letters. There are no solutions for kerning, except using graphics.

■ Another issue is anti-aliasing, known as *font smoothing* in the computer world. Without anti-aliasing, type can appear jagged. Figure 34.24 shows a non-graphical header—you can see the jagged edges on the type. I could use a graphic instead, and select an anti-aliasing option when preparing the type for the graphic. That's a good alternative. Another is controlling aliasing, as Microsoft has done with its font smoother, downloadable for PCs running Windows 95 at `http://www.microsoft.com/typography/grayscal/smoother.htm`. Figure 34.25 shows the same header, seen with font smoothing turned on.

FIGURE 34.24.

The header on this page without font smoothing.

FIGURE 34.25.

The same header with font smoothing on.

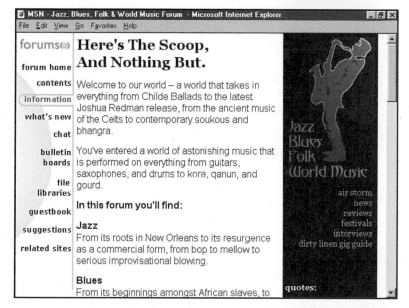

34

USING SPACE,
SHAPE, AND TYPE

If Web typography really interests you, here are some resources to get you started:

On the Net

DesktopPublishing.Com: A truly amazing place, at `http://www.desktoppublishing.com/`.

The World Wide Web Consortium: All kinds of HTML resources, at `http://www.w3.org/`. Visit `http://www.w3.org/style/` for an overview of cascading style sheets.

Microsoft's Typography on the Web: Excellent resource for all that's happening in Web typography, at `http://www.microsoft.com/typography/web/default.htm`.

Web Typography: A Moderated Digest, at `http://www.acdcon.com/webtyp.htm`.

Off the Net

The Mac is not a Typewriter (also *The PC is not a Typewriter*), Robin Williams, Peachpit Press.

Desktop Publisher's Easy Type Guide, Don Dewsnap, Rockport Publishing.

Alphabet: The History, Evolution, and Design of the Letters We Use Today, Allan Haley, Watson Guptill Publishing.

Type and Layout, Colin Wheildon, Strathmore Press.

Summary

Get your pages in shape, give them some space, and add a lot of style through appropriate design techniques! Most of the techniques in this chapter follow easy, standard HTML methods that you can put to use today. Others, like cascading style sheets, will take a bit more research, but either way, you're on the road to better-looking, more effective Web site design.

CHAPTER 35

Putting it All Together: The DisAbilities Forum on MSN

by Molly E. Holzschlag

IN THIS CHAPTER

Now that you've learned a variety of techniques to help improve your Web site, you're going to examine a Web site in detail to see those techniques in action.

I selected the DisAbilities Forum on the Microsoft Network (MSN) because it's one of the larger sites I've developed with several smaller content sections. It also uses a variety of media and programming, including RealAudio, VBScript, and Macromedia Flash, and plenty of interactivity, such as live chat rooms and bulletin boards. I want to show you how each of the sections maintains continuity, yet individuality, and demonstrate how the site, despite its interactive components, maintains integration through the interface, the navigation, and the design elements.

Introduction to the DisAbilities Forum Interface

As mentioned in Chapter 31, "Creating an Effective Interface," users must be welcomed, guided, and offered functional elements to successfully relate to the site through the interface.

Figure 35.1 shows the welcome page of the DisAbilities Forum. This functional page sets up the interface by immediately introducing a number of options that take visitors directly to areas that might be of interest to them. This page changes regularly to reflect a variety of activities offered on the site.

FIGURE 35.1.
The DisAbilities Forum welcome page.

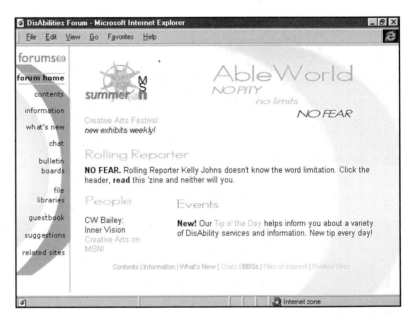

In this case, not only is the left-margin, frame-based navigation introduced, but sections of this static (non-scrolling) main page act as front door–style passages into other areas of the site. The smiling sun graphic at the top left of the welcome page links to the Summer Festival, a cross-promotional event that links to activities across the network. Below that, I have a link to the DisAbilities Forum's own summer activity, the Creative Arts Festival, which I'll be taking a closer look at throughout this chapter.

To the upper right is a welcome animation that tells the visitor where he or she is and makes a statement about what to expect from the content in the site by the site's main slogan: "No Fear, No Pity, No Limits."

Another important component of the forum is the Rolling Reporter, a travel and adventure magazine designed for people with disabilities. Its prominent place on this page draws the visitor to it, letting him or her know that it's an important place to visit! You'll get a closer look at the Rolling Reporter as this guided tour continues.

Along the bottom, two other "doors" offer up different activities. One is the Events section, which also changes regularly. In this case, it offers a link to the DisAbilities Forum's Tip o' the Day, an interactive, frames-based daily tip page, shown in Figure 35.2.

FIGURE 35.2.

The Tip o' the Day page.

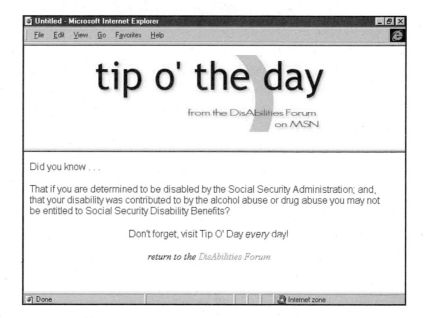

Another door featured on the welcome page is the People section, which has a changing link to information about different members and staff of the forum, as well as special guests of the forum. This example shows a link to photographer C.W. Bailey's work, showcased in the arts festival. Click on that link and voilà! You're visiting the start of C.W.'s exhibit, shown in Figure 35.3.

FIGURE 35.3.

From the People section, link to C.W. Bailey's photographic exhibit.

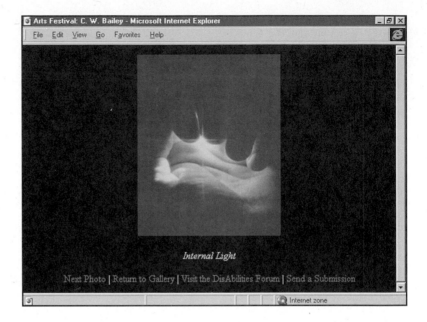

To sum it up, the main page interface welcomes visitors, guides them to popular and important places on the site through the left-margin navigation bar, and highlights areas with the virtual "doors" on the main page. This welcome page introduces visitors to the functional elements of the site, as well as the aesthetic ones.

Metaphor

The design metaphor used in the main tier of the DisAbilities Forum is very subtle. Icons aren't used for two primary reasons: First, the navigation was predetermined by the network, and second, for many disabled individuals, text explanations are more effective than visual cues. However, there are places where metaphor is used to great advantage.

The user interface of the site's Rolling Reporter magazine makes clear use of design metaphor. Take a look at the clever logo shown in Figure 35.4. Based on the international symbol for the DisAbled, a few changes were made to use metaphor in the logo. The wheel of the chair is the Earth, and the figure in the chair is leaning forward while the chair moves through space. This metaphor suggests that the world is accessible to all in some fashion, and that the subject matter in the site is forward-moving, forward-thinking, and progressive. Finally, the stars blinking quietly in the background behind the soaring figure suggest that the stars are reachable—a positive and powerful metaphor indeed.

Clarity and Consistency

Clarity is a critical aspect of interface design, so in the DisAbilities Forum, the buttons, maps, and links are predominantly text and described quite specifically. For example, if you want information about the forum, you click on information in the left-margin navigation bar. This action offers mail options that pull up a mail reader, as shown in Figure 35.5. The text is concise and descriptive and intentionally kept fairly short to maintain clarity.

FIGURE 35.4.

The Rolling Reporter.

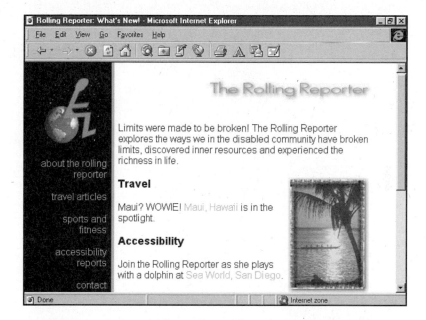

FIGURE 35.5.

A mailto option pulls up a mail reader.

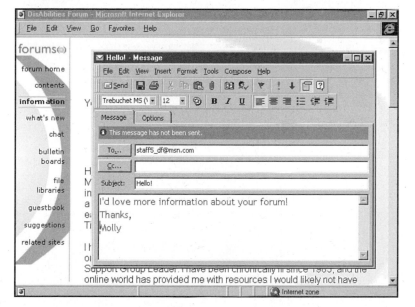

The design elements help produce the quality of consistency. On the main level of the forum, all the graphical headers, body text, colors, and background remain the same. Compare Figures 35.6. and 35.7. Although they are different pages with different content, the design elements are consistent, which conveys a sense of integration. Note, too, the left-margin navigation used in both pages.

FIGURE 35.6.

The BBS (bulletin boards) page.

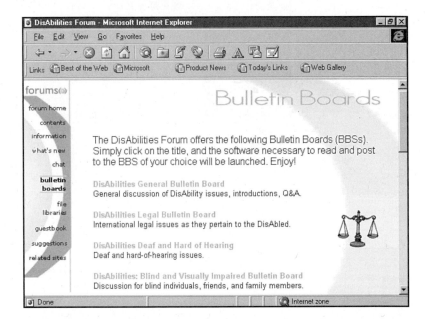

FIGURE 35.7.

The Related Sites page.

Consistency among the site sections is maintained by using the same font styles and colors for most areas of the forum. The Creative Arts Festival does deviate from this because to allow for creative license, some elements needed to be freed up. However, although elements such as backgrounds and fonts differ from the rest of the site, consistency is maintained by sticking to the site's color palette.

Orientation and Navigation

Orientation on this site is accomplished at the top level by the pervasive navigation bar, which keeps static throughout the site. As you can see in Figure 35.7, navigation on the top level also has a text component along the bottom, which helps with orientation by reinforcing the sections of the site.

The main navigation bar was created by MSN using Macromedia's Flash (`http://www.macromedia.com/`). Flash is also used to create active buttons on the main page. This compact and fun-to-use animation program makes creating active media easy, and the good news is that either Netscape or Internet Explorer 3.0 and above can manage these fast-loading files.

The rest of the navigation on the forum is text-based. If you refer back to Figure 35.4, you'll note how the navigation is based on the left margin. I'll show you how this was done later on in the chapter, when I discuss using tables and frames for layout control.

The Creative Arts Festival relies on a main menu (see Figure 35.8), which serves as an index for all the pages in the festival site. Navigation in the festival site is text-based, adding additional options in individual exhibits and always offering links back up to the index or to the top level of the forum.

FIGURE 35.8.

The Creative Arts Festival main menu.

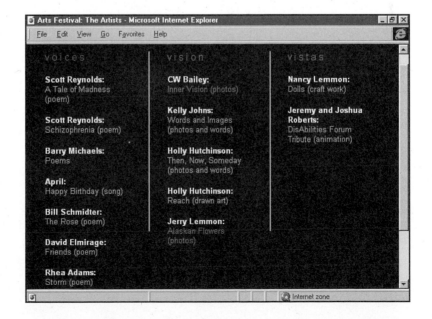

Finally, site visitors can orient themselves visually through the consistent palette and style, as well as the title bar and the text-based identification running along the bottom of the page. (See Figure 35.9.)

FIGURE 35.9.

Note the title and text-based orientation.

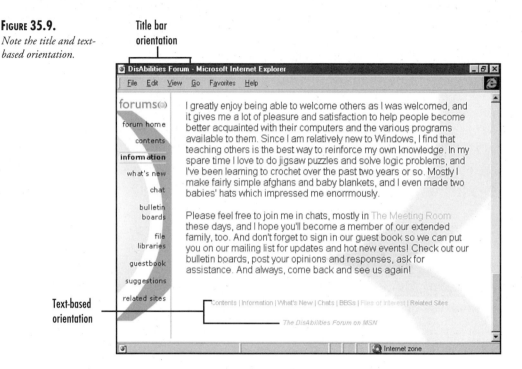

Title bar orientation

Text-based orientation

Site Planning Overview

Now that you have a good idea of the interface and basic design components of the forum, I'm going to step back for a moment and look more closely at the way the site was planned. Remember, it's careful planning that will ensure the type of consistent, integrated look and feel you're after with a design.

Design Intent

The intent of the DisAbilities Forum is to inform, educate, and provide support for people who have, or whose lives are somehow affected by, a disability. This intent is addressed by a number of options and services that create the *content* of the forum.

Design Content

At the top level, the content is primarily informational, with the interface opening doorways to activities and resources that are found throughout the site. The top-level information listed in the navigation bar includes the following:

Contents: This is an index of the site's offerings.

Information: The information area introduces the forum's staff and provides information on how to use the forum.

What's New: This section helps visitors quickly find out what's new and interesting on the DisAbilities Forum.

Chat: A listing of theme chats, chat rooms, and general information about chats is available on this page.

Bulletin Boards: Descriptions of individual BBSs within the forum are available, with links to each BBS.

File Libraries: Each available file library can be accessed from this page. Files on the forum site include informational documents on various disabilities, laws, benefits, and special software programs.

Guest Book: Members can introduce themselves in this area.

Suggestions: This area is the primary feedback section for the forum. Visitors with ideas or concerns about the forum can leave their ideas here.

Related Sites: This area offers links to other places on the Microsoft Network and specialized Web sites of interest to the community.

> **NOTE**
>
> This top-level setup is a good example to base your own sites on. Not everyone will have BBSs or file areas, but the general structure of this site is a sound one for typical Web projects.

Specialty content is delivered by the Arts Festival, the Rolling Reporter magazine, and the Tip o' the Day features.

Short- and Long-Term Goals

The short-term goal was simple: to provide a jumping-off point to the different aspects of the forum's content so members can get to the information they need quickly.

The long-term goal builds on the intent of the site. Content is aggregated by creating—and keeping—the results of activities and events. For example, the Creative Arts Festival began as part of a seasonal (in this case, summer) event, but the interesting content collected for that event remains available as an ongoing exhibit. Similarly, all articles and links added to the Rolling Reporter are archived so that interested parties can easily find them.

This collecting and archiving of content creates a growing, vital resource for the disabled community on MSN. Think about your own site's goals. You want people to come back to your

35

PUTTING IT ALL TOGETHER

site and to use it as a starting point, a reference, entertainment, or a point-of-sales mechanism. By offering information important to your audience, you maximize your Web site's effectiveness. In the case of the DisAbilities Forum, members come to know that if they are planning a trip to Disney World, for example, there's likely to be an article from the Rolling Reporter that will help them make decisions about their trip. (See Figure 35.10.)

FIGURE 35.10.

Want to learn about an accessible visit to Disney World? The Rolling Reporter is the place!

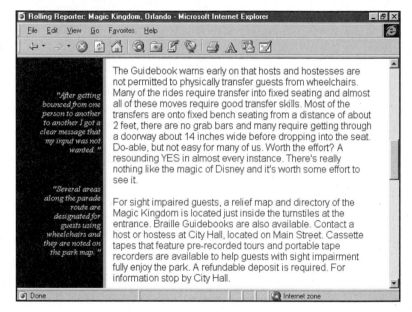

The Guidebook warns early on that hosts and hostesses are not permitted to physically transfer guests from wheelchairs. Many of the rides require transfer into fixed seating and almost all of these moves require good transfer skills. Most of the transfers are onto fixed bench seating from a distance of about 2 feet, there are no grab bars and many require getting through a doorway about 14 inches wide before dropping into the seat. Do-able, but not easy for many of us. Worth the effort? A resounding YES in almost every instance. There's really nothing like the magic of Disney and it's worth some effort to see it.

For sight impaired guests, a relief map and directory of the Magic Kingdom is located just inside the turnstiles at the entrance. Braille Guidebooks are also available. Contact a host or hostess at City Hall, located on Main Street. Cassette tapes that feature pre-recorded tours and portable tape recorders are available to help guests with sight impairment fully enjoy the park. A refundable deposit is required. For information stop by City Hall.

"After getting bounced from one person to another to another I got a clear message that my input was not wanted."

"Several areas along the parade route are designated for guests using wheelchairs and they are noted on the park map."

Audience Experience

Not only is the forum intended to be resourceful, it's also intended to be a place where a community can gather, support one another in times of difficulty, and learn skills and effective living methods from one another.

All these activities provide a sense of *community*, and as the Web becomes bigger and bigger, fostering and maintaining this sense of community becomes imperative. People aren't on the Internet or online services just looking for information—they want to interact with others! Interaction is a primary fascination of the Web, and you can bank on communities gathering around shared interests. This fascination and need for community can only help you in your quest for success with a Web site. Think about community and the audience experience as you plan and design your site.

The underlying theme of the DisAbilities Forum is promoting enlightenment. The audience experience should provide a sense of shared support as well as information access—ideally, an uplifting and life-enhancing experience.

> **CAUTION**
>
> As with almost any aspect of Web site design, knowledge of your audience is critical. If you haven't done your early analysis and determined *who* is visiting your site, it will be difficult to offer a sense of community. Know your audience first, and then seek to give them what they want and need.

Interactive and Multimedia Elements

Engaging, community-oriented resources are created on the Web with interactive elements and multimedia events. You want to grab your audience's attention, and then you want to keep it! The DisAbilities Forum achieves this with a variety of interactive and multimedia-oriented events, covered in the following sections.

Chats and Bulletin Boards

MSN has proprietary software for creating and using chat rooms and bulletin boards. In the case of the DisAbilities Forum, these areas are the true heart of the community—they are what keep people coming back. (See Figure 35.11.) Information and support can be exchanged, but more important, friendship ties develop.

FIGURE 35.11.

A BBS on the DisAbilities Forum.

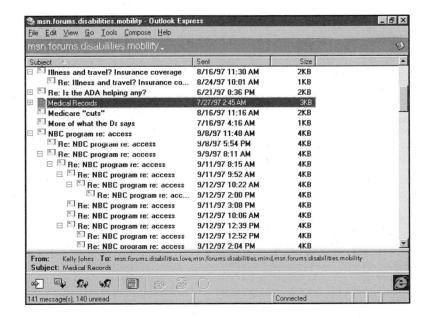

35

Many of the forum members meet each other in person, and their lives have been enriched by the online component of their relationships. In this way, a Web site can not only be good business, but give back to the community in important, lasting ways.

You might be thinking that there's no possible place for this sort of thing on your point-of-sales Web site. I'd caution you to think more creatively, as have many commercial sites, such as Saturn Cars (`http://www.saturncars.com/`) or Travelocity (`http://www.travelocity.com/`).

These are two Web sites with the primary intent of selling a product—cars or travel services—yet each one fosters community by offering BBSs to their visitors. I recently got involved in an online discussion about hotel rooms; people shared their experiences in a certain hotel I was going to stay at. When I got there, I was armed with knowledge about the hotel and how to maximize my time there, getting the best room possible, knowing who to talk to if I needed assistance, and the like.

Simply put, you can bet I'll go back to that Web site in the future. I know how much this interaction enhanced my travel experience. What a smart way to boost sales, too!

Multimedia and Programming

Another way to engage the audience is by offering interesting and fun elements that are programmed into the site. In the case of the DisAbilities Forum, multimedia is used carefully because the audience is very specific. For example, although Macromedia Flash and RealAudio (see Figure 35.12) are used in some sections of the site, audio and video are kept to a minimum because many forum members are blind or deaf. Still, these options enhance the audience experience for those who can access them, and care is taken to make certain the site's content isn't significantly altered because of the existence of multimedia.

FIGURE 35.12.
This RealAudio file of a breaching whale's cry adds a lot to the magazine's interactive experience.

Programming-based events also add interest to a site. The Tip o' the Day uses VBScript to deliver important information. Each day, this information automatically updates, which keeps the site fresh. Staff and management have very little maintenance overhead with this particular feature, and audiences enjoy coming to the site and finding something both new and useful.

Think about multimedia and programmed events that will enhance your site and your visitor's experience. There are many, many options, the most popular delivered by Macromedia Flash and Shockwave, Java and JavaScript, Visual Basic and VBScript, RealAudio and RealVideo, and a growing variety of other interactive options.

> **NOTE**
>
> More information on Macromedia products can be found at http://www.macromedia.com/. For Java and JavaScript, visit Sun Microsystem's home site at http://www.sun.com/. As the developers of Java, Sun offers updates, links, and other helpful resources for those interested in using it. Microsoft is the developer of Visual Basic and VBScript; more information can be found at http://www.microsoft.com/. Media options from Progressive Networks (RealAudio and Video) can be explored at http://www.realaudio.com/.

Navigation

You've already caught a glimpse of the navigation types on the forum. This section reviews the media used and gives you a look at the actual HTML code and programming used to produce the design.

Navigation Media

Two types of navigation media are prominent on the DisAbilities Forum Web site:

- **Text-based:** The most simple—but often most effective—option for Web sites, the top-level navigation choices are coded as follows:

```
<a href="contents.htm">Contents</a> ¦
<a href="info.htm">Information</a> ¦
<a href="whatsnew.htm">What's New</a> ¦
<a href="chatmain.htm">Chats</a> ¦
<a href="bbsmain.htm">BBSs</a> ¦
<a href="libmain.htm">Files of Interest</a> ¦
<a href="linksmain.htm">Related Sites</a>
```

> **TIP**
>
> You'll notice that I use a ¦ symbol as a separator between each selection. Other common text-based separators include a dash - or brackets [nav info here]. Whatever method you choose, it's helpful to create some kind of visual separation between the options.

■ **Macromedia Flash:** In the case of the left-margin navigation bar, the Microsoft Network offers designers a selection of navigation to be used at the top level of all internal sites.

The Flash navigation bar is then coded by using the <SCRIPT> tag, which handles the VBScript that controls the navigation and allows it to be customized from forum to forum, and the <OBJECT> tag, which manages the Flash file. (The <OBJECT> tag is covered in Chapters 11, "Adding Images to Your Web Page," and 16, "Embedding Objects in HTML"; the <SCRIPT> tag as it's used here is discussed in Chapter 24, "Using VBScript.") The code is as follows (note how the URLs are embedded into the code):

```
<script language="vbscript">

sub navbar_fscommand(byval command, byval args)
select case command
case "show_all" parent.location.href="http://forums.msn.com"
case "home" parent.forummain.location.href = "welcome.htm"
case "contents" parent.forummain.location.href = "contents.htm"
case "info" parent.forummain.location.href = "info.htm"
case "new" parent.forummain.location.href = "whatsnew.htm"
case "chat" parent.forummain.location.href = "chatmain.htm"
case "bbs" parent.forummain.location.href = "bbsmain.htm"
case "file" parent.forummain.location.href = "libmain.htm"
case "guestbook" parent.forummain.location.href
➥= "news://msnnews.msn.com/msn.forums.disabilities.guestbook"
case "suggestions" parent.forummain.location.href = "news://msnnews.msn.com/
➥msn.forums.disabilities.suggestbox"
case "sites" parent.forummain.location.href = "linksmain.htm"
end select
end sub

</script>


<object
  id="navbar"
  classid="clsid:d27cdb6e-ae6d-11cf-96b8-444553540000"
  width="100%" height="100%">
  <param name="movie" value="images/navbar.spl">
  <param name="quality" value="high">
  <param name="loop" value="false">
  <param name="play" value="false">
  <param name="scale" value="showall">
  <param name="devicefont" value="true">
  <param name="salign" value="tl">
  <param name="menu" value="false">
</object>
```

The results are an attractive, static navigation system that not only achieves its primary goal of getting visitors from page to page, but helps fulfill the interface goal of consistent design.

Navigation Styles

Typically, navigation is to the right, left, top, or bottom margin on a given page. The DisAbilities Forum's top level takes advantage of the left and bottom options by using the Flash navigation bar (left) and text-based navigation (bottom).

The Rolling Reporter uses left-based navigation as well, but in the form of text rather than graphics. Finally, the Creative Arts Festival uses very simple, bottom-based navigation throughout. (See Figure 35.13.)

FIGURE 35.13.
A simple, bottom-based navigation option in a Creative Arts Festival exhibit.

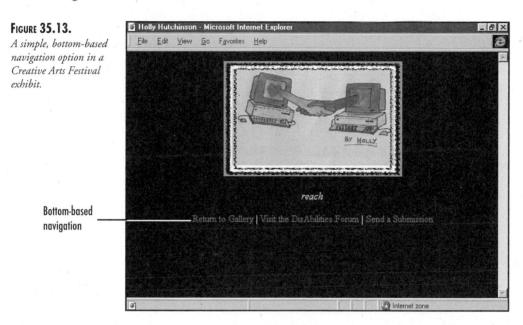

Bottom-based navigation

Left- and bottom-based styles prevail in this site, but they are produced differently. In the case of the top level, borderless frames are used to create the static, left-margin section where the Flash navigation bar sits. The Rolling Reporter, on the other hand, uses a table-based format to achieve a left-margin style.

Navigation Methods

Here's a look at how the different styles of navigation are coded.

■ **Frames-based navigation:** The frames-based navigation at the top level uses three files to create its interface:

The frame set   This is the "control" file of any frames-based design; its code is shown here:

```
<html>
<head>
```

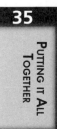

```
<title>DisAbilities Forum</TITLE>
</head>

<frameset cols="95,20%" framespacing="0" frameborder="0">
  <frame src="sidebar.htm" name="forum_sidebar" scrolling="no">
  <frame src="welcome.htm" name="forummain" noresize>
</frameset>

</html>
```

The HTML code calls for two columns, with a width of 95 pixels for the left margin. The frame borders are turned off in the frameset string, and scrolling is disabled. This simple frame set sets up the layout for the pages that will load in the right and left columns.

The first (left) frame   This is the frame that holds the navigation bar, with the scripting shown earlier in the chapter. Here's the page in its entirety:

```
<html>

<head>

<title> the disabilities forum </title>

<script language="vbscript">

sub navbar_fscommand(byval command, byval args)
select case command
case "show_all" parent.location.href="http://forums.msn.com"
case "home" parent.forummain.location.href = "welcome.htm"
case "contents" parent.forummain.location.href = "contents.htm"
case "info" parent.forummain.location.href = "info.htm"
case "new" parent.forummain.location.href = "whatsnew.htm"
case "chat" parent.forummain.location.href = "chatmain.htm"
case "bbs" parent.forummain.location.href = "bbsmain.htm"
case "file" parent.forummain.location.href = "libmain.htm"
case "guestbook" parent.forummain.location.href =
➥"news://msnnews.msn.com/msn.forums.disabilities.guestbook"
case "suggestions" parent.forummain.location.href = "news://
➥msnnews.msn.com/msn.forums.disabilities.suggestbox"
case "sites" parent.forummain.location.href = "linksmain.htm"
end select
end sub

</script>

</head>

<body
<bgcolor="#FFFFFF" leftmargin="0" topmargin="0">

<object
  id="navbar"
  classid="clsid:d27cdb6e-ae6d-11cf-96b8-444553540000"
  width="100%" height="100%">
  <param name="movie" value="images/navbar.spl">
```

```
<param name="quality" value="high">
<param name="loop" value="false">
<param name="play" value="false">
<param name="scale" value="showall">
<param name="devicefont" value="true">
<param name="salign" value="tl">
<param name="menu" value="false">

</object>

</body>
</html>
```

This HTML code loads the Flash navigation and its accompanying custom navigation calls into the left frame.

The second (right) frame   This is the welcome page, the main starting page of the forum that you viewed earlier in Figure 35.1. You'll see the Flash buttons, text, and other features, including style sheets, which I'll describe in the upcoming "Space, Shape, and Type" section. It's interesting to note the table-based layout of the page for optimum control. Here's the HTML code for the welcome page:

```
<html>
<head>

<title>

Welcome Page - AbleWorld: The DisAbilities Forum on MSN.

</title>

</head>

<style>

BODY {background: FFFFFF; color: 000000}
H3 {font: 14pt arial; color: 60099}
.1 {font: 11pt arial; color: 000000; text-align: right}
.2 {font: 12pt arial; color: 000000; text-align: left}
.3 {font: 10pt arial; color: 000000; text-align: left}
.4 {font: 11pt arial; color: 9966FF; text-align: right}
.5 {font: 8pt arial; color: FF9933; text-align: center}
A.p {color: FF9933; text-decoration: none}

</style>

<body bgcolor="#FFFFFF" text="#FFFFCC" link="#FFCC99"
vlink="#9999CC" alink="#FFFFCC" background="images/bak2.jpg">


<table border=0 width=510 cellpadding=5 cellspacing=5>
<tr>

<td class=3 valign=top width=200>
```

```
<OBJECT
classid="clsid:D27CDB6E-AE6D-11cf-96B8-444553540000"
codebase="http://active.macromedia.com/flash2/cabs/SWFLASH.CAB"
width="104" height="70">
<param NAME="Movie" VALUE="images/icon-wht.swf">
<param name="Loop" value="False">
<param NAME="Quality" VALUE="best">
<param name="Scale" value="showall">
</OBJECT>
<p>

<a class=p href="arts/default.htm" target=_top>Creative Arts Festival:</a>
<br>
<i>new exhibits weekly!</i>
</td>


<td class=1 valign=top width=300>

<img src="images/dis-ani1.gif" width=300 height=100 border=0 alt=" ">

</td>
</tr>

<tr>
<td class=3 width=500 colspan=2>

<object classid="clsid:D27CDB6E-AE6D-11CF-96B8-444553540000"
➥codebase="fsplash.cab" align="baseline" border="0" width="175"
➥height="35">
<param name="Movie" value="rr-but.swf">
<param name="Loop" value="False">
<param name="Play" value="True">
<param name="BGColor" value="ffffff">
<param name="Quality" value="high">
<param name="Scale" value="Showall">
</object>
<br>

<b>NO FEAR.</b> Rolling Reporter Kelly Johns doesn't know the word
➥limitation. Click the header, <b>read</b> this 'zine and neither
will you.

</td>
</tr>

<tr>
<td class=3 width=100>

<object classid="clsid:D27CDB6E-AE6D-11CF-96B8-444553540000"
➥codebase="fsplash.cab" align="baseline" border="0" width="83"
➥height="35">
<param name="Movie" value="pp-but.swf">
<param name="Loop" value="False">
<param name="Play" value="True">
<param name="BGColor" value="ffffff">
<param name="Quality" value="high">
<param name="Scale" value="Showall">
```

```
</object>
<br>
CW Bailey:
<br>
Inner Vision
<br>
<a class=p href="http://forums.msn.com/disabilities/arts/bails-1.htm"
➡target="_top">Creative Arts on MSN!</a>

</td>

<td class=3 width=400>

<object classid="clsid:D27CDB6E-AE6D-11CF-96B8-444553540000"
➡codebase="fsplash.cab" align="baseline" border="0" width="70"
➡height="35">
<param name="Movie" value="evt-but.swf">
<param name="Loop" value="False">
<param name="Play" value="True">
<param name="BGColor" value="ffffff">
<param name="Quality" value="high">
<param name="Scale" value="Showall">
</object>
<br clear="right">

<b>New! </b> Our <a class=p href="tip/daymain.htm" target=_top>Tip o' the
➡Day</a> helps inform you about a variety of DisAbility services and
➡information. New tip every day!
<p>
</td>
</tr>

<tr>
<td valign=top width=500 colspan=2>

<div class=5>

<a href="contents.htm">Contents</a> ¦
<a href="info.htm">Information</a> ¦
<a href="whatsnew.htm">What's New</a> ¦
<a href="chatmain.htm">Chats</a> ¦
<a href="bbsmain.htm">BBSs</a> ¦
<a href="libmain.htm">Files of Interest</a> ¦
<a href="linksmain.htm">Related Sites</a>

</div>

</tr>
</table>

</body>
</html>
```

The three files combined make up this left-margin navigation interface that
dominates the top-level design of the DisAbilities Forum.

35

PUTTING IT ALL
TOGETHER

■ **Table-based navigation:** On the Rolling Reporter site, the left-margin navigation is achieved with a table. Here's the code from the Rolling Reporter site's Contact page:

```
<html>
<head>
<title>Rolling Reporter: Contact</title>
</head>

<body bgcolor="#000000" text="#000000" link="#FF9933" vlink="#9966FF"
➥alink="#9966CC" background="images/rr-bak.gif">

<table width=600 cellpadding=0 cellspacing=20 border=0>
<tr>
```

This table cell creates the left-margin navigation:

```
<td valign=top align=right bgcolor="#000000" width=110>

<div align=center>
<img src="images/globe.gif" alt="globe graphic" width=100 height=109>
</div>
<p>

<font face=arial,helvetica size=3>

<a href="about.htm">about the rolling reporter</a>
<p>

<a href="articles.htm">travel articles</a>
<p>

<a href="sports.htm">sports and fitness</a>
<p>

<a href="access.htm">accessibility reports</a>
<p>

<a href="contact.htm">contact</a>
<p>

<a href="default.htm">home</a>

</font>

</td>
```

This table cell is the main content cell:

```
<td valign=top width=450>

<div align=right>
<img src="images/ct-hed.jpg" width=300 height=50 border=0 alt="contact
➥header">
</div>
<p>

<font face=arial,helvetica>

Want to get in touch? Have an article, link, or other item of interest for
The Rolling Reporter Web site?
```

```
Send email to <a href="mailto:kelly_df@MSN.com">the rolling reporter</a>.
<p>

The Rolling Reporter holds live events and discussions on the Microsoft
Network's DisAbilities Forum.
You can follow <a href="http://forums.MSN.com/disabilities/">this link</a> to
access the Forum and learn about all of our activities!
<p>

The Rolling Reporter is the concept of Kelly Johns.
<p>

All articles and photos are &copy; 1997, Kelly Johns unless otherwise noted.
Reprints are restricted, please write for permission for article reprints.
Design and graphics are &copy; 1997 The DisAbilities Forum.
<p>

</font>

</td>
</tr>
</table>
<p>

<div align=left>
<font size=-1>&copy; 1997<br> the rolling reporter</a>
</div>

</body>
</html>
```

At this point, you might be wondering which approach is better—tables or frames. I think it really boils down to what you're trying to achieve. Tables load faster and take up less space because there's only one file per page, but frames require at least three files to produce a page. Frames, however, can add static sections to your site, which is a strong, stable method of designing an interface. The choice depends on personal preference and application.

Managing Color and Graphics

Color is an important part of how the sections of the DisAbilities Forum maintain an integrated look.

The Individual Palette

One color palette dominates the entire forum, made up of black and white with a range of purples, oranges, and reds. The color *use* varies greatly, but these colors are maintained consistently throughout the site.

When developing sites, it's wise to use a main palette that dominates the entire site, even if you have sections that use the colors differently. For example, if you have white, black, pink, purple, yellow, and green in your palette, you might create a left-margin navigation system that uses different colors in the navigation area depending on where you are in the site. The look will be different, but the similar palette will lend some consistency. It's an effective way to gain visual texture and interest without losing precious consistency and orientation.

Safe Color

I always recommend using browser-safe color, which I discussed in Chapter 33, "Managing Web Color and Graphics." The DisAbilities Forum is no exception. All the colors used for backgrounds, text, and graphics were taken from the browser-safe palette.

Here's the <BODY> tag code for the top level of the forum:

```
<body bgcolor="#FFFFFF" text="#FFFFCC" link="#FFCC99"
vlink="#9999CC" alink="#FFFFCC" background="images/bak2.jpg">
```

Here's the code for the Rolling Reporter:

```
<body bgcolor="#000000" text="#000000" link="#FF9933" vlink="#9966FF"
➥alink="#9966CC" background="images/rr-bak.gif">
```

And here's the code for one of the Creative Arts Festival pages:

```
<body bgcolor="#FF9900" text="#000000" link="#CC3300" vlink="663333"
➥alink="#FFFFCC" background="images/af-p1bak.gif">
```

All these colors are browser-safe. As a little experiment, you can find these colors and put together the forum's palette on your own. Refer to Chapter 33 for information on where to get the resources to do this.

Graphics

All the graphics on the forum's top level are GIFs. There's a good reason for this: To combine the background with graphics, it was important to have transparencies. As Figure 35.14 shows, even the animated graphic on the welcome page is transparent.

FIGURE 35.14.

This animated GIF is transparent, too.

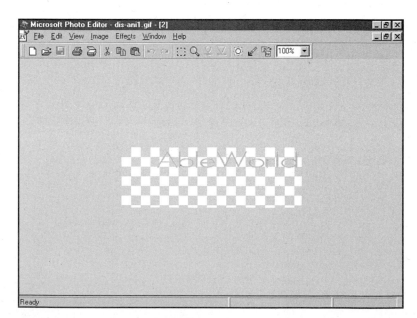

With the exception of face shots used in the staff area, there are no light-variable photographs used on the forum's main section. However, the Creative Arts Festival has several photographic exhibits (see Figure 35.15), as does the Rolling Reporter, shown in Figure 35.16. In these cases, the quality of the photos really demanded JPG quality.

FIGURE 35.15.

This photograph by C.W. Bailey required JPG quality.

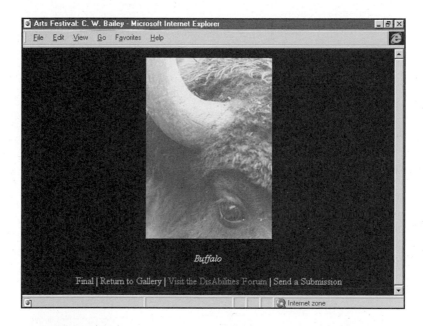

FIGURE 35.16.

Kelly John's exceptional photography on the Rolling Reporter Web site also demands JPG.

35

PUTTING IT ALL
TOGETHER

Space, Shape, and Type

The important design issues of space, shape, and type are addressed on the DisAbilities Forum in a variety of ways.

First, space is addressed on every content page in the site by using tables. Even a simple page such as the Creative Arts Festival index uses tables to manage both the columnar layout and the space:

```
<html>
<head>
<title>Arts Festival: The Artists</title>
</head>
<body bgcolor="#000000" text="#FFFFCC" link="#FF9900" vlink="CC3300"
➥ alink="#FFFFCC">

<table border=0 cellpadding=10 cellspacing=10 width=585>
<tr>
<td valign=top width=160>
<font face=arial color="#CC3300">v o i c e s</font>
<p>

<font face=arial size=2>

<b>Scott Reynolds: <a href="sr-1.htm"><br></b>A Tale of Madness (poem)</a>
<p>

<b>Scott Reynolds: <a href="schiz1.htm"><br></b>Schizophrenia (poem)</a>
<p>

<b>Barry Michaels: <a href="bm.htm"><br></b>Poems</a>
<p>

<b>April:</b> <br><a href="april.htm">Happy Birthday (song)</a>
<p>

<b>Bill Schmidter: <a href="bill1.htm"><br></b>The Rose (poem)</a>
<p>

<b>David Elmirage:<a href="david1.htm"><br></b> Friends (poem)</a>
<p>

<b>Rhea Adams:<a href="ra-1.htm"><br></b> Storm (poem)</a>
<p>

<b>Justin Roll:</b><br><a href="jr.htm">Poems</a>
<p>

</font>
</td>

<td width=2 valign=top>
<img src="images/org-bar.gif" alt="orange bar" width=2 height=300>
</td>
```

```
<td valign=top width=160>
<font face=arial color="#CC3300">v i s i o n</font>
<p>

<font face=arial size=2>
<b>CW Bailey:</b>
<br><a href="bails-1.htm">Inner Vision (photos)</a>
<p>

<b>Kelly Johns:</b> <br><a href="kelly.htm">Words and Images
(photos and words)</a>
<p>

<b>Holly Hutchinson:</b>
<br><a href="hol1.htm">Then, Now, Someday (photos and words)</a>
<p>

<b>Holly Hutchinson:</b>
<br><a href="hol2.htm">Reach (drawn art)</a>
<p>

<b>Jerry Lemmon:</b>
<br><a href="jer-1.htm">Alaskan Flowers (photos)</a>
<p>

</font>
</td>

<td width=2 valign=top>
<img src="images/org-bar.gif" alt="orange bar" width=2 height=300>
</td>

<td valign=top width-160>
<font face=arial color="#CC3300">v i s t a s</font>
<p>

<font face=arial size=2>
<b>Nancy Lemmon:</b>
<br><a href="nancy.htm">Dolls (craft work)</a>
<p>

<b>Jeremy and Joshua Roberts:</b>
<br><a href="jj.htm">DisAbilities Forum Tribute (animation)</a>
</font>
<p>

</td>
</tr>
</table>

<div align=center>
<a href="http://forums.MSN.com/disabilities/">Visit the DisAbilities Forum</a>
➡¦ <a href="mailto:kelly_df@MSN.com">Send a Submission </a>
</div>

</body>
</html>
```

Note the orange bars, created by GIFs and stretched vertically. This trick is a handy one for both horizontal and vertical spacing. You can do it with color or make the graphic transparent to create an invisible spacer.

Another way of gaining space is aligning images. Here's an HTML example from Jerry Lemmon's Alaskan Flowers page:

```
<img src="images/jer-fl2.jpg" alt="another flower" width=125 height=151
➥hspace=5 vspace=10 align=right>
```

In this case, you can see the use of alignment, as well as horizontal (hspace) and vertical (vspace) space, to produce additional space in the layout.

Shape is addressed in many places. You've probably already noticed the arc theme that runs through the top-level pages of the forum. Another interesting use of shape is found in the Creative Arts Festival entry (see Figure 35.17) and throughout festival exhibits, as shown in Figure 35.18. Shape adds a lot of interest for the forum, as it will for your designs, too!

FIGURE 35.17.

The entry to the Creative Arts Festival uses an unusual triangular treatment.

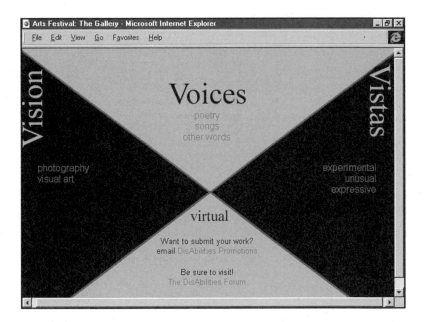

Finally, type is an integral part of the forum's consistency. With the exception of the Creative Arts Festival, where use of type is more liberal, font faces, colors, and sizes are very specific. The font face, called Espresso, used in headers for the top-level forum pages and the Rolling Reporter is the same, as you can see by comparing the two headers shown in Figure 35.19. The body text uses a sans serif type called Arial.

FIGURE 35.18.

This spiral accentuates the emotional aspect of the page's content.

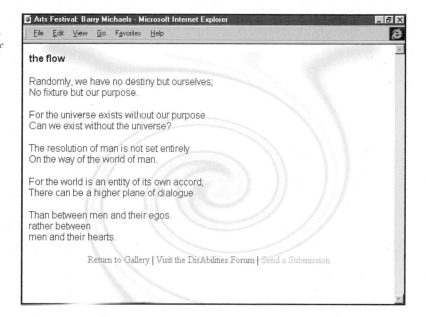

FIGURE 35.19.

Graphic headers for both the forum and the Rolling Reporter magazine use a font face called Espresso.

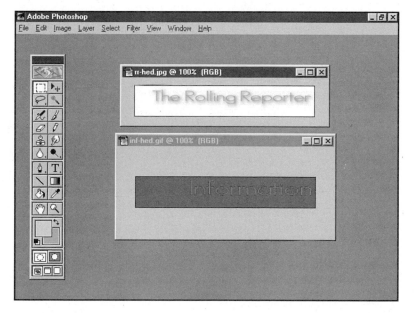

You'll note that fonts are controlled by style sheets embedded in individual pages of the forum. Here's an example:

```
<style>

BODY {background: FFFFFF; color: 000000}
H3 {font: 14pt arial; color: 60099}
.1 {font: 11pt arial; color: 000000; text-align: right}
.2 {font: 12pt arial; color: 000000; text-align: left}
.3 {font: 10pt arial; color: 000000; text-align: left}
.4 {font: 11pt arial; color: 9966FF; text-align: right}
.5 {font: 8pt arial; color: FF9933; text-align: center}
A.p {color: FF9933; text-decoration: none}

</style>
```

For more information about style sheets, visit Chapter 18, "Using Cascading Style Sheets."

> **NOTE**
>
> You can get the same results for type on your pages with the <FONT> tag and related attributes. Because everyone on MSN is using Internet Explorer, designing with style sheets caused no potential viewing problems for this site design. However, you'll need to weight the pros and cons of using style sheets or the <FONT> tag and attributes for each individual project.

Summary

This detailed examination of a professionally designed and implemented site gives you a working example of the techniques you've studied in the past four chapters. It's important to remember that interface design, graphic production, and management of color, space, and type should all be precluded by a thorough preproduction examination of your audience and intent. Without these, your direction will be haphazard at best. However, if you've done your groundwork, studied the techniques in these chapters carefully, and watched as these techniques are applied to the DisAbilities Forum on MSN, you're positioned to begin using these techniques. The results are certain to be better thought-out, more carefully designed, and—ultimately—more successful Web sites.

VIII

PART

IN THIS PART

XML

What Is XML?

by Simon North

IN THIS CHAPTER

XML, which stands for *Extensible Markup Language*, is a very simple dialect of SGML (the *Standard Generalized Markup Language*). XML has been developed to fill the gap between SGML's power and complexity and HTML's inadequacy and simplicity.

This chapter includes the following topics:

- The purpose and nature of XML
- XML's syntax and structure rules
- XML document type declarations (DTDs)
- XML's linking mechanisms (XLL)
- XML's style language (XSL)

After reading this chapter, you should be familiar with the core concepts of the XML language and have a basic understanding of XML's style language, XSL.

> **NOTE**
>
> Be warned that XML is not yet finished. The specification consists of three parts, and each part has reached a different stage. Part 1, covering the basic language, is now in its third revision, but is still only a draft. Part 2, covering linking, is now in its second draft version. Part 3, covering the style language, is a rough draft that has practically no formal status at all. Although the specification is already fairly stable, changes could still be made to any part of XML.

What Is XML?

As stated, XML is a very simple dialect of SGML, so to understand it properly, you need to know a little about SGML first.

Basically, SGML is a language that supplies the tools for defining markup languages. HTML is such a markup language, called an *SGML application*, consisting of a well-defined set of elements (enclosed in *tags*), attributes (such as color), and entities (such as ©).

Since its initial formalization as an ISO standard in 1986, SGML has consistently faced a problem of its own creation. In trying to be truly generalized, it had to be powerful. In being powerful, it became complex, and in becoming complex, it became difficult to learn, time-consuming to implement, and expensive.

The Internet (or more precisely, the World Wide Web) needed something simpler, something less demanding of both human and computer resources—so HTML was born.

HTML has been an excellent markup language for its purpose, but since its development, that purpose has grown and changed in ways no one could have foreseen. HTML is now being put to uses that push the boundaries of what's possible, and despite attempts to patch it with proprietary extensions, it's reaching its limits. Modern Web applications require more than what the simple addition of a few more tags can offer.

XML is an attempt to find a common ground between SGML and HTML. Instead of being another SGML application, another language like HTML, XML is—like SGML—a "metalanguage" for defining markup languages. XML applications are a toolkit for making your own HTML. You can use XML to define your own applications and define your own markup language so you can encode the information in your Web documents far more precisely than what can be done in HTML. Combine XML with the processing power that languages such as Java and ActiveX offer, and you have the means to produce "intelligent" documents, documents that can be understood by your applications so that the information can be processed in ways that would be absolutely impossible with HTML.

XML is not intended to be a replacement for HTML; it's meant to be a supplement and an alternative to HTML, when needed. XML and HTML can happily co-exist, each being used for what it's most suited: HTML for "quick and dirty" applications, such as Web pages, and XML for applications that need more intelligent documents and more processing ability.

XML Documents

An XML document doesn't need to look that different from an HTML document (and, as you see later in this chapter, it doesn't take much effort to convert an HTML document into an XML document). Just like an HTML document, an XML document consists of a mixture of text and markup (tags). Where XML documents differ is at the conceptual level—in particular, in validity and well-formedness.

Validity

Reflecting their closer relationship to SGML than HTML, XML documents can be validated to make sure their structure and content conform to the rules defined for that type of document. Like SGML, these rules are specified in a document called the *Document Type Declaration* (DTD).

Unlike other markup systems (such as HTML and TeX), using a DTD in SGML and XML means you can actually check, or validate, documents. *Validation* means you can make sure all the elements a document should contain are actually present, in the right order, and, to a limited extent, contain the data they should contain.

I cover the DTD again later in this chapter in the section "The XML Document Type Declaration," but it's enough for now to understand that for an XML document to be "valid," it must have a DTD, and its contents must conform to the rules expressed in that DTD. The specific rules for validity are explained in the following sections when the objects they apply to are described.

Well-Formedness

To save Internet bandwidth, to reduce the amount of processing required (and consequently the speed of interpretation), and to account for unknown, and unpredictable, delivery conditions, it's unreasonable—and even impossible—to insist that a DTD be always available. You might not even want the kind of control that validity would impose (after all, Web browsers don't check HTML documents for validity). To allow for a "looser" delivery of XML documents, a major departure from SGML's formality has been made, and XML introduces the new concept of *well-formedness*.

Well-formed XML documents don't require a DTD (that's why XML's reputation for being "DTD-less SGML" isn't really correct). Even if a DTD is present, XML documents don't need a reference to the DTD to be correctly processed. (XML's environment is thought of as a two-tier layer, which includes an XML processor module that reads XML documents for the application and gives access to their content and structure.) Of course, for an XML document to be correctly processed without reference to the information on its structure that would have been in its DTD, certain concessions have to be made. Well-formed XML documents must have the following features:

- Start with a required markup declaration (more on this later) that says that a DTD isn't required, such as:

  ```
  <?XML VERSION="1.0" RMD="NONE" ?>
  ```

- Contain one or more elements.

- Have all the elements nested inside each other and all the tags balanced (for every start tag, there's an end tag).

- Have all attribute values enclosed in quotes.

- Have empty element start tags closed with the special /> string, or they are made nonempty by adding a specific closing tag (such as <HR></HR>).

- Not have any markup characters in character data (markup characters must be escaped using the predefined entities).

- All element attributes are of the CDATA type (character data) because there's no way to define them as being otherwise without a DTD.

These well-formedness constraints will make more sense when you learn about the objects to which they apply. However, before you get too involved in the details of validity and well-formedness, take a look at some of the basic rules that apply to all XML documents.

XML Rules

An XML document has one entity called the *document entity*, which is the starting point for the XML processor and can contain the whole document, just as the HTML element contains a complete HTML document.

Entities must each contain an integral number of elements, comments, processing instructions, and references, possibly with character data not found in any element in the entity, or else they must contain nontextual data and no elements.

The logical and physical structures (elements and entities) in an XML document must be synchronous, which means that the tags and elements must each begin and end in the same entity, although they can refer to other entities internally.

Start Tags and End Tags

A start tag marks the beginning of every nonempty XML element. An end tag, with the same name found in the start tag, marks the end of every element, for example:

```
</TITLE>Simon's Home Page</TITLE>
```

If an element is empty, the start tag can be the whole element, and the tag can take a special form: *<name />*.

Comments

Comments use the same syntax as HTML:

```
<!-- this is a comment -->
```

However, they must be written using *exactly* this syntax. Comments have the following requirements:

- Spaces in the start (<!--) and end (-->) strings are forbidden.
- Comments can't be nested.
- The string -- (two hyphens) must not occur in comments.
- Comments can appear anywhere except in CDATA sections, in declarations, or in tags.

Declaring XML Documents

The first line of an XML document consists of an XML declaration that specifies the version of XML being used:

```
<?XML VERSION="1.0" ENCODING="UTF-8" RMD="NONE" ?>
```

Note the use of the question mark; this statement is technically a processing instruction. All ?XML processing instructions are reserved for use by XML itself.

The ENCODING declaration identifies the character set in which the document is coded. Unlike HTML, which favored ASCII, XML favors Unicode, which allows foreign character sets to be used far more easily than in HTML. (For more information on foreign character sets, see Chapter 40, "Internationalizing Your HTML.")

The required markup declaration (RMD) specifies whether DTD processing is necessary; in it, you can identify your document as being (potentially) valid or "just" well formed. These are the possible values of this declaration:

- **NONE:** The XML processor can parse the containing document correctly without first reading any part of the DTD.
- **INTERNAL:** The XML processor must read and process the internal subset of the DTD, if provided.
- **ALL (the default):** The XML processor must read and process the declarations in both subsets of the DTD, if they are provided.

The XML Document Type Declaration

The XML document type declaration (DTD) consists of element and attribute declarations that define the allowable element structure of an XML document of a specific type.

The DTD must appear before the first start tag in the document, as shown:

```
<!DOCTYPE letter SYSTEM "letter.dtd">
```

In this line, the DTD is contained in the file letter.dtd.

The part of the DTD that's in an external file is called the DTD's *external subset.* Just as with CSS1 style sheets, in which styles can be defined externally as a style sheet or internally in the same document, a DTD can also directly include another, internal subset:

```
<!DOCTYPE letter [
    <!ELEMENT address (#PCDATA)>

<!-- this part contains the entity, element and attribute -->
<!-- declarations using exactly the same syntax as an external -->
<!-- document type declaration -->

]>
<letter>
<!-- the body of the document comes here -->
</letter>
```

Together, these two subsets make up the document type declaration. One of the subsets can be empty (or simply absent), but both can't be empty.

If both the external and internal subsets are used, the internal subset is read first. Entity and attribute declarations in the internal subset take precedence over those in the external subset.

The name in the DTD must match the name of the root element in XML documents of that type.

The following sections examine the contents of the XML DTD more closely.

Element Declarations

Every element type that appears in a valid XML document must be declared once in the DTD. An element declaration constrains an element's type and its content, as shown in this example:

```
<!ELEMENT BOOK (FRONT, BODY, BACK)>
```

The element declaration states that the element BOOK contains a FRONT element followed by a BODY, which is followed by a BACK element. All three elements must be present, and they must appear in this order.

The element declarations that are allowed to be used in an element are called their *content models*. The contents of an element instance must match the content model declared for that element type.

The language for specifying the content models of elements uses the following syntax:

Table 36.1. Content model syntax.

Symbol	Description
( )	Surrounds a sequence or a set of alternatives.
,	Separates the element types in a sequence (read as "followed by"; A,B means "A followed by B").
¦	Separates alternative element types in a list of alternatives (A ¦ B means "A or B").
?	Follows an element or group of elements and indicates that it occurs zero times or once (A,B? means "A" or "A,B").
*	Follows an element or group of elements and indicates that it occurs zero or more times (A,B* means "A" or "A,B,B…").
+	Follows an element or group of elements and indicates that it occurs one or more times (A,B+ means "A,B" or "A,B,B,B…").

The content of an element can be "element content" (it can contain only other elements) or "mixed content" (it can contain character data mixed with elements).

Character data is declared as the #PCDATA (parsed character data) type. The # symbol (SGML's reserved name indicator) distinguishes this element type name from any other element type called PCDATA (which is a perfectly legal name that can be used anywhere). Parsed character data (or simply character data, as far as XML is concerned) needs to be processed to determine whether each character is markup or simply character data. Any markup characters (tags and entity symbols) in parsed character data will be interpreted. Markup characters that aren't meant to be interpreted must be *escaped* (using entity references) or *hidden* (using CDATA sections).

If an element contains mixed content, the character data part must be declared first, and the content model must use OR separators, like this:

```
<!ELEMENT address (#PCDATA | street | number )>
```

Empty elements are declared by using the keyword EMPTY, but be careful that they really are empty when they appear in the XML document.

An element declared by using the keyword ANY can contain child elements of any type and number, mixed with character data.

Attributes

Attributes assign certain properties (size, color, alignment, and so on) to a class of elements. Because many properties are often declared at the same time, attributes are declared in *attribute list declarations*, which specify the name, data type, and default value (if any) of each attribute associated with a given element type, as shown in this example:

```
<!ELEMENT person (#PCDATA)>
<!ATTLIST person
    forename    CDATA       #REQUIRED
    surname     CDATA       #REQUIRED
    age         NUMBER      #IMPLIED>
```

Attributes themselves can appear only within start tags, as shown here:

```
<person forename="Fred" surname="FLINTSTONE" age="5">
```

When more than one attribute list declaration is provided for a given element type, all their contents are merged. Also, when more than one definition is provided for the same attribute of a given element type, the first declaration counts and later declarations are ignored.

Attribute Remapping

To avoid conflicts with elements whose attributes have the same names (such as when an internal DTD subset and an external one declare the same attributes), attributes can be declared as equivalent by using the XML-ATTRIBUTES attribute.

This attribute must contain pairs of names. In each pair, the first name must be ROLE, HREF, TITLE, SHOW, INLINE, CONTENT-ROLE, CONTENT-TITLE, ACTUATE, BEHAVIOR, or STEPS. The second name is treated as though it were playing the role assigned to the first.

Attribute Types

XML attribute types are of three kinds: a string type, a set of tokenized types, and enumerated types.

A string type can take any literal string as a value, but a tokenized type has varying lexical and semantic constraints:

- An ID type must be a valid NAME symbol. The name must not appear more than once in an XML document as an ID.

- An IDREF must match the value of an ID attribute of some element in the XML document.
- ENTITY and ENTITIES types must exactly match the name of an external binary general entity declared in the DTD.
- NMTOKEN and NMTOKENS types must be a text string consisting of a letter or an underscore followed by one or more letters or digits.
- Notation attribute names must match one of the notation names included in the declaration.

Enumerated type values must match one of the NMTOKEN tokens in the declaration. The same NMTOKEN shouldn't occur more than once in the enumerated attribute types of a single element type.

Attribute Default Values

To avoid having to explicitly declare attributes for every element, you can declare default attribute values in the DTD. If a default value is declared and the attribute is omitted, the attribute is treated as though it were present; its value is the declared default value.

The attribute's declaration supplies information on whether its presence is required and, if not, how an XML processor should react if the declared attribute is absent in a document:

- **#FIXED:** The document is invalid if the attribute has a different value from the default.
- **#REQUIRED:** The document is invalid if there's a start tag for the element type that doesn't specify a value for the attribute.
- **#IMPLIED:** If the attribute is omitted, the XML processor must simply inform the application that no value was specified.

If the attribute is neither #REQUIRED nor #IMPLIED, the value contains the declared default value.

White Space Attribute

In HTML documents, multiple blank spaces (called *white spaces*) are reduced to a single white space. Sometimes extra white spaces mean something, however, so you want to keep them. The XML-SPACE attribute can be used to identify elements in which the white space is treated as significant by applications. The value of this attribute determines what's to be done with the white space in the element:

- **DEFAULT:** Means that the default white-space processing is acceptable.
- **PRESERVE:** Means that all the white space should be preserved.

Entities

Entities are similar to the sort of macros you would expect to find in a word processing package; they are short strings of characters that can be used as abbreviations for large pieces of text (or markup). When the XML processor encounters them, these abbreviations are expanded.

Entities can be either binary or text. A *text entity* contains text data, which is considered to be an integral part of the document. A *binary entity* contains binary data with an associated notation (notation declarations are explained later in the section "External Entities").

Only text entities can be referred to with entity references, and only the names of binary entities can be given as the value of entity attributes.

If the same entity is declared more than once, the first declaration encountered is binding.

In a well-formed XML document, the name given in an entity reference must exactly match the name given in the entity's declaration. Entity references must not contain the name of a binary entity, and binary entities can be referred to only in ENTITY or ENTITIES type attributes.

Parameter Entities

Parameter entity references can be used in a variety of places within the DTD. Parameter entities give you a convenient means of reusing markup code in many places, so you have to type the code once. For example, to declare a parameter entity, you would use something like this:

```
<!ENTITY % font (em¦tt¦bold¦strong)>
```

You would refer to it like this:

```
<!ELEMENT body (para, %font;)*>
```

Parameter entity references are always expanded immediately once they're recognized, and the DTD must match the relevant rules of the grammar after they have all been expanded.

In well-formed XML documents, parameter entities must not contain direct or indirect references to themselves.

General (Internal) Entities

If the definition of an entity is just a value, it's called a general entity (or internal entity) and its replacement text is given in the entity declaration, as shown in this example:

```
<!ENTITY Shortcut "This is a block of text that I am going to
use very often, but really want to type only once">
```

These entities are for use in the XML document; you refer to them like this:

```
&Shortcut;
```

External Entities

If an entity is not an internal entity, it's an external entity. External entities can be used to include text from another file, as shown in this example:

```
<!ENTITY commontext SYSTEM "http://my.home.com/text/block1.xml">
```

The keyword SYSTEM identifies a URL, which can be used to retrieve the entity. An external identifier can include the PUBLIC keyword and a public identifier, too. The XML processor might try to generate an alternative URL from this, but, if it can't, it must use the URL specified by the SYSTEM keyword.

Each external text entity in an XML document can use a different encoding for its characters. XML provides an encoding declaration processing instruction, which, if it occurs, must appear at the beginning of a system entity, before any other character data or markup. In the document entity, the encoding declaration is part of the XML declaration; in other entities, it's part of an encoding processing instruction.

To validate an XML document, an XML processor must include the content of an external text entity. If it's not trying to validate an XML document, the XML processor doesn't need to include the content of an external text entity.

External entities are also used to include nontext objects, such as graphics files. Nontext external entities must include a notation (NDATA) declaration, as shown:

```
<!ENTITY myface SYSTEM "../images/me.gif" NDATA GIF>
```

Notations identify by name the format of external binary entities or the application that can handle the format. Notation declarations supply a name for a notation and an external identifier that allows an XML processor or its client application (such as a browser plug-in) to find a helper application that can process data in the notation. The following example illustrates the declaration of two graphics files as external entities and identifies their format as PCX:

```
<!DOCTYPE BOOK SYSTEM "BOOK.DTD" [
<!-- Figures for this chapter: -->
<!ENTITY chap1.fig1 SYSTEM "0101.PCX" NDATA PCX>
<!ENTITY chap1.fig2 SYSTEM "0132.PCX" NDATA PCX>
]>
```

This ability to explicitly declare the notation for a file gives you much more freedom over the format than you get in HTML. The format is no longer tied to a specific file type (extension), but depends instead on what you declare it to be.

In a valid XML document, the name of the notation used in an entity declaration *must* be declared.

Predefined Entities

As I mentioned earlier, the ampersand character (&) and the left angle bracket (<), which are normally interpreted as markup, must be escaped by using either numeric character references or the strings & and <.

In addition, the right angle bracket (>) can be represented with the string >, the apostrophe or single-quote character (') can be represented as ', and the double-quote character (") can be represented as ".

Well-formed documents need not declare the amp, lt, gt, apos, and quot entities, but valid XML documents must declare them before using them. All XML processors must recognize these entities whether they are declared or not.

Conditional Sections

Parameter entities can also be used in DTDs to turn the sections of markup they enclose into *conditional sections*. These conditional sections can be used to allow DTDs to be "customized" for individual documents. You do this customizing by including the parameter entity declarations in the document's internal DTD subset so that they can be used as "switches":

```
<?XML VERSION "1.0" RMD="ALL"?>
<!DOCTYPE BOOK SYSTEM "strict.dtd" [
<!ENTITY % DRAFT "INCLUDE">
<!ENTITY % FINAL "IGNORE">
<![%DRAFT;[
<!ELEMENT BOOK (AUTHOR_COMMENTS*, FRONT, BODY, BACK)>
[[>
<![%FINAL;[
<!ELEMENT BOOK (FRONT, COPYRIGHT, BODY, BACK, SOFTWARE)>
]]>
]>
<BOOK> ...
```

This declaration sets the value of the parameter entity DRAFT to "INCLUDE" and the value of FINAL to "IGNORE" in this document. The final version of the document would simply swap the values of these two parameter entities.

CDATA Sections

CDATA sections (character data sections) allow you to enter large amounts of markup characters without having to escape every single & and < character and "hide" blocks of characters from the XML processor. CDATA sections can occur anywhere that character data might occur. They begin with the sequence <![CDATA[and end with the sequence]]>, as shown:

```
<![CDATA[ <P>This text will not be 'seen' & processed.</P> ]]>
```

In the special case of CDATA sections, *character data* is any string of characters not including the sequence]]>, which terminates the CDATA section.

CDATA sections can't be nested.

XML Linking

One aspect of XML that I have studiously avoided so far is linking. XML provides much more powerful links than either SGML or HTML and these links deserve to be treated separately to do them full justice. Built on years of research into linking, XML's linking mechanisms (known as *XLL, XML Link Language*) are based on ideas taken from HTML, HyTime (Hypermedia/Time-Based Structuring Language, ISO 10744:1992), and an SGML application extensively used in academia called the Text Encoding Initiative (TEI).

XML links are interoperable with HTML. They use the same HREF attribute and give its value the same general meaning as in HTML. The value of an HREF attribute is a URL identifying the *resource* that's the target of the link, optionally qualified by # and a *fragment identifier* or ?

and a query. XML links also conform to RFC 1738's conventions governing the characters that can appear within the URL.

However, XML's links extend HREF links with the following features:

- Allowing absolutely any element type to be the source of a link
- Defining additional properties and behaviors for all links
- Introducing the concept of out-of-line links
- Defining the precise meaning of the fragment identifier when the target of the link is an XML document

Link Types

XML allows any element type to act as a linking element by specifying the reserved attribute XML-LINK for each element that will act as a linking element. In addition, the value of the XML-LINK attribute indicates what type of link the element expresses, as shown in this example:

```
<A XML-LINK="SIMPLE" HREF="http://www.home.com/">Our Home Page</A>
```

This declaration tells an XML processor that it's dealing with a simple (inline) link.

An XML-LINK attribute can be a SIMPLE, EXTENDED, LOCATOR, GROUP, or DOCUMENT link type. Two of these types are described in the following sections.

Simple Links

A *simple* link can contain only one locator, and the locator attributes are attached directly to the linking element. Simple links are usually inline and always one-directional.

The following example shows the declaration for a simple link that mimics the behavior of the kind of link you're probably familiar with in HTML documents; the new content replaces the old when you click on the link:

```
<!ELEMENT SIMPLE ANY>
<!ATTLIST EXTENDED
    XML-LINK        CDATA               #FIXED "SIMPLE"
    ROLE            CDATA               #IMPLIED
    TITLE           CDATA               #IMPLIED
    INLINE          (TRUE|FALSE)        "TRUE"
    CONTENT-ROLE    CDATA               #IMPLIED
    CONTENT-TITLE   CDATA               #IMPLIED
    SHOW            (EMBED|REPLACE|NEW)  "REPLACE"
    ACTUATE         (AUTO|USER)         "USER"
    BEHAVIOR        CDATA               #IMPLIED>
```

Simple links are very much like HTML A elements.

Extended Links

An *extended* link can involve any number of resources and need not be located in the same physical document as any of them. An extended link's locators are stored in the elements it contains, each of which can have its own set of attributes. An application (such as a Web browser) is expected to follow all the links in the extended link, as shown in this example:

```
<!ELEMENT EXTENDED ANY>
<!ELEMENT LOCATOR ANY>
<!ATTLIST EXTENDED
     XML-LINK        CDATA                  #FIXED "EXTENDED"
     ROLE            CDATA                  #IMPLIED
     TITLE           CDATA                  #IMPLIED
     INLINE          (TRUE|FALSE)           "TRUE"
     CONTENT-ROLE    CDATA                  #IMPLIED
     CONTENT-TITLE   CDATA                  #IMPLIED
     SHOW            (EMBED|REPLACE|NEW)    "REPLACE"
     ACTUATE         (AUTO|USER)            "USER"
     BEHAVIOR        CDATA                  #IMPLIED>
<!ATTLIST LOCATOR
     XML-LINK        CDATA                  #FIXED "LOCATOR"
     ROLE            CDATA                  #IMPLIED
     HREF            CDATA                  #REQUIRED
     TITLE           CDATA                  #IMPLIED
     SHOW            (EMBED|REPLACE|NEW)    "REPLACE"
     ACTUATE         (AUTO|USER)            "USER"
     BEHAVIOR        CDATA                  #IMPLIED>
```

Extended links can be either inline (in the source document) or out-of-line (outside the source document) and can be used for multidirectional links, links into read-only data, and so on.

The attributes of the extended link element state how the elements within it behave, so that they can be given ROLE and TITLE attributes and their behaviors can be specified.

Note that many of the attributes can be provided for both the parent linking element and the locator elements it contains. If any such attribute is supplied in the linking element but not in a locator element, the value in the linking element is used to process the locator element.

Inline and Out-Of-Line Links

A link is identified as being inline or out-of-line by the value of its INLINE attribute. The value TRUE, which is the default, means that the linking element's entire content is considered part of the link, except for any child locator elements (which are considered part of the linking element machinery).

When the link is inline, the CONTENT-ROLE and CONTENT-TITLE attributes can be used to supply the title and role information for this "content" resource. If INLINE is FALSE, the CONTENT-TITLE and CONTENT-ROLE attributes have no effect.

Information Associated with Links

Like HTML, XML allows you to associate additional information with links. However, XML defines how key aspects of this information are actually used, which gives you more control over the way links behave.

This information is associated with links through the following attributes:

- **ROLE:** This is a string that identifies the meaning of the link to an application. Each participant in a link can be given its own role. There are no predefined values for link roles; the roles assigned, and their semantics, are specific to the particular XML application in which they're used.
- **HREF:** Identifies the target.
- **TITLE:** Labels the link. The XML application decides whether to use this label and what to use it for.
- **SHOW and ACTUATE:** Specify how and when the link is followed.
- **INLINE:** Specifies whether the linking element is inline.

Link Behavior

The timing and effects of following a link are expressed by the SHOW and ACTUATE attributes.

SHOW

The SHOW attribute specifies how a target should be displayed or processed; it has the following values:

- **EMBED:** On following the link, the target should be embedded in the body of the source where the link started.
- **REPLACE:** On following the link, the target should replace the source where the link started.
- **NEW:** On following the link, the target should be displayed or processed in a new context (such as a new browser window), without affecting the context of the source where the link started.

XML link behavior matches that specified by the EMBED attribute for IMG elements and the REPLACE attribute for A elements in HTML.

ACTUATE

The ACTUATE attribute specifies when a link should be followed; it has these two values:

- **AUTO:** When encountered, the display or processing of the source isn't considered complete until the link has been resolved.
- **USER:** The link isn't followed until there's an explicit external request to do so.

XML link behavior matches that specified by the AUTO attribute for IMG elements and the USER attribute for A elements in HTML.

Addressing

XML's HREF attributes are interoperable with HTML. However, XML supports more sophisticated addressing in the target resource when it's an XML document. You can use this special addressing from within HTML pages to address parts of XML documents.

When a locator identifies a target that's an XML document, the locator value can contain a URL, a fragment identifier, or both.

A URL, if present, is treated as a standard URL, and identifies the *containing resource* that's the target of the link (the document). If no URL is given, the document in which the link is found is considered the containing resource.

Any *fragment identifier* is treated as an *extended pointer.* If an extended pointer is provided, the target resource is a subresource of the containing resource. A fragment identifier is preceded by a *connector* that identifies how and where the fragment is to be located and processed:

- **#:** A standard HTML-style fragment; the entire containing resource is delivered to the client, which then must find the fragment.
- **?XML-PTR=:** An XML query; the server interprets the fragment identifier (extended pointer) and delivers *only* the requested fragment to the client.
- **¦:** An XML-specific connector; either of the preceding approaches can be used to fetch the requested resource.

Extended Pointers

Starting from the root element (the element named in the DTD), an element that contains other elements is considered their "parent" and they in turn are its "children." By expanding these parent-child relationships, you can map out a tree of an XML document's element structure. (Normally, you can't do this mapping out of element structures in HTML because there's little to prevent you from using, for example, H1, H2, H3, and H4 elements in any order you like, even though in a "structured" HTML document you should use them hierarchically.)

Extended pointers operate on the element tree defined by the elements in the XML document. They describe the elements within the document in terms of properties, such as their type or attribute values or just a count of them.

The basic form of an extended pointer is a series of location terms, each of which specifies either an absolute or a relative location.

Absolute Location Terms

In an absolute location, each *location term* works in the context of a location source. By default, the location source for the first location term is the root element of the XML document. Each extended pointer can start with one of the following location terms:

- **ROOT:** The ROOT keyword specifies that the location source is the root element of the source. This is the default behavior.

- ◼ **HERE:** The HERE keyword specifies that the location source for the first location term of the series is the linking element containing the locator rather than the default root element.

- ◼ **DITTO:** The DITTO keyword specifies that the location source for its first location term is the location source specified by the entire first pointer.

- ◼ **ID:** The ID keyword specifies that the location source for the first location term is the element in the source that has an attribute of type ID with a value matching the given name (for example, ID(*Name*)).

- ◼ **HTML:** The HTML keyword selects the first element whose type is A and that has a NAME attribute whose value is the same as the supplied NAME value (this is the same as the # in an HTML document).

Relative Location Terms

A relative location term consists of a keyword, followed by one or more steps. These are the allowed keywords:

- ◼ **CHILD:** Selects child elements of the location source.

- ◼ **DESCENDANT:** Selects elements appearing within the content of the location source (for example, the element tree beginning at this element).

- ◼ **ANCESTOR:** Selects elements in which the location source is found (for example, the element tree beginning at the parent of the current element).

- ◼ **PRECEDING:** Selects elements that appear before the location source.

- ◼ **PSIBLING:** Selects sibling elements that precede the location source (for example, the other children of the parent element that come before this element).

- ◼ **FOLLOWING:** Selects elements that appear after the location source.

- ◼ **FSIBLING:** Selects sibling elements that follow the location source (for example, the other children of the parent element that come after this element).

Selecting Targets

The elements that match a location reference are called *candidates*. Candidates can be selected by their occurrence number, element type, and attribute name and attribute value.

A keyword limits the possible candidates of a location reference to those elements that have the required property in relation to the location source. The keyword is followed by one or more steps. Each step defines an instance, an optional element type, and an optional attribute type and value.

The instance counts the candidates. It can be a positive number (counting forward from the first candidate), a negative number (counting backward from the last candidate), or the special value ALL to select all the candidates:

```
(4) - select the fourth candidate location
(-2) - select the second-to-last candidate location
```

The instance can be followed by a comma and an optional, but recommended, element type, which can take the following values:

- **Name:** Selects elements with the type Name
- ***:** Selects any element type
- ***CDATA:** Selects "pseudo-elements" containing only text

Here are some examples of how they're used:

- `(3,P)` Selects the third `<P>` element
- `(-1,*)` Selects the last element
- `(2,*CDATA)` Selects the second untagged span of text

The element type, if specified, can be qualified by an attribute name and value. The attribute name can take these two values:

- ***:** Matches any attribute name
- **Name:** Specifies the attribute type Name

The attribute value can take these values:

- ***IMPLIED:** Matches attributes for which no value was specified and no default exists
- ***:** Matches any value
- **Name:** Matches the value Name
- **"value":** Matches the value that's quoted

The following line selects the first child element of the location source that's a `<P>` element, for which the FONT attribute has been left unspecified:

```
CHILD(1,P,FONT,*IMPLIED)
```

Extended Pointer Ranges

A fragment identifier can contain a single extended pointer or two extended pointers separated by the string `..` to define a range or span of text.

The fragment is assumed to be everything from the start of the first extended pointer's target (the *location source*) to the end of the second one. You can select a range of elements as the target of the link, instead of the whole document, as you do in HTML.

The following fragment identifier selects the text that starts at the beginning of the first child element of the location source that's a `<P>` element and ends at the end of the last child that's a `<P>` element:

```
(CHILD(1,P) .. (CHILD(-1,P)
```

Extended Link Groups

An extended link group element is used to store a list of links to other documents that form an interlinked document group.

Each document is identified with the HREF attribute of an extended link document element, which is a child element of the GROUP. The value of the HREF attribute is a locator.

These elements are recognized by using the XML-LINK attribute with the value GROUP or DOCUMENT.

The GROUP element contains one or more DOCUMENT elements, each pointing to a resource (or a subresource, with the extended pointer syntax) that forms part of the document group.

For example, an XML document could contain the following:

```
<GROUP>
<DOCUMENT HREF="http://www.home.com/bookmarks1.xml"/>
<DOCUMENT HREF="http://www.home.com/bookmarks2.xml"/>
</GROUP>
```

In this declaration, GROUP and DOCUMENT are identified as linking elements, so documents bookmarks1.xml and bookmarks2.xml would be processed to look for links that point to this document.

Fixed XML-LINK Attributes

To avoid having to declare the special XML-LINK attribute every time you use an element, you can declare it once in the DTD as a fixed value:

```
<!ATTLIST MYLINK
          XML-LINK CDATA #FIXED "SIMPLE">
```

XML Style

In principle, CSS1 (cascading style sheets, level 1) can be used to apply simple formatting to XML documents. XML documents, like HTML documents, contain elements with names, IDs, and so on—the same blocks of text data CSS1 uses to define its formatting rules for HTML documents.

However, CSS1 is specifically designed around HTML, and some of its features rely on HTML-specific coding practice. For example, pseudo-classes, such as the A:link, A:visited, and A:active, allow links to look different when they're selected or after they have been followed. Pseudo-elements, such as :first-line and :first-letter, and normal classes used by CSS1 would also have to be added as attributes to elements in your XML DTDs to allow their values to be used in the CSS1 style sheets for XML documents.

XML has its own style language called *XSL* that's far more powerful than CSS1; whether it will be used along with CSS1 or used instead of CSS1 remains to be seen.

NOTE

XSL is still in a very early stage of development; at the time of this writing, the standard is available only as a preliminary proposal.

XSL is based on a profile of DSSSL, called DSSSL-o (*o* for *online*). DSSSL (Document Style and Semantics Specification Language: ISO/IEC Standard 10179:1996) is a language based on Scheme, a dialect of the LISP programming language, which supports transforming, querying, and processing SGML documents. DSSSL's transformation language is not used in XSL. Instead, XSL uses the official form of JavaScript as defined in the ECMA (European Association for Standardizing Information and Communication Systems) Standard 262 "ECMAScript." The style sheet part of DSSSL has also been cut down to the bare essentials needed to support printing Web pages.

How XSL Works

XSL is essentially a data-driven style mechanism. When an XML document is formatted (either for printing on paper or displaying on a screen), one or more XSL style sheets are read. The XSL style sheets can be specified in the XML document itself, or you can select them.

Processing the XML document is determined by scanning its structure and merging it with the *formatting specification* derived from the active style sheets. These instructions are then used to create *flow objects*, such as paragraphs and tables, which determine the coding applied to the document. This merging process produces a tree structure of flow objects called the *flow object tree*.

The basic statement in XSL is a *construction rule*, which declares what to do with an element. More precisely, it states what flow objects will be created and what characteristics each flow object will have. For example, an element construction rule for the P element might specify that a paragraph flow object is to be added to the flow object tree, with the following characteristics:

```
font-size: 12pt
first-line-start-indent: 18pt
quadding: left
```

This statement sets the characters in the paragraph to 12 points, with an 18-point indent at the start of the first line and left-justification applied to the whole paragraph.

XSL Processing

Even though XSL is a customization of DSSSL that has been reduced to its essentials, much as XML is considered a customization of SGML, XSL's adoption of ECMAScript gives you access to most of the features of a full programming language that you need for processing XML documents. ECMAScript can be used to perform calculations, test for conditions, and so on.

It can also be used to build up complex instructions for processing individual elements or even characters in an XML document.

Almost any aspect of an XML document's structure can be used to control its processing. Most construction rules operate at the element level, but you can easily refine their behavior by testing for properties of an element, such as its attributes and their values, or its ancestor elements.

Although by default the whole document will be processed, and in its original order, XSL gives you access to the full element structure at any point in the document. That means you can include parts of a document so that, for example, you can create a table of contents from the chapter headings and place it at the start of the document. It's also easy to suppress parts of the document that you don't want to be seen in this context, which allows features such as conditional content, dynamic content, and access-controlled content.

The Future of XML

So far, this discussion of XML has been fairly technical, so it seems only fair to breathe a little life back into the subject by quickly reviewing some of the applications XML is already being used for:

- Channel Definition Format (CDF) is the XML application behind *push technology* (see Chapter 39, "Understanding XSL," for more details on CDF). Instead of browsing from Web site to Web site, and from page to page within a site, you take out a "subscription" to a particular content provider. Instead of *pulling* Web pages to you, you allow someone else to *push* those pages to you when he or she decides. After you have made your subscription choices, you can sit back and passively enjoy the information as it's webcasted, or pushed, to your screen, almost as though you were watching television.

- Open Software Description (OSD) is an XML application for describing software components and their versions, structure, and relationships to other components. When combined with CDF, OSD allows software applications to be automatically installed and upgraded over the Internet.

- Sun's Answerbook is an application for distributing technical documentation. Using XML as the storage format, technical manuals are converted into HTML for publication on the Web.

- Chemical Markup Language (CML) is an XML application that, used with the Jumbo Java applet, allows chemical formulas and molecular models to be described and viewed with a Web browser.

- Mathematics Markup Language (MathML) is an XML application for marking up mathematics. It's an interesting application because it uses parallel markup structures to address both the presentation and the semantic structures of mathematics.

- OpenTag is an XML application for marking up text fragments for translation and localization independently of the software used to create the text. This application is an example of how XML can create useful applications that have even fewer elements than HTML.

- The Handheld Device Markup Language (HDML) is an XML application intended for displaying information (including Web pages) on pocket electronic devices, such as Personal Digital Assistants (PDAs) and mobile telephones equipped with display screens.

This list of XML applications is by no means complete; there are many more ranging from the simple (the FAQML, Frequently Asked Question Markup Language) to the extremely complex (XML/EDI, XML-based Electronic Data Interchange initiative).

Even though XML's specification hasn't been formalized yet, the applications it's already being used for are giving it an impressive track record. In less than a year, XML has developed from an idea to a mainstream language. Whatever form the final specification takes, there can be no doubt about the importance of XML to the future of not just the Web, but also all forms of electronic documentation.

Summary

In this chapter, you have learned the following:

- The purpose and nature of XML
- The basic XML syntax and structure rules
- The basics of XML document type declarations (DTDs)
- The essentials of XML's linking mechanisms (XLL)
- XML's style language (XSL)
- How and where XML is already being used

This chapter has focused on describing XML (and XSL) as a language, so it's inevitably been somewhat technical. In the following chapters, I'll compare XML with HTML on a more functional basis and then go on to translate these technical descriptions into more concrete discussions of XML in practice.

How XML Compares with HTML

by Simon North

IN THIS CHAPTER

In Chapter 36, "What Is XML?" I gave you a fairly technical description of XML (Extensible Markup Language). In this chapter, you use that knowledge to take a closer look at the differences between XML and HTML.

Trying to compare XML with HTML is, however, a little bit like trying to compare the U.S. Treasury Department with a $100 bill. HTML (the $100 dollar bill) is a markup language that's just one application of SGML. It consists of a fixed set of elements (tags) and a well-defined set of relationships between them. XML (the U.S. Treasury) is a dialect of SGML tuned for Internet use. XML is a sort of toolset that allows you to create as many markup languages as you like (not just a $100 bill, but $1, $5, $10, $50, or practically any denomination of bills).

As an SGML application, HTML is fundamentally different from an application produced using XML. To compare XML and HTML, then, you need to look at the differences between an XML application in general and HTML. The XML application could, however, be something far more sophisticated than HTML, such as the Mathematical Markup Language (MathML), or it could be something much simpler than HTML, such as the Handheld Device Markup Language (HDML). To make this a fair, meaningful comparison, you have to concentrate on the following general features, instead of specific characteristics:

- Extensibility
- Semantic markup
- Validation
- Linking
- Style language

After reading this chapter, you should have a general overview of the major differences between XML and HTML.

HTML Isn't Dead!

Before I get into a detailed comparison of XML and HTML, one point really does need emphasizing, even though you will probably hear it nauseatingly often in the coming months: *XML is not a replacement for HTML.*

HTML was intended to be simple and easy to learn and implement. Over the years, it has become more complex, but even with version 4.0, you can still teach someone the basic tag set in a few hours. Using one of the many available software packages, someone with no previous experience can still create a basic home page in a few minutes.

HTML does a wonderful job for simple Web pages—and there lies the major difference between XML and HTML. HTML is about user interfaces, and XML is about data. HTML describes presentation and user interaction; XML describes information. The two can happily live side-by-side because they perform different tasks, but having said this, take a look in the following sections at how much better XML is than HTML.

Intelligent Documents

HTML is the Swiss Army knife of markup languages. It gives you a general, multipurpose set of elements for displaying text in a Web browser. Officially, according to the HTML DTD (Document Type Definition), the only element in an HTML document that must be tagged is the TITLE element, even though it's probably one of the elements most often left out. The rest of the element tags are optional (or, more precisely, can be implied from their context), and there are few, if any, hard-and-fast rules about what element tags should be used where. One thing is certain, however; defined element tags are the only ones you can use.

XML is not called Extensible Markup Language for nothing. It is, as its name suggests, extensible, and that's one of the most important differences between XML and HTML. HTML has a finite, well-defined element set. In XML, you're totally free to define any elements you like. You can, if you want, simply use the existing HTML elements and add a few of your own; you would, of course, have to provide an XML-compliant version of the HTML DTD you want to use. On the other hand, you could use a completely different set of elements to suit your particular application.

In terms, there are two types of markup techniques. One is purely presentation oriented, defining paragraphs, lines, text characteristics, and so on. The other is content oriented and ignores the method of presentation completely, preferring to identify the information content. This kind of markup technique uses objects like warnings, procedures, introductions, chapters, and so forth. XML's extensibility allows you to introduce semantic meaning into your documents, turning them into "intelligent documents" that can describe their content in a meaningful way. You can, for example, say whether a list is actually a repair procedure or indicate that a paragraph set in red text is actually a warning message.

Probably no two HTML document authors can agree on the use of an H5 instead of an H6, and there's nothing to prevent you using them in any order you like. However, in XML you can identify them instead as section titles, chapter titles, and so on.

Validation

Although there is an HTML Document Type Definition (DTD), and software packages that actually check your HTML to make sure it's valid, validation is the exception rather than the rule. Of all the HTML pages currently on the Web, fewer than 1 percent are reckoned to be truly valid HTML.

Some authoring packages, such as SoftQuad's HoTMetaL packages, try to start you off on the right track to creating valid HTML documents. However, for every one of those packages, there are a hundred others that, under the blanket of offering a near-WYSIWYG environment (like the editor provided by Netscape as part of its complete Communicator suite), produce the HTML equivalent of spaghetti code. If the appearance of the final result is acceptable, it doesn't matter what kind of monstrous HTML code is created; after all, in a WYSIWYG environment, who cares what the code looks like?

This situation isn't entirely the fault of the software producers, though. One of the Web's first "unwritten" rules was that authoring packages should try to produce strictly valid HTML, but browsers should be free to accept anything and try to make sense of as much as they could. Unfortunately, some people interpreted this freedom just a little too broadly.

First, browser producers started adding in their own HTML elements, then individual authors started bending the rules by experimenting to see whether they could come up with some interesting effects, and then some Internet service providers started incorporating local elements that individual Web servers could understand. This is not meant as a condemnation of the efforts of these people. You could actually get an interesting scrolling effect in Netscape by using 40 or 50 TITLE elements at the start of an HTML document, and the "<META REFRESH=" statement used to be extremely useful for automatically redirecting Netscape browser users. To condemn these "hacks" would be to deny human nature by trying to curb the very inventiveness and resourcefulness that made the Web what it was.

However, the Web is no longer what it was a few years ago. It's perhaps an obvious point, but the Web is now a commercial platform. It has gone mainstream, and the people who are now considering putting material onto the Web have concerns that are a long way from those of college students who just want something that looks cool. These "industrial grade" users want guarantees that their HTML code will look and behave the same across all platforms (MacOS, Windows, IRIX, Solaris; different operating systems, different screen resolutions—the list of possible combinations is almost endless). These users also want those guarantees to be long lasting and, if possible, able to be implemented. In short, these users want a way to check that the HTML code is correct; they want formal validation mechanisms, and HTML can't provide them.

Validating HTML documents requires you to track down the particular DTD associated with a particular Web browser, or a particular version of HTML, or it requires you to get a separate validation package. The ability to validate HTML documents is very much an afterthought. In contrast, the ability to validate XML documents is an integral part of the language. You aren't forced to validate your XML documents, just as you aren't forced to validate your HTML documents, but XML's use of a DTD makes it easier to do so.

Instead of the DTD being "hard-wired" into the Web browser, as HTML's DTD is, you can either supply the XML DTD as an external document, or you can embed it at the start of the XML document. If you want, you can put a common part of the DTD, called the *external subset*, in an external document and include a local part of the DTD, called the *internal subset*, in each document. In Chapter 38, "Using XML," you will see a method for using this feature to reduce the amount of work involved in producing HTML pages by creating common libraries of graphic elements.

To specify whether your XML document requires validation, add an initial statement to the XML declaration (called the *Required Markup Declaration*, or *RMD*) at the start of the XML document:

```
<?XML VERSION="1.0" ENCODING="UTF-8" RMD="ALL" ?>
```

The keyword ALL means that the DTD must be used, the keyword INTERNAL specifies that only the internal subset must be used, and the keyword NONE indicates that the DTD is not required (even if it's present).

The Mechanics of Validation

So what exactly is validation? The DTD defines the structure of the elements that can be contained in a particular type or class of document. This structure says what elements there are, what elements are contained in other elements, and how many times they may appear. It identifies compulsory and optional elements, and, when the designer thinks it's necessary, defines the prescribed order in which the elements must appear.

Each element may have attributes declared for it, and these attributes are declared to have specific types of values. If you want, you can declare sets of values for attributes from which one can be chosen, or you can even declare default values for attributes when they're not declared in the document.

Using the declarations in the DTD, *validation* is the process of checking the particular document (technically known as an *instance*) to ensure that all the elements that must appear are present and appearing in the required order. Further, the declarations and values of any attributes are checked to make sure the values they have been given are allowed.

Validation can be a stringent process, depending on the nature of the DTD. HTML is an example of a very loose DTD because almost everything is optional and can be omitted or declared in any order; there's nothing to stop you, for example, from using an H1 tag, followed by an H6 tag, and then an H2 tag. If the DTD is strict (like some of the DTDs used for military applications), the content of an instance can be checked right down to the most minute detail. It's possible, for example, to even check that the date has been specified correctly as a year, followed by a month name written out in text form, followed by a day. In Chapter 38, you will see some practical examples of writing an XML DTD, but what's important is that the amount of control you exercise over what can be put in an XML document is, as the author of the DTD, completely in your own hands.

More Powerful Linking

Coding has come a long way over the past couple of years, from using a text editor to manually create HTML code to automatically generating HTML code from databases, spreadsheets, and user responses. With all this general progress, it seems strange that HTML's linking mechanisms haven't progressed. Have you ever thought about how ridiculously primitive HTML's linking mechanisms are? I don't want to sound insulting, but HTML's links really are dumb. You can use a mind-boggling array of tools to create code for Web pages (including HTML, Java, JavaScript, and ActiveX technologies, to name just a few), but when it comes down to creating links between pages, you're reduced to practically adding them by hand. It's hardly surprising that broken links are probably a Webmaster's greatest problem and almost certainly create the most work.

With links being directly embedded in HTML documents, it's not only nearly impossible to maintain the links, but an incredible amount of data and information lies outside the "reach" of these links. Yes, you can link from HTML pages to graphic files, and yes, you can use image maps to link from graphics in HTML pages to other HTML pages. Either way, to link to something, you must have write access because you need to be able to modify it to add the link. Try linking from read-only material (such as on a CD-ROM)—it can't be done.

If you want to link to some point inside another HTML document, you have to load that whole document and then move to the point you were addressing. This requirement alone must be responsible for a considerable waste of Internet bandwidth. You want to link to another HTML document, but you want to keep the current document open? Well, you can open another browser window, or you can open one or more frames. You pay the price in complicating the navigation and probably making your readers lose their overview of where they were.

XML changes all this by opening up exciting new possibilities for linking objects. When linking to an XML document (which means it should be possible to use these linking mechanisms in non-XML documents, even HTML documents, to address XML documents), XML radically extends the nature of the links that can be created with the following features:

- XML allows multi-ended links, either one-to-many or many-to-many.
- XML's links are bidirectional (this is much more than just the Back button in the Web browser).
- XML's link ends (the beginnings or the ends) don't need to be physically located inside one of the objects (documents) being linked. This feature means that the following are possible:
  - Links can be added to documents after they have been created, or added to the current Web, without forcing you to go back and hand-edit each of the documents.
  - Links can be generated automatically (by software), and, as a logical result, they can also be generated dynamically.
  - You can create "virtual" documents, like indexes, that consist of links to other documents.
- XML's links can behave in a far more sophisticated manner. By using the SHOW attribute, you can determine how the target of a link will be displayed. It can be embedded in the source document, it can replace the source document (as happens now with a simple HTML link), or it can be opened in a new "context" (a new frame or browser window). The link's activation can be specified as manual (as happens now with HTML links) or automatic, as soon as they are encountered.
- XML's links can select parts of XML documents. Using a highly sophisticated extended pointer syntax based on an academic application of SGML called the Text

Encoding Initiative (TEI), you can make use of the structure and hierarchy of elements to selectively pick out children of elements or their parents, or count the number of occurrences and pick out only specific elements.

■ XML's links can be labeled or named (using the ROLE and LABEL attributes) to identify their purpose or nature. The use of this feature isn't immediately obvious, but imagine using it in combination with XML's ability to apply semantic meaning to markup. You could, for example, use XML elements to identify the contents of a database and these link attributes to describe the relationships between them. Using Java, or some other processing language, you could then query a database and retrieve the results as a structured XML document. Because the XML document would be self-describing, you could then refine your query on the local data and reselect the data without necessarily making any more queries to the database. In this instance, it would mean you could divide the processing task between the Web server and local applications, dramatically increasing the speed of response.

In this comparison between XML and HTML, I can only skim over the general aspects of XML's linking mechanisms. However, in Chapter 38, I demonstrate a few practical examples of how to use these powerful tools.

Intelligent Styles

You will be able to use cascading style sheets (CSS1) with XML documents in almost exactly the same way they're used with HTML documents. In fact, CSS1 will probably still be widely used for simple XML documents, but it has some limitations when you try to use it for complex applications. However, you will be able to use XSL (Extensible Style Language) to format HTML documents.

Just as XML introduces its own language syntax and linking language, it also introduces its own style language: XSL. Briefly, XSL is based on the Document Style Semantics and Specification Language (DSSSL, ISO/OEC 10179: 1996) that was developed for specifying the formatting of structured (SGML) documents. In addition, it incorporates the official, standard form of JavaScript known as ECMA (the European Association for Standardizing Information and Communication Systems) Standard-262 "ECMAScript." For a more detailed description, see Chapter 36, "What Is XML?" and Chapter 39, "Understanding XSL."

> **NOTE**
>
> XSL is still in an early stage of development; at the time of this writing, the standard hasn't developed beyond it being a discussion document. Microsoft is rumored to be preparing its own proposal for an XML-style language, and there's no guarantee that any parts of the current XSL proposal won't change.

XSL is as different from CSS1 as XML is from HTML. Essentially, XSL is a full-blown programming language that allows you to perform complex conditional context and structure-sensitive processing on an XML document. Using XSL you can, for example, do the following:

- Extract elements from one place in a document and use them in another. This feature makes it possible, for example, to automatically generate such things as tables of contents, indexes, and cross-references.

- Apply formatting according to elements' structural relationships. You can do this in CSS1 by using pseudo-elements, but in XSL you could, for example, format alternate paragraphs in different styles.

- Calculate quantities and store variables. This feature allows you to pass parameter values when processing style sheets and generate such things as auto-numbering sequences, page numbers, and page headers and footers.

Apart from it "simply" being a programming language (it could be argued that Java or JavaScript, or even XML itself, could just as easily perform the preceding tasks), XSL is completely adapted to the needs of professional publishing. CSS1, on the other hand, is far more attuned to displaying HTML on a screen rather than on a piece of paper. XSL includes features for the following:

- Multiple printing directions (left-to-right, right-to-left, top-to-bottom); directions can be mixed arbitrarily

- Multiple column printing, including column spans and synchronized column layouts

- Floating-text objects (notes, footnotes, and so forth)

- Rotated text areas

- Margin attachments (sidebars, revision marks, and so forth)

It's difficult to exaggerate the power of XSL, and to do the topic full justice would require a separate book. However, the question of whether the final form of the XML-style language will look anything like the XSL language described here remains an open one. For the time being, much of the XSL language has already been implemented in software packages (such as Jade) as a cut-down form of its parent DSSSL language and can now be used to convert HTML documents into other formats. Examples of some of these conversions are described in Chapter 39.

Can't Java, JavaScript, or ActiveX Manage?

By using Java, JavaScript, ActiveX, CGI programming, or a combination of coding or scripting mechanisms, you could probably address the limitations of HTML that XML is designed to solve or produce many of the features that XML introduces. Using embedded scripts has certainly been placed on a firmer footing by adding the OBJECT element to HTML 4, and embedded scripts offer a powerful means of extending HTML beyond what its developers ever

How XML Compares with HTML

CHAPTER 37

717

37

How XML
Compares
with HTML

dreamed was possible. The problem isn't whether it can be done by embedding code in documents; the problem is whether it *should* be done.

The core notion of SGML is the separation of content and presentation. The way you present information has always been a major obstacle to the portability of text. Either the other platform didn't have the fonts, or it had a different encoding mechanism, or the software didn't understand the codes used.

Years ago, people were more willing to accept that a Macintosh document couldn't be viewed on a PC, or that an IBM DisplayWrite document couldn't be read in Lotus Manuscript. Recently, however, things got worse when you couldn't even guarantee being able to read a document across different versions of the same software package. It has been almost impossible to force all the software producers to agree on using a common format or to use a common interchange format. Some kind of neutral format had to be devised, so IBM (even now, the world's largest publisher of printed information) came up with GML, which grew into SGML.

SGML's basic premise is that the presentation of a piece of text (for example, whether it's set in bold type, in a larger font size, or on a separate line) is usually a function of its purpose within the document. Its function can usually be expressed in terms of its relation to the other parts of the document, which is another way of saying its position in the structure of the document. If you can identify something as simply being a heading, you can leave the local platform to resolve the matter of choosing suitable display characteristics.

Taking this theory even further, by identifying the structure of the document, you can even allow readers to choose presentation characteristics more suited to their own requirements (Braille, audio, very large type, and so on).

Embedding code in HTML documents to get "presentation effects" is tantamount to turning the clock back on everything SGML has been struggling to achieve and, by implication, undermining much of what HTML was developed to do. Ultimately, you turn documents into code fragments, which might be a good idea from a programmer's point of view, but for the rest of us nonprogrammer types, it transforms the task of creating HTML documents back into the preserve of the specially trained. Worse than this, it seriously threatens the portability of HTML documents and makes them very difficult to maintain.

Summary

In this chapter, I have tried to give you brief picture of some of the major differences between XML and HTML. Because HTML is an application of SGML, and XML is a version of SGML itself, the comparison is a little dishonest because it's comparing an application and an application toolkit. However, by seeing the comparison between some of the major features of HTML and an XML application in general, you should have some appreciation of the radical advances that XML heralds.

I have concentrated on features in general terms and skimmed over detail (such as XML's requirements that all element tags are properly nested and that all attribute values are enclosed in quotes), with the intention of giving a better global overview of the differences between XML and HTML. For those detailed aspects, see Chapter 36.

I have also intentionally skipped over some features of XML, such as its suitably for international applications through its use of Unicode (ISO 10646) because these features either already have been, or shortly will be, matched by developments in HTML. In Chapters 38 and 39, you get a chance to see practical examples of using these features.

Using XML

by Simon North

IN THIS CHAPTER

You have met the cool, technical side of XML in Chapters 36, "What Is XML?" and 37, "How XML Compares with HTML" (and you will see it again in Appendix D, "XML Quick Reference"). In this chapter, however, I take you on a short journey away from discussions of syntax and semantics to a look at the practical uses of XML.

With the help of copious examples, you will learn about the following topics:

- When to design a DTD and when one might not be needed
- The basic principles of XML DTD design
- The modeling of elements and attributes
- The use of text entities as shorthand
- The use of parameter entities as shorthand and for conditional sections
- The use of external binary entities and notation declarations
- The use, and dangers, of some of the features of XML's links

Well-Formed or Valid?

In Chapter 36, I explained about XML DTDs (document type definitions) and what they contain, but all that information begs the question: Do you need a DTD? It's an easy question to ask, but a very hard one to answer. Easy or hard, the question must be answered before you can go any further because it largely determines the nature and extent of the subsequent work you will have to do.

The easy answer, to quote the XML specification, is "only if the external subset contains any unspecified attributes that have default values, entity references, or if white space occurs directly within element types that have element content." Or, in plain English, only if the external part of the DTD contains attributes that aren't defined in the document but do have default values, if it contains entity references, or if you've included spaces in your document structure where elements would normally be expected.

The hard answer is, of course, much harder to give; it comes down to a matter of weighing some considerations rather than applying off-the-shelf rules.

Ask yourself, for example, what kind of checking you want to do on documents. If the documents are to be generated by a program, chances are you can tune the program to produce the correct XML code so that validity is not a concern.

Also, consider what you're going to do with the documents after they have been created. If you're going to reuse the content, or process it some way (such as converting it into HTML), a DTD gives you a formal structure that can be processed externally to derive rules for processing the documents.

Don't let the seeming complexity of a DTD put you off; a DTD needs to be only as complex as you want, or need, it to be. On the other hand, it can be as simple as you want or need it to be, consisting perhaps of only a few elements. For example, a proposed DTD is in circulation for Internet FAQs (frequently asked question documents) that has just three or four elements; a Q element for a question, an A element for an answer, and a few others to cover linking to other questions and answers.

As XML becomes more accepted, a ready supply of off-the-shelf XML DTDs should eventually be available, just as there is for SGML.

Creating a DTD

Having weighed the pros and cons of having a DTD, say that you have decided to write a DTD for your XML document. In the following sections, I highlight some of the tasks and problems you must address while you're developing a DTD. Before you rush off and start jotting down code, though, have a good look around on the Web to see if you can find another DTD that will serve your purpose. A little modification of an existing DTD can save you from wasting time by going over old ground that has already been covered by other people—and possibly covered better, too. If nothing else, use other people's DTDs as a learning resource; try to follow the logic of the design and understand the design decisions that played a role in the background.

A DTD is a plain ASCII file, and you can use whatever text editing or word processor package you like to actually create it provided you remember to save the file in ASCII format. As yet, there are no XML DTD development packages. There are, however, some specialized packages for developing SGML DTDs. They range from Microstar's top-end Near & Far graphic DTD modeling package to shareware and freeware packages such as EasyDTD, which converts an indented ASCII file into a correctly marked-up DTD element structure.

Choosing the Elements (Mapping the Tree)

If you're designing a DTD for a type of document that already exists in another form, your first job is to analyze the document to try to identify the elements in the document type. Make sure you analyze a representative selection of documents of the required type! Many a design has floundered while trying to accommodate special cases, when generalizing a common convention for all the variations of a particular document type had proved impossible. You might discover that the variety of content and structure in a document type could force you to design more than one DTD.

Your main concern is to try to abstract a general model of the information objects in the documents. Think of each document as a sort of database, and you will be thinking along the right lines because designing a good DTD shares many of the same concerns as designing parts of databases. It's important to remember that unless you have identified some piece of information in the DTD, either as an element or an attribute, you won't be able to process it by querying, formatting, and so on.

If you can manage to identify the function, rather than the appearance, of a piece of text, then you will be staying close to the essential philosophy of SGML—that of separating content and presentation. For example, in HTML, a list (OL or UL) is composed of list items (LI). This definition ties an LI element firmly into its context. In your XML DTD, you could take a far more abstract approach and refine this "content model." Suppose the basic element in which actual text (character data) is to appear is a PARA element. A UL would usually be defined as containing one or more list items, as shown here:

```
<!ELEMENT UL (LI)+ >
<!ELEMENT LI (#PCDATA) >
```

With your PARA element, however, you could instead subdivide the list item:

```
<!ELEMENT UL (LI)+ >
<!ELEMENT LI (PARA)+ >
<!ELEMENT PARA (#PCDATA) >
```

The advantage of this approach is that a PARA element, as a block of text, can now be easily moved into and out of a list item, and you can very easily merge and split list items. The end result makes it much simpler to manipulate PARA elements and reuse them in this or other documents.

Having chosen the elements you want to identify, place them into a tree structure. An absolute requirement of XML is this: There must be one element that serves as the root or parent of the whole tree, and that element's name should match the name of the DTD.

You will probably find, especially in the beginning, that sketching out an actual tree of the elements is a great help in developing the DTD. Later on, after you have discarded these sketches as being unnecessary, you will probably return to drawing them as the best tool for explaining the DTD to other people.

Avoiding Ambiguity

While building up the tree, make sure it's not ambiguous. XML processors are intended to be easy to create and fast, which means they are also not very sophisticated. In particular, they aren't supposed to (and probably even can't) look ahead to puzzle out what the next element is supposed to be and whether what it really sees is allowed. Being unambiguous means, therefore, being clear and explicit. A simple XML processor should be able to parse the DTD and quickly and easily confirm whether an XML document written to that DTD is valid.

Ambiguous content models can be a major problem in SGML, mostly because SGML allows you to define elements in a DTD so that it's possible to omit start and end tags. The SGML parser knows from the context where a start or an end tag would have appeared and can infer from the context what element is currently being processed. In XML, things are a little simpler because this shorthand method, called *tag optimization*, is not permitted; every XML element must have a start tag and an end tag. That doesn't mean the problem of ambiguity no longer exists, however.

In XML, you must be particularly wary of "mixed content" elements, which can contain character data and elements, as shown in this example:

```
<!ELEMENT P (#PCDATA ¦ A ¦ EM ¦ STRONG ¦ TT )* >
```

Note that, as required by the XML syntax, the character data (PCDATA) always comes first, and the content model uses only the OR (¦) condition. This might sound trivial, but think about what happens when the XML processor sees this:

```
<P>
    <EM>This is where the text starts</EM>   <A>and here we
have an anchor</A></P>
```

The XML processor will see the line feed (or line feed and carriage return) character (this is a character too) before the EM element, and it will see the white space between the EM and the A elements! If you don't keep to the rules, you can find yourself in a lot of trouble.

> **NOTE**
>
> The matter of white space, a touchy subject in XML circles, doesn't seem to have a very ready solution. In HTML, white space is simply ignored; in XML, it can be ignored or retained. The best method for handling it is the topic of many heated discussions.

Elements or Attributes?

Another question—one you will have to address—that causes a lot of head scratching in both SGML and XML circles is the choice between using elements or attributes.

The following example is a complete, but very simple, XML DTD for e-mail messages:

```
<!element email (to, from, date, subject, body) >
<!element to      (#PCDATA)>
<!element from    (#PCDATA)>
<!element date    (#PCDATA)>
<!element subject (#PCDATA)>
<!element body    (para)+ >
<!element para    (#PCDATA)>
```

The DTD simply identifies the basic information objects that you would expect to see in an e-mail message. But does it? A date is a date is a date... but you don't have to travel very far to appreciate that we all have different ways of expressing the date. In Britain, you'd expect to write the day of the month before the month; in America, you'd expect to write the month first.

The most important consideration facing you is to determine how the date information is to be used. For the purpose of displaying the e-mail message, you might want the date to be in a user-friendly form, such as this:

```
August 12th, 1997
```

However, from the information-modeling point of view, you might want to be able to find all the e-mail messages sent before or after a certain date or within a range of dates. For this purpose, you might prefer to express the date in a form that's more readily processed by a computer, as in this example:

```
19970812
```

At first glance, the two requirements might seem to conflict, but there are several ways to accommodate both of them. The simplest way to meet both of these needs is to *decompose* the date down into subelements containing a component of the date and turn the date element itself into a "container" element:

```
<!ELEMENT date (year, month, day)>
<!ELEMENT year (#PCDATA)>
<!ELEMENT month (#PCDATA)>
<!ELEMENT day (#PCDATA)>
```

In this case, the date would then be marked up as follows:

```
<date><year>1997</year><month>8</month><day>12</day></date>
```

For display, you would ask the style sheet to reorder the components of the date (first the month, then the day, and then the year), convert the numerical month into a word (August), and add a suitable suffix (st, nd, rd, or th) and a comma to the day:

```
August 12th, 1997
```

An alternative strategy is to use *attributes* to contain one of the forms in which the information is required. In this case, it's probably easier to have the "friendly" form of the date as the actual data content, and give the numerical form as a NUMBERFORM attribute value.

To do this, you need to declare an element type and an attribute list for date:

```
<!ELEMENT date (#PCDATA)>
<!ATTLIST date
          NUMBERFORM CDATA #IMPLIED>
```

The date would now be entered as follows:

```
<DATE NUMBERFORM="19970812">August 12th 1997</DATE>
```

Note that the default value for NUMBERFORM is #IMPLIED. If you had specified #REQUIRED instead, users would be forced to enter a value for the numerical form attribute (which actually might be a good idea).

Which should you choose? Ultimately, you are the only one who can really decide that because you're the only one close enough to your application to make a well-informed decision. The general consensus among XML developers is that, if there are no obvious application constraints, the choice is largely a matter of personal taste.

My own opinion is that it's marginally easier to validate and enforce the entry and content of attributes than it is the content of elements. XML (and SGML) has no way of ensuring that the content of an element is not empty, or not nonsense; at least you can exercise some control over the presence and content of an attribute value. On the other hand, as in this example, you would have to accept the risk of the attribute value and the value expressed in the element content not agreeing with each other. Further, you would, of course, burden the writer/user with entering the same information twice. However, for this last point, you might well consider the unlikelihood of a flesh-and-blood author actually creating bare XML code once XML becomes accepted.

Entities in the DTD

Entities are probably one of the most undervalued, but useful, items in SGML. In XML, they are just as handy. There are three main sorts of entities:

- **Text entities:** Identified by a &, these entities can be used in both the XML DTD and the XML document.
- **Parameter entities:** Identified by a %, they can be used only in an XML DTD.
- **Binary entities:** These Identified entities can be used only in an XML document.

I'll return to the subject of text and binary entities later in the discussion of XML documents (see "Inside the XML Document"). For now, take a look at parameter entities and how useful they can be in an XML DTD.

Parameter entities can be used as a sort of shorthand, macro language for markup. If you're going to use the same piece of markup several times in your XML DTD, you can declare it as a parameter entity:

```
<!entity % inline
    " (#pcdata ¦ f¦ x¦ %emph; ¦sq¦ %xref ¦ %index )* " >
```

Thereafter, any time you want to repeat that piece of markup, you simply reference it, as shown here:

```
<!element footnote  (%inline;)>
<!element subject   (%inline;) >
<!element closing   (%inline;) >
<!element cc (%inline;) +(newline) >
<!element encl (%inline;) +(newline) >
```

Parameter entities can also be used for provisional markup consisting of "conditional" sections. Suppose you're developing an XML document for a group of writers. Once the document has been finished, you want to be able to validate it fully. However, while it's being worked on, you want to leave the structure a little looser. For drafting, you might have this declaration:

```
<!ELEMENT document (title, abstract?, intro?, section*)>
```

In ordinary language, this declaration says: There must be a title, followed by an optional abstract, an optional introduction, and any number of sections (including none). Ideal for drafting purposes—you've got as much room as you need.

38

USING XML

However, for the document's final version, you want to be stricter:

```
<!ELEMENT document (title, abstract, intro, section+)>
```

This declaration says: There must be a title, followed by an abstract, an introduction, and at least one section. Now you've covered both situations—but there's more. You can put both these declarations in your XML DTD and use a parameter entity as a sort of "switch" to turn on the version you want and turn off the version you don't want:

```
<!ENTITY % draft "INCLUDE">
<!ENTITY % final "IGNORE">

<![ %draft; [
<!ELEMENT document (title, abstract?, intro?, section*)>
]]>

<![ %final; [
<!ELEMENT document (title, abstract, intro, section+)>
]]>
```

All you have to do now to activate the version you want is change the declaration of the one you want to INCLUDE and the other to IGNORE.

Inside the XML Document

So far in this chapter, you have examined just the XML DTD, but that's only part of the story. There's also a lot you can still do in the XML documents themselves.

As you might remember from Chapter 36, the XML DTD can be divided into two subsets: the external subset (kept in a separate document) and the internal subset, which is at the start of the XML document itself:

```
<!DOCTYPE EMAIL SYSTEM "EMAIL.DTD" [
<!-- internal DTD subset goes here -->
]>
<!-- and the document content starts here -->
```

In the following sections, you'll have a look at just what you can do with entities in this internal DTD subset.

Text Entities

XML text entities fall into two classes: internal entities, where the entity's content appears in the declaration, and external entities, where the content appears somewhere else (like in an external file).

Internal Text Entities

Internal text entities are a little like the parameter entities I described earlier (but note the different syntax) and can also be used as a sort of shorthand:

```
<!ENTITY W3C.home
```

```
'<a href="http://www.w3c.org/">The W3C Consortium</a>'>
<!ENTITY W3C.XML
'<a href="http://www.w3c.org/Activity/XML/">The W3C XML Page</a>'>
...
```

With that declaration, you can now use these entities as the shorthand for the A links in the text of your XML document:

```
<P>For an overview of the W3C's work see &W3C.home;. For
details of their work on XML see &W3C.XML;. ...
```

This code will be processed as though you had entered the A element in full each time:

```
<p>For an overview of the W3C's work see
<a href="http://www.w3c.org/"
>The W3C Consortium</a>. For details of
their work on XML see
<a href="http://www.w3c.org/Activity/XML/">The
W3C XML Page</a>. ...
```

External Text Entities

Instead of declaring the entities in the XML document itself, you could place them in a separate file, *not* in the DTD. Separating the entities like that gives you a handy way of keeping all the links from any number of XML documents in one place. This method won't stop other Web sites from changing their URLs, of course, but it will ease the administrative headache of making sure all your links to them are kept up to date.

Create a file that contains just the entity declarations, and give it the name /links/ext_lnks.ent. The contents of this file would then look exactly like the original declarations I described previously:

```
<!ENTITY W3C.home
'<a href="http://www.w3c.org/">The W3C Consortium</a>'>
<!ENTITY W3C.XML
'<a href="http://www.w3c.org/Activity/XML/">The W3C XML Page</a>'>
...
```

In the XML internal DTD subset, then, you declare this file instead of the entities. Note that although I used a SYSTEM identifier followed by a filename in the earlier example, I could just as easily have used a URL. Don't forget that you must also reference the entity (if you forget the entity reference, its content will be skipped):

```
<!DOCTYPE EMAIL SYSTEM "EMAIL.DTD" [

<!--declare the file as an entity -->
<!ENTITY % external.links SYSTEM "http://myhome.com/ext_lnks.ent">

<!--and now reference it -->
%external.links;

<!--any other local DTD subset content goes here -->
]>

<!--and the actual XML document starts here -->
```

Now you can use these entities just as though you had declared them locally in the internal DTD subset:

```
<P>For an overview of the W3C's work see &W3C.home;. For
details of their work on XML see &W3C.XML;. ...
```

The advantage of this approach is that all your external links can now be kept in one place, and you need to declare each link only once. If a URL changes—as it often does—you have to update it only once. You can then be sure that any of your pages with a link to that URL will continue to work.

External Binary Entities

External binary entities sound pretty exotic; in fact, they are just the binary images that you're probably used to referencing in HTML with the IMG element.

XML is slightly more demanding in its syntax for declaring external binary entities; you must follow these two rules:

- You must declare a notation.
- They can be referenced only through attribute values.

There are two ways to identify a notation:

- By identifying by name the format of external binary entities:

```
<!DOCTYPE HTML SYSTEM "HTML4.DTD" [
<!NOTATION GIF SYSTEM "Compuserve/Unisys Graphics Format">
```

- By identifying by name the application to which processing instructions are addressed:

```
<!DOCTYPE HTML SYSTEM "HTML4.DTD" [
<!NOTATION GIF SYSTEM "/gsworks.exe">
```

Whichever method you choose, once you have declared the notation, you use it in exactly the same way when you declare the external binary entity:

```
<!DOCTYPE HTML SYSTEM "HTML4.DTD" [

<!--here we declare the notation -->
<!NOTATION GIF SYSTEM "/gsworks.exe">

<!--and here we declare the entity -->
<!ENTITY lefthand SYSTEM "hand_pointing_left.gif" NDATA GIF>
]>
```

Now, in contrast to HTML, you reference the graphic (at least in this example) by making the SRC attribute specification point to the entity:

```
<PARA>This is the image we should see <FIG SRC="lefthand"/>
```

It probably seems like an awful lot of effort to go to just to define a link to a graphic, and maybe it is. Think, however, of the flexibility this method can introduce. Instead of worrying about whether the browser has been set up to recognize the right MIME type (which ties you to a particular naming convention), and trusting that the correct naming convention has been followed, the format of the graphic you reference is now what you say it is, regardless of what the file has been called.

As you have now seen, although XML does not require you to have a DTD, the full strength that distinguishes XML from HTML lies in the powerful features that you can embed in the DTD. DTDs can be an extremely complex subject, and in SGML circles, their development is almost a discipline in its own right. In XML, as you may begin to appreciate as you become more familiar with developing them, an admirable trade-off has been found between power and ease of development.

XML Links

To round off this chapter on using XML, I'd like to finish with a brief look at something that really makes XML special: linking. XML's links are what really sets it apart from both HTML and SGML. They are multi-ended, they can have user-readable labels, and they have extremely sophisticated mechanisms. Rather than drift off into a theoretical discussion of their syntax and resolution mechanisms (you can find these in Chapter 36, Appendix D, and in the official specification documents), I'll just examine a few practical examples in the following sections.

Using Extended Links

Extended links are simply links that use XML's extended pointers. These pointers can be used to make extremely powerful links, as shown in the following annotated example:

```
<!DOCTYPE CHESSGAME [

<!-- first we declare the elements -->
<!ELEMENT X ANY>
<!ELEMENT L ANY>

<!-- and then we declare their attributes -->
<!-- one as an extended link -->
  <ATTLIST X XML-LINK #FIXED "EXTENDED">
<!-- and one as a locator -->
  <ATTLIST L XML-LINK #FIXED "LOCATOR"
]>

<PARA>Karpov began a conventional game, starting with

<X>

<!-- this link opens an animation in a new window -->
<!-- Note how we can use the role to identify the link -->
<L ROLE="demonstration" LABEL="Animation"
   SHOW="NEW" HREF="/cgi-bin/qview?kpopen" />

<!-- this link embeds a picture -->
<L ROLE="picture" LABEL="Illustration"
   SHOW="EMBED"
   HREF="pix.xml#DESCENDANT(*,FIG,CAPTION,KP OPENING)"/>
```

```
<!-- This link selects a range; from the element whose -->
<!-- ID is Karpov.4.1 and the next two P elements -->
<!-- in the same document -->
<L ROLE="Game Report" LABEL="Game Report"
   HREF="report.xml#ID(Karpov.4.1)..DITTO,NEXT(2,P)" />

<!-- This link would move you to the specified point -->
<!-- In the HTML document -->
<L ROLE="ToMove" LABEL="Move to Game Transcript"
   SHOW="REPLACE" HREF="game4.html#Move1" />
a King's Pawn opening.</PARA>
```

Neither this example, nor a hundred examples, can give you a real idea of exactly what you can do with the power that these links place in your hands. It's up to you to explore their potential. One word of warning, though: Be careful—you might not get what you thought you would. Let me illustrate:

```
<PARA ID="a1">This is a simple paragraph taken from <CITE>A Famous Book</CITE>,
 showing just how clever the writer is
<EDITOR COMMENT>We beg to differ</EDITOR COMMENT>
in having read <CITE>Great Writer</CITE>.</PARA>
```

This is a simple paragraph containing three embedded elements, which is not so unusual, even in an HTML document. Be careful, though; it isn't quite as simple as it looks, especially in XML!

Now take a look at the structure of this element:

```
START PARA
    CDATA
      CITE
    CDATA
      EDITOR COMMENT
    CDATA
      CITE
    CDATA
END PARA
```

So, suppose you have a link to the following:

```
ID(a1)CHILD(4,*CDATA)
```

What am I going to get? The full stop at the end of the sentence (the fourth child that is character data)!

If you ask instead for the fourth child, as shown here, you will get the EDITOR COMMENT element:

```
ID(a1)CHILD(4)
```

As you will no doubt discover, increased power also means increased opportunities to make mistakes!

There are many more ways in which XML's links are so much more powerful than either HTML's or SGML's (such as extended linking groups). Unfortunately, the discussion of their features will have to be left to another author in a far more extensive book.

Summary

In this chapter, you have learned the following:

- What the considerations are that you must keep in mind when deciding whether you need to design a DTD, and the situations when one might not be needed
- The basic principles of document analysis—identifying the elements, attributes, and entities that will form the content of the XML DTD
- How to make your task of creating XML content simpler by using text entities in XML documents as a sort of shorthand
- How to use parameter entities in an XML DTD, either as a shorthand for larger pieces of code or for marking up conditional sections of code that you can easily turn on and off as the circumstances demand
- How to use external binary entities and notation declarations to include such things as graphics files, and to do so in a way that can save you a lot of link editing
- How to use some of the features of XML's linking mechanisms—and some of the dangers you might face in doing so

Understanding XSL

by Simon North

IN THIS CHAPTER

The Extensible Style Language (XSL) is a style sheet language designed for the Web community. It's the counterpart of XML in the same way that Cascading Style Sheets (CSS) are the counterpart of HTML.

In this chapter, you start by seeing a comparison of XSL with CSS and its parent, DSSSL. You then go on to looking at practical examples of using XSL statements in style sheets and conclude by learning what the XSL (ECMAScript) scripting language is.

XSL and CSS

XSL offers functionality beyond CSS's capabilities. It can handle advanced publishing functions, such as reordering elements or copying them to other locations, allowing you to perform tasks such as the following:

- Selectively format elements based on their ancestors, descendents, position, and uniqueness
- Create formatting constructs that include generated text and graphics
- Define reusable formatting macros
- Create style sheets that are independent of the writing direction
- Extend the set of formatting objects

CSS can still be used to display simply structured XML documents. XSL can be used when more powerful formatting capabilities are required or for formatting highly structured information, such as XML structured data or XML documents containing structured data.

XSL and DSSSL

XSL is based on a profile of DSSSL, called DSSSL-o (*o* for *online*). DSSSL (Document Style and Semantics Specification Language: ISO/IEC Standard 10179:1996) is a language based on Scheme, a dialect of the LISP programming language, which supports transforming, querying, and processing SGML documents. DSSSL's transformation aspect is not supported in XSL, and the style sheet part has been cut down to the basics required for displaying and printing XML (and HTML) documents.

XSL is compatible with DSSSL's fundamental design principles and processing model. However, just as the development of XML highlighted "improvements" that could be made to SGML (the language XML is derived from), the development of XSL has identified usability issues with the current DSSSL standard. Along with the development of the XSL specification, a proposal for an amendment to DSSSL has been announced. This proposal is intended to modify the DSSSL standard to "legalize" certain new XSL features, such as the CSS/HTML extensions. If and when this amendment is incorporated into the DSSSL standard, DSSSL will become a superset of XSL.

After amendment, the DSSSL standard should be compatible with the current DSSSL standard. The amended standard would have three additions:

- An alternative syntax compatible with the XSL (XML) syntax.

- Extensions to the flow object tree construction language to support the features of XSL that aren't included in DSSSL; these features would be available both with the current syntax and the alternative syntax.

- New (HTML) flow object classes and characteristics to support the formatting of Web pages.

> **NOTE**
>
> XSL is still in an early stage of development; at the time of this writing, it exists only in the form of a proposal that has been submitted to the World Wide Web Consortium (W3C) for consideration.
>
> Because of its novelty, and therefore a lack of support, many of the code examples used in this chapter are based on material in the XSL proposal. I have supplied some analysis and commentary to illustrate potential uses for XSL.

How XSL Works

XSL is essentially a data-driven style mechanism that allows formatting information to be associated with elements in the source document to produce formatted output.

An XSL style sheet describes this formatting process through its own small set of XML elements, called *XSL document elements*. The processing of an XML document is determined by scanning its structure and merging it with the *formatting specification* derived from the active style sheets. These instructions are then used to create *flow objects*, which determine the coding applied to the document. The merging process produces a tree structure of flow objects called the *flow object tree*. The formatted output—the results that will be printed or displayed—are created by formatting this tree of flow objects.

Flow Objects

Flow objects, which describe the layout of a document, represent layout components such as page sequences, paragraphs, tables, and graphic objects. They have characteristics such as page margins, font sizes, heights, and widths.

Illustrating its roots in DSSSL and its application in an HTML/CSS environment, XSL understands some (but not all) of the flow objects used in both DSSSL and HTML/CSS.

DSSSL Core Flow Objects

DSSSL flow objects are international in nature so that a single style sheet can be used to format documents in natural languages with different writing directions.

Not all the DSSSL flow objects are supported (for details of the flow object characteristics, refer to the DSSSL-o specification), but the following ones are:

- **scroll:** A scroll flow object class is used as the top-level flow object for online display that doesn't divide output into pages. It accepts displayed flow objects. The viewing environment determines the size of the flow object in the direction perpendicular to the filling direction.

- **paragraph:** A paragraph flow object class represents a paragraph. Its contents may be either inline or displayed. Inline flow objects are formatted to produce line areas. Displayed flow objects implicitly specify a break, and their areas are added to the resulting sequence of areas.

- **paragraph-break:** Used with the paragraph-break flow object class, a paragraph flow object can represent a sequence of paragraphs. The paragraphs are separated by paragraph-break flow objects, which are atomic. paragraph-break flow objects are allowed only in paragraph flow objects. All the characteristics that apply to a paragraph flow object are also applicable to a paragraph-break flow object. The characteristics of a paragraph-break flow object determine the formatting for the portion of the content of the paragraph flow object following that paragraph-break flow object up to the next paragraph-break flow object, if any.

- **character:** A character flow object class is formatted to produce a single inline area (character flow objects may only be inline). The area can be merged with adjacent inline areas.

- **line-field:** The line-field flow object class is inline and has inline content. It produces a single inline area. The width of this area is equal to the value of the field-width characteristic. If the content of the line-field area can't fit in this width, the area grows to accommodate the content. If the line-field occurs in the paragraph, there's a break after the line-field. You can use these objects to create fixed-width prefixes for items in a list, so that the start of the first character after the prefix doesn't depend on the size of the prefix.

- **external-graphic:** The external-graphic flow object class is used for graphics in an external entity. Flow objects of this class may be inline or displayed.

- **horizontal-rule and vertical-rule:** These rule flow objects specify horizontal rules and vertical rules; they may be inline or displayed.

- **score:** The score flow object class is used for underlining and ruling through (scoring) characters.

- **embedded-text:** The embedded-text flow object class is used for embedding right-to-left text within left-to-right text, or vice-versa. This flow object class can only be inline.

- **box:** The box flow object class is used to put a box around a sequence of flow objects; this flow object can be either displayed or inline. If the box is displayed, it accepts any displayed flow objects. If it's inline, it accepts any inline flow objects. A box flow object may result in more than one area, in which case the border of the box adjacent to the break may be omitted. If the box is inline, this border is perpendicular to the writing-mode, but if it's displayed, this border is parallel to the writing-mode. When the box is displayed, the size of the box (the distance between the positions of the borders) in the direction determined by the writing-mode is equal to the box's display size, less the start and end indents. The display size for the box's content is equal to the size of the box.

- **table:** A table flow object contains either all of class table-part or all of class table-column, table-row, or table-cell. If it contains flow objects of class table-column, they must appear before all the flow objects of other classes. A table flow object can only be displayed. A table has two directions associated with it: a row-progression direction and a column-progression direction.

- **table-part:** A table-part flow object class is allowed only within a table flow object. A table-part flow object consists of a table body, table header, and table footer. Only table-column flow objects are allowed in a table body. A table-row and a table-cell may be used anywhere in a table-part.

  The result of formatting a table-part flow object is a sequence of areas. Each area consists of the header's content (unless explicitly omitted), followed by some portion of the table body's content, followed by the table footer's content (unless explicitly omitted). Each row in the table body occurs exactly once, and the order of the rows is kept. The rows in the table header and footer are replicated for each result area.

- **table-column:** A table-column flow object class is an atomic flow object that specifies characteristics applicable to table cells that have the same column and span.

- **table-row:** A table-row flow object class groups table cells into rows; all table cells in a table-row start in the same geometric row. A table-row accepts flow objects of the table-cell class. A table-row flow object can occur only as the child of a table-part or table flow object.

- **table-cell:** A table-cell flow object class accepts any flow object that can be displayed. A table-cell flow object may occur only as the child of a table-row, table-part, or table flow object. The table's width is equal to the sum of the cells' widths.

- **table-border:** A table-border flow object is used to specify the border of a table cell or an entire table. However, a table-border flow object is not allowed in the content of any flow object. The width of borders doesn't affect the cells' widths, the positioning of the cells' contents, the table's width, or the size of the area produced by the table.

- **sequence:** A sequence flow object class is formatted to concatenate the areas produced by each of its children, which can be either inline or displayed. A sequence flow object is useful for specifying inherited characteristics. Another flow object accepts a `sequence` flow object only if it would accept each of the flow objects in that sequence.

- **display-group:** A `display-group` flow object class concatenates other flow objects in the same way `sequence` flow objects do, but it also creates a new display area by starting on a new line and being followed by a new line (even if it has no content). These flow groups are used for controlling the positioning of groups of displayed flow objects.

- **simple-page-sequence:** A `simple-page-sequence` flow object class is formatted to produce a sequence of page areas. This flow object accepts any displayed flow object, but it isn't allowed within the content of any other flow object class.

  A `simple-page-sequence` flow object may have a single line header and footer containing text that's constant except for a page number. A document can contain multiple `simple-page-sequences`. For example, each chapter of a document could be a separate `simple-page-sequence`, which would allow the chapter title to be used in a header or footer line.

  The page is filled from top to bottom. The display size for the contents of the `simple-page-sequence` is the page width, less the left and right margins.

- **link:** A `link` flow object class represents a hypertext link that can be interactively traversed, typically by clicking on the areas representing the flow object and its content. However, as you have seen, in XML you don't necessarily have to click on a link to traverse it. A link can contain both inline and displayed flow objects. `link` flow objects can be nested. If they are nested, the innermost link is effective.

HTML/CSS Core Flow Objects

XSL supports all the functionality of CSS so that an accurate mechanical translation from CSS to XSL is possible.

A core set of HTML flow objects is defined in addition to the core DSSSL flow objects:

A	FRAMESET	SCRIPT
AREA	HR	SELECT
BASE	HTML	SPAN
BODY	IMG	TABLE
BR	INPUT	TBODY
CAPTION	MAP	TD
COL	META	TEXTAREA
COLGROUP	OBJECT	TFOOT
DIV	PARAM	THEAD
FORM	PRE	TITLE
		TR

With these HTML/CSS flow objects, you can use XSL with HTML and CSS.

Flow Object Characteristics

XSL is easy enough that it's possible to make basic style sheets for simple XML DTDs just by learning the names of a few flow objects and listing their mapping to print through construction rules.

A flow object is really just a formatting object—a typographic component like a paragraph, a table, an area, a mathematical equation, and so on. Flow objects have characteristics, and most of the names for these characteristics are pretty obvious:

- **font-family-name:** A font family name.
- **font-size:** A quantity representing the size of the font, usually specified in points ("pt"), such as 10pt. You can also specify it in millimeters, inches, picas, and several other units.
- **line-spacing:** A quantity representing the amount of space from the bottom of one line to another.
- **space-before:** The space before an area, such as the space inserted before a paragraph.
- **start-after:** The space after an area, such as the space inserted after a paragraph. The actual space between objects is the sum of the previous space-after and the next space-before values.
- **start-indent:** The indentation, as in the space between the left margin of the text and the left margin of a page in left-to-right writing modes (English, for example).
- **quadding:** Word processors call quadding "justification" or "alignment."

All the DSSSL flow objects have specific characteristics; for details, you should initially refer to the DSSSL-o specification. However, a lot of DSSSL-o's more sophisticated flow objects (such as the column-set and page-sequence flow objects) have been dropped in XSL, which means that some of the characteristics described in the DSSSL-o specification can't be supported in XSL.

The characteristics applied to the HTML/CSS flow objects consist of the sum of the CSS property set, plus the original HTML attributes when the functionality isn't supplied by the CSS property set.

Construction Rules

Every style sheet language consists of a series of statements that map structural elements onto formatting objects. Even the Style menu in Microsoft Word consists of such a mapping. It takes paragraph elements and maps them to fonts, colors, and other typographic effects.

In XSL, the syntax for setting up this mapping is called a *construction rule* because it "constructs" a formatted document from an XML document. Construction rules contain a *pattern* to identify specific elements in the source tree and an *action* to specify a resulting sub-tree of flow objects. The style sheet processor recursively processes source elements to produce a complete flow object tree.

In addition to construction rules, XSL also supports *style rules,* which allow the merging of characteristics. Although only one construction rule can be invoked for a particular source element, *all* applicable style rules are invoked. Doing so allows characteristics to be merged in XML as they are in HTML by using CSS.

The following example shows a construction rule for simple lists, using the HTML/CSS core flow objects. The first rule provides margins and indenting for the entire list; the second supplies margins for individual list items. A negative indent and fixed width SPAN on a list item allows the item number to be generated and placed to the left of each item.

```
<rule>
  <target-element type="list"/>
  <DIV margin-left="36pt" margin-top="12pt">
    <children/>
  </DIV>
</rule>

<rule>
  <element type="list">
    <attribute name="type" value="enum"/>
    <target-element type="item"/>
  </element>
  <DIV margin-top="4pt"
       margin-bottom="4pt"
       text-indent="-24pt">
    <SPAN width="24pt" height="12pt">
      <eval>
        formatNumber(childNumber(element),"1") + "."
      </eval>
    </SPAN>
    <children/>
  </DIV>
</rule>
```

The empty children element is an instruction to the XSL processor to recursively processes the children of the element.

The following example contains a root rule, which creates the top-level HTML and BODY flow objects. It's followed by a rule that creates a DIV with certain style characteristics for each orders element, and a style-rule that applies the bold font weight style to all the customer elements.

```
<xsl>
  <rule>
    <root/>

    <HTML>
      <BODY>
        <children/>
      </BODY>
    </HTML>
  </rule>

  <rule>
```

```
      <target-element type="orders"/>
      <DIV font-size="14pt" font-family="serif">
        <children/>
      </DIV>
    </rule>

    <style-rule>
      <target-element type="customer"/>
      <apply font-weight="bold"/>
    </style-rule>
</xsl>
```

A rule is specified with the `rule` element that contains a pattern identifying the element to which the rule applies. A rule also contains an action that specifies the flow objects to construct.

For example, suppose an XML document contains the following:

```
   <P>This is a truly <emph>momentous</emph> occasion.</P>
```

The pattern in the following XSL rule identifies the elements of type `emph` and defines an action that produces a SPAN flow object with a bold `font-weight` characteristic:

```
<rule>
  <!-- pattern -->
  <target-element type="emph"/>
    <!-- action -->
  <SPAN font-weight="bold">
    <children/>
  </SPAN>
</rule>
```

More than one pattern can be associated with a single action. The following example constructs a SPAN for both `emph` and `strong` element patterns:

```
<rule>
  <target-element type="emph"/>
  <target-element type="strong"/>
  <SPAN font-weight="bold">
    <children/>
  </SPAN>
</rule>
```

Patterns

The pattern part of a construction rule must contain a `target-element` element that indicates the element to which the rule applies. The pattern also allows you to identify applicable elements by their context. The syntax is based on XML's extended pointer syntax. You can select elements according to the following:

> Their parents
>
> Their children
>
> By using wildcards in the parent/child hierarchy (to select arbitrary parents/children at any level above or below)

Their attributes

Their position in relation to sibling elements (for example, the third child)

Their uniqueness in relation to sibling elements

Element ancestry can be represented in the pattern by mirroring the document's hierarchy. The element has identical attributes to the `target-element`, but implies that the element named by its `type` attribute is part of the context of the applicable element in the document instead of the element to which this rule will be applied.

The nesting of the `element` elements in the pattern indicates their contextual relationship to the `target-element` element in the source. For example, the following pattern matches `title` elements that have a `section` element as a parent and a `chapter` element as a grandparent:

```
<element type="chapter">
  <element type="section">
    <target-element type="title"/>
  </element>
</element>
```

Children of an element can be specified similarly. The following pattern matches `table` source elements that have a `title` child element:

```
<target-element type="table">
  <element type="title"/>
</target-element>
```

More than one `element` element can be placed inside a `target-element` element. This placement indicates only that all these elements must be present, but not in any particular order. The following pattern matches `man` elements that contain both a `rich` element and an `old` element:

```
<target-element type="man">
  <element type="rich"/>
  <element type="old"/>
</target-element>
```

The root of the document tree can be identified within the special `root` pattern:

```
<rule>
  <root/>
  <HTML>
    <BODY>
      <children/>
    </BODY>
  </HTML>
</rule>
```

An element's parent element is the element containing it, and the element that's contained is the child element. This relationship is a direct one, but there's no direct concept of being a grandparent or grandchild. A grandparent relationship has to be expressed as being a parent of a parent, and a grandchild relationship has to be expressed as being the child of a child. To work around this, wildcards can be specified in the pattern with the any element used to select any elements in the element hierarchy.

The following example applies to any `para` element that has both a `chapter` ancestor and an `emph` descendant:

```
<element type="appendix">
  <any>
    <target-element type="para">
      <any>
        <element type="changed"/>
      </any>
    </target-element>
  </any>
</element>
```

Both the `target-element` and the `element` elements can be used as wildcards by omitting the `type` attribute. These elements then match exactly one element in the element hierarchy. The following pattern matches elements that have a grandparent of type `data-samples`, regardless of the type of the `target-element` or the parent element:

```
<element type="data-samples">
  <element>
    <target-element/>
  </element>
</element>
```

Attributes

The attributes of an element, or those of any of its ancestor or descendant elements, can also be used to determine whether a particular construction rule applies.

To select an element by a specific attribute and value, include the attribute with the value in an `element` or `target-element` element.

The following example matches an `item` element that's the child of a `list` element whose `type` attribute has the value `enum`:

```
<element type="list">
  <attribute name="type" value="enum"/>
  <target-element type="item"/>
</element>
```

You can also just test to see whether an attribute is present. When the `has-value` attribute has the value `"yes"`, an element matches the pattern if the attribute in question has been given a value (either by an explicit assignment or by receiving a default value). When the `has-value` attribute has the value `"no"`, an element matches the pattern if the default value of the attribute is `#IMPLIED` and a value hasn't been explicitly assigned. If the `value` attribute has been assigned, the `has-value` attribute is ignored.

The following example matches an `item` element that's the child of a `list` element whose `compact` attribute has some value (as opposed to being unassigned and therefore implied):

```
<element type="list">
  <attribute name="compact" has-value="yes"/>
  <target-element type="item"/>
</element>
```

More than one `attribute` element can be applied to a single `target-element` or `element` element, as shown here:

```
<target-element type="reference">
  <attribute type="href" has-value="yes"/>
  <attribute type="used-as" value="direct-quote"/>
</target-element>
```

Just like CSS, XSL treats ID attributes and CLASS attributes in a special way. An `element` attribute is an ID attribute if it's declared as an ID attribute in the XML DTD. Because XSL also has to work with XML documents that don't have a DTD, style sheets can specify the `element` attributes that should be treated as ID attributes. This is done by using an ID element, with an `attribute` attribute that specifies the name of the attribute that should be treated as an ID attribute. The following example indicates that a `name` attribute on any element should be treated as an ID attribute:

```
<id attribute="name"/>
```

A `target-element` or `element` element can specify an ID attribute to select an element that has an ID attribute with the same value.

In exactly the same way, a style sheet can use a `class` element to declare the name of an attribute that should be treated as a `class` attribute. The following example would make a `family` attribute on any element be treated as a `class` attribute:

```
<class attribute="family"/>
```

An `element` or `target-element` element can specify a `class` attribute to select an element that has a `class` attribute with the same value.

Qualifiers

As well as selecting XML elements according to their position in the document tree, you can also narrow a selection by choosing elements with specific positions or properties by using qualifiers with patterns.

There are two qualifiers, `position` and `only`; each is expressed as an attribute of the `element` and `target-element` elements.

The `position` qualifier specifies the position of an element among its siblings; its values are the following:

- **`first-of-type`:** The element must be the first sibling of its type.
- **`last-of-type`:** The element must be the last sibling of its type.
- **`first-of-any`:** The element must be the first sibling of any type.
- **`last-of-any`:** The element must be the last sibling of any type.

The `only` qualifier specifies whether the source element has any siblings; its values are the following:

- **of-type:** The element must have no element siblings of the same type.
- **of-any:** The element must have no element siblings at all.

The following pattern matches the first item in a list:

```
<element type="list">
  <target-element type="item" position="first-of-type"/>
</element>
```

The following pattern matches the only item in a list:

```
<element type="list">
  <target-element type="item" only="of-type"/>
</element>
```

Priority

It's possible for an element to match patterns in several different rules. When it does match more than one pattern, then the *most specific* pattern is used, according to the following order:

1. The pattern with the highest importance; the importance of a pattern is the value of the `importance` attribute on the rule that contains it.
2. The pattern with the most `ID` attributes.
3. The pattern with the most `class` attributes.
4. The pattern with the most `element` or `target-element` elements that have a `type` attribute.
5. The pattern with fewer wildcards (a wildcard is an `any` element, or a `target-element` or `element` element without a `type` attribute).
6. The pattern with the higher specified priority; a pattern's priority is the value of the `priority` attribute on the rule that contains it.
7. The pattern with the most `only` qualifiers.
8. The pattern with the most `position` qualifiers.
9. The pattern with the most attribute specifications.

To determine which of two matching patterns is more specific, the preceding criteria are applied in the order shown until one of the criteria identifies exactly *one* of the patterns.

There must always be a unique matching pattern for an element that's more specific than all the other matching patterns.

Actions

When the rule to be applied to an element has been identified, the *action* part of the rule is invoked. The structure of the elements making up the action represents the structure of the flow objects that will be created.

39

UNDERSTANDING XSL

Flow object elements can be combined with literal text (which generates character flow objects) and code-generated text (an eval element) to create a flow object sub-tree. The following example selects the chapter elements, puts a horizontal rule above and below each one, and adds the prefix "Chapter" followed by a chapter number and a colon:

```
<rule>
  <!-- pattern -->
  <target-element type="chapter"/>
  <!-- action -->
  <sequence>
    <horizontal-rule/>
    <paragraph space-before="2pt">
      Chapter
        <eval>formatNumber(element.childNumber(),'001')
        </eval>
      :
      <children/>
    </paragraph>
    <horizontal-rule/>
  </sequence>
</rule>
```

Applying Characteristics

Within formatting rules, in parallel with specifying formatting actions, you can set the characteristics of flow objects by applying them as attributes of the element that represents the flow object.

For the HTML core flow objects, CSS properties can be directly applied as attributes without using the HTML style attribute, as shown in the following example:

```
<rule>
  <target-element type="para"/>
  <DIV font-family="Courier"
       font-size="12pt"
       font-style="normal"
       text-align="justify"
       margin-top="10pt"
       margin-bottom="6pt">
    <children/>
  </DIV>
</rule>
```

Selection Within an Action

Selection within an action controls which elements are processed after a rule has identified an element. Selection uses two elements: the children element and the select element combined with a from attribute.

The children element processes the immediate children of the element. The following example creates a display-group flow object for a chapter element and then processes its immediate children:

```
<rule>
  <target-element type="chapter"/>
  <display-group>
```

```
      <children/>
  </display-group>
</rule>
```

The select element processes either the children or the descendants of the element and provides powerful filtering by using patterns. The previous example can be rewritten using the select element with the from attribute set to children to get the same effect:

```
<rule>
  <target-element type="chapter"/>
  <display-group>
    <select from="children"/>
  </display-group>
</rule>
```

These are the two values of the from attribute:

- **children:** The children of the element are processed (this is the default).
- **descendants:** The descendants of the element are processed.

The select element, by default, processes only the immediate children of the element. To process all the descendants of the source element (the children, their children, the children's children's children, and so on), the from attribute can be set to descendants. The following example processes all the title elements in the chapter element:

```
<rule>
  <target-element type="chapter"/>
  <paragraph>
    <select from="descendants">
      <target-element type="title"/>
    </select>
  </paragraph>
</rule>
```

Filters

Filters can be added to the select element so that only the elements that match the filter pattern are processed. The filter pattern uses the same syntax as the pattern part of the rule. In the following example, after creating a paragraph for the man element, only the rich children are selected for processing:

```
<rule>
  <target-element type="man"/>
  <paragraph>
    <select>
      <target-element type="rich"/>
    </select>
  </paragraph>
</rule>
```

More than one children or select element can be used in a single action to do simple reordering. The following example separates out the calls elements into two tables; the first table is filled with local calls and the second table is filled with foreign calls:

```
<rule>
  <target-element type="telephone"/>
```

```
<display-group>
  <table>
    <select from="descendants">
      <element type="calls">
        <target-element type="local"/>
      </element>
    </select>
  </table>
  <table>
    <select from="descendants">
      <element type="calls">
        <target-element type="foreign"/>
      </element>
    </select>
  </table>
</display-group>
</rule>
```

By default, the `children` and the `select` elements process the children of the element matched by the rule's pattern.

The `ancestor` attribute is used to process children in relation to an element higher up in the document. This example finds an employee's department and then processes the `group` children of the department:

```
<rule>
  <target-element type="employee"/>
  <paragraph>
    <select ancestor="department"/>
      <target-element type="group"/>
    </select>
  </paragraph>
</rule>
```

Flow Object Macros

Actions can also be separated out of rules and saved as *macros*, which allow you to collect flow objects together and refer to the composite as though it were a single flow object.

In this example, a macro is defined for a boxed paragraph with the word `Note:` preceding the contents. The macro is referenced from a rule for `note` elements:

```
<define-macro name="note">
  <box>
    <paragraph>
      Note:
      <contents/>
    </paragraph>
  </box>
</define-macro>

<rule>
  <target-element type="note"/>
  <note-para font-size="14pt">
    <children/>
  </note-para>
</rule>
```

The contents element in the macro refers to the contents of the macro reference (in this case, the children element).

The arguments and argument default values of a macro are specified with the arg element. The arguments can be accessed inside the macro with the expression syntax "=" + *argument name*. The following example defines a macro for a list-item with arguments that control the indentation and the string to be used as a marker:

```
<define-macro name="list-item">
  <arg name="marker" default=""/>
  <arg name="indent" default="0.25in"/>
  <paragraph
      first-line-start-indent="=-indent"
      start-indent="=indent">
    <line-field field-width="=indent">
      <eval>marker</eval>
    </line-field>
    <contents/>
  </paragraph>
</define-macro>

<rule>
  <target-element type="item"/>
  <list-item marker="+">
    <children/>
  </list-item>
</rule>
```

The Default Construction Rule

XSL has a built-in default construction rule that allows recursive processing to continue when a successful pattern match can't be made. You can override the default rule by specifying your own, as shown here:

```
<rule>
  <target-element/>
  <children/>
</rule>
```

Style Rules

An XML element can be associated with flow object characteristics through *style rules*. Style rules, like construction rules, consist of a pattern and an action. The pattern selects the element and the action specifies the flow object characteristics.

The following example shows a simple style rule that makes all the strong elements bold:

```
<style-rule>
  <target-element type="strong"/>
  <apply font-weight="bold"/>
</style-rule>
```

Style rules support the CSS feature that more than one style sheet rule can contribute properties (characteristics) to an element's presentation. For example, the following CSS rules would make the font-weight of strong elements within H1 elements bold, as well as making their color attributes red:

```
h1 {font-weight:bold; color:blue}
h1 strong {color:red}
```

Rewritten in XSL, the statement looks like this:

```
<style-rule>
  <target-element type="h1"/>
  <apply font-weight="bold" color="blue"/>
</style-rule>

<style-rule>
  <element type="h1">
    <any>
      <target-element type="strong"/>
    </any>
  </element>
  <apply color="red"/>
</style-rule>
```

> **NOTE**
>
> This example is a little unfair in that 12 lines of XSL code are needed to reproduce just 2 lines of CSS code. XSL selection and formatting syntax makes it far more powerful than CSS but, as this trivial example demonstrates, if your requirements are simple, CSS can even be preferable to XSL.

Named Styles

Instead of specifying the style for every element or set of elements that you select, you can name styles and then reuse them wherever you want.

You can label a set of characteristics by using a name attribute. The following example defines a style called title-style:

```
<define-style name="title-style"
              font-size="18pt"
              font-weight="bold"/>
```

Styles that have been named in this manner can be called by a flow object element by specifying the style name as the value of the use attribute. The following example applies the title-style defined in the preceding example to the heading elements in a chapter element:

```
<rule>
  <element type="chapter">
    <target-element type="heading"/>
  </element>
  <paragraph use="title-style">
    <children/>
  </paragraph>
</rule>
```

A style rule can use an element with the style name instead of apply as its action, which lets you supplement a named style with characteristics from the style rule.

Modes

Sometimes XML elements need to be displayed in several different places. For example, a `title` element might need to be displayed in a table of contents as well as in the body. In each place, the element might need to be formatted differently.

If you want to process a section (or all) of a document using some different construction rules, XSL has a simple way of doing so, called a "mode." Essentially, a *mode* is just a named formatting scheme.

An element can be processed with respect to a named mode. A rule is associated with a named mode by using the `mode` attribute of a rule. Such a rule can be invoked only when an element is being processed with the rule's mode.

Children and `select` elements can also change to a named mode by specifying a `mode` attribute:

```
<rule>
  <root/>
  <HTML>
    <BODY>
      <DIV name="table-of-contents">
        <children mode="toc-mode"/>
      </DIV>
      <children/>
    </BODY>
  </HTML>
</rule>

<rule>
  <target-element type="title"/>
  <DIV font-size="14pt" font-weight="bold">
    <children/>
  </DIV>
</rule>

<rule mode="toc-mode">
  <target-element type="title"/>
  <DIV font-size="12pt">
    <children/>
  </DIV>
</rule>
```

Referring to a Style Sheet from XML

The XML working group has yet to define the mechanisms for associating XML documents with XSL style sheets. Until this work has been completed, and some other proposal is made, you should use an XML style sheet processing instruction to associate a style sheet with an XML document. For example, include a line like the following at the start of the XML source file (after the XML declaration):

```
<?xml-stylesheet href="article.xsl" type="text/xsl" ?>
```

Importing a Style Sheet

An XSL style sheet may import other XSL style sheets by using an `import` element with an `href` attribute:

```
<import href="article.xsl"/>
```

Using an `import` element has exactly the same effect as though the style sheet located by the value of the `href` attribute were physically included at the point it's referred to.

Inline Styles

If you don't want to fully define the formatting style in the XSL style sheet, such as when you want to leave yourself room for local variations, XSL allows you to override the style characteristics in a document by including the style declarations in the document itself (inline).

Formatting Attributes

To override the XSL style sheet specifications for a particular element, add the style attributes to the element in the XML document. The following statement, for example, ensures that this `para` element is set in bold face, regardless of what the XSL style sheet specifies for all the others:

```
<para xsl::font-weight="bold">
```

Formatting Rules

To override the XSL style sheet specifications for groups of elements (in a somewhat similar way to using classes in CSS), include an XSL rule at the beginning of an XML document. To apply the rule and override what's in the style sheet, use the same ID attribute value for the style rule and for the elements to which the rule will be applied, as shown in this example:

```
<rule>
  <target-element id="local"/>
  <DIV font-weight="bold">
    <children/>
  </DIV>
</rule>
...
<para id="local">
```

Style Sheet Override

The two methods just described allow you to override the XSL style sheet specifications by including formatting instructions in the XML document. Looking from the other direction—from within the XSL style sheet—in the style sheet itself you can include a `use` attribute of a flow object element with a value of `#source` in the rule for an element type. This method causes any attributes whose name matches an inherited DSSSL characteristic to be applied to the element in the XML namespace (that is, the XML document):

```
<rule>
  <target-element type="para"/>
  <DIV use="#source">
```

```
    <children/>
  </DIV>
</rule>
```

The XSL Scripting Language

The ECMAScript standard supplies the basis for the XSL scripting language. ECMAScript—or more properly "Standard ECMA-262, ECMAScript: A general purpose scripting language"—is based mostly on JavaScript, as developed by Netscape. Netscape is said to have tried to formalize JavaScript by having it accepted as an ISO standard. Apparently, it was originally rejected as being unacceptable in its submitted form because of its incompleteness.

Officially founded in 1961, ECMA (formerly known as the European Computer Manufacturers' Association) was renamed the "European association for standardizing information and communication systems" in 1994. Since 1987, ECMA has been an A-liaison member of the ISO/IEC Joint Technical Committee 1 (JTC1), which is the same committee responsible for SGML.

The ECMA-262 specification is an extensive document, so it's rather outside the scope of this chapter. You can get the specification free of charge from the ECMA Web site `http://www.ecma.ch/` in either Adobe Acrobat (PDF) or Microsoft Word format. In the rest of this chapter, I will simply concentrate on the ways XSL extends and uses the ECMAScript language.

The XSL scripting language extends ECMAScript by providing a quantity data type that represents lengths and quantities derived from lengths, such as areas and volumes. The base unit is the SI meter (m).

The following derived units are defined:

- cm (0.01 m)
- mm (0.001 m)
- in (0.0254 m)
- pc (1/6 in)
- pt (1/12 pc)

Device-dependent quantities, such as pixels, are handled in XSL by using the DSSSL `length-spec` concept.

The XSL proposal states that a set of built-in functions will be included and that they will be a subset of those included in the DSSSL standard.

Scripting in XSL

The XSL (ECMAScript) scripting language can be used in XSL in a number of different ways:

- It can be used at the top level (outside any construction rules) to declare variables and define functions within a `define-script` element:

```
<define-script>
 var defaultFontSize = "12pt";
  function hierarchicalIndent(elementType, element)
  {
  return length(hierarchicalNumberRecursive
              (elementType, element)) * 12pt;
  }
</define-script>
```

The `hierarchicalNumberRecursive` function is a DSSSL function that returns an array representing the child numbers of the requested element type at each hierarchical level. Formatting this list produces a numbering system.

■ If the value of an attribute specifying a characteristic starts with an equals sign (=), the remainder of the attribute is interpreted as an ECMAScript expression:

```
<rule>
  <element type="list">
    <target-element type="item">
  </element>
  <DIV font-size="=defaultFontSize"
   <children/>
  </DIV>
</rule>
```

■ Within an action, an `eval` element containing an ECMAScript expression may be used to compute generated text. The value returned by the expression is converted to a string and then to a sequence of `character` flow objects.

The `eval` element can also contain a sequence of ECMAScript statements. The value returned by a `return` statement is converted to a string and then to a sequence of `character` flow objects, as shown:

```
<rule>
  <target-element type="title">
  <DIV>
    <eval>
      formatNumberList(
        hierarchicalNumberRecursive("title", element),
        "", ".")
    </eval>
    <children/>
  </DIV>
</rule>
```

■ A `select` element can filter an arbitrary node list specified by a script within the `from` attribute. This example finds the nearest `department` ancestor and returns the `manager` children of that element:

```
<select from='=ancestor("department",element)'>
  <target-element type="manager"/>
</select>
```

A Sample Style Sheet with Scripting

The following style sheet, taken from the XSL proposal, is an XSL translation of parts of the DSSSL style sheet that Jon Bosak wrote for reading HTML (an improved version of this script for creating hard copy in RTF (rich text format) from HTML 3.2 code is included in the public domain Jade DSSSL engine distribution).

This script shows how declarative constructs can be combined with a script to format lists:

```
<xsl>
  <define-script>

    var bfSize = 10pt;
    var paraSep = bfSize/2.0;
    var blockSep = paraSep*2.0;
    var bodyStartIndent = 6pc;
    var lineSpacingFactor = 1.1;

    function inlist(element)
    {
      return
        haveAncestor(element, "OL") |
        haveAncestor(element, "UL") |
        haveAncestor(element, "DIR") |
        haveAncestor(element, "MENU") |
        haveAncestor(element, "DL");
    }

    function olstep(element)
    {
      var x = length(hierarchicalNumberRecursive(element, "OL")) % 4;
      if (x == 1) return 1.2*bfSize;
      if (x == 2) return 1.2*bfSize;
      if (x == 3) return 1.6*bfSize;
      if (x == 0) return 1.4*bfSize;
    }
  </define-script>

  <define-style name="p-style"
    font-size="=bfSize"
    line-spacing="=bfSize * lineSpacingFactor"/>

  <rule>
    <target-element type="OL"/>

    <display-group
        space-before="=inlist(element) ? paraSep : blockSep"
        space-after="=inlist(element) ? paraSep : blockSep"
        start-indent="=inlist(element) ?
        inheritedStartIndent(element) : bodyStartIndent" >
      <children/>
    </display-group>
  </rule>

  <rule>
    <element type="OL">
      <target-element type="LI"/>
    </element>

    <paragraph use="p-style"
        space-before='=attributeString
          (ancestor("OL"), "compact") ? 0 : paraSep'
```

```
            start-indent="=inheritedStartIndent(element) + olstep(element)"
            first-line-start-indent="=-olstep(element)" >
        <line-field field-width="=olstep(element)">
          (
          <eval>
            var child = childNumber(element);
            var x = hierarchicalNumberRecursive("OL") % 4;
            if (x == 1) return formatNumber(child, "1");
            if (x == 2) return formatNumber(child, "a");
            if (x == 3) return formatNumber(child, "i");
            if (x == 0) return formatNumber(child, "a");
          </eval>
          )
        </line-field>
        <children/>
      </paragraph>
    </rule>

    <rule>
      <element type="OL">
        <element type="LI">
          <target-element type="P"/>
        </element>
      </element>
      <paragraph use="p-style"
       start-indent="=inheritedStartIndent(element)
       + olstep(element)"first-line-start-indent=
         "=-olstep(element)" >
      <children/>
      </paragraph>
    </rule>

</xsl>
```

Fixed Structure Style Sheets

If you want to create XSL code that's valid with respect to a single, fixed XML DTD for all
XSL style sheets (the DTD is included in the XSL proposal and shown in the next section),
there's an alternative syntax for using named styles:

```
<style-rule>
  <target-element type="title"/>
  <apply use="title-style" quadding="center"/>
</style-rule>
```

There's also an alternative syntax for macro invocation:

```
<rule>
  <target-element type="item"/>
  <invoke macro="list-item">
    <arg name="marker" value="+">
    <children/>
  </invoke>
</rule>
```

An XML DTD for XSL Rules

The following XML DTD is taken verbatim from the XSL proposal. Used with the alternative style rule and macro syntax described in the previous section, this XML DTD can be used to make sure an XSL style sheet is syntactically correct XML:

```
<!-- This DTD is for exegesis only.  It assumes that the
action parameter entity has been defined as an or-group
of flow object elements. The style parameter entity is
used to represent an or-group of the apply element
and styles defined with define-style. -->

<!ENTITY % pattern "(root ¦ (target-element ¦ element ¦ any)*)">

<!ELEMENT rule (%pattern;, %action;) >

<!ELEMENT style-rule (%pattern;, %style)>

<!ELEMENT root   EMPTY>

<!ATTLIST (rule ¦ style-rule)
        priority   NUMBER     #IMPLIED
        importance NUMBER     #IMPLIED
        mode       NAME       #IMPLIED>

<!ELEMENT target-element
        (attribute*, (element+ ¦ any)?)     -(target-element)>

<!ELEMENT element
        (attribute*, (target-element ¦ element ¦ any)?) >

<!ELEMENT any   EMPTY >

<!ATTLIST (target-element ¦ element)
        type      NAME         #IMPLIED
        id        NAME         #IMPLIED
        class     NAME         #IMPLIED
        only     (of-type¦of-any) #IMPLIED
        position (first-of-type¦last-of-type¦
                   first-of-any¦last-of-any)  #IMPLIED
>

<!ELEMENT attribute EMPTY >

<!ATTLIST attribute
        name     NAME         #REQUIRED
        value    CDATA        #IMPLIED
        has-value (yes¦no)     'yes'
```

Summary

In this chapter, you have learned the following:

- How XSL is intended to be a more powerful alternative to CSS to allow the sophisticated selection and formatting of elements
- The major differences between XSL as an XML and HTML style language and CSS as an HTML-only style language
- The major differences between XSL as an XML/HTML/SGML style language and DSSSL as an XML/HTML/SGML style and transformation language
- The basic syntax of the XSL langauge and how to construct XSL structure rules
- How to write an XSL style sheet and reference it from an XML document
- How to override XSL style sheet specifications by including inline style definitions in the XML documents themselves
- The essentials of the XSL (ECMAScript) scripting language

Although DSSSL itself is still very much in its infancy (despite having been around for several years, it didn't become an official ISO standard until 1996), it had already been largely written off as being simply too hard for anyone other than really dedicated programmers to use. DSSSL-o (and its short-lived predecessor DSSSL-lite) was an attempt to make DSSSL more suitable for everyday use. It's not being unfair to admit that DSSSL-o never really made it off the drawing board.

CSS, on the other hand, is a very useful tool for formatting HTML pages, but is far too limited for more sophisticated applications that require a more recognizable publishing model.

XML, although firmly rooted in DSSSL, is still a radical departure from DSSSL. It attempts to capitalize on DSSSL's strengths and power while incorporating CSS's ease and simplicity. In this alone, XSL is the perfect counterpart of XML, which in its turn tries to take advantage of SGML's strength and power while retaining HTML's ease and simplicity.

One feature that could be the deciding factor in XSL's success is that it can still be expressed in XML. The same editor you use to create XML documents can just as easily be used to create XSL style sheets.

IX
PART

IN THIS PART

Advanced Techniques

Internationalizing Your HTML

by Dmitry Kirsanov

IN THIS CHAPTER

No book on HTML is complete without a section on the ways to overcome the pronounced Western bias in the language and to provide for its fruitful application in the worldwide multilingual environment. This chapter covers the main approaches to this problem, both those used by practicing Webmasters all around the world and those suggested by standard-setting bodies.

The primary problem of HTML internationalization (or *i18n*, as it's often abbreviated: *i* plus 18 in-between letters plus *n*) is the correct rendering of characters used by other languages. That's why I start by examining different standards of character encoding (character sets). These standards are classified by the length of bit combinations they use, from 7-bit ASCII to Unicode and ISO 10646.

HTML internationalization issues were first crystallized in the important document RFC 2070 (`http://ds.internic.net/rfc/rfc2070.txt`). Then, RFC 2070 provisions were incorporated in HTML's version 4.0. Most of the discussion in this chapter is based on the draft of the HTML 4.0 specification (see `http://www.w3.org/TR/WD-html40/`).

The chapter continues by investigating the new document character set defined for HTML 4.0. You are introduced to the important distinction between the document character set and external character encoding. You also learn about existing methods of specifying external character encoding, proposed additions to handle multilanguage form input, as well as some real-world problems related to the HTML character set.

Another big part of the HTML internationalization problem is language markup—that is, specifying the language of a piece of text to help user agent software render it while observing that language's typography conventions. Some language-specific aspects of text presentation are also addressed by HTML 4.0, which introduces tools to control writing direction, cursive joining, rendering of quotation marks, text alignment, and hyphenation. As a conclusion, I briefly cover the font issues related to HTML internationalization.

Character Encoding Standards

It so happens that the computer industry has been flourishing in the country whose language uses one of the most compact alphabets in the world. However, not long after the first computers had learned to spell English, characters from other languages needed to be encoded, too. In fact, even the minimum set of Latin letters and basic symbols has been for some time the subject of controversy between two competing standards, ASCII and EBCDIC (now almost extinct). No wonder that for other languages' alphabets, a similar muddle has been around for much longer—and it's still far from over.

Each character encoding (often called *character set* or, more precisely, *coded character set*) is defined first, by the numerical range of codes; second, by the repertoire of characters; and third, by a mapping between these two sets. Therefore, the term *character set* is a bit misleading because it actually implies two sets and a relationship between them. Probably the most precise definition of a character encoding in mathematical terms is given by Dan Connolly in his paper "Character Set Considered Harmful" (`http://www.w3.org/pub/WWW/MarkUp/html-spec/charset-harmful.html`): "A function whose domain is a subset of integers, and whose range is a set of characters."

The range of codes is limited by the length of the sequence of bits (called *bit combination*) used to encode one character. For instance, a combination of 8 bits is enough to encode the total of 256 characters (although not all these code positions may actually be used). The smaller the bit combination size, the more compact the encoding (that is, less storage space is required for a given piece of text), but the fewer total characters you can encode.

It's quite logical to codify characters using bit combinations of the size most convenient for computers. Because modern computer architecture is based on bytes (also called *octets*) of 8 bits, all contemporary encoding standards use bit combinations of 8, 16, or 32 bits in length. The next sections survey the most important of these standards to see the roles they play in today's Internet.

7-Bit ASCII

The 7-bit ASCII, or US ASCII, encoding is equivalent to the international standard named ISO 646 (`ftp://dkuug.dk/i18n/ISO_646`) established by the International Organization for Standardization (ISO). This encoding actually uses octets of 8 bits per character, but it leaves the first, most significant, bit in each octet unused, so that it must always be zero. The 7 useful bits of ISO 646 are capable of encoding a total of 128 characters.

ISO 646 is the encoding standard used on the overwhelming majority of computers worldwide (either by itself or as a part of other encodings, as you'll see shortly). ISO 646 could be called "international" in the sense that there are precious few computers in the world that use other encodings for the same basic repertoire of characters. It's also used exclusively for keywords and syntax in all programming and markup languages (including SGML and HTML), as well as for all sorts of data that can be edited by humans but is essentially of a computer nature, such as configuration files or scripts.

However, with regard to the wealth of natural languages spoken around the world, ISO 646 is very restrictive. In fact, only English, Latin, and Swahili languages can use plain 7-bit ASCII with no additional characters. Most languages whose alphabets (also called *scripts* or *writing systems*) are based on the Latin alphabet use accented letters and ligatures.

The first 32 codes of ISO 646 are reserved for *control characters,* which means they invoke some functions or features in the device that reads the text rather than produce a visible shape (often called *glyph*) of a character for human readers. As a rule, character set standards are reluctant to precisely define the functions of control characters because these functions might vary considerably, depending on the nature of text-processing software.

For example, of the 32 control characters in ISO 646, only a few (carriage return, line feed, tabulation) have more or less established meanings. For use in texts, most of these codes are just useless. This wasted code space is a hangover from the ancient times when these control characters played the role of today's document formats and communication protocols.

40

INTERNATIONALIZ-ING YOUR HTML

8-Bit Encodings

The first natural step to accommodate languages that are more letter-hungry than English is to make use of the 8th bit in every byte. By doing so, you get an additional 128 codes that are enough to encode an alphabet of several dozen letters (for example, Cyrillic or Greek) or a set of additional Latin letters with diacritical marks and ligatures used in many European languages (such as ç in French or ß in German).

Unfortunately, there are many more 8-bit encodings in the world than are really necessary. Nearly every computer platform or operating system making its way onto a national market without a strong computer industry of its own has introduced a new encoding standard. For example, as many as three encodings for the Cyrillic alphabet are now widely used in Russia, one being left over from the days of MS-DOS, the second native to Microsoft Windows, and the third being popular in the UNIX community and on the Internet. A similar situation exists in many other national user communities.

ISO, being an authoritative international institution, has done its best to standardize the mess of 8-bit encodings. The ISO 8859 series of standards (see `http://wwwwbs.cs.tu-berlin.de/ ~czyborra/charsets/`) covers almost all extensions of the Latin alphabet as well as the Cyrillic (ISO 8859-5), Arabic (ISO 8859-6), Greek (ISO 8859-7), and Hebrew (ISO 8859-8) alphabets. All these encodings are backward-compatible with ISO 646; that is, the first 128 characters in each ISO 8859 code table are identical to 7-bit ASCII, and the national characters are always located in the upper 128 code positions.

Again, the first 32 code positions (128 to 159 decimal, inclusive) of the upper half in ISO 8859 are reserved for control characters and should not be used in texts. This time, however, many software manufacturers chose to disregard the taboo; for example, the majority of TrueType fonts for Windows conform to ISO 8859-1 in code positions from 160 upward, but use the range 128–159 for additional characters (notably the em-dash and the trademark sign). This leads to the endless confusion about whether these 32 characters can be accessed in HTML (the DTD, following ISO 8859, declares this character range unused). HTML internationalization extensions resolve this controversy by making it possible to address these characters by their Unicode codes.

ISO's authority was not, however, enough to position the entire 8859 series as a strong alternative to the ad hoc national encodings supported by popular operating systems and platforms. For example, ISO 8859-5 is hardly ever used to encode Russian texts except on a small share of UNIX workstations.

On the other hand, the first standard in the 8859 series, ISO 8859-1 (often called ISO Latin-1) which contains the most widespread Latin alphabet extensions serving many European languages, has been widely recognized as *the* 8-bit ASCII extension. Whenever there's a need for an 8-bit encoding standard that's as international as possible, you're likely to see ISO 8859-1 playing the role. For instance, ISO 8859-1 served as a basis for the document character set in HTML versions up to 3.2 (in 4.0, this role was taken over by Unicode, as discussed in the "HTML Character Set" section later in the chapter).

16-Bit Encodings

Not all languages in the world use small alphabets. Some writing systems (for example, Japanese and Chinese) use *ideographs*, or hieroglyphs, instead of letters, each corresponding not to a sound of speech but to an entire concept or word. Because there are many more words and especially conceivable ideas than there are sounds in a language, such writing systems usually contain many thousands of ideographs. An encoding for such a system needs at least 16 bits (2 octets) per character, which allows you to accommodate the total of $2^{16} = 65536$ characters.

Ideally, such a 16-bit encoding should be backward-compatible with the existing 8-bit (and especially 7-bit ASCII) encodings, which means that an ASCII-only device reading a stream of data in this encoding should be able to correctly interpret at least ASCII characters if they're present. This interpretation is achieved by using *code switching*, or *escaping* techniques: Special sequences of control characters are used to switch back and forth between ASCII mode with the one octet per character and 2-octet modes (also called *code pages*). Encodings based on this principle are now widely used for Far East languages.

Code switching works all right, but one interesting problem is that the technique makes it more ambiguous to determine character's coded representation—is it just its 2-octet code or the code preceded by the switching sequence? Obviously, the "extended" national symbols and ASCII characters are not treated equally in such systems, which might be justifiable in practical terms but is likely to pose problems in the future.

In the late 1980s, the need for a truly international 16-bit coding standard became apparent. The Unicode Consortium (`http://www.unicode.org`), formed in 1991, created such a standard, called *Unicode*. In Unicode, every character from the world's major writing systems is assigned a unique 2-octet code. According to the tradition I mentioned earlier, the first 128 codes of Unicode are identical to 7-bit ASCII, and the first 256 codes, to ISO 8859-1. However, strictly speaking, this standard is not backward-compatible with 8-bit encodings; for instance, Unicode for the Latin letter *A* is 0041 (hex), but ASCII code for the same letter is simply 41.

The Unicode standard deserves a separate book to describe it fully (in fact, its official specification is available in book form from the Unicode Consortium). Its many blocks and zones cover all literal and syllabic alphabets now in use, alphabets of many dead languages, lots of special symbols, and combined characters (such as letters with all imaginable diacritical marks, circled digits, and so on).

One downside to this plethora of characters is the problem of comparing text strings. For example, Unicode has both the accented letter é (code 00E9 hex) and the parts it consists of: the acute accent ´ (code 00B4 hex) and the small letter *e* (code 0065 hex). In principle, putting the accent mark and the accentless letter one after the other should give you the same visual result as the corresponding combined letterform, so the question arises whether the computer should consider these representations equal. The general solution accepted by HTML 4.0 is that text strings aren't treated as equal unless they consist of exactly the same Unicode characters in the same order, even if the case differences are disregarded.

Unicode provides space for more than 20 thousand unified ideographs used in Far East languages. Contrary to other alphabets, ideographic systems were treated on a language-independent basis. This means that an ideograph that has similar meanings and appearance across different Far East languages is represented by a single code, despite the fact that it corresponds to quite different *words* in each of the languages and that most such ideographs have country-specific glyph variants.

The resulting ideographic system carried out in Unicode is often abbreviated *CJK* after the names of the major languages covered by this system (Chinese, Japanese, Korean). CJK unification reduced the set of ideographs to be encoded to a manageable (and codeable) number, but the undesirable side-effect is that it's impossible to create a single Unicode font suitable for everyone; a Chinese text should be displayed using slightly different visual shapes of ideographs than a Japanese text, even if they use the same Unicode-encoded ideographs.

The work on Unicode is far from complete; about 34 percent of the total coding space remains unassigned. Working groups in both the Unicode Consortium and ISO are working on selection and codification of the most deserving candidates to colonize Unicode's as-of-yet wastelands. A good sign is that Unicode acceptance throughout the computer industry is taking off; for example, Unicode is used for internal character coding in the Java programming language and for font layout in Windows 95 and Windows NT operating systems.

ISO 10646

Although Unicode is still not widely used, ISO published in 1993 a new, 32-bit encoding standard named ISO/IEC 10646-1, or Universal Multiple-Octet Coded Character Set (abbreviated *UCS*; see `http://www.dkuug.dk/JTC1/SC2/WG2/docs/standards`). Just as 7-bit ASCII does, though, this standard leaves the most significant bit in the most significant octet unused, which makes it essentially a 31-bit encoding.

Still, the code space of ISO 10646 spans the tremendous amount of 2^{31} = 2147483648 code positions, which is much, much more than could be used by all the languages and writing systems that ever existed on Earth. What, then, is the rationale behind such a huge "Unicode of Unicodes?"

The main reason for developing a 4-octet encoding standard is that Unicode actually can't accommodate *all* the characters for which it would be useful to provide encoding. Although a significant share of Unicode codes is still vacant, the proposals for new character and ideograph groups that are now under consideration require several times more code positions than are available in 16-bit Unicode.

Extending Unicode seems inevitable, then, so it makes little sense to extend it by one octet because computers will have trouble dealing with 3-octet (24-bit) sequences; 32-bit encoding, on the other hand, is particularly convenient for modern computers, most of which process information in 32-bit chunks.

Just as Unicode extends ISO 8859-1, the new ISO 10646 is a proper extension of Unicode. In terms of ISO 10646, a chunk of 256 sequential code positions is called a *row*, 256 rows constitute a *plane*, and 256 planes make up a *group*. The whole code space is thus divided into 128 groups. In these terms, Unicode is simply plane 00 of group 00, the special plane that in the ISO 10646 standard is called the *Basic Multilingual Plane* (BMP). For example, the Latin letter *A* (Unicode 0041) is in ISO 10646 fully coded as 00000041. As of now, ISO 10646 BMP is absolutely identical to Unicode, and it's unlikely that these two standards will ever diverge.

ISO 10646 specifies some intermediate formats that don't require using the codes in the *canonical form* of 4 octets per character. For example, the UCS-2 (Universal Character Set, 2-octet format) is indistinguishable from Unicode as it uses 16-bit codes from the BMP. The UTF-8 format (UCS Transformation Format, 8 bits) can be used to incorporate, with a sort of code-switching technique, 32-bit codes into a stream consisting of mostly 7-bit ASCII codes. Finally, the UTF-16 method was developed to access more than a million 4-octet codes from within a Unicode/BMP 2-octet data stream, without making it incompatible with current Unicode implementations.

Most probably, ISO 10646 will rarely be used in its canonical 4-octet form. For most texts and text-processing applications, wasting 32 bits per character is beyond the acceptable level of redundancy. However, ISO 10646 is an important standard because it establishes a single authority on the vast lands lying beyond Unicode, thus preventing the problem of incompatible multi-octet encodings, even before this problem could possibly emerge.

MIME

MIME, which stands for *Multipurpose Internet Mail Extensions*, is a standard originally developed to extend the capabilities of electronic mail by allowing e-mail messages to include almost any type of data, not just plain text. However, MIME's mechanisms proved so useful and well-designed that they are now used in many other fields, including HTML. You can find the latest MIME specification in RFCs 2045 through 2049. (See `http://ds.internic.net/rfc/rfc2045.txt`, `http://ds.internic.net/rfc/rfc2046.txt`, and so forth.)

The existing e-mail transport systems, such as Simple Mail Transfer Protocol (SMTP) and Post Office Protocol 3 (POP3), don't accept anything but plain text in the body of a message. This means that a message should contain only printable (noncontrol) characters of 7-bit ASCII and the lines should not exceed some reasonable length. To overcome this limitation, MIME introduces methods to convert binary data or texts in more-than-7-bit encodings into "mail safe" plain ASCII text.

Special MIME header fields are added to such messages to specify what conversion method was used (if any) and what was the original type of the data sent in the message. For text messages, along with other parameters, the character encoding (character set, or *charset*) of the message body is specified. This mechanism is important because it's used not only in e-mail

messages, but also in HTTP headers for HTML documents transferred over the network. The
`charset` parameter is a part of the `Content-Type` header field and takes the following form:

```
Content-Type: text/html; charset=ISO-8859-1
```

Here, `text/html` is the standard identifier of the "HTML source" data type, and `ISO-8859-1`
indicates the character encoding used by the text of the HTML document. Both these values
are taken from the official registry of content data types, character sets, and other MIME-
related classifiers maintained by IANA (Internet Assigned Numbers Authority).

This official registry is what makes MIME so useful beyond the e-mail realm. For your purposes, it's especially important that MIME has developed a standard way of communicating
the character encoding of a document. You can get the list of registered MIME `charset` values
from `ftp://ftp.isi.edu/in-notes/iana/assignments/character-sets`.

HTML Character Set

Now that you're acquainted with character encoding standards and the MIME-supplied method
to indicate the standard in use, it's time to get to HTML and see how it has been tweaked in
version 4.0 to handle multilanguage data.

Document Character Set Versus External Character Encoding

First, an important distinction should be made. As you know from Chapter 4, "The HTML
Document Type Definition," HTML syntax is defined by the Document Type Definition
(DTD). The DTD is accompanied by another formal construct called the *SGML declaration*,
whose CHARSET section defines the single *document character set* to be used by all conforming
HTML documents.

On the one hand, this arrangement makes the choice of the document character set fairly obvious: It should be international, which means Unicode or, better yet, ISO 10646. Here's how
the SGML declaration for HTML 4.0 defines the document character set (see Chapter 4 for
syntax explanations):

```
CHARSET
     BASESET  "ISO 646:1983//CHARSET
               International Reference Version
               (IRV)//ESC 2/5 4/0"
     DESCSET  0    9    UNUSED
              9    2    9
              11   2    UNUSED
              13   1    13
              14   18   UNUSED
              32   95   32
              127  1    UNUSED
     BASESET  "ISO Registration Number 176//CHARSET
               ISO/IEC 10646-1:1993 UCS-2 with
               implementation level 3//ESC 2/5 2/15 4/5"
     DESCSET  128  32    UNUSED
              160  65375 160
```

Here, ISO 10646 is used in one of its transformation formats, namely the UCS-2, which is a 2-octet format identical to Unicode.

RFC 2070 takes a more thorough approach and bases the document character set on the canonical 4-octet form of ISO 10646 only, without a reference to ISO 646 (which is a subset of ISO 10646, anyway) and with the upper limit of the code space raised to as much as 2147483646.

On the other hand, it's unrealistic to expect—and fairly unreasonable to require—that all HTML authors and browser manufacturers switch to Unicode in the next couple of months (or years, for that matter). So how can we get the benefits of Unicode without making everybody change over to it?

This quandary is resolved by differentiating the document character set from the *external character encoding* of the document. The external encoding is applied to the document when it's stored on a server and transferred through the network; this encoding can be arbitrary, if it is sufficient to encode the document's character repertoire and if both server and user agent software can handle it properly.

After receiving the document, the user agent software should convert it from external encoding to the document character set, so that further SGML processing and markup parsing is performed in this character set only. Before displaying the parsed document, the user agent may recode it once again—for example, to comply with the encoding supported by the operating system (to call its display services) or to match the encoding of fonts that will be used for output.

Converting the document from external encoding to the SGML-specified document character set is done for two obvious purposes. First, it's necessary to make sure all characters that have special meaning in HTML, such as letters in element names and < and > characters, are correctly recognized (although it's unlikely, external encoding could remap some of these characters to other bit combinations).

Second, remember that users can invoke characters by using character references, such as © or © for the copyright sign. For these references to be unambiguous and not require changes when the document is recoded from one character set to another, the specification states that these explicit references must always refer to the document character set—that is, Unicode.

For example, to access the Cyrillic capital letter EF through a character reference, you should use its Unicode code, which yields Ф, regardless of what character encoding you work in when creating your document. It doesn't matter whether you use KOI8-R 8-bit Cyrillic encoding, in which this letter is coded 230 (decimal), or ISO 8859-1, which has no Cyrillic alphabet at all. A compliant HTML parser should always resolve character references in terms of the document character set (Unicode) simply because, at the time of HTML-specific processing, the document should already be converted into the document character set.

Here are some advantages of using Unicode as the document character set and separating it from external encoding of a document:

■ This solution is backward-compatible with previous versions of the HTML standard. Indeed, character references in, say, HTML 3.2 were supposed to refer to ISO 8859-1, which is a proper subset of Unicode. (Whether a code is 8 or 16 bits makes no difference in this case because padding zeros can be dropped in the code values of character references.)

■ The solution is also fairly flexible. International HTML authors can continue using the character sets that are widely supported by software and that minimize overhead for their languages. At the same time, they can directly access the entire character space of Unicode by character references.

■ Finally, implementing the technique shouldn't be too bothersome for browser manufacturers. The standard doesn't even require user agents (browsers) to be able to display *any* Unicode character, but offers instead some workarounds for the cases when a browser can't generate a glyph for a particular Unicode code (for example, displaying the hexadecimal code or some special icon in place of the character).

Specifying External Character Encoding

For an HTML browser to correctly translate the received document from external encoding into the document character set, it must know the external encoding beforehand. As of now, MIME is the only standard mechanism capable of communicating this information. As described earlier in this chapter, the charset parameter is included in the Content-Type field that must be part of any HTTP header—that is, must precede any document sent by HTTP protocol. This field should also be included in the header of an e-mail message containing an HTML document. Currently, there's no way to indicate character encoding for an HTML document retrieved through FTP or from a local or distributed file system.

Common browsers, such as Netscape or Internet Explorer, recognize the charset parameter and try to switch to the requested character set before displaying the document (in Netscape Communicator 4, for example, you can open the View | Encoding submenu to see the list of supported character sets). If no charset parameter is specified, ISO 8859-1 is assumed, and if it's not what the author planned for the document, the user must guess which encoding to switch to manually to read the document. (It's not unreasonable to claim that the very possibility of manually switching character sets in common browsers is to blame for the abundance of Web servers that never declare the character encoding of the documents they deliver.)

However, there's something more to character set negotiation. HTTP protocol allows a client program to list a number of character encodings it can handle, in the order of preference, right in an HTTP request by using the Accept-Charset field. With this listing, the server can select the appropriate version of the document among those available or translate it to a requested character set on-the-fly. The standard declares that if no Accept-Charset value is given in the request, the user agent thereby guarantees it can handle *any* character set. Unfortunately, the only browser (at this time) that allows a user to specify which `Accept-Charset` value to insert in HTTP requests is Lynx (see `http://lynx.browser.org`).

One more method to indicate a document's external character encoding is to emulate the `Content-Type` header field in a `META` element. For example, you should place the following tag within the `HEAD` block of your HTML document if you need to specify that your document is in KOI8-R Cyrillic encoding:

```
<META http-equiv="Content-Type" content="text/html; charset=KOI8-R">
```

This choice is handy for those who are unable or unwilling to change the setup of the server the document is stored on, but it has an obvious downside: Such a document, if automatically converted from one encoding to another, requires manually changing the `<META>` tag attributes. The `META` encoding indication is supported by most browsers, but beware of a pitfall: Contrary to the standard stating that the `charset` value in the HTTP header, if present, should override its `META` emulation, some browsers give preference to the `META`-supplied value.

Forms Internationalization

When browsing on the Web, you not only download information, but sometimes upload it as well, using the mechanism of HTML forms. Naturally, this mechanism needs adjustments to allow character set negotiation of the data submitted from the user agent software to the server. This section covers the new features introduced to meet this requirement.

In HTML 4.0, the `FORM` tag is given an additional `ACCEPT-CHARSET` attribute similar to the `Accept-Charset` HTTP field mentioned in the preceding section. The main difference is that the `ACCEPT-CHARSET` attribute in HTML works the other way around, specifying what character encodings the server can *receive* from the user. The value of the `ACCEPT-CHARSET` attribute is a list of MIME identifiers for character encodings the server can handle, in order of preference; usually this list contains at least the external character encoding of the document itself.

A browser could make use of the value of the `ACCEPT-CHARSET` attribute in several ways:

- A browser might configure the text input areas so that the text being typed in would display using appropriate glyphs. This level of support is minimal (it's implemented, for example, in Netscape Navigator 3.0, although this browser uses the main document encoding for this purpose instead of the `ACCEPT-CHARSET` attribute value) because it leaves the user with the problem of how to input text properly. If the operating system doesn't support the encoding, it might be necessary to use a specialized keyboard driver or copy and paste previously converted text. In certain cases, an HTML author could supply a clue right in the document about which encoding is accepted in a particular input field.

- Better yet, a browser might take into account the character encoding supported by the operating system and convert, if it's possible (if the encoding supported by the system and the encoding accepted by the server have identical character repertoires) and necessary (if these two encodings are not the same), the text typed in by the user before sending it out. This provision would make the preceding one unnecessary because the operating system itself takes care of the proper display of characters in text input areas, provided that they use the system's native encoding. This level of support is implemented in Microsoft Internet Explorer 4.0 and Netscape Communicator 4.0 (but here again, both these browsers ignore the ACCEPT-CHARSET value and consider the form charset the same as the document charset).

■ RFC 2070 suggests that a browser may restrict the range of characters that can be entered in the text area in accordance with the encoding specified. In my opinion, this is rather useless if not accompanied by one of the other two provisions.

The second part of the forms internationalization problem is how to submit the form data along with the information about its encoding. For the first of the two submission methods, POST, MIME is helpful once again. You can add the charset parameter to the Content-Type: application/x-www-form-urlencoded header field that precedes any data sent with the POST method, as in this example:

```
Content-Type: application/x-www-form-urlencoded; charset=KOI8-R
```

Such a header field must be used by the browser if the data from a POST form is being sent in KOI8-R encoding.

RFC 2070 gives preference to another technique that uses the multipart/form-data content type proposed in RFC 1867 (see http://ds.internic.net/rfc/rfc1867.txt) for form-based file uploads. (RFC 1867 provisions are also incorporated into HTML 4.0.) With this method, form data is not encapsulated in the form of a URL, and each name/value pair may have its own charset parameter attached. Currently, this technique isn't supported by common browsers, and HTML 4.0 recommends using multipart/form-data content type only if the form data contains files to be uploaded to the server.

With the other form submission method, GET, data is always encapsulated right in the URL that the browser submits to the server. In principle, URLs may contain any bit combinations, provided that they are encoded using the %HH notation (see Chapter 12, "Understanding Uniform Resource Locators"). However, quoting RFC 2070, "text submitted from a form is composed of *characters*, not octets," and there's no easy way to incorporate information about the encoding of text data into a URL (other than by providing an additional input field that the user will need to manually set, which would be pretty awkward).

Consequently, the HTML 4.0 specification states that the GET method is "deprecated for reasons of internationalization." RFC 2070 suggests that even with the GET method, user agent software could send the data in the body of the HTTP request instead of the URL, although currently no applications support this technique. Another solution with URLs might be using one of the special formats of ISO 10646; in particular, the UTF-8 format (see http://ds.internic.net/rfc/rfc2044.txt) preserves all 7-bit ASCII characters and encodes any non-ASCII characters using only the octets with the most significant bit set—that is, those outside the ASCII range. This feature makes UTF-8 completely backward-compatible with the current URL syntax. Because ISO 10646 is a superset of all other character encodings, a string in such a format doesn't require any further `charset` specifications (provided that, of course, the server is aware of using UTF-8).

Real-World Character Sets Problems

Differentiating the document character set from external encoding is not all that new in HTML. Any numerical character references in a document conforming to HTML 3.2 or an earlier version must refer to the characters from the Latin-1 (ISO 8859-1) set, regardless of the document's external character set. Unfortunately, this convention is ignored by many contemporary browsers, which leads to undesirable (although, admittedly, not too serious in the case of HTML 3.2 without internationalization extensions) consequences.

For instance, the KOI8-R character encoding, as defined in RFC 1489 (see `http://ds.internic.net/rfc/rfc1489.txt`), specifies code 191 (decimal) for the © character. In ISO 8859-1, the same symbol is coded 169. Ideally, when a mnemonic entity `&copy;` or character reference `&#169;` (which is what `&copy;` expands to, as defined by the HTML DTD) is used in a KOI8-R document, the browser must resolve it according to the ISO 8859-1 character set and display the copyright sign (for example, by accessing code position 191 in a KOI8-R font).

However, because most browsers can't remember anything about the ISO 8859-1 character set after being switched to KOI8-R or whatever external encoding is used for a document, an HTML author can't rely anymore on the table of Latin-1 mnemonic character entities. These entities or numeric character references are guaranteed to work only if the document itself is created (and viewed) in ISO 8859-1.

As a sort of a workaround, creators of several KOI8-R Cyrillic fonts for use on the Web chose to move the copyright sign from the standard-prescribed code 191 to the Latin-1–inspired 169. As Alan Flavell of CERN has put it, "Breaking your font in order to help a broken browser is a bad idea." Obviously, with the internationalized HTML gaining wide recognition, the problem might become more severe because Unicode character references in conforming documents are much more likely to go out of sync with the external character encoding of a document.

In essence, support for nonstandard document encodings in browsers such as Netscape Navigator 3.0 is reduced to the capability to switch display fonts, in response to either the `charset` parameter in the HTTP header or the user's having selected a command—and little else. As a result, Netscape Navigator 3.0 can't display Russian texts in KOI8-R without KOI8-R Cyrillic fonts installed, even if it's working under a Russian version of Windows that provides Cyrillic fonts in Windows encoding.

There are still more problems with document character encoding that many common browsers can't cope with and that HTML authors should, therefore, be aware of:

- Even when the text of a document is correctly displayed, its title, if it contains encoding-specific characters, could appear broken in the window title bar (apparently because the font used in window title bars is determined by the operating system, which might be completely unaware of the document's encoding).

- ALT texts in place of inline images, as well as button labels in forms, might not display correctly if they contain encoding-specific characters (again, the reason is that many browsers use system-provided fonts for these purposes).

- Text-oriented Java applets in Java-enabled browsers might have problems displaying text in a nonstandard encoding.

Language Identification

Character set problems are only a part of the whole HTML internationalization issue. Almost equally important is the problem of a document's language identification. Many aspects of document presentation depend not only on the character set, but also on the language of the text.

For example, as I've mentioned before, the same ideographs are used in many Far East languages, so that in each language they are rendered by slightly different glyphs and quite different sounds of speech. Also, different languages using the same character set might differ greatly in hyphenation, spacing, use of punctuation, and so on.

To this end, HTML 4.0 introduces the new lang attribute, which can be used with most HTML elements to describe the language of the element contents. A "language" in this context is defined as "spoken (or written) by human beings for communication of information to other human beings; computer languages are explicitly excluded." Here's an example of using the lang attribute:

```
<P lang="fr">Ce paragraphe est en Français</P>
```

The lang attribute may take as a value a two-letter abbreviated code (or *tag*) of the language. A list of these codes is defined by the ISO 639 standard (see ftp://dkuug.dk/i18n/ISO_639); these codes should not be confused with country codes (for example, uk as a language code means Ukrainian, not United Kingdom).

Also, *extended identifiers* can be used to designate different dialects or writing systems of a language, identify the country in which it's used, and so forth. These extended identifiers are based on two-letter codes with the addition of *subcodes* separated by a hyphen (-), as shown in the following examples:

- en-US

  English language of the USA (two-letter subcodes are always interpreted as country codes conforming to ISO 3166 standard)

- no-nynorsk

  Nynorsk variant of Norwegian

- az-cyrillic

  Azerbaijani language written in Cyrillic script

A registry of these extended language identifiers is maintained by IANA (see `ftp://ftp.isi.edu/in-notes/iana/assignments/languages/`). All `lang` values are case insensitive; their complete syntax is defined by RFC 1766 (see `http://ds.internic.net/rfc/rfc1766.txt`). Another useful resource is the document at `http://domen.uninett.no/~hta/ietf/lang-chars.txt`, where most known languages are listed along with the character sets they use.

Language specifications are inherited from parent elements. For example, if you add a `lang` attribute to the `<HTML>` tag of your document, all elements within the document are assigned the same language unless a different language is specified for some of them. Also, without explicit language specifications in the document, user agents should consult the `Content-Language` MIME header field if it's provided by the Web server for this document. For example, you can configure your server to send, along with your documents, the following header field:

```
Content-Language: en-US
```

The default value for the language of the element content is `unknown`.

Language-Specific Presentation Markup

In a multilanguage environment, you might need to specify some aspects of text presentation in HTML, such as the writing direction (left to right or right to left), punctuation peculiarities, and so on. These aspects can usually be derived from the language of the text (see the preceding section), but sometimes you might need to specify this information without specifying the language or to override the language default values. Also, some presentation aspects (such as quotation marks) require additional markup even if a language is specified.

RFC 2070 introduces, and HTML 4.0 adopts, a whole bouquet of new HTML elements, attributes, and entities for this sort of presentation markup. These new features are summarized in the following sections.

Writing Direction

Although most Western languages are written from left to right, languages such as Arabic and Hebrew are written from right to left. In situations where this text is intermingled with text of the opposite direction (resulting in a bidirectional, or *BIDI*, text), a special markup might be necessary to resolve ambiguity.

The Unicode standard has several direction-related provisions. Each Unicode character is assigned the *bidirectional category* parameter that may take a number of different values, such as left-to-right, right-to-left, number separator, or neutral (for example, white space). Some characters (such as parentheses) are marked as *mirrored*, depending on the text direction (in right-to-left text, an opening parenthesis should take the appearance of a closing one and vice versa).

To support this behavior, RFC 2070 introduces directional markup tools of three types. The first type consists of the left-to-right and right-to-left marks that behave exactly as zero-width spaces having corresponding direction properties. These marks are taken directly from Unicode inventory, so in HTML they are implemented as entities expanding into corresponding Unicode characters:

```
<!ENTITY lrm  CDATA "&#8206;" -- left-to-right mark -->
<!ENTITY rlm  CDATA "&#8207;" -- right-to-left mark -->
```

Direction marks can be used when, for example, a double quote (which doesn't have a direction of its own, but is not a mirrored character, either) sits between a Latin and a Hebrew character; in this situation, the actual place of the quote depends on whether it's assumed to belong to the left-to-right or right-to-left text stream. By placing an invisible direction mark (‎ or ‏) on one side of the quote, you can make sure the quote is surrounded by characters going in the same direction, thereby resolving the ambiguity.

The second type of direction markup is represented by the new dir attribute (not to be confused with the DIR element), which, like lang, can be used with nearly all HTML tags to indicate the writing direction of the text in the element's contents. Sometimes you might need to indicate the basic writing direction of a piece of text; also, explicit direction markup is critical when there are two or more levels of nested contra-directional text (for an example, refer to the HTML 4.0 specification).

The two possible values for the dir attribute are the strings RTL (right-to-left) and LTR (left-to-right). As is the case with CSS (Cascading Style Sheets) properties, you can use the dir attribute when no element is normally discriminated by using the SPAN element as a sort of a neutral container. If the dir attribute is omitted, block-level elements (but not inline elements) inherit the writing direction of their parent element. The entire HTML document's default direction is left to right. As stated in the specification, user agents must not use the value of a lang attribute to determine the directionality of the element's content.

For brevity, definitions of the dir and lang attributes are packed into one parameter entity in the HTML 4.0 DTD:

```
<!ENTITY % i18n
 "lang         NAME       #IMPLIED -- RFC 1766 language value --
  dir          (ltr|rtl)  #IMPLIED -- default directionality --"
  >
```

Later, the %i18n; entity is added to the ATTLIST declarations for the majority of HTML elements.

Finally, the third type of direction markup is represented by the new phrase-level BDO element (BDO stands for *bidirectional override*). It's used when a mix of left-to-right and right-to-left characters should be displayed in a single direction, overriding the intrinsic directional properties of the characters. For the BDO element, dir is the only obligatory attribute.

Cursive Joining Behavior

In some writing systems (most notably Arabic), a letter's glyph might be different depending on the context—whether the letter is preceded or followed by some other letters. Arabic letters are modeled after handwritten cursive prototypes, so a letter in a middle of a word is drawn joined to its neighbors, so it might look quite different when it's isolated.

As a rule, software capable of displaying Arabic letters handles these differences automatically, but sometimes it's necessary to control the joining behavior when you want to show, for example, a standalone letter with cursive joiners. For this situation, Unicode offers two special characters, both invisible with zero width; the first forces joining of adjacent characters where normally no joining would occur, and the second prevents joining that would normally take place. HTML 4.0 provides the means to access these characters in HTML with the ‍ and ‌ mnemonic character entities:

```
<!ENTITY zwnj CDATA "&#8204;" -- zero width non-joiner -->
<!ENTITY zwj  CDATA "&#8205;" -- zero width joiner      -->
```

Quotation Marks

Several different styles exist to render quotation marks around short, in-text quotations. Although the English language always uses quotes "like this," French has « comme ça », and German prefers „wie hier". Moreover, nested comments sometimes use different styles; for example, Russian tradition uses French quotes (without separating spaces) on the upper level and German quotes for quotations within quotations. Finally, it is desirable to be able to render the same text with "rich" quotes in a graphics environment but with plain double quotes of 7-bit ASCII in text-mode browsers.

To account for these differences, RFC 2070 proposed the new phrase-level Q element, whose content is surrounded by a pair of quotation marks rendered in accordance with the language of the text, the level of nesting, and the display capabilities available, as shown in this example:

```
<P lang="en">The English language always uses quotes <Q>like this</Q>,
French has <Q lang="fr">comme &ccedil;a</Q>,
and German prefers <Q lang="de">wie hier</Q>.</P>
```

Unfortunately, this solution is not backward-compatible; most existing software just ignores Q tags without displaying even the plain ASCII quotes, which can often damage the meaning of the text. Therefore, the HTML 4.0 specification, while adopting the new element, doesn't demand that user agents always put quotation marks around the content of a Q element, but passes on this functionality to style sheets, by declaring:

> "It is recommended that style sheets provide a way to insert quotation marks before and after a quotation delimited by Q or BLOCKQUOTE in a manner appropriate to the current language context…and the degree of nesting of quotations.

> However…it is recommended that user agents not insert quotation marks in the default style.

> Furthermore, if authors include quotation marks in a Q or BLOCKQUOTE element, user agents should not insert additional quotation marks."

40

INTERNATIONALIZ-
ING YOUR HTML

Alignment and Hyphenation

Traditions of using text justification modes in other languages can be quite different from those of English. That difference is why RFC 2070 introduces the optional align attribute that can be used with most block-level elements (namely P, HR, H1 to H6, OL, UL, DIV, MENU, LI, BLOCKQUOTE, and ADDRESS) with the values of left, right, center, and justify. RFC 2070 suggests that the default align value for texts with left-to-right writing direction should be left, and for right-to-left texts, right, although in the HTML 4.0 specification only left is marked as the default value.

This attribute is a significant improvement over HTML 3.2, in which the list of elements supporting the align attribute was shorter (only DIV, H1 to H6, HR, TD, and P) and the value justify was not allowed. HTML 4.0 takes a halfway approach in the matter: It adopts the justify option from RFC 2070 but leaves the list of elements accepting the align attribute almost the same as in HTML 3.2 (plus the additional table elements, such as COLGROUP, introduced in 4.0). Also, HTML 4.0 declares the align attribute deprecated in favor of using style sheets.

As for hyphenation, user agents are supposed to apply language-dependent rules to break words if this is necessary for proper display. In complex or critical cases, the HTML 4.0 specification suggests that HTML authors use the mnemonic entity ­ that invokes the soft hyphen character present in Unicode as well as all the ISO 8859 family and other character sets.

This invisible character marks the point where a word break can occur. If the word is indeed broken, the character is visualized as a usual hyphen (·) character. Unfortunately, common browsers don't implement this behavior; what's worse, both Netscape Navigator and Microsoft Internet Explorer (even in versions 4) *always* display a · in place of a soft hyphen, thus preventing you from using this character at all.

For better hyphenation control, the new HYPH element was proposed, which can handle complex cases when breaking a word is accompanied by a change in its spelling (for example, the German word *backen* becomes *bak-ken* when hyphenated). However, the HYPH element was not included in either RFC 2070 or HTML 4.0.

Font Issues

Fonts lie on the boundary between visual presentation aspects of HTML documents and the problems of HTML internationalization. It's of little use to have HTML supporting Unicode if you can't display its character repertoire (or at least, the part of Unicode that your document makes use of).

Of course, most users interested in non-English Web content already have corresponding fonts installed on their systems. Often, these fonts are supplied with localized versions of operating systems or other software and use encodings that are popular for a particular language. Common browsers such as Netscape Navigator allow using such fonts for viewing Web pages.

However, what's needed is a method to ensure the proper display of multilanguage data on any given system. One solution might be creating and distributing a free (or inexpensive) multilanguage font pack or a single font with Unicode character layout. A free Unicode font named Cyberbit is available from Bitstream at `http://www.bitstream.com/cyberbit.htm`.

The big downside to the single-font solution is that the file size of a typical Unicode font is several megabytes (even without the ideographs area). Probably the most practical solution for the Web today is a *glyph server*, a proxy server that substitutes inline bitmaps for all non-ASCII characters on the page you're viewing. Intermediation by such a server is a quick way to read a foreign-language page without any font headaches. Glyph servers now available include `http://www.lfw.org/shodouka/` (Japanese only) and `http://baka.aubg.bg`.

The latest versions of popular browsers offer yet another solution to this problem. Both Netscape Communicator 4 and Microsoft Internet Explorer 4 support some variations of *font embedding*, the technique allowing you to send, along with a Web page, the fonts needed to view it. The primary goal of this extension is to improve the typographic quality of Web pages, although font embedding, as you'll see shortly, might seriously affect the internationalization issue.

Microsoft's implementation of font embedding (see `http://www.microsoft.com/typography/web/embedding/default.htm`) uses the widely deployed TrueType font format. Embedded fonts can be efficiently compressed, subranged (only characters used on the page are included), and protected from unauthorized distribution. However, Internet Explorer relies heavily on the font display services of the operating system, thereby damaging portability. Netscape's solution, called *dynamic fonts*, is based on the TrueDoc technology from BitStream (see `http://www.bitstream.com/world/`); it's more portable because the browser itself takes care of the display.

So what does font embedding mean to internationalization? The possibility of ensuring the proper display of any characters in a document on any system capable of handling outline fonts is a big plus. However, there are some dangerous pitfalls along this path.

First, being able to rely on supplied fonts, some HTML authors (as well as browser manufacturers) might go wild in the area of character sets support. In fact, a character encoding of a document needs to comply only to that of the accompanying font, which makes nearly all HTML internationalization provisions described in this chapter redundant—and, as a result, puts them in danger of death by neglect without software support. Of course, fonts for Web distribution may use Unicode, but there's no guarantee that this will always be the case.

Second, the HTML font support puts additional emphasis on the visual presentation of a document, which is the aspect already being overemphasized with the current proprietary HTML extensions. Many documents on the Web today are created without any concern for portability or SGML compliance, and it's not very likely that font embedding in HTML documents, as implemented by the major browser companies, will ever improve the situation.

On the other hand, the urgent need for precise typographic control in HTML is obvious. In view of that, the W3 Consortium has recently proposed its own alternative to the proprietary font-embedding solutions. In accordance with the ideology of separating structure from presentation, this solution (see `http://www.w3.org/TR/WD-font`) is an extension of the CSS system, providing for detailed description, intelligent matching, and format-independent downloading of fonts. With this solution, user agents have four ways to select fonts for the presentation of HTML elements:

- *Exact matching* of the font specified in the style sheet with one of the fonts installed in the system.

- *Intelligent matching* of the specified font with a similar but different system font, if an exact match is unavailable.

- *Downloading* of the font file over the network, if the two preceding options are unavailable and if the font's URL is specified.

- As a last resort, some user agents may perform *font synthesis* to create necessary fonts on-the-fly based on the style sheet's font description.

The future of HTML internationalization is quite obscure now. The standards surveyed in this chapter have just been finalized, and their implementations in software are few. Also, the big software companies are particularly known for poor support of official standards and pursuing their own proprietary extensions instead.

However, most national webs are now growing much faster than the Web as a whole, so that Internet-related products without at least some international support are likely to become rare very soon. In view of this, the provisions of HTML 4.0 and related standards have, besides the thoughtful design, the clear advantage of being open, independent, and stable.

INTERNATIONALIZATION: AN UNPREMEDITATED CASE STUDY

It's not just HTML documents that are haunted by internationalization problems. Any computer-created document containing more than plain ASCII text, when copied from one computer to another, is prone to errors and incompatibilities. This very chapter of the book is an excellent illustration; I've prepared it as a Microsoft Word file and sent along to the editors. Although the chapter itself was in English, the few foreign characters I used as examples caused a lot of trouble to the editors. Here's a couple of the memos that the editors wrote to each other and to me trying to figure out what was the meaning of some of the more exotic bytes in my file, and my rather awkward descriptions of the intended characters' appearance—nothing better is available when one has no truly common standard to refer to.

Re: The ß German ligature

Dmitry: Is a beta close enough for the German letter? I don't see it on the chart of characters I have to choose from—ANSI characters. -- cm

CM: The "beta" character from ANSI is meant to be the German letter, not a Greek beta. ANSI has no Greek alphabet, so enough to make sure that you take the character from an ANSI font and not from a special font such as Symbol (which does have a full Greek alphabet). -- dk

Re: The examples of different quotation marks

RJ: I don't know what to do with the quote mark before *wie hier*. The code for the mark before *comme ça* is [171], and the one after is [167]—from the same list I faxed for Ch 3. -- cm

CM: I can't check out the list you mention here, but I guess you mean 187, not 167—in fact, the left (opening) guillemot is coded 171 and the right (closing) one is coded 187 in both ANSI and Latin-1. As for the German quotes, they're indeed absent in these charsets, but they can be emulated as follows: The opening German quote is a pair of commas („) kerned closely together and moved closely to the word they enclose, and the closing German quote is identical to an opening English quote (of the "66" sort). -- dk

Summary

In this chapter, I've examined the HTML internationalization provisions introduced in RFC 2070 and then adopted in HTML 4.0. This part of the HTML standard will allow you to create and serve Web content in any language and using any writing system, maximizing the chances of your audience getting your message and not a mess of indecipherable characters. In particular, I've covered the following topics:

- What a coded character set is, what character set standards exist, and how they are used

- What MIME is and how it helps to communicate information about the character set of a document

- Why it's important to differentiate the HTML document character set and the external character encoding of an HTML document

- What pitfalls of common browsers you should be aware of when working with international HTML documents

- What tools exist in HTML 4.0 to specify the language of any document fragment and its language-specific presentation parameters (writing direction, cursive joining, rendering of quotation marks, text alignment, hyphenation)

- How the font accessibility problem might affect the future of HTML internationalization

CHAPTER 41

Creating Widely Accessible Web Pages

by Dmitry Kirsanov

IN THIS CHAPTER

For those who haven't experienced any challenges to their physical or sensory abilities, it's very hard to imagine how those who do experience them perceive the world and exchange information. Admittedly, accessibility considerations are not what you're accustomed to taking into account for each step you make. Yet, as you enter the virtual realm of the Web, such an attitude might need readjusting.

It is difficult to overestimate the overall impact of the Web on human society. Not only is it a new mass medium, but also a tool capable of making each of us an information provider as well as an information consumer. The accessibility of this innovative technology is therefore a matter of ethics, even politics, much more than that of practicality or commercial profit. With 750 million disabled people worldwide, it's not irrelevant to compare the Web accessibility issue to the principle of equal rights regardless of race, color, sex, or age.

This understanding led to the launch, in April 1997, of the Web Accessibility Initiative (WAI), a project of the World Wide Web Consortium (W3C) aimed at improving Web standards from the accessibility viewpoint (see `http://www.w3.org/WAI/`). The following is from the official Statement of Support signed by U.S. President Bill Clinton:

> "Given the explosive growth in the use of the World Wide Web for publishing, electronic commerce, lifelong learning and the delivery of government services, it is vital that the Web be accessible to everyone. The Web Accessibility Initiative will develop the tools, technology, and guidelines to make it possible to display information in ways that are available to all users."

This chapter will acquaint you with the key considerations, existing solutions, and perspectives of development in the area of Web accessibility. You'll learn how your Web pages can be made more disabilities-friendly with today's technology and with minimal or no additional investment. Nearly every aspect of Web publishing needs to be addressed in this regard, so in this chapter you'll revisit, with the accessibility goals in mind, much of the book's material.

What We Need

The Web is primarily a visual medium, so vision problems are the most troublesome from the accessibility viewpoint. People with low (residual) vision and color-blind people use different techniques for improving visibility, such as increasing color contrast and using large fonts. Those who are blind have to resort to speech synthesizers or Braille (tactile) output. Needless to say, none of these methods can preserve anything but the very essence of Web pages' textual content.

Some people with physical disabilities have trouble using conventional input devices, most often the mouse. It requires much finer motor control to point-and-click with a mouse than to press keys on a keyboard, so providing a keyboard-only means of input and navigation is absolutely necessary for a Web interface. For the most part, this is an issue for browser developers to address, although HTML authors can help too (especially by proper coding of form elements; see "Forms and Links" later in the chapter).

Creating Widely Accessible Web Pages
CHAPTER 41

785

41

CREATING WIDELY
ACCESSIBLE WEB
PAGES

With other kinds of disabilities, accessibility considerations are relatively less onerous. Deaf users cannot receive audio information if it's not duplicated by visual means. Cognitive impairments sometimes impede using navigation mechanisms on a page, even if the content itself is accessible. The requirements of Web users with low-bandwidth or text-only access are also closely related to the accessibility issue.

There are also situations in which people with full sensory, physical, and cognitive abilities prefer a non-visual mode of delivering information—for instance, it might be convenient to listen to the news when driving a car or walking. Finally, you should remember about robots and intelligent agents that, in many aspects, could be likened to people with disabilities (for example, indexing robots usually cannot extract any useful information from images and have to rely on text only; for more on this, see Chapter 42, "Strategies for Indexing and Search Engines").

Of course, Web page authors aren't supposed to supply audio versions for all text on their pages. Users with disabilities commonly have the necessary software and hardware (usually called *assistive technologies*) to work with computer programs and data, including Web pages. For example, software for speech access to Web pages can be divided into *speech browsers* that interpret the HTML source of Web pages (for example, pwWebSpeak; see `http://www.prodworks.com`) and more general *screen readers* that just read out the text displayed on the screen or in a window (for example, the IBM Screen Reader, see `http://www.austin.ibm.com/sns/snssrd.html`).

Therefore, you could say that the most realistic goal of a Web page author is to present the content in a way that's easily accessible to the assistive technologies—in the hope that they will take more qualified care of the needs of the disabled. Admittedly, sometimes approaching this goal might involve some decisions justified purely by the features of particular access devices. Still, most accessibility recommendations can be derived from a couple of basic principles.

The Two Principles

The first accessibility principle is presenting your information in *alternative modalities*—that is, using as many different media and input/output techniques as possible. For example, the audio channel may work for the blind, and the visual channel would duplicate this information for the deaf. This principle is especially important for the "bottlenecks," the elements that are critical for delivering your message, for understanding what follows, or for navigating to other parts of the site.

In practice, the alternative modalities principle most often amounts to the imperative of supplying textual parallels for all non-textual information. This is because plain text is the most natural informational medium for the computer; it's easy to display with any sort of computer interface, easy to index and process automatically, and relatively easy to convert to speech. By presenting information as text, you take advantage of the "inherent accessibility" of this format and may not be concerned anymore about alternative modalities.

However, a page doesn't need to be text-only to be accessible. The principle of alternative modalities and the provisions of HTML allow you to produce pages that are both presentationally rich *and* accessible. If you need an audio clip, accompany it with a text transcript; if you want an image (as you most probably do), give it an `alt` text conveying as much of the image's information as possible (for more on `alt` texts, see "Images" later in the chapter); and if you feel an urge to use a Java applet or Shockwave object, make sure it's not *critically* necessary for navigating your pages or reading the text (and if that's not the case, provide an alternative access mechanism for the same information).

In other words, an accessible Web page can be *multi-modal* (that is, may use various input/output techniques) provided that all its critical parts are sufficiently *alt-modal* (no important part of its content is locked within one modality). The art of creating alt-modal Web pages while keeping them efficient, rich, and elegant enough to be competitive in today's Web might seem tricky, but actually, it's only a matter of obeying some simple and obvious guidelines (most of which are summarized in this chapter).

The second fundamental principle of accessibility is using *logical*, not *presentational*, markup for your content. (You might be familiar with these concepts from Chapter 4, "The HTML Document Type Definition," that deals with the SGML roots of HTML.) Logical markup means that for every element on your page, you should use HTML tags to describe what it *is* rather than how it's supposed to *look* (or sound, or print, or whatever).

The importance of logical markup reaches far beyond the problem of accessibility for the disabled; in fact, it's the best method to ensure the *general* accessibility, processibility, and, in the bottom line, longevity of your information. When the computer (not only your human reader) is aware of the logical structure of your data, the chances of its being able to successfully convert the data into another format or media are very much improved. And *accessibility* implies, for the most part, exactly this: the ease of transforming the document into another media or presentation mode to be able to communicate it to people with disabilities.

One example is the controversy of the `I` tag versus the `EM` tag. The former, being a tool of presentational markup, directs the browser to switch to an italic font and is thereby limited to visual presentation mode only. A speech browser has no "italic font," so it is likely to ignore this piece of markup altogether. Conversely, `EM` is a logical tag meaning *emphasis*; although a visual browser might interpret this element by switching to an italic font, a speech browser may read it aloud with a different tone of voice ("acoustic emphasis"). An additional advantage is that `EM` allows distinguishing italics for emphasis from other uses of italics, such as citations (to be marked up by the `CITE` logical tag).

Naturally, Web authors often need tools to adjust presentational aspects of their documents as well—for instance, to control font face, or size, or voice pitch. HTML's answer to this demand is *style sheets*, an external mechanism capable of specifying a multitude of presentational parameters in a flexible manner (see `http://www.w3.org/TR/REC-CSS1` and Chapter 18, "Using Cascading Style Sheets," of this book). The current specification of HTML style sheets supports only visual presentation parameters, but there is a proposed extension for handling aural (speech) parameters as well (see `http://www.w3.org/TR/WD-acss`).

Creating Widely Accessible Web Pages
Chapter 41

787

41

CREATING WIDELY
ACCESSIBLE WEB
PAGES

Text

As mentioned previously, from a computer's viewpoint, plain text is the most natural means of presenting information. Moreover, HTML as a language is inherently text-oriented (remember that in its abbreviation, *T* stands for "Text"). Therefore, by using plain text when possible, you will significantly increase the accessibility of your content even without any further efforts. Also, in several situations, plain text accessibility can be improved by following some simple guidelines.

The rest of this chapter draws largely from an important document, "Unified Web Site Accessibility Guidelines," prepared under the authority of member organizations of the Web Accessibility Initiative (see `http://www.trace.wisc.edu/HTMLgide/htmlgide.html`). I recommend that you consult this not-yet-finalized document for the most recent consensus and reference on the accessibility topics.

> **NOTE**
>
> To see if your document complies with accessibility requirements, use the online accessibility checker at `http://www.cast.org/bobby/`. This service rates all the elements of your page and gives recommendations on how to make it more accessible.

Text Markup and Formatting

The first thing to bear in mind when marking up text is to cling to logical tags describing what you *mean* rather than how you want it to *look*. This focus on logical tags drives out of favor a whole bunch of elements, including TT (monospaced font), I (italics), B (bold), BIG (enlarged font size), SMALL (reduced font size), STRIKE (strikethrough), S (same as STRIKE), and U (underline). Quoting the specification, "Although they are not all deprecated, their use is discouraged in favor of style sheets." (The BLINK element is not even included in the HTML 4.0 standard.)

The same applies to the notorious FONT element that has long been a bone of contention between the proponents and opponents of Netscape HTML extensions. The FONT and BASEFONT elements are deprecated in HTML 4.0, and all their attributes without exception are likely to pose accessibility problems. The face attribute is obviously limited to the visual presentation and might fail not only for users with text-only or speech browsers, but also for graphical browser users who don't have a particular font installed in their systems.

The size attribute of the FONT and BASEFONT tags is even more dangerous because, for inexperienced or frivolous users, the size of letters is likely to pass as a substitute for the missing logical markup. It's not uncommon to see sentences intended to be headings tagged by nothing but the FONT element with a large size value.

This formatting could look decent in a graphical browser, but for text-only or speech access, a sentence so tagged doesn't differ at all from body text, which results in its being rendered in the same manner as what precedes or follows it. Such a "heading" won't be marked by any pauses or tone change in the speech, nor by empty lines or character brightness in text mode. Also, automatic indexers or parsing applications won't have access to the structure of your document—they won't be able to tell where one section ends and another starts.

> **NOTE**
>
> Sometimes authors slip into visual, not logical, presentation even without writing a single tag. Borrowed from e-mail style, emoticons (such as : -)) as well as arrow-like compositions (for example, - ->) rely on how these punctuation characters *look*, not what they *mean*, and therefore aren't portable into a nonvisual medium. Imagine a blind user trying to make any sense out of "colon–hyphen–closing parenthesis" dispassionately read aloud by the speech browser. Not that it's going to sound very funny, so please avoid any unusual punctuation or fancy characters.
>
> There's a counterpoint to this recommendation, however: Many browsers (including Netscape Navigator and Microsoft Internet Explorer up to versions 3) do not allow accessing the Unicode character entity — to produce an em-dash (for reasons why you can't access this character by using the — entity, refer to Chapter 40, "Internation-alizing Your HTML"). Thus, for those who are tired of deciphering rebuses like "...*it is possible-even probable-to have...,*" the only way to produce something reasonably dash-like is to resort to - - or - - - in the hope that users of speech browsers can guess what this stands for.

Color Issues

The FONT and BASEFONT elements discussed in the previous section have one more attribute, color, that indicates the intended color of text. This attribute, along with the bgcolor, text, link, vlink, and alink attributes of the BODY element, poses another bunch of accessibility prob-lems. (Color-related properties of style sheets are also prone to similar problems, although they're easier for the user to turn off or override.)

Even sighted users are often embarrassed by the choice of colors that make some pages next to unreadable. If the background is a too-bright, flaming color or its contrast with the text is too low, reading the text becomes torture. Only one thing can be worse than that: reading a text in small font over an image background with lots of small crisp details.

Obviously, a bad color choice is more likely to hurt those with low vision and color blindness than full-sighted users. Therefore, you should be very careful in color selection and, if possible, use the default values that are unlikely to pose any problems. If you decide on an unusual color combination, you should not only check it for subjective readability, but also test it on a monochrome monitor to make sure you don't mistake contrasting hues (that might be indis-tinguishable for color-blind people) for true contrast (which is mostly represented by contrast in brightness, not hue).

A monochrome monitor (or a desaturated version of the page's screenshot) isn't a true model of human color-blindness because most color-blind people aren't incapable of perceiving *any* color, just some specific colors, usually green or red. Yet such a test is a must, given that there are many users of monochrome, laptop, or handheld Web access devices. (For further discussion of using color in Web design, refer to `http://www.webreference.com/dlab/9704/`.)

Last but not least, when setting nonstandard colors in the `<BODY>` tag, don't forget to explicitly specify *all* the color attributes, including background, text, links, and visited links. Some people set their own background or text colors in the browser, so any partial specification could result in a poor contrast of page author's text color with page viewer's background color (or vice versa). Also, never forget to set proper background color if you're using a background image, or your text might become unreadable for those users who have turned off auto-loading images in their browsers.

Lists

Lists are often used in HTML documents for presenting collections of one-level or nested elements. One common use of lists, namely the rows of links for navigating around the site (navigation panels), is now frequently implemented as graphics; also, lists of text elements sometimes use tables for layout and graphic images for bullets. However, even when marked up by the purely logical `<OL>` and `<UL>` tags, lists may present some accessibility problems.

When viewing a page in a browser window, you might not realize how heavily your perception relies on the two-dimensionality of the canvas. Even when reading plain linear text, your eyes not only follow the lines, but often leap back and forth (mostly unconsciously) in attempts to find out where the current paragraph or section ends, what goes next, and so on. The knowledge acquired from these eye leaps allows your brain to plan (again, unconsciously) for the near future, to make reading more efficient by skipping what seems unimportant and by "previewing" visually marked material even before you reach it in the flow of reading.

Now, try to imagine how a disabled user with a speech browser perceives the same information, being completely deprived of the visual clues. Such users have no means to skip forward (being totally unaware of where to skip) and to refer back to what has already been read; they have almost no means but their memory. For a sighted viewer, this limitation could be compared to reading a page through a tiny hole in a sheet of paper (so that only a couple of words can be seen through it) that's moving evenly and dispassionately along the lines of text.

All this helps to understand the two requirements set forth for lists in the "Unified Accessibility Guidelines" document mentioned previously: First, all items in a list should be numbered, and second, you should state beforehand how many items there are in a list. The following example shows how these two requirements could be used:

```
Now let me summarize the above in a list of 3 items:
<OL>
  <LI>Some item
  <LI>Another item; here follows a sublist of two items:
  <UL>
```

```
    <LI>First item
    <LI>Second item
  </UL>
  <LI>Last item
</OL>
```

As you can see, you don't have to always use OL elements (ordered lists) because sometimes it's more appropriate to "number" your items verbally by writing something like "First," "Second," and so on, in the text.

The same advice applies to stating the total number of items—you don't have to be pedantic and stick to the formulas given here. Follow the natural flow of your prose and just make it a little bit more self-explanatory when it comes to a list. For example, "The two principles of accessibility can be summarized as follows:" will work just fine before a two-item list. These provisions will make your lists much more friendly toward users with disabilities.

Layout

Layout is a totally alien concept for HTML (at least as it was envisioned by the creators of the language). Even though modern HTML allows you to specify some visual formatting parameters (font face, for example), the placement of an element on the page is defined only by where this element comes in the source HTML text. Exceptions (such as the align attribute for images and paragraphs) are rare and, in HTML 4.0, deprecated in favor of style sheets. (One of the extensions to style sheet mechanism does indeed provide for exact two-dimensional positioning of page elements; see http://www.w3.org/TR/WD-positioning.)

Yet, Web authors do require an effective means of arranging material on the page, and style sheets might not present a perfect solution because they aren't yet universally supported. This led to the "invention" and truly widespread deployment of "ad hoc" layout tools, most notably tables and invisible spacer images. For a long time, this question has been hotly debated: Is it allowable to use HTML elements not for their primary purpose but for the sake of their layout-related side-effects?

Now the consensus seems to be that some of these "hacks" are relatively harmless for the accessibility of documents as long as proper care is taken in their implementation. An example of such sensible use can be seen on the home page of World Wide Web Consortium itself (http://www.w3.org), whose layout is based on a two-column table. (See Figure 41.1.)

Tables

What are the right and wrong ways of using HTML tables for layout? The answer to this question depends on what kind of access devices you're taking into account. For most nongraphical user agents, including text-mode browsers, speech browsers, and automatic indexers, an HTML table is not a two-dimensional arrangement, but a linear sequence of cells showing up in the order in which they are coded in the HTML source file.

FIGURE 41.1.

The home page of the W3C uses tables for layout.

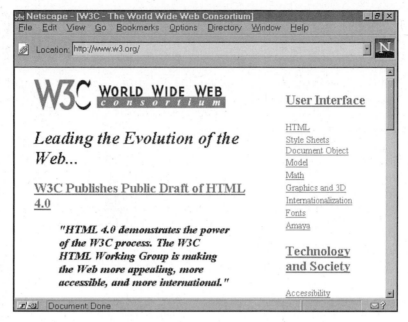

For your content to always make sense, then, you should keep the material as row-oriented as possible. Remember that only the cells that are next to each other *horizontally* will be read in sequence; *vertical* neighbors most probably will be separated by other cells.

For example, don't place a heading in one cell and the text it belongs to in another cell below that, as such placement is likely to result in the heading being separated from its text and making little sense on its own. Instead, place both the heading and the text in one cell, using the rowspan attribute, if necessary, to force the cell to stretch down as needed.

A quick way to check whether your layout meets this requirement is to strip away all HTML markup and read the remaining text in the source file looking for logical gaps and "hanging" material. The W3C home page you saw in Figure 41.1 is an example of sensible use of tables because all pieces that are logically connected go sequentially in the source file (for example, the rightmost column with the list of links is all contained in one cell).

Unfortunately, headings being separated from their text isn't the worst scenario of the tables-for-layout drama. Some people who need a Web page to be read aloud use, instead of specialized speech browsers, conventional graphical browsers combined with screen readers—programs that simply read out whatever is on the screen (or within a window). A screen reader has neither access to nor understanding of the HTML source of the page, so it can only read, from left to right and from top to bottom, all the content of a browser window, completely disregarding any tabular arrangement.

The "Unified Accessibility Guidelines" document suggests that Web authors attempt to imitate this behavior by holding a piece of paper up to the monitor, moving it slowly down, and reading what's revealed across the entire window (a simpler method could use another program's window being dragged down). Naturally, the W3C home page (see Figure 41.1) fails spectacularly when tested this way; what you'll hear from your screen reader will be a mess of fragments from different columns: "W3C... User Interface... HTML... Leading the Evolution of the... Style Sheets... Document Object... Web... Model... Math... W3C Publishes Public Draft of HTML... Graphics and 3D" and so on.

I don't know if it makes real sense to always pursue the "strict" accessibility with a consideration for screen reader users because that would totally eliminate any multicolumn layouts—a serious price indeed. Perhaps we should avoid columns (or provide a parallel text-only page without any layout tricks) only for those pages that are relatively likely to be accessed using screen readers.

Other Layout Tools

PREformatted text in monospaced font was widely used to present tabular material before the TABLE element was invented. Indeed it is, to some extent, an analog of the tabular layout because the PRE element allows you to control skips, indents, and alignments in the text. You must remember, however, that for disabled users with speech-only access, any positioning and white space are nonexistent; only the text itself can be perceived.

The practice of using BLOCKQUOTE elements for text indentation is also dangerous (in HTML 4.0 specification, this use is declared deprecated). Although in visual browsers BLOCKQUOTE is most often rendered with indents at both margins, you should remember that the real intended meaning of this logical tag is *quotation*, not indentation, and there are browsers that use other formatting conventions (such as starting each line with a >). And because a speech browser has almost no means of "formatting" at all, it's very likely that it will simply surround the BLOCKQUOTE element with something like "begin quotation... end quotation"—which is not what you might expect if you used it only for indentation.

One more dangerous layout feature is the align attribute, especially when it's used for images with alt texts (see "Images" later in the chapter). For a real-world example, analyze this fragment of a C|Net news article:

```
The media has portrayed the outcome of the UPS strike as an important
victory for U.S. trade unions. Certainly, the strikers were successful in
<img src="/Images/Perspectives/Stories/9_97/per_mission.gif"
width=132 height=121 border=0 align=left hspace=5 vspace=3
alt="Many businesses turned to email for mission critical delivery">
creating a brief moment in which we felt the stalemate, where a number of
people and businesses felt somewhat captive to the rebellion. But overall,
I think the strikers may lose out.
```

Here, an IMG element is inserted right in the middle of a sentence. When viewed on a graphical browser, the image with a pull-out quote is moved to the left margin, thanks to the align=left attribute. (See Figure 41.2.) However, for a speech or text-mode browser, image alignment makes little sense, so this attribute is ignored. Here's what you'd hear pronounced by a speech browser or see displayed by a text-mode one:

```
The media has portrayed the outcome of the UPS strike as an
important victory for U.S. trade unions. Certainly, the strikers
were successful in Many businesses turned to email for mission
critical delivery creating a brief moment in which we felt the
stalemate, where a number of people and businesses felt somewhat
captive to the rebellion. But overall, I think the strikers may
lose out.
```

FIGURE 41.2.

The image with a pull-out quote in this news article, although using a correct alt *text, produces a mess when rendered by a text-mode or speech browser.*

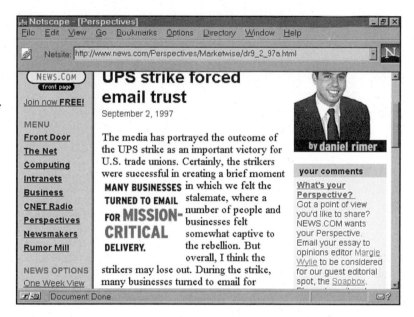

As you can see, the alt text gets intermingled with the body text, making it scarcely comprehensible. The correct solution would be to avoid the image alignment attribute (for example, by using tabular layout) or, at the very least, to surround the alt value with a pair of brackets to make the mishmash more decipherable.

Graphics

Using graphics is by far the most common device for "spicing up" Web pages. Usage patterns range from a couple of icons decorating a mostly textual page to a completely graphical site where the role of text is reduced to a copyright notice at the page bottom. The rest of Web pages lie somewhere in between these extremes.

Most images on the Web aren't intended to convey any really vital information, but to decorate, to amuse, to show off the site creator's design skills. Therefore, you don't need any special processing of images for the access of the disabled—if an image can't be replaced by a text string, it's probably a decoration and can be safely omitted altogether. (Although rare, there are situations when this isn't the case, that is, when an image carries some important information that can't be expressed by text).

Therefore, the primary accessibility requirement for using images is simple: Always accompany your images with an alternative textual representation (the alt text) or state explicitly that this image has no other meaning except as a decoration (for this, empty alt texts should be used, as shown in the following section). However, there are a number of related recommendations that are often left out, even by those who are well aware of this accessibility requirement.

alt Texts

The value of the alt attribute of the <IMG> tag is a string of characters defined as CDATA in the HTML DTD (see Chapter 4). This definition means it may contain both mnemonic (such as) and numeric (such as) character entities, but can't contain any markup tags. For example, you can't control linebreaks within an alt text because any <BR> will be displayed verbatim, instead of having the desired effect.

However, you can (and are even recommended to) surround the entire image with the necessary logical descriptive tags (for example, H1 if the image is meant to be the main heading on the page). In this way, the alt text of the image will be displayed or read aloud using the corresponding formatting (centering and highlighting in text mode, tone of voice in speech, and so on). This convention, however, is not followed by visual browsers (for more on the peculiarities of displaying alt texts in visual browsers, see "Real-World Character Sets Problems" in Chapter 40).

alt Writer's Guidelines

So what is the most important principle of writing alt texts? According to Alan Flavell, who has written an in-depth article on the topic (see http://ppewww.ph.gla.ac.uk/%7Eflavell/alt/alt-text.html), you should remember before all that an alt text is supposed to communicate the information contained *in* the image, not some meta-information *about* the image itself.

In the simplest case, when an image displays some text string (for example, a heading or a button on a navigation panel), its alt text should contain the very same text and *nothing more*. There's no need to write something like "Big red button," "Click here to go to...," or, God forbid, quote the size of the image in bytes or pixels. Such descriptions would present some meta-information about the image or its role on the page, and because this information is absent in the image itself, it's just as redundant in this image's alt text. For an example of a good alt text (although incorrectly formatted), refer back to the C|Net screenshot in the "Other Layout Tools" section earlier in the chapter; writing something like alt="pull-out quote" would be an obvious mistake in this case.

Of course, it's not always as simple as that. For a company logo, for instance, it's not so easy to decide what the image tells us. Are we always aware that it's a logo, or do we more often perceive it as just a fancy way of displaying the company name? I think that in most cases logos are

Creating Widely Accessible Web Pages

CHAPTER 41

795

41

CREATING WIDELY
ACCESSIBLE WEB
PAGES

used on Web pages simply as headings, so it's better to say alt="Foo Inc." than alt="Logo of Foo Inc." However, sometimes you need to emphasize the fact that the image represents a logo (for example, in an online logo design portfolio), so the second variant of the alt text could also have its uses.

In the following list, I've summarized the rules-of-thumb for choosing alt texts for different kinds of images:

- **Spacers and decorations:** For images with little or no importance to the page's meaning, *always* specify an empty alt text (alt="").

  You might think this is the default value anyway, but that's not the case. The HTML 4.0 specification lists a number of sources that a browser should use to make up an alt text for an image without the alt attribute, and the most probable outcome of the algorithm is the filename of the image (minus the extension). The most common text-mode browser, Lynx, uses [IMAGE] as a substitute for altless images. So alt="" is a must if you don't want to drive your readers crazy with this sort of junk.

- **List bullets:** Images of this kind might be considered decorative, but actually they're not; they serve a very practical purpose of separating items in a list. Therefore, the alt string should present what's conventionally used as bullets in text-only documents—most often the * character.

  Considering what has been said about lists (see "Lists" earlier in the chapter), it's a good idea to put consecutive numbers or letters as alt texts for a row of graphic bullets. This way, you don't distract users of visual browsers with redundant numeration, yet you provide a useful navigation aid for disabled users.

- **Dividing rules:** Again, an almost decorative element that nevertheless performs a useful function; plain ASCII substitutes for graphical rules can include =====, -----, *****, and so on. Note, however, that this recommendation clashes with the warning against using unusual punctuation (see the Note in the "Text Markup and Formatting" section, earlier in this chapter); imagine that you have to listen to the endless "hyphen hyphen hyphen..." mumbled by a speech browser in place of a graphical rule. Nevertheless, in the "Unified Accessibility Guidelines" document, graphical rules are preferred over HR elements precisely because they allow you to set alt values.

Simply put, an ideal alt text should be such that users of text-mode or speech browsers can't even guess that it's a substitute for an image, but perceive it as an integral part of the page text.

Presentation of alt Texts

As you've seen from the ClNet example in the "Other Layout Tools" section, nongraphical browsers do not treat alt texts any differently than they treat the usual text of the page; no separators are added, and an alt text is simply displayed in place of the image. For example, if two images are positioned immediately next to each other, their alt texts won't be separated by even a space. This is likely to seriously damage a navigation bar made of a row of adjacent images (for more on this, see "Just Say No to Image Maps" later in the chapter).

Therefore, in most cases it's advisable to provide some means of separation in the `alt` text itself. You could add a space at the end of the `alt` text, as shown here:

```
alt="text "
```

This solution may work but is not particularly elegant. The safest way is to surround the text with a pair of brackets:

```
alt="[text]"
```

You can also add a ¦ character, as follows (this variation can be used to separate the `alt` texts of several images in a row):

```
alt=" text ¦"
```

Visual browsers pose another problem. If you've specified `height` and `width` values for an image (and you should because this measure drastically improves the speed of downloading and displaying the page), its `alt` text might not fit into the allocated space. For users who have turned auto-loading images off, therefore, these `alt` texts might become unreadable. As a compromise, you can remove `height` and `width` attributes for those images that don't significantly affect the speed of page downloading; this will prompt the browser to allocate for each image a rectangle big enough to contain the `alt` text.

Alternatives to `alt` Texts

The use of the `alt` attribute with the `IMG` tag is widespread and universally supported, but has some serious limitations. The fact that `alt` texts cannot contain HTML markup and (for fear of breaking the display in some browsers) cannot exceed some reasonable length could become an obstacle when an image (such as a scientific diagram) contains a lot of data, most of which could be communicated in text form to those users who can't view graphics.

In such cases, the readily available solution is to provide a separate subpage for each image containing the necessary annotation. However, the remaining problem is how to link this page to the main page in a way that's obvious for non-graphics users and not distracting for graphics users. One suggested method is using a small capital *D* (standing for "Description") for the link, located near the image's upper-right corner.

A more elegant solution is to use a small transparent image for the link, one that's invisible in graphical browsers, positioned adjacent to the image being annotated, and given an `alt` text that makes its purpose obvious for non-graphics users.

In the future, other options of annotating images may become available. The new graphics format called PNG (Portable Network Graphics), intended to eventually replace GIF, has provisions for storing arbitrary text strings right in the image file. The HTML 4.0 specification suggests that with time, the `IMG` tag should be displaced by the `OBJECT` element whose content serves as an analog of the `alt` text:

```
<OBJECT data="TheEarth.gif">
 The <STRONG>Earth</STRONG> as seen from space.
</OBJECT>
```

Creating Widely Accessible Web Pages

CHAPTER 41

797

41

CREATING WIDELY
ACCESSIBLE WEB
PAGES

Here, the string between `<OBJECT>` and `</OBJECT>` will be rendered only by those user agents that can't display the image. In this way, any amount of text with any markup can be used as an alternative presentation for an image.

Just Say No to Image Maps

Image maps once were popularized as a significant improvement over the original HTML's one-link-per-element scheme. The capability to assign URLs to arbitrary areas of an image was indeed exciting in the era when images were still perceived as alien beings dispersed on graphics-poor Mosaic pages. Since those times, however, layout tools (or tricks?) have improved considerably, and for most design-conscious pages, images have become the foundation of the page composition.

Modern graphical browsers are able to position images with up-to-the-pixel precision (even without style sheets, such precise positioning can be achieved by using tables and spacer images). In fact, this feature makes image maps unnecessary: You can nearly always break your navigation panel into separate buttons with no more than one link per image and seamlessly arrange them on the canvas. However, you might feel reluctant to engage in this sort of handi-work without sufficient reasons. What are, at any rate, the disadvantages to image maps?

As you might guess, their most important disadvantage is poor accessibility to non-graphical user agents. This is especially true for server-side image maps that require a pair of coordinates to be sent to the server. Text-mode or speech browsers have no way to figure out any meaningful coordinate values, other than to attempt the "0,0" pair (that's why it is recommended to link this origin point to an alternative text-only page).

Client-side image maps that use MAP and AREA elements are much more disabilities-friendly because the HTML file itself contains all the information about the image map links and their URLs. An `alt` text for each of the links is now the only thing that's missing for a non-graphical browser to be able to build a working alternative for the image map. It's enough to display (or read out) the row of `alt` texts as links, and the user will never even suspect that they were extracted from an image map.

This is not a deficiency in the standard: The `alt` attribute is indeed provided for the AREA element and, what's more, is its only obligatory attribute. The following is an example of how it could be used:

```
<IMG src="navbar.gif" USEMAP="#navmap">

<MAP NAME="navmap">
  <AREA coords="0,0,50,50"
        href="page1.html" ALT="Previous Page">
  <AREA coords="51,0,100,50"
        href="/"           ALT="Home">
  <AREA coords="101,0,150,50"
        href="page3.html" ALT="Next Page">
</MAP>
```

However, the support for such gracefully degrading image maps is far from universal. Even those Web authors who are well aware of the necessity of setting alt texts for images, often forget to include alt texts in image maps' AREAs. Worse yet, far from all non-graphical browsers are smart enough to recognize the alt texts in AREAs and to present them as links. The same is true about the common graphical browsers with auto-loading images turned off.

Therefore, the main incentive to abandon image maps is accessibility: When each link is tied to its own IMG element with its own alt text, this link is guaranteed to work with any existing user agent or access technique. However, there are more reasons for preferring the one-link-per-image approach:

- If other pages of the site use similar but not identical navigation panels, you could reuse the buttons stored in separate graphics files, thereby reducing the total download time of the site.
- With GIF files that are limited to a maximum of 256 colors, breaking a navigation bar into pieces allows each button to have a separate palette of its own, thus improving the color rendering on high-color or true-color systems (systems that do not dither all images to one fixed palette).

Forms and Links

In essence, an HTML form is a device for collecting user input and sending it back to the server. As the input data is nearly always textual in nature, this process is unlikely to pose accessibility problems provided that disabled users have convenient means to navigate through forms and interact with form elements without using a mouse.

In HTML 4.0, some new elements and attributes were introduced to provide for a more comprehensive markup and to improve keyboard accessibility of forms. Some of the new attributes affect hypertext links as well as form elements. The big problem with all these enhancements, however, is that not all browsers support them yet.

The LABEL, FIELDSET, and LEGEND Elements

The new LABEL element associates a piece of content within a form with one of the form controls (see Chapter 15, "Building and Using HTML Forms"). As such, it supplies the functionality that HTML forms used to lack compared to, say, Windows dialog boxes where you can click on the text string next to a radio button to switch it on or off. Now if you mark a piece of text or other content as a LABEL for a form control, this label will pass the focus it's given (by mouse, keyboard, or other means) onto its corresponding control.

Therefore, the accessibility importance of the LABEL element is that it provides a sort of visible "alt text" for the control it's associated with. The INPUT element (but not the other form controls) might also have an alt attribute of its own; however, it's desirable that the same label value be accessible to all users of the form, not only to those using speech access or form-incapable browsers (who are supposed to be presented the alt string of an INPUT element).

Creating Widely Accessible Web Pages

CHAPTER 41

799

41

CREATING WIDELY
ACCESSIBLE WEB
PAGES

What is performed by LABEL for standalone controls, the FIELDSET and LEGEND elements can do for a group of controls. By enclosing a number of controls in a form into a FIELDSET, you're integrating them into a group that, in some respects, is treated as a whole. The LEGEND element, which is the obligatory first element within a FIELDSET, surrounds a piece of text that serves as a label for the entire group.

Keyboard Navigation

The keyboard being a much more disability-tolerant input device than the mouse, it's important, first, that all users have convenient means of keyboard navigation through the "hot spots" on the page, and second, that Web authors be able to redefine access sequences for their pages for maximum efficiency. These "hot spots" include form input controls and hypertext links. Note that with focus on a link, you still have to issue some additional command (such as pressing the Enter key) to activate it.

The two keyboard access modes provided by HTML 4.0 are access keys, or shortcuts, and tabbing order. *Access keys* are defined as characters that, when pressed on the keyboard along with a certain modifier key (Alt on Windows systems, Cmd on Macs), move focus onto the element associated with this access key. *Tabbing order* defines the order in which the elements receive focus when a certain "tabbing" key (usually the Tab key) is pressed repeatedly.

HTML elements differ in which keyboard access modes can be used with them. Setting the tabbing order position is available for the four input controls (INPUT, SELECT, TEXTAREA, and BUTTON) as well as for the A, AREA, and OBJECT elements. Access keys, on the other hand, can be assigned only to LABELs, LEGENDs, and A elements.

Thus, you can use shortcuts to switch to LABELed controls, groups of controls enclosed into FIELDSET elements, and stand-alone links, although tabbing will work for all form controls (it doesn't matter whether they're associated with LABELs or FIELDSETs or not) and for image maps and OBJECTs as well as stand-alone links.

To specify the tabbing order position for an element, use the tabindex attribute, as shown in this example:

```
<FORM action="..." method="post">
<INPUT tabindex="1" type="text" name="field1">
<INPUT tabindex="2" type="text" name="field2">
<INPUT tabindex="3" type="submit" name="submit">
</FORM>
```

Here is the complete algorithm that, according to the HTML 4.0 specification, user agents should follow to define the tabbing order on a page:

1. Those elements that support the tabindex attribute and assign a positive value to it are navigated first. Navigation proceeds from the element with the lowest tabindex value to the element with the highest value. Values need not be sequential or begin with any particular value. Elements that have identical tabindex should be navigated in the order they appear in the document.

2. Those elements that do not define the `tabindex` attribute or do not support it are navigated next. These elements are navigated in the order they appear in the document.

3. Those elements that support the `tabindex` attribute and assign a negative value to it do not participate in the tabbing order.

4. Elements that are disabled do not participate in the tabbing order.

Access keys are assigned by using the `accesskey` attribute, as follows:

```
<LABEL for="field1" accesskey="A">Enter Your <U>A</U>ge:</LABEL>
<INPUT type="text" id="field1">
```

The value of the `accesskey` attribute must be a single character (treated as case-insensitive) from the document's character encoding (see Chapter 40).

Miscellaneous Modalities

In this last section, I'll discuss the accessibility aspects of all other Web page elements and interfaces that didn't fit into the preceding "Text," "Graphics," "Layout," and "Forms" sections.

Frames

Documents using frames are really a scourge for disabled users (and, as you'll see in the next chapter, for search engines too). It's not that they're inaccessible in principle because of using a non-conventional medium or something; in fact, a root page of a frameset is nothing but a collection of links to frame pages, although these links are expressed by using FRAME tags instead of conventional hypertext anchors.

Of course, it's almost impossible for a blind person to really *use* a framed page—more difficult, perhaps, than playing chess without looking at the board. It's obvious, nevertheless, that at least *some* use could be made from framed pages by letting disabled users follow the FRAME references as though they were the usual hypertext links. Unfortunately, to my knowledge, no user agents currently implement this functionality.

For screen readers, a framed page is an aggravated example of the tabular layout (see "Tables" earlier in the chapter) with all its undesirable consequences galore. Other screen readers tend to treat each frame as a separate window, so sometimes it might be difficult to force the program to switch to another frame.

There is, however, a method of making framed sites accessible to people with disabilities: using the NOFRAMES tag. This technique is covered in detail in Chapter 42.

Audio and Video

Just like images, audio and video clips are inherently inaccessible to some categories of users. The methods of solving this problem are also similar to those developed for images (see "Images" earlier in the chapter).

If an audio or video clip carries important information that you want to be accessible to everyone, you should accompany it with a transcript (for speeches, conversations, and so on) or a general description (for nonverbal sounds or scenes). As with `alt` texts for images, you should try to convey the information contained *in* the clip, not meta-information *about* the clip itself. For instance, indicating file size for large audio or video files may be useful, but it doesn't belong in the alternative representation of a multimedia clip; it's those who *are* able to view/hear multimedia who may need this information, not those who are deprived of the possibility.

Technically, a transcript or description can be located in a separate page linked near the clip it belongs to. Also, as these types of data are likely to be embedded by using the `OBJECT` element, you can use its alternative rendering capability: All content enclosed between `<OBJECT>` and `</OBJECT>` will be rendered only by those user agents that can't render the `OBJECT` itself.

Java and JavaScript

These two Web-related programming languages are often considered to be something from the high-tech world of the latest graphical browsers, unlimited bandwidth, and sophisticated interfaces. It's true that only the major graphical browsers now support Java and JavaScript, but this doesn't mean you must completely abandon them for your pages to be universally accessible.

Java is not a tool for producing artful widgets for Web pages; it's a full-blown programming language with a great potential for building effective and portable information-processing applications. Java applets can be used—and *are* used—for a multitude of tasks that couldn't be performed with any other technology. There are situations in which the practicality of using Java is not in question; what may be in question is how to make Java applications accessible.

The basic principles (alternative modalities, logical rather than physical description of data) remain valid, but there are, of course, quite a number of Java-specific recommendations. Java accessibility is a huge topic, and an HTML book is perhaps not the place to discuss it in any detail. For the latest developments in the field of Java and JavaScript accessibility, refer to the site maintained by Trace R&D Center at `http://www.trace.wisc.edu/world/java/java.htm`.

A Final Remark

A relatively popular accessibility solution that I haven't mentioned so far in this chapter is a text-only version of an entire page or site, linked somewhere near the top of the "real" page as an emergency exit for those who can't bear anything more complicated than HTML 2.0.

It's not an omission; frankly, I left out this possibility rather consciously. As you can conclude from this long and diversified chapter, there are precious few situations that pose really tough accessibility challenges. After all, from its very beginning, HTML was intended to be an accessible, portable, and easily transformable medium, and no amount of "extensions" can rob it of this essential characteristic.

In the great majority of cases, inaccessible Web pages are a result not of the technologies applied, but rather of their incorrect implementation and lack of proper care. Setting up a text-only version is not only inefficient and prone to errors and desynchronization; it is, before all, a surrender, a capitulation, a betrayal of the very nature of HTML. On the contrary, sensible and accessible use of the entire inventory of HTML tools is a boon for site maintainers, users, and, as a final result, for the language itself.

Summary

In this chapter, I've discussed the ways to make HTML documents more accessible to people with physical and sensory disabilities, including both the proven techniques and the most recent developments of HTML 4.0. Most of the recommendations in this field can be derived from the two basic principles of accessibility: presenting information in alternative modalities and logical, rather than presentational, markup.

The following aspects of HTML authoring were discussed:

- **Text**: What tags should be avoided in text markup, what the major tips on selecting colors and presenting lists are
- **Layout**: How to properly use tables and other layout tools
- **Graphics**: Why `alt` texts are important, what the rules-of-thumb are for composing useful `alt` texts, and why you should avoid image maps
- **Forms**: What new means of keyboard navigation are provided in HTML 4.0 for forms and how to use them
- **Miscellany**: What the accessibility considerations are for using frames, multimedia clips, Java, and JavaScript

Strategies for Indexing and Search Engines

by Dmitry Kirsanov

CHAPTER 42

Some Webmasters claim that more than half the total traffic on their sites comes from search engines. This share, of course, will depend on the content of your site and the sort of audience you're after, but the importance of this free and efficient Web advertisement tool can't be denied.

Admittedly, traffic generated by search engines always contains a lot of "junk,"—that is, useless visits from people who were misled to your site by "keywords divination" in search of something completely different. However, those surfers who ended up finding what they were looking for are a very valuable category—maybe the most valuable of all your audience.

They might never have learned about your site from any other source, and having found it themselves, without any advertising or endorsement, they're more likely to be satisfied by the discovery. In fact, search engines are the closest possible approximation to the ideal of free, independent dissemination of information: You search for what you need, and you get what you searched for, with no marketing or political bias.

Of course, this ideal doesn't come easily. You'll have to learn some techniques to lure and welcome to your site first, automatic spiders indexing your page for search engines, and second, search engine users who might be interested in your content (these tasks are a bit different, although interrelated).

This chapter contains two major sections. In the first section, you'll get acquainted with how search engines work and what the main features of the major engines now in operation are. In the second section, I'll apply this knowledge to outline a set of specific recommendations for an efficient search-friendly HTML design.

How Search Engines Work

First off, I have bad news to tell you. When investigating the field, you're going to discover that search engines are, foremost, a proprietary technology in a very competitive market. Simply put, search engine companies keep their secrets well and reveal to the public only what they consider safe to reveal.

Given the importance—and necessity—of the special care and feeding of your site with regard to search engines, this behavior is really discouraging. The Webmasters who are interested in the matter have to rely mostly on their own research, which is often biased and incomplete. Rumors, gossips, and controversy are rampant.

Of course, there are sites whose maintainers are busy collecting information and doing research in this field (such as the Search Engine Watch at http://searchenginewatch.com), so this chapter drew much of its material from these useful sources. However, when it comes to the details of search engines' technology, you should take the conclusions of these third-party investigators with a grain of salt.

On the other hand, only research can provide the answers to certain questions because systems of this level of complexity tend to be ruled by multifactor statistics rather than by simple logic.

In fact, some peculiarities in the behavior of searching beasts might be as much of a surprise to their creators as to the general public. Huge information-processing systems sometimes behave as live beings, not soulless machines.

With these restrictions in mind, let's consider the principal gears that rotate inside a typical search engine.

Spiders

Indexing spiders (sometimes called robots, or bots, or crawlers) are the secret agents doing the work, the results of which you enjoy when you're performing searches. Spider programs, just like browsers, request and retrieve documents from Web servers, but unlike browsers, they do it not for viewing by humans but for automatic indexing and inclusion into their database. They do it tirelessly, in almost unimaginable amounts (millions of pages per day), around the clock and without days off.

Spiders are what sets apart search engines from *directories* (one of the most prominent directories is Yahoo!; see http://www.yahoo.com). Directories don't keep their pet spiders because all links in a directory are discovered (or submitted), examined, and annotated by humans. This difference makes the hand-picked resources of directories, on average, much more valuable but much less voluminous than the homogeneous heap of links in a search engine.

Each new document encountered by the spider is scanned for links, and these links are either traversed immediately or scheduled for later retrieval. Theoretically, by following all links starting from a representative initial set of documents, a spider will end up having indexed the whole Web.

In practice, however, this goal is unachievable. To begin with, lots of documents on the Web are generated *dynamically*, most often in response to input from a form. Naturally, although spiders can follow links, they have no idea what to put into the fields of a form, so any data retrieved on request is inherently inaccessible to search spiders (if no alternative access mechanism is provided). In this category belong various Web-accessible databases, including search engines themselves.

Also, spiders can never reach pages that are customized via cookies or pages using any JavaScript or Java tricks that affect their content. Some spiders can't even understand frames (see "Frames," later in this chapter). As you might have guessed, search engines cannot yet make heads or tails of any images or audio and video clips, so these bits of information are wasted (in fact, they aren't even requested by spiders). What remains is pure HTML source, of which spiders additionally strip off all markup and tags to get to the bare-bones plain text.

Even with these economizing assumptions, boxing up the entire Web into a single database turns out to be a practically unfeasible task. It might have been possible just a year ago, but not now when the Web has gotten *that* large. That's why search engines are now moving from the strategy of swallowing everything they see to various selection techniques.

Ideally, this selection should aim at improving the quality of the database by discarding junk and scanning only the premier Web content. In reality, of course, this kind of discernment is impossible because there are no automatic programs smart enough to separate wheat from chaff. The only way to sort out anything is by placing some rather arbitrary restrictions.

One search engine that admits "sampled spidering" is AltaVista (`http://altavista.digital.com`). It's been claimed that the quota for AltaVista's spider is not more than 600 documents per any single domain. If true, this means that large domains such as `geocities.com` or even `microsoft.com` are severely underrepresented in AltaVista's database. It remains open to speculation whether other search engines use similar sampling techniques or the size of their databases is limited only by their technical capacity.

All search engines allow users to add their URLs to the database for spidering. Some of them retrieve submitted documents immediately, and others schedule them for future scanning, but in any case this allows you to at least make sure your domain isn't missed. You're supposed to submit only the root URL of your site, and using this mechanism for registering each and every single page has been blamed as a sort of "spamming." On the other hand, given the selective nature of spidering, it's not a bad idea to register at least all key pages of your site. (Be careful, however: Some search engines limit the number of submissions per domain.)

Another important question is how often spiders update their databases by revisiting sites they've already indexed. This parameter varies significantly for different engines, with the update periods having been quoted from one week to several months. This aspect of search engines' performance allows some independent estimation: You can analyze your server's access logs to see when you were visited by spiders and what documents they requested. A helpful Perl script for this purpose, called BotWatch, is available at `http://www.tardis.ed.ac.uk/~sxw/robots/botwatch.html`.

Many search engines have problems with sites in languages other than English, especially if these languages use character sets different from ISO 8859-1 (see Chapter 40, "Internationalizing Your HTML"). For example, HotBot (`http://www.hotbot.com`) returns nothing when queried with keywords in Russian, nor can it properly display summaries for documents in Russian. This makes it useless for Russian surfers, despite the fact that HotBot's spider routinely scans a good share of all Web sites in Russia.

Search Interface

The *search interface* is the visible part of a search engine's iceberg. Every day millions of people enter myriads of keywords into search forms and get innumerable URLs in response. This is already one of the biggest and most intensively used information resources on Earth.

I'm not going to teach you how to *use* search engines, as that's beyond the scope of this book. However, to create search-friendly HTML documents, you must be aware of the range of features offered to the users of modern search engines.

Basic Options

All major search engines have, besides the simplest form of query with one or several keywords, some additional search options. However, the scope of these features varies significantly, and no standard syntax for invoking them is yet established. These are among the most common search options:

- **Boolean operators**: AND (find all), OR (find any), AND NOT (exclude) to combine keywords in queries
- **Phrase search**: Looking for the keywords only if they're positioned in the document next to each other, in this particular order
- **Proximity**: Looking for the keywords only if they're close enough to each other (the notion of "close enough" ranges from 2 in-between words for WebCrawler to 25 words for Lycos)
- **Media search**: Looking for pages containing Java applets, Shockwave objects, and so on
- **Special searches**: Looking for keywords or URLs within links, image names, document titles
- **Search constraints**: Limiting the search to a time span of document creation, specifying a document language (AltaVista), and so on

You should be aware that even with a full inventory of these bells and whistles, you can't expect from a search engine the capabilities that are comparable to, say, the Search dialog in Microsoft Word.

For example, AltaVista suggests using its database as a spelling dictionary: Search for CDROM and CD-ROM and see which will "win" by yielding more results. A bright idea, but you can't resolve in a similar fashion the controversy of World Wide Web versus World-Wide Web simply because the system treats both hyphens and spaces as "separators" and cannot differentiate between them. Those accustomed to regular expressions such as those used in Perl or awk can't even dream of using something similar with search engines.

In the future, search engines may offer more sophisticated options, although for now, their search interfaces seem to be developing in another direction, described in the following subsection.

Interactive Refining

Recently, several search engines developed schemes to categorize results of a search by combining them into groups with similar "keywords spectrum." By selecting the Refine button in AltaVista, you get a list of several categories that your results fall into, allowing you to specify whether you want to include or exclude any category for the next search iteration.

Similarly, Excite (http://www.excite.com) invites you to "Select words to add to your search," with these additional keywords extracted from the results just obtained. This selection allows you to narrow the search much more efficiently than you could do by blindly trying different keywords.

Northern Light Search (`http://www.nlsearch.com`) also sorts its search results into "folders" based on their content and the domain URL. All these features make really powerful searching possible by interactively detecting trends in the data.

Ranking

All search engines rank their results so that more relevant documents are at the top of the list. This sorting is based on, first, the frequency of keywords in a document, and second, the distance of keyword occurrences from the beginning of the document.

In other words, if one document contains two matches for a keyword and another is identical but contains only one, the first document will be closer to the top of list. If two documents are identical except that one has a keyword positioned closer to the top (especially in the document title), it will come first.

In addition to these principles, some search engines use extra factors, called *relevancy boosters*, to determine the ranking order. For instance, HotBot and Infoseek (`http://www.infoseek.com`) favor those documents that make use of <META> tags over their <META>-less peers.

WebCrawler (`http://www.webcrawler.com`) relies on *link popularity*. If a page is linked frequently from other pages and sites, it is considered "more authoritative" and gets some priority on the list of results. Excite, being a combination of a search engine and a directory, quite naturally gives preference to the pages reviewed in its directory.

Finally, all search engines try to fight unfair practices of some Webmasters who attempt to fool the ranking algorithm by repeating keywords to improve their effective frequency in the documents. You might have noticed pages with a tail of hundreds of repeated keywords (usually made invisible in browsers by changing font color, but still visible to search engines) or pages with multiple TITLE elements (again, only the first one is visible in browsers, but all are indexed by a spider). Now, not only do such "keyword spammers" not receive high rankings, but many search engines also automatically exclude them from the database. (For more on spamming, see "The Meta Controversy" later in this chapter.)

Results

Usually, lists of search results contain document titles, URLs, summaries, sometimes dates of the document creation (with other search engines, dates of their inclusion in the database), and document sizes. For compiling document summaries, several approaches have been developed.

Many search engines use META descriptions provided by page authors (see the next section for more on how this is done), but when META data is unavailable, they usually take the first 100 or 200 characters of page text. Excite stands apart by ignoring <META> tags altogether and using a sophisticated—but not particularly well-performing—algorithm that extracts sentences appearing to be the "theme" of the page and presents them as the page's summary.

However, the solution that seems optimal to me is that used by Aport, a Russian search engine (`http://russia.agama.com/aport/`). Instead of generating summaries, Aport just lists, for each document found, the sentences from the document that matched the query. Indeed, to decide whether a document is worth browsing, we're often more interested to see what the context of the keyword match is, not what sort of a document it is.

Aport has a number of other features unique among search engines. For example, it allows retrieving a text-only reconstruction of the document directly from the search engine's database, in case the original document (or the server it's stored on) is inaccessible.

How to Design for Search Engines

If you've read the previous chapter, "Creating Widely Accessible Web Pages," you might have noticed the similarity between search spiders and people with disabilities: Both have no access except to the text-only content of Web pages. Therefore, most of the HTML authoring recommendations from the chapter on disabilities apply to the search-friendly design as well.

Providing text-only alternatives for every piece of information on your page is an obvious requirement because spiders scan only plain text (although, unfortunately, not all of them index `alt` texts of images). Making your content fully comprehensible in text-only modality might be difficult (it's like trying to persuade somebody not in person but with a letter, without the powerful "multimedia" of gestures and facial expressions), but it's really rewarding in the long run.

Preserving the logical flow of the text, rather than sacrificing it for the sake of layout tricks, is also very important. It improves the chances of spiders extracting a better summary for your document and makes the text more suitable for automatic processing or categorizing.

Similarly, logical markup is an important requirement if you care about someone being able to *use* your document in any way, not just read it in a graphical browser. Besides the spiders of the major search engines, a great number of different robots and indexers wander along the roads of the Web, and many of them rely on the logical tags, such as `H1`, for figuring out the structure of your data.

Keyword Strategies

All searches on the Web are being done via keywords, so probably the most important requirement is making sure your documents contain all the keywords that are likely to be used to find the document. Two distinct strategies can be outlined for choosing keywords:

■ The first idea that comes to mind is simple: The more keywords you cram into a page, the better. Indeed, you can never predict what particular keywords will come to users' minds, so it's always a good idea to think about all possible synonyms, variants, generic inclusive terms, subterms, and related concepts for all the main subjects of your discourse.

Besides, remember that the keywords can be entered in a different grammatical form, such as plural instead of singular for nouns. And of the major search engines, only AltaVista provides the wildcard notation to look for *table* or *tables* by specifying `table*`. So, you'd better see to it yourself by including both forms in your document. (This problem is especially serious for languages other than English; for example, a verb in Russian might have up to 235 distinct forms. Therefore, most Russian search engines, such as Aport mentioned earlier, by default use word-inflection algorithms allowing to automatically match all word forms.)

Finally, if your main keyword is a relatively common word (such as *search*), it's likely that experienced search users will use the phrase searching feature to query for word combinations (such as *search engines*) rather than single words. Therefore, make sure your document contains the most common collocations of the main keyword with closely related nouns, adjectives, verbs, and so on.

■ However, one might think about an opposite to the strategy of maximizing "keyword coverage" just described. Remember that one of the factors in results ranking, as implemented by major search engines, is *frequency*, which is computed as the number of keyword occurrences divided by the document size.

One consequence of this calculation is that if two documents contain the same keyword (located at the same distance from the top of document), the one that is smaller in size will get a higher ranking. This gives you a clue: Select one of the root (introductory) pages on your site and try to make it as compact and concise as possible, so that it presents just the essence of your content with only the most common keywords. This page will get a boost with respect to searches for these keywords, thereby attracting more hits to the entire site.

Therefore, the best you can do is combine these two approaches by setting up both sorts of pages on your site: those with maximum keywords coverage and those with maximum relevance with respect to main keywords.

By the way, these two keyword strategies correspond to the two types of search queries, *specific* and *general* searches. Some search engine users are looking for very specific information; they use rare keywords, phrase searches, and advanced features such as Boolean operators. It's these "power users" that your keyword-rich pages should appeal to.

Other users, however, just need to find a good resource covering some fairly general topic; they enter a couple of simple keywords, get an avalanche of results, and browse the first several links found. For such general searches, Web directories (such as Yahoo!) usually perform better than search engines; however, a lot of users still employ search engines for the task. The relevance boosting technique described previously could be useful in attracting such users to your site.

You might be interested to see what keywords are entered most frequently by search engine users to better align your keyword spectrum with the public preferences. Unfortunately, this information (which would be immensely interesting from other viewpoints as well) is considered top-secret by major search engines—they never reveal their "top ten search words" lists for the (rather well-grounded) fear of spamming.

WebCrawler allows only a peek at the flow of search queries in real time, as they're entered on the search page (see `http://webcrawler.com/WebCrawler/Fun/SearchTicker.html`). However, minor search engines are usually less obsessed with confidentiality, and some of them show their search statistics (for example, a Russian search engine called Rambler presents its list of the top 100 search words at `http://www.rambler.ru/top.shtml.ru`).

The final piece of advice concerning keywords is rather obvious: Always check your spelling. Spiders, in contrast to human readers, can't "overlook" spelling errors, and you risk missing a good share of your potential audience by misspelling some important keyword. This suggestion is especially relevant given that in most cases you add your keywords into a <META> tag *after* the document itself is written, edited, and probably spellchecked.

The <META> Tag

Getting back to HTML, you might wonder what the syntax is for adding keywords to a document. Of course, the text of a page is the primary source of searchable material, but you may also need to add certain keywords without altering the page content. (Changing text color to make keywords invisible in the body of a document is a really ugly trick; please *never* resort to it!)

The <META> tag serves this purpose (as well as several other purposes). *Meta* is the Greek word for "over," and the <META> tag was intended to carry all sorts of *meta-information*—that is, information about (or "over") information. You should understand that using <META> for specifying keywords is not an HTML convention, but only one of the widely accepted uses of the tag.

A <META> tag usually takes the following form:

```
<META name="..." content="...">
```

As you can see, the names of the <META> tag attributes are rather generic, which allows you to use the tag to express virtually any information that can be represented as a name-value pair. For example, you could use <META> tags to supply information about yourself (`name="author"`), the program you used to create the HTML file (`name="generator"`), and so on.

Here's how the <META> tag is used for introducing your document to search engines:

```
<META name="keywords"
    content="searching, search engines, keywords, HTML">
<META name="description"
    content="A description of major web search engines, spiders,
        and search-friendly HTML authoring">
```

These tags should be placed within the HEAD element. Keywords and phrases in the content of the tag with the `name="keywords"` attribute can be separated by commas for better readability, although spiders usually ignore the separators. The maximum number of keywords depends on the search engine in question; for some of them, 25 words or 200 characters have been quoted as the upper limit.

Hopefully, the keywords thus specified will be added to the document's searchable representation in the engine's database, and the description will be stored as the summary to be displayed for the document in a list of results (in the absence of a description, most search engines take the first lines of text on the page).

Another use of the <META> tag is for excluding a page from spiders' attention. By adding the following tag, you instruct any spiders that run into your page to bypass it without indexing:

```
<META name="robots" content="noindex">
```

However, not all spiders support this convention. A more reliable solution is to add a robots.txt file to the root directory of your Web server, with a list of files that must be excluded from indexing. For example, your robots.txt file might contain these lines:

```
User-agent: *
Disallow: /dont_index_me.html
Disallow: /hidden_dir/
```

With these lines, no robot will scan the dont_index_me.html document or any document from the /hidden_dir/. For more information on robots exclusion, refer to http://info.webcrawler.com/mak/projects/robots/exclusion.html.

Frames

One of the features of HTML 4.0 deserves special attention with respect to search engines accessibility. About half of the major search engines can't penetrate framed sites. For them, the root page of a frameset is all that can be viewed and indexed on the site, and all the framed pages below the root are missed.

The best solution for this problem (as well as for the problem of frames accessibility to people with disabilities; see Chapter 41) is the NOFRAMES element. It should be placed within the FRAMESET element, usually before the first <FRAME> tag, and may contain any text, links, or other material. This is what search engines will see on the page and reflect in the database, and frame-capable browsers will ignore anything within a NOFRAMES element.

To make the rest of your content accessible, you should provide links to the framed pages from within the NOFRAMES element. Remember that you're doing this not only for spiders, but also for the users of non-graphical browsers, so accompany the links with proper descriptions. Usually, one of the frames contains a navigation bar with links to all other pages, so in the NOFRAMES element it may be enough to link to this document only.

For framed pages to be usable in the absence of frame context, remember to give them their own TITLE elements (this will improve their ranking in search engines as well).

The Meta Controversy

One of the major search engines, Excite, ignores any information in `<META>` tags, and does so on purpose. What could be the rationale for such a decision?

The reason stated on Excite's "Getting Listed" page (see `http://www.excite.com/Info/ listing.html`) is that `<META>` tags can be used by spammers to improve their rankings in an unfair way. For Excite, attempting to make a page appear any different to search spiders than to human users is an unfair practice. Indeed, nobody can guarantee that the keywords you enter are those describing your content, and in principle, you can easily use popular keywords to inflate your hits without any improvement of the page content.

At a first glance, this position might seem logical. But is it? Remember that I can easily put any number of "hot" keywords onto the page itself, and if I don't want to distract readers with this promotion machinery, I can make them invisible by painting them with the background color (as many spammers do already, simply because `<META>` tags don't allow them to enter too many keywords). After all, spiders will always index what I *want* them to, and banning one of the weapons can only ginger up the armaments race.

Excite's policy is based on the assumption that each page has its intrinsic "value," and that this value is evident from reading the text on the page. If this is true, then it's natural to require that spiders, to be able to assign a fair "relevance" value, would get exactly the same text as human readers. But it's also silently assumed that a spider can read, understand, and evaluate the text just as humans do—and this is where the main fallacy of this approach lies.

The main purpose of a `<META>` tag is to supply some information about the document, and the tag does it mostly for *computers* that can't deduce this information from the document itself. Keywords and descriptions, for example, are supposed to present the main concepts and subjects of the text, and no computer program can yet compile a meaningful summary or list of keywords for a given document. (In this context, it's interesting to note that Excite is the only search engine to use an artificial intelligence algorithm for compiling summaries based on the document text.)

True, the `<META>` mechanism is open to abuse, but so far it's the only technique capable of helping computers better understand human-produced documents. We won't have another choice but to rely on some sort of META information until computers achieve a level of intelligence comparable to that of human beings.

In view of this, it's interesting to discuss the latest development in the field of meta-information, the Meta Content Framework (MCF). This language is used for describing meta-information properties, connections, and interrelations of documents, sites, channels, subject categories, and other information objects. MCF was developed by Netscape and has been submitted as a draft standard to W3 Consortium (see `http://www.w3.org/TR/NOTE-MCF-XML/`).

MCF may be useful for maintainers of closed information systems, such as intranets, corporate and scientific databases, and so on. Its main promise, however, is the capability to build a meta-information network for the entire Web. Unfortunately, given the controversial position of the rather primitive <META> tags of today, it's not very likely that the sophisticated tools of MCF, even if approved by W3C, will gain any widespread recognition.

Summary

In this chapter, I've discussed search engines, an important tool for locating and publicizing information on the Web, and the techniques that can be used to build more efficient and search-friendly HTML pages. In particular, the following topics were covered:

- How search engines work, what search spiders are, and how they index the Web
- What search options and features are offered by the major search engines
- What the two strategies of selecting and grouping keywords on your Web pages are
- How to use the <META> tag to present keywords, summary, and other meta-information for a page
- Why the issue of authors building their own meta-information layers is controversial and what the possible implications of this controversy are

PART

X

IN THIS PART

Appendixes

HTML 4.0 Reference

by Lee Anne Phillips, Bob Correll,
and Will Kelly

IN THIS APPENDIX

APPENDIX

A

HTML 4.0 is a major upgrade to the HTML standard to meet the design and development needs of Web developers worldwide, both casual and professional. This appendix provides an extensive reference to the elements and attributes of the language as specified by the World Wide Web Consortium.

> **NOTE**
>
> This appendix is based on the information in the *HTML 4.0 Specification W3C Working Draft 17-Sep-1997*. The latest version of this document can be found at `http://www.w3.org/TR/WD-html40/`.

To make the information readily accessible, this appendix organizes HTML elements according to their function in the code you use to create your pages.

HTML Functionality

There are three basic types of elements: the "housekeeping" structure of each page, which doesn't actually alter the high-level rendering of the document directly; block-level tags that affect the layout of the document directly; and text-level tags that operate inline. In addition, there are mnemonic "entities" that allow you to access various characters commonly used in European languages and scientific works but not usually found on most keyboards. These entities are described in Appendix B, "Cross-Browser Reference Table," which also has information on browser differences. Because HTML is designed to display your page in a browser, we'll say a few words about them before we start.

Browsers and Platforms

Browsers are the power tools of the Web, and like all tools, they come in many different types and sizes to fit almost any pocketbook. No matter what you pay, or don't pay, none of them are perfect, none will display every tag exactly as you think it should, and some might have quirks that are annoying to live with. So you should look at several before you commit yourself. Appendix G, "Development Resources," has a small selection to choose from, but you should think about your intended purpose before you choose.

If you're on a tight budget, try one of the low-cost browsers that runs on a 386 or 486 with Windows, or an equivalent on the Mac Classic. The mainstream, heavily advertised browsers that everyone talks about will give little satisfaction on a machine like that, but Opera or Mosaic will run like a top. Likewise, if you want to look at your second cousin's site in China or Saudi Arabia, you'll probably want to try Tango or Internet with an Accent to allow you to see the glyphs properly.

If you want to see all the latest Java goodies and multimedia razzmatazz, you should probably figure on a Pentium or newer Mac platform with either Netscape Navigator or Microsoft Internet Explorer. Support for Netscape on the Web is better, but either will perform well.

If you have special needs, like a requirement for an audio or Braille browser, Appendix G has the URLs of a few links that might help you choose the most appropriate platform and software for this complex decision.

The resources of this book will also help, both the tags as listed in this appendix and the many discussions of resources throughout. Browsers will be a while catching up to the full power of the new HTML 4.0 specification, and as a Web designer, you should know that many people are happy with the browser they have and will never upgrade. Many Web developers have a collection of a dozen or more browsers on several platforms because they like to look at their work in all the many ways it will be displayed.

HTML 4.0 Philosophy and Practice

The World Wide Web is about communication. Like any medium of conversation, possibilities exist for misunderstanding and confusion. The new standards are designed to help make communication better and more inclusive for everyone. For a while, it was OK that the language of the Web was English by default, but that limitation restricted it to relatively few people worldwide. As you study the tags, you'll see how the additions have been carefully chosen to let more people in on the conversation and make it easier to allow for differences in the way people communicate and understand. It's really pretty cool.

> **NOTE**
>
> In the following list, some tags are placed for convenience with related tags and marked with an asterisk where they belong or are also appropriate. Some tags are placed where they do belong and are also referenced where many people might look for them, also for convenience.
>
> Some tags and attributes are deprecated, which means that they are not liked by the standards committee and should be avoided, if possible. Deprecated tags are marked with a little degree symbol (°).

HTML 4.0 tags are grouped in the following order in this appendix:

- ■ Structural (Housekeeping) Elements

    Basic structural elements: BODY, HEAD, HTML

    Header elements: BASE, ISINDEX°, LINK, META, NOSCRIPT, SCRIPT, STYLE, TITLE

    Frames: FRAMESET, FRAME, IFRAME, NOFRAMES

    SGML special tags: !-- (comment) --, !DOCTYPE

■ Block-level Elements

    Basic block elements: ADDRESS, BLOCKQUOTE, CENTER°, DIV, FIELDSET, H1–H6, HR, ISINDEX°*, P, PRE

    Lists: DD, DIR°, DL, DT, LI, MENU°, OL, UL

    Forms: BUTTON, FIELDSET, FORM, INPUT, LABEL, LEGEND, OPTION, SELECT, TEXTAREA

    Tables: CAPTION, COL, COLGROUP, TABLE, TBODY, TD, TFOOT, TH, THEAD, TR

■ Text-level Elements

    Text markup: B, BIG, I, S°, SMALL, STRIKE°, TT, U°

    Phrase markup: ACRONYM, ADDRESS*, BLOCKQUOTE*, CITE, CODE, DEL, DFN, EM, INS, KBD, PRE*, SAMP, STRONG, VAR

    Special markup: A, APPLET°, BASEFONT°, BDO, BR, FONT°, IFRAME*, IMG, NOSCRIPT*, OBJECT, Q, SCRIPT*, SPAN, SUB, SUP

    Client-side image maps: AREA, MAP

    Form control text: BUTTON*, INPUT*, LABEL*, SELECT*, TEXTAREA*

Within each section, the elements are listed alphabetically and the following information is given:

■ The tag itself and its closing tag, if it has one. If a tag is optional, it's surrounded by square brackets, but the brackets themselves are never part of any tag.

■ Usage: A general description of the element.

■ Syntax: A simple example of how the tag is written on the page. Optional elements are surrounded by square brackets. Optional attributes are shown with a placeholder in italics—*attributes*—to show that the actual attributes listed later in the section go in that position.

■ Start/End Tag: Indicates whether these tags are required, optional, or forbidden.

■ Attributes: Lists the attributes of the element with a short description of their effect. If a default value exists, it's printed in **bold**.

■ Intrinsics: Lists the intrinsic events that can be detected.

> **NOTE**
>
> HTML 4.0 introduces several new attributes and intrinsic events that apply to a large number of elements. They are called out by name at the end of the appropriate list but, because they always have exactly the same effect and description, please refer to the last section of this appendix, "Common Attributes and Intrinsic Events," for a more complete explanation.

■ Empty: Indicates that the element must be empty.

- Notes: Relates any special considerations when using the element and indicates whether the element is new or deprecated.
- Introduced: The version of HTML that standardized the element.
- Browsers: Indicates which versions of the popular Web browsers—Netscape Navigator and Microsoft Internet Explorer—support the HTML element.
- Example: Gives a short code example that illustrates how the tag is used.

> **NOTE**
>
> The element being highlighted appears in **bold**. For the purposes of illustration, deprecated elements and attributes are sometimes used in the example, but are rendered in *italics* to show that they're no longer recommended.

Structural (Housekeeping) Elements

HTML relies on several elements to give structure to a document (as opposed to structuring the text within the document) and supply information that's used by the browser or search engines.

Basic Structural Elements: BODY, HEAD, HTML

These are the basic tags on which all pages are founded. They are all unique in that they can almost always be inferred from the context, and many pages will work just fine without any of them. It's a very good habit to put them in, however, because they form a framework for your own thinking and help prevent mistakes that could cause some browsers to break your page.

[<BODY>]...[</BODY>]

Usage:	Contains the content of the document.
Syntax:	`<BODY [attributes]>the body of the HTML doc</BODY>`
Start/End Tag:	Optional/Optional
Attributes:	`background="..."` Deprecated. URL for the background image.
	`bgcolor="..."` Deprecated. Sets background color.
	`text="..."` Deprecated. Text color.
	`link="..."` Deprecated. Link color.
	`vlink="..."` Deprecated. Visited link color.
	`alink="..."` Deprecated. Active link color.
	`class=`, `id=`, `style=`, `title=`, `lang=`, `dir=` Common attributes.
Intrinsics:	`onload="..."` Intrinsic event.

	`onunload="..."` Intrinsic event triggered when document unloads.
	`onclick=, ondblclick=, onmousedown=, onmouseup=, onmouseover=,` `onmousemove=, onmouseout=, onkeypress=, onkeydown=,` `onkeyup=` Common intrinsic events.
Empty:	No
Notes:	There can be only one BODY element and it must follow the HEAD. The BODY element can be replaced by a FRAMESET element. The presentational attributes are deprecated in favor of setting these values with style sheets.
Introduced:	HTML 1.0
Browsers:	Netscape Navigator 0.9, 1.*x*, 2.*x*, 3.*x*, 4.*x*; Microsoft Internet Explorer 1.*x*, 2.*x*, 3.*x*, 4.*x*.

Example:

```
<BODY>
  <P align=center>
    In Scarlet town, where I was born<BR>
    There was a fair maid dwellin',<BR>
    Made every youth cry <I>Well-a-way!</I><BR>
    Her name was Barbara Allen.
</BODY>
```

[<HEAD>]...[</HEAD>]

Usage:	This is the document header; it contains other elements that provide information to users and search engines.
Syntax:	`[<HEAD [attributes]>]header information[</HEAD>]`
Start/End Tag:	Optional/Optional
Attributes:	`profile="..."` URL specifying the location of META data.
	`lang=, dir=` Common attributes.
Empty:	No
Notes:	There can be only one HEAD per document. It must follow the opening HTML tag and precede the BODY.
Introduced:	HTML 1.0
Browsers:	Netscape Navigator 0.9, 1.*x*,2.*x*, 3.*x*, 4.*x*; Microsoft Internet Explorer 2.*x*, 3.*x*, 4.*x*.

Example:

```
<HTML>
<HEAD>
    <TITLE>This is the text that will appear in the browser
    ➥title bar</TITLE>
</HEAD>
<BODY>
    <P>The title element contains the title text
       that appears in the subject line of the browser.
    <P>It should be accurate, descriptive, and give readers
       a reference to what is included on the page. Remember
```

```
          that most browsers place the title in the bookmark if
          the user wants to save your site and come back later.
          You can help her by making a snappy and distinctive
          title that identifies the site and tells who you are
          in a very few words.
        </BODY>
        </HTML>
```

[<HTML>]...[</HTML>]

Usage: The HTML element contains the entire document.

Syntax: `[<HTML [attributes]>]body and other HTML elements[</HTML>]`

Start/End Tag: Optional/Optional

Attributes: `version="..."`   URL of the document type definition specifying the HTML version used to create the document.

                       `lang=, dir=`   Common attributes.

Empty: No

Notes: The version information is duplicated in the `<!DOCTYPE...>` declaration, so it's not essential.

Introduced: HTML 1.0

Browsers: Netscape Navigator 0.9, 1.*x*, 2.*x*, 3.*x*, 4.*x*; Microsoft Internet Explorer 2.*x*, 3.*x*, 4.*x*.

Example:

```
<HTML>
  <HEAD>
    <TITLE>The Gallery</TITLE>
  </HEAD>
  <BODY bgcolor="#FFFFFF">
    <H1 align="center">The Gallery</H1>
  </BODY>
</HTML>
```

A

HTML 4.0 REFERENCE

Header Elements: BASE, ISINDEX°, LINK, META, NOSCRIPT, SCRIPT, STYLE, TITLE

Header elements occur in the head of an HTML document and have little, if any, effect on the direct formatting of the document; however, in the case of SCRIPT and STYLE, they can dynamically alter the default formatting.

<BASE>

Usage: All other URLs in the document are resolved against this location.

Syntax: `<BASE [attributes]>`

Start/End Tag: Required/Forbidden

Attributes: `href="..."`   The URL of the linked resource.

                       `target="..."`   Determines where the resource will be displayed (user-defined name, _blank, _parent, **_self**, _top).

Empty:	Yes, closing tag is forbidden.
Notes:	Located in the document HEAD.
Introduced:	HTML 2.0
Browsers:	Netscape Navigator 1.0, 2.*x*, 3.*x*, 4.*x*; Microsoft Internet Explorer 2.0, 3.0, 4.0. occur >
Example:	

```
<HTML>
  <HEAD>
    <TITLE>Base Tag Anatomy</TITLE>
    <BASE href="http://www.example.com/anatomy/">
  </HEAD>
  ...
```

<ISINDEX> °

Usage:	Creates a primitive form that prompts the user for input.
Syntax:	<ISINDEX [attributes]>
Start/End Tag:	Required/Forbidden
Attributes:	prompt="..." Deprecated. Provides a prompt string for the input field.
	class=, id=, style=, title=, lang=, dir= Common attributes.
Empty:	Yes, closing tag is forbidden.
Notes:	Deprecated. Use the INPUT element in a FORM instead.
Introduced:	HTML 3.2
Browsers:	Netscape Navigator 1.0, 2.*x*, 3.*x*, 4.*x*; Microsoft Internet Explorer 2.0, 3.0, 4.0.
Example:	

```
<HTML>
  <HEAD>
    <TITLE>Searchable Index</TITLE>
    <ISINDEX prompt="Enter your search string:">
  </HEAD>
  <BODY>
  ...
  </BODY>
</HTML>
```

<LINK>

Usage:	Defines the relationship between a link and a resource.
Syntax:	<LINK [attributes]>
Start/End Tag:	Required/Forbidden
Attributes:	href="..." The URL of the resource.
	rel="..." The forward link types.
	rev="..." The reverse link types.

type="..." The Internet content type.

media="..." Defines the destination medium (screen, print, projection, Braille, speech, all).

target="..." Determines where the resource will be displayed (user-defined name, _blank, _parent, **_self**, _top).

class=, id=, style=, title=, lang=, dir= Common attributes.

Intrinsics: onclick=, ondblclick=, onmousedown=, onmouseup=, onmouseover=, onmousemove=, onmouseout=, onkeypress=, onkeydown=, onkeyup= Common intrinsic events.

Link Types: contents Link refers to a document serving as a table of contents.

index Link refers to a document serving as an index for the current document.

glossary Link refers to a document serving as a glossary for the current document.

copyright Link refers to a copyright statement for the current document.

next Link refers to a document that's next in an ordered series of documents.

previous Link refers to the previous document in an ordered set of documents.

start Link refers to the first document in an ordered series of documents.

help Link refers to a document that includes help information.

bookmark Link refers to a bookmark included in a document.

Empty: Yes, closing tag is forbidden.

Notes: Located in the document HEAD. In theory, you could create quite sophisticated navigation systems with these attributes, including automatic language selection and other goodies. Unfortunately, most browsers don't actually do anything with the information.

Introduced: HTML 2.0

Browsers: Netscape Navigator 1.0, 2.0, 3.*x*, 4.*x*; Microsoft Internet Explorer 2.0, 3.0, 4.0.

Example:
```
...
<HEAD>
  <LINK href="contents.html" rel="next" rev="prev">
</HEAD>
... >
```

A

**HTML 4.0
REFERENCE**

`<META>`

Usage:	Supplies information about the document.
Syntax:	`<META [attributes]>`
Start/End Tag:	Required/Forbidden
Attributes:	`http-equiv="..."` HTTP response header name.
	`name="..."` Name of the meta-information.
	`content="..."` Content of the meta-information.
	`scheme="..."` Assigns a scheme to interpret the metadata.
	`lang=`, `dir=` Common attributes.
Empty:	Yes, closing tag is forbidden.
Notes:	The content of the `<META>` element is used for indexing purposes by many spiders and Web search engines.
Introduced:	HTML 2.0
Browsers:	Netscape Navigator 1.0, 2.*x*, 3.*x*, 4.*x*; Microsoft Internet Explorer 2.0, 3.0, 4.0.
Example:	```

```
<HTML>
  <HEAD>
    <TITLE>Author, Author</title>
    <META name="author" content="Joe Sample">
    <META name="keywords" content="research writing html">
  </HEAD>
  <BODY>
<H1>Example Page</H1>
<H2>by Joe Sample</H2>
...
  </BODY>
</HTML>
```

`<NOSCRIPT>...</NOSCRIPT>`

Usage:	The `NOSCRIPT` element provides alternative content for browsers unable to execute a script.
Syntax:	`<NOSCRIPT>alternative content</NOSCRIPT>`
Start/End Tag:	Required/Required
Attributes:	None
Empty:	No
Notes:	This is really an inline text element placed here for convenience so that both `<SCRIPT>` tags are together.
Introduced:	HTML 4.0
Browsers:	Netscape Navigator 3.0, 4.0; Microsoft Internet Explorer 4.0.

Example:
```
<HTML>
  <HEAD>
    <TITLE>Noscript Demonstration</TITLE>
  </HEAD>
  <BODY>
    <SCRIPT type ="text/javascript">
    <!--
      document.write ("<B>Hello, world.</B>")
     /-->
    </SCRIPT>
    <NOSCRIPT>
      <P>Hello, world.
    </NOSCRIPT>
  </BODY>
</HTML>
```

<SCRIPT>...</SCRIPT>

Usage: The SCRIPT element contains client-side command sequences that are executed by the browser.

Syntax: `<SCRIPT [attributes]>script commands</SCRIPT>`

Start/End Tag: Required/Required

Attributes: `type="..."` Script language Internet content type.

`language="..."` Deprecated. The scripting language, deprecated in favor of the type attribute.

`src="..."` The URL for the external script.

Empty: No

Notes: You can set the default scripting language in the META element.

Introduced: HTML 4.0

Browsers: Netscape Navigator 1.0, 2.0, 3.x, 4.0; Microsoft Internet Explorer 3.x, 4.0.

Example:
```
...
<SCRIPT type ="text/javascript">
<!--
  document.write ("<B>Hello, world.</B>")
 /-->
</SCRIPT>
...
```

<STYLE>...</STYLE>

Usage: Creates an internal style sheet.

Syntax: `<STYLE [attributes]>style sheet contents</STYLE>`

Start/End Tag: Required/Required

Attributes: `type="..."` The Internet content type.

	`media="..."` Defines the destination medium (`screen`, `print`, `projection`, `braille`, `speech`, `all`).
	`title="..."` The title of the style.
	`lang=, dir=` Common attributes.
Empty:	No
Notes:	Located in the HEAD element. It's a good idea to escape the style sheet with a comment, although not strictly necessary because some browsers, on seeing any text in the header, assume that the body has been reached and start rendering.
Introduced:	HTML 4.0
Browsers:	Netscape Navigator 4.0; Microsoft Internet Explorer 3.*x*, 4.0.

Example:

```
<HTML>
  <HEAD>
    <TITLE>Intro to Style Sheets</title>
    <STYLE type="text\css">
      <!--
          /* make all paragraphs red */
          p: (color: red : font-style: bold)
          -->
    </STYLE>
  </HEAD>
</HTML> occur
```

<TITLE>...</TITLE>

Usage:	This is the name you give your Web page. The TITLE element, located in the HEAD element, is displayed in the browser window title bar.
Syntax:	`<TITLE [attributes]>title of the page</TITLE>`
Start/End Tag:	Required/Required
Attributes:	`lang, dir`
Empty:	No
Notes:	This tag is required in every document. Only one title allowed per document.
Introduced:	HTML 1.0
Browsers:	Netscape Navigator 1.0, 2.*x*, 3.*x*, 4.*x*; Microsoft Internet Explorer 2.0, 3.0, 4.0.

Example:

```
...
<HEAD>
  <TITLE>The title appears in the browser title bar</TITLE>
</HEAD>
...
```

Frames: FRAMESET, FRAME, IFRAME, NOFRAMES

Frames create separate "panels" in the Web browser window that are used to display content from different source documents.

<FRAME>

Usage:	Defines a FRAME.
Syntax:	`<FRAME [attributes]>`
Start/End Tag:	Required/Forbidden
Attributes:	`name="..."` The name of a frame.
	`src="..."` The source to be displayed in a frame.
	`frameborder="..."` Toggles the border between frames (0, 1).
	`marginwidth="..."` Sets the space between the frame border and content.
	`marginheight="..."` Sets the space between the frame border and content.
	`noresize` Disables sizing.
	`scrolling="..."` Determines scrollbar presence (auto, yes, no).
Empty:	Yes, closing tag is forbidden.
Notes:	Frames first gained notice as one of the popular Netscape extensions released with Netscape Navigator 2.0. Netscape Communications Corporation then proposed it to the W3C to be part of the next HTML standard.
Introduced:	HTML 4.0
Browsers:	Netscape Navigator 2.0, 3.*x*, 4.*x*; Microsoft Internet Explorer 3.0, 4.0.
Example:	

A

HTML 4.0
REFERENCE

```
<!DOCTYPE html public "-//IETF//DTD HTML//EN">
<HTML>
  <HEAD>
    <TITLE>Technical Writing</TITLE>
    <META name="FORMATTER" content="Microsoft FrontPage 2.0">
  </HEAD>
  <FRAMESET rows="12%,*,12%">
    <FRAME src="frtop.htm" name="top" noresize>
    <FRAMESET cols="35%,65%">
      <FRAME src="frconten.htm" name="contents">
      <FRAME src="frmain.htm" name="main">
    </FRAMESET>
    <FRAME src="frbottom.htm" name="bottom" noresize>
  <NOFRAMES>
    <BODY>
      <P>This Web page uses frames, but your browser doesn't
      support them. Please go to my non-frames version of
      <A href="tw_nonf.htm">Technical Writing Resources</A>.
```

```
      </BODY>
    </NOFRAMES>
  </FRAMESET>
</HTML>
```

<FRAMESET>...</FRAMESET>

Usage:	Defines the layout of FRAMES within a window.
Syntax:	`<FRAMESET [attributes]>contents of frame set</FRAMESET>`
Start/End Tag:	Required/Required
Attributes:	`rows="..."` The number of rows.
	`cols="..."` The number of columns.
	`onload="..."` The intrinsic event triggered when the document loads.
	`onunload="..."` The intrinsic event triggered when the document unloads.
Empty:	No
Notes:	FRAMESETs can be nested.
Introduced:	HTML 4.0
Browsers:	Netscape Navigator 2.0, 3.*x*, 4.*x*; Microsoft Internet Explorer 3.0, 4.0.
Example:	

```
<HTML>
  <HEAD>
    <TITLE>Three Ages</TITLE>
  </HEAD>
  <FRAMESET rows="*,*,*">
    <FRAME src="childhood.htm">
    <FRAME src="maturity.htm">
    <FRAME src="oldage.htm">
  </FRAMESET>
  <NOFRAMES>
    <BODY>
      <P>
      This is the unframed version of the Three Ages page<BR>
      Please choose one of the following destinations:<BR>
      <A href="childhood.htm">Childhood</A><BR>
      <A href="maturity.htm">Maturity</A><BR>
      <A href="oldage.htm">Old Age</A><BR>
    </BODY>
  </NOFRAMES>
</HTML>
```

<IFRAME>...</IFRAME>

Usage:	Creates an inline frame.
Syntax:	`<IFRAME [attributes]>contents of inline frame</IFRAME>`
Start/End Tag:	Required/Required

Attributes: `name="..."` The name of the frame.

`src="..."` The source to be displayed in a frame.

`frameborder="..."` Toggles the border between frames (`0`, `1`).

`marginwidth="..."` Sets the space between the frame border and content.

`marginheight="..."` Sets the space between the frame border and content.

`scrolling="..."` Determines scrollbar presence (`auto`, `yes`, `no`).

`align="..."` Deprecated. Controls alignment (`left`, `center`, `right`, `justify`).

`height="..."` Height.

`width="..."` Width.

Empty: No

Notes: `IFRAME` is really an inline element but is placed here for convenience.

Introduced: HTML 4.0

Browsers: Microsoft Internet Explorer 3.0, 4.0.

Example:
```
<HTML>
  <HEAD>
    <TITLE>Three Ages</TITLE>
  </HEAD>
  <BODY>
    <P>These three ages, childhood,
      <IFRAME src="childhood.htm">
      maturity,
      <IFRAME src="maturity.htm">
      and old age
      <IFRAME src="oldage.htm">.
  </BODY>
</HTML>
```

`<NOFRAMES>...</NOFRAMES>`

Usage: Alternative content when frames are not supported.

Syntax: `<NOFRAMES>`*contents displayed in browsers that don't support frames*`</NOFRAMES>`

Start/End Tag: Required/Required

Attributes: None

Empty: No

Introduced: HTML 4.0

Browsers: Netscape Navigator 2.*x*, 3.*x*, 4.*x*; Microsoft Internet Explorer 3.0, 4.0.

Example: ...

```
<NOFRAMES>
  <BODY>
    <P>This Web page uses frames, but your browser doesn't
    support them. Please go to my non-frames version of <A
    href="tw_nonf.htm">Technical Writing Resources</a>.
  </BODY>
</NOFRAMES>
...
```

SGML Special Tags: !-- *(comment)* --, !DOCTYPE

These tags are both special cases: SGML (Standard Generalized Markup Language) markup that's also part of HTML. SGML comments, in particular, are a source of anomalous behavior in browsers because many programmers are confused about exactly how they work. It might be best to avoid using !DOCTYPE because none of the mainstream browsers support it and it could cause your pages to fail validation checks by online or local HTML validators, most of which do support it.

<!-- ... -->

Usage: SGML comment. Used to insert notes or scripts that aren't displayed by the browser.

Syntax: `<![-- ... --]*>`

Start/End Tag: N/A

Attributes: None

Empty: N/A

Notes: Comments are a special case. The actual comment tags are two dashes (--) surrounding each comment, but the comment must be enclosed in an SGML command: <! ... >. The first two dashes must follow the <! with no intervening spaces, and there must be a space immediately after. Comment dashes must occur in pairs, so if there are multiple comments, there will be four dashes (-- --) between each. Many browsers don't handle comments correctly; the most common errors are not allowing multiline comments, exiting the comment on the second set of dashes, or exiting the comment at the first >. All these behaviors are errors, but should be taken into account by the designer.

Introduced: HTML 2.0

Browsers: Netscape Navigator 1.0, 2.*x*, 3.*x*, 4.*x*; Microsoft Internet Explorer 1.*x*, 2.*x*, 3.*x*, 4.*x*.

Example:
```
<HTML>
<!-- Nobody ever seems to read comments anymore.-->
<!-- The same holds true for multiple-line comments like
     the one you're reading right now.-->
```

```
<!-- This is a series of comments --
  -- although many browsers --
  -- don't interpret them correctly -->
<!-- This is a <P> tag in a comment, which many browsers
     don't handle correctly.-->
</HTML>
```

<!DOCTYPE...>

Usage:	Version information appears on the first line of an HTML document and is an SGML declaration rather than an element.
Syntax:	`<!DOCTYPE html public "[standard DTD name]">`
Start/End Tag:	Required/None
Attributes:	None
Empty:	N/A
Notes:	This tag may be omitted because few browsers actually support it. In fact, it might cause problems unless you have particular reasons to validate against a certain DTD because there's no way to say you're trying to cover all bases by including elements from several.
Introduced:	HTML 1.0
Browsers:	Netscape Navigator 0.9, 1.*x*,2.*x*, 3.*x*, 4.*x*, Microsoft Internet Explorer 2.*x*, 3.*x*, 4.*x*.

Example:	`<!DOCTYPE html public "-//IETF//DTD HTML 4.0//EN">`
	`<HTML>`
	`...`

Block-level Elements

Block-level elements cause a break in the flow of text and affect the formatting of the document.

Basic Block Elements: ADDRESS, BLOCKQUOTE, CENTER°, DIV, FIELDSET, H1-H6, HR, ISINDEX°*, NOSCRIPT*, P, PRE

Basic block elements alter the document's formatting and cause a break in the flow of text but are not part of, nor do they contain, other block elements.

<ADDRESS>...</ADDRESS>

Usage:	Provides a special format for author or contact information or allows automatic extraction of an address by a process.
Syntax:	`<ADDRESS [attributes]>address or contact information` `➥</ADDRESS>`
Start/End Tag:	Required/Required

Attributes:	`class=`, `id=`, `style=`, `title=`, `lang=`, `dir=` Common attributes.
Intrinsics:	`onclick=`, `ondblclick=`, `onmousedown=`, `onmouseup=`, `onmouseover=`, `onmousemove=`, `onmouseout=`, `onkeypress=`, `onkeydown=`, `onkeyup=` Common intrinsic events.
Empty:	No
Notes:	This element causes a break in the flow of text, so it's included here. The BR element is commonly used inside the ADDRESS element to break the lines of an address. Some browsers render the contents as italic text.
Introduced:	HTML 2.0
Browsers:	Netscape Navigator 1.0, 2.0, 3.*x*, 4.*x*; Microsoft Internet Explorer 2.0, 3.0, 4.0.
Example:	

```
<ADDRESS>
  author@example.com<BR>
  123 Main Street<BR>
  Anytown, IN<BR>
  USA
</ADDRESS>
```

\<BLOCKQUOTE>...\</BLOCKQUOTE>

Usage:	Used to display long quotations.
Syntax:	`<BLOCKQUOTE [attributes]>text of blockquote</BLOCKQUOTE>`
Start/End Tag:	Required/Required
Attributes:	`cite="..."` The URL of the quoted text or the reason for the change.
	`class=`, `id=`, `style=`, `title=`, `lang=`, `dir=` Common attributes.
Intrinsics:	`onclick=`, `ondblclick=`, `onmousedown=`, `onmouseup=`, `onmouseover=`, `onmousemove=`, `onmouseout=`, `onkeypress=`, `onkeydown=`, `onkeyup=` Common intrinsic events.
Empty:	No
Notes:	Usually rendered with an offset from both margins. Related to but not the same as the \<Q> tag, which marks an inline quote.
Introduced:	HTML 2.0
Browsers:	Netscape Navigator 1.0, 2.0, 3.*x*, 4.*x*; Microsoft Internet Explorer 2.0, 3.0, 4.0.
Example:	

```
...
<BLOCKQUOTE cite="http://www.teresaofavila.com/">
  I only wish that I could write with both hands, so as not
➥to forget one thing while I am saying another. &mdash;
➥Teresa of Avila
</BLOCKQUOTE>
```

<CENTER>...</CENTER> °

Usage:	Used to center an HTML element.
Syntax:	`<CENTER [attributes]>centered text or elements</CENTER>`
Start/End Tag:	Required/Required
Attributes:	`class=`, `id=`, `style=`, `title=`, `lang=`, `dir=` Common attributes.
Intrinsics:	`onclick=`, `ondblclick=`, `onmousedown=`, `onmouseup=`, `onmouseover=`, `onmousemove=`, `onmouseout=`, `onkeypress=`, `onkeydown=`, `onkeyup=` Common intrinsic events.
Empty:	No
Notes:	Deprecated. Defined in HTML 4.0 as a synonym for `<DIV align="center">`, which should be used instead.
Introduced:	HTML 2.0
Browsers:	Netscape Navigator 1.1, 2.0, 3.*x*, 4.*x*; Microsoft Internet Explorer 2.0, 3.0, 4.0.

Example:	`<CENTER>`
	`  <A href="http://www.example.org/pancake/">Pancake Breakfast!</A>`
	`</CENTER>`

<DIV>...</DIV>

Usage:	The DIVISION element is used to add structure to a block of text.
Syntax:	`<DIV [attributes]>structured text</DIV>`
Start/End Tag:	Required/Required
Attributes:	`align="..."` Deprecated. Controls alignment (**left**, center, right, justify).
	`class=`, `id=`, `style=`, `title=`, `lang=`, `dir=` Common attributes.
Intrinsics:	`onclick=`, `ondblclick=`, `onmousedown=`, `onmouseup=`, `onmouseover=`, `onmousemove=`, `onmouseout=`, `onkeypress=`, `onkeydown=`, `onkeyup=` Common intrinsic events.
Empty:	No
Notes:	Cannot be used in a P element. The `align` attribute is deprecated in favor of controlling alignment through style sheets.
Introduced:	HTML 2.0
Browsers:	Netscape Navigator 2.0, 3.*x*, 4.*x*; Microsoft Internet Explorer 2.*x*, 3.*x*, 4.*x*.

Example:	`<HTML>`
	`  <DIV align="left">`
	`    <P>...for as ye think I fear too much,`
	`  </DIV>`

A

HTML 4.0 REFERENCE

```
        <DIV align="right">
          <P>be you well aware that you fear not as far too little.
        </DIV>
        <DIV align="center">
          <P>- Elizabeth Grey
        </DIV>
      </HTML>
```

<H1>...</H1> Through <H6>...</H6>

Usage: The six headings (H1 is the uppermost, or most important) are used in the BODY to structure information hierarchically.

Syntax: <H1 [attributes]>heading text</H1>

Start/End Tag: Required/Required

Attributes: align="..."   Deprecated. Controls alignment (**left**, center, right, justify).

                class=, id=, style=, title=, lang=, dir=   Common attributes.

Intrinsics: onclick=, ondblclick=, onmousedown=, onmouseup=, onmouseover=, onmousemove=, onmouseout=, onkeypress=, onkeydown=, onkeyup=   Common intrinsic events.

Empty: No

Notes: Visual browsers display the size of the headings in relation to their importance, with H1 being the largest and H6 the smallest. For compatibility, headings should start at H1 and proceed sequentially down to the lowest value. The align attribute is deprecated in favor of controlling alignment through style sheets.

Introduced: HTML 1.0

Browsers: Netscape Navigator 1.0, 2.*x*, 3.*x*, 4.*x*; Microsoft Internet Explorer 2.*x*, 3.*x*, 4.*x*.

Example:
```
<HTML>
  <HEAD>
    <TITLE>Heading examples</TITLE>
  </HEAD>
    <H1> This little piggy is heading style 1</H1>
    <H2> This little piggy is heading style 2</H2>
    <H3> This little piggy is heading style 3</H3>
    <H4> This little piggy is heading style 4</H4>
    <H5> This little piggy is heading style 5</H5>
    <H6> This little piggy is heading style 6</H6>
    <P> Header elements automatically create vertical white
        ➥space surrounding the header proportionally.
  </HTML>
```

<HR>

Usage: Horizontal rules can be used to separate sections of a Web page.

Syntax: <HR [attributes]>

Start/End Tag:	Required/Forbidden

Attributes: `align="..."` Deprecated. Controls alignment (**left**, center, right, justify).

`noshade="..."` Displays the rule as a solid color.

`size="..."` Deprecated. Controls the size of the rule.

`width="..."` Deprecated. Controls the width of the rule.

`class=, id=, style=, title=, lang=, dir=` Common attributes.

Intrinsics: `onclick=, ondblclick=, onmousedown=, onmouseup=, onmouseover=, onmousemove=, onmouseout=, onkeypress=, onkeydown=, onkeyup=` Common intrinsic events.

Empty: Yes, closing tag is forbidden.

Notes: There are many different schools of thought on using the <HR> tag, but some designers are straying away from this tag to make better use of white space to separate page elements.

Introduced: HTML 2.0

Browsers: Netscape Navigator 0.9, 1.*x*,2.*x*, 3.*x*, 4.*x*; Microsoft Internet Explorer 2.*x*, 3.*x*, 4.*x*.

Example:
```
...
  <H2>Section One</H2>
...
<HR>
  <H2>Section Two</H2>
...
```

A

HTML 4.0
REFERENCE

<ISINDEX>* °

Notes: Operates as a block-level element that creates a primitive form. It was discussed in the "Structural (Housekeeping) Elements" section as a header element. Deprecated. Use the INPUT element in a FORM instead.

<P>...[</P>]

Usage: Defines a paragraph.

Syntax: `<P [attributes]>paragraph text[</P>]`

Start/End Tag: Required/Optional

Attributes: `align="..."` Deprecated. Controls alignment (**left**, center, right, justify).

`class=, id=, style=, title=, lang=, dir=` Common attributes.

Intrinsics: `onclick=, ondblclick=, onmousedown=, onmouseup=, onmouseover=, onmousemove=, onmouseout=, onkeypress=, onkeydown=, onkeyup=` Common intrinsic events.

Empty:	No
Notes:	The closing tag is usually omitted.
Introduced:	HTML 1.0
Browser:	Netscape Navigator 1.0, 2.*x*, 3.*x*, 4.*x*; Microsoft Internet Explorer 2.0, 3.0, 4.0.
Example: >	

```
<P align=center>HTML 4 is a major upgrade to the HTML
    ➥standard.
```

`<PRE>...</PRE>`

Usage:	Displays preformatted text.
Syntax:	`<PRE [attributes]>formatted text</PRE>`
Start/End Tag:	Required/Required
Attributes:	`width="..."` The width of the formatted text.
	`class=, id=, style=, title=, lang=, dir=` Common attributes.
Intrinsics:	`onclick=, ondblclick=, onmousedown=, onmouseup=, onmouseover=,` `onmousemove=, onmouseout=, onkeypress=, onkeydown=,` `onkeyup=` Common intrinsic events.
Empty:	No
Note:	The `<PRE>` element is an excellent way to add already formatted text documents to a Web page because it preserves the document's original formatting.
Introduced:	HTML 2.0
Browsers:	Netscape Navigator 1.0, 2.0, 3.*x*, 4.*x*; Microsoft Internet Explorer 2.0, 3.0, 4.0.
Example:	

```
<PRE width ="80%">
Acquisitions Editors  Technical Editors  Editorial Assistant
  Development Editors  Office Manager     Mailroom Attendant
   Production Editors  Typist
          Copy Editors  Clerk            Other Workers
</PRE>
```

Lists: DD, DIR°, DL, DT, LI, MENU°, OL, UL

Like all block elements, list elements cause a break in the flow of the text, but they are special in that they can contain or be a part of other block elements. You can organize text into a more structured outline by creating lists, which can also be nested.

`<DD>...[</DD>]`

Usage:	The definition description used in a DL (definition list) element.
Syntax:	`<DD [attributes]>description of the word being defined[</DD>]`
Start/End Tag:	Required/Optional

Attributes:	`class=`, `id=`, `style=`, `title=`, `lang=`, `dir=` Common attributes.
Intrinsics:	`onclick=`, `ondblclick=`, `onmousedown=`, `onmouseup=`, `onmouseover=`, `onmousemove=`, `onmouseout=`, `onkeypress=`, `onkeydown=`, `onkeyup=` Common intrinsic events.
Empty:	No
Notes:	Can contain block-level content, such as the `<P>` element.
Introduced:	HTML 2.0
Browsers:	Netscape Navigator 1.0, 2.0, 3.*x*, 4.*x*; Microsoft Internet Explorer 2.0, 3.0, 4.0.

Example:

```
<DL>
  <DT> Publications Manager
    <DD> The person in charge of coordinating all
         ➥departmental activities.
  <DT> Technical Writer
    <DD> The person who writes a technical manual.
  <DT> Technical Editor
    <DD> The person who is responsible for the technical
         ➥accuracy of the finished manual.
</DL>
```

<DIR>...</DIR> °

Usage:	Creates a multi-column directory list (in theory).
Syntax:	`<DIR [attributes]>directory list contents</DIR>`
Start/End Tag:	Required/Required
Attributes:	`compact` Deprecated. May display the list in a compact form.
	`class=`, `id=`, `style=`, `title=`, `lang=`, `dir=` Common attributes.
Intrinsics:	`onclick=`, `ondblclick=`, `onmousedown=`, `onmouseup=`, `onmouseover=`, `onmousemove=`, `onmouseout=`, `onkeypress=`, `onkeydown=`, `onkeyup=` Common intrinsic events.
Empty:	No
Notes:	Must contain at least one list item. This element is deprecated in favor of the UL (unordered list) element. Originally, this element was to be used for listing files.
Introduced:	HTML 2.0
Browsers:	Netscape Navigator 1.0, 2.0, 3.*x*, 4.*x*; Microsoft Internet Explorer 2.0, 3.0, 4.0.

Example:

```
<DIR>
  <LI><CODE>README.</CODE>
  <LI><CODE>INSTALL</CODE>
  <LI><CODE>ERRATA</CODE>
</DIR>
```

A

HTML 4.0
REFERENCE

<DL>...</DL>

Usage:	Creates a definition list.
Syntax:	`<DL [attributes]>contents of definition list</DL>`
Start/End Tag:	Required/Required
Attributes:	`compact` Deprecated. May display the list in a compact form.
	`class=, id=, style=, title=, lang=, dir=` Common attributes.
Intrinsics:	`onclick=, ondblclick=, onmousedown=, onmouseup=, onmouseover=, onmousemove=, onmouseout=, onkeypress=, onkeydown=, onkeyup=` Common intrinsic events.
Empty:	No
Notes:	Must contain at least one `<DT>` or `<DD>` element in any order.
Introduced:	HTML 2.0
Browsers:	Netscape Navigator 1.0, 2.0, 3.*x*, 4.*x*; Microsoft Internet Explorer 2.0, 3.0, 4.0.

Example:

```
<DL>
   <DT> Publications Manager
     <DD> The person in charge of coordinating all
         ➥departmental activities.
   <DT> Technical Writer
     <DD> The person who writes a technical manual.
   <DT> Technical Editor
     <DD> The person who is responsible for the technical
         ➥accuracy of the finished manual.
</DL>
```

<DT>...[</DT>]

Usage:	The definition term (or label) used in a `DL` (definition list) element.
Syntax:	`<DT [attributes]>text of definition term[</DT>]`
Start/End Tag:	Required/Optional
Attributes:	`class=, id=, style=, title=, lang=, dir=` Common attributes.
Intrinsics:	`onclick=, ondblclick=, onmousedown=, onmouseup=, onmouseover=, onmousemove=, onmouseout=, onkeypress=, onkeydown=, onkeyup=` Common intrinsic events.
Empty:	No
Notes:	Must contain text (which can be modified by text markup elements).
Introduced:	HTML 2.0
Browsers:	Netscape Navigator 1.0, 2.0, 3.*x*, 4.*x*; Microsoft Internet Explorer 2.0, 3.0, 4.0.

Intrinsics:	`onclick=`, `ondblclick=`, `onmousedown=`, `onmouseup=`, `onmouseover=`, `onmousemove=`, `onmouseout=`, `onkeypress=`, `onkeydown=`, `onkeyup=` Common intrinsic events.
Empty:	No
Notes:	Must contain at least one list item.
Introduced:	HTML 2.0
Browsers:	Netscape Navigator 1.0, 2.0, 3.*x*, 4.*x*; Microsoft Internet Explorer 2.0, 3.0, 4.0.
Example:	

```
<UL>
    <LI>Item 1
    <LI>Item 2
    <LI>Item 3
</UL>
```

Forms: BUTTON, FIELDSET, FORM, INPUT, ISINDEX*, LABEL, LEGEND, OPTION, SELECT, TEXTAREA

Like other block elements, forms cause a break in the flow of the text and formatting. Forms are a special case because they may contain, or be a part of, other block elements and create an interface for the user to select options and submit data back to the Web server.

<BUTTON>...</BUTTON>

Usage:	Creates a button.
Syntax:	`<BUTTON [attributes]>the button</BUTTON>`
Start/End Tag:	Required/Required
Attributes:	`name="..."` The button name.
	`value="..."` The value of the button.
	`type="..."` The button type (button, submit, reset).
	`disabled="..."` Sets the button state to disabled.
	`tabindex="..."` Sets the tabbing order between elements with a defined tabindex.
	`class=`, `id=`, `style=`, `title=`, `lang=`, `dir=` Common attributes.
Intrinsics:	`onfocus="..."` The event that occurs when the element receives focus.
	`onblur="..."` The event that occurs when the element loses focus.
	`onclick=`, `ondblclick=`, `onmousedown=`, `onmouseup=`, `onmouseover=`, `onmousemove=`, `onmouseout=`, `onkeypress=`, `onkeydown=`, `onkeyup=` Common intrinsic events.
Empty:	No

A

HTML 4.0 REFERENCE

Introduced:	HTML 3.2
Browsers:	Netscape Navigator 3.*x* 4.*x*, Microsoft Internet Explorer 3.0, 4.0.
Example:	

```
<FORM action="..." method="...">
  <INPUT type="radio" name= sex value="M"> Male
  <INPUT type="radio" name= sex value="F"> Female
  <BUTTON type="submit" name="submit" value="submit">
    <IMG src="/icons/submit.gif" alt="submit"></BUTTON>
</FORM>
```

<FIELDSET>...</FIELDSET>

Usage:	Groups related controls.
Syntax:	`<FIELDSET [attributes]>related controls</FIELDSET>`
Start/End Tag:	Required/Required
Empty:	No
Introduced:	HTML 3.2
Browsers:	Netscape Navigator 3.*x*, 4.*x*, Microsoft Internet Explorer 3.0, 4.0.
Example:	

```
<HTML>
  <HEAD>
    <TITLE>Fieldset Legend</TITLE>
  </HEAD>
  <BODY>
    <FORM action="http://www.example.com/cgi-bin/testing.pl"
    ➥method="post">
      <FIELDSET>
        <LEGEND align="top">Customer Name</LEGEND>
        Last Name: <INPUT name="lastname" type="text"
        ➥tabindex="1">
        First Name: <INPUT name="firstname" type="text"
        ➥tabindex="2">
      </FIELDSET>
      <FIELDSET>
        <LEGEND align="top">Interests</LEGEND>
        <INPUT name="surfing"
               type="checkbox"
               value="surfing" tabindex="3">Surfing</INPUT>
        <INPUT name="hiking"
               type="checkbox"
               value="hiking" tabindex="4">Hiking</INPUT>
      </FIELDSET>
    </FORM>
  </BODY>
</HTML>
```

<FORM>...</FORM>

Usage:	Creates a form that holds controls for user input.
Syntax:	`<FORM [attributes]>contents of the form</FORM>`
Start/End Tag:	Required/Required

Attributes: `action="..."`   The URL for the server action.

`method="..."`   The HTTP method (`GET`, `POST`). `GET` is deprecated.

`enctype="..."`   Specifies the MIME (Internet media type).

`target="..."`   Determines where the resource will be displayed (user-defined name, `_blank`, `_parent`, `_self`, `_top`).

`accept-charset="..."`   The list of character encodings. Default value is `ISO-8859-1`.

`class=`, `id=`, `style=`, `title=`, `lang=`, `dir=`   Common attributes.

Intrinsics: `onsubmit="..."`   The intrinsic event that occurs when the form is submitted.

`onreset="..."`   The intrinsic event that occurs when the form is reset.

`onclick=`, `ondblclick=`, `onmousedown=`, `onmouseup=`, `onmouseover=`, `onmousemove=`, `onmouseout=`, `onkeypress=`, `onkeydown=`, `onkeyup=`   Common intrinsic events.

Empty: No

Introduced: HTML 2.0

Browsers: Netscape Navigator q.0, 2.*x*, 3.*x*, 4.*x*; Microsoft Internet Explorer 2.0, 3.0, 4.0.

Example: `<FORM action="http://www.example.com/cgi-bin/register.pl">`
`contents of form`
`</FORM>`

<INPUT>

Usage: Defines controls used in forms.

Syntax: `<INPUT [attributes]>`

Start/End Tag: Required/Forbidden

Attributes: `type="..."`   The type of input control (`text`, `password`, `checkbox`, `radio`, `submit`, `reset`, `file`, `hidden`, `image`, `button`).

`accept="..."`   File types allowed for upload.

`name="..."`   The name of the control (required except for `submit` and `reset`).

`value="..."`   The initial value of the control (required for radio buttons and checkboxes).

`checked="..."`   Sets the radio buttons to a checked state.

`disabled="..."`   Disables the control.

`readonly="..."`   For text password types.

`size="..."`   The width of the control in pixels except for text and password controls, which are specified in number of characters.

`maxlength="..."`   The maximum number of characters that can be entered.

`src="..."`   The URL to an image control type.

`alt="..."`   An alternative text description.

`usemap="..."`   The URL to a client-side image map.

`align="..."`   Deprecated. Controls alignment (**left**, `center`, `right`, `justify`).

`tabindex="..."`   Sets the tabbing order between elements with a defined `tabindex`.

`class=`, `id=`, `style=`, `title=`, `lang=`, `dir=`   Common attributes.

Intrinsics:
`onfocus="..."`   The event that occurs when the element receives focus.

`onblur="..."`   The event that occurs when the element loses focus.

`onselect="..."`   Intrinsic event that occurs when the control is selected.

`onchange="..."`   Intrinsic event that occurs when the control is changed.

`onclick=`, `ondblclick=`, `onmousedown=`, `onmouseup=`, `onmouseover=`, `onmousemove=`, `onmouseout=`, `onkeypress=`, `onkeydown=`, `onkeyup=`   Common intrinsic events.

Empty: Yes, closing tag is forbidden.

Input Types:
`text`   Creates a single-line text box.

`password`   Similar to text, but the entered text is rendered in the field in a way that hides the actual alpha and numeric characters that were entered.

`checkbox`   An on/off switch. When checked, it is on; when not checked, it's off.

`radio`   An on/off switch.

`submit`   Creates a submit button for submitting text.

`image`   Creates a graphical submit button.

`reset`   Creates a reset button.

`button`   Creates a button with no default behavior.

`hidden`   Creates an element not rendered by the user agent.

`file`   Prompts the user for a filename.

Introduced: HTML 2.0

| Browsers: | Netscape Navigator 1.0, 2.*x*, 3.*x*, 4.*x*; Microsoft Internet Explorer 2.0, 3.0, 4.0. |

Example:

```
<FORM ...>
  <INPUT type="radio" name="sex" value="M"> Male
  <INPUT type="radio" name="sex" value="F"> Female
</FORM>
```

`<ISINDEX>*` °

| Notes: | Operates as a block-level element that creates a primitive form. It was discussed in the "Structural (Housekeeping) Elements" section as a header element. Deprecated. Use the INPUT element in a FORM instead. |

`<LABEL>...</LABEL>`

Usage:	Labels a control.
Syntax:	`<LABEL [attributes]>labeled control</LABEL>`
Start/End Tag:	Required/Required
Attributes:	`for="..."` Associates a label with an identified control.
	`disabled="..."` Disables a control.
	`accesskey="..."` Assigns a hotkey to this element.
	`class=, id=, style=, title=, lang=, dir=` Common attributes.
Intrinsics:	`onfocus="..."` The event that occurs when the element receives focus.
	`onblur="..."` The event that occurs when the element loses focus.
	`onclick=, ondblclick=, onmousedown=, onmouseup=, onmouseover=, onmousemove=, onmouseout=, onkeypress=, onkeydown=, onkeyup=` Common intrinsic events.
Empty:	No
Introduced:	HTML 4.0
Browsers:	Netscape Navigator 4.*x*; Microsoft Internet Explorer 4.0.

Example:

```
<HTML>
  <FORM action="..." method="post">
    <TABLE>
      <TR>
        <TD><LABEL for="first">First name</LABEL>
            <TD><INPUT type="text" name="firstname"
            ⇥id="first">
        <TR>
          <TD><LABEL for="last">Last name</LABEL>
              <TD><INPUT type="text" name="lastname" id="last">
...
    </TABLE>
  </FORM>
</HTML>
```

A

HTML 4.0 REFERENCE

<LEGEND>...</LEGEND>

Usage:	Assigns a caption to a FIELDSET.
Syntax:	<LEGEND *[attributes]*>*fieldset caption*</LEGEND>
Start/End Tag:	Required/Required
Attributes:	class, id, style, title, lang, dir, onclick, ondblclick, onmousedown, onmouseup, onmouseover, onmousemove, onmouseout, onkeypress, onkeydown, onkeyup

align="..."   Deprecated. Controls alignment (**left**, center, right, justify).

accesskey="..."   Assigns a hotkey to this element.

Empty:	No
Introduced:	HTML 3.2
Browsers:	Netscape Navigator 3.*x*, 4.*x*; Microsoft Internet Explorer 3.0, 4.0.
Example:	

```
<HTML>
  <HEAD>
    <TITLE>Fieldset Legend</TITLE>
  </HEAD>
  <BODY>
    <FORM action="http://www.example.com/cgi-bin/testing.pl"
    ➥method="post">
      <FIELDSET>
        <LEGEND align="top">Customer Name</LEGEND>
        Last Name: <INPUT name="lastname" type="text"
        ➥tabindex="1">
        First Name: <INPUT name="firstname" type="text"
        ➥tabindex="2">
      </FIELDSET>
      <FIELDSET>
        <LEGEND align="top">Interests</LEGEND>
        <INPUT name="surfing"
               type="checkbox"
               value="surfing" tabindex="3">Surfing</INPUT>
        <INPUT name="hiking"
               type="checkbox"
               value="hiking" tabindex="4">Hiking</INPUT>
      </FIELDSET>
    </FORM>
  </BODY>
</HTML>
```

<OPTION>...</OPTION>

Usage:	Specifies choices in a SELECT element.
Syntax:	<OPTION *[attributes]*>*choices in a SELECT element*</OPTION>
Start/End Tag:	Required/Optional
Attributes:	selected="..." Specifies whether the option is selected.
	disabled="..." Disables control.

value="..." The value submitted if a control is submitted.

class=, id=, style=, title=, lang=, dir= Common attributes.

Intrinsics: onclick=, ondblclick=, onmousedown=, onmouseup=, onmouseover=, onmousemove=, onmouseout=, onkeypress=, onkeydown=, onkeyup= Common intrinsic events.

Empty: No

Introduced: HTML 2.0

Browsers: Netscape Navigator 1.0, 2.*x*, 3.*x*, 4.*x*; Microsoft Internet Explorer 2.0, 3.0, 4.0.

Example:
```
<HTML>
...
  <FORM action="..." method="post">
  ...
    <SELECT name="order" size="1">
        <OPTION value="one"> One potato
        <OPTION value="two"> Two potato
        <OPTION value="three"> Three potato
    </SELECT>
  ...
  </FORM>
...
</HTML>
```

<SELECT>...</SELECT>

Usage: Creates choices for the user to select.

Syntax: <SELECT *[attributes]*>choices</SELECT>

Start/End Tag: Required/Required

Attributes: name="..." The name of the element.

size="..." The width in number of rows.

multiple Allows multiple selections.

disabled="..." Disables the control.

tabindex="..." Sets the tabbing order between elements with a defined tabindex.

class=, id=, style=, title=, lang=, dir= Common attributes.

Intrinsics: onfocus="..." The event that occurs when the element receives focus.

onblur="..." The event that occurs when the element loses focus.

onselect="..." Intrinsic event that occurs when the control is selected.

onchange="..." Intrinsic event that occurs when the control is changed.

A

HTML 4.0 REFERENCE

```
onclick=, ondblclick=, onmousedown=, onmouseup=, onmouseover=,
onmousemove=, onmouseout=, onkeypress=, onkeydown=,
onkeyup=
```
Common intrinsic events.

Empty:	No
Introduced:	HTML 3.2
Browsers:	Netscape Navigator 1.0, 2.*x*, 3.*x*, 4.*x*; Microsoft Internet Explorer 3.0, 4.0.
Example:	

```
<HTML>
  ...
  <FORM action="..." method="post">
    ...
    <SELECT name="choice" size="2">
       <OPTION value="one">One fish
       <OPTION value="two">Two fish
       <OPTION value="red">Red fish
       <OPTION value="blue">Blue fish
    </SELECT>
    ...
  </FORM>
  ...
</HTML>
```

\<TEXTAREA>...\</TEXTAREA>

Usage:	Creates an area for user input with multiple lines.
Syntax:	`<TEXTAREA [attributes]>area for user input</TEXTAREA>`
Start/End Tag:	Required/Required
Attributes:	`name="..."` The name of the control.
	`rows="..."` The width in number of rows.
	`cols="..."` The height in number of columns.
	`disabled="..."` Disables the control.
	`readonly="..."` Sets the displayed text to read-only status.
	`tabindex="..."` Sets the tabbing order between elements with a defined `tabindex`.
	`class=, id=, style=, title=, lang=, dir=` Common attributes.
Intrinsics:	`onfocus="..."` The event that occurs when the element receives focus.
	`onblur="..."` The event that occurs when the element loses focus.
	`onselect="..."` Intrinsic event that occurs when the control is selected.
	`onchange="..."` Intrinsic event that occurs when the control is changed.

```
onclick=, ondblclick=, onmousedown=, onmouseup=, onmouseover=,
onmousemove=, onmouseout=, onkeypress=, onkeydown=,
onkeyup=   Common intrinsic events.
```

Empty:	No
Notes:	Text to be displayed is placed within the start and end tags.
Introduced:	HTML 3.2
Browsers:	Netscape Navigator 1.0, 2.*x*, 3.*x*, 4.*x*; Microsoft Internet Explorer 3.0, 4.0.
Example:	

```
<HTML>
  <HEAD>
    <TITLE>Form Demonstration</TITLE>
  </HEAD>
  <BODY>
    <FORM="http://www.example.com/sender" method="post">
      <TEXTAREA rows="30" cols="60">
        Text area preloaded content goes here
      </TEXTAREA>
  </BODY>
</HTML>
```

Tables: CAPTION, COL, COLGROUP, TABLE, TBODY, TD, TFOOT, TH, THEAD, TR

Tables are meant to display data in a tabular format. Before the introduction of HTML 4.0, tables were widely used for page layout purposes, but with the advent of style sheets, the W3C is discouraging that use.

<CAPTION>...</CAPTION>

Usage:	Displays a table caption.
Syntax:	`<CAPTION [attributes]>caption text</CAPTION>`
Start/End Tag:	Required/Required
Attributes:	`align="..."` Deprecated. Controls alignment (`left`, `center`, `right`, `top`, `bottom`).
	`class=, id=, style=, title=, lang=, dir=` Common attributes.
Intrinsics:	`onclick=, ondblclick=, onmousedown=, onmouseup=, onmouseover=, onmousemove=, onmouseout=, onkeypress=, onkeydown=, onkeyup=` Common intrinsic events.
Empty:	No
Notes:	Optional
Introduced:	HTML 3.2
Browsers:	Netscape Navigator 1.1, 2.0, 3.*x*, 4.*x*; Microsoft Internet Explorer 2.0, 3.0, 4.0.

Example:
```
<TABLE cellspacing="2" cellpadding="5">
<!-- Use IE valign= in addition to align= to achieve
    ➥the same --
-- effect on the page in spite of IE non-standard
    ➥syntax -->
<CAPTION align="bottom" valign="bottom">Holmes, 1997
    ➥</CAPTION>
```

<COL>

Usage: Groups columns within column groups in order to share attribute values.

Syntax: `<COL [attributes]>`

Start/End Tag: Required/Forbidden

Attributes: `span="..."` The number of columns the group contains.

`width="..."` The column width as a percentage, pixel value, or minimum value.

`align="..."` Horizontally aligns the contents of cells (**left**, center, right, justify, char).

`char="..."` Sets a character on which the column aligns. The default value is the decimal point character in the default language.

`charoff="..."` Offset to the first alignment character on a line.

`valign="..."` Vertically aligns the contents of a cell (top, middle, bottom, baseline).

`class=`, `id=`, `style=`, `title=`, `lang=`, `dir=` Common attributes.

Intrinsics: `onclick=`, `ondblclick=`, `onmousedown=`, `onmouseup=`, `onmouseover=`, `onmousemove=`, `onmouseout=`, `onkeypress=`, `onkeydown=`, `onkeyup=` Common intrinsic events.

Empty: Yes, closing tag is forbidden.

Introduced: HTML 4.0

Browsers: Netscape Navigator 3.*x*, 4.*x*; Microsoft Internet Explorer 2.0, 3.0, 4.0.

Example:
```
<TABLE cellspacing="2" cellpadding="5">
  <COLGROUP>
    <COL width="40">
    <COL width="0*">
    <COL width="2*">
  <COLGROUP align="center">
    <COL width="1*">
    <COL width="3*" align="char" char=":">
  <THEAD>
    <TR>
    ...
  </TABLE>
```

<COLGROUP>...[</COLGROUP>]

Usage:	Defines a column group.
Syntax:	`<COLGROUP [attributes]>columns group[</COLGROUP>]`
Start/End Tag:	Required/Optional
Attributes:	`span="..."` The number of columns in a group.

`width="..."` The width of the columns.

`align="..."` Horizontally aligns the contents of cells (**left**, center, right, justify, char).

`char="..."` Sets a character on which the column aligns. The default value is the decimal point character in the default language.

`charoff="..."` Offset to the first alignment character on a line.

`valign="..."` Vertically aligns the contents of a cell (top, middle, bottom, baseline).

`cellpadding="..."` Spacing in cells.

`class=, id=, style=, title=, lang=, dir=` Common attributes.

Intrinsics:	`onclick=, ondblclick=, onmousedown=, onmouseup=, onmouseover=, onmousemove=, onmouseout=, onkeypress=, onkeydown=, onkeyup=` Common intrinsic events.
Empty:	No
Introduced:	HTML 3.2
Browsers:	Netscape Navigator 3.x, 4.x; Microsoft Internet Explorer 2.0, 3.0, 4.0.
Example:	

```
<TABLE >
<COLGROUP span="2" width="200">
  <TR>
      <TH>Microsoft
          <TH>Corel
  <TR>
      <TD>MS Word 97
          <TD>WordPerfect 8
</TABLE>
```

A

HTML 4.0
REFERENCE

<TABLE>...</TABLE>

Usage	Defines a table.
Syntax	`[<TABLE [attributes]>]contents of table[</TABLE>]`
Start/End Tag	Required/Required
Attributes	`align="..."` Horizontally aligns the contents of cells (**left**, center, right, justify, char).

`bgcolor="..."` Deprecated. Sets the background color for the table.

border="..."   Width in pixels of the border surrounding the table.

cellpadding="..."   Defines the gutter surrounding each cell.

cellspacing="..."   Defines the gutter within each cell.

cols="..."   Defines the number of columns in the table.

frame="..."   Defines which sides of the table frame will be visible (**void**, above, below, hsides, lhs, rhs, vsides, box, border).

rules="..."   Defines which interior rules will be visible (**none**, groups, rows, cols, all).

width="..."   Defines the desired width of the table.

class=, id=, style=, title=, lang=, dir=   Common attributes.

Intrinsics:	onclick=, ondblclick=, onmousedown=, onmouseup=, onmouseover=, onmousemove=, onmouseout=, onkeypress=, onkeydown=, onkeyup= Common intrinsic events.
Empty	No
Introduced	HTML 3.2
Browsers	Netscape Navigator 3.*x*, 4.*x*; Microsoft Internet Explorer 2.0, 3.0, 4.0.

Example:

```
<TABLE>
  <TR>
     <TH>Microsoft
        <TH>Corel
  <TR>
     <TD>MS Word 97
        <TD>WordPerfect 8
</TABLE>
```

[<TBODY>]...[</TBODY>]

Usage:	Defines the table body.
Syntax:	[<TBODY *[attributes]*>]*contents of table body*[</TBODY>]
Start/End Tag:	Optional/Optional
Attributes:	align="..." Horizontally aligns the contents of cells (**left**, center, right, justify, char).

char="..."   Sets a character on which the column aligns. The default value is the decimal point character in the default language.

charoff="..."   Offset to the first alignment character on a line.

valign="..."   Vertically aligns the contents of cells (top, middle, bottom, baseline).

class=, id=, style=, title=, lang=, dir=   Common attributes.

Intrinsics: onclick=, ondblclick=, onmousedown=, onmouseup=, onmouseover=, onmousemove=, onmouseout=, onkeypress=, onkeydown=, onkeyup= Common intrinsic events.

Empty: No

Introduced: HTML 3.2

Browsers: Netscape Navigator 3.*x*, 4.*x*; Microsoft Internet Explorer 2.0, 3.0, 4.0.

Example:
```
<HTML>
<HEAD>
  <TITLE>Flange Manufacturing Statistics</TITLE>
</HEAD>
<BODY>
  ...
  <TABLE cellspacing="2" cellpadding="5">
    <CAPTION align="bottom" valign="bottom">Flange usage
          data from Holmes, 1997</CAPTION>
    <THEAD>
      <TR>
        <TH colspan="4" align="center">
          <B>Flange Market Share by Type</B>
      <TR>
        <TH>Closet
          <TH>Safety
            <TH>Stanchion
              <TH>Wheel
    <TBODY>
      <TR>
        <TD>21%
          <TD>48%
            <TD>12%
              <TD>73%
    <TFOOT>
      <TR>
        <TD colspan="4" align="center">
          <B>Note: These figures are entirely
          ➥fictional</B>
  </TABLE>
  ...
</BODY>
</HTML>
```

<TD>...[</TD>]

Usage: Defines a cell's contents.

Syntax: `<TD [attributes]>cell contents[</TD>]`

Start/End Tag: Required/Optional

Attributes: axis="..." Abbreviated name. The default value is the cell content.

axes="..." One or more axis names identifying row and/or column headers pertaining to the cell and separated by commas.

nowrap="..."   Deprecated. Turns off text wrapping in a cell.

bgcolor="..."   Deprecated. Sets the background color.

rowspan="..."   The number of rows spanned by a cell.

colspan="..."   The number of columns spanned by a cell.

align="..."   Horizontally aligns the contents of cells (**left**, center, right, justify, char).

char="..."   Sets a character on which the column aligns. The default value is the decimal point character in the default language.

charoff="..."   Offset to the first alignment character on a line.

valign="..."   Vertically aligns the contents of cells (top, **middle**, bottom, baseline).

class=, id=, style=, title=, lang=, dir=   Common attributes.

Intrinsics: onclick=, ondblclick=, onmousedown=, onmouseup=, onmouseover=, onmousemove=, onmouseout=, onkeypress=, onkeydown=, onkeyup=   Common intrinsic events.

Empty: No

Introduced: HTML 2.0

Browsers: Netscape Navigator 1.1, 2.0, 3.*x*, 4.*x*; Microsoft Internet Explorer 2.0, 3.0, 4.0.

Example:
```
<TR>
    <TD>MS Word 97
        <TD>FrameMaker
```

<TFOOT>...[</TFOOT>]

Usage: Defines the table footer.

Syntax: <TFOOT *[attributes]>contents of footer*[</TFOOT>]

Start/End Tag: Required/Optional

Attributes: align="..."   Horizontally aligns the contents of cells (**left**, center, right, justify, char).

char="..."   Sets a character on which the column aligns. The default value is the decimal point character in the default language.

charoff="..."   Offset to the first alignment character on a line.

valign="..."   Vertically aligns the contents of cells (top, middle, bottom, baseline).

class=, id=, style=, title=, lang=, dir=   Common attributes.

Intrinsics: onclick=, ondblclick=, onmousedown=, onmouseup=, onmouseover=, onmousemove=, onmouseout=, onkeypress=, onkeydown=, onkeyup=   Common intrinsic events.

Empty:	No
Introduced:	HTML 2.0
Browsers:	Netscape Navigator 2.*x*, 3.*x*, 4.*x*; Microsoft Internet Explorer 2.0, 3.0, 4.0.

Example:
```
<TFOOT>
  <TH>
    <TD colspan="4"
        align="center">Note: Data from Holmes, 1997
```

`<TH>...[</TH>]`

Usage:	Defines the table header data cells.
Syntax:	`<TH [attributes]>contents of table header[</TH>]`
Start/End Tag:	Required/Optional
Attributes:	`axis="..."` Abbreviated name. The default value is the cell content.
	`axes="..."` One or more axis names identifying row and/or column headers pertaining to the cell and separated by commas.
	`nowrap="..."` Deprecated. Turns off text wrapping in a cell.
	`bgcolor="..."` Deprecated. Sets the background color.
	`rowspan="..."` The number of rows spanned by a cell.
	`colspan="..."` The number of columns spanned by a cell.
	`align="..."` Horizontally aligns the contents of cells (`left`, **`center`**, `right`, `justify`, `char`).
	`char="..."` Sets a character on which the column aligns. The default value is the decimal point character in the default language.
	`charoff="..."` Offset to the first alignment character on a line.
	`valign="..."` Vertically aligns the contents of cells (`top`, **`middle`**, `bottom`, `baseline`).
	`class=`, `id=`, `style=`, `title=`, `lang=`, `dir=` Common attributes.
Intrinsics:	`onclick=`, `ondblclick=`, `onmousedown=`, `onmouseup=`, `onmouseover=`, `onmousemove=`, `onmouseout=`, `onkeypress=`, `onkeydown=`, `onkeyup=` Common intrinsic events.
Empty:	No
Notes:	Browsers should at least center the text content; many also boldface the header text.
Introduced:	HTML 2.0
Browsers:	Netscape Navigator 1.1, 2.0, 3.*x*, 4.*x*; Microsoft Internet Explorer 2.0, 3.0, 4.0.

A

HTML 4.0 REFERENCE

Example: ...
```
<TABLE>
  <TR>
      <TH>MS Word 97
          <TH>FrameMaker
  <TR>
      <TD>97
          <TD>102
</TABLE>
...
```

<THEAD>...[</THEAD>]

Usage: Defines the table header.

Syntax: `<THEAD [attributes]>contents of table header[</THEAD>]`

Start/End Tag: Required/Optional

Attributes: `align="..."`   Horizontally aligns the contents of cells (**left**, center, right, justify, char).

char="..."   Sets a character on which the column aligns. The default value is the decimal point character in the default language.

charoff="..."   Offset to the first alignment character on a line.

valign="..."   Vertically aligns the contents of cells (top, middle, bottom, baseline).

class=, id=, style=, title=, lang=, dir=   Common attributes.

Intrinsics: onclick=, ondblclick=, onmousedown=, onmouseup=, onmouseover=, onmousemove=, onmouseout=, onkeypress=, onkeydown=, onkeyup=   Common intrinsic events.

Empty: No

Introduced: HTML 2.0

Browsers: Netscape Navigator 3.x, 4.x; Microsoft Internet Explorer 2.0, 3.0, 4.0

Example:
```
<HTML>
  <HEAD>
    <TITLE>Tables Demonstration</TITLE>
  </HEAD>
  <BODY>
    <TABLE>
      <CAPTION>This is a caption</CAPTION>
    <THEAD>
      <TR>
          <TH>Column One
              <TH>Column Two
    <TBODY>
      <TR>
          <TD>Sample A
```

```
            <TD>Sample B
    </TABLE>
    </BODY>
</HTML>
```

<TR>...[</TR>]

Usage:	Defines a row of table cells.
Syntax:	`<TR [attributes]>contents of table row[</TR>]`
Start/End Tag:	Required/Optional
Attributes:	`align="..."` Horizontally aligns the contents of cells (**left**, center, right, justify, char).
	`char="..."` Sets a character on which the column aligns. The default value is the decimal point character in the default language.
	`charoff="..."` Offset to the first alignment character on a line.
	`valign="..."` Vertically aligns the contents of cells (top, middle, bottom, baseline).
	`bgcolor="..."` Deprecated. Sets the background color.
	`class=, id=, style=, title=, lang=, dir=` Common attributes.
Intrinsics:	`onclick=, ondblclick=, onmousedown=, onmouseup=, onmouseover=, onmousemove=, onmouseout=, onkeypress=, onkeydown=, onkeyup=` Common intrinsic events.
Empty:	No
Introduced:	HTML 2.0
Browsers:	Netscape Navigator 1.1, 2.*x*, 3.*x*, 4.*x*; Microsoft Internet Explorer 2.0, 3.0, 4.0.
Example:	

```
<HTML>
  <HEAD>
    <TITLE>File Formats</TITLE>
  </HEAD>
  <BODY>
    <TABLE>
      <TR>
          <TH>Graphics Formats
              <TH>Doc Formats
      <TR>
          <TD>.gif
              <TD>.doc
      <TR>
          <TD>.jpg
              <TD>.fm
    </TABLE>
  </BODY>
</HTML>
```

A

HTML 4.0
REFERENCE

Text-level Elements

Text-level elements flow like text and do not directly alter the layout or formatting of the document. Some of these tags affect the text's physical appearance; others are designed to mark text with lexical importance, meaning, or role. For example, both <I> and <EM> are usually rendered as italic type, but <EM> refers to emphasis, which might be available in languages that don't have any equivalent to italics.

Text Markup: B, BIG, I, S°, SMALL, STRIKE°, TT, U°

Text characteristics, such as the size, weight, and style, can be directly modified by using these elements, but the HTML 4.0 specification encourages you to use style sheets instead. However, these text characteristics will probably have a long life to support the needs of Web users who choose not to use "mainstream" browsers like Netscape Communicator 4.0 or Microsoft Internet Explorer 4.0. Access for the disabled, for example, is primarily by means of text-mode browsers, and many non-European languages are not well served by the browser market in general. All these people require another sort of browser, and it's thoughtful to be sensitive to their needs when designing almost any Web site.

<B>...</B>

Usage:	Bold text.
Syntax:	`<B [attributes]>bolded text</B>`
Start/End Tag:	Required/Required
Attributes:	`class=, id=, style=, title=, lang=, dir=` Common attributes.
Intrinsics:	`onclick=, ondblclick=, onmousedown=, onmouseup=, onmouseover=, onmousemove=, onmouseout=, onkeypress=, onkeydown=, onkeyup=` Common intrinsic events.
Empty:	No
Introduced:	HTML 1.0
Browsers:	Netscape Navigator 1.0, 2.0, 3.x, 4.x; Microsoft Internet Explorer 2.0, 3.0, 4.0.
Example:	`<P>The <B>virtual server name</B> should be the same name as your Web server.`

<BIG>...</BIG>

Usage:	Large text.
Syntax:	`<BIG [attributes]>large text</BIG>`
Start/End Tag:	Required/Required
Attributes:	`class=, id=, style=, title=, lang=, dir=` Common attributes.

Intrinsics:	`onclick=`, `ondblclick=`, `onmousedown=`, `onmouseup=`, `onmouseover=`, `onmousemove=`, `onmouseout=`, `onkeypress=`, `onkeydown=`, `onkeyup=` Common intrinsic events.
Empty:	No
Introduced:	HTML 3.2
Browsers:	Netscape Navigator 2.0, 3.*x*, 4.*x*; Microsoft Internet Explorer 2.0, 3.0, 4.0.
Example:	`<P><BIG>HEY</BIG>, come over here!`

`<I>...</I>`

Usage:	Italicized text.
Syntax:	`<I [attributes]>italicized text</I>`
Start/End Tag:	Required/Required
Attributes:	`class=`, `id=`, `style=`, `title=`, `lang=`, `dir=` Common attributes.
Intrinsics:	`onclick=`, `ondblclick=`, `onmousedown=`, `onmouseup=`, `onmouseover=`, `onmousemove=`, `onmouseout=`, `onkeypress=`, `onkeydown=`, `onkeyup=` Common intrinsic events.
Empty:	No
Introduced:	HTML 2.0
Browsers:	Netscape Navigator 1.0, 2.*x*, 3.*x*, 4.*x*; Microsoft Internet Explorer 2.0, 3.0, 4.0.
Example:	`<P><I>HTML 4 Unleashed, Professional Reference Edition</I> is available from Sams.net Publishing.`

`<S>...</S>` °

Usage:	Strikethrough text.
Syntax:	`<S [attributes]>strikethrough text</S>`
Start/End Tag:	Required/Required
Attributes:	`class=`, `id=`, `style=`, `title=`, `lang=`, `dir=` Common attributes.
Intrinsics:	`onclick=`, `ondblclick=`, `onmousedown=`, `onmouseup=`, `onmouseover=`, `onmousemove=`, `onmouseout=`, `onkeypress=`, `onkeydown=`, `onkeyup=` Common intrinsic events.
Empty:	No
Notes:	Deprecated. Use the `DEL` tag if possible.
Notes:	Same as the `STRIKE` element.
Introduced:	HTML 3.2
Browsers:	Netscape Navigator 3.0, 4.0; Microsoft Internet Explorer 3.0, 4.0.
Example:	`<P><S>The contract expires on October 7, 1997</S>`

A

HTML 4.0 REFERENCE

<SMALL>...</SMALL>

Usage:	Small text.
Syntax:	`<SMALL [attributes]>small text</SMALL>`
Start/End Tag:	Required/Required
Attributes:	`class=, id=, style=, title=, lang=, dir=` Common attributes.
Intrinsics:	`onclick=, ondblclick=, onmousedown=, onmouseup=, onmouseover=, onmousemove=, onmouseout=, onkeypress=, onkeydown=, onkeyup=` Common intrinsic events.
Empty:	No
Notes:	Same tasks now performed by style sheets.
Introduced:	HTML 3.2
Browsers:	Netscape Navigator 2.0, 3.0, 4.0; Microsoft Internet Explorer 2.0, 3.0, 4.0.
Example:	`<P><SMALL>This is fine print.</SMALL>`

<STRIKE>...</STRIKE>°

Usage:	Strikethrough text.
Syntax:	`<STRIKE [attributes]>strikethrough text</STRIKE>`
Start/End Tag:	Required/Required
Attributes:	`class=, id=, style=, title=, lang=, dir=` Common attributes.
Intrinsics:	`onclick=, ondblclick=, onmousedown=, onmouseup=, onmouseover=, onmousemove=, onmouseout=, onkeypress=, onkeydown=, onkeyup=` Common intrinsic events.
Empty:	No
Notes:	Deprecated. Use the DEL tag if possible.
Introduced:	HTML 3.2
Browsers:	Netscape Navigator 3.0, 4.0; Microsoft Internet Explorer 2.0, 3.0, 4.0.
Example:	`<P><STRIKE>The contract expires on October 7, 1997</STRIKE>`

<TT>...</TT>

Usage:	Teletype (monospaced) text.
Syntax:	`<TT [attributes]>teletype text</TT>`
Start/End Tag:	Required/Required
Attributes:	`class=, id=, style=, title=, lang=, dir=` Common attributes.

Intrinsics:	onclick=, ondblclick=, onmousedown=, onmouseup=, onmouseover=, onmousemove=, onmouseout=, onkeypress=, onkeydown=, onkeyup= Common intrinsic events.
Empty:	No
Notes:	Often thought of nowadays as "typewriter text."
Introduced:	HTML 3.2
Browsers:	Netscape Navigator 1.0, 2.0, 3.*x*, 4.*x*; Microsoft Internet Explorer 2.0, 3.0, 4.0.
Example:	`<P>The <TT>teletype element</TT> can be used to represent` `➥many things like code, directory listings, and other` `➥elements that need to stand out.`

`<U>...</U>` °

Usage:	Underlined text.
Syntax:	`<U [attributes]>underlined text</U>`
Start/End Tag:	Required/Required
Attributes:	class=, id=, style=, title=, lang=, dir= Common attributes.
Intrinsics:	onclick=, ondblclick=, onmousedown=, onmouseup=, onmouseover=, onmousemove=, onmouseout=, onkeypress=, onkeydown=, onkeyup= Common intrinsic events.
Empty:	No
Notes:	Deprecated.
Introduced:	HTML 3.2
Browsers:	Netscape Navigator 3.0, 4.0; Microsoft Internet Explorer 2.0, 3.0, 4.0.
Example:	`<P><U>HTML 4 Unleashed, Professional Reference Edition</U>` `is available from Sams.net Publishing.`

Phrase Markup: ACRONYM, ADDRESS*, BLOCKQUOTE*, CITE, CODE, DEL, DFN, EM, INS, KBD, PRE*, SAMP, STRONG, VAR

Phrase markup focuses on the lexical meaning of a phrase or word, identifying it by its place in the structure of the sentence, instead of by a physical font characteristic. This identification method makes them easy to search for using automated methods and simplifies creating foreign language equivalents.

`<ACRONYM...</ACRONYMN>`

Usage:	Used to define acronyms.
Syntax:	`<ACRONYM [attributes]>acronym text</ACRONYM>`

Start/End Tag:	Required/Required
Attributes:	`class=`, `id=`, `style=`, `title=`, `lang=`, `dir=` Common attributes.
Intrinsics:	`onclick=`, `ondblclick=`, `onmousedown=`, `onmouseup=`, `onmouseover=`, `onmousemove=`, `onmouseout=`, `onkeypress=`, `onkeydown=`, `onkeyup=` Common intrinsic events.
Empty:	No
Notes:	Use the `title` attribute to expand the acronym. This tag is particularly important for audio browsers because it tells the browser to spell out the acronym instead of trying to pronounce it. "Eff Bee Eye" is easier to hear and understand than "phbee."
Introduced:	HTML 4.0
Browsers:	Netscape Navigator 4.0; Microsoft Internet Explorer 3.0.
Example:	The `<ACRONYM title="Federal Bureau of Investigation">FBI ➥</ACRONYM>`

`<ADDRESS>...</ADDRESS>*`

Notes:	Operates as a block-level element; discussed in the "Block-level Elements" section as a basic block element.

`<BLOCKQUOTE>...</BLOCKQUOTE>*`

Notes:	Operates as a block-level element; discussed in the "Block-level Elements" section as a basic block element.

`<CITE>...</CITE>`

Usage:	Cites a reference.
Syntax:	`<CITE [attributes]>contents of the citation</CITE>`
Start/End Tag:	Required/Required
Attributes:	`class=`, `id=`, `style=`, `title=`, `lang=`, `dir=` Common attributes.
Intrinsics:	`onclick=`, `ondblclick=`, `onmousedown=`, `onmouseup=`, `onmouseover=`, `onmousemove=`, `onmouseout=`, `onkeypress=`, `onkeydown=`, `onkeyup=` Common intrinsic events.
Empty:	No
Introduced:	HTML 2.0
Browsers:	Netscape Navigator 1.0, 2.0, 3.*x*, 4.*x*; Microsoft Internet Explorer 2.0, 3.0, 4.0.

Example:	`<P>`
	`She drinks the honey of her vision.  <CITE>(Mira Bai, c.`
	`➥1530)</CITE>`

<CODE>...</CODE>

Usage:	Identifies a line or section of code for display.
Syntax:	`<CODE [attributes]>text in code format</CODE>`
Start/End Tag:	Required/Required
Attributes:	`class=`, `id=`, `style=`, `title=`, `lang=`, `dir=` Common attributes.
Intrinsics:	`onclick=`, `ondblclick=`, `onmousedown=`, `onmouseup=`, `onmouseover=`, `onmousemove=`, `onmouseout=`, `onkeypress=`, `onkeydown=`, `onkeyup=` Common intrinsic events.
Empty:	No
Introduced:	HTML 2.0
Browsers:	Netscape Navigator 1.0, 2.0, 3.*x*, 4.*x*; Microsoft Internet Explorer 2.0, 3.0, 4.0.
Example:	`<P> You need to save your files in the <CODE>c:\examples` `➥</CODE> directory.`

<DEL>...</DEL>

Usage:	Shows text as having been deleted from the document since the last change.
Syntax:	`<DEL [attributes]>deleted text</DEL>`
Start/End Tag:	Required/Required
Attributes:	`class=`, `id=`, `style=`, `title=`, `lang=`, `dir=` Common attributes.
Intrinsics:	`onclick=`, `ondblclick=`, `onmousedown=`, `onmouseup=`, `onmouseover=`, `onmousemove=`, `onmouseout=`, `onkeypress=`, `onkeydown=`, `onkeyup=` Common intrinsic events.
	`cite="..."` The URL of the source document.
	`datetime="..."` Indicates the date and time of the change.
Empty:	No
Notes:	New element in HTML 4.0.
Introduced:	HTML 4.0
Browsers:	Netscape Navigator 4.0; Microsoft Internet Explorer 4.0.
Example:	

```
<HTML>
  <BODY>
    <P>Type in<DEL cite="revision.html"
          datetime="1997-10-31T23:15:30-08:00">Enter</DEL>
          <KBD>red0202</KBD>
      as your password.
  </BODY>
</HTML>
```

<DFN>...</DFN>

Usage:	Defines an enclosed term.
Syntax:	`<DFN [attributes]>contents of the definition</DFN>`
Start/End Tag:	Required/Required
Attributes:	`class=, id=, style=, title=, lang=, dir=` Common attributes.
Intrinsics:	`onclick=, ondblclick=, onmousedown=, onmouseup=, onmouseover=, onmousemove=, onmouseout=, onkeypress=, onkeydown=, onkeyup=` Common intrinsic events.
Empty:	No
Introduced:	HTML 2.0
Browsers:	Netscape Navigator 3.*x*, 4.*x*; Microsoft Internet Explorer 2.0, 3.0, 4.0.
Example:	`<DFN>Security guard: An employee with responsibility` `➥for controlling access to an entryway or area</DFN>`

<EM>...</EM>

Usage:	Emphasized text.
Syntax:	`<EM [attributes]>emphasized text</EM>`
Start/End Tag:	Required/Required
Attributes:	`class=, id=, style=, title=, lang=, dir=` Common attributes.
Intrinsics:	`onclick=, ondblclick=, onmousedown=, onmouseup=, onmouseover=, onmousemove=, onmouseout=, onkeypress=, onkeydown=, onkeyup=` Common intrinsic events.
Empty:	No
Introduced:	HTML 3.2
Browsers:	Netscape Navigator 1.0, 2.0, 3.*x*, 4.*x*; Microsoft Internet Explorer 2.0, 3.0, 4.0.
Example:	`<P>This word is <EM>emphasized!</EM>`

<INS>...</INS>

Usage:	Shows text as having been inserted in the document since the last change.
Syntax:	`<INS [attributes]>inserted text</INS>`
Start/End Tag:	Required/Required
Attributes:	`cite="..."` The URL of the source document.
	`datetime="..."` Indicates the date and time of the change.
	`class=, id=, style=, title=, lang=, dir=` Common attributes.

Intrinsics:	onclick=, ondblclick=, onmousedown=, onmouseup=, onmouseover=, onmousemove=, onmouseout=, onkeypress=, onkeydown=, onkeyup= Common intrinsic events.
Empty:	No
Notes:	New element in HTML 4.0.
Introduced:	HTML 4.0
Browsers:	Netscape Navigator 4.0; Microsoft Internet Explorer 4.0.
Example:	`<INS cite="revision.html"` `    datetime="1997-10-31T23:15:30-08:00">Enter</INS>` `➥<KBD>red0202</KBD> as your password.`

<KBD>...</KBD>

Usage:	Indicates text a user would type.
Syntax:	`<KBD [attributes]>text to be typed</KBD>`
Start/End Tag:	Required/Required
Attributes:	class=, id=, style=, title=, lang=, dir= Common attributes.
Intrinsics:	onclick=, ondblclick=, onmousedown=, onmouseup=, onmouseover=, onmousemove=, onmouseout=, onkeypress=, onkeydown=, onkeyup= Common intrinsic events.
Empty:	No
Introduced:	HTML 2.0
Browsers:	Netscape Navigator 1.0, 2.0, 3.*x*, 4.*x*; Microsoft Internet Explorer 2.0, 3.0, 4.0.
Example:	`<P>Type in <KBD>red0202</KBD> as your password.`

<PRE>...</PRE>*

Notes:	Operates as a block-level element; discussed in the "Block-level Elements" section as a basic block element.

<SAMP>...</SAMP>

Usage:	Identifies sample output, as from a computer screen or printer.
Syntax:	`<SAMP [attributes]>sample output</SAMP>`
Start/End Tag:	Required/Required
Attributes:	class=, id=, style=, title=, lang=, dir= Common attributes.
Intrinsics:	onclick=, ondblclick=, onmousedown=, onmouseup=, onmouseover=, onmousemove=, onmouseout=, onkeypress=, onkeydown=, onkeyup= Common intrinsic events.
Empty:	No

Introduced:	HTML 3.2
Browsers:	Netscape Navigator 1.0, 2.0, 3.*x*, 4.*x*; Microsoft Internet Explorer 2.0, 3.0, 4.0.

Example:

```
<P>The ticket printer will eject the completed sales
    receipt containing the date and amount of
  ➥purchase:<BR><BR>
<SAMP>Oct 31, 1997<BR>
    Purchase Amount: $32.56<BR>
    Thank you for shopping at XYZ Market
</SAMP>
```

`<STRONG>...</STRONG>`

Usage:	Stronger emphasis.
Syntax:	`<STRONG [attributes]>text with strong emphasis</STRONG>`
Start/End Tag:	Required/Required
Attributes:	`class=, id=, style=, title=, lang=, dir=` Common attributes.
Intrinsics:	`onclick=, ondblclick=, onmousedown=, onmouseup=, onmouseover=, onmousemove=, onmouseout=, onkeypress=, onkeydown=, onkeyup=` Common intrinsic events.
Empty:	No
Introduced:	HTML 2.0
Browsers:	Netscape Navigator 1.0, 2.0, 3.*x*, 4.*x*; Microsoft Internet Explorer 2.0, 3.0, 4.0.

Example:

```
...
<P><STRONG>Warning:</STRONG>  Close cover before striking
match.
...
```

`<VAR>...</VAR>`

Usage:	A variable.
Syntax:	`<VAR [attributes]>variable</VAR>`
Start/End Tag:	Required/Required
Attributes:	`class=, id=, style=, title=, lang=, dir=` Common attributes.
Intrinsics:	`onclick=, ondblclick=, onmousedown=, onmouseup=, onmouseover=, onmousemove=, onmouseout=, onkeypress=, onkeydown=, onkeyup=` Common intrinsic events.
Empty:	No
Introduced:	HTML 2.0
Browsers:	Netscape Navigator, 2.*x*, 3.*x*, 4.*x*; Microsoft Internet Explorer 2.*x*, 3.*x*, 4.*x*.

Example: ...
                <P>The <VAR>virtual server name</VAR> should be the
                ↪same name as your Web server.
                ...

Special Markup: A, APPLET°, BASEFONT°, BDO, BR, FONT°, IFRAME*, IMG, NOSCRIPT*, OBJECT, Q, SCRIPT*, SPAN, SUB, SUP

`<A>...</A>`

Usage:	Used to define links and anchors.
Syntax:	`<A [attributes]>text of anchor</A>`
Start/End Tag:	Required/Required
Attributes:	`charset="..."` Character encoding of the resource. The default value is `ISO-8859-1`.
	`name="..."` Defines an anchor.
	`href="..."` The URL of the linked resource.
	`target="..."` Determines where the resource will be displayed (user-defined name, `_blank`, `_parent`, `_self`, `_top`).
	`rel="..."` Forward link types.
	`rev="..."` Reverse link types.
	`accesskey="..."` Assigns a hotkey to this element.
	`shape="..."` Allows you to define client-side image maps by using defined shapes (`default`, `rect`, `circle`, `poly`).
	`coords="..."` Sets the size of the shape using pixel or percentage lengths.
	`tabindex="..."` Sets the tabbing order between elements with a defined `tabindex`.
	`class=`, `id=`, `style=`, `title=`, `lang=`, `dir=` Common attributes.
Intrinsics:	`onclick=`, `ondblclick=`, `onmousedown=`, `onmouseup=`, `onmouseover=`, `onmousemove=`, `onmouseout=`, `onkeypress=`, `onkeydown=`, `onkeyup=` Common intrinsic events.
Empty:	No
Introduced:	HTML 1.0
Browsers:	Netscape Navigator 1.0, 1.1, 2.x, 3.x, 4.x; Microsoft Internet Explorer 2.0, 3.0, 4.0.

Example:
```
<HTML>
  <HEAD>
    <TITLE>Link Example</TITLE>
  </HEAD>
  <BODY>
    <P> Please reference: <A href="example.htm">Example</A>
  </BODY>
</HTML>
```

`<APPLET>...</APPLET>` °

Usage: Includes a Java applet.

Syntax: `<APPLET [attributes]>contents of the applet</APPLET>`

Start/End Tag: Required/Required

Attributes: `codebase="..."`   The URL base for the applet.

                `archive="..."`   Identifies the resources to be preloaded.

                `code="..."`   The applet class file.

                `object="..."`   The serialized applet file.

                `alt="..."`   Displays text while loading.

                `name="..."`   The name of the applet.

                `width="..."`   The height of the displayed applet.

                `height="..."`   The width of the displayed applet.

                `align="..."`   Deprecated. Controls alignment (**left**, center, right, justify).

                `hspace="..."`   The horizontal space separating the image from other content.

                `vspace="..."`   The vertical space separating the image from other content.

Empty: No

Notes: Applet is deprecated in favor of the OBJECT element. It was originally one of the proprietary Netscape extensions introduced to support embedding Java applets in HTML pages.

Introduced: HTML 3.2

Browsers: Netscape Navigator 2.0, 3.*x*, 4.*x*; Microsoft Internet Explorer 2.0, 3.0, 4.0.

Example: `<APPLET code="name.class" width="pixels" height="pixels"></APPLET>`

`<BASEFONT>` °

Usage: Sets the base font size.

Syntax: `<BASEFONT [attributes]>`

Start/End Tag:	Required/Forbidden
Attributes:	`size="..."` The font size (1 through 7, or relative, such as +3).
	`color="..."` The font color.
	`face="..."` The font type.
Empty:	Yes, closing tag is forbidden.
Notes:	Deprecated in favor of style sheets and because use of this element tends to cause huge problems for users who have non-European fonts loaded or disabled users who depend on certain font characteristics.
Introduced:	HTML 3.2
Browsers:	Netscape Navigator 1.0, 2.0, 3.*x*, 4.*x*; Microsoft Internet Explorer 2.0, 3.0, 4.0.
Example:	`<P><BASEFONT size ="2">  The <B>virtual server name</B>` `➥should be the same name as your Web server.`

`<BDO>...</BDO>`

Usage:	The `BDO` (bidirectional override) element is used to selectively alter the default text direction for inline text.
Syntax:	`<BDO [attributes]>content of BDO</BDO>`
Start/End Tag:	Required/Required
Attributes:	`lang="..."` The language of the document.
	`dir="..."` The text direction (`ltr`, `rtl`).
Empty:	No
Introduced:	HTML 4.0
Browsers:	Currently none.
Notes:	The `dir` attribute is mandatory. The `BDO` element is proposed as part of the enhancement to deal with the internationalization of HTML. It's needed for languages like Arabic and Hebrew, which are written from right to left but may have inline elements, such as included English words or numbers, which should read from left to right. This tag can also be used to include individual words in any language with a different writing order or to create a special effect.
Example:	`... <BDO dir="rtl">.rorrim a ni gnikool ton er'uoy ,siht daer` `➥nac uoy fI</BDO> ...`

`<BR>`

Usage:	Forces a line break.
Syntax:	`<BR [attributes]>`

Start/End Tag:	Required/Forbidden
Attributes:	clear="..." Sets the location where next line begins after a floating object (none, **left**, right, all).
	class=, id=, style=, title=, lang=, dir= Common attributes.
Intrinsics:	onclick=, ondblclick=, onmousedown=, onmouseup=, onmouseover=, onmousemove=, onmouseout=, onkeypress=, onkeydown=, onkeyup= Common intrinsic events.
Empty:	Yes, closing tag is forbidden.
Introduced:	HTML 1.0
Browsers:	Netscape Navigator 1.0, 2.0, 3.x, 4.x; Microsoft Internet Explorer 2.0, 3.0, 4.0.
Example:	...

```
<P>The &lt;BR&gt; tag is used to make a line break
   between each example.<BR>
   The &lt;BR&gt; tag is used to make a line break
   between each example.<BR>
   The &lt;BR&gt; tag is escaped in this code fragment
   so that it displays correctly on the page
   as well as being used to control line breaks.
   This technique is often valuable when creating
   tutorial pages that must display HTML without
   rendering it.
...
```

<FONT>...</FONT> °

Usage:	Changes the font size and color.
Syntax:	<FONT [attributes]>text</FONT>
Start/End Tag:	Required/Required
Attributes:	size="..." The font size (1 through 7, or relative, such as +3).
	color="..." The font color.
	face="..." The font type.
Empty	No
Notes:	Deprecated in favor of style sheets and because use of this element tends to cause huge problems for users who have non-European fonts loaded or disabled users who depend on certain font characteristics.
Introduced:	HTML 3.2
Browsers:	Netscape Navigator 1.1, 2.0, 3.x, 4.x; Microsoft Internet Explorer 2.0, 3.0, 4.0.
Example:	<P><FONT face="Arial">This is an example of using the deprecated FONT element to designate Arial type</FONT>

`<IFRAME>...</IFRAME>*`

Notes: Operates as an inline element within the body of the document but discussed for convenience in the "Structural (Housekeeping) Elements" section as a frames element, where it's actually not permitted.

`<IMG>`

Usage: Includes an image in the document.

Syntax: `<IMG [attributes]>`

Start/End Tag: Required/Forbidden

Attributes: `src="..."`   The URL of the image.

`alt="..."`   Alternative text to display.

`align="..."`   Deprecated. Controls alignment (**bottom**, middle, top, left, right).

`height="..."`   The height of the image.

`width="..."`   The width of the image.

`border="..."`   Border width.

`hspace="..."`   The horizontal space separating the image from other content.

`vspace="..."`   The vertical space separating the image from other content.

`usemap="..."`   The URL to a client-side image map.

`ismap`   Identifies a server-side image map.

`class=`, `id=`, `style=`, `title=`, `lang=`, `dir=`   Common attributes.

Intrinsics: `onclick=`, `ondblclick=`, `onmousedown=`, `onmouseup=`, `onmouseover=`, `onmousemove=`, `onmouseout=`, `onkeypress=`, `onkeydown=`, `onkeyup=`   Common intrinsic events.

Empty: Yes, closing tag is forbidden.

Introduced: HTML 2.0

Browsers: Netscape Navigator 1.0, 2.*x*, 3.*x*, 4.*x*; Microsoft Internet Explorer 2.0, 3.0, 4.0.

Example:
```
<HTML>
  <HEAD>
    <TITLE>Picture</TITLE>
  </HEAD>
  <BODY>
    <IMG src="picture1.jpg" alt="[Self-portrait]">
  </BODY>
</HTML>
```

A

HTML 4.0 REFERENCE

<NOSCRIPT>...</NOSCRIPT>*

Notes:
Operates as an inline element within the body of the document, but discussed for convenience in the "Structural Housekeeping Elements" section as a head element, where it's actually not permitted.

<OBJECT>...</OBJECT>

Usage:
Includes an object.

Syntax:
`<OBJECT [attributes]>contents of the object</OBJECT>`

Start/End Tag:
Required/Required

Attributes:
`declare`   A flag that declares but doesn't create an object.

`classid="..."`   The URL of the object's location.

`codebase="..."`   The URL for resolving URLs specified by other attributes.

`data="..."`   The URL to the object's data.

`type="..."`   The Internet content type for data.

`codetype="..."`   The Internet content type for the code.

`standby="..."`   Shows message while loading.

`align="..."`   Deprecated. Controls alignment (`texttop`, `middle`, `textmiddle`, `baseline`, `textbottom`, `left`, `center`, `right`, `justify`).

`height="..."`   The height of the object.

`width="..."`   The width of the object.

`border="..."`   Displays the border around an object.

`hspace="..."`   The space between the sides of the object and other page content.

`vspace="..."`   The space between the top and bottom of the object and other page content.

`usemap="..."`   The URL to an image map.

`shapes=`   Allows you to define areas to search for hyperlinks if the object is an image.

`name="..."`   The URL to submit as part of a form.

`tabindex="..."`   Sets the tabbing order between elements with a defined `tabindex`.

`class=`, `id=`, `style=`, `title=`, `lang=`, `dir=`   Common attributes.

Intrinsics:
`onclick=`, `ondblclick=`, `onmousedown=`, `onmouseup=`, `onmouseover=`, `onmousemove=`, `onmouseout=`, `onkeypress=`, `onkeydown=`, `onkeyup=`   Common intrinsic events.

Empty:
No

Notes:	This element can be nested to any level, with the outermost level that the browser is capable of stopping recursion. The innermost level should be plain text to allow the widest possible number of browsers to provide meaningful content.
Introduced:	HTML 4.0
Browsers:	Netscape Navigator 3.*x*, 4.*x*; Microsoft Internet Explorer 2.0, 3.0, 4.0.
Example:	

```
...
<OBJECT title="Barking Dog"
  classid="Barking.py">
  <OBJECT data="Barking.mpeg" type="application/mpeg">
    <OBJECT src="Barking.gif">
      [Barking Dog Logo]
    </OBJECT>
  </OBJECT>
</OBJECT>
...
```

\<PARAM>

Usage:	Initializes an object.
Syntax:	`<PARAM [attributes]>`
Start/End Tag:	Required/Forbidden
Attributes:	`name="..."` Defines the parameter name.
	`value="..."` The value of the object parameter.
	`valuetype="..."` Defines the value type (**data**, ref, object).
	`type="..."` The Internet media type.
Empty:	Yes, closing tag is forbidden.
Notes:	Must precede other object content. Used with `<OBJECT>` and deprecated `<APPLET>` tags.
Introduced:	HTML 3.2
Browsers:	Netscape Navigator 1.0, 2.0, 3.*x*, 4.*x*; Microsoft Internet Explorer 2.0, 3.0, 4.0.
Example:	

```
<HTML>
  <HEAD>
  </HEAD>
  <BODY>
    ...
    <APPLET code="tickertape.class" width="400" height="40">
      <PARAM name="message" value="This is a test message.">
      <PARAM name="speed" value="10">
      <PARAM name="textcolor" value="120,120,0">
    </APPLET>
    ...
  </BODY>
</HTML>
```

A

**HTML 4.0
REFERENCE**

<Q>...</Q>

Usage:	Used to display short quotations that don't require paragraph breaks.
Syntax:	`<Q [attributes]>short quotation</Q>`
Start/End Tag:	Required/Required
Attributes:	`cite="..."` The URL of the quoted text.
	`class=, id=, style=, title=, lang=, dir=` Common attributes.
Intrinsics:	`onclick=, ondblclick=, onmousedown=, onmouseup=, onmouseover=, onmousemove=, onmouseout=, onkeypress=, onkeydown=, onkeyup=` Common intrinsic events.
Empty:	No
Notes:	Some browsers insert language-appropriate quotation marks around the inline quote. New element in HTML 4.0.
Introduced:	HTML 4.0
Browsers:	Netscape Navigator 4.0; Microsoft Internet Explorer 4.0.
Example:	`<Q cite="http://www.enheduanna.com">O lady of all truths... ➥</Q>`

<SCRIPT>...</SCRIPT>*

Notes:	Operates as an inline element within the body of the document but discussed in the "Structural (Housekeeping) Elements" section as a head element, where it's also permitted.

<SPAN>...</SPAN>

Usage:	Organizes the document by defining an inline span of text.
Syntax:	`<SPAN [attributes]>defined span of text</SPAN>`
Start/End Tag:	Required/Required
Attributes:	`class=, id=, style=, title=, lang=, dir=` Common attributes.
Intrinsics:	`onclick=, ondblclick=, onmousedown=, onmouseup=, onmouseover=, onmousemove=, onmouseout=, onkeypress=, onkeydown=, onkeyup=` Common intrinsic events.
Empty:	No
Notes:	Equivalent to `<DIV>` but operates as an inline text element instead of forcing a break.
Introduced:	HTML 3.2
Browsers:	Netscape Navigator 3.0, 4.x; Microsoft Internet Explorer 2.0, 3.0, 4.0.

Example:
```
<P>
<DIV id="Books-HTML" class="Books">
  Book Title: <SPAN class="Books-Title">HTML 4 Unleashed,
  Professional Reference Edition</SPAN>
  ISBN: <SPAN class="Books-ISBN">1-57521-380-X</SPAN>
</DIV>
```

_{...}

Usage:	Creates subscript.
Syntax:	`<SUB [attributes]>text in subscript</SUB>`
Start/End Tag:	Required/Required
Attributes:	`class=, id=, style=, title=, lang=, dir=` Common attributes.
Intrinsics:	`onclick=, ondblclick=, onmousedown=, onmouseup=, onmouseover=, onmousemove=, onmouseout=, onkeypress=, onkeydown=, onkeyup=` Common intrinsic events.
Empty:	No
Notes:	Used in scientific notations and some languages.
Introduced:	HTML 3.2
Browsers:	Netscape Navigator 2.0, 3.*x*, 4.*x*; Microsoft Internet Explorer 2.0, 3.0, 4.0.
Example:	`<P>The chemical formula for water is: H<SUB>2</SUB>O`

^{...}

Usage:	Creates superscript.
Syntax:	`<SUP [attributes]>text in superscript</SUP>`
Start/End Tag:	Required/Required
Attributes:	`class=, id=, style=, title=, lang=, dir=` Common attributes.
Intrinsics:	`onclick=, ondblclick=, onmousedown=, onmouseup=, onmouseover=, onmousemove=, onmouseout=, onkeypress=, onkeydown=, onkeyup=` Common intrinsic events.
Empty:	No
Notes:	Used for superscript abbreviations, certain languages, and exponentiation.
Introduced:	HTML 3.2
Browsers:	Netscape Navigator 2.0, 3.*x*, 4.*x*; Microsoft Internet Explorer 2.*x*, 3.*x*, 4.*x*.
Example:	`<P>M<SUP>lle</SUP> Robards and W<SUP>m</SUP> Shakespeare met on 3<SUP>rd</SUP> Street` `<P>This is a simple equation: 3<SUP>3</SUP> = 27`

A

HTML 4.0
REFERENCE

Client-side Image Maps: AREA, MAP

<AREA>

Usage:	The AREA element is used to define links and anchors.
Syntax:	`<AREA [attributes]>`
Start/End Tag:	Required/Forbidden
Attributes:	`shape="..."` Allows you to define client-side image maps by using defined shapes (`default`, `rect`, `circle`, `poly`).
	`coords="..."` Sets the size of the shape using pixel or percentage lengths.
	`href="..."` The URL of the linked resource.
	`target="..."` Determines where the resource will be displayed (user-defined name, `_blank`, `_parent`, `_self`, `_top`).
	`nohref="..."` Indicates that the region has no action.
	`alt="..."` Displays alternative text.
	`tabindex="..."` Sets the tabbing order between elements with a defined `tabindex`.
Empty:	Yes, closing tag is forbidden.
Notes:	Only valid within a MAP container.
Introduced:	HTML 3.2
Browsers:	Netscape Navigator 1.0, 2.0, 3.x, 4.x; Microsoft Internet Explorer 2.0, 3.0, 4.0.
Example:	

```
<HTML>
<MAP name="page1">
  <AREA shape="circle" coords="70,70,35">
  <AREA shape="rectangle" coords="65,65,80,80">
</MAP>
```

<MAP>...</MAP>

Usage:	When used with the AREA element, creates a client-side image map.
Syntax:	`<MAP [attributes]>contents of image map</MAP>`
Start/End Tag:	Required/Required
Attributes:	`name="..."` The name of the image map to be created.
	`class=`, `id=`, `style=`, `title=` Common attributes.
Empty:	No
Introduced:	HTML 3.2
Browsers:	Netscape Navigator 1.0, 2.x, 3.x, 4.x; Microsoft Internet Explorer 2.0, 3.0, 4.0.

Example:

```
<HTML>
<MAP name="page1">
<AREA shape="circle" coords=",70,70,35">
<AREA shape="rectangle" coords="65,65,80,80">
</MAP>
```

Form Control Text: BUTTON*, INPUT*, LABEL*, SELECT*, TEXTAREA*

<BUTTON>...</BUTTON>*

Notes: Operates as an inline element within the body of a form; discussed in the "Block-level Elements" section as a form element, where it is permitted.

<INPUT>...</INPUT>*

Notes: Operates as an inline element within the body of a form; discussed in the "Block-level Elements" section as a form element, where it is permitted.

<LABEL>...</LABEL>*

Notes: Operates as an inline element within the body of a form; discussed in the "Block-level Elements" section as a form element, where it is permitted.

<SELECT>...</SELECT>*

Notes: Operates as an inline element within the body of a form; discussed in the "Block-level Elements" section as a form element, where it is permitted.

<TEXTAREA>...</TEXTAREA>*

Notes: Operates as an inline element within the body of a form; discussed in the "Block-level Elements" section as a form element, where it is permitted.

Common Attributes and Intrinsic Events

Four core attributes apply to many elements:

- ■ `id="..."`   A unique global identifier that allows the element to be individually acted on by a style sheet or other process.
- ■ `class="..."`   A list of classes, non-unique identifiers separated by spaces, which allows the element to be acted on as a group by a style sheet or other process.
- ■ `style="..."`   Inline style information.

■ `title="..."`   Provides more information for a specific element, as opposed to the `TITLE` element, which creates a title for the entire Web page.

Two attributes for internationalization apply to many elements:

■ `lang="..."`   The ISO language identifier.

■ `dir="..."`   The text direction (**ltr**, `rtl`).

The following intrinsic events apply to many elements:

■ `onclick="..."`   A pointing device (such as a mouse) was single-clicked.

■ `ondblclick="..."`   A pointing device (such as a mouse) was double-clicked.

■ `onmousedown="..."`   A mouse button was clicked and held down.

■ `onmouseup="..."`   A mouse button that was clicked and held down was released.

■ `onmouseover="..."`   A mouse moved the cursor over an object.

■ `onmousemove="..."`   The mouse was moved.

■ `onmouseout="..."`   A mouse moved the cursor off an object.

■ `onkeypress="..."`   A key was pressed and released.

■ `onkeydown="..."`   A key was pressed and held down.

■ `onkeyup="..."`   A key that was pressed has been released.

APPENDIX B

Cross-Browser Reference Table

by Lee Anne Phillips

The World Wide Web is about communication; out of a bewildering cacophony of differing standards, browser capabilities, languages, and design styles, we're trying to form information and entertainment channels between people and machines, between vendors and their customers, between information providers and their users, between the widely scattered members of a distributed community, and between machines and processes on the Web and their human users. This appendix aims to make that job a little easier by pointing out tags and attributes that are widely supported, as well as those with only marginal utility.

Why a Cross-Browser Table Is Important

Why should you care about HTML standards and which tag works where? Isn't the coming XML (Extensible Markup Language) standard going to make all this stuff irrelevant and obsolete anyway?

In a word, no. XML is going to be a long time coming, and even longer before it becomes a standard on the Web. There are literally millions of syntactically incorrect Web pages out there—most of them, in fact. XML depends on being able to actually parse a DTD to figure out how a document is structured, a rather quaint conceit to anyone who has spent much time actually looking at other people's code, as opposed to the pure perfection that one generates herself, of course.

Fixing all that existing HTML is a project that makes Year 2000 look like a weekend outing. Every browser manufacturer has had to deal with the simple fact that you can't force good code onto the Web; you have to deal with what's there.

If your shiny new browser makes a page look trashy when it's been running fine for years, guess whose fault it is? So they have all pretty much given up even trying to parse HTML, opting instead to grab tags out of "tag soup" and try to do something sensible with them. It's harder than it looks.

HTML Today

What's a Web designer to do? The proliferation of tags, inline scripting languages, plug-ins, and other tools for creating Web pages is starting to make coding a page look more like programming than design, and the sheer number of tags is becoming a daunting task just to memorize, much less use. The size of this table is a case in point, and it doesn't include the really special-purpose WebTV tags or other ultra-proprietary extensions.

Aside from corporate intranets where you can be fairly certain of the desktop configuration, however, the number of tags and attributes supported across all (or mostly all) platforms is still fairly manageable. New technologies are insinuating themselves into sites instead of overwhelming them, letting the judicious Webmaster add some "pizzazz" to her site without making it terribly inconvenient for everyone else.

In spite of what well-meaning people may tell you, the new draft standards will probably change, if only slightly, during the process of going from a draft proposal to a recommendation and then an RFC, so you needn't rush into anything. No matter what your intended audience might be, the existence of millions of older machines on the Internet running older software and browsers, as well as the disabled and other important market segments, means that your page probably has to be visible and useful to a wider range of browsers than are represented in your office or workplace. The safest policy is to make sure your pages look readable in a text-only browser like Lynx, even if it loses a lot in the translation. With that ultimate fallback position covered, you can be fairly sure that almost all browsers will do something reasonable with your page.

You'll have that time to master the new techniques, perhaps reinventing the task of Web design and making room for both programmers and traditional graphic artists, and possibly forming teams to incorporate the best of both worlds.

Cross-Browser Differences

Unfortunately, the browser wars have heated up lately. Microsoft and Netscape are battling it out with different object models, event handling, Dynamic HTML tags, and other incompatibilities to tax the ingenuity and patience of the beleaguered Webmaster. At its heart, these differences make possible different behaviors in the two browsers.

In MSIE 4.0, for example, events "bubble up" through the object most closely associated with an event toward the parent window and data binding is dynamic. That means that every element on the page can access events like onClick, offering the possibility of making almost everything "clickable" or "mouseoverable," including headers, horizontal rules, and other elements that have been traditionally static. It also means that the entire page can be dynamically rendered again at any time using new data. The very idea of a page is pushed to the limit because it can be reprinted with new information on-the-fly, and the underlying structure is amorphous, sort of like the liquid metal robot in *Terminator 2*.

In Netscape Communicator and Navigator 4.0, by way of contrast, events are captured first by the window. The number of potentially interactive elements is more or less restricted to images and links, those elements that have long been associated in people's minds with the possibility of performing actions. Once the page has been rendered, it's basically static, more like a printed book or other objects in your everyday experience.

Both strategies have strengths and weaknesses, although it looks like the Microsoft bubbling-up, all-elements-navigable model will prevail, based on the latest Document Object Model (DOM) thinking from the W3C.

An MSIE/W3C Document Object Model page is potentially either a feature-rich multimedia experience or a confusing jack-in-the-box of shape-shifting characters "morphing" into new bodies at will, instead of the sedate and predictable text we're all used to, depending on your viewpoint. Creating the page requires both restraint and mastery of new ways of thinking about data and the mechanics of page display.

A Netscape page is more like a familiar book (perhaps a pop-up book), but with the possibility of unique multimedia adventures lurking at the turn of every page. Traditional page-display methods have been extended with a few new tags and attributes that are comparatively easy to use and understand. The difference seems to be that the Microsoft/W3C Document Object Model has more or less abandoned the traditional "markers" for links off the page and "triggers" in favor of interacting with almost everything, whether visible or not, and perhaps controlling every aspect of the browsing experience dynamically. Freedom and innovation versus responsibility and stability: a classic intergenerational confrontation.

But the incompatibility of these two approaches means that, until Netscape releases a browser with this capability, most pages will use restricted subsets of features that work across both platforms, and developers will have to exercise special care to create designs that will translate gracefully between platforms, learning two (or even more) methodologies in the process and further fragmenting the browser world. There will also undoubtedly be instances of page designers grabbing focus and forcing viewers to sit through a "commercial" of razzle-dazzle special effects before returning control to the user. Hmmm…

We live in interesting times.

Cross-Browser Table Legend

■ The table is arranged alphabetically for convenient reference, but the Structure/Block/Text types of the tags are identified following the tag itself as Ⓢ, Ⓑ, and Ⓣ.

■ Tags and attributes in **bold** are included in the HTML 4.0 draft, and tags in square brackets are optional.

■ Values for some attributes are placed in parentheses under the attribute they correspond to.

■ The following abbreviations are used:

MSIE = Microsoft Internet Explorer

Netscp = Netscape Navigator or Communicator

NCSA = NCSA Mosaic

Opera = Opera

Lynx = Lynx

SM = Sun Microsystems

Emacs = Emacs (W3 mode)

HTML = HTML version number or proprietary

Sponsor = Promulgating organization

Status = Status of element in standards process

W3C = World Wide Web Consortium

MS = Microsoft Corp.

N = Netscape, Inc.

Tag	MSIE	Netscp	NCSA	Opera	Lynx	Emacs	HTML	Sponsor Status
<!-- *comment* -->	✓	✓	✓	✓	✓	✓	2	W3C

WARNING: The SGML comment syntax is not an HTML-style container, but can contain multiple comments enclosed by double dashes, one comment, or none. The first comment, if present, must follow the exclamation mark with no intervening space. Many browsers don't implement this element correctly, so use it with caution. Avoid enclosing HTML tags and keep multiline comments to a minimum. These are legal comments:

<!>, <!-- x -->, <!-- x -- -- y -->

Tag	MSIE	Netscp	NCSA	Opera	Lynx	Emacs	HTML	Sponsor Status
<!DOCTYPE>	✓	✓	✓	✓	✓	✓	2	W3C
html	✓	✓	✓	✓	✓	✓	2	W3C
<A></A> T	✓	✓	✓	✓	✓	✓	2	W3C
accesskey=	4	-	-	-	-	-	4	W3C
charset=	4	-	-	-	-	-	4	W3C
class=	-	✓3/4	-	-	✓*	✓	3/4	W3C
coords=	4	-	-	-	-	-	4	W3C
dir=	-	-	-	-	-	-	4	W3C
href=	✓	✓	✓	✓	✓	✓	2-4	W3C

WARNING: Netscape introduced a ?subject=xxx postfix to a mailto URL to automatically insert a subject line in those browsers that support it, Netscape Navigator and MSIE among others. Be aware, though, that this extension is specific to a few mainstream browsers. Using this URL type and extension could cause an incorrect e-mail address to be used in other browsers, such as NCSA Mosaic and Lynx, that are less commonly used. It might even cause the browser to crash.

Tags and attributes in **bold** are included in the HTML 4.0 draft, and tags in square brackets are optional. The table is arranged alphabetically for convenient reference, but the Structure/Block/Text types of the tags are identified following the tag itself as S, B, and T.

2, 3, 4, etc. = Condensed HTML version number; 3+ = HTML version 3.2; ✓ = Available in all current versions; ↓ = Deprecated—HTML version; **✗** = Obsolete; P = Proprietary/nonconforming; * = Partial or partially nonconforming implementation.

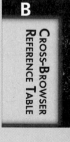

B

CROSS-BROWSER REFERENCE TABLE

<A></A> *continued*

If you're concerned with wide accessibility, you might want to avoid this feature or exercise special care in constructing the subject line so it will work in more browsers. For certain applications, though, it can be a real benefit to know automatically which page the sender was mailing from. As an example, here is a link that will work in most browsers, although the subject line may or may not be filled in:

E-mail Address: `<A HREF="mailto:myname@mycompany.com?subject=Re:`
`myname@mycompany.com (LocationID)">myname@mycompany.com</A>`

Either way, you will probably get some indication of where the message originated, either in the subject line or as a comment in the e-mail address, if an automatic link to e-mail is supported at all. Be sure to retain the exact format shown because it's quite sensitive to changes and the code is inherently dicey, since it depends on browser behavior that may change over time.

This e-mail link format has been tested in recent versions of MSIE, Netscape Navigator, NCSA Mosaic, Opera, and Lynx. Inserting a line break within the quotes might cause a malformed but legal address to be inserted. Browsers that don't support mailto links have a plain text equivalent, which they can copy into their own mailer.

Tag	MSIE	Netscp	NCSA	Opera	Lynx	Emacs	HTML	Sponsor	Status
id=	✓3/4	✓3/4	-	-	-	✓*	3/4	W3C	
lang=	✓3/4	✓3/4	-	-	-	✓*	3/4	W3C	
language= (javascript,vbscript)	✓3/4	✓3/4	-	-	-	-	℗	MS	✗3+
md=	-	-	-	-	✓*	✓	3	W3C	✗3+
methods=	✓2-4	✓	-	-	✓	✓	2	W3C	✗3+
name=	✓	✓	✓	✓	✓	✓	2-4	W3C	
rel=	✓	✓2-4	✓	✓	✓	✓	2-4	W3C	
rev=	-	✓2-4	✓	✓	✓	✓	2-4	W3C	
shape=	✓3/4	-	-	-	✓*	✓*	3/4	W3C	
style=	✓3/4	4	-	-	-	-	4	W3C	
tabindex=	✓3/4	4*	-	-	-	-	4	W3C	

Tag	MSIE	Netscp	NCSA	Opera	Lynx	Emacs	HTML	Sponsor	Status
target=	✓3/4	✓2-4	-	3	✓*	✓	4	W3C	
title=	✓2-4	✓2-4	✓	✓	✓	✓	2-4	W3C	
urn=	✓2-4	✓2-4	-	-	✓	✓	2	W3C	✗3+
event=	✓3/4	✓	-	✓	-	-	4	W3C	✗3+
<ABBREV></ABBREV>Ⓣ	-	-	-	-	✓*	✓	3	W3C	✗3+
class=	-	-	-	-	✓*	✓	3	W3C	✗3+
id=	-	-	-	-	✓	✓	3	W3C	✗3+
lang=	-	-	-	-	✓	✓	3	W3C	✗3+
<ACRONYM>Ⓣ **...</ACRONYM>**	-	-	-	-	✓*	✓	3/4	W3C	
class=	-	-	-	-	✓*	✓	3/4	W3C	
dir=	-	-	-	-	-	-	4	W3C	
id=	-	-	-	-	✓*	✓	3/4	W3C	
lang=	-	-	-	-	✓*	✓	3/4	W3C	
style=	-	-	-	-	✓*	✓	3/4	W3C	
title=	-	-	-	-	✓*	✓	3/4	W3C	
event=	-	-	-	-	-	-	3/4	W3C	

Tags and attributes in **bold** are included in the HTML 4.0 draft, and tags in square brackets are optional.
The table is arranged alphabetically for convenient reference, but the Structure/Block/Text types of the tags are identified following the tag itself as Ⓢ, Ⓑ, and Ⓣ.

2, 3, 4, etc. = Condensed HTML version number; 3+ = HTML version 3.2; ✓ = Available in all current versions; ↓ = Deprecated—HTML version;
✗ = Obsolete; Ⓟ = Proprietary/nonconforming; * = Partial or partially nonconforming implementation.

B

CROSS-BROWSER REFERENCE TABLE

Tag	MSIE	Netscp	NCSA	Opera	Lynx	Emacs	HTML	Sponsor	Status
<ADDRESS>[T] **...</ADDRESS>**	✓	✓	✓	✓	✓*	✓	2-4	W3C	
align= (center, left, right)	✓3/4	-	-	-	-	-	(P)	W3C	
class=	-	✓3/4	-	-	✓*	✓	3/4	W3C	
clear= (left, right, all)	-	✓3/4	-	-	✓*	✓	3	W3C	✗3+
dir=	-	-	-	-	-	-	4	W3C	
id=	✓	✓3/4	-	-	✓*	✓	3/4	W3C	
lang=	-	✓3/4	-	-	✓*	✓	3/4	W3C	
nowrap	-	✓	-	-	✓*	✓	3	W3C	✗3+
style=	✓3/4	4	-	-	-	-	4	W3C	
title=	✓3/4	-	-	-	-	-	4	W3C	
event=	✓3/4	-	-	-	-	-	4	W3C	
<APP><APP>[B]	4	-	-	-	-	-	(P)	SM	
class=	4	-	-	-	-	-	(P)	SM	
src=	4	-	-	-	-	-	(P)	SM	
align= (bottom, top, middle)	4	-	-	-	-	-	(P)	SM	
width=	4	-	-	-	-	-	(P)	SM	
height=	4	-	-	-	-	-	(P)	SM	

WARNING: The <APP> tag is used by Sun Microsystems for HotJava, but mostly unsupported elsewhere.

Tag	MSIE	Netscp	NCSA	Opera	Lynx	Emacs	HTML	Sponsor	Status
<APPLET></APPLET> B	✓3/4	✓2-4	-	3	✓*	✓	3+/4	W3C	↓4
align=	✓3/4	✓2-4	-	3	-	-	3+	W3C	
(left, center, right, top, middle, bottom)									
alt=	✓3/4	✓2-4	-	3	✓*	✓	3+	W3C	
archive=	-	-	-	-	-	-	4	W3C	
code=	✓3/4	✓2-4	-	✓	✓*	✓	3+	W3C	
codebase=	✓3/4	✓2-4	-	✓	✓*	✓	3+	W3C	
download=	✓3/4	-	-	-	-	-	P	MS	✗3+
height=	✓3/4	✓2-4	-	3	✓*	✓	3+	W3C	
hspace=	✓3/4	✓2-4	-	3	✓*	✓	3+	W3C	
name=	✓3/4	✓2-4	-	3	✓*	✓	3+	W3C	
object=	-	4	-	-	-	-	4	W3C	
title=	✓3/4	-	-	-	✓*	-	3	MS	✗3+
vspace=	✓3/4	✓2-4	-	3	✓*	✓	3+	W3C	
width=	✓3/4	✓2-4	-	3	✓*	✓	3+	W3C	
<AREA>[</AREA>] B	✓ P	✓	✓	✓	✓*	✓	3+/4	W3C	

TIP: Lynx doesn't actually display the image; it creates a reference list of all the destinations in a client-side image map. If the destination names are meaningful, people without access to the map can still navigate by using the constructed text-mode analog.

Tags and attributes in **bold** are included in the HTML 4.0 draft, and tags in square brackets are optional.
The table is arranged alphabetically for convenient reference, but the Structure/Block/Text types of the tags are identified following the tag itself as S, B, and T.

2, 3, 4, etc. = Condensed HTML version number; 3+ = HTML version 3.2; ✓ = Available in all current versions; ↓ = Deprecated—HTML version;
✗ = Obsolete; P = Proprietary/nonconforming; * = Partial or partially nonconforming implementation.

Tag	MSIE	Netscp	NCSA	Opera	Lynx	Emacs	HTML	Sponsor	Status
<AREA>[</AREA>] *continued*									
alt=	-	✓2-4	✓	✓	✓*	✓	3+/4	W3C	
coords=	✓2-4	✓2-4	✓	✓	✓*	✓	3+/4	W3C	
href=	✓2-4	✓2-4	✓	✓	✓*	✓	3+/4	W3C	
id=	✓3/4	✓3	-	-	✓*	✓	3	W3C	✗3+
name=	✓3/4	-	-	-	✓*	✓	3	W3C	✗3+
nohref=	✓2-4	✓2-4	3	✓	✓*	✓	3+/4	W3C	
shape=	✓2-4	✓2-4	3	✓	✓*	✓	3+/4	W3C	
(circ, circle, poly, polygon, rect, rectangle)									
style=	✓3/4	4	-	-	-	-	3	W3C	✗3+
tabindex=	4	4*	-	-	-	-	4	W3C	
target=	✓3/4	✓2-4	-	-	-	-	4	W3C	
title=	✓3/4	✓2-4	-	-	-	-	3	W3C	✗3+
event=	✓3/4	-	-	-	-	-	3	W3C	✗3+
<AU></AU>Ⓣ	-	-	-	-	✓*	✓	3	W3C	✗3+
class=	-	-	-	-	✓*	✓	3	W3C	
id=	-	-	-	-	✓*	✓	3	W3C	
lang=	-	-	-	-	✓*	✓	3	W3C	
<B></B>Ⓣ	✓	✓	✓	✓	✓*	✓	2-4	W3C	
class=	-	✓3/4	-	-	✓*	✓	3/4	W3C	
dir=	-	-	-	-	-	-	4	W3C	
id=	✓3/4	✓3/4	-	-	✓*	✓	3/4	W3C	
lang=	-	✓3/4	-	-	✓*	✓	3/4	W3C	

Tag	MSIE	Netscp	NCSA	Opera	Lynx	Emacs	HTML	Sponsor	Status
style=	✔3/4	4	-	-	-	✔	4	W3C	
title=	✔3/4	4	-	-	-	-	4	W3C	
event=	✔3/4	-	-	-	-	-	4	W3C	
<BANNER></BANNER> Ⓑ	-	-	✔	-	✔*	✔	3	W3C	✘3+
class=	-	-	-	-	✔*	✔	3	W3C	
id=	-	-	-	-	✔*	✔	3	W3C	
lang=	-	-	-	-	✔*	✔	3	W3C	
<BASE>[</BASE>] Ⓢ	✔	✔2-4	✔	✔	✔	✔	2-4	W3C	
href=	✔ Ⓟ	-	✔	✔	✔*	✔	2-4	W3C	
target=	✔3/4	✔2-4	-	3	✔*	✔	4	W3C	
title=	✔3/4	-	-	-	-	-	Ⓟ	MS	
<BASEFONT> Ⓑ **...[</BASEFONT>]**	✔	✔	-	✔	✔*	✔	3+/4	W3C	↓4
color=	✔3/4	✔2-4	-	3	✔*	✔	3+/4	W3C	↓4
face=	✔3/4	✔2-4	-	3	✔*	✔	4	W3C	↓4
id=	✔3/4	✔3/4	-	-	✔*	✔	3	W3C	✘3+
size=	✔3/4	✔2-4	-	✔	✔*	✔	3+	W3C	↓4
title=	✔3/4	-	-	-	-	-	-	MS	✘3+

Tags and attributes in **bold** are included in the HTML 4.0 draft, and tags in square brackets are optional.
The table is arranged alphabetically for convenient reference, but the Structure/Block/Text types of the tags are identified following the tag itself as Ⓢ, Ⓑ, and Ⓣ.

2, 3, 4, etc. = Condensed HTML version number; 3+ = HTML version 3.2; ✔ = Available in all current versions; ↓ = Deprecated—HTML version;
✘ = Obsolete; Ⓟ = Proprietary/nonconforming; * = Partial or partially nonconforming implementation.

B
CROSS-BROWSER REFERENCE TABLE

Tag	MSIE	Netscp	NCSA	Opera	Lynx	Emacs	HTML	Sponsor	Status
<BDO>[T]	-	-	-	-	-	-	4	W3C	
dir=	-	-	-	-	-	-	4	W3C	
lang=	-	-	-	-	-	-	4	W3C	
<BGSOUND>[B]	✓	✓2-4	-	-	-	-	[P]	MS	✗3+
...[</BGSOUND>]									
loop=	✓	✓2-4	-	-	-	-			
src=	✓	✓2-4	-	-	-	-			
id=	✓	-	-	-	-	-			
title=	✓	-	-	-	-	-			
<BIG></BIG>[T]	✓	✓	-	✓	✓*	✓	3+/4	W3C	
class=	-	✓3/4	-	-	✓*	✓	3/4	W3C	
dir=	-	-	-	-	-	-	4	W3C	
id=	✓3/4	✓3/4	-	-	✓*	✓	3/4	W3C	
lang=	-	✓3/4	-	-	✓*	✓	3/4	W3C	
style=	✓3/4	4	-	-	-	-	4	W3C	
title=	✓3/4	-	-	-	-	-	4	W3C	
event=	✓3/4	-	-	-	-	-	4	W3C	
<BLINK></BLINK>[T]	-	✓2-4	-	-	-	[P]	NS	[P]	
<BLOCKQUOTE>[S]	✓	✓	✓	✓	✓	✓	2	W3C	
...</BLOCKQUOTE>									

TIP: MSIE and Netscape handle the "white space" around a blockquote differently, especially when nesting blocks. This tag can't be counted on to consistently indent or offset text from a background margin, although it's often used for that purpose.

Tag	MSIE	Netscp	NCSA	Opera	Lynx	Emacs	HTML	Sponsor	Status
cite=	-	-	-	-	-	-	4	W3C	
class=	-	-	-	-	-	-	4	W3C	
dir=	-	-	-	-	-	-	4	W3C	
id=	3/4	✔3/4	-	-	-	-	4	W3C	
lang=	-	-	-	-	-	-	4	W3C	
style=	✔3/4	4	-	-	-	-	4	W3C	
title=	✔3/4	-	-	-	-	-	4	W3C	
event=	✔3/4	-	-	-	-	-	4	W3C	
[<BODY>]|[</BODY>] Ⓢ	✔	✔	✔	✔	✔	✔	2-4	W3C	

NOTE: The <BODY> tag is optional and can be inferred.

Tag	MSIE	Netscp	NCSA	Opera	Lynx	Emacs	HTML	Sponsor	Status
align= (center, left, right)	✔3/4	-	-	-	-	-	4	W3C	↓4
alink=	✔	✔	-	-	-	-	3+/4	W3C	↓4
background=	✔	✔	-	-	-	-	3+/4	W3C	↓4
bgcolor=	✔	✔	-	-	-	-	3+/4	W3C	↓4
bgproperties= (fixed)	✔3/4	-	-	-	-	-	Ⓟ	MS	✗3+
class=	-	-	-	-	-	-	4	W3C	

Tags and attributes in **bold** are included in the HTML 4.0 draft, and tags in square brackets are optional.

The table is arranged alphabetically for convenient reference, but the Structure/Block/Text types of the tags are identified following the tag itself as Ⓢ, Ⓑ, and Ⓣ.

2, 3, 4, etc. = Condensed HTML version number; 3+ = HTML version 3.2; ✔ = Available in all current versions; ↓ = Deprecated—HTML version; ✗ = Obsolete; Ⓟ = Proprietary/nonconforming; * = Partial or partially nonconforming implementation.

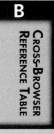

B

CROSS-BROWSER REFERENCE TABLE

Tag	MSIE	Netscp	NCSA	Opera	Lynx	Emacs	HTML	Sponsor	Status
[<BODY>||</BODY>] *continued*									
dir=	-	-	-	-	-	-	4	W3C	
id=	✓3/4	✓3/4	-	-	-	-	4	W3C	
lang=	-	-	-	-	-	-	4	W3C	
leftmargin=	✓	-	-	-	-	-	Ⓟ	MS	
link=	✓3/4	✓2-4	-	-	-	-	3+/4	W3C	↓4
scroll=	✓3/4	-	-	-	-	-	Ⓟ	MS	
style=	✓3/4	4	-	-	-	-	4	W3C	
text=	✓3/4	✓2-4	-	-	-	-	3+/4	W3C	↓4
title=	✓3/4	-	-	-	-	-	4	W3C	
topmargin=	✓3/4	-	-	-	-	-	Ⓟ	MS	
vlink=	✓3/4	✓2-4	-	-	-	-	3+/4	W3C	↓4
event=	✓3/4	-	-	-	-	-	4	W3C	
** ** Ⓢ Ⓣ	✓	✓	✓	✓	✓	✓	2-4	W3C	

WARNING: The practice of inserting multiple <BR> or <P> tags to insert "white space" is nonstandard and prone to error. The HTML standard can be interpreted as implying that excess white space should be ignored. Some browsers do ignore multiple tags, although most browser makers have interpreted the standard to mean that each <BR> inserts another line feed.

Tag	MSIE	Netscp	NCSA	Opera	Lynx	Emacs	HTML	Sponsor	Status
class=	✓	✓3/4	-	-	-	-	3	W3C	
clear=	✓	✓2-4	-	-	-	-	3	W3C	
(left, right, all)									
none	-	-	-	-	-	-	3+	W3C	
dir=	-	-	-	-	-	-	4	W3C	
id=	✓	✓3/4	-	-	-	-	3	W3C	

Tag	MSIE	Netscp	NCSA	Opera	Lynx	Emacs	HTML	Sponsor	Status
lang=	-	✔3/4	-	-	-	-	3	W3C	
style=	✔3/4	4	-	-	-	-	4	W3C	
title=	✔3/4	-	-	-	-	-	4	W3C	
<BQ></BQ> Ⓢ	-	-	-	-	✔	✔	3	W3C	✗3+

WARNING: <BQ> is the HTML 3.0 synonym for <BLOCKQUOTE>, but it's no longer widely supported.

Tag	MSIE	Netscp	NCSA	Opera	Lynx	Emacs	HTML	Sponsor	Status
<BUTTON></BUTTON> Ⓢ	✔3/4	-	-	-	-	-	4	W3C	
accesskey=	✔3/4	-	-	-	-	-	Ⓟ	MS	
class=	4	-	-	-	-	-	4	W3C	
dir=	-	-	-	-	-	-	4	W3C	
disabled	✔3/4	-	-	-	-	-	4	W3C	
id=	4	-	-	-	-	-	4	W3C	
lang=	-	-	-	-	-	-	4	W3C	
name=	-	-	-	-	-	-	4	W3C	
style=	4	-	-	-	-	-	4	W3C	
tabindex=	4	-	-	-	-	-	4	W3C	
title=	✔3/4	-	-	-	-	-	4	W3C	
type=	4	-	-	-	-	-	4	W3C	
value=	4	-	-	-	-	-	4	W3C	
event=	✔3/4	-	-	-	-	-	4	W3C	

Tags and attributes in **bold** are included in the HTML 4.0 draft, and tags in square brackets are optional.

The table is arranged alphabetically for convenient reference, but the Structure/Block/Text types of the tags are identified following the tag itself as Ⓢ, Ⓑ, and Ⓣ.

2, 3, 4, etc. = Condensed HTML version number; 3+ = HTML version 3.2; ✔ = Available in all current versions; ↓ = Deprecated—HTML version; ✗ = Obsolete; Ⓟ = Proprietary/nonconforming; * = Partial or partially nonconforming implementation.

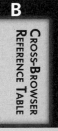

B

CROSS-BROWSER REFERENCE TABLE

Tag	MSIE	Netscp	NCSA	Opera	Lynx	Emacs	HTML	Sponsor	Status
<CAPTION>⑤ **...</CAPTION>**	✔	✔	✔	✔	✔	✔	3	W3C	
align= (center, left, right)	✔	✔	-	✔	✔	✔	3+/4	W3C	
(top, bottom)									
class=	-	-	-	-	-	-	4	W3C	
dir=	-	-	-	-	-	-	4	W3C	
id=	✔	✔3/4	-	-	✔	✔	3/4	W3C	
lang	-	-	-	-	✔	✔	3/4	W3C	
style=	✔3/4	4	-	-	-	-	4	W3C	
title=	✔3/4	-	-	-	-	-	4	W3C	
valign= (top, bottom)	✔2-4	✔	✔	-	✔	✔	3+	W3C	✗4
event=	✔3/4	-	-	-	-	-	4	W3C	
<CENTER></CENTER>⑤	✔	✔	✔	✔	✔	✔	3+	W3C	↓4

NOTE: HTML 3.2 defined the widely supported <CENTER> tag as a shorthand for <DIV ALIGN="CENTER">, although its use is deprecated now.

Tag	MSIE	Netscp	NCSA	Opera	Lynx	Emacs	HTML	Sponsor	Status
class=	-	-	-	-	-	-	4	W3C	
dir=	-	-	-	-	-	-	4	W3C	
id=	✔3/4	✔3/4	-	-	✔	✔	3	W3C	
lang=	-	-	-	-	-	-	4	W3C	
style=	✔3/4	4	-	-	-	-	4	W3C	

Tag	MSIE	Netscp	NCSA	Opera	Lynx	Emacs	HTML	Sponsor	Status
title=	✔3/4	-	-	-	-	-	4	W3C	
event=	✔3/4	-	-	-	-	-	4	W3C	
<CITE></CITE> [T]	✔	✔	✔	✔	✔*	✔	2-4	W3C	
class=	-	✔3/4	-	-	✔	✔	3/4	W3C	
dir=	-	-	-	-	-	-	4	W3C	
id=	✔3/4	✔3/4	-	-	✔	✔	3/4	W3C	
lang=	-	✔3/4	-	-	✔	✔	3/4	W3C	
style=	✔3/4	4	-	-	-	-	4	W3C	
title=	✔3/4	-	-	-	-	-	4	W3C	
event=	✔3/4	-	-	-	-	-	4	W3C	
<CODE></CODE> [T]	✔	✔	✔	✔	✔*	✔	2	W3C	
class=	-	✔3/4	-	-	✔	✔	3	W3C	
dir=	-	-	-	-	-	-	4	W3C	
id=	✔3/4	✔3/4	-	-	✔	✔	3	W3C	
lang=	-	✔3/4	-	-	✔	✔	3	W3C	
style=	✔3/4	4	-	-	-	-	4	W3C	
title=	✔3/4	-	-	-	-	-	4	W3C	
event=	✔3/4	-	-	-	-	-	4	W3C	

Tags and attributes in **bold** are included in the HTML 4.0 draft, and tags in square brackets are optional.

The table is arranged alphabetically for convenient reference, but the Structure/Block/Text types of the tags are identified following the tag itself as [S], [B], and [T].

2, 3, 4, etc. = Condensed HTML version number; 3+ = HTML version 3.2; ✔ = Available in all current versions; ↓ = Deprecated—HTML version; ✘ = Obsolete; [P] = Proprietary/nonconforming; * = Partial or partially nonconforming implementation.

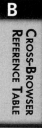

B

CROSS-BROWSER
REFERENCE TABLE

Tag	MSIE	Netscp	NCSA	Opera	Lynx	Emacs	HTML	Sponsor	Status
<COL></COL> Ⓢ	4	-	-	-	-	-	4	W3C	
align=	4	-	-	-	-	-	4	W3C	
(center, left, right)									
char=	-	-	-	-	-	-	4	W3C	
charoff=	-	-	-	-	-	-	4	W3C	
class=	-	-	-	-	-	-	4	W3C	
dir=	-	-	-	-	-	-	4	W3C	
id=	4	-	-	-	-	-	4	W3C	
span=	4	-	-	-	-	-	4	W3C	
style=	4	-	-	-	-	-	4	W3C	
title=	4	-	-	-	-	-	4	W3C	
valign=	4	-	-	-	-	-	4	W3C	
(baseline, bottom, center, top)									
width=	4	-	-	-	-	-	4	W3C	
event=	4	-	-	-	-	-	4	W3C	
<COLGROUP> Ⓢ	✔3/4	-	-	-	-	-	4	W3C	
align=	4	-	-	-	-	-	4	W3C	
(center, left, right)									
char=	-	-	-	-	-	-	4	W3C	
charoff=	-	-	-	-	-	-	4	W3C	
class=	-	-	-	-	-	-	4	W3C	
id=	4	-	-	-	-	-	4	W3C	
span=	4	-	-	-	-	-	4	W3C	

Tag	MSIE	Netsp	NCSA	Opera	Lynx	Emacs	HTML	Sponsor	Status
style=	4	-	-	-	-	-	4	W3C	
title=	4	-	-	-	-	-	4	W3C	
valign=	-	-	-	-	-	-	4	W3C	
(baseline, bottom, center, top)									
width=	4	-	-	-	-	-	4	W3C	
<COMMENT>[T]	✔	-	-	-	✔	-	[P]		✗2
...</COMMENT>	✔	-	-	-	✔	-			
title=									

WARNING: Any information entered between the <COMMENT> start and end tags is treated as a comment by MSIE and Lynx, but the tags are ignored by most other browsers, so the text or code between them is rendered as though the tags were not there.

Tag	MSIE	Netsp	NCSA	Opera	Lynx	Emacs	HTML	Sponsor	Status
<CREDIT></CREDIT>[T]	-	-	-	-	✔*	✔	3	W3C	
<DD>[S]	✔	✔	✔	✔	✔	✔	2-4	W3C	
align=	4	-	-	✔	-	-	3	W3C	✗4
(center, left, right)									
class=	4	3	-	-	-	-	4	W3C	
dir=	-	-	-	-	-	-	4	W3C	
id=	4	3	-	-	-	-	3	W3C	✗4

Tags and attributes in **bold** are included in the HTML 4.0 draft, and tags in square brackets are optional.

The table is arranged alphabetically for convenient reference, but the Structure/Block/Text types of the tags are identified following the tag itself as [S], [B], and [T].

2, 3, 4, etc. = Condensed HTML version number; 3+ = HTML version 3.2; ✔ = Available in all current versions; ↓ = Deprecated—HTML version; ✗ = Obsolete; [P] = Proprietary/nonconforming; * = Partial or partially nonconforming implementation.

Tag	MSIE	Netscp	NCSA	Opera	Lynx	Emacs	HTML	Sponsor	Status
<DD> Ⓢ *continued*									
lang=	-	3	-	-	-	-	3	W3C	✗4
style=	4	4	-	-	-	-	3	W3C	✗4
title=	4	-	-	-	-	-	3	W3C	✗4
event=	4	-	-	-	-	-	-	-	✗4
<DEL></DEL> Ⓣ	-	-	-	-	✓*	✓	3	W3C	✗3+
cite=	-	-	-	-	-	-	4	W3C	
class=	-	-	-	-	✓	✓	3/4	W3C	
datetime=	-	-	-	-	-	-	4	W3C	
dir=	-	-	-	-	-	-	4	W3C	
id=	-	-	-	-	✓	✓	3/4	W3C	
lang=	-	-	-	-	✓	✓	3/4	W3C	
style=	-	-	-	-	✓	✓	3/4	W3C	
title=	-	-	-	-	✓	✓	3/4	W3C	
event=	-	-	-	-	-	-	3/4	W3C	
<DFN><DFN> Ⓣ	✓	✓	✓	✓	✓*	✓	3/4	W3C	
class=	-	-	-	-	✓	✓	3/4	W3C	
dir=	-	-	-	-	-	-	4	W3C	
id=	✓3/4	-	-	-	✓	✓	3/4	W3C	
lang=	-	-	-	-	✓	✓	3/4	W3C	
style=	4	-	-	-	-	-	4	W3C	
title=	4	-	-	-	-	-	4	W3C	
event=	4	-	-	-	-	-	4	W3C	

Tag	MSIE	Netscp	NCSA	Opera	Lynx	Emacs	HTML	Sponsor	Status
\<DIR>\<DIR> (S)	✔	✔	✔	✔	✔	✔	2	W3C	↓4
class=	-	-	-	-	-	-	4	W3C	
compact	✔	✔	✔	✔	✔*	✔	2	W3C	↓4
dir=	-	-	-	-	-	-	4	W3C	
id=	4	✔3/4	-	-	-	-	4	W3C	
lang=	4	-	-	-	-	-	3/4	W3C	
style=	4	4	-	-	-	-	4	W3C	
title=	4	-	-	-	-	-	4	W3C	
event=	4	-	-	-	-	-	4	W3C	
\<DIV> (S)	✔	✔	✔	✔	✔	✔	3/4	W3C	
align=	4	✔	✔	✔	✔	✔	3/4	W3C	
(center, left, right)							3/4		
(justify)	✔	-	-	-	-	-	3	W3C	✗3+
class=	-	✔3/4	-	✔	✔	✔	3/4	W3C	
clear=	-	✔	-	-	✔	✔	3	W3C	✗3+
(left, right, all)	✔	-	-	✔*	✔	-			
datafld=	4	-	-	-	-	-	(P)		
dataformats=	4	-	-	-	-	-	(P)		
datasrc=	4	-	-	-	-	-	(P)		

Tags and attributes in **bold** are included in the HTML 4.0 draft, and tags in square brackets are optional.
The table is arranged alphabetically for convenient reference, but the Structure/Block/Text types of the tags are identified following the tag itself as (S), (B), and (T).

2, 3, 4, etc. = Condensed HTML version number; 3+ = HTML version 3.2; ✔ = Available in all current versions; ↓ = Deprecated—HTML version; ✗ = Obsolete; (P) = Proprietary/nonconforming; * = Partial or partially nonconforming implementation.

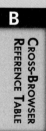

B

CROSS-BROWSER
REFERENCE TABLE

Tag	MSIE	Netscp	NCSA	Opera	Lynx	Emacs	HTML	Sponsor	Status
<DIV> S *continued*									
dir=	-	-	-	-	-	-	4	W3C	
id=	4	✓3/4	-	-	✓	✓	3/4	W3C	
lang=	-	✓3/4	-	-	✓	✓	3/4	W3C	
nowrap	-	✓3/4	-	-	✓	✓	3	W3C	✗3+
style=	4	4	-	-	-	-	4	W3C	
title=	4	-	-	-	-	-	4	W3C	
event=	4	-	-	-	-	-	4	W3C	
<DL> S	✓	✓	✓	✓	✓	✓	2-4	W3C	
align=	4	-	-	-	-	-			
(center, left, right)									
class=	-	3	-	-	✓	✓	3/4	W3C	
clear=	-	✓	-	✓*	✓*	✓	3	W3C	
(left, right, all)	✓	-	-	✓	✓	-			
compact	✓	✓	✓	✓	✓	✓	2-4	W3C	
dir=	-	-	-	-	-	-	4	W3C	
id=	4	✓3/4	-	-	✓	✓	3/4	W3C	
lang=	-	✓3/4	-	-	-	-	3/4	W3C	
style=	4	4	-	-	-	-	4	W3C	
title=	4	-	-	-	-	-	4	W3C	
event=	4	-	-	-	-	-	4	W3C	

Tag	MSIE	Netscp	NCSA	Opera	Lynx	Emacs	HTML	Sponsor	Status
<DT> S	✔	✔	✔	✔	✔	✔	2-4	W3C	
align=	4	-	-	-	-	-	3	W3C	✘3+
(center, left, right)									
class=	-	-	-	-	-	-	4		
dir=	-	-	-	-	-	-	4		
id=	4	-	-	-	✔	✔	3	W3C	
lang=	-	-	-	-	-	-	4	W3C	
style=	4	-	-	-	-	-	4	W3C	
title=	4	-	-	-	-	-	4	W3C	
event=	4	-	-	-	-	-	4	W3C	
<EM></EM> T	✔	✔	✔	✔	✔*	✔	2-4	W3C	
class=	-	-	-	-	✔	✔	3/4	W3C	
dir=	-	-	-	-	-	-	4	W3C	
id=	✔3/4	-	-	-	-	-	3/4	W3C	
lang=	-	-	-	-	-	-	3/4	W3C	
style=	4	-	-	-	-	-	4	W3C	
title=	4	-	-	-	-	-	4	W3C	
event=	4	-	-	-	-	-	4	W3C	

Tags and attributes in **bold** are included in the HTML 4.0 draft, and tags in square brackets are optional.

The table is arranged alphabetically for convenient reference, but the Structure/Block/Text types of the tags are identified following the tag itself as S, B, and T.

2, 3, 4, etc. = Condensed HTML version number; 3+ = HTML version 3.2; ✔ = Available in all current versions; ↓ = Deprecated—HTML version; ✘ = Obsolete; P = Proprietary/nonconforming; * = Partial or partially nonconforming implementation.

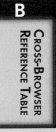

B

CROSS-BROWSER
REFERENCE TABLE

Tag	MSIE	Netscp	NCSA	Opera	Lynx	Emacs	HTML	Sponsor	Status
<EMBED></EMBED> [B]	✔3/4	✔	–	–	–	–	[P]	NS	
NOTE: <EMBED> was included in MSIE for backward compatibility. Use <OBJECT>, if possible.									
accesskey=	4	–	–	–	–	–			
align=	4	✔	–	–	–	–			
(absbottom, absmiddle, baseline, bottom, left, middle, right, texttop, top)									
height=	4	–	–	–	–	–			
hidden=	4	–	–	–	–	–			
id=	4	–	–	–	–	–			
palette=	4	–	–	–	–	–			
pluginspage=	4	–	–	–	–	–			
src=	4	–	–	–	–	–			
style=	4	–	–	–	–	–			
title=	4	–	–	–	–	–			
width=	4	–	–	–	–	–			
event=	4	–	–	–	–	–			
<FIELDSET> [S]	4	–	–	–	–	–	4	W3C	
...</FIELDSET>									
class=	–	–	–	–	–	–	4	W3C	
dir=	–	–	–	–	–	–	4	W3C	
id=	–	–	–	–	–	–	4	W3C	
lang=	–	–	–	–	–	–	4	W3C	
style=	–	–	–	–	–	–	4	W3C	

Tag	MSIE	Netscp	NCSA	Opera	Lynx	Emacs	HTML	Sponsor	Status
title=	-	-	-	-	-	-	4	W3C	
event=	-	-	-	-	-	-	4	W3C	
<FIG></FIG> Ⓢ	-	-	-	-	✔*	✔	3	W3C	✗3+
align=	-	-	-	-	✔*	✔	3	W3C	✗3+
(left, center, right)									
(justify, bleedleft, bleedright)									
class=					✔	✔	3	W3C	✗3+
clear=					✔	✔	3	W3C	✗3+
(left, right, all)									
height=	-	-	-	-	-	-	3	W3C	✗3+
id=	-	-	-	-	-	-	3	W3C	✗3+
imagemap=	-	-	-	-	-	-	3	W3C	✗3+
lang=	-	-	-	-	-	-	3	W3C	✗3+
md=	-	-	-	-	-	-	3	W3C	✗3+
noflow	-	-	-	-	-	-	3	W3C	✗3+
src=	-	-	-	-	-	-	3	W3C	✗3+
units=	-	-	-	-	-	-	3	W3C	✗3+
width=	-	-	-	-	-	-	3	W3C	✗3+

Tags and attributes in **bold** are included in the HTML 4.0 draft, and tags in square brackets are optional.

The table is arranged alphabetically for convenient reference, but the Structure/Block/Text types of the tags are identified following the tag itself as Ⓢ, Ⓑ, and Ⓣ.

2, 3, 4, etc. = Condensed HTML version number; 3+ = HTML version 3.2; ✔ = Available in all current versions; ↓ = Deprecated—HTML version; ✗ = Obsolete; Ⓟ = Proprietary/nonconforming; * = Partial or partially nonconforming implementation.

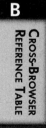

Tag	MSIE	Netscp	NCSA	Opera	Lynx	Emacs	HTML	Sponsor	Status
<FN></FN> [S]	-	-	-	-	✓	✓	3	W3C	✗3+
class=	-	-	-	-	✓	✓	3	W3C	
dir=	-	-	-	-	-	-	4	W3C	
id=	-	-	-	-	✓	✓	3	W3C	
lang=	-	-	-	-	✓	✓	3	W3C	
<FONT></FONT> [T]	✓3/4	✓	-	✓	✓*	✓	3+	W3C	↓4

WARNING: Use of the <FONT> tag can cause anomalous behavior in browsers that use a non-Roman character set, or even use a different set of fonts than what's on the developer's machine. Use CSS, if at all possible.

Tag	MSIE	Netscp	NCSA	Opera	Lynx	Emacs	HTML	Sponsor	Status
color=	✓	✓	-	✓	✓+	✓	3+	W3C	↓4
face=	✓	-	-	-	-	✓	4	W3C	↓4
id=	✓	-	-	-	-	-	-		✗3+
size=	✓	✓	-	✓	✓*	✓	3+	W3C	↓4
style=	-	-	-	-	-	-	-	W3C	✗3+
title=	-	-	-	-	-	-	-	W3C	✗3+
event=	-	-	-	-	-	-	-	W3C	✗3+
<FORM></FORM> [S]	✓	✓	✓	✓	✓*	✓	2-4	W3C	
accept-charset=	-	-	-	-	-	-	4	W3C	
action=	✓	✓	✓	✓	✓	✓	2-4	W3C	
class=	-	-	-	-	-	-	4	W3C	
dir=	-	-	-	-	-	-	4	W3C	
enctype=	✓	✓	✓	✓	✓	✓	2-4	W3C	

WARNING: Some older browsers do not support enctype, which causes the contents to be transferred in a default type, usually enctype="application/x-www-form-urlencoded" or some close variant. The resulting text must be decoded by a CGI or other script on the server before processing. Some browsers allow enctype="text/plain" to send the data as plain text. This method can be useful when using the mailto: feature to avoid needing a CGI script at the server; however, it can cause security and data corruption problems if not handled carefully.

In addition, some browsers support enctype="application/sgml-form-urlencoded", which is similar to the default enctype mentioned previously, but sends separators between name/value pairs as a semicolon (;) instead of an ampersand (&). This format is preferred when using method="GET" because using ampersands can lead to corruption of the transferred data in certain circumstances.

Netscape introduced additional data types to support "enhanced" features that aren't supported by all browsers. When using these data types, you must use caution to avoid breaking most other browsers. In particular, using enctype="multipart/form-data" with an <INPUT> requesting a filename is problem-prone. Although MSIE and others are adding this support, proper handling of this data type is by no means universal.

Tag	MSIE	Netscp	NCSA	Opera	Lynx	Emacs	HTML	Sponsor	Status
id=	4	-	-	-	-	-	4	W3C	
lang=	-	-	-	-	-	-	4	W3C	
method=	✔	✔	✔	✔	✔	✔	2-4	W3C	
(get, post)	✔	✔	✔	✔	✔	✔	2-4	W3C	
name=	4	-	-	-	-	-	-		✘3+
script=	-	-	-	-	-	-	3	W3C	✘3+
style=	4	-	-	-	-	-	4	W3C	
target=	4	-	-	-	-	-	-	W3C	
title=	4	-	-	-	-	-	4	W3C	
event=	4	-	-	-	-	-	4	W3C	

Tags and attributes in **bold** are included in the HTML 4.0 draft, and tags in square brackets are optional.

The table is arranged alphabetically for convenient reference, but the Structure/Block/Text types of the tags are identified following the tag itself as Ⓢ, Ⓑ, and Ⓣ.

2, 3, 4, etc. = Condensed HTML version number; 3+ = HTML version 3.2; ✔ = Available in all current versions; ↓ = Deprecated—HTML version; ✘ = Obsolete; Ⓟ = Proprietary/nonconforming; * = Partial or partially nonconforming implementation.

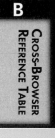

B
CROSS-BROWSER
REFERENCE TABLE

<FRAME></FRAME> Ⓢ

Tag	MSIE	Netscp	NCSA	Opera	Lynx	Emacs	HTML	Sponsor	Status
<FRAME></FRAME> Ⓢ	✓	✓	-	✓	✓*	✓	4	W3C	

TIP: The <FRAME> tag is still controversial and should be used carefully, especially because it affects accessibility for people using audio or Braille text-mode browsers. Always use the <NOFRAMES> container to enclose meaningful content, such as a list of ordinary navigation elements, to allow use by all. Inserting a terse message that tells visitors to use another, more "modern" browser is possibly just a little insensitive.

Tag	MSIE	Netscp	NCSA	Opera	Lynx	Emacs	HTML	Sponsor	Status
bordercolor=	✓3/4	✓3/4	-	-	-	-	-	W3C	✗4
class=	-	-	-	-	-	-	4	W3C	
dir=	-	-	-	-	-	-	4	W3C	
frameborder=	✓3/4	4	-	-	-	-	4	W3C	✗4
framespacing	✓3/4	✓	-	-	-	-	-	W3C	✗4
height=	4	-	-	-	-	-	-	W3C	
id=	4	-	-	-	-	-	4	W3C	
marginheight=	✓3/4	✓	-	-	-	-	4	W3C	
marginwidth=	✓3/4	✓	-	-	-	-	4	W3C	
method=	-	-	-	-	-	-	4	W3C	
name= (window_name, _blank, _parent, _self, _top)	✓3/4	✓2-4	-	✓	✓*	✓	4	W3C	
noresize= (noresize, resize)	✓3/4	✓	-	-	-	-	4	W3C	
scrolling= (auto, no, yes)	✓3/4	✓2-4	-	-	-	-	Ⓟ	MS	✗4
src=	✓3/4	✓2-4	-	✓	✓*	✓	4	W3C	
style	-	-	-	-	-	-	-	W3C	✗4

Tag	MSIE	Netscp	NCSA	Opera	Lynx	Emacs	HTML	Sponsor	Status
target=	✔	✔	-	✔	✔*	✔	4	W3C	
title=	4	-	-	-	-	-	4	W3C	
width=	4	-	-	-	-	-	-	W3C	✘4
event=	4	-	-	-	-	-	4	W3C	
<FRAMESET> Ⓢ	✔3/4	✔2-4	-	✔	✔*	✔	4	W3C	
...</FRAMESET>									
border=	4	-	-	-	-	-	-		✘4
bordercolor=	4	-	-	-	-	-	-		✘4
cols=	4	✔	-	-	-	-	4	W3C	
frameborder=	4	-	-	-	-	-	-		✘4
framespacing=	4	-	-	-	-	-	-		✘4
id=	4	✔	-	-	-	-	-	W3C	✘4
rows=	4	✔	-	-	-	-	4	W3C	
title=	4	-	-	-	-	-	-	W3C	✘4
event=	4	-	-	-	-	-	4	W3C	
(onload, onunload)									

Tags and attributes in **bold** are included in the HTML 4.0 draft, and tags in square brackets are optional.

The table is arranged alphabetically for convenient reference, but the Structure/Block/Text types of the tags are identified following the tag itself as Ⓢ, Ⓑ, and Ⓣ.

2, 3, 4, etc. = Condensed HTML version number; 3+ = HTML version 3.2; ✔ = Available in all current versions; ↓ = Deprecated—HTML version; ✘ = Obsolete; Ⓟ = Proprietary/nonconforming; * = Partial or partially nonconforming implementation.

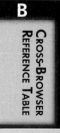

B

CROSS-BROWSER
REFERENCE TABLE

Tag	MSIE	Netscp	NCSA	Opera	Lynx	Emacs	HTML	Sponsor	Status
[<HEAD>][</HEAD>] S	✓	✓	✓	✓	✓	✓	2-4	W3C	

NOTE: The <HEAD> tag is optional and can be inferred. Although <BASE>, <ISINDEX>, <LINK>, and <META> are not containers in the head, Microsoft and probably others allow closing container tags. This practice is forbidden by the specifications, but because it doesn't affect behavior in any case, it doesn't really matter whether you use closing container tags.

Tag	MSIE	Netscp	NCSA	Opera	Lynx	Emacs	HTML	Sponsor	Status
id=	4	-	-	-	-	-	-	W3C	✗4
dir=	-	-	-	-	-	-	4	W3C	
lang=	-	-	-	-	-	-	4	W3C	
profile=	-	-	-	-	-	-	4	W3C	
style=	4	-	-	-	-	-	-	W3C	✗4
title=	4	-	-	-	-	-	4	W3C	
<H1></H1> S	✓	✓	✓	✓	✓*	✓	2-4	W3C	
align= (left, center, right) (justify)	✓	✓	✓	✓	✓	✓	3	W3C	↓4
class=	-	✓	-	-	-	-	3/4	W3C	✗3+
clear= (left, right, all)	✓	✓	-	-	-	-	3	W3C	
color=	✓	-	-	-	-	✓	P		✗3+
dingbat=	-	-	-	-	✓*	✓	3	W3C	✗3+
dir=	-	-	-	-	-	✓	4	W3C	
id=	-	-	-	-	✓	✓	3/4	W3C	✗3+
lang=	-	-	-	-	✓	✓	3/4	W3C	✗3+
md=	-	-	-	-	✓	✓	3	W3C	✗3+

Tag	MSIE	Netscp	NCSA	Opera	Lynx	Emacs	HTML	Sponsor	Status
nowrap	-	-	-	-	✓	✓	3	W3C	✗3+
seqnum=	-	-	-	-	-	-	3	W3C	✗3+
skip=	-	-	-	-	-	-	3	W3C	
style=	-	-	-	-	-	-	4	W3C	
title=	-	-	-	-	-	-	4	W3C	

<H2>, <H3>, <H4>, <H5>, <H6> Same as **<H1>**

Tag	MSIE	Netscp	NCSA	Opera	Lynx	Emacs	HTML	Sponsor	Status
<HR> Ⓑ	✓	✓	✓	✓	✓*	✓	2	W3C	
align=	✓*	✓	✓	✓	✓*	✓	3	W3C	
(center, left, right)									
(justify)	-	-	-	-	-	-	3	W3C	✗3+
class=	-	-	-	-	-	-	4	W3C	
clear=	-	-	-	-	-	-	3	W3C	✗3+
(left, right, all)									
color=	4	-	-	-	-	-	Ⓟ	MS	✗3+
id=	4	-	-	-	-	-	3/4	W3C	
md=	-	-	-	-	-	-	3	W3C	✗3+
noshade=	✓	✓	✓	✓	✓*	✓	3+/4	W3C	✗3+
nowrap	-	-	-	-	-	-	3	W3C	

Tags and attributes in **bold** are included in the HTML 4.0 draft, and tags in square brackets are optional.

The table is arranged alphabetically for convenient reference, but the Structure/Block/Text types of the tags are identified following the tag itself as Ⓢ, Ⓑ, and Ⓣ.

2, 3, 4, etc. = Condensed HTML version number; 3+ = HTML version 3.2; ✓ = Available in all current versions; ↓ = Deprecated—HTML version;

✗ = Obsolete; Ⓟ = Proprietary/nonconforming; * = Partial or partially nonconforming implementation.

Tag	MSIE	Netscp	NCSA	Opera	Lynx	Emacs	HTML	Sponsor	Status
<HR> *continued*									
size=	4	✓	-	✓	✓	✓	3+	W3C	↓4
src=	4	-	-	-	-	-	3	W3C	✗3+
style=	4	-	-	-	-	-	4	W3C	
title=	4	-	-	-	-	-	4	W3C	
width=	✓	✓	✓	✓	✓	✓	3+	W3C	↓4
event=	4	-	-	-	-	-	4	W3C	
<HTML>...[</HTML>] Ⓢ	✓	✓	✓	✓	✓	✓	2-4	W3C	
dir=	-	-	-	-	-	-	4	W3C	
lang=	-	-	-	-	-	-	4	W3C	
title=	4	-	-	-	-	-	4	W3C	✗4
version=	-	-	-	-	-	-	4	W3C	
<I></I> Ⓣ	✓	✓	✓	✓	✓*	✓	2-4	W3C	
class=	-	-	-	-	✓	✓	3/4	W3C	
dir=	-	-	-	-	-	-	4	W3C	
id=	✓3/4	-	-	-	✓	✓	3/4	W3C	
lang=	-	-	-	-	✓	✓	3/4	W3C	
style=	4	-	-	-	-	-	4	W3C	
title=	4	-	-	-	-	-	4	W3C	
event=	4	-	-	-	-	-	4	W3C	

Tag	MSIE	Netscp	NCSA	Opera	Lynx	Emacs	HTML	Sponsor	Status
<IFRAME></IFRAME> Ⓢ	✔3/4	✔	-	-	-	-	4	W3C	
align=	✔3/4	-	-	-	-	-	4	W3C	
(absbottom, absmiddle, baseline, bottom, left, middle, right, texttop, top)									
border=	4	4	-	-	-	-			✗4
bordercolor=	4	-	-	-	-	-			✗4
frameborder=	✔	4	-	-	-	-	4	W3C	
framespacing=	4	-	-	-	-	-			✗4
height=	4	-	-	-	-	-		W3C	✗4
hspace=	4	-	-	-	-	-		W3C	✗4
id=	4	-	-	-	-	-		W3C	✗4
marginheight=	4	4	-	-	-	-	4	W3C	
marginwidth=	4	-	-	-	-	-		W3C	
name=	4	✔	-	-	-	-	4	W3C	
(window_name._blank,_parent,_self,_top)									
noresize=	✔	4	-	-	-	-	4	W3C	
(noresize, resize)									
scrolling=	4	-	-	-	-	-	4	W3C	
(auto, no, yes)									
src=	4	-	-	-	-	-	4	W3C	

Tags and attributes in **bold** are included in the HTML 4.0 draft, and tags in square brackets are optional.
The table is arranged alphabetically for convenient reference, but the Structure/Block/Text types of the tags are identified following the tag itself as Ⓢ, Ⓑ, and Ⓣ.

2, 3, 4, etc. = Condensed HTML version number; 3+ = HTML version 3.2; ✔ = Available in all current versions; ↓ = Deprecated—HTML version; ✗ = Obsolete; Ⓟ = Proprietary/nonconforming; * = Partial or partially nonconforming implementation.

B

CROSS-BROWSER REFERENCE TABLE

Tag	MSIE	Netscp	NCSA	Opera	Lynx	Emacs	HTML	Sponsor	Status
<IFRAME></IFRAME> *continued*									
style=	4	-	-	-	-	-			✗4
title=	4	-	-	-	-	-			✗4
vspace=	4	-	-	-	-	-			✗4
width=	4	-	-	-	-	-	4	W3C	
event=	4	-	-	-	-	-	4	W3C	
<ILAYER></ILAYER> Ⓢ	-	4	-	-	-	-	Ⓟ	NS	

NOTE: <ILAYER> is similar to the <LAYER> tag.

Tag	MSIE	Netscp	NCSA	Opera	Lynx	Emacs	HTML	Sponsor	Status
<IMG> Ⓑ	✓	✓	✓	✓	✓*	✓*	2	W3C	

NOTE: Text-mode browsers like Lynx always render the alt= attribute, although they might (or might not) make the image itself available for rendering with a separate utility. In general, it's best to always include an ALT= value, explicitly setting it to null for purely decorative images that shouldn't be labeled.

Tag	MSIE	Netscp	NCSA	Opera	Lynx	Emacs	HTML	Sponsor	Status
align=	✓	✓	✓*	✓	✓*	✓	2	W3C	
(bottom, left, middle, right, top)									
(absbottom, absmiddle, baseline, texttop)									
alt=	✓	✓	✓	✓	✓	✓	2-4	W3C	
border=	✓	✓	✓	✓	-	-	3+/4	W3C	
class=	-	-	-	-	-	-	3/4	W3C	
controls=	✓	-	-	-	-	-	Ⓟ		✗4
dir=	-	-	-	-	-	-	4	W3C	
datafld=	4	-	-	-	-	-	Ⓟ		✗4
datasrc=	4	-	-	-	-	-	Ⓟ		✗4
dynsrc=	4	-	-	-	-	-	Ⓟ		✗4

Tag	MSIE	Netscp	NCSA	Opera	Lynx	Emacs	HTML	Sponsor	Status
height=	✔	✔	-	✔	-	✔*	2-4	W3C	
hspace=	✔3/4	✔	-	✔	-	-	3+/4	W3C	
id=	✔3/4	-	✔	✔	-	-	3/4	W3C	
ismap=	✔	✔	✔	✔	✔*	✔*	2-4	W3C	
lang=	-	-	-	-	-	-	3/4	W3C	
loop=	4	✔	-	-	-	-	Ⓟ		✗4
lowsrc=	4	✔	-	-	-	-	Ⓟ		✗4
md=	-	-	-	-	-	-	3	W3C	✗3+
name=	4	-	-	✔	-	-		W3C	
src=	✔	✔	✔	✔	✔*	✔*	2-4	W3C	
style=	4	-	-	-	-	-	4	W3C	
title=	4	-	-	-	-	-	4	W3C	
units= (pixels, en)	-	-	-	-	-	-	3	W3C	✗3+
usemap=	✔	✔	-	✔	✔*	✔*	3+/4	W3C	
vrml=	4	-	-	✔	-	-	3+/4	W3C	✗4
vspace=	✔3/4	✔	-	✔	-	✔	3+/4	W3C	
width=	✔	✔	-	✔	-	-	2	W3C	
event=	4	-	-	-	-	-	4	W3C	

Tags and attributes in **bold** are included in the HTML 4.0 draft, and tags in square brackets are optional.
The table is arranged alphabetically for convenient reference, but the Structure/Block/Text types of the tags are identified following the tag itself as Ⓢ, Ⓑ, and Ⓣ.

2, 3, 4, etc. = Condensed HTML version number; 3+ = HTML version 3.2; ✔ = Available in all current versions; ↓ = Deprecated—HTML version; ✗ = Obsolete; Ⓟ = Proprietary/nonconforming; * = Partial or partially nonconforming implementation.

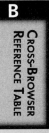

B
CROSS-BROWSER
REFERENCE TABLE

Tag	MSIE	Netscp	NCSA	Opera	Lynx	Emacs	HTML	Sponsor	Status
<INPUT>[</INPUT>] S	✓	✓	✓	✓	✓	✓	2-4	W3C	
accesskey=	4	-	-	-	*	-	Ⓟ	MS	
accept=	-	-	-	-	-	-	4	W3C	
align=	✓	✓	-	✓	-	-	3/4	W3C	
(bottom, left, middle, right, top)									
(absbottom, absmiddle, baseline, texttop)									
alt=	-	-	-	-	-	-	4	W3C	
checked	✓	✓	✓	✓	✓	✓	3/4	W3C	
class=	-	-	-	-	-	-	3/4	W3C	
datafld=	4	-	-	-	-	-	Ⓟ		✗4
datasrc=	4	-	-	-	-	-	Ⓟ		✗4
dir=	-	-	-	-	-	-	4	W3C	
disabled	4	-	-	-	-	-	3/4	W3C	
error	-	-	-	-	-	-	3	W3C	✗3+
id=	4	-	-	-	-	-	3/4	W3C	
lang=	-	-	-	-	-	-	3/4	W3C	
language=	4	-	-	-	-	-			✗4
(javascript, vbscript)									
max=	✓	✓	-	✓	✓	-	3	W3C	✗3+
maxlength=	✓	✓	✓	✓	✓	✓	2-4	W3C	
md=	-	-	-	-	-	-	3	W3C	✗3+
min=	✓	✓	-	-	-	-	3	W3C	✗3+
name=	✓	✓	✓	✓	✓	✓	2-4	W3C	

Tag	MSIE	Netsp	NCSA	Opera	Lynx	Emacs	HTML	Sponsor	Status
readonly=	4	-	-	-	-	-	4	W3C	
size=	✓	✓	✓	✓	✓	✓	2-4	W3C	
src=	-	-	-	-	-	-	2-4	W3C	
style=	4	-	-	-	-	-	4	W3C	
tabindex=	4	4*	-	-	-	-	4	W3C	
title=	4	-	-	-	-	-	4	W3C	
type=	✓	✓	✓	✓	✓*	✓	2-4	W3C	
(button, checkbox, hidden, image, password, radio, reset, select-multiple, select-one, submit, text, textarea)									
usemap=	-	-	-	-	-	-	4	W3C	
value=	✓	✓	✓	✓	✓	✓	2	W3C	✗4
event=	4	-	-	-	-	-	4	W3C	
<INS></INS> Ⓣ	-	-	-	-	✓*	✓	3/4	W3C	✗3+
cite=	-	-	-	-	-	-	4	W3C	
class=	-	-	-	-	✓	✓	3/4	W3C	
datetime=	-	-	-	-	-	-	4	W3C	
dir=	-	-	-	-	-	-	4	W3C	
id=	-	-	-	-	-	-	3	W3C	
lang=	-	-	-	-	-	-	3	W3C	

Tags and attributes in **bold** are included in the HTML 4.0 draft, and tags in square brackets are optional.

The table is arranged alphabetically for convenient reference, but the Structure/Block/Text types of the tags are identified following the tag itself as Ⓢ, Ⓑ, and Ⓣ.

2, 3, 4, etc. = Condensed HTML version number; 3+ = HTML version 3.2; ✓ = Available in all current versions; ↓ = Deprecated—HTML version; ✗ = Obsolete; Ⓟ = Proprietary/nonconforming; * = Partial or partially nonconforming implementation.

B
CROSS-BROWSER
REFERENCE TABLE

Tag	MSIE	Netscp	NCSA	Opera	Lynx	Emacs	HTML	Sponsor	Status
<INS></INS> [T] *continued*									
style=	-	-	-	-	-	-	-	W3C	
title=	-	-	-	-	-	-	-	W3C	
event=	-	-	-	-	-	-	-	W3C	
<ISINDEX> [B]									
action=	✔	✔	✔	✔	✔	✔	2-4	W3C	↓4

NOTE: Use <FORM> instead of <ISINDEX>, if possible. ✘3+

Tag	MSIE	Netscp	NCSA	Opera	Lynx	Emacs	HTML	Sponsor	Status
class=	-	-	-	-	-	-	4	W3C	
dir=	-	-	-	-	-	-	4	W3C	
id=	-	-	-	-	-	-	4	W3C	
lang=	-	-	-	-	-	-	4	W3C	
prompt=	✔	✔	-	✔	-	-	4	W3C	
style=	-	-	-	-	-	-	4	W3C	
title=	-	-	-	-	-	-	4	W3C	
<KBD></KBD> [T]	✔	✔	✔	✔	✔*	✔	2-4	W3C	
class=	-	-	-	-	✔	✔	3/4	W3C	
dir=	✔3/4	-	-	-	-	-	4	W3C	
id=	-	-	-	-	✔	✔	3/4	W3C	
lang=	-	-	-	-	✔	✔	3/4	W3C	
style=	4	-	-	-	-	-	4	W3C	
title=	4	-	-	-	-	-	4	W3C	
event=	4	-	-	-	-	-	4	W3C	

Tag	MSIE	Netscp	NCSA	Opera	Lynx	Emacs	HTML	Sponsor	Status
<KEYGEN></KEYGEN> (S)	-	✔	-	-	-	-	(P)	NS	
<LABEL></LABEL> (T)	✔3/4	-							
accesskey=	4	-	-	-	-	-	4	W3C	
class=	-	-	-	-	-	-	4	W3C	
dir=	-	-	-	-	-	-	4	W3C	
disabled	-	-	-	-	-	-	4	W3C	
for=	4	-	-	-	-	-	4	W3C	
id=	4	-	-	-	-	-	4	W3C	
lang=	-	-	-	-	-	-	4	W3C	
style=	4	-	-	-	-	-	4	W3C	
title=	4	-	-	-	-	-	4	W3C	
event=	4	-	-	-	-	-	4	W3C	
<LAYER></LAYER> (S)	-	4	-	-	-	-	(P)	NS	
id=									
left=									
top=									
pagex=									
pagey=									

Tags and attributes in **bold** are included in the HTML 4.0 draft, and tags in square brackets are optional.
The table is arranged alphabetically for convenient reference, but the Structure/Block/Text types of the tags are identified following the tag itself as (S), (B), and (T).

2, 3, 4, etc. = Condensed HTML version number; 3+ = HTML version 3.2; ✔ = Available in all current versions; ↓ = Deprecated—HTML version;
✘ = Obsolete; (P) = Proprietary/nonconforming; * = Partial or partially nonconforming implementation.

B

**CROSS-BROWSER
REFERENCE TABLE**

Tag	MSIE	Netscp	NCSA	Opera	Lynx	Emacs	HTML	Sponsor	Status
<LAYER></LAYER> (S) *continued*									
src=									
z-index=									
above=									
below=									
width=									
height=									
clip=									
visibility=									
(show, hidden, inherit)									
bgcolor=									
background=									
onmouseover=									
onmouseout=									
onfocus=									
onblur=									
onload=									
<LEGEND> (S)	4	-	-	-	-	-	4	W3C	
accesskey=	4	-	-	-	-	-	4	W3C	
align=	-	-	-	-	-	-	4	W3C	
class=	-	-	-	-	-	-	4	W3C	
dir=	-	-	-	-	-	-	4	W3C	

Tag	MSIE	Netscp	NCSA	Opera	Lynx	Emacs	HTML	Sponsor	Status
id=	4	–	–	–	–	–	4	W3C	
lang=	–	–	–	–	–	–	4	W3C	
style=	4	–	–	–	–	–	4	W3C	
title=	4	–	–	–	–	–	4	W3C	
event=	4	–	–	–	–	–	4	W3C	
<LI>[</LI>] [S]	✔	✔	✔	✔	✔	✔	2	W3C	
align=	4	–	–	–	–	–			
(center, left, right)									
class=	–	–	–	–	–	–	4	W3C	
dir=	–	–	–	–	–	–	4	W3C	
id=	4	–	–	–	–	–	4	W3C	
lang=	–	–	–	–	–	–	4	W3C	
style=	4	–	–	–	–	–	4	W3C	
title=	4	–	–	–	–	–	4	W3C	
type=	✔	✔	–	✔	✔	✔	3+/4	W3C	
(1, a, A, i, I)									
value=	4	–	–	–	–	–	3+/4	W3C	
event=	4	–	–	–	–	–	4	W3C	

Tags and attributes in **bold** are included in the HTML 4.0 draft, and tags in square brackets are optional.

The table is arranged alphabetically for convenient reference, but the Structure/Block/Text types of the tags are identified following the tag itself as [S], [B], and [T].

2, 3, 4, etc. = Condensed HTML version number; 3+ = HTML version 3.2; ✔ = Available in all current versions; ↓ = Deprecated—HTML version; **✗** = Obsolete; [P] = Proprietary/nonconforming; * = Partial or partially nonconforming implementation.

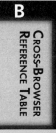

B
CROSS-BROWSER
REFERENCE TABLE

Tag	MSIE	Netscp	NCSA	Opera	Lynx	Emacs	HTML	Sponsor	Status
<LINK>[</LINK>] Ⓢ	✓ Ⓟ	✓	✓	✓	✓	✓	2-4	W3C	
class=	-	-	-	-	-	-	4	W3C	
dir=	-	-	-	-	-	-	4	W3C	
href=	✓	✓	✓	✓	✓	✓	2-4	W3C	
id=	-	-	-	-	-	-	4	W3C	
lang=	-	-	-	-	-	-	4	W3C	
media=	-	-	-	-	-	-	4	W3C	
methods=	✓	✓	✓	✓	✓	✓	2	W3C	✗3+
name=	✓	-	-	-	-	-	2	W3C	✗3+
rel=	✓	✓	✓	✓	✓	✓	2-4	W3C	
(contents, home, toc, index, glossary, copyright, up, next, previous, start, help, bookmark, banner, **stylesheet, alternate)**									
rev=	✓	✓	✓	✓	✓	✓	2-4	W3C	
style=	-	-	-	-	-	-	4	W3C	
target=	✓	-	-	-	-	-	4	W3C	
title=	✓	✓	✓	✓	✓	✓	2-4	W3C	
type=	-	-	-	-	-	-	4	W3C	
urn=	✓	✓	✓	✓	✓	✓	2	W3C	✗3+

Tag	MSIE	Netscp	NCSA	Opera	Lynx	Emacs	HTML	Sponsor	Status
<LISTING></LISTING> ⊤	✔	✔	✔	✔	✔	✔	2	W3C	↓2✗4
align=	4	-	-	-	-	-			
(center, left, right)									
class=	-	-	-	-	✔	✔	3	W3C	
id=	✔3/4	-	-	-	✔	✔	3	W3C	
lang=	-	-	-	-	-	-	3	W3C	
style=	4	-	-	-	-	-		W3C	
title=	4	-	-	-	-	-		W3C	
event=	4	-	-	-	-	-		W3C	
<MAP></MAP> ⑬	✔3/4	✔	✔	✔	✔*	✔*	3+/4	W3C	

TIP: Lynx doesn't actually display the image; it creates a reference list of all the destinations in a client-side image map. If the destination names are meaningful, people without access to the map can still navigate by using the constructed text-mode analog.

Tag	MSIE	Netscp	NCSA	Opera	Lynx	Emacs	HTML	Sponsor	Status
class=	-	-	-	-	-	-	4	W3C	
id=	4	-	-	-	-	-	4	W3C	
name=	✔	✔	-	-	✔	✔	3+/4	W3C	
style=	4	-	-	-	-	-	4	W3C	
title=	4	-	-	-	-	-	4	W3C	
event=	4	-	-	-	-	-	4	W3C	

Tags and attributes in **bold** are included in the HTML 4.0 draft, and tags in square brackets are optional.

The table is arranged alphabetically for convenient reference, but the Structure/Block/Text types of the tags are identified following the tag itself as Ⓢ, Ⓑ, and ⊤.

2, 3, 4, etc. = Condensed HTML version number; 3+ = HTML version 3.2; ✔ = Available in all current versions; ↓ = Deprecated—HTML version; ✗ = Obsolete; Ⓟ = Proprietary/nonconforming; * = Partial or partially nonconforming implementation.

B

CROSS-BROWSER REFERENCE TABLE

Tag	MSIE	Netscp	NCSA	Opera	Lynx	Emacs	HTML	Sponsor	Status
<MARQUEE> [B]	✓	-	-	-	✓*	-	[P]	MS	✓
...</MARQUEE>									

NOTE: Lynx treats the Microsoft <MARQUEE> as a synonym for <BANNER> and renders it statically (as plain text). In practice, most browsers just ignore the tag and render the contents as plain text.

Tag	MSIE	Netscp	NCSA	Opera	Lynx	Emacs
align=		-	-	-	-	-
(absbottom, absmiddle, baseline, bottom, left, middle, right, texttop, top)						
behavior=	✓	-	-	-	-	-
(alternate, scroll, slide)						
bgcolor=	✓	-	-	-	-	-
datafld=	4	-	-	-	-	-
dataformats=	4	-	-	-	-	-
datasrc=	4	-	-	-	-	-
direction=	✓	-	-	-	-	-
(down, left, right, up)						
height=	✓	-	-	-	-	-
hspace=	✓	-	-	-	-	-
id=	4	-	-	-	-	-
loop=	✓	-	-	-	-	-
scrollamount=	4	-	-	-	-	-
scrolldelay=	4	-	-	-	-	-
style=	4	-	-	-	-	-
title=	4	-	-	-	-	-
vspace=	✓	-	-	-	-	-

Tag	MSIE	Netscp	NCSA	Opera	Lynx	Emacs	HTML	Sponsor	Status
width=	✓	-	-	-	-	-			
event=	4	-	-	-	-	-			
$$Ⓣ							3	W3C	✗3+

NOTE: The many HTML 3.0 math elements are not included in this table because they were never really used and were dropped from HTML 3.2. The W3C is working on a new math markup standard.

Tag	MSIE	Netscp	NCSA	Opera	Lynx	Emacs	HTML	Sponsor	Status
<MENU></MENU>Ⓢ	✓	✓	✓	✓	✓	✓	2-4	W3C	↓4
compact	✓	✓	✓	✓	✓*	✓	2-4	W3C	↓4
dir=	-	-	-	-	-	-	4	W3C	
id=	4	-	-	-	-	-	4	W3C	
lang=	-	-	-	-	-	-	4	W3C	
style=	4	-	-	-	-	-	4	W3C	
title=	4	-	-	-	-	-	4	W3C	
event=	4	-	-	-	-	-	4	W3C	
<META>[</META>]Ⓢ	✓ Ⓟ	✓	✓	✓	✓	✓	2-4	W3C	
content=	✓	✓	✓	✓	✓	✓	2-4	W3C	
dir=	-	-	-	-	-	-	4	W3C	
http-equiv=	✓	✓	✓	✓	✓	✓	2-4	W3C	

Tags and attributes in **bold** are included in the HTML 4.0 draft, and tags in square brackets are optional.

The table is arranged alphabetically for convenient reference, but the Structure/Block/Text types of the tags are identified following the tag itself as Ⓢ, Ⓑ, and Ⓣ.

2, 3, 4, etc. = Condensed HTML version number; 3+ = HTML version 3.2; ✔ = Available in all current versions; ↓ = Deprecated—HTML version;
✗ = Obsolete; Ⓟ = Proprietary/nonconforming; * = Partial or partially nonconforming implementation.

B

CROSS-BROWSER REFERENCE TABLE

Tag	MSIE	Netscp	NCSA	Opera	Lynx	Emacs	HTML	Sponsor	Status
<META>[</META>] *continued*									
lang=	-	-	-	✓	-	-	4	W3C	
name=	✓	✓	✓	✓	✓	✓	2-4	W3C	

TIP: NAME and HTTP-EQUIV probably shouldn't both be used at once because NAME is assumed to be the same as HTTP-EQUIV. HTTP-EQUIV should avoid names that correspond to built-in HTTP headers as these values are passed by HTTP and are usually silently ignored if they infringe on HTTP "reserved words."

Tag	MSIE	Netscp	NCSA	Opera	Lynx	Emacs	HTML	Sponsor	Status
scheme=	-	-	-	-	-	-	4	W3C	
title=	4	-	-	-	-	-	-	W3C	✗4
url]=	4	-	-	-	-	-	-	W3C	✗4
<MULTICOL> S	-	✓	-	-	-	-	(P)	NS	
<NEXTID> S	✓	✓	✓	✓	✓	✓	2	W3C	✗3+

NOTE: Nobody actually seems to do anything with the <NEXTID> tag, and it has disappeared from the standard.

Tag	MSIE	Netscp	NCSA	Opera	Lynx	Emacs	HTML	Sponsor	Status
n=	✓	✓	✓	✓	✓	✓	2	W3C	
(znnn)									
<NOBR>[</NOBR>] S	✓	✓	-	✓	-	✓	-	NS	
id=	4	-	-	-	-	-	4	W3C	
style=	4	-	-	-	-	-	4	W3C	
title=	4	-	-	-	-	-	4	W3C	
<NOEMBED> B	-	✓	-	-	-	-	(P)	NS	

Tag	MSIE	Netscp	NCSA	Opera	Lynx	Emacs	HTML	Sponsor	Status
<NOFRAMES> Ⓢ	✓3/4	✓2-4	-	✓	✓*	✓	4	W3C	
...**</NOFRAMES>**									
id=	4	✓	-	-	-	-	4	MS	
style=	4	-	-	-	-	-	4	MS	
title=	4	-	-	-	-	-	4	MS	
<NOLAYER> Ⓢ	-	4	-	-	-	-	Ⓟ	NS	
...</NOLAYER>									
<NOSCRIPT> Ⓑ	✓3/4	✓3/4	-	✓	✓	✓	4	W3C	
...</NOSCRIPT>									
title=	4	-	-	-	-	-	4	W3C	
<NOTE></NOTE> Ⓢ	-	-	-	-	✓*	✓	3	W3C	✗3+
class=	-	-	-	-	✓*	✓	3	W3C	
clear=	-	-	-	-	✓*	✓	3	W3C	
(left, right, all)									
id=	-	-	-	-	✓	✓	3	W3C	
lang=	-	-	-	-	✓	✓	3	W3C	
md=	-	-	-	-	-	-	3	W3C	
src=	-	-	-	-	✓*	✓	3	W3C	

Tags and attributes in **bold** are included in the HTML 4.0 draft, and tags in square brackets are optional.

The table is arranged alphabetically for convenient reference, but the Structure/Block/Text types of the tags are identified following the tag itself as Ⓢ, Ⓑ, and Ⓣ.

2, 3, 4, etc. = Condensed HTML version number; 3+ = HTML version 3.2; ✓ = Available in all current versions; ↓ = Deprecated—HTML version; ✗ = Obsolete; Ⓟ = Proprietary/nonconforming; * = Partial or partially nonconforming implementation.

B

CROSS-BROWSER REFERENCE TABLE

Tag	MSIE	Netscp	NCSA	Opera	Lynx	Emacs	HTML	Sponsor	Status
\<OBJECT\>\</OBJECT\> Ⓑ	✔3/4	-	-	-	✔	✔	4	W3C	
accesskey=	4	-	-	-	-	-	4	MS	
align=	✔3/4	-	-	-	-	-	4	W3C	↓4
(absbottom, absmiddle, baseline, bottom, left, middle, right, texttop, top)									
border=	✔3/4	-	-	-	-	-	4	W3C	
class=	✔3/4	-	-	-	-	-	4	W3C	
classid=	4	-	-	-	-	-	4	W3C	
code=	4	-	-	-	-	-	4	W3C	✗4
codebase=	4	-	-	-	-	-	4	W3C	
codetype=	4	-	-	-	-	-	4	W3C	
data=	✔3/4	-	-	-	-	-	4	W3C	
datafld=	4	-	-	-	-	-			✗4
datasrc=	4	-	-	-	-	-			✗4
declare=	-	-	-	-	-	-	4	W3C	
dir=	-	-	-	-	-	-	4	W3C	
disabled	4	-	-	-	-	-			✗4
height=	✔3/4	-	-	-	-	-	4	W3C	
hspace=	-	-	-	-	-	-	4	W3C	
id=	4	-	-	-	-	-	4	W3C	
lang=	-	-	-	-	-	-	4	W3C	
name=	✔3/4	-	-	-	-	-	4	W3C	
shapes=	-	-	-	-	-	-	4	W3C	
standby=	-	-	-	-	-	-	4	W3C	

Tag	MSIE	Netscp	NCSA	Opera	Lynx	Emacs	HTML	Sponsor	Status
style=	4	-	-	-	-	-	4	W3C	
tabindex=	4	-	-	-	-	-	4	W3C	
title=	4	-	-	-	-	-	4	W3C	
type=	✓3/4	-	-	-	-	-	4	W3C	
usemap=	-	-	-	-	-	-	4	W3C	
vspace=	-	-	-	-	-	-	4	W3C	
width=	✓3/4	-	-	-	-	-	4	W3C	
event=	4	-	-	-	-	-	4	W3C	
<OL></OL> Ⓢ									
align= (center, left, right)	✓ 4	✓	✓*	✓	✓	✓	2-4	W3C	
class=	-	-	-	-	✓	✓	3/4	W3C	
clear= (left, right, all)	-	-	-	-	✓*	✓	3	W3C	✗3+
compact	-	-	-	✓	✓	✓	2	W3C	↓4
continue	-	-	-	-	✓	✓	3	W3C	✗3+
dir=	-	-	-	-	-	-	4	W3C	
id=	4	-	-	-	✓	✓	3/4	W3C	
lang=	-	-	-	-	✓	✓	3/4	W3C	

Tags and attributes in **bold** are included in the HTML 4.0 draft, and tags in square brackets are optional.
The table is arranged alphabetically for convenient reference, but the Structure/Block/Text types of the tags are identified following the tag itself as Ⓢ, Ⓑ, and Ⓣ.

2, 3, 4, etc. = Condensed HTML version number; 3+ = HTML version 3.2; ✓ = Available in all current versions; ↓ = Deprecated—HTML version; ✗ = Obsolete; Ⓟ = Proprietary/nonconforming; * = Partial or partially nonconforming implementation.

B

CROSS-BROWSER REFERENCE TABLE

Tag	MSIE	Netscp	NCSA	Opera	Lynx	Emacs	HTML	Sponsor	Status
<OL></OL> *continued*									
seqnum=	✓	✓	-	✓	✓	✓	3	W3C	✗3+
start=	✓3/4	✓	-	✓	✓	✓	3+/4	W3C	
style=	4	-	-	-	-	-	4	W3C	
title=	4	-	-	-	-	-	4	W3C	
type= (1, a, A, i, I)	✓	✓	-	✓	✓	✓	2-4	W3C	
event=	4	-	-	-	-	-	4	W3C	
<OPTION> Ⓢ	✓	✓	✓	✓	✓*	✓	2-4	W3C	
...[</OPTION>]								W3C	
class=	-	-	-	-	-	-	4	W3C	
dir=	-	-	-	-	-	-	4	W3C	
disabled	-	-	-	-	-	-	4	W3C	
id=	4	-	-	-	-	-	4	W3C	
lang=	-	-	-	-	-	-	4	W3C	
name=	✓	✓	✓	✓	✓	✓	2-4	W3C	
selected=	✓	✓	✓	✓	✓*	✓	2-4	W3C	
style=	-	-	-	-	-	-	4	W3C	
title=	4	-	-	-	-	-	4	W3C	
value=	✓	✓	✓	✓	✓*	✓	2-4	W3C	
<OVERLAY>	-	-	-	-	✓*	✓	3	W3C	✗3+

NOTE: The <OVERLAY> tag was part of the HTML 3.0 <FIG> figure specification and is no longer used.

Tag	MSIE	Netscp	NCSA	Opera	Lynx	Emacs	HTML	Sponsor	Status
<P>[**</P>**] Ⓢ	✔	✔	✔	✔	✔	✔	2-4	W3C	

TIP: Some older browsers insert an extra line feed on seeing the closing </P> tag, so it's best to leave it out, even though the standard lists it as optional. This behavior is nonconforming when seen, but rarely matters because most HTML authors ignore the closing tag.

Tag	MSIE	Netscp	NCSA	Opera	Lynx	Emacs	HTML	Sponsor	Status
align=	✔	✔	✔*	✔	✔	✔	3+	W3C	↓4
(center, **left**, right)									
(justify)				-	-	-	3	W3C	✗3+
class=	-	-	-	-	-	-	3/4	W3C	
clear=	-	✔	-	-	-	-	3	W3C	✗3+
(left, right, all)									
dir=	-	-	-	-	-	-	4	W3C	
id=	4	-	-	-	-	-	3/4	W3C	
lang=	-	-	-	-	-	-	3/4	W3C	
style=	4	-	-	-	-	-	4	W3C	
title=	4	-	-	-	-	-	4	W3C	
width=	4	-	-	-	-	-	2	W3C	✗3+
event=	4	-	-	-	-	-	4	W3C	

Tags and attributes in **bold** are included in the HTML 4.0 draft, and tags in square brackets are optional.

The table is arranged alphabetically for convenient reference, but the Structure/Block/Text types of the tags are identified following the tag itself as Ⓢ, Ⓑ, and Ⓣ.

2, 3, 4, etc. = Condensed HTML version number; 3+ = HTML version 3.2; ✔ = Available in all current versions; ↓ = Deprecated—HTML version; ✗ = Obsolete; Ⓟ = Proprietary/nonconforming; * = Partial or partially nonconforming implementation.

B

CROSS-BROWSER
REFERENCE TABLE

Tag	MSIE	Netscp	NCSA	Opera	Lynx	Emacs	HTML	Sponsor	Status
<PARAM>[</PARAM>] B	✔3/4	✔	-	-	-	-	3+	W3C	
data=	4	-	-	-	-	-			
datafld=	4	-	-	-	-	-			
datasrc=	4	-	-	-	-	-			
name=	4	✔	-	-	-	-	3+/4	W3C	
object=	4	-	-	-	-	-			
ref=	4	-	-	-	-	-			
title=	4	-	-	-	-	-			
type=	-	-	-	-	-	-	4	W3C	
value=	4	✔	-	-	-	-	3+/4	W3C	
valuetype=	-	-	-	-	-	-	4	W3C	
(data, ref, object)									
<PERSON><PERSON> T	-	-	-	-	✔*	✔	3	W3C	✗3+
class=	-	-	-	-	✔	✔	3	W3C	
id=	-	-	-	-	✔	✔	3	W3C	
lang=	-	-	-	-	✔	✔	3	W3C	
<PLAINTEXT> S	✔	✔	✔	✔	✔	✔	2	W3C	↓2✗4

NOTE: Both MSIE and NCSA Mosaic allowed a nonconforming `</PLAINTEXT>` end tag. The syntax implied should have been this:

`<HTML> ... <BODY> ... [</BODY>] [</HTML>] <PLAINTEXT> ...`

Tag	MSIE	Netscp	NCSA	Opera	Lynx	Emacs	HTML	Sponsor	Status
id=	4	-	-	-	-	-		W3C	
style=	4	-	-	-	-	-		W3C	

Tag	MSIE	Netscp	NCSA	Opera	Lynx	Emacs	HTML	Sponsor	Status
title=	4	-	-	-	-	-	-	W3C	
event=	4	-	-	-	-	-	-	W3C	
PRE></PRE> Ⓢ	✔	✔	✔	✔	✔	✔	2-4	W3C	
class=	-	-	-	-	-	-	3/4	W3C	
clear= (left, right, all)	-	-	-	-	-	-	3	W3C	✘3+
dir=	-	-	-	-	-	-		W3C	
id=	✔3/4	-	-	-	-	-	3/4	W3C	
lang=	-	-	-	-	-	-	3/4	W3C	
style=	4	-	-	-	-	-	4	W3C	
title=	4	-	-	-	-	-	4	W3C	
width=	4	-	-	-	-	-	2-4	W3C	
event=	4	-	-	-	-	-	4	W3C	
<Q></Q> Ⓣ	4	-	-	-	✔ˣ	✔	3/4	W3C	
cite=	-	-	-	-	-	-	4	W3C	
class=	-	-	-	-	✔	✔	3/4	W3C	
dir=	-	-	-	-	-	-	4	W3C	
id=	✔3/4	-	-	-	✔	✔	3/4	W3C	

Tags and attributes in **bold** are included in the HTML 4.0 draft, and tags in square brackets are optional.

The table is arranged alphabetically for convenient reference, but the Structure/Block/Text types of the tags are identified following the tag itself as Ⓢ, Ⓑ, and Ⓣ.

2, 3, 4, etc. = Condensed HTML version number; 3+ = HTML version 3.2; ✔ = Available in all current versions; ↓ = Deprecated—HTML version; ✘ = Obsolete; Ⓟ = Proprietary/nonconforming; ˣ = Partial or partially nonconforming implementation.

B

CROSS-BROWSER REFERENCE TABLE

Tag	MSIE	Netsp	NCSA	Opera	Lynx	Emacs	HTML	Sponsor	Status
`<Q></Q>` *continued*									
lang=	-	-	-	-	✓	✓	3/4	W3C	
style=	4	-	-	-	-	-	4	W3C	
title=	4	-	-	-	-	-	4	W3C	
event=	4	-	-	-	-	-	4	W3C	
`<RANGE>`	-	-	-	-	-	-	3	W3C	✗3+
class=	-	-	-	-	-	-	3	W3C	
from=	-	-	-	-	-	-	3	W3C	
id=	-	-	-	-	-	-	3	W3C	
until=	-	-	-	-	-	-	3	W3C	
`<S></S>` T	✓	✓	✓	✓	✓*	✓	2	W3C	✗3+✓4
class=	-	✓3/4	-	-	✓	✓	3/4	W3C	
dir=	-	-	-	-	-	-	4	W3C	
id=	✓3/4	✓3/4	-	-	✓	✓	3/4	W3C	
lang=	-	✓3/4	-	-	✓	✓	3/4	W3C	
style=	4	-	-	-	-	-	4	W3C	
title=	4	-	-	-	-	-	4	W3C	
event=	4	-	-	-	-	-	4	W3C	
`<SAMP></SAMP>` T	✓	✓	✓	✓	✓*	✓	2-4	W3C	
class=	-	✓	-	-	✓	✓	3/4	W3C	
dir=	-	-	-	-	-	-	4	W3C	
id=	✓3/4	-	-	-	✓	✓	3/4	W3C	

Tag	MSIE	Netscp	NCSA	Opera	Lynx	Emacs	HTML	Sponsor	Status
lang=	–	–	–	–	✔	✔	3/4	W3C	
style=	4	–	–	–	–	–	4	W3C	
title=	4	–	–	–	–	–	4	W3C	
event=	4	–	–	–	–	–	4	W3C	

<SCRIPT></SCRIPT> Ⓑ

	MSIE	Netscp	NCSA	Opera	Lynx	Emacs	HTML	Sponsor	Status
	✔*	✔	–	3	–	–	3+/4	W3C	

WARNING: Microsoft's implementation of Netscape's JavaScript, JScript, was incompatible with the Netscape "standard." This unfortunate situation is said to be improving, but Microsoft JScript code still regularly breaks Netscape and vice versa, unless special care is taken to account for differences.

Tag	MSIE	Netscp	NCSA	Opera	Lynx	Emacs	HTML	Sponsor	Status
event=	4	–	–	–	–	–	–		✘4
for=	4	–	–	–	–	–	–		✘4
id=	4	–	–	–	–	–	–		✘4
in=	4	–	–	–	–	–	–		✘4
language=	✔*	✔	–	3	–	–	4	W3C	
(javascript, vbscript)									
library=	4	–	–	–	–	–	–		✘4
src=	✔	✔	–	–	–	–	4	W3C	
title=	4	–	–	–	–	–	4	W3C	
type=	–	–	–	–	–	–	4	W3C	

Tags and attributes in **bold** are included in the HTML 4.0 draft, and tags :n square brackets are optional.

The table is arranged alphabetically for convenient reference, but the Structure/Block/Text types of the tags are identified following the tag itself as Ⓢ, Ⓑ, and Ⓣ.

2, 3, 4, etc. = Condensed HTML version number; 3+ = HTML version 3.2; ✔ = Available in all current versions; ↓ = Deprecated—HTML version; ✘ = Obsolete; Ⓟ = Proprietary/nonconforming; * = Partial or partially nonconforming implementation.

Tag	MSIE	Netscp	NCSA	Opera	Lynx	Emacs	HTML	Sponsor	Status
<SELECT></SELECT> (S)	✓	✓	✓	✓	✓	✓	2-4	W3C	
accesskey=	4						(P)	MS	
align=	4						3	W3C	✗3+
(bottom, left, middle, right, top, absbottom, absmiddle, baseline, texttop)									
class=		✓3/4					3/4	W3C	
datafld=	✓						(P)		
datasrc=							(P)		
dir=							4	W3C	
disabled	4						3/4	W3C	
height=							3	W3C	✗3+
id=	4	✓3/4					4	W3C	
lang=		✓3/4					3/4	W3C	
language=	4							W3C	✗4
(javascript, vbscript)									
md=							3	W3C	✗3+
multiple	✓	✓		✓			2-4	W3C	
name=	✓	✓		✓			2-4	W3C	
readonly=	4						3	W3C	✗4
size=	✓	✓		✓			2-4	W3C	
style=	4	4					4	W3C	
tabindex=	4	4*					4	W3C	
title=	4						4	W3C	
units=							3	W3C	✗3+

Tag	MSIE	Netscp	NCSA	Opera	Lynx	Emacs	HTML	Sponsor	Status
width=	-	-	-	-	-	-	3	W3C	✗3+
event=	4	-	-	-	-	-	4	W3C	-
<SERVER>	-	✔	-	-	-	-	[P]	NS	-
<SMALL></SMALL> [T]	✔	✔	-	✔	✔*	✔	3/4	W3C	
class=	-	3	-	-	✔	✔	3/4	W3C	
dir=	-	-	-	-	-	-	4	W3C	
id=	✔3/4	3	-	-	✔	✔	3/4	W3C	
lang=	-	3	-	-	✔	✔	3/4	W3C	
style=	4	4	-	-	-	-	4	W3C	
title=	4	-	-	-	-	-	4	W3C	
event=	4	-	-	-	-	-	4	W3C	
<SPACER> [T]	-	✔3/4	-	-	-	-	[P]	NS	
<SPAN></SPAN> [T]	✔3/4	4	-	-	-	-	4	W3C	
align=	-	4	-	-	-	-	4	W3C	
class=	-	-	-	-	-	-	4	W3C	
datafld=	4	-	-	-	-	-	[P]		✗4
dataformats=	4	-	-	-	-	-	[P]		✗4
datasrc=	4	-	-	-	-	-	[P]		✗4

Tags and attributes in **bold** are included in the HTML 4.0 draft, and tags in square brackets are optional.

The table is arranged alphabetically for convenient reference, but the Structure/Block/Text types of the tags are identified following the tag itself as (S), (B), and (T).

2, 3, 4, etc. = Condensed HTML version number; 3+ = HTML version 3.2; ✔ = Available in all current versions; ↓ = Deprecated—HTML version; ✗ = Obsolete; (P) = Proprietary/nonconforming; * = Partial or partially nonconforming implementation.

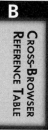

B

CROSS-BROWSER REFERENCE TABLE

Tag	MSIE	Netscp	NCSA	Opera	Lynx	Emacs	HTML	Sponsor	Status
<SPAN></SPAN> continued									
dir=	-	-	-	-	-	-	4	W3C	
id=	4	3	-	-	-	-	4	W3C	
style=	4	4	-	-	-	-	4	W3C	
title=	4	-	-	-	-	-	4	W3C	
event=	4	-	-	-	-	-	4	W3C	
<SPOT> [T]	-	-	-	-	-	-	3	W3C	✗3+
id=	-	-	-	-	-	-	3	W3C	
<STRIKE></STRIKE> [T]	✓	✓	✓	✓	*	✓	3+/4	W3C	↓4
class=	-	✓3/4	-	-	✓	✓	4	W3C	
dir=	-	-	-	-	-	-	4	W3C	
id=	4	✓3/4	-	-	✓	✓	4	W3C	
lang=	-	✓3/4	-	-	✓	✓	4	W3C	
style=	4	4	-	-	-	✓	4	W3C	
title=	4	-	-	-	-	-	4	W3C	
event=	4	-	-	-	-	-	4	W3C	
<STRONG></STRONG> [T]	✓	✓	✓	✓	*	✓	2-4	W3C	
class=	-	3	-	-	✓	✓	3/4	W3C	
dir=	-	-	-	-	-	-	4	W3C	
id=	✓3/4	3	-	-	✓	✓	3/4	W3C	
lang=	-	3	-	-	✓	✓	3/4	W3C	
style=	4	4	-	-	-	-	4	W3C	

Tag	MSIE	Netscp	NCSA	Opera	Lynx	Emacs	HTML	Sponsor	Status
title=	4	-	-	-	-	-	4	W3C	
event=	4	-	-	-	-	-	4	W3C	
<STYLE></STYLE> [T]	✔3/4	4	-	✔	✔*	✔	3+/4	W3C	
dir=	-	-	-	-	-	-	4	W3C	
lang=	-	-	-	-	-	-	4	W3C	
media=	-	-	-	-	-	-	4	W3C	
title=	4	-	-	-	-	-	4	W3C	
type=	4	-	-	-	✔	-	4	W3C	
<SUB> [T]	✔	✔	✔	✔	✔*	✔	3/4	W3C	
class=	-	3	-	-	✔	✔	3/4	W3C	
dir=	-	-	-	-	-	-	4	W3C	
id=	3/4	3	-	-	✔	✔	3/4	W3C	
lang=	-	3	-	-	✔	✔	3/4	W3C	
style=	4	4	-	-	-	-	4	W3C	
title=	4	-	-	-	-	-	4	W3C	
event=	4	-	-	-	-	-	4	W3C	
<SUP> [T]	✔	✔	✔	✔	✔*	✔	3/4	W3C	
class=	-	3	-	-	✔	✔	3/4	W3C	

Tags and attributes in **bold** are included in the HTML 4.0 draft, and tags in square brackets are optional.
The table is arranged alphabetically for convenient reference, but the Structure/Block/Text types of the tags are identified following the tag itself as Ⓢ, Ⓑ, and Ⓣ.

2, 3, 4, etc. = Condensed HTML version number; 3+ = HTML version 3.2; ✔ = Available in all current versions; ↓ = Deprecated—HTML version;
✗ = Obsolete; Ⓟ = Proprietary/nonconforming; * = Partial or partially nonconforming implementation.

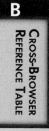

B
CROSS-BROWSER
REFERENCE TABLE

Tag	MSIE	Netscp	NCSA	Opera	Lynx	Emacs	HTML	Sponsor	Status
<SUP> continued									
dir=	-	-				-	4	W3C	
id=	3/4	3	-	-	✓	✓	3/4	W3C	✗4
lang=	-	3			✓	✓	3/4	W3C	✗4
style=	4	4			-	-	4	W3C	✗4
title=	4	-			-	-	4	W3C	✗4
event=	4	-			-	-	4	W3C	✗4
<TAB> Ⓑ Ⓣ	-	-	-	-	✓	-	3	W3C	✗4
align=	-	-	-	-	✓	-	3	W3C	✗4
dp=	-	-	-	-	✓	-	3	W3C	✗4
id=	-	-	-	-	✓	-	3	W3C	✗4
indent=	-	-	-	-	✓	-	3	W3C	✗4
to=	-	-	-	-	✓	-	3	W3C	✗4
<TABLE></TABLE> Ⓢ	✓	✓	✓	✓	✓*	✓	3+/4	W3C	
align=	✓	✓	-	✓	✓*	✓	3+/4	W3C	
(left, center, right)									
(justify, bleedleft, bleedright)									
class=	-	3	-	-	-	-	3	W3C	✗3+
background=	✓3/4	4*	-	3	-	-	3/4	W3C	✗4
bgcolor=	✓3/4	4	-	3	-	-	4	W3C	
border=	✓	✓	✓	✓	✓*	✓	3+/4	W3C	
bordercolor=	✓3/4	-	-	-	-	-	Ⓟ	MS	✗4

Tag	MSIE	Netsp	NCSA	Opera	Lynx	Emacs	HTML	Sponsor	Status
bordercolordark=	✔3/4	–	–	–	–	–	(P)	MS	✘4
bordercolorlight=	✔3/4	–	–	–	–	–	(P)	MS	✘4
cellpadding=	4	✔	–	✔	–	–	3+/4	W3C	
cellspacing=	4	✔	–	✔	–	–	3+/4	W3C	
class=	–	✔3/4	–	–	–	–	3/4	W3C	✘3+
clear=	–	–	–	–	–	–	3	W3C	
(left, right, all)									
cols=	4	–	–	–	–	–	4	W3C	
colspec=	–	–	–	–	–	–	3	W3C	✘3+
datasrc=	4	–	–	–	–	–	(P)	W3C	✘3+
dir=	–	–	–	–	–	–	4	W3C	
dp=	–	–	–	–	–	–	3	W3C	✘3+
frame=	4	–	–	–	–	–	4	W3C	
(above, below, border, box, insides, lhs, rhs, void, vsides)									
height=	4	–	–	–	–	–			✘4
id=	4	✔3/4	–	–	–	–	3/4	W3C	
lang=	–	✔3/4	–	–	–	–	3/4	W3C	
noflow	–	–	–	–	–	–	3	W3C	✘3+
nowrap	✔	✔	–	–	–	–	3	W3C	✘3+

Tags and attributes in **bold** are included in the HTML 4.0 draft, and tags in square brackets are optional.

The table is arranged alphabetically for convenient reference, but the Structure/Block/Text types of the tags are identified following the tag itself as (S), (B), and (T).

2, 3, 4, etc. = Condensed HTML version number; 3+ = HTML version 3.2; ✔ = Available in all current versions; ↓ = Deprecated—HTML version; ✘ = Obsolete; (P) = Proprietary/nonconforming; * = Partial or partially nonconforming implementation.

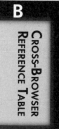

B

**CROSS-BROWSER
REFERENCE TABLE**

Tag	MSIE	Netscp	NCSA	Opera	Lynx	Emacs	HTML	Sponsor	Status
<TABLE></TABLE> *continued*									
rules=	4	-	-	-	-	-	4	W3C	
(all, cols, groups, none, rows)									
style=	4	4	-	-	-	-	4	W3C	
title=	4	-	-	-	-	-	4	W3C	
units=	-	-	-	-	-	-	3	W3C	✗3+
width=	4	-	-	-	-	-	3+/4	W3C	
event=	4	-	-	-	-	-	4	W3C	
<TBODY>...[**</TBODY>**] B	✔3/4	4	-	✔	-	-	4	W3C	
align=	4	-	-	-	-	-	4	W3C	
(center, left, right)									
bgcolor=	4	-	-	-	-	-		W3C	
char=	-	-	-	-	-	-		W3C	
charoff=	-	-	-	-	-	-		W3C	
class=	-	-	-	-	-	-	4	W3C	
dir=	-	-	-	-	-	-	4	W3C	
id=	4	-	-	-	-	-	4	W3C	
lang=	-	-	-	-	-	-	4	W3C	
style=	4	-	-	-	-	-	4	W3C	
title=	4	-	-	-	-	-	4	W3C	
valign=	4	-	-	-	-	-	4	W3C	
(baseline, bottom, center, top)									
event=	4	-	-	-	-	-	4	W3C	

Tag	MSIE	Netscp	NCSA	Opera	Lynx	Emacs	HTML	Sponsor	Status
<TD>[</TD>] [S]	✔	✔	✔	✔	✔*	✔	3+/4	W3C	
align=	✔3/4*	✔	✔	✔	-	-	3+/4	W3C	
(center, left, right)									
(decimal)							3	W3C	✗3+
(justify)							3	W3C	✗3+
axis=	-	-	-	-	-	-	3/4	W3C	
axes=	-	-	-	-	-	-	3/4	W3C	✗4
background=	4	-	-	-	-	-			✗4
bgcolor=	4	4	-	3	-	-	4	W3C	
bordercolor=	4	-	-	-	-	-			✗4
bordercolordark=	4	-	-	-	-	-		MS	✗4
bordercolorlight=	4	-	-	-	-	-		MS	✗4
char=	-	-	-	-	-	-	4	W3C	
charoff=	-	-	-	-	-	-	4	W3C	
class=	-	-	-	-	-	-	4	W3C	
colspan=	✔	✔	-	✔	-	-	3+/4	W3C	
dir=	-	-	-	-	-	-	4	W3C	
dp=	-	-	-	-	-	-	3	W3C	✗3+
height=	4	-	-	-	-	-	3+	W3C	✗4

Tags and attributes in **bold** are included in the HTML 4.0 draft, and tags in square brackets are optional.

The table is arranged alphabetically for convenient reference, but the Structure/Block/Text types of the tags are identified following the tag itself as (S), (B), and (T).

2, 3, 4, etc. = Condensed HTML version number; 3+ = HTML version 3.2; ✔ = Available in all current versions; ↓ = Deprecated—HTML version; ✗ = Obsolete; (P) = Proprietary/nonconforming; × = Partial or partially nonconforming implementation.

Tag	MSIE	Netscp	NCSA	Opera	Lynx	Emacs	HTML	Sponsor	Status
<TD>[</TD>] continued									
id=	4	3	-	-	-	-	3/4	W3C	
lang=	-	3	-	-	-	-	3/4	W3C	
nowrap	✓	✓	✓	✓	-	-	3+	W3C	✗4
rowspan=	4	✓	✓	✓	-	-	3+	W3C	✗4
style=	4	4	-	-	-	-	4	W3C	
title=	4	-	-	-	-	-	4	W3C	
valign=	✓	✓	✓	✓	-	-	3+/4	W3C	
(baseline, **bottom, center, top**)									
width=	4	-	-	✓	-	-	3+	W3C	✗4
event=	4	-	-	-	-	-	4	W3C	
<TEXTAREA> Ⓢ	✓	✓	✓	✓	✓*	✓	2-4	W3C	
...**</TEXTAREA>**									
accesskey=	4	-	-	-	-	-	Ⓟ	MS	
align=	4	-	-	-	-	-	3	W3C	
(bottom, left, middle, right, top)									
(absbottom, absmiddle, baseline, texttop)									
class=	-	✓3/4	-	-	-	-	3/4	W3C	
cols=	✓	✓	✓	✓	✓*	✓	2	W3C	
datafld=	✓	-	-	-	-	-	Ⓟ	MS	
datasrc=	✓	-	-	-	-	-	Ⓟ	MS	
dir=	-	-	-	-	-	-	4	W3C	
disabled	4	-	-	-	-	-	3/4	W3C	

Tag	MSIE	Netscp	NCSA	Opera	Lynx	Emacs	HTML	Sponsor	Status
error=	-	-	-	-	-	-	3	W3C	
id=	4	3	-	-	-	✔	3/4	W3C	
lang=	-	✔3/4	-	-	✔	✔	3/4	W3C	
name=	✔	✔	✔	✔	✔	✔	2-4	W3C	
readonly=	4	-	-	-	-	-	4	W3C	
rows=	✔	✔	✔	✔	✔*	✔	2-4	W3C	
style=	4	4	-	-	-	-	4	W3C	
tabindex=	4	4*	-	-	-	-	4	W3C	
title=	4	-	-	-	-	-	4	W3C	
wrap= (virtual, physical, none)	-	✔	-	✔	-	-	Ⓟ	NS	✗4
event=	4	-	-	-	-	-	4	W3C	
<TFOOT>[</TFOOT>] Ⓢ	✔3/4	4	-	3	-	-	4	W3C	
align= (center, left, right)	4	-	-	-	-	-	4	W3C	
bgcolor=	4	-	-	-	-	-	Ⓟ	MS	
char=	-	-	-	-	-	-	4	W3C	
charoff=	-	-	-	-	-	-	4	W3C	
dir=	-	-	-	-	-	-	4	W3C	

Tags and attributes in **bold** are included in the HTML 4.0 draft, and tags in square brackets are optional.

The table is arranged alphabetically for convenient reference, but the Structure/Block/Text types of the tags are identified following the tag itself as Ⓢ, Ⓑ, and Ⓣ.

2, 3, 4, etc. = Condensed HTML version number; 3+ = HTML version 3.2; ✔ = Available in all current versions; ↓ = Deprecated—HTML version;
✗ = Obsolete; Ⓟ = Proprietary/nonconforming; * = Partial or partially nonconforming implementation.

B

CROSS-BROWSER
REFERENCE TABLE

<TFOOT>[</TFOOT>] *continued*

Tag	MSIE	Netscp	NCSA	Opera	Lynx	Emacs	HTML	Sponsor	Status
id=	4	-	-	-	-	-	4	W3C	
lang=	-	-	-	-	-	-	4	W3C	
style=	4	-	-	-	-	-	4	W3C	
title=	4	-	-	-	-	-	4	W3C	
valign=	4	-	-	-	-	-	4	W3C	
(baseline, bottom, center, top)									
event=	4	-	-	-	-	-	4	W3C	
<TH>[</TH>] [S]	✓	✓	✓	✓	✓	✓	3+/4	W3C	
align=	✓*	✓	✓*	✓	✓*	✓	3+/4	W3C	
(center, left, right)									
(decimal)	-	-	-	-	-	-	3	W3C	✗3+
(justify)	-	-	-	-	-	-	3	W3C	✗3+
axes=	-	-	-	-	-	-	3/4	W3C	
axis=	-	✓	-	-	-	-	3/4	W3C	
background=	✓	✓	-	-	-	-	℗	W3C	✗4
bgcolor=	✓	-	-	✓	-	-	4	W3C	
bordercolor=	4	-	-	-	-	-	℗	MS	
bordercolordark=	4	-	-	-	-	-	℗	MS	
bordercolorlight=	4	-	-	-	-	-	℗	MS	
char=	-	-	-	-	-	-	4	W3C	
charoff=	-	-	-	-	-	-	4	W3C	
class=	-	-	-	-	-	-	4	W3C	

Tag	MSIE	Netscp	NCSA	Opera	Lynx	Emacs	HTML	Sponsor	Status
colspan=	✔	✔	✔	✔	–	–	3+/4	W3C	
dir=	–	–	–	–	–	–	4	W3C	
dp=	–	–	–	–	–	–	3	W3C	✗3+
height=	✔	✔	–	✔	–	–	3+	W3C	✗4
id=	4	3	–	–	–	–	3	W3C	
lang=	–	3	–	–	–	–	3	W3C	
nowrap	✔	✔	✔	✔	–	–	3+	W3C	
rowspan=	✔	✔	✔	✔	–	–	3+	W3C	
style=	4	4	–	–	–	–	4	W3C	
title=	4	–	–	–	–	–	4	W3C	
valign=	✔	✔	–	✔	–	–	3+	W3C	
(baseline, bottom, center, top)									
width=	✔	✔	✔	✔	–	–	3+	W3C	✗4
event=	4	–	–	–	–	–	4	W3C	
<THEAD>...[</THEAD>] Ⓢ	✔3/4	–	–	–	–	–	4	W3C	
align=	4	4	–	3	–	–	4	W3C	
(center, left, right)									
bgcolor=	4	–	–	–	–	–	Ⓟ	MS	
char=	–	–	–	–	–	–	4	W3C	

Tags and attributes in **bold** are included in the HTML 4.0 draft, and tags in square brackets are optional.

The table is arranged alphabetically for convenient reference, but the Structure/Block/Text types of the tags are identified following the tag itself as Ⓢ, Ⓑ, and Ⓣ.

2, 3, 4, etc. = Condensed HTML version number; 3+ = HTML version 3.2; ✔ = Available in all current versions; ↓ = Deprecated—HTML version;
✗ = Obsolete; Ⓟ = Proprietary/nonconforming; * = Partial or partially nonconforming implementation.

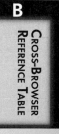

B
CROSS-BROWSER
REFERENCE TABLE

Tag	MSIE	Netscp	NCSA	Opera	Lynx	Emacs	HTML	Sponsor	Status
<THEAD>...[</THEAD>] *continued*									
charoff=	-	-	-	-	✔	-	4	W3C	
class=	-	-	-	-	✔	-	4	W3C	
dir=	-	-	-	-	✔	-	4	W3C	
id=	4	-	-	-	✔	-	4	W3C	
lang=	-	-	-	-	✔	-	4	W3C	
style=	4	-	-	-	✔	-	4	W3C	
title=	4	-	-	-	✔	-	4	W3C	
valign=	4	-	-	-	✔	-	4	W3C	
(baseline, bottom, center, top)									
event=	4	-	-	-	-	-	4	W3C	
<TITLE></TITLE> [S]	✔	✔	✔	✔	✔	✔	2-4	W3C	

NOTE: As of HTML 3.2, one and only one <TITLE> container is required for every HTML document, although most browsers don't enforce this requirement. It's a good idea to include a meaningful title on every document, but avoid "tricks" like pseudo-animated multiple titles.

Tag	MSIE	Netscp	NCSA	Opera	Lynx	Emacs	HTML	Sponsor	Status
dir=	-	-	-	-	✔	-	4	W3C	
lang=	-	-	-	-	✔	-	4	W3C	
<TR>[</TR>] [S]	✔	✔	✔	✔	✔*	✔	3+/4	W3C	
align=	4*	-	-	-	-	-	3+/4	W3C	
(center, left, right)									
(justify)	-	4	-	3	-	-	3	W3C	**✗**3+
bgcolor=	4	4	-	3	-	-	4	W3C	

Tag	MSIE	Netscp	NCSA	Opera	Lynx	Emacs	HTML	Sponsor	Status
bordercolor=	4	-	-	-	-	-	ⓟ	MS	
bordercolordark=	4	-	-	-	-	-	ⓟ	MS	
bordercolorlight=	4	-	-	-	-	-	ⓟ	MS	
char=	-	-	-	-	-	-	4	W3C	
charoff=	-	-	-	-	-	-	4	W3C	
class=	-	✔	-	-	-	-	3/4	W3C	
dir=	-	-	-	-	-	-	4	W3C	
dp=	-	-	-	-	-	-	3	W3C	✘3+
height=	4	✔	-	-	-	-	3+	W3C	✘4
id=	4	✔	-	-	-	-	3/4	W3C	
lang=	-	✔	-	-	-	-	3/4	W3C	
nowrap	-	✔	-	✔	-	-	3	W3C	✘4
style=	4	4	-	-	-	-	4	W3C	
title=	4	-	-	-	-	-	4	W3C	
valign=	✔	✔	✔	✔	✔*	✔	3/4	W3C	
(baseline, bottom, center, top)									
vspace=	✔	✔	✔	✔	-	-	ⓟ	NS	✘4
event=	4	-	-	-	-	-	4	W3C	

Tags and attributes in **bold** are included in the HTML 4.0 draft, and tags in square brackets are optional.
The table is arranged alphabetically for convenient reference, but the Structure/Block/Text types of the tags are identified following the tag itself as Ⓢ, Ⓑ, and Ⓣ.

2, 3, 4, etc. = Condensed HTML version number; 3+ = HTML version 3.2; ✔ = Available in all current versions; ↓ = Deprecated—HTML version;
✘ = Obsolete; ⓟ = Proprietary/nonconforming; * = Partial or partially nonconforming implementation.

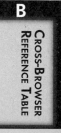

B
CROSS-BROWSER
REFERENCE TABLE

Tag	MSIE	Netscp	NCSA	Opera	Lynx	Emacs	HTML	Sponsor	Status
<TT></TT> [T]	✓	✓	✓	✓	✓*	✓	2-4	W3C	
class=	-	✓	-	-	✓	✓	3/4	W3C	
dir=	-	-	-	-	-	-	4	W3C	
id=	3/4	✓	-	-	✓	✓	3/4	W3C	
lang=	-	✓	-	-	✓	✓	3/4	W3C	
style=	4	4	-	-	-	-	4	W3C	
title=	4	-	-	-	-	-	4	W3C	
event=	4	-	-	-	-	-	4	W3C	
<U></U> [T]	✓	✓	✓	✓	✓*	✓	3/4	W3C	↓4
class=	-	✓	-	-	✓	✓	3/4	W3C	
dir=	-	-	-	-	-	-	4	W3C	
id=	✓	✓	-	-	✓	✓	3/4	W3C	
lang=	-	✓	-	-	✓	✓	3/4	W3C	
style=	4	4	-	-	-	-	4	W3C	
title=	4	-	-	-	-	-	4	W3C	
event=	4	-	-	-	-	-	4	W3C	
<UL></UL> [S]	✓	✓	✓	✓	✓	✓	2-4	W3C	
align= (center, left, right)	4	-	-	-	-	-	4		✗4
class=	-	3	-	-	✓	✓	3/4	W3C	
clear= (left, right, all)	-	-	-	-	-	-	3	W3C	✗3+

Tag	MSIE	Netscp	NCSA	Opera	Lynx	Emacs	HTML	Sponsor	Status
compact	✔*	✔*	✔*	✔*	✔*	✔*	2-4	W3C	↓4
dingbat+	-	-	-	-	✔*	✔	3	W3C	✗3+
dir=	-	-	-	-	-	-	4	W3C	
id=	4	3	-	-	-	-	3/4	W3C	
lang=	-	3	-	-	-	-	3/4	W3C	
md=	-	-	-	-	-	-	3	W3C	✗3+
plain	-	-	-	-	-	-	3	W3C	✗3+
src=	4	-	-	-	-	-	3	W3C	✗3+
style=	4	4	-	-	-	-	4	W3C	
title=	4	-	-	-	-	-	4	W3C	
type=	4	-	-	-	✔*	✔	3+/4	W3C	✗3+
(disk, square, circle)									
wrap=	-	-	-	-	-	-	3	W3C	✗3+
(vert, horiz)									
event=	4	-	-	-	-	-	4	W3C	
<VAR></VAR> Ⓣ	✔	✔	✔	✔	✔*	✔	3+/4	W3C	
class=	-	✔	-	-	✔	✔	3/4	W3C	
dir=	-	-	-	-	-	-	4	W3C	
id=	✔	✔	-	-	✔	✔	3/4	W3C	

Tags and attributes in **bold** are included in the HTML 4.0 draft, and tags in square brackets are optional.

The table is arranged alphabetically for convenient reference, but the Structure/Block/Text types of the tags are identified following the tag itself as Ⓢ, Ⓑ, and Ⓣ.

2, 3, 4, etc. = Condensed HTML version number; 3+ = HTML version 3.2; ✔ = Available in all current versions; ↓ = Deprecated—HTML version;
✗ = Obsolete; Ⓟ = Proprietary/nonconforming; * = Partial or partially nonconforming implementation.

Tag	MSIE	Netscp	NCSA	Opera	Lynx	Emacs	HTML	Sponsor	Status
\<VAR>\</VAR> *continued*									
lang=	-	✔	-	-	✔	✔	3/4	W3C	
style=	✔	✔	-	-	-	-	4	W3C	
title=	4	-	-	-	-	-	4	W3C	
event=	4	-	-	-	-	-	4	W3C	
\<WBR> Ⓢ Ⓣ	✔	✔	-	✔	-	✔	Ⓟ	NS	
id=	4	3	-	-	-	✔			
style=	4	4	-	-	-	✔			
title=	4	-	-	-	-	✔			
\<XMP>\</XMP> Ⓢ	✔	✔	✔	✔	✔	✔	2	W3C	↓2✗4
id=	4	3	-	-	-	-	3	W3C	
style=	4	4	-	-	-	-	3	W3C	
title=	4	-	-	-	-	-	3	W3C	
event=	4	-	-	-	-	-	4	W3C	

Tags and attributes in **bold** are included in the HTML 4.0 draft, and tags in square brackets are optional.

The table is arranged alphabetically for convenient reference, but the Structure/Block/Text types of the tags are identified following the tag itself as Ⓢ, Ⓑ, and Ⓣ.

2, 3, 4, etc. = Condensed HTML version number; 3+ = HTML version 3.2; ✔ = Available in all current versions; ↓ = Deprecated—HTML version; ✗ = Obsolete; Ⓟ = Proprietary/nonconforming; * = Partial or partially nonconforming implementation.

Intrinsic Events

Intrinsic Event	MSIE	Netscp	NCSA	Opera	Lynx	Emacs	HTML	Sponsor	Status
onafterupdate	4								
onbeforeupdate	4								
onblur	4	4					4	W3C	
onchange	-	4					4	W3C	
onclick	4	4					4	W3C	
ondblclick	4	4					4	W3C	
onfocus	4	4					4	W3C	
onhelp	4								
onkeydown	4	4					4	W3C	
onkeypress	4	4					4	W3C	
onkeyup	4	4					4	W3C	
onmousedown	4	4					4	W3C	
onmousemove	4	4					4	W3C	
onmouseout	4	4					4	W3C	
onmouseover	4	4					4	W3C	
onmouseup	4	4					4	W3C	
onsubmit	4	4					4	W3C	
onreset	4	4					4	W3C	

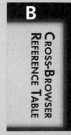

B

CROSS-BROWSER
REFERENCE TABLE

> **NOTE**
>
> Not all events are defined for every tag.

> **NOTE**
>
> For the latest official information on HTML 4.0, consult the World Wide Web Consortium at `http://www.w3.org/`.
>
> For current browser capabilities, visit these Web sites:
>
> **Emacs W3:**
>
> `http://www.cs.indiana.edu/elisp/w3/docs.html`
>
> **Lynx:**
>
> `http://www.crl.com/~subir/lynx.html`
>
> **Microsoft Internet Explorer:**
>
> `http://www.microsoft.com/ie/`
>
> **Netscape Navigator:**
>
> `http://www.netscape.com/`
>
> **NCSA Mosaic:**
>
> `http://www.ncsa.uiuc.edu/SDG/Software/Mosaic/`
>
> **Opera:**
>
> `http://www.operasoftware.com`

HTML 4.0 Escaped Entities

The following characters should always be escaped in your code to avoid hard-to-find problems because they are significant to HTML markup:

Named Entity	Numeric Entity	Description
&quot;	&#34;	" (double quote mark)
&amp;	&#38;	& (ampersand)
&gt;	&#62;	> (greater than)
&lt;	&#60;	< (less than)

Although the problem might not display as an error in your own browser, other browsers could have less "error recovery" built in.

HTML 4.0 Named Colors

The colors in the following list are approximations of the standard Windows colors as displayed on a 16-color monitor, a sort of lowest common denominator. The full gamut of colors available on your display are available through the hex pair syntax to specify the named color.

I've also added the process color (print) names often used to refer to the pure subtractive colors (CYMK) as well as the additive (monitor) primary colors (RGB) in the USA. However, they aren't official names in the standard; in fact, they partially conflict with it. Because of the confusing different naming spaces for colors used by browser manufacturers, it's probably best to use the unambiguous numeric values rather than the superficially more self-explanatory names, so I haven't shown them as escaped.

Color Name	Hex Pair Syntax	Process Color
Black	= #000000	K = (Black)
Navy	= #000080	
Blue	= #0000FF	B = (Blue)
Green	= #008000	
Teal	= #008080	
Lime	= #00FF00	G = (Green)
Aqua	= #00FFFF	C = (Cyan)
Maroon	= #800000	
Purple	= #800080	
Olive	= #808000	
Gray	= #808080	
Silver	= #C0C0C0	
Red	= #FF0000	
Fuchsia	= #FF00FF	M = (Magenta)
Yellow	= #FFFF00	Y = (Yellow)
White	= #FFFFFF	

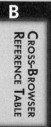

B

CROSS-BROWSER
REFERENCE TABLE

HTML 4.0 Character Entities

The following table offers the same data in two different ways, in ASCII order (capitals sort before lowercase letters) and in numeric order. The reason for doing so is that if you know the name of the character, you can find the numeric equivalent that matches; conversely, if you know the number, you can figure out what it does.

TIP

The general rule in HTML is that letter case doesn't matter, but character names are exceptions because they belong to another standard—ISO. Few browsers support all the characters, however, so if you have your heart set on one particular but obscure glyph, it's probably safer to use the numeric value and test it in many browsers before passing it onto the Web.

NOTE

Portions © International Organization for Standardization, 1986.

Permission to copy in any form is granted for use with conforming SGML systems and applications as defined in ISO 8879, provided this notice is included in all copies.

ASCII Order

Name	*Value*	*Description*
Æ	Æ	capital AE diphthong (ligature)
Á	Á	capital A, acute accent
Â	Â	capital A, circumflex accent
À	À	capital A, grave accent
Α	Α	Greek capital letter alpha, Unicode: 0391
Å	Å	capital A, ring
Ã	Ã	capital A, tilde
Ä	Ä	capital A, dieresis or umlaut mark
Β	Β	Greek capital letter beta, Unicode: 0392
Ç	Ç	capital C, cedilla
Χ	Χ	Greek capital letter chi, Unicode: 03A7
‡	‡	double dagger, Unicode: 2021
Δ	Δ	Greek capital letter delta, Unicode: 0394
Ð	Ð	capital Eth, Icelandic
É	É	capital E, acute accent
Ê	Ê	capital E, circumflex accent
È	È	capital E, grave accent
Ε	Ε	Greek capital letter epsilon, Unicode: 0395

Name	*Value*	*Description*
&Eta;	&#919;	Greek capital letter eta, Unicode: 0397
&Euml;	&#203;	capital E, dieresis or umlaut mark
&Gamma;	&#915;	Greek capital letter gamma, Unicode: 0393
&Iacute;	&#205;	capital I, acute accent
&Icirc;	&#206;	capital I, circumflex accent
&Igrave;	&#204;	capital I, grave accent
&Iota;	&#921;	Greek capital letter iota, Unicode: 0399
&Iuml;	&#207;	capital I, dieresis or umlaut mark
&Kappa;	&#922;	Greek capital letter kappa, Unicode: 039A
&Lambda;	&#923;	Greek capital letter lambda, Unicode: 039B
&Mu;	&#924;	Greek capital letter mu, Unicode: 039C
&Ntilde;	&#209;	capital N, tilde
&Nu;	&#925;	Greek capital letter nu, Unicode: 039D
&OElig;	&#338;	Latin capital ligature oe, Unicode: 0152
&Oacute;	&#211;	capital O, acute accent
&Ocirc;	&#212;	capital O, circumflex accent
&Ograve;	&#210;	capital O, grave accent
&Omega;	&#937;	Greek capital letter omega, Unicode: 03A9
&Omicron;	&#927;	Greek capital letter omicron, Unicode: 039F
&Oslash;	&#216;	capital O, slash
&Otilde;	&#213;	capital O, tilde
&Ouml;	&#214;	capital O, dieresis or umlaut mark
&Phi;	&#934;	Greek capital letter phi, Unicode: 03A6
&Pi;	&#928;	Greek capital letter pi, Unicode: 03A0
&Prime;	&#8243;	double prime, seconds, inches, Unicode: 2033
&Psi;	&#936;	Greek capital letter psi, Unicode: 03A8
&Rho;	&#929;	Greek capital letter rho, Unicode: 03A1
&Scaron;	&#352;	Latin capital letter s with caron, Unicode: 0160
&Sigma;	&#931;	Greek capital letter sigma, Unicode: 03A3
&THORN;	&#222;	capital THORN, Icelandic
&Tau;	&#932;	Greek capital letter tau, Unicode: 03A4
&Theta;	&#920;	Greek capital letter theta, Unicode: 0398

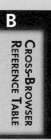

B

CROSS-BROWSER
REFERENCE TABLE

continues

Name	*Value*	*Description*
Ú	Ú	capital U, acute accent
Û	Û	capital U, circumflex accent
Ù	Ù	capital U, grave accent
Υ	Υ	Greek capital letter upsilon, Unicode: 03A5
Ü	Ü	capital U, dieresis or umlaut mark
Ξ	Ξ	Greek capital letter xi, Unicode: 039E
Ý	Ý	capital Y, acute accent
Ÿ	Ÿ	Latin capital letter y with dieresis, Unicode: 0178
Ζ	Ζ	Greek capital letter zeta, Unicode: 0396
á	á	small a, acute accent
â	â	small a, circumflex accent
´	´	acute accent
æ	æ	small ae diphthong (ligature)
à	à	small a, grave accent
ℵ	ℵ	alef symbol, first transfinite cardinal, Unicode: 2135
α	α	Greek small letter alpha, Unicode: 03B1
&	&	ampersand, Unicode: 0026
∧	⊥	logical and, wedge, Unicode: 2227
∠	∠	angle, Unicode: 2220
å	å	small a, ring
≈	≈	almost equal to, asymptotic to, Unicode: 2248
ã	ã	small a, tilde
ä	ä	small a, dieresis or umlaut mark
„	„	double low-9 quotation mark, Unicode: 201E
β	β	Greek small letter beta, Unicode: 03B2
¦	¦	broken (vertical) bar
•	•	bullet, black small circle, Unicode: 2022
∩	∩	intersection, cap, Unicode: 2229
ç	ç	small c, cedilla
¸	¸	cedilla
¢	¢	cent sign
χ	χ	Greek small letter chi, Unicode: 03C7
ˆ	ˆ	modifier letter circumflex accent, Unicode: 02C6

Name	Value	Description
♣	♣	black club suit, shamrock, Unicode: 2663
≅	≅	approximately equal to, Unicode: 2245
©	©	copyright sign
↵	↵	downwards arrow with corner leftwards, carriage return, Unicode: 21B5
∪	∪	union, cup, Unicode: 222A
¤	¤	general currency sign
⇓	⇓	downwards double arrow, Unicode: 21D3
†	†	dagger, Unicode: 2020
↓	↓	downwards arrow, Unicode: 2193
°	°	degree sign
δ	δ	Greek small letter delta, Unicode: 03B4
♦	♦	black diamond suit, Unicode: 2666
÷	÷	division sign
é	é	small e, acute accent
ê	ê	small e, circumflex accent
è	è	small e, grave accent
∅	∅	empty set, null set, diameter, Unicode: 2205
		em space, Unicode: 2003
		en space, Unicode: 2002
ε	ε	Greek small letter epsilon, Unicode: 03B5
≡	≡	identical to, Unicode: 2261
η	η	Greek small letter eta, Unicode: 03B7
ð	ð	small eth, Icelandic
ë	ë	small e, dieresis or umlaut mark
∃	∃	there exists, Unicode: 2203
ƒ	ƒ	Latin small f with hook, function, florin, Unicode: 0192
∀	∀	for all, Unicode: 2200
½	½	fraction one-half
¼	¼	fraction one-quarter
¾	¾	fraction three-quarters
⁄	⁄	fraction slash, Unicode: 2044

continues

Name	Value	Description
&gamma;	&#947;	Greek small letter gamma, Unicode: 03B3
&ge;	&#8805;	greater-than or equal to, Unicode: 2265
&gt;	&#62;	greater-than sign, Unicode: 003E
&hArr;	&#8660;	left right double arrow, Unicode: 21D4
&harr;	&#8596;	left right arrow, Unicode: 2194
&hearts;	&#9829;	black heart suit, valentine, Unicode: 2665
&hellip;	&#8230;	horizontal ellipsis, three dot leader, Unicode: 2026
&iacute;	&#237;	small i, acute accent
&icirc;	&#238;	small i, circumflex accent
&iexcl;	&#161;	inverted exclamation mark
&igrave;	&#236;	small i, grave accent
&image;	&#8465;	blackletter capital I, imaginary part, Unicode: 2111
&infin;	&#8734;	infinity, Unicode: 221E
&int;	&#8747;	integral, Unicode: 222B
&iota;	&#953;	Greek small letter iota, Unicode: 03B9
&iquest;	&#191;	inverted question mark
&isin;	&#8712;	element of, Unicode: 2208
&iuml;	&#239;	small i, dieresis or umlaut mark
&kappa;	&#954;	Greek small letter kappa, Unicode: 03BA
&lArr;	&#8656;	leftwards double arrow, Unicode: 21D0
&lambda;	&#955;	Greek small letter lambda, Unicode: 03BB
&lang;	&#9001;	left-pointing angle bracket, bra, Unicode: 2329
&laquo;	&#171;	angle quotation mark, left
&larr;	&#8592;	leftwards arrow, Unicode: 2190
&lceil;	&#8968;	left ceiling, apl upstile, Unicode: 2308,
&ldquo;	&#8220;	left double quotation mark, Unicode: 201C
&le;	&#8804;	less-than or equal to, Unicode: 2264
&lfloor;	&#8970;	left floor, apl downstile, Unicode: 230A,
&lowast;	&#8727;	asterisk operator, Unicode: 2217
&loz;	&#9674;	lozenge, Unicode: 25CA
&lrm;	&#8206;	left-to-right mark, Unicode: 200E RFC 2070
&lsaquo;	&#8249;	single left-pointing angle quotation mark, Unicode: 2039

Name	Value	Description
‘	‘	left single quotation mark, Unicode: 2018
<	<	less-than sign, Unicode: 003C
¯	¯	macron
—	—	em dash, Unicode: 2014
µ	µ	micro sign
·	·	middle dot
−	−	minus sign, Unicode: 2212
μ	μ	Greek small letter mu, Unicode: 03BC
∇	∇	nabla, backward difference, Unicode: 2207
		no-break space
–	–	en dash, Unicode: 2013
≠	≠	not equal to, Unicode: 2260
∋	∋	contains as member, Unicode: 220B
¬	¬	not sign
∉	∉	not an element of, Unicode: 2209
⊄	⊄	not a subset of, Unicode: 2284
ñ	ñ	small n, tilde
ν	ν	Greek small letter nu, Unicode: 03BD
ó	ó	small o, acute accent
ô	ô	small o, circumflex accent
œ	œ	Latin small ligature oe, Unicode: 0153
ò	ò	small o, grave accent
‾	‾	overline, spacing overscore, Unicode: 203E
ω	ω	Greek small letter omega, Unicode: 03C9
ο	ο	Greek small letter omicron, Unicode: 03BF
⊕	⊕	circled plus, direct sum, Unicode: 2295
∨	⊦	logical or, vee, Unicode: 2228
ª	ª	ordinal indicator, feminine
º	º	ordinal indicator, masculine
ø	ø	small o, slash
õ	õ	small o, tilde
⊗	⊗	circled times, vector product, Unicode: 2297

continues

Name	Value	Description
ö	ö	small o, dieresis or umlaut mark
¶	¶	pilcrow (paragraph sign)
∂	∂	partial differential, Unicode: 2202
‰	‰	per mille sign, Unicode: 2030
⊥	⊥	up tack, orthogonal to, perpendicular, Unicode: 22A5
φ	φ	Greek small letter phi, Unicode: 03C6
π	π	Greek small letter pi, Unicode: 03C0
ϖ	ϖ	Greek pi symbol, Unicode: 03D6
±	±	plus-or-minus sign
£	£	pound sterling sign
′	′	prime, minutes, feet, Unicode: 2032
∏	∏	n-ary product, product sign, Unicode: 220F
∝	∝	proportional to, Unicode: 221D
ψ	ψ	Greek small letter psi, Unicode: 03C8
"	"	quotation mark, apl quote, Unicode: 0022
⇒	⇒	rightwards double arrow, Unicode: 21D2
√	√	square root, radical sign, Unicode: 221A
⟩	〉	right-pointing angle bracket, ket, Unicode: 232A
»	»	angle quotation mark, right
→	→	rightwards arrow, Unicode: 2192
⌉	⌉	right ceiling, Unicode: 2309,
”	”	right double quotation mark, Unicode: 201D
ℜ	ℜ	blackletter capital R, real part symbol, Unicode: 211C
®	®	registered sign
⌋	⌋	right floor, Unicode: 230B,
ρ	ρ	Greek small letter rho, Unicode: 03C1
‏	‏	right-to-left mark, Unicode: 200F RFC 2070
›	›	single right-pointing angle quotation mark, Unicode: 203A
’	’	right single quotation mark, Unicode: 2019
‚	‚	single low-9 quotation mark, Unicode: 201A
š	š	Latin small letter s with caron, Unicode: 0161
⋅	⋅	dot operator, Unicode: 22C5

Name	Value	Description
&sect;	&#167;	section sign
&shy;	&#173;	soft hyphen
&sigma;	&#963;	Greek small letter sigma, Unicode: 03C3
&sigmaf;	&#962;	Greek small letter final sigma, Unicode: 03C2
&sim;	&#8764;	tilde operator, varies with, similar to, Unicode: 223C
&spades;	&#9824;	black spade suit, Unicode: 2660
&sub;	&#8834;	subset of, Unicode: 2282
&sube;	&#8838;	subset of or equal to, Unicode: 2286
&sum;	&#8721;	n-ary summation, Unicode: 2211
&sup;	&#8835;	superset of, Unicode: 2283
&sup1;	&#185;	superscript one
&sup2;	&#178;	superscript two
&sup3;	&#179;	superscript three
&supe;	&#8839;	superset of or equal to, Unicode: 2287
&szlig;	&#223;	small sharp s, German (sz ligature)
&tau;	&#964;	Greek small letter tau, Unicode: 03C4
&there4;	&#8756;	therefore, Unicode: 2234
&rheta;	&#952;	Greek small letter theta, Unicode: 03B8
&thetasym;	&#977;	Greek small letter theta symbol, Unicode: 03D1
		thin space, Unicode: 2009
&thorn;	&#254;	small thorn, Icelandic
&tilde;	&#732;	small tilde, Unicode: 02DC
&times;	&#215;	multiply sign
&trade;	&#8482;	trademark sign, Unicode: 2122
&uArr;	&#8657;	upwards double arrow, Unicode: 21D1
&uacute;	&#250;	small u, acute accent
&uarr;	&#8593;	upwards arrow, Unicode: 2191
&ucirc;	&#251;	small u, circumflex accent
&ugrave;	&#249;	small u, grave accent
&uml;	&#168;	umlaut (dieresis)
&upsih;	&#978;	Greek upsilon with hook symbol, Unicode: 03D2
&upsilon;	&#965;	Greek small letter upsilon, Unicode: 03C5

continues

Name	Value	Description
ü	ü	small u, dieresis or umlaut mark
℘	℘	script capital P, power set, Weierstrass p, Unicode: 2118
ξ	ξ	Greek small letter xi, Unicode: 03BE
ý	ý	small y, acute accent
¥	¥	yen sign
ÿ	ÿ	small y, dieresis or umlaut mark
ζ	ζ	Greek small letter zeta, Unicode: 03B6
‍	‍	zero width joiner, Unicode: 200D
‌	‌	zero width non-joiner, Unicode: 200C

Numeric Order

Name	Value	Description
"	"	quotation mark, apl quote, Unicode: 0022
&	&	ampersand, Unicode: 0026
<	<	less-than sign, Unicode: 003C
>	>	greater-than sign, Unicode: 003E
		no-break space
¡	¡	inverted exclamation mark
¢	¢	cent sign
£	£	pound sterling sign
¤	¤	general currency sign
¥	¥	yen sign
¦	¦	broken (vertical) bar
§	§	section sign
¨	¨	umlaut (dieresis)
©	©	copyright sign
ª	ª	ordinal indicator, feminine
«	«	angle quotation mark, left
¬	¬	not sign
­	­	soft hyphen
®	®	registered sign
¯	¯	macron
°	°	degree sign

Name	Value	Description
&plusmn;	&#177;	plus-or-minus sign
&sup2;	&#178;	superscript two
&sup3;	&#179;	superscript three
&acute;	&#180;	acute accent
&micro;	&#181;	micro sign
&para;	&#182;	pilcrow (paragraph sign)
&middot;	&#183;	middle dot
&cedil;	&#184;	cedilla
&sup1;	&#185;	superscript one
&ordm;	&#186;	ordinal indicator, masculine
&raquo;	&#187;	angle quotation mark, right
&frac14;	&#188;	fraction one-quarter
&frac12;	&#189;	fraction one-half
&frac34;	&#190;	fraction three-quarters
&iquest;	&#191;	inverted question mark
&Agrave;	&#192;	capital A, grave accent
&Aacute;	&#193;	capital A, acute accent
&Acirc;	&#194;	capital A, circumflex accent
&Atilde;	&#195;	capital A, tilde
&Auml;	&#196;	capital A, dieresis or umlaut mark
&Aring;	&#197;	capital A, ring
&AElig;	&#198;	capital AE diphthong (ligature)
&Ccedil;	&#199;	capital C, cedilla
&Egrave;	&#200;	capital E, grave accent
&Eacute;	&#201;	capital E, acute accent
&Ecirc;	&#202;	capital E, circumflex accent
&Euml;	&#203;	capital E, dieresis or umlaut mark
&Igrave;	&#204;	capital I, grave accent
&Iacute;	&#205;	capital I, acute accent
&Icirc;	&#206;	capital I, circumflex accent
&Iuml;	&#207;	capital I, dieresis or umlaut mark
&ETH;	&#208;	capital Eth, Icelandic

continues

Name	*Value*	*Description*
&Ntilde;	&#209;	capital N, tilde
&Ograve;	&#210;	capital O, grave accent
&Oacute;	&#211;	capital O, acute accent
&Ocirc;	&#212;	capital O, circumflex accent
&Otilde;	&#213;	capital O, tilde
&Ouml;	&#214;	capital O, dieresis or umlaut mark
&times;	&#215;	multiply sign
&Oslash;	&#216;	capital O, slash
&Ugrave;	&#217;	capital U, grave accent
&Uacute;	&#218;	capital U, acute accent
&Ucirc;	&#219;	capital U, circumflex accent
&Uuml;	&#220;	capital U, dieresis or umlaut mark
&Yacute;	&#221;	capital Y, acute accent
&THORN;	&#222;	capital THORN, Icelandic
&szlig;	&#223;	small sharp s, German (sz ligature)
&agrave;	&#224;	small a, grave accent
&aacute;	&#225;	small a, acute accent
&acirc;	&#226;	small a, circumflex accent
&atilde;	&#227;	small a, tilde
&auml;	&#228;	small a, dieresis or umlaut mark
&aring;	&#229;	small a, ring
&aelig;	&#230;	small ae diphthong (ligature)
&ccedil;	&#231;	small c, cedilla
&egrave;	&#232;	small e, grave accent
&eacute;	&#233;	small e, acute accent
&ecirc;	&#234;	small e, circumflex accent
&euml;	&#235;	small e, dieresis or umlaut mark
&igrave;	&#236;	small i, grave accent
&iacute;	&#237;	small i, acute accent
&icirc;	&#238;	small i, circumflex accent
&iuml;	&#239;	small i, dieresis or umlaut mark
&eth;	&#240;	small eth, Icelandic
&ntilde;	&#241;	small n, tilde

Name	*Value*	*Description*
&ograve;	&#242;	small o, grave accent
&oacute;	&#243;	small o, acute accent
&ocirc;	&#244;	small o, circumflex accent
&otilde;	&#245;	small o, tilde
&ouml;	&#246;	small o, dieresis or umlaut mark
&divide;	&#247;	divide sign
&oslash;	&#248;	small o, slash
&ugrave;	&#249;	small u, grave accent
&uacute;	&#250;	small u, acute accent
&ucirc;	&#251;	small u, circumflex accent
&uuml;	&#252;	small u, dieresis or umlaut mark
&yacute;	&#253;	small y, acute accent
&thorn;	&#254;	small thorn, Icelandic
&yuml;	&#255;	small y, dieresis or umlaut mark
&OElig;	&#338;	Latin capital ligature oe, Unicode: 0152
&oelig;	&#339;	Latin small ligature oe, Unicode: 0153
&Scaron;	&#352;	Latin capital letter s with caron, Unicode: 0160
&scaron;	&#353;	Latin small letter s with caron, Unicode: 0161
&Yuml;	&#376;	Latin capital letter y with diaeresis, Unicode: 0178
&fnof;	&#402;	Latin small f with hook, function, florin, Unicode: 0192
&circ;	&#710;	modifier letter circumflex accent, Unicode: 02C6
&tilde;	&#732;	small tilde, Unicode: 02DC
&Alpha;	&#913;	Greek capital letter alpha, Unicode: 0391
&Beta;	&#914;	Greek capital letter beta, Unicode: 0392
&Gamma;	&#915;	Greek capital letter gamma, Unicode: 0393
&Delta;	&#916;	Greek capital letter delta, Unicode: 0394
&Epsilon;	&#917;	Greek capital letter epsilon, Unicode: 0395
&Zeta;	&#918;	Greek capital letter zeta, Unicode: 0396
&Eta;	&#919;	Greek capital letter eta, Unicode: 0397
&Theta;	&#920;	Greek capital letter theta, Unicode: 0398
&Iota;	&#921;	Greek capital letter iota, Unicode: 0399
&Kappa;	&#922;	Greek capital letter kappa, Unicode: 039A

B

CROSS-BROWSER
REFERENCE TABLE

continues

Name	*Value*	*Description*
&Lambda;	&#923;	Greek capital letter lambda, Unicode: 039B
&Mu;	&#924;	Greek capital letter mu, Unicode: 039C
&Nu;	&#925;	Greek capital letter nu, Unicode: 039D
&Xi;	&#926;	Greek capital letter xi, Unicode: 039E
&Omicron;	&#927;	Greek capital letter omicron, Unicode: 039F
&Pi;	&#928;	Greek capital letter pi, Unicode: 03A0
&Rho;	&#929;	Greek capital letter rho, Unicode: 03A1
&Sigma;	&#931;	Greek capital letter sigma, Unicode: 03A3
&Tau;	&#932;	Greek capital letter tau, Unicode: 03A4
&Upsilon;	&#933;	Greek capital letter upsilon, Unicode: 03A5
&Phi;	&#934;	Greek capital letter phi, Unicode: 03A6
&Chi;	&#935;	Greek capital letter chi, Unicode: 03A7
&Psi;	&#936;	Greek capital letter psi, Unicode: 03A8
&Omega;	&#937;	Greek capital letter omega, Unicode: 03A9
&alpha;	&#945;	Greek small letter alpha, Unicode: 03B1
&beta;	&#946;	Greek small letter beta, Unicode: 03B2
&gamma;	&#947;	Greek small letter gamma, Unicode: 03B3
&delta;	&#948;	Greek small letter delta, Unicode: 03B4
&epsilon;	&#949;	Greek small letter epsilon, Unicode: 03B5
&zeta;	&#950;	Greek small letter zeta, Unicode: 03B6
&eta;	&#951;	Greek small letter eta, Unicode: 03B7
&theta;	&#952;	Greek small letter theta, Unicode: 03B8
&iota;	&#953;	Greek small letter iota, Unicode: 03B9
&kappa;	&#954;	Greek small letter kappa, Unicode: 03BA
&lambda;	&#955;	Greek small letter lambda, Unicode: 03BB
&mu;	&#956;	Greek small letter mu, Unicode: 03BC
&nu;	&#957;	Greek small letter nu, Unicode: 03BD
&xi;	&#958;	Greek small letter xi, Unicode: 03BE
&omicron;	&#959;	Greek small letter omicron, Unicode: 03BF
&pi;	&#960;	Greek small letter pi, Unicode: 03C0
&rho;	&#961;	Greek small letter rho, Unicode: 03C1
&sigmaf;	&#962;	Greek small letter final sigma, Unicode: 03C2
&sigma;	&#963;	Greek small letter sigma, Unicode: 03C3

Name	*Value*	*Description*
τ	τ	Greek small letter tau, Unicode: 03C4
υ	υ	Greek small letter upsilon, Unicode: 03C5
φ	φ	Greek small letter phi, Unicode: 03C6
χ	χ	Greek small letter chi, Unicode: 03C7
ψ	ψ	Greek small letter psi, Unicode: 03C8
ω	ω	Greek small letter omega, Unicode: 03C9
ϑ	ϑ	Greek small letter theta symbol, Unicode: 03D1
ϒ	ϒ	Greek upsilon with hook symbol, Unicode: 03D2
ϖ	ϖ	Greek pi symbol, Unicode: 03D6
		en space, Unicode: 2002
		em space, Unicode: 2003
		thin space, Unicode: 2009
‌	‌	zero width non-joiner, Unicode: 200C
‍	‍	zero width joiner, Unicode: 200D
‎	‎	left-to-right mark, Unicode: 200E RFC 2070
‏	‏	right-to-left mark, Unicode: 200F RFC 2070
–	–	en dash, Unicode: 2013
—	—	em dash, Unicode: 2014
‘	‘	left single quotation mark, Unicode: 2018
’	’	right single quotation mark, Unicode: 2019
‚	‚	single low-9 quotation mark, Unicode: 201A
“	“	left double quotation mark, Unicode: 201C
”	”	right double quotation mark, Unicode: 201D
„	„	double low-9 quotation mark, Unicode: 201E
†	†	dagger, Unicode: 2020
‡	‡	double dagger, Unicode: 2021
•	•	bullet, black small circle, Unicode: 2022
…	…	horizontal ellipsis, three dot leader, Unicode: 2026
‰	‰	per mille sign, Unicode: 2030
′	′	prime, minutes, feet, Unicode: 2032
″	″	double prime, seconds, inches, Unicode: 2033
‹	‹	single left-pointing angle quotation mark, Unicode: 2039

B

CROSS-BROWSER
REFERENCE TABLE

continues

Name	Value	Description
›	›	single right-pointing angle quotation mark, Unicode: 203A
‾	‾	overline, spacing overscore, Unicode: 203E
⁄	⁄	fraction slash, Unicode: 2044
ℑ	ℑ	blackletter capital I, imaginary part, Unicode: 2111
℘	℘	script capital P, power set, Weierstrass p, Unicode: 2118
ℜ	ℜ	blackletter capital R, real part symbol, Unicode: 211C
™	™	trademark sign, Unicode: 2122
ℵ	ℵ	alef symbol, first transfinite cardinal, Unicode: 2135
←	←	leftwards arrow, Unicode: 2190
↑	↑	upwards arrow, Unicode: 2191
→	→	rightwards arrow, Unicode: 2192
↓	↓	downwards arrow, Unicode: 2193
↔	↔	left-right arrow, Unicode: 2194
↵	↵	downwards arrow with corner leftwards, carriage return, Unicode: 21B5
⇐	⇐	leftwards double arrow, Unicode: 21D0
⇑	⇑	upwards double arrow, Unicode: 21D1
⇒	⇒	rightwards double arrow, Unicode: 21D2
⇓	⇓	downwards double arrow, Unicode: 21D3
⇔	⇔	left-right double arrow, Unicode: 21D4
∀	∀	for all, Unicode: 2200
∂	∂	partial differential, Unicode: 2202
∃	∃	there exists, Unicode: 2203
∅	∅	empty set, null set, diameter, Unicode: 2205
∇	∇	nabla, backward difference, Unicode: 2207
∈	∈	element of, Unicode: 2208
∉	∉	not an element of, Unicode: 2209
∋	∋	contains as member, Unicode: 220B
∏	∏	n-ary product, product sign, Unicode: 220F
∑	∑	n-ary sumation, Unicode: 2211
−	−	minus sign, Unicode: 2212
∗	∗	asterisk operator, Unicode: 2217

Name	Value	Description
√	√	square root, radical sign, Unicode: 221A
∝	∝	proportional to, Unicode: 221D
∞	∞	infinity, Unicode: 221E
∠	∠	angle, Unicode: 2220
∩	∩	intersection, cap, Unicode: 2229
∪	∪	union, cup, Unicode: 222A
∫	∫	integral, Unicode: 222B
∴	∴	therefore, Unicode: 2234
∼	∼	tilde operator, varies with, similar to, Unicode: 223C
≅	≅	approximately equal to, Unicode: 2245
≈	≈	almost equal to, asymptotic to, Unicode: 2248
≠	≠	not equal to, Unicode: 2260
≡	≡	identical to, Unicode: 2261
≤	≤	less-than or equal to, Unicode: 2264
≥	≥	greater-than or equal to, Unicode: 2265
⊂	⊂	subset of, Unicode: 2282
⊃	⊃	superset of, Unicode: 2283
⊄	⊄	not a subset of, Unicode: 2284
⊆	⊆	subset of or equal to, Unicode: 2286
⊇	⊇	superset of or equal to, Unicode: 2287
⊕	⊕	circled plus, direct sum, Unicode: 2295
⊗	⊗	circled times, vector product, Unicode: 2297
∧	⊥	logical and, wedge, Unicode: 2227
⊥	⊥	up tack, orthogonal to, perpendicular, Unicode: 22A5
∨	⊦	logical or, vee, Unicode: 2228
⋅	⋅	dot operator, Unicode: 22C5
⌈	⌈	left ceiling, apl upstile, Unicode: 2308,
⌉	⌉	right ceiling, Unicode: 2309,
⌊	⌊	left floor, apl downstile, Unicode: 230A,
⌋	⌋	right floor, Unicode: 230B,
⟨	〈	left-pointing angle bracket, bra, Unicode: 2329
⟩	〉	right-pointing angle bracket, ket, Unicode: 232A

continues

Name	*Value*	*Description*
◊	◊	lozenge, Unicode: 25CA
♠	♠	black spade suit, Unicode: 2660
♣	♣	black club suit, shamrock, Unicode: 2663
♥	♥	black heart suit, valentine, Unicode: 2665
♦	♦	black diamond suit, Unicode: 2666

Notes on the Tables

Although this appendix was current while this book was in production, HTML 4.0 was still in draft form, and browser capabilities are constantly changing. In addition, specifications published by browser manufacturers are sometimes more hopeful than accurate, so claims of complete support for this or that standard are usually less than strictly true. As mentioned before, no manufacturer actually adheres to any of the DTDs as written.

As much as possible, I've verified the manufacturer's existing documentation by testing actual code, but there are no guarantees that a slightly different browser version won't reveal small differences in attribute or tag support, nor was my testing exhaustive enough to discover every unexpected behavior that might exist.

Only the more recent versions of each browser are listed in the interest of clarity and saving space. If the more recent versions of freely available browsers support a given feature, a checkmark is used to indicate support, instead of cluttering the table with too many hard-to-read version numbers. In addition, HTML standards references start at 2.0 because compliance with HTML 1.0 is no longer recommended.

The entries for Lynx and Emacs W3 require some explanation. For the most part, both browsers have internal parsing engines that recognize almost everything in a superset of HTML tags and attributes across every platform. Whether the maker or modifier of any particular version of these powerful tools has elected to make that recognition visible on the page is entirely another matter. Neither Lynx nor Emacs has a central configuration management authority to control what goes into any particular version and "missing features" can be "easily" added by anyone at all. In fact, that's how the program evolves. What organization does exist is that of consensus, with a worldwide community of developers donating their time and energy freely to create something that serves a common purpose. It's a brave new world that has such people in it.

Cascading Style Sheets Level 1 Quick Reference

by Rick Darnell

IN THIS APPENDIX

This appendix gives you an overview of the attributes you can use to control the appearance of your HTML documents through style sheets. The World Wide Web Consortium (W3C) set the current standard for style sheets as Cascading Style Sheets Level 1 (CSS1). The W3C's complete recommendation for CSS is located at its Web site at `http://www.w3.org/pub/WWW/TR/REC-CSS1`.

Basic Syntax

All styles in a style sheet definition follow the same basic syntax. You'll notice that there are a lot of opportunities to add other attributes or members of a group:

```
SELECTOR[.class] [,SELECTOR2[.class2]] ...
{ attribute1: value1 [;
  attribute2: value2] [;
  ... ]            [;
  attributen: valuen] }
```

The `SELECTOR` is how the style is referenced within the rest of the HTML page. It uses one of the existing HTML tags, such as `<CODE>` or `<P>`, along with an optional `class` to create additional substyles. A `class` is a subset of a selector, allowing the same element to have a variety of styles. For example, you could color-code blockquotes to identify sources or speakers.

In addition to the standard HTML tags, you can use two other values for a selector: `first-line` and `first-letter`. The `first-line` value sets the style for the first line of text in a document or several passages within a document, such as a paragraph or blockquote. The `first-letter` value creates drop caps and other special effects on the first letter in a document or passage.

Groups of selectors and their classes are separated by commas. Any member of the group receives the same style as any other member in the group. For example, if you wanted all headings to be displayed in red, you could list H1 through H6 with the attributes to set the color to red. All other tag attributes, such as size, would remain unaffected.

Another option is contextual selectors, which tell the browser what to do with a certain tag when it's found nested within the parent tag, as shown in this example:

```
OUTER_SELECTOR INNER_SELECTOR {attribute:value}
```

This means that when the `INNER_SELECTOR` is used within the `OUTER_SELECTOR`, the style is used. Otherwise, other occurrences of `INNER_SELECTOR` are handled according to the browser default.

After making all the selector and group definitions, use a curly bracket along with a series of attributes and their values. Mate each attribute with its value with a colon, and separate each pair from the next pair by a semicolon. The values in a definition, such as the name of a typeface or a color value, are not case-sensitive. For example, for `font-family`, you can have `Garamond`, `garamond`, or `GARAMOND`, and they all work out the same in the browser.

As with all good syntax, you can place style definitions in three ways within a document: with an embedded style sheet, with a linked style sheet, and with an inline style sheet.

Embedded Style Sheet

The `<STYLE>` tags contain an embedded style sheet. As a matter of structure, the format of an HTML page with an embedded style sheet is as follows:

```
<HTML>
<HEAD>...</HEAD>
<STYLE>...</STYLE>
<BODY>...</BODY>
</HTML>
```

The `<STYLE>` tags contain the list of selectors and styles.

Linked Style Sheet

The linked style sheet is a `.css` file that contains nothing but a set of `<STYLE>` tags and their contents. Identify the style file in an HTML document by using the `<LINK>` tag in the head, as shown here:

```
<HEAD>
<LINK rel=stylesheet href="filename.css" type="text/css">
</HEAD>
```

At runtime, the browser will load the style in the `.css` file and use it to format the document. If the HTML page also includes an embedded style sheet that conflicts with the linked style sheet, the embedded version takes precedence.

Inline Style Sheet

The last option, inline style sheets, uses style sheet syntax, although it's technically not a style sheet implementation. This option uses the style sheet nomenclature to customize single incidents of tags in the document:

```
<TAG style="attribute1:value1; ...">
```

Essentially, this is a way to customize HTML tags on a case-by-case basis. When you use all three forms of syntax, they occur in a cascading form of precedence. The highest priority is inline, followed by embedded, and then linked.

Style Attributes

Several classes of attributes are used in the definition for a selector. The following sections cover each of the attributes within a class.

There's a predictable way the rules are applied when faced with conflicts between styles on a page. To determine how an element will appear on the page, follow these rules, in order:

1. First, find all the declarations that apply to the element in question. Style declarations apply if the selector matches the element in question. If no declarations apply, the element's style is inherited from its parent. Any unspecified values are handled according to browser defaults.

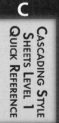

2. For multiple declarations, any styles marked `!important` carry more weight than unmarked declarations.

3. Next comes origin priority. The author's style sheets override the reader's style sheets, which override the browser's default values. Linked styles are considered to have the same origin as the author.

4. Next comes specificity. A more specific selector overrides less specific selectors. For example, if you set `BODY` as black text on a white background, then set `BLOCKQUOTE` as red text on a white background, then a blockquote within the body will be red because `BLOCKQUOTE` is more specific than `BODY`.

5. Sort by the order in which the styles are specified. If two rules have the same weight, the last definition wins, so a linked style sheet at the beginning of the document sets the first style. Any discrepancies between the linked style and an embedded style default to the embedded style. If for some reason the embedded style includes two definitions for the same element, such as two sets of properties for `BLOCKQUOTE`, then the last `BLOCKQUOTE` wins.

Using these rules, you can accurately predict how your style sheet will be applied when interpreted by a browser.

Fonts

There are no current standards for typefaces and their use on different user machines, so you'll need to choose carefully and include several options to get the effect you want for the user.

The `font-family` Attribute

The `font-family` attribute lists font families in order of preference, separated by commas. Two types of variables are used: family name and generic family. Here's an example of how the `font-family` attribute is used:

```
BODY {font-family: Garamond, Palatino, Serif}
```

A family name is the name of a specific typeface, such as Helvetica, Garamond, Palatino, or Optima. Enclose font names with spaces in quotes, such as `"Gil Sans"`. The generic family is one of five choices that classifies the typeface by its style and is recommended as the last option in a `font-family` list:

- Serif: Fonts with accents at the tips of the lines (for example, Times New Roman)
- Sans serif: Fonts without finishing accents (for example, Helvetica)
- Cursive: Scripts that more closely resemble hand-drawn calligraphy (for example, Zapf Chancery)
- Fancy: Special-use decorative fonts (for example, ITC Jambalaya or Bazooka)
- Monospace: Fonts that maintain uniform spacing despite letter width (for example, Courier)

The font-style Attribute

This attribute specifies the type of treatment a font gets and is represented by the values normal, italic, or oblique. The normal value is also referred to as *Roman* in some typeface references. The oblique value is similar to italic except that it's usually slanted manually by the system rather than by a separate style of the font, like italic. The font-style attribute is used like this:

```
BODY {font-style: italic}
```

The font-variant Attribute

Similar to font-style, this attribute sets small caps. Its two values are normal and small-caps. Here's an example of using the font-variant attribute:

```
BODY {font-variant: small-caps}
```

If there's no true small caps version of the typeface, the system tries to scale the capital letters to a smaller size for lowercase letters. As a last resort, the text appears in all uppercase letters.

The font-weight Attribute

A number of values for this attribute set the darkness or lightness of a typeface. The primary values are normal and bold. You can substitute these values with one of a list of values from 100 to 900. If a typeface includes a "medium" weight, its value corresponds to 500. Bold is represented by 700. Here's the syntax for the font-weight attribute:

```
BODY {font-weight: bold}
```

Two additional values are bolder and lighter, which increase the weight from the current parent weight by one level, such as 200 to 300 for bolder or 700 to 600 for lighter.

The font-size Attribute

Four methods can define the size of a font in a style: absolute size, relative size, length, or percentage.

■ **Absolute size:** This method is represented in several ways. The first is with a value that represents its size in relation to other sizes in the family (xx-small, x-small, small, medium, large, x-large, xx-large). You can also use a numerical value, such as 12pt (12 points), as shown here:

```
BODY {font-size: 18pt}
```

■ **Relative size:** This method sets the size in relation to the parent style. It can be one of two values, smaller or larger, and it adjusts the size up or down the scale of sizes, as shown here:

```
P {font-size: smaller}
```

If a font doesn't include a mapping to size names, a scaling of 1.5 is recommended between sizes. For example, a 10pt font would be scaled larger to 15pt or smaller to 7pt.

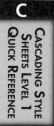

- **Length:** This method is another form of relative size that sets the size by the scale factor of the width of an em, such as `1.5em`, as shown in this example:

```
P {font-size: 1.5em}
```

- **Percentage:** This method is also a relative specification that multiplies the size of the parent font by the percentage value to produce the new size, such as `150%`, as shown in this example:

```
H3 {font-size: 150%}
```

The font Attribute

This attribute provides a shorthand for setting all the previous attributes under one umbrella. The order of the attributes should be `font-style`, `font-variant`, `font-weight`, `font-size`, `line-height`, `font-family`. Place no commas between each of the attribute values, except for listed font families:

```
BODY {font: small-caps bold 14pt garamond, palatino, serif}
```

Color and Background

These elements set the color values for the text (foreground) and the area behind the text (background). In addition to setting a background color, you can also define a background image. All color values are defined by using the same choices (color names or hexadecimal triplet) as the `color` property.

The color Attribute

This attribute defines the color of the text element and is specified by using one of the color keywords (such as `red`). You can also define the color with a hexadecimal triplet or decimal values separated by commas, denoting a mix of red, green, and blue (such as `rgb(255,0,0)`):

```
BLOCKQUOTE {color: rgb(0,255,255)}
```

The background-color Attribute

This attribute sets the background color for a style. You can set this attribute independently of a background color for the document to allow you to highlight text in a different manner:

```
BLOCKQUOTE {background-color: blue}
```

The background-image Attribute

This attribute specifies a background image for a style element. Use it with `background-color` to ensure a substitute effect if the image becomes unavailable. If the image is available, it's displayed on top of the background color. Here's an example of how this attribute is used:

```
BLOCKQUOTE {background-image: url(logo.gif)}
```

The background-repeat Attribute

If the background image should be repeated (tiled), use this attribute to define how. Its values include repeat, repeat-x, and repeat-y. The repeat value indicates that the image should be tiled normally. The repeat-x value repeats the image in a single horizontal line, as shown in the following example, and the repeat-y value repeats the image in a vertical line:

```
BLOCKQUOTE {background-image: url(logo.gif);
           background-repeat: repeat-x}
```

The background-attachment Attribute

This attribute, an extended feature of background images not seen in HTML before, specifies whether the background image is attached to the foreground text (scroll) or anchored to the background (fixed). This feature is apparent only when the user scrolls across a selection of text. Here's an example of how to use this attribute:

```
BLOCKQUOTE {background-image: url(logo.gif);
           background-attachment: fixed}
```

The background-position Attribute

When you use a background image in normal HTML, the starting point is always the top left of the screen. With a style sheet, you can specify a starting point anywhere within the box that contains the style content.

You can specify the image's starting position in three ways. The first way is with keyword locations. For horizontal placement, your choices are left, center, or right. For vertical placement, your choices are top, center, or bottom. Or, you can represent the position as a percentage of the available area, with 0% 0% being the top left (default) and 100% 100% being the bottom right. The last option is to specify an actual measurement in centimeters or inches.

If only one value for the placement is given, it's used as the horizontal position. If both values are given, the first is evaluated as horizontal and the second as vertical.

Here's an example of using keyword locations to specify the position for a background image:

```
BLOCKQUOTE {background-image: url(logo.gif);
           Background-repeat: repeat-y;
           background-position: right top; }
```

The background Attribute

This shorthand attribute, similar to font, lets you define a set of values for the background in one step. The order is background-color, background-image, background-repeat, background-attachment, background-position, as shown in this example:

```
P { background: black url(logo.gif) repeat-y fixed right top }
```

Text

This set of style attributes covers the values that can affect the appearance of text, but not by directly changing the typeface. This set includes values for spacing, underlining, blinking, and strikethrough. It also supports some of the positioning attributes, including left- and right-justification and indents.

The word-spacing Attribute

This attribute, which indicates an addition to the default amount of space between individual words, is specified in *ems*. An *em* is the space occupied by the letter *m* and is the baseline for determining widths within a font. To return the value to its default, use `0em` or `normal`. Here's an example of setting the spacing to 1 em:

```
BODY { word-spacing: 1em }
```

The letter-spacing Attribute

The `letter-spacing` attribute is similar to `word-spacing`, except that `letter-spacing` adds an extra bit of spacing between individual letters, as shown:

```
BODY { letter-spacing: 0.2em }
```

In addition to the default method the browser uses to determine spacing, additional letter spacing is also affected by text alignment.

The text-decoration Attribute

This attribute is more closely related to its cousins in the `font` family. It specifies extra text flourishes, such as underline, strikethrough, and blinking. The five values are `none`, `underline`, `overline`, `line-through`, and `blink`. The following is an example of using `text-decoration`:

```
STR.blink { text-decoration: underline blink }
```

The vertical-align Attribute

This attribute sets the vertical position of the text either to an absolute reference or in relation to the parent element. It supports a range of values and keywords:

- **baseline:** Aligns the baseline of the style with the baseline of the parent element
- **sub:** Assigns the style to a subscript relative to the parent element
- **super:** Assigns the style to a superscript relative to the parent element
- **text-top:** Aligns the top of the text with the top of the parent's text
- **text-bottom:** Aligns the bottom of the text with the bottom of the parent's text
- **middle:** Aligns the vertical halfway point of the element with the baseline of the parent plus half of the x-height of the parent (x-height is the height of the font's lowercase *x*)
- **top:** Aligns the top of the element with the tallest element on the current line
- **bottom:** Aligns the bottom of the element with the lowest element on the current line

■ **(percentage):** Using a positive or negative percentage value, raises or lowers the element beyond the baseline of the parent

```
SUB { vertical-align: -10% }
```

The text-transform Attribute

This attribute sets the capitalization of the affected text to one of four choices: `capitalize` (first letter of every word), `uppercase` (all letters in capitals), `lowercase` (all letters in lowercase), and `none`. Here's an example of using the `text-transform` attribute:

```
STR.caps { text-transform: uppercase }
```

The text-align Attribute

This attribute moves beyond the standard HTML `left-right-center` alignment to provide full justification (`justify` both left and right), as shown here:

```
BLOCKQUOTE { text-align: justify }
```

If a browser doesn't support `justify`, it typically substitutes `left`.

The text-indent Attribute

The `text-indent` attribute, specified in an absolute value measured in ems or inches, defines the amount of space added before the first line, as shown in this example:

```
P { text-indent: 5em }
```

The line-height Attribute

This attribute sets the distance between adjacent baselines using a length (in ems), multiplication factor, or percentage. Factors are indicated without any units, such as `1.5`. When you use this method, the child inherits the factor, not the resulting value. In the following example, the line height becomes 18 points and the font size remains at 12 points:

```
DIV { line-height: 1.5; font-size: 12pt }
```

Now if there's a paragraph that's a child of the division, and the default text size of the paragraph is 10 points, then the child inherits the factor of 1.5, making its size 15 points.

Margins, Padding, and Borders

Each element created in a style sheet is presented in its own "box." All the styles from the element inside the box are applied, although the box itself can have its own properties that define how it relates to adjoining elements on the page. Length is specified in inches (`in`), centimeters (`cm`), ems (`em`), points (`pt`), or pixels (`px`).

Box properties are divided into three basic categories. Margin properties set the border around the outside of the box, padding properties determine how much space to insert between the border and the content, and border properties define graphical lines around an element.

Additional properties of the box include its width, height, and physical position.

The `margin-top`, `margin-bottom`, `margin-right`, and `margin-left` Attributes

These four attributes set the amount of space between the element and adjoining elements, whether defined by length or percentage of the parent text's width or handled automatically, as shown in this example:

```
BLOCKQUOTE { margin-top: 4em;
             margin-bottom: auto }
```

The `margin` Attribute

The `margin` attribute gives you a shorthand method for setting the four margin values. When you specify the four values, they are applied, in order, to the top, right, bottom, and left. If you supply only one value, it applies to all sides. If you use two or three values, the missing values are copied from the opposite sides. Here's an example of how to use the `margin` attribute:

```
BLOCKQUOTE {margin: 4em 2em}
```

The `padding-top`, `padding-bottom`, `padding-right`, and `padding-left` Attributes

These attributes set the distance between the boundaries of the box and the elements inside the box. It can use any of the physical measurements or a percentage of the parent's width, as shown here:

```
BLOCKQUOTE {padding-top: 110%; padding-bottom: 115%}
```

The `padding` Attribute

The `padding` attribute provides a shorthand way to set the four padding values. When you specify the four values, they are applied, in order, to the top, right, bottom, and left. If you provide only one value, it applies to all sides; if you use two or three values, the missing values are copied from the opposite sides. This is an example of how the `padding` attribute is used:

```
BLOCKQUOTE {padding: 10pt 12pt}
```

The `border-top`, `border-bottom`, `border-right`, and `border-left` Attributes

These four attributes set the style and color of each border around an element. Specify styles with one of the border style keywords: `none`, `dotted`, `dashed`, `solid`, `double`, `groove`, `ridge`, `inset`, and `outset`. For more information on these keywords, see the information on `border-style` later in this chapter.

Specify colors by using a color keyword. For more information, see the `border-color` section later in this chapter.

```
BLOCKQUOTE {border-left: solid red}
```

The `border-top-width`, `border-bottom-width`, `border-right-width`, and `border-left-width` Attributes

These attributes define a physical border around the box, similar to the border used for HTML tables. In addition to defining a specific width in ems, points, or inches, you can also use the keywords `thin`, `medium`, and `thick`. Using a measurement in ems results in a border whose width changes in relation to the size of the current font. Here's an example of setting the border attributes:

```
STR {border-right-width: 2pt;
     border-left-width: 2pt }
```

The `border-width` Attribute

The `border-width` attribute provides a shorthand method for setting the width of the four borders around a box. When you specify the four values, they are applied, in order, to the top, right, bottom, and left. If you supply only one value, it applies to all sides. If you use two or three values, the missing values are copied from the box's opposite sides.

```
BLOCKQUOTE {border-width: medium 0pt 0pt thick}
```

The `border-color` Attribute

This attribute sets the color of all four borders and uses one color keyword as its value. You can't set the color of each side independently. Here's an example of using the `border-color` attribute:

```
BLOCKQUOTE {border-color: yellow}
```

The `border-style` Attribute

The border's appearance can take on several different settings, represented by `none`, `dotted`, `dashed`, `solid`, `double`, `groove`, `ridge`, `inset`, and `outset`. The last four values are represented in 3-D, if the browser supports it, or the browser also can present all the variations as a solid line, except `none`.

Like `border-color`, the style is applied uniformly to all four sides. The attribute is set as follows:

```
BLOCKQUOTE {border-style: groove}
```

The border Attribute

The border attribute gives you a shorthand method for setting all the border variables, including width, style, and color, as shown here:

```
BLOCKQUOTE {border: 1.5pt double black}
```

It sets the values for all four sides at the same time, overriding any individual settings that might have been set previously for the same element.

The height Attribute

This attribute sets the overall height of the bounding box that contains either the text or image element. If the content is text, scrollbars are added as needed so that all the material is still available to the user. If the content is an image, it's scaled to fit inside the area. You can set a physical value, as shown in the following value, or use auto to let the browser allocate space as needed:

```
BLOCKQUOTE {height: 100px}
```

The width Attribute

Similar to height, the width attribute sets the overall width of the bounding box that contains the element. If the content is text, scrollbars are added as needed so that all the material is still available for the user. If both elements are used with an image and the value of one element is auto, as shown in the following example, the aspect ratio for the image is maintained:

```
BLOCKQUOTE {width: auto}
```

The float Attribute

This attribute sets a value similar to the align attribute used in HTML. The three possible values are left, right, and none. The none value allows the element to fall where it may, and the other two values force the element to the left or right of the screen with text wrapping around the opposite side. Here's an example of setting the float attribute for a BLOCKQUOTE element:

```
BLOCKQUOTE {float: right}
```

The clear Attribute

This attribute mimics the clear attribute used with the HTML <BR> tag and uses the same keywords as float. If you use it with right or left, elements will move below any floating element on that respective side, as shown here:

```
BLOCKQUOTE {clear: left right}
```

If you set it to none, floating elements are allowed on both sides.

Classification

These attributes control the general behavior of other elements more than actually specifying an appearance. In addition, classification includes the attributes for list items, identified in HTML with the `<LI>` tag.

The `display` Attribute

This attribute identifies when and if a style element should be used. Four keywords determine its behavior:

- **`inline`:** A new box is created within the same line as adjoining text items and is formatted according to the size and amount of content within its borders, such as an image (`IMG`) or text (`STR`).

- **`block`:** A new box is created in relation to the surrounding elements. This is common with elements, such as `H1` and `P`.

- **`list-item`:** Similar to `block`, only list item markers, which behave more like inline content, are added.

- **`none`:** Turns off the display of the element in any situation, including for children of the element.

The following example shows how the `inline` and `block` keywords are used:

```
IMG {display: inline}
BLOCKQUOTE {display: block}
```

The `white-space` Attribute

The name of this attribute is a bit misleading because it relates to how spaces and line breaks are handled. The choices are `normal` (in which extra spaces are ignored), `pre` (as in preformatted HTML text), and `nowrap` (in which lines are broken only with `<BR>`). Here's an example of using this attribute:

```
BLOCKQUOTE {white-space: pre}
```

The `list-style-type` Attribute

This element sets a list. Your choices are `disc`, `circle`, `square`, `decimal`, `lower-roman`, `upper-roman`, `lower-alpha`, `upper-alpha`, and `none`. For more information on how each of these is represented onscreen, see Chapter 8, "Using Lists to Organize Information." The following are some examples of using this attribute:

```
LI.outline1 {list-style-type: upper-roman}
LI.outline2 {list-style-type: upper-alpha}
LI.outline3 {list-style-type: decimal}
```

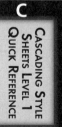

The `list-style-image` Attribute

In lieu of a text marker for the list item, you can also specify the URL of an image to use. If the image is unavailable, the text marker is used as the default. This attribute can be used as follows:

```
LI.general {list-style-image: url(bullet.jpg)}
```

The `list-style-position` Attribute

The two values for this attribute, `inside` and `outside`, determine the formatting of text following the list item marker. The `outside` value, the default value, lines up the additional lines of text beyond the first line with the first character in the first line. If you use the `inside` value, as shown in the following example, the second and following lines are justified with the list item marker:

```
LI {list-style-position: inside}
```

The `list-style` Attribute

This property provides a shorthand method for the `list-style-type`, `list-style-image`, and `list-style-position` attributes, as shown in the following examples:

```
OL {list-style: lower-alpha outside}
UL {list-style: square url(bullet.jpg) inside}
```

XML Quick Reference

by Simon North

APPENDIX D

This appendix is a very heavily edited version of the two standards governing the XML language ("Part 1: Syntax" and "Part 2: Linking") that have been officially released to date.

This version of the specifications has no authority and is not intended to replace the official documents. It's intended to give you a quick reference to the essential rules in the specifications without any grammar and syntax rules and without any clarification or examples. These parts of the standards are extremely useful when you're first becoming acquainted with XML, but in the long-term, their level of detail can become an obstacle to ready reference. By eliminating the introductory explanations and examples, I hope this quick reference helps you as a long-term resource by allowing you to concentrate on the essentials you need to remember.

The original section headings have been kept intact so you can quickly refer to the official documents.

XML Syntax

The following sections distill the XML "Syntax" specification.

Documents

A piece of text is considered an XML document, if it's either valid or well-formed.

Logical and Physical Structure

Each XML document has a logical structure containing *declarations, elements, comments, character references*, and *processing instructions*, all indicated by explicit markup and a physical structure composed of *entities*.

Well-Formed XML Documents

A piece of text qualifies as a well-formed XML document if it meets the following requirements:

- It contains one or more elements.
- It meets all the well-formedness constraints.
- All the elements are nested inside each other.

Characters

The data stored in an XML entity is either text or binary. Binary data has an associated notation, identified by name.

Comments

Comments may appear anywhere except in a CDATA section, in declarations, or in tags. The string - - (two hyphens) must not occur in comments.

Processing Instructions

Processing instructions with names beginning with the string XML are reserved.

CDATA Sections

- CDATA sections can occur anywhere character data may occur.

- Left angle brackets (<) and ampersands (&) may occur in their literal form.

- CDATA sections cannot be nested.

White Space Handling

The XML-SPACE attribute identifies elements in which white space should be treated as significant by applications:

- **DEFAULT:** Means that the default white-space processing is acceptable.

- **PRESERVE:** Means that all the white space should be preserved.

Prolog and Document Type Declaration

- XML documents should begin with an XML declaration that specifies the version of XML being used.

- The document type declaration must appear before the first start tag in the document.

- The XML document type declaration may include a pointer to an external entity containing a subset of the necessary markup declarations, and may also directly include another, internal subset. These two subsets make up the document type definition (DTD), and both subsets can't be empty.

- If both the external and internal subsets are used, an XML processor must read the internal subset first. Entity and attribute declarations in the internal subset take precedence over those in the external subset.

- The name in the DTD must match the element type of the root element.

Required Markup Declaration

The required markup declaration (RMD) specifies whether DTD processing is necessary:

- **NONE:** The XML processor can parse the containing document correctly without first reading any part of the DTD.

- **INTERNAL:** The XML processor must read and process the internal subset of the DTD, if provided.

- **ALL (the default):** The XML processor must read and process the declarations in both subsets of the DTD, if provided.

The RMD must indicate that the entire DTD is required if the external subset contains any unspecified attributes that have default values or entity references, or if white space occurs within element types that have element content.

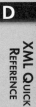

Logical Structures

- An XML document contains one or more elements, which are delimited either by start tags and end tags or, for empty elements, by only start tags.
- Each element has a type, identified by name, and may have a set of attributes.
- Each attribute has a name and a value.

Start Tags and End Tags

- The beginning of every XML element is marked by a start tag.
- The end of every element is marked by an end tag containing the same name name that's in the start tag.
- If an element is empty, it must be closed off with an end tag, or the start tag is the whole element and the tag takes a special form: `<name/>`.
- Each element type used must be declared. The content of an element instance must match the content model declared for that element type.

Element Declarations

- The element structure of an XML document may, for validation purposes, be constrained by using element and attribute declarations.
- An element declaration constrains the element's type and its content. In a valid XML document, no element type can be declared more than once.
- The content of an element may be *element content* (containing only other elements) or *mixed content* (containing character data mixed with elements).
- An element declared with the keyword EMPTY must be empty when it appears in the document.
- An element declared with the keyword ANY may contain child elements of any type and number, mixed with character data.

Attribute List Declarations

- Attributes may appear only within start tags.
- Attribute list declarations specify the name, data type, and default value (if any) of each attribute associated with a given element type.
- When more than one attribute list declaration is supplied for a given element type, all of their contents are merged.
- When more than one definition is provided for the same attribute of a given element type, the first declaration counts and later declarations are ignored.

Attribute Types

- XML attribute types are of three kinds: a string type, a set of tokenized types, and enumerated types.

- The string type may take any literal string as a value.
- The tokenized types have varying lexical and semantic constraints:

    An ID type must be a valid NAME symbol. The name must not appear more than once in an XML document as an ID.

    An IDREF must match the value of an ID attribute on some element in the XML document.

    Entity name values of this type must exactly match the name of an external binary general entity declared in the DTD.

    A name token type must consist of a string matching the NMTOKEN type (a letter or an underscore followed by one or more letters or digits).

    Notation attribute names must match one of the notation names included in the declaration.

- Enumeration values must match one of the NMTOKEN tokens in the declaration. The same NMTOKEN should not occur more than once in the enumerated attribute types of a single element type.

Attribute Defaults

An attribute declaration provides information on whether the attribute's presence is required, and if not, how an XML processor should react if a declared attribute is absent in a document:

- **#FIXED:** The document is invalid if the attribute has a different value from the default.
- **#REQUIRED:** The document is invalid if there's a start tag for the element type that doesn't specify a value for the attribute.
- **#IMPLIED:** If the attribute is omitted, the XML processor must simply inform the application that no value was specified.

If the attribute is neither #REQUIRED nor #IMPLIED, the value contains the declared default value. If a default value is declared and the attribute is omitted, the attribute is treated as though it were present, with its value being the declared default value.

Conditional Sections

Conditional sections are portions of the DTD external subset that are included in, or excluded from, the DTD's logical structure, according to the keyword that controls them. A conditional section may contain one or more complete declarations, comments, processing instructions, or nested conditional sections, intermingled with white space.

If the keyword of the conditional section is INCLUDE, the conditional section is read and processed normally. If the keyword is IGNORE, the declarations in the conditional section are ignored. If a conditional section with a keyword of INCLUDE occurs within a larger conditional section with a keyword of IGNORE, both the outer and the inner conditional sections are ignored.

D

XML QUICK REFERENCE

If the keyword of the conditional section is a parameter entity reference, the parameter entity is replaced by its value before the processor decides whether to include or ignore the conditional section.

Physical Structures

An XML document has one entity, called the *document entity*, which serves as the starting point for the XML processor (and may contain the whole document).

Entities can be either binary or text. A *text entity* contains text data that's considered an integral part of the document. A *binary entity* contains binary data with an associated notation. Only text entities may be referred to by using entity references, and only the names of binary entities may be given as the value of entity attributes.

Logical and Physical Structures

The logical and physical structures (elements and entities) in an XML document must be synchronous. Tags and elements must each begin and end in the same entity, but may refer to other entities internally. Comments, processing instructions, character references, and entity references must each be contained entirely within a single entity.

Entities must each contain an integral number of elements, comments, processing instructions, and references, possibly with character data not found in any element in the entity, or else they must contain nontextual data and no elements.

Character and Entity References

The following rules apply to character and entity references in well-formed XML documents:

- The name given in the entity reference must exactly match the name given in the declaration of the entity.
- You don't need to declare the amp, lt, gt, apos, and quot entities in well-formed documents. However, in valid documents, these entities must be declared. The declaration of parameter entities must precede the reference.
- An entity reference must not contain the name of a binary entity. Binary entities may be referred to only in ENTITY or ENTITIES type attributes.
- A text or parameter entity must not contain a direct or indirect reference to itself.

Entity Declarations

If the same entity is declared more than once, the first declaration encountered is binding.

Internal Entities

If the definition of an entity is just a value, it's called an *internal entity*, and its replacement text is given in the declaration.

Parameter entity and character references are recognized within the entity value and expanded immediately. General entity references in the replacement text aren't recognized when the entity declaration is parsed, though they may be recognized when the entity itself is referred to.

External Entities

- If the entity is not internal, it's an external entity.

- In a valid XML document, the name must match the declared name of a notation.

- The keyword SYSTEM identifies a URL, which can be used to retrieve the entity.

- In addition, an external identifier may include the PUBLIC keyword and a public identifier. The XML processor might try to generate an alternative URL from this identifier, but if it can't, it must use the URL specified with the SYSTEM keyword.

Character Encoding in Entities

Each external text entity in an XML document may use a different encoding for its characters. XML provides an encoding declaration processing instruction, which, if it occurs, must appear at the beginning of a system entity, before any other character data or markup. In the document entity, the encoding declaration is part of the XML declaration; in other entities, it's part of an encoding processing instruction.

Document Entity

The document entity serves as the root of the entity tree and a starting point for an XML processor.

XML Processor Treatment of Entities

When an XML processor encounters character and general entity references, or the name of an external binary entity as the value of an ENTITY or ENTITIES attribute, the following rules apply:

- It may always inform the application of the reference's occurrence and its identifier.

- It must remove character and entity references from the text data before passing the data to the application.

- It must pass the character indicated to the application in place of a character reference.

- It must inform the application of an external entity's system and public identifier, if any.

- It must inform the application of a binary external entity's associated notation name and the notation's associated system and public identifier, if any.

- It must include an internal (text) entity and process it as part of the document.

- To validate an XML document, the processor must include the content of an external text entity.

- If it's not trying to validate an XML document, the processor may include the content of an external text entity, but it's not required to.

Parameter entity references can be used in a variety of places in the DTD. They are always expanded immediately on being recognized, and the DTD must match the relevant rules of the grammar after they have all been expanded.

Predefined Entities

■ The ampersand character (&) and the left angle bracket (<) must be escaped by using either numeric character references or the strings & and <.

■ The right angle bracket (>) may be represented by using the string >. The apostrophe or single-quote character (') may be represented as ', and the double-quote character (") as ".

All XML processors must recognize these entities whether they are declared or not. Valid XML documents must declare these entities before using them.

Notation Declarations

Notations identify by name the format of external binary entities. Notation declarations supply a name for the notation, for use in entity and attribute list declarations and in attribute value specifications. They also supply an external identifier for the notation that may allow an XML processor or its client application to find a helper application capable of processing data in the given notation.

Conformance

Conforming XML processors fall into two classes: validating and non-validating.

Validating and non-validating systems alike must report violations of the well-formedness constraints given in the specification.

Validating processors must report locations where the document doesn't comply with the constraints expressed by the declarations in the DTD. They must also report all failures to fulfill the validity constraints.

XML Linking

The following sections distill the XML "Linking" specification, which specifies a method for describing links between objects and addressing parts of XML documents.

Link Recognition

The existence of a link is asserted by a linking element. XML linking elements are recognized by their XML-LINK. Possible values are SIMPLE, EXTENDED, LOCATOR, GROUP, and DOCUMENT, signalling that the element is to be treated as being of that type.

Attribute Remapping

To avoid conflicts with elements whose attributes have the same names, attributes can be declared as equivalent by using the XML-ATTRIBUTES attribute.

This attribute must contain pairs of names. In each pair, the first name must be ROLE, HREF, TITLE, SHOW, INLINE, CONTENT-ROLE, CONTENT-TITLE, ACTUATE, BEHAVIOR, or STEPS. The second name is treated as though it were playing the role assigned to the first.

To avoid having to explicitly declare attributes for every element, default attribute values can be declared.

Linking Elements

Simple links are usually inline and always one-directional. Extended links can be either inline (in the source document) or out-of-line (outside the source document) and can be used for multi-directional links, links into read-only data, and so on.

Information Associated with Links

Information can be associated with links through these attributes:

- **ROLE:** A string that identifies the meaning of the link to an application program. Each participant in a link may be given its own role.
- **HREF:** Identifies the target.
- **TITLE:** Labels the link.
- **SHOW and ACTUATE:** Specifies the behavior on following the link.
- **INLINE:** Specifies whether the linking element is inline.

Content of Linking Elements

Any element can be recognized as a linking element based on use of the XML-LINK attribute. In a valid XML document, each linking element must conform to the constraints expressed in its governing DTD.

Simple Links

A simple link may contain only one locator; the locator attributes are attached directly to the linking element.

Extended Links

An extended link can involve any number of resources, but it doesn't need to be co-located with any of them. An application can be expected to follow links among all of them. An extended link's locators are stored in child elements of the linking element, each with its own set of attributes.

Note that many of the attributes can be supplied for both the parent linking element and the child locator element. If any such attribute is provided in the linking element but not in a locator element, the value given in the linking element is to be used in processing the locator element.

Inline and Out-Of-Line Links

The INLINE attribute can take the values TRUE and FALSE. The value TRUE, which is the default, means that the entire content of the linking element is to be considered as part of the link, except for any child locator elements (which are considered part of the linking element machinery).

When the link is inline, the CONTENT-ROLE and CONTENT-TITLE attributes may be used to supply the title and role information for this "content" resource. If INLINE is FALSE, the CONTENT-TITLE and CONTENT-ROLE attributes have no effect.

Link Behavior

The timing and effects of following a link can be expressed by the SHOW and ACTUATE attributes.

SHOW

The SHOW attribute specifies how a target should be displayed or processed on following the link:

- **EMBED:** The target should be embedded in the body of the source where the link started.
- **REPLACE:** The target should replace the source where the link started.
- **NEW:** The target should be displayed or processed in a new context, not affecting that of the source where the link started.

ACTUATE

The ACTUATE attribute specifies when a link should be followed:

- **AUTO:** When encountered, and the display or processing of the source isn't considered complete until this is done.
- **USER:** Not until there's an explicit external request to do so.

Addressing

A locator always contains a URL. When a locator identifies a target that is an XML document, the locator value may contain a URL, a fragment identifier, or both.

Extended Pointers

Extended pointers operate on the element tree defined by the elements in the XML document. The basic form is a series of location terms, each specifying either an absolute or a relative location. Each term has a keyword and can be qualified by parameters such as an instance number, element type, or attribute.

Absolute Location Terms

Absolute locations are specified by using one of the following keywords.

ROOT

The ROOT keyword specifies that the location source is the root element of the source. This is the default behavior.

HERE

The HERE keyword specifies that the location source for the first location term of that series is the linking element containing the locator rather than the default root element.

DITTO

The DITTO keyword specifies that the location source for its first location term is the one specified by the entire first pointer.

ID

The ID keyword specifies that the location source for the first location term is the element in the source that has an attribute of type ID with a value matching the given name.

HTML

The HTML keyword selects the first element whose type is A that has a NAME attribute with the same value as the supplied NAME value (this is the same as the # in an HTML document).

Relative Location Terms

Relative locations are specified by using one of the following keywords.

- **CHILD:** Selects child elements of the location source.
- **DESCENDANT:** Selects elements appearing in the content of the location source.
- **ANCESTOR:** Selects elements where the location source is found.
- **PRECEDING:** Selects elements that appear before the location source.
- **PSIBLING:** Selects preceding sibling elements of the location source.
- **FOLLOWING:** Selects elements that appear after the location source.
- **FSIBLING:** Selects following sibling elements of the location source.

Candidates can be selected by occurrence number, element type, attribute name, and attribute value.

Extended Link Groups

An extended link group element is used to store a list of links to other documents that form an interlinked document group.

Each document is identified by using the HREF attribute of an extended link document element, which is a child element of the GROUP. The value of the HREF attribute is a locator.

These elements are recognized by the use of the XML-LINK attribute with the value GROUP or DOCUMENT.

JavaScript Reference

APPENDIX

E

The first part of this reference is organized by object, with properties and methods listed by the object to which they apply. The second part covers independent functions in JavaScript not connected with a particular object, as well as operators in JavaScript.

A Note About JavaScript 1.2

JavaScript 1.2 is designed to interface seamlessly with Netscape Navigator 4.0. New features have been introduced in various areas of the language model, including but not limited to the following:

- Events
- Objects
- Properties
- Methods

Netscape Navigator 4.0 has been coded to support these new features, but earlier versions of Navigator have not. Backward compatibility is, therefore, an issue.

In this appendix, techniques that work only in Netscape Navigator 4.0 and above are clearly marked. At each heading, the words "Navigator 4.0 Only" will appear.

Finally, note that when developing, you should now clearly identify which version of JavaScript you're using. If you don't, your scripts might not work. You identify the version by using the LANGUAGE attribute in the <SCRIPT> tag. The following are some examples:

```
<Script Language = "JavaScript"> - Compatible with 2.0 and above

<Script Language = "JavaScript 1.1"> - Compatible with 3.0 and above

<Script Language = "JavaScript 1.2"> - Compatible with 4.0 and above
```

The following codes are used next to section headings to indicate where objects, methods, properties, and event handlers are implemented:

- **C:** Client JavaScript (Server JavaScript is not covered in this appendix)
- **2:** Netscape Navigator 2
- **3:** Netscape Navigator 3
- **4:** Netscape Navigator 4 only (that's not to say Navigator 4 works with these items only; Navigator 4 will handle all implementations)
- **I:** Microsoft Internet Explorer 3

The anchor Object [C|2|3|4|I]

The anchor object reflects an HTML anchor.

Properties

- **name:** A string value indicating the name of the anchor. [Not 2|3]

The applet Object [C|3]

The applet object reflects a Java applet included in a Web page with the <APPLET> tag.

Properties

- **name:** A string reflecting the NAME attribute of the <APPLET> tag.

The area Object [C|3]

The area object reflects a clickable area defined in an image map; area objects appear as entries in the links array of the document object.

Properties

- **hash:** A string value indicating an anchor name from the URL.
- **host:** A string value reflecting the host and domain name portion of the URL.
- **hostname:** A string value indicating the host, domain name, and port number from the URL.
- **href:** A string value reflecting the entire URL.
- **pathname:** A string value reflecting the path portion of the URL (excluding the host, domain name, port number, and protocol).
- **port:** A string value indicating the port number from the URL.
- **protocol:** A string value indicating the protocol portion of the URL, including the trailing colon.
- **search:** A string value specifying the query portion of the URL (after the question mark).
- **target:** A string value reflecting the TARGET attribute of the <AREA> tag.

Methods

- **getSelection:** Gets the current selection and returns this value as a string.

Event Handlers

- **onDblClick:** Specifies JavaScript code to execute when the user double-clicks the area. (Not implemented on Macintosh) Netscape Navigator 4.0 only. [4]

- **onMouseOut:** Specifies JavaScript code to execute when the mouse moves outside the area specified in the `<AREA>` tag.

New Properties with JavaScript 1.2

type	Indicates a `MouseOut` event.
target	Indicates the object to which the event was sent.
layer[n]	Where [n] represents X or Y, used (with page[n] and screen[n]) to describe the cursor location when the `MouseOut` event occurred.
page[n]	Where [n] represents X or Y, used (with layer[n] and screen[n]) to describe the cursor location when the `MouseOut` event occurred.
screen[n]	Where [n] represents X or Y, used (with layer[n] and page[n]) to describe the cursor location when the `MouseOut` event occurred.

- **onMouseOver:** Specifies JavaScript code to execute when the mouse enters the area specified in the `<AREA>` tag.

New Properties with JavaScript 1.2

type	Indicates a `MouseOver` event.
target	Indicates the object to which the event was sent.
layer[n]	Where [n] represents X or Y, used (with page[n] and screen[n]) to describe the cursor location when the `MouseOver` event occurred.
page[n]	Where [n] represents X or Y, used (with layer[n] and screen[n]) to describe the cursor location when the `MouseOver` event occurred.
screen[n]	Where [n] represents X or Y, used (with layer[n] and page[n]) to describe the cursor location when the `MouseOver` event occurred.

The array Object [C|3|I]

The array object provides a mechanism for creating arrays and working with them. New arrays are created with *arrayName* = new Array() or *arrayName* = new Array(*arrayLength*).

Properties

- **length:** An integer value reflecting the number of elements in an array.
- **prototype:** Used to add properties to an array object.

Methods

- **concat(*arrayname*):** Combines elements of two arrays and returns a third, one level deep, without altering either of the derivative arrays. (Netscape Navigator 4.0 only.)
- **join(*string*):** Returns a string containing each element of the array separated by *string*. (Not I)
- **reverse():** Reverses the order of an array. (Not I)
- **slice(arrayName, beginSlice, endSlice):** Extracts a portion of some array and derives a new array from it. The beginSlice and endSlice parameters specify the target elements at which to begin and end the slice. (Netscape Navigator 4.0 only.)
- **sort(*function*):** Sorts an array based on function, which indicates a *function* defining the sort order. *function* can be omitted, in which case the sort defaults to dictionary order. Note: sort now works on all platforms.

The button Object [C | 2 | 3 | I]

The button object reflects a pushbutton from an HTML form in JavaScript.

Properties

- **enabled:** A Boolean value indicating whether the button is enabled. (Not 2|3)
- **form:** A reference to the form object containing the button. (Not 2|3)
- **name:** A string value containing the name of the button element.
- **type:** A string value reflecting the TYPE attribute of the <INPUT> tag. (Not 2|I)
- **value:** A string value containing the value of the button element.

Methods

- **click():** Emulates the action of clicking the button.
- **focus():** Gives focus to the button. (Not 2|3)

Event Handlers

- **onMouseDown:** Specifies JavaScript code to execute when a user presses a mouse button.
- **onMouseUp:** Specifies JavaScript code to execute when the user releases a mouse button.
- **onClick:** Specifies JavaScript code to execute when the button is clicked.
- **onFocus:** Specifies JavaScript code to execute when the button receives focus. (Not 2|3)

E

JAVASCRIPT REFERENCE

The checkbox Object [c | 2 | 3 | I]

The checkbox object makes a checkbox in an HTML form available in JavaScript.

Properties

- ■ **checked:** A Boolean value indicating whether the checkbox element is checked.
- ■ **defaultChecked:** A Boolean value indicating whether the checkbox element was checked by default (that is, it reflects the CHECKED attribute).
- ■ **enabled:** A Boolean value indicating whether the checkbox is enabled. (Not 2|3)
- ■ **form:** A reference to the form object containing the checkbox. (Not 2|3)
- ■ **name:** A string value containing the name of the checkbox element.
- ■ **type:** A string value reflecting the TYPE attribute of the <INPUT> tag. (Not 2|I)
- ■ **value:** A string value containing the value of the checkbox element.

Methods

- ■ **click():** Emulates the action of clicking the checkbox.
- ■ **focus():** Gives focus to the checkbox. (Not 2|3)

Event Handlers

- ■ **onClick:** Specifies JavaScript code to execute when the checkbox is clicked.
- ■ **onFocus:** Specifies JavaScript code to execute when the checkbox receives focus. (Not 2|3)

The combo Object [C | I]

The combo object reflects a combo field in JavaScript.

Properties

- ■ **enabled:** A Boolean value indicating whether the combo box is enabled. (Not 2|3)
- ■ **form:** A reference to the form object containing the combo box. (Not 2|3)
- ■ **listCount:** An integer reflecting the number of elements in the list.
- ■ **listIndex:** An integer reflecting the index of the selected element in the list.
- ■ **multiSelect:** A Boolean value indicating whether the combo field is in multiselect mode.
- ■ **name:** A string value reflecting the name of the combo field.
- ■ **value:** A string containing the value of the combo field.

Methods

- **addItem(*index*):** Adds an item to the combo field before the item at *index*.
- **click():** Simulates a click on the combo field.
- **clear():** Clears the contents of the combo field.
- **focus():** Gives focus to the combo field.
- **removeItem(*index*):** Removes the item at *index* from the combo field.

Event Handlers

- **onClick:** Specifies JavaScript code to execute when the mouse clicks the combo field.
- **onFocus:** Specifies JavaScript code to execute when the combo field receives focus.

The date Object [C | 2 | 3 | I]

The date object provides mechanisms for working with dates and times in JavaScript. Instances of the object can be created with the following syntax:

newObjectName = new Date(*dateInfo*)

Here, *dateInfo* is an optional specification of a particular date and can be one of the following:

"*month day, year hours:minutes:seconds*"

year, month, day

year, month, day, hours, minutes, seconds

The latter two options represent integer values.

If no *dateInfo* is specified, the new object represents the current date and time.

Properties

- **prototype:** Provides a mechanism for adding properties to a date object. (Not 2)

Methods

- **getDate():** Returns the day of the month for the current date object as an integer from 1 to 31.
- **getDay():** Returns the day of the week for the current date object as an integer from 0 to 6 (0 is Sunday, 1 is Monday, and so on).
- **getHours():** Returns the hour from the time in the current date object as an integer from 0 to 23.
- **getMinutes():** Returns the minutes from the time in the current date object as an integer from 0 to 59.

- **getMonth():** Returns the month for the current date object as an integer from 0 to 11 (0 is January, 1 is February, and so on).

- **getSeconds():** Returns the seconds from the time in the current date object as an integer from 0 to 59.

- **getTime():** Returns the time of the current date object as an integer representing the number of milliseconds since 1 January 1970 at 00:00:00.

- **getTimezoneOffset():** Returns the difference between the local time and GMT as an integer representing the number of minutes.

- **getYear():** Returns the year for the current date object as a two-digit integer representing the year less 1900.

- **parse(*dateString*):** Returns the number of milliseconds between January 1, 1970 at 00:00:00 and the date specified in *dateString*, which should take the following format: (Not I)

  Day, DD Mon YYYY HH:MM:SS TZN

  Mon DD, YYYY

- **setDate(*dateValue*):** Sets the day of the month for the current date object. *dateValue* is an integer from 1 to 31.

- **setHours(*hoursValue*):** Sets the hours for the time for the current date object. *hoursValue* is an integer from 0 to 23.

- **setMinutes(*minutesValue*):** Sets the minutes for the time for the current date object. *minutesValue* is an integer from 0 to 59.

- **setMonth(*monthValue*):** Sets the month for the current date object. *monthValue* is an integer from 0 to 11 (0 is January, 1 is February, and so on).

- **setSeconds(*secondsValue*):** Sets the seconds for the time for the current date object. *secondsValue* is an integer from 0 to 59.

- **setTime(*timeValue*):** Sets the value for the current date object. *timeValue* is an integer representing the number of milliseconds since January 1, 1970 at 00:00:00.

- **setYear(*yearValue*):** Sets the year for the current date object. *yearValue* is an integer greater than 1900.

- **toGMTString():** Returns the value of the current date object in GMT as a string using Internet conventions in the following form:

  Day, DD Mon YYYY HH:MM:SS GMT

- **toLocaleString():** Returns the value of the current date object in the local time using local conventions.

- **UTC(*yearValue, monthValue, dateValue, hoursValue, minutesValue, secondsValue*):** Returns the number of milliseconds since January 1, 1970 at 00:00:00 GMT. *yearValue* is an integer greater than 1900. *monthValue* is an integer from 0 to 11.

dateValue is an integer from 1 to 31. *hoursValue* is an integer from 0 to 23. *minutesValue* and *secondsValue* are integers from 0 to 59. *hoursValue*, *minutesValue*, and *secondsValue* are optional. (Not I)

The document Object [C | 2 | 3 | I]

The document object reflects attributes of an HTML document in JavaScript.

Properties

■ **alinkColor:** The color of active links as a string or a hexadecimal triplet.

■ **anchors:** Array of anchor objects in the order they appear in the HTML document. Use anchors.length to get the number of anchors in a document.

■ **applets:** Array of applet objects in the order they appear in the HTML document. Use applets.length to get the number of applets in a document. (Not 2)

■ **bgColor:** The color of the document's background.

■ **cookie:** A string value containing cookie values for the current document.

■ **embeds:** Array of plugin objects in the order they appear in the HTML document. Use embeds.length to get the number of plug-ins in a document. (Not 2|I)

■ **fgColor:** The color of the document's foreground.

■ **forms:** Array of form objects in the order the forms appear in the HTML file. Use forms.length to get the number of forms in a document.

■ **images:** Array of image objects in the order they appear in the HTML document. Use images.length to get the number of images in a document. (Not 2|I)

■ **lastModified:** String value containing the last date of the document's modification.

■ **linkColor:** The color of links as a string or a hexadecimal triplet.

■ **links:** Array of link objects in the order the hypertext links appear in the HTML document. Use links.length to get the number of links in a document.

■ **location:** A string containing the URL of the current document. Use document.URL instead of document.location. This property is expected to disappear in a future release.

■ **referrer:** A string value containing the URL of the calling document when the user follows a link.

■ **title:** A string containing the title of the current document.

■ **URL:** A string reflecting the URL of the current document. Use instead of document.location. (Not I)

■ **vlinkColor:** The color of followed links as a string or a hexadecimal triplet.

Event Handlers

- **onMouseDown:** Specifies JavaScript code to execute when a user presses a mouse button.

- **onMouseUp:** Specifies JavaScript code to execute when the user releases a mouse button.

- **onKeyUp:** Specifies JavaScript code to execute when the user releases a specific key. (Netscape Navigator 4.0 only.) (4)

- **onKeyPress:** Specifies JavaScript code to execute when the user holds down a specific key. (Netscape Navigator 4.0 only.) (4)

- **onKeyDown:** Specifies JavaScript code to execute when the user presses a specific key. (Netscape Navigator 4.0 only.) (4)

- **onDblClick:** Specifies JavaScript code to execute when the user double-clicks the area. (Not implemented on Macintosh.) (Netscape Navigator 4.0 only.) (4)

Methods

- **captureEvents():** Used in a window with frames (along with enableExternalCapture), it specifies that the window will capture all specified events. New in JavaScript 1.2.

- **clear():** Clears the document window. (Not I)

- **close():** Closes the current output stream.

- **open(*mimeType*):** Opens a stream that allows write() and writeln() methods to write to the document window. *mimeType* is an optional string that specifies a document type supported by Navigator or a plug-in (for example, text/html or image/gif).

- **releaseEvents(*eventType*):** Specifies that the current window must release events (as opposed to capture them) so that these events can be passed to other objects, perhaps further on in the event hierarchy. New in JavaScript 1.2.

- **routeEvent(event):** Sends or routes an event through the normal event hierarchy.

- **write():** Writes text and HTML to the specified document.

- **writeln():** Writes text and HTML to the specified document followed by a newline character.

The fileUpload Object [C|3]

Reflects a file upload element in an HTML form.

Properties

- **name:** A string value reflecting the name of the file upload element.

- **value:** A string value reflecting the file upload element's field.

The form Object [C | 2 | 3 | I]

The form object reflects an HTML form in JavaScript. Each HTML form in a document is reflected by a distinct instance of the form object.

Properties

- **action:** A string value specifying the URL to which the form data is submitted.
- **elements:** Array of objects for each form element in the order in which they appear in the form.
- **encoding:** String containing the MIME encoding of the form as specified in the ENCTYPE attribute.
- **method:** A string value containing the method of submission of form data to the server.
- **target:** A string value containing the name of the window to which responses to form submissions are directed.

Methods

- **reset():** Resets the form. (Not 2|I)
- **submit():** Submits the form.

Event Handlers

- **onReset:** Specifies JavaScript code to execute when the form is reset. (Not 2|I)
- **onSubmit:** Specifies JavaScript code to execute when the form is submitted. The code should return a true value to allow the form to be submitted. A false value prevents the form from being submitted.

The frame Object [C | 2 | 3 | I]

The frame object reflects a frame window in JavaScript.

Properties

- **frames:** An array of objects for each frame in a window. Frames appear in the array in the order in which they appear in the HTML source code.
- **onblur:** A string reflecting the onBlur event handler for the frame. New values can be assigned to this property to change the event handler. (Not 2)
- **onfocus:** A string reflecting the onFocus event handler for the frame. New values can be assigned to this property to change the event handler. (Not 2)
- **parent:** A string indicating the name of the window containing the frame set.
- **self:** An alternative for the name of the current window.

- **top:** An alternative for the name of the topmost window.
- **window:** An alternative for the name of the current window.

Methods

- **alert(*message*):** Displays *message* in a dialog box.
- **blur():** Removes focus from the frame. (Not 2)
- **clearInterval(*intervalID*):** Cancels timeouts created with the setInterval method. New in JavaScript 1.2.
- **close():** Closes the window.
- **confirm(*message*):** Displays *message* in a dialog box with OK and Cancel buttons. Returns true or false based on the button clicked by the user.
- **focus():** Gives focus to the frame. (Not 2)
- **open(*url*,*name*,*features*):** Opens *url* in a window named *name*. If *name* doesn't exist, a new window is created with that name. *features* is an optional string argument containing a list of features for the new window. The feature list contains any of the following name-value pairs separated by commas and without additional spaces:

toolbar=[yes,no,1,0]	Indicates whether the window should have a toolbar
location=[yes,no,1,0]	Indicates whether the window should have a location field
directories=[yes,no,1,0]	Indicates whether the window should have directory buttons
status=[yes,no,1,0]	Indicates whether the window should have a status bar
menubar=[yes,no,1,0]	Indicates whether the window should have menus
scrollbars=[yes,no,1,0]	Indicates whether the window should have scrollbars
resizable=[yes,no,1,0]	Indicates whether the window should be resizable
width=*pixels*	Indicates the width of the window in pixels
height=*pixels*	Indicates the height of the window in pixels

- **print():** Prints the contents of a frame or window. This is the equivalent of the user clicking the Print button in Netscape Navigator. New in JavaScript 1.2.
- **prompt(*message*,*response*):** Displays *message* in a dialog box with a text entry field with the default value of *response*. The user's response in the text entry field is returned as a string.
- **setInterval(*function*, msec, [*args*]):** Repeatedly calls a function after the period specified by the msec parameter. New in JavaScript 1.2.
- **setInterval(*expression*, msec):** Evaluates *expression* after the period specified by the msec parameter. New in JavaScript 1.2.

■ **setTimeout(*expression*,*time*):** Evaluates *expression* after *time*; *time* is a value in milliseconds. The timeout can be named with the following structure:

```
name = setTimeOut(expression,time)
```

■ **clearTimeout(*name*):** Cancels the timeout with the name *name*.

Event Handlers

■ **onBlur:** Specifies JavaScript code to execute when focus is removed from a frame. (Not 2)

■ **onFocus:** Specifies JavaScript code to execute when focus is removed from a frame. (Not 2)

■ **onMove:** Specifies JavaScript code to execute when the user moves a frame. (Netscape Navigator 4.0 only.)

■ **onResize:** Specifies JavaScript code to execute when a user resizes the frame. (Netscape Navigator 4.0 only.)

The function Object [C | 3]

The function object provides a mechanism for indicating JavaScript code to compile as a function. This is the syntax to use the function object:

```
functionName = new Function(arg1, arg2, arg3, ..., functionCode)
```

This is similar to the following:

```
function functionName(arg1, arg2, arg3, ...) {
    functionCode
}
```

However, in the former, *functionName* is a variable with a reference to the function, and the function is evaluated each time it's used instead of being compiled once.

Properties

■ **arguments:** An integer reflecting the number of arguments in a function.

■ **prototype:** Provides a mechanism for adding properties to a function object.

The hidden Object [C | 2 | 3 | I]

The hidden object reflects a hidden field from an HTML form in JavaScript.

Properties

■ **name:** A string value containing the name of the hidden element.

■ **type:** A string value reflecting the TYPE property of the <INPUT> tag. (Not 2|I)

■ **value:** A string value containing the value of the hidden text element.

The history Object [C|2|3|I]

The history object allows a script to work with the Navigator browser's history list in JavaScript. For security and privacy reasons, the actual content of the list isn't reflected into JavaScript.

Properties

■ **length:** An integer representing the number of items on the history list. (Not I)

Methods

■ **back():** Goes back to the previous document in the history list. (Not I)

■ **forward():** Goes forward to the next document in the history list. (Not I)

■ **go(*location*):** Goes to the document in the history list specified by *location*, which can be a string or integer value. If it's a string, it represents all or part of a URL in the history list. If it's an integer, *location* represents the relative position of the document on the history list. As an integer, *location* can be positive or negative. (Not I)

The image Object [C|3]

The image object reflects an image included in an HTML document.

Properties

■ **border:** An integer value reflecting the width of the image's border in pixels.

■ **complete:** A Boolean value indicating whether the image has finished loading.

■ **height:** An integer value reflecting the height of an image in pixels.

■ **hspace:** An integer value reflecting the HSPACE attribute of the <IMG> tag.

■ **lowsrc:** A string value containing the URL of the low-resolution version of the image to load.

■ **name:** A string value indicating the name of the image object.

■ **prototype:** Provides a mechanism for adding properties as an image object.

■ **src:** A string value indicating the URL of the image.

■ **vspace:** An integer value reflecting the VSPACE attribute of the <IMG> tag.

■ **width:** An integer value indicating the width of an image in pixels.

Event Handlers

■ **onKeyUp:** Specifies JavaScript code to execute when the user releases a specific key. (Netscape Navigator 4.0 only.) (4)

■ **onKeyPress:** Specifies JavaScript code to execute when the user holds down a specific key. (Netscape Navigator 4.0 only.) (4)

- **onKeyDown:** Specifies JavaScript code to execute when the user presses a specific key. (Netscape Navigator 4.0 only.) (4)

- **onAbort:** Specifies JavaScript code to execute if the attempt to load the image is aborted. (Not 2)

- **onError:** Specifies JavaScript code to execute if there's an error while loading the image. Setting this event handler to null suppresses error messages if an error occurs while loading. (Not 2)

- **onLoad:** Specifies JavaScript code to execute when the image finishes loading. (Not 2)

The layer Object [4] (Netscape Navigator 4.0 Only)

The layer object is used to embed layers of content within a page; they can be hidden or not. Either type is accessible through JavaScript code. The most common use for layers is in developing Dynamic HTML (DHTML). With layers, you can create animations or other dynamic content on a page by cycling through the layers you have defined.

Properties

- **above:** Places a layer on top of a newly created layer.

- **background:** Used to specify a tiled background image of the layer.

- **below:** Places a layer below a newly created layer.

- **bgColor:** Sets the background color of the layer.

- **clip(left, top, right, bottom):** Specifies the visible boundaries of the layer.

- **height:** Specifies the height of the layer, expressed in pixels (integer) or by a percentage of the instant layer.

- **ID:** Previously called NAME. Used to name the layer so that it can be referred to by name and accessed by other JavaScript code.

- **left:** Specifies the horizontal positioning of the top-left corner of the layer. Used with the Top property.

- **page[n]:** Where [n] is X or Y. Specifies the horizontal (X) or vertical (Y) positioning of the top-left corner of the layer, in relation to the overall, enclosing document. (Note: This is different from the Left and Top properties.)

- **parentLayer:** Specifies the layer object that contains the present layer.

- **SRC:** Specifies HTML source to be displayed with the target layer. (This source can also include JavaScript.)

- **siblingAbove:** Specifies the layer object immediately above the present one.

- **siblingBelow:** Specifies the layer object immediately below the present one.

- **top:** Specifies the vertical positioning of the top-left corner of the layer. (Used with the Left property.)

- **visibility:** Specifies the visibility of the layer. There are three choices: show (it is visible), hidden (it is not visible), and inherit (the layer inherits the properties of its parent.)

- **width:** Specifies the width of the layer. Used for wrapping procedures; that is, the width denotes the boundary after which the contents wrap inside the layer.

- **z-index:** Specifies the z-order (or stacking order) of the layer. Used to set the layer's position within the overall rotational order of all layers. Expressed as an integer. (Used where there are many layers.)

Events

- **onBlur:** Specifies JavaScript code to execute when the layer loses focus.

- **onFocus:** Specifies JavaScript code to execute when the layer gains focus.

- **onLoad:** Specifies JavaScript code to execute when a layer is loaded.

- **onMouseOut:** Specifies JavaScript code to execute when the mouse cursor moves off the layer.

New Properties

type	Indicates a MouseOut event.
target	Indicates the object to which the event was sent.
layer[n]	Where [n] represents X or Y, used (with page[n] and screen[n]) to describe the cursor location when the MouseOut event occurred.
page[n]	Where [n] represents X or Y, used (with layer[n] and screen[n]) to describe the cursor location when the MouseOut event occurred.
screen[n]	Where [n] represents X or Y, used (with layer[n] and page[n]) to describe the cursor location when the MouseOut event occurred.

- **onMouseover:** Specifies the JavaScript code to execute when the mouse cursor enters the layer.

New Properties with JavaScript 1.2

type	Indicates a MouseOver event.
target	Indicates the object to which the event was sent.
layer[n]	Where [n] represents X or Y, used (with page[n] and screen[n]) to describe the cursor location when the MouseOver event occurred.
page[n]	Where [n] represents X or Y, used (with layer[n] and screen[n]) to describe the cursor location when the MouseOver event occurred.
screen[n]	Where [n] represents X or Y, used (with layer[n] and page[n]) to describe the cursor location when the MouseOver event occurred.

Methods

- **captureEvents():** Used in a window with frames (along with enableExternalCapture), it specifies that the window will capture all specified events. New in JavaScript 1.2.

- **load(*source*, *width*):** Alters the source of the layer by replacing it with HTML (or JavaScript) from the file specified in *source*. Using this method, you can also pass a width value (in pixels) to accommodate the new content.

- **moveAbove(*layer*):** Places the layer above *layer* in the stack.

- **moveBelow(layer):** Places the layer below *layer* in the stack.

- **moveBy(x,y):** Alters the position of the layer by the specified values, expressed in pixels.

- **moveTo(x,y):** Alters the position of the layer (within the containing layer) to the specified coordinates, expressed in pixels.

- **moveToAbsolute(x,y):** Alters the position of the layer (within the page) to the specified coordinates, expressed in pixels.

- **releaseEvents(*eventType*):** Specifies that the current window should release events instead of capturing them so that these events can be passed to other objects, perhaps further on in the event hierarchy. New in JavaScript 1.2.

- **resizeBy(*width*,*height*):** Resizes the layer by the specified values, expressed in pixels.

- **resizeTo(*width*,*height*):** Resizes the layer to the specified height and size, expressed in pixels.

- **routeEvent(event):** Sends or routes an event through the normal event hierarchy.

The link Object [C | 2 | 3 | I]

The link object reflects a hypertext link in the body of a document.

Properties

- **hash:** A string value containing the anchor name in the URL.

- **host:** A string value containing the host name and port number from the URL.

- **hostname:** A string value containing the domain name (or numerical IP address) from the URL.

- **href:** A string value containing the entire URL.

- **pathname:** A string value specifying the path portion of the URL.

- **port:** A string value containing the port number from the URL.

- **protocol:** A string value containing the protocol from the URL (including the colon, but not the slashes).

■ **search:** A string value containing any information passed to a GET CGI-BIN call (such as any information after the question mark).

■ **target:** A string value containing the name of the window or frame specified in the TARGET attribute.

Event Handlers

■ **onMouseDown:** Specifies JavaScript code to execute when a user presses a mouse button. (JavaScript 1.2 and Netscape Navigator 4.0 only.) (4)

■ **onMouseOut:** Specifies JavaScript code to execute when the user moves the mouse cursor out of an object. (JavaScript 1.2 and Netscape Navigator 4.0 only.) (4)

New Properties with JavaScript 1.2

type	Indicates a MouseOut event.
target	Indicates the object to which the event was sent.
layer[n]	Where [n] represents X or Y, used (with page[n] and screen[n]) to describe the cursor location when the MouseOut event occurred.
page[n]	Where [n] represents X or Y, used (with layer[n] and screen[n]) to describe the cursor location when the MouseOut event occurred.
screen[n]	Where [n] represents X or Y, used (with layer[n] and page[n]) to describe the cursor location when the MouseOut event occurred.

■ **onMouseUp:** Specifies the JavaScript code to execute when the user releases a mouse button.

■ **onKeyUp:** Specifies the JavaScript code to execute when the user releases a specific key. (Netscape Navigator 4.0 only.) (4)

■ **onKeyPress:** Specifies the JavaScript code to execute when the user holds down a specific key. (Netscape Navigator 4.0 only.) (4)

■ **onKeyDown:** Specifies the JavaScript code to execute when the user presses a specific key. (Netscape Navigator 4.0 only.) (4)

■ **onDblClick:** Specifies the JavaScript code to execute when the user double-clicks the area. (Not implemented on Macintosh.) (Netscape Navigator 4.0 only.) (4)

■ **moveMouse:** Specifies the JavaScript code to execute when the mouse pointer moves over the link. (Not 2|3)

■ **onClick:** Specifies the JavaScript code to execute when the link is clicked.

■ **onMouseOver:** Specifies the JavaScript code to execute when the mouse pointer moves over the hypertext link.

New Properties with JavaScript 1.2

type	Indicates a MouseOver event.
target	Indicates the object to which the event was sent.

layer[n]   Where [n] represents X or Y, used (with page[n] and screen[n]) to describe the cursor location when the MouseOver event occurred.

page[n]   Where [n] represents X or Y, used (with layer[n] and screen[n]) to describe the cursor location when the MouseOver event occurred.

screen[n]   Where [n] represents X or Y, used (with layer[n] and page[n]) to describe the cursor location when the MouseOver event occurred.

The location Object [C | 2 | 3 | I]

The location object reflects information about the current URL.

Properties

- ◼ **hash:** A string value containing the anchor name in the URL.
- ◼ **host:** A string value containing the host name and port number from the URL.
- ◼ **hostname:** A string value containing the domain name (or numerical IP address) from the URL.
- ◼ **href:** A string value containing the entire URL.
- ◼ **pathname:** A string value specifying the path portion of the URL.
- ◼ **port:** A string value containing the port number from the URL.
- ◼ **protocol:** A string value containing the protocol from the URL (including the colon, but not the slashes).
- ◼ **search:** A string value containing any information passed to a GET CGI-BIN call (such as information after the question mark).

Methods

- ◼ **reload():** Reloads the current document. (Not 2|I)
- ◼ **replace(*url*):** Loads *url* over the current entry in the history list, making it impossible to navigate back to the previous URL with the Back button. (Not 2|I)

The math Object [C | 2 | 3 | I]

The math object provides properties and methods for advanced mathematical calculations.

Properties

- ◼ **E:** The value of Euler's constant (roughly 2.718) used as the base for natural logarithms.
- ◼ **LN10:** The value of the natural logarithm of 10 (roughly 2.302).
- ◼ **LN2:** The value of the natural logarithm of 2 (roughly 0.693).

- **LOG10E:** The value of the base 10 logarithm of e (roughly 0.434).
- **LOG2E:** The value of the base 2 logarithm of e (roughly 1.442).
- **PI:** The value of Π; used to calculate the circumference and area of circles (roughly 3.1415).
- **SQRT1_2:** The value of the square root of one-half (roughly 0.707).
- **SQRT2:** The value of the square root of two (roughly 1.414).

Methods

- **abs(*number*):** Returns the absolute value of *number*. The absolute value is the value of a number with its sign ignored, so abs(4) and abs(-4) both return 4.
- **acos(*number*):** Returns the arc cosine of *number* in radians.
- **asin(*number*):** Returns the arc sine of *number* in radians.
- **atan(*number*):** Returns the arc tangent of *number* in radians.
- **atan2(*number1*,*number2*):** Returns the angle of the polar coordinate corresponding to the Cartesian coordinate (*number1*,*number2*). (Not I)
- **ceil(*number*):** Returns the next integer greater than *number*; in other words, rounds up to the next integer.
- **cos(*number*):** Returns the cosine of *number*, which represents an angle in radians.
- **exp(*number*):** Returns the value of E to the power of *number*.
- **floor(*number*):** Returns the next integer less than *number*; in other words, rounds down to the nearest integer.
- **log(*number*):** Returns the natural logarithm of *number*.
- **max(*number1*,*number2*):** Returns the greater of *number1* and *number2*.
- **min(*number1*,*number2*):** Returns the smaller of *number1* and *number2*.
- **pow(*number1*,*number2*):** Returns the value of *number1* to the power of *number2*.
- **random():** Returns a random number between zero and 1 (at press time, this method was available only on UNIX versions of Navigator 2.0).
- **round(*number*):** Returns the closest integer to *number*; in other words, rounds to the closest integer.
- **sin(*number*):** Returns the sine of *number*, which represents an angle in radians.
- **sqrt(*number*):** Returns the square root of *number*.
- **tan(*number*):** Returns the tangent of *number*, which represents an angle in radians.

The `mimeType` Object [C | 3]

The `mimeType` object reflects a MIME type supported by the client browser.

Properties

- ▪ **type:** A string value reflecting the MIME type.
- ▪ **description:** A string containing a description of the MIME type.
- ▪ **enabledPlugin:** A reference to `plugin` object for the plug-in supporting the MIME type.
- ▪ **suffixes:** A string containing a comma-separated list of file suffixes for the MIME type.

The `navigator` Object [C | 2 | 3 | I]

The `navigator` object reflects information about the version of Navigator being used.

Properties

- ▪ **appCodeName:** A string value containing the code name of the client (for example, "Mozilla" for Netscape Navigator).
- ▪ **appName:** A string value containing the name of the client (for example, "Netscape" for Netscape Navigator).
- ▪ **appVersion:** A string value containing the version information for the client in the following form:

  `versionNumber (platform; country)`

  For example, Navigator 2.0, beta 6 for Windows 95 (international version), would have an `appVersion` property with the value `"2.0b6 (Win32; I)"`.

- ▪ **language:** Specifies the translation of Navigator. (A read-only property.) New in JavaScript 1.2.
- ▪ **mimeTypes:** An array of `mimeType` objects reflecting the MIME types supported by the client browser. (Not 2|I)
- ▪ **platform:** Specifies the platform for which Navigator was compiled. (For example, Win32, MacPPC, UNIX.) New in JavaScript 1.2.
- ▪ **plugins:** An array of `plugin` objects reflecting the plug-ins in a document in the order of their appearance in the HTML document. (Not 2|I)
- ▪ **userAgent:** A string containing the complete value of the user-agent header sent in the HTTP request. The following contains all the information in `appCodeName` and `appVersion`:

  `Mozilla/2.0b6 (Win32; I)`

Methods

- **javaEnabled():** Returns a Boolean value indicating whether Java is enabled in the browser. (Not 2|I)

- **preference(*preference.Name*, setValue):** In signed scripts, this method allows the developer to set certain browser preferences. Preferences available with this method are the following:

`general.always_load_images`	`true`/`false` value that sets whether images are automatically loaded.
`security.enable_java`	`true`/`false` value that sets whether Java is enabled.
`javascript.enabled`	`true`/`false` value that sets whether JavaScript is enabled.
`browser.enable_style_sheets`	`true`/`false` value that sets whether style sheets are enabled.
`autoupdate.enabled`	`true`/`false` value that sets whether `autoinstall` is enabled.
`network.cookie.cookieBehavior`	(`0`,`1`,`2`) Value that sets the manner in which cookies are handled. There are three parameters. `0` accepts all cookies; `1` accepts only those that are forwarded to the originating server; `2` denies all cookies.
`network.cookie.warnAboutCookies`	`true`/`false` value that sets whether the browser will warn you about accepting cookies.

The option Object [C|3]

The option object is used to create entries in a select list by using the following syntax:

optionName = new Option(*optionText*, *optionValue*, *defaultSelected*, *selected*)

Then the following line is used:

selectName.options[*index*] = *optionName*.

Properties

- **defaultSelected:** A Boolean value specifying whether the option is selected by default.

- **index:** An integer value specifying the option's index in the select list.

- **prototype:** Provides a mechanism to add properties to an option object.

- **selected:** A Boolean value indicating whether the option is currently selected.

- **text:** A string value reflecting the text displayed for the option.

■ **value:** A string value indicating the value submitted to the server when the form is submitted.

The password Object [C | 2 | 3 | I]

The password object reflects a password text field from an HTML form in JavaScript.

Properties

■ **defaultValue:** A string value containing the default value of the password element (such as the value of the VALUE attribute).

■ **enabled:** A Boolean value indicating whether the password field is enabled. (Not 2|3)

■ **form:** A reference to the form object containing the password field. (Not 2|3)

■ **name:** A string value containing the name of the password element.

■ **value:** A string value containing the value of the password element.

Methods

■ **focus():** Emulates the action of focusing in the password field.

■ **blur():** Emulates the action of removing focus from the password field.

■ **select():** Emulates the action of selecting the text in the password field.

Event Handlers

■ **onBlur:** Specifies JavaScript code to execute when the password field loses focus. (Not 2|3)

■ **onFocus:** Specifies JavaScript code to execute when the password field receives focus. (Not 2|3)

The plugin Object

The plugin object reflects a plug-in supported by the browser.

Properties

■ **name:** A string value reflecting the name of the plug-in.

■ **filename:** A string value reflecting the filename of the plug-in on the system's disk.

■ **description:** A string value containing the description supplied by the plug-in.

The radio Object [C | 2 | 3 | I]

The radio object reflects a set of radio buttons from an HTML form in JavaScript. To access individual radio buttons, use numeric indexes starting at zero. For example, individual

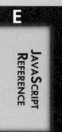

buttons in a set of radio buttons named `testRadio` could be referenced by `testRadio[0]`, `testRadio[1]`, and so on.

Properties

- **checked:** A Boolean value indicating whether a specific radio button is checked. Can be used to select or deselect a button.
- **defaultChecked:** A Boolean value indicating whether a specific radio button was checked by default (that is, it reflects the CHECKED attribute). (Not I)
- **enabled:** A Boolean value indicating whether the radio button is enabled. (Not 2|3)
- **form:** A reference to the `form` object containing the radio button. (Not 2|3)
- **length:** An integer value indicating the number of radio buttons in the set. (Not I)
- **name:** A string value containing the name of the set of radio buttons.
- **value:** A string value containing the value of a specific radio button in a set (that is, it reflects the VALUE attribute).

Methods

- **click():** Emulates the action of clicking a radio button.
- **focus():** Gives focus to the radio button. (Not 2|3)

Event Handlers

- **onClick:** Specifies the JavaScript code to execute when a radio button is clicked.
- **onFocus:** Specifies the JavaScript code to execute when a radio button receives focus. (Not 2|3)

The `regExp` Object

The `regExp` object is relevant to searching for regular expressions. Its properties are set before or after a search is performed. They don't generally exercise control over the search itself, but instead articulate a series of values that can be accessed throughout the search.

Properties

- **input:** The string against which a regular expression is matched. New in JavaScript 1.2.
- **multiline [true, false]:** Sets whether the search continues beyond line breaks on multiple lines (`true`) or not (`false`). New in JavaScript 1.2.
- **lastMatch:** Property that indicates the characters last matched. New in JavaScript 1.2.
- **lastParen:** Property that indicates the last matched string that appeared in parentheses. New in JavaScript 1.2.

■ `leftContext:` Property that indicates the string just before the most recently matched regular expression. New in JavaScript 1.2.

■ `rightContext:` Property that indicates the remainder of the string, beyond the most recently matched regular expression. New in JavaScript 1.2.

■ `$1,..$9:` Property that indicates the last nine substrings in a match; those substrings are enclosed in parentheses. New in JavaScript 1.2.

The Regular Expression Object

The Regular Expression object contains the pattern of a regular expression.

Parameters

■ `regexp:` Parameter that specifies the name of the regular expression object. New in JavaScript 1.2.

■ `pattern:` Parameter that specifies the text of the regular expression. New in JavaScript 1.2.

Flags

■ `i:` Option specifying that during the regular expression search, case is ignored (that is, the search is not case sensitive).

■ `g:` Option specifying that during the regular expression search, the match (and search) should be global.

■ `gi:` Option specifying that during the regular expression search, case is ignored and that during the regular expression search, the match (and search) should be global.

Properties

■ `global [true,false]:` A property that sets the g flag value in code, such as whether the search is global (`true`) or not (`false`). New in JavaScript 1.2.

■ `ignoreCase [true,false]:` A property that sets the i flag value in code, such as whether the search is case sensitive (`true`) or not (`false`). New in JavaScript 1.2.

■ `lastIndex:` A property (integer value) that indicates the index position at which to start the next matching procedure (for example, `lastIndex == 2`). New in JavaScript 1.2.

■ `source:` A property (read-only) that contains the pattern's text. New in JavaScript 1.2.

Methods

■ `compile:` Compiles the regular expression. This method is usually invoked at script startup, when the regular expression is already known and will remain constant. New in JavaScript 1.2.

- **exec(str):** Executes a search for a regular expression within the specified string (str). New in JavaScript 1.2. Note: It uses the same properties as the RegExp object.
- **test(str):** Executes a search for a regular expression and a specified string (str). New in JavaScript 1.2. Note: It uses the same properties as the RegExp object.

The reset Object [C | 2 | 3 | I]

The reset object reflects a reset button from an HTML form in JavaScript.

Properties

- **enabled:** A Boolean value indicating whether the reset button is enabled. (Not 2|3)
- **form:** A reference to the form object containing the reset button. (Not 2|3)
- **name:** A string value containing the name of the reset element.
- **value:** A string value containing the value of the reset element.

Methods

- **click():** Emulates the action of clicking the reset button.
- **focus():** Specifies the JavaScript code to execute when the reset button receives focus. (Not 2|3)

Event Handlers

- **onClick:** Specifies the JavaScript code to execute when the reset button is clicked.
- **onFocus:** Specifies the JavaScript code to execute when the reset button receives focus. (Not 2|3)

The screen Object (New in JavaScript 1.2)

The screen object describes (or specifies) the characteristics of the current screen.

Properties

- **availHeight:** Property that specifies the height of the screen in pixels (minus static display constraints set forth by the operating system). New in JavaScript 1.2.
- **availWidth:** Property that specifies the width of the current screen in pixels (minus static display constraints set forth by the operating system). New in JavaScript 1.2.
- **height:** Property that specifies the height of the current screen in pixels. New in JavaScript 1.2.
- **width:** Property that specifies the width of the current screen in pixels. New in JavaScript 1.2.

- **pixelDepth:** Property that specifies the number of bits (per pixel) in the current screen. New in JavaScript 1.2.
- **colorDepth:** Property that specifies the number of possible colors to display in the current screen. New in JavaScript 1.2.

The select Object [C | 2 | 3]

The select object reflects a selection list from an HTML form in JavaScript.

Properties

- **length:** An integer value containing the number of options in the selection list.
- **name:** A string value containing the name of the selection list.
- **options:** An array reflecting each of the options in the selection list in the order they appear. The options property has its own properties:

defaultSelected	A Boolean value indicating whether an option was selected by default (that is, it reflects the SELECTED attribute).
index	An integer value reflecting the index of an option.
length	An integer value reflecting the number of options in the selection list.
name	A string value containing the name of the selection list.
selected	A Boolean value indicating whether the option is selected. Can be used to select or deselect an option.
selectedIndex	An integer value containing the index of the currently selected option.
text	A string value containing the text displayed in the selection list for a particular option.
value	A string value indicating the value for the specified option (that is, reflects the VALUE attribute).

- **selectedIndex:** Reflects the index of the currently selected option in the selection list.

Methods

- **blur():** Removes focus from the selection list. (Not 2|3)
- **focus():** Gives focus to the selection list. (Not 2|3)

Event Handlers

- **onBlur:** Specifies the JavaScript code to execute when the selection list loses focus.
- **onFocus:** Specifies the JavaScript code to execute when focus is given to the selection list.
- **onChange:** Specifies the JavaScript code to execute when the selected option in the list changes.

The `string` Object [C | 2 | 3 | I]

The `string` object provides properties and methods for working with string literals and variables.

Properties

■ **`length`:** An integer value containing the length of the string expressed as the number of characters in the string.

■ **`prototype`:** Provides a mechanism for adding properties to a `string` object. (Not 2)

Methods

■ **`anchor(name)`:** Returns a string containing the value of the `string` object surrounded by an A container tag with the NAME attribute set to *name*.

■ **`big()`:** Returns a string containing the value of the `string` object surrounded by a BIG container tag.

■ **`blink()`:** Returns a string containing the value of the `string` object surrounded by a BLINK container tag.

■ **`bold()`:** Returns a string containing the value of the `string` object surrounded by a B container tag.

■ **`charAt(index)`:** Returns the character at the location specified by *index*.

■ **`charCodeAt(index)`:** Returns a number representing an ISO-Latin-1 codeset value at the instant *index*. (Netscape Navigator 4.0 and above only.)

■ **`concat(string2)`:** Combines two strings and derives a third, new `string`. (Netscape Navigator 4.0 and above only.)

■ **`fixed()`:** Returns a string containing the value of the `string` object surrounded by a FIXED container tag.

■ **`fontColor(color)`:** Returns a string containing the value of the `string` object surrounded by a FONT container tag with the COLOR attribute set to *color*, which is a color name or an RGB triplet. (Not I)

■ **`fontSize(size)`:** Returns a string containing the value of the `string` object surrounded by a FONTSIZE container tag with the size set to *size*. (Not I)

■ **`fromCharCode(num1, num2, ...)`:** Returns a string constructed of ISO-Latin-1 characters. Those characters are specified by their codeset values, which are expressed as *num1*, *num2*, and so on.

■ **`indexOf(findString, startingIndex)`:** Returns the index of the first occurrence of *findString*, starting the search at *startingIndex*, which is optional; if it's not provided, the search starts at the start of the string.

■ **`italics()`:** Returns a string containing the value of the `string` object surrounded by an I container tag.

- **lastIndexOf(*findString*, *startingIndex*):** Returns the index of the last occurrence of *findString*. This is done by searching backward from *startingIndex*. *startingIndex* is optional and is assumed to be the last character in the string if no value is provided.

- **link(*href*):** Returns a string containing the value of the string object surrounded by an A container tag with the HREF attribute set to *href*.

- **match(*regular_expression*):** Matches a regular expression to a string. The parameter *regular_expression* is the name of the regular expression, expressed either as a variable or a literal.

- **replace(*regular_expression*, newSubStr):** Finds and replaces *regular_expression* with newSubStr.

- **search(*regular_expression*):** Finds *regular_expression* and matches it to some string.

- **slice(*beginSlice*, [*endSlice*]):** Extracts a portion of a given string and derives a new string from that excerpt. *beginSlice* and *endSlice* are both zero-based indexes that can be used to grab the first, second, and third character, and so on.

- **small():** Returns a string containing the value of the string object surrounded by a SMALL container tag.

- **split(*separator*):** Returns an array of strings created by splitting the string at every occurrence of *separator*. (Not 2|I) split has additional functionality in JavaScript 1.2 and for Navigator 4.0 and above. That new functionality includes the following elements:

Regex and Fixed String Splitting	One can now split the string string by both regular expression argument and fixed string.
Limit Count	One can now add a limit count to prevent including empty elements within the string.
White Space Splitting	The ability to split on a white space (including any white space, such as space, tab, newline, and so forth).

- **strike():** Returns a string containing the value of the string object surrounded by a STRIKE container tag.

- **sub():** Returns a string containing the value of the string object surrounded by a SUB container tag.

- **substr(start, [length]):** Used to extract a set number (length) of characters within a string. Use start to specify the location at which to begin this extraction process. New in JavaScript 1.2.

- **substring(*firstIndex*, *lastIndex*):** Returns a string equivalent to the substring beginning at *firstIndex* and ending at the character before *lastIndex*. If *firstIndex* is greater than *lastIndex*, the string starts at *lastIndex* and ends at the character before *firstIndex*. Note: In JavaScript 1.2, x and y are no longer swapped. To get this result, you must specify JavaScript 1.2 with the language attribute within the <SCRIPT> tag.

- **sup():** Returns a string containing the value of the string object surrounded by a SUP container tag.
- **toLowerCase():** Returns a string containing the value of the string object with all characters converted to lowercase.
- **toUpperCase():** Returns a string containing the value of the string object with all characters converted to uppercase.

The submit Object [C | 2 | 3 | I]

The submit object reflects a submit button from an HTML form in JavaScript.

Properties

- **enabled:** A Boolean value indicating whether the submit button is enabled. (Not 2|3)
- **form:** A reference to the form object containing the submit button. (Not 2|3)
- **name:** A string value containing the name of the submit button element.
- **type:** A string value reflecting the TYPE attribute of the <INPUT> tag. (Not 2|I)
- **value:** A string value containing the value of the submit button element.

Methods

- **click():** Emulates the action of clicking the submit button.
- **focus():** Gives focus to the submit button. (Not 2|3)

Event Handlers

- **onClick:** Specifies the JavaScript code to execute when the submit button is clicked.
- **onFocus:** Specifies the JavaScript code to execute when the submit button receives focus. (Not 2|3)

The text Object [C | 2 | 3 | I]

The text object reflects a text field from an HTML form in JavaScript.

Properties

- **defaultValue:** A string value containing the default value of the text element (that is, the value of the VALUE attribute).
- **enabled:** A Boolean value indicating whether the text field is enabled. (Not 2|3)
- **form:** A reference to the form object containing the text field. (Not 2|3)
- **name:** A string value containing the name of the text element.
- **type:** A string value reflecting the TYPE attribute of the <INPUT> tag. (Not 2|I)
- **value:** A string value containing the value of the text element.

Methods

- **focus():** Emulates the action of focusing in the text field.
- **blur():** Emulates the action of removing focus from the text field.
- **select():** Emulates the action of selecting the text in the text field.

Event Handlers

- **onBlur:** Specifies the JavaScript code to execute when focus is removed from the field.
- **onChange:** Specifies the JavaScript code to execute when the content of the field is changed.
- **onFocus:** Specifies the JavaScript code to execute when focus is given to the field.
- **onSelect:** Specifies the JavaScript code to execute when the user selects some or all of the text in the field.

The textarea Object [C | 2 | 3 | I]

The textarea object reflects a multiline text field from an HTML form in JavaScript.

Properties

- **defaultValue:** A string value containing the default value of the textarea element (that is, the value of the VALUE attribute).
- **enabled:** A Boolean value indicating whether the textarea field is enabled. (Not 2I3)
- **form:** A reference to the form object containing the textarea field. (Not 2I3)
- **name:** A string value containing the name of the textarea element.
- **type:** A string value reflecting the type of the textarea object. (Not 2II)
- **value:** A string value containing the value of the textarea element.

Methods

- **focus():** Emulates the action of focusing in the textarea field.
- **blur():** Emulates the action of removing focus from the textarea field.
- **select():** Emulates the action of selecting the text in the textarea field.

Event Handlers

- **onKeyUp:** Specifies the JavaScript code to execute when the user releases a specific key. (Netscape Navigator 4.0 only.) (4)
- **onKeyPress:** Specifies the JavaScript code to execute when the user holds down a specific key. (Netscape Navigator 4.0 only.) (4)
- **onKeyDown:** Specifies the JavaScript code to execute when the user presses a specific key. (Netscape Navigator 4.0 only.) (4)

- **onBlur:** Specifies the JavaScript code to execute when focus is removed from the field.
- **onChange:** Specifies the JavaScript code to execute when the content of the field is changed.
- **onFocus:** Specifies the JavaScript code to execute when focus is given to the field.
- **onSelect:** Specifies the JavaScript code to execute when the user selects some or all of the text in the field.

The window Object [C | 2 | 3 | I]

The window object is the top-level object for each window or frame and the parent object for the document, location, and history objects.

Properties

- **defaultStatus:** A string value containing the default value displayed in the status bar.
- **frames:** An array of objects for each frame in a window. Frames appear in the array in the order in which they appear in the HTML source code.
- **innerHeight():** Specifies the vertical size of the content area (in pixels). New in JavaScript 1.2.
- **innerWidth():** Specifies the horizontal size of the content area (in pixels). New in JavaScript 1.2.
- **length:** An integer value indicating the number of frames in a parent window. (Not I)
- **name:** A string value containing the name of the window or frame.
- **opener:** A reference to the window object containing the open() method used to open the current window. (Not 2|I)
- **pageXOffset:** Specifies the current X position of the viewable window area (expressed in pixels). New in JavaScript 1.2.
- **pageYOffset:** Specifies the current Y position of the viewable window area (expressed in pixels). New in JavaScript 1.2.
- **parent:** A string indicating the name of the window containing the frameset.
- **personalbar [visible=true,false]:** Represents the Directories bar in Netscape Navigator and whether it's visible. New in JavaScript 1.2.
- **scrollbars [visible=true,false]:** Represents the scrollbars of the instant window and whether they are visible. New in JavaScript 1.2.
- **self:** An alternative for the name of the current window.
- **status:** Used to display a message in the status bar; it's done by assigning values to this property.
- **statusbar=[true,false,1,0]:** Specifies whether the status bar of the target window is visible.

■ **toolbar=[true,false,1,0]:** Specifies whether the toolbar of the target window is visible.

■ **top:** An alternative for the name of the topmost window.

■ **window:** An alternative for the name of the current window.

Methods

■ **alert(*message*):** Displays *message* in a dialog box.

■ **back():** Sends the user back to the previous URL stored in the history list. (Simulates a click on the Back button in Navigator.) New in JavaScript 1.2.

■ **blur():** Removes focus from the window. On many systems, it sends the window to the background. (Not 2|I)

■ **captureEvents():** Used in a window with frames (along with enableExternalCapture), it specifies that the window will capture all specified events.

■ **clearInterval(*intervalID*):** Cancels timeouts created with the setInterval method. New in JavaScript 1.2.

■ **close():** Closes the window. (Not I)

■ **confirm(*message*):** Displays *message* in a dialog box with OK and Cancel buttons. Returns true or false based on the button clicked by the user.

■ **disableExternalCapture():** Prevents the instant window with frames from capturing events occurring in pages loaded from a different location. New in JavaScript 1.2.

■ **enableExternalCapture():** Allows the instant window (with frames) to capture events occurring in pages loaded from a different location. New in JavaScript 1.2.

■ **find([string], [true, false], [true, false]):** Finds string in the target window. There are two true/false parameters: The first specifies the Boolean state of case sensitivity in the search; the second specifies whether the search is performed backward. New in JavaScript 1.2.

■ **focus():** Gives focus to the window. On many systems, it brings the window to the front. (Not 2|I)

■ **forward():** Sends the user to the next URL in the history list. (Simulates a user clicking the Forward button in Navigator.) New in JavaScript 1.2.

■ **home():** Sends the user to the user's Home Page URL. (Example: In a default configuration of Netscape Navigator, it sends the user to http://home.netscape.com.) New in JavaScript 1.2.

■ **moveBy(horizontal, vertical):** Moves the window according to the specified values horizontal and vertical. New in JavaScript 1.2.

■ **moveTo(*x*, *y*):** Moves the top-left corner of the window to the specified location; *x* and *y* are screen coordinates. New in JavaScript 1.2.

■ **navigator(*url*):** Loads *url* in the window. (Not 2|3)

■ **open(*url*,*name*,*features*)**: Opens *url* in a window named *name*. If *name* doesn't exist, a new window is created with that name. *features* is an optional string argument containing a list of features for the new window. The feature list contains any of the following name-value pairs separated by commas and without additional spaces: (Not I)

`toolbar=[yes,no,1,0]`	Indicates whether the window should have a toolbar.
`location=[yes,no,1,0]`	Indicates whether the window should have a location field.
`directories=[yes,no,1,0]`	Indicates whether the window should have directory buttons.
`status=[yes,no,1,0]`	Indicates whether the window should have a status bar.
`menubar=[yes,no,1,0]`	Indicates whether the window should have menus.
`scrollbars=[yes,no,1,0]`	Indicates whether the window should have scrollbars.
`resizable=[yes,no,1,0]`	Indicates whether the window should be resizable.
`width=pixels`	Indicates the width of the window in pixels.
`alwaysLowered=[yes,no,1,2]`	Indicates (if true) that the window should remain below all other windows. (This feature has varying results on varying window systems.) New in JavaScript 1.2. Note: The script must be signed to use this feature.
`alwaysRaised=[yes,no,1,2]`	Indicates (if true) that the window should always remain the top-level window. (This feature has varying results on varying window systems.) New in JavaScript 1.2. Note: The script must be signed to use this feature.
`dependent[yes,no,1,2]`	Indicates that the current child window will die (or close) when the parent window does. New in JavaScript 1.2.
`hotkeys=[yes,no,1,2]`	Indicates (if true) that most hot keys are disabled within the instant window. New in JavaScript 1.2.
`innerWidth=pixels`	Indicates the width (in pixels) of the instant window's content area. New in JavaScript 1.2.
`innerHeight=pixels`	Indicates the height (in pixels) of the instant window's content area. New in JavaScript 1.2.

`outerWidth=pixels`	Indicates the instant window's horizontal outside width boundary. New in JavaScript 1.2.
`outerHeight=pixels`	Indicates the instant window's horizontal outside height boundary. New in JavaScript 1.2.
`screenX=pixels`	Indicates the distance that the new window is placed from the left side of the screen (horizontally). New in JavaScript 1.2.
`screenY=pixels`	Indicates the distance that the new window is placed from the top of the screen (vertically). New in JavaScript 1.2.
`z-lock=[yes,no,1,2]`	Indicates that the instant window does not move through the cycling of the z-order; that is, it doesn't rise above other windows, even if activated. New in JavaScript 1.2. Note: The script must be signed for this feature to work.
`height=pixels`	Indicates the height of the window in pixels.

- `print()`: Prints the contents of a frame or window. It's the equivalent of the user pressing the Print button in Netscape Navigator. New in JavaScript 1.2.

- `prompt(message,response)`: Displays *message* in a dialog box with a text entry field with the default value of *response*. The user's response in the text entry field is returned as a string.

- `releaseEvents(eventType)`: Specifies that the current window should release events instead of capturing them so that these events can be passed to other objects, perhaps further on in the event hierarchy. New in JavaScript 1.2.

- `resizeBy(horizontal, vertical)`: Resizes the window, moving from the bottom-right corner. New in JavaScript 1.2.

- `resizeTo(outerWidth, outerHeight)`: Resizes the window, using `outerWidth` and `outerHeight` properties. New in JavaScript 1.2.

- `routeEvent(event)`: Sends or routes an event through the normal event hierarchy. New in JavaScript 1.2.

- `scrollBy(horizontal, vertical)`: Scroll the viewing area of the current window by the specified amount. New in JavaScript 1.2.

- `scrollTo(x, y)`: Scrolls the current window to the specified position, calculated in x and y coordinates, starting at the top-left corner of the window. New in JavaScript 1.2.

- `setInterval(function, msec, [args])`: Repeatedly calls a function after the period specified by the `msec` parameter. New in JavaScript 1.2.

- `setInterval(expression, msec)`: Evaluates *expression* after the period specified by the `msec` parameter. New in JavaScript 1.2.

- **setTimeout(*expression*,*time*):** Evaluates *expression* after *time*, which is a value in milliseconds. The timeout can be named with the following structure:

  name = setTimeOut(*expression*,*time*)

- **scrollTo(*x*,*y*):** Scrolls the window to the coordinate *x*,*y*. (Not 2|I)

- **stop():** Stops the current download. It's the equivalent of the user pressing the Stop button in Netscape Navigator.

- **clearTimeout(*name*):** Cancels the timeout with the name *name*.

Event Handlers

- **onDragDrop:** Specifies the JavaScript code to execute when the user drops an object onto the window. (Netscape Navigator 4.0 and above only.) (4.0)

- **onBlur:** Specifies the JavaScript code to execute when focus is removed from a window. (Not 2|I)

- **onError:** Specifies the JavaScript code to execute when a JavaScript error occurs while loading a document. It can be used to intercept JavaScript errors. Setting this event handler to null effectively prevents JavaScript errors from being displayed to the user. (Not 2|I)

- **onFocus:** Specifies the JavaScript code to execute when the window receives focus. (Not 2|I)

- **onLoad:** Specifies the JavaScript code to execute when the window or frame finishes loading.

- **onMove:** Specifies the JavaScript code to execute when the user moves a window. (Netscape Navigator 4.0 only.)

- **onResize:** Specifies the JavaScript code to execute when a user resizes the window.

- **onUnload:** Specifies the JavaScript code to execute when the document in the window or frame is exited.

Independent Functions, Operators, Variables, and Literals

Independent Functions

- **escape(*character*):** Returns a string containing the ASCII encoding of *character* in the form %xx; xx is the numeric encoding of the character. (C|2|3|I)

- **eval(*expression*):** Returns the result of evaluating *expression*, which is an arithmetic expression. (C|2|3|I)

- **isNaN(*value*):** Evaluates *value* to see if it's NaN. Returns a Boolean value. (C|2|3|I) (On UNIX platforms, not 2.)

- **parseFloat(*string*):** Converts *string* to a floating-point number and returns the value. It continues to convert until it hits a nonnumeric character and then returns the result. If the first character can't be converted to a number, the function returns NaN (zero on Windows platforms). (C|2|3|I)

- **parseInt(*string*,*base*):** Converts *string* to an integer of base *base* and returns the value. It continues to convert until it hits a nonnumeric character and then returns the result. If the first character can't be converted to a number, the function returns NaN (zero on Windows platforms). (C|2|3|I)

- **taint(*propertyName*):** Adds tainting to *propertyName*. (C|3)

- **toString():** This is a method of all objects. It returns the object as a string or returns "[object *type*]" if no string representation exists for the object. (C|2|3) Note: In JavaScript 1.2, it converts objects and strings into literals.

- **unescape(*string*):** Returns a character based on the ASCII encoding contained in *string*. The ASCII encoding should take the form "%integer" or "hexadecimalValue". (C|2|3|I)

- **untaint(*propertyName*):** Removes tainting from *propertyName*. (C|3)

Statements

- **break:** Terminates a while or for loop and passes program control to the first statement following the loop. (2|3|4) Note: In JavaScript 1.2, break has the added functionality of being able to break out of labeled statements.

- **comment:** Used to add a comment within the script. This comment is ignored by Navigator. Comments in JavaScript work similarly to those in C. They are enclosed in a /* (start), */ (end) structure. (2|3|4)

- **continue:** Terminates execution of statements in a while or for loop and continues iteration of the loop. (2|3|4) Note: In JavaScript 1.2, continue has added functionality that allows you to continue within labeled statements.

- **do while:** Scts up a loop that continues to execute statements and code until the condition evaluates to false. New in JavaScript 1.2.

- **export:** Used with the import statement. In secure, signed scripts, it allows the developer to export all properties, functions, and variables to another script. New in JavaScript 1.2.

- **for([*initial-expression*]; [*condition*]; [*incremental-expression*];)):** Specifies the opening of a for loop. The arguments are these: initialize a variable (*initial-expression*), create a condition to test for (*condition*), and specify an incrementation scheme (*incremental-expression*). (2|3|4)

- **for...in:** Imposes a variable to all properties of an object and executes a block of code for each. (2|3|4)

- **function [name]():** Declares a function so that it can be referred to or reached by event handlers (or other processes). (2|3|4)

■ **if...else:** A structure used to test whether a certain condition is true. `If...else` blocks can contain nested statements and functions (and call them) if a condition is either true or false. (2|3|4)

■ **import:** Used with the `export` statement. In secure, signed scripts, it allows the developer to import all properties, functions, and variables from another script. New in JavaScript 1.2.

■ **label (labeled statements):** Statement that creates a label or pointer to code elsewhere in the script. By calling this label, you redirect the script to the labeled statement.

■ **new:** Creates an instance of a user-defined object. (It can also be used to create an instance of built-in objects, inherent to JavaScript, such as `new Date`.) (2|3|4)

■ **return [value]:** Specifies a value to be returned by a given function. For example, `return x` returns the variable value associated with *x*. (2|3|4)

■ **switch:** Evaluates an expression and attempts to match it to a `case` pattern or label. If the expression matches the `case`, trailing statements associated with that label are executed. New in JavaScript 1.2. (Operates similarly to the `switch` statement in C shell syntax.)

■ **this:** A statement used to refer to a specific object, as shown in this example: [2|3|4]

```
onClick = 'javascript:my_function(this.form)'
```

■ **var [name]:** Declares a variable by name. (2|3|4)

■ **while:** Statement that begins a `while` loop. `while` loops specify that as long as (while) a condition is true, execute some code. (2|3|4)

■ **with:** Statement that sets the value for the default object, a method that's similar to creating a global variable with a function. (2|3|4)

Operators

■ **Assignment Operators:** See Table E.1. (C|2|3|I)

Table E.1. Assignment operators in JavaScript.

Operator	Description
=	Assigns the value of the right operand to the left operand.
+=	Adds the left and right operands and assigns the result to the left operand.
-=	Subtracts the right operand from the left operand and assigns the result to the left operand.
*=	Multiplies the two operands and assigns the result to the left operand.
/=	Divides the left operand by the right operand and assigns the value to the left operand.
%=	Divides the left operand by the right operand and assigns the remainder to the left operand.

■ **Arithmetic Operators:** See Table E.2. (C|2|3|I)

Table E.2. Arithmetic operators in JavaScript.

Operator	Description
+	Adds the left and right operands.
-	Subtracts the right operand from the left operand.
*	Multiplies the two operands.
/	Divides the left operand by the right operand.
%	Divides the left operand by the right operand and evaluates to the remainder.
++	Increments the operand by one (can be used before or after the operand).
- -	Decreases the operand by one (can be used before or after the operand).
-	Changes the sign of the operand.

■ **Bitwise Operators:** Bitwise operators deal with their operands as binary numbers, but return JavaScript numerical value. (See Table E.3.) (C|2|3|I)

Table E.3. Bitwise operators in JavaScript.

Operator	Description
AND (or &)	Converts operands to integers with 32 bits, pairs the corresponding bits, and returns one for each pair of ones. Returns zero for any other combination.
OR (or ¦)	Converts operands to integers with 32 bits, pairs the corresponding bits, and returns one for each pair when one of the two bits is one. Returns zero if both bits are zero.
XOR (or ^)	Converts operands to integer with 32 bits, pairs the corresponding bits, and returns one for each pair when only one bit is one. Returns zero for any other combination.
<<	Converts the left operand to an integer with 32 bits and shifts bits to the left the number of bits indicated by the right operand. Bits shifted off to the left are discarded, and zeros are shifted in from the right.
>>>	Converts the left operand to an integer with 32 bits and shifts bits to the right the number of bits indicated by the right operand. Bits shifted off to the right are discarded, and zeros are shifted in from the left.
>>	Converts the left operand to an integer with 32 bits and shifts bits to the right the number of bits indicated by the right operand. Bits shifted off to the right are discarded, and copies of the leftmost bit are shifted in from the left.

■ **Logical Operators:** See Table E.4. (C|2|3|I)

Table E.4. Logical operators in JavaScript.

Operator	Description
&&	Logical "and." Returns `true` when both operands are true; otherwise, it returns `false`.
¦¦	Logical "or." Returns `true` if either operand is true. It returns `false` only when both operands are false.
!	Logical "not." Returns `true` if the operand is false and `false` if the operand is true. This is a unary operator and precedes the operand.

■ **Comparison Operators:** See Table E.5. [C|2|3|I]

Table E.5. Logical (comparison) operators in JavaScript.

Operator	Description
==	Returns `true` if the operands are equal.
!=	Returns `true` if the operands are not equal.
>	Returns `true` if the left operand is greater than the right operand.
<	Returns `true` if the left operand is less than the right operand.
>=	Returns `true` if the left operand is greater than or equal to the right operand.
<=	Returns `true` if the left operand is less than or equal to the right operand.

■ **Conditional Operators:** Conditional expressions take one form:

```
(condition) ? val1 : val2
```

If `condition` is true, the expression evaluates to `val1`; otherwise, it evaluates to `val2`. (C|2|3|I)

■ **String Operators:** The concatenation operator (+) is one of two string operators. It evaluates to a string combining the left and right operands. The concatenation assignment operator (+=) is also available. (C|2|3|I)

■ **The `typeof` Operator:** The `typeof` operator returns the type of its single operand. Possible types are `object`, `string`, `number`, `boolean`, `function`, and `undefined`. (C|3|I)

■ **The `void` Operator:** The `void` operator takes an expression as an operand but returns no value. (C|3)

■ **Operator Precedence:** JavaScript applies the rules of operator precedence as follows (from lowest to highest precedence):

Comma (,)

Assignment operators (=, +=, -=, *=, /=, %=)

Conditional (? :)

Logical OR (¦¦)

Logical AND (&&)

Bitwise OR (¦)

Bitwise XOR (^)

Bitwise AND (&)

Equality (==, !=)

Relational (<, <=, >, >=)

Shift (<<, >>, >>>)

Addition/subtraction (+, -)

Multiply/divide/modulus (*, /, %)

Negation/increment (!, -, ++, --)

Call, member ((), [])

VBScript Reference

This appendix summarizes the statements, functions, and operators used in the Visual Basic Scripting Edition.

Category/Keyword	Type	Usage
		Arithmetic
Atn	Function	Returns the arctangent of a number
		Atn(*number*)
Cos	Function	Returns the cosine of an angle
		Cos(*number*)
Exp	Function	Returns a number raised to a power
		Exp(*number*)
Log	Function	Returns the logarithm of a number
		Log(*number*)
Randomize	Statement	Primes the internal random-number generator
		Randomize
Rnd	Function	Returns a random number
		Rnd
Sin	Function	Returns the sine of an angle
		Sin(*number*)
Sqr	Function	Returns the square root of a number
		Sqr(*number*)
Tan	Function	Returns the tangent of an angle
		Tan(*number*)
		Array Handling
Dim	Statement	Declares an array
		Dim *arrayname([subscripts])*
Erase	Statement	Clears the contents of an array
		Erase *arrayname*
IsArray	Function	Returns True if *var* is an array, and False if not
		IsArray(*var*)
LBound	Function	In VBScript, always returns 0
		Lbound(*arrayname*)

Category/Keyword	Type	Usage
Preserve	Statement	Copies the contents of a dynamic array to a resized dynamic array
		`Redim Preserve arrayname(subscripts)`
ReDim	Statement	Declares a dynamic array or redimensions a dynamic array (see `Preserve`)
		`ReDim arrayname()`
		or
		`ReDim arrayname([subscripts])`
UBound	Statement	Returns the largest subscript of an array
		`Ubound(arrayname)`

Assignment

=	Operator	Assigns a value to a variable or property
		`variable = value`
Set	Statement	Assigns an object reference to a variable
		`Set variable = object`

Comment

Rem	Statement	Declares the following line as a comment to be ignored by the language engine
		`Rem comment_text`

Constants/Literals

Empty	Literal	Declares a special uninitialized variable value
		`variable = Empty`
False	Constant	A Boolean value representing 0
		`variable = False`
Nothing	Literal	Used to disassociate an object reference from a variable; used with `Set`
		`Set variable = Nothing`
Null	Literal	Represents no valid data
		`variable = Null`

continues

F

VBScript
REFERENCE

Category/Keyword	*Type*	*Usage*
True	Constant	Boolean value representing -1
		variable = True

Conversions

Abs	Function	Returns the unsigned (absolute) value of a number
		Abs(*number*)
Asc	Function	Returns the ANSI/ASCII code of a character
		Asc(*string*)
CBool	Function	Returns a Boolean subtype Variant value from any valid expression
		CBool(*expression*)
CByte	Function	Returns a Byte subtype Variant value from any valid expression
		CByte(*expression*)
CDate	Function	Returns a Date subtype Variant value from any valid date expression
		CDate(*expression*)
CDbl	Function	Returns a Double Precision subtype Variant value from any valid numeric expression
		CDbl(*expression*)
Chr	Function	Returns the character corresponding to the ANSI or ASCII code
		Chr(*number*)
CInt	Function	Returns an Integer subtype Variant value from any valid numeric expression
		CInt(*expression*)
CLng	Function	Returns a Long Integer subtype Variant value from any valid numeric expression
		CLng(*expression*)
CSng	Function	Returns a Single Precision subtype Variant value from any valid numeric expression
		CSng(*expression*)
CStr	Function	Returns a String subtype Variant value from any valid expression
		CStr(*expression*)

Category/Keyword	Type	Usage
DateSerial	Function	Returns a date subtype Variant from valid year, month, and day values DateSerial(*year*,*month*,*day*)
DateValue	Function	Returns a Date subtype Variant value from any valid date expression DateValue(*expression*)
Hex	Function	Returns a string subtype Variant representing the hexadecimal value of a number Hex(*number*)
Int	Function	Returns an Integer subtype Variant rounded down from the number supplied Int(*number*)
Fix	Function	Returns an Integer subtype Variant rounded up from the number supplied Fix(*number*)
Oct	Function	Returns a string subtype Variant representing the octal value of a number Oct(*number*)
Sgn	Function	Returns an integer subtype Variant representing the sign of a number Sgn(*number*) values > 0 return 1 values = 0 return 0 values < 0 return -1
TimeSerial	Function	Returns a Date subtype Variant from valid hour, minute, and second values TimeSerial(*hour*,*minute*,*second*)
TimeValue	Function	Returns a Date subtype Variant value from any valid time expression TimeValue(*expression*)

Dates and Times

Date	Function	Returns the current system date Date()

continues

F

**VBSCRIPT
REFERENCE**

Category/Keyword	Type	Usage
DateSerial	Function	Returns a Date subtype `Variant` from valid year, month, and day values
		`DateSerial(year,month,day)`
DateValue	Function	Returns a Date subtype `Variant` value from any valid date expression
		`DateValue(expression)`
Day	Function	Returns an Integer subtype `Variant` representing the day (`1-31`) from a valid date expression
		`Day(dateexpression)`
Hour	Function	Returns an Integer subtype `Variant` representing the hour (`0-23`) from a valid time expression
		`Hour(timeexpression)`
Minute	Function	Returns an Integer subtype `Variant` representing the minute (`0-60`) from a valid time expression
		`Minute(timeexpression)`
Month	Function	Returns an Integer subtype `Variant` representing the month (`1-12`) from a valid date expression
		`Month(dateexpression)`
Now	Function	Returns the current date and time of the system
		`Now()`
Second	Function	Returns an Integer subtype `Variant` representing the second (`0-60`) from a valid time expression
		`Second(timeexpression)`
Time	Function	Returns the current system time
		`Time()`
TimeSerial	Function	Returns a Date subtype `Variant` from valid hour, minute, and second values
		`TimeSerial(hour,minute,second)`
TimeValue	Function	Returns a Date subtype `Variant` value from any valid time expression
		`TimeValue(expression)`
Weekday	Function	Returns an Integer subtype `Variant` between 1 and 7 representing the day of the week, starting at Sunday, from a date expression
		`Weekday(dateexpression)`

Category/Keyword	Type	Usage
Year	Function	Returns an Integer subtype `Variant` representing the year from a valid date expression `Year(dateexpression)`

Declarations

Category/Keyword	Type	Usage
Dim	Statement	Declares a variable `Dim variable`

End	Statement	Declares the end of a `Sub` procedure or function
		
		`End Sub`
		
		`End Function`

Exit	Statement	Use with `Do`, `For`, `Function`, or `Sub` to prematurely exit the routine `Exit Do/For/Function/Sub`

Function	Statement	Declares a function and the argument list passed into the function, and declares the end of a function; also used with `Exit` to prematurely end a function
		
		`Function functionname(argumentlist)`
		
		`Exit Function`
		
		`End Function`
		
		`Public variable`

Sub	Statement	Declares a custom procedure or event handler and the argument list, if any, and declares the end of a custom procedure or event handler; also used with `Exit` to prematurely end a custom procedure or event handler
		
		`Sub subroutinename([argumentlist])`
		
		`Exit Sub`
		
		`End Sub`

Error Handling

Category/Keyword	Type	Usage
Clear	Method	A method of the `Err` object to reset the `Err.Number` property to 0 `Err.Clear`

continues

Category/Keyword	Type	Usage
Description	Property	A property of the `Err` object that contains a description of the last error, as specified in the `Err.Number` property
		`Err.Description`
Err	Object	An object containing information about the last error
		`Err.property|method`
On Error	Statement	Used with `Resume Next` to continue execution with the line directly following the line in which the error occurred
		`On Error Resume Next`
Raise	Method	A method of the `Err` object used to simulate the occurrence of an error specified by number
		`Err.Raise(errornumber)`
Number	Property	A property of the `Err` object that contains the error code for the last error, or `0` if no error has occurred
		`Err.Number`
Source	Property	Returns the name of the object or application that raised the error
		`Err.Source`

Input/Output

InputBox	Function	Displays a dialog box to allow user input
		`InputBox(caption[,title][,value][,x][,y])`
MsgBox	Function	Displays a dialog box
		`MsgBox(prompt[, definition][, title])`

Operators

+	Operator	Addition of two numerical expressions
		`result = expr1 + expr2`
And	Operator	Logical conjunction operator
		`If expression AND expression Then`
/	Operator	Division operator
		`result = expression / expression`

Category/Keyword	Type	Usage
=	Operator	Equality operator
		If *expression* = *expression* Then
Eqv	Operator	Logical-equivalence operator
		If *expression* Eqv *expression* Then
^	Operator	Exponentiation operator
		result = *expression* ^ *expression*
>	Operator	Greater-than comparison
		If *expression* > *expression* Then
>=	Operator	Greater-than or equal-to comparison
		If *expression* >= *expression* Then
Imp	Operator	Logical implication
		If *expression* Imp *expression* Then
<>	Operator	Inequality comparison
		If *expression* <> *expression* Then
\	Operator	Integer-division operator
		result = *expression* \ *expression*
<	Operator	Less-than comparison
		If *expression* < *expression* Then
<=	Operator	Less-than or equal-to comparison
		If *expression* <= *expression* Then
Mod	Operator	Modulus arithmetic; returns only the remainder of a division of two numbers
		result = *expression* mod *expression*
*	Operator	Multiplication
		result = *expression* * *expression*
-	Operator	Subtraction
		result = *expression* - *expression*
Or	Operator	Logical disjunction
		If *expression* Or *expression* Then
&	Operator	Concatenation of two string values
		result = *string* & *string*
Xor	Operator	Logical exclusion
		If expression Xor expression Then

Category/Keyword	Type	Usage
		Options
Option Explicit	Statement	Forces a compile-time error if an undeclared variable is found
		`Option Explicit`

Category/Keyword	Type	Usage
		Program Flow
Call	Statement	Passes execution to a subroutine or event handler; also can be used to replicate the actions of the user
		`Call myroutine()`
		`Call cmdbutton_OnClick()`
Do...Loop	Statement	Repeats code while a condition is met or until a condition is met
		`Do While condition`
		`        ...`
		`        Loop`
		or
		`Do Until condition`
		`        ...`
		`        Loop`
		or
		`Do`
		`        ...`
		`        Loop While condition`
		or
		`Do`
		`        ...`
		`        Loop Until condition`
For...Next	Statement	Repeats a block of code until the counter reaches a given number
		`For counter = lower to upper [step]`
		`        ...`
		`        Next`
If...Then...Else	Statement	Conditional execution of code
		`If condition Then`
		`        ... (if condition met)`
		`        Else`
		`        ... (if condition not met)`
		`        End If`

Category/Keyword	*Type*	*Usage*

`Select Case`	Statement	Selective execution of code; `testexpression` must match `expression`
		
		`Select Case testexpression`
		`        Case expression`
		`        ...`
		`        Case expression`
		`        ...`
		`        Case Else`
		`        End Select`

`While...Wend`	Statement	Execution of a code block while a condition is met
		
		`While expression`
		`        ...`
		`        Wend`

Strings

`InStr`	Function	Returns the starting point of one string within another string, or `0` if not found `result = InStr(start,searched,sought)`
`LCase`	Function	Converts a string to lowercase `result = LCase(string)`
`Left`	Function	Returns the leftmost *n* characters of a string `result = Left(string, length)`
`Len`	Function	Returns the length of a string `result = Len(string)`
`LTrim`	Function	Removes all leading spaces `result = LTrim(string)`
`Mid`	Function	Returns a string of length `L`, starting at `S` within `string` `result = Mid(string, S, L)`
`Right`	Function	Returns the rightmost *n* characters of a string `result = Right(string, n)`
`RTrim`	Function	Removes all trailing spaces from a string `result = RTrim(string)`

continues

Category/Keyword	*Type*	*Usage*
Space	Function	Returns a string consisting of *n* spaces
		result = Space(*n*)
StrComp	Function	Returns an integer subtype Variant representing the result of a comparison of two strings
		result = StrComp(*string1, string2*)
		string1 < *string2* returns -1
		string1 < *string2* returns 0
		string1 < *string2* returns 1
String	Function	Returns a string consisting of character *c*, of length *L*
		result = String(*L, C*)
Trim	Function	Removes both leading and trailing spaces
		result = Trim(*string*)
UCase	Function	Returns a string as uppercase alphabetical characters
		result = UCase(*string*)

Variants

IsArray	Function	Returns True (-1) if *expression* is an array and False (0) if not
		result = IsArray(*expression*)
IsDate	Function	Returns True (-1) if *expression* is a valid date and False (0) if not
		result = IsDate(*expression*)
IsEmpty	Function	Returns True (-1) if *expression* equates to an Empty subtype and False (0) if not
		result = IsEmpty(*expression*)
IsNull	Function	Returns True (-1) if *expression* equates to a Null subtype and False (0) if not
		result = IsNull(*expression*)
IsNumeric	Function	Returns True (-1) if *expression* is a valid numeric expression and False (0) if not
		result = IsNumeric(*expression*)
VarType	Function	Returns an integer representing the sub data type of a Variant
		result = VarType(*expression*)

Development Resources

by Lee Anne Phillips

APPENDIX G

If you're expecting the usual bookmark list of everything under the sun, with no attempt to separate the wheat from the chaff, you won't find it here. This is an opinionated list with detailed references to the best of the software available for creating Web pages, as well as lists of the commonly used servers and other "infrastructures," so that it forms an annotated reference and Web bibliography covering a large, if not the greater, part of this book. Like everything else worthwhile in life, writing is a cooperative effort involving many people, some of whose names you'll see listed in the front matter of this book. I'd especially like to thank David and Rhonda Crowder, Robert McDaniel, and Kelly Murdock, who generously shared some of their favorite URLs to make this appendix even more useful, and Lisa Lord, who helped make it more readable.

I've divided the list rather arbitrarily into the following sections, although some of them overlap a little at the edges:

- Web browsers
- HTML editors
- Web site tools: Web publishers, site managers, site maps, and miscellaneous shareware
- Graphics
- Multimedia for professionals and for the rest of us
- Scripting/platform-independent languages
- Web servers
- HTML validators
- Common Gateway Interface (CGI)
- Firewalls, proxy servers, and security
- Libraries and other resources on the Web
- Notes for further research, including search engines

Some of the following general headings are broken down into subcategories for the actual discussion, just to add a little bit of organization to a lot of data in one place.

Web Browsers

Web browsers are the heart of the Web and—at the machine level—the justification for HTTP servers and all the rest of the complicated technology that puts the content on your desktop. They are what translates the raw bits and bytes of electricity into words, pictures, sound, or other things you can understand. They are also your servant and intermediary, automatically deciding the best way to get and render any given piece of information while hiding the messy details that would interfere with your enjoyment.

It's an important job, and the attention paid by the major software manufacturers shows just how important they think Web browsers will be in the future. Table G.1 offers a selection of browsers, not only the most popular, but also the ones addressing specific needs not truly served by the mainstream bells and whistles.

Table G.1. HTML browsers.

Product	Type/Support	Minimal System Req.	Price Range	Platforms
Microsoft Internet Explorer 3.0	Graphical HTML 3.2 plus extensions	Mid	Free to $$	Win95 Mac WinNT
Microsoft Internet Explorer 4.0	Graphical HTML 4.0 plus extensions	Mid	Free to $$	Win95
Netscape Navigator 3.0	Graphical HTML 3.2 plus extensions	Mid	Free to $$	Win95 Windows Mac/UNIX
Netscape Navigator 4.0	Graphical HTML 3.2 plus extensions, plus part of HTML 4.0	Mid	Free to $$	Win95 Mac UNIX
NCSA Mosaic 3.0	Graphical HTML 3.0	Mid	Free	Win95 Windows
Opera 3.0	Graphical HTML 3.2	Low	$$	Win95 Windows
Tango	Graphical Multilingual HTML 3.2	Low	$$	Win95/NT Windows
Lynx	Text-mode HTML 3.2*	Low	Free	UNIX DOS
Emacs W3	Graphical/ Text-mode HTML 3.2*	Low	Free	UNIX Win95 Mac
Ariadna	Graphical Russian HTML 3.2	Mid	$$	Win95/NT

G

DEVELOPMENT RESOURCES

continues

Table G.1. continued

Product	Type/Support	Minimal System Req.	Price Range	Platforms
Grail	Graphical Extensible HTML 3.2	Mid	Free	UNIX Mac Win95/NT
HotJava	Graphical HTML 3.2	Mid	Free	Any
Amaya	Graphical HTML 3.2+	Mid	Free	UNIX Win95/NT
Cyberdog	Graphical	Mid	$$$	Mac
Cello	Graphical	Low	Free	Windows

NOTE

Throughout this appendix's tables, computers are described in terms of their Intel equivalent, just because most people seem to know how their particular box compares to the ubiquitous standard:

> High: Pentium Pro workstation, server, or equivalent

> Mid: High-end 486, Pentium, or equivalent

> Low: 386 to low-end 486 or equivalent

Dollar signs are roughly equivalent to digits in decimal notation, but fudged a little based on how much it might hurt an average user's pocketbook:

> $$: Less than $75

> $$$: Around $100 or more

> $$$$: Around $1,000

> $$$$$: $5,000 or more

Microsoft Internet Explorer 4.0

`http://www.microsoft.com/ie/`

With the release of IE 4.0, Microsoft has taken one giant step toward integrating Internet Explorer with the operating system. In fact, with its tight integration with the Windows 95+ desktop, the "upgrade" could almost be described as an operating system replacement. Quirky implementations of standard tags and supporting technologies have given Microsoft a bit of a "bad boy" reputation, but it's a force to reckon with, based on its control of most of the desktop market. If you've ever tried to get rid of the Windows 95 Inbox encouraging you to use Microsoft Exchange (and MSN), you'll know what "persistence" really means. Its latest version has come to terms with many compatibility issues, although its implementation of Java and JavaScript still leaves something to be desired. In fact, its implementation of Dynamic HTML is closer to the draft W3C standard than any other browser. A good choice for Microsoft-standardized offices and intranets, but Microsoft has less commitment to Macintosh and practically none to UNIX; sites supporting more than one platform should keep that in mind.

Internet Explorer has graduated to the status of a true innovator, and its integration with the Windows desktop is second to none. No other platform gives you as much access to Visual Basic, VBScript, ActiveX, and other Microsoft tools, which is of course a two-edged sword. For corporate intranets on Microsoft and Intel platforms, there's complete integration with many legacy applications using proprietary access methods; for the developer, there's instant availability of extensive libraries of prewritten code and widgets to perform almost any function, code that would have to be written from scratch or ported to go to any other platform.

On the other hand, if your customers are on the Internet, you can't depend on the Windows platform being available, so many of the tools and widgets are of less value or have to be made available in alternative ways, a possible duplication of effort. Any large-scale Internet development project will have to take into account both IE and Netscape, but short-term "80% of functionality" efforts might get a big boost up from the use of IE as a prototyping tool, and every project may benefit from judicious use of WinNT and IE tools on the server side if a database or other resource resides on that platform.

In today's marketplace, Internet Explorer shares with Netscape Navigator pride of place in being the premier browsers offering the latest and greatest of everything, including Dynamic HTML (code that can rewrite itself on-the-fly without server intervention), virtual reality, scripting and other client-side functionality, multimedia, and all the other goodies that make Web developer's hearts beat faster. This book largely concentrates on what you can do with both IE and Netscape, so a glance at the table of contents will give you a far better overview of their capabilities than I can provide in this short space.

Win95/NT platforms primarily, but it does also support Macs, usually a bit later in the year or with different feature sets.

Netscape Navigator 4.0

`http://www.netscape.com/`

The grand old man of commercial Web browser makers and still having by far the larger market share and Web site support, Netscape has been an innovator with a conscience for the most part. Although properly criticized for many of the extensions it unilaterally made available to HTML developers, for quite some time it drove the standards development process by sheer demand from users, and its extensions were designed to create very few problems for other browsers. Its initial foray into Dynamic HTML, implemented with a proprietary <LAYER> tag as well as the approved style sheets is, as usual for Netscape, going a little against the flow but is very easy to work with compared to the W3C object model. It will be augmented with a W3C implementation as the draft HTML 4.0 standard develops.

Navigator has changed almost beyond recognition from the simple collection of a few dozen tags and boring gray displays of a few years ago. Today's Web designer needs to master a dizzying array of new technologies, interactive scripting, client-side programming, downloadable program snippets in Java or other languages, multimedia, virtual reality, extensible markup (soon), and other methods of making their pages stand out from the crowd. This is both an opportunity and a problem. Designing cutting-edge pages is no longer a part-time sort of job, or even something that one person can do on his or her own in many cases. This is the era of professional design teams and truly dynamic pages that are sensitive to the merest passage of the mouse cursor over almost every element and require programming skills to create and maintain. Win95/NT, Macintosh, and UNIX platforms.

Netscape Communicator 4.0

http://www.netscape.com/

Netscape Navigator with the addition of e-mail, conferencing, scheduling, and other business productivity tools, creating a suite of network-based applications that cover many necessary workgroup-enhancement functions. Communicator/Navigator 4.0 adds keyboard navigation and other HTML 4.0–style innovations to remain a strong but slightly outgunned competitor to Microsoft. Its latest browser, like the latest version of Internet Explorer, is pushing the limits of multimedia and interactivity on the Web, with a dazzling array of features available for audio, video, pop-up windows, rollover graphics, and other advanced features to add real sizzle to leading-edge Web sites. Win95/NT, Macintosh, and UNIX platforms.

NCSA Mosaic 3.0

http://www.ncsa.uiuc.edu/SDG/Software/Mosaic/

One of the originals and still going strong after all these years, Mosaic is the mother of all (well, most) graphical browsers in a very literal sense. Both IE and Navigator were originally based on Mosaic code and functionality and still inherit fossilized resemblances. NCSA (National Center for Supercomputing Applications) Mosaic is no longer being directly supported, but remains a good test of what a "vanilla" browser can do. Source code is available with some restrictions because of licensing arrangements with Spyglass, and UNIX X Window source is available free for individual noncommercial use. UNIX X Window, Windows, and Macintosh platforms.

Opera 3.0

http://www.operasoftware.com/

An innovative and compact browser from Norway with many passionate adherents, Opera is under active development. It's one of the few modern browsers that runs quite happily on a 386 with 8M RAM and a disk footprint of about 1.5M! Multiple windows, good user control over the size and layout of the user interface (including audible feedback for many events), keyboard navigation, and even zoom enlargement of the page (up to 10x) make this a good choice for people with limited vision. You can zoom in reverse to make a field of tiny thumbnails of a series of pages or request the browser to load all of a page's "children," making Opera a good choice for comparative browsing of a Web site. Very quick and responsive, especially so on faster machines. The latest version has JavaScript support and other enhancements. Windows/Win95 platform.

Alis Technologies' Tango Browser

http://www.alis.com/

The Tango browser seems impossible when you first use it to access one of the many international sites that display "alphabet soup" on your screen when you follow a link. The hodgepodge of extended characters is magically transformed into neat rows of perfectly formed characters in whatever language is being used. In the case of pages that don't identify their language, a simple trial process quickly narrows it down until the soup turns into text. For foreign language students, or Web designers, I can think of no other browser with such versatility. It handles Arabic and Devangari scripts, Chinese characters, Japanese characters and Kanji syllabary, as well as the complex Korean writing system and a host of other scripts with ease. A mail program is built in, and a companion program, Tango Creator, allows you to create a foreign language Web site on your own, without the help of a special version of the operating system. Language lessons are not included. Windows platforms.

Lynx

http://www.crl.com/~subir/lynx.html http://lynx.browser.org http://sol.slcc.edu/lynx/

Widely used in the student and "shell account" world, Lynx is a text-mode–only browser available on almost any UNIX system. It's widely used by visually impaired or mobility-impaired Web surfers because of its easy-to-use keyboard interface and its ability to be integrated with audio or Braille output devices. Source code available from multiple sources worldwide. Almost all UNIX platforms, and ports to Windows, Win95, Amiga, Macintosh, and others.

Emacs (W3 mode) Version 4.0

http://www.cs.indiana.edu/elisp/w3/docs.html

Another browser from the UNIX world, Emacs W3 (GNUscape) is an extremely powerful tool you could wander around in for years without ever discovering its limits or even needing to leave except perhaps to log off. Long-time users tend to be both dedicated and partisan. It supports both text and graphics modes and has been used to develop many accessibility tools, including audio browsers. The documentation has explicit instructions on how to use Emacs W3 as an audio browser. Direct access to a powerful programming language, Emacs Lisp, and the innate power of the UNIX shell make this browser capable, in theory, of doing almost anything your heart desires and that you have the spare time to develop. Source code available. UNIX, X Window, Win95, Windows, and Macintosh platforms. Limited Windows and Macintosh support.

AMSD Ariadna (Beta)

http://www.kd.qd.se/iii/amsd/Ariadna/ariadna.htm

Full-featured, inexpensive Russian language browser available for Windows and Russian Win95 platforms. I really included this because I liked the name, but it does illustrate the browsers that hardly anyone has heard of, but that are vitally important to a smaller community of users. Such specialized browsers exist for Arabic, Chinese, and other non-European languages, some of which have writing systems that differ from the one in which you're reading this text. Win95/NT platform.

Grail 0.3

http://monty.cnri.reston.va.us/grail/

Extensible Web browser written in Python, an object-oriented programming language, and requiring Tcl/Tk support on UNIX platforms for the most part. Full HTML 2.0 support plus much of 3.2. For the user who wants full control of her browser platform, including the ability to fix bugs as they crop up. Not for the faint-hearted or technically intimidated. Source code available. UNIX platforms, with Windows and Macintosh ports available.

HotJava 1.0

http://java.sun.com/products/hotjava/

Sun Microsystems platform-independent extensible browser, supporting all the latest in Java goodies, including JavaBeans. Design your own GUI using HTML, create your own custom Web-aware applications, download and execute Java applets even from behind corporate firewalls, and add new multimedia protocols whenever you want them. If you like Java, you'll love HotJava. UNIX, Windows, and Macintosh platforms.

Amaya 1.1

http://www.w3.org/Amaya/

The W3C testbed for new features and functionality. Usually supports their latest standards and proposals, but there is some lag. Source code available. WYSIWYG editor and browser combination available for UNIX and Windows platforms.

Cyberdog 2.0

http://cyberdog.apple.com/

Integrated Web browser from Apple that includes access e-mail, QTVR movies, Telnet, and specialized Apple toolkits, including OpenDoc and Bosco, a Web project for kids. It also offers a paid referral program (as of this writing) that might encourage you to recruit your friends to the Apple/Cyberdog cause. Macintosh platform.

Cello 1.01a

`http://www.law.cornell.edu/cello/cellotop.html`

No longer under active development, but with a small community of users, including academic users and others with limited access to the more powerful hardware needed by modern browsers. Cello will run on a 386, but a more powerful chip improves performance. Lest they feel too terribly superior to an "antique" piece of software from 1994, most modern browsers will find that they can't display a Windows bitmap file found on the Cello site, but Cello handles it quite nicely. Windows platform.

HTML Editors

An HTML editor is the basic tool of the Web designer. The best of them can make life easy for you, either hiding the details of code or helping you control its complexity with syntax-checking and other intelligent "helpers." Table G.2 gives you an overall view of the editors that are described in more detail in this section.

Table G.2. HTML editors.

Product	Type/Features	Audience	Price Range	Platforms
Netscape Composer	Semi-WYSIWYG	Novice	Free to $$	Win95, Mac, UNIX
HoTMetaL Pro	Code-based WYSIWYG			Win95/NT UNIX* Mac*
Hot Dog Express	WYSIWYG	Novice	$$	Win95
HotDog Pro	Code-based Site Manager Expert Helpers	Intermediate to Expert	$$$	Win95
Amaya	WYSIWYG	Intermediate	Free	UNIX Win95/NT
BBEdit	Code-based	Novice to Expert	$$	Mac
PageMill	WYSIWYG	Novice to Intermediate	$$$	Mac Win95/NT
HomeSite	Code-based	Intermediate	$$	Win95/NT
Home Page	Semi-WYSIWYG	Novice	$$	Windows
WebEdit Pro	Code-based	Intermediate	$$	Win95/NT

G

DEVELOPMENT RESOURCES

continues

Table G.2. continued

Product	Type/Features	Audience	Price Range	Platforms
Webber 32	Code-based HTML modes	Intermediate	$$	Win95/NT
Vis. SlickEdit	Code-based HTML modes Extensible Project- Management Interface	Intermediate to Expert	$$$	Win95/NT UNIX
Multi-Edit	Code-based HTML modes Extensible Site Manager Project Management Interface	Intermediate	$$$	Win95/NT
Emacs	Code-based HTML modes Extensible	Expert	Free or ??	UNIX Win95/NT Many
Vi	Code-based HTML modes Extensible	Expert	Free or ??	UNIX Win95/NT Many

Novice: Imperfect control over HTML code/appearance, but relatively easy to use.

Intermediate: Good control over HTML code/appearance, but requires some skill and experience to use.

Expert: Excellent control over HTML code/appearance, but requires considerable skill or experience to use.

NOTE

Many editors could suitably, or at least arguably, be assigned to several categories. In every succinct table, some overlaps and fuzzy boundaries are inevitable.

Netscape Composer 4.0

`http://www.netscape.com`

Part of the Communicator package, a semi-WYSIWIG editor that lets you include arbitrary tags by typing them into a special tag element on the page. Easy to use, but limited in scope. Good for quickly throwing a page onto the Web, but it's quickly outgrown for serious work.

HoTMetaL Pro 4.0

`http://www.softquad.com/`

The mother of all HTML editors in a new incarnation that includes lots of goodies for almost everyone, from built-in support for Microsoft and Netscape-style Dynamic HTML to accessibility tutors to help make sure your pages can be easily used by Braille, text, and audio browsers. AdaptAble Technology, including a Visual Dynamic Keyboard to allow people with limited dexterity to access all the program's features, provides an interface for differently-abled users to design and code their own Web pages. This is a very cool thing to do, and HoTMetaL Pro is to be highly commended for its attention to a market almost everyone else ignores.

HoTMetaL Pro includes Web site overviews and management, syntax and link checking, WYSIWYG editing, Tag Icon editing, raw code editing, and automatic conversion from major word processors and spreadsheets, in addition to everything else you can think of for the Web page designer. It's a good choice for beginners as well as professionals. Not to be confused with HoTMetaL, a freely available older version that has substantially less power. Latest version is Win95 platform only (so far), but it also supports UNIX and Macs with older versions.

Hot Dog Express

`http://www.sausage.com/`

Designed for beginning Web developers, HDE offers an extremely simple drag-and-drop (WYSIWYG) interface to let you quickly develop a home page or other straightforward tasks. It can't edit HTML directly, but it's a quick-and-dirty way to fiddle with a layout or look, leaving more complex tasks to its more powerful sibling. Win95 platform.

Hot Dog Pro 4.0

`http://www.sausage.com/`

The big dog, a professional Web developer's toolkit with available "Supertoolz" (hey, I can't be held responsible for Australian "humour," but at least the latest incarnation has dropped the howling dog startup screen in favor of a green doggy flasher) to create everything from RealAudio/Video out of `.wav` or `.avi` files to a little grab bag of Java applets.

Tag colors by HTML level, IE and Netscape extensions, syntax and link checking, extensible tags, and other goodies make it a good choice for serious development. An automated update facility makes keeping track of the latest revisions to the program simple, but the code is licensed to each individual machine, a potential problem for people who hop around a lot and a hassle if your machine dies.

Site management, inline macros, automated upload of a finished site, and other features make managing large Web sites an easy task, which is what I use it for mostly. Code-based editing. Win95 platform.

Amaya

`http://www.w3.org/Amaya/`

WYSIWYG HTML editing from W3 Corp. See the short discussion of Amaya in the preceding HTML browsers section.

BBEdit 4.5

`http://www.barebones.com/`

A code-based HTML editor in an easy-to-use format. Multiple-language support, color-coding of tags, extensible tag support, built-in checking, and other features make this an excellent first choice for Mac users and advanced HTML coders. Macintosh platform.

Adobe PageMill 2.0

`http://www.adobe.com/internet/`

A commercial editor that automates the process of putting up a good-looking site with as little hassle as possible. Step-by-step drag-and-drop (WYSIWYG) interface makes it easy to create what it calls a "museum quality" Web site very quickly, even for novices. Photoshop LE is included for manipulating graphics directly. A good starting point for people already committed to the Macintosh environment, but not as powerful as code-based environments for advanced users. Latest version for Macintosh includes Site Mill, covered later in the "Web Publishers and Site Managers" section. Macintosh and Win 95/NT platforms.

Allaire's HomeSite 2.5

`http://www.allaire.com/`

A simple but powerful code-based editor from the makers of Cold Fusion. Win95/NT platform.

Claris Home Page 3.0

`http://www.claris.com/products/clarispage/`

A semi-WYSIWYG editor for beginners with quite a few built-in tools, including Java applets, multimedia gadgets, and other features you can use to put your first pages into the big leagues. The name says it all, though—this is mainly for home use, not for serious Web work. Windows platform.

WebEdit Pro 2.03

`http://www.luckman.com`
A code-based editor for Win95/NT platforms.

ExperTelligence's Webber 32

`http://www.webbase.com/`
A code-based editor with excellent support for built-in restriction of tags and attributes to predefined standards, either W3C proposals or proprietary extended tag sets. Win95/NT platform.

MicroEdge's Visual SlickEdit 2.0

`http://www.slickedit.com/`
A real programmer's editor, and one I use myself (with the addition of my own custom-built extensions and toolbars), that supports true code-based development. Support for most of the major programming languages is built in, including direct access to API Apprentice for figuring out difficult API calls, syntax checkers and/or compilers, and other programming "dream" features. Among the supported languages are Java, JavaScript, and Perl, so the applicability to the Web is obvious. Some HTML support is built in as well, with direct access to your favorite Web browser to view your code "in progress." Further enhancements to the HTML feature set, including full color-coding and smart spellchecking, are planned and should be available by the time you read this.

New code can be highlighted in a different color so it's easy to keep track of changed lines. A highly extensible command set with an object-oriented C++-like programming language built in make customizing the editor for any purpose simple for people with programming experience. It emulates several editors in common use, such as Emacs, Vi, and Brief, as well as its own native CUA mode, and understands "regular expressions."

Extreme speed compared to the graphical editors makes SlickEdit a fabulous choice for people who want to get serious work done without waiting for the screen to finish updating. Interface to project management and source-code control systems, including merge and difference editing to help keep track of simultaneous code changes by several programmers on one source and maintain a code history, also make it a good choice for large shops committed to code and standard code formats, although there are no specific Web site management tools included. Text-mode–only version available for DOS. Windows, Win95/NT, OS/2, UNIX, and X Window platforms. Alas, no Macintosh support is planned.

American Cybernetics Multi-Edit

`http://www.amcyber.com/`
Another true programmer's editor with a roughly similar feature set and range of applicability to the Web, but with an optional WebLair site-management component that adds considerably to its power for total Web site development. Special HTML programming modes,

G

DEVELOPMENT RESOURCES

optional site management, context-sensitive attribute editing, and the full power of an editor that knows about Java, JavaScript, Perl, and VBScript, in addition to HTML and other major programming languages, make it a powerful competitor to Visual SlickEdit, although not available on as many platforms, and the equal of any code-based editor on the market today. Emulates Brief, but not Emacs or Vi. Text-mode–only version available for DOS. Win95/NT platforms only.

Emacs and Vi

`http://www.gnu.org/`

Of course, the quintessential programmers' editors are Emacs and, perhaps to a lesser extent, Vi. Although neither has direct access to the HTML validation and other nice features of the dedicated graphical editors, extensive knowledge of one or possibly both editors is widespread in the programming world, and custom packages (*modes* in Emacs) exist (or have been created by finicky users) to speed almost any programming task, including validation.

Notice that I didn't say "simplify" programming tasks; both programs are extremely complex, offer little or no help for beginners, and have dedicated followings of fans (fanatics?) who are contemptuous of lesser editors. Watching a skilled Emacs or Vi guru write code is sort of like trying to keep track of a magician's hands—you get confused easily but the trick astonishes you. The price for this speed and power is an extremely long learning curve. Versions have been created for almost every major platform, and both free and commercial versions are widely available. On UNIX machines, both are usually present by default or can be obtained from the Free Software Foundation (GNU) Web site listed above. Win95/NT, Windows, DOS, Macintosh, UNIX, VMS, and other platforms.

Web Site Tools: Web Publishers and Site Managers

One step up from an editor is a publisher or site manager, although there's considerable overlap. Some of the editors mentioned in the preceding sections can also be considered publishers or site managers, and I've listed them in Table G.3 as well.

Table G.3. Web publishers and site managers.

Product	Type/Features	Audience	Price Range	Platforms
HotDog Pro 4.0	Code-based Site Manager Expert Helpers	Intermediate to Expert	$$$	Win95
NetObjects Fusion	WYSIWYG Site Manager	Intermediate to Expert	$$$	Win95/NT Mac

Product	Type/Features	Audience	Price Range	Platforms
SiteMill	WYSIWYG Site Manager	Beginner to Intermediate	$$$	Mac
HoTMetaL Pro	WYSIWYG Code-Based	Novice to Expert	$$$	Win95/NT UNIX Mac
Cold Fusion	Tag-based Server-side	Intermediate to Expert	$$$	Win95/NT
WebberActive	Site Manager			Win95/NT
FrontPage 98	WYSIWYG Expert Helpers Site Manager	Novice to Intermediate	$$$	Win95/NT

Hot Dog Pro 4.0

http://www.sausage.com/

See the discussion in the previous section under "HTML Editors."

NetObjects Fusion 2.0

http://www.netobjects.com/

A WYSIWYG editor and publisher that has some people swearing by it and some swearing at it. Its strengths are a good drag-and-drop interface, a snazzy feature set, and great site-management tools, making it easy to centralize decision making and control on large projects or distributed development teams and also simple enough to allow a novice user to set up a well-designed Web site without a lot of learning and thrashing before the first page goes up.

Fabulous site architecture tools make overall design simple; you just lay out pages on an overall plan, and it makes all the links for you. Cool. Great control over placement of graphics and text with good palette control and other features of interest to serious designers. The code produced can't be tweaked by hand, however, and is incredibly "messy" to look at, so it will offend Web purists and HTML gurus who like to get their hands dirty. Win95 and Macintosh platforms.

Adobe SiteMill 2.0

http://www.adobe.com/internet/

Simple, easy-to-use site management for right-brained people and the companion product to Adobe PageMill. When you move a page, it automatically repairs links that break and does other housekeeping chores for you with little or no effort other than dragging little icons around with your mouse. It also checks off-site links and uploads an entire site at the click of your forefinger, so it fits well with the Apple Macintosh philosophy. Macintosh platform only, so if you got it as part of the Windows package, it doesn't do you much good.

G

DEVELOPMENT RESOURCES

HoTMetaL Pro 4.0

`http://www.softquad.com/`
See the discussion in the section "HTML Editors."

Cold Fusion 3.0

`http://www.allaire.com/`
Have you ever wished there was a tag to do…? Cold Fusion doesn't fit easily into any category, but it's a dedicated environment to speed and simplify Web site development, "extending" HTML with special non-HTML tags that do database access "directly," e-mail, credit card processing, and almost everything else the HTML fanatic's heart desires. It's really part of a package deal, requiring the Cold Fusion Application Server (NT platform only) to work with any standard HTTP server and perform the dynamic tasks that give Cold Fusion its power.

There's little here that couldn't be done with custom CGI scripts, but who has time to develop all the code required to cover the Cold Fusion territory? Not only that, who has time to learn all the APIs required to fully use ActiveX or ODBC or whatever? If the "canned" interfaces aren't enough, you can even write your own tag interfaces to your required functionality and tell the Application Server about them. Presto! An off-the-shelf Web browser that finally seems to understand the `<PIRATE>` and `<PINHEAD>` tags, although you'll have to call them `<CF_PIRATE>` and `<CF_PINHEAD>`. Of course it doesn't really understand them, but we'll never tell. Win95/NT platform.

ExperTelligence's WebberActive 1.1

`http://www.webbase.com/`
A site-management and editing utility that also includes support for Microsoft's Dynamic HTML and Active Channels. Tied very closely to Microsoft standards and browsers, although the current version is still supporting primarily HTML 3.2 tags. Win95/NT platform.

Microsoft FrontPage 98

`http://www.microsoft.com/sitebuilder/`
`http://www.microsoft.com/products/developer.htm`
Another WYSIWYG editor/site manager with wizards that take you through setting up your first Web pages. As with most of the feature-rich Microsoft products, it takes up a lot of room on your disk, but includes some very cool gadgets, such as Active Channels and other Microsoft proprietary goodies, as well as database wizards to grab content from existing databases. Very well integrated with Microsoft products, but the designs it comes up with can be a little on the pedestrian side. On the other hand, they are lots better than half the pages you see on the Net, so this is an excellent choice for beginners or those without a clear sense of their own style. It has good site-management tools, too, but quite not as good as NetObjects Fusion. Win95 and Macintosh platforms.

Web Site Tools: Site Maps

Most of the site managers have decent site maps available, but sometimes you want something that stands on its own, either because the site manager isn't flexible enough or because you want something that automatically keeps itself updated, so you don't have to be constantly updating the map as the site changes. There are two basic models for site-mapping: a hierarchical one, which maps well onto a typical directory tree, and a non-hierarchical graphic representation that more closely reflects how many sites, and the Web itself, are actually organized. The future seems to be in the multidimensional graphical tools, as humans can't easily grasp or navigate any but a simple directory tree.

The "cyberspace" virtual realities so lovingly described by Peter Gibson and others are all essentially extraordinarily detailed and interactive site mappers that create an interface, through the magic of future technologies, directly to the brain. This seems a peculiarly male fantasy to me; wouldn't it be easier just to stop and ask for directions?

Of course, the major search engines could be regarded as site-mapping tools, but they are well-known enough to need no discussion here. However, several can be installed on a local site, providing some level of search/site-mapping functionality. Here are a few more specialized candidates, including several that can be included on your own pages for the cost of a link to the developer. Such a deal! Table G.4 gives you a quick comparison of the site-mapping tools.

Table G.4. Site-mapping tools.

Product	Type/Features	Audience	Price Range	Platforms
MapXsite	Geographic	Expert	$$$	WinNT
SiteAnalyst	Site Map	Intermediate	$$$	Win95/NT
CLEARWeb	Site Map	Everyone	$$	Win95/NT
MAPA	Map Service	N/A	$$$$	Any
WebAnalyzer	Site Map Statistics	Everyone	$$	Win95/NT
SiteCommand	Site Map Statistics	Intermediate	$$$	WinNT
HotSauce	Site Map 3-D Views	Everyone	$$$	Mac Win95/NT
Webcutter	Site Map 3-D Views	Everyone	???	Any
Visual SiteMap	Site Map	Expert	N/A	UNIX
WebCollection	Paper	Everyone	Free	N/A
Site Map	Site Map	Everyone	Free	Any

continues

Table G.4. continued

Product	Type/Features	Audience	Price Range	Platforms
Web Site Expl.	Site Map	Everyone	Free	Any
Governor	Site Map	Everyone	Free	Any
Exploder	Site Map	Everyone	$$$	Any

MapInfo's MapXsite

`http://www.mapxsite.com/ WinNT platform`
A commercial product for WinNT platforms that allows the creation of clickable, zoomable, navigable 2-D maps and locale searches based on real geography. Although not specifically applicable to mapping a logical site, for sites with a strong geographic metaphor, it's a very powerful tool, with built-in access to geographic information databases (Geographical Information Systems—GIS) and other features that make it easy to go between physical reality and logical features. WinNT platform.

Microsoft SiteAnalyst (Formerly NetCarta's WebMapper)

`http://backoffice.microsoft.com/products/features/SiteAnalyst/SiteServerE.asp`
A 2-D tool for analyzing and maintaining Web sites, not providing a navigation map for users; it's part of the BackOffice suite of programs for network administrators and Webmasters. Win95/NT platform.

CLEARWeb

`http://www.clearweb.com/`
A Java-based site-mapping tool that displays both a directory structure and a graphical map. This tool is aimed at Webmasters and people who might need to organize their own collection of bookmarks and references. IE and Netscape browsers. Windows, Win95/WinNT platforms.

Dynamic Diagrams' MAPA Service

`http://www.dynamicdiagrams.com/`
A slick, Java-based, pseudo–3-D site mapper, which can bring up a "street map" view of a site and popup windows to display more information as you investigate the site using a mouse. Visually very pleasing, but still only a visual analogue and overview of a simple hierarchical directory tree. It's sold only as a monthly fee-for-service package, so platform is irrelevant. The company also does 3-D modeling, so it's not terribly clear whether that possibility exists for site mapping, but it doesn't seem so. Maps exist on its server and are visible in any browser that supports Java.

InContext's WebAnalyzer 2.0 and SiteCommand 1.01

`http://www.incontext.com/`

A text-based and graphical toolkit for visualizing a Web site as a hierarchy of linked pages or a "wavefront" of related nodes on a directed graph with the ability to pick any node as the central point. Recently merged with EveryWare Development Canada, so the Web address might change. The SiteCommand kernel (a "Pro" version is soon to be released) runs on a limited number of Netscape and Microsoft servers and allows text-based site maps and extensive statistical data to be dynamically constructed and analyzed by the Webmaster, but is not necessary for occasional or intermittent use on a small site. WebAnalyzer is also aimed toward the Webmaster, offering multiple views of a site, including graphical displays, to allow tracking down broken links, duplicated files, files with too much content, and other information of limited use to users, although the maps themselves might be useful. Win95/NT platform.

Apple's HotSauce

`http://hotsauce.apple.com/`

A graphical 3-D "fly-through" browser plug-in that requires building an MCF (Meta Content Framework) file to describe the 3-D interactive model that HotSauce navigates. Nice concept, but a lot of work for most Webmasters, and, of course, you can't do much astral projection without the out-of-body plug-in. However, it forms part of the offerings of others, including NetObjects Fusion, which can generate an MCF description on the fly, and several other systems. For an in-house environment or other restricted audience, it has real possibilities as a user overview, but as a general-purpose tool to entice people further into your site, it leaves something to be desired because it requires a plug-in. Mac and Win95/NT platforms.

WebCutter (Lotus Domino)

`http://www-ee.technion.ac.il/W3C/abstract.html`
`http://www-ee.technion.ac.il/W3C/WebCutter.html`

A Java-based tool to display both directory-style (tree) and logical-geography (directed graphs or networks) site maps dynamically, based on ASCII text files created by a dedicated Webcrawler that describe the site. Context-sensitive mapping provides a pseudo–3-D view of the site as a collection of graphs whose nodes are grouped by equating visual distance with logical relevance from the node picked as a starting point. Very cool stuff that could eventually become part of the Lotus Notes/Domino package. Any Java platform.

Visual Site Map

`http://lislin.gws.uky.edu/Sitemap/Sitemap.html`

University of Kentucky's Visual Site Map Research Prototype—a neural-network–based offline tool for analyzing and presenting logical relationships between portions of a site, based on content rather than mere links. It's an experimental project only, but interesting because it probably represents one future direction out of the many places site mapping is going. No platform dependency.

G

DEVELOPMENT RESOURCES

WebCollection (W3C Draft)

http://www-ee.technion.ac.il/W3C/WebCollection.html

A background paper on some of the work being done on site mapping by W3C. No platform dependency.

Joe Bart's Site Map

http://junior.apk.net/~jbarta/

Very slick Explorer-style 2-D site map in JavaScript with "you are here" indication and link exchange-style banner. The map appears in a floating window so you can move it around. Any platform.

Rabbit Internet's Web Site Explorer

http://www.rabbitnet.com/

Another Explorer-style 2-D site map tool in JavaScript. Any platform.

Governor Site Map

http://www.governor.co.uk/

A freely available Explorer-style 2-D site map in Java. Very quick and flexible. Any platform.

Beach Software's Exploder Site Map Tool

http://www.halcyon.com/beach/products/applets/

Here's another 2-D site map in Java, also very portable although the background is dull gray for some reason; more impressed by cool code than aesthetics, I suppose. A commercial product, but Java source code is included in the purchase price, so you can make it as pretty as you like. Any Java-enabled platform.

Web Site Tools: Miscellaneous Shareware

There are many good tools available at low cost as shareware, far too many to list here and bound to be outdated by the time you read this because new programs come on the market all the time. They are available for downloading at several sites, but I rather like the TUCOWS site as they actually rate the programs and give you a capsule summary. The other two mentioned in this section (and listed in Table G.5) have ratings, too, and a broader range.

Table G.5. Miscellaneous shareware.

Product	Type/Features	Audience	Price Range	Platforms
TUCOWS	WinSock Ware	Everyone	Varies	Win95/NT
ZDNet	Shareware	Everyone	Varies	Many
C|Net	Shareware	Everyone	Varies	Many

TUCOWS Central

`http://www.tucows.com/`

This site specializes in WinSock tools, so it has rather poor coverage of graphics editors and the like. The name stands for The Ultimate Collection Of Winsock Software, although they have made much of the obvious play on words by prominently featuring pictures of cows, bad "moo" puns, and other cow jokes on their site. Because WinSock is usually seen with nerd capitalization, I suspect they thought of the pun first and then tweaked around their name until it came out right so they could use cute cow pictures on their site. Windows and Macintosh platforms.

ZDNet's Software Library

`http://www.hotfiles.com/need description`

Ziff-Davis, the publisher of *PC Magazine*, *PC Week*, *MacWEEK*, and other computer-oriented magazines, regularly features reviews and comparisons of software in the pages of its magazines. It has, in fact, a staff that's constantly testing new products, and they place these reviews on their Web site for anyone to read. Cool! The magazines are by far the better (and more timely) place to find the reviews, as they delay publication on the Web so they don't cannibalize their newsstand sales and usually include more data, but if you're in a hurry for information and haven't had the time to read, it's a good second choice. All platforms are covered, but with an emphasis on Intel and Macintosh platforms.

C | Net's Download.com

`http://www.download.com/ditto`

C|Net is the widely known producer of high-tech information shows on TV, including "The New Edge," "C|Net Central," "TV.COM," and "The Web." They also have a Web radio show and the NEWS.COM Web news site. As part of this potpourri of technospeak, they offer Download.com, a site for getting the latest in shareware, demoware, and other tidbits to stuff into spare corners of your hard drive, some of which have been reviewed and rated. All platforms are available, but with an emphasis on Intel and Macintosh.

Graphics

If a picture is worth a thousand words, why do comic strips have words? Seriously, cool graphics can make a good Web site great, but great pictures aren't worth a lot without words. You need both, and you need good tools to make pictures that work well on the Web.

There are a few handy and inexpensive utilities available to get you started (see Table G.6), like GIF Construction Set (especially for simple animation on Windows platforms) and LView Pro, both widely available as shareware from the major download sites. There are even credible photo-editing programs like Paint Shop Pro that won't set you back too much. You can do a lot with them. More important, you can learn.

But when the rubber meets the road, you'll want to start thinking about Adobe Photoshop, Illustrator, and other professional graphics tools. It's not just because these tools are insanely great, which they are, but they are so widespread in the serious graphic design world that most of the add-on utilities are written to work with them. They are also great timesavers, which as you probably know is what separates the people who sleep at night from the people who are up at 4 a.m. trying to finish a job in time for the client presentation in exactly six hours.

Table G.6. Graphics resources.

Product	Type/Features	Audience	Price Range	Platforms
Photoshop	Photo Editor	Professionals	$$$$	Win95/NT Mac
Illustrator	Line Art Editor	Professionals	$$$$	Win95/NT Mac
Fractal Paint	Photo Editor	Professionals	$$$	Win95/NT Mac
CorelDRAW!	Line Art Editor	Professionals	$$$	Win95/NT
PHOTO-PAINT	Photo Editor	Professionals	$$$	Win95/NT
DeBabelizer	Graphics Tool	Professioanls	$$$	Win95/NT Mac
The GIMP	Photo Editor	Professionals	Free	UNIX X Window
Freehand 7	Line Art Editor	Professionals	$$$	Win95/NT Mac
GIF Construct	GIF Utility	Everyone	$$	Win95/NT
Colorworks W3	Photo Editor	Everyone	$$$	Win95/NT
Paint Shop Pro	Photo Editor	Everyone	$$	Win95/NT
LView Pro	Image Utility	Everyone	$$	Win95/NT
GIFTool	GIF Utility	Everyone	Free	UNIX
GIFTrans	GIF Utility	Everyone	Free	UNIX
XV Image View	Image Utility	Everyone	Free	UNIX X Window
Imaging Mach.	Online Utility	Everyone	Free	Any
Dmitry's Labs	Tutorials	Everyone	Free	Any
Web Wonk	Tutorials	Everyone	Free	Any
Photoshop Tips	Tutorials	Everyone	Free	Any

Product	Type/Features	Audience	Price Range	Platforms
Homegurrrl	Tutorials	Everyone	Free	Any
Top Ten Mistakes	Tutorials	Everyone	Free	Any
Free Icons	Icons	Limited	Free	Any
Wagon Train	Icons	Everyone	Free	Any
GIFs	Clipart			
	Links			
Encyclopedia	Reference	Everyone	Free	Any
Barry's Clip Art Server	Clipart	Everyone	Free	Any

Adobe Photoshop/Illustrator

`http://www.adobe.com/prodindex/`

There are two basic kinds of artwork used on the Web: line art (vector graphics) and photographs (bitmaps or raster graphics). Adobe makes the Cadillac tools for both types—Photoshop, which does photographic image touch-up and manipulation, and Illustrator, which handles line art.

Both tools have a place on your desktop, but the most recent version of Photoshop has a ton of new features for professional Web artists, including support for PNG, the new graphics file format that might eventually replace GIFs, and digital watermarking (steganography), so you can secretly place copyright information in every image that can be retrieved, even after printing and rescanning the image!

Add features like the Actions palette, which allows you to record the steps needed to create an effect and reapply it to many photos automatically, and the availability of third-party packages, such as Kai's Power Tools or Alien Skin, and you have a truly wonderful platform for production artwork.

Illustrator is equally powerful for creating line art (the sort you draw with pen and ink as opposed to a paintbrush), and these two tools work very well together because line art typically has to be converted to a bitmap format before publication on the Web.

If you have any plans for taking your graphics to a graphics shop to turn them into slides or professional hardcopy, or even "farm out" part of your work, most of the pros have only Adobe software available and can accept only Adobe file formats. Macintosh and Win95 platforms.

Fractal Design Painter

http://www.fractal.com/

This is another photo-style graphics package aimed toward the production of "painterly" effects and the actual creation of digital artwork, instead of touching up or manipulating scanned-in images. A pressure-sensitive graphics tablet is a real advantage with this tool, as it is with most high-end graphics editors. Painter accepts and creates Adobe and other file formats, so you can move easily from one to the other. They also do Ray Dream Studio for 3-D modeling and animation. Macintosh and Win95 platforms.

CorelDRAW!/PHOTO-PAINT

http://www.corel.com/

A good second choice (some would say the only second choice) for professional designers. Although support is not as widespread as for Adobe, it does exist, so you won't be stuck in limbo with a file nobody else can use if you decide to go outside for printing or subcontracting.

Corel file formats have a reputation for being a little quirky, but one attraction is that CorelDRAW!/PHOTO-PAINT is a lot less expensive and still offers enough power to be useful. In fact, many designers have both on their desktops because each tool has particular strengths. You can often trade files back and forth to make tasks easier than they would have been on one or the other.

The current edition comes as a package with both in a single bundle, as well as CorelDREAM 3D, a three-dimensional rendering package, and a few other very cool things. Corel supports digital watermarks, Kai's Power Tools, and quite a few of the goodies you'll find in Photoshop, as well as a raft of "free" clip art images. It's a great tool, so get both if you can. Win95/NT platforms.

DeBabelizer

http://www.equil.com/

An essential tool for production Web work, allowing you to do batch manipulations on many files at once, including finding an optimum palette for a set of images and imposing that palette on all of them. You can have the program watch while you perform a complex task on one file, and it then knows how to do the same thing to all the rest. It's almost as good as having a sorcerer's apprentice to do the bulk of your work for you, but not nearly as dangerous. A very cool tool. Macintosh and Win95 platforms.

The GIMP

http://scam.xcf.berkeley.edu/~gimp/

The GIMP (Gnu Image Manipulation Program) is a graphic editor and photo-retouching tool for the UNIX X Window world, with the same general features you'll find in Photoshop, including filters, plug-ins, and effects to perform quite complicated image transformations. Examples on the site of available effects are Mosaic, which renders a photo as though it had been tiled with little bits of ceramic; Carving, for incising a graven Dragnet-style 3-D effect into a photo; IFS, which evidently creates dendritic patterns automatically, simulating plant growth; and Chrome, which gives an image a metallic look. UNIX X Window platforms.

Macromedia Freehand Graphics Studio 7

`http://www.macromedia.com/`

A powerful tool for creating animated vector (line art) Web graphics, well integrated with other Macromedia products. Win95/NT and Macintosh platforms.

GIF Construction Set by Alchemy Mindworks

`http://www.mindworkshop.com/alchemy/alchemy.html`

Alchemy Mindworks also makes the Graphics Workshop, which allows you to convert many types of graphics formats back and forth, as well as other tricks. Both can create transparent GIFs and perform simple image manipulation, but only GIF Construction Set lets you create animated GIFs for the Web, a low-cost alternative to streaming video in many cases and supported by almost all modern browsers without the need for plug-ins or special viewers. Windows and Win95 platforms.

SPG's ColorWorks: Web 3

`http://www.spg-net.com/`

An innovative new graphics package that calls itself "the Mother of all Web Graphics Suites," Web 3 offers a lot of Web-aware functionality, including GIF animation optimization that can automatically shrink your animated files by 50 percent or more, an image-mapping utility, JPEG "image repair," an image library browser, and (I don't recommend this for casual use on copyrighted sites without prior permission) a Web graphics spider that automatically snatches all the images off a site for later use—way cool.

They offer free plug-ins to download from their site and plan to offer Adobe Photoshop plug-in support in the near future. They also have a free upgrade offer, good within 30 days from the date of purchase, for people who bought a soon-to-be-updated version. And get this—you don't have to find out for yourself! They e-mail to ask if you want it and if your shipping address is still correct. You can skip upgrades without a penalty, too. Incredible (and unusual) social responsibility toward its loyal customers! Not only that, but one of its superheroic Ultimate Web designer "mascots" is a woman. I wish Web 3 would put her on the splash page, but it's not a perfect world. Win95/NT platform.

Paint Shop Pro

`http://www.jasc.com/`

A good choice for occasional use or "hobby" Web page design, Paint Shop Pro is widely available as shareware with a moderate registration fee or can be ordered from the maker. It supports a surprising number of features and even accepts Adobe Photoshop plug-ins, so much of the power of the professional tools can be yours for a far lower price tag. Windows and Win95 platforms.

G

DEVELOPMENT
RESOURCES

LView Pro

`http://www.lview.com/`

Shareware graphics file format converter and image manipulator that includes creating transparent GIFs and animation and simple editing. Often available on shareware download sites, or refer to its home page. Windows and Win95/NT platforms.

GIFTool

`http://www.homepages.com/tools`

A command-line–driven GIF tool for making interlaced GIFs. Unfortunately, the home page listed here has disappeared, perhaps permanently, but it's still available in the FreeBSD UNIX source code. You'll need access to a C compiler (usually cc on most UNIX systems) to compile it. Here is one source in Russia, but you might be able to find a copy locally:

`http://www.cronyx.ru/pub/pub/FreeBSD/distfiles/giftool.tar.gz`

Some versions also do transparency, for which you might need a color indexing tool, such as John Bradley's XV Image Viewer (listed later in this section). Your graphic editor probably has a way to identify the color of your background, although you might have to convert to hex by hand. However, for command-line–driven programs, it can be a difficult trick because the interface is text-only and you can't actually see the graphic. UNIX platform.

Andreas Ley's GIFTrans

`ftp://ftp.rz.uni-karlsruhe.de/pub/net/www/tools/`

A command-line–driven GIF transparency maker. You might need something like John Bradley's XV Image Viewer to select your transparency color, unless you know it already, although almost any graphics program will let you see the actual color. You might have to convert from an RGB decimal value to hex, though, depending on the tool. Source code available, as well as a DOS-executable .exe file. UNIX and DOS platforms.

John Bradley's XV Image Viewer

`http://www.trilon.com/xv/`

If you're running X Window under UNIX, this tool might already be available on your system, or you can get it from the author's site. Lots of cool things to fool around with, including getting the color index of any given pixel in an image. Multiple file formats supported and conversions performed. He also has a binary of GIFTrans available for download. Source code available, but it's not freeware. UNIX X Window platforms.

The Imaging Machine

`http://www.vrl.com/Imaging/`

If you have access to your own Web page, you can feed file URLs to this service and it converts them to transparent, interlaced GIFs or animations of up to 25 images. You get the images back by capturing the image from the screen. Any platform, but you do need access to a Web page.

Dmitry Kirsanov's Design Lab

http://www.webreference.com/dlab/

A site by one of the contributors to this book that explores the use of photography in Web design and other graphic design issues. An eclectic assortment of links, called his "dessert links," are a fitting part of this well-balanced meal. No platform dependencies.

David Siegel's Web Wonk

http://www.dsiegel.com/tips/

A page of tips and tricks from one of the most famous designers on the Web. He covers a lot of bases, from typography to what color to set your backgrounds to for the best-looking images, and has a wry sense of humor to boot. Well worth looking at for both Web novices and old hands. No platform dependencies.

Laurie McCanna's Photoshop Tips

http://www.mccannas.com/pshop/photosh0.htm

Laurie's large site, of which this page is only a small part, has lots of information on design, free art, link lists, and other swell articles to read or grab. Feel free to explore. No platform dependencies.

Lynda's Homegurrrl Page

http://www.lynda.com/

This site has loads of information available, including her mailing list, discussions of animated GIFs and color, an eclectic assortment of links, and other nifty items for the Web designer. No platform dependencies.

Top Ten Mistakes in Web Design

http://www.useit.com/alertbox/9605.html

Jakob Nielsen's cogent essay on the problems of orphan pages, nonstandard link colors, and so on. This is only one of many good articles on Web page design, graphics, accessibility, page layout, typography, and other issues of interest to Web designers, which can all be accessed through this site. No platform dependencies.

Free Icons by Goff

http://members.aol.com/tedgoff/icons.html

Some novelty icons in a large size by a professional cartoonist whose work has appeared in *The Saturday Evening Post, The Wall Street Journal, Better Homes & Gardens, Good Housekeeping, Air & Space,* and *Harvard Magazine.* If you've ever pined for a nose icon, or a green-faced icon of a man about to be sick, this is the place for you. UNIX, Macintosh, and Win95/NT platforms.

G

DEVELOPMENT
RESOURCES

Wagon Train Animated GIFs

`http://dreamartists.com/animated.htm`

Carol Waggoner's delightful and exuberant site contains a grab bag of original artwork you can use on your own Web sites or just admire. This is real Americana, as homey and cluttered as an old country store and as much a labor of the heart as a display of her work. She also has a lot of links to other sites where you can find still more clip art, unlike some of the less generous "free" artwork sites you'll find out there on the Web. UNIX, Macintosh, and Win95/NT platforms.

Encyclopedia of Graphics File Formats

`http://www.ipahome.com/gff/textonly/book.htm`

An indispensable guide to the Web professional. Covers in detail every aspect of GIFs, JPEGs, PNGs, and other graphic formats. There are lots of other graphics resources available on Bob MacDonald's site, so it would pay to snoop around. No platform dependencies.

Barry's Clip Art Server

`http://www.barrysclipart.com/mdex.html`

There are so many sites offering free clip art that it's hard to know where to either stop or start. The examples in this section are only a few of the large number available. The index alone is on this one is five pages long—a really gigantic collection of clip art for Web pages. No platform dependencies.

Plug-ins from Various Sources

There are literally dozens, perhaps hundreds, of special-purpose plug-ins available for the major browsers, each of which has a mission in the world, but each of which limits your audience to those who have the plug-in installed or don't mind loading it onto their hard drive. If your task demands one of them, perhaps because you have to distribute a particular file format or achieve a certain "look," by all means use them, but the nearer you can come to "vanilla" formats that are supported directly by the major browsers, the better off you'll be if your audience is general. Plug-ins take time to download and space on the disk; many people don't have much of either to spare.

You can find a good list of currently available plug-ins for Netscape at this site:

`http://home.netscape.com/comprod/products/navigator/version_2.0/plugins/index.html`

Most of these plug-ins have IE versions as well.

Many of the download sites mentioned in the previous sections on graphics tools also have lengthy lists of plug-ins. Try them, too.

Multimedia for Professionals

When you think of multimedia on the Web, the two that spring to mind most quickly are Macromedia and RealAudio, whose Shockwave, Director, and RealAudio products almost define the term *multimedia* for many. Although all these technologies work better over higher-speed connections, they can generate smallish files that load quickly, allowing the multimedia content to display or be heard before the viewer gives up in disgust. Both these vendors offer free viewers to the general public (perhaps with a paid "premium" version as well) and sell the tools needed to create their proprietary data formats. An important advantage of these formats is that almost everyone who's at all interested in multimedia over the Web has already downloaded and installed these two in particular. Some browsers even come with them pre-installed. Table G.7 lists some of the best tools and products for professional Web site use.

Table G.7. Multimedia for professionals.

Product	Type/Features	Audience	Price Range	Platforms
RealAudio and RealVideo	Audio/Video Server	Professionals	$$$$$	WinNT UNIX
Macromedia	Authoring Tool Animation	Professionals	$$$$	Win95/NT Mac
Asymetrix	Authoring Tool Animation Education	Professionals	$$$	Win95/NT
3D Studio Max	Graphic Design 3-D Rendering 3-D Animation	Professionals	$$$$	WinNT

RealAudio/Video

`http://www.realaudio.com/`

Streaming audio/video presentations and content provider, offering Web "radio" as well as slow-scan TV. It has both free and commercial plug-ins available. Its server package is quite expensive, but can put you into the Web broadcasting business as a turnkey package. This company also makes free utilities available to convert common audio file formats to their proprietary streaming ones. The resulting files can be served up by any HTTP server as a pseudo-streaming file that will be recognized by its players. Macintosh and Win95 platforms.

Macromedia

`http://www.macromedia.com/`

The famous "Shocked" enhancements to many Web sites, offering the potential of interactive content, games, and the like. They also offer free trials of some programs and low-cost versions supplying some of the same functionality, so don't give up on them just because you know that they "cost too much for me." A little taste might whet your appetite for more. Dozens of products, including the flagship products Director 6 Multimedia Studio and Authorware 4 Interactive Studio. More affordable products exist, such as Flash 2 and Backstage Internet Studio-Desktop Edition. Latest enhancements are streaming ShockWave, live Internet authoring, and Shocked CDs. Macintosh and Win95 platforms.

Asymetrix Multimedia Toolbook

`http://www.asymetrix.com/`

A multimedia company specializing in online learning, with tools and expertise in creating interactive courseware for educators or corporate intranets. If you need this kind of knowledge, Asymetrix is one good place to start. They offer tools to create 3-D images on the Web, visual on-the-fly Java development, digital video production, a scripting language for courseware, and other utilities to support teaching on the Web. Some are available as demos. Win95/NT platforms.

3D Studio Max from Autodesk/Kinetix

`http://www.ktx.com/`

Prepare for sticker shock on this one—well into four figures, but incredibly powerful. It's the sort of software you dream about if you want to do studio-quality 3-D animation or videos. Rendering is superb, rivaling dedicated UNIX graphics workstations, and the feature set is very rich, allowing the lucky user to view the project at hand in any of four views, selecting the one that seems most appropriate for a given task.

Plug-ins are available to perform tasks like bipedal motion and muscle movement, so it's an environment for really cool effects and custom animation features. Even if you can't afford it yourself, it's the sort of resource you might want to ask an outside graphic design firm about if you want "photo-realistic animation" on your site. Anyone with this tool on her desktop is really serious about animation and 3-D graphic design. Free demo CD-ROM available on the Web site as of this writing. High-end Pentium Pro (preferably more than a single processor and gobs of RAM). WinNT platforms only.

Multimedia for Casual Use

But what about the rest of us, who can't afford the thousand-dollar-or-more price tags on these specialized tools? There are several inexpensive technologies for creating sound, at least, including the familiar .WAV, .AU, and .MID files, which have "viewers" built into the major browsers. If the content is small in file size, the load times are no more apparent than that of the lead times on the streaming techniques. Once again, shareware utilities have much to offer, but you often pay for the low cost in a less integrated environment that requires several steps in different programs to do a given task. Table G.8 gives you an overview of good sources of tested and rated graphics and multimedia shareware.

Table G.8. Multimedia resources for casual use.

Product	Type/Features	Audience	Price Range	Platforms
MacWorld	Resource List	Everybody	Free	Mac
PCWorld	Resource List	Everybody	Free	Win95/NT
Hotfiles	Resource List	Everybody	Free	Many
Sound Forge	Sound Editor	Professionals	$$$	Win95/NT
NoteWorthy	MIDI Composer	Professionals	$$	Win95/NT
GoldWave	Sound Editor	Everybody	$$	Win95/NT
WebShot	Live Video	Everybody	$$$	Win95/NT
Movie Cleaner	Movie Utility	Everybody	$$	Mac
RealAudio	Audio Encoder	Everybody	Free	Win95 Mac
RealVideo	Video Encoder	Everybody	Free	Win95 Mac
Personal AVI	Video Editor	Everybody	$$	Windows
Sirius Multi-media Links	Resource List	Everybody	Free	Many
Cross Platform	Resource List	Everybody	Free	Many
3DSite	Resource List	Everybody	Free	Many
WDVL Graphics	Resource List	Everybody	Free	Many
Grafica	Resource List	Everybody	Free	Many
Obscura	Tidbits			

MacWorld

`http://www.macworld.com/`

A good source for software for the Mac platform. Some software reviews are available from the splash page index, but most are offered without ratings. Search engine makes it fairly easy to find reviews, and a list of the top downloads gives you an idea of what other people think is worthwhile. Macintosh platform.

PCWorld

`http://www.pcworld.com/`

A similar site offering hardware and software reviews and ratings for Windows/Intel platforms. Same ownership makes these sites not quite clones of each other, but very close in concept. Windows/Intel platforms.

ZDNet's Hotfiles Software Library

`http://www.hotfiles.com/graphics.html`

Great selection of rated and reviewed shareware and demoware, well organized by category. Many platforms.

Here are a few examples from the preceding sites showing the range of what's available, but please remember that there are hundreds of programs in any given category. What's covered in the following sections is only a small sampling of the "best of breed."

Sound Forge

`http://www.sfoundry.com/`

A high-end sound editor for putting together your own audio tracks. A little pricey, but the Sound Forge XP version is much more affordable. Windows/Win95 platform.

NoteWorthy Composer

`http://www.ntworthy.com/`

Create your own MIDI files with an inexpensive MIDI composer. Windows/Win95 platforms.

GoldWave

`http://www.goldwave.com/`

Shareware sound recorder and editor that you might want to consider if Sound Forge is a little too steep. The user interface is not quite as nice as Sound Forge, but it's lots more affordable. Windows/Win95 platforms.

WebShot

`http://www.cinecom.com/products/webshot.htm`

Install your own live Net camera! Amaze your friends! If you ever had a hankering to expose the details of your office or home on the World Wide Web, this is your chance. Win95/NT platform.

Movie Cleaner Pro

`http://www.terran-int.com/`

Compress and clean your videos for presentation on the Web. Macintosh platform.

RealAudio and RealVideo Encoders

`http://www.realaudio.com/products/encoder/`

Produce your own multimedia Web performances using the RealAudio and RealVideo formats and pseudo-streaming from any Web server. Free utilities convert common source files into the "Real" format. Win95 and Macintosh platforms.

Personal AVI Editor

`http://www.flickerfree.com/`

Video editor for AVI files. Windows platforms.

Sirius Multimedia Links

`http://ardvark.com/mm.htm`

Links from people who are in the business of multimedia, so they know what they're talking about; however, the page is obviously dated. A good starting point for any multimedia search. No platform dependencies.

The Cross Platform Page

`http://www.mcad.edu/Guests/EricB/xplat.html`

Excellent collection of multimedia links with particular emphasis on translating file formats between platforms. The trade-offs between some formats are clearly explained, so this page might serve as a brief introduction for some viewers. All platforms.

3DSite

`http://www.3dsite.com/`

Great page with resources for 3-D Web design and VRML information. Online resources (mainly Mac), jobs board, and classified ads make this an interesting gathering place for Web artists and animators. Mainly Macintosh platforms, but resources cross platforms.

The World-Wide Web Virtual Library—Computer Graphics and Visualization

`http://www.dataspace.com/WWW/vlib/comp-graphics.html`

Enough links to commercial companies offering graphics and multimedia tools to let you while away an afternoon looking through them, as well as online research papers and other cutting-edge stuff for the graphics professional. No platform dependency.

Paul Haeberli's Grafica Obscura

`http://www.sgi.com/grafica/`

An interesting site by a Web artist offering examples of his work, cool tools, articles, tutorials on producing graphics and multimedia for the Web, and the sort of stuff you might find laying around gathering dust in a studio. Very simple, but very nice. Some of it is incredibly cool in spite of the no-nonsense linear presentation. No particular platform dependency, although he is associated with SGI.

Scripting/Platform-Independent Languages

Scripting is the hard part, where many designers call for assistance from a programmer. It's difficult to master every skill needed to create a modern Web page, just as few people could build a car from scratch nowadays. In fact, many people who are skilled, competent designers refuse to look "under the hood" of Web pages and deal only with the surface, leaving tinkering to "Web mechanics."

It's not that scripting is impossible to learn; in fact, the following references, listed in Table G.9, will show you that many tasks are surprisingly easy. However, you have time for only so much learning in life, and some people draw the line at any form of programming.

Table G.9. Scripting/platform-independent languages.

Language	Type/Features	Audience	Price Range	Platforms
Java	Compiled	Developers	Free	Any
JavaScript	Interpreted	Everyone	Free	Any
JScript	Interpreted	IE Users	Free	IE
VBScript	Interpreted	IE Users	Free	IE

Java

Java is Sun Microsystem's answer to the increasing dominance of Intel/Windows desktops. It's a fully platform-independent language that will run quite happily on any machine incorporating a Java Virtual Machine, a special sort of interpreter that pretends to be an ideal machine everyone has, as opposed to the many different hardware and operating system combinations that actually exist. You may create, use, and distribute Java applets rather freely in a noncommercial setting, although you need a noncommercial license, which Sun will grant at no charge. If you plan on incorporating the interpreter into a commercial product, however, you have to negotiate a commercial license; in that case, expect to spend some money.

Java is a very productive language for developers, as the strong typing and excellent control structures make it very easy to create clean code that runs correctly right off the bat. In addition, "garbage collection" of unused memory removes one of the prime source of errors for C/C++ programmers—memory leaks and incorrect references to memory locations given back to the system by mistake.

One of the most exciting developments in Java is servlets, server-side Java programs that can partially replace CGI scripts for heavily accessed sites. Because the servlet is always resident in memory, the overhead involved in starting a new process for every request is eliminated, and because the Java Virtual Machine executes Java much faster than Perl is interpreted on most servers, the overall performance boost can be tremendous. Even more important, because the servlet runs on the server, there's no problem with using Java power with any browser, regardless of whether a Java engine is available on the client-side.

The following table, G.10, is a capsule summary of the sort of information you can find on the Web to help you develop Java code or find prewritten Java to solve a particular problem. Although the resources themselves are free, they might point to a commercial or shareware site with price tags attached to their code, so be cautious about what you use and how you use it. It's not uncommon for software licenses and costs to vary depending on what purpose the code is used for.

Table G.10. Java resources.

Site	Type/Features	Audience	Price Range	Platforms
Sun Java Home	Tutorials Examples Vendors	Developers	Free	Any
Gamelan	Tutorials Examples Vendors	Developers	Free	Any
Haifa Research	Servlet Engine	Developers	Free	Any
Sun Servlets	Tutorials	Developers	Free	Any
Programmers Source	Tutorials Examples	Developers	Free	Any

Sun's Java Home Page

`http://java.sun.com/`
The source for the latest (company-approved) news about Java and supporting technologies, as well as software (Software Development Kit and examples) to download. No platform dependencies, by design.

Gamelan

`http://www.gamelan.com/`
A Web site devoted to Java and JavaScript, although exactly how a gamelan (percussion and gong) orchestra is related to Java, other than originating from the same part of the world as gourmet coffee does, is hard to fathom. One of those obscure allusions that sophisticated people are fond of, I suppose. Great resource, though. No platform dependencies.

IBM's Haifa Research Institute

`http://www.haifa.il.ibm.com/servlet_express/`
An IBM Web site with a downloadable Java servlet engine, Servlet Express. Servlets are very hot in the Java world because they allow a developer to add CGI-type functionality directly to

the server without the overhead of starting a new process for every request. Servlet Express is an engine that allows a developer to extend the functionality of almost any server, but especially those that have no servlet support built-in or whose servlet support is outdated. Very cool technology; check it out. No platform dependencies.

Sunsoft's Servlet Page

`http://jserv.javasoft.com/products/java-server/servlets/index.html`
The definitive source for information about Java servlets, the downloadable Servlet Development Kit (SDK) allows developers to get up and running quickly in this exciting new technology. Links to commercial developers who support servlets allow even the nonprogrammer to purchase off-the-shelf components to allow almost any Web designer to take advantage of the speed and platform-independence of servlets for his or her Web site projects. No platform dependencies.

The Programmer's Source—Java Resources

`http://www.progsource/java/`
An extensive single-page link list of tutorials, developers' resources, and other links of interest to Java professionals. No platform dependencies.

JavaScript

Java has one big problem. You need to know how to program to use it, and you need a compiler and other stuff that isn't laying around on most desktops, although Sun will give you one for free. That's a big hurdle for many people (although Java is much easier to learn than C or C++), so Netscape invented a Java-like language that didn't need any special tools—just the editor you wrote the rest of your page with—and that had a much simpler set of commands, so almost anyone could do useful "programming" without special knowledge or training. JavaScript does have weaknesses; Netscape's definition of the language didn't include a version mechanism to account for changes and differences between implementations, which has caused problems as its own definition has evolved and requires users to upgrade their browsers periodically or risk being left behind. An overview of JavaScript resources is listed in Table G.11.

Table G.11 JavaScript resources.

Site	Type/Features	Audience	Price Range	Platforms
Web Reference	Tutorials Examples Vendors	Everyone	Free	Any
JavaScript	Tutorials Examples Vendors	Everyone	Free	Any

Site	Type/Features	Audience	Price Range	Platforms
JavaScript Planet	Tutorials Examples Vendors	Everyone	Free	Any
JavaScript World	Tutorials Examples	Everyone	Free	Any
Cut-N-Paste JavaScript	Examples	Everyone	Free	Any
JavaScript Debugger	Tool	Everyone	Free	Any
Visual JavaScript	Tool	Everyone	Free	Any
JavaScript Index	Examples	Everyone	Free	Any
Snark Hunt JavaScript	Example	Everyone	Free	Any
Voodoo JavaScript	Tutorial	Everyone	Free	Any

Web Reference's JavaScript Page

`http://www.webreference.com/javascript/`

No longer being updated, but still interesting, with tutorials and other information. No platform dependencies.

JavaScript

`http://javascript.developer.com/`

Similar in concept to Gamelan, also hosted on `developer.com`, which features sub-sites devoted to other languages and technologies, including ActiveX. You can link to it from Gamelan (also known as `java.developer.com`), but the URL given here is the direct link. No platform dependencies.

JavaScript Planet

`http://www.geocities.com/SiliconValley/7116/`

A small site with big aspirations, a newsletter, and hundreds of JavaScript samples. A nice feature is a visible warning next to scripts that don't work in IE and other browser/platform incompatibilities. No hardware platform dependencies.

G

DEVELOPMENT RESOURCES

JavaScript World

`http://www.jsworld.com.`

This popular site includes an extensive archive, as well as news and discussion groups. No platform dependencies.

Cut-N-Paste JavaScript

`http://www.infohiway.com/javascript.`

This site specializes in prewritten JavaScript that you can cut and paste into your own pages to perform common tasks. Their scripts range from simple scripts to scroll text to complex calculators and graphic slideshows. No platform dependencies.

Netscape JavaScript Debugger

`http://search.netscape.com/eng/Tools/JSDebugger/relnotes/relnotespr1.html`

This is a general-purpose debugging tool that can help users track down bugs by allowing them to walk through the code step-by-step and examine values. No platform dependencies.

Netscape's Visual JavaScript 1.0

Visual development environment for JavaScript. This powerful tool will help you create scripts by means of a layout editor with drag-and-drop capability. No platform dependencies.

JavaScript Index

`http://www.cob.ohio-state.edu/~lindeman/javascript/andrew.html`

Good source for lots of scripts, ranging from calculators and spreadsheets to the Web Prophet. No platform dependencies.

Hunting the SNARK with JavaScript

`http://www.cs.cmu.edu/~jab/snark/`

How to put a JavaScript search engine on your Web site. No platform dependencies.

Voodoo's Introduction to JavaScript

`http://rummelplatz.uni-mannheim.de/~skoch/js/tutorial.htm`

Stefan Koch's excellent tutorial covers just about everything you can do with JavaScript. No platform dependencies.

JScript

Microsoft's JScript has been a source of confusion among JavaScript coders since Microsoft chose to go its own way with the language. The most recent version is far more conforming, but still has significant differences that have to be accounted for in Internet development. In the meantime, because many older versions of IE are still in use and will be for quite some time, code should either be limited to a compatible subset or Explorer should be explicitly tested for—and code written to account for—the differences without throwing error messages onto the screen.

Win95/NT platforms and eventual support for the PowerMac. Third parties may supply UNIX support for JScript on their own, although this is becoming less important as JScript comes closer to JavaScript.

Microsoft's JScript 2.0 Web Page

`http://www.microsoft.com/jscript/`
A good reference for JScript and Microsoft toolkits; also includes tutorials and tips for creating JScript scripts for IE browsers. In general, Microsoft JScript can't be trusted not to throw out JavaScript errors on the screen when viewed in other browsers, nor can JavaScript itself be fully trusted to run on IE without testing for the presence of Microsoft Internet Explorer and coding around certain features. It's a shame, really, although Microsoft's adherence to standards is getting much better recently. On the other hand, in an exclusive Microsoft environment, such as a platform-controlled corporate intranet, the access to Microsoft proprietary tools is superb, although VBScript is arguably better in that environment.

VBScript

Microsoft's answer to JavaScript. Because JavaScript and JScript are partially incompatible, the "safer" way to do similar tasks (at least in Internet Explorer) is to use VBScript, which is completely under Microsoft control. It interfaces well with ActiveX and other Microsoft technologies and is a good choice for intranets with a Win95/NT standard configuration. Many developers use both JavaScript and VBScript on the page so that they can force IE to choose VBScript, which Netscape doesn't recognize, and ignore the immediately following JavaScript, but it does mean that some functions have to be coded twice.

Win95/NT platforms mainly, but support for the PowerMac usually follows after Win95/NT versions have been on the market for some time. Third parties may supply UNIX support on their own, but there are no guarantees.

Microsoft's VBScript 2.0 Web Page

`http://www.microsoft.com/vbscript/`
A good reference for VBScript, with free downloads, tutorials, documentation, and other goodies to make it easy to write VBScript code. It interfaces well with ActiveX and other Microsoft technologies. Win95/NT platforms.

HTML Validators

Now that you've designed and coded your page, does it work? Is it really correct? How can you trust the validity check, if any, performed by your editing program? Would it tell you if it were wrong? It never hurts to have a second opinion, or even a third. I usually test in at least two or three validators and also look at my pages using many different browsers, but I'm paranoid and cherish my independence.

Just because a validator tells you a combination of tags doesn't pass a standard, it doesn't mean your page is bad. Sometimes you have to use "extra" tags or attributes to make sure your pages look pretty much the same in different browsers, but the validator flags it as being "non-compliant." Tsk, tsk, tsk! None of the validators knows anything at all about the skills involved in balancing the requirements of the many conflicting "standards" on the Web, so my advice is to take warning messages with a grain of salt, as long as you pass the basic tests of validity. Table G.12 summarizes some of the available validation tools and resources.

Table G.12. HTML validators.

Product	Type/Features	Audience	Price Range	Platforms
CSE 3310	Desktop Many options	Developers	$$	Win95/NT
WebTechs	Online/Desktop Many options	Developers	Free	N/A or UNIX
Weblint	Online/Desktop Many options	Developers	Free	N/A or Many
Bobby	Online/Desktop Many options	Developers	Free	Many or Any

CSE 3310 HTML Validator 2.0

`http://www.htmlvalidator.com/`
Currently supports DTDs up to HTML 3.2 plus unspecified Netscape and Microsoft extensions. A flexible standalone validator for use on the desktop. Win95/NT platform.

WebTechs Validation Service

`http://www.webtechs.com/html-val-svc/`
An online resource for validating either an entire page on the Web or snippets of code using a form. Includes many options, such as strict interpretations of IETF 2.0, IETF 3.0 (now withdrawn), W3C 3.2 (Wilbur), W3C 3.2 + CSS1, and W3C 4.0 (draft). It also supports DTDs describing the behavior, more or less, of proprietary extensions for Mozilla (Netscape Navigator), SoftQuad, AdvaSoft, Microsoft IE, and Microsoft IE 3.0 Beta. Very temperamental in the face of certain types of errors. Various interpretations of the same code, originally a service of HaL Software (Dave?), exist around the Web and many are freely available for download. WebTechs supplies the HTML Check Toolkit, which is a command-line version of the program for UNIX systems at no cost. No platform dependencies.

Neil Bowers' Weblint

`http://www.cre.canon.co.uk/~neilb/weblint/`

A Perl script that "picks the fluff off Web pages" and available freely on the Net. This is one of several versions out there, but all share a common heritage in the grandmother of all fluff pickers, Lint, which was made for C code on UNIX systems. Weblint doesn't "know" HTML and doesn't supply the extensive error reports of the WebTechs service, but is more robust in that it keeps generating meaningful messages even after stumbling on a first serious mistake. Many validators quickly start generating page after page of relatively meaningless error messages based on one missing tag or quote mark. This site also contains a very good list of other validation and coding resources, including Web gateways to the Weblint software itself. Runs on any platform that supports a Perl interpreter, including UNIX, Win95/NT, and Macintosh.

CAST's Bobby 2.0

`http://www.cast.org/bobby/`

This is a special kind of validator that tests your page for compliance with accessibility guidelines as well as adherence to external standards. It's harder than you might think but, once you've passed the Bobby test, you can put its cute little Bobby logo on your page as a certification of your design prowess. Unlike most other validators, Bobby validates WebTV, Lynx, and AOL compliance and extends the vague "proprietary extensions" checkbox found in most external validation suites to specific releases of IE and Navigator. Unfortunately, it doesn't do IE 4.0 or Navigator 4.0 yet, but it's early yet.

As designers, it's our social responsibility to be aware of the needs of the disabled, but Web accessibility is also fairly likely to become a legal mandate for large businesses and all government entities in the USA and elsewhere, just as accessibility in public accommodations is mandated for physical and telephone access. Paying attention to these issues now may well save your client or business an expensive lawsuit later on, as well as giving you the warm and fuzzy feeling that comes from doing the right thing.

The source to Bobby 1.2.1 is available for download as a Perl script, so it should be possible to run it on any system with a Perl engine available, although they promise only UNIX compatibility. You might have to tweak the script to eliminate UNIX dependencies. A Java version of release 2.0 that will run without tweaking should be available by the time you read this book. It's a very cool product and it's free, so you might consider a donation. No platform dependencies.

Web Servers

A Web server is what sits on your server, or your service provider's server, and actually responds to the requests made by your browser or the many browsers of the people visiting your Web site. They form a team, with you or some other human (usually) on one end, the data you want to get on the other, and these two cooperating agents figuring out how to get from there to here, and vice versa.

G

DEVELOPMENT RESOURCES

The cooperation is made possible by a special language that they both know, the HyperText Transfer Protocol (HTTP), which is the scheme that makes data and content available on your desktop as though it were right inside your own machine when it might be half a world away. Table G.13 summarizes some of the more popular Web servers.

Table G.13. HTTP servers.

Product	Type/Features	Audience	Price Range	Platforms
CERN HTTPD	HTTP 1.0	Expert	Free	Many
NCSA HTTPD	HTTP 1.0	Expert	Free	Many
NCSA HTTPD/Win	HTTP 1.0	Expert	Free	Windows
ORA WebSite	HTTP 1.1	Intermediate	$$$	Win95/NT
MacHTTP	HTTP 1.0	Intermediate	$$	Mac
WebStar	HTTP 1.1	Intermediate	$$$	Mac
Microsoft	HTTP 1.1	Intermediate	$$$$	Win95/NT
Netscape	HTTP 1.1	Intermediate	$$$$	Win95/NT UNIX
Jigsaw	HTTP 1.1	Expert	Free	Any
CL-HTTP	HTTP 1.1	Expert	Free	Linux, Mac
Apache	HTTP 1.1	Expert	Free	UNIX, Win95/NT
Sun Servers	HTTP 1.1	Expert	$$$$	Sun UNIX Solaris
Lotus Domino	N/A	Expert	$$$$$	N/A
Cold Fusion AS	N/A	Intermediate	$$$	WinNT

CERN HTTPD

`http://www.w3.org/pub/WWW/Daemon/`

This is the famous CERN server that formed the basis, along with the NCSA server, for much of the initial Web and still runs quite a lot of it. The last release was in 1996 and all future work will be on the Jigsaw Java server, which is covered later in this section. UNIX platform, but it has been ported with name changes to several other platforms.

NCSA HTTPD

`http://hoohoo.ncsa.uiuc.edu/index.html`

This is the other "big name" in servers. Both of these vanilla Web servers offer a basic medley of services and are well-known in the community. Like buying a Ford or a Chevy, spare parts are easy to come by and there are a lot of Web mechanics around who know how to work on them. They are nice stable "family" servers. Also on UNIX platforms, but a Windows port/recode exists (see the next section).

NCSA HTTPD for Windows

`http://tech.west.ora.com/win-httpd/`

This is probably the last Windows update for this software. It's no longer completely freeware but a more-or-less commercial product from O'Reilly that has been superseded by WebSite (see the next section). Windows platform only.

O'Reilly WebSite 2.0

`http://website.ora.com/`

A 32-bit Web server with all the bells and whistles, secure commerce, and other nice features that let you put a real Web server on the air in jig time without an awful lot of expertise. This is the O'Reilly server being worked on now and where you can expect to see even more improvement over time. A particularly exciting development is built-in support for Java servlets in WebSite Pro 2.0. Win95/NT platforms.

MacHTTP

`http://www.starnine.com/machttp/`

A shareware Web server for the Mac OS, superseded by WebStar from the same company, which is much faster and under active development. The MacHTTP page is still bragging about Mosaic compatibility, so it evidently doesn't put much effort into keeping current. Macintosh platform.

WebStar 2.1

`http://www.starnine.com/`

A modern server with such improvements as speed and dynamic caching. Shipped by Apple in its Apple Internet Server Solution Version 2.1, WebSTAR is a full-featured HTTP server for the Apple world. Macintosh platform.

Microsoft Web Servers

`http://www.microsoft.com/products/os.htm`

Microsoft's various Web servers. All have great integration with Microsoft products and the Microsoft worldview, but can be difficult to manage for very large sites and reportedly have an awkward Microsoft-centered interface to the rest of the Web. Still, if you run a Microsoft/Intel site, this one is probably the easiest to use because it fits right in with everything else and you don't have to learn a new operating system. Microsoft WinNT platforms, either Intel or DEC Alpha.

Netscape SuiteSpot Servers

`http://www.netscape.com/comprod/server_central/`

The central source for the whole array of Netscape servers and Web-centered development tools, including Visual JavaScript, NetObjects Fusion, Symantec Visual Café Pro, and other tools designed to work with Netscape servers and clients. They have many partners offering products that extend the functionality of their servers as well, offering such things as virus scanning at the proxy server or firewall, search engines, database tools, and administrative utilities. UNIX and WinNT platforms.

Jigsaw

`http://www.w3.org/Jigsaw/`

A full-featured Web server from the W3C, replacing the CERN HTTPD server in the W3C's fond heart of hearts and development effort. Written entirely in Java, so it will run on any machine that has a virtual Java engine available. Jigsaw also supports Java servlets, the server-side equivalent of Java applets and a faster way to execute CGI-type tasks with much less overhead. The current version is alpha code only, but this is something to keep track of, at the very least. Any platform by design.

Common Lisp Hypermedia Server (CL-HTTP)

`http://www.ai.mit.edu/projects/iiip/doc/cl-http/home-page.html`

A Web server written in Common Lisp with source code freely available for Linux and Macintosh platforms. Excellent resource for programmers and others who want to really experiment with servers and push the edge of the envelope. Linux and Macintosh platforms.

Apache

`http://www.apache.org/`

Freeware HTTP Server including SSL option. Like much of the freeware, open-development world, things are constantly changing based on the amount of free time the disparate community of authors has at hand in any given span of moments. Check the site for availability. UNIX platform but source-code–only WinNT port to be released at some point in the future.

Sun Server Family

`http://www.sun.com/servers/`

An extremely capable line of HTTP servers from Sun, designed to be as "hands-free" as possible, that run on many of their boxes from the NetraJ line to the Ultra Enterprise Server. A fault-tolerant SPARC line is specifically targeted at the telecommunications industry or anyone who needs true reliability. Superb integration with Java makes this line a good choice for shops with a Java focus, but the servers run only on Sun UNIX platforms so UNIX-phobes will not be pleased. Great products, though, and sure to please the tech-heads among you. Sun UNIX platforms only.

Lotus Notes/Domino

`http://www.lotus.org/`

I should say something about IBM/Lotus and Domino here, although they are currently outside the purview of most users of this book because their browser interface is at least partly (mostly?) proprietary and the platform requires a corporate monetary and cultural commitment of great magnitude. Their worldview is approaching that of a generalized Web browser/server combination, though, and I would be remiss not to mention it, at least in passing, and the IBM push toward Java may let them break out of the corporate box and onto the small-business desktop. The Lotus Notes/Domino business productivity paradigm is all-inclusive, subsuming the vagaries of other proprietary browsers and servers with a well-defined environment in which proprietary extensions to standard capabilities are the rule rather than the exception.

If your audience is on the intranet of a large corporation, governmental organization, or consortium, the Lotus approach makes a lot of sense as it successfully integrates messaging, conferencing, scheduling, database access, and a host of other functions that mere Internetizens can only admire from afar. Not only that, but the administration tools were designed for sites with a thousand or more users, not cobbled together like some I could name. That's not to say you couldn't do it all on the cheap and on the fly by doing your own integration and development, but hey, who has the time? Complete platform dependency.

Cold Fusion Application Server

`http://www.allaire.com/`

This is the other end of the Cold Fusion partnership and not really a server, even though I stuck it here. In spite of the name, the CF Application Server is not an HTTP server at all, but rather a sort of interpreter (like a CGI, which is discussed in the following section) for the special tags and attributes created in Cold Fusion. I include it in servers because it's at least closely associated with servers, making it possible to "pretend" that the HTTP server understands quite a bit more than it does and taking the functionality of multiple scripts and making their content available to the Web designer in the form of special tags and attributes that hide the underlying complexity under the familiar tag/attribute interface. It also precompiles Cold Fusion pages so they serve up quickly. See the preceding discussion of Cold Fusion under "Web Site Tools: Web Publishers and Site Managers." WinNT platform.

Common Gateway Interface (CGI)

Well, now that we have Web pages zipping all over the planet, somebody thought it would be nice if you could actually talk back to the server and ask for other stuff—things that couldn't be described as pages and things that you wanted to write or say, as opposed to read or hear. Neat problem; HTTP was essentially a one-way street. You could ask for things and have them returned to you with no problem, but HTTP had no way of keeping track of who you were from moment to moment or any way to store anything it did learn.

Another protocol was called for, the Common Gateway Interface or CGI, which lets you write special code to ask for and receive almost anything you want from the server end and makes yet another language and set of tools to learn. Table G.14 contains references to general tools for making the most of the CGI protocol.

Table G.14. CGI resources.

Resource	Type/Features	Audience	Price Range	Platforms
NCSA CGI	Resource List Tutorials	Developers	Free	Any
CGI Resources	Resource List Tutorials Tools	Developers	Free	Any
CGI Collection	Resource List Tools	Developers	Free	Any
CGI Made Easy	Resource List Tutorials Tools	Developers	Free	Any
Matt's Script Archive	Resource List Tools	Developers	Free	Any
Selena Sol's Script Archive	Resource List Tutorials Tools Social Commentary	Developers	Free	Any

General Information

Here is some useful background information on the CGI dealing with a wide range of issues and tools, from "How to program the CGI" to "Here's something you can use today."

The Common Gateway Interface at NCSA

`http://hoohoo.ncsa.uiuc.edu/cgi/`

Excellent introduction to CGI, from the people who invented it or were around, at least, when it was being invented, including an introduction, a primer, and tutorials, as well as specifications and other information to get you started on CGI programming quickly.

CGI Resources

`http://www.halcyon.com/sanford/cgi/index.html`

Great collection of tutorials, debugging tools, and other resources for the beginning CGI scriptwriter. Assumes knowledge of Perl, the most common CGI scripting language. No particular platform dependency, although most CGI gateways reside on UNIX machines, so you might find some assumptions in the actual code examples.

The CGI Collection

`http://www.selah.net/cgi.html`

A fairly well-organized but smallish collection of resources from a Washington State access provider, Selah.net, who advertises World Wide Mart's CGI Resource Index on the splash page. Scripts address access counters, chat rooms, password protection, and so on, but the tutorials all seem to be off-site. With all the reciprocal advertising going on, it's hard to tell who actually has the final responsibility for any given page sometimes.

Most of the actual scripts seem to be in Perl, but there are some in C, too. One of the nice features is a CGI-Bot that will search multiple CGI resource pages for information. As with many of these small sites, the content seems almost like an excuse to lure people in to look at ads, and not like the labors of love that some of the older private CGI sites were. There are valuable things on the page, nonetheless. UNIX, Macintosh, and Win95/NT platforms.

CGI Made Really Easy

`http://www.jmarshall.com/easy/cgi/`

A straight, no-nonsense guide that strips the mysticism and supposed complexity from the Common Gateway Interface with examples in both Perl and C. There are links to other CGI information on the same site and elsewhere. UNIX, Macintosh, and Win95/NT platforms.

CGI Resource Index

`http://www.cgi-resources.com/`

Over 800 different links to CGI resources from another access provider, World Wide Mart. The resources range from ready-to-use form processors to professional CGI programmers you can hire. Lots of scripts on this site, written in Perl and C++, and many seem genuinely useful. It's also the home of Matt's Script Archive (see the following item). UNIX, Macintosh, and Win95/NT platforms.

Matt's Script Archive

`http://worldwidemart.com/scripts/`

One of the best sources of CGI scripts in the world, this site has a few dozen Perl and C++ scripts online, with search engines, random link generators, animation, clocks, credit card verifiers, and several more really useful items. One of the best ways to use sites like this, if you can't use the actual code, is to study how a professional programmer attacks a given task. Often, you can capture enough of the strategy to be able to approach your own problem with more confidence. UNIX, Macintosh, and Win95/NT platforms.

Selena Sol's Script Archive

`http://selena.mcp.com/Scripts/`

Selena Sol, the feminine alter ego of Eric Tachibana, has a really meaningful collection of scripts, thoughts, philosophy, and resources collected here and on mirror sites around the world. From password protection to database searching to an automated fortune cookie, Selena Sol's site has one of the greatest collections of CGI routines ever put together, and the author is well worth getting to know through her work and pages. UNIX, Macintosh, and Win95/NT platforms.

Perl (The Practical Extraction and Report Language)

You can actually use any computer language to write a CGI "script." In fact, they don't have to be "scripts" at all. You could use COBOL if you wanted to, as long as you can make it behave and speak like the CGI wants it to behave and speak. Most CGI scripts have been written in Perl, a true "scripting" language especially designed as a report language to process text easily and quickly with a minimum of programmer effort. It was and is ideal for the task, although many people are using Java, C/C++, or other languages for specific tasks. Java is especially interesting because a vendor can supply a single module for an application that will run on any machine. Table G.15 summarizes some Perl-specific resources and tools available on the Web.

Table G.15. Perl resources.

Resource	Type/Features	Audience	Price Range	Platforms
Web Toolbox	Tutorial	Novice	Free	Any
Perl Language	Resource List	Developers	Free	Any
MKS Toolkit	UNIX Emulation Utilities Editor Etc.	Developers	$$$	Win95/NT MIPS, Alpha, PowerPC
Perl/Tk FAQ	Tutorial	Developers	Free	Any
NCSA Perl	Tutorial	Developers	Free	Any
Perl CGI	Examples	Developers	Free	Any

Jacqueline Hamilton's Web Engineer's Toolbox

`http://lightsphere.com/dev/class/`

Simply superb tutorial Perl lessons in small doses for very beginning Web people. Assumes only a general knowledge of HTML and probably the best starting point if you don't know a programming language already. No platform dependencies.

The Perl Language Homepage

`http://www.perl.com/`

Central source for information about Perl, a powerful object-oriented language specifically designed for dealing with text and lexical manipulation. Although visually dense compared to Visual Basic and some other scripting languages, there's little that can't be done quickly and easily in Perl once you get past a steep learning curve. For programmers already familiar with C or C++, Perl comes easily. There are more resources and links here than you could shake a stick at, so be prepared to spend quite a lot of time exploring from this site. Many platforms with no particular dependencies.

Mortice Kern Systems (MKS) Toolkit

`http://www.mks.com/`

The MKS Toolkit provides utilities and commands based on UNIX that ease the transition either way. If you know UNIX well, the Toolkit lets you use UNIX commands on DOS/Windows machines. If you know DOS/Windows, it can let you practice in the privacy of your own home before braving the terse world of UNIX without a safety net. Includes Perl, Awk, Vi, Tar, CPIO, Ksh, and many other UNIX look-alikes. Optional PScript utility includes Perlized ActiveX functions for Win95/NT. Win95, WinNT, and OS/2 platforms, including Intel, MIPS, Alpha, and PowerPC hardware.

Perl/Tk FAQ

`http://w4.lns.cornell.edu/~pvhp/ptk/ptkTOC.html`

This site has information on merging Perl and Tcl/Tk, a "widget" toolkit of visual terminal controls. Basically, it allows you to add a graphical user interface to Perl, which is text-based. Primarily UNIX X Window platform, but Win95/NT ports have been made.

Perl Tutorial from NCSA

`http://www.ncsa.uiuc.edu/General/Training/PerlIntro/`

A simple introduction to all the basic functions of Perl using a simple mailto function as a learning tool. At the end of the self-paced course, you have a working tool.

PERL CGI Examples

`http://www.panix.com/~wizjd/test.html`

Free CGI programs meant for the CGI professional to study. UNIX, Macintosh, and Win95/NT platforms.

C/C++

Where to start? C/C++ is a world of its own, with a culture, language, C-itizens, and customs of worldwide range. C and C++ give you direct access to the complete facilities of any UNIX machine, for which it is the preferred systems programming language. If you can't do something in any other way that you can think of, C/C++ is almost guaranteed to work. It won't walk the dog yet, but the C/C++ gurus are working on that. Table G.16 lists a few good places to begin contacting the inhabitants of the C-ontinuum.

Table G.16. C/C++ resources.

Resource	Type/Features	Audience	Price Range	Platforms
C++ Lite FAQ	Tutorial/FAQ	Developers	Free	Any
Prog. Source	Resource List Tutorials	Developers	Free	Any
C Prog by Nerd	Resource List Product Reviews Tutorials Job Referrals	Developers	Free	Any
Lysator C Prog	Resource List Scholarly Papers Tutorials	Developers	Free	Any

C++-Lite FAQ

`http://www.cerfnet.com/~mpcline/c++-faq-lite/`
A small tutorial on C++ and a few links are its major claims to fame other than the FAQ itself, which is excellent. No platform dependencies.

The Programmer's Source

`http://www.progsource.com/`
An extensive resource link list covering not only C/C++, but also Java, CGI, Perl, and other items of interest to developers. Contents include references to compilers, tutorials, discussion groups, and software archives. No platform dependencies.

C Programming by Nerd World

`http://www.nerdworld.com/users/dstein/nw93.html`
A small but decent collection of tutorials and links. No platform dependencies.

Lysator C Programming

`http://www.lysator.liu.se/c/`

An extensive list of references, some light-hearted but most very earnest indeed. If it isn't here, it might not be very important. (I'm being facetious, so please don't jump on me for it.) No platform dependencies.

Visual Basic

Visual Basic (VB) is the language of choice for many Windows/Win95 programmers. It has great access to Windows resources, and there are many toolkits of widgets available to do almost anything you want. A quick overview of Visual Basic resources is listed in Table G.17.

Table G.17. Visual Basic resources.

Resource	Features	Audience	Price Range	Platforms
MSDN	Resources Press Releases Tutorials	Developers	Free	Win95/NT
MS Visual Basic	Resources Press Releases Tutorials	Developers	Free	Win95/NT
IR for Win Developers	Resources Product Reviews Tutorials	Developers	Free	Win95/NT
Visual Basic IR	Resources Product Reviews Tutorials	Developers	Free	Win95/NT

The Microsoft Developers Network (MSDN)

`http://www.microsoft.com/msdn/`

This is a central source for information on Microsoft compilers, SDKs, and other tools for developers. If you want to know what's cooking in the Microsoft kitchen, this is the place to smell the bacon. Microsoft platform dependencies abound.

The Microsoft Visual Basic Site

`http://www.microsoft.com/vbasic/`

A short skip away from MSDN and more specific to Visual Basic development. Extensive coverage of tools and techniques for VB developers. Microsoft platform dependencies.

G

DEVELOPMENT
RESOURCES

Internet Resources for Windows Developers

`http://www.r2m.com/windev/`

This is a page of links from an independent Internet Resources for Windows Developers site, which has much on it besides Visual Basic and is worth exploring for other reasons. Microsoft platform dependencies.

Visual Basic Internet Resources

`http://www.r2m.com/windev/visual-basic.html`

Good independent site for Windows developers and the child of the preceding more general site. You can also find lots of resources at the Microsoft Developers Network sites mentioned previously. Microsoft platform dependencies.

Firewalls, Proxy Servers, and Security

Internet security is in the news and on almost everyone's mind today. You can hardly open the paper without hearing about confidential data illicitly obtained or some scam targeting businesses and even individuals—credit card numbers stolen, identities stolen, even stealthy Java or ActiveX programs that hang up your phone and redial some overseas site to run up your telephone bill in return for a kickback from an unscrupulous overseas telephone company.

How do you keep your data safe? It's bad enough to open your mail and see that you somehow spent five hours on the phone to Faroutistan, unbeknownst to you and while you were asleep, but if someone breaks into your Web site and replaces all your databases with garbage, or steals the information on your top-secret new spring line of bathing suits to sell to a competitor, we're talking about something that can destroy businesses and even lives.

Firewalls are the Internet's answer to padlocks and barred gates, keeping unwanted visitors out while letting people with the proper keys pass freely back and forth. A proxy server is sort of like your "dorm mother" in college, at least if you're old enough to remember them, telling you what you can do and when you can do it, and requiring all calls from boys to be screened at the front desk. The purpose is to protect you from unwise decisions you might make by trusting people (and strange machines) too much.

In general, proprietary OS packages offer the best security and the least exposure, if only because the majority of hacking tools are available for the common systems—UNIX, WinNT, and so on. On the other hand, they have high upfront costs. For Webmasters who want to create their own security systems, the widely available UNIX firewall and proxy implementations offer the resourceful Web site administrator the ability to create a custom secure system on the cheap. Table G.18 lists security resources available on the Web.

Table G.18. Firewalls, proxies, and security.

Product	Type	Audience	Price Range	Platforms
WWW Sec. FAQ	Information	Novice to Expert	Free	Any
I-Pad	Secure Server	Intermediate	$$$$	WinNT
Border Manager	Firewall	Advanced	$$$$$	Proprietary
MS Proxy	Proxy Server	Advanced	$$$$	WinNT
Netscape Proxy	Proxy Server	Advanced	$$$$	WinNT/ UNIX
Cisco PIX	Firewall	Advanced	$$$$$	Proprietary
Checkpoint	Firewall	Advanced	$$$$$	WinNT/ UNIX
SSLeay	Secure Sockets	Advanced	Free	UNIX
Apache SSL	Secure Server	Advanced	Free	UNIX

The WWW Security FAQ

`http://www-genome.wi.mit.edu/WWW/faqs/www-security-faq.html`

Introduction to WWW security with a step-by-step, Q&A format discussion of the implications of security on the World Wide Web.

I-Pad eSoft

`http://www.esoft.com/`

A self-contained "server in a box" with TCP/IP router and HTTP, FTP, DNS, SMTP, POP3, and Dial-up SLIP/PPP servers. A limited number of CGI gateways are built in, but off-the-shelf packages can't be added. Firewall functionality is also built in. Good for small to medium sites requiring a simple system up and running "yesterday." Intel WinNT platform is part of the package.

Novell Border Manager

`http://www.novell.com/`

NCSA-certification–pending firewall for medium to large businesses. Claims lowest cost of ownership through centralized management and clean, well-optimized code. Proprietary IntranetWare Intel-based platform.

Microsoft Proxy

`http://www.microsoft.com/proxy/` `http://www.microsoft.com/`
Server-oriented proxy server that's easy to use and relatively powerful for small to medium sites using primarily Microsoft operating systems, but shares WinNT Server's scalability, standardization, and security problems when trying to extend to larger organizations. Well-integrated with Microsoft Internet Information Server. WinNT Server platform.

Netscape Proxy Server

`http://www.netscape.com/comprod/netscape_products.html` `http://www.netscape.com/`
This is a widely used proxy server for common platforms that requires much less investment in knowledge and skills to set up a decent system than the "roll-your-own" UNIX varieties. Integrates well with Netscape Commerce Server and other Netscape servers. WinNT Server, Alpha NT Server, and UNIX platforms.

Cisco Systems PIX

`http://www.cisco.com/pix/`
NCSA-certified flexible hardware-based firewall solution for medium to large businesses. Claims lowest cost of ownership. Proprietary embedded OS platform.

Check Point Firewall

`http://www.checkpoint.com/`
With two-fifths of the world firewall market, Check Point must be doing something right. It's a full-featured, software-only firewall and security system offering a full range of features and options for the demanding Webmaster. WinNT and UNIX platforms.

SSLeay and SSLapps

`http://www.psy.uq.oz.au/~ftp/Crypto/`
`http://apache.org/`
`http://www.algroup.co.uk/Apache-SSL/`
Secure Sockets Layer for UNIX and WinNT platforms. The combination of SSLeay and Apache SSL make it possible to run a "home-brewed" secure server on almost any machine. It might be necessary to buy a site certificate from a trusted authority (like Verisign, for example), but an active and worldwide development community might solve the problem by the time you read this. Source code available.

Apache SSL

`http://www.apache.org/`
`http://www.algroup.co.uk/Apache-SSL/`
A modification of the Apache server discussed in the preceding "Web Servers" section. See the discussion and needed patches to Apache code at the second URL. The server itself is available from the first URL. Another valuable discussion is found in the section "International Cryptography," later in this chapter.

Libraries and Other Resources on the Web

Well, where do you go from here? This book has told you a lot about HTML, and this appendix has covered a lot of ground as well. But there's a lot we haven't had time or space to mention, even in a huge book such as this one, and things are constantly changing. Luckily, there are sites on the Web dedicated to keeping up-to-date information available to you 24 hours a day and seven days a week. Some are labors of love by people who have a particular interest in a special topic, and some are commercial sites publishing the Web equivalent of a magazine, giving you access to articles and information in return for reading the advertisements they want to show you. Table G.19 contains summarized references to a host of information that doesn't fit easily anywhere else.

Table G.19. Web resources.

Resource	Type	Audience	Price Range	Platforms
W3C	Standards Body	The Whole Web	N/A	Any
HTML	HTML DTDs	Developers	N/A	Any
CSS	Style Sheets	Developers	N/A	Any
DOM	Object Model	Developers	N/A	Any
Math	Math Markup	Developers	N/A	Any
Graphics	GFX Standards	Developers	N/A	Any
Access	Accessibility	Developers	N/A	Any
XML	Extending HTML	Developers	N/A	Any
NS DevEdge	NS Resources	Developers	Free to $$$$	Any
Site Builder	MS Resources	Developers	Free to $$$$	MS
Web Reference	Library	Developers	Free	Any
Macmillan	Library	Developers	Free	Any
HTML Guru	Library	Developers	Free	Any
HTML WG	Guild/Library	Developers	Free	Any
WDVL	Library	Developers	Free	Any
Stars.com	WDVL clone	Developers	Free	Any
Webmaster	Library	Developers	Free	Any
WebABLE!	Resource List	Anyone	Free	Any
CAST	Resource List	Anyone	Free	Any
Low Vision	Resource List	Anyone	Free	Any
Blindness	Resource List	Anyone	Free	Any

continues

Table G.19. continued

Resource	Type	Audience	Price Range	Platforms
Cryptography	Resource List	Developers	Free	Any
Spiderwoman	Mailing List	Developers	Free	Any
VBScript	Mailing List	Developers	Free	MS
ActiveX	Mailing List	Developers	Free	MS
CGI List	Mailing List	Developers	Free	Any
Advanced CGI	Mailing List	Developers	Free	Any

World Wide Web Consortium (W3C)

`http://w3c.org/`

The central source for information about what's going on in the real world, as opposed to the hothouses of the major browser makers. Although Microsoft and Netscape have come to dominate a good portion of the input to this standards-promulgating body, if only because they can afford to dedicate staff to working on their many projects, they are both still in thrall to it in the long run. This is where new standards come from and where old standards go to die. The W3C also runs several research and test efforts, including the Amaya testbed browser and the Jigsaw Java-based server. No platform dependencies.

HTML 3.2 and 4.0

`http://w3.org/MarkUp/`

This is the page that should be bookmarked because subpages have been known to move around or even disappear. It contains references to all current incarnations of the W3C documents held on site, as well as beaucoup links to outside sources of information, a traditional strength of W3C pages. No platform dependencies.

Cascading Style Sheets (CSS)

`http://w3c.org/Style/`

This is the start of the tree for style sheets that includes the current specification as well as links to working documents on Dynamic HTML and Cascading Style Sheets. This is also a starting point for the ISO standard style sheet document that's more theoretically advanced (and complex): DSSSL (Document Style Semantics and Specification Language).

Document Object Model (DOM)

`http://w3c.org/MarkUp/DOM/`

Speaking of Dynamic HTML, here is the W3C's starting point for the DOM Working Group, which is trying to reconcile the incompatible visions of Microsoft and Netscape (primarily) and ensure that everyone's Dynamic HTML actually works without crashing everyone else. A neat trick if it works. It looks like some version of the Microsoft architecture will prevail, but one never knows; HTML 3.0 was hot stuff for a while, but nobody brags about it today. No platform dependencies.

Math on the Web

`http://www.w3.org/Math/`

And speaking of HTML 3.0, here is where the fabled HTML 3.0 math elements wound up, having suffered a sea change into something far more rich and strange. This is the center of the HTML Math Working Group and the place to go if you've ever had the quixotic desire to publish geometric monodromy matrices, or other esoterica, to a worldwide audience doubtless waiting in breathless anticipation for an easy way to view these sublime revelations. I have absolutely no idea what monodromy is, so please don't ask, but it's probably the culmination and pinnacle of billions of years of evolution and forms the very basis of Life As We Know It. No platform dependencies.

Graphics on the Web

`http://w3c.org/Graphics/`

Everything you always wanted to know about graphic file formats but were afraid to ask. GIF, TIFF, JPEG, PNG, PostScript, CGM—they're all here (or links at least) with discussions of what their future role on the Web may be. The latest thoughts are that GIFs are on the way out because of Unisys's belated insistence on enforcing its (disputed) patent rights in LZW compression, which GIF is based on. PNG (Portable Network Graphics), the favored replacement, is currently in development and propagation on the Web. None of the references on the site are very recent, so I'm guessing that the issue has sort of died down. Obviously, if PNG completely replaces GIF, the Unisys patent isn't worth much except for Web historians. On the other hand, replacing all those GIFs floating around on the Web would be a major chore, so maybe the nuisance is worth what Unisys is charging. What's certain is that as a Web designer, you should look very carefully at what graphics formats you use because it could come back to haunt you if you operate a commercial site. No platform dependencies.

The Web Accessibility Initiative

`http://w3c.org/WAI/`

This is Accessibility Central, where they take into account the millions of people in the world with permanent or temporary disabilities. Their Reference page is an excellent starting place for research. It looks like accessibility is finally becoming a real part of the HTML standards, as the WAI had some influence on certain features of the new HTML 4.0 draft, but there is still more to be done. This is a good place to find sites that support accessibility as well as specialized browsers often used by the disabled, although this appendix gives you a good overview.

Extensible Markup Language (XML)

`http://w3c.org/XML/`

This is where you'll find links to information about XML, the Extensible Markup Language that will let us all design our own DTDs and have our own tags and attributes. They claim this will make documents more readable, but I have just the barest smidgen of doubt because few seem able to handle the handful of tags that make up existing HTML standards all that well. On the other hand, XML is the greatest thing since the invention of sliced bread that always lands butter-side up, according to the markup gurus. No platform dependencies.

Other W3C Issues

`http://w3c.org/`

Other issues addressed by the W3C are the Amaya testbed browser and Jigsaw HTTP server mentioned previously, internationalization (especially font and character set issues), fonts (propagating fonts on the Web but also internationalization), the Digital Signature Initiative, electronic commerce, metadata (a generalized activity for figuring out how to express opinions—assertions, rather—about the identity of individuals, the content of Web sites, and distributed authoring and versioning mechanisms), PICS (content rating systems), intellectual property rights, privacy and preferences, security, HTTP 1.1, object technology (CORBA, DCE, Microsoft COM, Plan 9), audio, video, and synchronized multimedia. All these issues can be found by links from their home page.

Netscape DevEdge

`http://developer.netscape.com/`

The Netscape developer's salon for those with a Netscape horizon. Many links to outside and internal resources. Multiple levels of membership. No particular platform dependencies—although they don't seem to have a lot of links to Microsoft!

Microsoft Site Builder Network

`http://www.microsoft.com/sitebuilder/`

A Microsoft-centered site with tons of good information about Microsoft tools and products. If you live in a Microsoft world, this is the place to find out what might be possible in it, but the vision turns myopic when looking beyond the virtual walls. Multiple levels of membership. Microsoft (Win95/NT) platforms.

Web Reference

`http://www.webreference.com/`

A good general introduction to lots of topics and tutorials on common technologies, such as JavaScript.

Macmillan's HTML Workshop and Survival Guide

`http://www.mcp.com/general/workshop/`

Very good tutorials and introduction to HTML from the famous publisher of many computer reference works of truly stunning value, especially this one. No platform dependencies.

Chuck Musciano's The HTML Guru

`http://members.aol.com/htmlguru/`

A small collection of tips and tricks from an individual author and columnist. Some of this site's strengths, especially for novices, are the uniform and well-organized data space in which to search and the Q&A pattern of much of the material. Only one viewpoint is available, though, so you should balance opinions from this site with others. No platform dependencies.

The HTML Writer's Guild

`http://hwg.org/`

This site is the home of one of the premier organizations for Web professionals as well as a good source of information on all aspects of the profession, job referrals, forums, and other good stuff. Various membership levels available. No platform dependencies.

Web Developer's Virtual Library (WDVL)

`http://www.wdvl.com/`

An excellent and up-to-date resource for anyone involved in developing or maintaining Web sites. Contains a very thorough treatment of HTML 4.0 with tutorial examples and links to many additional resources, including most of the specifications from the W3C and elsewhere. Almost every subject you could think of is presented in a well-organized index on the splash page, so searching for what you're interested in is extremely simple. No platform dependencies.

The Virtual Library of WWW Development

`http://www.stars.com/Vlib/`

Another version of the WDVL discussed previously.

Webmaster Resources

`http://www.cio.com/resources/`

A well-organized compendium of tools and resources for Webmasters, including discussions of the profession, professional societies, tutorials, HTML, graphics, publicizing sites, search engines, technologies, and other topics of interest to Web professionals. No platform dependencies.

Yuri Rubinsky Insight Foundation WebABLE!

`http://www.yuri.org/webable/`

At some point in your life, you are very likely to be disabled, perhaps temporarily and perhaps not so temporarily. This is an excellent collection of links and design guidelines for inclusive Web sites, to support the real people who live in the world with all sorts of disabilities and perhaps even the person you are or might become. I talked about this before in connection with the Bobby HTML validator, but it bears repeating; now that the W3C has made accessibility possible to code for, it's only a matter of time before it's expected on any professional project. Now is an excellent time to study the issues involved before they become regulated as matters of law. No platform dependencies.

CAST—Center for Applied Special Technology

`http://www.cast.org/`

Home of the Bobby HTML and accessibility validator, CAST is also an excellent resource for design guidelines, and links to other organizations, and papers relating to inclusive design. No platform dependencies.

Low Vision and Deaf/Blind

`http://home.earthlink.net/~robinpow/blind.htm`

An excellent and extensive link list of resources for the sight and hearing disabled. No platform dependencies and aggressively Lynx-compatible.

Blindness Resource Center

`http://www.nyise.org/speech/blind.htm`

An excellent list of links for the blind with a more hierarchical structure than the preceding Low Vision and Deaf/Blind site. Very good coverage of commercial vendors that offer products for the blind and links to interest everyone, including a good resource on the History of Writing Codes for the Blind, which is marred only by the extensive use of graphics (although it's hard to imagine how the early Braille variants, New York Point, and embossed Roman letter systems could be represented in ASCII characters). Better `alt` text would help. A large print version is available in contrasting white on black. No platform dependencies.

International Cryptography

`http://www.cs.hut.fi/crypto/`

Extensive resources on cryptography and security from Finland that concentrates on software available outside the United States to avoid our short-sighted export restrictions. Good tutorial references and access to all the information you need to set up SSH (Secure Shell), SSLeay/Apache-SSL, electronic purses, and other secure applications. Note that the techniques and products described may not be legal, or legal to re-export, in your country. Many platforms, but much of the freeware is on UNIX.

Stephanie Brail's Spiderwoman Mailing List at Amazon City

http://www.amazoncity.com/spiderwoman/

An excellent resource for women in Web design, with tips, resources, a chat room, and other stuff of particular interest to women—and, of course, the excellent list itself. No platform dependencies.

VBScript Mailing List

A great resource for VBScript programmers on Microsoft platforms. This is one place where the heavyweights in the VBScript world hang out, answer questions, and share experiences. Microsoft platforms.

To subscribe, send e-mail to: Listserv@listserv.msn.com

In the body of the message, type:

```
Subscribe VBScript Firstname Lastname
```

ActiveX Controls Mailing List

A similar resource for programmers writing or using ActiveX controls on Microsoft platforms. This is where you might turn for answers to vexing questions, advice, or even to show off your own knowledge a bit. Microsoft platforms.

To subscribe, send e-mail to: Listserv@listserv.msn.com

In the body of the message, type:

```
Subscribe ActiveXControls Firstname Lastname
```

Common Gateway Interface List

A list for CGI developers to ask questions and share experiences with writing to this popular interface. No platform dependencies.

To subscribe, send e-mail to: listserv@vm.ege.edu.tr

In the body of the message, type:

```
Subscribe CGI-L Firstname Lastname
```

Advanced CGI Discussion List

Discussions and inquiries about the Common Gateway Interface and creating programs or scripts that access this interface. No platform dependencies.

To subscribe, send e-mail to: listproc@lists.nyu.edu

In the body of the message, type:

```
Subscribe ADV-CGI Firstname Lastname
```

Libraries and Other Resources: Mainly HTML

There are so many great resources available on the Web that it's hard to know when to stop; at the suggestion of some dedicated partisans of the Web sites here, I've included yet another section of miscellaneous resources so that you won't be jealous of resource lists with more numbers but less substance. Like those people selling fancy Ginsu™ knives on TV, today's Blue Light Special includes not one, but two great resource lists: the handy general list in the previous section, "Libraries and Other Resources on the Web," and this one, which concentrates on HTML.

HTML is such a large subject, in spite of being a little overshadowed by the many dazzling multimedia extensions that seem to be appearing faster than we can cope with sometimes, that it's worth pausing to consider that this is where it all started, and no-frills HTML is still capable of presenting an exciting and informative page. In addition (or rather, to start with, because I've presented them at the top of the list), I'm including some interesting references to some of our collective history, my aim being to make this list useful as a cultural resource for the sophisticated Net citizen as well as a guide for dedicated HTML wonks.

Table G.20 summarizes HTML resources, primarily, but is almost as much a grab bag as the preceding section.

Table G.20. HTML resources.

Resource	Type	Audience	Price Range	Platforms
As We Think	Essay	Everyone	Free	Any
Xanadu	Essay/Project	Everyone	Free	Any
Berners-Lee	Talks	Everyone	Free	Any
WebTools	Tutorials	Developers	Free	Any
Compendium of HTML	Index	Developers	Free	Any
Ultimate Tag Reference	Index	Developers	Free	Any
HTML 4.0 DTD	Documentation	Developers	Free	Any
HTML Station	Tutorials	Developers	Free	Any
DOT.html	Tutorials	Developers	Free	Any
Netcaster	Tutorial	Developers	Free	Any
Style Guide	Guide	Developers	Free	Any
Web Help	Tutorials	Developers	Free	Any
Yale Guide	Tutorials	Developers	Free	Any
Joe Barta	Tutorials	Developers	Free	Any

Resource	Type	Audience	Price Range	Platforms
Guide to Publishing	Tutorials	Developers	Free	Any
HTML Card	Reference Card	Developers	Free	Any
Jan's Guide	Tutorials	Developers	Free	Any
HTML by Example	Tutorials	Developers	Free	Any
Netscape Cookies	Tutorial	Developers	Free	Any
Malcolm's Cookies	Tutorial	Developers	Free	Any
Andy's Cookies	Tutorial	Developers	Free	Any
Advanced HTML	Mailing List	Developers	Free	Any
Newsgroups	News	Developers	Free	Any

As We May Think

`http://www.isg.sfu.ca/~duchier/micc/vbush/`
`http://www.ausbcomp.com/~bbott/wik/vbush.htm`

This is the article by Vannevar Bush that many believe was a prescient vision of what the World Wide Web is today. It's written from the perspective of 1945, just after a devastating World War, yet filled with the bright optimism of those years when many U.S. citizens felt like they were emerging from a long dark tunnel and into the sunlight. It's a rallying cry and exhortation to "men of science" (and lest we wax too terribly nostalgic about those years, that's exactly what they were) to make the knowledge and new sciences invented during the war years accessible to everyone by using new technologies that hadn't even been invented yet, but that he could foresee. No platform dependencies.

Ted Nelson's Xanadu

`http://www.xanadu.net/xanadu/`
`http://jefferson.village.virginia.edu/elab/hfl0155.html`
`http://www.wired.com/wired/3.06/features/xanadu.html`
`http://www.xanadu.net/ararat`
`http://www.w3.org/Xanadu.html`

This is a small part of the story of Xanadu, the conceptual hypertext library and "docuverse" by the man who invented the word *hypertext* and is responsible for many of the ideas that other people later borrowed or reinterpreted to create the Web we know and love today. Like many gifted visionaries, Theodor Holm Nelson sometimes got bogged down when trying to communicate with the rest of us, so a lot of the interpretation was necessary to let ordinary people understand what was going on. Nonetheless, there's a lot of innovation whose antecedents are clearly in Xanadu but whose ancestry and debt of gratitude is unacknowledged, and a lot of sniping by Monday-morning quarterbacks whose last truly original thought was deciding on the salad bar instead of the surf 'n' turf for dinner. No platform dependencies.

Tim Berners-Lee

```
http://www.w3.org/Talks/9510_Bush/Talk.html
http://www.taponline.com/rant/download/berners/page1.html
http://www-unix.oit.umass.edu/~abhu000/rp593m.disc.tbl.html
```

No discussion of Web history is complete with mentioning Tim Berners-Lee, who brought all the tentative theoretical threads together (try saying *that* ten times fast) into an actual working HTTP server and browser in 1990 through 1991. At last! Not only is he a clever and practical man, but one with some surprising and insightful views of what the world has made of his creation. The last Web reference is an interesting collaborative project that illustrates the power of the Web for some types of research. Check it out. No platform dependencies.

WebTools.org

```
http://www.webtools.org
http://www.webtools.org/counter/
```

A nice collection of general HTML resources, including the WebTools.org HTML Access Counter 4.0 script. No platform dependencies.

Compendium of HTML Elements

```
http://www.htmlcompendium.org/sitemap.htm
```

This exhaustive listing of every known HTML tag ever used includes everything from specialized WebTV tags to the latest HTML 4.0 elements. The compendium includes all the attributes for every tag, as well as specific examples of usage for each of the elements and attributes. You can download it for use on your own system, or you can use the online version to make sure you're as up to date as it is. No platform dependencies.

D.J. Quad's Ultimate Tag Reference List

```
http://www.quadzilla.com/reference/reference.htm
```

This site has all the elements organized into neat reference packets, each with an example of how it's used in actual code. No platform dependencies.

Guide to Web Style

`http://www.sun.com/styleguide/`

This handy reference from Sun Microsystems (the developers of the Java language) covers everything from deciding on the purpose of your site and its intended audience to using graphics. No platform dependencies.

HTML 4.0 Document Type Definition HTML Version

`http://www.webtechs.com/sgml/HTML4/`

This public service site from WebTechs has every element in the new HTML specification from W3C in an easily accessible format. No platform dependencies.

HTML Station

`http://www.december.com/html/`

A complete reference resource for the Web developer. Covers all aspects of the HTML language, from version 0 to version 4.0. Includes sections on CGI, forms, tables, character sets, Netscape and Internet Explorer extensions, and cookies. On top of all this, it also has an excellent Web design tutorial. No platform dependencies.

Index DOT HTML

`http://www.blooberry.com/html/index.html`

Available in both online and downloadable versions, this site has a thumb-nail history of the Hypertext Markup Language, Netscape, and Internet Explorer versions. The Tag History breaks down exactly what was available in which version. In addition to this considerable achievement, the site boasts a Tag Tree, which clearly shows the container relationships among HTML's elements. Detailed examples of each element show how it's used, what browsers it works with (and any quirks those browsers have in handling this element), and just about anything else you would want to know. As if this weren't enough, there's also a tutorial on Cascading Style Sheets. No platform dependencies.

Netcaster Developers Guide

`http://developer.netscape.com/library/documentation/netcast/devguide/index.html`

The official guide to developing channel broadcasts with Netscape Netcaster. No platform dependencies, but oriented toward the Netscape browser.

Style Guide for Online Hypertext

`http://www.w3.org/Provider/Style/Overview.html`

Although it's a bit old, the theme of this work is still valid. Tim Berners-Lee, the primary architect of the World Wide Web, gives his thoughts on good Web site design. No platform dependencies.

Web Designer Help Desk

`http://web.canlink.com/helpdesk/`
This site has sections on HTML authoring, Web site design, tables, frames, Java, search engines, and Netiquette. No platform dependencies.

Yale C/AIM Web Style Guide

`http://info.med.yale.edu/caim/manual/`
One of the most important, but least covered, areas of Web design. This site covers layout, typography, multimedia, the works. Requires a JavaScript-compatible browser to view or download the entire guide as an Adobe PDF file:

`ftp://info.med.yale.edu/pub/caim/pdf/s_guide.pdf`
No platform dependencies.

Joe Barta's Form, Frame, Table, and HTML Tutorials

`http://junior.apk.net/~jbarta/tutor/forms/index.html`
`http://junior.apk.net/~jbarta/tutor/frames/index.html`
`http://junior.apk.net/~jbarta/tutor/tables/index.html`
`http://junior.apk.net/~jbarta/tutor/makapage/index.html`
Joe Barta's marvelous suite of Web authoring tutorials have something to offer to practically anyone working with HTML. Whether you're just getting started or are looking for a good source of tips and tricks, he has put just about everything you would want to know about using forms, frames, tables, and general Web design into a clear, concise format. Use the online version or download them. No platform dependencies.

Guide to Publishing HTML and Forms

`http://www.2kweb.net/guide-to-publishing-html.html`
An excellent tutorial with visual presentation of how different attribute values affect the look of a page. It's still expanding, and future sections will cover the implementation of MIDI files in both Netscape and Internet Explorer. No platform dependencies.

HTML Quick Reference

`http://sdcc8.ucsd.edu/%7Em1wilson/htmlref.html`
Though not yet updated for HTML 4.0, this makes a great reference card. No platform dependencies.

Jan's Guide to HTML

`http://www.ftech.net/~dutch/guide/`
A comprehensive guide to the language, including some JavaScript, forms, tables, and an overview of available software for Web developers. No platform dependencies.

Learning HTML by Example

`http://jeffco.k12.co.us/high/awest/learnhtml/00conten.htm`
One of the best-designed HTML tutorials around. No platform dependencies.

Netscape's Persistent Cookies Documentation

`http://home.netscape.com/newsref/std/cookie_spec.html`
Netscape's documentation on how to use cookies to save information from session to session or during a transaction. No platform dependencies.

Malcolm's Guide to Persistent Cookies

`http://www.emf.net/~mal/cookiesinfo.html`
Similar information from another source. No platform dependencies.

Andy's Netscape HTTP Cookie Notes

`http://www.illuminatus.com/cookie`
Similar information from another source. No platform dependencies.

Advanced HTML Discussion List

An excellent source of advice about HTML, the problems Web developers face and overcome in creating a Web site, and other topics of interest to the Web page developer community. No platform dependencies.

To subscribe, send e-mail to: `listserv@ua1vm.ua.edu`

In the body of the message, type:

`Subscribe ADV-HTML Firstname Lastname`

Newsgroups

Here are a few of the hundreds, or even thousands, of newsgroups that address issues of concern to Web developers. The best way to discover which group works for you is to follow a link from a site or a recommendation from a friend. Personally, I don't use newsgroups because I've noticed that I get far too many extraneous comments from people with axes to grind. I prefer the more controlled environment of a mailing list, where disruptive people can be kicked off easily; that measure of control tends to elevate the general level of discourse. But many people love newsgroups and read lots of them every day.

```
comp.infosystems.www.authoring.html
comp.infosystems.www.authoring.cgi
comp.infosystems.www.authoring.misc
comp.infosystems.www.browsers.mac
comp.infosystems.www.browsers.ms-windows
comp.infosystems.www.browsers.x
comp.infosystems.www.browsers.misc
```

G

**DEVELOPMENT
RESOURCES**

Notes for Further Research

This is just an introduction to the vast amount of information freely available on the Web and a starting point for your own studies. Of course, no list can be complete, so a given program or resource, possibly your favorite, being missing from this list is no reflection on its quality, nor is every resource here listed without flaws. What is true is that each of the programs and utilities mentioned has an audience for whom it seems ideal or at least well-suited. I've tried to tell you enough about each so that you can decide for yourself before haring off over the Web to find yet another item of no earthly use to you.

When you have to hare off, though, there are strategies and techniques you can use to make sure your labors are not in vain. The link lists and libraries listed in this appendix are excellent starting points for a focused search of your own, but sometimes you want to know something about a topic nobody seems to have heard of, at least as far as you know.

This is where the big search engines and Web spiders come into their own. There are basically two types: those based on keyword searches and those based on topical organization. An example of a keyword site is Alta Vista, and Yahoo! is perhaps the best-known topical site. However, the issue is a little confused by Yahoo! now providing Alta Vista word searches on its site.

Searching by categories works best when you know something about a subject and can guess what category the information might be filed under. In that situation, you'd simply walk down the list until you reach your topic. This method has the great advantage that everything fitting that topic will be gathered in one place where you can see it.

But what about those times when you don't know anything at all? Nothing but a concept, or even a word perhaps. How do you find something then?

As an experiment, try thinking about a problem, one already addressed in this appendix so you can see where you're going and know enough already to be fairly sure I didn't "cook" the results. Say you're a Web designer with original artwork on your site, and you want to be sure that some unscrupulous individual can't steal your work and pass it off as his own. What to do? You can't lock the artwork up—it has to be visible on your site or what's the point? You don't want to put a big sign plastered across its face because that would be ugly—and again, what's the point? You decide to try searching the Web for an answer to your problem. You use Alta Vista because it's well known.

Where to start? You try searching for the word *art* and discover 7,542,680 matches, not very encouraging. You try *art* and *protect*, not much better at 439,330 documents, far too many to search through. But wait, you're interested in digital art, not art in general, so you decide to add the word *digital*. Dang! 499,580 matches! More, not less! What's going on? Hang on—the very first matches have some interesting words in them: "Watermarking and Digital Signature: Protect your work!" It looks like you found your reference.

There are a lot of ways to refine a search; adding words is just one way. You could also be more specific, instructing the engine to demand certain words or phrases by adding a plus sign in front of the word or to exclude other words by putting a minus sign in front although the syntax is sometimes different on different engines. Experiment with +watermark +digital signature. These are words discovered in your search, not ones you knew about already. You end up with 39 documents, and all of them seem to be right on target. You're not especially interested in offerings from commercial companies, though, so you narrow the field by adding some minus signs based on the first page, and bingo! You've got a list of 28 documents, an easy three pages to search.

AltaVista also has smart agents that let you construct complex searches based on associations by simply checking boxes, but usually I find that you can do about as well and get results more quickly by simply refining the initial idea. There are lots of search engines, each with strengths; some are covered in the following section. Good hunting!

Search Engines

Search engines! How do we love thee, let us count the ways… A good search engine can help feed users to your site, if you have anything worth seeing, and construct a good introduction. Be aware that many spiders use meta-information to construct a description, but many just take the first few lines of text and resolve to do both things right. Treat a Web page like a newspaper article with a rock'em sock'em headline and lead story in addition to a formal description.

Also, be aware that many unscrupulous individuals engage in Web spamming, larding their pages with completely unrelated or duplicative terms, often invisible, to increase the number of times a hit occurs and making hundreds of copies of their pages so they will get page after page of listings when people look for common terms. This is a dishonest, destructive, and pernicious practice, and people who do it deserve to be ostracized, if not soundly thrashed. You can avoid many of these jerks in your searches by including the negation of a small selection of trigger words, usually vulgar and sexual, which the "clever" dimwits include in their pages.

Among the practitioners of this deceptive scam, you will find everyone from lawyers (tell me it isn't so!) to authors (for shame!) and golf ball salesmen. Don't buy anything from any spammer, and maybe they will wither away eventually. Of course you, dear reader, would never, ever spam, but consider that a person who deliberately wastes your time is not your friend, no matter how much he says he is. It doesn't take a rocket scientist to realize this, and you'd be surprised how very many mild-mannered people hate such shifty tactics and wish the practitioners ill.

Table G.21 summarizes the strengths of the search engines discussed in this section.

G

DEVELOPMENT RESOURCES

Table G.21. Search engines.

Product	Type	Audience	Price Range	Platforms
AltaVista	Keyword	All	Free	Any
Excite	Keyword	All	Free	Any
Infoseek	Topic/Keyword	All	Free	Any
Lycos	Keyword	All	Free	Any
Yahoo!	Topic/Keyword	All	Free	Any
Magellan	Keyword/Rated	All	Free	Any
Lexis-Nexis	Keyword	Professionals	$$/month	Any
Reuters	Feed/Keyword	Professionals	Varies	Any

The following sections offer a small sampling of a few of the most notable search engines.

AltaVista

http://www.altavista.digital.com/

Huge keyword search site with the main problem being how to limit your search to bring the total number of hits down to the point that you could read them in your lifetime. Offers very good ways to include what are advanced options in many engines as quick little additions to the command line. Don't like typing quotes to bracket a phrase? Try an underscore instead. Add or subtract words with plus and minus symbols. Trés logical.

Excite

http://www.excite.com/

Excite is much like AltaVista, a keyword search site with a method of excluding or including terms built in. It differs in that it shows a small selection of ways to limit the search on the result page and offers its opinion about the relevance (a slippery term) of the page to your search. They all do this, trying to put the "best" results at the top, but Excite actually tells you how confident it is. Excite does something more, though; it has a smart engine that will broaden your search to related terms, so if you type in `elderly people`, it will think of retired people and senior citizens, too. Whether this is maddening or wonderful depends entirely on how you're feeling that day.

Infoseek

http://www.infoseek.com/

Infoseek is both topic and keyword-oriented and offers little red checkmarks in front of sites it particularly recommends, whatever that means. Although it doesn't allow negation at the "command line" (since it uses the hyphen to represent a non-breaking space), it does allow you to pipe the results of one search to another, so you can search for `dog ¦ Dalmatian` to make sure you don't see too many references to Dalmatia in what used to be Yugoslavia and is now Croatia or Hrvatska, depending on how close you are.

Lycos

http://www.lycos.com/

Lycos is a keyword search engine with a sort of online topical magazine on the side. It can be a very good resource because you can often find an article that tells you enough about your subject to give you the right buzzwords to look for in a search. Like Alta Vista, you can include or exclude words by prefacing them with plus or minus signs.

Yahoo!

http://www.yahoo.com/

The definitive topical site and a very good starting place if you know a lot about the subject of your search and can traverse the subject tree easily. Yahoo! offers a way of opting out of categories by means of an AltaVista keyword search, or you can go part way down a tree and then search the rest of the leaves. I know that sounds upside down, but nobody ever said programmers (and I am one) had common sense. It actually has a sort of twisted logic (in a virtual sort of way) and is very convenient for display, so almost every time you see a logical tree, the root is at the top. It all started with Alice in Wonderland...

Magellan

http://www.mckinley.com/

This is an interesting search engine, because it's one of the few that offers the option of looking at rated and reviewed sites, as well as what it calls "green light" sites that are, in its opinion, suitable for children. Actually, I think most people understand and agree about what the phrase means, but one never knows. This is a sub-engine of Excite, but is not currently accepting new sites for review. Darn! Like Excite, it gives a relevance measure.

Lexis-Nexis

http://www.lexis.com/

This is an entirely different league of search engines, and only the most well-known among many value-added purveyors of full-text articles and research on the Web. This particular engine specializes in legal research, offering the full text of appellate cases, legal decisions, patent applications, legal news, and every other tidbit of information that might make a lawyer's heart go pitterpat. You subscribe at a monthly charge per lawyer in your office, so it's a relatively expensive way to search. They do have a few free services, such as a nationwide lawyer locator, that are available to the public. The advantage of subscribing is that most of the information available on Lexis-Nexis isn't available on the Web at all, although you could traipse down to your local law library and find most of it at no cost, paying only for copying the pages you need or even writing them out by hand for free.

Reuters

`http://www.reuters.com/`
`http://www.reutershealth.com/`

This is another value-added service with some free offerings, like top news stories, as teasers. Reuters, as one might expect from the largest news agency in the world, specializes in news of all sorts. It has offerings for financial wizards as well as health professionals, advertising and marketing people, transportation executives, the insurance industry, and other categories, not to mention its bread-and-butter product, news feeds to newspapers, radio and television stations, and other media markets, including the Web.

Typically, you access Reuters through a site that uses its feeds, although you can subscribe on your own for very large dollars. As opposed to the more-or-less pay-per-recipient model of Lexis-Nexis, Reuters is primarily subscription-based. Some portions, however, like the Reuters Health site, allow searches of health-related information. When you sign up for a Reuters feed, you get everything that comes down the pipe and can use it or toss it, using internal criteria. Many large sites use Reuters or another such agency to supply a continuous feed of news that they can post to draw people looking for everything from sports scores and late-breaking medical news to the latest dirt on the movers and shakers in Silicon Valley.

There are many, many more, some with quite sharply delimited subject areas, as well as the versions of these engines you often find on private sites that index local content only.

What's on the CD-ROM?

APPENDIX H

IN THIS APPENDIX

On the *HTML 4 Unleashed, Professional Reference Edition* CD-ROM, you will find sample files that have been presented in this book along with a wealth of other applications and utilities.

> **NOTE**
>
> Please refer to the `readme.wri` file on the CD-ROM (Windows) or the Guide to the CD-ROM (Macintosh) for the latest listing of software.

Windows 95 Software

ActiveX

- Microsoft ActiveX Control Pad and HTML Layout Control

Book

- HTML version of Appendix A
- Source code and examples used throughout the book

Graphics

- HyperSnap screen capture tool
- Sampler of over 500 graphics
- MapThis! image map utility
- Paint Shop Pro 4.12 shareware graphics tool
- SnagIt
- Web graphics from The Rocket Shop

HTML

- NetObjects Fusion demo
- HotDog Express HTML Editor
- 14-Day trial version of HotDog 4 Professional
- ATRAX HTML editor
- HTMLed HTML editor
- Net-It Now! Intranet tool
- HTML assistant HTML editor

MISC

- Adobe Acrobat viewer
- WinZip for Windows NT/95
- WinZip Self-Extractor
- Microsoft Internet Explorer 4
- Goldwave sound editor, player, and recorder
- Macromedia's Shockwave media player

Sprint

- Complete Internet connection package including Internet account software and web browser

Windows 3.1 Software

Book

- HTML version of Appendix A
- Source code and examples used throughout the book

Graphics

- Sampler of over 500 graphic images
- Web graphics from The Rocket Shop

HTML

- HTMLed HTML editor
- HTML assistant HTML editor
- HotDog Express 16-bit HTML editor

MISC

- Adobe Acrobat viewer
- Macromedia's Shockwave media player
- WinZip for Windows 3.1
- Microsoft Internet Explorer 3.03

Sprint

- Complete Internet connection package including Internet account software and web browser

Macintosh Software

Book

- HTML version of Appendix A
- Source code and examples used throughout the book

Graphics

- Graphic Converter
- Sampler of over 500 graphic images
- Web graphics from The Rocket Shop

HTML

- NetObjects Fusion demo
- Grinder 3.3 HTML tool from Matterform Media
- BBEdit LITE
- HTML Colormeister shareware tool
- PageSpinner HTML editing tool demo

MISC

- StuffIt Expander and ShrinkWrap both from Aladdin Systems
- Sound App
- Adobe Acrobat reader software

Sprint

- Complete Internet connection package including Internet account software and web browser

About the Software

Please read all documentation associated with a third-party product (usually found in files named readme.txt or license.txt), and follow all installation guidelines.

Notes

_____

_____

_____

_____

_____

_____

_____

_____

_____

_____

_____

_____

_____

_____

Notes

Notes

_____

_____

_____

_____

_____

_____

_____

_____

_____

_____

_____

_____

_____

Notes

Notes

_____

_____

_____

_____

_____

_____

_____

_____

_____

_____

_____

_____

Notes

Notes

Notes

_____

_____

_____

_____

_____

_____

_____

_____

_____

_____

_____

_____

_____

I

INDEX

W

Presenting XML

Richard Light

Presenting XML teaches you about XML (Extensible Markup Language) and how it can be used to speed up the Web through greater use of client-side processing, better indexing, search and retrieval, richer link types, and more complex structures. The book covers what XML is, how it relates to HTML and SGML, how it will affect the Web, and the kinds of applications possible. It explains in detail what the XML specification is and describes the basics of writing XML code and creating XML-aware applications.

$24.99 US; $35.95 CDN   *1-57521-334-6*
350 pp.   *Casual—Accomplished*

Dynamic HTML Unleashed

Michael Van Hoozer

Dynamic HTML Unleashed is an all-in-one guide to using Dynamic HTML and Web scripting languages to create Web pages and Web applications that change in response to user actions. Real-world examples show how Dynamic HTML enhances static Web pages. It covers the following:

Dynamic styles—showing or hiding elements, changing the size or color of fonts, changing the position of elements; the Dynamic HTML Object Model—describing an object model and explaining how to use it on a page; positioning—placing elements anywhere on x, y, and z planes; dynamic content—changing, inserting or deleting elements; filter, transition, and animation—adding multimedia controls; data awareness—making HTML a better environment for displaying and collecting data.

$39.99 US; $56.95 CDN   *1-57521-353-2*
800 pp.   *Casual—Accomplished*

Sams' Teach Yourself Java 1.1 in 21 Days, Second Edition

Laura Lemay and Charles Perkins

This updated best-seller is the definitive guide to learning Java 1.1, carefully stepping you through the fundamental concepts of the Java language, the basics of applet design, and integration with Web presentations. Add interactivity and animation to your Web sites with Java applets. CD-ROM includes Sun's Java Development Kit 1.1, Sun's Java Development Kit 1.02 for Macintosh, and Sun's Bean Development Kit for Windows 95, Windows NT, and Solaris.

$39.99 US; $56.95 CDN   *1-57521-142-4*
782 pp.   *New—Casual*

Designing Web Graphics.2

Lynda Weinman

Designing Web Graphics.2 is the completely updated and expanded version of the original best-seller. World-renowned author Lynda Weinman makes this book the cornerstone of any well-read designer's library. Includes updated coverage on file formats, file sizes, file translation, resolution, and more. Gives you step-by-step instructions from the master teacher Lynda Weinman.

$55.00 US; $77.95 CDN   *1-56205-715-4*
480 pp.   *All User Levels*

Add to Your Sams.net Library Today
with the Best Books for Internet Technologies

ISBN	Quantity	Description of Item	Unit Cost	Total Cost
1-57521-334-6		Presenting XML	$24.99	
1-57521-353-2		Dynamic HTML Unleashed	$39.99	
1-57521-142-4		Sams' Teach Yourself Java 1.1 in 21 Days, 2E	$39.99	
1-56205-715-4		Designing Web Graphics.2	$55.00	
		Shipping and Handling: See information below.		
		TOTAL		

Shipping and Handling: $4.00 for the first book and $1.75 for each additional book. If you need to have it NOW, we can ship product to you in 24 hours for an additional charge of approximately $18.00, and you will receive your item overnight or in two days. Overseas shipping and handling adds $2.00. Prices subject to change. Call between 9:00 a.m. and 5:00 p.m. EST for availability and pricing information on latest editions.

201 W. 103rd Street, Indianapolis, Indiana 46290

1-800-428-5331 — Orders   1-800-835-3202 — Fax   1-800-858-7674 — Customer Service

Book ISBN 1-57521-380-X

Technical Support

If you need assistance with the information in this book or with the CD-ROM accompanying this book, you can check out this title's book information page on our Web site at this address:

http://www.mcp.com/info

Just enter the ISBN for this title to get late-breaking information.

> **NOTE**
>
> If you're having trouble reading from the CD-ROM, try to clean the data side of the CD-ROM with a clean, soft cloth; dirt can disrupt accessing the data on the disc. If the problem still persists, try inserting this CD-ROM into another computer to determine whether the problem is with the disc or your CD-ROM drive.
>
> Another common cause of problems could be outdated CD-ROM drivers. To update your drivers on a Windows-based machine, first verify the manufacturer of your CD-ROM drive from your system's documentation. Or, under Windows 95/NT 4.0, you can check your CD-ROM manufacturer by clicking the Start button, choosing Settings | Control Panel | System, and then selecting the Device Manager. Double-click on the CD-ROM option to see the information on the manufacturer of your drive.
>
> You can download the latest drivers from your manufacturer's Web site or from this site:
>
> http://www.windows95.com

Windows 95 Installation Instructions

1. Insert the CD-ROM disc into your CD-ROM drive.

   If Windows 95 is installed on your computer, and you have the AutoPlay feature enabled, a Program Group for this book is automatically created when you insert the disc into your CD-ROM drive.

2. If AutoPlay is not enabled, using Windows Explorer, choose Setup from the CD drive to create the Program Group for this book.

3. Double-click any icon in the newly created Program Group to access the installation program for the desired application.

4. To review the latest information about this CD-ROM, double-click on the icon "About this CD-ROM."

NOTE

For best results, set your Windows-based computer monitor to display between 256 and 64,000 colors. A screen resolution of 640×480 pixels is also recommended. If necessary, adjust your monitor settings before using the CD-ROM.

Macintosh Installation Instructions

1. Insert the CD-ROM disc into your CD-ROM drive.

2. If the CD-ROM contents window doesn't appear on your desktop, open the disc by double-clicking on the CD-ROM icon.

3. Double-click on the icon named "Guide to the CD-ROM," and follow the directions.

Installation Instructions

What's on the Disc

The companion CD-ROM contains software developed by the authors, plus an assortment of third-party tools, shareware software, and product demos.

Many programs included on the disc are designed for use with an HTML-based Web browser. You *must* have either a Web browser or another program that recognizes .htm files in order to preview many of the files on this CD-ROM.

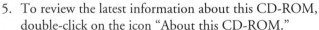

> **NOTE**
>
> A 16-bit, 32-bit, and Macintosh version of Internet Explorer are included on this CD-ROM for your convenience.

Windows 3.1 Installation Instructions

To run the browser program, follow these steps:

1. Insert the CD-ROM disc into your CD-ROM drive.
2. From File Manager or Program Manager, choose Run from the File menu.
3. Type `<drive>\setup` and press Enter; `<drive>` corresponds to the drive letter of your CD-ROM. For example, if your CD-ROM is drive D:, type `D:\SETUP` and press Enter.
4. Double-click on any icon in the newly created Program Group to access the installation program for the desired application.
5. To review the latest information about this CD-ROM, double-click on the icon "About this CD-ROM."